Access® 2013 BIBLE

Michael Alexander and Dick Kusleika

Access® 2013 Bible

Published by
John Wiley & Sons, Inc.
10475 Crosspoint Boulevard
Indianapolis, IN 46256
www.wiley.com

Published simultaneously in Canada

ISBN 978-1-118-49035-8 (pbk); ISBN 978-1-118-49034-1 (ebk); ISBN 978-1-118-49155-3 (ebk); ISBN 978-1-118-49154-6 (ebk)

Manufactured in the United States of America

10 9 8 7 6 5 4 3 2

For general information on our other products and services or to obtain technical support, please contact our Customer Care Department within the U.S. at (877) 762-2974, outside the U.S. at (317) 572-3993 or fax (317) 572-4002.

Library of Congress Control Number: 2013933952

Wiley publishes in a variety of print and electronic formats and by print-on-demand. Some material included with standard print versions of this book may not be included in e-books or in print-on-demand. If this book refers to media such as a CD or DVD that is not included in the version you purchased, you may download this material at http://booksupport.wiley.com. For more information about Wiley products, visit www.wiley.com.

Credits

Sr. Acquisitions Editor
Katie Mohr

Project Editor
Elizabeth Kuball

Technical Editor
Doug Steele

Copy Editor
Elizabeth Kuball

Editorial Manager
Jodi Jensen

Editorial Director
Mary Corder

Vice President and Executive Group Publisher
Richard Swadley

Vice President and Publisher
Andy Cummings

Senior Project Coordinator
Kristie Rees

Graphics and Production Specialists
Andrea Hornberger
Jennifer Mayberry

Quality Control Technician
Lindsay Amones

Proofreading and Indexing
Evelyn Wellborn
BIM Indexing & Proofreading Services

Vertical Websites Project Manager and Producer
Rich Graves

About the Authors

Michael Alexander is a Microsoft Certified Application Developer (MCAD) and author of several books on advanced business analysis with Microsoft Access and Microsoft Excel. He has more than 15 years of experience consulting and developing Microsoft Office solutions. Mike has been named a Microsoft MVP for his ongoing contributions to the Excel community. In his spare time, he runs a free tutorial site, www.datapigtechnologies.com, where he shares Excel and Access tips.

Dick Kusleika has been awarded as a Microsoft MVP for 12 consecutive years and has been working with Microsoft Office for more than 20. Dick develops Access- and Excel-based solutions for his clients and has conducted training seminars on Office products in the United States and Australia. Dick also writes a popular Excel-related blog at www.dailydoseofexcel.com.

To the memory of Mike Groh, the author of this book's previous two editions.

Acknowledgments

Our deepest thanks to the professionals at John Wiley & Sons for all the hours of work put into bringing this book to life. Thanks also to Doug Steele for suggesting numerous improvements to the examples and text in this book. Finally, a special thank you goes out to our families for putting up with all the time spent locked away on this project.

Contents at a Glance

Contents

Part II: Understanding Access Tables 31

Introduction

Welcome to *Access 2013 Bible,* your personal guide to the most powerful desktop database management system available today.

If you've picked up this book, you've probably already recognized that Microsoft Access can help you manage your data in ways that no other application can. Even the king of applications, Microsoft Excel, can't do what Access can. Now, it may seem silly to compare Access (a database management application) with Excel (a spreadsheet application), but there is no doubt that Excel is being used every day to manage and analyze large amounts of data in all kinds of organizations. Indeed, you may be opening this book because you need to get past the limitations of Excel.

Access is an excellent (many would say logical) next step for the analyst who faces an ever-increasing data pool. Access takes very few performance hits with larger datasets. It has no predetermined row limitations. And it can effectively manage the relationships between disparate data tables. In addition, Access comes with tools that help you build your own distributable applications.

Today, when we have more data than ever and more demands for complex data analysis, power analysts need to add some tools to their repertoire in order to get away from being simply "spreadsheet mechanics." That's why this book is such an important step in the evolution of your skillset. Throughout this book, not only will you get an introduction to Access, but you'll also learn various ways in which you can use Access to improve your daily data management and analysis.

Is This Book for You?

This book contains everything you need in order to learn Access 2013 to a mid-advanced level. The book starts off with database basics and builds, chapter by chapter.

This book is designed to enhance the skillset of users at all levels (beginning, intermediate, and even advanced users of Access). Start at the beginning if you're new to Access. If you're already familiar with Access and comfortable building Access applications, you may want to start with the later parts of this book.

If you're new to the world of database management, this book has everything you need to get started with Access 2013. It also offers advanced topics for reference and learning. Beginning developers should pay particular attention to Part I, where we cover the essential skills necessary for building successful and efficient databases. Your ability as a database designer is constantly judged by how well the applications you build perform and how well they handle data entrusted to them by their users.

If you've been working an earlier version of Access, this book is for you. Although you may already be familiar with the workings of Access, every new version has changes not only in features, but also in the mechanics of how certain actions are performed. This book will help you navigate through all these changes.

If you want to learn the basics of Visual Basic for Applications (VBA) programming, you'll find what you need in this book. Although the topic of VBA is a rich one that deserves its own book, this book offers a robust set of chapters that will get you started leveraging VBA to enhance your Access databases. Part VI of this book explains the nuts and bolts — with a lot of gritty technical details — of writing VBA procedures and building Access applications around the code you add to your databases.

Conventions Used in This Book

We use the following conventions in this book:

- When you're instructed to press a key combination (press and hold down one key while pressing another key), the key combination is separated by a plus sign. For example, Ctrl+Esc indicates that you must hold down the Ctrl key and press the Esc key; then release both keys.
- *Point the mouse* refers to moving the mouse so that the mouse pointer is on a specific item. *Click* refers to pressing the left mouse button once and releasing it. *Double-click* refers to pressing the left mouse button twice in rapid succession and then releasing it. *Right-click* refers to pressing the right mouse button once and releasing it. *Drag* refers to pressing and holding down the left mouse button while moving the mouse.
- We use *italics* for new terms and for emphasis.
- We use **bold** for material that you need to type directly into the computer.
- We use `monofont` for code and for on-screen messages.

How This Book Is Organized

This book is divided into nine parts:

- **Part I: Access Building Blocks:** Part I provides a solid understanding of the basic elements of databases, introduces you to the keywords of database management, and teaches you how to plan tables and work with Access data types. In this part, you'll also get your first look into Access and the Access interface.

- **Part II: Understanding Access Tables:** In Part II, you get the skills you need to build Access tables, manage relationships between tables, and link to disparate data sources like Excel files, text files, SQL Server, and other Access databases.
- **Part III: Working with Access Queries:** Part III introduces you to some of the basic analytical tools available in Access. Here, you'll explore the Query Builder, as well as techniques to create both simple and advanced analytical outputs from your Access tables. We cover query basics, aggregate queries, action queries, and crosstab queries.
- **Part IV: Analyzing Data in Access:** Part IV demonstrates many of the advanced techniques that truly bring data analysis to the next level. Here, you'll explore how to transform your data via queries, create custom calculations, perform conditional analysis, build powerful subqueries, and apply statistical analysis to your queries.
- **Part V: Working with Access Forms and Reports:** Part V focuses on building forms and reports using Access. Here, we cover the basics of turning data into slick-looking user interfaces and PDF-style Access reports. You'll also explore how to enhance the look and feel of your Access applications via advanced form controls.
- **Part VI: Access Programming Fundamentals:** In Part VI, you'll take the next step and dive into programming. The chapters in this part start you with Access macros, take you into VBA fundamentals, and eventually work up to leveraging VBA to improve your Access database. This part helps you understand the complex object and event models that drive Access applications and how to construct the VBA code necessary to take advantage of this rich programming environment.
- **Part VII: Advanced Access Programming Techniques:** Part VII turns your attention to automation and integration, showing you how your reporting mechanisms can be enhanced by leveraging other programs and platforms. In these chapters, you'll not only learn the fundamental skills required to become more proficient in VBA, but you'll also discover many insider tricks to apply to your Access application development projects. You'll also explore advanced techniques, such as customizing the Access 2013 Ribbon.
- **Part VIII: Access and Windows SharePoint Services:** In Part VIII, we cover the topic of Microsoft Windows SharePoint Services. Here, you'll discover the extended Microsoft SharePoint integration capabilities in Access that allow you to publish Access tables, forms, and reports on SharePoint sites. Although somewhat limited when compared with strictly Access applications, publishing Access objects to the SharePoint platform provides a powerful way of sharing Access data with remote users.
- **Part IX: Appendixes:** Part IX includes useful reference materials that will assist you in your everyday dealings with Access. Appendix A documents the Access 2013 specifications, including maximum and minimum sizes of databases and many of the controls in Access. Appendix B offers ideas on how to improve speed and performance of your Access applications. Appendix C shows you how to avoid and handle corruption issues when working with Access databases. Appendix D details many of the built-in Access functions that are available to data analysts.

How to Use This Book

Although each chapter is an integral part of the book as a whole, each chapter can also stand on its own and has its own example files, available on the book's website. You can read the book in any order you want, skipping from chapter to chapter and from topic to topic. This book's index is particularly thorough; you can refer to the index to find the location of a particular topic you're interested in.

What's on the Website

The examples demonstrated throughout this book can be found on this book's website. The URL is `www.wiley.com/go/access2013bible`.

Getting Additional Help with Access

As you experiment with the new functions and tools you learn here in this book, you may sometimes need an extra push in the right direction. The first place you should look is Access's Help system. The Help system in Access isn't perfect. To a new user, the Help system may seem like a clunky add-in that returns a perplexing list of topics that has nothing to do with the original topic being searched. The truth is, however, once you learn how to use the Access Help system effectively, it's often the fastest and easiest way to get extra help on a topic.

Following are some tips that will help you get the most out of Access's Help system:

- **Location matters when asking for help.** You may remember the Help system in older versions of Access being a lot more user-friendly and more effective than newer versions of Access. Well, rest assured that you aren't just imagining it. The fact is, Microsoft fundamentally changed the mechanics of the Access Help system.

  In Access 2013, there are actually two Help systems: one providing help on Access features and another providing help on VBA programming topics. Instead of doing a global search with your criteria, Access throws your search criteria only against the Help system that is relevant to your current location. This essentially means that the help you get is determined by the area of Access in which you're working. So, if you need help on a topic that involves VBA programming, you'll need to be in the VBA Editor while performing your search. On the other hand, if you need help on building a query, it's best to be in the Query Design view. This will ensure that your keyword search is performed on the correct Help system.

- **Online help is better than offline help.** When you search for help on a topic, Access checks to see if you're connected to the Internet. If you are, Access returns help results based on online content from Microsoft's website. If you aren't, Access uses the Help files that are locally stored with Microsoft Office. One way to maximize the help you get in Access is to use the online help. Online help is generally better than offline help because the content you find with online help is often more detailed and includes updated information, as well as links to other resources not available offline.
- **Diversify your knowledge base with online resources.** Familiarize yourself with a handful of websites and forums dedicated to Access. These resources can serve as supplemental help, not only for basic Access topics, but also to give you situation-specific tips and tricks. The following list of sites should get you started.
  - `www.allenbrowne.com`
  - `www.microsoft.com/office/community/en-us/default.mspx`
  - `www.mvps.org/access`
  - `www.utteraccess.com`

  These sites are free to use and are particularly helpful when you need an extra push in the right direction.

Part I

Access Building Blocks

Each part of this book builds on previous parts, and the chapters in each part contain examples that draw on techniques explained in previous parts and chapters. As a developer, your applications will benefit from the skills you acquire by reading the chapters and practicing the examples contained in this book.

But everyone has to start somewhere when approaching a new discipline, and Part I of this book presents the essential skills necessary for anyone to succeed at database development with Access. The topics covered in this part explain the concepts and techniques that are necessary to successfully use database environments and give you the skills necessary to normalize data and plan and implement effective tables.

If you're already familiar with the concepts involved in database design, you may want to skim these chapters. If you're new to the world of databases, spend some time here gaining a thorough understanding of these important topics.

IN THIS PART

CHAPTER 1

An Introduction to Database Development

IN THIS CHAPTER

Examining the differences between databases, tables, records, fields, and values

Discovering why multiple tables are used in a database

Exploring Access database objects

Designing a database system

Database development is unlike most other ways you work with computers. Unlike Microsoft Word or Excel, where the approach to working with the application is relatively intuitive, good database development requires prior knowledge. You have to learn a handful of fundamentals, including database terminology, basic database concepts, and database best practices.

Throughout this chapter, we cover the fundamentals of database development.

If your goal is to get right into Access, you might want to skip to Chapter 2.

The Database Terminology of Access

Access follows most, but not all, traditional database terminology. The terms *database, table, record, field,* and *value* indicate a hierarchy from largest to smallest. These same terms are used with virtually all database systems.

Databases

Generally, the word *database* is a computer term for a collection of information concerning a certain topic or business application. Databases help you organize this related information in a logical fashion for easy access and retrieval.

NOTE
Some older database systems used the term *database* to describe individual tables; current use of *database* applies to all elements of a database system.

Databases aren't only for computers. There are also manual databases; we sometimes refer to these as *manual filing systems* or *manual database systems*. These filing systems usually consist of people, papers, folders, and filing cabinets — paper is the key to a manual database system. In manual database systems, you typically have in and out baskets and some type of formal filing method. You access information manually by opening a file cabinet, taking out a file folder, and finding the correct piece of paper. Users fill out paper forms for input, perhaps by using a keyboard to input information that's printed on forms. You find information by manually sorting the papers or by copying information from many papers to another piece of paper (or even into an Excel spreadsheet). You may use a spreadsheet or calculator to analyze the data or display it in new and interesting ways.

An Access database is nothing more than an automated version of the filing and retrieval functions of a paper filing system. Access databases store information in a carefully defined structure. Access tables store a variety of different kinds of data, from simple lines of text (such as name and address) to complex data such as pictures, sounds, or video images. Storing data in a precise format enables a database management system (DBMS) like Access to turn data into useful information.

Tables serve as the primary data repository in an Access database. Queries, forms, and reports provide access to the data, enabling a user to add or extract data, and presenting the data in useful ways. Most developers add macros or Visual Basic for Applications (VBA) code to forms and reports to make their Access applications easier to use.

A relational database management system (RDBMS), such as Access, stores data in *related* tables. For example, a table containing employee data (names and addresses) may be related to a table containing payroll information (pay date, pay amount, and check number).

Queries allow the user to ask complex questions (such as "What is the sum of all paychecks issued to Jane Doe in 2012?") from these related tables, with the answers displayed as onscreen forms and printed reports.

In fact, one of the fundamental differences between a relational database and a manual filing system is that, in a relational database system, data for a single person or item may be stored in separate tables. For example, in a patient management system, the patient's name, address, and other contact information is likely to be stored in a different table from the table holding patient treatments. In fact, the treatment table holds all treatment information for all patients, and a patient identifier (usually a number) is used to look up an individual patient's treatments in the treatment table.

In Access, a *database* is the overall container for the data and associated objects. It's more than the collection of tables, however — a database includes many types of objects, including queries, forms, reports, macros, and code modules.

As you open an Access database, the objects (tables, queries, and so on) in the database are presented for you to work with. You may open several copies of Access at the same time and simultaneously work with more than one database, if needed.

Many Access databases contain hundreds, or even thousands, of tables, forms, queries, reports, macros, and modules. With a few exceptions, all the objects in an Access database reside within a single file with an extension of ACCDB, ACCDE, MDB, MDE, or ADP.

Tables

A table is just a container for raw information (called *data*), similar to a folder in a manual filing system. Each table in an Access database contains information about a single entity, such as a person or product, and the data in the table is organized into rows and columns.

In Chapters 3 and 4, you learn the very important rules governing relational table design and how to incorporate those rules into your Access databases. These rules and guidelines ensure that your applications perform well while protecting the integrity of the data contained within your tables.

In Access a table is an entity. As you design and build Access databases, or even when working with an existing application, you must think of how the tables and other database objects represent the physical entities managed by your database and how the entities relate to one another.

After you create a table, you can view the table in a spreadsheet-like form, called a *datasheet,* comprising rows and columns (known as *records* and *fields,* respectively — see the following section, "Records and fields"). Although a datasheet and a spreadsheet are superficially similar, a datasheet is a very different type of object.

Chapter 5 discusses Access datasheets and the differences between datasheets and spreadsheets. You can find much more about fields and field properties in Chapter 3.

Records and fields

A datasheet is divided into rows (called *records*) and columns (called *fields*), with the first row (the heading on top of each column) containing the names of the fields in the database.

Each row is a single record containing fields that are related to that record. In a manual system, the rows are individual forms (sheets of paper), and the fields are equivalent to the blank areas on a printed form that you fill in.

Each column is a field that includes many properties that specify the type of data contained within the field, and how Access should handle the field's data. These properties include the name of the field (Company) and the type of data in the field (Text). A field may include other properties as well. For example, the Address field's Size property tells Access the maximum number of characters allowed for the address.

NOTE

When working with Access, the term *field* is used to refer to an attribute stored in a record. In many other database systems, including Microsoft SQL Server, *column* is the expression you'll hear most often in place of *field. Field* and *column* mean the same thing. The terminology used relies somewhat on the context of the database system underlying the table containing the record.

Values

At the intersection of a record and a field is a *value* — the actual data element. For example, if you have a field called Company, a company name entered into that field would represent one data value. Certain rules govern how data is contained in an Access table.

See Chapters 3 and 4 for more on these rules.

Relational Databases

Access is a relational database management system. Access data is stored in related tables, where data in one table (such as customers) is related to data in another table (such as orders). Access maintains the relationships between related tables, making it easy to extract a customer and all the customer's orders, without losing any data or pulling order records not owned by the customer.

Multiple tables simplify data entry and reporting by decreasing the input of redundant data. By defining two tables for an application that uses customer information, for example, you don't need to store the customer's name and address every time the customer purchases an item.

After you've created the tables, they need to be related to each other. For example, if you have a Customer table and a Sales table, you can relate the two tables using a common field between them. In this case, Customer Number would be a good field to have in both tables. This will allow you to see sales in the Sales table where the Customer Number matches the Customer table.

The benefit of this model is that you don't have to repeat key attributes about a customer (like customer name, address, city, state, zip) each time you add a new record to the Sales table. All you need is the customer number. When a customer changes address, for example, the address changes only in one record in the Customers table.

Why Create Multiple Tables?

The prospect of creating multiple tables almost always intimidates beginning database users. Most often, beginners want to create one huge table that contains all the information they need — for example, a Customer table with all the sales placed by the customer and the customer's name, address, and other information. After all, if you've been using Excel to store data so far, it may seem quite reasonable to take the same approach when building tables in Access.

A single large table for all customer information quickly becomes difficult to maintain. You have to input the customer information for every sale a customer makes (repeating the name and address information over and over in every row). The same is true for the items purchased for each sale when the customer has purchased multiple items as part of a single purchase. This makes the system more inefficient and prone to data-entry mistakes. The information in the table is inefficiently stored — certain fields may not be needed for each sales record, and the table ends up with a lot of empty fields.

You want to create tables that hold a minimum of information while still making the system easy to use and flexible enough to grow. To accomplish this, you need to consider making more than one table, with each table containing fields that are related only to the focus of that table. Then, after you create the tables, you link them so that you're able to glean useful information from them. Although this process sounds extremely complex, the actual implementation is relatively easy.

Separating data into multiple tables within a database makes a system easier to maintain because all records of a given type are within the same table. By taking the time to properly segment data into multiple tables, you experience a significant reduction in design and work time. This process is known as *normalization*.

You can read about normalization in Chapter 4.

Access Database Objects

If you're new to databases (or even if you're an experienced database user), you need to understand a few key concepts before starting to build Access databases. The Access database contains six types of top-level objects, which consist of the data and tools that you need to use Access:

- **Table:** Holds the actual data.
- **Query:** Searches for, sorts, and retrieves specific data.
- **Form:** Lets you enter and display data in a customized format.
- **Report:** Displays and prints formatted data.

- **Macro:** Automates tasks without programming.
- **Module:** Contains programming statements written in the VBA programming language.

Datasheets

Datasheets are one of the many ways by which you can view data in Access. Although not a permanent database object, a datasheet displays a table's content in a row-and-column format similar to an Excel worksheet. A datasheet displays a table's information in a raw form, without transformations or filtering. The Datasheet view is the default mode for displaying all fields for all records.

You can scroll through the datasheet using the directional keys on your keyboard. You can also display related records in other tables while in a datasheet. In addition, you can make changes to the displayed data.

Queries

Queries extract information from a database. A query selects and defines a group of records that fulfill a certain condition. Most forms and reports are based on queries that combine, filter, or sort data before it's displayed. Queries are often called from macros or VBA procedures to change, add, or delete database records.

An example of a query is when a person at the sales office tells the database, "Show me all customers, in alphabetical order by name, who are located in Massachusetts and bought something over the past six months" or "Show me all customers who bought Chevrolet car models within the past six months and display them sorted by customer name and then by sale date."

Instead of asking the question in plain English, a person uses the query by example (QBE) method. When you enter instructions into the Query Designer window and run the query, the query translates the instructions into Structured Query Language (SQL) and retrieves the desired data.

Chapter 8 discusses the Query Designer window and building queries.

Data-entry and display forms

Data-entry forms help users get information into a database table quickly, easily, and accurately. Data-entry and display forms provide a more structured view of the data than what a datasheet provides. From this structured view, database records can be viewed, added, changed, or deleted. Entering data through the data-entry forms is the most common way to get the data into the database table.

Data-entry forms restrict access to certain fields within the table. Forms can also be enhanced with data validation rules or VBA code to check the validity of your data before it's added to the database table.

Most users prefer to enter information into data-entry forms rather than into Datasheet views of tables. Forms often resemble familiar paper documents and can aid the user with data-entry tasks. Forms make data entry easy to understand by guiding the user through the fields of the table being updated.

Read-only forms are often used for inquiry purposes. These forms display certain fields within a table. Displaying some fields and not others means that you can limit a user's access to sensitive data while allowing access to other fields within the same table.

Reports

Reports present your data in printed format. Access allows for an extraordinary amount of flexibility when creating reports. For instance, you can configure a report to list all records in a given table (such as a Customers table) or you can have the report contain only the records meeting certain criteria (such as all customers living in Arizona). You do this by basing the report on a query that selects only the records needed by the report.

Reports often combine multiple tables to present complex relationships among different sets of data. An example is printing an invoice. The customers table provides the customer's name and address (and other relevant data) and related records in the sales table to print the individual line-item information for each product ordered. The report also calculates the sales totals and prints them in a specific format. Additionally, you can have Access output records into an *invoice report,* a printed document that summarizes the invoice.

TIP

When you design your database tables, keep in mind all the types of information that you want to print. Doing so ensures that the information you require in your various reports is available from within your database tables.

Database objects

To create database objects, such as tables, forms, and reports, you first complete a series of design tasks. The better your design is, the better your application will be. The more you think through your design, the faster and more successfully you can complete any system. The design process is not some necessary evil, nor is its intent to produce voluminous amounts of documentation. The sole intent of designing an object is to produce a clear-cut path to follow as you implement it.

A Five-Step Design Method

The five design steps described in this section provide a solid foundation for creating database applications — including tables, queries, forms, reports, macros, and simple VBA modules.

The time you spend on each step depends entirely on the circumstances of the database you're building. For example, sometimes users give you an example of a report they want printed from their Access database, and the sources of data on the report are so obvious that designing the report takes a few minutes. Other times, particularly when the users' requirements are complex, or the business processes supported by the application require a great deal of research, you may spend many days on Step 1.

As you read through each step of the design process, *always* look at the design in terms of outputs and inputs.

Step 1: The overall design – from concept to reality

All software developers face similar problems, the first of which is determining how to meet the needs of the end-user. It's important to understand the overall user requirements before zeroing in on the details.

For example your users may ask for a database that supports the following tasks:

- Entering and maintaining customer information (name, address, and financial history)
- Entering and maintaining sales information (sales date, payment method, total amount, customer identity, and other fields)
- Entering and maintaining sales line-item information (details of items purchased)
- Viewing information from all the tables (sales, customers, sales line items, and payments)
- Asking all types of questions about the information in the database
- Producing a monthly invoice report
- Producing a customer sales history
- Producing mailing labels and mail-merge reports

When reviewing these eight tasks, you may need to consider other peripheral tasks that weren't mentioned by the user. Before you jump into designing, sit down and learn how the existing process works. To accomplish this, you must do a thorough needs analysis of the existing system and how you might automate it.

Prepare a series of questions that give insight to the client's business and how the client uses his data. For example, when considering automating any type of business, you might ask these questions:

- What reports and forms are currently used?
- How are sales, customers, and other records currently stored?
- How are billings processed?

As you ask these questions and others, the client will probably remember other things about the business that you should know.

A walkthrough of the existing process is also helpful to get a feel for the business. You may have to go back several times to observe the existing process and how the employees work.

As you prepare to complete the remaining steps, keep the client involved — let the users know what you're doing and ask for input on what to accomplish, making sure it's within the scope of the user's needs.

Step 2: Report design

Although it may seem odd to start with reports, in many cases, users are more interested in the printed output from a database than they are in any other aspect of the application. Reports often include every bit of data managed by an application. Because reports tend to be comprehensive, they're often the best way to gather important information about a database's requirements.

When you see the reports that you'll create in this section, you may wonder, "Which comes first — the chicken or the egg?" Does the report layout come first, or do you first determine the data items and text that make up the report? Actually, these items are considered at the same time.

It isn't important how you lay out the data in a report. The more time you take now, however, the easier it will be to construct the report. Some people go so far as to place gridlines on the report to identify exactly where they want each bit of data to be.

Step 3: Data design

The next step in the design phase is to take an inventory of all the information needed by the reports. One of the best methods is to list the data items in each report. As you do so, take careful note of items that are included in more than one report. Make sure that you keep the same name for a data item that is in more than one report because the data item is really the same item.

For example, you can start with all the customer data you'll need for each report, as shown in Table 1.1.

TABLE 1.1 Customer-Related Data Items Found in the Reports

Customers Report	Invoice Report
Customer Name	Customer Name
Street	Street
City	City
State	State
ZIP Code	ZIP Code
Phone Numbers	Phone Numbers
E-Mail Address	
Web Address	
Discount Rate	
Customer Since	
Last Sales Date	
Sales Tax Rate	
Credit Information (four fields)	

As you can see by comparing the type of customer information needed for each report, there are many common fields. Most of the customer data fields are found in both reports. Table 1.1 shows only some of the fields that are used in each report — those related to customer information. Because the related row and field names are the same, you can easily make sure that you have all the data items. Although locating items easily isn't critical for this small database, it becomes very important when you have to deal with large tables containing many fields.

After extracting the customer data, you can move on to the sales data. In this case, you need to analyze only the Invoice report for data items that are specific to the sales. Table 1.2 lists the fields in the report that contain information about sales.

TABLE 1.2 Sales Data Items Found in the Reports

Invoice Report	Line Item Data
Invoice Number	Product Purchased
Sales Date	Quantity Purchased
Invoice Date	Description of Item Purchased

Invoice Report	Line Item Data
Payment Method	Price of Item
Salesperson	Discount for Each Item
Discount (overall for sale)	
Tax Location	
Tax Rate	
Product Purchased (multiple lines)	
Quantity Purchased (multiple lines)	
Description of Item Purchased (multiple lines)	
Price of Item (multiple lines)	
Discount for each item (multiple lines)	
Payment Type (multiple lines)	
Payment Date (multiple lines)	
Payment Amount (multiple lines)	
Credit Card Number (multiple lines)	
Expiration Date (multiple lines)	

As you can see when you examine the type of sales information needed for the report, a few items (fields) are repeating (for example, the Product Purchased, Quantity Purchased, and Price of Item fields). Each invoice can have multiple items, and each of these items needs the same type of information — number ordered and price per item. Many sales have more than one purchased item. Also, each invoice may include partial payments, and it's possible that this payment information will have multiple lines of payment information, so these repeating items can be put into their own grouping.

You can take all the individual items that you found in the sales information group in the preceding section and extract them to their own group for the invoice report. Table 1.2 shows the information related to each line item.

Step 4: Table design

Now for the difficult part: You must determine what fields are needed for the tables that make up the reports. When you examine the multitude of fields and calculations that make up the many documents you have, you begin to see which fields belong to the various tables in the database. (You already did much of the preliminary work by arranging the fields into logical groups.) For now, include every field you extracted. You'll need to add others later (for various reasons), although certain fields won't appear in any table.

It's important to understand that you don't need to add every little bit of data into the database's tables. For example, users may want to add vacation and other out-of-office days to the database to make it easy to know which employees are available on a particular day. However, it's very easy to burden an application's initial design by incorporating too many ideas during the initial development phases. Because Access tables are so easy to modify later on, it's probably best to put aside noncritical items until the initial design is complete. Generally speaking, it's not difficult to accommodate user requests after the database development project is under way.

After you've used each report to display all the data, it's time to consolidate the data by purpose (for example, grouped into logical groups) and then compare the data across those functions. To do this step, first look at the customer information and combine all its different fields to create a single set of data items. Then do the same thing for the sales information and the line-item information. Table 1.3 compares data items from these three groups of information.

TABLE 1.3 Comparing the Data Items

Customer Data	Invoice Data	Line Items
Customer Company Name	Invoice Number	Product Purchased
Street	Sales Date	Quantity Purchased
City	Invoice Date	Description of Item Purchased
State	Payment Method	Price of Item
ZIP Code	Discount (overall for this sale)	Discount for Each Item
Phone Numbers (two fields)	Tax Rate	Taxable?
E-Mail Address	Payment Type (multiple lines)	
Web Address	Payment Date (multiple lines)	
Discount Rate		
Customer Since	Payment Amount (multiple lines)	
Last Sales Date	Credit Card Number (multiple lines)	
Sales Tax Rate	Expiration Date (multiple lines)	
Credit Information (four fields)		

Consolidating and comparing data is a good way to start creating the individual table, but you have much more to do.

As you learn more about how to perform a data design, you also learn that the customer data must be split into two groups. Some of these items are used only once for each customer, while other items may have multiple entries. An example is the Sales column — the payment information can have multiple lines of information.

You need to further break these types of information into their own columns, thus separating all related types of items into their own columns — an example of the *normalization* part of the design process. For example, one customer can have multiple contacts with the company or make multiple payments toward a single sale. Of course, we've already broken the data into three categories: customer data, invoice data, and line items.

Keep in mind that one customer may have multiple invoices, and each invoice may have multiple line items on it. The invoice-data category contains information about individual sales and the line-items category contains information about each invoice. Notice that these three columns are all related; for example, one customer can have multiple invoices, and each invoice may require multiple line items.

The relationships between tables can be different. For example, each sales invoice has one and only one customer, while each customer may have multiple sales. A similar relationship exists between the sales invoice and the line items of the invoice.

Database table relationships require a unique field in both tables involved in a relationship. A unique identifier in each table helps the database engine to properly join and extract related data.

Only the Sales table has a unique identifier (Invoice Number), which means that you need to add at least one field to each of the other tables to serve as the link to other tables. For example, adding a Customer ID field to the Customer table, adding the same field to the Invoice table, and establishing a relationship between the tables through Customer ID in each table. The database engine uses the relationship between customers and invoices to connect customers with their invoices. Relationships between tables is done through key fields.

We cover creating and understanding relationships and the normalization process in Chapter 4.

With an understanding of the need for linking one group of fields to another group, you can add the required key fields to each group. Table 1.4 shows two new groups and link fields created for each group of fields. These linking fields, known as *primary keys* and *foreign keys,* are used to link these tables together.

The field that uniquely identifies each row in a table is the *primary key.* The corresponding field in a related table is the *foreign key.* In our example, Customer ID in the Customers table is a primary key, while Customer ID in the Invoices table is a foreign key.

Let's assume a certain record in the Customers table has 12 in its Customer ID field. Any record in the Invoices table with 12 as its Customer ID is "owned" by customer 12.

TABLE 1.4 Tables with Keys

Customers Data	Invoice Data	Line Items Data	Sales Payment Data
Customer ID	Invoice ID	Invoice ID	Invoice ID
Customer Name	Customer ID	Line Number	Payment Type
Street	Invoice Number	Product Purchased	Payment Date
City	Sales Date	Quantity Purchased	Payment Amount
State	Invoice Date	Description of Item Purchased	Credit Card Number
ZIP Code	Payment Method	Price of Item	Expiration Date
Phone Numbers (two fields)	Salesperson	Discount for Each Item	
E-Mail Address	Tax Rate		
Web Address			
Discount Rate			
Customer Since			
Last Sales Date			
Sales Tax Rate			

With the key fields added to each table, you can now find a field in each table that links it to other tables in the database. For example, Table 1.4 shows Customer ID in both the Customers table (where it's the primary key) and the Invoice table (where it's a foreign key).

You've identified the three core tables for your system, as reflected by the first three columns in Table 1.4. This is the general, or first, cut toward the final table designs. You've also created an additional fact table to hold the sales payment data. Normally, payment details (such as the credit card number) are not part of a sales invoice.

Taking time to properly design your database and the tables contained within it is arguably the most important step in developing a database-oriented application. By designing your database efficiently, you maintain control of the data — eliminating costly data-entry mistakes and limiting your data entry to essential fields.

Although this book is not geared toward teaching database theory and all its nuances, this is a good place to briefly describe the art of database normalization. You'll read the details of normalization in Chapter 4, but in the meantime you should know that *normalization* is the process of breaking data down into constituent tables. Earlier in this chapter you read about how many Access developers add dissimilar information, such as customers, invoice data, and invoice line items, into one large table. A large table containing dissimilar data quickly becomes unwieldy and hard to keep updated. Because a customer's phone number appears in every row containing that customer's data, multiple updates must be made when the phone number changes.

Step 5: Form design

After you've created the data and established table relationships, it's time to design your forms. *Forms* are made up of the fields that can be entered or viewed in Edit mode. Generally speaking, your Access screens should look a lot like the forms used in a manual system.

When you're designing forms, you need to place three types of objects onscreen:

- **Labels and text-box data-entry fields:** The fields on Access forms and reports are called *controls*.
- **Special controls (multiple-line text boxes, option buttons, list boxes, check boxes, business graphs, and pictures).**
- **Graphical objects to enhance the forms (colors, lines, rectangles, and three-dimensional effects).**

Ideally, if the form is being developed from an existing printed form, the Access data-entry form should resemble the printed form. The fields should be in the same relative place on the screen as they are in the printed counterpart.

Labels display messages, titles, or captions. Text boxes provide an area where you can type or display text or numbers that are contained in your database. Check boxes indicate a condition and are either unchecked or checked. Other types of controls available with Access include list boxes, combo boxes, option buttons, toggle buttons, and option groups.

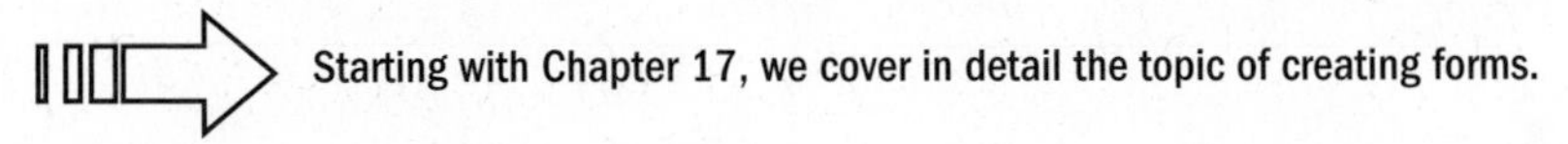

Starting with Chapter 17, we cover in detail the topic of creating forms.

CHAPTER 2

Getting Started with Access

IN THIS CHAPTER

Looking at the Access welcome screen

Creating a database from scratch

Opening a new database

Getting acquainted with the Access interface

In this chapter, you'll gain an understanding of the major components of the user interface. Even if you're an experienced Access user, you may be surprised at how different the Access 2013 interface is from previous versions.

The Access Welcome Screen

If you open Access 2013 via Windows (Start➪Programs➪Access 2013), you'll see the default welcome screen shown in Figure 2.1. The welcome screen gives you several options for opening an existing Access database or creating a new database.

NOTE

If you open an Access database directly from Windows Explorer (by double-clicking it), you won't see the welcome screen. Instead, you'll go directly to the database interface covered later in this chapter.

In the upper-left corner of the welcome screen, you'll notice the Recent section. The files listed here are databases that you've previously opened through Access 2013. You can click any of the database files listed there to open them.

NOTE

Access does not distinguish existing databases from deleted databases when populating the Recent section. This means you could see a database in the Recent list that you know for a fact you've deleted. Clicking an already deleted database in the Recent list will simply activate an error message stating that Access could not find the database.

FIGURE 2.1

The Access welcome screen provides a number of ways to start working with Access.

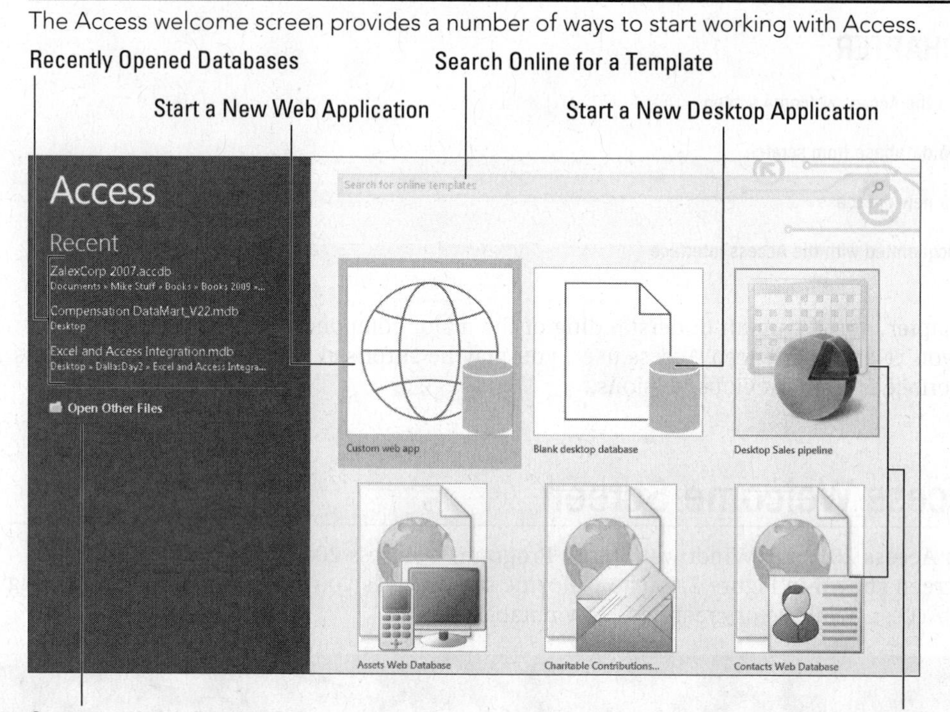

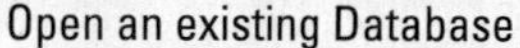

Below the Recent section, you'll see the Open Other Files check box. Click this box to browse for and open databases on your computer or network.

At the top of the welcome screen, you can search for Access database templates online. These templates are typically starter databases that have various purposes. Microsoft makes them available free of charge.

In the center of the welcome screen, you'll see various predefined templates that you can click on to download and use. Microsoft established the online templates repository as a way to provide people with the opportunity to download partially or completely built

Access applications. The template databases cover many common business requirements such as inventory control and sales management. You may want to take a moment to explore the online templates, but they aren't covered in this book.

In the center of the welcome screen, you'll also see two commands: Custom Web App and Blank Desktop Database. These two options allow you to create a database from scratch. If your aim is to create a new Access database that will be used on a PC (either yours or your users'), choose Blank Desktop Database. If you'll eventually be publishing your Access application via SharePoint, choose the Custom Web App database.

We cover custom web apps in Part VIII of this book.

How to Create a Blank Desktop Database

To create a new blank database, you can click Blank Desktop Database option on the welcome screen (refer to Figure 2.1). When you do, the dialog box shown in Figure 2.2 appears, allowing you to specify the name and location of your database.

NOTE

The default location of the new database will be your `Documents` folder. If you want to use a different folder, click the Browse button (it looks like a Windows Explorer folder) to the right of the File Name box to browse to the location you want to use.

FIGURE 2.2

Enter the name of the new database in the File Name box.

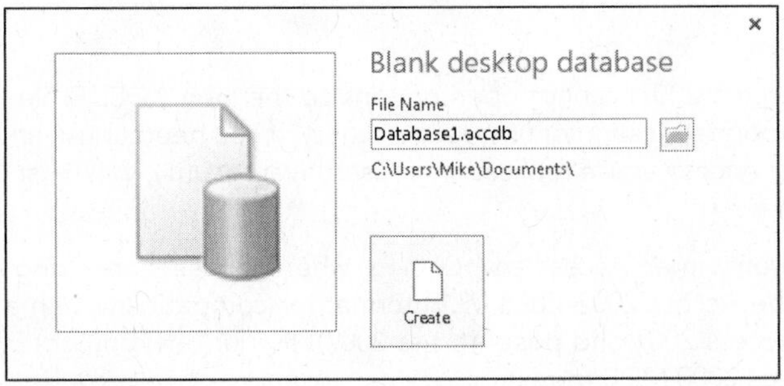

Blank desktop database
File Name
Database1.accdb
C:\Users\Mike\Documents\
Create

When the new database is created, Access automatically opens it for you. In Figure 2.3, notice that Access opens the new database with a blank table already added to the database, ready to be filled in with fields and other design details.

FIGURE 2.3

Your new database is created.

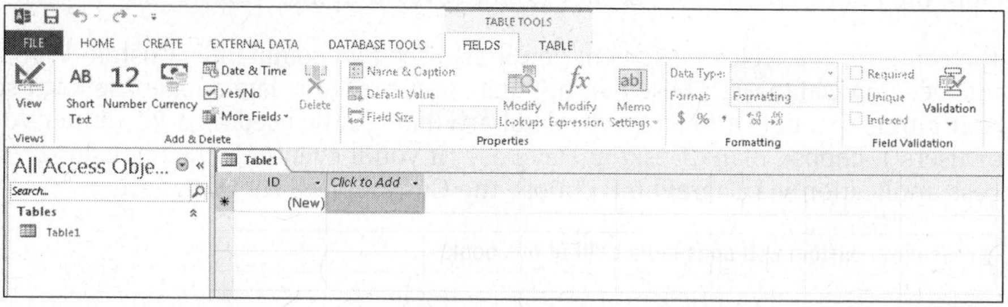

Access File Formats

Since Access 2007, the default file format for Access database files has been ACCDB instead of MDB. It's worth a moment of your time to understand why this changed and how it affects how Access 2013 works with older Access database files.

Since its inception, Access has used a database engine named Jet (an acronym for Joint Engine Technology). With Access 2007, the Access development team wanted to add significant new features to Access, such as multivariable and attachment fields. Because the new features were so significant, they couldn't retrofit Jet with the code necessary to support the new features. As a result, Microsoft developed an entirely new database engine, the Access Connectivity Engine (ACE).

Access 2013 supports several file formats, including the following:

- Access 2007–2013 ACCDB format
- Access 2002–2003 MDB format
- Access 2000 MDB format
- Access 97 MDB format

Earlier versions of Access (before Access 2007) cannot open nor link to the new ACCDB file format. Also, the ACCDB format doesn't support replication or user-level security. If you need to use an Access 2013 database with earlier versions of Access or use replication or user-level security, you must use the MDB format.

The ACCDB format should be used only in an Access environment where all users are using Access 2007 or higher versions. Stick with the Access 2002–2003 MDB format for compatibility with a mixed environment of Access users (pre–Access 2007 and post–Access 2007). If your environment includes Access 2000 users, stay with the Access 2000 MDB format.

In Access 2013, you can open Access 2002–2003 and Access 2000 MDB files and make any desired changes to them, but you'll only be able to use features specific to those versions. Some of the new Access features won't be available, particularly those features that rely on the ACE database engine. You can open and even run Access 97 MDB files, but you can't make any design changes in Access 97 MDB files.

You can convert a database saved in a previous format by opening the database in Access 2013, choosing File➪Save As, and then, in the Save As dialog box, choosing any one of the different Access formats.

The Access 2013 Interface

After you create or open a new database, the Access screen will look similar to Figure 2.4. Across the top of the screen is the Ribbon, which was introduced in Access 2007. On the left, you see the Navigation pane. These two components make up the bulk of the Access interface. In addition, you have at your disposal the Quick Access toolbar, which you can customize with the commands you use most frequently.

FIGURE 2.4

The Access interface starts with the Ribbon at the top and the Navigation pane at the left.

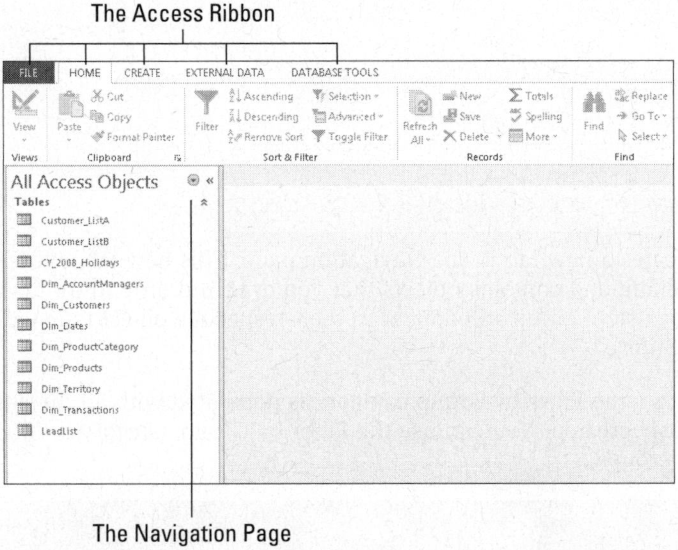

The Access Ribbon

The Navigation Page

The Navigation pane

The Navigation pane, at the left of the screen, is your primary navigation aid when working with Access. The Navigation pane shows queries, forms, reports, and other Access object types. It can also display a combination of different types of objects.

Click the drop-down list in the Navigation pane's title bar to reveal the navigation options (see Figure 2.5).

The navigation options are divided into two categories: Navigate to Category and Filter by Group. First, you choose an option under Navigate to Category, and then you choose an option under Filter by Group. The Filter by Group options you're presented with depend on the Navigate to Category option you select. We cover each of the Navigate to Category options in the following sections, along with the corresponding Filter by Group options.

FIGURE 2.5

Choosing an alternate display for the Navigation pane.

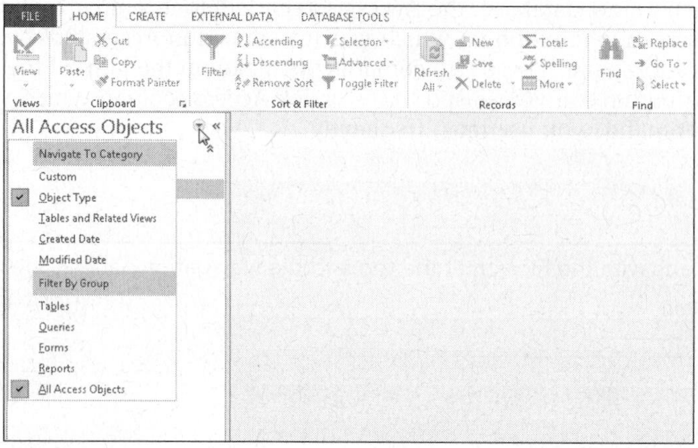

Custom

The Custom option creates a new tab in the Navigation pane. This new tab is titled Custom Group 1 by default and contains objects that you drag and drop into the tab's area. Items added to a custom group still appear in their respective object type view, as described in the next bullet.

When you select Custom, the Filter by Group category is populated with all the custom groups you've previously created. You can use the Filter by Group category to filter to any of the created custom groups.

TIP

Custom groups are a great way to group dissimilar objects (like tables, queries, and forms) that are functionally related. For example, you could create a Customers custom group and add all the database objects related to customer activities. Items contained in a custom group can appear in other groups as well.

Object Type

The Object Type option is most similar to previous versions of Access.

When you select Object Type, you have the following options under Filter by Group:

- Tables
- Queries
- Forms
- Reports
- All Access Objects

By default, the Navigation pane shows all objects in the current database. Select All Access Objects when you've been working with one of the filtered view and want to see every object in the database.

Tables and Related Views

The Tables and Related Views option requires a bit of explanation. Access tries very hard to keep the developer informed of the hidden connections between objects in the database. For example, a particular table may be used in a number of queries or referenced from a form or report. In previous versions of Access, these relationships were very difficult to determine, and no effective tool was built into Access to help you understand these relationships. Selecting Tables and Related Views allows you to understand which objects are affected by each table.

When you select Tables and Related View, the Filter by Group category is populated with the objects in your database. Clicking each object in the Filter by Group category will filter the list to that object and all the other dependent and precedent objects related to it.

Created Date

This option groups the database objects by the created date. This setting is useful when you need to know when an object was created.

When you select Created Date, you have the following options under Filter by Group:

- Today
- Yesterday
- Last Week
- Two Weeks Ago
- Older

Modified Date

This option groups the database objects by the modified date. This setting is useful when you need to know when an object was modified.

When you select Modified Date, you have the following options under Filter by Group:

- Today
- Yesterday
- Last Week
- Two Weeks Ago
- Older

Tabbed Windows

A common complaint among some developers with earlier versions of Access was the fact that when multiple objects were simultaneously opened in the Access environment, the objects would often overlap and obscure each other, making it more difficult to navigate between the objects.

Microsoft has added a tabbed document interface to Access, preventing objects from obscuring other objects that are open at the same time. In the accompanying figure, multiple objects are open (one query and four tables). As you can see, switching between them is very easy — just select a tab associated with an object, and the object is brought to the top.

Query1 | Customer_ListA | Customer_ListB | Dim_AccountManagers | **Dim_Customers**

CustomerID	Customer_Name	Address	City	State	Pc
9933	MALBUS Corp.	2583 Pine Circle	MULBERRY	FL	33
9934	KUYDAS Corp.	3240 Eighth Road	OLDSMAR	FL	34
9935	FRUUMA Corp.	2502 Cedar Avenue	ST PETERSBURG	FL	33
9937	BUNDEA Corp.	2629 Fifth Circle	TAMPA	FL	33
9939	FLATOU Corp.	4064 First Street	LAKELAND	FL	33
9941	SLOGLE Corp.	218 Washington Circle	DUNNELLON	FL	34
9942	DATAPR Corp.	83 Lake Blvd.	TAMPA	FL	33
9943	RUDUNA Corp.	782 Park Circle	TAMPA	FL	33
9946	JUNIAN Corp.	4536 Eighth Blvd.	BROOKVILLE	FL	34
9947	LUUNS Corp.	443 Seventh Circle	TAMPA	FL	33
9948	THEWUT Corp.	180 Washington Road	CLEARWATER	FL	33
9950	WHATLU Corp.	547 Hill Street	TAMPA	FL	33
9957	BLECKD Corp.	2612 Second Road	LECANTO	FL	34

TIP

Don't like the new tabbed windows configuration? You can go back to the old overlapping windows by choosing File ➪ Options. In the Access Options dialog box, select the Current Database tab, and change the Document Window Options from Tabbed Documents to Overlapping Windows. You'll have to close and reopen your database to have the change take effect.

The Ribbon

The Ribbon occupies the top portion of the main Access screen. Starting with Access 2007, the Ribbon replaced the menus and toolbars seen in previous versions of Access.

The Ribbon is divided into five tabs, each tab containing any number of controls and commands (refer to Figure 2.5):

- **File:** Confusingly, Microsoft refers to the File tab as the "File button." Regardless of what you call it, when you click it, the Office Backstage view opens. Backstage view contains a number of options for creating databases, opening databases, saving databases, and configuring databases. We delve deeper into the Office Backstage view in the nearby sidebar.

- **Home:** The theme of the Home tab is "frequently used." Here, you find generally unrelated commands that are repeatedly called upon during the course of working with Access. For example, there are commands for formatting, copying and pasting, sorting, and filtering.
- **Create:** The Create tab contains commands that create the various objects in Access. This tab is where you'll spend most of your time. Here, you can initiate the creation of tables, queries, forms, reports, and macros. As you read this book, you'll be using the Create tab all the time.
- **External Data:** The External Data tab is dedicated to integrating Access with other sources of data. On this tab, you find commands that allow you to import and export data, establish connections to outside databases, and work with SharePoint or other platforms.
- **Database Tools:** The Database Tools tab contains the commands that deal with the inner workings of your database. Here, you find tools to create relationships between tables, analyze the performance of your database, document your database, and compact and repair your database.

In addition to the standard five tabs on the Access Ribbon, you'll also see contextual tabs. *Contextual tabs* are special types of tabs that appear only when a particular object is selected. For example, when you're working with the query builder, you'll see the Query Tools Design tab shown in Figure 2.6.

FIGURE 2.6

Contextual tabs contain commands that are specific to whichever object is active.

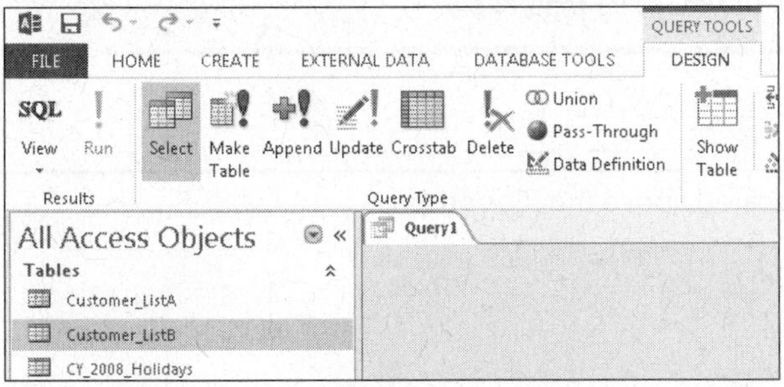

The Quick Access toolbar

The Quick Access toolbar (shown in Figure 2.7) is a customizable toolbar that allows you to add commands that are most important to your daily operations. By default, the Quick Access toolbar contains three commands: Save, Undo, and Redo.

Office Backstage View

Office Backstage view (shown in the accompanying figure) is the gateway to a number of options for creating, opening, or configuring Access databases. You get to Backstage view by clicking the File button on the Ribbon (see the preceding section).

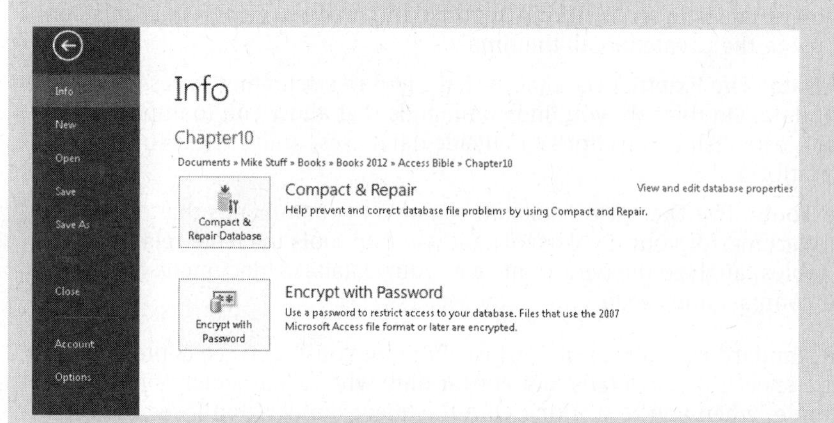

Backstage view is shared by all the Office 2013 applications, and it features similar options in Access, Word, Excel, and Microsoft Outlook. The Backstage options include activities that are used infrequently when you're working within the main Access window, but that are necessary for saving, printing, or maintaining Access databases. Putting these options into the Backstage area means they don't have to appear anywhere on the Ribbon as you're working with Access.

We cover the Backstage commands in the chapters that follow.

FIGURE 2.7

The Quick Access toolbar is located above the Ribbon.

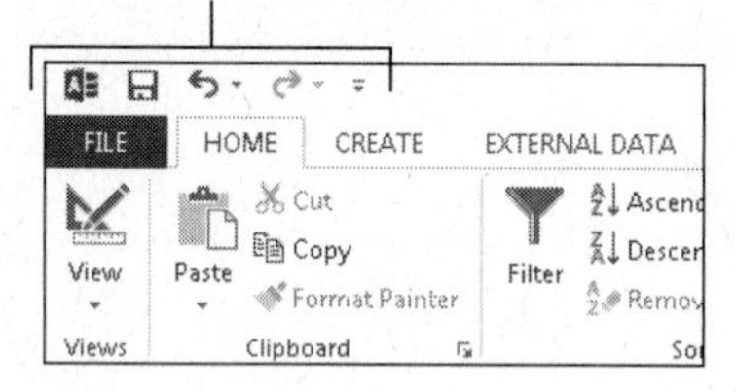

If you click the drop-down arrow next to the Quick Access toolbar, you'll see that many more commands are available (see Figure 2.8). Place a check mark next to any of these options to add it to the Quick Access toolbar.

FIGURE 2.8

Commands you can add to the Quick Access toolbar.

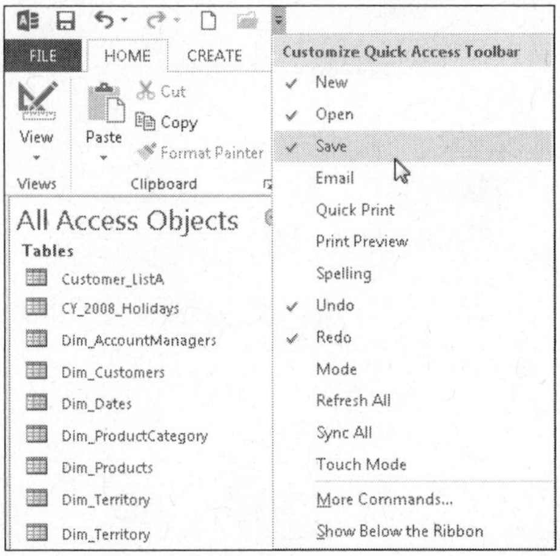

You're not limited to the commands shown in this drop-down list. You can add all kinds of commands. To add a command to the Quick Access toolbar, follow these steps:

1. **Click the drop-down arrow next to the Quick Access toolbar, and select the More Commands option.** The Quick Access tab of the Access Options dialog box (shown in Figure 2.9) appears.
2. **In the Choose Commands From drop-down list on the left, select All Commands.**
3. **From the alphabetical list of commands, select the one you're interested in and click the Add button.**
4. **When you're done, press OK.**

FIGURE 2.9

Adding more commands to the Quick Access toolbar.

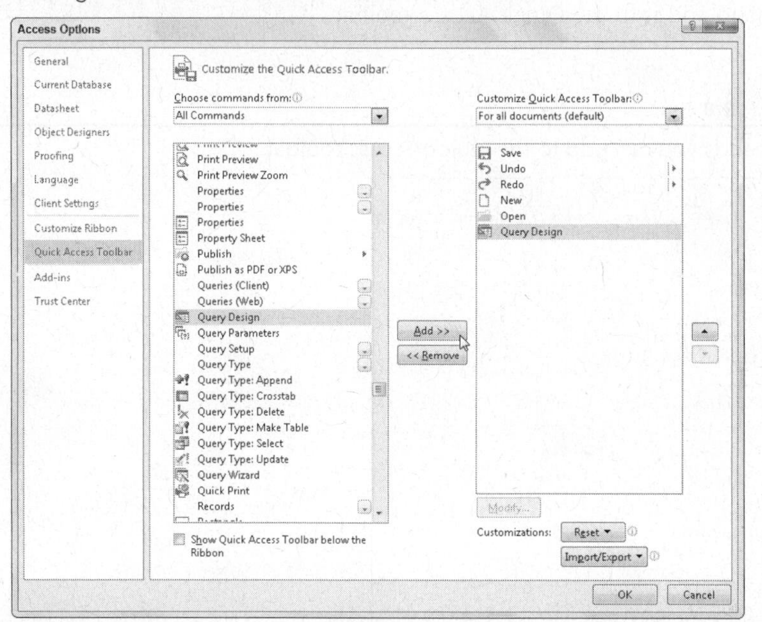

TIP

To change the order of the icons on the Quick Access toolbar, select the Quick Access tab of the Access Options dialog box (refer to Figure 2.9). The list on the right shows all the commands that are currently in the Quick Access toolbar. You can click each command and click the up and down arrow buttons on the right to move the command up or down in the list. This will change the order of the commands.

Part II

Understanding Access Tables

The topics covered in this part explain the techniques for creating and managing Access database tables, the core of any application you build in Access.

These chapters go well beyond simply describing how to build tables. Here, you learn fundamental concepts that are key to utilizing the capabilities documented in the remaining parts of this book.

Chapter 3 lays the foundation by defining tables and their component parts. In Chapter 4, you learn the importance of table relationships and how to effectively build and manage the relationships between the tables in your database. Chapter 5 demonstrates the techniques to effectively sort, filter, and work with your raw tables and datasheets. Finally, Chapters 6 and 7 explain how you can reach outside your database and create tables from imported or linked external data sources.

IN THIS PART

Creating Access Tables

IN THIS CHAPTER

Creating a new table

Modifying the design of a table

Working with field properties

Specifying the primary key

Adding indexes

Documenting a table's design

Saving a new table

Working with tables

Adding data to a table

Using attachment fields

In this chapter, you learn how to create a new Access database and its tables. You establish the database container to hold your tables, forms, queries, reports, and code that you build as you learn Access. Finally, you create the actual tables used by the Collectible Mini Cars database.

ON THE WEB

This chapter uses the examples in the database named `Chapter03.accdb`. If you haven't yet downloaded this file from the book's website, please do so now.

Table Types

To Access, a table is always just a table. But to your Access application, different tables serve different purposes. A database table fits into one of three types: object, transaction, or join. Knowing what type of table you're creating helps to determine how you create it.

Object tables

Object tables are the most common. Each record of this type of table holds information that relates to a real-world object. A customer is a real-world object and a record in a table named tblCustomers holds information about that customer. The fields in an object table reflect the characteristics of the object they represent. A City field that says Detroit maps to the actual city where the customer is. When creating an object table, think about the characteristics of that object that make it unique or that are important.

Transaction tables

The next most common type of table is a transaction table. Each record of a transaction table holds information about an event. Placing an order for a book is an example of an event. To hold the details of all the orders, you might have a table named tblBookOrders. Transaction tables almost always have a Date/Time field because when the event happened is usually an important piece of information to record. Another common type of field is a field that refers to an object table, such as a reference to the customer in tblCustomers that placed the order. When creating a transaction table, think about the information created by the event and who was involved.

Join tables

Join tables are the easiest to create and are vitally important to a well-designed database. Usually relating two tables is a simple process: A customer orders a book, for instance, and you can easily relate that order to that customer. But sometimes the relationship isn't so clear. A book may have many authors. And an author may have many books. When this relationship exists, called a many-to-many relationship, a join table sits in the middle of the two tables. A join table usually has a name that reflects the association, such as tblAuthorBook. A join table generally has only three fields: a unique field to identify each record, a reference to one side of the association, and a reference to the other side of an association.

Creating a New Table

Creating database tables is as much art as it is science. Acquiring a good working knowledge of the user's requirements is a fundamental step for any new database project.

Chapter 4 covers the details of applying database design rules to the creation of Access tables.

In this chapter, I show you the steps required to create basic Access tables. In the following sections, you'll study the process of adding tables to an Access database, including the relatively complex subject of choosing the proper data type to assign to each field in a table.

It's always a good idea to plan tables on paper first, before you use the Access tools to add tables to the database. Many tables, especially small ones, really don't require a lot of forethought before adding them to the database. After all, not much planning is required to design a table holding lookup information, such as the names of cities and states. However, more complex entities, such as customers and products, usually require considerable thought and effort to implement properly.

Although you can create the table interactively without any forethought, carefully planning a database system is a good idea. You can make changes later, but doing so wastes time; generally, the result is a system that's harder to maintain than one that you've planned well from the beginning.

In the following sections, I explore the new, blank table added to the `Chapter03.accdb` database. It's important to understand the steps required to add new tables to an Access database. Because the steps required to add tables have changed so dramatically from earlier versions of Access, even experienced Access developers will want to read the following sections.

The Importance of Naming Conventions

Most Access developers eventually adopt a naming convention to help identify database objects. Most naming conventions are relatively simple and involve nothing more than adding a prefix indicating an object's type to the object's name. For example, an employees form might be named frmEmployees.

As your databases grow in size and complexity, the need to establish a naming convention for the objects in your databases increases. Even with the Name AutoCorrect option turned on (click the File button and choose Options ➪ Current Database ➪ Name AutoCorrect), Access only corrects the most obvious name changes. Changing the name of a table breaks virtually every query, form, and report that uses the information from that table. Your best defense is to adopt reasonable object names, use a naming convention early on as you begin building Access databases, and stick with the naming convention throughout the project.

Access imposes very few restrictions on the names assigned to database objects. Therefore, it's entirely possible to have two distinctly different objects (for example, a form and a report, or a table and a macro) with the same name. (You can't, however, have a table and a query with the same name, because tables and queries occupy the same namespace in the database.)

Although simple names like Contacts and Orders are adequate, as a database grows in size and complexity, you might be confused about which object a particular name refers to. For example, later in this book, you'll read about manipulating database objects through code and macros. When working with Visual Basic for Applications (VBA), the programming language built into Access, there must be no ambiguity or confusion between referenced objects. Having both a form and a report named Contacts might be confusing to you *and* your code.

continued

continued

The simplest naming convention is to prefix object names with a three- or four-character string indicating the type of object carrying the name. Using this convention, tables are prefixed with tbl and queries with qry. The generally accepted prefixes for forms, reports, macros, and modules are frm, rpt, mcr, and bas or mod, respectively.

In this book, most compound object names appear in *camel case*: tblBookOrders, tblCustomers, and so on. Most people find camel-case names easier to read and remember than names that appear in all-uppercase or all-lowercase characters (such as TBLBOOKORDERS or tblbookorders).

Also, at times, we use informal references for database objects. For example, the formal name of the table containing contact information in the previous examples is tblContacts. An informal reference to this table might be "the Contacts table."

In most cases, your users never see the formal names of database objects. One of your challenges as an application developer is to provide a seamless user interface that hides all data-management and data-storage entities that support the user interface. You can easily control the text that appears in the title bars and surfaces of the forms, reports, and other user-interface components to hide the actual names of the data structures and interface constituents.

Access allows table names up to 64 characters. Take advantage of this to give your tables, queries, forms, and reports descriptive, informative names. There is no reason why you should confine a table name to BkOrd when tblBookOrders is handled just as easily and is much easier to understand.

Descriptive names can be carried to an extreme, of course. There's no point in naming a form frmUpdateContactInformation if frmUpdateInfo does just as well. Long names are more easily misspelled or misread than shorter names, so use your best judgment when assigning names.

Although Access lets you use spaces in database object names, you should avoid spaces at all costs. Spaces don't add to readability and can cause major headaches, particularly when upsizing to client/server environments or using OLE automation with other applications. Even if you don't anticipate extending your Access applications to client/server or incorporating OLE or DDE automation into your applications, get into the habit of not using spaces in object names.

Finally, you can use some special characters, like an underscore, in your table names. Some developers use an underscore to separate words in a table name as part of a larger naming convention. Unless you use a specific convention that includes special characters, you should avoid them.

Designing tables

Designing a table is a multistep process. By following the steps in order, your table design can be created readily and with minimal effort:

1. **Create the new table.**
2. **Enter field names, data types, properties, and (optionally) descriptions.**

3. **Set the table's primary key.**
4. **Create indexes for appropriate fields.**
5. **Save the table's design.**

Generally speaking, some tables are never really finished. As users' needs change or the business rules governing the application change, you might find it necessary to open an existing table in Design view. This book, like most books on Access, describes the process of creating tables as if every table you ever work on is brand new. The truth is, however, that most of the work that you do on an Access application is performed on existing objects in the database. Some of those objects you've added yourself, while other objects may have been added by another developer at some time in the past. However, the process of maintaining an existing database component is exactly the same as creating the same object from scratch.

TIP

Just a quick note about modifying tables once they're built: Adding a *new* field to a table almost never causes problems. Existing queries, forms, reports, and even VBA code will continue using the table as before. These objects won't reference the new field because the field was added *after* their creation. The new field will not be automatically added to existing objects, but you can add the new field where needed in your application, and everything works as expected.

The trouble comes when you remove or rename a field in a table. Even with AutoCorrect turned on, Access won't update field name references in VBA code, in control properties, and in expressions throughout the database. Changing an existing field (or any other database object, for that matter) is always a bad idea. You should always strive to provide your tables, fields, and other database objects with good, strong, descriptive names when you add them to the database, instead of planning to go back later and fix them.

TIP

Many Access developers routinely turn off AutoCorrect. (Use the File tab to access the Backstage, select Options, and then select Current Database. In the Name AutoCorrect Options, make sure Track Name AutoCorrect Info is unchecked.) The AutoCorrect feature negatively affects performance because it constantly watches for name changes in an application and takes corrective action when needed. Furthermore, because AutoCorrect never quite corrects all the names in an application, there is always more work to perform when you change the name of a database object.

Begin by selecting the Create tab on the ribbon at the top of the Access screen. The Create tab (shown in Figure 3.1) contains all the tools necessary to create not only tables, but also forms, reports, and other database objects.

ON THE WEB

The following examples use the `Chapter03.accdb` database found on this book's website.

FIGURE 3.1

The Create tab contains tools necessary for adding new objects to your Access database.

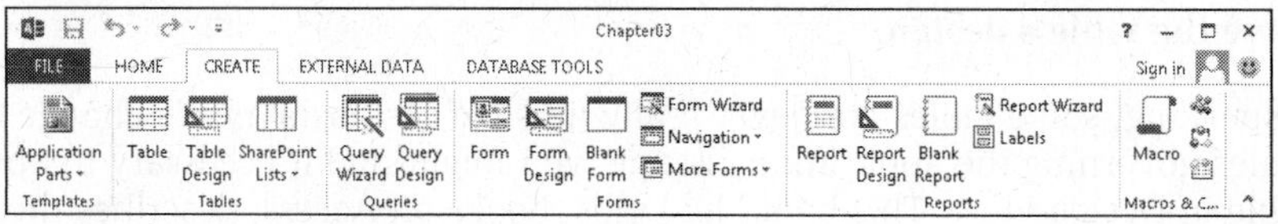

There are two main ways to add new tables to an Access database, both of which are invoked from the Tables group on the Create tab:

- **Clicking the Table button:** Adds a table in Datasheet view to the database with one AutoNumber field named ID.
- **Clicking the Table Design button:** Adds a table in Design view to the database.

For this example, I'll be using the Table Design button, but first, let's take a look at the Table button.

Clicking the Table button adds a new table to the Access environment. The new table appears in Datasheet view in the area to the right of the Navigation Pane. The new table is shown in Figure 3.2. Notice that the new table appears in Datasheet view, with an ID column already inserted and a Click to Add column to the right of the ID field.

FIGURE 3.2

The new table in Datasheet view.

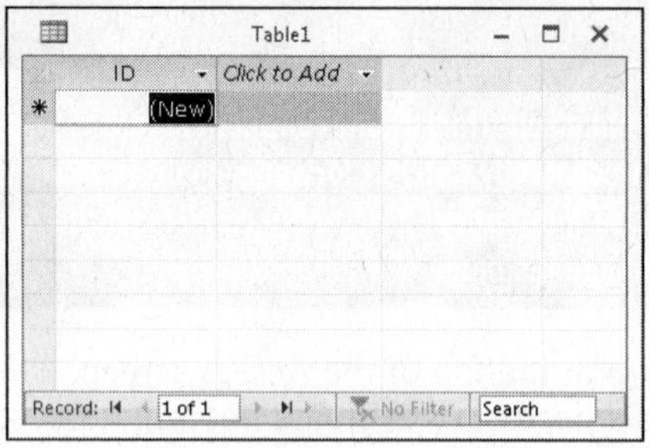

The Click to Add column is intended to permit users to quickly add fields to a table. All you have to do is begin entering data in the new column. You assign the field a name by right-clicking the field's heading, selecting Rename Field, and entering a name for the field. In other words, building an Access table can be very much like creating a spreadsheet in Excel.

NOTE

In previous versions of Access, this approach was usually referred to as "creating a table in Datasheet view."

Once you've added the new column, the tools on the Fields tab of the Ribbon (shown in Figure 3.3) allow you to set the specific data type for the field, along with its formatting, validation rules, and other properties.

FIGURE 3.3

Field design tools are located on the Fields tab of the Ribbon.

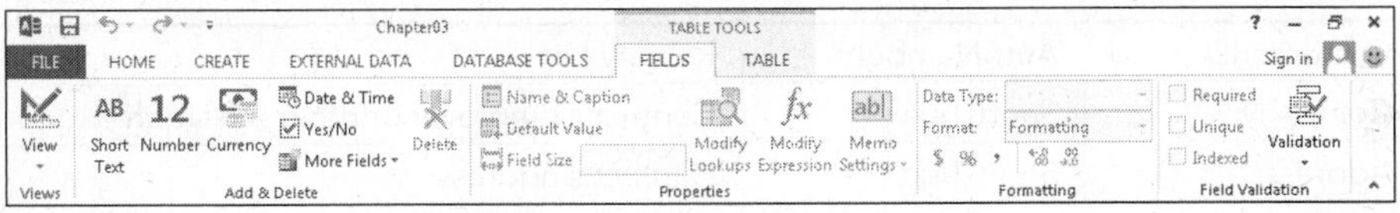

The second method of adding new tables is to click the Table Design button in the Tables group on the Create tab. Access opens a new table in Design view, allowing you to add fields to the table's design. Figure 3.4 shows a new table's design after a few fields have been added. Table Design view provides a somewhat more deliberate approach to building Access tables.

FIGURE 3.4

A new table added in Design view.

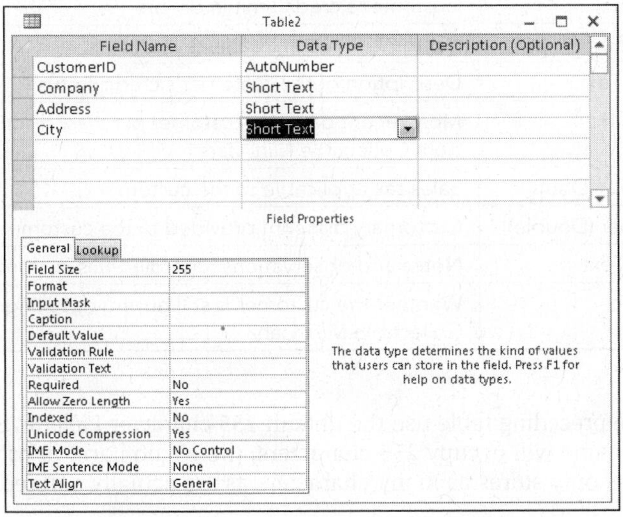

The Table Designer is quite easy to understand, and each column is clearly labeled. At the far left is the Field Name column, where you input the names of fields you add to the table. You assign a data type to each field in the table and (optionally) provide a description for the field.

For this exercise, you create the Customers table for the Collectible Mini Cars application. The basic design of this table is outlined in Table 3.1. I cover the details of this table's design in the "Creating tblCustomers" section, later in this chapter.

TABLE 3.1 The Collectible Mini Cars Customers Table

Field Name	Data Type	Description
CustomerID	AutoNumber	Primary key
Company	Short Text	Contact's employer or other affiliation
Address	Short Text	Contact's address
City	Short Text	Contact's city
State	Short Text	Contact's state
ZipCode	Short Text	Contact's zip code
Phone	Short Text	Contact's phone
Fax	Short Text	Contact's fax
Email	Short Text	Contact's e-mail address
WebSite	Short Text	Contact's web address
OrigCustDate	DateTime	Date the contact first purchased something from Collectible Mini Cars
CreditLimit	Currency	Customer's credit limit in dollars
CurrentBalance	Currency	Customer's current balance in dollars
CreditStatus	Short Text	Description of the customer's credit status
LastSalesDate	DateTime	Most recent date the customer purchased something from Collectible Mini Cars
TaxRate	Number (Double)	Sales tax applicable to the customer
DiscountPercent	Number (Double)	Customary discount provided to the customer
Notes	Long Text	Notes and observations regarding this customer
Active	Yes/No	Whether the customer is still buying or selling to Collectible Mini Cars

The Short Text fields in the preceding table use the default 255 character Field Size. While it's unlikely that anyone's name will occupy 255 characters, there's no harm in providing for very long names. Access only stores as many characters as are actually entered into a text field. So, allocating 255 characters doesn't actually *use* 255 characters for every name in the database.

Looking once again at Figure 3.4, you see that the Table Design window consists of two areas:

- **The field entry area:** Use the field entry area, at the top of the window, to enter each field's name and data type. You can also enter an optional description.
- **The field properties area:** The area at the bottom of the window is where the field's properties are specified. These properties include field size, format, input mask, and default value, among others. The actual properties displayed in the properties area depend upon the data type of the field. You learn much more about these properties in the "Assigning field properties" section, later in this chapter.

TIP

You can switch between the upper and lower areas of the Table Designer by clicking the mouse when the pointer is in the desired pane or by pressing F6. The F6 key cycles through all open panes, such as the Navigation pane and the Property search, so you may have to press it multiple times to get where you're going.

Using the Design tab

The Design tab of the Access Ribbon (shown in Figure 3.5) contains many controls that assist in creating a new table definition.

FIGURE 3.5

The Design tab of the Ribbon.

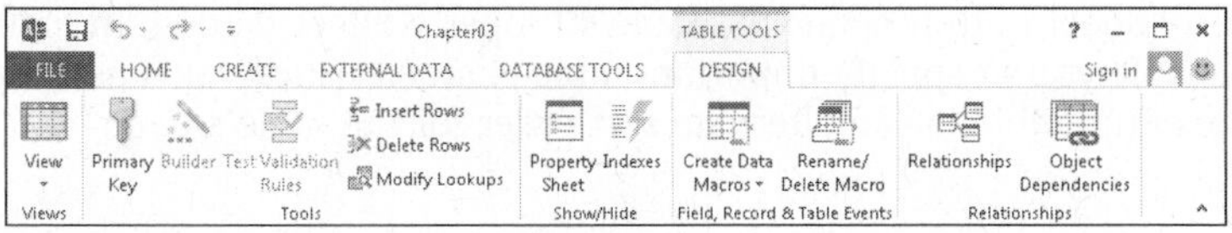

The controls on the Design tab affect the important table design considerations. Only a few of the controls shown in Figure 3.5 are described in the following sections. You'll learn much more about the other buttons in the "Creating tblCustomers" section, later in this chapter, and in subsequent chapters of this book.

Primary Key

Click this button to designate which of the fields in the table you want to use as the table's primary key. Traditionally, the primary key appears at the top of the list of fields in the table, but it could appear anywhere within the table's design.

TIP
To move a field, simply left-click the selector to the left of the field's name to highlight the field in the Table Designer, and drag the field to its new position.

Insert Rows

Although it makes very little difference to the database engine, many developers are fussy about the sequence of fields in a table. Many of the wizards in Access display the fields in the same order as the table. Keeping an address field above a city field, for example, can make development easier.

Composite keys, consisting of multiple fields combined as a single key, are discussed in detail in Chapter 4.

Clicking the Insert Rows button inserts a blank row just *above* the position occupied by the mouse cursor. For example, if the cursor is currently in the second row of the Table Designer, clicking the Insert Row button inserts an empty row in the second position, moving the existing second row to the third position.

Delete Rows

Clicking the Delete Rows button removes a row from the table's design.

CAUTION
Access doesn't ask you to confirm the deletion before actually removing the row.

Property Sheet

Clicking the Property Sheet button opens the table's Property Sheet (shown in Figure 3.6). These properties enable you to specify important table characteristics, such as a validation rule to apply to the entire table, or an alternate sort order for the table's data.

Indexes

Indexes are discussed in much more detail in the "Indexing Access Tables" section, later in this chapter. Clicking the Indexes button opens the Indexes dialog box, which enables you to specify the details of indexes on the fields in your table.

Working with fields

You create fields by entering a field name and a field data type in the upper entry area of the Table Design window. The (optional) Description property indicates the field's purpose. The description appears in the status bar at the bottom of the screen during data entry and may be useful to people working with the application. After entering each field's name and data type, you can further specify how each field is used by entering properties in the property area.

FIGURE 3.6

The Property Sheet.

Property Sheet

Selection type: Table Properties

General

Subdatasheet Expanded	No
Subdatasheet Height	0"
Orientation	Left-to-Right
Description	
Default View	Datasheet
Validation Rule	
Validation Text	
Filter	
Order By	
Subdatasheet Name	[Auto]
Link Child Fields	
Link Master Fields	
Filter On Load	No
Order By On Load	Yes
Order By On	0

Naming a field

A field name should be descriptive enough to identify the field to you as the developer, to the user of the system, and to Access. Field names should be long enough to quickly identify the purpose of the field, but not overly long. (Later, as you enter validation rules or use the field name in a calculation, you'll want to save yourself from typing long field names.)

To enter a field name, position the pointer in the first row of the Table Design window under the Field Name column. Then type a valid field name, observing these rules:

- Field names can be from 1 to 64 characters in length.
- Field names can include letters, numbers, and many special characters.
- Field names can include spaces. Spaces should be avoided in field names for some of the same reasons you avoid them in table names.
- Field names can't include a period (.), exclamation point (!), brackets ([ ]), or accent grave (`).
- You can't use low-order ASCII characters — for example Ctrl + J or Ctrl + L (ASCII values 0 through 31).
- You can't start with a blank space.
- You can't use a double quotation mark ("") in the name of a Microsoft Access project file.

You can enter field names in uppercase, lowercase, or mixed case. If you make a mistake while typing the field name, position the cursor where you want to make a correction and type the change. You can change a field name at any time, even if the table contains data.

NOTE

Access is not case sensitive, so the database itself doesn't care whether you name a table tblCustomers or TblCustomers. Choosing uppercase, lowercase, or mixed case characters is entirely your decision and should be aimed at making your table names descriptive and easy to read.

CAUTION

After your table is saved, if you change a field name that is also used in queries, forms, or reports, you have to change it in those objects as well. One of the leading causes of errors in Access applications stems from changing the names of fundamental database objects such as tables and fields, but neglecting to make all the changes required throughout the database. Overlooking a field name reference in the control source of a control on the form or report, or deeply embedded in VBA code somewhere in the application, is far too easy.

Specifying a data type

When you enter a field, you must also decide what type of data each of your fields will hold. In Access, you can choose any of several data types (these data types are detailed in the "Assigning field data types" section, later in this chapter). The available data types are shown in Table 3.2.

TABLE 3.2 Data Types Available in Microsoft Access

Data Type	Type of Data Stored	Storage Size
Short Text	Alphanumeric characters	255 characters or less
Long Text	Alphanumeric characters	1GB of characters or less
Number	Numeric values	1, 2, 4, or 8 bytes; 16 bytes for Replication ID (GUID)
Date/Time	Date and time data	8 bytes
Currency	Monetary data	8 bytes
AutoNumber	Automatic number increments	4 bytes; 16 bytes for Replication ID (GUID)
Yes/No	Logical values: Yes/No, True/False	1 bit (0 or –1)
OLE Object	Pictures, graphs, sound, video	Up to 1GB (disk space limitation)
Hyperlink	Link to an Internet resource	1GB of characters or less
Attachment	A special field that enables you to attach external files to an Access database	Varies by attachment
Lookup Wizard	Displays data from another table	Generally 4 bytes

Figure 3.7 shows the Data Type drop-down list used to select the data type for the field you just created.

FIGURE 3.7

The Data Type drop-down list.

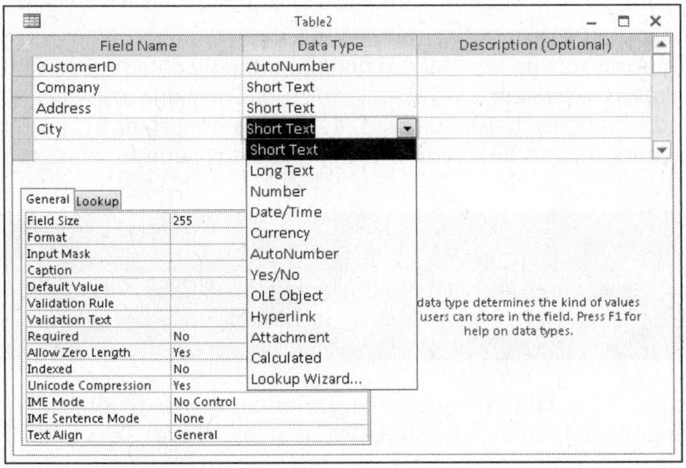

One of these data types must be assigned to each of your fields. Some of the data types have addition options, such as Field Size for Short Text fields and Number fields.

Here are the basic questions to consider when choosing the data type for new fields in your tables:

- **What is the data type?** The data type should reflect the data stored in the field. For example, you should select one of the numeric data types to store numbers like quantities and prices. Don't store data like phone numbers or Social Security numbers in numeric fields, however; your application won't be performing numeric operations like addition or multiplication on phone numbers. Instead, use text fields for common data, such as Social Security numbers and phone numbers.

NOTE

Numeric fields never store leading zeros. Putting a zip code such as 02173 into a numeric field means only the last four digits (2173) are actually stored.

- **What are the storage requirements of the data type you've selected?** Although you can use the Long Integer data type in place of Integer or Byte, the storage requirements of Long Integer (4 bytes) is twice that of Integer. This means that twice as much memory is required to use and manipulate the number and twice as much disk space is required to store its value. Whenever possible, use Byte or Integer data types for simple numeric data.

- **Will you want to sort or index the field?** Because of their binary nature, Long Text and OLE Object fields can't be sorted or indexed. Use Long Text fields sparingly. The overhead required to store and work with Long Text fields is considerable.
- **What is the impact of the data type on sorting requirements?** Numeric data sorts differently from sorting text data. Using the numeric data type, a sequence of numbers will sort as expected: 1, 2, 3, 4, 5, 10, 100. The same sequence stored as text data will sort like this: 1, 10, 100, 2, 3, 4, 5. If it's important to sort text data in a numeric sequence, you'll have to first apply a conversion function to the data before sorting.

TIP

If it's important to have text data representing numbers to sort in the proper order, you might want to prefix the numerals with zeros (001, 002, and so on). Then the text values will sort in the expected order: 001, 002, 003, 004, 005, 010, 100.

- **Is the data text or date data?** When working with dates, you're almost always better off storing the data in a Date/Time field than as a Short Text field. Text values sort differently from dates (dates are stored internally as numeric values), which can upset reports and other output that rely on chronological order.

  Don't be tempted to store dates in one Date/Time field and time in another Date/Time field. The Date/Time field is specifically designed to handle both dates and times, and, as you'll see throughout this book, it's quite easy to display only the date or time portion of a Date/Time value.

  A Date/Time field is also meant to store a discrete date and time, and not a time interval. If keeping track of durations is important, you could use two Date/Time fields — one to record the start and the other at the end of a duration — or one Long Integer field to store the number of elapsed second, minutes, hours, and so forth.
- **What reports will be needed?** You won't be able to sort or group memo or OLE data on a report. If it's important to prepare a report based on memo or OLE data, add a Tag field like a date or sequence number, which can be used to provide a sorting key, to the table.

Short Text data type

The Short Text data type holds information that is simply characters (letters, numbers, punctuation). Names, addresses, and descriptions are all text data, as are numeric data that are not used in a calculation (such as telephone numbers, Social Security numbers, and zip codes).

Although you specify the size of each Short Text field in the property area, you can enter no more than 255 characters of data in any Short Text field. Access uses variable length fields to store text data. If you designate a field to be 25 characters wide and you use only 5 characters for each record, then only enough room to store 5 characters is used in your database.

You'll find that the ACCDB database file might quickly grow quite large, but text fields are not the usual cause. However, it's good practice to limit Short Text field widths to the maximum you believe is likely for the field. Names can be quite tricky because fairly long names are common in some cultures. However, it's a safe bet that a postal code will be less than 12 characters, while a U.S. state abbreviation is always 2 characters. By limiting a Short Text field's width, you also limit the number of characters users can enter when the field is used in a form.

Long Text data type

The Long Text data type holds a variable amount of data up to 1GB. Long Text fields use only as much memory as necessary for the data stored. So, if one record uses 100 characters, another requires only 10, and yet another needs 3,000, you use only as much space as each record requires.

You don't specify a field size for the Long Text data type. Access allocates as much space as necessary for the data.

New Feature

In versions prior to Access 2013, the Short Text data type was called simply Text and the Long Text data type was called Memo. If you're working in previous versions, you'll need to refer to the old data type names. The properties and limitations of those data types did not change; only the name has.

Number data type

The Number data type enables you to enter *numeric* data — that is, numbers that will be used in mathematical calculations or represent scalar quantities such as inventory counts. (If you have data that will be used in monetary calculations, you should use the Currency data type, which performs calculations without rounding errors.)

The exact type of numeric data stored in a number field is determined by the Field Size property. Table 3.3 lists the various numeric data types, their maximum and minimum ranges, the decimal points supported by each numeric data type, and the storage (bytes) required by each numeric data type.

TABLE 3.3 Numeric Field Settings

Field Size Setting	Range	Decimal Places	Storage Size
Byte	0 to 255	None	1 byte
Integer	–32,768 to 32,767	None	2 bytes
Long Integer	–2,147,483,648 to 2,147,483,647	None	4 bytes
Double	–1.797 × 10308 to 1.797 × 10308	15	8 bytes
Single	–3.4 × 1038 to 3.4 × 1038	7	4 bytes
Replication ID	N/A	N/A	16 bytes
Decimal	1–28 precision	15	8 bytes

CAUTION

Many errors are caused by choosing the wrong numeric type for number fields. For example, notice that the maximum value for the Integer data type is 32,767. We once saw a database that ran perfectly for several years and then started crashing with overflow errors. It turned out that the overflow was caused by a particular field being set to the Integer data type, and when the company occasionally processed very large orders, the 32,767 maximum was exceeded.

Be aware that overflow may occur simply by adding two numbers together or by performing any mathematical operation that results in a value too large to be stored in a field. Some of the most difficult bugs occur only when circumstances (such as adding or multiplying two numbers) cause an overflow condition at runtime.

Design your tables very conservatively, and allow for larger values than you ever expect to see in your database. This is not to say that using the Double data type for all numeric fields is a good idea. The Double data type is very large (8 bytes) and might be somewhat slow when used in calculations or other numeric operations. Instead, the Single data type is probably best for most floating-point calculations, and Long Integer is a good choice where decimal points are irrelevant.

Date/Time data type

The Date/Time data type is a specialized number field for holding dates or times (or dates *and* times). When dates are stored in a Date/Time field, it's easy to calculate days between dates and other calendar operations. Date data stored in Date/Time fields sort and filter properly as well. The Date/Time data type holds dates from January 1, 100, to December 31, 9999.

Currency

The Currency data type is another specialized number field. Currency numbers are not rounded during calculations and preserve 15 digits of precision to the left of the decimal point and 4 digits to the right. Because Currency fields use a fixed decimal point position, they're faster in numeric calculations than doubles.

AutoNumber

The AutoNumber field is another specialized Number data type. When an AutoNumber field is added to a table, Access automatically assigns a long integer (32-bit) value to the field (beginning at 1) and increments the value each time a record is added to the table. Alternatively (determined by the New Values property), the value of the AutoNumber field is a random integer that is automatically inserted into new records.

Only one AutoNumber field can appear in a table. Once assigned to a record, the value of an AutoNumber field can't be changed programmatically or by the user. AutoNumber fields are stored as a Long Integer data type and occupy 4 bytes. The range of possible values for AutoNumber fields is from 1 to 4,294,967,296 — more than adequate as the primary key for most tables.

NOTE

An AutoNumber field is not guaranteed to generate a continuous, unbroken set of sequential numbers. For example, if the process of adding a new record is interrupted (such as the user pressing the Esc key while entering the new record's data) an AutoNumber field will "skip" a number. AutoNumber fields should not be used to provide a stream of sequential numbers. Instead, sequential numbers can be easily added to a table through a data macro (data macros are explained in Chapter 22) or VBA code.

TIP

When you create a relationship between two tables and one of the fields in that relationship is an AutoNumber field, the other field should be made a Long Integer data type to prevent overflow errors. Creating relationships between tables is explained in Chapter 4.

Yes/No

Yes/No fields accept only one of two possible values. Internally stored as 1 (Yes) or 0 (No), the Yes/No field is used to indicate yes/no, on/off, or true/false. A Yes/No field occupies a single bit of storage.

OLE Object

The OLE Object field stores OLE data, highly specialized binary objects such as Word documents, Excel spreadsheets, sound or video clips, and images. The OLE object is created by an application that Windows recognizes as an OLE server and can be linked to the parent application or embedded in the Access table. OLE objects can only be displayed in bound object frames in Access forms and reports. OLE fields can't be indexed.

Attachment

The Attachment data type was introduced in Access 2007. In fact, the Attachment data type is one of the reasons Microsoft changed the format of the Access data file. The older MDB format is unable to accommodate attachments.

The Attachment data type is relatively complex, compared to the other types of Access fields, and it requires a special type of control when displayed on Access forms. For details on this interesting type of field, turn to "Understanding Attachment Fields," later in this chapter.

Hyperlink data type

The Hyperlink data type field holds combinations of text and numbers stored as text and used as a hyperlink address. It can have up to three parts:

- The text that appears in a control (usually formatted to look like a clickable link).
- The Internet address — the path to a file or web page.
- Any sub-address within the file or page. An example of a sub-address is a picture on a web page. Each part of the hyperlink's address is separated by the pound sign (#).

Access hyperlinks can even point to forms and reports in other Access databases. This means that you can use a hyperlink to open a form or report in an external Access database and display the form or report on the user's computer.

Lookup Wizard

The Lookup Wizard data type inserts a field that enables the end-user to choose a value from another table or from the results of a SQL statement. The values may also be presented as a combo box or list box. At design time, the Lookup Wizard leads the developer through the process of defining the lookup characteristics when this data is assigned to a field.

As you drag an item from the Lookup Wizard field list, a combo box or list box is automatically created on the form. The list box or combo box also appears on a query data sheet that contains the field.

Entering a field description

The field description is completely optional; you use it only to help you remember a field's uses or to let another developer understand the field's purpose. Often, you don't use the Description column at all, or you use it only for fields whose purpose is not obvious. If you enter a field description, it appears in the status bar whenever you use that field in Access — in the datasheet or in a form. The field description can help clarify a field whose purpose is ambiguous or give the user a more complete explanation of the appropriate values for the field during data entry.

Specifying data validation rules

The last major design decision concerns data validation, which becomes important as users enter data. You want to make sure that only good data (data that passes certain defined tests) gets into your system. You have to deal with several types of data validation. You can test for known individual items, stipulating that the Gender field can accept only the values Male, Female, or Unknown, for example. Or you can test for ranges, specifying that the value of Weight must be between 0 and 1,500 pounds. You'll read more about validation rules in the "Validation Rule and Validation Text" section, later in this chapter.

Creating tblCustomers

Working with the different data types, you should be ready to create the final working copy of tblCustomers.

Using AutoNumber fields

Access gives special considerations to AutoNumber fields. You can't change a previously defined field from another type to AutoNumber if any data has been added to the table. If you try to change an existing field to an AutoNumber, you'll see an error that says

```
Once you enter data in a table, you can't change the data type of
   any field to AutoNumber, even if you haven't yet added data to
   that field.
```

You'll have to add a new AutoNumber field and begin working with it instead of changing an existing field to AutoNumber.

NOTE
Only one AutoNumber field can be added to an Access table. Generally speaking, it's better to use AutoNumber fields where their special characteristics are needed by an application.

Completing tblCustomers

With tblCustomers in Design view, you're ready to finalize its design. Table 3.1, shown earlier in this chapter, lists the field definitions for tblCustomers. Enter the field names and data types as shown in Table 3.1. The next few pages explain how to change existing fields (which includes rearranging the field order, changing a field name, and deleting a field).

Here are the steps for adding fields to a table structure:

1. **Place the cursor in the Field Name column in the row where you want the field to appear.**
2. **Enter the field name and press Enter or Tab to move to the Data Type column.**
3. **Select the field's data type from the drop-down list in the Data Type column.**
4. **If desired, add a description for the field in the Description column.**

Repeat each of these steps to create each of the data entry fields for tblCustomers. You can press the down arrow (↓) key to move between rows, or use the mouse and click on any row. Pressing F6 switches the focus from the top to the bottom of the Table Design window, and vice versa.

Changing a Table Design

Even the best planned table will require changes from time to time. You might find that you want to add another field, remove a field, change a field name or data type, or simply rearrange the order of the field names.

Although a table's design can be changed at any time, special considerations must be given to tables containing data. Be careful of making changes that damage data in the table, such as making text fields smaller or changing the Field Size property of Number fields. You can always add new fields to a table without problems, but changing existing fields might be an issue. And, with very few exceptions, it's almost always a bad idea to change a field's name after a table has been put into use in an application.

Inserting a new field

To insert a new field, in the Table Design window, place your cursor on an existing field, right-click on a field in the table's design surface, and select Insert ⇨ Rows, or just click the Insert Rows button in the Ribbon. A new row is added to the table, and existing fields are pushed down. You can then enter a new field definition. Inserting a field doesn't disturb other fields or existing data. If you have queries, forms, or reports that use the table, you might need to add the field to those objects as well.

Deleting a field

There are three ways to delete a field. While the table is in Design view:

- Select the field by clicking the row selector and then press Delete.
- Right-click the selected field and choose Delete Rows from the shortcut menu.
- Select the field and click the Delete Rows button from the Tools group on the Design tab of the Ribbon.

When you delete a field containing data, you'll see a warning that you'll lose data in the table for the selected field. If the table contains data, make sure that you want to eliminate the data for that field (column). You'll also have to delete the same field from queries, forms, reports, macros, and VBA code that use the field name.

TIP

When you delete a field, you can immediately click the Undo button and return the field to the table. But you must undo changes before you save the table's definition or make any other changes to the table's design.

TIP

If you try to delete a field that's part of a relationship (a primary or secondary key field), Access informs you that you can't delete the field until you remove the relationship in the Relationships window.

Table relationships and the Relationships window are discussed in Chapter 4.

If you delete a field, you must also fix up all references to that field throughout Access. Because you can use a field name in forms, queries, reports, and even table data validation, you must examine your system carefully to find any instances in which you might have used the specific field name.

Changing a field location

The order of your fields, as entered in the table's Design view, determines the left-to-right column sequence in the table's Datasheet view. If you decide that your fields should be rearranged, click on a field selector and use the mouse to drag the field to its new location.

Changing a field name

You change a field's name by selecting the field's name in the Table Design window and entering a new name; Access updates the table design automatically. As long as you're creating a new table, this process is easy.

Changing a field size

Making a field size larger is simple in a table design. However, only text and number fields can be increased in size. You simply increase the Field Size property for text fields or specify a different field size for number fields. You must pay attention to the decimal-point property in number fields to make sure that you don't select a new size that supports fewer decimal places than you currently have.

CAUTION

When you want to make a field size smaller, make sure that none of the data in the table is larger than the new field width. Choosing a smaller field size may result in data loss.

TIP

Remember that each text field uses only the number of characters actually entered in the field. You should still try to make your fields only as large as the largest value so that Access can stop someone from entering a value that might not fit on a form or report.

Handling data conversion issues

If, in spite of your best efforts, it becomes necessary to change the data type of a field containing data, you might suffer data loss as the data-type conversion occurs. You should be aware of the effects of a data-type conversion on existing data:

- **Any data type to AutoNumber:** Can't be done. The AutoNumber field type must be created fresh in a new field.
- **Short Text to Number, Currency, Date/Time, or Yes/No:** In most cases, the conversion will be made without damaging the data. Inappropriate values are automatically deleted. For instance, a Text field containing "January 28, 2012" will be faithfully converted to a Date/Time field. If, however, you change a field containing "January 28, 2012" to a Yes/No data type, its value will be deleted.
- **Long Text to Short Text:** A straightforward conversion with no loss or corruption of data. Any text longer than the field size specified for the Short Text field is truncated and lost.
- **Number to Short Text:** No loss of information. The number value is converted to text using the General Number format.
- **Number to Currency:** Because the Currency data type uses a fixed decimal point, some precision may be lost as the number is truncated.
- **Date/Time to Short Text:** No loss of information. Date and time data are converted to text with the General Date format.
- **Currency to Short Text:** No loss of information. The currency value is converted to text without the currency symbol.
- **Currency to Number:** Simple, straightforward conversion. Some data may be lost as the currency value is converted to fit the new number field. For example, when converting Currency to Long Integer, the decimal portion is truncated (cut off).
- **AutoNumber to Short Text:** Conversion occurs without loss of data, except in a case where the width of the text field is inadequate to hold the entire AutoNumber value. In this case, the number is truncated.
- **AutoNumber to Number:** Simple, straightforward conversion. Some data may be lost as the AutoNumber value is converted to fit the new number field. For example, an AutoNumber larger than 32,767 will be truncated if it is converted to an Integer field.
- **Yes/No to Short Text:** Simple conversion of Yes/No value to text. No loss of information.

Note

The OLE Object data type can't be converted to any other type of data.

Assigning field properties

The field properties built into Access tables are powerful allies that can help you manage the data in your tables. In most cases, the field property is enforced by the database engine, which means the property is consistently applied wherever the field's value is used. For example, if you've set the Default Value property in the table design, the default value is available in the table's Datasheet view, on forms, and in queries.

In fact, field properties are among the many differences between Access tables and Excel worksheets. Understanding field properties is just one of several skills necessary to begin using Access tables to store data, rather than Excel worksheets.

Each field data type has its own set of properties. For example, Number fields have a Decimal Places property, and Text fields have a Text Align property. Although many data types share a number of properties (such as Name) in common, there are enough different field properties to make it easy to become confused or to incorrectly use the properties. The following sections discuss some of the more important and frequently used field properties.

NOTE

The following sections include many references to properties, and property settings in the Access Table Designer. The formal name for a property (such as DefaultValue) never contains a space, while the property's expression in the Table Designer usually contains a space for readability (Default Value). These relative minor differences become important when referencing properties in expressions, VBA code, and macros. When making a formal reference to a property in code or a macro, always use the "spaceless" version of the property's name, not the property reference you see in the Access user interface.

Common properties

Here's a list of all the general properties (note that they may not all be displayed, depending on which data type you chose):

- **Field Size:** When applied to Short Text fields, limits the size of the field to the specified number of characters (1–255). The default is 255.
- **New Values:** Applies to AutoNumber fields. Allows specification of Increment or Random type.
- **Format:** Changes the way data appears after you enter it (uppercase, dates, and so on). There are many different types of formats that may be applied to Access data. Many of these differences are explained in the "Format" section, later in this chapter.
- **Input Mask:** Used for data entry into a predefined format (phone numbers, zip codes, Social Security numbers, dates, customer IDs). Applicable to both Number and Text data types.

- **Decimal Places:** Specifies the number of decimal places for the Currency and the Single, Double, and Decimal Number data types.
- **Caption:** Optional label for form and report fields. Access uses the Caption property instead of the field name when creating a control on a form or report.
- **Default Value:** The value automatically provided for new data entry into the field. This value can be any value appropriate for the field's data type. A default is no more than an initial value; you can change it during data entry. To specify a default value, simply enter the desired value into the DefaultValue property setting. A default value can be an expression, as well as a number or a text string.

NOTE

Because the Default Value for Number and Currency data types is set to 0 by default, these fields are set automatically to 0 when you add a new record. In many situations, such as medical test results and many financial applications, 0 is not an appropriate default value for numeric fields. Be sure to verify that 0 is an appropriate default value in your Access applications.

- **Validation Rule:** Ensures that data entered into the field conforms to some business rule, such as "greater than zero," "date must occur after January 1, 2000," and so on.
- **Validation Text:** The message displayed when data fails validation.
- **Required:** Specifies whether you must enter a value into a field.
- **Allow Zero Length:** Determines whether you may enter an empty string ("") into a text field to distinguish it from a null value.
- **Indexed:** Speeds up data access and (if desired) limits data to unique values. Indexing is explained in greater detail later in this chapter.
- **Unicode Compression:** Used for multilanguage applications. Requires about twice the data storage but enables Office documents, including Access reports, to be displayed correctly no matter what language or symbols are used. Generally speaking, Unicode is of no value unless the application is likely to be used in Asian environments.
- **IME Mode:** Also known as the Kanji conversion mode property, this is used to show whether the Kanji mode is maintained when the control is lost. The setting has no relevance in English or European-language applications.
- **IME Sentence Mode:** Used to determine the Sequence mode of fields of a table or controls of a form that switch when the focus moves in or out of the field. The setting has no relevance in English or European-language applications.

Format

The Format property specifies how the data contained in table fields appears whenever the data is displayed or printed. When set at the table level, the format is in effect throughout the application. There are different format options for each data type.

Access provides built-in format option for most field data types. The exact format used to display field values is influenced by the Region and Language settings in the Control Panel.

The Format property affects only the way a value is displayed and not the value itself or how the value is stored in the database.

If you elect to build a custom format, construct a string in the field's Format property box. There are a number of different symbols you use for each data type. Access provides global format specifications to use in any custom format:

- **(space):** Display spaces as characters.
- ***"SomeText"*:** Display the text between the quotes as literal text.
- **! (exclamation point):** Left-aligns the display.
- *** (asterisk):** Fills empty space with the next character.
- **\ (backslash):** Displays the next character as literal text. Use the backslash to display characters that otherwise have special meaning to Access.
- **[color]:** Displays the output in the color (black, blue, green, cyan, red, magenta, yellow, or white) indicated between the brackets.

The Format property takes precedence when both a format and an input mask have been defined.

Number and Currency field formats

There is a wide variety of valid formats for Number and Currency fields. You can use one of the built-in formats or construct a custom format of your own:

- **General Number:** The number is displayed in the format in which it was entered. (This is the default format for numeric data fields.)
- **Currency:** Add a thousands separator (usually a comma), add a decimal point with two digits to the right of the decimal, and enclose negative numbers in parentheses. A Currency field value is shown with the currency symbol (such as a dollar sign or euro sign) specified by the Region and Language settings in the Control Panel.
- **Fixed:** Always display at least one digit to the left and two digits to the right of the decimal point.
- **Standard:** Use the thousands separator with two digits to the right of the decimal point.
- **Percent:** The number value is multiplied by 100 and a percent sign is added to the right. Percent values are displayed with two decimal places to the right of the decimal point.
- **Scientific:** Scientific notation is used to display the number.
- **Euro:** Prefixes the euro currency symbol to the number.

The built-in numeric formats are summarized in Table 3.4.

TABLE 3.4 Numeric Format Examples

Format Type	Number as Entered	Number as Displayed	Format Defined
General	987654.321	987654.3	######.#
Currency	987654.321	$987,654.32	$###,##0.00
Euro	987654.321	€987,654.32	€###,##0.00
Fixed	987654.321	987654.32	######.##
Standard	987654.321	987,654.32	###,###.##
Percent	.987	98.7%	###.##%
Scientific	987654.321	9.88E+05	###E+00

All the previous formats are the default formats based on setting the Decimal Places property to AUTO. The exact format applied also depends on the Region and Language settings in the Control Panel.

Custom numeric formats

Custom formats are created by combining a number of symbols to create a format. The symbols used with Number and Currency fields are listed here:

- **. (period):** Specifies where the decimal point should appear.
- **, (comma):** The thousands separator.
- **0 (zero):** A placeholder for 0 or a digit.
- **# (pound sign):** A placeholder for nothing or a digit.
- **b (dollar sign):** Displays the dollar sign character.
- **% (percent sign):** Multiplies the value by 100 and adds a percent sign.
- **E– or e–:** Uses scientific notation to display the number. Uses a minus sign to indicate a negative exponent and no sign for positive exponents.
- **E+ or e+:** Uses scientific notation to display the number. Uses a plus sign to indicate positive exponent.

You create custom formats by composing a string made up of one to four sections separated by semicolons. Each section has a different meaning to Access:

- **First section:** The format for positive values
- **Second section:** The format for negative values
- **Third section:** The format for zero values
- **Fourth section:** The format for null values

Each section is a combination of a numeric formatting string and an optional color specification. Here's an example of a custom format:

```
0,000.00[Green];(0,000.00)[Red];"Zero";"—"
```

This format specifies showing the number with zeros in all positions (even if the number is less than 1,000), using the comma thousands separator, enclosing negative numbers in parentheses, using `"Zero"` to indicate zero values, and using a dash for null values.

Built-in Date/Time formats

The following are the built-in Date/Time formats (these examples are based on the "English (United States)" Region and Language settings in the Control Panel.):

- **General Date:** If the value contains a date only, don't display a time value, and vice versa. Dates are displayed in the built-in Short Date format (mm/dd/yy), while time data is displayed in the Long Time format.
- **Long Date:** Sunday, May 13, 2012.
- **Medium Date:** 13-May-12.
- **Short Date:** 5/13/12.
- **Long Time:** 9:21:17 AM.
- **Medium Time:** 09:21 AM.
- **Short Time:** 09:21.

Date and time formats are influenced by the Region and Language settings in the Control Panel.

Custom Date/Time formats

Custom formats are created by constructing a specification string containing the following symbols:

- **: (colon):** Separates time elements (hours, minutes, seconds)
- **/ (forward slash):** Separates date elements (days, months, years)
- **c:** Instructs Access to use the built-in General Date format
- **d:** Displays the day of the month as one or two digits (1–31)
- **dd:** Displays the day of the month using two digits (01–31)
- **ddd:** Displays the day of the week as a three-character abbreviation (Sun, Mon, Tue, Wed, Thu, Fri, Sat)
- **dddd:** Uses the full name of the day of the week (Sunday, Monday, Tuesday, Wednesday, Thursday, Friday, Saturday)
- **ddddd:** Uses the built-in Short Date format
- **dddddd:** Uses the built-in Long Date format

3

- **w:** Uses a number to indicate the day of the week
- **ww:** Shows the week of the year
- **m:** Displays the month of the year using one or two digits
- **mm:** Displays the month of the year using two digits (with leading zero if necessary)
- **mmm:** Displays the month as a three-character abbreviation (Jan, Feb, Mar, Apr, May, Jun, Jul, Aug, Sep, Oct, Nov, Dec)
- **mmmm:** Displays the full name of the month (for example, January)
- **q:** Displays the date as the quarter of the year
- **y:** Displays the day of the year (1 through 366)
- **yy:** Displays the year as two digits (for example, 12)
- **yyyy:** Displays the year as four digits (2012)
- **h:** Displays the hour using one or two digits (0–23)
- **hh:** Displays the hour using two digits (00–23)
- **n:** Displays the minutes using one or two digits (0–59)
- **nn:** Displays the minutes using two digits (00–59)
- **s:** Displays the seconds using one or two digits (0–59)
- **ss:** Displays the seconds using two digits (00–59)
- **tttt:** Uses the built-in Long Time format
- **AM/PM:** Uses a 12-hour format with uppercase AM or PM
- **am/pm:** Uses a 12-hour format with lowercase am or pm
- **A/P:** Uses a 12-hour format with uppercase A or P
- **a/p:** Uses a 12-hour format with lowercase a or p
- **AMPM:** 12-hour format using the morning or after designator specified in the Region and Language settings in the Control Panel

Short Text and Long Text field formats

When applied to Short Text fields, formats help clarify the data contained within the fields. tblCustomers uses several formats. The State text field has a > in the Format property to display the data entry in uppercase. The Active field has a Yes/No format with lookup Display Control property set to Text Box.

Short Text and Long Text fields are displayed as plain text by default. If a particular format is to be applied to Short Text or Long Text field data, use the following symbols to construct the format:

- **@:** A character or space is required.
- **&:** A character is optional (not required).

- <: Force all characters to their lowercase equivalents.
- >: Force all characters to their uppercase equivalents.

The custom format may contain as many as three different sections, separated by semicolons:

- **First section:** Format for fields containing text
- **Second section:** Format for fields containing zero-length strings
- **Third section:** Format for fields containing null values

If only two sections are given, the second section applies to both zero-length strings and null values. For example, the following format displays `None` when no string data is contained in the field and `Unknown` when a null value exists in the field. Otherwise, the simple text contained in the field is displayed:

```
@;"None";"Unknown"
```

Several examples of custom text formats using the "English (United States)" Regional Settings are presented in Table 3.5.

TABLE 3.5 Format Examples

Format Specified	Data as Entered	Formatted Data as Displayed
>	Adam Smith	ADAM SMITH
<	Adam Smith	adam smith
-	Adam	Ad-am
&-	Ad	-Ad
@;"Empty"	""	Empty
@;"Empty"	Null	Empty

Yes/No field formats

A Yes/No field displays `Yes`, `No`, `True`, `False`, `On`, or `Off`, depending on the value stored in the field and the setting of the Format property for the field. Access predefines these rather obvious format specifications for the Yes/No field type:

- **Yes/No:** Displays `Yes` or `No`
- **True/False:** Displays `True` or `False`
- **On/Off:** Displays `On` or `Off`

Yes, True, and On all indicate the same "positive" value, while No, False, and Off indicate the opposite ("negative") value.

Access stores Yes/No data in a manner different from what you might expect. The Yes data is stored as –1, whereas No data is stored as 0. You'd expect it to be stored as 0 for No and 1 for Yes, but this isn't the case. Without a format setting, Access will display `-1` or `0`, and it will be stored and displayed that way.

Regardless of the format set, you can enter data into a Yes/No field using any of the words in the built-in formats or as numbers. To enter No, you can enter **False**, **No**, **Off**, or **0**. To enter Yes, you can enter **True**, **Yes**, **On**, or any number other than zero. If you enter a number other than 0 or –1, Access converts it to –1.

You're also able to specify a custom format for Yes/No fields. For example, assume you've got a table with a field that indicates whether the employee has attended an orientation meeting. Although a yes or no answer is appropriate, you might want to get a little fancy with the field's display. By default, a check box is used to indicate the value of the Yes/No field (checked means Yes). To customize the appearance of the Yes/No field, set its Format property according to the following pattern:

```
;"Text for Yes values";"Text for No values"
```

Notice the placeholder semicolon at the front of this string. Also, notice that each text element must be surrounded by quotes. In the case of the employee table, you might use the following Format property specifier:

```
;"Attendance OK";"Must attend orientation"
```

You must also set the Yes/No field's Display Control property to Text Box in order to change the default check box display to text.

Hyperlink field format

Access also displays and stores hyperlink data in a manner different from what you would expect. The format of this type is comprised of up to three parts, separated by pound signs (#):

- **Display Text:** The text that is displayed as a hyperlink in the field or control
- **Address:** The path to a file (UNC) or page (URL) on the Internet
- **Sub-Address:** A specific location within a file or page

The Display Text property is the text that is visible in the field or control, while the address and sub-address are hidden. In the following example, "Microsoft MSN Home Page" is the displayed text, while `http://www.msn.com` is the hyperlink's address.

```
Microsoft MSN Home Page#http://www.msn.com
```

Input Mask

The Input Mask property makes it easier for users to enter the data in the correct format. An input mask limits the way the user inputs data into the application. For example, you can restrict entry to only digits for phone numbers, Social Security numbers, and employee IDs. An input mask for a Social Security number might look like "000-00-0000." This mask requires input into every space, restricts entry to digits only, and does not permit characters or spaces.

A field's input mask is applied anywhere the field appears (query, form, report).

The Input Mask property value is a string containing as many as three semicolon-separated sections:

- **First section:** Contains the mask itself, comprised of the symbols shown later.
- **Second section:** Tells Access whether to store the literal characters included in the mask along with the rest of the data. For example, the mask might include dashes to separate the parts of the Social Security number, while a phone number might include parentheses and dashes. Using a zero tells Access to store the literal characters as part of the data while 1 tells Access to store only the data itself.
- **Third section:** Defines the "placeholder" character that tells the user how many characters are expected in the input area. Many input masks use pound signs (#) or asterisks (*) as placeholders.

The following characters are used to compose the input mask string:

- **0:** A digit is required, and plus (+) and minus (–) signs are not permitted.
- **9:** A digit is optional, and plus (+) and minus (–) signs are not permitted.
- **#:** Optional digit or space. Spaces are removed when the data is saved in the table. Plus and minus signs are allowed.
- **L:** A letter from A to Z is required.
- **?:** A letter from A to Z is optional.
- **A:** A character or digit is required.
- **a:** A character or digit is optional.
- **&:** Permits any character or space (required).
- **C:** Permits any character or space (optional).
- **. (period):** Decimal placeholder.
- **, (comma):** Thousands separator.
- **: (colon):** Date and time separator.
- **; (semicolon):** Separator character.

- - **(dash):** Separator character.
- / **(forward slash):** Separator character.
- < **(less-than sign):** Converts all characters to lowercase.
- > **(greater-than sign):** Converts all characters to uppercase.
- ! **(exclamation point):** Displays the input mask from right to left. Characters fill the mask from right to left.
- \ **(back slash):** Displays the next character as a literal.

The same masking characters are used on a field's Property Sheet in a query or form.

An input mask is ignored when importing data or adding data to a table with an action query.

An input mask is overridden by the Format property assigned to a field. In this case, the input mask is in effect only as data is entered and reformatted according to the Format when the entry is complete.

The Input Mask Wizard

Although you can manually enter an input mask, you can easily create an input mask for Text or Date/Time type fields with the Input Mask Wizard. When you click the Input Mask property, a Builder button (three periods) appears in the property's input box. Click the Builder button to start the wizard. Figure 3.8 shows the first screen of the Input Mask Wizard.

FIGURE 3.8

The Input Mask Wizard for creating input masks for Text and Date field types.

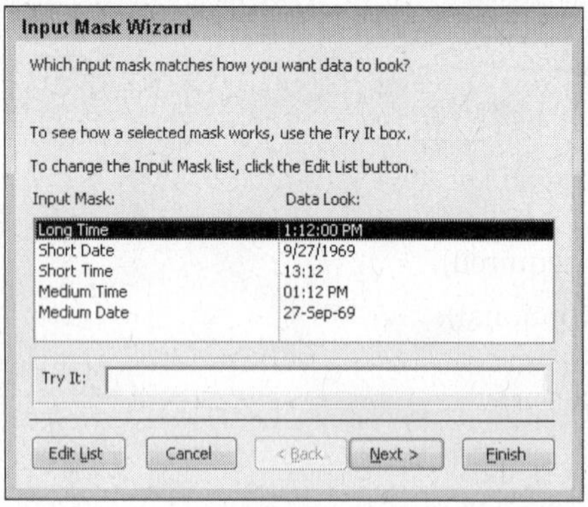

The Input Mask Wizard shows not only the name of each predefined input mask, but also an example for each name. You can choose from the list of predefined masks. Click in the Try It text box and enter a test value to see how data entry will look. After you choose an input mask, the next wizard screen enables you to refine the mask and specify the placeholder symbol (perhaps a # or @). Another wizard screen enables you to decide whether to store special characters (such as the dashes in a Social Security number) with the data. When you complete the wizard, Access adds the input mask characters in the field's Property Sheet.

TIP

You can create your own Input Mask properties for Text and Date/Time fields by simply clicking the Edit List button in the Input Mask Wizard, and entering a descriptive name, input mask, placeholder character, and sample data content. Once created, the new mask will be available the next time you use the Input Mask Wizard.

Enter as many custom masks as you need. You can also determine the international settings so that you can work with multiple country masks. A custom input mask you create in one database is available in other databases.

Caption

The Caption property determines what appears in the default label attached to a control created by dragging the field from the field list onto a form or report. The caption also appears as the column heading in Datasheet view for tables or queries that include the field.

CAUTION

Be careful using the Caption property. Because the caption text appears as the column heading in Datasheet view, you might be misled by a column heading in a query's Datasheet view. When the field appears in a query, you don't have immediate access to the field's properties, so you must be aware that the column heading is actually determined by the Caption property and may not reflect the field's name. To be even more confusing, the caption assigned in the table's Design view and the caption assigned in a field's Property Sheet in the Query Design view are different properties and can contain different text.

Captions can be as long as 2,048 characters, more than adequate for all but the most verbose descriptions.

Validation Rule and Validation Text

The Validation Rule property establishes requirements for input into the field. Enforced by the ACE database engine, the Validation Rule ensures that data entered into the table conforms to the requirements of the application.

Validation properties are a great way to enforce business rules, such as ensuring that a product is not sold for zero dollars, or requiring that an employee review date comes after her hire date. And, like other field properties, validation rules are enforced wherever the field is used in the application.

The value of the Validation Rule property is a string containing an expression that is used to test the user's input. The expression used as a field's Validation Rule property can't contain user-defined functions or any of the Access domain or aggregate functions (`DCount`, `DSum`, and so on). A field's Validation Rule property can't reference forms, queries, or other tables in the application. (These restrictions don't apply to validation rules applied to controls on a form, however.) Field validation rules can't reference other fields in the table, although a rule applied to a record in a table can reference fields in the same table (a record-level validation rule is set in the table's Property Sheet, rather than in an individual field).

The Validation Text property contains a string that is displayed in a message box when the user's input doesn't satisfy the requirements of the Validation Rule property. The maximum length of the Validation Text property value is 255 characters.

When using the Validation Rule property, you should always specify a Validation Text value to avoid triggering the generic message box Access displays when the rule is violated. Use the Validation Text property to provide users with a helpful message that explains acceptable values for the field. Figure 3.9 shows the message box displayed when the value specified by the Validation Rule attached to the CreditLimit field is exceeded.

FIGURE 3.9

A data-validation warning box. This appears when the user enters a value in the field that does not match the rule specified in the design of the table.

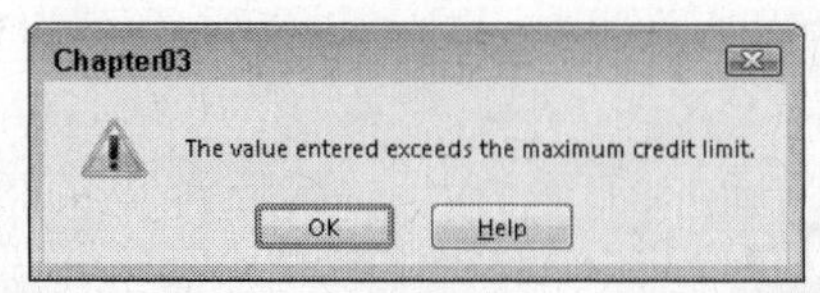

The Validation Rule property doesn't apply to check boxes, option buttons, or toggle buttons within an option group on a form. The option group itself has a Validation Rule property that applies to all the controls within the group.

Validation properties are often used to ensure that certain dates fall after other dates (for example, an employee's retirement date must fall after his starting date), that nonnegative numbers are entered for values such as inventory quantities, and that entries are restricted to different ranges of numbers or text.

Dates used in Access expressions, such as a Validation Rule property, are surrounded, or *delimited,* by pound signs (#). If you want to limit the LastSalesDate data entry to dates between January 1, 2013, and December 31, 2014, enter **Between #1/1/2013# And #12/31/2014#**.

TIP

If you want to limit the upper end to the current date, you can enter a different set of dates, such as Between #1/1/2013# And Date(). `Date()` is a built-in VBA function that returns the current date; it's completely acceptable as part of a validation rule or other expression.

When a field is dragged onto a form, the Validation Rule property of the new control is not set to the field's Validation Rule. Unless you enter a new Validation Rule value in the control's Property Sheet, Access enforces the rule set at the table level.

Field and control Validation Rule properties are enforced when the focus leaves the table field or form control. Validation Rule properties applied to both a field and a control bound to the field are enforced for both entities. The table-level rule is applied as data is edited on the bound control and as focus leaves the control.

You can't create table-level Validation Rule properties for linked "foreign" tables, such as FoxPro, Paradox, or dBASE. Apply Validation Rule properties to controls bound to fields in linked foreign tables.

Required

The Required property instructs Access to require input into the field. When set to Yes, input is required in the field within a table or in a control on a form bound to the field. The value of a required field can't be Null.

The Required property is invalid for AutoNumber fields. By default, all AutoNumber fields are assigned a value as new records are created.

The Access database engine enforces the Required property. An error message is generated if the user tries to leave a text box control bound to a field with its Required property set to Yes.

The Required property can be used in conjunction with the AllowZeroLength property to determine when the value of a field is unknown or doesn't exist.

AllowZeroLength

The AllowZeroLength property specifies whether you want a zero-length string (`""`) to be a valid entry for a Short Text or Long Text field. AllowZeroLength accepts the following values:

- **Yes:** A zero-length string is a valid entry.
- **No:** The table will not accept zero-length strings, and instead, inserts a Null value into the field when no valid text data is supplied.

Combining the AllowZeroLength and Required properties enables you to differentiate between data that doesn't exist (which you'll probably want to represent as a zero-length string) and data that is unknown (which you'll want to store as a null value). In some cases, you'll want to store the proper value in the Short Text or Long Text field.

An example of data that doesn't exist is the case of a customer who doesn't have an e-mail address. The e-mail address field should be set to an empty (zero-length) string indicating that you know the user has an e-mail address, but you don't know what it is. Another customer who is entirely new to the company should have a null value in the e-mail address field, indicating that you don't know whether the customer has an e-mail address.

An input mask can help your application's users distinguish when a field contains a null value. For example, the input mask could be set to display `Ask customer` when the field contains a zero-length string and `Unknown` when the value is null.

The Required property determines whether a null value is accepted by the field, while the AllowZeroLength property permits zero-length strings in the field. Together, these independent properties provide the means to determine whether a value is unknown or absent for the field.

The interaction between Required and AllowZeroLength can be quite complicated. Table 3.6 summarizes how these two properties combine to force the user to input a value, or to insert either a null or zero-length string into a field.

TABLE 3.6 Required and AllowZeroLength Property Combinations

AllowZeroLength	Required	Data Entered by User	Value Stored in Table
No	No	Null	Null
No	No	Space	Null
No	No	Zero-length string	Disallowed
Yes	No	Null	Null
Yes	No	Space	Null
Yes	No	Zero-length string	Zero-length string
No	Yes	Null	Disallowed
No	Yes	Space	Disallowed
No	Yes	Zero-length string	Disallowed
Yes	Yes	Null	Disallowed
Yes	Yes	Space	Zero-length string
Yes	Yes	Zero-length string	Zero-length string

Indexed

The Indexed property tells Access that you want to use a field as an index in the table. Indexed fields are internally organized to speed up queries, sorting, and grouping operations. If you intend to frequently include a certain field in queries (for example, the employee ID or Social Security number) or if the field is frequently sorted or grouped on reports, you should set its Indexed property to Yes.

The valid settings for the Indexed property are as follows:

- **No:** The field is not indexed (default).
- **Yes (Duplicates OK):** The field is indexed and Access permits duplicate values in the column. This is the appropriate setting for values such as names, where it's likely that names like Smith will appear more than once in the table.
- **Yes (No Duplicates):** The field is indexed and no duplicates are permitted in the column. Use this setting for data that should be unique within the table, such as Social Security numbers, employee IDs, and customer numbers.

Indexes are discussed in more detail later in this chapter.

In addition to the primary key, you can index as many fields as necessary to provide optimum performance. Access accepts as many as 32 indexes per table. Keep in mind that each index extracts a small performance hit as new records are added to the table. Access dynamically updates the indexing information each time a new record is added. If a table includes an excessive number of indexes, a noticeable delay might occur as each new record is added.

The Indexed property is set in the field's Property Sheet or on the table's Property Sheet. You must use the table's Property Sheet to set multi-field indexes. Multifield indexes are discussed later in this chapter.

The AutoIndex option

The Access Options dialog box (File➪Options➪Object Designers) contains an entry (AutoIndex on Import/Create) that directs Access to automatically index certain fields as they're added to a table's design. By default, fields that begin or end with ID, key, code, or num (for example, EmployeeID or TaskCode) are automatically indexed as the field is created. Every time a new record is added to the table, the field's value is added to the field's index. If there are other field name patterns you'd like Access to automatically index, add new values to the `Auto Index on Import/Create` checkbox on the Object Designers tab in the Access Options dialog box (see Figure 3.10).

FIGURE 3.10

The Table Design View area on the Options screen contains a box for setting the AutoIndex on Import/Create options.

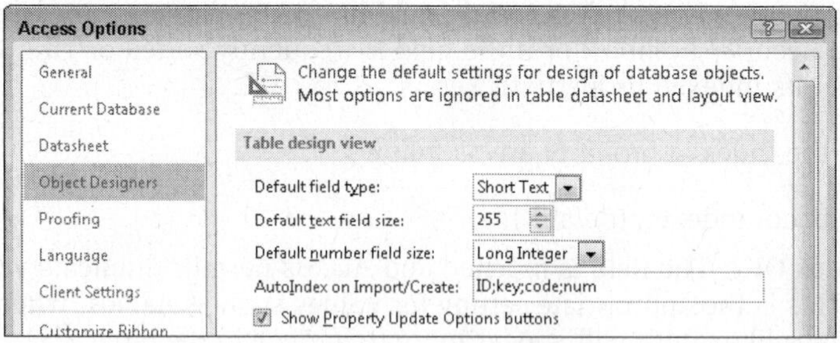

When to index

Generally speaking, you should index fields that are frequently searched or sorted. Remember that indexes slow down certain operations such as inserting records and some action queries.

Long Text and OLE Object fields can't be indexed. It would be impossible for Access to maintain an index on these complex data types.

An index should not be used if a field contains very few unique values. For example, you won't see a significant benefit from indexing a field containing a person's sex or state, or a Yes/No field. Because there is a limited range of values in such fields, Access easily sorts the data in these fields.

Use a multiple-field index in situations where sorts are often simultaneously performed on multiple fields (for example, first and last names). Access will have a much easier time sorting such a table.

Understanding tblCustomers Field Properties

After you enter the field names, data types, and field descriptions, you may want to go back and further refine each field. Every field has properties, and these are different for each data type. In tblCustomers, you must enter properties for several data types. Figure 3.11 shows the property area for the field named CreditLimit. Notice that there are two tabs on the property box — General and Lookup.

Pressing F6 switches between the field entry grid and the Field Properties pane (you may have to press F6 several times before you reach the desired pane). You can also move between panes by clicking the desired pane. Some properties display a list of possible values, along with a downward-pointing arrow when you move the pointer into the field. When you click the arrow, the values appear in a drop-down list.

FIGURE 3.11

The property area for the Currency field named CreditLimit.

General | Lookup

Format	Currency
Decimal Places	2
Input Mask	
Caption	
Default Value	0
Validation Rule	<=2500
Validation Text	The value entered exceeds the maximum credit limit.
Required	No
Indexed	No
Text Align	General

TIP

Figure 3.11 shows ten properties available for the CreditLimit Currency field. Other types, such as Number, Date/Time, Short Text, or Yes/No show more or fewer options.

The Field Properties pane of the Table Design window has a second tab: the Lookup tab. After clicking this tab, you may see a single property, the Display Control property. This property is used for Short Text, Number, and Yes/No fields.

Figure 3.12 shows the Lookup Property window for the Active Yes/No field where Display Control is the only property. This property has three choices: Check Box, Text Box, and Combo Box. Choosing one of these determines which control type is used when a particular field is added to a form. Generally, all controls are created as text boxes except Yes/No fields, which are created as check boxes by default. For Yes/No data types, however, you may want to use the Text Box setting to display Yes/No, True/False, or another choice that you specifically put in the format property box.

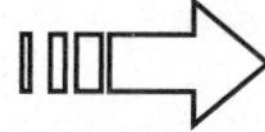

You learn about combo boxes in Chapter 19.

FIGURE 3.12

The Lookup tab for a Yes/No field.

General | Lookup

Display Control	Check Box
	Check Box
	Text Box
	Combo Box

If you're working with Short Text fields instead of a Yes/No field and know a certain Short Text field can only be one of a few combinations, select the combo box choice for the display control. Figure 3.13 shows the Lookup tab when combo box has been selected as the display control for the Credit Status field. There are only two acceptable values for Credit Status: OK and Not OK. These two values (separated by a semicolon) are specified as the combo box's Row Source, and the Row Source Type is set to Value List.

FIGURE 3.13

Setting up a combo box as the display control for Credit Status.

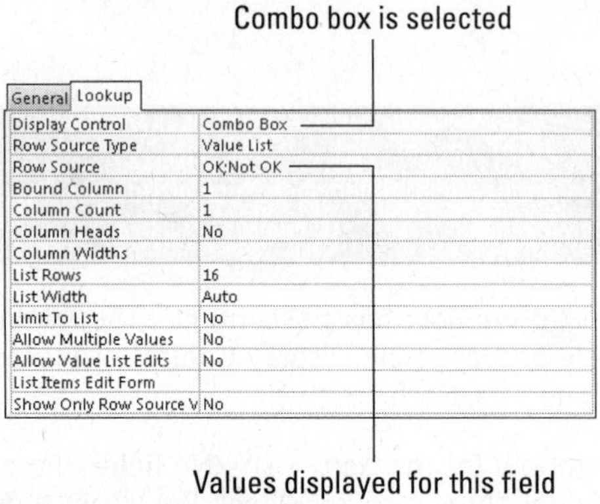

Combo box is selected

General | Lookup

Display Control	Combo Box
Row Source Type	Value List
Row Source	OK;Not OK
Bound Column	1
Column Count	1
Column Heads	No
Column Widths	
List Rows	16
List Width	Auto
Limit To List	No
Allow Multiple Values	No
Allow Value List Edits	No
List Items Edit Form	
Show Only Row Source V	No

Values displayed for this field

Although Figure 3.13 shows a combo box using a value list for its items, you could also specify a query or SQL statement as the combo box's Row Source.

Figure 3.14 shows how the Credit Status field appears when tblCustomers is displayed as a datasheet. The user can select only OK or Not OK as the credit status, and the same combo box appears when the field is added to an Access form.

The properties for a Lookup field are different for each data type. The Yes/No data type fields differ from Text fields or Number fields. Because a Lookup field is really a combo box, the standard properties for a combo box are displayed when you select a Lookup field data type.

FIGURE 3.14

Using a combo box as a lookup control to restrict user input on a field.

tblCustomers

OrigCustom	CreditLimit	CurrentBalai	CreditStatus	LastSalesDat	TaxRate
$41,044.00	$2,000.00	$0.00	OK	3/28/2012	0.06
$40,766.00	$2,500.00	$57.00	OK	3/28/2012	0.05
$40,976.00	$750.00	$0.00	OK	2/26/2007	0.05
$41,613.00	$900.00	$958.00	OK	3/28/2012	0.07
$41,060.00	$1,400.00	$168.00	OK	3/28/2012	0.06
$41,167.00	$1,500.00	$1,599.00	OK		0.05
	$0.00	$0.00	OK		0.05
	$0.00	$0.00	OK		0.06
	$0.00	$0.00	Not OK		0.07
	$0.00	$0.00			0.06
	$0.00	$0.00			0.07
$0.00	$0.00	$0.00			
$0.00	$0.00	$0.00			

Record: 28 of 33 No Filter Search

Setting the Primary Key

Every table should have a *primary key* — one or a combination of fields with a unique value for each record. (This principle is called *entity integrity* in the world of database management.) In tblCustomers, the CustomerID field is the primary key. Each customer has a unique CustomerID value so that the database engine can distinguish one record from another. CustomerID 17 refers to one and only one record in the Contacts table. If you don't specify a primary key (unique value field), Access can create one for you.

Choosing a primary key

Without the CustomerID field, you'd have to rely on another field or combination of fields for uniqueness. You couldn't use the `Company` field because two customers could easily have the same company name. In fact, you couldn't even use the Company and City fields together (in a multi-field key), for the same reason — it's entirely possible that two customers with the same name exist in the same city. You need to come up with a field or combination of fields that makes every record unique.

The easiest way to solve this problem is to add an AutoNumber field to serve as the table's primary key. The primary key in tblCustomers is CustomerID, an AutoNumber field.

If you don't designate a field as a primary key, Access can add an AutoNumber field and designate it as the table's primary key. AutoNumber fields make very good primary keys because Access creates the value for you, the number is never reused within a table, and you can't change the value of an AutoNumber field.

3

Good primary keys

- Uniquely identify each record.
- Cannot be null.
- Must exist when the record is created.
- Must remain stable. (You should never change a primary key value once it's established.)
- Should be simple and contain as few attributes as possible.

In addition to uniquely identifying rows in a table, primary keys provide other benefits:

- A primary key is always an index.
- An index maintains a presorted order of one or more fields that greatly speeds up queries, searches, and sort requests.
- When you add new records to your table, Access checks for duplicate data and doesn't allow any duplicates for the primary key field.
- By default, Access displays a table's data in the order of its primary key.

By designating a field such as CustomerID as the primary key, data is displayed in a meaningful order. In our example, because the CustomerID field is an AutoNumber, its value is assigned automatically by Access in the order that a record is put into the system.

The ideal primary key is, then, a single field that is immutable and guaranteed to be unique within the table. For these reasons, the Collectible Mini Cars database uses the AutoNumber field exclusively as the primary key for all tables.

Creating the primary key

The primary key can be created in any of three ways. With a table open in Design view:

- Select the field to be used as the primary key and click the Primary Key button (the key icon) in the Tools group on the Design tab of the Ribbon.
- Right-click the field and select Primary Key from the shortcut menu.
- Save the table without creating a primary key, and allow Access to automatically create an AutoNumber field.

After you designate the primary key, a key icon appears in the gray selector area to the left of the field's name to indicate that the primary key has been created.

Creating composite primary keys

You can designate a combination of fields to be used as a table's primary key. Such keys are often referred to as *composite primary keys*. As indicated in Figure 3.15, select the fields that you want to include in the composite primary key; then click the key icon on the Tools tab of the Ribbon. It helps, of course, if the fields lie right next to each other in the table's design.

FIGURE 3.15

Creating a composite primary key.

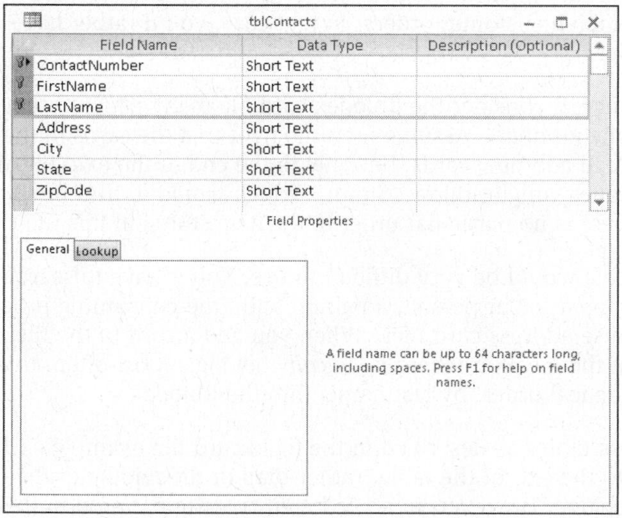

tblContacts

Field Name	Data Type	Description (Optional)
ContactNumber	Short Text	
FirstName	Short Text	
LastName	Short Text	
Address	Short Text	
City	Short Text	
State	Short Text	
ZipCode	Short Text	

Field Properties

General Lookup

A field name can be up to 64 characters long, including spaces. Press F1 for help on field names.

Composite primary keys are primarily used when the developer strongly feels that a primary key should be comprised of data that occurs naturally in the database. There was a time when all developers were taught that every table should have a *natural primary key* (data that occurs naturally in the table).

Composite primary keys are seldom used these days because developers have come to realize that data is highly unpredictable. Even if your users promise that a combination of certain fields will never be duplicated in the table, things have a way of turning out differently from planned. Using a *surrogate primary key* (a key field that does not naturally occur in the table's data, such as a Social Security Number or Employee ID), such as an AutoNumber, separates the table's design from the table's data. The problem with natural primary keys is that, eventually, given a large enough data set, the values of fields chosen as the table's primary key are likely to be duplicated.

Furthermore, when using composite keys, maintaining relationships between tables becomes more complicated because the fields comprising the primary key must be duplicated in all the tables containing related data. Using composite keys simply adds to the complexity of the database without adding stability, integrity, or other desirable features.

Indexing Access Tables

Data is rarely, if ever, entered into tables in a meaningful order. Usually, records are added to tables in random order (with the exception of time-ordered data). For example, a busy order-entry system will gather information on a number of different customer orders in a single day. Most often, this data will be used to report orders for a single customer for billing purposes or for extracting order quantities for inventory management. The records in the Orders table, however, are in chronological order, which is not necessarily helpful when preparing reports detailing customer orders. In that case, you'd rather have data entered in customer ID order.

To further illustrate this concept, consider the Rolodex card file many people use to store names, addresses, and phone numbers. Assume for a moment that the cards in the file were fixed in place. You could add new cards, but only to the end of the card file. This limitation would mean that "Jones" might follow "Smith," which would in turn be followed by "Baker." In other words, there is no particular order to the data stored in this file.

An unsorted Rolodex like this would be very difficult to use. You'd have to search each and every card looking for a particular person, a painful and time-consuming process. Of course, this isn't how you use address card files. When you add a card to the file, you insert it into the Rolodex at the location where it *logically* belongs. Most often, this means inserting the card in alphabetical order, by last name, into the Rolodex.

Records are added to Access tables as described in the fixed card file example earlier. New records are always added to the end of the table, rather than in the middle of the table where they may logically belong. However, in an order-entry system, you'd probably want new records inserted next to other records on the same customer. Unfortunately, this isn't how Access tables work. The *natural order* of a table is the order in which records were added to the table. This order is sometimes referred to as *entry order* or *physical order* to emphasize that the records in the table appear in the order in which they were added to the table.

Using tables in natural order is not necessarily a bad thing. Natural order makes perfect sense if the data is rarely searched or if the table is very small. Also, there are situations where the data being added to the table is highly ordered to start with. If the table is used to gather sequential data (like readings from an electric meter) and the data will be used in the same sequential order, there is no need to impose an index on the data.

But for situations where natural order doesn't suffice, Access provides *indexing* to help you find and sort records faster. You specify a *logical* order for the records in a table by creating an *index* on that table. Access uses the index to maintain one or more internal sort orders for the data in the table. For example, you may choose to index the LastName field that will frequently be included in queries and sorting routines.

Access uses indexes in a table as you use an index in a book: To find data, Access looks up the data's location in the index. Most often, your tables will include one or more *simple indexes*. A simple index is one that involves a single field in the table. Simple indexes may arrange the table's records in ascending or descending order. Simple indexes are created by setting the field's Indexed property to one of the following values:

- Yes (Duplicates OK)
- Yes (No Duplicates)

By default, Access fields are not indexed, but it's hard to imagine a table that doesn't require some kind of index. The next section discusses why indexing is important to use in Access tables.

The importance of indexes

Microsoft's data indicates that more than half of all tables in Access databases contain *no* indexes. This number doesn't include the tables that are improperly indexed — it includes only those tables that have no indexes at all. It appears that a lot of people don't appreciate the importance of indexing the tables in an Access database.

ON THE WEB

As a demonstration of the power and value of indexes, this book's website includes a database named `IndexTest.accdb`. This database includes two identical tables containing approximately 355,000 random words. One table is indexed on the Word field, and the other is not. A small form (shown in Figure 3.16) lets you query either the indexed or unindexed table and shows the number of milliseconds the search takes.

FIGURE 3.16

frmIndexTest provides a quick and easy way to verify the importance of indexes.

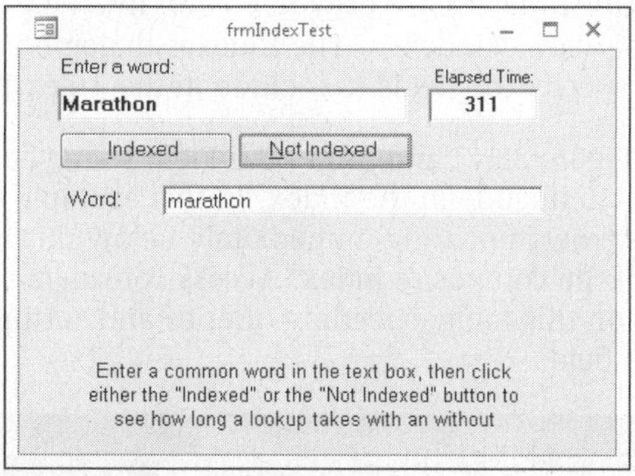

In a number of repeated tests, the indexed table consistently finds a word in less than 20 milliseconds, while the unindexed search takes between 200 and 350 milliseconds.

Displaying the results you see in Figure 3.16 takes almost no time at all and doesn't contribute to the overall time required to run the query. It goes without saying that the actual time required to run a query depends very much on the computer's hardware, but performance enhancements of 500 percent and more are not at all uncommon when adding an index to a field.

Because an index means that Access maintains an internal sort order on the data contained in the indexed field, you can see why query performance is enhanced by an index. You should index virtually every field that is frequently involved in queries or is frequently sorted on forms or reports.

Without an index, Access must search each and every record in the database looking for matches. This process is called a *table scan* and is analogous to searching through each and every card in Rolodex file to find all the people who work for a certain company. Until you reach the end of the deck, you can't be sure you've found every relevant card in the file.

As mentioned earlier in this chapter, a table's primary key field is always indexed. This is because the primary key is used to locate records in the table. Indexing the primary key makes it much easier for Access to find the required tables in either the current table or a foreign table related to the current table. Without an index, Access has to search all records in the related table to make sure it has located all the related records.

TIP

The performance losses due to unindexed tables can have a devastating effect on the overall performance of an Access application. Anytime you hear a complaint about the performance of an application, consider indexing as a possible solution.

Multiple-field indexes

Multiple-field indexes (also called *composite indexes*) are easy to create. In Design view, click the Indexes toolbar button or choose View⇨Indexes. The Indexes dialog box (shown in Figure 3.17) appears, allowing you to specify the fields to include in the index.

Enter a name for the index (CityState in Figure 3.17) and tab to the Field Name column. Use the drop-down list to select the fields to include in the index. In this example City and State are combined as a single index. Any row appearing immediately below this row that does not contain an index name is part of the composite index. Access considers both these fields when creating the sort order on this table, speeding queries and sorting operations that include both the City and State fields.

NOTE

The order of the fields in a composite index is important. The CityState index described in this chapter will be used by Access when only the City is provided in a query, but it'll provide no benefit when only the State is provided.

FIGURE 3.17

Multiple-field (composite) indexes can enhance performance.

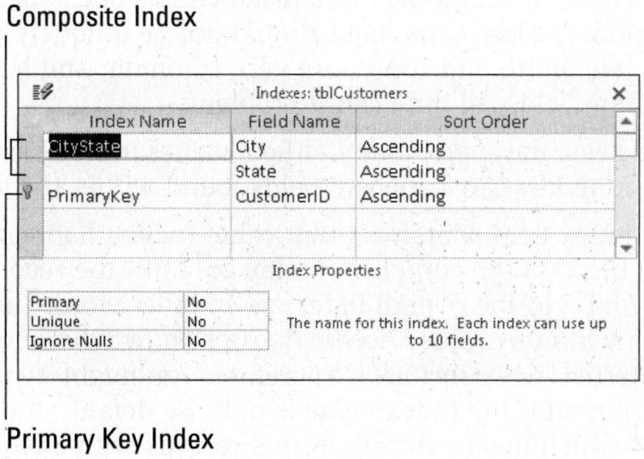

Composite Index

Indexes: tblCustomers

Index Name	Field Name	Sort Order
CityState	City	Ascending
	State	Ascending
PrimaryKey	CustomerID	Ascending

Index Properties

Primary	No
Unique	No
Ignore Nulls	No

The name for this index. Each index can use up to 10 fields.

Primary Key Index

As many as ten fields can be included in a composite index. As long as the composite index is not used as the table's primary key, any of the fields in the composite index can be empty.

Figure 3.18 shows how to set the properties of an index. The cursor is placed in the row in the Indexes dialog box containing the name of the index. Notice the three properties appearing below the index information in the top half of the Indexes dialog box.

FIGURE 3.18

It's easy to set the properties of an index.

Indexes: tblCustomers

Index Name	Field Name	Sort Order
PrimaryKey	CustomerID	Ascending
CityState	City	Ascending
	State	Ascending

Index Properties

Primary	No
Unique	No
Ignore Nulls	No

The name for this index. Each index can use up to 10 fields.

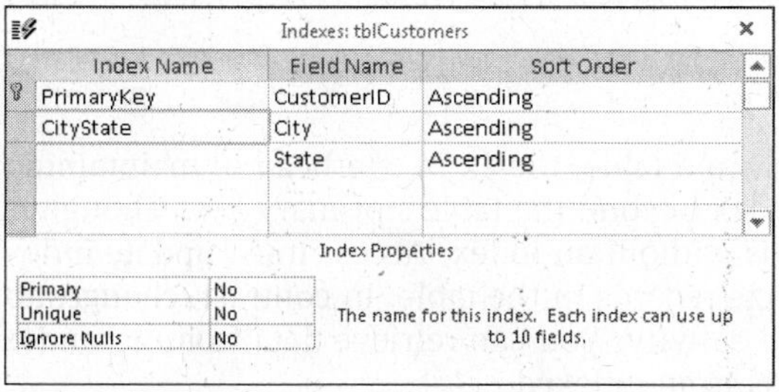

The index properties are quite easy to understand (these properties apply to single-field and composite indexes equally):

- **Primary:** When set to Yes, Access uses this index as the table's primary key. More than one field can be designated as the primary key, but keep the rules governing primary keys in mind, particularly those requiring each primary key value to be unique and that no field in a composite primary key can be empty. The default for the Primary property is No.

- **Unique:** When set to Yes, the index must be unique within a table. A Social Security number field is a good candidate for a unique index because the application's business rules may require one and only one instance of a Social Security number in the table. In contrast, a last name field should not be uniquely indexed, because many last names, like Smith and Jones, are very common, and having a unique index on the last name field will only cause problems.

  When applied to composite keys, the *combination* of field values must be unique — each field within the composite key can duplicate fields found within the table.
- **Ignore Nulls:** If a record's index field contains a null value (which happens in a composite index only if all fields in the composite index are null) the record's index won't contribute anything to the overall indexing. In other words, unless a record's index contains some kind of value, Access doesn't know where to insert the record in the table's internal index sort lists. Therefore, you might want to instruct Access to ignore a record if the index value is null. By default, the Ignore Nulls property is set to No, which means Access inserts records with a Null index value into the indexing scheme along with any other records containing Null index values.

You should test the impact of the index properties on your Access tables and use the properties that best suit the data handled by your databases.

A field can be both the primary key for a table and part of a composite index. You should index your tables as necessary to yield the highest possible performance without worrying about over-indexing or violating some arcane indexing rules. For example, in a database such as Collectible Mini Cars, the invoice number in tblSales is frequently used in forms and reports and should be indexed. In addition, there are many situations in which the invoice number is used in combinations with other fields, such as the sales date or salesperson ID. You should consider adding composite indexes combining the invoice number with sales date, and salesperson ID, to the sales table.

When to index tables

Depending on the number of records in a table, the extra overhead of maintaining an index may not justify creating an index beyond the table's primary key. Though data retrieval is somewhat faster than it is without an index, Access must update index information whenever you enter or change records in the table. In contrast, changes to nonindexed fields do not require extra file activity. You can retrieve data from nonindexed fields as easily (although not as *quickly*) as from indexed fields.

Generally speaking, it's best to add secondary indexes when tables are quite large and when indexing fields other than the primary key speeds up searches. Even with large tables, however, indexing can slow performance if the records in tables will be changed often or new records will be added frequently. Each time a record is changed or added, Access must update all indexes in the table.

Given all the advantages of indexes, why not index everything in the table? What are the drawbacks of indexing too many fields? Is it possible to over-index tables?

First, indexes increase the size of the Access database somewhat. Unnecessarily indexing a table that doesn't really require an index eats up a bit of disk space for each record in the table. More important, indexes extract a performance hit for each index on the table every time a record is added to the table. Because Access automatically updates indexes each time a record is added (or removed), the internal indexing must be adjusted for each new record. If you have ten indexes on a table, Access makes ten adjustments to the indexes each time a new record is added or an existing record is deleted, causing a noticeable delay on large tables (particularly on slow computers).

Sometimes changes to the data in records cause adjustments to the indexing scheme. This is true if the change causes the record to change its position in sorting or query activities. Therefore, if you're working with large, constantly changing data sets that are rarely searched, you may choose *not* to index the fields in the table, or to minimally index by indexing only those few fields that are likely to be searched.

As you begin working with Access tables, you'll probably start with the simplest one-field indexes and migrate to more complex ones as your familiarity with the process grows. Do keep in mind, however, the trade-offs between greater search efficiency and the overhead incurred by maintaining a large number of indexes on your tables.

It's also important to keep in mind that indexing does not modify the physical arrangement of records in the table. The natural order of the records (the order in which the records were added to the table) is maintained after the index is established.

NOTE

A compact and repair cycle on an Access database forces Access to rebuild the indexes in all the tables, and physically rearranges tables in primary key order in the ACCDB file. The maintenance operations ensure that your Access databases operate at maximum efficiency.

Printing a Table Design

You can print a table design by clicking the Database Documenter button in the Analyze group on the Database Tools tab of the Ribbon. The Analyze group contains a number of tools that make it easy to document your database objects. When you click the Database Documenter button, the Documenter dialog box appears, letting you select objects to print. In Figure 3.19, tblCustomers is selected on the Tables tab of the Documenter dialog box.

FIGURE 3.19

The Documenter dialog box.

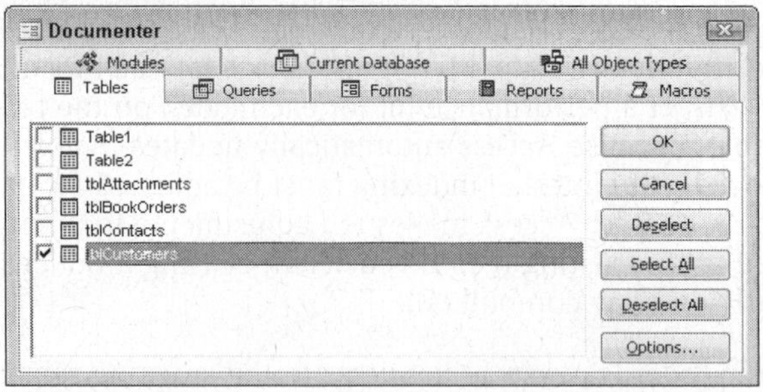

You can also set various options for printing. When you click the Options button, the Print Table Definition dialog box (shown in Figure 3.20) appears, enabling you to select which information from the Table Design to print. You can print the various field names, all their properties, the indexes, and even network permissions.

FIGURE 3.20

Printing options in the Print Table Definition dialog box.

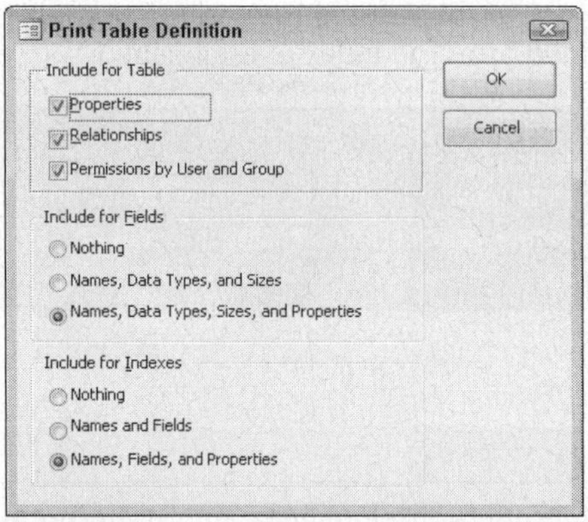

> **CAUTION**
>
> Don't select too many options in the Print Table Definition dialog box. Printing every detail of a table's design can take many pages to output. It's probably best to print just a few items for a table, and add to the options when necessary.

After you select which data you want to view, Access generates a report. You can view the report in a Print Preview window or send it to a printer. You may want to save the report within the database as part of the application's documentation.

TIP

The Database Documenter creates a table of all the objects and object properties you specify. You can use this utility to document such database objects as forms, queries, reports, macros, and modules.

Saving the Completed Table

You can save the completed table design by choosing File➪Save or by clicking the Save button on the Quick Access toolbar in the upper-left corner of the Access environment. If you're saving the table for the first time, Access asks for its name. Table names can be up to 64 characters long and follow standard Access object naming conventions — they may include letters and numbers, can't begin with a number, and can't include punctuation. You can also save the table when you close it.

If you've saved this table before and you want to save it with a different name, choose File➪Save Object As and enter a different table name. This action creates a new table design and leaves the original table with its original name untouched. If you want to delete the old table, select it in the Navigation pane and press the Delete key.

Manipulating Tables

As you add many tables to your database, you may want to use them in other databases or make copies of them as backups. In many cases, you may want to copy only the table's design and not include all the data in the table. You can perform many table operations in the Navigation pane, including

- Renaming tables
- Deleting tables
- Copying tables in a database
- Copying a table to another database

You perform these tasks by direct manipulation or by using menu items.

Renaming tables

Rename a table by right-clicking its name in the Navigation pane and selecting Rename from the shortcut menu. After you change the table name, it appears in the Tables list, which re-sorts the tables in alphabetical order.

CAUTION

If you rename a table, you must change the table name in any objects in which it was previously referenced, including queries, forms, and reports.

Deleting tables

Delete a table by right-clicking its name in the Navigation pane and selecting Delete from the shortcut menu or by selecting the table in the Navigation pane and pressing the Delete key. Like most delete operations, you have to confirm the delete by clicking Yes in a confirmation box.

CAUTION
Be aware that holding down the Shift key while pressing the Delete key deletes the table (or any other database object, for that matter) *without* confirmation. You'll find the Shift+Delete key combination useful for removing items but also dangerous if not carefully applied.

Copying tables in a database

The copy and paste options in the Clipboard group on the Home tab allow you to copy any table in the database. When you paste the table back into the database, the Paste Table As dialog box appears, asking you to choose from three options:

- **Structure Only:** Clicking the `Structure Only` button creates a new, empty table with the same design as the copied table. This option is typically used to create a temporary table or an archive table to which you can copy old records.
- **Structure and Data:** When you click `Structure and Data`, a complete copy of the table design and all its data is created.
- **Append Data to Existing Table:** Clicking the `Append Data to Existing Table` button adds the data of the selected table to the bottom of another table. This option is useful for combining tables, such as when you want to add data from a monthly transaction table to a yearly history table.

Follow these steps to copy a table:

1. **Right-click the table name in the Navigation pane and choose Copy from the shortcut menu, or click the Copy button in the Clipboard group on the Home tab.**
2. **Choose Paste from the shortcut menu, or click the Paste button in the Clipboard group on the Home tab.** The Paste Table As dialog box (shown in Figure 3.21) appears.
3. **Enter the name of the new table.** When you're appending data to an existing table (see the next step), you must type the name of an existing table.
4. **Choose one of the Paste options — Structure Only, Structure and Data, or Append Data to Existing Table — from the Paste Table As dialog box.**
5. **Click OK to complete the operation.**

FIGURE 3.21

Pasting a table opens the Paste Table As dialog box.

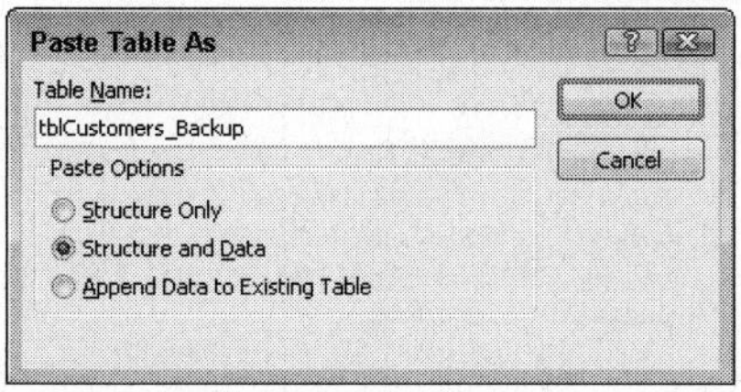

Copying a table to another database

Just as you can copy a table within a database, you can copy a table to another database. There are many reasons why you may want to do this. Maybe you share a common table among multiple systems, or maybe you need to create a backup copy of your important tables within the system.

When you copy tables to another database, the relationships between tables are not copied. Access copies only the table design and the data to the other database. The method for copying a table to another database is essentially the same as for copying a table within a database:

1. **Right-click the table name in the Navigation pane and choose Copy from the shortcut menu, or click the Copy button in the Clipboard group on the Home tab.**
2. **Open the other Access database and choose Edit Paste from the shortcut menu, or click the Copy button in the Clipboard group on the Home tab.** The Paste Table As dialog box appears.
3. **Enter the name of the new table.**
4. **Choose one of the Paste options: Structure Only, Structure and Data, or Append Data to Existing Table.**
5. **Click OK to complete the operation.**

Adding Records to a Database Table

Adding records to a table is as simple as clicking the table in the Navigation pane to open the table in Datasheet view. Once the table is opened, enter values for each field. Figure 3.22 shows adding records in datasheet mode to the table.

You can enter information into all fields except CustomerID. AutoNumber fields automatically provide a number for you.

FIGURE 3.22

Using Datasheet view to add records to a table.

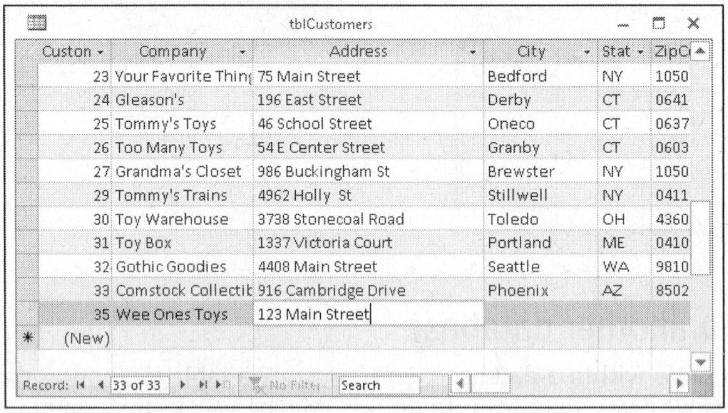

tblCustomers

Custon	Company	Address	City	Stat	ZipC
23	Your Favorite Thin	75 Main Street	Bedford	NY	1050
24	Gleason's	196 East Street	Derby	CT	0641
25	Tommy's Toys	46 School Street	Oneco	CT	0637
26	Too Many Toys	54 E Center Street	Granby	CT	0603
27	Grandma's Closet	986 Buckingham St	Brewster	NY	1050
29	Tommy's Trains	4962 Holly St	Stillwell	NY	0411
30	Toy Warehouse	3738 Stonecoal Road	Toledo	OH	4360
31	Toy Box	1337 Victoria Court	Portland	ME	0410
32	Gothic Goodies	4408 Main Street	Seattle	WA	9810
33	Comstock Collecti	916 Cambridge Drive	Phoenix	AZ	8502
35	Wee Ones Toys	123 Main Street			
* (New)					

Record: 33 of 33 No Filter Search

Although you can add records directly into the table through the Datasheet view, it isn't the most efficient way. Adding records using forms is better because code behind a form can dynamically provide default values (perhaps based on data already added to the form) and communicate with the user during the data entry process.

Understanding Attachment Fields

Microsoft recognizes that database developers must deal with many different types of data. Although the traditional Access data types (Text, Currency, OLE Object, and so on) are able to handle many different types of data, until recently there was no way to accommodate *complete files* as Access data without performing some transformation on the file (such as conversion to OLE data).

Since Access 2010, Access has included the Attachment data type, enabling you to bring entire files into your Access database as "attachments" to a table. When you click an attachment field, a small Attachments dialog box (shown in Figure 3.23) appears, enabling you to locate files to attach to the table.

The Add button in Figure 3.23 opens the familiar Choose File dialog box, enabling you to search for one or more files to attach to the field. The selected files are added to the list you see in Figure 3.23. Notice also that the Attachments dialog box includes buttons for removing attachments from the field, and for saving attachments back to the computer's disk.

The significant thing to keep in mind about the Attachment data type is that a single attachment field in a table can contain multiple files of different types. It's entirely possible to store a Word document, several audio or video clips, and a number of photographs, within a single attachment field.

FIGURE 3.23

Managing attachments in an Attachment field.

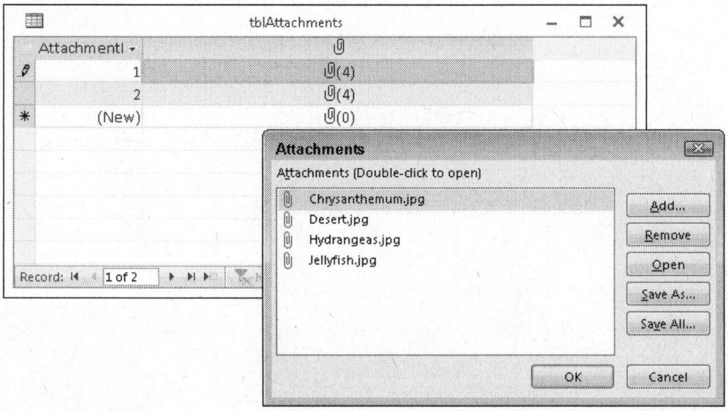

CAUTION

Obviously, because the attached data is incorporated into the database, the ACCDB file will quickly grow if many attachments are added. You should use the Attachment data type only when its benefits outweigh the burden it places on an Access application.

Understanding Table Relationships

IN THIS CHAPTER

Understanding bulletproof database design

Normalizing database data

Looking at common table relationships

Understanding integrity rules

Adding key fields to tables

We've already covered one of the most basic assumptions about relational database systems — that is, that data is spread across a number of tables that are related through primary and foreign keys. Although this basic principle is easy to understand, it can be much more difficult to understand why and when data should be broken into separate tables.

Because the data managed by a relational database such as Access exists in a number of different tables, there must be some way to connect the data. The more efficiently the database performs these connections, the better and more flexible the database application as a whole will function.

Although databases are meant to model real-world situations, or at least manage the data involved in real-world situations, even the most complex situation is reduced to a number of relationships between pairs of tables. As the data managed by the database becomes more complex, you may need to add more tables to the design. For example, a database to manage employee affairs for a company will include tables for employee information (name, Social Security number, address, hire date, and so on), payroll information, benefits programs the employee belongs to, and so on.

This chapter uses a variety of data from different business situations, including Northwind Traders (the traditional Access example database), a small bookstore, and the Collectible Mini Cars application used in other chapters of this book. Each data set has somewhat different objectives from the others and is used to emphasize different aspects of relational theory. All the tables described in this chapter are contained in the `Chapter04.accdb` database.

When working with the actual data, however, you concentrate on the relationship between two tables at a time. You might create the Employees and Payroll tables first, connecting these tables with a relationship to make it easy to find all the payroll information for an employee.

ON THE WEB

This chapter uses a variety of data from the database named `Chapter04.accdb`. If you haven't already downloaded it, you'll need to do so now. If you're following the examples, you can use the tables in this database or create the tables yourself in another database.

Building Bulletproof Databases

In Chapters 1, 2, and 3, you saw examples of common relationships found in many Access databases. By far the most common type of table relationship is the one-to-many. The Collectible Mini Cars application has many such relationships: Each record in the Customers table is related to one or more records in the Sales table (each contact may have purchased more than one item through Collectible Mini Cars). (We cover one-to-many relationships in detail in the "Table Relationships" section, later in this chapter.)

You can easily imagine an arrangement that would permit the data contained in the Customers and Sales tables to be combined within a single table. All that would be needed is a separate row for each order placed by each of the contacts. As new orders come in, new rows containing the customer and order information would be added to the table.

The Access table shown in Figure 4.1, tblCustomersAndOrders, is an example of such an arrangement. In this figure, the OrderID column contains the order number placed by the contact (the data in this table has been sorted by CustomerID to show how many orders have been placed by each contact). The table in Figure 4.1 was created by combining data from the Customers and Orders tables in the Northwind Traders sample database and is included in the `Chapter04.accdb` database file on this book's website.

Notice the OrderID column to the right of the CompanyName column. Each contact (like Alfreds Futterkiste) has placed a number of orders. Columns to the far right in this table (beyond the right edge of the figure) contain more information about each contact, including address and phone numbers, while columns beyond the company information contain the specific order information. In all, this table contains 24 different fields.

The design shown in Figure 4.1 is what happens when a spreadsheet application such as Excel is used for database purposes. Because Excel is entirely spreadsheet oriented, there is no provision for breaking up data into separate tables, encouraging users to keep everything in one massive spreadsheet.

FIGURE 4.1

An Access table containing contact *and* orders data.

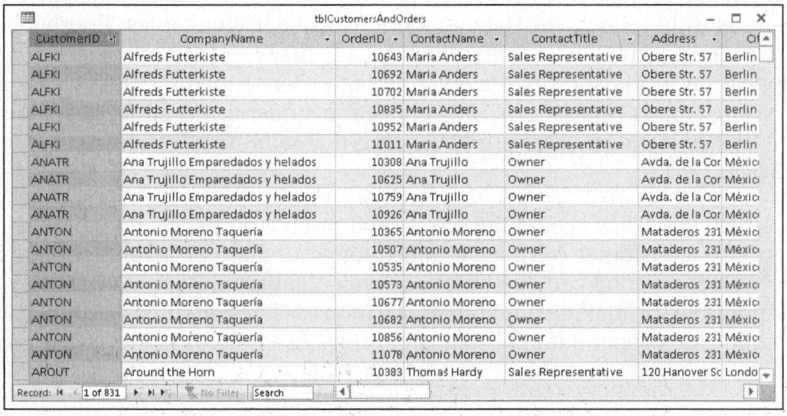

tblCustomersAndOrders

CustomerID	CompanyName	OrderID	ContactName	ContactTitle	Address	Ci
ALFKI	Alfreds Futterkiste	10643	Maria Anders	Sales Representative	Obere Str. 57	Berlin
ALFKI	Alfreds Futterkiste	10692	Maria Anders	Sales Representative	Obere Str. 57	Berlin
ALFKI	Alfreds Futterkiste	10702	Maria Anders	Sales Representative	Obere Str. 57	Berlin
ALFKI	Alfreds Futterkiste	10835	Maria Anders	Sales Representative	Obere Str. 57	Berlin
ALFKI	Alfreds Futterkiste	10952	Maria Anders	Sales Representative	Obere Str. 57	Berlin
ALFKI	Alfreds Futterkiste	11011	Maria Anders	Sales Representative	Obere Str. 57	Berlin
ANATR	Ana Trujillo Emparedados y helados	10308	Ana Trujillo	Owner	Avda. de la Cor	Méxic
ANATR	Ana Trujillo Emparedados y helados	10625	Ana Trujillo	Owner	Avda. de la Cor	Méxic
ANATR	Ana Trujillo Emparedados y helados	10759	Ana Trujillo	Owner	Avda. de la Cor	Méxic
ANATR	Ana Trujillo Emparedados y helados	10926	Ana Trujillo	Owner	Avda. de la Cor	Méxic
ANTON	Antonio Moreno Taquería	10365	Antonio Moreno	Owner	Mataderos 231	Méxic
ANTON	Antonio Moreno Taquería	10507	Antonio Moreno	Owner	Mataderos 231	Méxic
ANTON	Antonio Moreno Taquería	10535	Antonio Moreno	Owner	Mataderos 231	Méxic
ANTON	Antonio Moreno Taquería	10573	Antonio Moreno	Owner	Mataderos 231	Méxic
ANTON	Antonio Moreno Taquería	10677	Antonio Moreno	Owner	Mataderos 231	Méxic
ANTON	Antonio Moreno Taquería	10682	Antonio Moreno	Owner	Mataderos 231	Méxic
ANTON	Antonio Moreno Taquería	10856	Antonio Moreno	Owner	Mataderos 231	Méxic
ANTON	Antonio Moreno Taquería	11078	Antonio Moreno	Owner	Mataderos 231	Méxic
AROUT	Around the Horn	10383	Thomas Hardy	Sales Representative	120 Hanover Sc	Londo

Record: 1 of 831 No Filter Search

Such an arrangement has several problems:

- **The table quickly becomes unmanageably large.** The Northwind Traders Contacts table contains 11 different fields, while the Orders table contains 14 more. One field — OrderID — overlaps both tables. Each time an order is placed, all 24 data fields in the combined table would be added for each record added to the table, including a lot of data (such as the Contact Name and Contact Title) not directly relevant to an order.
- **Data are difficult to maintain and update.** Making simple changes to the data in the large table — for example, changing a contact's phone or fax number — involves searching through all records in the table and changing every occurrence of the phone number. It's easy to make an erroneous entry or miss one or more instances. The fewer records needing changes, the better off the user will be.
- **A monolithic table design is wasteful of disk space and other resources.** Because the combined table contains a huge amount of redundant data (for example, a contact's address is repeated for every sale), a large amount of hard disk space is consumed by the redundant information. In addition to wasted disk space, network traffic, computer memory, and other resources would be poorly utilized.

A much better design — the relational design — moves the repeated data into a separate table, leaving a field in the first table to serve as a reference to the data in the second table. The additional field required by the relational model is a small price to pay for the efficiencies gained by moving redundant data out of the table.

A second huge advantage of normalizing data and applying strict database design rules to Access applications is that the data becomes virtually bulletproof. In an appropriately designed and managed database, users are ensured that the information displayed on forms and reports truly reflects the data stored in the underlying tables. Poorly designed databases are prone to data corruption, which means that records are sometimes "lost" and never appear on forms and reports, even though users added the data to the application, or the wrong data is returned by the application's queries. In either case, the database can't be trusted because users are never sure that what they're seeing in forms and reports is correct.

Users tend to trust what they see on the screen and printed on paper. Imagine the problems that would occur if a customer were never billed for a purchase or inventory were incorrectly updated. Nothing good can come from a weak database design. As database developers, we're responsible for making sure the applications we design are as strong and resilient as possible. Following proper data normalization rules can help us achieve that goal.

Data Normalization and Denormalization

The process of splitting data across multiple tables is called *normalizing* the data. There are several stages of normalization; the first through the third stages are the easiest to understand and implement and are generally sufficient for the majority of applications. Although higher levels of normalization are possible, they're usually ignored by all but the most experienced and fastidious developers.

To illustrate the normalization process, I'll use a little database that a book wholesaler might use to track book orders placed by small bookstores in the local area. This database must handle the following information:

- The dates on which the books were ordered
- The customers who placed the orders
- The quantity of each book ordered
- The title of each book ordered

Although this data set is very simple, it's typical of the type of data you might manage with an Access database application, and it provides a valid demonstration of normalizing a set of data.

First normal form

The initial stage of normalization, called *first normal form* (1NF), requires that the table conform to the following rule:

> Each cell of a table must contain only a single value, and the table must not contain repeating groups of data.

A table is meant to be a two-dimensional storage object, and storing multiple values within a field or permitting repeating groups within the table implies a third dimension to the data. Figure 4.2 shows the first attempt at building a table to manage bookstore orders (tblBookOrders1). Notice that some bookstores have ordered more than one book. A value like 7 Cookie Magic in the BookTitles field means that the contact has ordered seven copies of the cookbook titled *Cookie Magic*. Storing both a quantity and the item's name in the same cell is just one of several ways that this table violates first normal form.

FIGURE 4.2

An unnormalized tblBookOrders table.

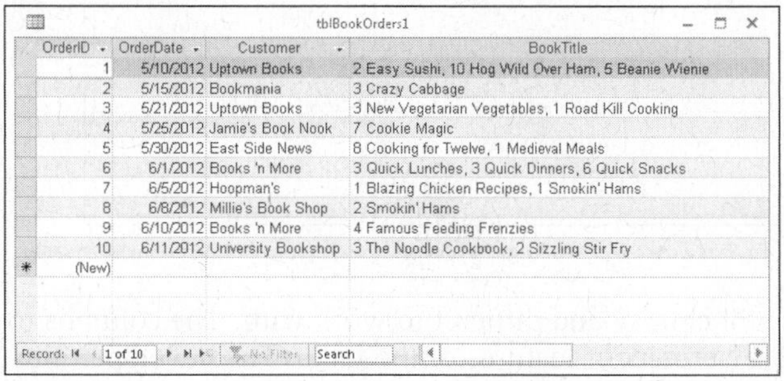

tblBookOrders1

OrderID	OrderDate	Customer	BookTitle
1	5/10/2012	Uptown Books	2 Easy Sushi, 10 Hog Wild Over Ham, 5 Beanie Wienie
2	5/15/2012	Bookmania	3 Crazy Cabbage
3	5/21/2012	Uptown Books	3 New Vegetarian Vegetables, 1 Road Kill Cooking
4	5/25/2012	Jamie's Book Nook	7 Cookie Magic
5	5/30/2012	East Side News	8 Cooking for Twelve, 1 Medieval Meals
6	6/1/2012	Books 'n More	3 Quick Lunches, 3 Quick Dinners, 6 Quick Snacks
7	6/5/2012	Hoopman's	1 Blazing Chicken Recipes, 1 Smokin' Hams
8	6/8/2012	Millie's Book Shop	2 Smokin' Hams
9	6/10/2012	Books 'n More	4 Famous Feeding Frenzies
10	6/11/2012	University Bookshop	3 The Noodle Cookbook, 2 Sizzling Stir Fry
(New)			

Record: 1 of 10 No Filter Search

The table in Figure 4.2 is typical of a *flat-file approach* to building a database. Data in a flat-file database is stored in two dimensions (rows and columns) and neglects the third dimension (related tables) possible in a relational database system such as Access.

Notice how the table in Figure 4.2 violates the first rule of normalization. Many of the records in this table contain multiple values in the BookTitle field. For example, the book titled *Smokin' Hams* appears in records 7 and 8. There is no way for the database to handle this data easily — if you want to cross-reference the books ordered by the bookstores, you'd have to parse the data contained in the BookTitle field to determine which books have been ordered by which contacts.

A slightly better design is shown in Figure 4.3 (tblBookOrders2). The books' quantities and titles have been separated into individual columns. Each row still contains all the data for a single order. This arrangement makes it somewhat easier to retrieve quantity and title information, but the repeating groups for quantity and title (the columns Quant1, Title1, Quant2, Title2, and so on) continue to violate the first rule of normalization. (The row height in Figure 4.3 has been adjusted to make it easier to see the table's arrangement.)

FIGURE 4.3

Only a slight improvement over the previous design.

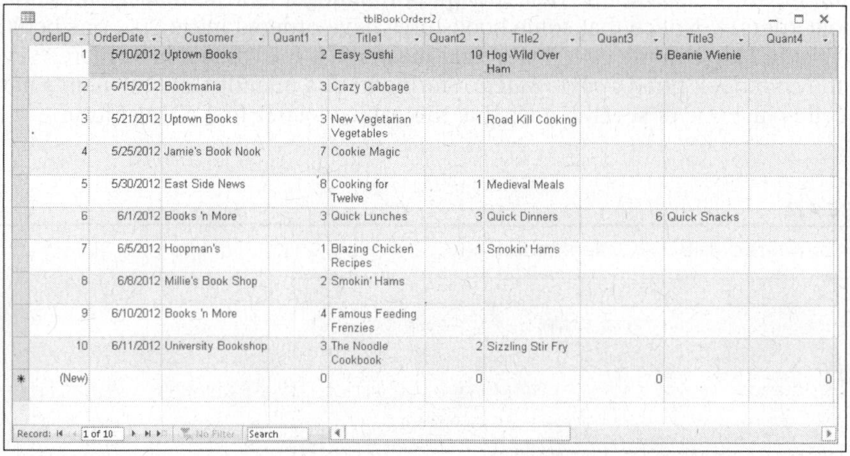

tblBookOrders2

OrderID	OrderDate	Customer	Quant1	Title1	Quant2	Title2	Quant3	Title3	Quant4
1	5/10/2012	Uptown Books	2	Easy Sushi	10	Hog Wild Over Ham	5	Beanie Wienie	
2	5/15/2012	Bookmania	3	Crazy Cabbage					
3	5/21/2012	Uptown Books	3	New Vegetarian Vegetables	1	Road Kill Cooking			
4	5/25/2012	Jamie's Book Nook	7	Cookie Magic					
5	5/30/2012	East Side News	8	Cooking for Twelve	1	Medieval Meals			
6	6/1/2012	Books 'n More	3	Quick Lunches	3	Quick Dinners	6	Quick Snacks	
7	6/5/2012	Hoopman's	1	Blazing Chicken Recipes	1	Smokin' Hams			
8	6/8/2012	Millie's Book Shop	2	Smokin' Hams					
9	6/10/2012	Books 'n More	4	Famous Feeding Frenzies					
10	6/11/2012	University Bookshop	3	The Noodle Cookbook	2	Sizzling Stir Fry			
(New)			0		0		0		0

Record: 1 of 10 No Filter Search

The design in Figure 4.3 is still clumsy and difficult to work with. The columns to hold the book quantities and titles are permanent features of the table. The developer must add enough columns to accommodate the maximum number of books that could be purchased on a single order. For example, let's assume that the developer anticipates that no bookstore will ever order more than 50 books at a time. This means that 100 columns are added to the table (two columns — Quantity and Title — are required for each book title ordered). If a bookstore orders a single book, 98 columns would sit empty in the table, a very wasteful and inefficient situation.

Based on the design shown in Figure 4.3, it would be exceedingly difficult to query tblBookOrders2 to get the sales figure for a particular book. The quantity sold for any book is scattered all over the table, in different rows and different columns, making it very difficult to know where to look for a book's sales data.

Also, if any book order exceeds 50 books, the table has to be redesigned to accommodate the additional columns needed by the order. Of course, the user might add a second row for the order, making the data in the table more difficult to work with than intended.

Figure 4.4 shows tblBookOrders3, a new table created from the data in Figure 4.3 in first normal form. Instead of stacking multiple book orders within a single record, in tblBookOrders3 each record contains a single book ordered by a customer. More records are required, but the data is handled much more easily. First normal form is much more efficient because the table contains no unused fields. Every field is meaningful to the table's purpose.

FIGURE 4.4

First normal form at last!

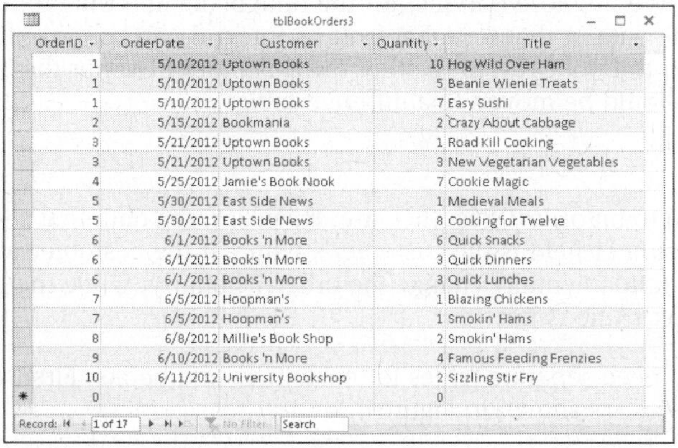

tblBookOrders3

OrderID	OrderDate	Customer	Quantity	Title
1	5/10/2012	Uptown Books	10	Hog Wild Over Ham
1	5/10/2012	Uptown Books	5	Beanie Wienie Treats
1	5/10/2012	Uptown Books	7	Easy Sushi
2	5/15/2012	Bookmania	2	Crazy About Cabbage
3	5/21/2012	Uptown Books	1	Road Kill Cooking
3	5/21/2012	Uptown Books	3	New Vegetarian Vegetables
4	5/25/2012	Jamie's Book Nook	7	Cookie Magic
5	5/30/2012	East Side News	1	Medieval Meals
5	5/30/2012	East Side News	8	Cooking for Twelve
6	6/1/2012	Books 'n More	6	Quick Snacks
6	6/1/2012	Books 'n More	3	Quick Dinners
6	6/1/2012	Books 'n More	3	Quick Lunches
7	6/5/2012	Hoopman's	1	Blazing Chickens
7	6/5/2012	Hoopman's	1	Smokin' Hams
8	6/8/2012	Millie's Book Shop	2	Smokin' Hams
9	6/10/2012	Books 'n More	4	Famous Feeding Frenzies
10	6/11/2012	University Bookshop	2	Sizzling Stir Fry
* 0			0	

Record: 1 of 17 No Filter Search

The table in Figure 4.4 contains the same data as shown in Figure 4.2 and Figure 4.3. The new arrangement, however, makes it much easier to work with the data. For example, queries are easily constructed to return the total number of a particular book ordered by contacts, or to determine which titles have been ordered by a particular bookstore.

TIP

Your tables should *always* be in first normal form. Make sure each cell of the table contains a single value, don't mix values within a cell, and don't have repeating groups (as you saw in Figure 4.3).

The table design optimization is not complete at this point, however. Much remains to be done with the BookOrders data and the other tables in this application. In particular, the table shown in Figure 4.4 contains a lot of redundant information. The book titles are repeated each time customers order the same book, and the order number and order date are repeated for all the rows for an order.

A more subtle issue is the fact that the OrderID can no longer be used as the table's primary key. Because the OrderID is duplicated for each book title in an order, it can't be used to identify individual records in the table. Instead, the OrderID field is now a key field for the table and can be used to locate all the records relevant to a particular order. The next step of optimization corrects this situation.

Second normal form

A more efficient design results from splitting the data in tblBookOrders into multiple tables to achieve *second normal form* (2NF). The second rule of normalization states the following:

> Data not directly dependent on the table's primary key is moved into another table.

This rule means that a table should contain data that represents a single entity. Because we're gradually turning one unnormalized table into normalized data, tblBookOrders3 doesn't have a primary key. We'll ignore that fact for the time being and think of each row in a table as an entity. All the data in that row that isn't an integral part of the entity is moved to a different table. In tblBookOrders3, neither the Customer field nor the Title field is integral to the order and should be moved to a different table.

Identifying entities

But aren't customers integral to an order? Yes, they are. However, the data that's stored in tblBookOrders3 in the Customer field is the customer's name. If the customer were to change names, it would not fundamentally change the order. Similarly, while the book is integral to the order, the book's title is not.

To remedy this situation, we need separate tables for customers and books. First, create a new table named tblBookStores, as shown in Figure 4.5.

FIGURE 4.5

Moving customer data to its own table.

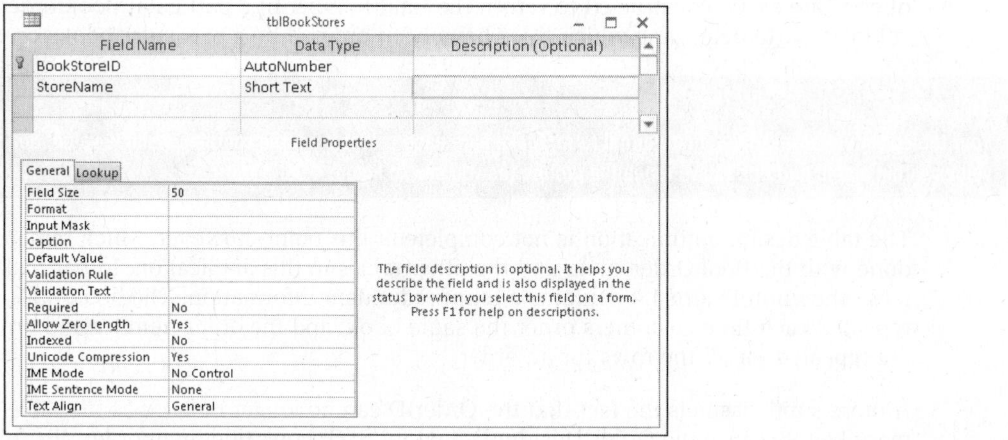

tblBookStores

Field Name	Data Type	Description (Optional)
BookStoreID	AutoNumber	
StoreName	Short Text	

Field Properties

General | Lookup

Field Size	50
Format	
Input Mask	
Caption	
Default Value	
Validation Rule	
Validation Text	
Required	No
Allow Zero Length	Yes
Indexed	No
Unicode Compression	Yes
IME Mode	No Control
IME Sentence Mode	None
Text Align	General

The field description is optional. It helps you describe the field and is also displayed in the status bar when you select this field on a form. Press F1 for help on descriptions.

To create tblBookStores follow these steps:

1. **Click Table Design on the Create tab of the Ribbon.**
2. **Add an AutoNumber field named BookStoreID.**
3. **Click Primary Key on the Table Tools Design tab of the Ribbon.**
4. **Add a Short Text field named StoreName.**
5. **Set the length of StoreName to 50.**
6. **Save the table as tblBookStores.**

You can imagine that we want to store some more information about customers, such as their mailing addresses and phone numbers. For now, we're getting our data into 2NF by moving data that isn't integral to an order to its own table.

Next create a table for books by following these steps:

1. **Click Table Design on the Create tab of the Ribbon.**
2. **Add an AutoNumber field named BookID.**
3. **Click Primary Key on the Table Tools Design tab of the Ribbon.**
4. **Add a Short Text field named BookTitle.**
5. **Save the table as tblBooks.**

The customer and the book are still integral to the order (just not the name and title) and we need a way to relate the tables to each other. While the customer may change names, the customer can't change the BookStoreID because we created it and we control it. Similarly, the publisher may change the book's title but not the BookID. The primary keys of tblBookStores and tblBooks are reliable pointers to the objects they identify, regardless of what other information may change.

Figure 4.6 shows our three tables, but instead of a customer name and a book title, tblBookOrder3 now contains the primary key of its related record in both tblBookStores and tblBooks. When the primary key of one table is used as a field in another table, it's called a *foreign key*.

FIGURE 4.6

The first step in making our table 2NF.

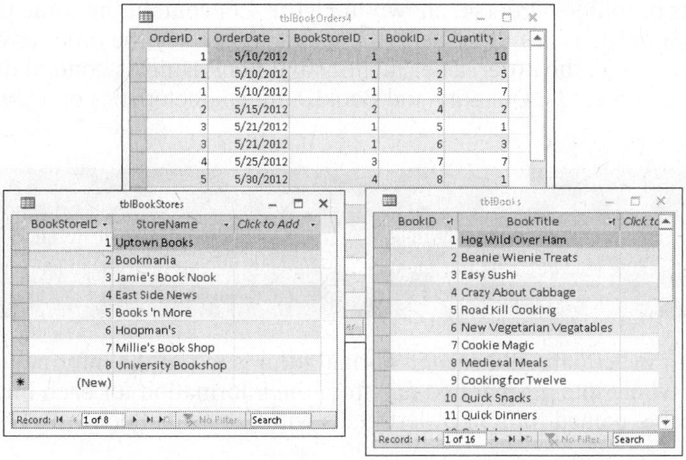

tblBookOrders4

OrderID	OrderDate	BookStoreID	BookID	Quantity
1	5/10/2012	1	1	10
1	5/10/2012	1	2	5
1	5/10/2012	1	3	7
2	5/15/2012	2	4	2
3	5/21/2012	1	5	1
3	5/21/2012	1	6	3
4	5/25/2012	3	7	7
5	5/30/2012	4	8	1

tblBookStores

BookStoreID	StoreName	Click to Add
1	Uptown Books	
2	Bookmania	
3	Jamie's Book Nook	
4	East Side News	
5	Books 'n More	
6	Hoopman's	
7	Millie's Book Shop	
8	University Bookshop	
(New)		

Record: 1 of 8 No Filter Search

tblBooks

BookID	BookTitle	Click to Add
1	Hog Wild Over Ham	
2	Beanie Wienie Treats	
3	Easy Sushi	
4	Crazy About Cabbage	
5	Road Kill Cooking	
6	New Vegetarian Vegatables	
7	Cookie Magic	
8	Medieval Meals	
9	Cooking for Twelve	
10	Quick Snacks	
11	Quick Dinners	

Record: 1 of 16 No Filter Search

Before we split out the customer data to its own table, if Uptown Books changed its name to Uptown Books and Periodicals, we would have to identify all the rows in tblBookOrders3 that had a customer of Uptown Books and change the field's value for each row identified.

Overlooking an instance of the customer's name during this process is called an *update anomaly* and results in records that are inconsistent with the other records in the database. From the database's perspective, Uptown Books and Uptown Books and Periodicals are two completely different organizations, even if we know that they're the same store. A query to retrieve all the orders placed by Uptown Books and Periodicals will miss any records that still have Uptown Books in the Customer field because of the update anomaly.

Another advantage of removing the customer name from the orders table is that the name now exists in only one location in the database. If Uptown Books changes its name to Uptown Books and Periodicals, we now only have to change its entry in the tblBookStores table. This single change is reflected throughout the database, including all forms and reports that use the customer name information.

Identifying separate entities and putting their data into separate tables is a great first step to achieving second normal form. But we're not quite done. Our orders table still doesn't have a unique field that we can use as the primary key. The OrderID field has repeating values that provide a clue that there is more work to be done to achieve 2NF.

Less obvious entities

Customers and books are physical objects that are easy to identify as separate entities. The next step is a little more abstract. Our orders table, now called tblBookOrders4, still contains information about two separate, but related, entities. The order is one entity, and the order details (the individual lines on the order) are entities all their own.

The first three records of tblBookOrders4, shown in Figure 4.6, contain the same OrderID, OrderDate, and BookStoreID. These three fields are characteristics of the order as a whole, not of each individual line on the order. The Quantity and BookID fields contain different values in those three first records. Quantity and BookID are characteristics of a particular line on the order.

TIP

Values that repeat in multiple records, like OrderID in tblBookOrders2 shown in Figure 4.6, is an indicator that your data is not yet in second normal form. Some data, like foreign keys, are meant to repeat. Other data, like dates and quantities, repeat naturally and aren't indicative of a problem.

The last step to get our order data into second normal form is to put the information integral to the order as a whole into a separate table from the information for each line on the order. Create a new table named tblBookOrderDetails with the fields BookOrderDetailID,

Quantity, and BookID. BookOrderDetailID is an AutoNumber field that will serve as the primary key, and BookID is a foreign key field that we use to relate the two tables. Figure 4.7 shows our new orders table, tblBookOrders5, and our new details table, tblBookOrderDetails.

FIGURE 4.7

We have achieved second normal form.

tblBookOrders5

OrderID	OrderDate	BookStoreID	Click to Add
1	5/10/2012	1	
2	5/15/2012	2	
3	5/21/2012	1	
4	5/25/2012	3	
5	5/30/2012	4	
6	6/1/2012		
7	6/5/2012		
8	6/8/2012		
9	6/10/2012		
10	6/11/2012		
(New)			

Record: 1 of 10

tblBookOrderDetails

BookOrderDetailID	OrderID	Quantity	BookID
1	1	10	1
2	1	5	2
3	1	7	3
4	2	2	4
5	3	1	5
6	3	3	6
7	4	7	7
8	5	1	8
9	5	8	9
10	6	6	10
11	6	3	11
12	6	3	12
13	7	1	13

Record: 1 of 17 No Filter Search

The OrderID field in tblBookOrders5 was deleted and a new AutoNumber field named OrderID was created. Now that we have a unique field in the orders table, we can set OrderID as the primary key. All the data in each record of tblBookOrders5 directly relates to an order entity. Or, in 2NF language, all the data is directly dependent on the primary key.

The OrderID field in tblBookOrderDetails is a foreign key that is used to relate the two tables together. Figure 4.7 shows that the first three records in tblBookOrderDetails show an OrderID of 1 that maps to the first record of tblBookOrders5.

All the fields in tblBookOrderDetails are directly dependent on the primary key BookOrderDetailID. The quantity from the first record, 10, relates directly to that line item on the order. It only relates to the order as a whole indirectly, just as the quantities from the next two records, 5 and 7, do. That indirect relationship is created by including the OrderID foreign key in the record.

The original table, tblBookOrders1, contained data about several different entities in each record. Through a series of steps, we split the data into four tables — tblBookOrders5, tblBookOrderDetails, tblCustomers, and tblBooks — each of which contains data about one entity. Our data is finally in the second normal form.

Breaking a table into individual tables, each of which describes some aspect of the data, is called *decomposition*. Decomposition is a very important part of the normalization process. Even though the tables appear smaller than the original table (refer to Figure 4.2), the data contained within the tables is the same as before.

A developer working with the bookstore tables is able to use queries to recombine the data in the four tables in new and interesting ways. It'd be quite easy to determine how many books of each type have been ordered by the different customers, or how many times a particular book has been ordered. When coupled with a table containing information such as book unit cost, book selling price, and so on, the important financial status of the book wholesaler becomes clear.

Notice also that the number of records in tblBookOrders5 has been reduced. This is one of several advantages to using a relational database. Each table contains only as much data as is necessary to represent the entity (in this case, a book order) described by the table. This is far more efficient than adding duplicate field values (refer to Figure 4.2) for each new record added to a table.

Breaking the rules

From time to time, you might find it necessary to break the rules. For example, let's assume that the bookstores are entitled to discounts based on the volume of purchases over the last year. Strictly following the rules of normalization, the discount percentage should be included in the tblBookStores table. After all, the discount is dependent on the customer, not on the order.

But maybe the discount applied to each order is somewhat arbitrary. Maybe the book wholesaler permits the salespeople to cut special deals for valued customers. In this case, you might want to include a Discount column in the table containing book orders information, even if it means duplicating information in many records. You could store the traditional discount as part of the customer's record in tblBookStores, and use it as the default value for the Discount column but permit the salesperson to override the discount value when a special arrangement has been made with the customer.

In fact, it only appears that this breaks the second normal form. The default discount is directly dependent on the customer. The actual discount given is directly dependent on the order. A similar situation might exist with shipping addresses. A customer may have most of their orders shipped to them, but occasionally they may want to have an order shipped directly to their customer. The customer's shipping address directly relates to the customer, and the address where the order was actually shipped relates directly to the order. Values in object tables that serve as default values in transaction tables are common in large databases.

See Chapter 3 for a discussion of object tables and transaction tables.

Third normal form

The last step of normalization, called third normal form (3NF), requires removing all fields that can be derived from data contained in other fields in the table or other tables in the database. For example, let's say the sales manager insists that you add a field to contain the total number of books in an order in the Orders table. This information, of course, would be calculated from the Quantity field in tblBookOrderDetails.

It's not really necessary to add the new OrderTotal field to the Orders table. Access easily calculates this value from data that is available in the database. The only advantage of storing order totals as part of the database is to save the few milliseconds required for Access to retrieve and calculate the information when the calculated data is needed by a form or report.

Removing calculated data maintains the integrity of the data in your database. Figure 4.7 shows three records in tblBookOrderDetails that relate to the order with OrderID of 1. Summing the Quantity field, you can see that 22 books were ordered. If there were an OrderTotal field and the total were incorrectly entered as 33 instead of 22, the data would be inconsistent. A report showing total books ordered using the OrderTotal field would show a different number than a report based on the Details table.

Depending on the applications you build, you might find good reasons to store calculated data in tables, particularly if performing the calculations is a lengthy process, or if the stored value is necessary as an audit check on the calculated value printed on reports. It might be more efficient to perform the calculations during data entry (when data is being handled one record at a time) instead of when printing reports (when many thousands of records are manipulated to produce a single report).

As you'll read in the "Denormalization" section, later in this chapter, there are some good reasons why you might choose to include calculated fields in a database table. As you'll read in this section, most often the decision to denormalize is based on a need to make sure the same calculated value is stored in the database as is printed on a report.

TIP

Although higher levels of normalization are possible, you'll find that, for most database applications, third normal form is more than adequate. At the very least, you should always strive for first normal form in your tables by moving redundant or repeating data to another table.

More on Anomalies

This business about update anomalies is important to keep in mind. The whole purpose of normalizing the tables in your databases is to achieve maximum performance with minimum maintenance effort.

Three types of errors can occur from an unnormalized database design. Following the rules outlined in this chapter will help you avoid the following pitfalls:

- **Insertion anomaly:** An error occurs in a related table when a new record is added to another table. For example, let's say you've added the OrderTotal field described in the previous section. After the order has been processed, the customer calls and changes the number of books ordered or adds a new book title to the same order. Unless you've carefully designed the database to automatically update the calculated OrderTotal field, the data in that field will be in error as the new data is inserted into the table.

  If insertion anomalies are a problem in your applications, you may be able to use macros (see Chapter 22) to help synchronize the data in your tables when changes are made.
- **Deletion anomaly:** A deletion anomaly causes the accidental loss of data when a record is deleted from a table. Let's assume that the tblBookOrders3 table contains the name, address, and other contact information for each bookstore. Deleting the last remaining record containing a particular customer's order causes the customer's contact information to be unintentionally lost. Keeping the customer contact information in a separate table preserves and protects that data from accidental loss. Avoiding deletion anomalies is one good reason not to use cascading deletes in your tables. (See the "Table Relationships" section, later in this chapter, for more on cascading deletes.)
- **Update anomaly:** Storing data that is not dependent on the table's primary key causes you to have to update multiple rows anytime the independent information changes. Keeping the independent data (such as the bookstore information) in its own table means that only a single instance of the information needs to be updated. (For more on update anomalies, see "Further optimization: Adding tables to the scheme" earlier in this chapter.)

Denormalization

After hammering you with all the reasons why normalizing your databases is a good idea, let's consider when you might deliberately choose to denormalize tables or use unnormalized tables.

Generally speaking, you normalize data in an attempt to improve the performance of your database. For example, in spite of all your efforts, some lookups will be time consuming. Even when using carefully indexed and normalized tables, some lookups require quite a bit of time, especially when the data being looked up is complicated or there's a large amount of it.

Similarly, some calculated values may take a long time to evaluate. You may find it more expedient to simply store a calculated value than to evaluate the expression on the fly. This is particularly true when the user base is working on older, memory-constrained, or slow computers.

Another common reason for denormalizing data is to provide the ability to exactly reproduce a document as it was originally produced. For example, if you need to reprint an invoice from a year ago but the customer's name has changed in the last year, reprinting the invoice will show the new name in a perfectly normalized database. If there are business reasons that dictate the invoice be reproducible precisely, the customer's name may need to be stored in the invoice record at the time the invoice is created.

Be aware that most steps to denormalize a database schema result in additional programming time required to protect the data and user from the problems caused by an unnormalized design. For example, in the case of the calculated OrderTotal field, you must insert code that calculates and updates this field whenever the data in the fields underlying this value change. This extra programming, of course, takes time to implement and time to process at runtime.

CAUTION
Make sure that denormalizing the design does not cause other problems. If you know you've deliberately denormalized a database design and you're having trouble making everything work (particularly if you begin to encounter any of the anomalies discussed in the previous section), look for workarounds that permit you to work with a fully normalized design.

Finally, always document whatever you've done to denormalize the design. It's entirely possible that you or someone else will be called in to provide maintenance or to add new features to the application. If you've left design elements that seem to violate the rules of normalization, your carefully considered work may be undone by another developer in an effort to "optimize" the design. The developer doing the maintenance, of course, has the best of intentions, but he may inadvertently reestablish a performance problem that was resolved through subtle denormalization.

One thing to keep in mind is that denormalization is almost always done for reporting purposes, rather than simply to maintain data in tables. Consider a situation in which a customer has been given a special discount that doesn't correspond to his traditional discount. It may be very useful to store the actual amount invoiced to the customer, instead of relying on the database to calculate the discount each time the report is printed. Storing the actual amount ensures that the report always reflects the amount invoiced to the customer, instead of reporting a value that depends on other fields in the database that may change over time.

Table Relationships

Many people start out using a spreadsheet application like Excel or Lotus 1-2-3 to build a database. Unfortunately, a spreadsheet stores data as a two-dimensional worksheet (rows and columns) with no easy way to connect individual worksheets together. You must manually connect each cell of the worksheet to the corresponding cells in other worksheets — a tedious process at best.

Two-dimensional storage objects like worksheets are called *flat-file databases* because they lack the three-dimensional quality of relational databases. Figure 4.8 shows an Excel worksheet used as a flat-file database.

FIGURE 4.8

An Excel worksheet used as a flat-file database.

	A	B	C	D	E	F	G
1	EmployeeID	LastName	FirstName	Title	PayrollDate	CheckNumber	CheckAmount
2	1	Davolio	Nancy	Marketing Manager	8/23/2014	10344	1417.38
3	2	Fuller	Andrew	Vice President, Sales	8/23/2014	10345	3327.56
4	3	Leverling	Janet	Sales Representative	8/23/2014	10346	1952.19
5	4	Peacock	Margaret	Sales Representative	8/23/2014	10347	1417.38
6	5	Buchanan	Steven	Sales Manager	8/23/2014	10348	2113.76
7	6	Suyama	Michael	Sales Representative	8/23/2014	10349	2113.76
8	7	King	Robert	Sales Representative	8/23/2014	10350	978.55
9	8	Callahan	Laura	Inside Sales Coordinator	8/23/2014	10351	1952.19
10	9	Dodsworth	Anne	Sales Representative	8/23/2014	10352	1952.19
11	1	Davolio	Nancy	Marketing Manager	8/30/2014	10353	1417.38
12	2	Fuller	Andrew	Vice President, Sales	8/30/2014	10354	3327.56
13	3	Leverling	Janet	Sales Representative	8/30/2014	10355	1952.19
14	4	Peacock	Margaret	Sales Representative	8/30/2014	10356	1417.38
15	5	Buchanan	Steven	Sales Manager	8/30/2014	10357	1215.92
16							

Sheet1

The problems with flat-file databases should be immediately apparent from viewing Figure 4.8. Notice that the employee information is duplicated in multiple rows of the worksheet. Each time a payroll check is issued to an employee, a new row is added to the worksheet. Obviously, this worksheet would rapidly become unmanageably large and unwieldy.

Consider the amount of work required to make relatively simple changes to the data in Figure 4.8. For example, changing an employee's title requires searching through numerous records and editing the data contained within individual cells, creating many opportunities for errors.

Through clever programming in the Excel VBA language, it would be possible to link the data in the worksheet shown in Figure 4.8 with another worksheet containing paycheck detail information. It would also be possible to programmatically change data in individual rows. But such Herculean efforts are needless when you harness the power of a relational database such as Access.

Connecting the data

A table's primary key uniquely identifies the records in a table. In a table of employee data, the employee's Social Security number, a combination of first and last names, or an employee ID might be used as the primary key. Let's assume the employee ID is selected as the primary key for the Employees table. When the relationship to the Payroll table is formed, the EmployeeID field is used to connect the tables together. Figure 4.9 shows this sort of arrangement (see the "One-to-many" section, later in this chapter).

Some of the issues related to using natural keys (such as Social Security number) are discussed in the "Natural versus surrogate primary keys" section, later in this chapter.

FIGURE 4.9

The relationship between the Employees and Payroll tables is an example of a typical one-to-many relationship.

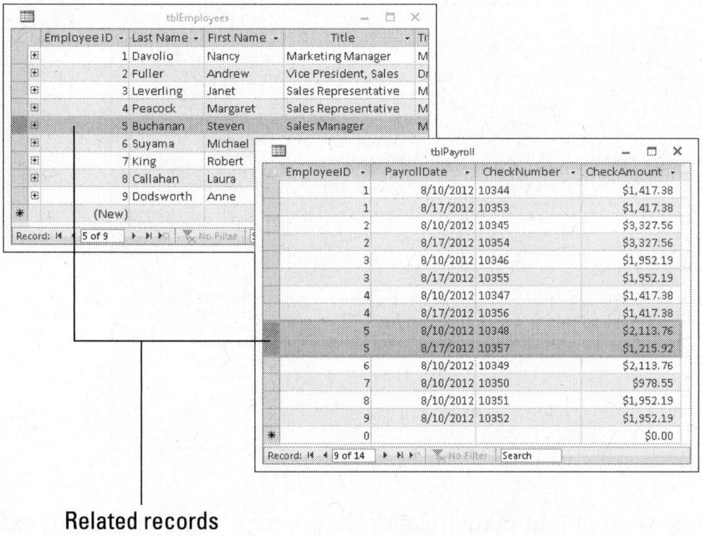

tblEmployees

Employee ID	Last Name	First Name	Title	Ti
1	Davolio	Nancy	Marketing Manager	M
2	Fuller	Andrew	Vice President, Sales	Dr
3	Leverling	Janet	Sales Representative	M
4	Peacock	Margaret	Sales Representative	M
5	Buchanan	Steven	Sales Manager	M
6	Suyama	Michael		
7	King	Robert		
8	Callahan	Laura		
9	Dodsworth	Anne		
(New)				

Record: 5 of 9 No Filter

tblPayroll

EmployeeID	PayrollDate	CheckNumber	CheckAmount
1	8/10/2012	10344	$1,417.38
1	8/17/2012	10353	$1,417.38
2	8/10/2012	10345	$3,327.56
2	8/17/2012	10354	$3,327.56
3	8/10/2012	10346	$1,952.19
3	8/17/2012	10355	$1,952.19
4	8/10/2012	10347	$1,417.38
4	8/17/2012	10356	$1,417.38
5	8/10/2012	10348	$2,113.76
5	8/17/2012	10357	$1,215.92
6	8/10/2012	10349	$2,113.76
7	8/10/2012	10350	$978.55
8	8/10/2012	10351	$1,952.19
9	8/10/2012	10352	$1,952.19
0			$0.00

Record: 9 of 14 No Filter Search

Related records

Although you can't see the relationship in Figure 4.9, Access knows it's there because a formal relationship has been established between tblEmployees and tblPayroll (this process is described in the "Creating relationships and enforcing referential integrity" section, later in this chapter). Because of the relationship between these tables, Access is able to instantly retrieve all the records from tblPayroll for any employee in tblEmployees.

The relationship example shown in Figure 4.9, in which each record of tblEmployees is related to several records in tblPayroll, is the most common type found in relational database systems, but it's by no means the only way that data in tables is related. This book, and most books on relational databases such as Access, discuss the three basic types of relationships between tables:

- One-to-one
- One-to-many
- Many-to-many

Figure 4.10 shows most of the relationships in the Collectible Mini Cars database.

FIGURE 4.10

Most of the Collectible Mini Cars table relationships.

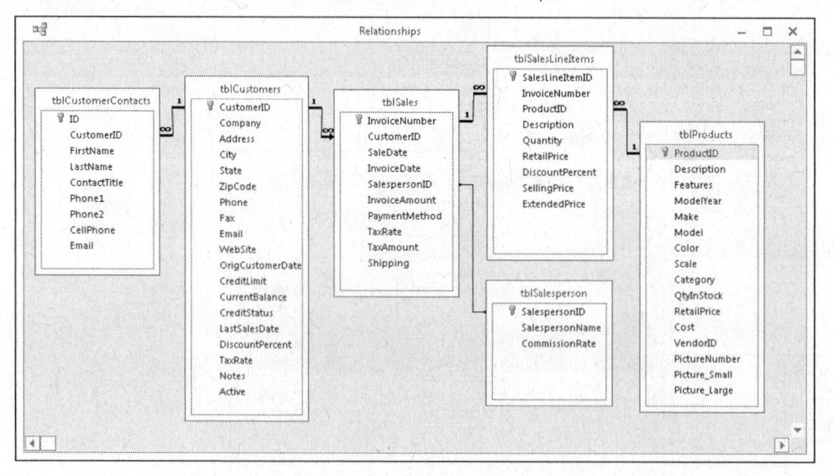

Notice that there are several one-to-many relationships between the tables (for example, tblSales-to-tblSalesPayments, tblSales-to-tblSalesLineItems, and tblCustomers-to-tblSales). The relationship that you specify between tables is important. It tells Access how to find and display information from fields in two or more tables. The program needs to know whether to look for only one record in a table or look for several records on the basis of the relationship. tblSales, for example, is related to tblCustomers as a many-to-one relationship. This is because the focus of the Collectible Mini Cars system is on sales. This means that there will *always* be only one customer related to every sales record. That is, many sales can be associated with a single customer. In this case, the Collectible Mini Cars system is actually using tblCustomers as a lookup table.

NOTE

Relationships can be very confusing — they depend upon the focus of the system. For example, when working with tblCustomers and tblSales, you can always create a query that has a one-to-many relationship to tblSales from tblCustomers. Although the system is concerned with sales (invoices), sometimes you'll want to produce reports or views that are customer related instead of invoice related. Because one customer can have more than one sale, there will always be one record in tblCustomers and at least one record in tblSales. In fact, there could be many related records in tblSales. So, Access knows to find only one record in the Customers table and to look for any records in the Sales table (one or more) that have the same customer number.

One-to-one

A one-to-one relationship between tables means that for every record in the first table, one and only one record exists in the second table. Figure 4.11 illustrates this concept.

FIGURE 4.11

A one-to-one relationship.

tblBusinesses

CustomerID	CustomerName
1	Suncoast Cinema
2	Decorating Elements, Inc.
3	Drawbridge Travel
4	Flammer Ford
5	Hyatt Legal Services
6	Cooler Air Conditioning
7	Timmerman Chevrolet
8	Lexus of Clearwater
9	Keller and Company
10	Homer's Funeral Home
11	Genie, Inc.
12	Fisher Trailers
13	Rising Waters
14	Shady Grove Nursery
15	Western Wear USA
16	Express Cleaners
17	Henry's Car Care
18	Technology Resources
19	Frank Realtors
20	Quick Auto Detail

Record: 9 of 20 No Filter Se

tblSecurityIDs

CustomerID	SecurityCode
1	1040
2	3125
3	1171
4	4669
5	7424
6	2765
7	7928
8	5588
9	8519
10	0187
11	2977
12	7394
13	4865
14	5223
15	3034
16	1014
17	0079
18	3999
19	7811
20	7446

Record: 9 of 20

Pure one-to-one relationships are not common in relational databases. In most cases, the data contained in the second table is included in the first table. As a matter of fact, one-to-one relationships are generally avoided because they violate the rules of normalization. Following the rules of normalization, data should not be split into multiple tables if the data describe a single entity. Because a person has one and only one birth date, the birth date should be included in the table containing a person's other data.

There are times, however, when storing certain data along with other data in the table isn't a good idea. For example, consider the situation illustrated in Figure 4.11. The data contained in tblSecurityIDs is confidential. Normally, you wouldn't want anyone with access to the public customer information (name, address, and so on) to have access to the confidential security code that the customer uses for purchasing or billing purposes. If necessary, tblSecurityIDs could be located on a different disk somewhere on the network, or even maintained on removable media to protect it from unauthorized access.

Another instance of a one-to-one relationship is a situation in which the data in a table exceeds the 255-field limit imposed by Access. Although rare, there could be cases in which you might have too many fields to be contained within a single table. The easiest solution is simply to split the data into multiple tables and connect the tables in a one-to-one relationship through the primary key (using the same key value, of course, in each table).

A common situation for one-to-one relationships is when data are being transferred or shared among databases. Perhaps the shipping clerk in an organization doesn't need to see all of a customer's data. Instead of including irrelevant information such as job titles, birth dates, alternate phone numbers, and e-mail addresses, the shipping clerk's database contains only the customer's name, address, and other shipping information. A record in the Customers table in the shipping clerk's database has a one-to-one relationship with the corresponding record in the master Customers table located on the central computer somewhere within the organization. Although the data is contained within separate ACCDB files, the links between the tables can be *live* (meaning that changes to the master record are immediately reflected in the shipping clerk's ACCDB file).

Tables joined in a one-to-one relationship will almost always have the same primary key — for example, OrderID or EmployeeNumber. There are very few reasons you would create a separate key field for the second table in a one-to-one relationship.

One-to-many

A far more common relationship between tables in a relational database is the one-to-many. In one-to-many relationships, each record in the first table (the *parent*) is related to one or more records in the second table (the *child*). Each record in the second table is related to one and only one record in the first table.

Without a doubt, one-to-many relationships are the most common type encountered in relational database systems. Examples of one-to-many situations abound:

- **Customers and orders:** Each customer (the "one" side) has placed several orders (the "many" side), but each order is sent to a single customer.
- **Teacher and student:** Each teacher has many students, but each student has a single teacher (within a particular class, of course).
- **Employees and paychecks:** Each employee has received several paychecks, but each paycheck is given to one and only one employee.
- **Patients and treatments:** Each patient receives zero or more treatments for a disease, but each treatment is given to multiple patients.

As we discuss in the "Creating relationships and enforcing referential integrity" section, later in this chapter, Access makes it very easy to establish one-to-many relationships between tables. A one-to-many relationship is illustrated in Figure 4.12. This figure, using tables from the Northwind Traders database, clearly demonstrates how each record in the Customers table is related to several different records in the Orders table. An order can be sent to only a single customer, so all requirements of one-to-many relationships are fulfilled by this arrangement.

FIGURE 4.12

The Northwind Traders database contains many examples of one-to-many relationships.

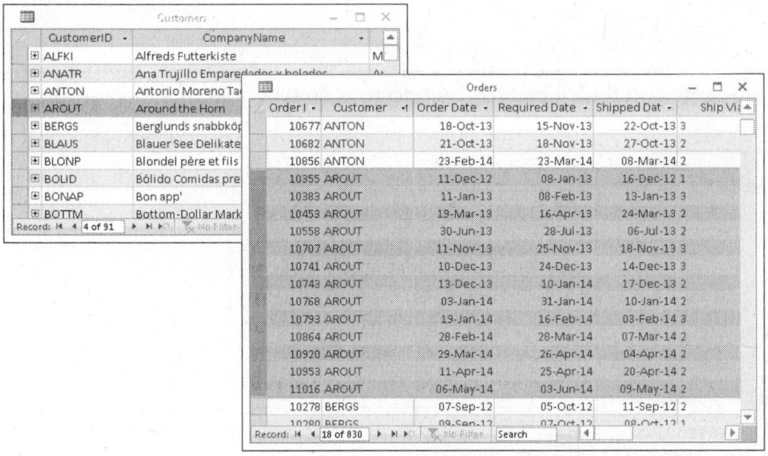

Although the records on the "many" side of the relationship illustrated in Figure 4.12 are sorted by the Customer field in alphabetical order, there is no requirement that the records in the "many" table be arranged in any particular order.

NOTE

Although *parent-child* is the most common expression used to explain the relationship between tables related in a one-to-many relationship, you may hear other expressions used, such as *master-detail,* applied to this design. The important thing to keep in mind is that the intent of referential integrity is to prevent lost records on the "many" side of the relationship. Referential integrity guarantees that there will never be an *orphan* (a child record without a matching parent record). As you work with related tables, it's important to keep in mind which table is on the "one" side and which is on the "many" side.

Notice how difficult it would be to record all the orders for a customer if a separate table were not used to store the order's information. The flat-file alternative discussed earlier in this section requires much more updating than the one-to-many arrangement shown in Figure 4.12. Each time a customer places an order with Northwind Traders, a new record is added to the Orders table. Only the Customer (for example, Around the Horn) is added to the Orders table as the foreign key back to the Customers table. Keeping the customer information is relatively trivial because each customer record appears only once in the Customers table.

Many-to-many

You'll come across many-to-many situations from time to time. In a many-to-many arrangement, each record in both tables can be related to zero, one, or many records in the other table. An example is shown in Figure 4.13. Each student in tblStudents can belong to more than one club, while each club in tblClubs has more than one member.

FIGURE 4.13

A database of students and the clubs they belong to is an example of a many-to-many relationship.

tblStudents

StudentID	LastName	FirstName
1	Hunter	Beth
2	Barde	Michael
3	Wilson	Patty
4	Casey	Kathleen
5	Smith	Victor
6	Mingus	Edgar
7	Williams	Barry
8	Pilgrim	Billy
9	Berry	David
10	Cohen	Frederick
11	Cesnick	Kevin
12	Walker	Jeffrey
13	Dakel	Colleen
14	Yurkak	
15	Lian	
16	Reisinger	
17	Henly	
18	Porte	

Record: 12 of 20

tblClubs

ClubID	ClubName	FacultyAdvisor
1	Astronomy	Wiggens, J.
2	Horticulture	Smith, P.
3	Photography	Williams, B.
4	French	Beuvier, L.
5	Science	Newton, I.
6	Art	McMinn, L.
7	Music	DeLong, J.
8	4-H	O'Dell, F.

Record: 2 of 8

tblStudentToClubJoin

StudentID	ClubID	DateJoined
6	2	
6	2	
7	2	
7	4	5/12/2012
7	1	2/9/2012
9	4	5/12/2012
12	3	9/24/2012
12	2	
13	1	2/9/2012
17	1	2/9/2012

Record: 12 of 15

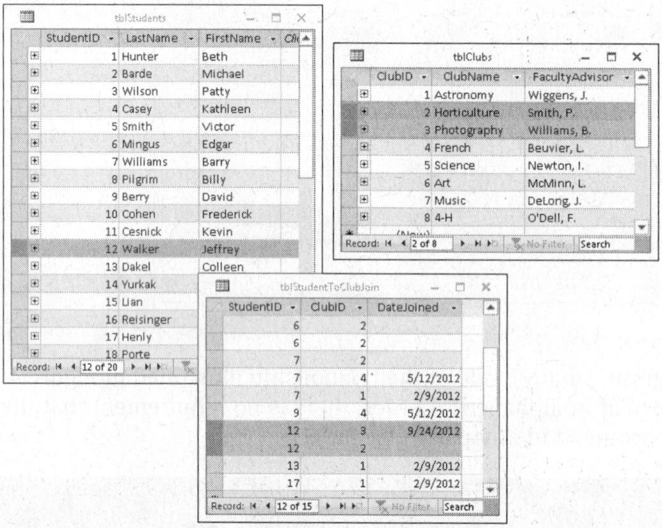

As indicated in Figure 4.13, many-to-many relationships are somewhat more difficult to understand because they can't be directly modeled in relational database systems like Access. Instead, the many-to-many relationship is broken into two separate one-to-many relationships, joined through a linking table (called a *join table*). The join table has one-to-many relationships with both of the tables involved in the many-to-many relationship. This principle can be a bit confusing at first, but close examination of Figure 4.13 soon reveals the beauty of this arrangement.

In Figure 4.13, you can see that Jeffrey Walker (StudentID 12) belongs to both the Horticulture and Photography clubs (ClubID = 2 and ClubID = 3), an example of one student belonging to many clubs. You can also see that the Horticulture Club (ClubID = 2) has Edgar Mingus, Barry Williams, and Jeffrey Walker (StudentIDs 6 ,7, and 12), an example of one club having many students. Each student belongs to multiple clubs, and each club contains multiple members.

Because of the additional complication of the join table, many-to-many relationships are often considered more difficult to establish and maintain. Fortunately, Access makes such relationships quite easy to establish, if a few rules are followed. These rules are explained in various places in this book. For example, in order to update either side of a many-to-many relationship (for example, to change club membership for a student), the join table must contain the primary keys of both tables joined by the relationship.

Many-to-many relationships are quite common in business environments:

- **Lawyers to clients (or doctors to patients):** Each lawyer may be involved in several cases, while each client may be represented by more than one lawyer on each case.
- **Patients and insurance coverage:** Many people are covered by more than one insurance policy. For example, if you and your spouse are both provided medical insurance by your employers, you have multiple coverage.
- **Video rentals and customers:** Over a year's time, each video is rented by several people, while each customer rents more than one video during the year.
- **Magazine subscriptions:** Most magazines have circulations measured in the thousands or millions. Most people subscribe to more than one magazine at a time.

The Collectible Mini Cars database has a many-to-many relationship between tblCustomers and tblSalesPayments, linked through tblSales. Each customer might have purchased more than one item, and each item might be paid for through multiple payments. In addition to joining contacts and sales payments, tblSales contains other information, such as the sale date and invoice number. The join table in a many-to-many relationship often contains information regarding the joined data.

Given how complicated many-to-many joins can be to construct, it's fortunate that many-to-many relationships are quite a bit less common than straightforward one-to-many situations.

As shown in Figure 4.13 join tables can contain information other than the primary keys of the tables they join. The tblStudentToClubJoin table includes a field to record the date that the related student joined the related club.

Integrity Rules

Access permits you to apply referential integrity rules that protect data from loss or corruption. *Referential integrity* means that the relationships between tables are preserved during updates, deletions, and other record operations. The relational model defines several rules meant to enforce the referential integrity requirements of relational databases. In addition, Access contains its own set of referential integrity rules that are enforced by the ACE database engine.

Imagine a payroll application that contained no rules regulating how data in the database is used. It'd be possible to issue payroll checks that aren't linked to an employee, for instance. From a business perspective, issuing paychecks to "phantom" employees is a very serious situation. Eventually, the issue will be noticed when the auditors step in and notify management of the discrepancy.

Referential integrity operates strictly on the basis of the tables' key fields. Referential integrity means that the database engine checks each time a key field (whether primary or foreign) is added, changed, or deleted. If a change to a value in a key field invalidates a relationship, it is said to violate referential integrity. Tables can be set up so that referential integrity is automatically enforced.

Figure 4.14 illustrates a relationship between a Customers table and a Sales table. tblCustomers is related to tblSales through the CustomerID field. The CustomerID field in tblCustomers is the primary key, while the CustomerID field in tblSales is a foreign key. The relationship connects each customer with a sales invoice. In this relationship, tblCustomers is the parent table, while tblSales is the child table.

FIGURE 4.14

A typical database relationship.

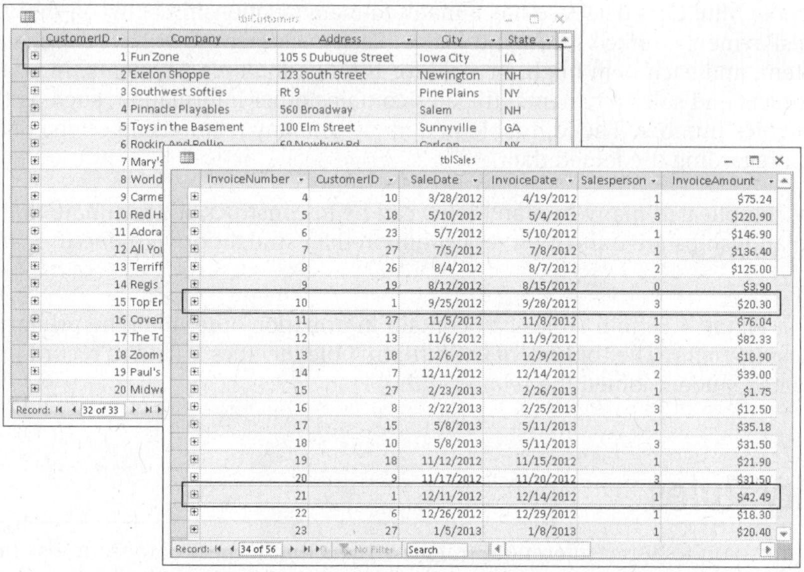

tblCustomers

CustomerID	Company	Address	City	State
1	Fun Zone	105 S Dubuque Street	Iowa City	IA
2	Exelon Shoppe	123 South Street	Newington	NH
3	Southwest Softies	Rt 9	Pine Plains	NY
4	Pinnacle Playables	560 Broadway	Salem	NH
5	Toys in the Basement	100 Elm Street	Sunnyville	GA
6	Rockin And Rollin	60 Newbury Rd	Carlson	NY
7	Mary's			
8	World			
9	Carme			
10	Red H			
11	Adora			
12	All Yo			
13	Terriff			
14	Regis			
15	Top Er			
16	Coven			
17	The To			
18	Zoom			
19	Paul's			
20	Midw			

Record: 32 of 33

tblSales

InvoiceNumber	CustomerID	SaleDate	InvoiceDate	Salesperson	InvoiceAmount
4	10	3/28/2012	4/19/2012	1	$75.24
5	18	5/10/2012	5/4/2012	3	$220.90
6	23	5/7/2012	5/10/2012	1	$146.90
7	27	7/5/2012	7/8/2012	1	$136.40
8	26	8/4/2012	8/7/2012	2	$125.00
9	19	8/12/2012	8/15/2012	0	$3.90
10	1	9/25/2012	9/28/2012	3	$20.30
11	27	11/5/2012	11/8/2012	1	$76.04
12	13	11/6/2012	11/9/2012	3	$82.33
13	18	12/6/2012	12/9/2012	1	$18.90
14	7	12/11/2012	12/14/2012	2	$39.00
15	27	2/23/2013	2/26/2013	1	$1.75
16	8	2/22/2013	2/25/2013	3	$12.50
17	15	5/8/2013	5/11/2013	1	$35.18
18	10	5/8/2013	5/11/2013	3	$31.50
19	18	11/12/2012	11/15/2012	1	$21.90
20	9	11/17/2012	11/20/2012	3	$31.50
21	1	12/11/2012	12/14/2012	1	$42.49
22	6	12/26/2012	12/29/2012	1	$18.30
23	27	1/5/2013	1/8/2013	1	$20.40

Record: 34 of 56 No Filter Search

Orphaned records are very bad in database applications. Because sales information is almost always reported as which products were sold to which customers, a sales invoice that is not linked to a valid customer will not be discovered under most circumstances. It's easy to know which products were sold to Fun Zone, but given an arbitrary sales record, it may not be easy to know that there is no valid customer making the purchase. In Figure 4.14, the invoice records related to Fun Zone are indicated by boxes drawn around the data in tblSales.

Because the referential integrity rules are enforced by the Access database engine, data integrity is ensured wherever the data appear in the database: in tables, queries, or forms. Once you've established the integrity requirements of your applications, you don't have to be afraid that data in related tables will become lost or disorganized.

We can't overemphasize the need for referential integrity in database applications. Many developers feel that they can use VBA code or user interface design to prevent orphaned records. The truth is that, in most databases, the data stored in a particular table may be used in many different places within the application, or even in other applications that use the data. Also, given the fact that many database projects extend over many years, and among any number of developers, it's not always possible to recall how data should be protected. By far, the best approach to ensuring the integrity of data stored in any database system is to use the power of the database engine to enforce referential integrity.

The general relational model referential integrity rules ensure that records contained in relational tables are not lost or confused. For obvious reasons, it's important that the primary keys connecting tables be protected and preserved. Also, changes in a table that affect other tables (for example, deleting a record on the "one" side of a one-to-many relationship) should be rippled to the other tables connected to the first table. Otherwise, the data in the two tables will quickly become unsynchronized.

No primary key can contain a null value

The first referential integrity rule states that no primary key can contain a null value. A *null value* is one that simply does not exist. The value of a field that has never been assigned a value (even a default value) is null. No row in a database table can have null in its primary key field because the main purpose of the primary key is to guarantee uniqueness of the row. Obviously, null values cannot be unique and the relational model would not work if primary keys could be null. Access will not allow you to set a field that already contains null values as the primary key.

Furthermore, Access can't evaluate a null value. Because a null value doesn't exist, it can't be compared with any other value. It isn't larger or smaller than any other value; it simply doesn't exist. Therefore, a null value can't be used to look up a record in a table or to form a relationship between two tables.

4

Access automatically enforces the first referential integrity rule. As you add data to tables, you can't leave the primary key field empty without generating a warning (one reason the AutoNumber field works so well as a primary key). Once you've designated a field in an Access table as the primary key, Access won't let you delete the data in the field, nor will it allow you to change the value in the field so that it duplicates a value in another record.

When using a composite primary key made up of several fields, all the fields in the composite key must contain values. None of the fields is allowed to be empty. The combination of values in the composite primary key must be unique.

All foreign key values must be matched by corresponding primary keys

The second referential integrity rule says that all foreign key values must be matched by corresponding primary keys. This means that every record in a table on the "many" (or child) side of a one-to-many relationship must have a corresponding record in the table on the "one" (or parent) side of the relationship. A record on the "many" side of a relationship without a corresponding record on the "one" side is said to be *orphaned* and is effectively removed from the database schema. Identifying orphaned records in a database can be very difficult, so you're better off avoiding the situation in the first place.

The second rule means the following:

- **Rows cannot be added to a "many" side table (the child) if a corresponding record does not exist on the "one" side (the parent).** If a child record contains a ParentID field, the ParentID value *must* match an existing record in the parent table.
- **The primary key value in a "one" side table cannot be changed if the change would create orphaned child records.**
- **Deleting a row on the "one" side must not orphan corresponding records on the "many" side.**

For example, in the sales example, the foreign key in each record in tblSales (the "many" side) must match a primary key in tblCustomers. You can't delete a record in tblCustomers (the "one" side) without deleting the corresponding records in tblSales.

One of the curious results of the rules of referential integrity is that it's entirely possible to have a parent record that isn't matched by any child records. Intuitively, this makes sense. A company may certainly have employees who haven't yet been issued paychecks. Or the Collectible Mini Cars company may hire a new employee who hasn't made any sales yet. Eventually, of course, most parent records are matched by one or more child records, but this condition is not a requirement of relational databases.

As you'll see in the next section, Access makes it easy to specify the integrity rules you want to employ in your applications. You should be aware, however, that not using the referential integrity rules means that you might end up with orphaned records and other data integrity problems.

Keys

When you create database tables, like those created in Chapter 3, you should assign each table a primary key. This key is a way to make sure that the table records contain only one unique value; for example, you may have several contacts named Michael Heinrich, and you may even have more than one Michael Heinrich (for example, father and son) living at the same address. So, in a case like this, you have to decide how you can create a record in the Customers database that will let you identify each Michael Heinrich separately.

Uniquely identifying each record in a table is precisely what a primary key field does. For example, using the Collectible Mini Cars as an example, the CustomerID field (a unique number that you assign to each customer placing an order) is the primary key in tblCustomers — each record in the table has a different CustomerID number. (No two records have the same number.) This is important for several reasons:

- You don't want to have two records in tblCustomers for the same customer, because this can make updating the customer's record virtually impossible.
- You want assurance that each record in the table is accurate so that the information extracted from the table is accurate.
- You don't want to make the table (and its records) any larger than necessary. Adding redundant or duplicate fields and records just complicates the database without adding value.

The ability to assign a single, unique value to each record makes the table clean and reliable. This is known as *entity integrity*. By having a different primary key value in each record (such as the CustomerID in tblCustomers), you can tell two records (in this case, customers) apart, even if all other fields in the records are the same. This is important because you can easily have two individual customers with a common name, such as Fred Smith, in your table.

Theoretically, you could use the customer's name and address, but two people named Fred D. Smith could live in the same town and state, or a father and son (Fred David Smith and Fred Daniel Smith) could live at the same address. The goal of setting primary keys is to create individual records in a table that *guarantees* uniqueness.

If you don't specify a primary key when creating Access tables, Access asks whether you want one. If you say yes, Access uses the AutoNumber data type to create a primary key for the table. An AutoNumber field is automatically inserted each time a record is added to the table, and it can't be changed once its value has been established. Furthermore, once an AutoNumber value has appeared in a table, the value will never be reused, even if the record containing the value is deleted and the value no longer appears in the table. In fact, because an AutoNumber field is added to a new record before any of the other data, if the new row is not saved for some reason, the new AutoNumber is never used in the table at all.

Deciding on a primary key

As you learned earlier, a table normally has a unique field (or combination of fields) — the primary key for that table — which makes each record unique. The primary key is an identifier that is often a text or AutoNumber data type. To determine the contents of this ID field, you specify a method for creating a unique value for the field. Your method can be as simple as letting Access automatically assign an AutoNumber value or using the first letter of the real value you're tracking along with a sequence number (such as A001, A002, A003, B001, B002, and so on). The method may rely on a random set of letters and numbers for the field content (as long as each field has a unique value) or a complicated calculation based on information from several fields in the table.

However, there is no reason why the primary key value has to be *meaningful* to the application. A primary key exists in a table solely to ensure uniqueness for each row and to provide an anchor for table relationships. Many Access developers routinely use AutoNumber fields as primary keys simply because they meet all the requirements of a primary key without contributing to an application's complexity.

In fact, meaningful primary keys can cause confusion as the data in the table changes. For example, if the primary key for a table of employee information is the first letter of the employee's last name plus a sequential number, then Jane Doe might have an EmployeeID of D001. If Jane were to get married and change her last name, her EmployeeID would no longer be consistent with the data in her record. Her EmployeeID may still be unique, but it may also cause confusion if someone were to rely on that data.

Table 4.1 lists the Collectible Mini Cars tables and describes one *possible* plan for deriving the primary key values in each table. As this table shows, it doesn't take a great deal of work (or even much imagination) to derive a plan for key values. Any rudimentary scheme with a good sequence number always works. Access automatically tells you when you try to enter a duplicate key value. To avoid duplication, you can simply add the value of 1 to the sequence number.

TABLE 4.1 Deriving the Primary Key

Table	Possible Derivation of Primary Key Value
tblCustomers	Companies: AutoNumber field assigned by Access
tblSales	Invoice Number: AutoNumber field
tblSalesLineItems	Invoice Number (from Sales) and an AutoNumber field
tblProducts	Product Number, entered by the person putting in a new product
tblSalesPayments	Invoice Number (from Sales) and an AutoNumber field
tblSalesperson	Sales Person ID: AutoNumber field
tblCategories	Category of Items: Entered by the person putting in a new record

Even though it isn't difficult to use logic (implemented, perhaps, though VBA code) to generate unique values for a primary key field, by far the simplest and easiest approach is to use AutoNumber fields for the primary keys in your tables. The special characteristics of the AutoNumber field (automatic generation, uniqueness, the fact that it can't be changed, and so on) make it the ideal candidate for primary keys. Furthermore, an AutoNumber value is nothing more than a 4-byte integer value, making it very fast and easy for the database engine to manage. For all these reasons, the Collectible Mini Cars exclusively uses AutoNumber fields as primary keys in its tables.

NOTE

AutoNumber fields are guaranteed to be unique, but they are not guaranteed to be sequential. There are a number of reasons why gaps in AutoNumbers can be introduced, such as deleting records, and you should never rely on AutoNumbers being sequential.

You may be thinking that all these sequence numbers make it hard to look up information in your tables. Just remember that, in most case, you never look up information by an ID field. Generally, you look up information according to the *purpose* of the table. In tblCustomers, for example, you would look up information by customer name — last name, first name, or both. Even when the same name appears in multiple records, you can look at other fields in the table (zip code, phone number) to find the correct customer. Unless you just happen to know the customer ID number, you'll probably never use it in a search for information.

Looking at the benefits of a primary key

Have you ever placed an order with a company for the first time and then decided the next day to increase your order? When you call the people at the order desk, they may ask you for your customer number. You tell them that you don't know your customer number. Next, they ask you for some other information — generally, your zip code and last name. Then, as they narrow down the list of customers, they ask your address. Once they've located you in their database, they can tell you your customer number. Some businesses use phone numbers or e-mail addresses as starting points when searching for customer records.

Primary and foreign keys are discussed in Chapter 1, but because these concepts are so important in database applications, they're covered again in this chapter.

Database systems usually have more than one table, and the tables are related in some manner. For example, in the Collectible Mini Cars database, tblCustomers and tblSales are related to each other through the CustomerID field. Because each customer is *one* person or organization, you only need one record in tblCustomers.

Each customer can make many purchases, however, which means you need to set up a second table to hold information about each sale — tblSales. Again, each invoice is *one* sale (on a specific day at a specific time). CustomerID is used to relate the customer to the sales.

The *primary key* in the parent table (CustomerID in tblCustomers) is related to a *foreign key* in the child table (the CustomersID field in the tblSales table).

Besides being a common link field between tables, the primary key field in an Access database table has the following advantages:

- Primary key fields are always indexed, greatly speeding up queries, searches, and sorts that involve the primary key field.
- Access forces you to enter a value (or automatically provides a value, in the case of AutoNumber fields) every time you add a record to the table. You're guaranteed that your database tables conform to the rules of referential integrity.
- As you add new records to a table, Access checks for duplicate primary key values and prevents duplicates entries, thus maintaining data integrity.
- By default, Access displays your data in primary key order.

TIP

An index is a special internal file that is created to put the records in a table in some specific order. For example, the primary key field in tblCustomers is an index that puts the records in order by CustomerID field. Using an indexed table, Access uses the index to quickly find records within the table.

Designating a primary key

From the preceding sections, you're aware that choosing a table's primary key is an important step toward bulletproofing a database's design. When properly implemented, primary keys help stabilize and protect the data stored in your Access databases. As you read the following sections, keep in mind that the cardinal rule governing primary keys is that the values assigned to the primary key field within a table must be unique. Furthermore, the ideal primary key is stable.

Single-field versus composite primary keys

Sometimes, when an ideal primary key doesn't exist within a table as a single value, you may be able to combine fields to create a *composite* primary key. For example, it's unlikely that a first name or last name alone is enough to serve as a primary key, but by combining first and last names with birth dates, you may be able to come up with a unique combination of values to serve as the primary key. As you'll see in the "Creating relationships and enforcing referential integrity" section, later in this chapter, Access makes it very easy to combine fields as composite primary keys.

There are several practical considerations when using composite keys:

- **None of the fields in a composite key can be null.**
- **Sometimes composing a composite key from data naturally occurring within the table can be difficult.** Sometimes records within a table differ by one or two fields, even when many other fields may be duplicated within the table.
- **Each of the fields can be duplicated within the table, but the combination of composite key fields cannot be duplicated.**

However, as with so many other issues in database design, composite keys have a number of issues:

- **Composite keys tend to complicate a database's design.** If you use three fields in a parent table to define the table's primary key, the same three fields must appear in every child table.
- **Ensuring that a value exists for all the fields within a composite key (so that none of the fields is null) can be quite challenging.**

TIP

Most developers avoid composite keys unless absolutely necessary. In many cases, the problems associated with composite keys greatly outweigh the minimal advantage of using composite keys generated from data within the record.

Natural versus surrogate primary keys

Many developers maintain that you should use only natural primary keys. A *natural primary key* is derived from data already in the table, such as a Social Security number or employee number. If no single field is enough to uniquely identify records in the table, these developers suggest combining fields to form a *composite primary key*.

However, there are many situations where no "perfect" natural key exists in database tables. Although a field like SocialSecurityNumber may seem to be the ideal primary key, there are a number of problems with this type of data:

- **The value is not universal.** Not everyone has a Social Security number.
- **The value may not be known at the time the record is added to the database.** Because primary keys can never be null, provisions must be made to supply some kind of "temporary" primary key when the Social Security number is unknown, and then other provisions must be made to fix up the data in the parent and child tables once the value becomes known.
- **Values such as Social Security number tend to be rather large.** A Social Security number is at least nine characters, even omitting the dashes between groups of numbers. Large primary keys unnecessarily complicate things and run more slowly than smaller primary keys.

4

- **Legal and privacy issues inhibit its use.** A Social Security number is considered "personally identifiable information" and (in the United States) its use is limited under the Social Security Protection Act of 2005.

CAUTION

By far the largest issue is that adding a record to a table is impossible unless the primary key value is known at the time the record is committed to the database. Even if temporary values are inserted until the permanent value is known, the amount of fix-up required in related tables can be considerable. After all, unless Cascade Update is enabled on the relationship, you can't change the value of a primary key if related child records exist in other tables.

Although an AutoNumber value does not naturally occur in the table's data, because of the considerable advantages of using a simple numeric value that is automatically generated and cannot be deleted or changed, in most cases an AutoNumber is the ideal primary key candidate for most tables.

Creating primary keys

A primary key is created by opening a table in Design view, selecting the field(s) that you want to use as a primary key, and clicking the Primary Key button on the Table Tools Design tab of the Ribbon. If you're specifying more than one field to create a composite key, hold down the Ctrl key while using the mouse to select the fields before clicking on the Primary Key button.

Setting a table's primary key is covered in detail in Chapter 3.

Creating relationships and enforcing referential integrity

The Relationships window lets you establish the relationships and referential integrity rules that you want to apply to the tables involved in a relationship. Creating a permanent, managed relationship that ensures referential integrity between Access tables is easy:

1. **Select Database Tools⇨Relationships.** The Relationships window appears.
2. **Click the Show Table button on the Ribbon, or right-click the Relationships window and select Show Table from the shortcut menu.** The Add Table dialog box (shown in Figure 4.15) appears.
3. **Add tblBookOrders5 and tblOrderDetails to the Relationships window (double-click each table in the Show Table dialog box, or select each table and click the Add button).**
4. **Create a relationship by dragging the primary key field in the "one" table and dropping it on the foreign key in the "many" table.** Alternatively, drag the foreign key field and drop it on the primary key field.

FIGURE 4.15

Double-click to add tables to the Relationships window.

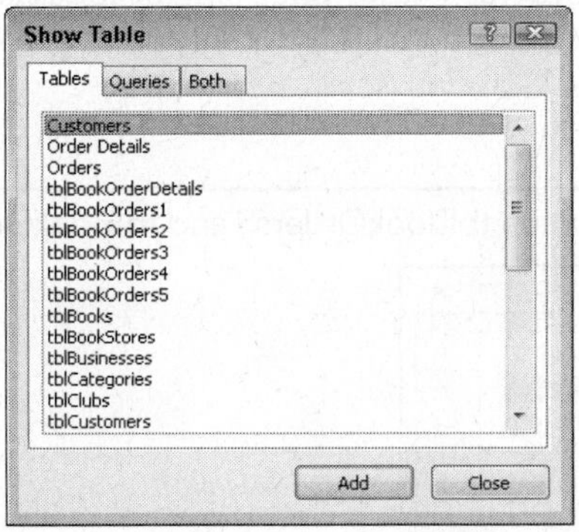

For this example, drag OrderID from tblBookOrders5 and drop it on OrderID in tblBookOrderDetails. Access immediately opens the Edit Relationships dialog box (shown in Figure 4.16) to enable you to specify the details about the relationship you intend to form between the tables. Notice that Access recognizes that the relationship between the tblBookOrders5 and tblBookOrderDetails as a one-to-many.

5. **Specify the referential details you want Access to enforce in the database.** In Figure 4.16, notice the Cascade Delete Related Records check box. If this check box is left unchecked, Access won't permit you to delete records in tblBookOrders5 (the "one" table) until all the corresponding records in tblBookOrderDetails (the "many" table) are first deleted. With this box checked, deletions across the relationship "cascade" automatically. Cascading deletes can be a dangerous operation because the deletions in the "many" table occur without confirmation.

FIGURE 4.16

You enforce referential integrity in the Edit Relationships dialog box.

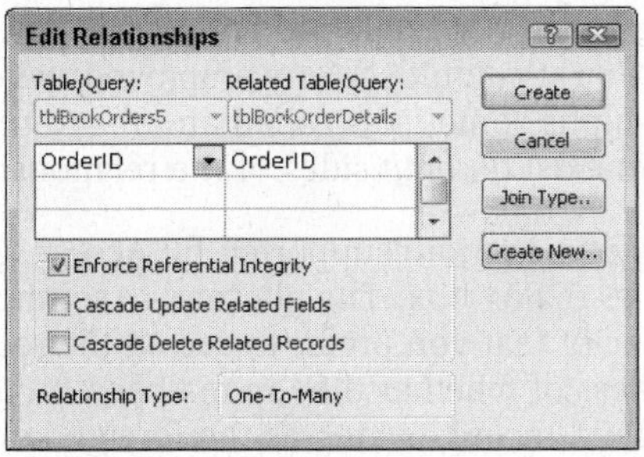

6. **Click the Create button.** Access draws a line between the tables displayed in the Relationships window, indicating the type of relationship. In Figure 4.17, the 1 symbol indicates that tblBookOrders5 is the "one" side of the relationship while the infinity symbol (∞) designates tblBookOrderDetails as the "many" side.

FIGURE 4.17

A one-to-many relationship between tblBookOrders5 and tblBookOrderDetails.

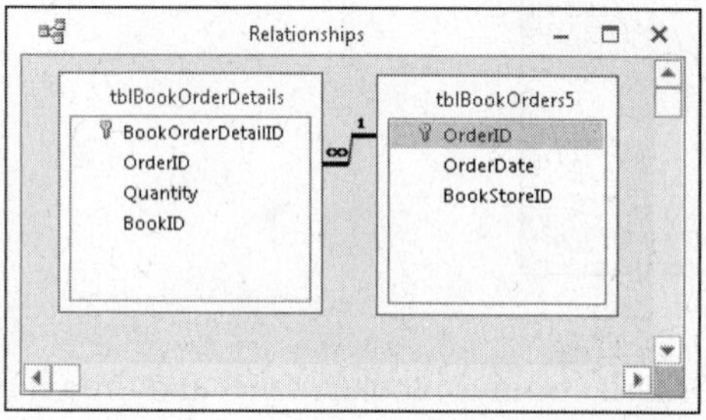

Specifying the join type between tables

The right side of the Edit Relations window has four buttons:

- **Create:** Clicking the Create button returns you to the Relationships window with the changes specified.
- **Cancel:** The Cancel button cancels the current changes and returns you to the Relationships window.
- **Join Type:** The Join Type button opens the Join Properties dialog box.
- **Create New:** The Create New button lets you specify an entirely new relationship between the two tables and fields.

By default, when you process a query on related tables, Access only returns records that appear in both tables. Considering the payroll example from the "Integrity Rules" section, earlier in this chapter, this means that you would only see employees that have valid paycheck records in the paycheck table. You wouldn't see any employees who haven't yet received a paycheck. Such a relationship is sometimes called an *inner join* because the only records that appear are those that exist on *both* sides of the relationship.

However, the inner join is not the only type of join supported by Access. Click the Join Type button to open the Join Properties dialog box. The alternative settings in the Join Properties dialog box allow you to specify that you prefer to see all the records from either the parent table or child table, regardless of whether they're matched on the other side. (It's possible to have an unmatched child record as long as the foreign key in the child table is null.) Such a join (called an *outer join*) can be very useful because it accurately reflects the state of the data in the application.

In the case of the Collectible Mini Cars example, seeing all the customers, regardless of whether they have records in the Sales table, is what you're shooting for. To specify an outer join connecting customers to sales, perform these steps:

1. **From the Relationships window, add tblCustomers and tblSales.**
2. **Drag the CustomerID from one table and drop it on the other.** The Edit Relationships dialog box appears.
3. **Click the Join Type button.** The Join Properties dialog box (shown in Figure 4.18) appears.
4. **Select the Include ALL Records from 'tblCustomers' and Only Those Records from 'tblSales' Where the Joined Fields Are Equal option button.**

FIGURE 4.18

The Join Properties dialog box, used to set up the join properties between tblCustomers and tblSales. Notice that it specifies all records from the Contacts table.

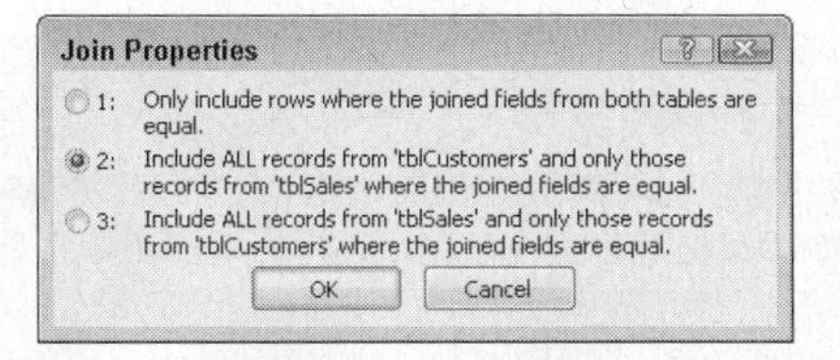

5. **Click OK.** You're returned to the Edit Relationships dialog box.
6. **Click OK.** You're returned to the Relationships window. The Relationships window should now show an arrow going from the Contacts table to the Sales table. At this point, you're ready to set referential integrity between the two tables on an outer join relationship.

TIP

To change an existing relationship, double-click the line in the Relationships window for the relationship you'd like to change. The Edit Relationships dialog box appears, and you can change referential integrity and join type settings.

Given the join properties shown in Figure 4.18, any time the Customers and Sales tables are involved in a query, all the customer records are returned, even if a customer hasn't yet placed any orders. This setting should give a more complete impression of the company's customer base instead of restricting the returned records to customers who've placed orders.

Establishing a join type for every relationship in your database isn't absolutely necessary. In the following chapters, you'll see that you can specify outer joins for each query in your application. Many developers choose to use the default inner join for all the relationships in their databases and to adjust the join properties on each query to yield the desired results.

Enforcing referential integrity

After using the Edit Relationships dialog box to specify the relationship, to verify the table and related fields, and to specify the type of join between the tables, you should set referential integrity between the tables. Select the Enforce Referential Integrity check box in the lower portion of the Edit Relationships dialog box to indicate that you want Access to enforce the referential integrity rules on the relationship between the tables.

CAUTION

If you choose not to enforce referential integrity, you can add new records, change key fields, or delete related records without warnings about referential integrity violations — thus, making it possible to change critical fields and damaging the application's data. With no integrity active, you can create tables that have orphans (Sales without a Contact). With normal operations (such as data entry or changing information), referential integrity rules should be enforced.

Enforcing referential integrity also enables two other options (cascading updates and cascading deletes) that you may find useful. These options are near the bottom of the Edit Relationships dialog box (refer to Figure 4.16).

NOTE

You might find, when you select Enforce Referential Integrity and click the Create button (or the OK button if you've reopened the Edit Relationships window to edit a relationship), that Access won't allow you to create a relationship and enforce referential integrity. The most likely reason for this behavior is that you're asking Access to create a relationship that violates referential integrity rules, such as a child table with orphans in it. In such a case, Access warns you by displaying a dialog box similar to the one shown in Figure 4.19. The warning happens in this example because there are some records in the Sales table with no matching value in the Salesperson table. This means that Access can't enforce referential integrity between these tables because the data within the tables already violates the rules.

FIGURE 4.19

A dialog box warning that referential integrity can't be enforced because of integrity violations.

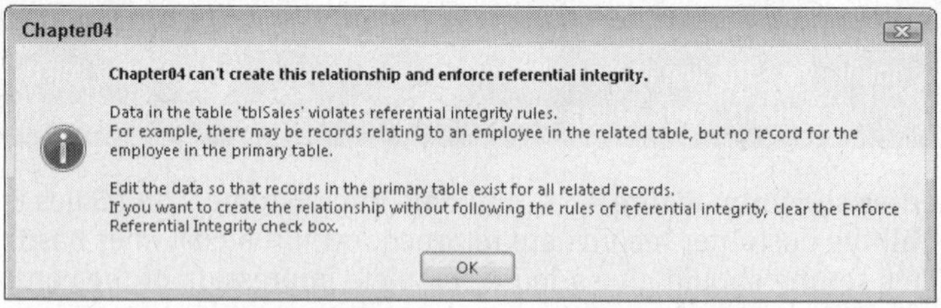

Chapter04

Chapter04 can't create this relationship and enforce referential integrity.

Data in the table 'tblSales' violates referential integrity rules.
For example, there may be records relating to an employee in the related table, but no record for the employee in the primary table.

Edit the data so that records in the primary table exist for all related records.
If you want to create the relationship without following the rules of referential integrity, clear the Enforce Referential Integrity check box.

OK

TIP

To solve any conflicts between existing tables, you can create a Find Unmatched query by using the Query Wizard to find the records in the "many" table that violate referential integrity. Then you can convert the Unmatched query to a Delete query to delete the offending records or add the appropriate value to the SalespersonID field.

You could remove the offending records, return to the Relationships window, and set referential integrity between the two tables. Whether it's appropriate to clean up data by deleting records depends entirely on the business rules governing the application. Deleting orders just because referential integrity can't be enforced would be considered a bad idea in most environments.

Choosing the Cascade Update Related Fields option

If you specify Enforce Referential Integrity in the Edit Relationships dialog box, Access enables the Cascade Update Related Fields check box. This option tells Access that, as a user changes the contents of a related field (the primary key field in the primary table — CustomerID, for example), the new CustomerID is rippled through all related tables.

NOTE

If the primary key field in the primary table is a related field between several tables, the Cascade Update Related Fields option must be selected for all related tables or it won't work.

Generally speaking, however, there are very few reasons why the value of a primary key may change. The example I give in the "Connecting the data" section, earlier in this chapter, of a missing Social Security number, is one case where you may need to replace a temporary Social Security number with the permanent Social Security number after employee data has been added to the database. However, when using an AutoNumber or another surrogate key value, there is seldom any reason to have to change the primary key value once a record has been added to the database.

Choosing the Cascade Delete Related Records option

The Cascade Delete Related Records option instructs Access to delete all related child records when a parent record is deleted. Although there are instances in which this option can be quite useful, as with so many other options, cascading deletes comes with a number of warnings.

For example, if you've chosen Cascade Delete Related Records and you try to delete a particular customer (who moved away from the area), Access first deletes all the related records from the child tables — Sales and SalesLineItems — and then deletes the customer record. In other words, Access deletes all the records in the sales line items for each sale for each customer — the detail items of the sales, the associated sales records, and the customer record — with one step.

Perhaps you can already see the primary issue associated with cascading deletes. If all of a customer's sales records are deleted when the customer record is deleted, you have no way of properly reporting sales for the period. You couldn't, for instance, reliably report on the previous year's sales figures because all the sales records for "retired" customers have been deleted from the database. Also, in this particular example, you would lose the opportunity to report on sales trends, product category sales, and a wide variety of other uses of the application's data.

It would make much more sense to use an Active field (Yes/No data type) in the Customers table to indicate which customers are still active. It would be quite easy to include the Active field in queries where only current customers are needed (Active = Yes), and ignore the Active field in queries where all sales (regardless of the customer's active status) are required.

TIP

To use the Cascade Delete Related Records option, you must specify Cascade Delete Related Records for all the table's relationships in the database. If you don't specify this option for all the tables in the chain of related tables, Access won't cascade deletions.

In general, it's probably not a good idea to enable cascading deletes in a database. It's far too easy to accidentally delete important data. Consider a situation where a user accidentally deletes a customer, wiping out the customer's entire sales history, including payments, shipping, backorders, promotions, and other activities. There are very few situations where users should be permitted to delete many different types of data as a single action.

Viewing all relationships

With the Relationships window open, click All Relationships on the Relationship Tools Design tab of the Ribbon to see all the relationships in the database. If you want to simplify the view you see in the Relationships window, you can "hide" a relationship by deleting the tables you see in the Relationships window. Click a table, press the Delete key, and Access removes the table from the Relationships window. Removing a table from the Relationships window doesn't delete any relationships between the table and other tables in the database.

When building database tables, make sure that the Required property of the foreign key field in the related table (in the case of tblBookOrders5 and tblBookOrderDetails, the foreign key is OrderID in tblBookOrderDetails) is set to Yes. This action forces the user to enter a value in the foreign key field, providing the relationship path between the tables.

The relationships formed in the Relationships window are permanent and are managed by Access. When you form permanent relationships, they appear in the Query Design window by default as you add the tables (queries are discussed in detail in Part III). Even without permanent relationships between tables, you form temporary relationships any time you include multiple tables in the Query Design window.

Deleting relationships

From time to time, you might find it necessary to delete relationships between tables. The Relationships window is simply a picture of the relationships between tables. If you open the Relationships window, click each of the tables in the relationship, and press the Delete key, you delete the picture of the tables in the relationship, but not the relationship itself.

You must first click the line connecting the tables and press Delete to delete the relationship, and then delete each of the table pictures to completely remove the relationship.

Following application-specific integrity rules

In addition to the referential integrity rules enforced by the ACE Database Engine, you can establish a number of business rules that are enforced by the applications you build in Access. In many cases, your clients or users will tell you the business rules that must be enforced by the application. It's up to you as the developer to compose the Visual Basic code, table design, field properties, and so on that implement the business rules expected by your users.

Typical business rules include items such as the following:

- The order-entry clerk must enter his ID number on the entry form.
- Quantities can never be less than zero.
- The unit selling price can never be less than the unit cost.
- The order ship date must come after the order date.

Most often, these rules are added to a table at design time. Enforcing such rules goes a long way toward preserving the value of the data managed by the database. For example, in Figure 4.20, the ValidationRule property of the Quantity field (> =0) ensures that the quantity can't be a negative number. If the inventory clerk tries to put a negative number into the Quantity field, an error message box pops up containing the validation text: `Must not be a negative number.`

FIGURE 4.20

A simple validation rule goes a long way toward preserving the database's integrity.

tblInventory

Field Name	Data Type	Description (Optional)
InventoryID	AutoNumber	
ISBN	Short Text	
BinLocation	Short Text	
Quantity	Number	

Field Properties

General | Lookup

Field Size	Long Integer
Format	
Decimal Places	Auto
Input Mask	
Caption	
Default Value	0
Validation Rule	>=0
Validation Text	Must not be a negative number
Required	No
Indexed	No
Text Align	General

A field name can be up to 64 characters long, including spaces. Press F1 for help on field names.

You can also establish a tablewide validation rule using the Validation Rule property on the table's Property Sheet that provides some protection for the data in the table. Unfortunately, only one rule can be created for the entire table, making it difficult to provide specific validation text for all possible violations.

The Validation Rule property has some limitations. For instance, you can't use user-defined functions in a rule. Also, you can't reference other fields, data in other records, or other tables in your rules. Validation rules prevent user entry rather than provide warnings that the user can bypass. If you need to provide a warning but still allow the user to continue, you shouldn't use a validation rule.

You can read examples of using VBA to enforce business rules throughout this book.

CHAPTER

5

Working with Access Tables

IN THIS CHAPTER

- Understanding datasheets
- Looking at the Datasheet window
- Opening a datasheet
- Entering new data
- Navigating records
- Changing values in a datasheet
- Using the Undo feature
- Copying and pasting values in a datasheet
- Replacing values in a datasheet
- Adding records in a datasheet
- Deleting records in a datasheet
- Displaying records in a datasheet
- Sorting and filtering records
- Aggregating data
- Printing records

In this chapter, you'll use a datasheet to enter data into an Access table and display the data many different ways. Using Datasheet view allows you to see many records at once, in the familiar spreadsheet-style format. In this chapter, you'll work with tblContacts and tblProducts to add, change, and delete data, as well as learn about different features available in Datasheet view.

ON THE WEB

This chapter uses the database named `Chapter05.accdb`. If you haven't already downloaded it from this book's website, you'll need to do so now.

Understanding Datasheets

Using a datasheet is just one of the ways to view data in Access. A datasheet is visually similar to a spreadsheet in that it displays data as a series of rows and columns. Figure 5.1 shows a typical Datasheet view of a table. Each row represents a single record, and each column represents a single field in the table. Scroll up or down in the datasheet to see the rows (records) that don't fit on the screen; scroll left or right to see the columns (fields) that don't fit.

NOTE

Many of the behaviors described in this chapter apply equally to Access forms. Most Access forms display data from a single record at a time, and interacting with the data on such a form is much like working with data in a single row of a datasheet.

Datasheets are completely customizable, which allows you to view data in many ways. Changing the font size, column widths, and row heights makes more or less of the data fit on the screen. Rearranging the order of the rows and/or columns lets you organize the records and fields logically. Locking columns makes them stay in position as you scroll to other parts of the datasheet, and hiding columns makes them disappear. Filtering the data hides records that don't match specific criteria.

NOTE

Datasheet view displays data from a number of different data sources: tables, queries, and forms displayed as datasheets. Depending on the data source, some of the datasheet behaviors described in this chapter may not work exactly as described. This is particularly true when the underlying data source is a query or form. With these data sources, you might frequently find the datasheet is read only.

FIGURE 5.1

A typical Datasheet view. Each row represents a single record in the table; each column represents a single field (like Description or ModelYear) in the table.

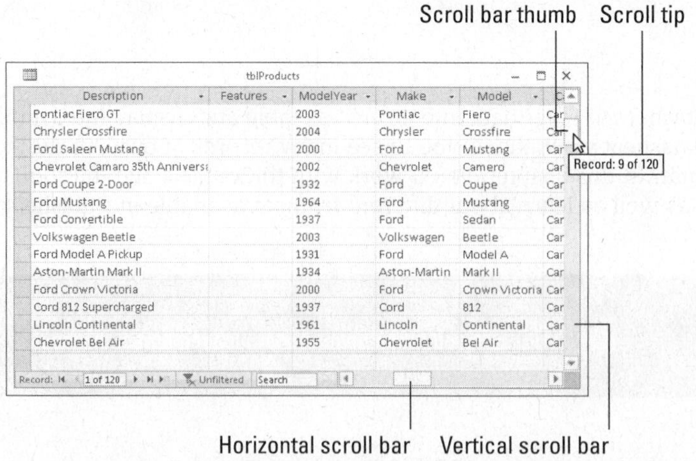

Scroll bar thumb Scroll tip

tblProducts

Description	Features	ModelYear	Make	Model	C
Pontiac Fiero GT		2003	Pontiac	Fiero	Car
Chrysler Crossfire		2004	Chrysler	Crossfire	Car
Ford Saleen Mustang		2000	Ford	Mustang	Car
Chevrolet Camaro 35th Annivers		2002	Chevrolet	Camero	Car
Ford Coupe 2-Door		1932	Ford	Coupe	Car
Ford Mustang		1964	Ford	Mustang	Car
Ford Convertible		1937	Ford	Sedan	Car
Volkswagen Beetle		2003	Volkswagen	Beetle	Car
Ford Model A Pickup		1931	Ford	Model A	Car
Aston-Martin Mark II		1934	Aston-Martin	Mark II	Car
Ford Crown Victoria		2000	Ford	Crown Victoria	Car
Cord 812 Supercharged		1937	Cord	812	Car
Lincoln Continental		1961	Lincoln	Continental	Car
Chevrolet Bel Air		1955	Chevrolet	Bel Air	Car

Record: 9 of 120

Record: 1 of 120 Unfiltered Search

Horizontal scroll bar Vertical scroll bar

A Quick Review of Records and Fields

A *table* is a container for storing related information — patient records, a card list (birthday, holiday), birthday reminders, payroll information, and so on. Each table has a formal structure comprised of fields, each with a unique name to identify and describe the stored information and a specific data type — text, numeric, date, time, and so on — to limit what users enter in these fields. When displayed in a *datasheet* (a two-dimensional sheet of information), Access displays these fields in columns.

The table is comprised of records, which hold information about a single entity (like a single customer or a single product). One record is made up of information stored in all the fields of the table structure. For example, if a table has three fields — name, address, and phone number — then the first record only has one name, one address, and one phone number in it. The second record also has one name, one address, and one phone number in it.

A datasheet is an ideal way of looking at all the table's contents at once. A single record appears as a row in the datasheet; each row contains information for that specific record. The fields appear as columns in the datasheet; each column contains an individual field's contents. This row-and-column format lets you see lots of data at once.

Looking at the Datasheet Window

The datasheet arranges the records initially by primary key and arranges the fields by the order in the table design. At the top of the Access window, you see the title bar (displaying the database filename), the Quick Access toolbar, and the Ribbon. At the bottom of the Access window, you see the status bar, which displays information about the datasheet. For example, it might contain field description information, error messages, warnings, or a progress bar.

Generally, error messages and warnings appear in dialog boxes in the center of the screen rather than in the status bar. If you need help understanding the meaning of a button in the toolbar, move the mouse over the button, hovering over it, and an explanatory tooltip appears with a one- or two-word explanation.

The right side of the Datasheet window contains a scroll bar for moving vertically between records. As you scroll between records, a scrolltip (shown in Figure 5.1) tells you precisely where the scroll bar takes you. The size of the scroll bar "thumb" (the small rectangle on the scroll bar) gives you a proportional look at how many of the total number of records are being displayed. The bottom of the Datasheet window also contains a scroll bar for moving among fields (left to right). The Navigation buttons for moving between records also appear in the bottom-left corner of the Datasheet window.

Moving within a datasheet

You easily move within the Datasheet window using the mouse to indicate where you want to change or add to your data — just click a field within a record. In addition, the ribbons, scroll bars, and Navigation buttons make it easy to move among fields and records. Think of a datasheet as a spreadsheet without the row numbers and column letters. Instead, columns have field names, and rows are unique records that have identifiable values in each cell.

Table 5.1 lists the navigational keys you use for moving within a datasheet.

TABLE 5.1 Navigating in a Datasheet

Navigational Direction	Keystrokes
Next field	Tab
Previous field	Shift+Tab
First field of current record	Home
Last field of current record	End
Next record	Down arrow (↓)
Previous record	Up arrow (↑)
First field of first record	Ctrl+Home
Last field of last record	Ctrl+End
Scroll up one page	PgUp
Scroll down one page	PgDn

Using the Navigation buttons

The *Navigation buttons* (shown in Figure 5.2) are the six controls located at the bottom of the Datasheet window, which you click to move between records. The two leftmost controls move you to the first record or the previous record in the datasheet. The three rightmost controls position you on the next record, last record, or new record in the datasheet. If you know the record number (the row number of a specific record), you can click the record-number box, enter a record number, and press Enter.

FIGURE 5.2

The Navigation buttons of a datasheet.

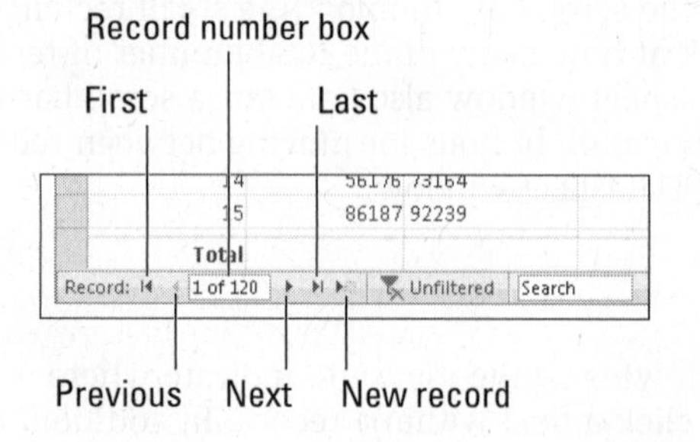

NOTE

If you enter a record number greater than the number of records in the table, an error message appears stating that you can't go to the specified record.

Examining the Datasheet Ribbon

The Datasheet Ribbon (shown in Figure 5.3) provides a way to work with the datasheet. The Home Ribbon has some familiar objects on it, as well as some new ones. This section provides an overview of the groups on the Ribbon; the individual commands are described in more detail later in this chapter.

I explain the Ribbon in Chapter 30.

FIGURE 5.3

The Datasheet Ribbon's Home tab.

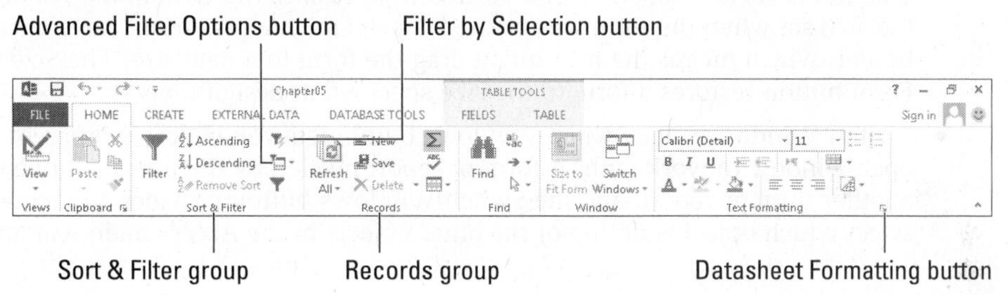

Views

The Views group allows you to switch between Datasheet view, PivotTable view, PivotChart view, and Design view. You can see all four choices by clicking the View command's downward-pointing arrow. Clicking Design View permits you to make changes to the object's design (table, query, and so on). Clicking Datasheet View returns you to the datasheet.

Clipboard

The Clipboard group contains the Cut, Copy, and Paste commands. These commands work like the commands in other applications (such as Word and Excel). The Paste command's down arrow gives you three choices: Paste, Paste Special, and Paste Append. Paste Special gives you the option of pasting the contents of the Clipboard in different formats (text, CSV, records, and so on). Paste Append pastes the contents of the Clipboard as a new record — as long as a row with a similar structure was copied to the Clipboard.

Sort & Filter

The Sort & Filter group lets you change the order of the rows, as well as limit the rows being displayed — based on criteria you want.

Records

The Records group lets you save, delete, or add a new record to the datasheet. It also contains commands to show totals, check spelling, freeze and hide columns, and change the row height and cell width.

Find

The Find group lets you find and replace data and go to specific records in the datasheet. Use the Select command to select a record or all records.

Window

The Window group includes two buttons that help you control the items (forms, reports, tables, and so on) that are open in the main Access window:

- **Size to Fit Form:** The Size to Fit Form button resizes the form in the window to fit the size set when the form was created. By default, Access forms have a sizeable border, which means the user might drag the form to a new size. The Size to Fit Form button restores a form to the size specified at design time.
- **Switch Windows:** The Switch Windows button lets you choose a different open window to work with. A form or report needed by the user might be under another form or report, and the Switch Windows button provides a quick way to select which object is on top of the other objects in the Access main window.

Text Formatting

The Text Formatting group lets you change the look of text fields in the datasheet. Use these commands to change the font, size, bold, italic, color, and so on. Selecting a font attribute (such as bold) applies the attribute to all fields in the datasheet (see the Note just below this paragraph for the only exception to this rule). Use the Align Left, Align Right, and Align Center commands to justify the data in the selected column. Click the Gridlines command to toggle gridlines on and off. Use the Alternate Fill/Back Color command to change the colors of alternating rows or to make them all the same. All the controls in the Text Formatting group are disabled when the focus is on a field that is not either the Short Text or Long Text data types.

NOTE

The controls in the text formatting group behave differently when the currently selected field in the datasheet happens to be the Long Text data type. When a Long Text field is selected, you can change the font attributes (bold, underline, italics, and so on) of individual characters and words in the field, but only if the Text Format property is set to Rich Text. The Text Format property (which applies only to the Long Text data type) is set to Plain Text by default.

Opening a Datasheet

Follow these steps to open a datasheet from the Database window:

1. **Using the Chapter05.accdb database from this book's website, click Tables in the Navigation pane.**
2. **Double-click the table name you want to open (in this example, tblProducts).**

An alternative method for opening the datasheet is to right-click tblProducts and select Open from the pop-up menu.

> **TIP**
>
> If you're in any of the design windows, click the Datasheet View command in the View group of the Ribbon to view your data in a datasheet.

Entering New Data

All the records in your table are visible when you first open it in Datasheet view. If you just created your table, the new datasheet doesn't contain any data. Figure 5.4 shows an empty datasheet and a portion of the Modify Fields tab of the Ribbon. When the datasheet is empty, the first row contains an asterisk (*) in the record selector — indicating it's a new record.

FIGURE 5.4

An empty datasheet. Notice that the first record is blank and has an asterisk in the record selector.

Add & Delete group

Validation rules

New record indicator

Field properties

Formatting group

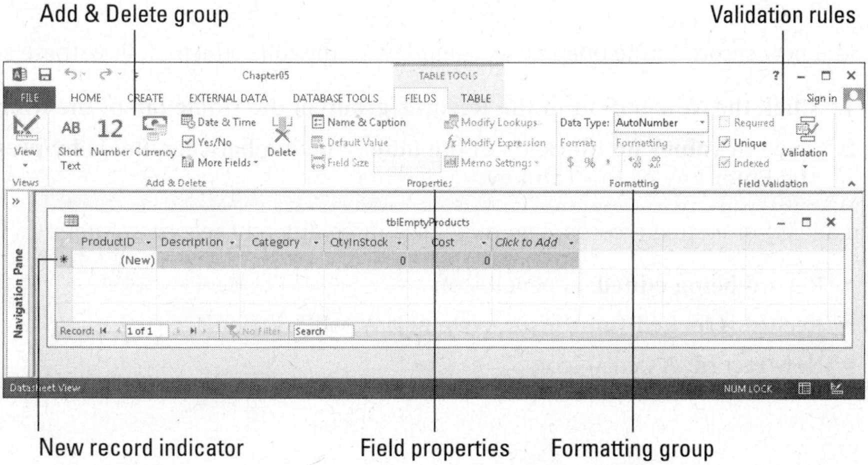

The Table Tools tab group of the Ribbon includes virtually all the tools needed to build a complete table. You can specify the data type, default formatting, indexing, field and table validation, and other table construction tasks from the controls in the Table Tools tab group.

The new row appears at the bottom of the datasheet when the datasheet already contains records. Click the New Record command in the Record group of the Ribbon, or click the New Record button in the group of navigation buttons at the bottom of the datasheet to move the cursor to the new row — or simply click on the last row, which contains the asterisk. The asterisk turns into a pencil when you begin entering data, indicating that the record is being edited. A new row — containing an asterisk — appears below the one you're entering data into. The new record pointer always appears in the last row of the datasheet. Figure 5.5 shows adding a new record to tblProducts.

FIGURE 5.5

Entering a new record into the Datasheet view of tblProducts.

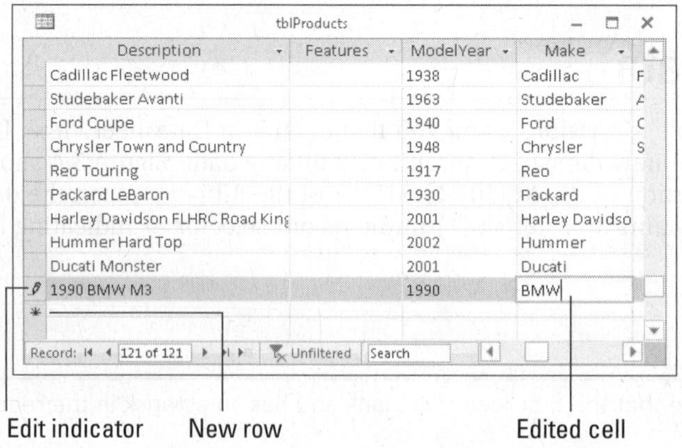

tblProducts

Description	Features	ModelYear	Make
Cadillac Fleetwood		1938	Cadillac
Studebaker Avanti		1963	Studebaker
Ford Coupe		1940	Ford
Chrysler Town and Country		1948	Chrysler
Reo Touring		1917	Reo
Packard LeBaron		1930	Packard
Harley Davidson FLHRC Road Kin		2001	Harley Davidso
Hummer Hard Top		2002	Hummer
Ducati Monster		2001	Ducati
1990 BMW M3		1990	BMW

Record: 121 of 121 Unfiltered Search

Edit indicator New row Edited cell

To add a new record to the open Datasheet view of the tblProducts, follow these steps:

1. **Click the New button in the Records group of the Home tab of the Ribbon.**
2. **Type in values for all fields of the table, moving between fields by pressing the Enter key or the Tab key.**

When adding or editing records, you might see three different record pointers:

- **Record being edited:** A pencil icon
- **Record is locked (multiuser systems):** A padlock icon
- **New record:** A pencil icon

CAUTION
If the record contains an AutoNumber field, Access shows the name (New) in the field. You can't enter a value in this type of field; instead, simply press the Tab or Enter key to skip the field. Access automatically puts the number in when you begin entering data.

Saving the record

Moving to a different record saves the record you're editing. Tabbing through all the fields, clicking on the Navigation buttons, clicking Save in the Record group of the Ribbon, and closing the table all write the edited record to the database. You'll know the record is saved when the pencil disappears from the record selector.

To save a record, you must enter valid values into each field. The fields are validated for data type, uniqueness (if indexed for unique values), and any validation rules that you've entered into the Validation Rule property. If your table has a primary key that's not an AutoNumber field, you'll have to make sure you enter a unique value in the primary key field to avoid the error message shown in Figure 5.6. One way to avoid this error message while entering data is to use an AutoNumber field as the table's primary key.

FIGURE 5.6

The error message Access displays when attempting to save a record with a duplicate primary key value entered into the new record. Use an AutoNumber field as your primary key to avoid this error.

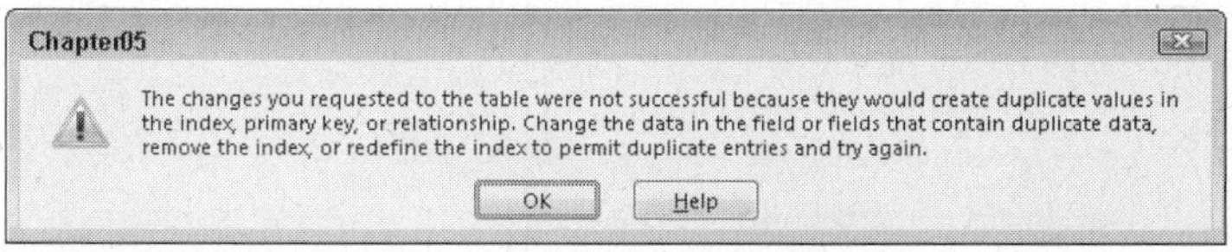

Chapter05

The changes you requested to the table were not successful because they would create duplicate values in the index, primary key, or relationship. Change the data in the field or fields that contain duplicate data, remove the index, or redefine the index to permit duplicate entries and try again.

OK Help

TIP
The Undo button in the Quick Access toolbar reverses changes to the current record and to the last saved record. After you change a second record, you can't undo the saved record.

TIP
You can save the record to disk without leaving the record by pressing Shift+Enter.

Now you know how to enter, edit, and save data in a new or existing record. In the next section, you learn how Access validates your data as you make entries into the fields.

Understanding automatic data-type validation

Access validates certain types of data automatically. Therefore, you don't have to enter any data validation rules for these data types when you specify table properties. The data types that Access automatically validates include

- Number/Currency
- Date/Time
- Yes/No

Access validates the data type when you move off the field. When you enter a letter into a Number or Currency field, you don't initially see a warning not to enter these characters. However, when you tab out of or click on a different field, you get a warning like the one shown in Figure 5.7. This particular warning lets you choose to enter a new value or change the column's data type to Text. You'll see this message if you enter other inappropriate characters (symbols, letters, and so on), enter more than one decimal point, or enter a number too large for the specified numeric data type.

FIGURE 5.7

The warning Access displays when entering data that doesn't match the field's data type. Access gives you a few choices to correct the problem.

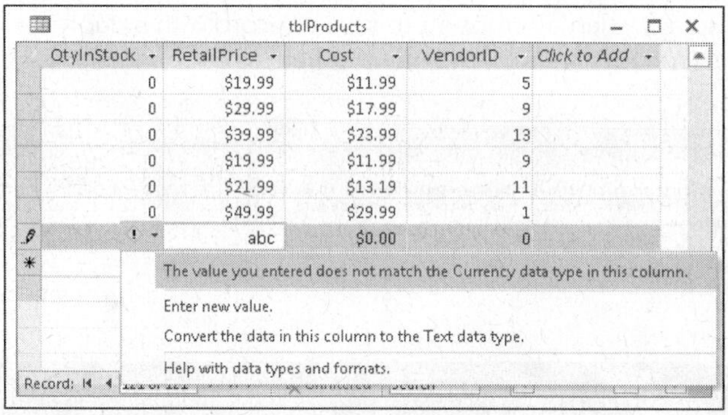

Access validates Date/Time fields for valid date or time values. You'll see a warning similar to the one shown in Figure 5.7 if you try to enter a date such as 14/45/05, a time such as 37:39:12, or an invalid character in a Date/Time field.

Yes/No fields require that you enter one of these defined values:

- **Yes:** Yes, True, On, –1, or a number other than 0 (which displays as –1)
- **No:** No, False, Off, or 0

Of course, you can define your own acceptable values in the Format property for the field, but generally these values are the only acceptable ones. If you enter an invalid value, the warning appears with the message to indicate an inappropriate value.

TIP

The default value of a Yes/No field's Display Control is Check Box. Displaying a check box in Yes/No fields prevents users from entering invalid data.

Knowing how properties affect data entry

Because field types vary, you use different data-entry techniques for each type. In the "Saving the record" section, earlier in this chapter, you learned that some data-type validation is automatic. Designing tblContacts, however, means entering certain user-defined format and data validation rules. The following sections examine the types of data entry.

Standard text data entry

The first field — ContactID — in tblContacts is an AutoNumber field, while other fields in the table are Short Text fields. After skipping ContactID, you simply enter a value in each field and move on. The ZipCode field uses an input mask (00000\-9999;0;) for data entry. The Phone and Fax fields also use an input mask (!\(999") "000\-0000;0;). A 0 in an input mask represents a required numeric entry. A 9 in an input mask represents an optional numeric entry. The ZipCode input mask requires the first five digits, but the plus 4 portion is optional. Short Text fields accept any characters, unless you restrict them with an input mask.

TIP

To enter multiple lines in a Short Text or Long Text field, press Ctrl+Enter to add a new line. This is useful, for example, in large text strings for formatting a multiple-line address field.

Date/Time data entry

The OrigCustDate and LastSalesDate fields in tblContacts are Date/Time data types, which both use a Short Date format (3/16/2015). However, you could've defined the format as Medium Date (16-Mar-15) or Long Date (Monday, March 16, 2015). Using either of these formats simply means that no matter how you type in the date — using month and year; day, month, and year; or month, day, and year — the date always displays in the specified format (short date [3/16/2015], medium date [16-Mar-15], or long date [Monday, March 16, 2015]). Therefore, if you type **4/8/13** or **8 Apr 13**, Access displays the value in the specified format as you leave the field. Dates are actually stored in the database without any formatting, so the format you select for a field doesn't affect how the data is stored.

TIP

Formats affect only the display of the data. They don't change storage of data in the table.

CAUTION
In general, it isn't a good idea to apply an input mask on Date/Time data. Microsoft Access does a more than adequate job of validating date and time values. You're far more likely to encounter data entry problems with an input mask on a date-containing control than you are to avoid trouble by using an input mask.

Number/Currency data entry with data validation

The CreditLimit field in tblContacts has a validation rule assigned to it. It has a Validation Rule property to limit the amount of credit to $250,000. If the rule is violated, a dialog box appears with the validation text entered for the field. If you want to allow a contact to have more than $250,000 of credit, change the validation rule in the table design.

The exact currency character used by Access (in this case, the dollar sign) is determined by the regional options set in the Region and Language Settings of the Control Panel.

OLE object data entry

You can enter Object Linking and Embedding (OLE) object data into a datasheet, even though you don't see the object. An OLE Object field holds many different item types, including

- Bitmap pictures
- Sound files
- Business graphs
- Word or Excel files

Any object that an OLE server supports can be stored in an Access OLE Object field. OLE objects are generally entered into a form so you can see, hear, or use the value. When OLE objects appear in datasheets, you see text that tells what the object is (for example, you may see Bitmap Image in the OLE Object field). You can enter OLE objects into a field in two ways:

- By pasting from the Clipboard
- By right-clicking on the OLE Object field and selecting Insert Object from the pop-up menu

Long Text field data entry

The second-to-last field in the table is Notes, which is a Long Text data type. This type of field allows up to 1GB of text for each field. As you enter text into a Long Text field, you see only a few characters at a time — the rest of the string scrolls out of sight. Pressing Shift + F2 displays a Zoom window with a scroll bar (see Figure 5.8) that lets you see more characters at a time. Click the Font button at the bottom of the window to view all the text in a different font or size. (The font in Figure 5.8 has been enlarged considerably over the 8-point default font size for the Zoom window.)

FIGURE 5.8

The Zoom window. Notice that you can see a lot more of the field's data — not all of it, but still quite a lot.

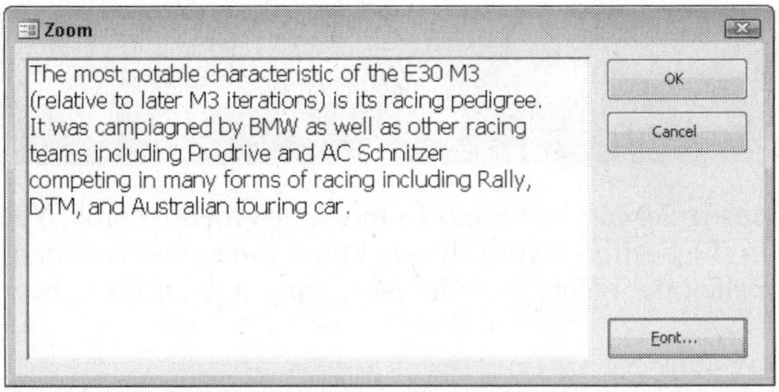

When you first display text in the Zoom window, all the text is selected. You can deselect the text by clicking anywhere in the window. If you accidentally delete all the text or change something you didn't want to, click Cancel to exit back to the datasheet with the field's original data.

TIP

Use the Zoom window (Shift+F2) when designing Access objects (tables, forms, reports, queries) to see text that normally scrolls out of view.

Navigating Records in a Datasheet

Wanting to make changes to records after you've entered them is not unusual. You might need to change records because you receive new information that changes existing values or you discover errors in existing values.

When you decide to edit data in a table, the first step is to open the table, if it isn't already open. From the list of tables in the Navigation pane, double-click tblProducts to open it in Datasheet view. If you're already in Design view for this table, click the Datasheet View button to switch views.

When you open a datasheet in Access that has related tables, a column with a plus sign (+) is added to indicate the related records, or subdatasheets. Click a row's plus sign to open the subdatasheet for the row.

Moving between records

You can move to any record by scrolling through the records and positioning your cursor on the desired record. With a large table, scrolling through all the records might take a while, so you'll want to use other methods to get to specific records quickly.

Use the vertical scroll bar to move between records. The scroll bar arrows move one record at a time. To move through many records at a time, drag the scroll box or click the areas between the scroll thumb and the scroll bar arrows.

TIP

Watch the scrolltips when you use scroll bars to move to another area of the datasheet. Access doesn't update the record number box until you click a field.

Use the five Navigation buttons (refer to Figure 5.2) to move between records. You simply click these buttons to move to the desired record. If you know the record number (the row number of a specific record), click the record number box, enter a record number, and press Enter.

Also, use the Go To command in the Find group of the Ribbon to navigate to the First, Previous, Next, Last, and New records.

Finding a specific value

Although you can move to a specific record (if you know the record number) or to a specific field in the current record, usually you'll want to find a certain value in a record. You can use one of these methods for locating a value in a field:

- Select the Find command (a pair of binoculars) from the Find group of the Ribbon.
- Press Ctrl + F.
- Use the Search box at the bottom of the Datasheet window.

The first two methods display the Find and Replace dialog box (shown in Figure 5.9). To limit the search to a specific field, place your cursor in the field you want to search before you open the dialog box. Change the Look In combo box to Current Document to search the entire table for the value.

FIGURE 5.9

The Find and Replace dialog box. The fastest way to activate it is to simply press Ctrl+F.

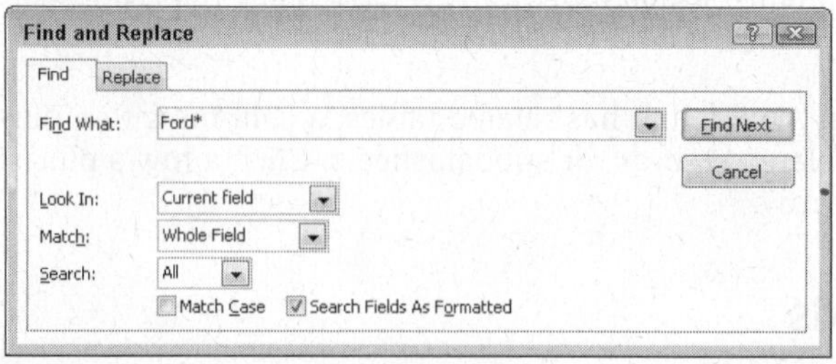

TIP

If you highlight the entire record by clicking the record selector (the small gray box next to the record), Access automatically searches through all fields.

The Find and Replace dialog box lets you control many aspects of the search. Enter the value you want to search for in the Find What combo box — which contains a list of recently used searches. You can enter a specific value or choose to use wildcard characters. Table 5.2 lists the wildcard characters available in the Find dialog box.

TABLE 5.2 Wildcard Characters

Character	Description	Example
* (asterisk)	Matches any number of characters	Ford* finds Ford Mustang
? (question mark)	Matches any single character	F?rd finds Ford
[ ] (brackets)	Matches one of a list of characters	19[67]1 finds 1961 and 1971
! (exclamation point)	With brackets, excludes a list of characters	19[!67]1 finds 1951 but not 1961
- (hyphen)	With brackets, matches a range of characters	196[2–8] finds 1962 to 1968
# (hash)	Matches one number	1:## finds 1:18 but not 1:9

You can combine wildcard characters for more robust searches. For example, 196[!2–8] will find 1961 and 1969, but nothing in between.

The Match drop-down list contains three choices that eliminate the need for wildcards:

- **Any Part of Field:** If you select Any Part of Field, Access searches to see whether the value is contained anywhere in the field. This search finds the Ford anywhere in the field, including values like Ford Mustang, 2008 Ford F-150, and Ford Galaxy 500.
- **Whole Field:** The default is Whole Field, which finds fields containing exactly what you've entered. For example, the Whole Field option finds Ford only if the value in the field being searched is exactly Ford, and nothing else.
- **Start of Field:** A search for Ford using the Start of Field option searches from the beginning of the field and returns all the rows containing Ford as the first four characters of the description.

In addition to these combo boxes, you can use two check boxes at the bottom of the Find and Replace dialog box:

- **Match Case:** Match Case determines whether the search is case sensitive. The default is not case sensitive (not checked). A search for SMITH finds smith, SMITH, or Smith. If you check the Match Case check box, you must then enter the search string in the exact case of the field value. (The data types Number, Currency, and Date/Time don't have any case attributes.)

  If you've checked Match Case, Access doesn't use the value Search Fields As Formatted (the second check box), which limits the search to the actual values displayed in the table. (If you format a field for display in the datasheet, you should check the box.)
- **Search Fields As Formatted:** The Search Fields As Formatted check box, the selected default, finds only text that has the same pattern of characters as the text specified in the Find What box. Clear this box to find text regardless of the formatting. For example, if you're searching the Cost field for a value of $16,500, you must enter the comma if Search Fields as Formatted is checked. Uncheck this box to search for an unformatted value (16500.)

CAUTION
Checking Search Fields As Formatted may slow the search process.

The search begins when you click the Find Next button. If Access finds the value, the cursor highlights it in the datasheet. To find the next occurrence of the value, click the Find Next button again. The dialog box remains open so that you can find multiple occurrences. Choose one of three search direction choices (Up, Down, or All) in the Search drop-down list to change the search direction. When you find the value that you want, click Close to close the dialog box.

Use the search box at the bottom of the Datasheet window (refer to Figure 5.1) to quickly search for the first instance of a value. When using the search box, Access searches the entire datasheet for the value in any part of the field. If you enter **FORD** in the search box, the datasheet moves to the closest match as you type each letter. First, it finds a field with *F* as the first character, then it finds *FO*, and so on. Once it finds the complete value, it stops searching. To find the next instance, press the Enter key.

Changing Values in a Datasheet

If the field that you're in has no value, you can type a new value into the field. When you enter new values into a field, follow the same rules as for a new record entry.

Manually replacing an existing value

Generally, you enter a field with either no characters selected or the entire value selected. If you use the keyboard (Tab or Arrow keys) to enter a field, you select the entire value. (You know that the entire value is selected when it's displayed in reverse video.) When you begin to type, the new content replaces the selected value automatically.

When you click in a field, the value is not selected. To select the entire value with the mouse, use any of these methods:

- Click just to the left of the value when the cursor is shown as a large plus sign.
- Click to the left of the value, hold down the left mouse button, and drag the mouse to select the whole value.
- Click in the field and press F2.

TIP

You may want to replace an existing value with the value from the field's Default Value property. To do so, select the value and press Ctrl+Alt+Spacebar. To replace an existing value with that of the same field from the preceding record, press Ctrl+' (apostrophe). Press Ctrl+; (semicolon) to place the current date in a field.

CAUTION

Pressing Ctrl+– (minus sign) deletes the current record.

Changing an existing value

If you want to change an existing value instead of replacing the entire value, use the mouse and click in front of any character in the field to activate Insert mode; the existing value moves to the right as you type the new value. If you press the Insert key, your entry changes to Overstrike mode; you replace one character at a time as you type. Use the arrow keys to move between characters without disturbing them. Erase characters to the left by pressing Backspace, or to the right of the cursor by pressing Delete.

Table 5.3 lists editing techniques.

TABLE 5.3 Editing Techniques

Editing Operation	Keystrokes
Move the insertion point within a field	Press the right-arrow (→) and left-arrow (←) keys.
Insert a value within a field	Select the insertion point and type new data.
Toggle entire field and insertion point	Press F2.
Move insertion point to the beginning of the field	Press Ctrl+left-arrow (←) key or press the Home key.

continued

5

TABLE 5.3 *(continued)*

Editing Operation	Keystrokes
Move insertion point to the end of the field	Press Ctrl+right-arrow (→) key or press the End key.
Select the previous character	Press Shift+left-arrow (←) key.
Select the next character	Press Shift+right-arrow (→) key.
Select from the insertion point to the beginning	Press Ctrl+Shift+left-arrow (←) key.
Select from the insertion point to the end	Press Ctrl+Shift+right-arrow (→) key.
Replace an existing value with a new value	Select the entire field and type a new value.
Replace a value with the value of the previous field	Press Ctrl+' (apostrophe).
Replace the current value with the default value	Press Ctrl+Alt+Spacebar.
Insert a line break in a Short Text or Long Text field	Press Ctrl+Enter.
Save the current record	Press Shift+Enter or move to another record.
Insert the current date	Press Ctrl+; (semicolon).
Insert the current time	Press Ctrl+: (colon).
Add a new record	Press Ctrl++ (plus sign).
Delete the current record	Press Ctrl+– (minus sign).
Toggle values in a check box or option button	Press Spacebar.
Undo a change to the current field	Press Esc or click the Undo button.
Undo a change to the current record	Press Esc or click the Undo button a second time after you undo the current field.

Fields That You Can't Edit

Some fields can't be edited, such as:

- **AutoNumber fields:** Access maintains AutoNumber fields automatically, calculating the values as you create each new record. AutoNumber fields can be used as the primary key.
- **Calculated fields:** Forms or queries may contain fields that are the result of expressions. These values are not actually stored in your table and are not editable.
- **Fields in multiuser locked records:** If another user is editing a record, it can be locked and you can't edit any fields in that record.

Using the Undo Feature

The Undo button on the Quick Access toolbar is often dimmed because there's nothing to undo. As soon as you begin editing a record, however, you can use this button to undo the typing in the current field. You can also undo a change with the Esc key; pressing Esc cancels any changes to a field that you're actively editing or cancels the changes to the last field you edited if you're not currently editing a field. Pressing Esc twice undoes changes to the entire current record.

After you type a value into a field, click the Undo button to undo changes to that value. After you move to another field, you can undo the change to the preceding field's value by clicking the Undo button. You can also undo all the changes to an unsaved current record by clicking the Undo button after you undo a field. After you save a record, you can still undo the changes by clicking the Undo button. However, after the next record is edited, changes to the previous record are permanent.

Caution

Don't rely on the Undo command to save you after you edit multiple records. When working in a datasheet, changes are saved when you move from record to record and you can only undo changes to the current record.

Copying and Pasting Values

Copying or cutting data to the Clipboard is performed by Microsoft Office or Microsoft Windows, depending on the type of data; it isn't a specific function of Access. After you cut or copy a value, you can paste into another field or record by using the Paste command in the Clipboard group of the Ribbon. You can cut, copy, or paste data from any Windows application or from one task to another in Access. Using this technique, you can copy entire records between tables or databases, and you can copy datasheet values to and from Word and Excel.

The Paste command's down arrow gives you three choices:

- **Paste:** Inserts the contents of the Clipboard into one field
- **Paste Special:** Gives you the option of pasting the contents of the Clipboard in different formats (text, CSV, records, and so on)
- **Paste Append:** Pastes the contents of the Clipboard as a new record — provided a row with a similar structure was copied

Tip

Select a record or group of records using the record selector to cut or copy one or more records to the Clipboard. Then use Paste Append to add them to a table with a similar structure.

Replacing Values

To replace an existing value in a field, you can manually find the record to update or you can use the Find and Replace dialog box. Display the Find and Replace dialog box using these methods:

- Select the Replace command from the Find group of the Ribbon.
- Press Ctrl + H.

The Find and Replace dialog box allows you to replace a value in the current field or in the entire table. Use it to find a certain value and replace it with a new value everywhere it appears in the field or table.

After the Find and Replace dialog box is active, select the Replace tab and type in the value that you want to find in the Find What box. After you've selected all the remaining search options (turn off Search Fields As Formatted, for example), click the Find Next button to find the first occurrence of the value. To change the value of the current found item (under the cursor), enter a value in the Replace With box and click the Replace button. For example, Figure 5.10 shows that you want to find the value Mini Vans in the Category field of tblProducts and change it to Minivans.

FIGURE 5.10

The Find and Replace dialog box with the Replace tab showing. In this case, you want to replace Mini Vans with Minivans.

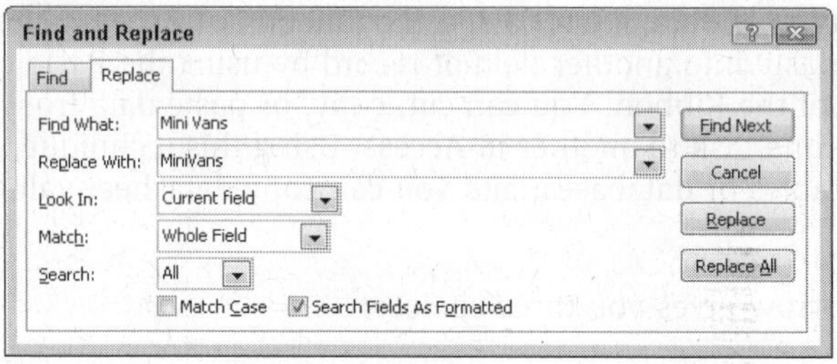

You can select your search options on the Find tab and then select the Replace tab to continue the process. However, it's far easier to simply do the entire process using the Replace tab. Enter the value you want to find and the value that you want to replace it with. After you've completed the dialog box with all the correct information, select one of the command buttons on the side:

- **Find Next:** Finds the next field that has the value in the Find What field.
- **Cancel:** Closes the form and performs no find and replace.

- **Replace:** Replaces the value in the current field only. (***Note:*** You must click the Find Next button first.)
- **Replace All:** Finds all the fields with the Find What value and replaces them with the Replace With value. Use this if you're sure that you want to replace all the values; double-check the Look In box to make sure you don't replace the values in the entire datasheet if you don't want to.

Adding New Records

There are a number of ways to add a record to a datasheet:

- Click the datasheet's last line, where the record pointer is an asterisk.
- Click the new record Navigation button (the furthest button on the right).
- Click the New command from the Records group of the Ribbon.
- Choose Go To⇨New from the Find group of the Ribbon.
- Move to the last record and press the down-arrow (↓) key.
- Press Ctrl + + (plus sign).
- Right-click any record selector and choose New Record from the context menu. The new record is still appended to the bottom regardless of which record's selector you click.

Once you move to a new record, enter data into the desired fields and save the record.

Deleting Records

To delete records, select one or more records using the record selectors, and then press the Delete key, click the Delete command in the Records group of the Ribbon, or right-click a record's selector. The Delete command's drop-down list contains the Delete Record command, which deletes the current record, even if it isn't selected. When you delete a record, a dialog box asks you to confirm the deletion (see Figure 5.11). If you select Yes, the records are deleted; if you select Cancel, no changes are made.

CAUTION

The Default value for this dialog box is Yes. Pressing the Enter key automatically deletes the records. If you accidentally erase records using this method, the action can't be reversed.

FIGURE 5.11

The Delete Record dialog box warns you that you're about to delete a specific number of records — the default response is Yes (okay to delete) so be careful when deleting records.

Chapter05

You are about to delete 2 record(s).

If you click Yes, you won't be able to undo this Delete operation.
Are you sure you want to delete these records?

Yes No

CAUTION

If you have relations set between tables and checked Enforce Referential Integrity — for example, the tblContacts (Customer) table is related to tblSales — then you can't delete a parent record (tblContacts) that has related child records (in tblSales) unless you also check the Cascade Delete check box. Otherwise, you receive an error message dialog box that reports `The record can't be deleted or changed because the table '<tablename>' includes related records.`

To select multiple contiguous records, click the record selector of the first record that you want to select and drag the mouse to the last record that you want to select. Or click to select the first record, and then hold the Shift key and click on the last record that you want in the selection.

TIP

To select multiple contiguous records with the keyboard, press Shift+Spacebar to select the current record and Shift+down-arrow (↓) key or Shift+up-arrow (↑) key to extend the selection to neighboring records.

Displaying Records

A number of techniques can increase your productivity when you add or change records. Change the field order, hide and freeze columns, change row height or column width, change display fonts, and change the display or remove gridlines to make data entry easier.

Changing the field order

By default, Access displays the fields in a datasheet in the same order in which they appear in the table design. Sometimes, you want to see certain fields next to each other in order to better analyze your data. To rearrange your fields, select a column by clicking the column heading, and then drag the column to its new location (as shown in Figure 5.12).

FIGURE 5.12

Selecting and dragging a column to change the field order.

tblProducts

Description	Features	ModelYear	Make	Model	Category
Buick Skylark	The 1953 Skylar	1953	Buick	Skylark	Cars
Cord 810	What the make	1936	Cord	810	Cars
Chevrolet Corvette Convertible	Every year, mo	1959	Chevrolet	Corvette	Cars
Chevrolet Corvette Convertible	One noteworth	1957	Chevrolet	Corvette	Cars
Chevrolet Bel Air Convertible		1953	Chevrolet	Bel Air	Cars
Ford Fairlane		1967	Ford	Fairlane	Cars
Buick T-Type		1968	Buick	T-Type	Cars
Pontiac Vibe		2003	Pontiac	Vibe	Cars
Pontiac Fiero GT		2003	Pontiac	Fiero	Cars
Chrysler Crossfire		2004	Chrysler	Crossfire	Cars
Ford Saleen Mustang		2000	Ford	Mustang	Cars
Chevrolet Camaro 35th Annivers		2002	Chevrolet	Camero	Cars
Ford Coupe 2-Door		1932	Ford	Coupe	Cars
Ford Mustang		1964	Ford	Mustang	Cars
Ford Convertible		1937	Ford	Sedan	Cars
Volkswagen Beetle		2003	Volkswagen	Beetle	Cars

Record: 1 of 121 Unfiltered Search

You can select and drag columns one at a time, or select multiple columns to move at the same time. Suppose you want ModelYear to appear before Features in the tblProducts datasheet. Follow these steps to make this change:

1. **Position the mouse pointer over the QtyInStock column heading.** The cursor changes to a down arrow.
2. **Click to select the column.** The entire QtyInStock column is now highlighted.
3. **Release the mouse button.**
4. **Click the mouse button on the column heading again.** The pointer changes to an arrow with a box under it.
5. **Drag the column to the left edge of the datasheet between the Description and Features fields.** A thin black column appears between them (refer to Figure 5.12).
6. **Release the mouse button.** The column moves in front of the Description field of the datasheet.

With this method, you can move any individual field or contiguous field selection. To select multiple fields, click and drag the mouse across multiple column headings. Then you can move the fields left or right or past the right or left boundary of the window.

NOTE

Moving fields in a datasheet does not affect the field order in the table design.

5

Changing the field display width

You can change the *field display width* (column width) either by specifying the width in a dialog box (in number of characters) or by dragging the column border. When you drag a column border, the cursor changes to the double-arrow symbol.

To widen a column or to make it narrower, follow these steps:

1. **Place the mouse pointer between two column names on the field separator line.** The mouse pointer turns into a small line with arrows pointing to the left and right — if you have it in the correct location.
2. **Drag the column border to the left to make the column smaller or to the right to make it larger.**

TIP

You can instantly resize a column to the best fit (based on the longest visible data value) by double-clicking the right column border after the cursor changes to the double arrow.

NOTE

Resizing the column doesn't change the number of characters allowed in the table's field size. You're simply changing the amount of viewing space for the data contained in the column.

Alternatively, you can resize a column by right-clicking the column header and selecting Field Width from the pop-up menu to display the Column Width dialog box, as shown in Figure 5.13. Set the Column Width box to the number of characters you want to fit in the column or click the Standard Width check box to set the column to its default size. Click Best Fit to size the column to the widest visible value.

FIGURE 5.13

The Column Width dialog box.

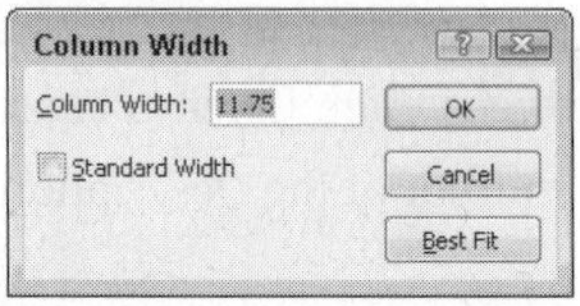

CAUTION

You can hide a column by dragging the column gridline to the gridline of the next column to the left, or by setting the column width to 0 in the Column Width dialog box. If you do this, you must choose More ➪ Unhide Fields in the Records group of the Ribbon to redisplay the hidden columns.

Changing the record display height

You might need to increase the row height to accommodate larger fonts or text that uses multiple lines. Change the record (row) height of all rows by dragging a row's border to make the row height larger or smaller, or you can choose More⇨Row Height in the Records group of the Ribbon.

When you drag a record's border, the cursor changes to the vertical two-headed arrow you see at the left edge of Figure 5.14.

FIGURE 5.14

Changing a row's height. Position the mouse as shown, and drag to the desired height.

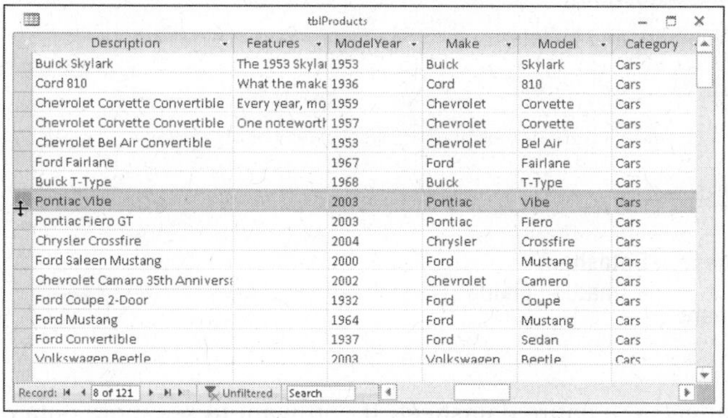

tblProducts

Description	Features	ModelYear	Make	Model	Category
Buick Skylark	The 1953 Skylar	1953	Buick	Skylark	Cars
Cord 810	What the make	1936	Cord	810	Cars
Chevrolet Corvette Convertible	Every year, mo	1959	Chevrolet	Corvette	Cars
Chevrolet Corvette Convertible	One notewortl	1957	Chevrolet	Corvette	Cars
Chevrolet Bel Air Convertible		1953	Chevrolet	Bel Air	Cars
Ford Fairlane		1967	Ford	Fairlane	Cars
Buick T-Type		1968	Buick	T-Type	Cars
Pontiac Vibe		2003	Pontiac	Vibe	Cars
Pontiac Fiero GT		2003	Pontiac	Fiero	Cars
Chrysler Crossfire		2004	Chrysler	Crossfire	Cars
Ford Saleen Mustang		2000	Ford	Mustang	Cars
Chevrolet Camaro 35th Annivers		2002	Chevrolet	Camero	Cars
Ford Coupe 2-Door		1932	Ford	Coupe	Cars
Ford Mustang		1964	Ford	Mustang	Cars
Ford Convertible		1937	Ford	Sedan	Cars
Volkswagen Beetle		2003	Volkswagen	Beetle	Cars

Record: 8 of 121 Unfiltered Search

To increase or decrease a row's height, follow these steps:

1. **Place the mouse pointer between record selectors of two rows.** The cursor changes to the double-pointing arrow (up and down).
2. **Drag the row border up to shrink all row heights or down to increase all row heights.**

NOTE

The procedure for changing row height changes the row size for all rows in the datasheet. You can't have rows with different heights.

You can also resize rows by choosing More⇨Row Height in the Records group of the Ribbon. The Row Height dialog box appears; there you enter the row height in point size. Check the Standard Height check box to return the rows to their default size.

CAUTION

If you drag a record's gridline up to meet the gridline immediately above it in the previous record, all rows are hidden. This also occurs if you set the row height close to 0 (for example, a height of 0.1) in the Row Height dialog box. In that case, you must use the Row Height dialog box to set the row height to a larger number to redisplay the rows.

Changing display fonts

By default, Access displays all data in the datasheet in the Calibri 11-point Regular font. Use the commands and drop-down lists in the Text Formatting group of the Ribbon (shown in Figure 5.15) to change the datasheet's text appearance.

FIGURE 5.15

Changing the datasheet's font directly from the Ribbon. Choose font type style, size, and other font attributes for the entire datasheet.

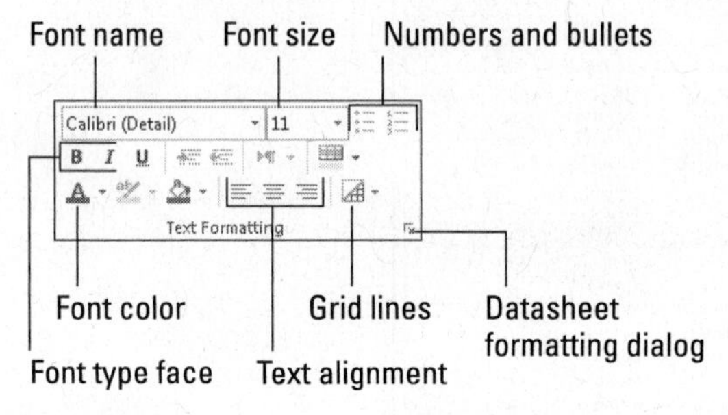

Setting the font display affects the entire datasheet. If you want to see more data on the screen, you can use a very small font. You can also switch to a higher-resolution display size if you have the necessary hardware. If you want to see larger characters, you can increase the font size or click the Bold button.

Displaying cell gridlines and alternate row colors

Normally gridlines appear between fields (columns) and between records (rows). You can set how you want the gridlines to appear using the Gridlines command in the Text Formatting group of the Ribbon (shown in Figure 5.15). Choose from the following options in the Gridlines drop-down list:

- Gridlines: Both
- Gridlines: Horizontal
- Gridlines: Vertical
- Gridlines: None

Use the Background Color and Alternate Row Color drop-down lists, also in the Text Formatting group, to change the background colors of the datasheet. The Background Color palette changes the color of all the rows in the datasheet. The Alternate Row Color palette changes the color of the even-numbered rows. When Alternate Row Color is set, the Background Color palette only affects the odd-numbered rows. To remove coloring from alternate rows, set Alternate Row Color to No Color.

After changing the gridline settings or alternate row colors, Access will ask whether to save the changes to the datasheet's layout. Be sure to click Yes if you want to make the changes permanent.

The Datasheet Formatting dialog box (shown in Figure 5.16) gives you complete control over the datasheet's look. Open this dialog box using the Datasheet Formatting command in the bottom-right corner of the Text Formatting group of the Ribbon. Use the Flat, Sunken, and Raised radio buttons under Cell Effect to change the grid to a 3-D look. Click the Horizontal and Vertical check boxes under Gridlines Shown to toggle which gridlines you want to see. Change the Background Color, Alternate Background Color, and Gridline Color using the available color palettes. The sample in the middle of the dialog box shows you a preview of changes.

FIGURE 5.16

The Datasheet Formatting dialog box. Use this dialog box to customize the look of the datasheet.

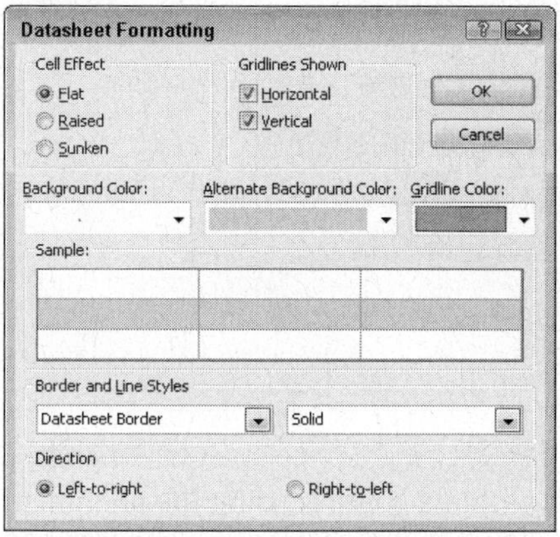

Use the Border and Line Styles drop-down lists to change the look of the gridlines. You can change the styles for the Datasheet Border and the Column Header Underline. Choose a different line style for each of the selections in the first drop-down list. The different line styles you can select from include

- Transparent Border
- Solid
- Dashes
- Short Dashes
- Dots

- Sparse Dots
- Dash-Dot
- Dash-Dot-Dot
- Double Solid

Figure 5.17 shows a datasheet with dashes instead of solid lines and a higher contrast between alternating rows. You can use the various colors and styles to customize the datasheet's look to your liking.

FIGURE 5.17

Different line styles and row colors for the datasheet.

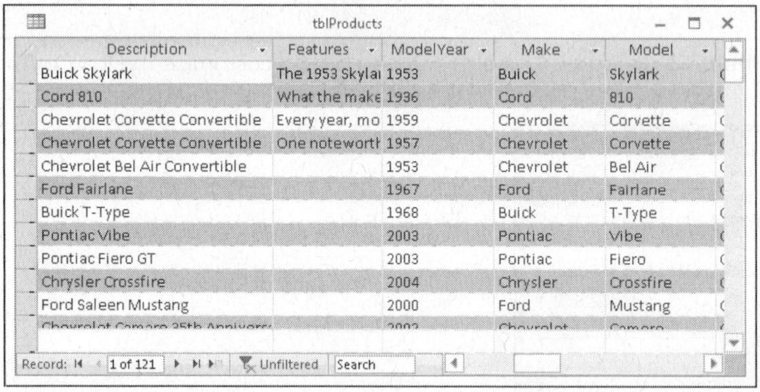

tblProducts

Description	Features	ModelYear	Make	Model
Buick Skylark	The 1953 Skylai	1953	Buick	Skylark
Cord 810	What the make	1936	Cord	810
Chevrolet Corvette Convertible	Every year, mo	1959	Chevrolet	Corvette
Chevrolet Corvette Convertible	One noteworth	1957	Chevrolet	Corvette
Chevrolet Bel Air Convertible		1953	Chevrolet	Bel Air
Ford Fairlane		1967	Ford	Fairlane
Buick T-Type		1968	Buick	T-Type
Pontiac Vibe		2003	Pontiac	Vibe
Pontiac Fiero GT		2003	Pontiac	Fiero
Chrysler Crossfire		2004	Chrysler	Crossfire
Ford Saleen Mustang		2000	Ford	Mustang

Record: 1 of 121 Unfiltered Search

Aligning data in columns

Align the data to the left or right, or center it within a column using the alignment buttons. Choose alignments different from the default alignments Access chooses based on a field's data type (text aligns left, numbers/dates align right). Follow these steps to change the alignment of the data in a column:

1. **Position the cursor anywhere within the column that you want to change the alignment.**
2. **Click the Align Left, Align Center, or Align Right commands in the Text Formatting group of the Ribbon (refer to Figure 5.15) to change the alignment of the column's data.**

Hiding and unhiding columns

Hide columns by dragging the column gridline to the preceding field or by setting the column width to 0:

1. **Position the cursor anywhere within the column that you want to hide.**
2. **Choose More➪Hide Fields in the Records group of the Ribbon.** The column disappears because the column width is simply set to 0. You can hide multiple columns by first selecting them and then choosing More➪Hide Fields.

After you've hidden a column, you can redisplay it by choosing More➪Unhide Fields in the Records group of the Ribbon. A dialog box appears, letting you selectively unhide columns by checking next to each field (see Figure 5.18). Click Close to return to the datasheet showing the desired columns. You can also use this dialog box to hide one or more columns by unchecking the check box next to each field you want to hide.

FIGURE 5.18

Hide and unhide columns using the Unhide Columns dialog box.

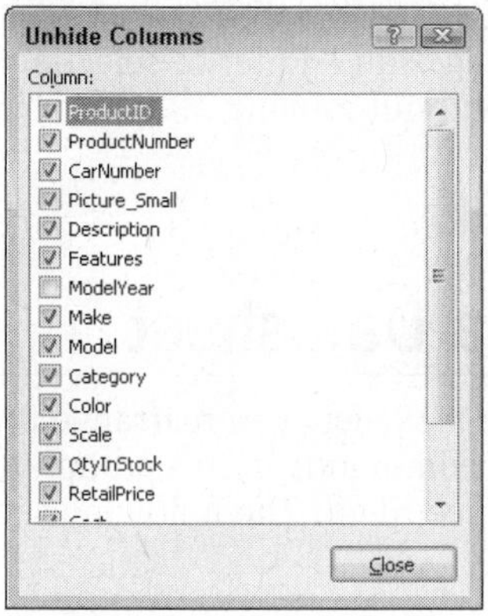

Freezing columns

When you want to scroll left and right among many columns but want to keep certain columns from scrolling out of view, choose More➪Freeze Fields in the Records group of the Ribbon. With this command, for example, you can keep the ProductID and Description fields visible while you scroll through the datasheet to find the product's features. The frozen columns are visible on the far-left side of the datasheet while other fields scroll horizontally out of sight. The fields must be contiguous if you want to freeze more than one at a time. (Of course, you can first move your fields to place them next to each other.) When you're ready to unfreeze the datasheet columns, simply choose More➪Unfreeze All Fields.

TIP

When you unfreeze columns, the column doesn't move back to its original position. You must move it back manually.

Saving the changed layout

When you close the datasheet, you save all your data changes but you might lose all your layout changes. As you make all these display changes to your datasheet, you probably won't want to make them again the next time you open the same datasheet. If you make any layout changes, Access prompts you to save the changes to the layout when you close the datasheet. Choose Yes to save the changes. You can also save the layout changes manually by clicking Save on the Quick Access toolbar.

CAUTION

If you're following the example, don't save the changes to tblProducts if you want your screen to match the figures in the rest of this chapter.

Saving a record

Access saves each record when you move off it. Pressing Shift + Enter or selecting Save from the Records group of the Ribbon saves a record without moving off it. Closing the datasheet also saves a record.

Sorting and Filtering Records in a Datasheet

The Sort & Filter group of the Ribbon (shown in Figure 5.19) lets you rearrange the order of the rows and reduce the number of rows. Using the commands in this group, you'll display the records you want in the order you want to see them. The following sections demonstrate how to use these commands.

FIGURE 5.19

The Sort & Filter group lets you change the record order and narrow the number of rows.

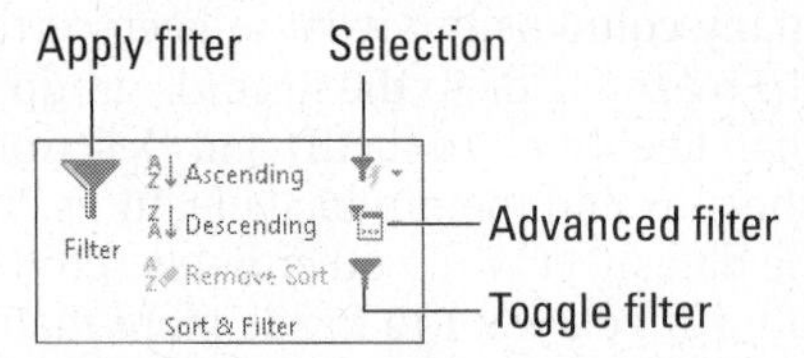

Sorting your records with QuickSort

Sometimes you might simply want to sort your records in a desired order. The QuickSort Ribbon commands let you sort selected columns into either ascending or descending order. To use these commands, click in a field you want to sort by, and then click Ascending or Descending. The data redisplays instantly in the sorted order. Right-clicking on a column and selecting either of the Sort buttons also sorts the data. The captions on the right-click menu change depending on the data type of the field. Short Text fields display Sort A to Z and Sort Z to A, while numeric fields display Sort Smallest to Largest and Sort Largest to Smallest. Some fields, such as OLE and Long Text fields, can't be sorted.

To sort your data on the basis of values in multiple fields, highlight more than one column: Highlight a column (see the "Changing the field order" section, earlier in this chapter), hold down the Shift key, and drag the cursor to the right. When you select one of the QuickSort commands, Access sorts the records into major order (by the first highlighted field) and then into orders within orders (based on subsequent fields). If you need to select multiple columns that aren't contiguous (next to each other), you can move them next to each other (see the "Changing the field order" section, earlier in this chapter).

TIP

To display the records in their original order, use the Remove Sort command in the Sort & Filter group of the Ribbon.

Filtering a selection

Filter by Selection lets you select records on the basis of the current field value. For example, using tblProducts, move your cursor to the Category column and click the Ascending command. Access sorts the data by the vehicle's category. Now place your cursor in a row containing Trucks in the Category column. Press the Selection command in the Sort & Filter group of the Ribbon and choose Equals "Trucks." Access filters the datasheet to show only those records where the Category is trucks.

Access gives you four choices when you click the Selection command:

- Equals "Trucks"
- Does Not Equal "Trucks"
- Contains "Trucks"
- Does Not Contain "Trucks"

The area to the right of the Navigation buttons — at the bottom of the Datasheet window — tells you whether the datasheet is currently filtered; in addition, the Toggle Filter command on the Ribbon is highlighted, indicating that a filter is in use. When you click this command, it removes the filter. The filter specification doesn't go away; it's simply turned off. Click the Toggle Filter command again to apply the same filter.

Filtering by selection is additive. You can continue to select values, each time pressing the Selection command.

TIP

Right-click the field content that you want to filter by and then select from the available menu choices.

If you want to further specify a selection and then see everything that *doesn't* match that selection (for example, where the Make field isn't Chevrolet), move the cursor to the field (the Make field where the value is Chevrolet), right-click the datasheet, and then select Does Not Equal "Chevrolet" from the filter options that appear in the right-click shortcut menu.

When using the Selection command on numeric or date fields, select Between from the available command to enter a range of values. Enter the smallest and largest numbers or oldest and newest dates to limit the records to values that fall in the desired range.

Imagine using this technique to review sales by salespeople for specific time periods or products. Filtering by selection provides incredible opportunities to drill down into successive layers of data. Even when you click the Toggle Filter command to redisplay all the records, Access still stores the query specification in memory. Figure 5.20 shows the filtered datasheet, with the Filter by Select list still open on the Category field.

FIGURE 5.20

Using Filter by Selection. In this case, you see all trucks that are not Chevrolet models.

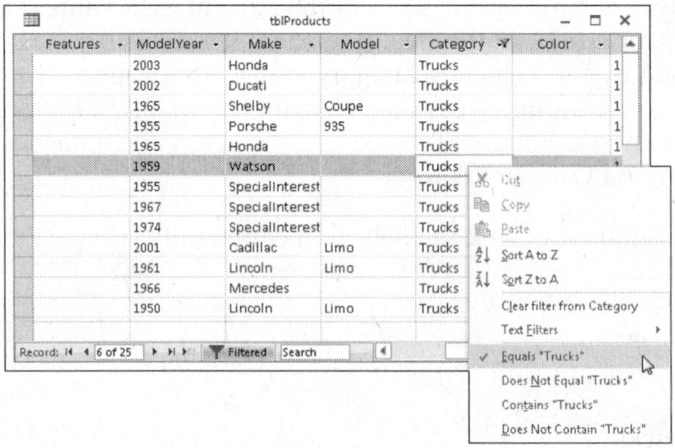

When a datasheet is filtered, each column has an indicator in the column heading letting you know if a filter is applied to that column. Hover the mouse over the indicator to see a tooltip displaying the filter. Click the indicator to specify additional criteria for the column using the pop-up menu shown in Figure 5.21. Click the column heading's down-arrow for an unfiltered column to display a similar menu.

The menu contains commands to sort the column ascending or descending, clear the filter from the field, select a specific filter, and check values you want to see in the datasheet. The available commands change based on the data type of the column. In this case, Text Filter lets you enter a criterion that filters the data based on data you type in.

FIGURE 5.21

Filtering the Category field. Use the column filter menu to select criteria for a field.

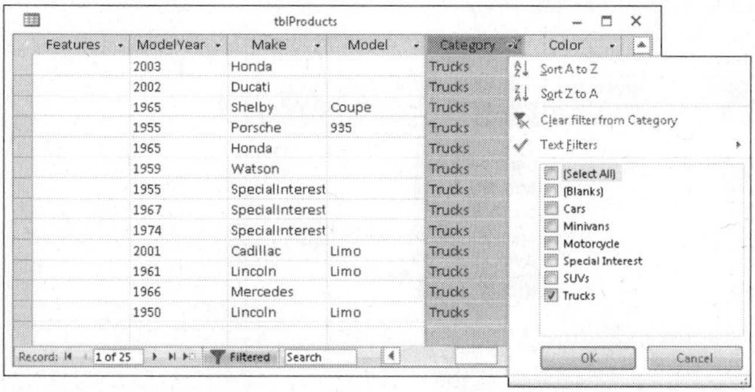

The check boxes in this menu contain data that appear in the column. In this case, the choices are: (Select All), (Blanks), Cars, Minivans, Motorcycle, Special Interest, SUVs, and Trucks. Click (Select All) to see all the records regardless of this field's value. Click (Blanks) to see the records that don't contain data. Select any of the data values to limit the records where the field contains the selected values. Click Minivans and Cars to display the records where Category is equal to Minivans or Cars.

If you want to filter data but you can't find the value that you want to use and you know the value, click the Text Filters (or Number Filters, Date Filters, and so on) command and choose one of the available commands (Equals, Does Not Equal, Begins With, and so on) to display a dialog box where you type in the desired value.

Filtering by form

Filter by Form lets you enter criteria into a single row on the datasheet. Clicking the Filter by Form button transforms the datasheet into a single row containing a drop-down list in every column. The drop-down list contains all the unique values for the column. An Or tab at the bottom of the window lets you specify *OR* conditions for each group. Choose Advanced ➪ Filter by Form in the Sort & Filter group of the Ribbon to enter Filter by Form mode, shown in Figure 5.22.

Select values from the combo boxes or type values you want to search for in the field. If you want to see records where the Category is Trucks or SUVs, select Trucks from the Category drop-down list, select the Or tab at the bottom of the window, and then select SUVs from the Category drop-down list. To see records where Category is SUV and QtyInStock is 1, select SUV from the Category drop-down and type **1** in QtyInStock. Once you enter the desired criteria, click the Toggle Filter command to apply the filter. (The Toggle Filter button is shown in Figure 5.19.)

FIGURE 5.22

Using Filter by Form lets you set multiple conditions for filtering at one time. Notice the Or tab at the bottom of the window.

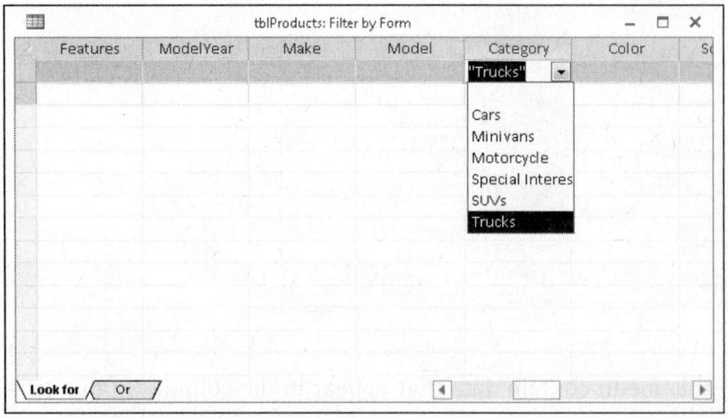

Enter as many conditions as you need using the Or tab. If you need even more advanced manipulation of your selections, you can choose Advanced ➪ Advanced Filter/Sort from the Sort & Filter group of the Ribbon to get an actual Query by Example (QBE) screen that you can use to enter more-complex criteria.

Chapters 8 and 9 discuss queries and using operators and expressions.

Aggregating Data

Historically, Access datasheets have always borne a close resemblance to Excel worksheets. Not only do worksheets and datasheets look alike, but in many ways they work alike, as well. As you've seen in this chapter, Access datasheets support sorting, searching, freezing columns, and other features mirrored in Excel worksheets. But, until recently, Access datasheets and Excel worksheets had little else in common.

Unlike Excel worksheets, Access datasheets haven't supported row and column summation and other types of data aggregation. Beginning with Access 2007, Access datasheets support a Totals row at the bottom of datasheets. The Totals row is opened by clicking the Totals button in the Records group on the Home tab of the Ribbon (the Totals button is marked with a Greek sigma character, much like the AutoSum button in Excel). Each column in the totals row can be set to a different aggregate calculation (Sum, Average, Minimum, Maximum, Count, Standard Deviation, or Variance).

To use the Totals row, open a table or form in Datasheet view and click the Totals button in the Records group (see Figure 5.23) on the Home tab of the Ribbon. Access adds a Totals row at the bottom of the datasheet, just below the New row.

FIGURE 5.23

The datasheet Totals row.

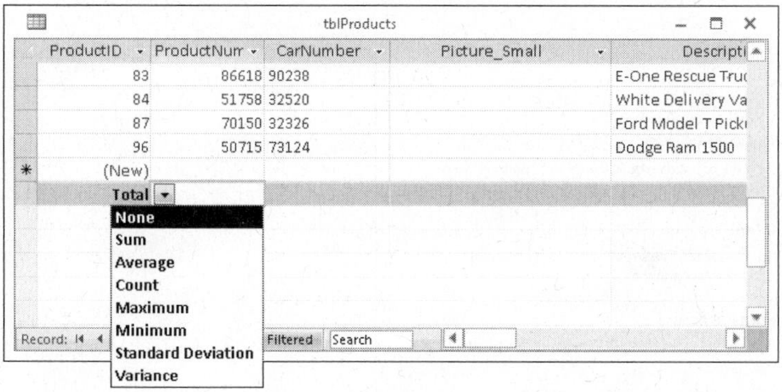

Clicking a column in the Totals row transforms the datasheet cell to a drop-down list. The items in the drop-down list are specific to the column's data type. For example, in text columns, the drop-down list shows only None and Count, while a numeric column contains a full complement of totals calculations (Sum, Average, Count, and so on). DateTime columns include None, Average, Count, Minimum, and Maximum.

The Totals calculation you choose is dynamic. As you change data in the datasheet or underlying table, the calculation results displayed in the Totals row are automatically updated after a very short delay. Recalculating a lot of totals extracts a small performance penalty, so you might want to hide the Totals row when its special features aren't needed.

The Totals options you choose for the columns in a datasheet persist. If you close the datasheet and re-open it, the Totals row is still there.

To remove the Totals row, open the datasheet and click the Totals button in the Records group on the Ribbon. Here's one interesting behavior of the Totals row: If you choose to remove it, you can restore it later (by clicking the Totals button again). The row is restored to its original setting.

Printing Records

You can print all the records in your datasheet in a simple row-and-column layout. In Chapter 20, you learn to produce formatted reports. For now, the simplest way to print is to click the Print button on the Quick Access toolbar. This prints the datasheet to the

Windows default printer. Choose the File menu to view other print options, shown in Figure 5.24.

FIGURE 5.24

The Microsoft Office Print menu.

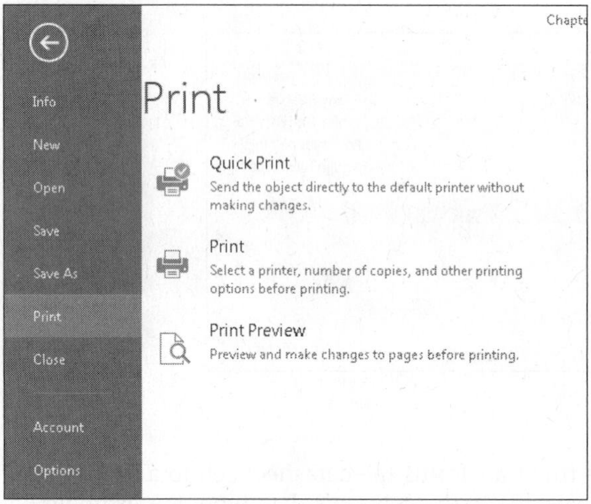

The printout reflects all layout options that are in effect when the datasheet is printed. Hidden columns don't print. Gridlines print only if the cell gridline properties are on. The printout also reflects the specified row height and column width.

Only so many columns and rows can fit on a page; the printout takes up as many pages as required to print all the data. Access breaks up the printout as necessary to fit on each page. For example, the tblProducts printout might be six pages — three pages across are needed to print all the fields in tblProducts, and all the records require three pages in length. The records of tblContacts might need four pages in length. The number of pages depends on your layout and your printer.

Printing the datasheet

You can also control printing from the Print dialog box, which you open by choosing File➪Print. From the Print dialog box, customize your printout by selecting from several options:

- **Print Range:** Prints the entire datasheet or only selected pages or records
- **Copies:** Determines the number of copies to be printed
- **Collate:** Determines whether multiple copies are collated

You can also change the printer, click the Properties button, and set options for the selected printer. The Setup button allows you to set margins and print headings.

Using the Print Preview window

Although you may have all the information in the datasheet ready to print, you may be unsure of whether to change the width or height of the columns or rows, or whether to adjust the fonts to improve your printed output. To preview your print job, click the Print Preview command under the Print menu to display the Print Preview window. The default view is the first page in single-page preview. Use the Ribbon commands to select different views and zoom in and out. Click Print to print the datasheet to the printer. Click the Close Print Preview command on the right side of the Ribbon to return to Datasheet view.

CHAPTER

6

Importing and Exporting Data

IN THIS CHAPTER

Understanding external data

Selecting the import and export options that are right for you

Creating import specifications

Exporting to external tables and files

In this chapter, I show you how to bring data into your Access database from an outside source by importing. I also show you how to create external files from the data by exporting. An import process adds data to an Access database from some external source, such as an XML file. An export from Access means you create something outside the Access database, like an XML or Excel file containing data stored in Access.

ON THE WEB

This chapter uses various files for importing, plus two Access databases: `Chapter06_1.accdb` and `Chapter06_2.accdb`. Both databases are used for importing and exporting examples. If you haven't already downloaded these files onto your machine from this book's website, you'll need to do so now. The website contains the two databases and a number of auxiliary files in different formats (XLS, XML, TXT, and so on). Be sure to copy these files to your computer.

How Access Works with External Data

Exchanging information between Access and another program is an essential capability in today's database world. Information is usually stored in a wide variety of application programs and data formats. Access, like many other products, has its own native file format, designed to support referential integrity and provide support for rich data types, such as OLE objects. Most of the time, Access alone is sufficient for the job. Occasionally, however, you need to move data from one Access database file to another or use data from another program's format.

Types of external data

Access can use and exchange data among a wide range of applications. For example, you may need to get data from other database files (such as FoxPro or dBASE files) or get information from a SQL Server, Oracle, or even a text file. Access can move data among several categories of applications, including other Windows applications, Macintosh applications, database management systems, text files, and even mainframe files.

Ways of working with external data

Often, you need to move data from another application or file into your Access database, or vice versa. You might need to get information you already have in an external spreadsheet file. You can reenter all that information by hand or have it automatically imported into your database.

Access has tools that enable you to exchange data with another database or spreadsheet file. In fact, Access can exchange data with many different file types, including the following:

- Access database objects (all types)
- Text files
- Excel files
- ODBC databases (SQL Server, Sybase Server, Oracle Server, and other ODBC-compliant databases)
- HTML tables, lists, and documents
- XML documents
- Outlook
- Microsoft Exchange documents
- SharePoint
- Word documents
- Rich Text Format (RTF) documents

Access works with these external data sources in several ways:

- **Linking:** Linking to data creates a connection to a table in another Access database or links to the data from a different format. Linking uses the data in the source file format (such as Excel or XML). The linked data remains in its original file. The file containing the link data should not be moved, deleted, or renamed; otherwise, Access won't be able to locate the data the next time it's needed. If moving or renaming the linked data source is unavoidable, Access provides tools for relinking to the source.

- **Importing:** Importing copies data from a data source, another Access database, or another application's database file into an Access table. The imported data is converted to the appropriate Access data type, stored in a table, and managed by Access from that point on.
- **Exporting:** Exporting copies data from an Access table into a text file, another Access database, or another application's file. Like importing, changing the source data does not affect the exported data.

Linking between Access and external data is discussed in Chapter 7.

Each method has clear advantages and disadvantages, covered in the following sections.

When to link to external data

Linking in Access enables you to work with the data in another application's format — thus, sharing the file with the existing application. If you leave data in another database format, Access can read the data while the original application is still using it. This capability is useful when you want to work with data in Access that other programs also need to work with. However, there are limitations as to what you can do with linked data. For example, you can't update data in a linked Excel spreadsheet or a linked text file. The ability to work with external data is also useful when you use Access as a front end for a SQL Server database — you can link to a SQL Server table and directly update the data, without having to batch-upload it to a SQL Server.

Access databases are often linked to external data so that people can use Access forms to add and update the external data or to use the external data in Access reports.

You can link to the following types of data in Access:

- Other Access tables (ACCDB, ACCDE, ACCDR, MDB, MDA, MDE)
- Excel spreadsheets
- Outlook folders
- Text files
- XML files
- HTML documents
- SharePoint lists
- ODBC databases

CAUTION

Access is capable of linking to certain formats (like HTML tables, text files, Excel files, and XML documents) for read-only access. You can use and look at tables in HTML or text format; however, the tables can't be updated and records can't be added to them using Access.

A big disadvantage of working with linked tables is that you lose the capability to enforce referential integrity between tables (unless all the linked tables are in the same external Access database or all are in some other database management system that supports referential integrity). Linked tables may exhibit somewhat poorer performance than local tables. Depending on the source, and the location of the source data, users might experience a noticeable delay when they open a form or report that is based on linked data.

Performance issues become more pronounced when joining linked and local data in a query. Because Access is unable to apply optimization techniques to foreign data, many joins are inefficient and require a lot of memory and CPU time to complete. However, Access can work with many different types of external data, which makes it the ideal platform for applications requiring these features.

When to import external data

Importing data enables you to bring an external table or data source into a new or existing Access table. By importing data, Access automatically converts data from the external format and copies it into Access. You can even import data objects into a different Access database or Access project than the one that is currently open. If you know that you'll use your data in Access only, you should import it. Generally, Access works faster with its own local tables.

NOTE

Because importing makes another copy of the data, you might want to delete the old file after you import the copy into Access. Sometimes, however, you'll want to preserve the old data file. For example, the data might be an Excel spreadsheet still in use. In cases such as this, simply maintain the duplicate data and accept that storing it will require more disk space (and that the two files are going to get out of sync).

One of the principal reasons to import data is to customize it to meet your needs. After a table has been imported into an Access database, you can work with the new table as if you'd built it in the current database. With linked tables, on the other hand, you're greatly limited in the changes you can make. For example, you can't specify a primary key or assign a data entry rule, which means that you can't enforce integrity against the linked table. Also, because linked tables point to external files, which Access expects to find in a specific location, it can make distributing your application more difficult.

Data is frequently imported into an Access database from an obsolete system being replaced by a new Access application. When the import process is complete, the obsolete application can be removed from the user's computer.

TIP

If you'll be importing data from the same source frequently, you can automate the process with a macro or a VBA procedure. This can be very helpful for those times when you have to import data from an external source on a regular schedule or when you have complex transformations that must be applied to the imported data.

Working with Data in Unsupported Programs

Although uncommon, you might occasionally need to work with data from a program that isn't stored in a supported external database or file format. In cases such as this, the programs usually can export or convert their data into one of the formats recognized by Access. To use the data in these programs, export it into a format recognized by Access and then import it into Access.

For example, many applications can export to the XML file format. If the XML format is not available, most programs, even those on different operating systems, can export data to delimited or fixed-width text files, which you can then import into Access.

When to export internal data

Exporting data enables you to pass data to other applications. By exporting data, Access automatically converts data to the external format and copies it to a file that can be read by the external application. As we've already mentioned, sometime you have to import data into Access as opposed to just linking to the external data source if you want to be able to modify the data. If you still need to be able to work with the modified data in the external application, you have little choice but to create a new file by exporting the modified data.

A common reason to export data is because you want to share the data with other users who don't have Access installed.

Options for Importing and Exporting

Before examining the processes of importing and exporting, let's take a brief look at the various options for importing and exporting data with Access.

Access is often described as a "landing pad" for many types of data. What this means is that Access can use and exchange data among a wide range of applications. For example, you might need to get data from other databases, such as FoxPro or dBASE. Or you might need to obtain information from SQL Server or Oracle, a text file, or even an XML document. Access can move data among several categories of applications, database engines, and even platforms (mainframes and Macintosh computers).

Open the `Chapter06_1.accdb` database in Access, and click the External Data tab of the Ribbon (see Figure 6.1). You'll see the following groups: Import & Link, Export, and Web Linked Lists.

FIGURE 6.1

The External Data tab of the Ribbon hints at the variety of external data sources available to Access.

The Import & Link group includes the following options:

- **Saved Imports**
- **Linked Table Manager**
- **Excel**
- **Access**
- **ODBC Database**
- **Text File**
- **XML File**
- **More:** Click this button to open the More drop-down list, which has the following options:
  - SharePoint List
  - Data Services
  - HTML document
  - Outlook folder

The Export group includes the following options:

- **Saved Exports**
- **Excel**
- **Text File**
- **XML File**
- **PDF or XPS**
- **E-mail**
- **Access**
- **Word Merge**

- **More:** Click this button to open the More drop-down list, which has the following options:
  - Word
  - SharePoint List
  - ODBC Database
  - HTML Document

Obviously, Microsoft has prepared Access well for its role as a "landing pad" for data.

How to Import External Data

An import copies external data into an Access database. The external data remains in its original state, but, after the import, a copy exists within Access. When you import a file (unlike when you link tables), Access converts a copy of the data from an external source into records in an Access table. The external data source is not changed during the import. No connection to the external data source is maintained once the import process is complete.

You can import information to new or existing tables. Every type of data can be imported to a new table. However, some types of imports — such as spreadsheets and text files — may have to be imported into existing tables, because text files and spreadsheets don't necessarily have a table structure compatible with Access.

Importing from another Access database

You can import items from a source database into the current database. The objects you import can be tables, queries, forms, reports, macros, or modules. Import an item into the current Access database by following these steps:

1. **Open the destination database you want to import into.** In this case, open the `Chapter06_1.accdb` database.
2. **Select the External Data tab.**
3. **Click the Access option in the Import section, and then click the Browse button to select the filename of the source database (Chapter06_2.accdb).**
4. **Select the Import Tables, Queries, Forms, Reports option button and click OK.** The Import Objects dialog box (shown in Figure 6.2) appears. It gives you options for importing a database object.

NOTE

When working with an external Access database, you can import any type of object, including tables, queries, forms, reports, macros, and VBA code modules.

FIGURE 6.2

Many types of Access database objects can be imported from one Access database into another.

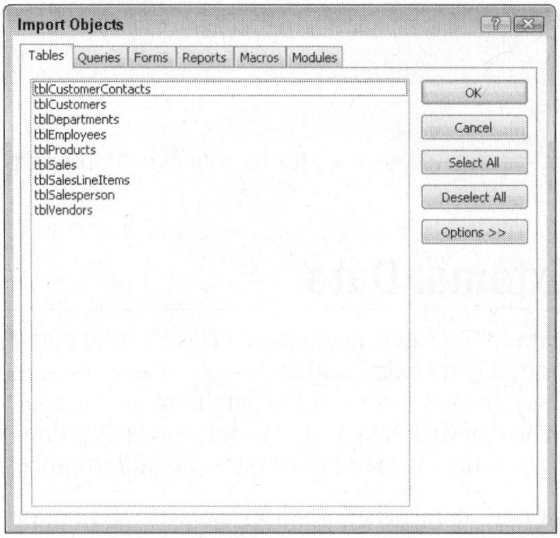

5. **Select a table, and click OK.** If an object already exists in the destination database, then a sequential number is added to the name of the imported object, distinguishing it from the original item. For example, if tblDepartments already exists, the new imported table is named tblDepartments1.

   The Get External Data - Save Import Steps dialog box appears, with a very useful feature that allows you to store the import process as a saved import, as shown in Figure 6.3.

6. **Provide a name for the import process to make it easy to recall the saved import's purpose.** You can execute the saved import again at a later date by clicking the Saved Imports button in the Import group of the External Data tab of the Ribbon (see Figure 6.4). From the Manage Data Tasks dialog box, you can change the name of the saved import, the location of the source file, and the description of the saved import. All other information about the saved import (such as the destination table name) can't be changed. If you need to change other information, create a new saved import with the proper parameters.

TIP

The Manage Data Tasks dialog box includes the Create Outlook Task button to set up the import procedure as a scheduled Outlook Task. This is a very convenient way to automatically execute the import process on a regular schedule.

FIGURE 6.3

The Saved Import Steps feature lets you save frequently executed import processes for future use.

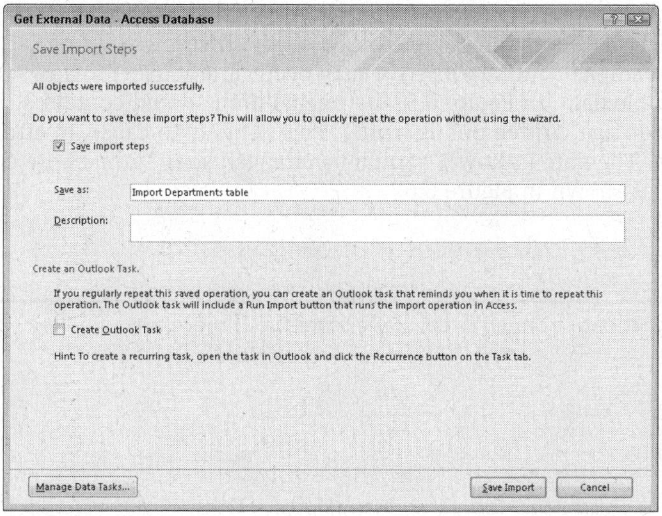

Get External Data - Access Database

Save Import Steps

All objects were imported successfully.

Do you want to save these import steps? This will allow you to quickly repeat the operation without using the wizard.

☑ Save import steps

Save as: Import Departments table

Description:

Create an Outlook Task.

If you regularly repeat this saved operation, you can create an Outlook task that reminds you when it is time to repeat this operation. The Outlook task will include a Run Import button that runs the import operation in Access.

☐ Create Outlook Task

Hint: To create a recurring task, open the task in Outlook and click the Recurrence button on the Task tab.

Manage Data Tasks... | Save Import | Cancel

FIGURE 6.4

The Saved Imports feature lets you rerun previous saved import processes.

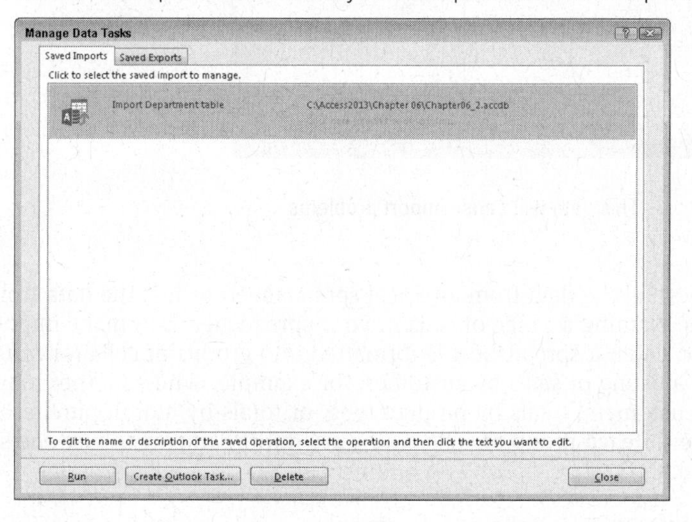

Importing from an Excel spreadsheet

You can import data from Excel spreadsheets to a new or existing table. The primary rule when importing Excel data is that each cell in a column must contain the same type of data. When you're importing Excel data into a new table, Access guesses at the data type to assign to each field in the new table based on the first few rows of Excel data (other than column headings). An import error may occur if any Excel row past the first row contains incompatible data. In Figure 6.5, the Age column should contain all numeric data, but it contains an age written out as words. This is likely to cause an error during the import process. The data in Row 5 should be changed so that the entire column contains numeric data (as shown in Figure 6.6).

FIGURE 6.5

Access can import data from an Excel spreadsheet, but there are some restrictions.

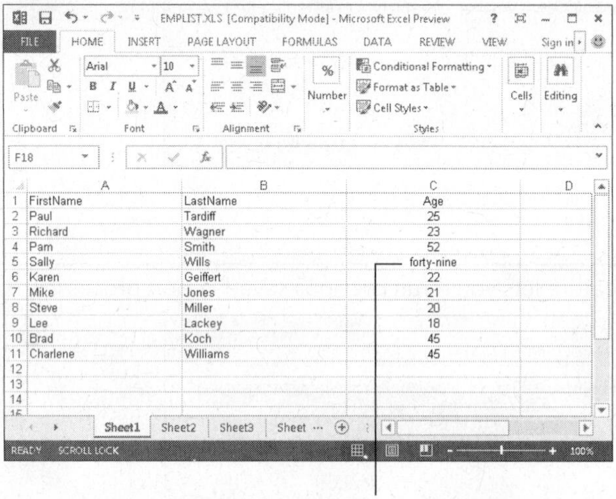

	A	B	C	D
1	FirstName	LastName	Age	
2	Paul	Tardiff	25	
3	Richard	Wagner	23	
4	Pam	Smith	52	
5	Sally	Wills	forty-nine	
6	Karen	Geiffert	22	
7	Mike	Jones	21	
8	Steve	Miller	20	
9	Lee	Lackey	18	
10	Brad	Koch	45	
11	Charlene	Williams	45	

This data will cause import problems

You can import all the data from an Excel spreadsheet, or just the data from a named range of cells. Naming a range of cells in your spreadsheet can make importing into Access easier. Often a spreadsheet is formatted into groups of cells (or *ranges*). One range may contain a listing of sales by customer, for example, while another may include total sales for all customers, totals by product type, or totals by month purchased. By providing a range name for each group of cells, you can limit the import to just one section of the spreadsheet data.

To import `EMPLIST.xls`, follow these steps:

1. **Click the Excel button in the Import group on the External Data tab.**
2. **Browse to the Excel file.**

3. **Select Import the Source Data into a New Table in the Current Database and click OK.**

   The first Import Spreadsheet Wizard screen (shown in Figure 6.7) shows lists of worksheets or named ranges, and a preview of the data, in the Excel spreadsheet.

FIGURE 6.6

Excel worksheet columns should contain consistent data.

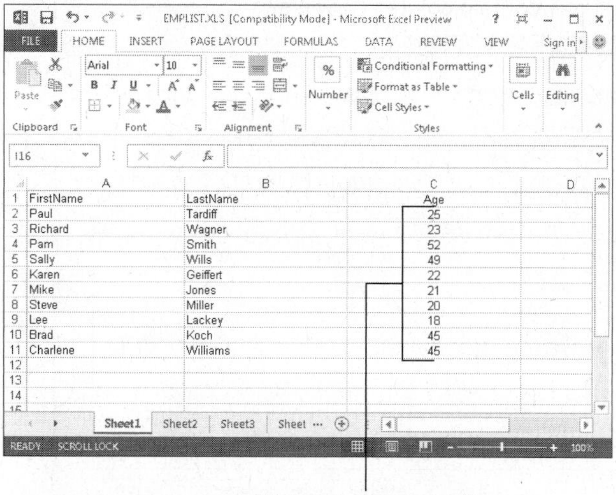

All data is now numeric

FIGURE 6.7

The Import Spreadsheet Wizard.

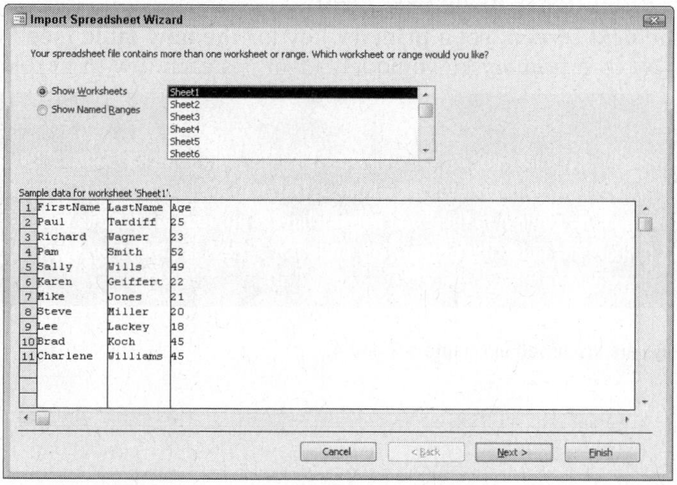

4. **Select a worksheet or named range and click Next.**
5. **On the next screen (shown in Figure 6.8), select the First Row Contains Column Headings check box and click Next.** Normally you don't want the Excel column headings stored as field data. Access uses the column headings as the field names in the new table.

FIGURE 6.8

Does the first row contain column headers?

Import Spreadsheet Wizard

Microsoft Access can use your column headings as field names for your table. Does the first row specified contain column headings?

☑ First Row Contains Column Headings

	FirstName	LastName	Age
1	Paul	Tardiff	25
2	Richard	Wagner	23
3	Pam	Smith	52
4	Sally	Wills	49
5	Karen	Geiffert	22
6	Mike	Jones	21
7	Steve	Miller	20
8	Lee	Lackey	18
9	Brad	Koch	45
10	Charlene	Williams	45

Cancel | < Back | Next > | Finish

6. **On the next screen (shown in Figure 6.9), you can override the default field name and data type, remove fields from the import, and create an index on a field; when you're done, click Next.**
7. **On the next screen, set a primary key for the new table (see Figure 6.10) and click Next.** A primary key uniquely identifies each row in a table.

CAUTION

Be somewhat wary when choosing a primary key for the imported file. The field you choose must conform to the rules of primary keys: No value can be null and no duplicates are allowed. The purpose of a table's primary key is to uniquely identify the rows in the table, so if no column in the Excel spreadsheet is appropriate for this purpose, it's probably best to let Access add a default primary key field. The primary key added by Access is always an AutoNumber and always conforms to data normalization rules.

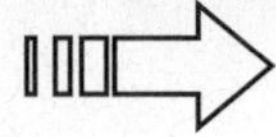

Primary keys are discussed in Chapters 3 and 4.

FIGURE 6.9

You can override any of the default settings Access has chosen.

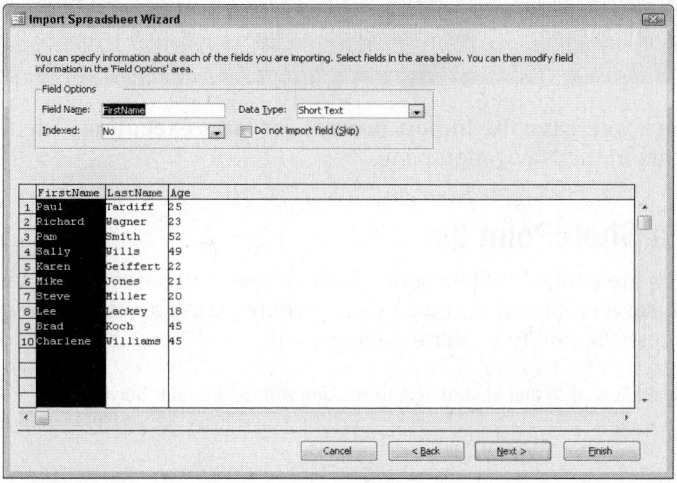

Import Spreadsheet Wizard

You can specify information about each of the fields you are importing. Select fields in the area below. You can then modify field information in the 'Field Options' area.

Field Options

Field Name: FirstName Data Type: Short Text

Indexed: No Do not import field (Skip)

	FirstName	LastName	Age
1	Paul	Tardiff	25
2	Richard	Wagner	23
3	Pam	Smith	52
4	Sally	Wills	49
5	Karen	Geiffert	22
6	Mike	Jones	21
7	Steve	Miller	20
8	Lee	Lackey	18
9	Brad	Koch	45
10	Charlene	Williams	45

Cancel < Back Next > Finish

FIGURE 6.10

Specify a primary key for the new table.

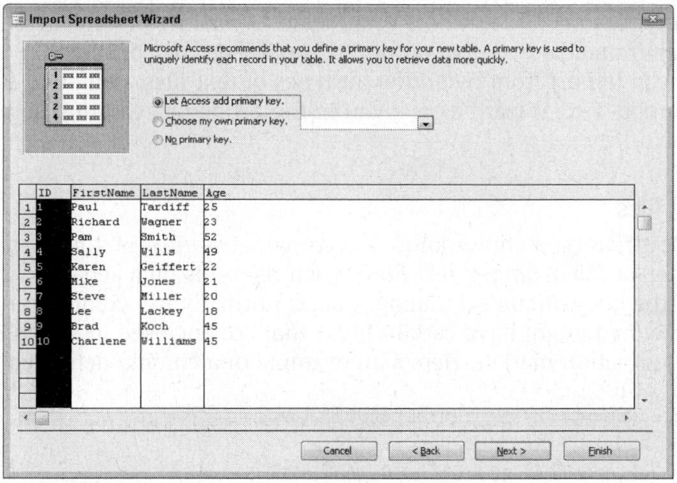

Import Spreadsheet Wizard

Microsoft Access recommends that you define a primary key for your new table. A primary key is used to uniquely identify each record in your table. It allows you to retrieve data more quickly.

Let Access add primary key.

Choose my own primary key.

No primary key.

	ID	FirstName	LastName	Age
1	1	Paul	Tardiff	25
2	2	Richard	Wagner	23
3	3	Pam	Smith	52
4	4	Sally	Wills	49
5	5	Karen	Geiffert	22
6	6	Mike	Jones	21
7	7	Steve	Miller	20
8	8	Lee	Lackey	18
9	9	Brad	Koch	45
10	10	Charlene	Williams	45

Cancel < Back Next > Finish

8. **Specify the new table's name and click Finish.**

CAUTION
If you import an Excel file with the same name as an Excel file you've already linked, Access will ask if you want to overwrite the existing file. Unless you actually intend to replace the linked table, you must give the newly imported table a new name.

9. **If you want, save the import process for later execution.** The new table now appears in the Navigation pane.

Importing a SharePoint list

SharePoint lists are candidate data sources for Access databases. Because SharePoint lists reside on web servers, SharePoint data is accessible across a network to qualified users. This gives Access the ability to share data virtually anywhere in the world.

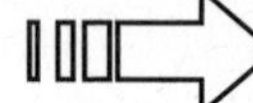

Part VIII is dedicated to understanding and working with Sharepoint Services.

Because SharePoint is increasingly deployed on corporate intranets, Access is guaranteed to continue as a major player in enterprise environments.

Importing data from text files

There are many reasons for text file output, such as business-to-business (B2B) data transfers. Also, mainframe data is often output as text files to be consumed in desktop applications. Access can import from two different types of text files: delimited and fixed width. The Access Import Text Wizard assists you in importing or exporting both delimited and fixed-width text files.

Delimited text files

In *delimited text files* (sometimes known as *comma-delimited text files, comma-separated-values text files,* or *tab-delimited text files*), each record is on a separate line in the text file. The fields on the line contain no trailing spaces, normally use commas or tab characters as field separators, and might have certain fields that are enclosed in *delimiters* (such as single or double quotation marks). Here's an example of a comma-delimited text file:

```
1,Davolio,Nancy,5/1/14 0:00:00,4000
2,Fuller,Andrew,8/14/14 0:00:00,6520
3,Leverling,Janet,4/1/14 0:00:00,1056
4,Peacock,Margaret,5/3/15 0:00:00,4000
5,Buchanan,Steven,10/17/15 0:00:00,5000
6,Suyama,Michael,10/17/15 0:00:00,1000
7,King,Robert,1/2/14 0:00:00,1056
8,Callahan,Laura,3/5/14 0:00:00,1056
9,Dodsworth,Joeseph,11/15/14 0:00:00,1056
```

Notice that the file has nine records (rows of text) and five fields. A comma separates each field. In this example, text fields are not delimited with double quotation marks. Notice also that the rows are different lengths because of the variable data within each row.

To import a delimited text file named `ImportDelim.txt`, follow these steps:

1. **Open the Chapter06_1.accdb database.**
2. **Select the External Data tab.**
3. **Click Text File in the Import & Link group.**
4. **Browse to the ImportDelim.txt file, select the Import option button, and click OK.** The first screen of the Import Text Wizard (shown in Figure 6.11) appears. The Import Text Wizard displays the data in the text file and lets you choose between delimited or fixed width.

FIGURE 6.11

The first screen of the Import Text Wizard.

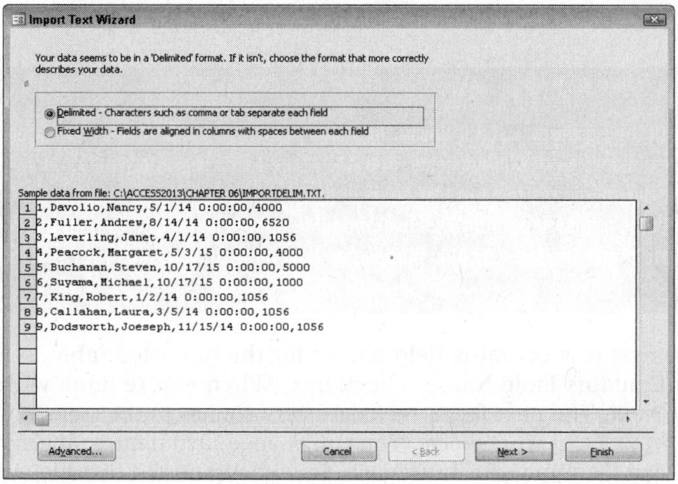

5. **Select Delimited and click Next.** The next screen of the Import Text Wizard (shown in Figure 6.12) appears. As you can see in Figure 6.12, this screen enables you to specify the separator used in the delimited file. A *separator* is the character placed between fields in a delimited text file. The separator is often a comma or semicolon, although it can be another character.
6. **Select the delimiter that separates your fields; if an uncommon delimiter is used, select Other and enter the delimiter in the Other box.**

FIGURE 6.12

The second Import Text Wizard screen.

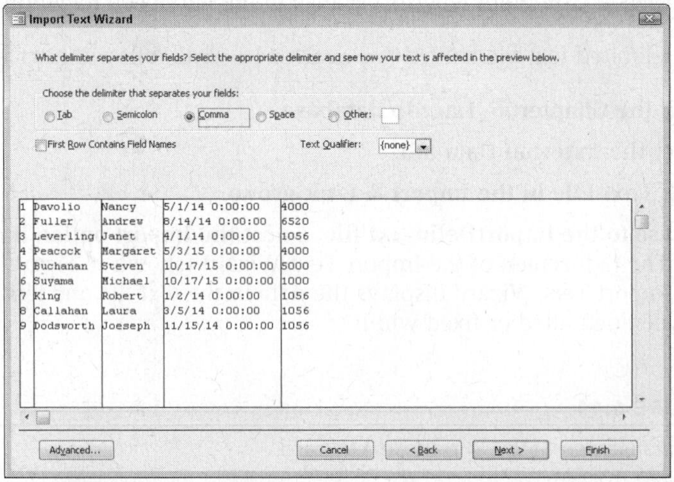

CAUTION

There can be a problem with the separator used if any of the fields in the text file contains the separator character as data. For example, if you use a comma to delimit fields, and one of the fields is Acme Widgets, Inc., Access will have a problem importing the file. The solution is to wrap text fields in double quotes ("Acme Widgets, Inc.") so that the comma is not misinterpreted as a field separator. This use of double quotes is referred to as the *text qualifier.* Most often single- or double-quote marks are used for this purpose and usually resolve issues with special characters contained within data fields.

7. **If the first row contains field names for the imported table, select the First Row Contains Field Names check box. When you're done with this screen, click Next.** The next few screens are very similar to the steps involved when importing Excel worksheets. You can change field names, specify a primary key, and save the import for future use. Save the imported text file with a descriptive Access table name. Access creates the new table, using the text file's name by default. The new table appears in the Navigation pane.

TIP

To specify a field containing no data in a delimited file, leave no characters between the commas (not even a space character). An empty field at the end of a row is indicated by a comma at the end of the line.

Fixed-width text files

Fixed-width text files also place each record on a separate line. However, the fields in each record are fixed in length. Fields are padded with trailing spaces to maintain spacing within each line, as shown in Figure 6.13.

FIGURE 6.13

A typical fixed-width text file.

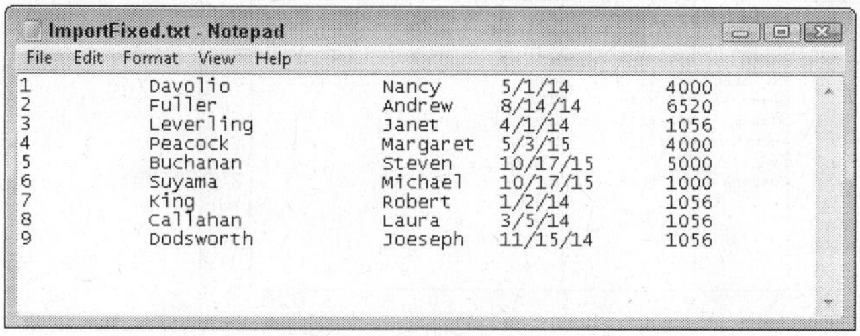

```
ImportFixed.txt - Notepad
File  Edit  Format  View  Help
1          Davolio            Nancy      5/1/14       4000
2          Fuller             Andrew     8/14/14      6520
3          Leverling          Janet      4/1/14       1056
4          Peacock            Margaret   5/3/15       4000
5          Buchanan           Steven     10/17/15     5000
6          Suyama             Michael    10/17/15     1000
7          King               Robert     1/2/14       1056
8          Callahan           Laura      3/5/14       1056
9          Dodsworth          Joeseph    11/15/14     1056
```

Notice that the fields in a fixed-width text file are not separated by delimiters. Instead, they start at exactly the same position in each record, and each record has exactly the same length.

Text values, such as first and last names, are not surrounded by quotation marks. There is no need for delimiting text values because each field is a specific width. Anything within a field's position in a row is considered data and does not require delimiters.

NOTE

If the Access table being imported has a primary key field, the text file cannot have any duplicate primary key values. If duplicate primary keys are found, the import will report an error and fail to import rows with duplicate primary keys.

To import a fixed-width text file, follow these steps:

1. **Open the Chapter06_1.accdb database.**
2. **Select the External Data tab.**
3. **Click Text File in the Import group.**
4. **Browse to ImportFixed.txt, select the Import option button, and click OK.** The first screen of the Import Text Wizard (refer to Figure 6.11) appears. The Import Text Wizard displays the data in the text file and lets you choose between delimited or fixed width.
5. **Select Fixed Width and click Next.** The next screen of the Import Text Wizard (shown in Figure 6.14) appears.

FIGURE 6.14

The Import Text Wizard screen for fixed-width text files.

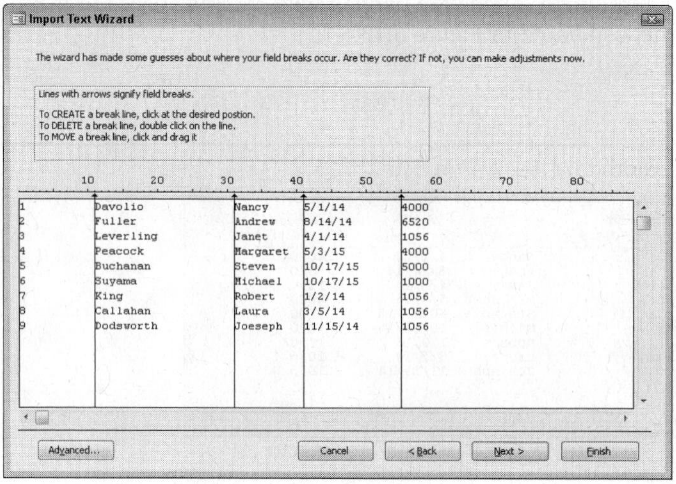

6. **Adjust field widths as needed.** Access guesses at the best breaks to use for fields, based on the most consistent spacing across rows. In this case, the field breaks are very consistent. If necessary, however, use the mouse to grab a dividing line and move it left or right to change the width of fields in the file.
7. **Click the Advanced button at the bottom of the wizard.** The Import Specification dialog box (shown in Figure 6.15) appears. The Import Specification dialog box lets you specify formats for dates, times, field names, indexing, and data types. It also provides an option for skipping fields you don't want to import. (For detailed information on this dialog box, see the nearby sidebar.)
8. **Ensure that the Date Order is set to MDY and the Four Digit Years check box is selected.**
9. **Select the Leading Zeros in Dates check box.**
10. **Click OK to dismiss the Import Specification dialog box.**
11. **Continue through the remaining Import Text Wizard screens.**

FIGURE 6.15

The Import Specification dialog box for importing a fixed-width text file.

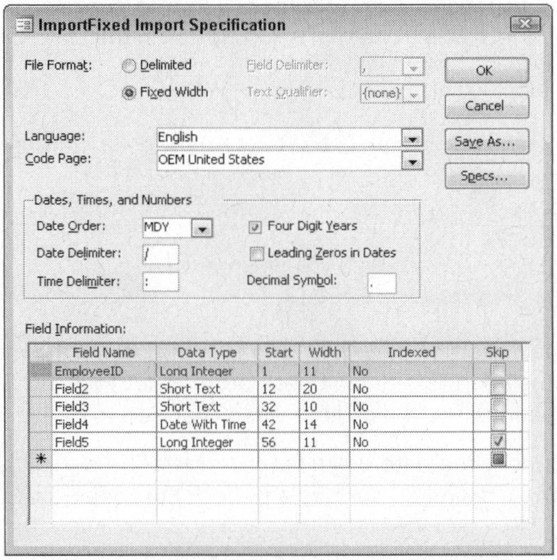

Using the Import Specification Dialog Box

One advantage of using the Import Specification dialog box is the fact that you can specify the type of file to be imported from or exported to. The Language and Code Page drop-down lists determine the fundamental type of format. The Code Page drop-down list displays the code pages that are available for the selected language.

You can also specify the Field Delimiter option for delimited text files. Four built-in field-separator choices (semicolon, tab, space, and comma) are available in this combo box, or you can specify another character by typing into the combo box, if needed.

You can also specify the text qualifier used to surround text fields. Normally, text fields in a delimited file are enclosed by characters such as quotation marks that set the text data apart from other fields. This is useful for specifying numeric data like Social Security and phone numbers as text data rather than numeric.

The Text Qualifier drop-down list is actually a combo box, so you can enter a different delimiter in the text area.

continued

continued

When Access imports or exports data, it converts dates to a specific format (such as MMDDYY). You can specify how date fields are to be converted, using one of the six choices in the Date Order combo box:

- DMY
- DYM
- MDY
- MYD
- YDM
- YMD

These choices specify the order for each portion of a date. The D is the day of the month (1–31), M is the calendar month (1–12), and Y is the year. The default date order is set to the U.S. format (month, day, year). When you work with European dates, the order is often changed to day, month, and year.

You use the Date Delimiter field to specify the date delimiter character. The default is a forward slash (/), but you can change this to any other delimiter, such as a period. European dates are often separated by periods, as in 22.10.12.

NOTE

When you import text files with Date-type data, you must have a separator between the month, day, and year. Access reports an error if the field is specified as a Date/Time type and no delimiter is used. When you're exporting date fields, the separator is not needed.

With the Time Delimiter option, you can specify a separator (usually a colon) between the parts of time values in a text file. To change the separator, simply enter another in the Time Delimiter box.

Select the Four Digit Years check box to specify that the year portion of a date field is formatted with four digits. By checking this box, you can import dates that include the century (such as in 1981 or 2001). The default is to use four-digit years.

The Leading Zeros in Dates option specifies that date values include leading zeros. This means that date formats include leading zeros (as in 02/04/03), if needed.

Importing and exporting XML documents

Importing XML documents is easy with Microsoft Access. XML is often used to transfer information between disparate platforms, databases, operating systems, applications, companies, planets, universes — you name it! XML is used for raw data, *metadata* (data descriptions), and even processing data. It's safe to say that most Access developers eventually import or export data in XML format.

Presenting XML in Access needs to be done in an odd way. You could easily import a simple XML document in your Access database. But the best way to find out how well Access uses XML is to begin by exporting something into XML.

Follow these steps to export data from Access to an XML file:

1. **Open the Chapter06_1.accdb database.**
2. **Open tblDepartments in Datasheet view.**
3. **Select the External Data tab, and click XML File in the Export section.**
4. **Name the XML file tblDepartments.xml, and click OK.** The Export XML dialog box (shown in Figure 6.16) appears.

FIGURE 6.16

The Export XML dialog box.

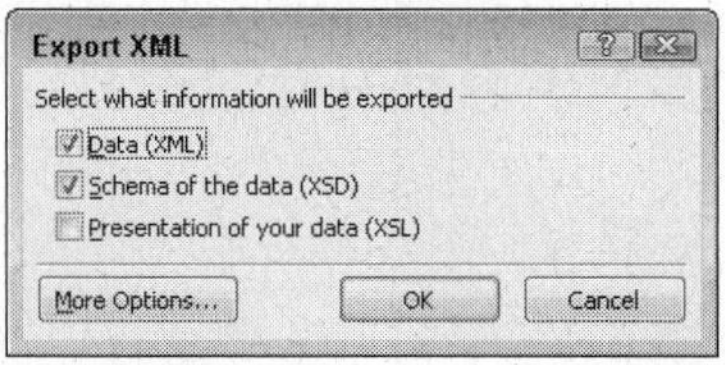

The Export XML Wizard includes options for specifying advanced options for the XML export process. Clicking the More Options button opens a dialog box (see Figure 6.17) with several important XML settings.

FIGURE 6.17

Advanced XML export options.

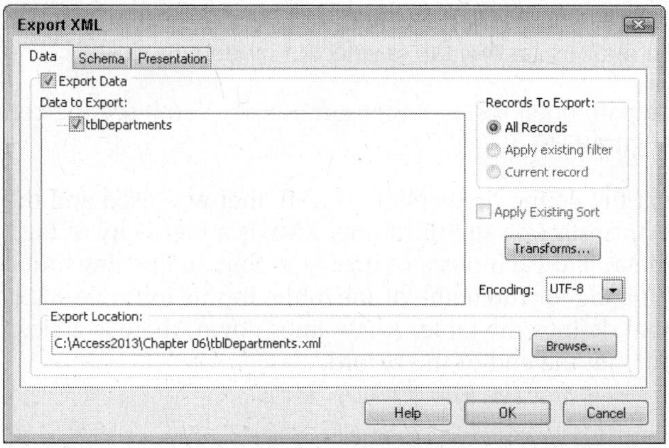

The data contained in an XML file may be relational or hierarchical. For example, a single XML file might contain information on both product categories and the products themselves. A *schema file* is needed for complex XML to be understood by other applications. Access automatically produces a schema file (XSD extension) for data exported in XML format. Figure 6.18 shows the Schema tab of the Export XML dialog box.

FIGURE 6.18

Exporting XML schema information.

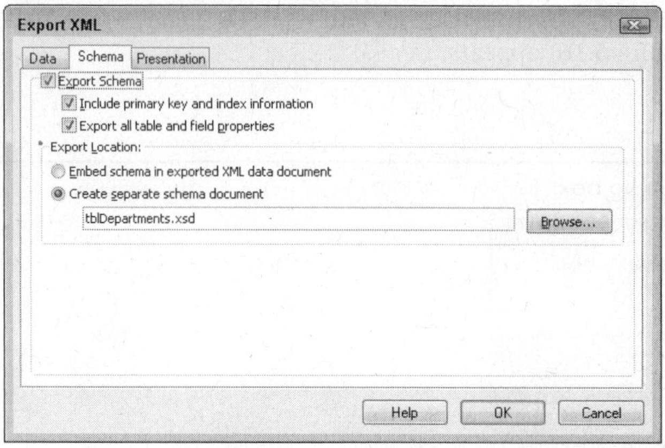

The XML schema file includes information such as the data type of each field and the source table's primary key and indexes.

A further refinement of the XML export process is to specify how the XML data should be presented in an application using the exported data. (The presentation is specified using HTML conventions.) In most cases, the XML presentation file (XSL extension) is not needed because the application that is designed to use the XML file displays the data as required by its users. Figure 6.19 shows the Presentation tab of the Export XML dialog box. Notice that none of the options on this tab is selected by default.

In a text editor, such as Notepad, open tblDepartments.xml. You'll see the contents of the XML file, as shown in Figure 6.20.

The first two lines of the text file define the version of XML that was used and the schema. The exported data and structure start on the third line. XML is a hierarchy of tags that define the structure of the data, and each piece of data is within an opening and closing tag. Each record begins with a tag for the name of the table. In this example <tbl Departments> is the tag that defines the table. A few lines down, there is a closing tag, </tblDepartments>, signifying the end of the record.

FIGURE 6.19

XML presentation options.

Export XML

Data | Schema | Presentation

Export Presentation (HTML 4.0 Sample XSL)

Run from:

Client (HTML)

Server (ASP)

Include report images:

Put images in:

Images

Browse...

Don't include images

Export Location:

tblDepartments.xsl

Browse...

Help | OK | Cancel

FIGURE 6.20

An exported XML file in plain text.

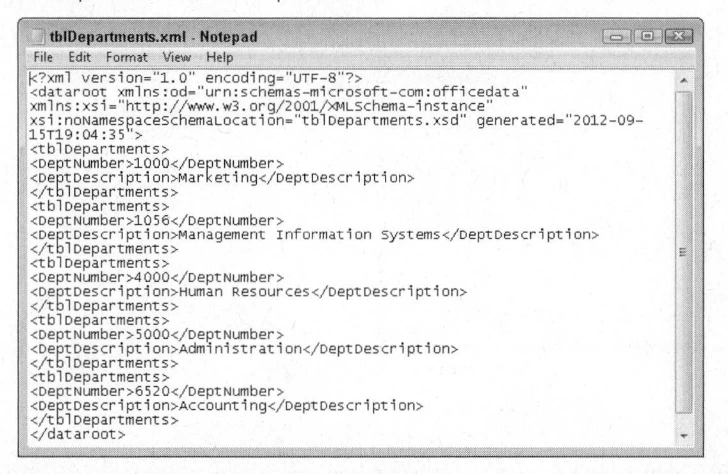

```
tblDepartments.xml - Notepad
File  Edit  Format  View  Help
<?xml version="1.0" encoding="UTF-8"?>
<dataroot xmlns:od="urn:schemas-microsoft-com:officedata"
xmlns:xsi="http://www.w3.org/2001/XMLSchema-instance"
xsi:noNamespaceSchemaLocation="tblDepartments.xsd" generated="2012-09-
15T19:04:35">
<tblDepartments>
<DeptNumber>1000</DeptNumber>
<DeptDescription>Marketing</DeptDescription>
</tblDepartments>
<tblDepartments>
<DeptNumber>1056</DeptNumber>
<DeptDescription>Management Information Systems</DeptDescription>
</tblDepartments>
<tblDepartments>
<DeptNumber>4000</DeptNumber>
<DeptDescription>Human Resources</DeptDescription>
</tblDepartments>
<tblDepartments>
<DeptNumber>5000</DeptNumber>
<DeptDescription>Administration</DeptDescription>
</tblDepartments>
<tblDepartments>
<DeptNumber>6520</DeptNumber>
<DeptDescription>Accounting</DeptDescription>
</tblDepartments>
</dataroot>
```

NOTE

Like HTML, XML uses tags to give context to the data. Opening tags define the start of a structure and consist of text between a less-than symbol (<) and a greater-than symbol (>). Closing tags define the end of the structure. Closing tags are formatted similarly to opening tags except that a forward slash is included after the less-than symbol (<).

In between these two tags are the fields and data for that record. The first field of the first record is recorded as `<DeptNumber>1000</DeptNumber>`. An application that understands XML will interpret that line to mean there is a field named DeptNumber and this record has 1000 in that field. This hierarchy of tags and data continues for each field in the record and for each record in the table.

Just as Access can export to XML, it can also import it. To import the `tblDepartments.xml` file that we just exported, follow these steps:

1. **Click on the XML File button on the Import & Link group of the External Data tab.**
2. **Browse to tblDepartments.xml and click OK.** The Import XML dialog, shown in Figure 6.21, displays how Access interprets the XML data.

FIGURE 6.21

Access understands XML data.

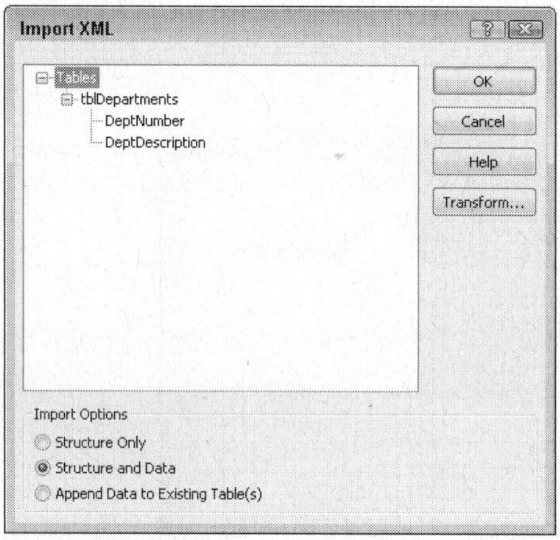

3. **Click OK.**

Access converted the well-formed XML into a table. The `<tblDepartments>` tag determine what the imported table will be named, the tags within the `<tblDepartments>` tag and its closing tag define the fields, and the data in between the field tags will become data in the new table.

Importing and exporting HTML documents

Access enables you to import HTML tables as easily as any other database, Excel spreadsheet, or text file. You simply select an HTML file to import and use the HTML Import

Wizard. The HTML Import Wizard works exactly like the other import wizards described earlier in this chapter.

And just like demonstrating XML in the previous section, we'll do an HTML import in reverse, as well. First, you export a table to generate an HTML file; then you import the file back into Access to create a new table:

1. **Open the Chapter06_1.accdb database.**
2. **Select the External Data tab, click the More drop-down button in the Export group, and select HTML Document.**
3. **Specify an HTML file as the export destination in the Export HTML dialog box (see Figure 6.22).**

FIGURE 6.22

The HTML Export dialog box.

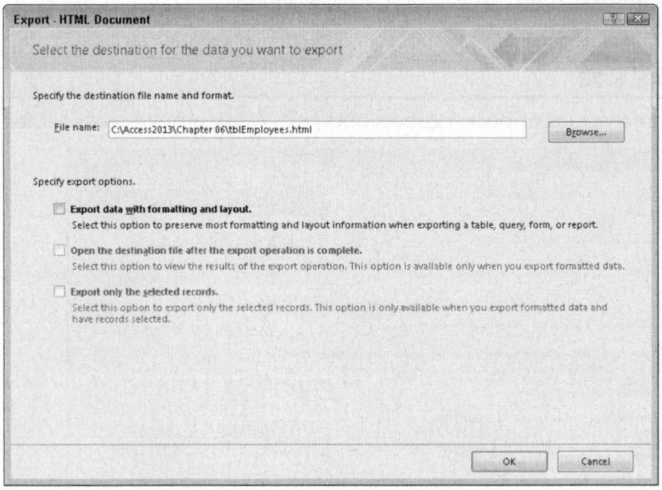

4. **Select your HTML output options and click OK.** The HTML export is completed as soon as you click the OK button. Unless you check Export Data with Formatting and Layout, no options other that what you see in Figure 6.22 are available when exporting HTML data.

Exporting data with formatting and layout, an option in the Export – HTML Document dialog box, presents additional exporting options. The most important option is that it allows you to specify an HTML template for your export. An HTML template is a normal HTML file, except that it includes special tags that Access recognizes. These tags instruct Access where to place certain data when exporting, allowing you to define the other aspects of the HTML document, such as styling and logos.

Importing the HTML is much like importing a text file shown previously in this chapter. In fact, the Import HMTL Wizard has most of the same screens and options as the Import Text Wizard, such as defining data types for fields and identifying the primary key.

Importing Access objects other than tables

You can import other Access database tables or any other object in another database, which means you can import an existing table, query, form, report, macro, or module from another Access database. You can also import custom toolbars and menus.

As a simple demonstration, follow these steps:

1. **Open the Chapter06_1.accdb database.**
2. **Select the External Data tab, and in the Import section click the option to import from another Access database.** The screen in Figure 6.23 appears. Notice that this dialog box enables you to specify whether to import database objects or link to tables in an external Access database.

FIGURE 6.23

The same wizard imports objects and links to external Access tables.

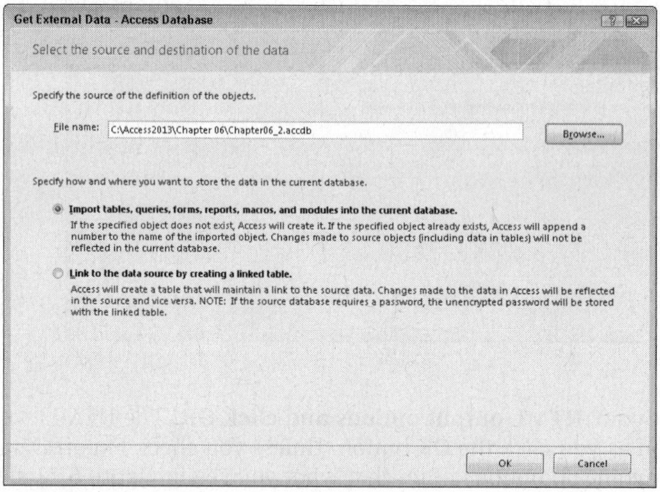

3. **Browse to the Chapter06_2.accdb database and click OK.** Figure 6.24 shows that you can import every type of Access object.

FIGURE 6.24

Importing Access objects.

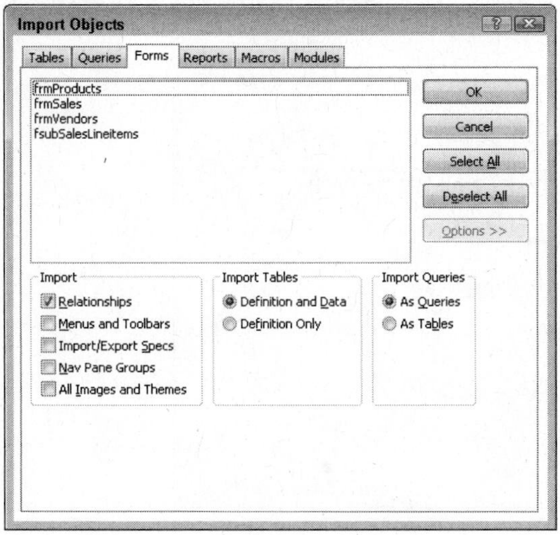

When including tables, queries, forms, reports, macros, or modules — all in the same import — you can select objects from each tab and then import all the objects at once.

Figure 6.24 shows the Import Object dialog box with the Options button clicked. Clicking Options shows the options for importing table relationships, menus, toolbars, and other Access database objects. Importing (and exporting, for that matter) is an excellent way of backing up objects prior to making changes to them.

Importing an Outlook folder

An interesting Access import capability is the option to import data directly from Outlook. Although most people think of Outlook as an e-mail system, it supports a number of important business needs, such as scheduling and contact management.

When working with Outlook data, Access doesn't care whether an imported item is an e-mail or contact. Access handles all types of Outlook objects with equal ease.

Select Outlook Folder from the More drop-down list in the Import group to open the initial Outlook Folder import dialog box (shown in Figure 6.25). Access provides options for importing Outlook data, adding it to an existing Access table, or linking to it from the current Access database.

FIGURE 6.25

The initial Outlook import options.

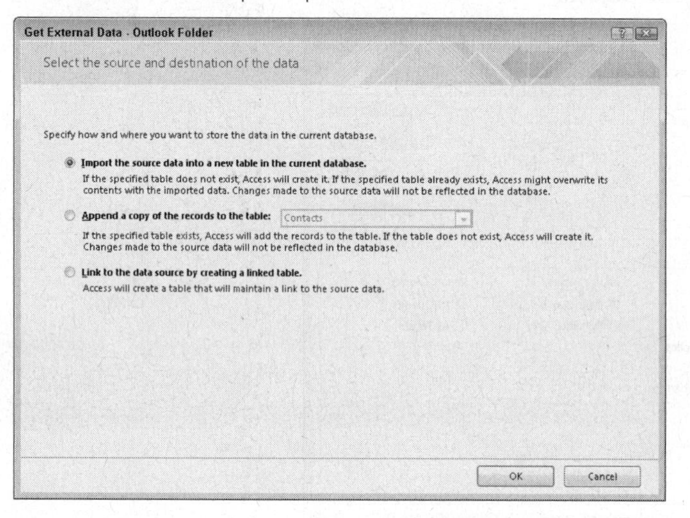

Selecting the import option opens the Import Exchange/Outlook Wizard (shown in Figure 6.26). As shown in this dialog box, Access can import Outlook e-mail, contacts, calendars, journals, and other folders.

FIGURE 6.26

Importing Outlook objects into Access.

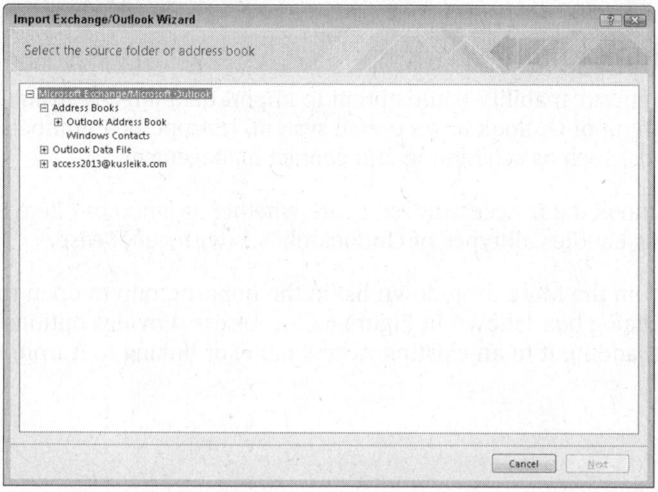

Import Exchange/Outlook Wizard
Select the source folder or address book
Microsoft Exchange/Microsoft Outlook
Address Books
Outlook Address Book
Windows Contacts
Outlook Data File
access2013@kusleika.com
Cancel
Next

Depending on which item you select in the Import Exchange/Outlook Wizard, the remaining wizard screens walk you through the process of bringing Outlook data into Access. You can import Outlook data into a new or existing table, add a primary key, specify data types, and save the import process for later execution.

How to Export to External Formats

An export copies data from an Access table to some other application or data source, such as an XML document. The exported result uses the format of the destination data source and not the format of an Access database. You can copy data from an Access table or query into a new external file. You can export tables to several different sources.

> **NOTE**
> In general, anything imported can also be exported, unless otherwise stated in this chapter.

Exporting objects to other Access databases

When the destination of an export process is an Access database, you can export every type of Access object (tables, queries, forms, reports, and so on). Unlike importing, which allows you to import many objects at once, exporting only allows you to export one object at a time. To export an object to another Access database, follow these generic steps:

1. **Open the source database and select an object to export.**
2. **Click the Access button under the Export section of the External Data tab.** The Export – Access Database dialog box appears.
3. **Use the Browse button to locate the destination Access database.**

> **NOTE**
> Ensure that the target database isn't open when attempting to export to it. If it is, a locking conflict will occur.

4. **Click OK.** The export process proceeds.

> **NOTE**
> Tables can be exported as definition and data or data only.

   If an object already exists in the target database, you'll be asked whether you want to replace the object in the target database. If you don't, you can create a new object in the target database.

5. **The last step of the wizard enables you to save the export configuration for future use.** This option can be quite handy if you'll be frequently performing the same export process.

NOTE
If you try to export an object to another Access database that has an object of the same type and name, Access warns you before copying. You then have the option to cancel or overwrite.

Exporting through ODBC drivers

Exporting using an ODBC driver connection to another relational database is a simple process. You connect to the external database (in our case, an Oracle database). You then select a table to export, as shown in Figure 6.27.

FIGURE 6.27

Exporting Access tables to an ODBC destination.

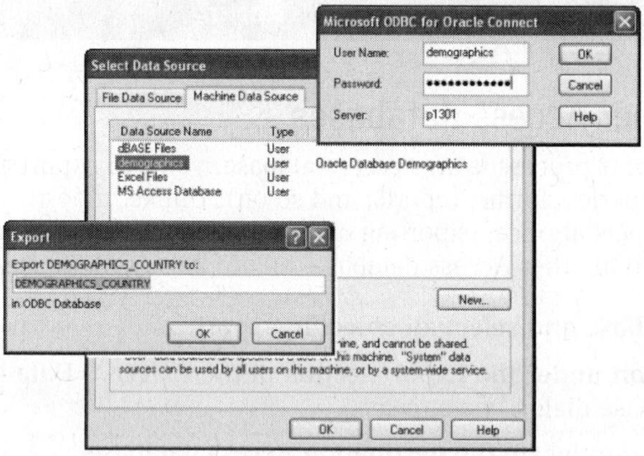

Exporting to Word

Access provides two ways to transfer data to Word: Export to Rich Text Format and Word Merge. Rich Text Format (RTF) is a plain text file with special characters that define the formatting. Exporting to RTF creates a document with an RTF extension, not a native Word document. But Word can read RTF as can WordPad and many other text editors.

Merging data into Word

The real power of exporting to Word is through Word Merge. With Word Merge, you can control where your data ends up inside the Word document. This is useful for sending letters, addressing envelopes, producing reports, and creating file folder labels.

To create file folder labels for each department in tblDepartments, follow these steps:

1. **Open tblDepartments in Datasheet view.**
2. **Click the Word Merge button in the Export group on the External Data tab.**
3. **On the first screen of the Microsoft Word Mail Merge Wizard, shown in Figure 6.28, select Create a New Document and Then Link the Data to It, and click OK.** Word opens to a new document and the Mail Merge task pane appears on the right.

FIGURE 6.28

The Microsoft Word Mail Merge Wizard allows you to export data to existing or new documents.

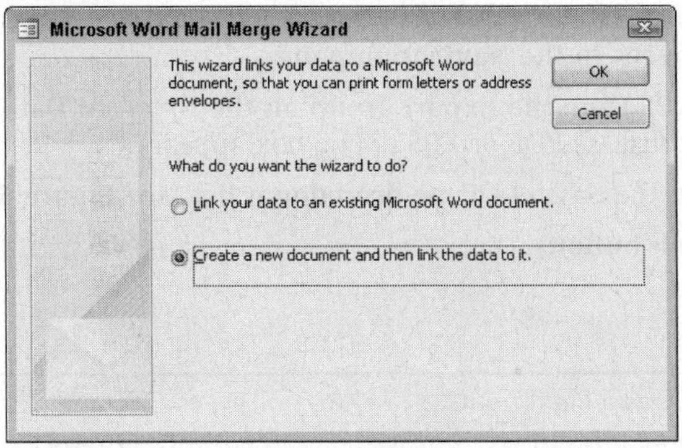

Microsoft Word Mail Merge Wizard

This wizard links your data to a Microsoft Word document, so that you can print form letters or address envelopes.

OK

Cancel

What do you want the wizard to do?

Link your data to an existing Microsoft Word document.

Create a new document and then link the data to it.

4. **Follow the Mail Merge wizard for the type of labels you have. On step 3 of the wizard, Microsoft Word has already selected tblDepartments as the data source.**
5. **Arrange the DeptNumber and DeptDescription on the label and template and complete the merge.** Figure 6.29 shows the results of a merge where the department number and description are separated by a hyphen.

FIGURE 6.29

A completed Word Merge.

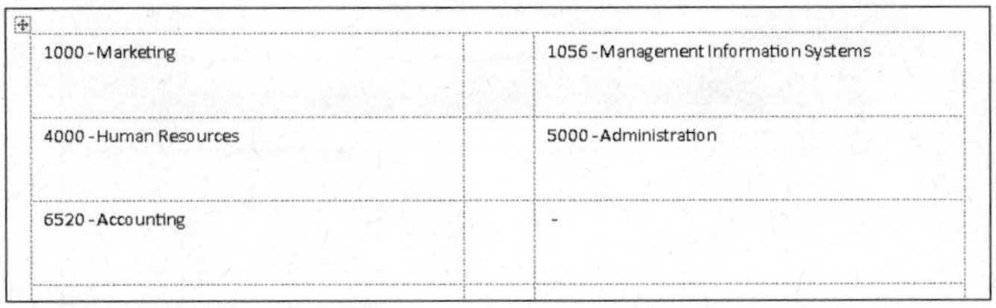

1000 - Marketing	1056 - Management Information Systems
4000 - Human Resources	5000 - Administration
6520 - Accounting	-

NOTE
You can import from Word into Access by converting the Word document into a text file first. You could even use Word in combination with Excel to produce a delimited text file.

Publishing to PDF or XPS

The PDF and XPS file formats were developed to display data as it would appear on a printed page. Data displayed in these formats are generally not editable. Publishing to PDF or XPS outputs a relatively small file and is useful when you want to share data but don't want the other person to be able to change it. To export tblEmployees to a PDF, follow these steps

1. **Select tblEmployees in the Navigation pane.**
2. **Select PDF or XPS from the Export group on the External Data tab of the Ribbon.** The Publish as PDF or XPS dialog box appears.
3. **Select PDF from the Save As Type drop-down list (see Figure 6.30).**
4. **Click the Publish button.**

FIGURE 6.30

Select PDF or XPS as a file format.

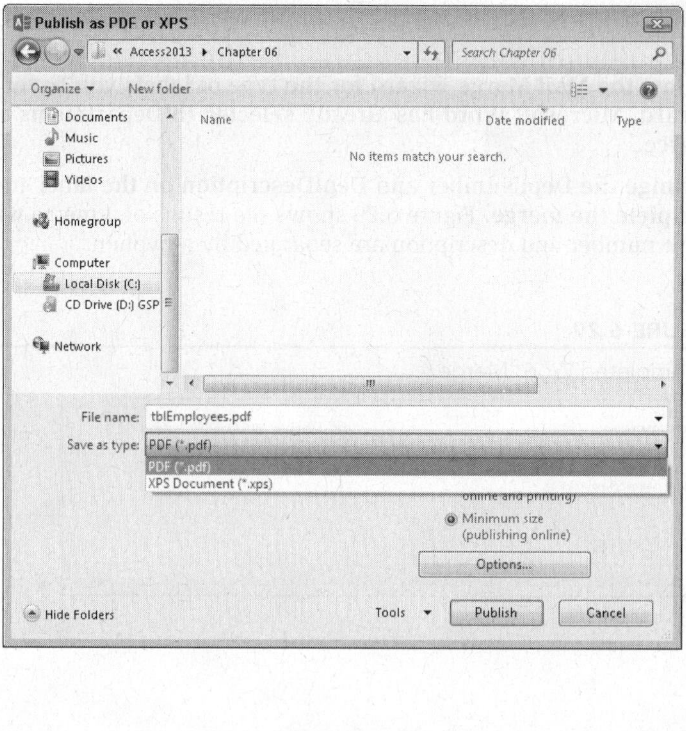

The result, as shown in Figure 6.31, is a PDF file that can be opened by many different PDF reader programs. Most computers have some PDF reader software installed, which makes it a great format for sharing data you don't want changed.

FIGURE 6.31

A table published in the PDF file format.

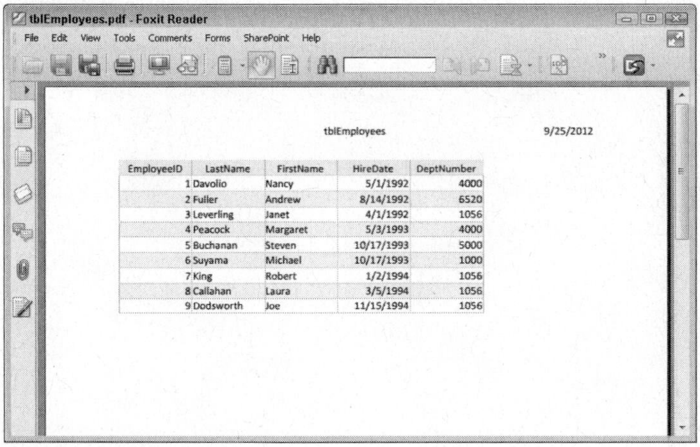

tblEmployees.pdf - Foxit Reader

File Edit View Tools Comments Forms SharePoint Help

tblEmployees 9/25/2012

EmployeeID	LastName	FirstName	HireDate	DeptNumber
1	Davolio	Nancy	5/1/1992	4000
2	Fuller	Andrew	8/14/1992	6520
3	Leverling	Janet	4/1/1992	1056
4	Peacock	Margaret	5/3/1993	4000
5	Buchanan	Steven	10/17/1993	5000
6	Suyama	Michael	10/17/1993	1000
7	King	Robert	1/2/1994	1056
8	Callahan	Laura	3/5/1994	1056
9	Dodsworth	Joe	11/15/1994	1056

Linking to External Data

IN THIS CHAPTER

Looking at the types of external data and methods for working with them

Linking your Access database to external data

Using linked tables

Splitting an Access database

In Chapter 6, you learned about the types of external data that you can import and export to and from Access. You also learned when to import and export and when to link. This chapter describes the methods for using external data in Access through a live, updating link to the data.

> **ON THE WEB**
> This chapter uses the `Chapter07.accdb` database, as well as several other files that you'll use for linking. If you haven't already downloaded these files onto your machine from this book's website, you'll need to do so now.

Note that, because the point of this chapter is to show how Access works with external data, there are examples of external data that you need to copy to your machine. Unfortunately, when working with external data, Access requires an exact path to each file — it can't work with relative paths. That means that when you copy `Chapter07.accdb` to your machine, it won't work until you relink the various external files. I show you how to do that in this chapter. For now, be aware that the following tables are linked to the files indicated:

Table	External File Type	Filename(s)
ContactsFixed	Text File	`ContactsFixed.txt`
Customers	Excel	`CollectibleMiniCars.xls`
CustomerTypes	HTML	`CustomerTypes.html`
Products	Excel 8.0	`CollectibleMiniCars.xls`
tblSales	Access	`Chapter07_Link.accdb`
tblSalesLineItems	Excel 8.0	`tblSalesLineItems.xls`
tblSalesPayments	Access	`Chapter07_Link.accdb`

Fixing Links

We'll discuss the Linked Table Manager later in this chapter in detail. For now, follow these steps to fix the linked tables in Chapter07.accdb:

1. **Copy the** Chapter 07 **folder to your computer and make a note of the location.**
2. **Open** Chapter07.accdb.
3. **Click Linked Table Manager in the Import & Link group on the External Data tab of the Ribbon.** The Linked Table Manager appears.
4. **Click the Select All button and then click OK.** You'll be prompted for the new location for each of the linked tables.
5. **Using the table of filenames provided earlier in this chapter, browse to each file.** The Linked Table Manager displays a message that all selected linked tables were successfully refreshed.

Now you can follow along with the examples in this chapter.

The data linked to Access applications comes in a bewildering variety of formats. There is no practical way to document every possible type of linking operation in a single chapter. So, this chapter discusses the essential steps required to link to external data and gives a few examples demonstrating how these processes are performed in Access, instead of filling page after page with examples that may or may not be relevant to your work.

As you'll soon see, knowledge of the external data format is critical to a successful linking operation. You must have some notion of the external data format before you can successfully import data into your Access application or incorporate the data into an Access database through linking. This chapter points out many of the issues involved if you choose to link to external data; it's intended to serve as a guide as you perform these operations in your Access applications.

Linking External Data

As the database market continues to grow, the need to work with information from many different sources will escalate. If you have information captured in a SQL Server database or an old Excel spreadsheet, you don't want to reenter the information from these sources into Access. Ideally, you want to open an Access table containing the data and use the information in its native format, without having to copy it or write a translation program to access it. In many cases, the capability of accessing information from one database format while working in another is often an essential starting point for many business projects.

Using code to copy or translate data from one application format to another is both time consuming and costly. The time it takes can mean the difference between success and failure. Therefore, you want an intermediary between the different data sources in your environment.

Access can simultaneously link to multiple tables contained within other database systems. After an external file is linked, Access stores the link specification and uses the external data as if it were contained in a local table. Access easily links to other Access database tables as well as to non-Access database tables, such as dBASE and FoxPro. A recommended practice is to split an Access database into two separate databases for easier use in a multiuser or client-server environment.

Identifying linked tables

In the "Ways of working with external data" section in Chapter 6, you saw a list of database tables and other types of files that Access links to. Access displays the names of linked tables in the object list and uses a special icon to indicate that the table is linked and not local. An arrow pointing to an icon indicates that the table name represents a link data source. Figure 7.1 shows several linked tables in the list. (The icon indicates that the file is linked. The icon also indicates which type of file is linked to the current Access database. For example, Excel has an *X* in a box and HTML tables have a globe symbol.)

FIGURE 7.1

Linked tables in an Access database. Notice that each linked table has an icon indicating its status as a linked table.

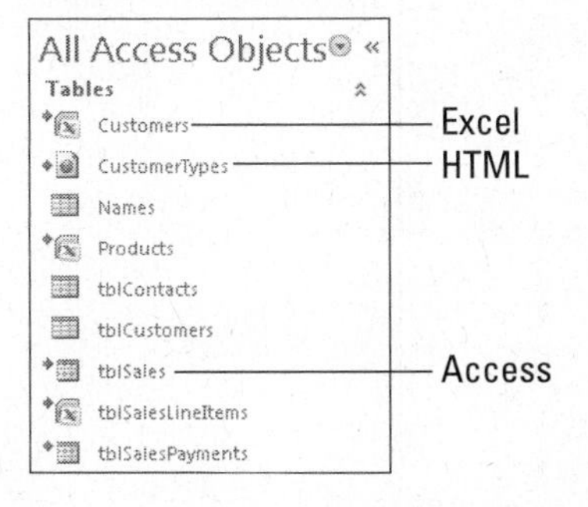

After you link an external database table to your Access database, you use it as you would any other table. For example, Figure 7.2 shows a query using several linked tables: tblCustomers (a local Access table), tblSales (a linked Access table), tblSaleLineItems (from an Excel file), and xlsProducts (from another Excel file). As you can see, there's nothing that distinguishes the fact that the tables are from external sources — Access treats them no differently from any other tables.

FIGURE 7.2

A query using externally linked tables.

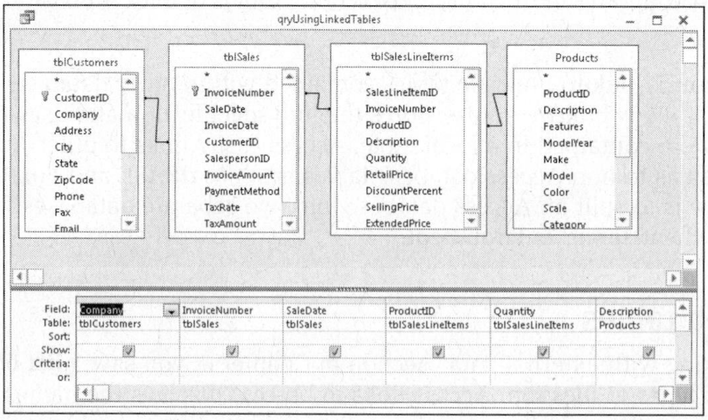

This query shows the potential benefit of linking to a variety of data sources and seamlessly displays data from internal and linked tables. Figure 7.3 shows the datasheet returned by this query. Each column in this datasheet comes from a different data source.

FIGURE 7.3

The Datasheet view of externally linked data.

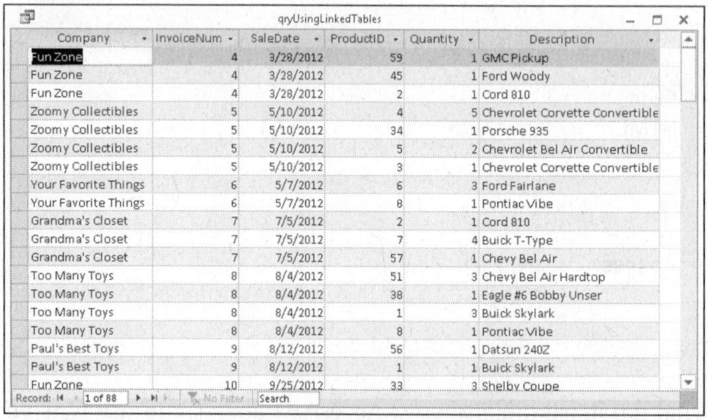

Company	InvoiceNum	SaleDate	ProductID	Quantity	Description
Fun Zone	4	3/28/2012	59	1	GMC Pickup
Fun Zone	4	3/28/2012	45	1	Ford Woody
Fun Zone	4	3/28/2012	2	1	Cord 810
Zoomy Collectibles	5	5/10/2012	4	5	Chevrolet Corvette Convertible
Zoomy Collectibles	5	5/10/2012	34	1	Porsche 935
Zoomy Collectibles	5	5/10/2012	5	2	Chevrolet Bel Air Convertible
Zoomy Collectibles	5	5/10/2012	3	1	Chevrolet Corvette Convertible
Your Favorite Things	6	5/7/2012	6	3	Ford Fairlane
Your Favorite Things	6	5/7/2012	8	1	Pontiac Vibe
Grandma's Closet	7	7/5/2012	2	1	Cord 810
Grandma's Closet	7	7/5/2012	7	4	Buick T-Type
Grandma's Closet	7	7/5/2012	57	1	Chevy Bel Air
Too Many Toys	8	8/4/2012	51	3	Chevy Bel Air Hardtop
Too Many Toys	8	8/4/2012	38	1	Eagle #6 Bobby Unser
Too Many Toys	8	8/4/2012	1	3	Buick Skylark
Too Many Toys	8	8/4/2012	8	1	Pontiac Vibe
Paul's Best Toys	9	8/12/2012	56	1	Datsun 240Z
Paul's Best Toys	9	8/12/2012	1	1	Buick Skylark
Fun Zone	10	9/25/2012	33	3	Shelby Coupe

Record: 1 of 88

Figure 7.3 illustrates an important concept regarding using linked data in Access: Users won't know, nor will they care, where the data resides. All they want is to see the data in a format they expect. Only you, the developer, understand the issues involved in bringing this data to the user interface (UI). Other than the limitations of linked data (explained in the next section), users won't be able to tell the difference between native and linked data.

NOTE

After you link an external table to an Access database, don't move the source table to another drive or directory. Access doesn't bring the external data file into the ACCDB file; it maintains the link via the filename and file path. If you move the external table, you have to update the link using the Linked Table Manager, explained in the "Viewing or changing information for linked tables" section, later in this chapter.

Limitations of linked data

Although this chapter describes using linked data as if it existed as native Access tables, certain operations can't be performed on linked data. Plus, the prohibited operations depend, to a certain extent, on the type of data linked to Access.

These limitations are relatively easy to understand. Linked data is never "owned" by Access. External files that are linked to Access are managed by their respective applications. For example, an Excel worksheet is managed by Excel. It would be presumptive — and dangerous — for Access to freely modify data in an Excel worksheet. For example, because many Excel operations depend on the relative positions of rows and columns in a worksheet, inserting a row into a worksheet might break calculations and other operations performed by Excel on the data. Deleting a row might distort a named range in the Excel worksheet, causing similar problems. Because there is no practical way for Access to understand all the operations performed on an external data file by its respective owner, Microsoft has chosen to take a very conservative route and not allow Access to modify data that might cause problems for the data's owner.

The following list describes the limitations of linked data:

- **Access data:** There are no limitations to what you can do with the data in linked tables. You can't delete or rename the source table. Nor can you change the fields or data types of the source table.
- **Excel data:** Existing data in an Excel worksheet can't be changed, nor can rows be deleted or new rows be added to a worksheet. Excel data is essentially treated in a read-only fashion by Access.
- **Text files:** For all practical purposes, data linked to text files is treated as read-only in Access. Although the data can be used in forms and reports, you can't simply and easily update rows in a linked text file, nor can you delete existing rows in a text file. Oddly enough, you can *add* new rows to a text file; presumably, this is because new rows won't typically break existing operations the way that deleting or changing the contents of an existing row might.
- **HTML:** HTML data is treated exactly as Excel data. You can't modify, delete, or add rows to an HTML table.
- **Outlook contacts:** Outlook contacts can be displayed in Access forms and reports, but they can't be added, deleted, or changed.

- **ODBC:** ODBC is a data access technology that uses a driver between an Access database and an external database file, such as SQL Server or Oracle. Generally speaking, because the linked data source is a database table, you can perform whatever database operations (modifying, deleting, adding) you would with a native Access table, provided you've defined a unique index in Access. (We discuss ODBC database tables in some detail in the "Linking to ODBC data sources" section, later in this chapter.)

Linking to other Access database tables

Access easily incorporates data located in the other Access files by linking to those tables. This process makes it easy to share data among Access applications across the network or on the local computer. The information presented in this section applies to virtually any Access data file you linked to from an Access database. Later in this chapter, you'll see short sections explaining the differences between linking to an Access table and linking to each of the other types of data files recognized by Access.

NOTE

A very common practice among Access developers is splitting an Access database into two pieces. One piece contains the forms, reports, and other UI components of an application, while the second piece contains the tables, queries, and other data elements. There are many advantages to splitting Access databases, including certain performance benefits, as well as easier maintenance. You can read about splitting Access databases later in this chapter. The process of linking to external Access tables described in this section is an essential part of the split database paradigm.

After you link to another Access table, you use it just as you use any table in the open database (with the exception that it can't be used in a relationship to other tables not in the source database). Follow these steps to link to tblSalesPayments in the `Chapter07_Link.accdb` database from the `Chapter07.accdb` database file:

1. **Open Chapter07.accdb.**
2. **Select the External Data tab of the Ribbon, and then choose Access as the type of data you want to link.** The Get External Data – Access Database dialog box (shown in Figure 7.4) appears.
3. **Click the Browse button.** The File Open dialog box appears.
4. **Locate Chapter07_Link.accdb, and click Open.** The File Open dialog box closes and you're taken back to the Get External Data – Access Database dialog box.
5. **Select the option button for linking and click OK in the Get External Data – Access Database dialog box.** The Link Tables dialog box enables you to select one or more tables from the selected database (in this case, Chapter07_Link). Figure 7.5 shows the Link Tables dialog box open on `Chapter07_Link.accdb`.

FIGURE 7.4

Use the Get External Data dialog box to select the type of operation you want to perform on the external data sources.

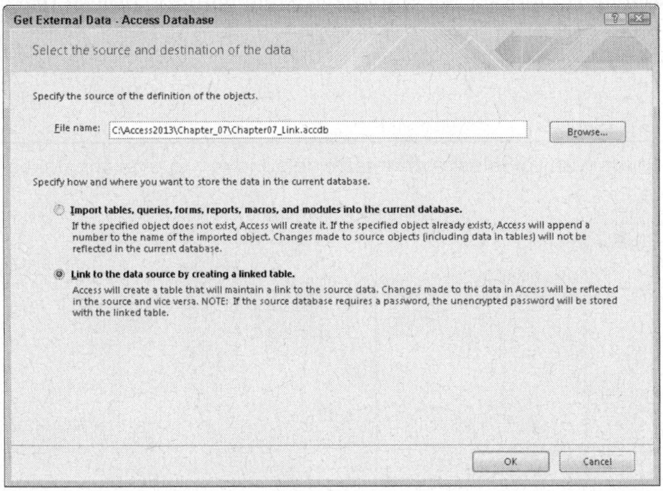

FIGURE 7.5

Use the Link Tables dialog box to select the Access table(s) for linking.

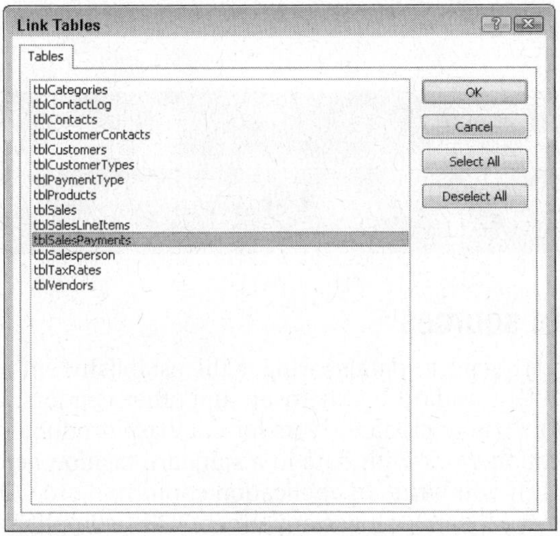

6. **Select tblSalesPayments and click OK.** Double-clicking the table name won't link the table — you have to highlight it and then click OK.

After you link tblSalesPayments, Access returns to the object list and shows you the newly linked table. Figure 7.6 shows tblSalesPayments linked to the current database. Notice the special icon attached to tblSalesPayments. This icon indicates that this table is linked to an external data source. Hovering over the linked table with the mouse reveals the linked table's data source.

FIGURE 7.6

The Navigation pane with tblSalesPayments added. Hovering over the linked table icon reveals its source.

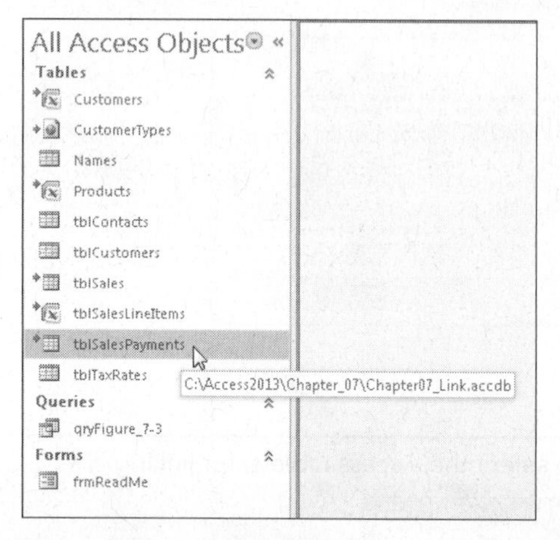

TIP

You can link more than one table at a time by selecting multiple tables before you click the OK button in the Link Tables dialog box. Clicking the Select All button selects all the tables. Once you've selected all the tables, you can click individual selections to unselect them.

Linking to ODBC data sources

One significant advance with regard to data sharing is the establishment of the Open Database Connectivity (ODBC) standard by Microsoft and other vendors. ODBC is a specification that software vendors use to create drivers for database products. This specification lets your Access application work with data in a standard fashion across many different database platforms. If you write an application conforming to ODBC specifications, then your application will be able to use any other ODBC-compliant back end.

For example, say you create an Access application that uses a SQL Server database back end. The most common way to accomplish this requirement is to use the SQL Server

ODBC driver. After developing the application, you find that one of your branch offices would like to use the application as well, but they're using Oracle as a database host. If your application has conformed closely to ODBC syntax, then you should be able to use the same application with Oracle by acquiring an Oracle ODBC driver. Not only are vendors supplying drivers for their own products, but there are now software vendors who only create and supply ODBC drivers.

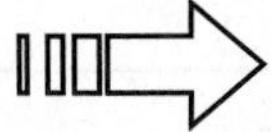

Linking to ODBC sources is discussed in detail in Chapter 29. In that chapter, you'll learn about setting up ODBC data sources and linking to those sources. Although SQL Server is used as the example in Chapter 29, the same principles apply to all ODBC data sources.

7

Linking to non-database data

You can also link to non-database data, such as Excel, HTML, and text files. When you select one of these types of data sources, Access runs a Link Wizard that prompts you through the process.

Linking to Excel

Here are the main issues to keep in mind when linking to Excel data:

- An Excel XLS spreadsheet file might contain multiple worksheets. You must choose which worksheet within a workbook file to link to (unless you're using named ranges).
- You may link to named ranges within an Excel worksheet. Each range becomes a separate linked table in Access.
- Excel columns may contain virtually any type of data. Just because you've successfully linked to an Excel worksheet doesn't mean that your application will be able to use all the data contained in the worksheet. Because Excel doesn't limit the types of data contained in a worksheet, your application may encounter multiple types of data within a single column of a linked Excel worksheet. This means that you may have to add code or provide other strategies for working around the varying types of data contained in an Excel worksheet.

On the Web

This book's website contains an Excel spreadsheet created by exporting the Products table from the Collectible Mini Cars application. Use this file to practice linking to Excel data, keeping in mind that, in practice, the data you're likely to encounter in Excel spreadsheets is far more complex and less orderly than the data contained in `Products.xls`.

Follow these steps to link to the Excel `CollectibleMiniCars.xls` spreadsheet:

1. **In the Chapter07.accdb database, click the Excel button on the External Data tab of the Ribbon.** The Get External Data dialog box (shown in Figure 7.7) appears.

2. **Select Link to the Data Source by Creating a Linked Table, and then click Browse.** The same Get External Data dialog box is used for both import and link operations, so be sure the correct operation is selected before continuing.

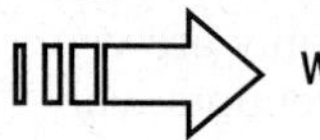

We cover importing data into Access in Chapter 6.

FIGURE 7.7

The first screen of the Get External Data – Excel Spreadsheet dialog box.

Get External Data - Excel Spreadsheet

Select the source and destination of the data

Specify the source of the definition of the objects.

File name: C:\Access2013\Chapter_07\CollectibleMiniCars.xls Browse...

Specify how and where you want to store the data in the current database.

Import the source data into a new table in the current database.
If the specified table does not exist, Access will create it. If the specified table already exists, Access might overwrite its contents with the imported data. Changes made to the source data will not be reflected in the database.

Append a copy of the records to the table: Names
If the specified table exists, Access will add the records to the table. If the table does not exist, Access will create it. Changes made to the source data will not be reflected in the database.

Link to the data source by creating a linked table.
Access will create a table that will maintain a link to the source data in Excel. Changes made to the source data in Excel will be reflected in the linked table. However, the source data cannot be changed from within Access.

OK Cancel

3. **Click the Browse button to the right of the File Name box.** The File Open dialog box appears.
4. **Locate and open the Excel file.** You're returned to the Link Spreadsheet Wizard (see Figure 7.8). Notice that the Link Spreadsheet Wizard contains options for selecting either worksheets or named ranges within the workbook file. In this example, there are three different worksheets (named Products, Sales, and Customers) within the spreadsheet file.
5. **Select the Products worksheet for this demonstration.** The Link Spreadsheet Wizard walks you through a number of different screens where you specify details such as First Row Contains Column Headings and the data type you want to apply to each column in the Excel worksheet. The last screen of the Link Spreadsheet Wizard asks for the name of the newly linked table.
6. **Click Finish.** The linked table is established and you're returned to the Access environment.

FIGURE 7.8

The main Link Spreadsheet Wizard screen.

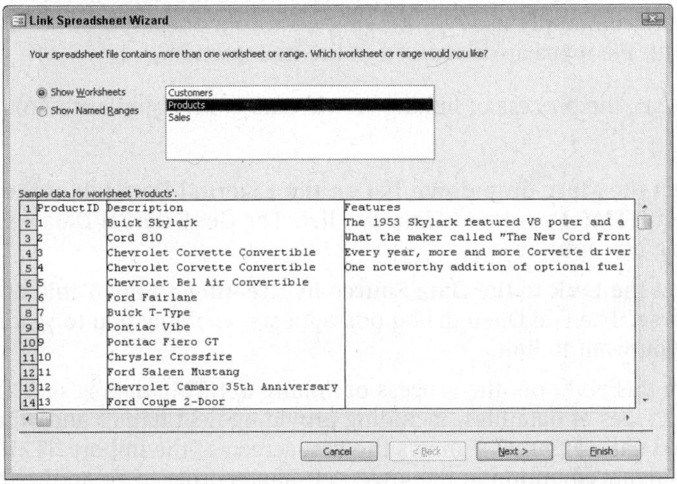

As with so many other things in database development, many decisions involved in linking to external data sources are based on how the data is to be used in the application. Also, the names you provide for fields and other details have a direct impact on your application.

Linking to HTML files

Linking to data contained in HTML documents is not covered in detail in this book because of the rather severe limitations imposed by Access on this process. For example, Access is unable to retrieve data from an arbitrary HTML file. The data must be presented as an HTML table, in a row-and-column format, and the data has to be relatively clean (absent any unusual data or mix of data, such as text, image, and numeric data combined within a single HTML table).

You're likely to encounter problems if more than one HTML table appears on the page, or if the data is presented in a hierarchical fashion (parent and child data).

TIP

Linking to arbitrary HTML documents is hit or miss at best. You're much better off linking to an HTML document specifically prepared as a data source for your Access application than trying to work with arbitrary HTML files.

If someone is going to the trouble of creating specialized HTML documents to be used as Access data sources, producing comma-separated values (CSV) or fixed-width text files is probably a better choice than HTML. CSV files, where the fields in each row are separated by commas, are commonly used for moving data from one application to another. CSV and fixed-width file types are discussed in the next section.

Having said that, the process of linking HTML data is very similar to linking to Excel spreadsheets:

1. **Select the More drop-down list on the External Data tab of the Ribbon and select HTML Document from the list.** The Get External Data – HTML Document dialog box appears.
2. **Select the Link to the Data Source by Creating a Link Table option, and click Browse.** The File Open dialog box appears, enabling you to search for the HTML file you want to link.

   From this point on, the process of linking to HTML data is similar to linking to other types of data files, including providing field names and other details of the linked data. Figure 7.9 shows the first screen of the Import HTML Wizard. Click the Advanced button in the lower-left hand corner to get to the Import Specification screen (shown in Figure 7.10), where you can provide the field names and other details.

FIGURE 7.9

The Import HTML Wizard screen showing the data in the HTML file.

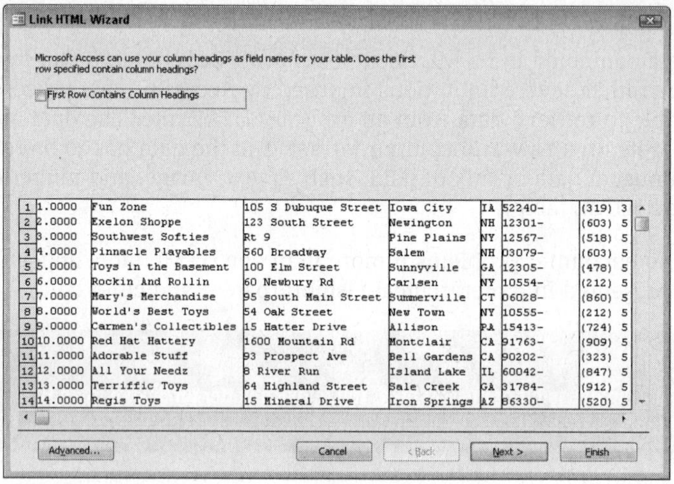

Link HTML Wizard

Microsoft Access can use your column headings as field names for your table. Does the first row specified contain column headings?

First Row Contains Column Headings

1	1.0000	Fun Zone	105 S Dubuque Street	Iowa City	IA	52240-	(319) 3
2	2.0000	Exelon Shoppe	123 South Street	Newington	NH	12301-	(603) 5
3	3.0000	Southwest Softies	Rt 9	Pine Plains	NY	12567-	(518) 5
4	4.0000	Pinnacle Playables	560 Broadway	Salem	NH	03079-	(603) 5
5	5.0000	Toys in the Basement	100 Elm Street	Sunnyville	GA	12305-	(478) 5
6	6.0000	Rockin And Rollin	60 Newbury Rd	Carlsen	NY	10554-	(212) 5
7	7.0000	Mary's Merchandise	95 south Main Street	Summerville	CT	06028-	(860) 5
8	8.0000	World's Best Toys	54 Oak Street	New Town	NY	10555-	(212) 5
9	9.0000	Carmen's Collectibles	15 Hatter Drive	Allison	PA	15413-	(724) 5
10	10.0000	Red Hat Hattery	1600 Mountain Rd	Montclair	CA	91763-	(909) 5
11	11.0000	Adorable Stuff	93 Prospect Ave	Bell Gardens	CA	90202-	(323) 5
12	12.0000	All Your Needz	8 River Run	Island Lake	IL	60042-	(847) 5
13	13.0000	Terriffic Toys	64 Highland Street	Sale Creek	GA	31784-	(912) 5
14	14.0000	Regis Toys	15 Mineral Drive	Iron Springs	AZ	86330-	(520) 5

Advanced... Cancel < Back Next > Finish

FIGURE 7.10

The Import HTML Wizard screen that is used to name the column headings (field names) for the linked table.

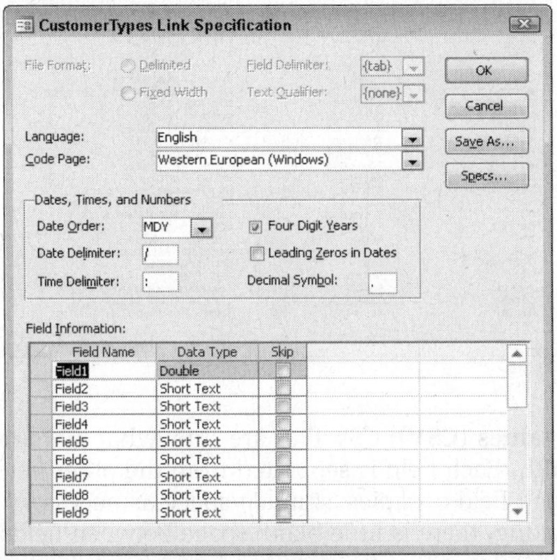

> **ON THE WEB**
>
> This book's website includes a very simple HTML file named `CustomerTypes.html`. The data in this file may be overly simplistic, but it gives you the opportunity to practice linking to HTML documents. Because of the wide variety of ways that data is stored in HTML documents, it isn't possible to generalize an approach to linking to HTML data. However, as you gain proficiency with the ability to link to external data sources, you might find linking to HTML a valuable addition to your Access skills.

Linking to text files

A far more common situation than linking to HTML files is linking to data stored in plain text files. Most applications, including Word and Excel, are able to publish data in a variety of text formats. The most common formats you're likely to encounter are

- **Fixed width:** In a fixed-width text file, each line represents one row of a database table. Each field within a line occupies exactly the same number of characters as the corresponding field in the lines above and below the current line. For example, a Last Name field in a fixed-width text file might occupy 20 characters, while a phone number field may only use 10 or 15 characters. Each data field is padded with spaces to the right to fill out the width allocated to the field. Figure 7.11 shows a typical fixed-width file open in Notepad.

FIGURE 7.11

A typical fixed-width text file.

```
Contacts_FixedWidth.txt - Notepad
File  Edit  Format  View  Help
1         Buyer          John           Jones          Nopa Auto Parts
2         Seller         Hank           Masters        Jiffy Auto Sales
3         Both           Larry          Minkler        All Start Autos
11        Both           Joe            Hammerman      Columbia Chevy
12        Buyer          Cary           James          James Auto Parts
13        Buyer          Mark           Uno            Fillion Sales And Service
14        Buyer          Brandon        Aley           Tip Top Chevy
15        Both           Michael        Dennis         Newbury Auto
16        Both           Mark           Martin         Peekskill Sales
17        Both           Karl           Johnson        KJ Auto Repair
18        Both           William        Gleason        R & G Monda Inc
19        Both           Alex           Tomaso         Tires National
20        Both           Karla          Hayes          Hayes Auctions
21        Seller         Teresa         Aikins         Middletown Auto Parts
22        Both           John           Marino         Bill Thomas Sales, Inc
23        Both           Donald         Peterson       Yantic Auto Parts
24        Seller         Dennie         Parkson        ACC Car Sales
25        Buyer          Ann            Bond           A-1 Auto Sales
26        Seller         Joe            Crook          Main Street Used Auto Parts
27        Both           Jeffrey        Lan            LAN Trucking
28        Buyer          Matt           Smith          ABC Trucking
29        Both           David          Smith          Fordman Colonial Times
30        Both           Cindy          Casey          Circle Auto Sales
31        Both           Karen          Bailey         Sammy Fordman
```

- **Comma-separated values (CSV):** CSV files are somewhat more difficult to understand than fixed width. Each field is separated from the other fields by a comma character (,), and each field occupies as much space as necessary to contain the data. Generally speaking, there is little blank space between fields in a CSV file. The advantage of CSV files is that the data can be contained in a smaller file because each field occupies only as much disk space as necessary to contain the data.

  CSV files can be difficult to read when opened in Notepad. Figure 7.12 shows a typical CSV text file.

FIGURE 7.12

CSV data is more compact than fixed-width text, but it's more difficult to read.

```
Contacts_CSV.txt - Notepad
File  Edit  Format  View  Help
1,"Buyer","John","Jones","Nopa Auto Parts","11253 Main Street","Springfield","MA","01111-1253","Parts Sto
2,"Seller","Hank","Masters","Jiffy Auto Sales","623 Field Road","Springfield","MO","12345-","Dealer","(57
3,"Both","Larry","Minkler","All Start Autos","971 E Main St","Detroit","MI","12345-6767","Wholesaler","(9
11,"Both","Joe","Hammerman","Columbia Chevy","105 Main Street","Columbia","MA","12237-","Dealer","(413) 5
12,"Buyer","Cary","James","James Auto Parts","59 South Street","Portland","CT","06480-","Wholesaler","(86
13,"Buyer","Mark","Uno","Fillion Sales And Service","8908 North Park Ave","South Windsor","CT","06074-","
14,"Buyer","Brandon","Aley","Tip Top Chevy","1916 Erickson Drive","Fairbanks","MA","12333-","Other Retail
15,"Both","Michael","Dennis","Newbury Auto","75 Main Street","Bedford","NY","10506-","Other Retail","(518
16,"Both","Mark","Martin","Peekskill Sales","51 Tolland Tnpk","Lake Peekskill","NY","10537-","Wholesaler"
17,"Both","Karl","Johnson","KJ Auto Repair","350 Broadway St","Rye","NY","10580-","Wholesaler","(315) 555
18,"Both","William","Gleason","R & G Monda Inc","196 East Street","Derby","CT","06418-","Dealer","(860) 5
19,"Both","Alex","Tomaso","Tires National","46 School Street","Oneco","CT","06373-","Wholesaler","(203) 5
20,"Both","Karla","Hayes","Hayes Auctions","54 E Center Street","Granby","CT","06035-","Auctioneer","(860
21,"Seller","Teresa","Aikins","Middletown Auto Parts","100 Northfield Dr","Middletown","CT","06457-","Par
22,"Both","John","Marino","Bill Thomas Sales, Inc","986 Buckingham St","Brewster","NY","10509-","Dealer",
23,"Both","Donald","Peterson","Yantic Auto Parts","8 Oak Street","Yantic","CT","06389-","Parts Store","(8
24,"Seller","Dennie","Parkson","ACC Car Sales","963 New England Turnpike","Peekskill","NY","10566-","Whol
25,"Buyer","Ann","Bond","A-1 Auto Sales","54 South Main","Colchester","CT","06415-","Dealer","(860) 555-6
26,"Seller","Joe","Crook","Main Street Used Auto Parts","61 North Main Street","Windsor","CT","06095-","P
27,"Both","Jeffrey","Lan","LAN Trucking","108 Thomas Road","North Branch","NJ","08876-","Dealer","(609) 5
28,"Buyer","Matt","Smith","ABC Trucking","7 Depot Rd","Stratford","CT","06615-","Dealer","(860) 555-3255"
29,"Both","David","Smith","Fordman Colonial Times","123 Federal Street","Quincy","MA","12301-","Dealer","
30,"Both","Cindy","Casey","Circle Auto Sales","123 South Street","Newington","NH","12301-","Wholesaler","
31,"Both","Karen","Bailey","Sammy Fordman","59 West Church","Westbourgh","MA","01581-","Wholesaler","(413
```

Text files are often used as intermediate data-transfer vehicles between dissimilar applications. For example, there might be an obsolete data management system in your environment that's incompatible with any of the link or import data types in Access. If you're lucky, the obsolete system is able to output either fixed-width or CSV files. Linking to or importing the fixed-width or CSV files might be the best option for sharing data with the obsolete system. At the very least, much less time is required to link or import the data than would be involved in rekeying all the information from the obsolete system into Access.

Follow these steps to link to `Contacts_FixedWidth.txt` or `Contacts_CSV.txt`:

1. **Open Chapter07.accdb and select the External Data tab of the Ribbon.**
2. **Click the Text File button.** The Get External Data – Text File dialog box appears.
3. **Be sure the Link to the Data Source by Creating a Link Table option is selected, and then click Browse.** The File Open dialog box appears.
4. **Locate the text file (either Contacts_FixedWidth.txt or Contacts_CSV.txt) and click Open.**
5. **Click OK on the Get External Data – Text File dialog box.** You'll be taken to the Link Text Wizard.

   Generally speaking, Access makes a pretty good guess at how the data in the file is delimited. Linking to text data involves nothing more than clicking Next and verifying that Access has correctly identified the data in the file.

On the Web

Rather than show or describe each of the dialog boxes in the Link Text Wizard, link to `Contacts_CSV.txt` and `Contacts_FixedWidth.txt`, both included on this book's website.

As you'll see when you link to these files, about the only input required from you is to provide a name for each of the fields Access finds in the text files. If you're lucky, the text file includes field names as the first row in the text file. Otherwise, linking to text files will likely require that you specify names for each field.

Working with Linked Tables

After you link to an external table from another database, you use it just as you would any another Access table. You use linked tables with forms, reports, and queries just as you would native Access tables. When working with external tables, you can modify many of their features (for example, setting view properties and relationships, setting links between tables in queries, and renaming the tables).

One note on renaming linked tables: Providing a different name for the table inside Access doesn't change the name of the file that's linked to the application. The name that Access refers to in a linked table is maintained within the Access application and doesn't influence the physical table that's linked.

Setting view properties

Although an external table is used like another Access table, you can't change the structure (delete, add, or rearrange fields) of an external table. You can, however, set several properties for the fields in a linked table:

- Format
- Decimal places
- Caption
- Input mask
- Unicode compressions
- IME sequence mode
- Display control

To change these properties, open the linked table in Design view. When you open a linked table in Design view, Access warns you that the design can't be modified. Figure 7.13 shows a warning when the Products table is opened in Design view. Despite that warning, the above properties can be changed.

FIGURE 7.13

Opening linked tables in Design view comes with a warning.

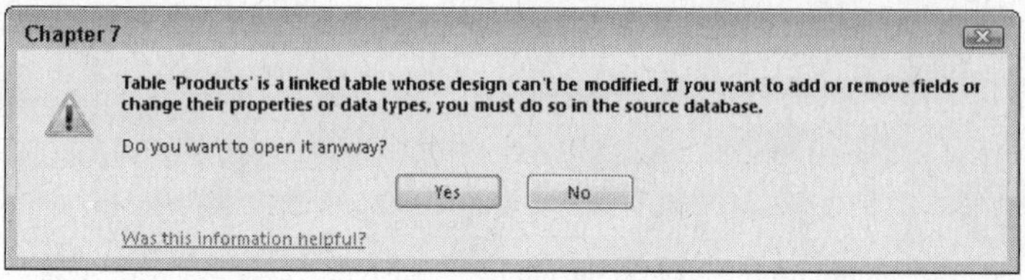

Chapter 7

Table 'Products' is a linked table whose design can't be modified. If you want to add or remove fields or change their properties or data types, you must do so in the source database.

Do you want to open it anyway?

Yes No

Was this information helpful?

Setting relationships

TIP

Access enables you to set permanent relationships at the table level between linked non-Access tables and native Access tables through the Relationships Builder. You can't, however, set referential integrity between linked tables, or between linked tables and internal tables. Access enables you to create forms and reports based on relationships set up in the Relationships Builder, such as building a SQL statement used as the RecordSource property of a form or report.

Linking to external Access tables maintains the relationships that might exist between the external tables. Therefore, when linking to a back-end database, the relationships you've established in the back end are recognized and honored by the front-end database. This is a good thing, because it means that the rules you've defined will be enforced regardless of how many front ends are created to use the tables.

We discuss relationships in detail in Chapter 4.

Optimizing linked tables

When working with linked tables, Access has to retrieve records from another file. This process takes time, especially when the table resides on a network or in a SQL database. When working with external data, optimize performance by observing these basic rules:

- **Avoid using functions in query criteria.** This is especially true for aggregate functions, such as `DTotal` or `DCount`, which retrieve all records from the linked table before performing the query operation.
- **Limit the number of external records to view.** Create a query using criteria that limit the number of records from an external table. This query can then be used by other queries, forms, or reports.
- **Avoid excessive movement in datasheets.** View only the data you need to in a datasheet. Avoid paging up and down and jumping to the first or last record in very large tables. (The exception is when you're adding records to the external table.)
- **If you add records to external linked tables, create a form to add records and set the DataEntry property to True.** This makes the form an entry form that starts with a blank record every time it's executed. Data entry forms are not pre-populated with data from the bound table. Using a dedicated data entry form is much more efficient than building a normal form, populating it with data from the linked source, and then moving to the end of the linked data just to add a new record.

Deleting a linked table reference

Deleting a linked table from the object list is a simple matter of performing three steps:

1. **In the object list, select the linked table you want to delete.**
2. **Press the Delete key, or right-click the linked table and select Delete from the shortcut menu.**
3. **Click OK in the Access dialog box to delete the file.**

NOTE

Deleting an external table deletes only its name from the database object list. The actual data is not deleted from its source location.

Viewing or changing information for linked tables

Use the Linked Table Manager to update the links when you move, rename, or modify tables or indexes associated with linked tables. Otherwise, Access won't be able to find the data file referenced by the link.

1. **Select the External Data tab of the Ribbon and click the Linked Table Manager button.** The Linked Table Manager (shown in Figure 7.14) appears, enabling you to locate the data files associated with the linked tables in the database.

FIGURE 7.14

The Linked Table Manager enables you to relocate external tables that have been moved.

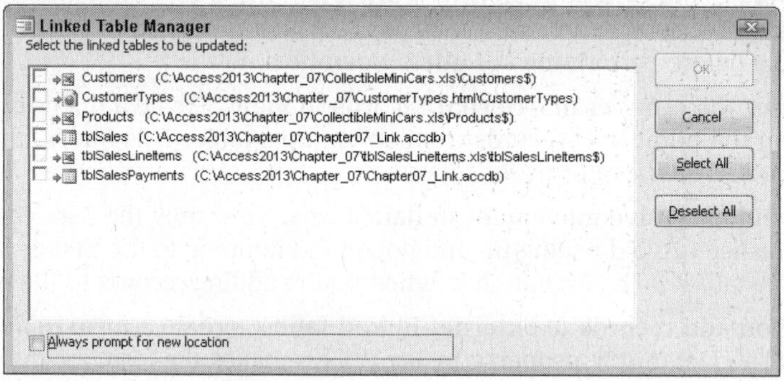

2. **Click the check box next to a linked table and click OK.**
3. **Find the missing file and relink to Access.** If all the files are already linked correctly, clicking OK makes Access verify all the linkages associated with all the selected tables.
4. **If you know all of the linked data sources have been moved, select the Always Prompt for a New Location check box, and then click OK.** Access then prompts you for the new location, and links all the tables as a batch process. You'll find this operation much faster than linking one or two tables at a time.

NOTE

If the Linked Table Manager is not present on your computer, Access automatically prompts you to provide the original Office CD so that Access can install the wizard. This might happen if you didn't instruct Office to install the Additional Wizards component during the initial installation process.

Refreshing linked tables

Linked tables are kept in sync with the source data automatically by Access. No user intervention is required to have up-to-date data. When a linked table is open in Datasheet view or otherwise being used, Access attempts to restrict access to the source data depending on what kind of data it is. For instance, Access locks linked text files that are in use so that you can't open it in a text editor.

To demonstrate how linked data is synchronized automatically, create a linked table to a text file and edit that text file by following these steps:

1. **Click Text File from the Import & Link group on the External Data tab of the Ribbon.**
2. **Create a linked text file from the file named ContactsFixed.txt, a fixed-length text file.** The file is well formatted so Access will guess correctly about where the fields begin. Don't worry about field names for this exercise.
3. **Open the linked table ContactsFixed.** Note that it contains 12 records. If you attempt to open `ContactFixed.txt` in a text editor, Windows will tell you that it's being used by another process and won't allow you to open it.
4. **Close the ContactsFixed table.**
5. **Add a new row to the text file using your favorite plain text editor, such as Notepad.** Don't use Word for this process because you'll risk saving it in a format that's not plain text. Figure 7.15 shows the new `ContactsFixed.txt` file.

FIGURE 7.15

Linked tables are synchronized automatically.

ContactsFixed.txt - Notepad

File Edit Format View Help

```
01   Jones       John     Nopa Auto Parts     Springfield     MA 1994/02/22
02   Masters     Hank     Jiffy Auto Sales    Springfield     MO 2005/01/01
03   Minkler     Larry    All Start Autos     Detroit         MI 2011/06/17
04   Hammerman   Joe      Columbia Chevy      Columbia        MA 2003/03/13
05   James       Cary     James Auto Parts    Portland        CT 2011/04/04
06   Uno         Mark     Fillion Sales And   South Windsor   CT 2004/07/08
07   Aley        Brandon  Tip Top Chevy       Fairbanks       MA 1999/05/25
08   Dennis      Michael  Newbury Auto        Bedford         NY 2013/06/26
09   Martin      Mark     Peekskill Sales     Lake Peekskill  NY 2010/10/20
10   Johnson     Karl     KJ Auto Repair      Rye             NY 2001/09/29
11   Gleason     William  R & G Monda Inc     Derby           CT 2009/01/10
12   Tomaso      Alex     Tires National      Oneco           CT 2011/02/01
13   Smith       Jerry    Smith Service       Detroit         MI 2012/03/01
```

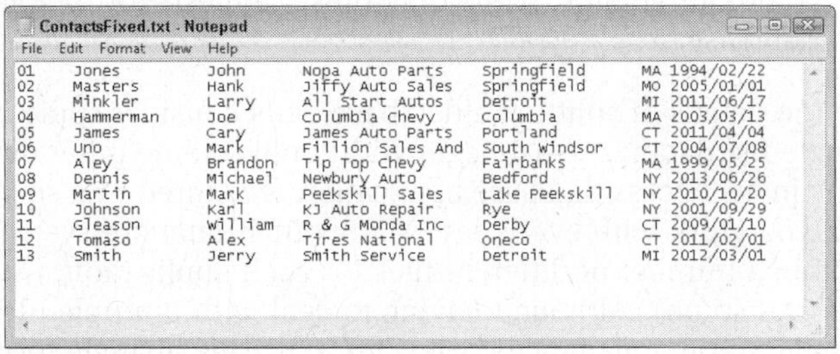

6. **Save the file and close the text editor.**
7. **In Access, open the ContactsFixed linked table.** The linked table now contains a 13th row.

Splitting a Database

There are many great reasons to link tables between Access databases. One of the best, and most common, reasons is to split the database. Splitting a database means creating two ACCDB files from one. One of the files, generally called the *back end,* contains only tables. The other file, the *front end,* contains queries, macros, code, and UI elements, such as forms and reports. The front end also contains links to all the tables in the back end.

The benefits of splitting a database

There is at least one extremely good reason why you should consider splitting your Access databases. Although you can place a single copy of an ACCDB or MDB file onto a shared computer on the network, the performance degradation from such a design is considerable.

Using an Access database stored on a remote computer involves much more than simply moving data from the remote computer to the local machine. All the form, menu, and Ribbon definitions must be transported to the local computer so that Windows can "construct" the UI on the local computer's monitor. The Windows installation on the local computer must intercept and transmit any keyboard and mouse events to the remote computer so that the proper code will run in response to these events. Finally, the single copy of Access on the remote computer must fulfill all data requests, no matter how trivial or demanding. The impact of all these actions is compounded by increasing the number of users working with the same remotely installed copy of the database.

Fortunately, most of these issues disappear when the database application is split into front-end and back-end components. The local Windows installation handles the UI from information stored in the front-end database. All code is run on the user's desktop computer, rather than on the remote machine. Also, the locally installed copy of Access is able to handle all local data requirements, while only those requests for remote data are passed on to the back-end database.

Before getting into the details of splitting a database, let's consider some of the problems associated with single-file databases. To begin with, unlike some other development systems, all the objects in an Access database application are stored in a single file, the familiar ACCDB or MDB you work with every day. Many other database systems like FoxPro for Windows maintain a number of different files for each application, usually one file per object (form, table, and so on). Although having to deal with multiple files complicates database development and maintenance somewhat, updating a single form or query involves nothing more than replacing the related file with the updated form or query file.

Updating an Access database object is somewhat more complicated. As you've probably discovered, replacing a form or query in an Access database used by a large number of users can be quite a problem. Replacing a form or other database object often requires hours of work importing the object into each user's copy of the database.

A second consideration is the network traffic inherent in single-file Access databases. Figure 7.16 shows an example of the problem. This figure illustrates a common method of sharing an Access database. The computer in the upper-left corner of the figure is the file server and holds the Access database file. Assume for a moment that the entire database is contained within a single ACCDB on the file server, and the database has been enabled for shared data access. Each workstation in Figure 7.16 has a full copy of Access (or the Access runtime) installed.

FIGURE 7.16

A database kept on a file server can generate a large amount of traffic on the network.

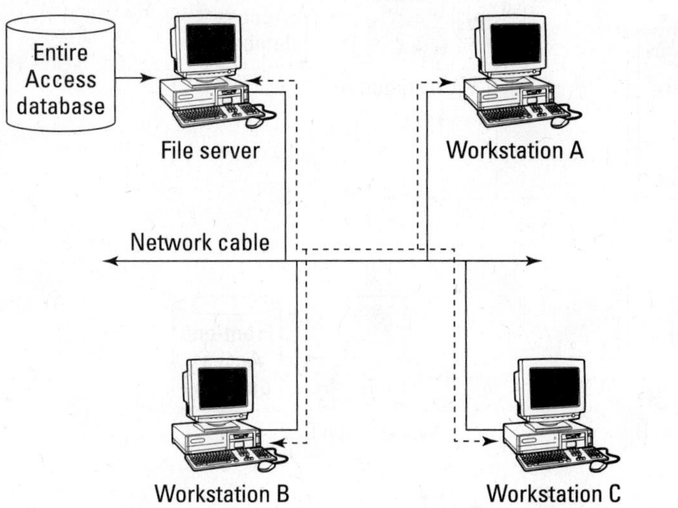

Now, what happens when the user on Workstation C opens the database? The Access installation on that machine must locate the ACCDB on the file server, open that file, and start up the application. This means that any splash forms, queries, and other startup activities must take place across the network before the user is able to work with the database. Any time a form is opened or a query is run, the information necessary to fulfill the query must travel across the network, slowing the operation. (In Figure 7.16, the network load is indicated by a thick dashed line.)

The situation shown in Figure 7.16 is made even worse when more than one user is using the same database. In this case, the network traffic is increased by the queries, opening of forms, and other operations performed by each additional user's copy of Access. Imagine the dashed line getting thicker with each operation across the network.

The split-database model is illustrated in Figure 7.17. Notice that the back-end database resides on the server while individual copies of the front-end database are placed on each workstation. Each front-end database contains links to the tables stored in the back-end ACCDB file. The front-end databases also contain the forms, reports, queries, and other user-interface components of the application.

FIGURE 7.17

A database kept on a file server can generate a large amount of traffic on the network.

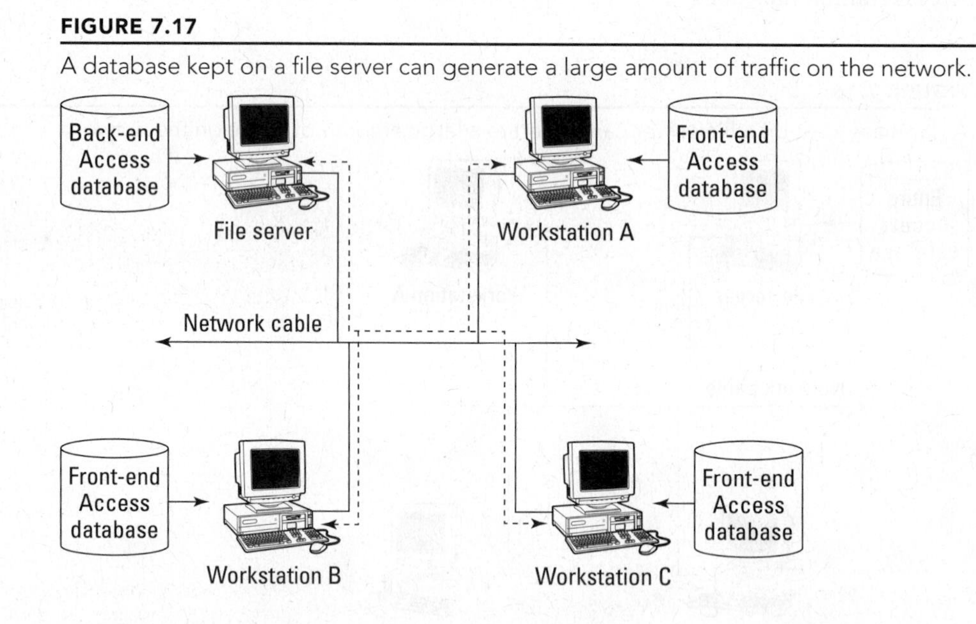

The network traffic is reduced in Figure 7.17 because only linking information and data returned by queries is moved across the network. A user working with the database application uses the forms, queries, reports, macros, and code stored in the local front-end ACCDB file. Because the front end is accessed by a single user, response time is much improved because the local copy of Access is able to instantly open the database and begin the startup operations. Only when actually running queries does the network traffic increase.

The second major benefit of the split database design is that updating the forms, reports, and other application components requires nothing more than replacing the front-end database on each user's computer and reestablishing the links to the table in the back-end database. In fact, the design in Figure 7.17 supports the notion of customized front ends, depending on the requirements of the user sitting at each workstation. For example, a manager sitting at Workstation A might need access to personnel information that is not available to the people sitting at workstations B and C. In this case, the front-end database on Workstation A includes the forms, queries, and other database objects necessary to view the personnel information.

Knowing where to put which objects

The local ACCDB contains all the UI objects, including forms, reports, queries, macros, and modules. Keeping the UI components on the local machine dramatically improves performance. You don't need to move forms, queries, or reports across the network — these objects are much more easily manipulated on the local machine than when accessed across the network.

All shared tables should be placed in the back-end database kept on the server. The server database is opened in Shared mode, making all its objects accessible to multiple users. The tables in the server database are linked to the front-end ACCDB on each user's Desktop. (There is no problem with simultaneously linking the same table to multiple databases.)

Obviously, with more than one person using the data within a table, the possibility exists that the same record will be edited by multiple users. The Access database engine handles this problem by locking a record as it's edited by a user. A lock contention occurs when more than one user tries to update the same record. Only one user will have "live" access to the record — all other users will either be locked or have their changes held up until the record holder is done making changes.

Using the Database Splitter add-in

The Database Splitter helps you split an application into front-end and back-end databases. This wizard enables you to build and test your database to your heart's content, and then lightens the burden of preparing the application for multiuser access.

As an experiment, let's take a look at splitting the Northwind Traders database into front-end and back-end ACCDB files. You start the Database Splitter by selecting the Database Tools tab of the Ribbon and then clicking the Access Database button in the Move Data group. The opening wizard screen (shown in Figure 7.18) explains the actions of the Database Splitter and suggests that you make a backup of the database before proceeding.

FIGURE 7.18

The Database Splitter is a very simple wizard.

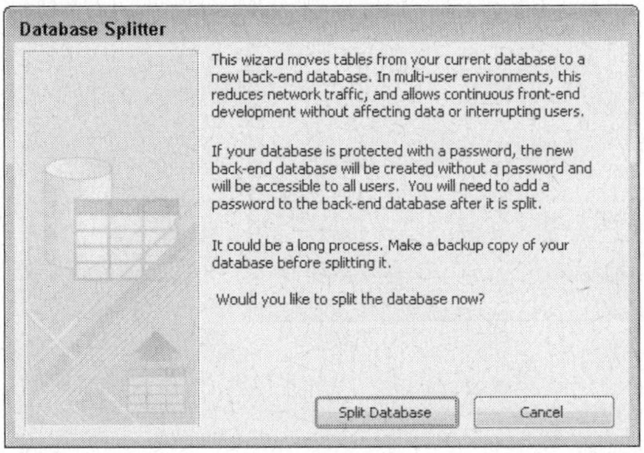

Database Splitter

This wizard moves tables from your current database to a new back-end database. In multi-user environments, this reduces network traffic, and allows continuous front-end development without affecting data or interrupting users.

If your database is protected with a password, the new back-end database will be created without a password and will be accessible to all users. You will need to add a password to the back-end database after it is split.

It could be a long process. Make a backup copy of your database before splitting it.

Would you like to split the database now?

Split Database | Cancel

The only other information that the Database Splitter requires is where you want to put the back-end database. Figure 7.19 shows the familiar Explorer-style Create Back-end Database dialog box that lets you specify the location of the back-end ACCDB file. By default, the back-end database has the same name as the original database with a `_be` suffix added to the name (for example, `MyDB_be.accdb`).

CAUTION

You can access a network location through a Universal Naming Convention (UNC) path or through a mapped drive. A UNC path starts with two back slashes, the server name, and the path to the network location. An example of a UNC path is `\\MyServer\MyDatashare\MyFolder\`. A mapped drive assigns a letter to a particular UNC path (such as `S:`). Mapped drives are unique to each computer and there is no guarantee that a mapped drive on one computer will be the same on another. When creating a back-end database, always use a UNC path to link the tables because UNC paths are the same for all computers on the same network. To use UNC paths, navigate to the network location through the Network shortcut (called My Network Places in older versions of Windows).

TIP

Plan to put the back end exactly where it will reside in the production environment. Because the front-end database will contain links to the back-end database, and because links are path specific, the links would have to be refreshed if the back end were moved after being built by the Database Splitter.

FIGURE 7.19

Specify the permanent location of the back-end database in the Create Back-end Database dialog box.

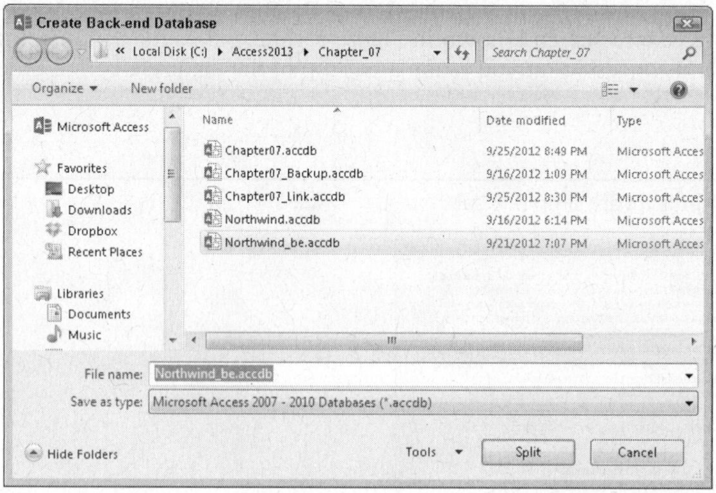

When you click the Split button (refer to Figure 7.19), the Database Splitter creates the back-end database, exports all tables to it, deletes the tables in the local database, and creates links to the back-end tables. In other words, the Database Splitter performs precisely the same steps you'd have to perform manually if the Database Splitter weren't available.

NOTE

Be prepared for this process to take a little while, especially on large databases. Because Access has to create the new database, transfer tables to it, and create the links back to the original database, the splitting process can easily require more than a few minutes. Don't worry if the process appears to be taking longer than you expect — you'll be well rewarded for your efforts!

Also, keep in mind that the Database Splitter is rather simplistic and tends to ignore system considerations such as available disk space. Make sure adequate disk space exists on the target machine to accommodate the back-end database.

Figure 7.20 shows the Access Database Explorer after splitting the Northwind Traders database. The back-end database contains only the tables exported from `Northwind.accdb`. Notice that the icons associated with all the tables in `Northwind.accdb` have been changed, indicating that they're now pointing to copies in the back-end database. You'll have to import any local tables from the back-end database before distributing the front end to the users.

FIGURE 7.20

The Database Splitter creates links for all tables in the database.

Part III

Working with Access Queries

The chapters in Part III introduce you to some of the basic analytical tools and techniques available in Access. Specifically, you get a solid foundation in building Access queries.

Queries draw various data sources together and present the combined information in useful views. They enable you to synthesize the raw data in your Access tables into meaningful analysis.

Chapter 8 starts by exploring the query builder along with techniques to create simple analytical outputs from your Access tables. Chapter 9 outlines the various operators and expressions that can be used to add complexity to your Access data analysis. Finally, in Chapter 10, you dive deeply into more advanced query concepts; here, you learn how to go beyond simply selecting data from your tables and explore how to aggregate query outputs, how to perform action queries, and how to create versatile crosstab queries.

IN THIS PART

CHAPTER 8

Selecting Data with Queries

IN THIS CHAPTER

- Understanding what queries are and what they can do for you
- Creating queries
- Specifying the fields in a query
- Displaying a query's results
- Adding and removing fields from a query's design
- Sorting a query's results
- Filtering records returned by a query
- Printing records returned by a query
- Saving a query
- Including more than one table in a query
- Adding, deleting, and moving tables in a query
- Joining tables in a query's design
- Understanding the options for joining tables in a query

Queries are an essential part of any database application. Queries are the tools that enable you and your users to extract data from multiple tables, combine it in useful ways, and present it to the user as a datasheet, on a form, or as a printed report.

You may have heard the old cliché, "Queries convert data to information." To a certain extent, this statement is true — that's why it's a cliché. The data contained within tables is not particularly useful because, for the most part, the data in tables appears in no particular order. Also, in a properly normalized database, important information is spread out among a number of different tables. Queries are what draw these various data sources together and present the combined information in such a way that users can actually work with the data.

On the Web

The starting database for this walkthrough, `Chapter08.accdb`, can be downloaded from this book's website.

Introducing Queries

A database's primary purpose is to store and extract information. Information can be obtained from a database immediately after the data is added, or days, weeks, or even years later. Of course, retrieving information from database tables requires knowledge of how the database is designed.

For example, consider printed reports kept in a traditional filing cabinet, arranged by date and by a sequence number that indicates when the report was produced. To find a specific report, you must know its year and sequence number. In a good filing system, you might have a cross-reference book to help you find a specific report. This book might have all reports categorized alphabetically by type of report and, perhaps, by date. Such a book can be helpful, but if you know only the report's topic and approximate date, you still have to search through all the sections of the book to find out where to get the report.

Unlike manual filing systems, databases like Access quickly and easily retrieve information to meet virtually any criteria you specify.

This is the real power of a database — the capacity to examine the data in more ways than you can imagine. Queries, by definition, ask questions about the data stored in the database. Most queries are used to drive forms, reports, and graphical representations of the data contained in a database.

What queries are

Let's start with the basics. The word *query* comes from the Latin word *quaerere,* which means "to ask or inquire." Over the years, the word *query* has become synonymous with *quiz, challenge, inquire,* or *question.*

An Access query is a question that you ask about the information stored in Access tables. You build queries with the Access query tools, and then save it as a new object in the Access database. Your query can be a simple question about data in a single table, or it can be a more complex question about information stored in several tables. For example, you might ask your database to show you only trucks that were sold in the year 2012. After you submit the question in the form of a query, Access returns only the information you requested.

What queries can do

Queries are flexible. They allow you to look at your data in virtually any way you can imagine. Most database systems are continually evolving and changing over time. Very often, the original purpose of a database is very different from its current use.

Here's just a sampling of what you can do with Access queries:

- **Choose tables.** You can obtain information from a single table or from many tables that are related by some common data. Suppose you're interested in seeing the customer name along with the items purchased by each type of customer. When using several tables, Access combines the data as a single recordset.
- **Choose fields.** Specify which fields from each table you want to see in the recordset. For example, you can select the customer name, zip code, sales date, and invoice number from tblCustomers and tblSales.
- **Provide criteria.** Record selection is based on selection criteria. For example, you might want to see records for only a certain category of products.
- **Sort records.** You might want to sort records in a specific order. For example, you might need to see customer contacts sorted by last name and first name.
- **Perform calculations.** Use queries to perform calculations such as averages, totals, or counts of data in records.
- **Create tables.** Create a brand-new table based on data returned by a query.
- **Display query data on forms and reports.** The recordset you create from a query might have just the right fields and data needed for a report or form. Basing a report or form on a query means that, every time you print the report or open the form, you see the most current information contained in the tables.
- **Use a query as a source of data for other queries (subquery).** You can create queries that are based on records returned by another query. This is very useful for performing ad hoc queries, where you might repeatedly make small changes to the criteria. In this case, the second query filters the first query's results.
- **Make changes to data in tables.** Action queries modify multiple rows in the underlying tables as a single operation. Action queries are frequently used to maintain data, such as updating values in specific fields, archiving old records, or deleting obsolete information.

What queries return

Access combines a query's records and, when executed, displays them in Datasheet view by default. The set of records returned by a query is commonly called (oddly enough) a *recordset*. A recordset is a dynamic set of records. The recordset returned by a query is not stored within the database, unless you've directed Access to build a table from those records.

You can read much more about Datasheet view in Chapter 5.

When you save a query, only the structure of the query is saved, not the returned records. That is to say, only the SQL syntax used to build the query is stored.

We cover SQL Syntax behind queries in Chapter 14.

Consider these benefits of *not* saving the recordset to a physical table:

- A smaller amount of space on a storage device (usually a hard disk) is needed.
- The query uses updated versions of records.

Every time the query is executed, it reads the underlying tables and re-creates the recordset. Because recordsets themselves are not stored, a query automatically reflects any changes to the underlying tables made since the last time the query was executed — even in a real-time, multiuser environment. Depending on your needs, a query's recordset can be viewed as a datasheet, or in a form or report. When a form or report is based on a query, the query's recordset is re-created and bound to the form or report each time it's opened.

A query's recordset can also be used in macros and VBA procedures to help drive any number of automated tasks.

Creating a Query

After you create your tables and place data in them, you're ready to work with queries. To begin a query, select the Create tab on the Ribbon, and click the Query Design button in the Queries group. This opens the query designer shown in Figure 8.1.

Figure 8.1 shows two windows. The underlying window is the query designer. Floating on top of the designer is the Show Table dialog box. The Show Table dialog box is *modal,* which means that you must do something in the dialog box before continuing with the query. Before you continue, you add the tables required for the query. In this case, tblProducts is highlighted and ready to be added.

The Show Table dialog box (refer to Figure 8.1) displays the tables and queries in your database. Double-click tblProducts to add it to the query design, or highlight tblProducts in the list and click the Add button. Close the Show Table dialog box after adding tblProducts. Figure 8.2 shows tblProducts added to the query.

FIGURE 8.1

The Show Table dialog box and the query design window.

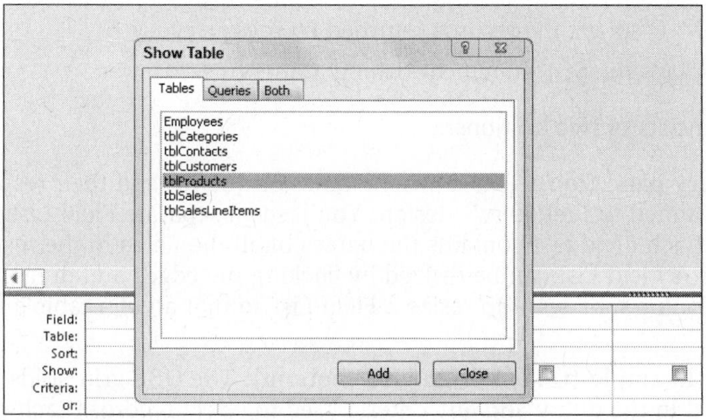

FIGURE 8.2

The query design window with tblProducts added.

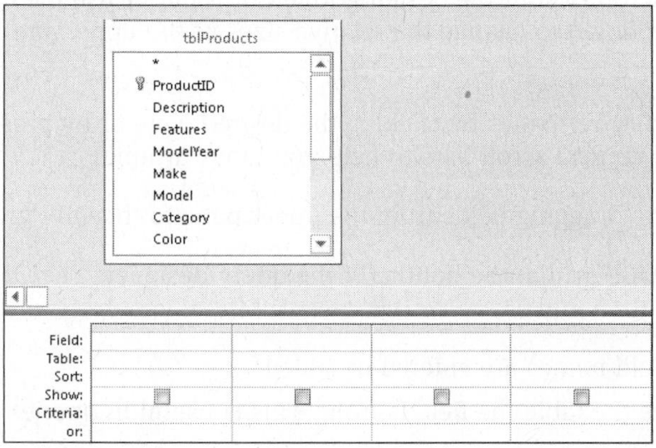

To add additional tables to the query, right-click anywhere in the upper portion of the query designer and select Show Table from the shortcut menu that appears. Alternatively, drag tables from the Navigation pane to the upper portion of the query designer. There is also a Show Table button on the Design tab of the Ribbon.

Removing a table from the query designer is easy. Just right-click the table in the query designer and select Remove Table from the shortcut menu.

The query design window has three primary views:

- **Design view:** Where you create the query
- **Datasheet view:** Displays the records returned by the query
- **SQL view:** Displays the SQL statement behind a query

The query designer consists of two sections:

- **The table/query pane (top):** This is where tables or queries and their respective Field Lists are added to the query's design. You'll see a separate Field List for each object to add. Each Field List contains the names of all the fields in the respective table or query. A Field List can be resized by clicking the edges and dragging it to a different size. You may want to resize a Field List so that all of a table's fields are visible.
- **The Query by Example (QBE) design grid (bottom):** The QBE grid holds the field names involved in the query and any criteria used to select records. Each column in the QBE grid contains information about a single field from a table or query contained within the upper pane.

The two window panes are separated horizontally by a pane-resizing scroll bar (refer to Figure 8.2). You can use the scroll to shift the design grid left or right, or use the mouse to click and drag the bar up or down to change the relative sizes of the upper and lower panes.

Switch between the upper and lower panes by clicking the desired pane or by pressing F6. Each pane has horizontal and vertical scroll bars to help you move around.

You actually build the query by dragging fields from the upper pane to the QBE grid.

Figure 8.2 displays an empty QBE grid at the bottom of the query designer. The QBE grid has six labeled rows:

- **Field:** This is where field names are entered or added.
- **Table:** This row shows the table the field is from. This is useful in queries with multiple tables.
- **Sort:** This row enables sorting instructions for the query.
- **Show:** This row determines whether to display the field in the returned recordset.
- **Criteria:** This row consists of the criteria that filter the returned records.
- **Or:** This row is the first of a number of rows to which you can add multiple query criteria.

You learn more about these rows as you create queries in this chapter.

The Query Tools Design Ribbon (shown in Figure 8.3) contains many different buttons specific to building and working with queries. Although each button is explained as it's used in the chapters of this book, here are the main buttons:

FIGURE 8.3

The Query Tools Design Ribbon.

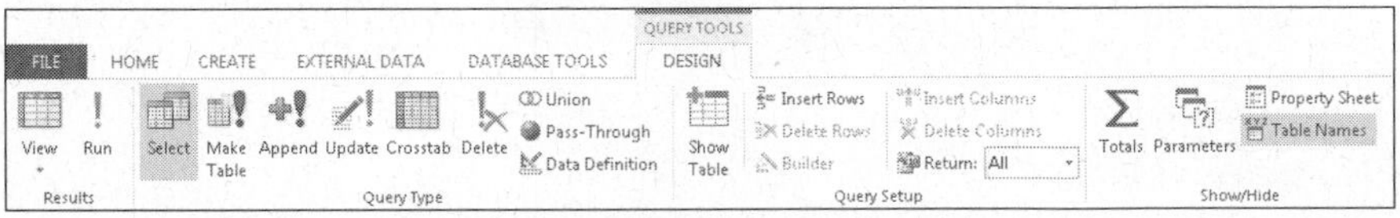

- **View:** Switches between the Datasheet view and Design view in the query design window. The View drop-down control also enables you to display the underlying SQL statement behind the query.
- **Run:** Runs the query. Displays a select query's datasheet, serving the same function as selecting Datasheet View from the View button. However, when working with action queries, the Run button performs the operations (append, make-table, and so on) specified by the query.
- **Select:** Clicking the Select button transforms the opened query into a Select query.
- **Make Table, Append, Update, Crosstab, and Delete:** Each of these buttons specifies the type of query you're building. In most cases, you transform a select query into an action query by clicking one of these buttons.
- **Show Table:** Opens the Show Table dialog box.

The remaining buttons are used for creating more-advanced queries, printing the contents of the query, and displaying a query's Property Sheet.

Adding fields to your queries

There are several ways to add fields to a query. You can add fields one at a time, select and add multiple fields, or select all the fields in a field list.

Adding a single field

You add a single field in several ways. One method is to double-click the field name in the table in the top pane of the query designer. The field name immediately appears in the first available column in the QBE pane. Alternatively, drag a field from a table in the top pane of the query designer, and drop it on a column in the QBE grid. Dropping a field between two fields in the QBE grid pushes other fields to the right.

In Figure 8.4 you can see that the Cost field was brought into the QBE grid. Once a field is added, you can simply add the next field you need to see in the query.

FIGURE 8.4

To add fields from your table to the QBE grid, simply double-click or drag the field.

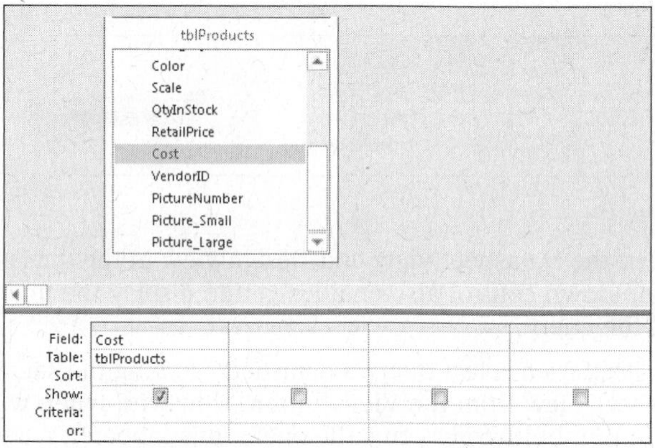

Each cell in the Table row of the QBE grid contains a drop-down list of the tables contained in the upper pane of the query designer.

Adding multiple fields

You can add multiple fields in a single action by selecting the fields from the Field List window and dragging them to the QBE grid. The selected fields don't have to be contiguous (one after the other). Hold down the Ctrl key while selecting multiple fields. Figure 8.5 illustrates the process of adding multiple fields.

The fields are added to the QBE grid in the order in which they occur in the table.

You can also add all the fields in the table by double-clicking the Field List's header (where it says tblProducts in Figure 8.6) to highlight all the fields in the table. Then drag the highlighted fields to the QBE grid.

Alternatively, you can click and drag the asterisk (*) from the Field List to the QBE grid (or double-click the asterisk to add it to the QBE grid). Although this action doesn't add all the fields to the QBE grid, the asterisk directs Access to include all fields in the table in the query.

FIGURE 8.5

Selecting multiple fields to add to the QBE grid.

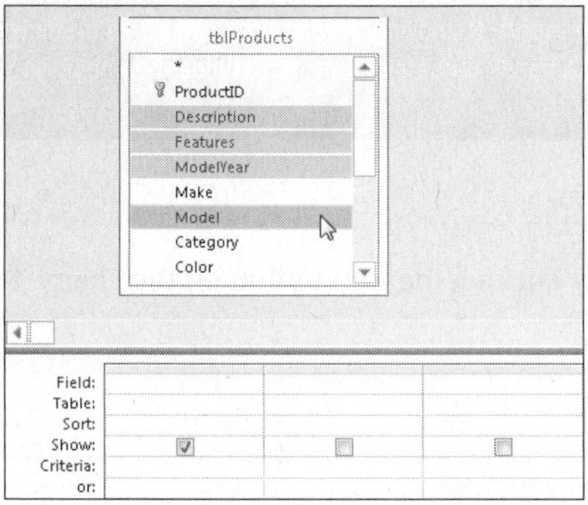

FIGURE 8.6

Adding the asterisk to the QBE grid selects all fields in the table.

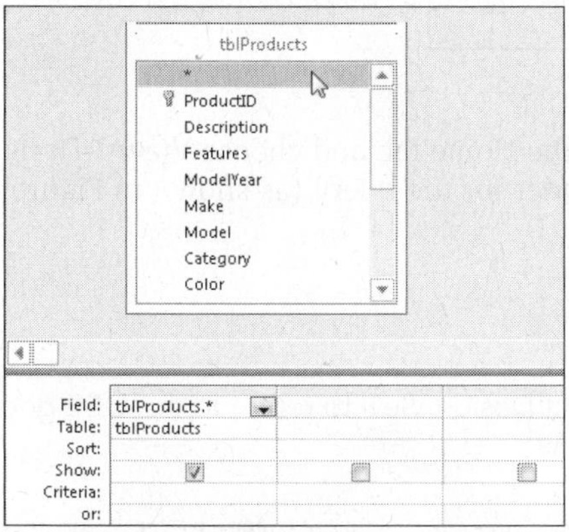

TIP

Unlike selecting all the fields, the asterisk places a reference to all the fields in a single column. When you drag multiple columns, as in the preceding example, you drag names to the QBE grid. If you later change the design of the table, you also have to change the design of the query. The advantage of using the asterisk for selecting all fields is that changes to the underlying tables don't require changes to the query. The asterisk means to select all fields in the table, regardless of the field names or changes in the number of fields in the table.

CAUTION

The downside of using the asterisk to specify all fields in a table is that the query, as instructed, returns all the fields in a table, regardless of whether every field is used on a form or report. Retrieving unused data can be an inefficient process. Very often, performance problems can be traced to the asterisk returning many more fields than necessary to a form or report.

Running your query

After selecting the fields, run the query by clicking the Run button on the Query Tools Design Ribbon (see Figure 8.7).

FIGURE 8.7

Click the Run button to display the results of your query.

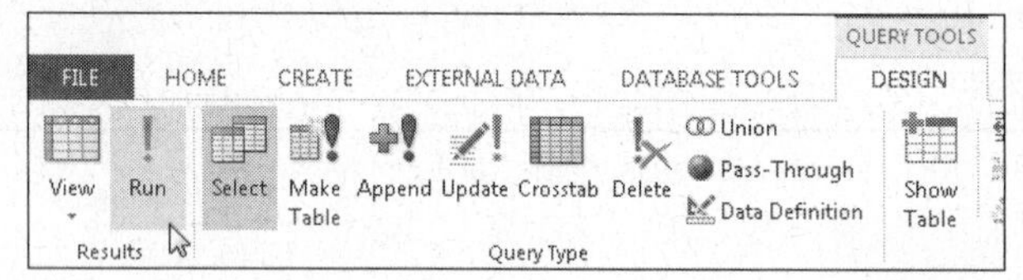

To return to the QBE grid, you can go up to the Home tab and choose View ➪ Design View. Alternatively, you can right-click the tab header for the query (as shown in Figure 8.8) and select Design View.

FIGURE 8.8

Right-click on the queries tab header and select Design View to return to the QBE grid.

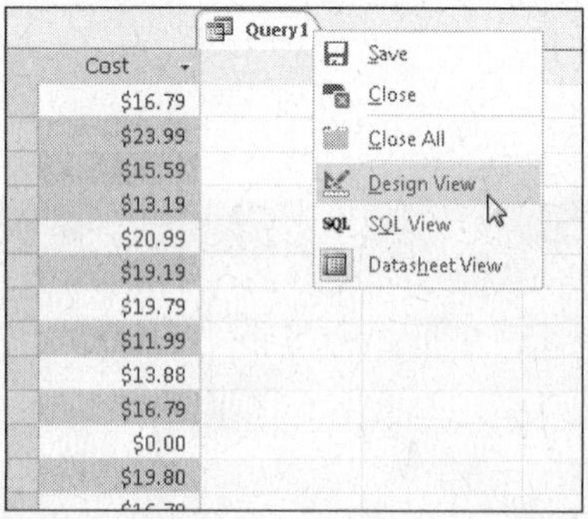

Working with Query Fields

Sometimes you'll want to work with the fields you've already selected — rearranging their order, inserting a new field, or deleting an existing field. You may even want to add a field to the QBE grid without showing it in the datasheet. Adding a field without showing it enables you to sort on the hidden field or to use the hidden field as criteria.

Selecting a field in the QBE grid

Before you can move a field's position, you must first select it. To select it, you will work with the field selector row.

The *field selector* is the thin gray area at the top of each column in the QBE grid at the bottom of the query designer. Each column represents a field. To select the Category field, move the mouse pointer until a small selection arrow (in this case, a dark downward arrow) is visible in the selector row and then click and drag the column. Figure 8.9 shows the selection arrow above the Category column just before it's selected.

FIGURE 8.9

Selecting a column in the QBE grid. The pointer changes to a downward-pointing arrow when you move over the selection row.

Field:	ProductID	Description	Category	QtyInStock	Cost
Table:	tblProducts	tblProducts	tblProducts	tblProducts	tblProducts
Sort:					
Show:	☑	☑	☑	☑	☑
Criteria:					

TIP

Select multiple contiguous fields by clicking the first field you want to select, and then dragging across the field selector bars of the other fields.

Changing field order

The left-to-right order in which fields appear in the QBE grid determines the order in which they appear in Datasheet view. You might want to move the fields in the QBE grid to achieve a new sequence of fields in the query's results. With the fields selected, you can move the fields on the QBE design by simply dragging them to a new position.

Left-click a field's selector bar, and, while holding down the left mouse button, drag the field into a new position in the QBE grid.

Figure 8.10 shows the Category field highlighted. As you move the selector field to the left, the column separator between the fields ProductID and Description changes (gets wider) to show you where Category will go.

FIGURE 8.10

Moving the Category field to between ProductID and Description. Notice the QBE field icon below the arrow near the Description column.

Field:	ProductID	Description	Category	QtyInStock	Cost
Table:	tblProducts	tblProducts	tblProducts	tblProducts	tblProducts
Sort:					
Show:	☑	☑	☑	☑	☑
Criteria:					

TIP

The field order in a query is irrelevant to how the data appears on a form or report. Normally, you'll arrange the controls on a form or report in response to user requirements.

Resizing columns in the QBE grid

The QBE grid generally shows five or six fields in the viewable area of your screen. The remaining fields are viewed by moving the horizontal scroll bar at the bottom of the window.

You might want to shrink some fields to be able to see more columns in the QBE grid. You adjust the column width to make them smaller (or larger) by moving the mouse pointer to the margin between two fields, and dragging the column resizer left or right (see Figure 8.11).

FIGURE 8.11

Resizing columns in the QBE grid.

Field:	ProductID	Category	Description	QtyInStock	Cost
Table:	tblProducts	tblProducts	tblProducts	tblProducts	tblProducts
Sort:					
Show:	☑	☑	☑	☑	☑
Criteria:					

TIP

An easier way to resize columns in the QBE grid is to double-click the line dividing two columns in the grid. Access auto-sizes the column to fit the data displayed in the column.

The width of a column in the QBE grid has no affect on how the field's data is displayed in a datasheet, form, or report. The column width in the QBE grid is just a convenience to you, the developer. Also, QBE column width is not preserved when you save and close the query.

Removing a field

Remove a field from the QBE grid by selecting the field and pressing the Delete key. You can also right-click on a field's selector bar and choose Cut from the shortcut menu.

Inserting a field

Insert new fields in the QBE grid by dragging a field from a Field List window in the tables pane above the QBE grid and dropping it onto a column in the QBE grid. The new column is inserted to the left of the column on which you dropped the field. Double-clicking a field in a Field List adds the new column at the far-right position in the QBE grid.

Hiding a field

While you're performing queries, you might want to show only some of the fields in the QBE grid. Suppose, for example, you've chosen FirstName, LastName, Address, City, and State. Then you decide that you want to temporarily look at the same data, without the State field. Instead of completely removing the State field, you can simply hide it by unchecking the Show check box in the State column (see Figure 8.12).

FIGURE 8.12

The Show check box is unchecked for the State field so that field will not show in the results.

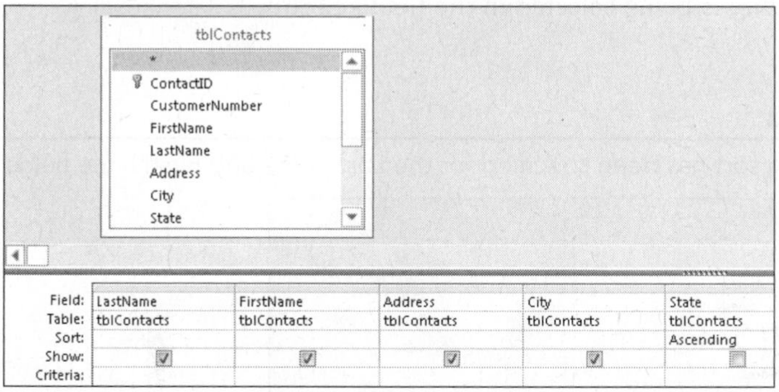

Field:	LastName	FirstName	Address	City	State
Table:	tblContacts	tblContacts	tblContacts	tblContacts	tblContacts
Sort:					Ascending
Show:	☑	☑	☑	☑	☐
Criteria:					

A common reason to hide a field in the query is because the field is used for sorting or as criteria, but its value is not needed in the query. For example, consider a query involving invoices. For a number of reasons, the users might want to see the invoices sorted by the order date, even though the actual order date is irrelevant for this particular purpose. You could simply include the OrderDate field in the QBE grid, set the sort order for the OrderDate field, and uncheck its Show box. Access sorts the data by the OrderDate field even though the field is not shown in the query's results.

> **NOTE**
> If you save a query that has an unused field (its Show box is unchecked and no criteria or sort order is applied to the field), Access eliminates the field from the query as part of the query optimization process. The next time you open the query, the field won't be included in the query's design.

Changing the sort order of a field

When viewing a recordset, you often want to display the data in a sorted order to make it easier to analyze the data. For example, you may want to review the results from the tblProducts table sorted by category.

Sorting places the records in alphabetical or numeric order. The sort order can be ascending or descending. You can sort on a single field or multiple fields.

You input sorting directions in the Sort row in the QBE grid. To specify a sort order on a particular field (such as LastName), perform these steps:

1. **Position the cursor in the Sort cell in the LastName column.**
2. **Click the drop-down list that appears in the cell, and select the sort order (Ascending or Descending) you want to apply.** Figure 8.13 shows the QBE grid with ascending sorts specified for the LastName and FirstName fields. Notice that the LastName field is still showing the sort options available. Also notice that the word *Ascending* is being selected in the field's Sort cell.

FIGURE 8.13

An ascending sort has been specified for the LastName and FirstName fields.

tblContacts
*
ContactID
CustomerNumber
FirstName
LastName
Address
City
State

Field:	LastName	FirstName	City	State
Table:	tblContacts	tblContacts	tblContacts	tblContacts
Sort:	Ascending	Ascending		
Show:	☑	☑	☑	☑
Criteria:				

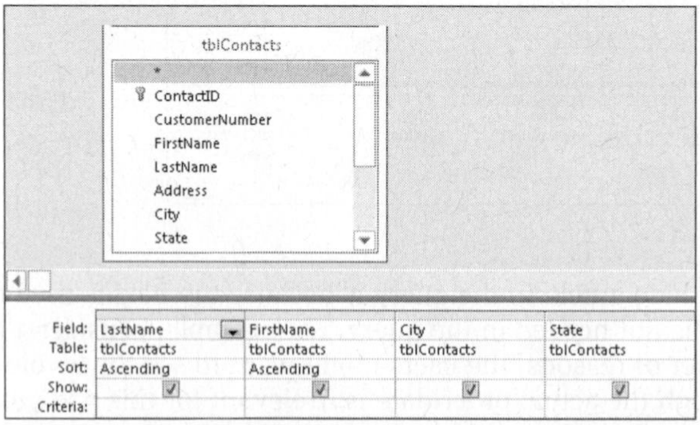

> **NOTE**
> You can't sort on a Memo or an OLE object field.

The left-to-right order in which fields appear in the QBE grid is important when sorting on more than one field. Not only do the fields appear in the datasheet in left-to-right order, but they're sorted in the same order; this is known as *sort order precedence*. The leftmost field containing sort criteria is sorted first, the first field to the right containing sort criteria is sorted next, and so on. In the example shown in Figure 8.13, the LastName field is sorted first, followed by the FirstName field.

Figure 8.14 shows the results of the query shown in Figure 8.13. Notice that the data is sorted by LastName and then by FirstName. This is why Ann Bond appears before John Bond, and John Jones appears before Kevin Jones in the query's data.

FIGURE 8.14

The order of the fields in the QBE grid is critical when sorting on multiple fields.

LastName	FirstName	City	State
Aikins	Teresa	Middletown	CT
Aley	Brandon	Fairbanks	MA
Bailey	Karen	Westbourgh	MA
Baker	Harry	Mohegan Lake	NY
Bond	Ann	Colchester	CT
Bond	John	Colchester	CT
Calson	Larry	Chicota	TX
Casey	Debbie	Jackhorn	KY
Crook	Joe	Windsor	CT
Jackson	Harry	Tuskahoma	OK
James	Cary	Portland	CT
Johnson	Karl	Rye	NY

Adding Criteria to Your Queries

Most often users want to work only with records conforming to some criteria. Otherwise, too many records may be returned by a query, causing serious performance issues. For example, you might want to look only at customers who haven't bought any products within the last six months. Access makes it easy for you to specify a query's criteria.

Understanding selection criteria

Selection criteria are filtering rules applied to data as they're extracted from the database. Selection criteria tell Access which records you want to look at in the recordset. A typical criterion might be "all sellers," or "only those vehicles that are not trucks," or "products with retail prices greater than $75."

Selection criteria limit the records returned by a query. Selection criteria aid the user by selecting only the records a user wants to see, and ignoring all the others.

You specify criteria in the Criteria row of the QBE grid. You designate criteria as an expression. The expression can be simple (like "trucks" or "not trucks"), or it can take the form of complex expressions using built-in Access functions.

Proper use of query criteria is critical to an Access database's success. In most cases, the users have no idea what data is stored in a database's tables and accept whatever they see on a form or report as truthfully representing the database's status. Poorly chosen criteria might hide important information from the application's users, leading to bad business decisions or serious business issues later on.

Entering simple string criteria

Character-type criteria are applied to Text-type fields. Most often, you'll enter an example of the text you want to retrieve. Here is a small example that returns only product records where the product type is "Cars":

1. **Add tblProducts and choose the Description, Category, and Cost fields.**
2. **Type** CARS **into the Criteria cell under the Category column (see Figure 8.15).** Notice that Access adds double quotes around the value. Access, unlike many other database systems, automatically makes assumptions about what you want.
3. **Run the query.** Note that only cars are displayed in the query's results.

FIGURE 8.15

Specifying Cars as the query's criteria.

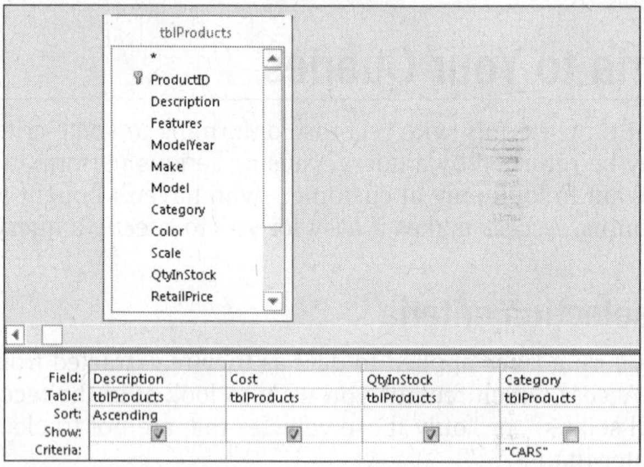

tblProducts: *, ProductID, Description, Features, ModelYear, Make, Model, Category, Color, Scale, QtyInStock, RetailPrice

Field:	Description	Cost	QtyInStock	Category
Table:	tblProducts	tblProducts	tblProducts	tblProducts
Sort:	Ascending			
Show:	☑	☑	☑	☐
Criteria:				"CARS"

When looking at the results of the query, you may argue that there is no point in displaying Cars in every row. In fact, because this query only returns information about cars, the user can very well assume that every record references a car, and there's no need to display a product category in the query. Unchecking the Category field's Show box in the query's design removes Category from the datasheet, making the data easier to understand.

You could enter the criteria expression in any of these other ways:

CARS

= CARS

"CARS"

= "Cars"

By default, Access is *not* case sensitive, so any form of the word *cars* works just as well as this query's criteria.

Figure 8.15 is an excellent example for demonstrating the options for various types of simple character criteria. You could just as well enter **Not Cars** in the criteria column, to return all products that are not cars (trucks, vans, and so on).

Generally, when dealing with character data, you enter equalities, inequalities, or a list of acceptable values.

This capability is a powerful tool. Consider that you only have to supply an example, and Access not only interprets it but also uses it to create the query recordset. This is exactly what *Query by Example* means: You enter an example and let the database build a query based on the example.

To erase the criteria in the cell, select the contents and press Delete, or select the contents and right-click Cut from the shortcut menu that appears.

Entering other simple criteria

You can also specify criteria for Numeric, Date, and Yes/No fields. Simply enter the example data in the criteria field just as you did for text fields. In almost every case, Access understands the criteria you enter and adjusts to correctly apply the criteria to the query's fields.

It's also possible to add more than one criteria to a query. For example, suppose that you want to look only at contacts who live in Connecticut and have been customers since January 1, 2012 (where OrigCustDate is greater than or equal to January 1, 2012). This query requires criteria in both the State and OrigCustDate fields. To do this, it's critical that you place both examples on the same criteria row. Follow these steps to create this query:

1. **Create a new query starting with tblCustomers.**
2. **Add ContactType, FirstName, LastName, State, and OrigCustDate to the QBE grid.**

3. **Enter** ct **or** CT **in the Criteria cell in the State column.**
4. **Enter** > = 01/01/2012 **in the Criteria cell in the OrigCustDate column.** Access adds pound sign characters (#) around the date in the criteria box.
5. **Run the query.** Figure 8.16 shows how the query should look.

FIGURE 8.16

Specifying text and date criteria in the same query.

tblContacts
*
ContactID
CustomerNumber
FirstName
LastName
Address
City
State

Field:	OrigCustDate	LastName	FirstName	State
Table:	tblContacts	tblContacts	tblContacts	tblContacts
Sort:	Ascending			
Show:	☑	☑	☑	☑
Criteria:	>=#1/1/2010#			"CT"

Access displays records of customers who live in Connecticut and who became customers after January 1, 2012.

Access uses comparison operators to compare Date fields to a value. These operators include less than (<), greater than (>), equal to (=), or a combination of these operators.

Notice that Access automatically adds pound sign (#) delimiters around the date value. Access uses these delimiters to distinguish between date and text data. The pound signs are just like the quote marks Access added to the "Cars" criteria. Because OrigCustDate is a DateTime field, Access understands what you want and inserts the proper delimiters for you.

Be aware that Access interprets dates according to the region and language settings in the Control Panel. For example, in most of Europe and Asia, #5/6/2012# is interpreted as June 5, 2012, while in the United States this date is May 6, 2012. It's very easy to construct a query that works perfectly but returns the wrong data because of subtle differences in regional settings.

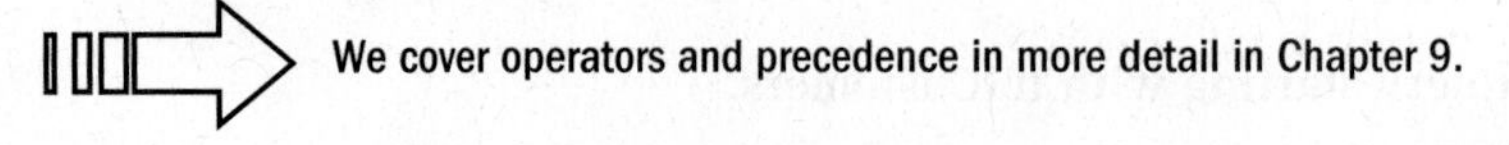

We cover operators and precedence in more detail in Chapter 9.

Printing a Query's Recordset

After you create your query, you can easily print all the records in the recordset. Although you can't specify a type of report, you can print a simple matrix-type report (rows and columns) of the recordset created by your query.

You do have some flexibility when printing a recordset. If you know that the datasheet is set up just as you want, you can specify some options as you follow these steps:

1. **Use the query you just created for Connecticut customers who've been active since January 1, 2012.**
2. **If you aren't in the Datasheet view, run the query by clicking the Run button in the Results group on the Ribbon.**
3. **Choose File⇨Print from the Query Datasheet window's Ribbon.**
4. **Specify the print options that you want in the Print dialog box and click OK.**

The printout reflects all layout options in effect when you print the dataset. Hidden columns don't print, and gridlines print only if the Gridlines option is on. The printout reflects the specified row height and column width.

8

Saving a Query

To save your query, click the Save button on the Quick Access toolbar at the top of the Access screen. Access asks you for the name of the query if this is the first time the query has been saved.

After saving the query, Access returns you to the mode you were working in. Occasionally, you'll want to save and exit the query in a single operation. To do this, click the Close Window button in the upper-right corner of the query designer. Access always asks you to confirm saving the changes before it actually saves the query.

Creating Multi-Table Queries

Using a query to get information from a single table is common; often, however, you need information from several related tables. For example, you might want to obtain a buyer's name and product purchased by the customer. This query requires four tables: tblCustomers, tblSales, tblSalesLineItems, and tblProducts.

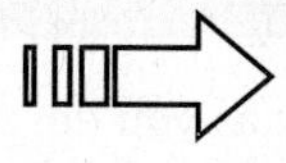

In Chapter 3, you learned the importance of primary and foreign keys and how they link tables together. You learned how to use the Relationships window to create relationships between tables. Finally, you learned how referential integrity affects data in tables.

After you create the tables for your database and decide how the tables are related to one another, you're ready to build multi-table queries to obtain information from several related tables. A multi-table query presents data as if it existed in one large table.

The first step in creating a multi-table query is to add the tables to the query design window:

1. **Create a new query by clicking the Query Design button on the Create tab of the Ribbon.**
2. **Add tblCustomers, tblSales, tblSalesLineItems, and tblProducts by double-clicking each table's name in the Show Table dialog box.**
3. **Click the Close button.**

NOTE
You can also add each table by highlighting the table in the list separately and clicking Add.

Figure 8.17 shows the top pane of the query design window with the four tables you just added. Because the relationships were set at table level, the join lines are automatically added to the query.

FIGURE 8.17

The query design window with four tables added. Notice that the join lines are already present.

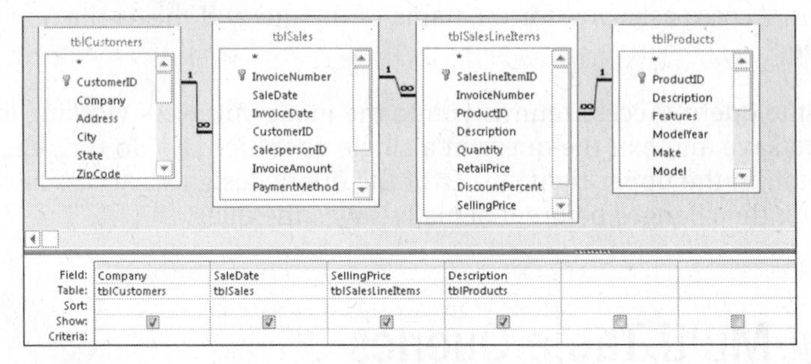

NOTE
You can add more tables, at any time, by choosing Query ➪ Show Table from the Query Tools Design Ribbon. Alternatively, you can right-click the design window and select the Show Table option from the context menu.

You add fields from more than one table to the query in exactly the same way as you do when you're working with a single table. You can add fields one at a time, multiple fields as a group, or all the fields from a table.

When you select a field that has a common name in multiple tables, Access adds the table's name, followed by a period and the field name. For example, if ProductID is a field found in more than one table used in the query design window (let's say tblProducts and tblSalesLineItems), adding the ProductID field from tblSalesLineItems will display that field in the design grid as tblSalesLineItems.ProductID. This helps you select the correct field name. Using this method, you can select a common field name from a specific table.

TIP

The easiest way to select fields is still to double-click the field names in the top half of the query designer. To do so, you might have to resize the Field List windows to see the fields that you want to select.

Viewing table names

When you're working with multiple tables in a query, the field names in the QBE grid can become confusing. You might find yourself asking, for example, just which table the Description field is from.

Access automatically maintains the table name that is associated with each field displayed in the QBE grid. Figure 8.18 shows the query designer with the name of each table displayed under the field name in the QBE grid.

FIGURE 8.18

The QBE grid with table names displayed. Notice that it shows all four table names.

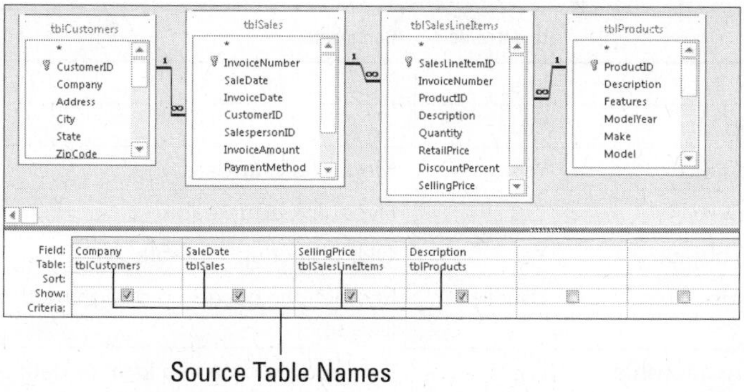

Source Table Names

Adding multiple fields

The process of adding multiple fields in a multi-table query is identical to adding multiple fields in a single-table query. When you're adding fields from several tables, you must add them from one table at a time. The easiest way to do this is to select multiple fields and drag them together down to the QBE grid.

Select multiple contiguous fields by clicking the first field of the list and then clicking the last field while holding down the Shift key. You can also select noncontiguous fields in the list by holding down the Ctrl key while clicking individual fields.

CAUTION

Selecting the asterisk (*) does have one drawback: You can't specify criteria on the asterisk column itself. You have to add an individual field from the table and enter the criterion. If you add a field for a criterion (when using the asterisk), the query displays the field twice — once for the asterisk field and a second time for the criterion field. Therefore, you might want to deselect the Show cell of the criterion field.

Recognizing the limitations of multi-table queries

When you create a query with multiple tables, there are limits to which fields can be edited. Generally, you can change data in a query's recordset, and your changes are saved in the underlying tables. The main exception is a table's primary key — a primary key value can't be edited if referential integrity is in effect and if the field is part of a relationship.

There may be instances when you will want to make manual edits to the resulting recordset of a query. In Access, the records in your tables might not always be updateable. Table 8.1 shows when a field in a table is updateable. As Table 8.1 shows, queries based on one-to-many relationships are updateable in both tables (depending on how the query was designed).

TABLE 8.1 Rules for Updating Queries

Type of Query or Field	Updateable	Comments
One table	Yes	
One-to-one relationship	Yes	
Results contains Memo field	Yes	Memo field updateable
Results contain a hyperlink	Yes	Hyperlink updateable
Results contain an OLE object	Yes	OLE object updateable
One-to-many relationship	Usually	Restrictions based on design methodology (see text)
Many-to-one-to-many relationship	No	Can update data in a form or data access page if Record Type = Recordset
Two or more tables with no join line	No	Must have a join to determine updateability
Crosstab	No	Creates a snapshot of the data
Totals query (Sum, Avg, and so on)	No	Works with grouped data creating a snapshot
Unique Value property is Yes	No	Shows unique records only in a snapshot

Type of Query or Field	Updateable	Comments
SQL-specific queries	No	Union and pass-through work with ODBC data
Calculated field	No	Will recalculate automatically
Read-only fields	No	If opened read-only or on read-only drive (CD-ROM)
Permissions denied	No	Insert, replace, or delete not granted
ODBC tables with no unique identifier	No	Unique identifier must exist
Paradox table with no primary key	No	Primary key file must exist
Locked by another user	No	Can't be updated while a field is locked by another

Overcoming query limitations

Table 8.1 shows that there are times when queries and fields in tables are not updateable. As a general rule, any query that performs aggregate operations or uses an ODBC data source is not updateable; most other queries can be updated. When your query has more than one table and some of the tables have a one-to-many relationship, some fields might not be updateable (depending on the design of the query).

8

Updating a unique index (primary key)

If a query uses two tables involved in a one-to-many relationship, the query must include the primary key from the "one" table. Access must have the primary key value so that they can find the related records in the two tables.

Replacing existing data in a query with a one-to-many relationship

Normally, all the fields in the "many" table (such as the tblSales table) are updateable in a one-to-many query. All the fields (*except* the primary key) in the "one" table (tblCustomers) can be updated. This is sufficient for most database application purposes. Also, the primary key field is rarely changed in the "one" table because it's the link to the records in the joined tables.

Updating fields in queries

If you want to add records to both tables of a one-to-many relationship, include the foreign key from the "many" table and show the field in the datasheet. After doing this, records can be added starting with either the "one" or "many" table. The "one" table's primary key field is automatically copied to the "many" table's join field.

If you want to add records to multiple tables in a form (covered in Chapters 17 and 18), remember to include all (or most) of the fields from both tables. Otherwise, you won't have a complete set of the record's data on your form.

Working with the Table Pane

The upper (table) pane of the query designer contains information that's important to your query. Understanding the table pane and how to work with Field Lists is critically important to building complex queries.

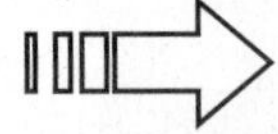

These lines were predrawn because you already set the relationships between the tables as described in Chapter 4.

Looking at the join line

A *join line* connects tables in the query designer (refer to Figure 8.17). The join line connects the primary key in one table to the foreign key in another table. The *join line* represents the relationship between two tables in the Access database. In this example, a join line goes from tblSales to tblCustomers, connecting ContactID in tblCustomers to the Buyer field in tblSales. The join line is added by Access because relationships were set in the Relationship Builder.

If referential integrity is set on the relationship, Access uses a somewhat thicker line for the join connecting to the table in the query designer. A one-to-many relationship is indicated by an infinity symbol (∞) on the "many" table end of the join line.

Access auto-joins two tables if the following conditions are met:

- Both tables have fields with the same name.
- The same-named fields are the same data type (text, numeric, and so on). Note that the AutoNumber data type is the same as Numeric (Long Integer).
- One of the fields is a primary key in its table.

Note

After a relationship is created between tables, the join line remains between the two fields. As you move through a table selecting fields, the line moves relative to the linked fields. For example, if you scroll downward, towards the bottom of the window in tblCustomers, the join line moves upward with the customer number, eventually stopping at the top of the table window.

When you're working with many tables, these join lines can become confusing as they cross or overlap. As you scroll through the table, the line eventually becomes visible, and the field it's linked to becomes obvious.

Moving a table

Move the Field Lists by grabbing the title bar of a Field List window (where the name of the table is) with the mouse and dragging the Field List window to a new location. You may want to move the Field Lists for a better working view or to clean up a confusing query diagram.

You can move and resize the Field Lists anywhere in the top pane. Access saves the arrangement when you save and close the query. Generally speaking, the Field Lists will appear in the same configuration the next time you open the query.

Removing a table

You might need to remove tables from a query. Use the mouse to select the table you want to remove in the top pane of the query design window and press the Delete key. Or right-click the Field List window and choose Remove Table from the shortcut menu.

Removing a table from a query's design does not remove the table from the database, of course.

Caution

When you remove a table from a query design, join lines to that table are deleted as well. There is no warning or confirmation before removal. The table is simply removed from the screen, along with any of the table's fields added to the QBE grid. Be aware, however, that deleted tables referenced in calculated fields will not be removed. The "phantom" table references may cause errors when you try to run the query.

8

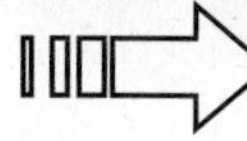

Calculated fields are discussed in detail in Chapter 12.

Adding more tables

You might decide to add more tables to a query or you might accidentally delete a table and need to add it back. You accomplish this task by clicking the Show Table button on the Query Setup group in the Design Ribbon. The Show Table dialog box appears in response to this action.

Creating and Working with Query Joins

You'll often need to build queries that require two or more related tables be joined to achieve the desired results. For example, you may want to join an employee table to a transaction table in order create a report that contains both transaction details and information on the employees who logged those transactions. The type of join used will determine the records that will be output.

Understanding joins

There are three basic types of joins: inner joins, left outer joins, and right outer joins:

- **Inner joins:** An *inner join* operation tells Access to select only those records from both tables that have matching values. Records with values in the joined field that do not appear in both tables are omitted from the query results. Figure 8.19 represents the inner join operation visually.

FIGURE 8.19

An inner join operation will select only the records that have matching values in both tables. The arrows point to the records that will be included in the results.

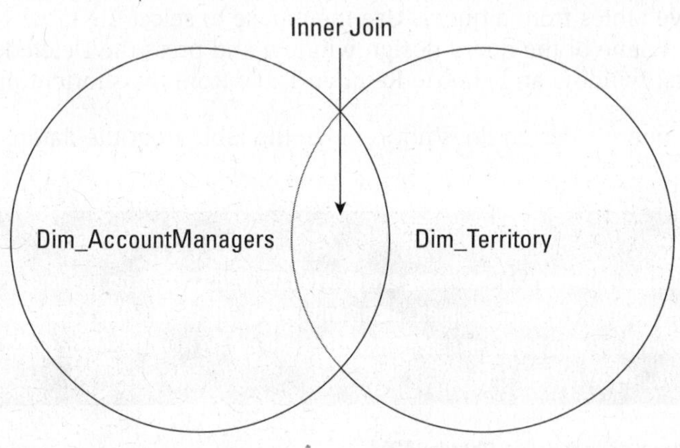

- **Left outer joins:** A *left outer join* operation (sometimes called a "left join") tells Access to select all the records from the first table regardless of matching *and* only those records from the second table that have matching values in the joined field. Figure 8.20 represents the left join operation visually.
- **Right outer joins:** A *right outer join* operation (sometimes called a "right join") tells Access to select all the records from the second table regardless of matching *and* only those records from the first table that have matching values in the joined field (see Figure 8.21).

By default, an Access query returns only records where data exists on both sides of a relationship (inner join). For example, a query that extracts data from the Contacts table and the Sales table only returns records where contacts have actually placed sales and will not show contacts who haven't yet placed a sale. If a contact record isn't matched by at least one sales record, the contact data isn't returned by the query. This means that, sometimes, the query might not return all the records you expect.

FIGURE 8.20

A left outer join operation will select all records from the first table and only those records from the second table that have matching values in both tables. The arrows point to the records that will be included in the results.

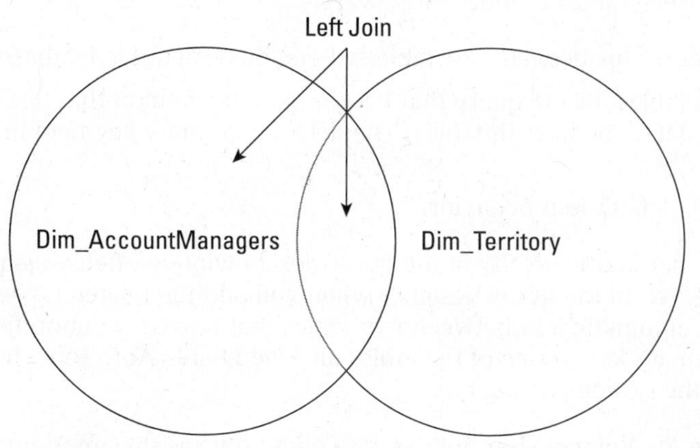

FIGURE 8.21

A right outer join operation will select all records from the second table and only those records from the first table that have matching values in both tables. The arrows point to the records that will be included in the results.

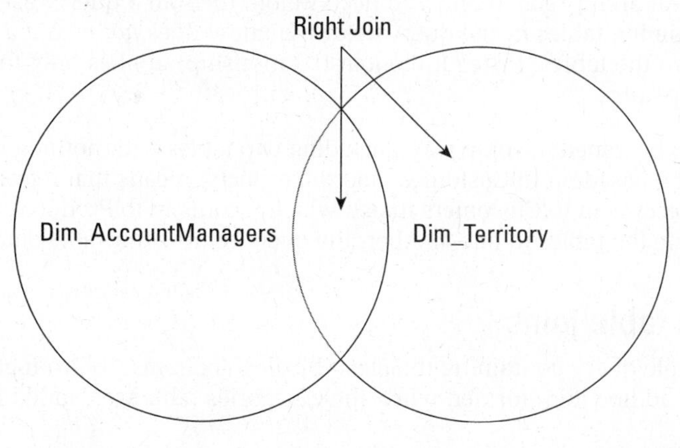

Although this is the most common join type between tables in a query, users sometimes want to see all the data in a table (like tblCustomers in the preceding example), regardless of whether those records are matched in another table. In fact, users often want to specifically see records that are *not* matched on the other side of the join. Consider a sales department that wants to know all the contacts who have *not* made a sale in the last year. You must modify the default query join characteristics in order to process this type of query.

You can create joins between tables in these three ways:

- By creating relationships between the tables when you design the database.
- By selecting two tables for the query that have a field in common that has the same name and data type in both tables. The field is a primary key field in one of the tables.
- By modifying the default join behavior.

The first two methods occur automatically in the query design window. Relationships between tables are displayed in the query designer when you add the related tables to a query. It also creates an automatic join between two tables that have a common field, as long as that field is a primary key in one of the tables and the Enable Auto Join choice is selected (by default) in the Options dialog box.

If relationships are set in the Relationship Builder, you might not see the auto-join line if

- The two tables have a common field, but it isn't the same name.
- A table isn't related and can't be logically related to the other table (for example, tblCustomers can't directly join the tblSalesLineItems table).

If you have two tables that aren't related and you need to join them in a query, use the query design window. Joining tables in the query design window does *not* create a permanent relationship between the tables; instead, the join (relationship) applies only to the tables while the query operates.

Tables in a query have to be joined in some way. Including two tables with nothing in common (for example, a query based on tblCustomers and tblProducts) means that Access has no way to know which records in tblCustomers match which records in tblProducts. Unless there is some way to relate the tables to one another, the query returns unusable data.

Leveraging ad hoc table joins

Figure 8.22 shows a simple query containing tblSales, tblSalesLineItems, tblProducts, and tblCategories. This is an ad hoc join, formed when the Categories table was added to the query.

No direct relationship yet exists between tblProducts and tblCategories. However, Access found the Category field in both the tables, determined that the Category data type is the same in both tables, and determined that the Category field in tblCategories is the primary key. Therefore, Access added an ad hoc join between the tables.

FIGURE 8.22

An ad hoc join between tblProducts and tblCategories.

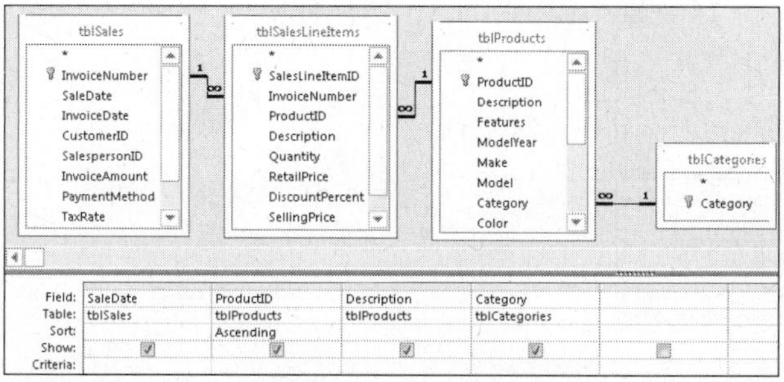

NOTE

Tables are not joined automatically in a query if they aren't already joined at the table level, if they don't have a common named field for a primary key, or if the AutoJoin option is off.

If Access hasn't auto-joined tblProducts and tblCategories (perhaps because the Category field was named differently in the tables), you can easily add an ad hoc join by dragging the Category field from one table and dropping it on the corresponding field in the other table.

Specifying the type of join

The problem with most joins is that, by default, they exhibit equi-join behavior as the query executes. In the case of the query in Figure 8.19, if a product record exists that doesn't have an assigned category (for example, a car that was never assigned to a category), the query doesn't return any records where a product record isn't matched by a category.

The problem is that you can't even tell records are missing. The only way you'd ever determine that there should be more records returned by this query is by carefully examining the sales records, by composing another query that counts all sales, or by performing some other audit operation.

You must modify the join characteristics between tblProducts and tblCategories to get an accurate picture of sales. Carefully right-click on the thin join line between tblProducts and tblCategories, and select the Join Properties command from the shortcut menu. This action opens the Join Properties dialog box (see Figure 8.23), enabling you to specify an alternate join between the tables.

FIGURE 8.23

Selecting an outer join for the query.

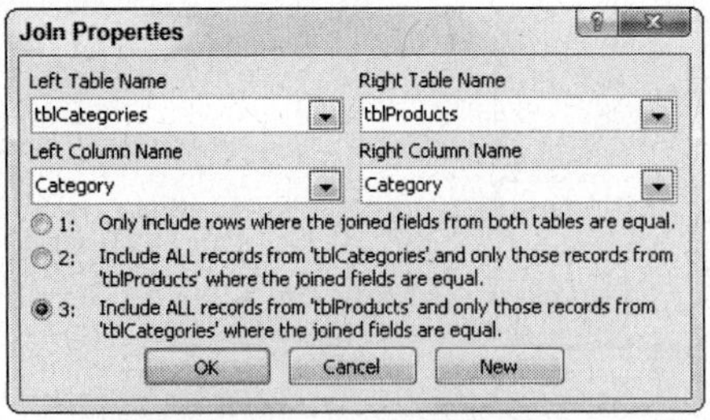

In Figure 8.23, the third option (Include All Records from 'tblProducts') has been selected (the first option is the default). Options 2 and 3 are left outer join and right outer join, respectively. These options direct Access to retrieve all records from the left (or right) table involved in the join, regardless of whether those records are matched on the other side of the join.

Figure 8.24 shows the result of the new join. In the lower-right corner of this figure you see how an outer join appears in the Access query designer, while the rest of the figure shows the recordset returned by the query.

FIGURE 8.24

A right outer join corrects the "missing products" problem in Figure 8.23.

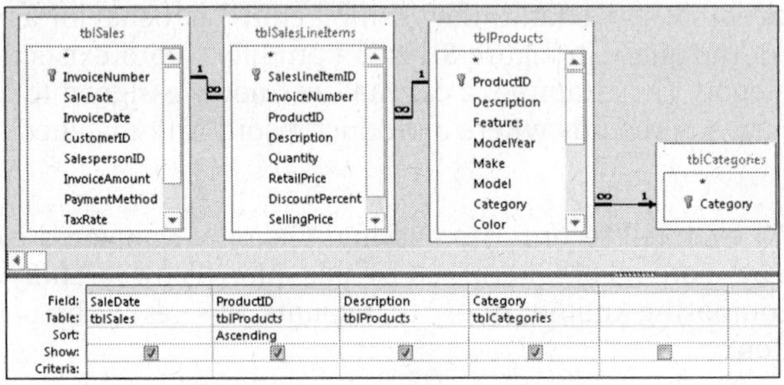

Of course, you can easily create joins that make no sense, but when you view the data, it'll be pretty obvious that you got the join wrong. If two joined fields have no values in common, you'll have a datasheet in which no records are selected.

You would never want to create a meaningless join. For example, you wouldn't want to join the City field from tblCustomer to the SalesDate field of tblSales. Although Access enables you to create this join, the resulting recordset will have no records in it.

Deleting joins

To delete a join line between two tables, select the join line and press the Delete key. Select the join line by placing the mouse pointer on any part of the line and clicking once.

CAUTION
If you delete a join between two tables and the tables remain in the query design window unjoined to any other tables, the solution will have unexpected results because of the Cartesian product that Access creates from the two tables. The Cartesian product is effective for only this query. The underlying relationship remains intact.

Access enables you to create multi-field joins between tables (more than one line can be drawn). The two fields must have data in common; if not, the query won't find any records to display.

CHAPTER

9

Using Operators and Expressions in Access

IN THIS CHAPTER

Understanding operators in expressions

Creating complex queries

Building queries with simple criteria

Using multiple criteria in a query

Composing complex query criteria

In the preceding chapter, you created queries using selected fields from one or more tables. You also sorted the data and set criteria to limit the results of a query. This chapter focuses on using operators and expressions to calculate information, compare values, and display data in a different format — using queries to build examples.

This chapter uses queries to demonstrate the use of operators and functions, but the principles in this chapter's exercises apply anywhere operators and expressions appear in Access.

ON THE WEB

The starting database for this walkthrough, `Chapter09.accdb`, can be downloaded from this book's website.

Introducing Operators

Operators let you compare values, put text strings together, format data, and perform a wide variety of tasks. You use operators to instruct Access to perform a specific action against one or more *operands*. The combination of operators and operands is known as an *expression*.

NOTE
You'll see the term *evaluate* a lot in this chapter. When you present Access with a field, expression, variable, and so on, Access *evaluates* the item and (internally) represents the item as a value. It's very important to compose expressions in such a way that Access evaluates them as we expect. If Access incorrectly evaluates an expression, the application won't perform as expected. Understanding how Access evaluates a query's criteria or an expression used in VBA code is critically important to success as an Access developer.

You'll use operators every time you create an equation in Access. For example, operators specify data validation rules in table properties, create calculated fields in forms and reports, and specify criteria in queries.

Types of operators

Operators can be grouped into the following types:

- Mathematical operators
- Comparison operators
- String operators
- Boolean (logical) operators
- Miscellaneous operators

Mathematical operators

Mathematical operators are also known as arithmetic operators, because they're used for performing numeric calculations. By definition, you use mathematical operators to work with numbers as operands. When you work with mathematical operators, numbers can be any numeric data type. The number can be a constant value, the value of a variable, or a field's contents. You use these numbers individually or combine them to create complex expressions.

There are seven basic mathematical operators:

+	Addition
–	Subtraction
*	Multiplication
/	Division
\	Integer division
^	Exponentiation
`Mod`	Modulo

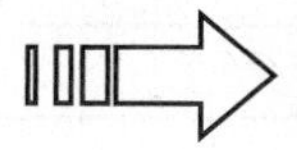

The mathematical operators discussed in this section are typically used in calculated fields. Calculated fields are covered in detail in Chapter 12.

The addition operator: +

If you want to create a calculated field in a query for adding the value of tax to the price, use an expression similar to the following:

```
[TaxAmt]+[Price]
```

The subtraction operator: –

The subtraction operator (–) performs simple subtraction, such as calculating a final invoice amount by subtracting a discount from the price:

```
[Price] - ([Price] * [DiscountPercent])
```

NOTE

Although parentheses are not mathematical operators, they play an important role in many expressions, as discussed in the "Operator precedence" section, later in this chapter.

*The multiplication operator: **

A simple example of when to use the multiplication operator (`*`) is to calculate the total price of several items. You could design a query to display the number of items purchased and the price for each item. Then you could add a calculated field containing the value of the number of items purchased times the price per item. In this case, the expression would be

```
[Quantity] * [Price]
```

The division operator: /

Use the division operator (`/`) to divide two numbers. Suppose, for example, that a pool of 212 people win a $1,000,000 lottery. The expression to determine each individual's payoff of $4,716.98 is

```
1000000 / 212
```

NOTE

Notice that the `1000000` value does not contain commas. Access is not able to perform a mathematical operation on numeric values containing punctuation.

*The integer division operator: *

The integer division operator (`\`) takes any two numbers (`number1` and `number2`), rounds them up or down to integers, divides the first by the second (`number1 / number2`), and then drops the decimal portion, leaving only the integer value. Here are some examples of how integer division differs from normal division:

Normal Division	Integer Conversion Division
100 / 6 = 16.667	100 \ 6 = 16
100.9 / 6.6 = 19.288	100.9 \ 6.6 = 14
102 / 7 = 14.571	102 \ 7 = 14

NOTE

Access rounds whole numbers based on a principle known as "banker's rounding" or "round half to even." Rounding is always done to the nearest even number: 6.5 becomes 6, and 7.5 becomes 8. This can produce unexpected results only when the rounded value is exactly midway between two whole numbers. As you'd expect, 6.51 rounds to 7, and 6.49 rounds to 6. Access does this to minimize round-off errors.

The exponentiation operator: ^

The exponentiation operator (`^`) raises a number to the power of an exponent. Raising a number simply means multiplying a number by itself. For example, multiplying the value `4 x 4 x 4` (that is, 43) is the same as entering the formula `4^3`.

The exponent does not have to be a whole number; it can even be negative. For example, `2^2.1` returns `4.28709385014517`, and `4^-2` is `0.0625`.

The modulo division operator: Mod

The modulo operator (`Mod`) takes any two numbers (`number1` and `number2`), rounds them up or down to integers, divides the first by the second (`number1 / number2`), and then returns the remainder. Here are some examples of how modulo division compares to normal division:

Normal Division	Modulo Division	Explanation
10 / 5 = 2	10 Mod 5 = 0	10 is evenly divided by 5
10 / 4 = 2.5	10 Mod 4 = 2	10 / 4 = 2 with a remainder of 2
22.24 / 4 = 9.56	22.24 Mod 4 = 2	22 / 4 = 5 with a remainder of 2
22.52 / 4 = 9.63	22.52 Mod 4 = 3	23 / 4 = 5 with a remainder of 3

The tricky thing about modulo division is that the returned value is the remainder after integer division is performed on the operands. The `Mod` operator is often used to determine whether a number is even or odd by performing modulo division with 2 as the divisor:

```
5 Mod 2 = 1
4 Mod 2 = 0
```

If `Mod` returns `1`, the dividend is odd. `Mod` returns `0` when the dividend is even.

Comparison operators

Comparison operators compare two values or expressions in an equation. There are six basic comparison operators:

=	Equal
<>	Not equal
<	Less than
<=	Less than or equal to
>	Greater than
>=	Greater than or equal to

The expressions built from comparison operators always return `True`, `False`, or `Null`. Null is returned when the expression can't be evaluated.

As you read the following descriptions, please keep in mind that Access is case insensitive in most situations. When comparing strings, for example, "CAR," "Car," and "car" are the same to Access.

NOTE

Access actually returns a numeric value for comparison operator expressions. Access uses `-1` to represent `True` and `0` to represent `False`.

If either side of an equation is a null value, the result is always null.

The equal operator: =

The equal operator (=) returns `True` if the two expressions are the same. For example,

`[Category] = "Car"`	Returns `True` if `Category` is `Car`; returns `False` for any other category
`[SaleDate] = Date()`	Returns `True` if the date in `SaleDate` is today; returns `False` for any other date

The not-equal operator: <>

The not-equal operator (<>) is the opposite of the equal operator. For example,

`[Category] <> "Car"`	Returns `True` if `Category` is anything but `Car` and `False` only when `Category` is `Car`.

The less-than operator: <

The less-than operator (<) returns a logical True if the left side of the equation is less than the right side, as in this example:

`[Price] < 1000`	Returns True if the Price field contains a value of less than 1,000; returns False whenever Price is greater than or equal to 1,000.

Interestingly, the less-than operator is easily applied to string values (the same is true for most comparison operators). For example, the following expression is False:

```
"Man" > "Woman"
```

Without getting philosophical about the expression, what actually happens is that Access does a character-by-character comparison of the strings. Because *M* appears before *W* in the alphabet, the word *Man* is not greater than *Woman*. The ability to compare strings can be of significant value when sorting string data or arranging names in a particular order.

Again, because Access string comparisons are not case sensitive, *XYZ* is not greater than *xyz*.

Note

You may not get the results you were expecting when doing string-based comparisons on numbers. For instance, 10 will come before 9 because textually, 1 comes before 9.

The less-than-or-equal-to operator: <=

The less-than-or-equal-to operator (<=) returns True if the operand on the left side of the equation is either less than or equal to the right-side operand, as in this example:

`[Price] <= 2500`	Returns True if Price equals 2500 or is less than 2500; returns False for any Price that is more than 2500

Caution

Comparison operators must be composed properly. Access reports an error if you enter =<. The order of the characters in this operator is important. It must be less than or equal to: <=.

The greater-than operator: >

The greater-than operator (>) is the opposite of less than. This operator returns True when the left-side operand is greater than the operand on the right side. For example,

`[TaxRate] > 3.5`	Returns True if TaxRate is greater than 3.5; returns False whenever TaxRate is less than or equal to 3.5

The greater-than-or-equal-to operator: >=

The greater-than-or-equal-to operator (>=) returns `True` if the left side is greater than or equal to the right side. For example,

`[TaxRate] >= 5`	Returns `True` if `TaxRate` is 5 or greater; returns `False` when `TaxRate` is less than 5

String operators

Access has three string operators for working with strings. Unlike the mathematical and logical operators, the string operators are specifically designed to work with the string data type:

`&`	Concatenates operands
`Like`	Operands are similar
`Not Like`	Operands are dissimilar

The concatenation operator: &

The concatenation operator joins two or more strings into a single string. In some ways, concatenation is similar to addition. Unlike addition, however, concatenation always returns a string:

```
[FirstName] & [LastName]
```

However, there is no space between the names in the returned string. If `[FirstName]` is "Fred" and `[LastName]` is "Smith," the returned string is `FredSmith`. If you want a space between the names, you must explicitly add a space between the strings, as follows:

```
[FirstName] & " " & [LastName]
```

The concatenation operator easily joins a string with a numeric- or date-type value. Using the `&` eliminates the need for special functions to convert numbers or dates to strings.

Suppose, for example, that you have a number field (HouseNumber) and a text field (StreetName), and you want to combine both fields:

```
[HouseNumber] & " " & [StreetName]
```

If `HouseNumber` is "1600" and `StreetName` is "Pennsylvania Avenue N.W.," the returned string is

```
"1600 Pennsylvania Avenue N.W."
```

NOTE
Quotes are added around the returned string to clarify the result.

Maybe you want to print the OperatorName and current date at the bottom of a report page. This can be accomplished with the following:

```
"This report was printed " & Now() & " by " & [OperatorName]
```

Notice the spaces after the word *printed* and before and after the word *by*. If the date is March 21, 2012, and the time is 4:45 p.m., this expression looks like:

```
This report was printed 3/21/12 4:45:40 PM by Jim Rosengren
```

The addition operator (+) also concatenates two character strings. For example, to combine FirstName and LastName from tblContacts to display them as a single string, the expression is

```
[FirstName] + " " + [LastName]
```

TIP

Knowing how the concatenation operator works makes maintaining your database expressions easier. If you always use the concatenation operator (&) — instead of the addition operator (+) — when working with strings, you won't have to be concerned with the data types of the concatenation operands. Any expression that uses the concatenation operator converts all operands to strings for you. Using the addition operator to concatenate strings can sometimes lead to unpredictable results because Access must decide whether the operands are numbers or strings and act accordingly. The concatenation operator forces Access to treat the operands as strings and always returns a string as a result.

Although & and + both serve as concatenation operators, using + might exhibit unexpected results in some situations. & *always* returns a string when concatenating two values. The operands passed to & may be strings, numeric or date/time values, field references, and so on, and a string is always returned.

Because it always returns a string, & is often used to prevent `Invalid use of null` errors when working with data that might be null. For example, let's assume a particular text box on an Access form may or may not contain a value because we can't be sure the user has entered anything in the text box. When assigning the contents of the text box to a variable (see Chapter 10), some developers concatenate an empty string to the text box's contents as part of the assignment:

```
MyVariable = txtLastName & ""
```

& ensures that, even if the text box contains a null value, the variable is assigned a string and no error is raised.

+, on the other hand, returns a null value when one of the operands is null:

```
MyVariable = txtLastName + ""
```

In this case, if txtLastName is truly null, the user may encounter an `Invalid use of null` error because the result of the concatenation is null (assuming, once again, that txtLastName contains a null value).

Most experienced Access developers reserve + for arithmetical operations and always use & for string concatenation.

The Like and Not Like operators

The Like operator, and its opposite, the Not Like operator, compare two string expressions. These operators determine whether one string matches, or doesn't match, the pattern of another string. The returned value is True, False, or Null. The Like and Not Like operators are case insensitive.

The Like operator uses the following syntax:

```
expression Like pattern
```

Like looks for the expression in the pattern; if it's present, the operation returns True. For example:

[FirstName] Like "John"	Returns True if the first name is John.
[LastName] Like "SMITH*"	Returns True if the last name is Smith, Smithson, or any other name beginning with "Smith," regardless of capitalization. (Wildcards like * are discussed in the "Using wildcards" sidebar.)
[State] Not Like "NY"	Returns True for any state other than New York.

NOTE
If either operand in a Like operation is null, the result is null.

The Like and Not Like operators provides powerful and flexible tools for string comparisons. Wildcard characters extend the flexibility of the Like operator.

9

Using Wildcards

The following table shows the five wildcards you can use with the Like operator:

Wildcard	Purpose
?	A single character (0–9, Aa–Zz)
*	Any number of characters (0–*n*)
#	Any single digit (0–9)
[list]	Any single character in the list
[!list]	Any single character *not* in the list

continued

continued

Both `[list]` and `[!list]` can use the hyphen between two characters to signify a range.

Here are some wildcard examples:

`[tblContacts].[LastName] Like "Mc*"`	Returns `True` for any last name that begins with "Mc" or "MC," such as "McDonald," "McJamison," and "MCWilliams." Anything that doesn't start with "Mc" or "MC" returns `False`.
`[Answer] Like "[A-D]"`	Returns `True` if the Answer is A, B, C, D, a, b, c, or d. Any other character returns `False`.
`"AB1989" Like "AB####"`	Returns `True` because the string begins with "AB" and is followed by four digits.
`[LastName] Not Like "[A,E,I,O,U]*"`	Returns `True` for any last name that does *not* begin with a vowel. "Smith" and "Jones" return `True` while "Adams" and "O'Malley" return `False`.
`[City] Like "?????"`	Returns `True` for any city that is exactly five characters long.

TIP

If the pattern you're trying to match contains a wildcard character, you must enclose the wildcard character in brackets. In the following example, the `[*]` in the pattern treats asterisks in the third position as data:

```
"AB*Co" Like "AB[*]C*"
```

Since the asterisk character is enclosed in brackets, it won't be mistaken for an asterisk wildcard character.

Boolean (logical) operators

Boolean operators (also referred to as *logical operators*) are used to create multiple conditions in expressions. Like comparison operators, these operators always return `True`, `False`, or `Null`. Boolean operators include the following:

`And`	Returns `TRUE` when both `Expression1` and `Expression2` are true
`Or`	Returns `TRUE` when either `Expression1` or `Expression2` is true
`Not`	Returns `TRUE` when the `Expression` is not true
`Xor`	Returns `TRUE` when either `Expression1` or `Expression2` is true, but not both
`Eqv`	Returns `TRUE` when both `Expression1` and `Expression2` are true or both are false
`Imp`	Performs bitwise comparisons of identically positioned bits in two numerical expressions

The And operator

Use the `And` operator to perform a logical *conjunction* of two expressions. The operator returns `True` if both expressions are `True`. The general syntax of `And` is

```
Expression1 And Expression2
```

For example:

`[tblContacts].[State] = "MA" And [tblContacts].[ZipCode] = "02379"`	Returns `True` only if both expressions are true

The logical `And` operator depends on how the two operands are evaluated by Access. Table 9.1 describes all the possible results when the operands are `True` or `False`. Notice that `And` returns `True` only when *both* operands are true.

TABLE 9.1 And Operator Results

Expression1	Expression2	Expression1 And Expression2
True	True	True
True	False	False
True	Null	Null
False	True	False
False	False	False
False	Null	False
Null	True	Null
Null	False	False
Null	Null	Null

The Or operator

The `Or` operator performs a logical *disjunction* of two expressions. `Or` returns `True` if *either* condition is true. The general syntax of `Or` is

```
Expression1 Or Expression2
```

The following examples show how the `Or` operator works:

`[LastName] = "Casey" Or [LastName] = "Gleason"`	Returns `True` if `LastName` is either Casey or Gleason
`[TaxLocation] = "TX" Or [TaxLocation] = "CT"`	Returns `True` if `TaxLocation` is either TX or CT

The `Or` operator (like `And`) returns `True` or `False` depending on how Access evaluates its operands. Table 9.2 shows all possible combinations with two operands. Notice that `Or` returns `False` only when *both* operands are false.

TABLE 9.2 Or Expression Results

Expression1	Expression2	Expression1 Or Expression2
True	True	True
True	False	True
True	Null	True
False	True	True
False	False	False
False	Null	Null
Null	True	True
Null	False	Null
Null	Null	Null

The Not operator

The `Not` operator negates a numeric or Boolean expression. The `Not` operator returns the `True` if the expression is false, and `False` if the expression is true. The general syntax of `Not` is

```
Not [numeric|boolean] expression
```

The following examples show how to use the `Not` operator:

`Not [Price] <= 100000`	Returns `True` if `Price` is greater than 100,000
`If Not (City = "Seattle") Then`	Returns `True` for any city that is not Seattle

If the operand is null, the `Not` operator returns `Null`. Table 9.3 shows all the possible values.

TABLE 9.3 Not Operator Results

Expression	Not Expression
True	False
False	True
Null	Null

Miscellaneous operators

Access has three very useful miscellaneous operators:

`Between...And`	Range
`In`	List comparison
`Is`	Reserved word

The Between...And operator

`Between...And` determines whether an expression's value falls within a range of values:

```
expression Between value1 And value2
```

If the value of the expression falls within *value1* and *value2*, or is the same as *value1* or *value2*, the result is `True`; otherwise, it's `False`. Note that the `Between...And` operator is inclusive, the equivalent of >= and <=.

The following examples show how to use the `Between...And` operator:

`[TotalCost] Between 10000 And 19999`	Returns `True` if the `TotalCost` is between 10,000 and 19,999, or equal to 10,000 or 19,999.
`[SaleDate] Between #1/1/2012# And #12/31/2012#`	Returns `True` when the `SaleDate` occurs within the year 2012.

The `Between...And` operator can also be used with `Not` operator to negate the logic:

`Not [SaleDate] Between #1/1/2012# And #3/31/2012#`	Returns `True` only when `SaleDate` is *not* within the first quarter of 2012.

9

The In operator

The `In` operator determines whether an expression's value is the same as any value within a list. The general syntax of `In` is:

```
Expression In (value1, value2, value3, ...)
```

If the expression's value is found within the list, the result is `True`; otherwise, the result is `False`.

The following example uses the `In` operator as a query's criteria in the Category column:

```
In ('SUV','Trucks')
```

This query displays only those models that are SUVs or trucks.

The `In` operator is also used in VBA code:

```
If [tblCustomers].[City] In("Seattle", "Tacoma") Then
```

In this case the body of the If...Then...Else statement executes only if the City field is either Seattle or Tacoma.

The return value of the `In` operator can be negated with `Not`:

```
If strCity Not In ("Pittsburgh", "Philadelphia") Then
```

In this case, the body of the If...Then...Else statement executes only if strCity is not set to either Pittsburgh or Philadelphia.

The Is operator

The `Is` operator is generally used with the keyword `Null` to determine whether the value of an object is null:

```
expression Is Null
```

In the VBA environment, the `Is` operator can be used to compare various objects to determine if they represent the same entity.

The following example uses the `Is` operator:

`[LastName] Is Null`	Returns `True` if the LastName field is null; returns `False` if the `LastName` field contains any value.

It is important to note that the `Is` operator applies only to objects and object variables, such as fields in tables. The `Is` operator can't be used with simple variables such as strings or numbers.

Operator precedence

When you work with complex expressions that have many operators, Access must determine which operator to evaluate first, and then which is next, and so forth. Access has a built-in predetermined order for mathematical, logical, and Boolean operators, known as *operator precedence*. Access always follows this order unless you use parentheses to override its default behavior.

Operations within parentheses are performed before operations outside parentheses. Within parentheses, Access follows the default operator precedence.

Precedence is determined first according to category of the operator. The operator rank by order of precedence is

1. Mathematical
2. Comparison
3. Boolean

Each category contains its own order of precedence, which we explain in the following sections.

The mathematical precedence

Mathematical operators follow this order of precedence:

1. Exponentiation
2. Negation
3. Multiplication and/or division (left to right)
4. Integer division
5. Modulus division
6. Addition and/or subtraction (left to right)
7. String concatenation

The comparison precedence

Comparison operators observe this order of precedence:

1. Equal
2. Not equal
3. Less than
4. Greater than
5. Less than or equal to
6. Greater than or equal to
7. Like

The Boolean precedence

The Boolean operators follow this order of precedence:

1. Not
2. And
3. Or
4. Xor
5. Eqv
6. Imp

Using Operators and Expressions in Queries

One of the most common uses of operators and expressions is when building complex query criteria. A thorough understanding of how these constructs work can ease the process of building sophisticated, useful queries. This section deals specifically with building query criteria using operators and expressions. Some of the information in the remainder of this chapter parallels earlier discussions, but the context is specifically query design.

Knowing how to specify criteria is critical to designing and writing effective queries. Although queries can be used against a single table for a single criterion, many queries extract information from several tables using more complex criteria.

Because of this complexity, your queries are able to retrieve only the data you need, in the order that you need it. You might, for example, want to select and display data from the database to get the following information:

- All buyers of Chevy car or Ford truck models
- All buyers who have purchased something during the past 60 days
- All sales for items greater than $90
- The number of customers in each state
- Customers who have made comments or complaints

As your database system evolves, you'll want to retrieve subsets of information like these examples. Using operators and expressions, you create complex select queries to limit the number of records returned by the query. This section discusses select queries that use operators and expressions. Later, you'll apply this knowledge when working with forms, reports, and VBA code.

Chapter 8 gives an in-depth explanation of working with queries.

Using query comparison operators

When working with select queries, you may need to specify one or more criteria to limit the scope of information shown. You specify criteria by using comparison operators in equations and calculations. The categories of operators are mathematical, relational, logical, and string. In select queries, operators are used in either the Field cell or the Criteria cell of the Query by Example (QBE) pane.

Table 9.4 shows the most common operators used with select queries.

TABLE 9.4 Common Operators Used in Select Queries

Mathematical	Relational	Logical	String	Miscellaneous
* (multiply)	= (equal)	`And`	& (concatenate)	`Between...And`
/ (divide)	<> (not equal)	`Or`	`Like`	`In`
+ (add)	> (greater than)	`Not`	`Not Like`	`Is Null`
– (subtract)	< (less than)			`Is Not Null`

Using these operators, you can ferret out groups of records like these:

- Product records that include a picture
- A range of records, such as all sales between November and January
- Records that meet both `And` *and* `Or` criteria, such as all records that are cars and are not either a truck or an SUV
- All records that do *not* match a value, such as any category that is not a car

When you add criteria to a query, use the appropriate operator with an example of what you want. In Figure 9.1, the example is `Cars`. The operator is equal (=). Notice that the equal sign is *not* shown in the figure because it's the default operator for select queries.

FIGURE 9.1

The QBE pane shows a simple criterion asking for all models where the category is Cars.

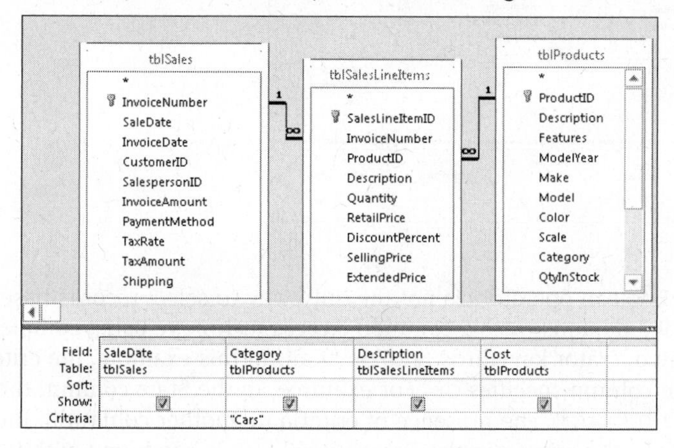

Understanding complex criteria

You build complex query criteria using any combination of the operators shown in Table 9.4. For many queries, complex criteria consist of a series of `And`s and `Or`s, as in these examples:

- State must be Connecticut *or* Texas.
- City must be Sunnyville *and* state must be Georgia.
- State must be MA *or* MO *and* city must be Springfield.

These examples demonstrate the use of both logical operators: `And/Or`. Many times, you can create complex criteria by entering example data in different cells of the QBE pane, as shown in Figure 9.2. In Figure 9.2, criteria is specified in both the State and Category columns. Within the State column, the criteria specifies "either California or Arizona," while the additional criteria in the Category column adds "not Cars." When combined, the criteria in the two columns limits the returned records to those where the customer state is either California or Arizona, and the product category is not cars.

FIGURE 9.2

Using `And` and `Or` criteria in a query.

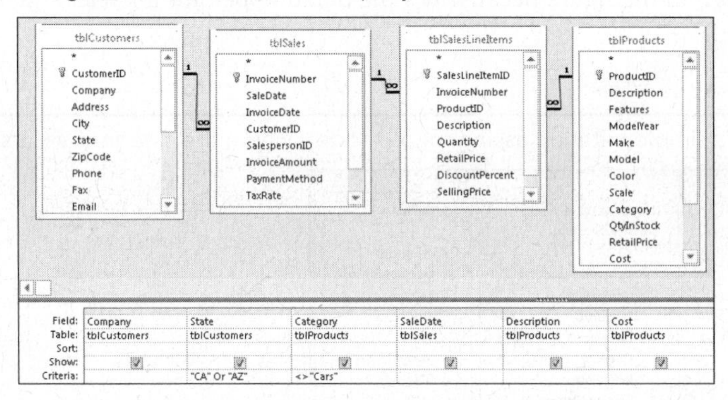

However, using explicit Boolean operators is not the only way to select records based on multiple criteria. Figure 9.3 demonstrates a common Access technique using complex criteria without entering the operator keywords `And/Or` at all. In this example, the criteria "stacked" within a single column specifies `Or`. For example, in the State column, the criteria is interpreted as `"CA" Or "AZ"`. The presence of criteria in another column in the QBE grid implies `And`. Therefore, the criteria in the Category column is combined with the state criteria and is interpreted as

```
(State = "CA" And Category <> "Cars") Or (State = "AZ" And Category <> "Cars")
```

In any case, the queries in Figures 9.2 and 9.3 are equivalent and return the same data.

FIGURE 9.3

Creating complex criteria without using the And/Or operators.

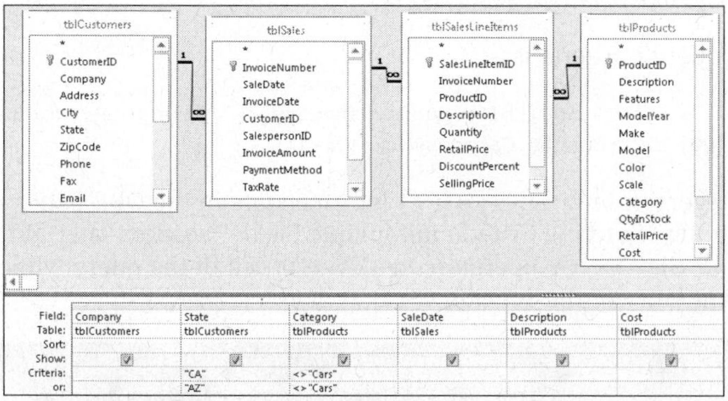
tblCustomers
CustomerID
Company
Address
City
State
ZipCode
Phone
Fax
Email
tblSales
InvoiceNumber
SaleDate
InvoiceDate
CustomerID
SalespersonID
InvoiceAmount
PaymentMethod
TaxRate
tblSalesLineItems
SalesLineItemID
InvoiceNumber
ProductID
Description
Quantity
RetailPrice
DiscountPercent
SellingPrice
tblProducts
ProductID
Description
Features
ModelYear
Make
Model
Color
Scale
Category
QtyInStock
RetailPrice
Cost
Field: Company State Category SaleDate Description Cost
Table: tblCustomers tblCustomers tblProducts tblSales tblProducts tblProducts
Sort:
Show:
Criteria: "CA" <> "Cars"
or: "AZ" <> "Cars"

One confusing aspect about the query in Figure 9.3 is that the criteria in the Category column must appear twice, once for each value in the State column. If the Category criteria appeared only once, perhaps in the same row as "AZ" in the State column, the combined criteria would be interpreted as

```
(State = "AZ" and Category <> "Cars") Or (State = "CA")
```

You learn how to create this type of complex query in the "Entering Criteria in Multiple Fields" section, later in this chapter.

TIP

In the QBE pane, enter And criteria in the same row and Or criteria in different rows.

Access takes your graphical query and creates a single SQL SELECT statement to actually extract the information from your tables. Click the drop-down in the ribbon's View group and select SQL View to change the window's contents to display the SQL SELECT statement (shown in Figure 9.4), which Access creates from the fields and criteria placed in the QBE pane in Figure 9.3.

9

FIGURE 9.4

The SQL view for the query in Figure 9.3. Notice that it contains a single OR and two AND operators (in the WHERE clause).

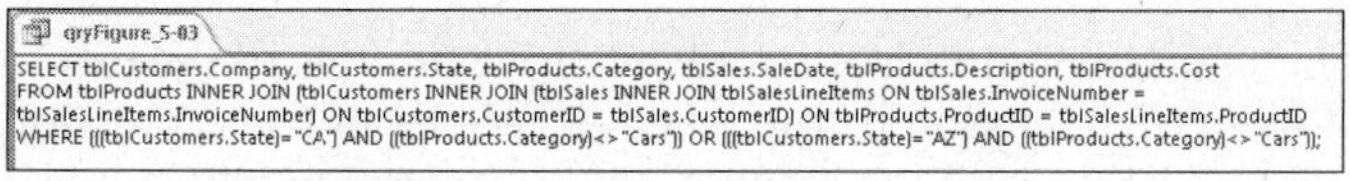
qryFigure_5-03
SELECT tblCustomers.Company, tblCustomers.State, tblProducts.Category, tblSales.SaleDate, tblProducts.Description, tblProducts.Cost
FROM tblProducts INNER JOIN (tblCustomers INNER JOIN (tblSales INNER JOIN tblSalesLineItems ON tblSales.InvoiceNumber =
tblSalesLineItems.InvoiceNumber) ON tblCustomers.CustomerID = tblSales.CustomerID) ON tblProducts.ProductID = tblSalesLineItems.ProductID
WHERE (((tblCustomers.State)="CA") AND ((tblProducts.Category)<>"Cars")) OR (((tblCustomers.State)="AZ") AND ((tblProducts.Category)<>"Cars"));

The SQL statement in Figure 9.4 has been slightly rearranged by the author for clarification purposes. When you switch to SQL view in your database, you'll see one long multiline statement with no breaks between sections.

An expression for this query's criteria is

```
(tblCustomers.State = "CT" AND tblProducts.Category <> "Cars") OR (tblCustomers.
  State = "MA" AND tblProducts.Category <> "Cars")
```

You must enter the category criteria (`<> "Cars"`) for each state in the QBE pane, as shown in Figure 9.3. In the "Entering Criteria in Multiple Fields" section, later in this chapter, you learn to use the `And/Or` operators in a Criteria cell of the query, which eliminates the redundant entry of these fields.

TIP

In this example, you looked for all models that didn't contain cars in the Category field. To find records that *do* match a value, drop the <> operator with the value. For example, enter Cars to find all records with Cars as the category. You don't have to use the equal sign in the QBE pane when working with select queries.

The `And/Or` operators are the most common operators when working with complex criteria. The operators consider two different expressions (one on each side of the `And/Or` operators) and then determine whether the expressions are true or false. Then the operators compare the results of the two expressions against each other for a logical true/false answer. For example, take the first `And` statement in the expression given in the preceding paragraph:

```
(tblCustomers.State = "CA" AND tblProducts.Category <> "Cars")
```

The right side of the criteria (`tblProducts.Category <> "Cars"`) evaluates to `True` if the Category is anything other than Cars. The `And` operator compares the logical true/false from the left and right expressions to return a true/false answer.

NOTE

A field has a null value when it has no value at all. Null indicates the lack of entry of information in a field. Null is neither true nor false, nor is it the same as a space character or 0. Null simply has no value. If you never enter a name in the City field and just skip it, Access leaves the field empty (unless a default value is provided in the table's design). This state of emptiness is known as null.

When the result of an `And/Or` operation is `True`, the overall condition is true, and the query displays the records meeting the true condition.

Notice that the result of an `And` operation is true only when *both* sides of the expression are true, whereas the result of an `Or` operation is true when *either* side of the expression is true. In fact, one side can be a null value, and the result of the `Or` operation will still be true if the other side is true. This is the fundamental difference between `And/Or` operators.

Using functions in select queries

When you work with queries, you might want to use built-in Access functions to display information. For example, you might want to display items such as

- The day of the week for sales dates
- All customer names in uppercase
- The difference between two date fields

You can display all this information by creating calculated fields for the query.

We discuss calculated fields in depth in detail in Chapter 12 (and throughout this book).

Referencing fields in select queries

When you work with a field's name in queries, most often you should enclose the name in square brackets ([]). Access requires brackets around any field name that's used as a query's criteria and around field names that contain spaces or punctuation characters. An example of a field name in brackets is

```
[tblSales].[SaleDate] + 30
```

In this example, 30 days is added to the SaleDate field in tblSales.

CAUTION

If you omit the brackets ([]) around a field name in the QBE grid, Access might place quotes around the field name and treat it as literal text instead of a field name.

9

Entering Single-Value Field Criteria

You'll encounter situations in which you want to limit the query records returned on the basis of a single field criterion, such as in these queries:

- Customer (buyer) information for customers living in New York
- Sales of truck models
- Customers who bought anything in the month of January

Each of these queries requires a single-value criterion. Simply put, a *single-value criterion* is the entry of only one expression in the QBE grid. The expression can be example data, such as `"CA"`, or a function, such as `DatePart("m",[SaleDate]) = 1`. Criteria expressions can be specified for virtually any data type: Text, Numeric, Date/Time, and so forth. Even OLE Object and Counter field types can have criteria specified.

Entering character (Text or Memo) criteria

You use character criteria for Text or Memo data-type fields. These are either examples or patterns of the contents of the field. To create a query that returns customers who live in New York, for example, follow these steps:

1. **Open a new query in Design view based on tblCustomers and add the FirstName, LastName, and State fields to the QBE pane.**
2. **Click the Criteria cell for State field.**
3. **Type** NY **in the cell.** Your query should look like Figure 9.5. Notice that only one table is open and only three fields are selected. Click the Datasheet View button in the Home Ribbon's Views group to see this query's results.

FIGURE 9.5

The query design window showing tblCustomers open.

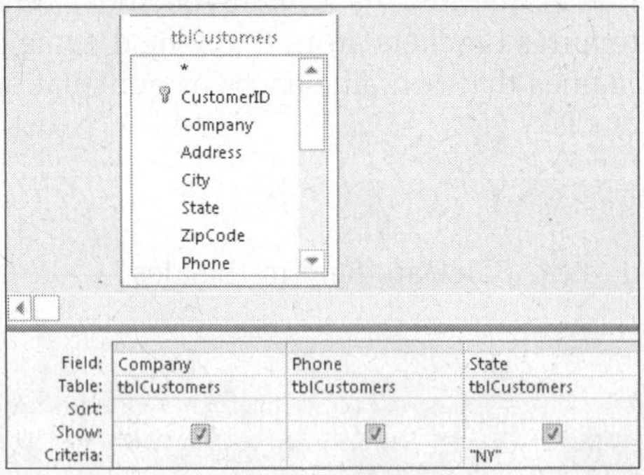

You don't have to enter an equal sign before the literal word NY because this is a select query. To see all states except New York, you must enter either the <> (not equal) or the `Not` operator before NY.

You also don't have to type quotes around NY. Access assumes that you're using a literal string NY and adds the quotes for you automatically.

Special considerations apply when data in the field contains quotation marks. For example, consider a query to find a person whose name is given as Robert "Bobby" Jones. Ideally, the contacts table would include a nickname field to capture "Bobby," but, in the absence of a nickname field, the data entry clerk may enter the first name as Robert "Bobby," using the quotation marks around "Bobby."

In this case, Access sees the double-quotation characters as data, and you may want to include the quotes in the criteria. The simplest solution is to use a criteria expression such as the following:

```
'Robert "Bobby"'
```

Notice the single quotes surrounding the criteria string. Access correctly interprets the single quotes as delimiting characters, and understands that the double quotes within the single quotes are just data. You shouldn't use an expression such as the following:

```
"Robert 'Bobby'"
```

This is, of course, the opposite use of quotation marks as the previous example. In this case, Access expects to find single quotes around "Bobby" in the first name field, and no records will be returned.

The Like operator and wildcards

In previous sections, you worked with *literal* criteria. You specified the exact field contents for Access to find, which was NY in the previous example. Access used the literal to retrieve the records. Sometimes, however, you know only a part of the field contents, or you might want to see a wider range of records on the basis of a pattern.

For example, you might want to see all product information for items with "convertible" in the description. Many different makes and models may be convertibles, and there's no field where "convertible" will work by itself as the query's criteria. You'll need to use wildcards to make sure you successfully select all records containing "convertible" in the description.

Here's another example: Suppose you have a buyer who has purchased a couple of red models in the last year. You remember making a note of it in the Notes field about the color, but you don't remember which customer it was. To find these records, you're required to use a wildcard search against the Notes field in tblCustomers to find records that contain the word *red*.

Use the `Like` operator in the Criteria cell of a field to perform wildcard searches against the field's contents. Access searches for a pattern in the field; you use the question mark (`?`) to represent a single character or the asterisk (`*`) for several characters. In addition to `?` and `*`, Access uses three other characters for wildcard searches. The table in the "Using Wildcards" sidebar, earlier in this chapter, lists the wildcards that the `Like` operator can use.

The question mark (`?`) stands for any single character located in the same position as the question mark in the example expression. An asterisk (`*`) stands for any number of characters in the same position in which the asterisk is placed. The pound sign (`#`) stands for a single digit (0–9) found in the position occupied by the pound sign. The brackets (`[]`) and the list they enclose stand for any single character that matches any one character in the list located within the brackets. Finally, the exclamation point (`!`) inside the brackets represents the `Not` operator for the list — that is, any single character that does *not* match any character in the list.

9

These wildcards can be used alone or in conjunction with each other. They can even be used multiple times within the same expression.

To create an example using the `Like` operator, let's suppose you want to find the customer who likes red model cars. You know that *red* is used in one of the Notes field in tblCustomers. To create the query, follow these steps:

1. **Add tblCustomers, tblSales, tblSalesLineItems, and tblProducts to the query.**
2. **Add Company and Notes from tblCustomers, SalesDate from tblSales, and Description from tblProducts to the QBE pane.**
3. **Click the Criteria cell of the Notes field and enter** * red * **as the criteria.** Be sure to put a space between the first asterisk and the *r* and the last asterisk and the *d* — in other words, put spaces before and after the word *red.*

TIP

In the preceding steps, you put a space before and after the word *red.* If you didn't, Access would find all words that have the word *red* in them — like *aired, bored, credo, fired, geared, restored,* and on and on. By placing a space before and after the word *red,* Access is being told to look for the word *red* only.

You may point out that if the Notes field starts with the word *Red* (as in "Red cars are the customer's preference"), Access would not include this record because the word *Red* is not preceded by a space. You're right!

You should expect to have to experiment a bit when you build the criteria for your queries. Because the data in your tables (especially text fields) can be unpredictable, you may have to create several queries to capture every scenario. In this case, you could create a supplemental query with the criteria to `"red *"` to try to capture this record.

There is, however, one issue with this example. Notice that the criteria (`"* red *"`) requires a space after the word *red.* This means that a record containing the following note will not be returned by this query:

> Customer wants any model of car, as long as it's red!

Because there is no space immediately after *red,* this record will be missed. The proper criteria to use is

```
Like "* red[ ,.!?]"
```

The brackets around " ,.!?" instruct Access to select records when the Notes field ends with the word *red,* followed by a space or punctuation character. Obviously, there may be other characters to consider within the brackets, and you must have a good idea of the variety of data in the queried field.

When you click outside the Criteria cell, Access automatically adds the `Like` operator and the quotation marks around the expression. Your query QBE pane should look like Figure 9.6.

FIGURE 9.6

Using the `Like` operator in a select query.

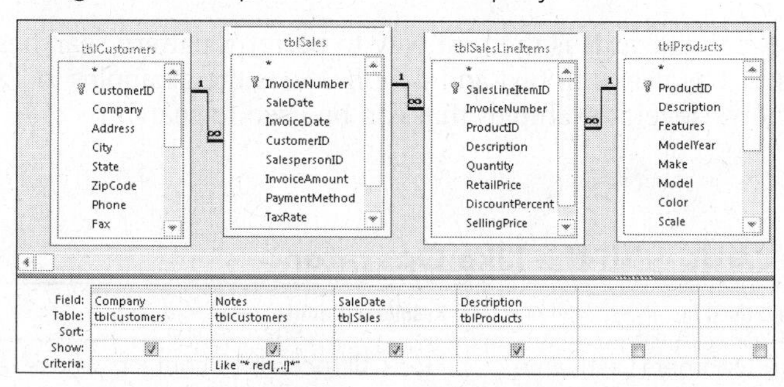

After creating this query, click on the Datasheet View command to view the query's results. It should look like Figure 9.7.

FIGURE 9.7

The results of using the `Like` operator with a select query in a Memo field. The query looks for the word *red* in the Features field.

Company	Notes	SaleDate	Description
Terriffic Toys	I'd prefer cars that were red, blue or yellow.	11/6/2012	Ford Fairlane
Carmen's Collectibles	Customer wants any model of car, as long as it's red!	11/17/2012	Chevrolet Bel Air
Carmen's Collectibles	Customer wants any model of car, as long as it's red!	11/17/2012	Chevrolet 150
Carmen's Collectibles	Customer wants any model of car, as long as it's red!	11/17/2012	Volkswagen Beetle
Rockin And Rollin	Seems to like red models.	12/26/2012	Ford Galaxy 500
Rockin And Rollin	Seems to like red models.	12/26/2012	Ford Convertible
Rockin And Rollin	Seems to like red models.	12/26/2012	Ford Galaxy 500
Rockin And Rollin	Seems to like red models.	1/13/2013	Buick T-Type
Carmen's Collectibles	Customer wants any model of car, as long as it's red!	3/29/2013	Ford Convertible
Carmen's Collectibles	Customer wants any model of car, as long as it's red!	5/9/2013	Honda F1 RA272
Terriffic Toys	I'd prefer cars that were red, blue or yellow.	6/30/2013	Chevrolet Bel Air
Terriffic Toys	I'd prefer cars that were red, blue or yellow.	6/30/2013	Lincoln Continental Limo
Terriffic Toys	I'd prefer cars that were red, blue or yellow.	6/30/2013	Honda F1 RA272
Terriffic Toys	I'd prefer cars that were red, blue or yellow.	7/13/2013	Lincoln Presidental Limo

If you click the Datasheet View command on the Ribbon, you see that a number of records match your query's criteria. The recordset returned by this query includes redundant information in the Company and Notes columns, but the redundancy is the result of asking for this information along with the sales and product data.

Access automatically adds the `Like` operator and quotation marks if you meet these conditions:

- Your expression contains no spaces.
- You use only the wildcards `?`, `*`, or `#`.
- You use brackets (`[]`) inside quotation marks (`" "`).

If you use the brackets without quotation marks, you must supply the `Like` operator and the quotation marks.

Using the `Like` operator with wildcards is the best way to perform pattern searches through memo fields. It's just as useful in text and date fields as the examples in Table 9.5 demonstrate. Table 9.5 shows several examples that can be used to search records in the tables of the database.

TABLE 9.5 Using Wildcards with the Like Operator

Expression	Field Used In	Results of Criteria
`Like "Ca*"`	tblCustomers.LastName	Finds all records of contacts whose last name begins with Ca (for example, Carson and Casey).
`Like "* red *"`	tblProducts.Features	Finds all records of products with the word *red* anywhere within the Features field.
`Like "C*"`	tblSales.PaymentMethod	Finds all sales that were paid for by check or credit card.
`Like "## South Main"`	tblCustomers.Address	Finds all records of contacts with houses containing house numbers between 10 and 99 inclusively (for example, 10, 22, 33, 51 on South Main).
`Like "[CDF]*"`	tblCustomers.City	Finds all records of contacts for customers who live in any city with a name beginning with *C*, *D*, or *F*.
`Like "[!EFG]*"`	tblCustomers.City	Finds all records of contacts who live in any city with a name beginning with any letter except *E*, *F*, or *G*.

Specifying non-matching values

To specify a non-matching value, you simply use either the `Not` or the <> operator in front of the expression that you don't want to match. For example, you might want to see all contacts who have purchased a vehicle, but you want to exclude buyers from New York. Follow these steps to see how to specify this non-matching value:

1. **Open a new query in Design view, and add tblCustomers.**
2. **Add Company and State from tblCustomers.**
3. **Click in the Criteria cell of State.**
4. **Type** < > NY **in the cell.** Access automatically places quotation marks around NY if you don't do so before you leave the field. The query should look like Figure 9.8. The query selects all records *except* those for buyers who live in the state of New York.

FIGURE 9.8

Using the `Not` operator in criteria.

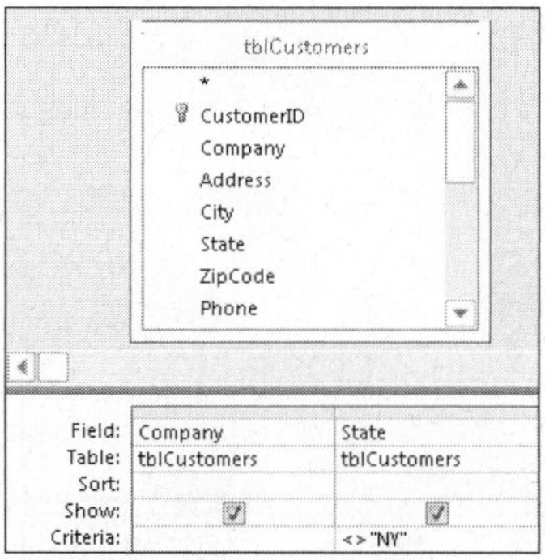

> **NOTE**
> You can use the `Not` operator instead of <> in Step 4 of the previous instructions to exclude New York (NY). The result is the same with either operator. These two operators are interchangeable except with the use of the keyword `Is`. You can't say `Is <> Null`. Instead, you must say `Not Is Null` or, more accurately, `Is Not Null`.

Entering numeric criteria

You use numeric criteria with numeric or currency data-type fields. You simply enter the numbers and the decimal symbol — if required — following the mathematical or comparison operator (but don't use commas!). For example, you might want to see all sales where the product's inventory count is less than six:

1. **Open a new query in Design view, and add tblProducts.**
2. **Add ProductID, Description, Make, Model, and QtyInStock from tblProducts to the QBE grid.**
3. **Click in the Sort cell for Make and select Ascending from the drop-down list.**
4. **Click in the Criteria cell for QtyInStock and enter** < 10 **in the cell.** Your query looks like Figure 9.9. When working with numeric data, Access doesn't enclose the expression with quotes, as it does with string criteria.

The criteria applied to numeric fields usually includes comparison operators, such as less than (<), greater than (>), or equal to (=). If you want to specify a comparison other than equal, you must enter the operator as well as the value. Remember that Access defaults to equal when running a select query. That's why you needed to specify `<10` in the QtyInStock column in the example shown in Figure 9.9.

FIGURE 9.9

Criteria set for products with low inventory.

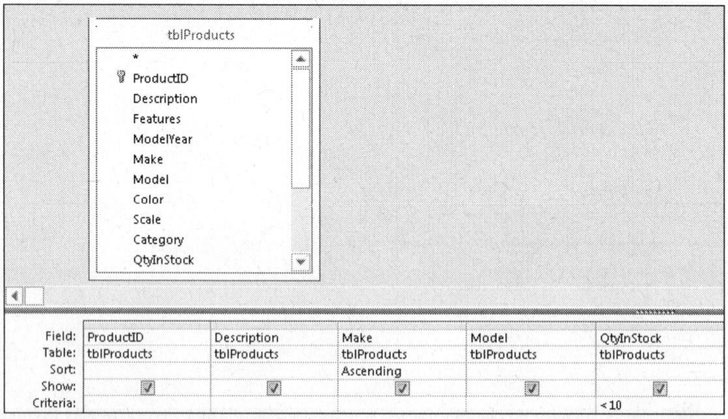

Access does not surround the criteria with quotes because QtyInStock is numeric and requires no delimiter.

Entering true or false criteria

True and false criteria are used with Yes/No type fields. The example data that you supply as criteria must evaluate to true or false. You can also use the `Not` and the <> operators to signify the opposite, but the Yes/No data also has a null state that you might want to consider. Access recognizes several forms of true and false.

Thus, instead of typing **Yes**, you can type any of these in the Criteria: cell: **On**, **True**, **Not No**, **< > No**, **< No**, or **-1**.

NOTE

A Yes/No field can have three states: Yes, No, and Null. Null only occurs when no default value was set in a table and the value has not yet been entered. Checking for `Is Null` displays only records containing `Null` in the field, and checking for `Is Not Null` always displays all records with `Yes` or `No` in the field. After a Yes/No field check box is checked (or checked and then deselected), it can never be `Null`. It must be either `Yes` or `No` (-1 or 0).

Entering OLE object criteria

You can specify criteria for OLE objects: `Is Null` or `Is Not Null`. For example, suppose you don't have pictures for all the products and you want to view only those records that have a picture — that is, those in which the picture is not null. You specify the `Is Not Null` criterion for the Picture field of tblProducts.

TIP

Although `Is Not Null` is the correct syntax, you can also use `Not Null` in the QBE grid and Access supplies the `Is` operator for you.

Using Multiple Criteria in a Query

In previous sections of this chapter, you worked with single-condition criteria on a single field. As you learned in those sections, you can specify single-condition criteria for any field type. In this section, you work with multiple criteria based on a single field. For example, you might be interested in seeing all records in which the buyer comes from New York, California, or Arizona. Or maybe you want to view the records of all the products sold during the first quarter of the year 2012.

The QBE pane has the flexibility to solve these types of problems. You can specify criteria for several fields in a select query. Using multiple criteria, for example, you can determine which products were sold for the past 90 days. Either of the following expressions could be used as criteria in the SaleDate field's criteria:

```
Between Date() And Date() - 90
Between Date() And DateAdd("d",-90,Date())
```

Of these, the expression using the `DateAdd` function is less ambiguous and more specific to the task.

We delver deeper into the topic of creating calculations with dates in Chapter 12.

Understanding an Or operation

You use an `Or` operator in queries when you want a field to meet either of two conditions. For example, you might want to see all the records where the customer lives in either New York or California. In other words, you want to see all records where a customer lives in NY, in CA, or both. The general expression for this operation is

```
[State] = "NY" Or [State] = "CA"
```

If either side of this expression is true, the resulting answer is also true. To clarify this point, consider these conditions:

- Customer 1 lives in NY — the expression is true.
- Customer 2 lives in CA — the expression is true.
- Customer 3 lives in NY and CA — the expression is true.
- Customer 4 lives in CT — the expression is false.

9

Specifying multiple values with the Or operator

The `Or` operator is used to specify multiple values for a field. For example, you use the `Or` operator if you want to see all records of buyers who live in CT or NJ or NY. To do this, follow these steps:

1. **Open a new query in Design view, and add tblCustomers and tblSales.**
2. **Add Company and State from tblCustomers and SalesDate from tblSales.**
3. **Click in the Sort cell of State.**
4. **Select Ascending from the drop-down list.**
5. **Click in the Criteria cell of State.**
6. **Type** AZ Or CA Or NY **in the cell.** Your QBE pane should resemble the one shown in Figure 9.10. Access automatically places quotation marks around your example data — AZ, CA, and NY.

FIGURE 9.10

Using the `Or` operator. Notice the two `Or` operators under the State field — `AZ Or CA Or NY`.

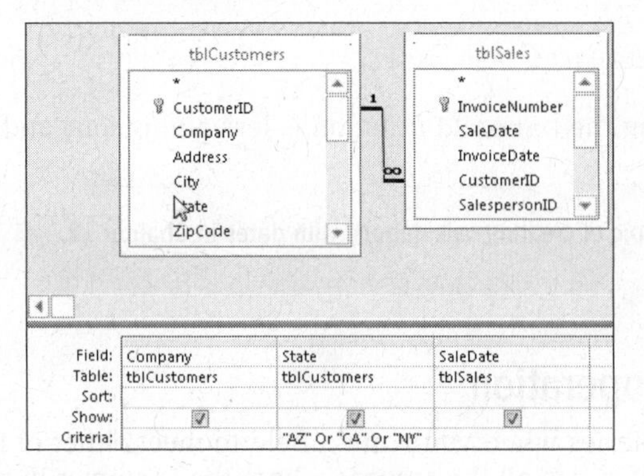

Using the Or cell of the QBE pane

Besides using the literal `Or` operator as a single expression on the Criteria row under the `State` field, you can supply individual criteria for the field vertically on separate rows of the QBE pane, as shown in Figure 9.11.

FIGURE 9.11

Using the Or cell of the QBE pane. You can place criteria vertically in the QBE grid.

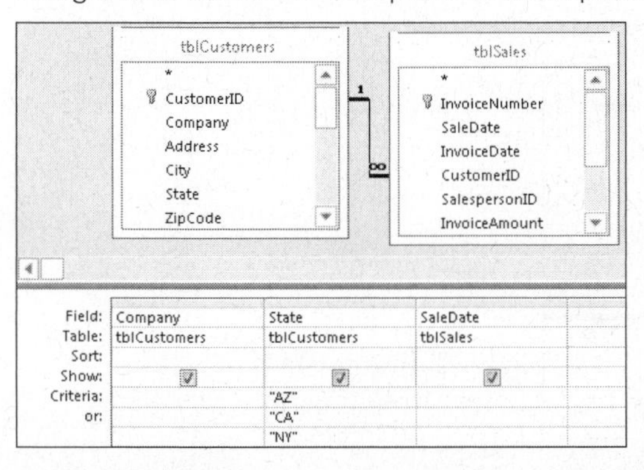

TIP

Access allows up to nine Or cells for each field. If you need to specify more `Or` conditions, use the `Or` operator between conditions (for example, `AZ Or CA Or NY Or PA`).

Access rearranges the design shown in Figure 9.11 when the query is saved to match the query in Figure 9.10. In fact, when you open `qryFigure_9-11` in the `Chapter09.accdb` example database, you'll see that it is exactly the same as `qryFigure_9-10` because of the way Access rearranged the criteria when `qryFigure_9-11` was originally saved. When you build a query using "vertical" `Or` criteria, Access optimizes the SQL statement behind the query by placing all the `Or` criteria into a single expression.

Using a list of values with the In operator

Another method for specifying multiple values of a single field is using the `In` operator. The `In` operator finds a value from a list of values. For example, use the expression `IN(AZ, CA, NY)` under the `State` field in the query used in Figure 9.11. The list of values in the parentheses becomes an example criterion. Your query should resemble the query shown in Figure 9.12.

Access automatically adds quotation marks around AZ, CA, and NY.

NOTE

When you work with the `In` operator, each value (example data) must be separated from the others by a comma.

FIGURE 9.12

Using the `In` operator to find all records for buyer state being either AZ, CA, or NY.

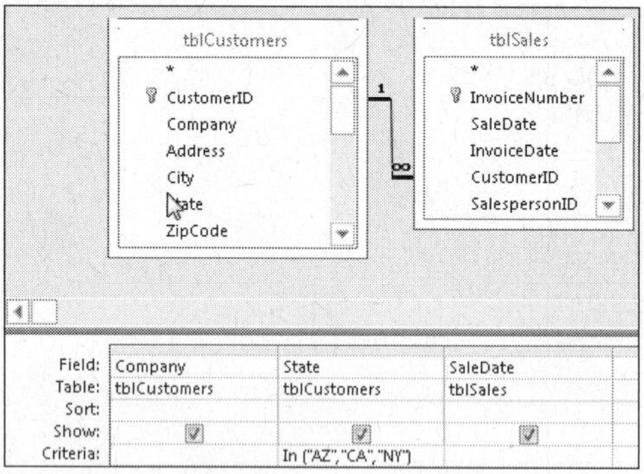

Using And to specify a range

The `And` operator is frequently used in fields that have numeric or date/time data types. It's seldom used with text data types, although it can be this way in some situations. For example, you might be interested in viewing all buyers whose names start with the letters *d*, *e*, or *f*. The `And` operator can be used here (`>="D" And <="F"`), although the `Like` operator is better (`Like "[DEF]*"`) because it's much easier to understand.

You use the `And` operator in queries when you want a field to meet two or more conditions that you specify. For example, you might want to see records of buyers that have purchased products between October 1, 2012, and March 31, 2013. In other words, the sale had to have occurred during the last quarter of the year 2012 and the first quarter of 2013. The general expression for this example is

```
(SaleDate >= 10/1/2012) And (SaleDate <= 3/31/2013)
```

NOTE

Parentheses are included in this example for clarity.

Unlike the `Or` operation (which has several conditions under which it is true), the `And` operation is true only when *both* sides of the expression are true. To clarify use of the `And` operator, consider these conditions:

- `SaleDate` (9/22/2012) is not greater than 10/01/2012 but is less than 3/31/2013 — the result is false.
- `SaleDate` (4/11/2013) is greater than 10/01/2012 but is not less than 3/31/2013 — the result is false.
- `SaleDate` (11/22/2012) is greater than 10/01/2012 and less than 3/31/2013 — the result is true.

Using an And operator with a single field sets a range of acceptable values in the field. Therefore, the key purpose of an And operator in a single field is to define a range of records to be viewed. For example, you can use the And operator to create a range criterion to display all buyers who have purchased products between October 1, 2012, and March 31, 2013, inclusively. To create this query, follow these steps:

1. **Create a new query using tblCustomers and tblSales.**
2. **Add Company from tblCustomers and SaleDate from tblSales.**
3. **Click in the Criteria cell of SaleDate.**
4. **Type** > = #10/1/2012# And < = #3/31/2013# **in the cell.** The query should resemble Figure 9.13.

FIGURE 9.13

Using an And operator to specify complex query criteria.

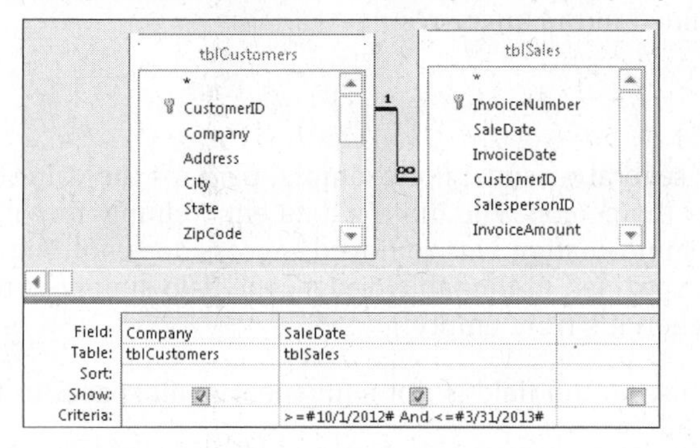

Notice the pound signs (#) used to delimit the dates in the expressions on both sides of the And operator. Access recognizes pound signs as delimiters for date and time values. Without the pound signs, Access evaluates the date values as numeric expressions (10 divided by 1 divided by 2012, for example).

Using the Between...And operator

You can request a range of records using another method — the Between...And operator. With Between...And, you can find records that meet a range of values — for example, all sales where the list price of the product was $50 or $100. Using the previous example, create the query shown in Figure 9.14.

9

FIGURE 9.14

Using the `Between...And` operator. The results are the same as the query in Figure 9.13.

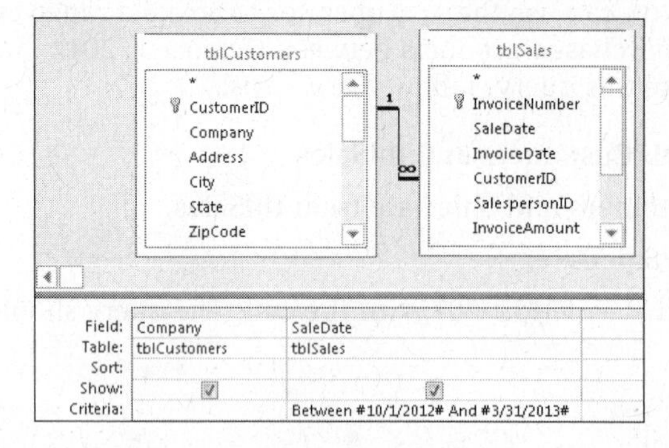

The operands for the `Between...And` operator are inclusive. This means that sales on 10/1/2012 and 3/31/2013 are included in the query results.

Searching for null data

A field might have no contents for several reasons: For example, perhaps the value wasn't known at the time of data entry, or the person who did the data entry simply forgot to enter the information, or the field's information was removed. Access does nothing with this field. Unless a default value is specified in the table design, the field simply remains empty. (A field is said to be *null* when it's truly empty.)

Logically, null is neither true nor false. A full field is not equivalent to all spaces or to zero. A null field simply has no value.

What Is a Null Value?

Databases must work with all kinds of information. We're all familiar with text, numeric, date, and other types of data, and in most cases, the value is known. For example, we almost certainly know a new employee's first and last name, but we may not yet know his middle name. How does a database represent a value that is unknown and that may, in fact, not exist? That's where *null* comes in. By default, most fields in a database table are null until a value is provided. The value may come from a user entering a value on a form, or it may be provided through the field's default value property. If we learn that the employee doesn't have a middle name, we may enter an empty string (" ") in the field holding the middle name. In this case, an empty string means that there is no middle name. But as long as the value is unknown, the field is null.

Access lets you work with null value fields by means of two special operators:

```
Is Null                 Is Not Null
```

You use these operators to limit criteria based on the null state of a field. Earlier in this chapter, you learned that a null value can be used to query for products having a picture on file. In the next example, you look for buyers that don't have the Notes field filled in:

1. **Create a new query using tblCustomers and tblSales.**
2. **Add Notes and Company from tblCustomers, and SaleDate from tblSales.**
3. **Enter** Is Null **as the criteria in the Notes field.**
4. **Uncheck the Show box in the Notes field.**

Your query should look like Figure 9.15. Select the Datasheet View command to see the records that don't have a value in the Notes field.

You unchecked the Show box because there is no need to display the Notes field in the query results. The criteria selects only those rows where the Notes field is null, so there is, quite literally, nothing to see in the Notes field and no reason to display it in the results.

FIGURE 9.15

Use `Is Null` to select rows containing fields that contain no data.

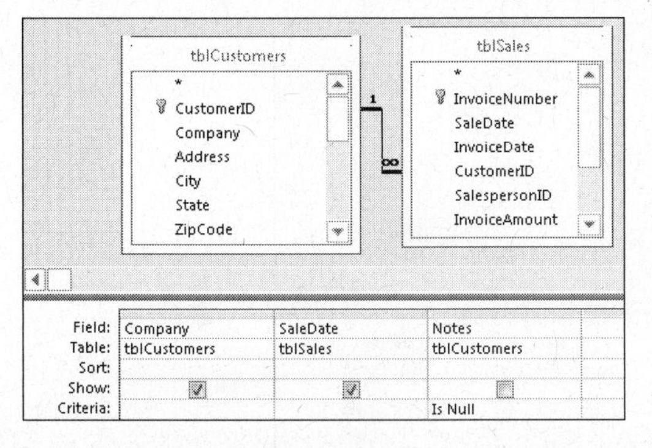

TIP

When using the `Is Null` and `Is Not Null` operators, you can enter Null or Not Null and Access automatically adds the `Is` to the Criteria field.

Entering Criteria in Multiple Fields

Earlier in this chapter, you worked with single and multiple criteria specified in single fields. In this section, you work with criteria across several fields. When you want to limit the records based on several field conditions, you do so by setting criteria in each of the fields that will be used for the scope. Suppose you want to search for all sales of models to resellers in Kansas. Or suppose you want to search for motorcycle model buyers in Massachusetts or Connecticut. Or suppose you want to search for all motorcycle buyers in Massachusetts or trucks in Connecticut. Each of these queries requires placing criteria in multiple fields and on multiple lines.

Using And and Or across fields in a query

To use the `And` operator and the `Or` operator across fields, place your example or pattern data in the Criteria cells (for the `And` operator) and the Or cells of one field relative to the placement in another field. When you want to use `And` between two or more fields, you place the example or pattern data across the same row in the QBE pane. When you want to use `Or` between two fields, you place the criteria on different rows in the QBE pane. Figure 9.16 shows the QBE pane and a rather extreme example of this placement.

FIGURE 9.16

The QBE pane with `And`/`Or` criteria between fields using the Criteria and Or rows.

tblProducts
*
ProductID
Description
Features
ModelYear
Make
Model
Color

Field:	ModelYear	Make	Model	Color	Category
Table:	tblProducts	tblProducts	tblProducts	tblProducts	tblProducts
Sort:					
Show:	☑	☑	☑	☑	☑
Criteria:	"1932"	"Ford"	"Coupe"		
or:				"Green"	
					"Cars"

The query in Figure 9.16 displays a record if a value matches any of the following criteria:

- ModelYear = 1932 `And` Make = Ford `And` Model = Coupe (all must be true).
- Color = Green (this can be true even if and either or both of the other two lines are false).
- Category = Cars (this can be true even if and either or both of the other two lines are false).

As long as one of these three criteria is true, the record appears in the query's results.

Here's the SQL statement behind the query in Figure 9.16:

```
SELECT ModelYear, Make, Model, Color, Category
FROM tblProducts
WHERE ((ModelYear="1932") AND (Make="Ford") AND (Model="Coupe"))
OR (Color="Green")
OR (Category="Cars")
```

The locations of the parentheses in this SQL statement are significant. One set of parentheses surrounds the criteria for Field1, Field2, and Field3, while parentheses surround each of the criteria applied to Field4 and Field5. This means, of course, that ModelYear, Make, and Model are applied as a group, while Color and Category are included individually.

Specifying Or criteria across fields of a query

Although the `Or` operator isn't used across fields as commonly as the `And` operator, occasionally `Or` is very useful. For example, you might want to see records of any models bought by contacts in Connecticut or you might want to see records on truck models, regardless of the state the customers live in. To create this query, follow these steps:

1. **Add tblCustomers, tblSales, tblSalesLineItems, and tblProducts to a new query.**
2. **Add Company and State from tblCustomers, and Description and Category from tblProducts.**
3. **Enter** `CT` **as the criteria for State.**
4. **Enter** Trucks **in the Or cell under Category.** Your query should resemble Figure 9.17. Notice that the criteria entered are not in the same row of the QBE pane for State and Category. When you place criteria on different rows in the QBE grid, Access interprets this as an `Or` between the fields. This query returns customers who either live in Connecticut or have bought truck models.

9

FIGURE 9.17

Using the `Or` operator between fields.

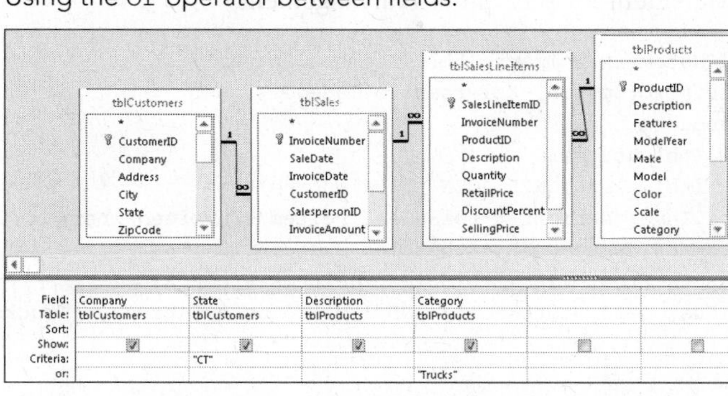

Here's the SQL statement behind the query in Figure 9.17:

```
SELECT tblCustomers.Company, tblCustomers.State,
tblProducts.Description, tblProducts.Category
FROM tblProducts
INNER JOIN (tblCustomers
INNER JOIN (tblSales INNER JOIN tblSalesLineItems
ON tblSales.InvoiceNumber = tblSalesLineItems.InvoiceNumber)
ON tblCustomers.CustomerID = tblSales.CustomerID)
ON tblProducts.ProductID = tblSalesLineItems.ProductID
WHERE (tblCustomers.State="CT") OR (tblProducts.Category="Trucks")
```

Notice the placement of parentheses in the `WHERE` clause. Either condition (`State = "CT"` or `Category="Trucks"`) can be true, and the record is returned by the query.

Moving "Trucks" to the same row as "CT" in the QBE grid changes the query's logic to return customers who live in Connecticut *and* have bought truck models. The rearranged query is shown in Figure 9.18.

FIGURE 9.18

A simple rearrangement in the QBE grid results in a very different query.

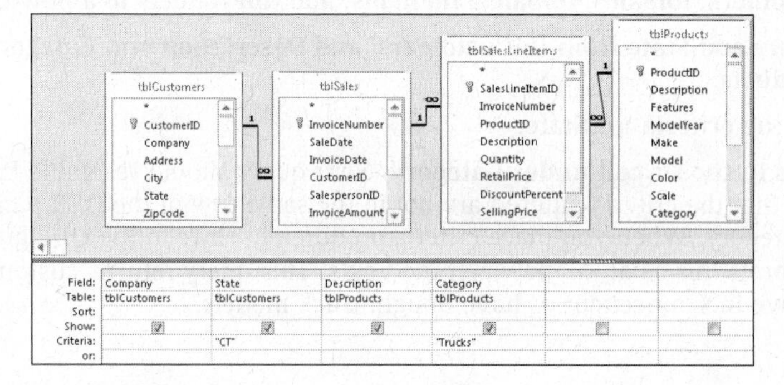

Here's the SQL statement for this minor rearrangement:

```
SELECT tblCustomers.Company, tblCustomers.State,
tblProducts.Description, tblProducts.Category
FROM tblProducts
INNER JOIN (tblCustomers
INNER JOIN (tblSales INNER JOIN tblSalesLineItems
ON tblSales.InvoiceNumber = tblSalesLineItems.InvoiceNumber)
ON tblCustomers.CustomerID = tblSales.CustomerID)
ON tblProducts.ProductID = tblSalesLineItems.ProductID
WHERE (tblCustomers.State="CT") AND (tblProducts.Category="Trucks")
```

The difference is significant because the rearrangement is considerably more restrictive when returning records. Only one record is returned by `qryFigure_5-18`, while `qryFigure5-17` returns 17 rows.

Using And and Or together in different fields

After you've worked with `And` and `Or` separately, you're ready to create a query using `And` and `Or` in different fields. In the next example, the query displays records for all buyers of motorcycle models in Connecticut and buyers of truck models in New York:

1. **Use the query from the previous example, emptying the two criteria cells first.**
2. **Enter** CT **in the Criteria row in the State column.**
3. **Enter** NY **in the or row under CT in QBE grid.**
4. **Type** Motorcycles **as criteria in the Category field.**
5. **Enter** Trucks **under Motorcycles in the Category field.** Figure 9.19 shows how the query should look. Notice that CT and Motorcycle are in the same row; NY and Trucks are in another row. This query represents two `And`s across fields, with an `Or` in each field.

FIGURE 9.19

Using `Ands` and `Ors` in a select query.

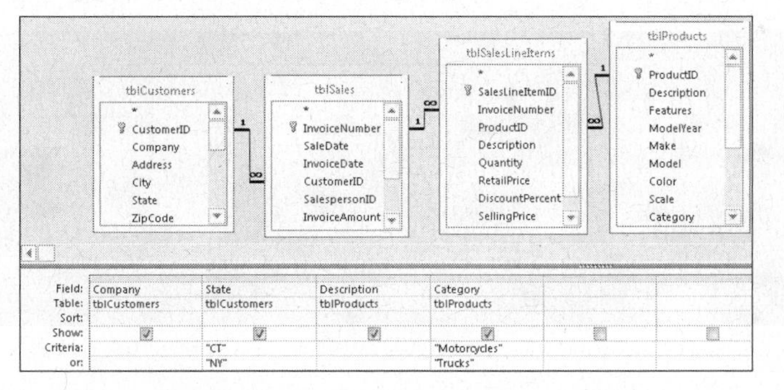

The important thing to notice about this query is that Access returns, essentially, two sets of data: motorcycle model owners in Connecticut and truck model owners in New York. All other customers and model combinations are ignored.

A complex query on different lines

Suppose you want to view all records of Chevy models bought in the first six months of 2012 where the buyer lives in Massachusetts or any type of vehicle from buyers in

California. In this example, you use two fields for setting criteria: tblCustomers.State and tblSales.SaleDate. Here's the expression for setting these criteria:

```
((tblSales.SaleDate Between #1/1/2012# And #6/30/2012#) And (tblProducts.
   Description = Like "*Chev*" ) And (tblCustomers.State = "MA")) OR
   (tblCustomers.State = "CA")
```

The query design is shown in Figure 9.20.

FIGURE 9.20

Using multiple Ands and Ors across fields. This is a rather complex select query.

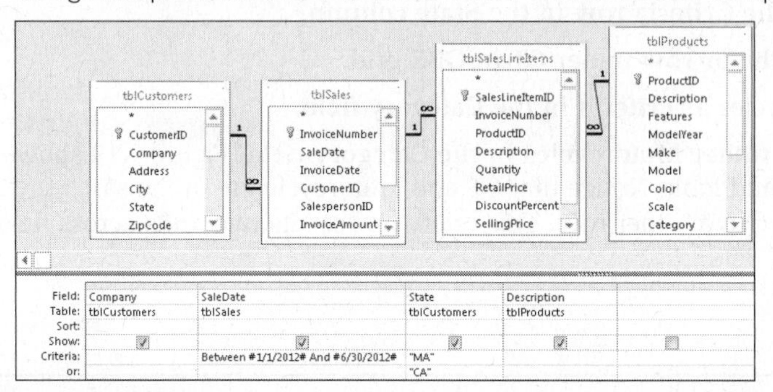

> **CAUTION**
>
> Be aware that Access interprets dates based on the region and language settings in the Control Panel. Those settings could tell Access to interpret short dates as mm/dd/yyyy or dd/mm/yyyy depending on the region. Make sure that you account for these regional differences when working with dates.
>
> Also, keep in mind that Access, by default, interprets two-digit years from 00 to 30 as 2000 to 2030, while all two-digit years between 31 and 99 are taken to be 1931 to 1999. This is one reason why consistently using four-digit years during data entry is always a good idea.

CHAPTER

10

Going Beyond Select Queries

IN THIS CHAPTER

Working with aggregate queries

Using action queries

Considering crosstab queries

Retrieving and displaying specific records with a select query is indeed a fundamental task when analyzing data in Access. However, it's just a small portion of what makes up data analysis. The scope of data analysis is broad and includes grouping and comparing data, updating and deleting data, performing calculations on data, and shaping and reporting data. Access has built-in tools and functionalities designed specifically to handle each one of these tasks.

In this chapter, we give you an in-depth look at the various tools available to you in Access and how they can help you go beyond select queries.

On the Web

The starting database for this walkthrough, `Chapter10.accdb`, can be downloaded from this book's website.

Aggregate Queries

An aggregate query, sometimes referred to as a group-by query, is a type of query you can build to help you quickly group and summarize your data. With a select query, you can retrieve records only as they appear in your data source. But with an aggregate query, you can retrieve a summary snapshot of your data that shows you totals, averages, counts, and more.

Creating an aggregate query

To get a firm understanding of what an aggregate query does, take the following scenario as an example: You've just been asked to provide the sum of total revenue by period. In response to this request, start a query in Design view and bring in the Period and LineTotal fields as shown in Figure 10.1. If you run this query as is, you'll get every record in your dataset instead of the summary you need.

FIGURE 10.1

Running this query will return all the records in your dataset, not the summary you need.

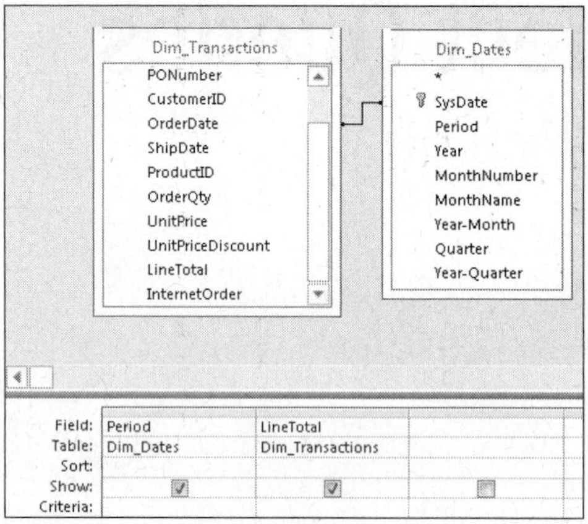

> **TIP**
>
> Here's a quick reminder on how to start a query in Design view: Go to the Ribbon and select the Create tab. From there, select Query Design. The Show Table Dialog box opens on top of a blank Query Design view. Select the table(s) you need to work with.

If you need more information, refer back to Chapter 8 for a quick refresher on the basics of Access queries.

In order to get a summary of revenue by period, you'll need to activate Totals in your design grid. To do this, go up to the Ribbon and select the Design tab and then click the Totals button. As you can see in Figure 10.2, after you've activated Totals in your design grid, you'll see a new row in your grid called Totals. The Totals row tells Access which aggregate function to use when performing aggregation on the specified fields.

Notice that the Totals row contains the words *group by* under each field in your grid. This means that all similar records in a field will be grouped to provide you with a unique data item. We'll cover the different aggregate functions in depth later in this chapter.

The idea here is to adjust the aggregate functions in the Totals row to correspond with the analysis you're trying perform. In this scenario, you need to group all the periods in your dataset, and then sum the revenue in each period. Therefore, you'll need to use the `Group By` aggregate function for the Period field, and the `Sum` aggregate function for the LineTotal field.

Since the default selection for Totals is the `Group By` function, no change is needed for the Period field. However, you'll need to change the aggregate function for the LineTotal field from `Group By` to `Sum`. This tells Access that you want to sum the revenue figures in the

LineTotal field, not group them. To change the aggregate function, simply click the Totals drop-down list under the LineTotal field, shown in Figure 10.3, and select Sum. At this point, you can run your query.

FIGURE 10.2

Activating Totals in your design grid adds a Totals row to your query grid that defaults to "group by."

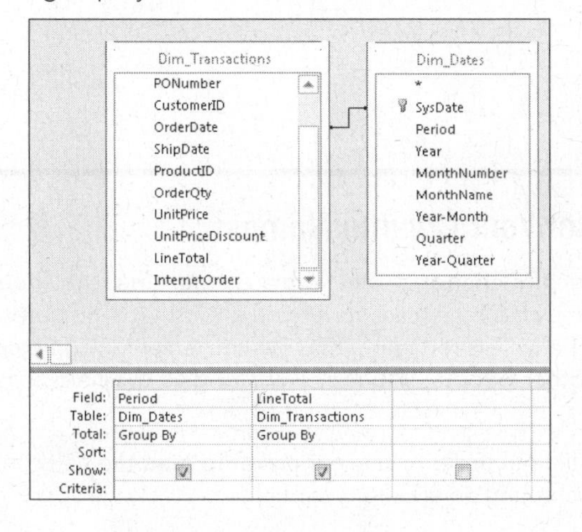

FIGURE 10.3

Change the aggregate function under the LineTotal field to `Sum`.

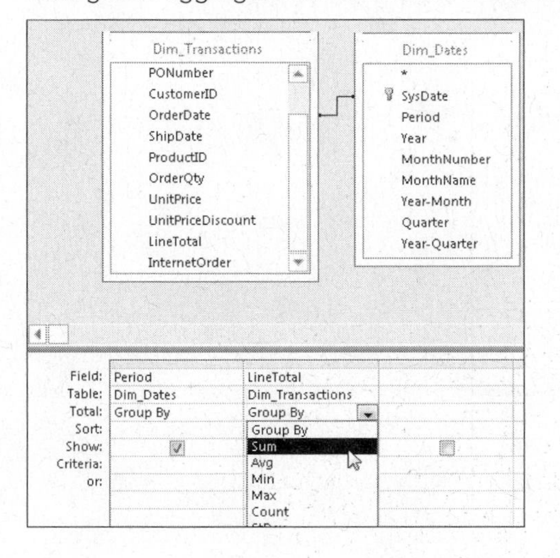

As you can see in Figure 10.4, the resulting table gives a summary of your dataset, showing total revenue by period.

FIGURE 10.4

After you run your query, you have a summary showing your total revenue by period.

Period	SumOfLineTotal
200607	$1,282,530.35
200608	$3,008,547.90
200609	$2,333,985.05
200610	$1,982,360.35
200611	$4,338,025.75
200612	$3,457,253.40
200701	$1,928,725.30
200702	$3,712,032.10
200703	$3,109,211.70
200704	$2,224,498.50

Creating Aliases for Your Column Names

Notice that in Figure 10.4, Access automatically changed the name of the LineTotal field to SumOfLineTotal. This is a common courtesy extended by Access to let you know that the figures you see here are a result of summing the LineTotal field. This renaming may be convenient in some cases, but if you need to distribute these results to other people, you may want to give the field a better name. This is where aliases come in handy.

An alias is an alternate name you can give to a field in order to make it easier to read the field's name in the query results. There are two methods for creating an alias for your field:

- **Method 1:** Preface the field with the text you would like to see as the field name, followed by a colon. The following figure demonstrates how you would create aliases to ensure that your query results have user-friendly column names. Running this query will result in a dataset with a column called Period and column called Total Revenue.

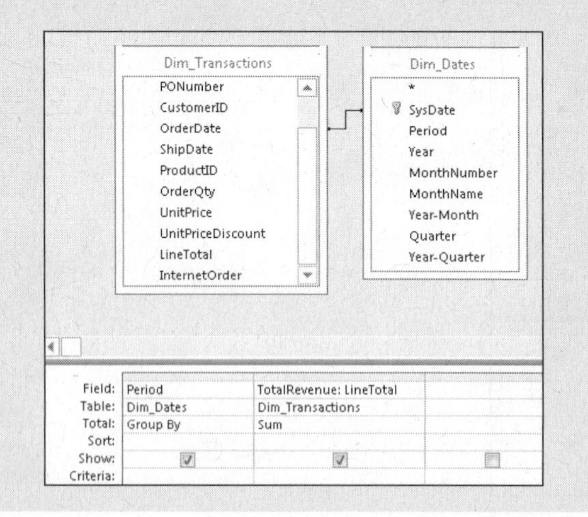

- **Method 2:** Right-click the field name and select Properties. The Property Sheet dialog box for Field Properties appears. In this dialog box, enter the desired alias in the Caption input, as shown in the following figure.

Property Sheet
Selection type: Field Properties
General | Lookup

Description	
Format	
Decimal Places	
Input Mask	
Caption	TotalRevenue

CAUTION
Be aware that if you use the Field Properties dialog box to define your alias, there will be no clear indication in either your query's Design view or your query's SQL string that you're using an alias. This may lead to some confusion for anyone using your queries. For this reason, it's generally better to use the first method to define an alias.

About aggregate functions

In the example shown in Figure 10.3, you selected the `Sum` aggregate function from the Totals drop-down list. Obviously, you could've selected any one of the 12 functions available. Indeed, you'll undoubtedly come across analyses where you'll have to use a few of the other functions available to you. So, it's important to know what each one of these aggregate functions means for your data analysis.

Group By

The `Group By` aggregate function aggregates all the records in the specified field into unique groups. Here are a few things to keep in mind when using the `Group By` aggregate function:

- **Access performs the Group By function in your aggregate query before any other aggregation.** If you're performing a `Group By` along with another aggregate function, the `Group By` function will be performed first. The example shown in Figure 10.4 illustrates this concept. Access groups the Period field before summing the LineTotal field.
- **Access sorts each group-by field in ascending order.** Unless otherwise specified, any field tagged as a group-by field will be sorted in ascending order. If your query has multiple group-by fields, each field will be sorted in ascending order starting with the leftmost field.

- **Access treats multiple group-by fields as one unique item.** To illustrate this point, create a query that looks similar to the one shown in Figure 10.5. This query counts all the transactions that were logged in the 200701 period.

FIGURE 10.5

This query returns only one line showing total records for the 200701 period.

Field:	Period	Period	
Table:	Dim_Dates	Dim_Dates	
Total:	Group By	Count	
Sort:			
Show:	☑	☑	☐
Criteria:	"200701"		

Period	CountOfPeriod
200701	503

Now return to the Query Design view and add ProductID, as shown here in Figure 10.6. This time, Access treats each combination of Period and Product Number as a unique item. Each combination is grouped before the records in each group are counted. The benefit here is that you've added a dimension to your analysis. Not only do you know how many transactions per ProductID were logged in 200701, but if you add up all the transactions, you'll get an accurate count of the total number of transactions logged in 200701.

FIGURE 10.6

This query results in a few more records, but if you add up the counts in each group, they'll total 4,164.

Field:	Period	ProductID	Period
Table:	Dim_Dates	Dim_Transactions	Dim_Dates
Total:	Group By	Group By	Count
Sort:			
Show:	☑	☑	☑
Criteria:	"200701"		

Period	ProductID	CountOfPeriod
200701	710	22
200701	732	4
200701	753	164
200701	755	9
200701	756	8
200701	757	5
200701	759	7
200701	760	15
200701	761	15
200701	762	17

Sum, Avg, Count, StDev, Var

These aggregate functions all perform mathematical calculations against the records in your selected field. It's important to note that these functions exclude any records that are set to null. In other words, these aggregate functions ignore any empty cells.

- **Sum:** Calculates the total value of all the records in the designated field or grouping. This function will work only with the following data types: AutoNumber, Currency, Date/Time, and Number.
- **Avg:** Calculates the average of all the records in the designated field or grouping. This function will work only with the following data types: AutoNumber, Currency, Date/Time, and Number.
- **Count:** Counts the number of entries within the designated field or grouping. This function works with all data types.
- **StDev:** Calculates the standard deviation across all records within the designated field or grouping. This function will work only with the following data types: AutoNumber, Currency, Date/Time, and Number.
- **Var:** Calculates the amount by which all the values within the designated field or grouping vary from the average value of the group. This function will work only with the following data types: AutoNumber, Currency, Date/Time, and Number.

Min, Max, First, Last

Unlike other aggregate functions, these functions evaluate all the records in the designated field or grouping and return a single value from the group.

- **Min:** Returns the value of the record with the lowest value in the designated field or grouping. This function will work only with the following data types: AutoNumber, Currency, Date/Time, Number, and Text.
- **Max:** Returns the value of the record with the highest value in the designated field or grouping. This function will work only with the following data types: AutoNumber, Currency, Date/Time, Number, and Text.
- **First:** Returns the value of the first record in the designated field or grouping. This function works with all data types.
- **Last:** Returns the value of the last record in the designated field or grouping. This function works with all data types.

Expression, Where

One of the steadfast rules of aggregate queries is that every field must have an aggregation performed against it. However, in some situations you'll have to use a field as a utility. That is, use a field to simply perform a calculation or apply a filter. These fields are a means to get to the final analysis you're looking for, rather than part of the final analysis. In these situations, you'll use the `Expression` function or the `Where` clause. The `Expression` function and the `Where` clause are unique in that they don't perform any grouping action per se.

- **Expression:** The Expression aggregate function is generally applied when you're utilizing custom calculations or other functions in an aggregate query. Expression tells Access to perform the designated custom calculation on each individual record or group separately.
- **Where:** The Where clause allows you to apply a criterion to a field that is not included in your aggregate query, effectively applying a filter to your analysis.

To see the Expression aggregate function in action, create a query in Design view that looks like the one shown in Figure 10.7. Note that you're using two aliases in this query, "Revenue" for the LineTotal field and "Cost" for the custom calculation defined here. Using an alias of "Revenue" gives the sum of LineTotal a user-friendly name.

Now you can use [Revenue] to represent the sum of LineTotal in your custom calculation. The Expression aggregate function ties it all together by telling Access that [Revenue]*.33 will be performed against the resulting sum of LineTotal for each individual Period group. Running this query will return the total Revenue and Cost for each Period group.

FIGURE 10.7

The Expression aggregate function allows you to perform the designated custom calculation on each Period group separately.

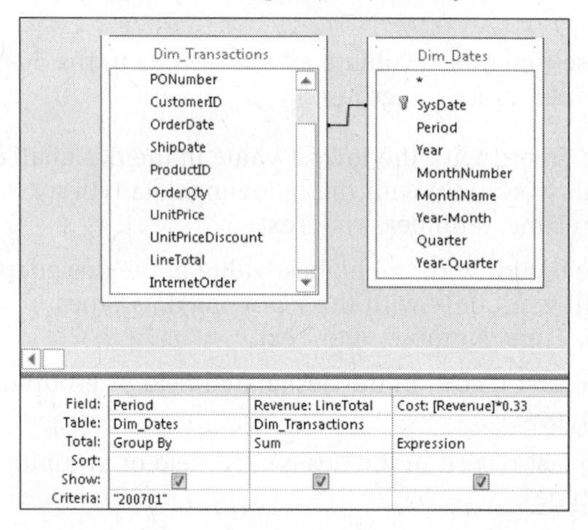

To see the Where clause in action, create a query in Design view that looks like the one shown in Figure 10.8. As you can see in the Total row, you're grouping ProductID and summing LineTotal. However, Period has no aggregation selected because you only want to use it to filter out one specific period. You've entered **200701** in the criteria for Period. If you run this query as is, you'll get the following error message: You tried to execute a query that does not include the specified expression 'Period' as part of an aggregate function.

FIGURE 10.8

Running this query will cause an error message because you have no aggregation defined for Period.

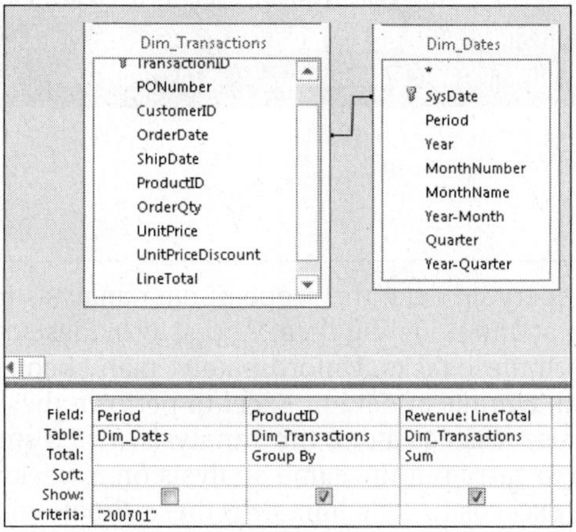

Field:	Period	ProductID	Revenue: LineTotal
Table:	Dim_Dates	Dim_Transactions	Dim_Transactions
Total:		Group By	Sum
Sort:			
Show:		✓	✓
Criteria:	"200701"		

To run this query successfully, click the Totals drop-down list for the Period field and select Where. At this point, your query should look similar to the one shown here in Figure 10.9. With the `Where` clause specified, you can successfully run this query.

FIGURE 10.9

Adding a `Where` remedies the error and allows you to run the query.

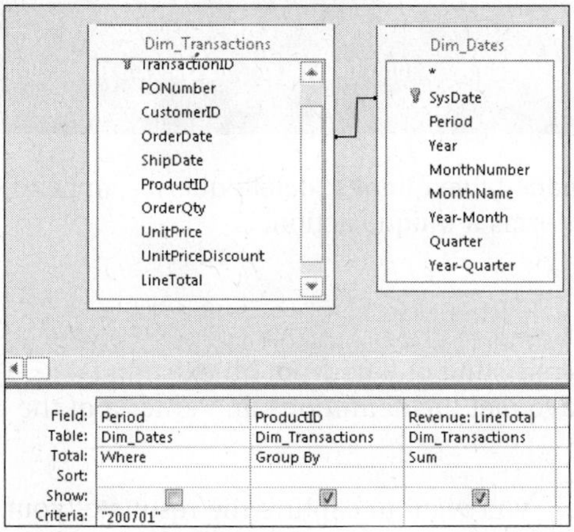

Field:	Period	ProductID	Revenue: LineTotal
Table:	Dim_Dates	Dim_Transactions	Dim_Transactions
Total:	Where	Group By	Sum
Sort:			
Show:		✓	✓
Criteria:	"200701"		

NOTE

Here is one final note about the `Where` clause. Notice in Figure 10.9 that the check box in the Show row has no check in it for the Period. This is because fields that are tagged with the `Where` clause can't be shown in an aggregate query. Therefore, this check box must remain empty. If you check the Show check box of a field with a `Where` clause, you'll get an error message stating that you can't display the field for which you entered `Where` in the Total row.

Action Queries

As we mentioned earlier, in addition to querying data, the scope of data analysis includes shaping data, changing data, deleting data, and updating data. Access provides action queries as data analysis tools to help you with these tasks. Unfortunately, many people don't use these tools; instead, they export small chunks of data to Excel to perform these tasks. That may be fine if you're performing these tasks as a one-time analysis with a small dataset. But what do you do when you have to carry out the same analysis on a weekly basis, or if the dataset you need to manipulate exceeds Excel's limits? In these situations, it would be impractical to routinely export data into Excel, manipulate the data, and then re-import the data back into Access. Using action queries, you can increase your productivity and reduce the chance of errors by carrying out all your analytical process within Access.

You can think of an action query the same way you think of a select query. Like a select query, an action query extracts a dataset from a data source based on the definitions and criteria you pass to the query. The difference is that when an action query returns results it doesn't display a dataset; instead, it performs some action on those results. The action it performs depends on its type.

NOTE

Unlike select queries, you can't use action queries as a data source for a form or a report, as they do not return a dataset that can be read.

There are four types of action queries: make-table queries, delete queries, append queries, and update queries. Each query type performs a unique action.

Make-table queries

A *make-table query* creates a new table consisting of data from an existing table. The table that is created consists of records that have met the definitions and criteria of the make-table query.

In simple terms, if you create a query, and you want to capture the results of your query in its own table, you can use a make-table query to create a hard table with your query results. Then you can use your new table in some other analytical process.

CAUTION

When you build a make-table query, you have to specify the name of the table that will be made when the make-table query is run. If you give the new table the same name as an existing table, the existing table will be overwritten. If you accidentally write over another table with a make-table query, you won't be able to recover the old table. Be sure that you name the tables created by your make-table queries carefully to avoid overwriting existing information.

NOTE

The data in a table made by a make-table query is not, in any way, linked to its source data. This means that the data in your new table will not be updated when data in the original table is changed.

Let's say you've been asked to provide the marketing department with a list of customers, along with information on each customer's sales history. A make-table query will get you the data you need. To create a make-table query, follow these steps:

1. **Create a query in the Query Design view that looks similar to the one shown in Figure 10.10.**

FIGURE 10.10

Create this query in Design view.

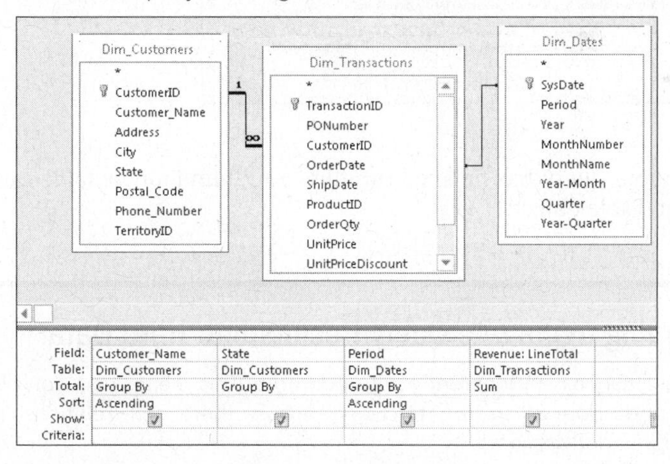

2. **Select the Design tab of the Ribbon, and then click the Make Table button.** The Make Table dialog box (shown in Figure 10.11) appears.
3. **In the Table Name field, enter the name you want to give to your new table.** For this example, type **SalesHistory**. Be sure not to enter the name of a table that already exists in your database, because it'll be overwritten.

FIGURE 10.11

Enter the name of your new table.

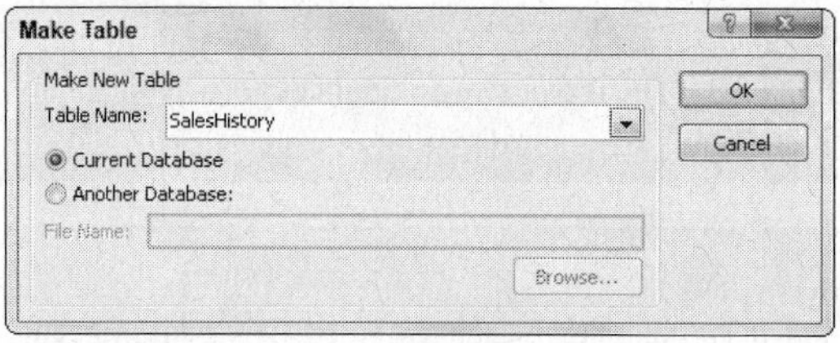

4. **Click OK to close the dialog box, and then run your query.** Access throws up the warning message shown in Figure 10.12, letting you know that you won't be able to undo this action.
5. **Click Yes to confirm and create your new table.**

FIGURE 10.12

Click Yes to run your query.

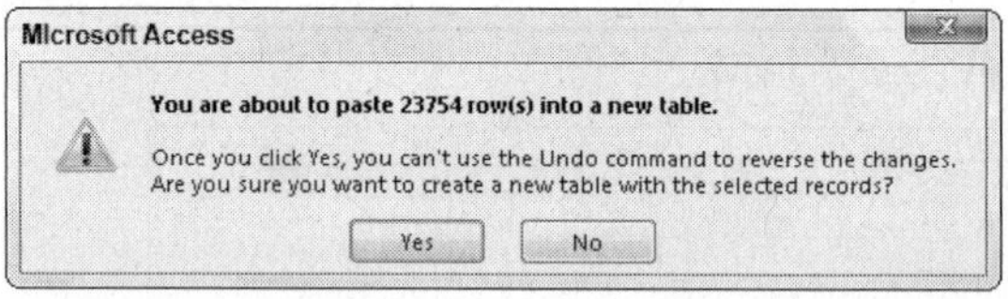

When your query has finished running, you'll find a new table called SalesHistory in your Table objects.

Turning Aggregate Query Results into Hard Data

The results of aggregate queries are inherently not updatable. This means you won't be able to edit any of the records returned from an aggregate query because there is no relationship between the aggregated data and the underlying data.

However, you can change your aggregate query into a Make Table query and create a hard table with your aggregate query's results. With your new hard table, you'll be able to edit to your heart's content.

To illustrate how this works, create the query shown in the following figure in Design view. Then change the query into a make-table query, enter a name for your new table, and run it.

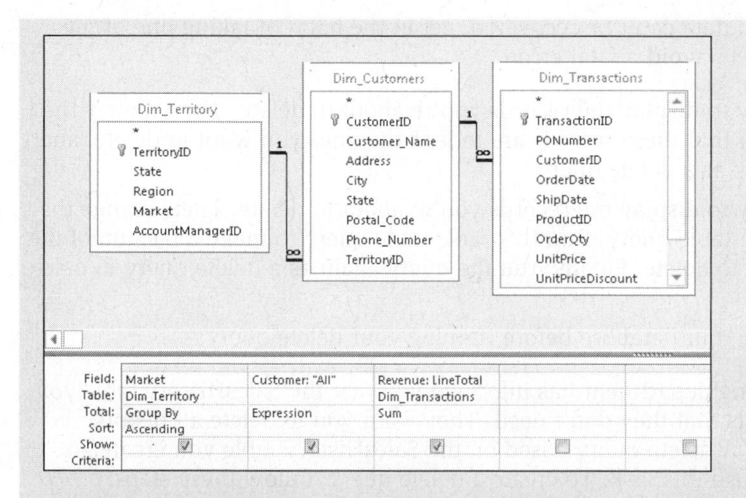

TIP

Notice that in the figure you defined a column with an alias of "Customer." After the alias, you simply enter "All" (in quotes). When you run the query, you'll notice that your new table has a column named Customer in which the value for every record is All. This example illustrates that when running a make-table query, you can create your own columns on the fly simply by creating an alias for the column and defining its contents after the colon.

Delete queries

A *delete* query deletes records from a table based on the definitions and criteria you specify. That is, a delete query affects a group of records that meet a specified criterion that you apply.

Although you can delete records by hand, in some situations using a delete query is more efficient. For example, if you have a very large dataset, a delete query deletes your records faster that a manual delete can. In addition, if you want to delete certain records based on several complex criteria, you'll want to use a delete query. Finally, if you need to delete records from one table based on a comparison to another table, a delete query is the way to go.

CAUTION

Like all other action queries, you can't undo the effects of a delete query. However, a delete query is much more dangerous than the other action queries because there is no way to remedy accidentally deleted data.

Given the fact that deleted data can't be recovered, get in the habit of taking one of the following actions in order to avoid a fatal error:

- Run a select query to display the records you're about to delete. Then review the records to confirm that these records are indeed the ones you want to delete, and then run the query as a delete query.
- Run a select query to display the records you're about to delete. Then change the query into a make-table query. Run the make-table query to make a backup of the data you're about to delete. Finally, run the query again as a delete query to delete the records.
- Make a backup of your database before running your delete query.

Now let's say the marketing department has informed you that the SalesHistory table you gave them includes records that they don't need. They want you to delete all history before the 200806 Period. A delete query based on the SalesHistory table you created a moment ago will accomplish this task. To create a delete query, follow these steps:

1. **Bring in the Period field and enter** < 200806 **in the Criteria row.** Your design grid should look like the one shown in Figure 10.13.

FIGURE 10.13

This query will select all records with a Period earlier than 200806.

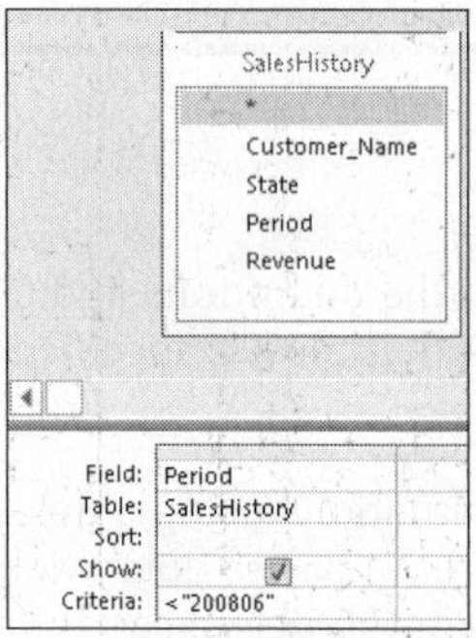

2. **Perform a test by running the query.**
3. **Review the records that are returned, and take note that 6,418 records meet your criteria.** You now know that 6,418 records will be deleted if you run a delete query based on these query definitions.
4. **Return to Design view.**
5. **Select the Design tab of the Ribbon, and then click the Delete button.**
6. **Run your query again.** Access throws up the message shown in Figure 10.14, telling you that you're about to delete 6,418 rows of data and warning you that you won't be able to undo this action. This is the number you were expecting to see, because the test you ran earlier returned 6,418 records.

7. **Because everything checks out, click Yes to confirm and delete the records.**

FIGURE 10.14

Click Yes to continue with your delete action.

Microsoft Access

You are about to delete 6418 row(s) from the specified table.

Once you click Yes, you can't use the Undo command to reverse the changes.
Are you sure you want to delete the selected records?

Show Help >>

Yes No

> **NOTE**
>
> If you're working with a very large dataset, Access may throw up a message telling you that the undo command won't be available because the operation is too large or there isn't enough free memory. Many people mistakenly interpret this message as meaning that the operation can't be done because there isn't enough memory. But this message is simply telling you that Access won't be able to give the option of undoing this change if you choose to continue with the action. This is applicable to delete queries, append queries, and update queries.

Deleting Records from One Table Based on the Records from Another Table

You'll encounter many analyses in which you'll have to delete records from one table based on the records from another table. This task is relatively easy. However, many users get stuck on it because of one simple mistake.

The query in the following figure looks simple enough. It's telling Access to delete all records from the Customer_ListA table if the customer is found in the Customer_ListB table.

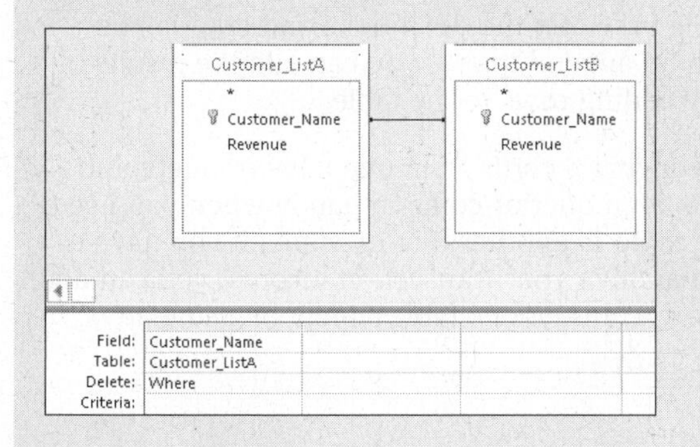

continued

continued

If you run this query, Access throws up the message shown in the following figure. This message is asking you to specify which table contains the records you want to delete.

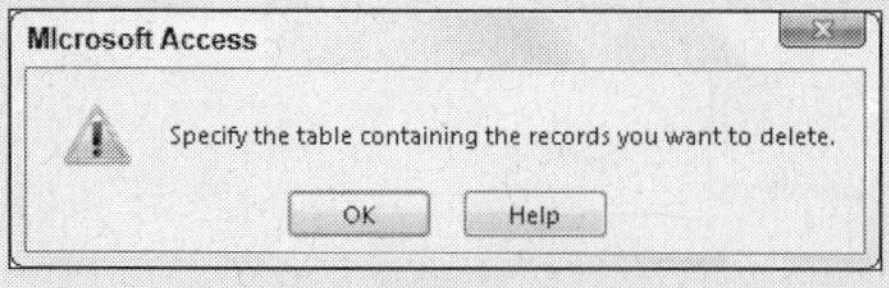

This message stumps many Access users. Unfortunately, this message doesn't clearly state what you need in order to remedy the mistake. Nevertheless, the remedy is a simple one: First, clear the query grid by deleting the CustomerName field. Next, double-click the asterisk (*) in the Customer_ListA table. This explicitly tells Access that the Customer_ListA table contains the records you want to delete. The following figure demonstrates the correct way to build this query.

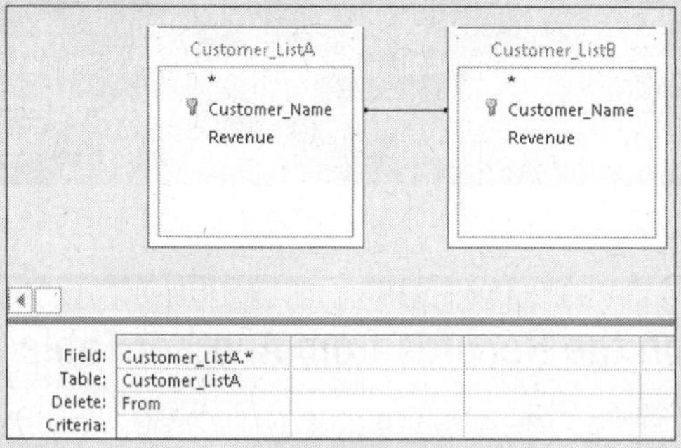

Append queries

An append query appends records to a table based on the definitions and criteria you specify in your query. In other words, with an append query, you can add the results of your query to the end of a table, effectively adding rows to the table.

With an append query, you're essentially copying records from one table or query and adding them to the end of another table. Append queries come in handy when you need to transfer large datasets from one existing table to another. For example, if you have a table called Old Transactions in which you archive your transaction records, you can add the latest batch of transactions from the New Transactions table simply by using an append query.

CAUTION
The primary hazard of an append query is losing records during the append process. Not all the records you think you're appending to a table actually make it to your table. Also, you'll want to be wary of running the same append query more than once, so that data is duplicated.

There are generally two reasons why records can get lost during an append process:

- **Type conversion failure:** This failure occurs when the character type of the source data doesn't match that of the destination table column. For example, imagine that you have a table with a field call Cost. Your Cost field is set as a Text character type because you have some entries that are tagged as TBD (to be determined), because you don't know the cost yet. If you try to append that field to another table whose Cost field is set as a Number character type, all the entries that have TBD will be changed to null, effectively deleting your TBD tag.
- **Key violation:** This violation occurs when you're trying to append duplicate records to a field in the destination table that is set as a primary key or is indexed as No Duplicates. In other words, when you have a field that prohibits duplicates, Access won't let you append any record that is a duplicate of an existing record in that field.

Another hazard of an append query is that the query will simply fail to run. There are five reasons why an append query will fail:

- **Lock violation:** This violation occurs when the destination table is open in Design view or is opened by another user on the network.
- **Validation rule violation:** This violation occurs when a field in the destination table has one of the following properties settings:
- **Required field is set to Yes:** If a field in the destination table has been set to Required Yes and you don't append data to this field, your append query will fail.
- **Allow Zero Length is set to No:** If a field in the destination table has been set to Zero Length No and you don't append data to this field, your append query will fail.
- **Validation rule set to anything:** If a field in the destination table has a validation rule and you break the rule with your append query, your append query will fail. For example, if you have a validation rule for the Cost field in your destination table set to >0, you can't append records with a quantity less than or equal to zero.

Luckily, Access will clearly warn you if you're about to cause any of these errors. Figure 10.15 demonstrates this warning message, which tells you that you can't append all the records due to errors. It also tells you exactly how many records won't be appended because of each error. In this case, 5,979 records won't be appended because of key violations. You have the option of clicking Yes or No. If you click Yes, the warning is ignored and all records are appended, minus the records with the errors. If you click No, the query will be canceled, which means that no records will be appended.

FIGURE 10.15

The warning message tells you that you'll lose records during the append process.

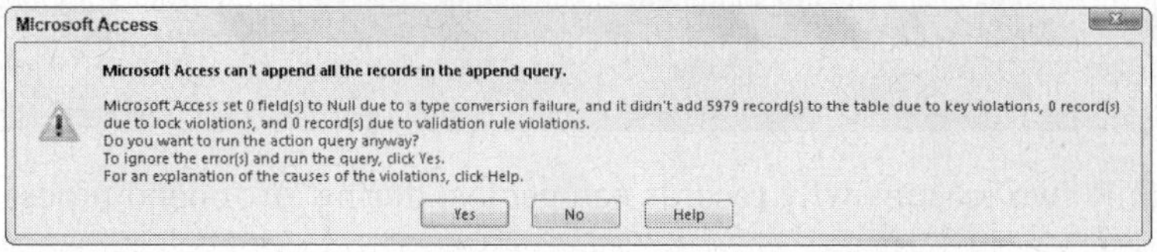

> **CAUTION**
>
> Keep in mind that like all other action queries, you won't be able to undo your append query once you've pulled the trigger.

> **TIP**
>
> If you can identify the records you recently appended in your destination table, you could technically undo your append action simply by deleting the newly appended records. This would obviously be contingent upon your providing yourself a method of identifying appended records. For example, you could create a field that contains some code or tag that identifies the appended records. This code can be anything from a date to a simple character.

Let's say the marketing department tells you that they made a mistake — they actually need all the sales history for the 2008 fiscal year. So, they need periods 200801 thru 200805 added back to the SalesHistory report. An append query is in order.

In order to get them what they need, follow these steps:

1. **Create a query in the Query Design view that looks similar to the one shown in Figure 10.16.**

FIGURE 10.16

This query selects all records contained in Periods 200801 thru 200805.

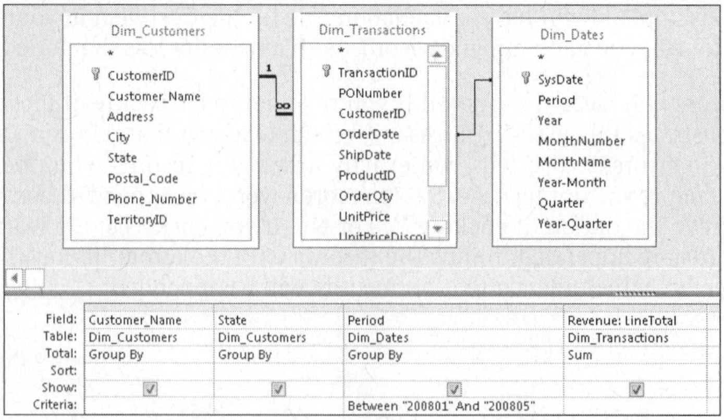

2. **Select the Design tab of the Ribbon, and then click the Append button.** The Append dialog box (shown in Figure 10.17) appears.
3. **In the Table Name field, enter the name of the table to which you would like to append your query results.** In this example, enter **SalesHistory**.

FIGURE 10.17

Enter the name of the table to which you want to append your query results.

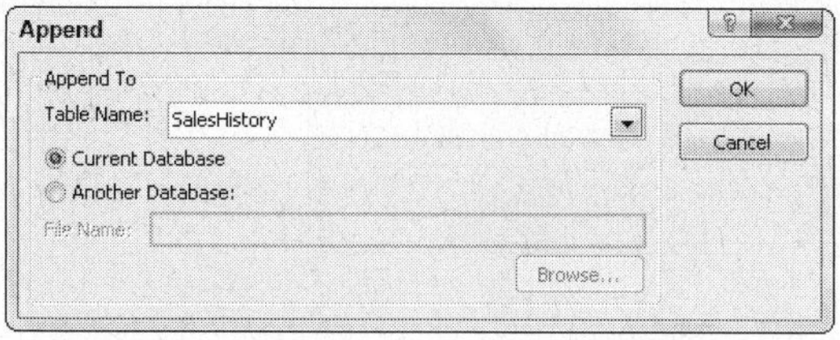

4. **Once you've entered your destination table's name, click OK.** Your query grid has a new row called Append To under the Sort row (see Figure 10.18). The idea is to select the name of the field in your destination table where you want to append the information resulting from your query. For example, the Append To row under the Period field shows the word *Period*. This means that the data in the Period field of this query will be appended to the Period field in the SalesHistory table.

FIGURE 10.18

In the Append To row, select the name of the field in your destination table where you want to append the information resulting from your query.

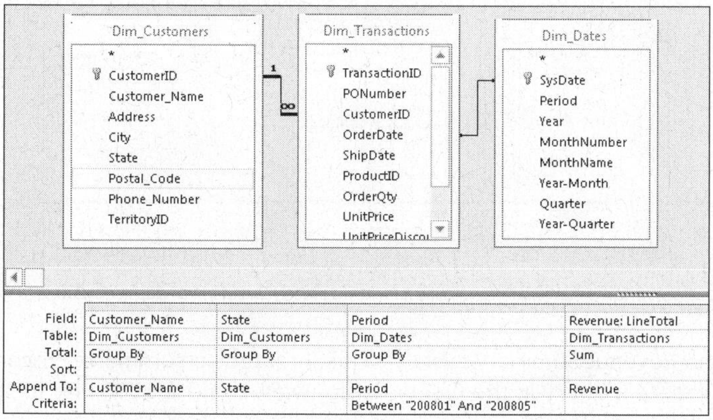

5. **Run your query.** Access throws up a message, as shown in Figure 10.19, telling you that you're about to append 1,760 rows of data and warning you that you won't be able to undo this action.
6. **Click Yes to confirm and append the records.**

FIGURE 10.19

Click Yes to continue with your append action.

Microsoft Access

You are about to append 1760 row(s).

Once you click Yes, you can't use the Undo command to reverse the changes.
Are you sure you want to append the selected rows?

Yes No

Adding a Totals Row to Your Dataset

Your manager wants you to create a revenue summary report that shows the total revenue for each account manager in each market. He also wants to see the total revenue for each market. Instead of giving your manager two separate reports, you can give him one table that has account manager details and market totals. This is an easy process:

1. **Create a query in the Query Design view that looks similar to the one shown here in the following figure.** Note that you're creating an alias for the LineTotal Field.
2. **Change the query into a make-table query and name your table RevenueSummary.**
3. **Run this query.**

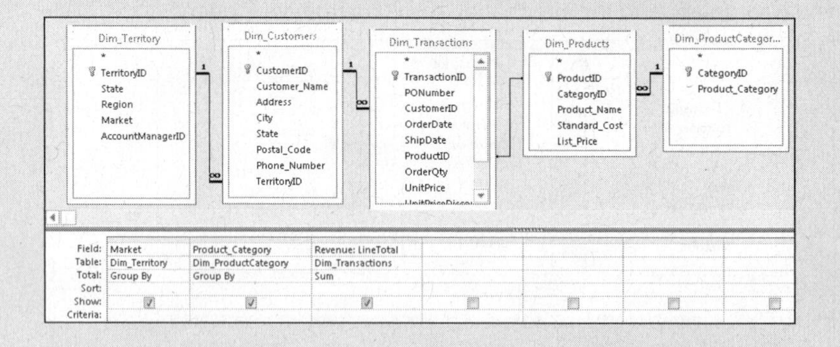

4. **Now use the RevenueSummary table you just created to summarize revenue by Market; to do this, create a query in the Query Design view that looks similar to the one shown here in the following figure.**

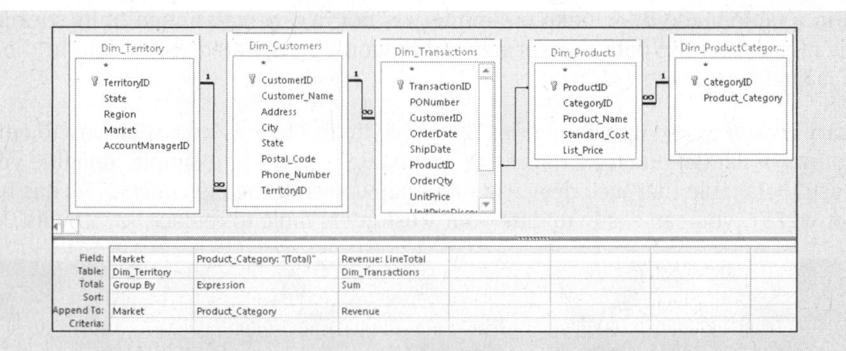

Take a moment and look at the query in this figure. You'll notice that you're making a custom Product_Category field, filling it with "(Total)". This will ensure that the summary lines you append to the RevenueSummary table will be clearly identifiable, as they'll have the word "Total" in the Product_Category field.

5. **Change the query into an append query and append these results to the RevenueSummary table.**

Now you can open the RevenueSummary table and sort by Market and Product_Category. As you can see in the following figure, you've successfully created a table that has a total revenue line for every product category and a total revenue line for each market, all in one table.

Market	Product_Category	Revenue
Baltimore	(Total)	$19,387.00
Baltimore	Bar Equipment	$80.00
Baltimore	Fryers	$352.00
Baltimore	Ovens and Ranges	$7,470.00
Baltimore	Refrigerators and Coolers	$10,730.00
Baltimore	Warmers	$755.00
Buffalo	(Total)	$5,283,983.55
Buffalo	Bar Equipment	$37,397.90
Buffalo	Commercial Appliances	$237,297.85
Buffalo	Concession Equipment	$187,711.00
Buffalo	Fryers	$127,287.70
Buffalo	Ovens and Ranges	$1,654,376.65
Buffalo	Refrigerators and Coolers	$2,030,464.50
Buffalo	Warmers	$1,009,447.95
California	(Total)	$11,363,506.25

Update queries

When you build a make-table query, you will have to specify the name of the table that will be made when the make-table query is run. If you give the new table the same name as an existing table, the existing table will be overwritten. If you accidentally write over another table with a make-table query, you won't be able to recover the old table. Be sure that you name the tables created by your make-table queries carefully so as to avoid overwriting existing information.

The data in a table made by a make-table query is not in any way linked to its source data. This means that the data in your new table won't be updated when data in the original table is changed.

The primary reason to use update queries is to save time. There is no easier way to edit large amounts of data at one time than with an update query. For example, imagine you have a Customers table that includes customers' zip codes. If the zip code 32750 has been changed to 32751, you can easily update your Customers table to replace 32750 with 32751.

CAUTION

As is the case with all other action queries, you must always take precautions to ensure that you aren't in a situation where you can't undo the effects of an update query. To give yourself a way back to the original data in the event of a misstep, make a backup of your database before running your update query. Alternatively, you can run a select query to display, and then change the query into a make-table query; run the make-table query to make a backup of the data you're about to update; and then run the query again as an update query to delete the records.

Let's say you've just received word that the zip code for all customers in the 33605 zip code has been changed to 33606. In order to keep your database accurate, you'll have to update all the 33605 zip codes in your Dim_Customers table to 33606. Here's how:

1. **Create a query in the Query Design view that looks similar to the one shown in Figure 10.20.**

FIGURE 10.20

This query will select all customers that are in the 33605 zip code.

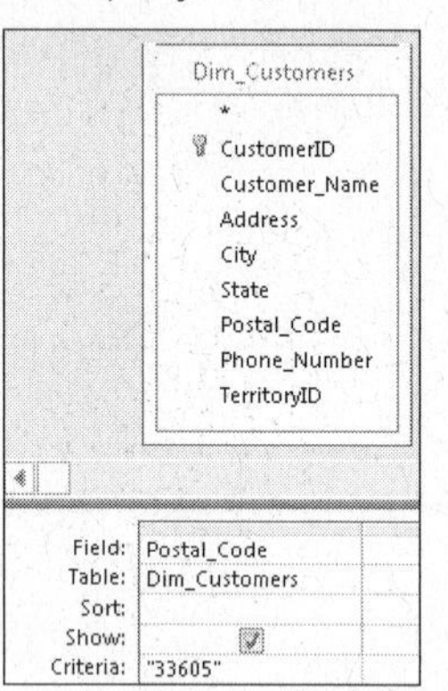

2. **Perform a test by running the query.**
3. **Review the records that are returned, and take note that six records meet your criteria.** You now know that six records will be updated if you run an update query based on these query definitions.

4. **Return to the Design view.**
5. **Select the Design tab of the Ribbon, and click the Update button.** Your query grid now has a new row called Update To. The idea is to enter the value to which you would like to update the current data. In this scenario, shown in Figure 10.21, you want to update the zip code for the records you're selecting to 33606.

FIGURE 10.21

In this query, you are updating the zip code for all customers that have a code of 33605 to 33606.

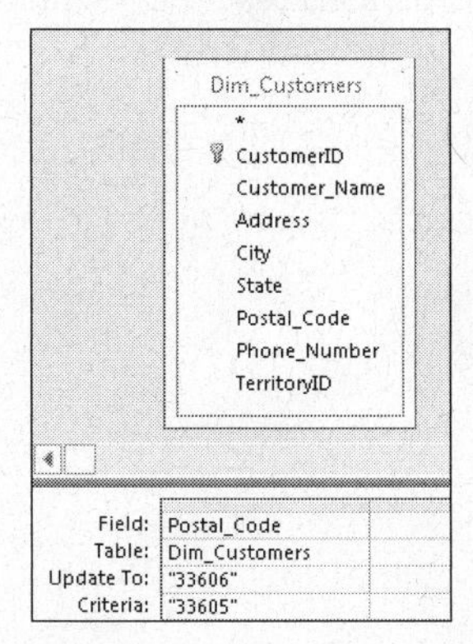

6. **Run the query.** Access throws up the message shown in Figure 10.22, telling you that you're about to update six rows of data and warning you that you won't be able to undo this action. This is the number you were expecting to see, because the test you ran earlier returned six records.
7. **Since everything checks out, click Yes to confirm and update the records.**

FIGURE 10.22

Click Yes to continue with your update action.

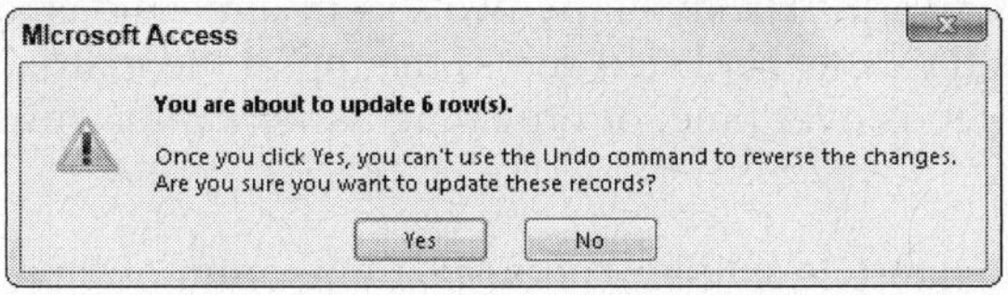

Microsoft Access

You are about to update 6 row(s).

Once you click Yes, you can't use the Undo command to reverse the changes.
Are you sure you want to update these records?

Yes No

Using Expressions in Your Update Queries

You'll come across situations in which you'll have to execute record-specific updates. That is, you aren't updating multiple records with one specific value; instead, you're updating each record individually based on an expression.

To demonstrate this concept, start a query in Design view based on the SalesHistory table you created in the "Make-table queries" section, earlier in this chapter. Build your query like the one shown in the following figure.

This query is telling Access to update the Period to the concatenated text "PD " with the value in the Period field.

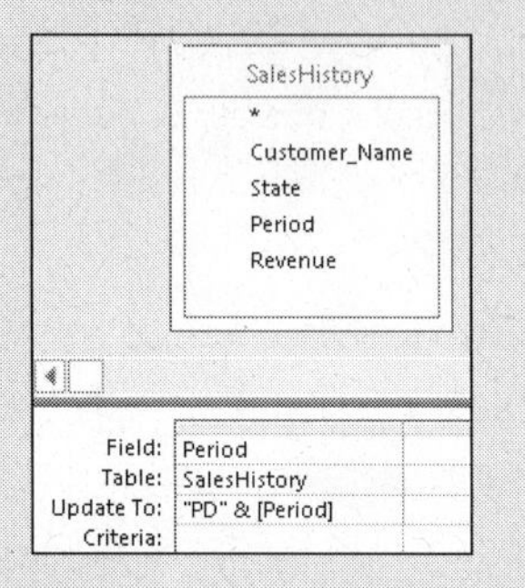

After you run this query, all the values in the Period field will have a prefix of PD. For example, 200801 will be updated to PD 200801.

Remember: This is just one example of an expression you can use to update your records. You can use almost any expression with an update query, ranging from mathematical functions to string operations.

Crosstab Queries

A *crosstab query* is a special kind of aggregate query that summarizes values from a specified field and groups them in a matrix layout by two sets of dimensions, one set down the left side of the matrix and the other set listed across the top of the matrix. Crosstab queries are perfect for analyzing trends over time, or providing a method for quickly identifying anomalies in your dataset.

The anatomy of a crosstab query is simple. You need a minimum of three fields in order to create the matrix structure that will become your crosstab. The first field makes up the row headings, the second field makes up the column headings, and the third field makes up the aggregated data in the center of the matrix. The data in the center can represent a `Sum`, `Count`, `Average`, or any other aggregate function. Figure 10.23 demonstrates the basic structure of a crosstab query.

A Word on Updatable Datasets

Not all datasets are updatable. That is, you may have a dataset that Access can't update for one reason or another. If your update query fails, you'll get one of these messages: `Operation must use an updatable query` or `This recordset is not updateable`.

Your update query will fail if any one of the following applies:

- **Your query is using a join to another query.** To work around this issue, create a temporary table that you can use instead of the joined query.
- **Your query is based on a crosstab query, an aggregate query, a union query, or a sub query that contains aggregate functions.** To work around this issue, create a temporary table that you can use instead of the query.
- **Your query is based on three or more tables and there is a many-to-one-to-many relationship.** To work around this issue, create a temporary table that you can use without the relationship.
- **Your query is based on a table where the Unique Values property is set to Yes.** To work around this issue, set the Unique Values property of the table to No.
- **Your query is based on a table that's locked by another user.** To work around this issue, ensure the table is not in Design view or locked by another user.
- **Your query is based on a table in a database that is open as read-only or is located on a read-only drive.** To work around this issue, obtain write access to the database or drive.
- **Your query is based on a linked ODBC table with no unique index or a paradox table without a primary key.** To work around this issue, add a primary key or a unique index to the linked table.
- **Your query is based on a SQL pass-through query.** To work around this issue, create a temporary table that you can use instead of the query.

FIGURE 10.23

The basic structure of a crosstab query.

Region Name	QTR1	QTR2	QTR3	QTR4
Region A	data	data	data	data
Region B	data	data	data	data
Region C	data	data	data	data

There are two methods to create a crosstab query. You can use the Crosstab Query Wizard or create a crosstab query manually using the query design grid.

Using the Crosstab Query Wizard

To use the Crosstab Query Wizard to create a crosstab query, follow these steps:

1. **Select the Create tab of the Ribbon and then click the Query Wizard button.** The New Query dialog box, shown in Figure 10.24, appears.
2. **Select Crosstab Query Wizard from the selection list, and then click OK.**

FIGURE 10.24

Select Crosstab Query Wizard from the New Query dialog box.

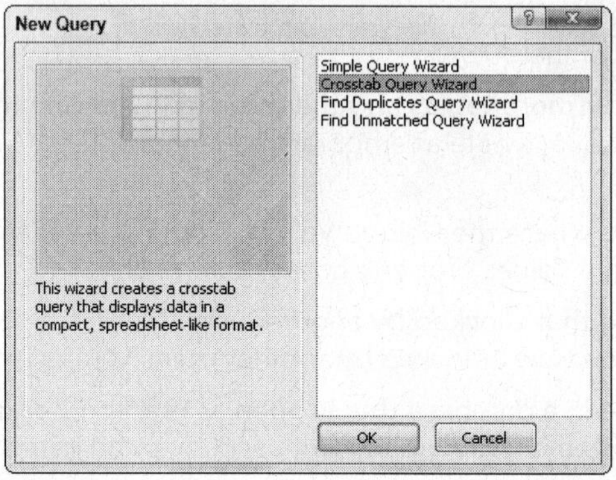

The first step in the Crosstab Query Wizard is to identify the data source you'll be using. As you can see in Figure 10.25, you can choose either a query or a table as your data source. In this example, you'll be using the Dim_Transactions table as your data source.

3. **Select Dim_Transactions and then click the Next button.**

   The next step is to identify the fields you want to use as the row headings.

4. **Select the ProductID field and click the button with the > symbol on it to move it to the Selected Items list.** The dialog box should look like Figure 10.26. Notice that the ProductID field is shown in the sample diagram at the bottom of the dialog box.

   You can select up to three fields to include in your crosstab query as row headings. Remember that Access treats each combination of headings as a unique item. That is, each combination is grouped before the records in each group are aggregated.

FIGURE 10.25

Select the data source for your crosstab query.

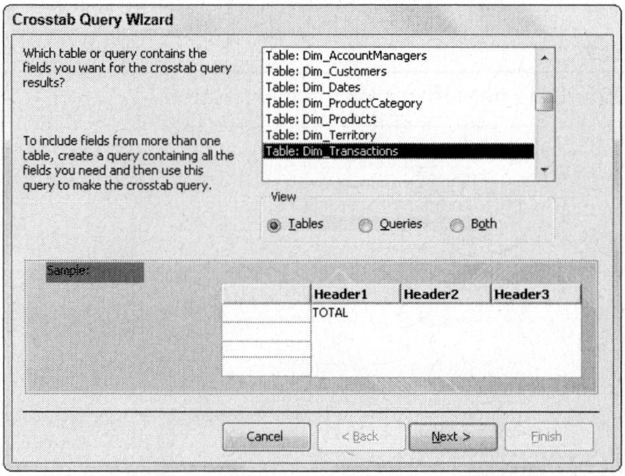

FIGURE 10.26

Select the ProductID field and then click the Next button.

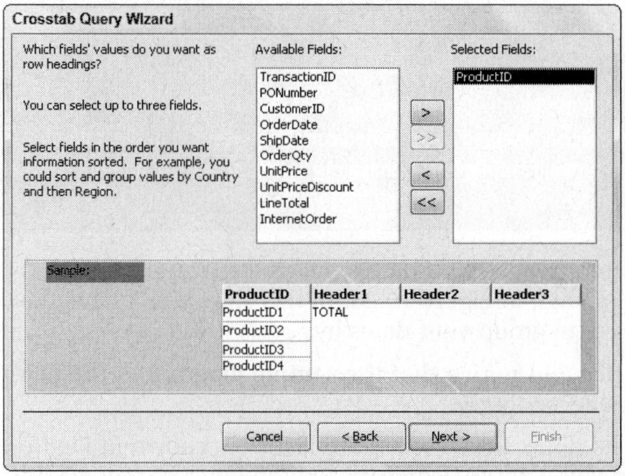

The next step is to identify the field you want to use as the column heading for your crosstab query. Keep in mind that there can be only one column heading in your crosstab.

5. **Select the OrderDate field from the field list.** Notice in Figure 10.27 that the sample diagram at the bottom of the dialog box updates to show the OrderDate.

FIGURE 10.27

Select the OrderDate field then click the Next button.

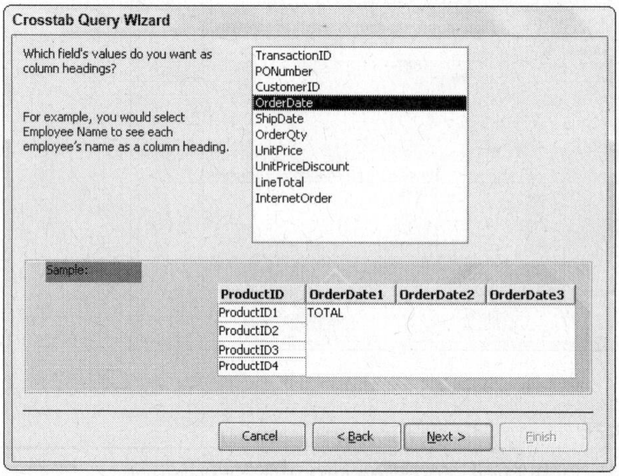

NOTE

If the field that is being used as a column heading includes data that contains a period (.), an exclamation point (!), or a bracket ([or]), those characters will be changed to an underscore character (_) in the column heading. This does not happen if the same data is used as a row heading. This behavior is by design, as the naming convention for field names in Access prohibits use of these characters.

If your Column Heading is a date field, as the OrderDate is in this example, you'll see the step shown in Figure 10.28. In this step, you'll have the option of specifying an interval to group your dates by.

6. **Select Quarter and notice that the sample diagram at the bottom of the dialog box updates accordingly.**

   You're almost done. In the second-to-last step, shown in Figure 10.29, you'll identify the field you want to aggregate and the function you want to use.

7. **Select the LineTotal field from the Fields list, and then select Sum from the Functions list.** Notice the Yes, Include Row Sums check box. This box is checked by default to ensure that your crosstab query includes a Total column that contains the sum total for each row. If you don't want this column, simply remove the check from the check box.

If you look at the sample diagram at the bottom of the dialog box, you will get a good sense of what your final crosstab query will do. In this example, your crosstab will calculate the sum of the LineTotal field for each ProductID by Quarter.

FIGURE 10.28

Select Quarter and then click Next.

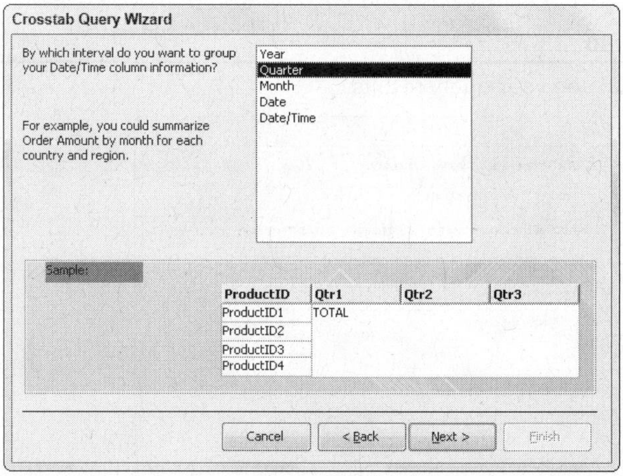

FIGURE 10.29

Select the LineTotal and Sum, and then click the Next button.

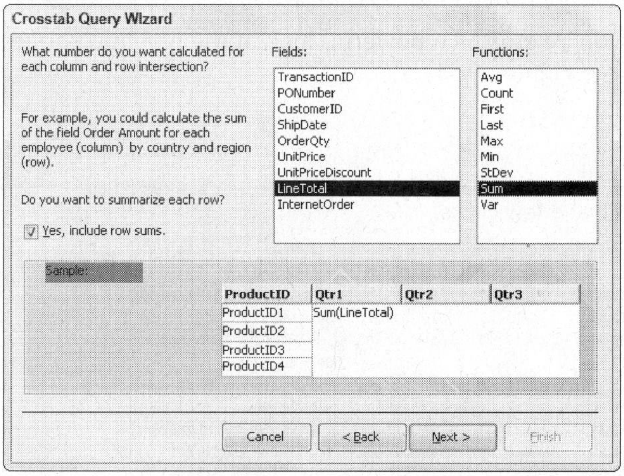

The final step, shown in Figure 10.30, is to name your crosstab query.

8. **In this example, name your crosstab Product Summary by Quarter.** After you name your query, you have the option of viewing your query or modifying the design.
9. **In this case, you want to view your query results so simply click the Finish button.**

FIGURE 10.30

Click Finish to see your query results.

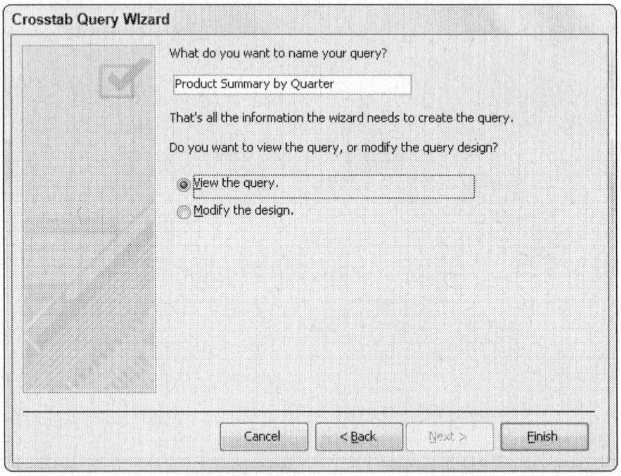

In just a few clicks, you've created a powerful look at the revenue performance of each product by quarter (see Figure 10.31).

FIGURE 10.31

A powerful analysis in just a few clicks.

ProductID	Total Of LineTotal	Qtr 1	Qtr 2	Qtr 3	Qtr 4
709	$28,663.80	$3,787.20	$8,000.40	$9,485.40	$7,390.80
710	$353,507.05	$69,334.85	$64,463.10	$62,870.60	$156,838.50
718	$732,725.50		$171,432.25	$414,166.75	$147,126.50
719	$5,853,748.80	$1,244,884.20	$1,541,942.70	$1,616,661.00	$1,450,260.90
720	$495,413.50			$495,413.50	
732	$160,733.00	$23,115.00	$49,948.50	$36,247.00	$51,422.50
733	$57,352.00		$22,411.50	$13,065.00	$21,875.50
753	$9,373,695.50	$2,286,041.00	$2,949,132.00	$1,824,659.50	$2,313,863.00
755	$582,601.20	$145,650.30	$166,482.60	$103,370.40	$167,097.90
756	$526,095.55	$133,975.65	$155,210.75	$85,507.75	$151,401.40
757	$250,742.10	$82,378.10	$83,924.30		$84,439.70
759	$517,812.55	$116,694.85	$147,762.65	$124,890.65	$128,464.40
760	$1,680,850.20	$340,321.65	$439,951.80	$489,024.00	$411,552.75
761	$1,609,727.40	$346,173.30	$433,207.60	$433,159.70	$397,186.80
762	$1,970,584.00	$412,384.00	$521,899.00	$558,061.00	$478,240.00
763	$1,381,724.40	$298,040.80	$374,013.60	$373,272.00	$336,398.00
764	$953,558.70	$211,096.10	$263,555.85	$245,037.80	$233,868.95

Turning Your Crosstab Query into Hard Data

You'll undoubtedly encounter scenarios in which you'll have to convert your crosstab query into hard data in order to use the results on other analyses. A simple trick for doing this is to use your saved crosstab query in a make-table query to create a new table with your crosstab results.

Start by creating a new select query in Design view and add your saved crosstab query. In the following figure, you'll notice that you're using the Product Summary by Quarter crosstab you just created. Bring in the fields you want to include in your new table.

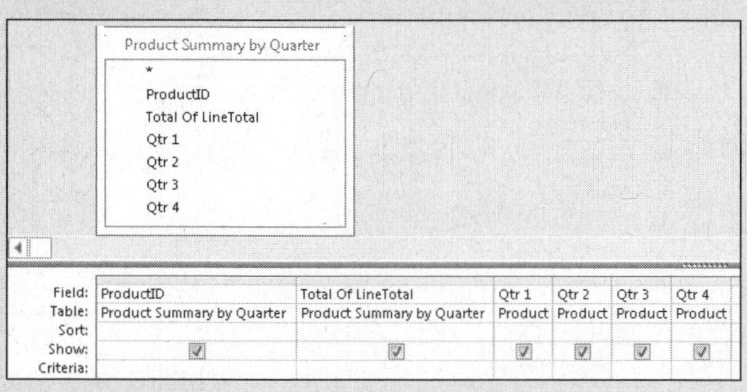

Product Summary by Quarter
*
ProductID
Total Of LineTotal
Qtr 1
Qtr 2
Qtr 3
Qtr 4

Field:	ProductID	Total Of LineTotal	Qtr 1	Qtr 2	Qtr 3	Qtr 4
Table:	Product Summary by Quarter	Product Summary by Quarter	Product	Product	Product	Product
Sort:						
Show:	☑	☑	☑	☑	☑	☑
Criteria:						

At this point, simply convert your query into a make-table query and run it. After you run your make-table query, you'll have a hard table that contains the results of your crosstab.

Manually creating a crosstab query

Although the Crosstab Query Wizard makes it easy to create a crosstab in just a few clicks, it does have limitations that may inhibit your data analysis efforts:

- **You can select only one data source on which to base your crosstab.** This means that if you need to crosstab data residing across multiple tables, you'll need to take extra steps to create a temporary query to use as your data source.
- **There is no way to filter or limit your crosstab query with criteria from the Crosstab Query Wizard.**
- **You're limited to only three row headings.**
- **You can't explicitly define the order of your column headings from the Crosstab Query Wizard.**

The good news is that you can create a crosstab query manually through the query design grid. Manually creating your crosstab query allows you greater flexibility in your analysis.

Using the query design grid to create your crosstab query

Here's how to create a crosstab query using the query design grid:

1. **Create the aggregate query shown in Figure 10.32.** Notice that you're using multiple tables to get the fields you need. One of the benefits of creating a crosstab query manually is that you don't have to use just one data source — you can use as many sources as you need in order to define the fields in your query.

FIGURE 10.32

Create an aggregate query as shown here.

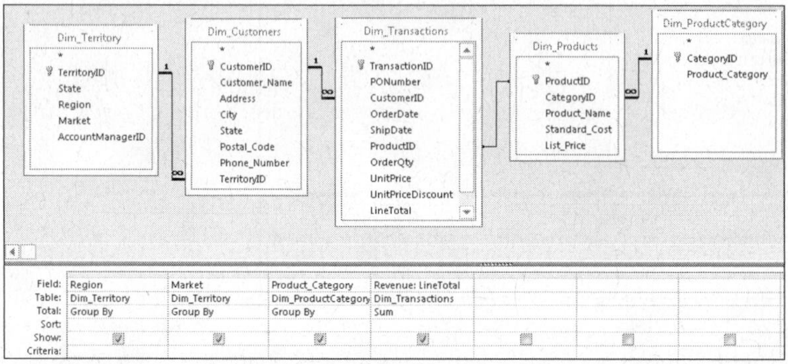

2. **Select the Design tab of the Ribbon and click the Crosstab button.** A row has been added to your query grid called Crosstab (see Figure 10.33). The idea is to define what role each field will play in your crosstab query.
3. **Under each field in the Crosstab row, select whether the field will be a row heading, a column heading, or a value.**
4. **Run the query to see your crosstab in action.**

FIGURE 10.33

Set each field's role in the Crosstab row.

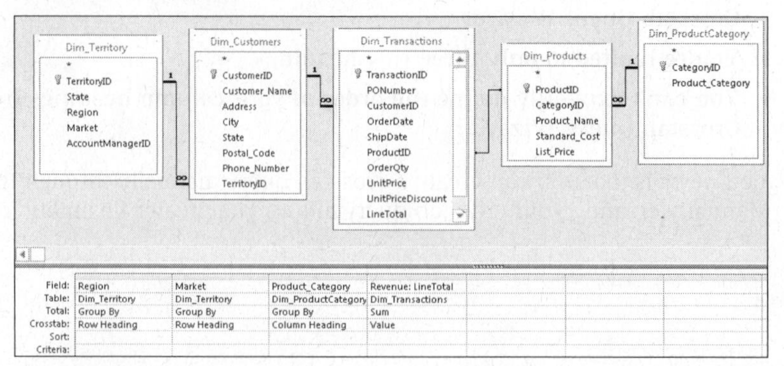

When building your crosstab in the query grid, keep the following in mind:

- You must have a minimum of one row heading, one column heading, and one value field.
- You can't define more than one column heading.
- You can't define more than one value heading.
- You are *not* limited to only three row headings.

Creating a Crosstab View with Multiple Value Fields

One of the rules of a crosstab query is that you can't have more than one value field. However, you can work around this limitation and analyze more than one metric with the same data groups. To help demonstrate how this works, create a crosstab query as shown in the following figure and save it as Crosstab-1. Your column heading is a custom field that will give you the region name and the word *Revenue* next to it.

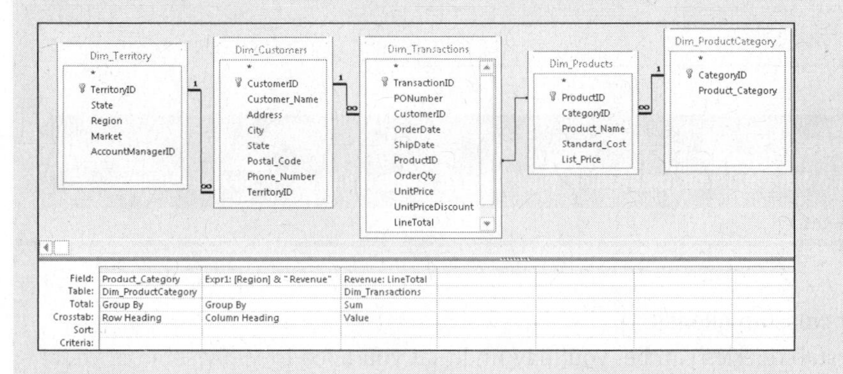

Next, create another crosstab query as shown in the following figure and save it as Crosstab-2. Again, your column heading is a custom field that will give you the region name and the word *Transactions* next to it.

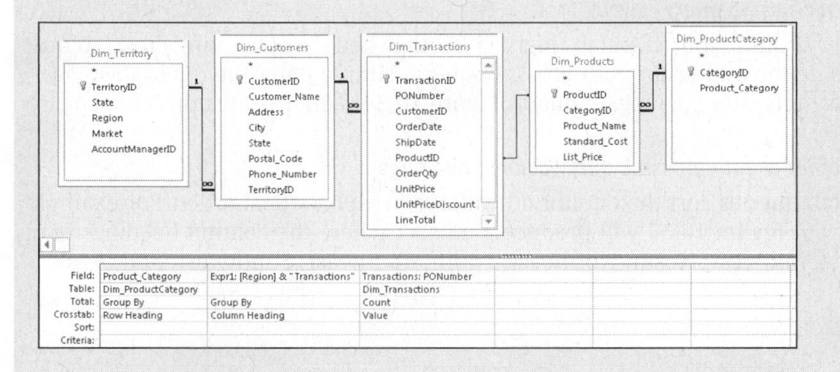

continued

continued

Finally, create a select query that will join the two crosstab queries on the row heading. In the example shown in the following figure, the row heading is the Product_Category field. Bring in all the fields in the appropriate order. When you run this query, the result will be an analysis that incorporates both crosstab queries, effectively giving you multiple value fields.

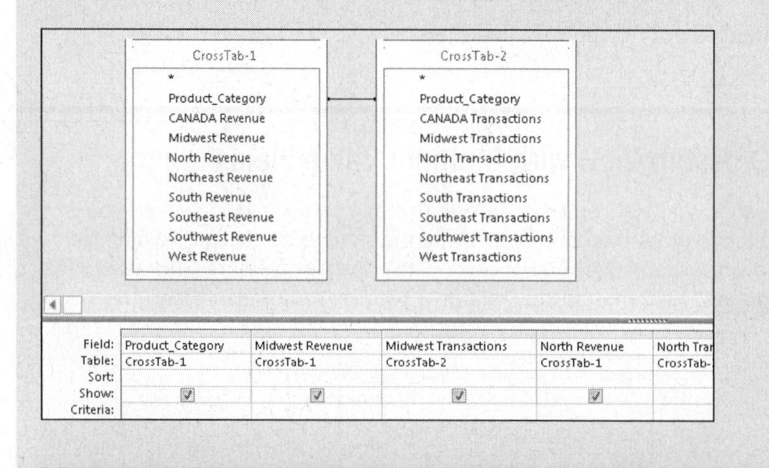

NOTE

Keep in mind that if you have more than one row heading, you'll have to create a join on each row heading.

Customizing your crosstab queries

As useful as crosstab queries can be, you may find that you need to apply some of your own customizations in order to get the results you need. In this section, we explain a few of the ways you can customize your crosstab queries to meet your needs.

Defining criteria in a crosstab query

The ability to filter or limit your crosstab query is another benefit of creating crosstab queries manually. To define a filter for your crosstab query, simply enter the criteria as you normally would for any other aggregate query. Figure 10.34 demonstrates this concept.

Changing the sort order of your crosstab query column headings

By default, crosstab queries sort their column headings in alphabetical order. For example, the crosstab query in Figure 10.35 will produce a dataset where the column headings read this order: Canada, Midwest, North, Northeast, South, Southeast, Southwest, and West.

FIGURE 10.34

You can define a criterion to filter your crosstab queries.

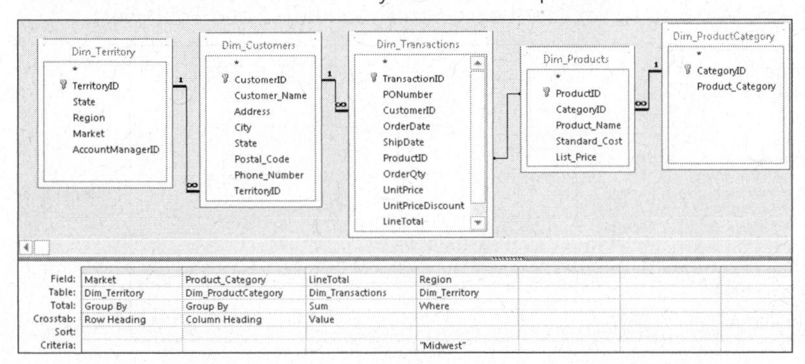

FIGURE 10.35

This crosstab query will display all regions as columns in alphabetical order.

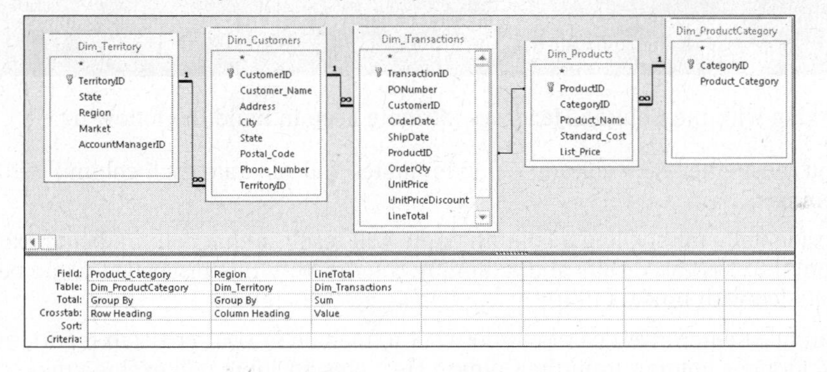

This may be fine in most situations, but if your company headquarters is in California, the executive management may naturally want to see the West region first. You can specify the column order of a crosstab query by changing the Column Headings attribute in the Query Properties.

To get to the Column Headings attribute:

1. **Open the query in Design view.**
2. **Right-click in the gray area above the white query grid and select Properties.** The Query Properties dialog box, shown in Figure 10.36, appears.
3. **Enter the order in which you want to see the column headings by changing the Column Headings attribute.**

10

FIGURE 10.36

The Column Headings attribute is set to have the column read in this order: West, Canada, Midwest, North, Northeast, South, Southeast, and Southwest.

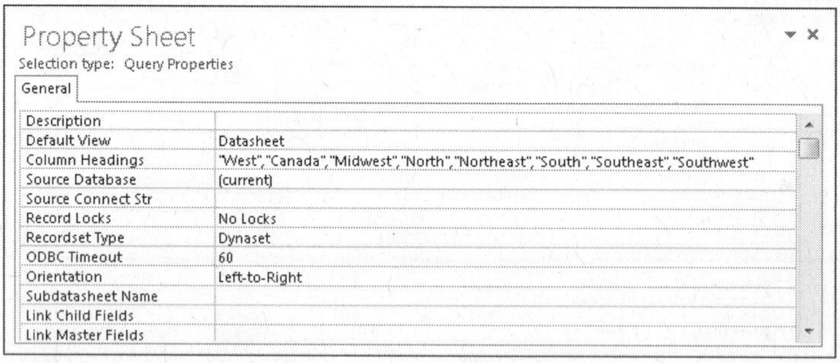

Property Sheet

Selection type: Query Properties

General

Description	
Default View	Datasheet
Column Headings	"West","Canada","Midwest","North","Northeast","South","Southeast","Southwest"
Source Database	(current)
Source Connect Str	
Record Locks	No Locks
Recordset Type	Dynaset
ODBC Timeout	60
Orientation	Left-to-Right
Subdatasheet Name	
Link Child Fields	
Link Master Fields	

TIP

Adjusting the Column Headings attribute comes in handy when you're struggling with showing months in month order instead of alphabetical order. Simply enter the month columns in the order you want to see them. For example: "Jan", "Feb","Mar","Apr","May","Jun", "Jul","Aug","Sep","Oct","Nov","Dec".

When working with the Column Headings attribute keep in mind the following:

- You must enter each column name in quotes and separate each column with commas.
- Accidentally misspelling a column name will result in that column being excluded from the crosstab results and a dummy column with the misspelled name being included with no data in it.
- You must enter every column you want to include in your crosstab report. Excluding a column from the Column Headings attribute will exclude that column from the crosstab results.
- Clearing the Column Headings attribute will ensure that all columns are displayed in alphabetical order.

Part IV

Analyzing Data in Access

Now that you know how to organize the data into tables and how to use queries to interact with that data, the chapters in this part highlight the tools and functionalities in Access 2013 that can drive more meaningful data analysis. Indeed, using Access for your data analysis needs can help you streamline your analytical processes, increase your productivity, and analyze the larger datasets.

Chapter 11 covers data transformation, providing examples of how to clean and shape raw data into staging areas. Chapter 12 provides in-depth instruction on how to create and utilize custom calculations in analysis; this chapter also shows you how to work with dates, using them in simple date calculations. Chapter 13 introduces you to some conditional analysis techniques that allow for the addition of business logic into analytical processes. Chapter 14 explores SQL syntax and some of the SQL-specific queries that can be leveraged to improve analytics. Chapter 15 introduces you to powerful subquery and domain aggregate functionality. Chapter 16 demonstrates many of the advanced statistical analyses that can be performed using subqueries and domain aggregate functions.

IN THIS PART

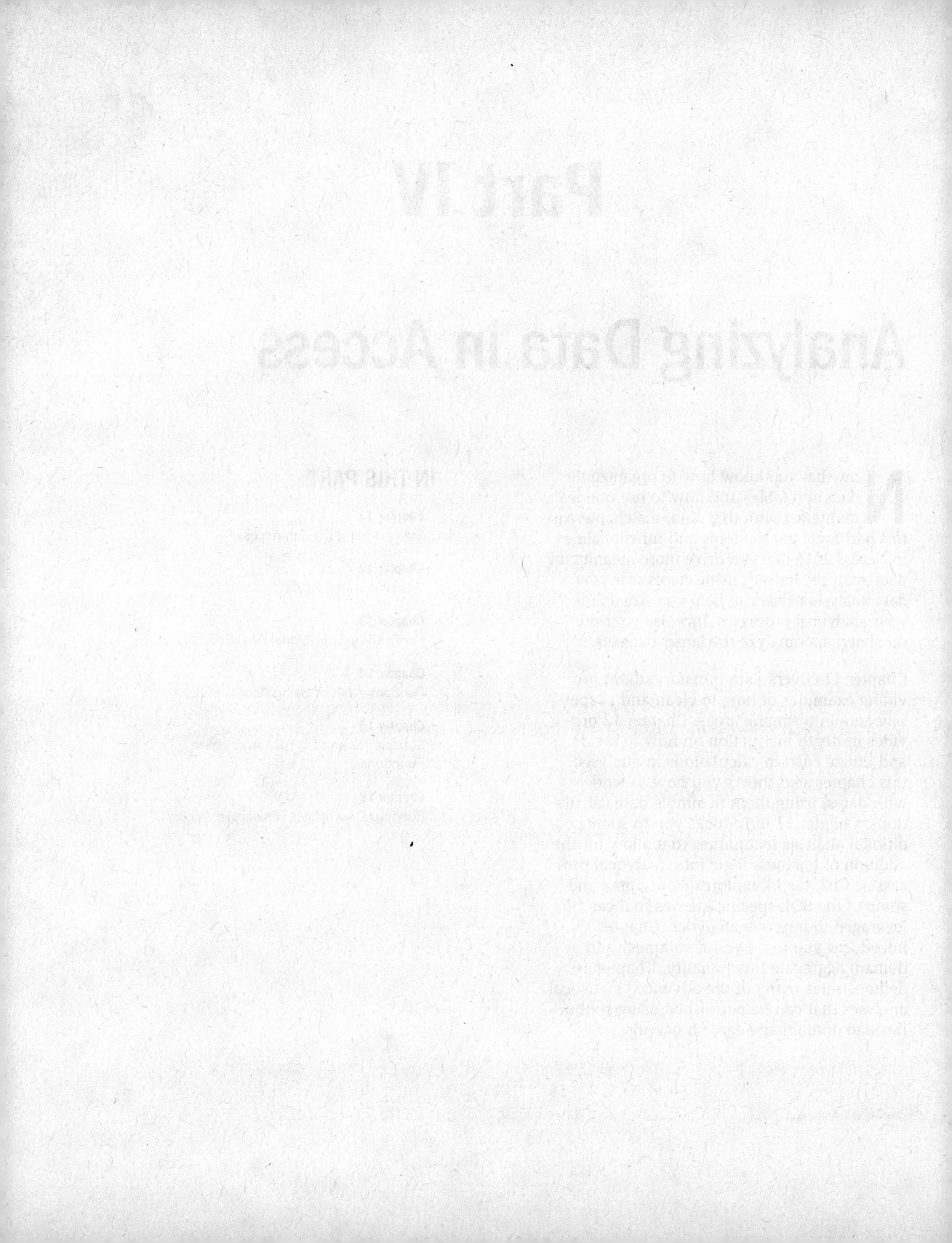

CHAPTER

11

Transforming Data in Access

IN THIS CHAPTER

- Finding and removing duplicate records
- Filling in blank fields
- Concatenating
- Changing case
- Removing leading and trailing spaces
- Finding and replacing specific text
- Padding strings
- Parsing strings

Data transformation generally entails certain actions that are meant to "clean" your data — actions such as establishing a table structure, removing duplicates, cleaning text, removing blanks, and standardizing data fields.

You'll often receive data that is unpolished or raw. That is to say, the data may have duplicates, there may be blank fields, there may be inconsistent text, and so on. Before you can perform any kind of meaningful analysis on data in this state, it's important to go through a process of data transformation or data cleanup.

Many people store their data in Access, but few use Access for data transformation purposes, oftentimes preferring to export the data to Excel, perform any necessary cleanup there, and then import the data back to Access. The obvious motive for this behavior is familiarity with the flexible Excel environment. However, exporting and importing data simply to perform such easy tasks can be quite inefficient, especially if you're working with large datasets.

In this chapter, we introduce you to some of the tools and techniques in Access that make it easy for you to clean and massage your data without turning to Excel.

ON THE WEB

The starting database for this walkthrough, `Chapter11.accdb`, can be downloaded from this book's website.

Finding and Removing Duplicate Records

Duplicate records are absolute analysis killers. The effect duplicate records have on your analysis can be far reaching, corrupting almost every metric, summary, and analytical assessment you produce. For this reason, finding and removing duplicate records should be your first priority when you receive a new dataset.

Defining duplicate records

Before you jump into your dataset to find and remove duplicate records, it's important to consider how you define a *duplicate record.* To demonstrate this point, look at the table shown in Figure 11.1, where you see 11 records. Out of the 11 records, how many are duplicates?

FIGURE 11.1

Are there duplicate records in this table? It depends on how you define one.

SicCode	PostalCode	CompanyNumber	DollarPotential	City	State	Address
1389	77032	11147805	$9,517.00	houston	tx	6000 n sem heirten pkwy e
1389	77032	11147848	$9,517.00	houston	tx	43410 e herdy rd
1389	77042	11160116	$7,653.00	houston	tx	40642 rachmend ave ste 600
1389	77051	11165400	$9,517.00	houston	tx	5646 helmis rd
1389	77057	11173241	$9,517.00	houston	tx	2514 san filape st ste 6600
1389	77060	11178227	$7,653.00	houston	tx	100 n sem heirten pkwy e ste 100
1389	77073	11190514	$9,517.00	houston	tx	4660 rankan rd # 400
1389	77049	11218412	$7,653.00	houston	tx	4541 mallir read 6
1389	77040	13398882	$18,379.00	houston	tx	3643 wandfirn rd
1389	77040	13399102	$18,379.00	houston	tx	3643 wandfirn rd
1389	77077	13535097	$7,653.00	houston	tx	44160 wisthiamir rd ste 100

If you were to define a duplicate record in Figure 11.1 as a duplication of just SicCode, you would find 11 duplicate records. Now, if you were to expand your definition of a duplicate record to a duplication of both SicCode and PostalCode, you'd find only two duplicates: the duplication of PostalCodes 77032 and 77040. Finally, if you were to define a duplicate record as a duplication of the unique value of SicCode, PostalCode, and CompanyNumber, you would find no duplicates.

This example shows that having two records with the same value in a column doesn't necessarily mean that you have a duplicate record. It's up to you to determine which field or combination of fields will best define a unique record in your dataset.

Once you have a clear idea what field(s) best make up a unique record in your table, you can easily test your table for duplicate records by attempting to set them as a primary or combination key. To demonstrate this test, open the LeadList table in Design view, and then tag the CompanyNumber field as a primary key. If you try to save this change, you'll get the error message shown in Figure 11.2. This message means there is some duplication of records in your dataset that needs to be dealt with.

Revisit Chapter 3 to get a refresher on designing tables.

FIGURE 11.2

If you get this error message when trying to set a primary key, you have duplicate records in your dataset.

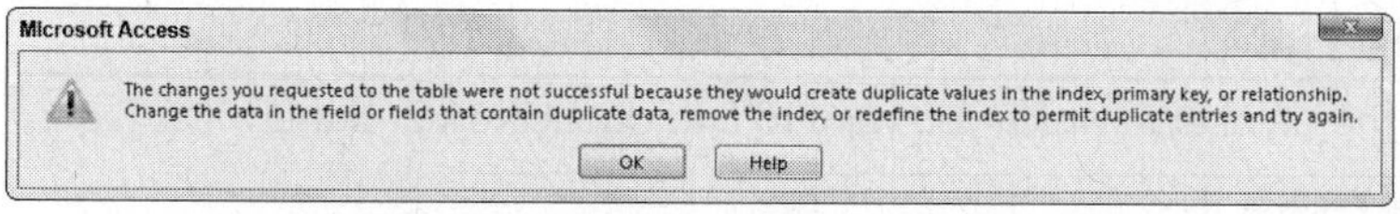

Finding duplicate records

If you've determined that your dataset does, indeed, contain duplicates, it's generally a good idea to find and review the duplicate records before removing them. Giving your records a thorough review will ensure you don't mistake a record as a duplicate and remove it from your analysis. You may find that you're mistakenly identifying valid records as duplicates, in which case you'll need to include another field in your definition of what makes a unique record.

The easiest way to find the duplicate records in your dataset is to run the Find Duplicates Query Wizard.

1. **Select the Create tab of the Ribbon and click the Query Wizard button.** The New Query dialog box, shown in Figure 11.3, appears.
2. **Select Find Duplicates Query Wizard and then click OK.**

FIGURE 11.3

Select the Find Duplicates Query Wizard and then click OK.

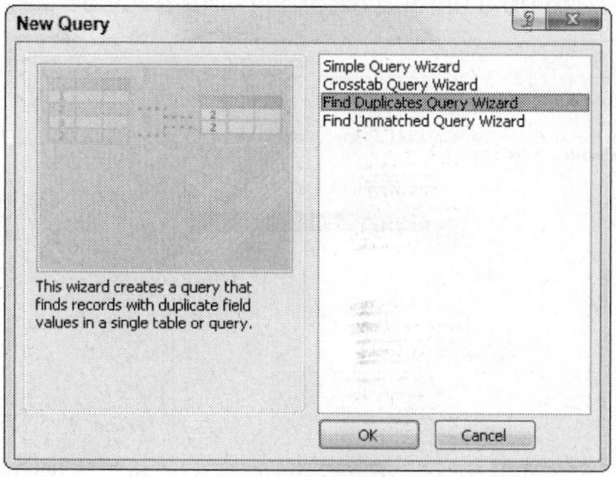

3. **Select the particular dataset you will use in your Find Duplicate query (see Figure 11.4).**

FIGURE 11.4

Select the dataset in which you want to find duplicates, and then click Next.

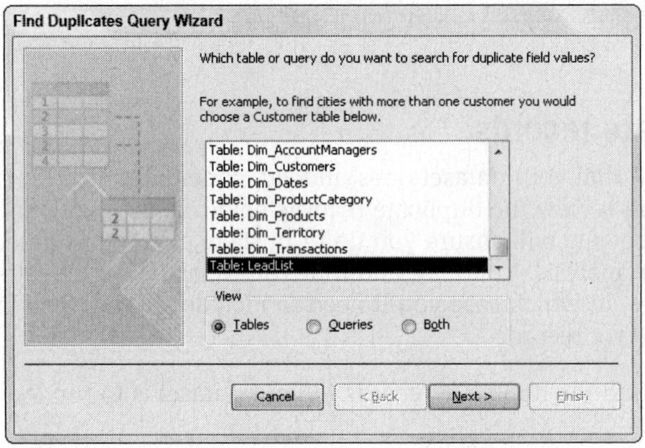

4. **Identify which field, or combination of fields, best defines a unique record in your dataset, and then click Next.** In the example shown in Figure 11.5, the CompanyNumber field alone defines a unique record.

FIGURE 11.5

Select the field(s) that make up a unique record in your dataset.

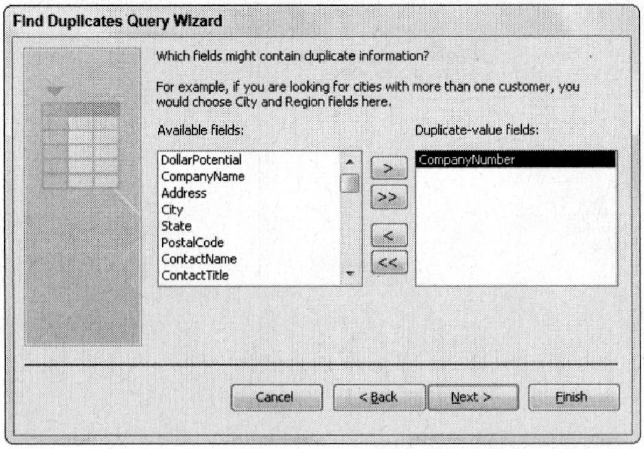

5. **Identify any additional fields you would like to see in your query (see Figure 11.6), and then click Next.**

FIGURE 11.6

Select the field(s) you want to see in your query.

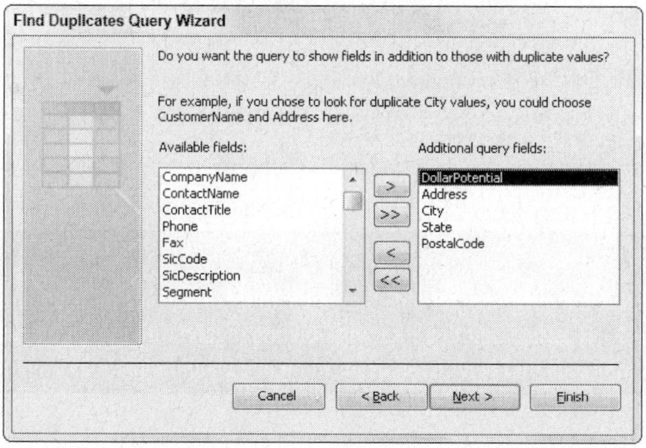

6. **Name your query and click Finish (see Figure 11.7).** Your new Find Duplicates query will immediately open for your review. Figure 11.8 shows the resulting query. Now that Access has found the records that are repeating, you can remove duplicates simply by deleting the duplicate records.

FIGURE 11.7

Name your query and click Finish.

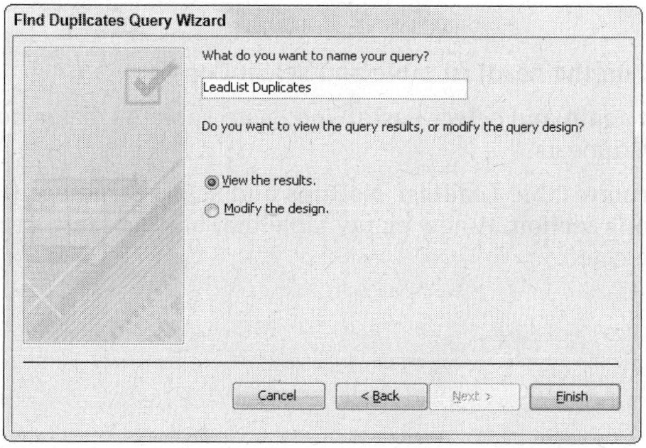

FIGURE 11.8

Your Find Duplicates query.

CompanyNumber	DollarPotential	Address	City	State	PostalCode
10625840	$47,039.00	1100 landirs rd	n little rock	ar	72117
10625840	$47,039.00	1100 landirs rd	n little rock	ar	72117
11145186	$60,770.00	5364 iost fwy	houston	tx	77029
11145186	$60,770.00	5364 iost fwy	houston	tx	77029
11145186	$60,770.00	5364 iost fwy	houston	tx	77029
11145186	$60,770.00	5364 iost fwy	houston	tx	77029
11166089	$60,770.00	6632 biffalo spiidway	houston	tx	77054
11166089	$60,770.00	6632 biffalo spiidway	houston	tx	77054
11166089	$60,770.00	6632 biffalo spiidway	houston	tx	77054
11166089	$60,770.00	6632 biffalo spiidway	houston	tx	77054
11220179	$60,770.00	40420 tilge rd	houston	tx	77095
11220179	$60,770.00	40420 tilge rd	houston	tx	77095
11220179	$60,770.00	40420 tilge rd	houston	tx	77095
11220179	$60,770.00	40420 tilge rd	houston	tx	77095

NOTE

The records shown in your Find Duplicates query are not only the duplications. They include one unique record plus the duplication. For example, in Figure 11.8, notice that there are four records tagged with the CompanyNumber 11145186. Three of the four are duplicates that can be removed, while one should remain as a unique record.

Removing duplicate records

If you're working with a small dataset, removing the duplicates can be as easy as manually deleting records from your Find Duplicates query. However, if you're working with a large dataset, your Find Duplicates query may result in more records than you care to manually delete. Believe it when someone tells you that manually deleting records from a 5,000-row Find Duplicates query is an eyeball-burning experience. Fortunately, there is an alternative to burning out your eyeballs.

The idea is to remove duplicates en masse by taking advantage of the built-in protections Access has against duplicate primary keys. To demonstrate this technique, follow these steps:

1. **Right-click on the LeadList table and select Copy.**
2. **Right-click again and select Paste.** The Paste Table As dialog box, shown in Figure 11.9, appears.
3. **Name your new table LeadList_NoDups and select Structure Only from the Paste Options section.** A new empty table that has the same structure as your original is created.

FIGURE 11.9

Activate the Paste Table As dialog box to copy your table's structure into a new table called LeadList_NoDups.

Paste Table As
Table Name:
LeadList_NoDups
OK
Cancel
Paste Options
Structure Only
Structure and Data
Append Data to Existing Table

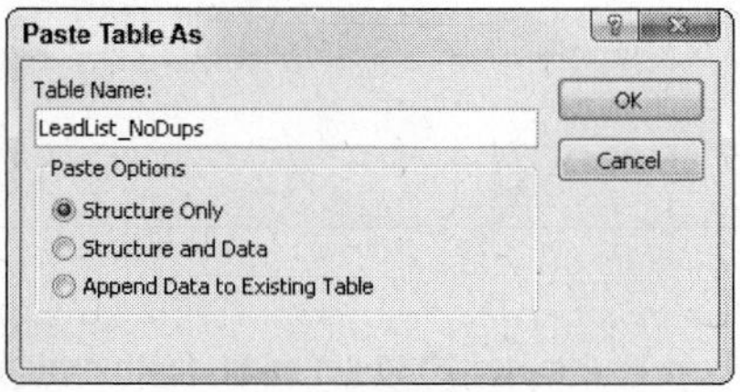

4. **Open your new LeadList_NoDups table in Design view and set the appropriate field or combination of fields as primary keys.** It's up to you to determine which field or combination of fields will best define a unique record in your dataset. As you can see in Figure 11.10, the CompanyNumber field alone defines a unique record; therefore, only the CompanyNumber field will be set as a primary key.

FIGURE 11.10

Set as a primary key the field(s) that best define a unique record.

Field Name	Data Type
CompanyNumber	Short Text
DollarPotential	Currency
CompanyName	Short Text
Address	Short Text
City	Short Text
State	Short Text
PostalCode	Short Text
ContactName	Short Text
ContactTitle	Short Text
Phone	Short Text
Fax	Short Text
SicCode	Short Text
SicDescription	Short Text

Pause here a moment and review what you have so far. At this point, you should have a table called LeadList and a table called LeadList_NoDups. The LeadList_NoDups table is empty and has the CompanyNumber field set as a primary key.

5. **Create an Append query that appends all records from the LeadList table to the LeadList_NoDups table.** When you run the Append query, you'll get a message similar to the one shown in Figure 11.11.

FIGURE 11.11

Now you can append all records excluding the duplicates.

Microsoft Access
Microsoft Access can't append all the records in the append query.
Microsoft Access set 0 field(s) to Null due to a type conversion failure, and it didn't add 1617 record(s) to the table due to key violations, 0 record(s) due to lock violations, and 0 record(s) due to validation rule violations.
Do you want to run the action query anyway?
To ignore the error(s) and run the query, click Yes.
For an explanation of the causes of the violations, click Help.
Yes
No
Help

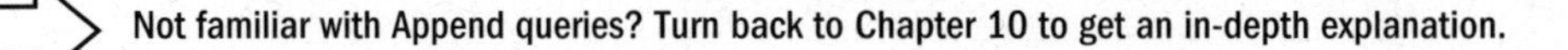

Not familiar with Append queries? Turn back to Chapter 10 to get an in-depth explanation.

Because the CustomerNumber field in the LeadList_NoDups table is set as the primary key, Access won't allow duplicate customer numbers to be appended. In just a few clicks, you've effectively created a table free from duplicates. You can now use this duplicate-free table as the source for any subsequent analysis!

Removing Duplicates with One Make-Table Query

Here's a trick that will allow you to remove duplicates by running a make-table query.

1. **Select the Create tab and choose Query Design.**
2. **In the Show Table dialog box, select your table that contains duplicates.**
3. **On the Query Tools Design tab, select the Properties Sheet command.** The Property Sheet dialog box, shown in the following figure, appears.

All you have to do here is change the Unique Values property to Yes. Close the Property Sheet dialog box and change the query type to a Make Table Query.

CAUTION

Be aware that Access makes no fuzzy logical determination to see if records may duplicate. It processes your request literally. For instance, a simple mistyping of an address or phone number would mean that rows that actually are duplicates would be allowed. You'll want to keep this in mind, especially when working with textual fields where data entry is manual.

Common Transformation Tasks

Besides duplicate records, you'll find that many of the unpolished datasets that come to you will require other types of transformation actions. This section covers some of the more common transformation tasks you'll have to perform.

Filling in blank fields

Often, you'll have fields that contain empty values. These values are considered null — a value of nothing. Nulls are not necessarily a bad thing. In fact, if used properly, they can be an important part of a well-designed relational database. That said, you may find that you need to fill in blank fields with some logical code that indicates a missing value.

Filling in the null fields in your dataset is as simple as running an update query. In the example shown in Figure 11.12, you're updating the null values in the DollarPotential field to zero.

FIGURE 11.12

This query will update the null values in the DollarPotential field to a value of 0.

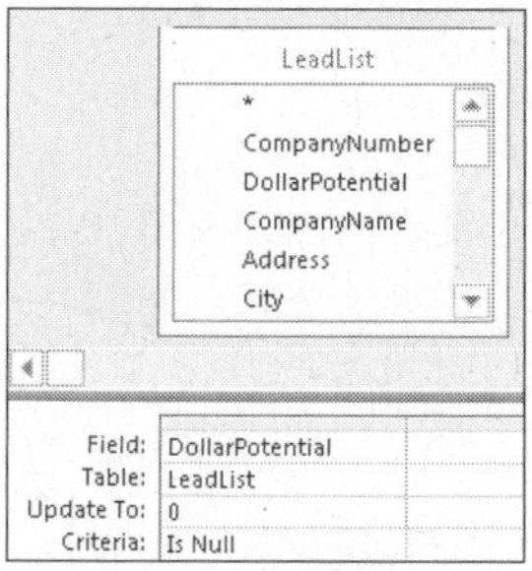

LeadList
*
CompanyNumber
DollarPotential
CompanyName
Address
City

Field:	DollarPotential
Table:	LeadList
Update To:	0
Criteria:	Is Null

It's important to note that there are actually two kinds of blank values: null and empty string (""). When filling in the blank values of a text field, include the empty string as a criterion in your update query to ensure that you don't miss any fields. In the example shown in Figure 11.13, you're updating the blank values in the Segment field to "Other."

FIGURE 11.13

This query will update blank values in the Segment field to a value of "Other."

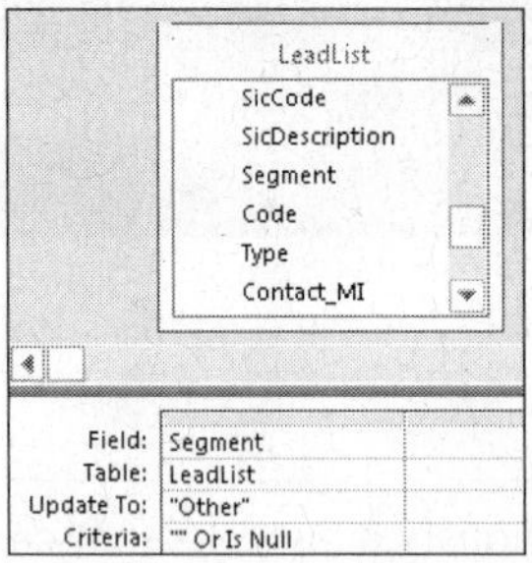

Concatenating

It's always amazing to see anyone export data out of Access and into Excel, only to concatenate (join two or more character strings end to end) and then re-import the data back into Access. You can easily concatenate any number of ways in Access with a simple Update query.

Concatenating fields

Look at the update query shown in Figure 11.14. In this query, you're updating the MyTest field with the concatenated row values of the Type field and the Code field.

FIGURE 11.14

This query concatenates the row values of the Type field and the Code field.

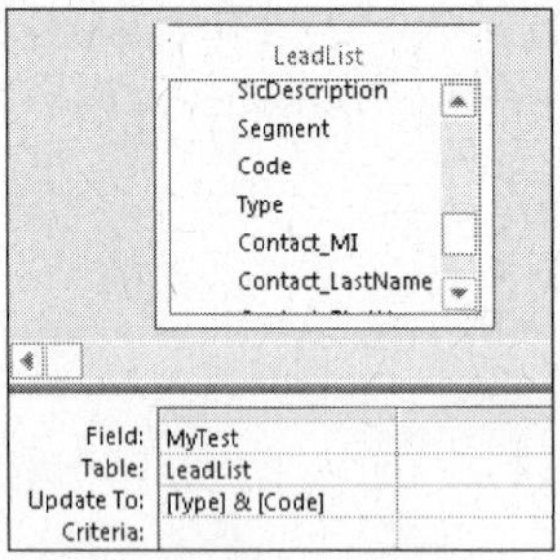

TIP

It's a good idea to create a test field in order to test the effects of your data transformation actions before applying changes to the real data.

Take a moment to analyze the following query breakdown:

- **[Type]:** This tells Access to use the row values of the Type field.
- **&:** The ampersand is a character operator that joins strings together.
- **[Code]:** This tells Access to use the row values of the Code field.
- **&:** The ampersand is a character operator that joins strings together.

Figure 11.15 shows the results of this query.

FIGURE 11.15

The MyTest field now contains the concatenated values of the Type field and the Code field.

Type	Code	MyTest
DB	100199	DB100199
DB	200	DB200
DB	100199	DB100199
DB	100199	DB100199
DB	100199	DB100199
DB	100199	DB100199
DB	100199	DB100199
DB	100199	DB100199
DB	100199	DB100199
DB	100199	DB100199
DB	200	DB200
DB	100199	DB100199

CAUTION

When running update queries that perform concatenations, make sure the field you're updating is large enough to accept the concatenated string. For example, if the length of your concatenated string is 100 characters long, and the field size of the field you're updating is 50 characters long, your concatenated string will be cut short without warning.

Augmenting field values with your own text

You can augment the values in your fields by adding your own text. For example, you may want to concatenate the row values of the Type field and the Code field, but separate them with a colon. The query in Figure 11.16 does just that.

FIGURE 11.16

This query concatenates the row values of the Type field and the Code field and separates them with a colon.

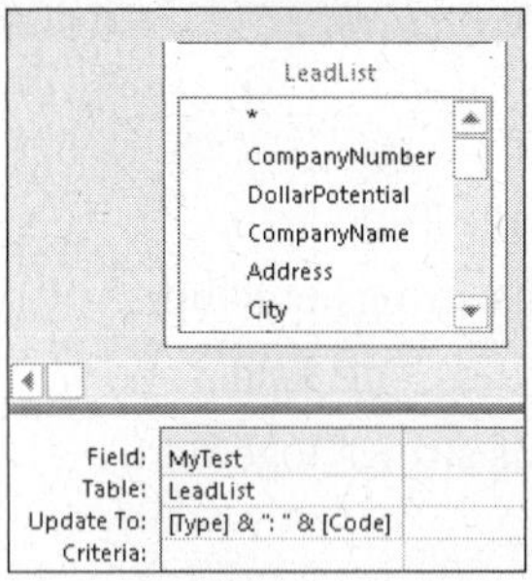

LeadList
*
CompanyNumber
DollarPotential
CompanyName
Address
City

Field:	MyTest
Table:	LeadList
Update To:	[Type] & ": " & [Code]
Criteria:	

Take a moment to analyze the following query breakdown:

- **[Type]:** This tells Access to use the row values of the Type field.
- **&:** The ampersand is a character operator that joins strings together.
- **": ":** This text will add a colon and a space to the concatenated string.
- **&:** The ampersand is a character operator that joins strings together.
- **[Code]:** This tells Access to use the row values of the Code field.

Figure 11.17 shows the results of this query.

FIGURE 11.17

The MyTest field now contains the concatenated values of the Type field and the Code field, separated by a colon.

Type	Code	MyTest
DB	100199	DB: 100199
DB	200	DB: 200
DB	100199	DB: 100199
DB	100199	DB: 100199
DB	100199	DB: 100199
DB	100199	DB: 100199
DB	100199	DB: 100199
DB	100199	DB: 100199
DB	100199	DB: 100199
DB	100199	DB: 100199

NOTE

When specifying your own text in a query, you must enclose the text in quotes.

Changing case

Making sure the text in your database has the correct capitalization may sound trivial, but it's important. Imagine you receive a customer table that has an address field where all the addresses are lowercase. How is that going to look on labels, form letters, or invoices? Fortunately, for those who are working with tables containing thousands of records, Access has a few built-in functions that make changing the case of your text a snap.

The LeadList table shown in Figure 11.18 contains an Address field that is in all lowercase letters.

FIGURE 11.18

The Address field is in all lowercase letters.

Address	City	State	PostalCode
46 gin criaghten w ebrems dr	agawam	ma	01001
426 bewlis rd	agawam	ma	01001
651 sheimekir ln	agawam	ma	01001
44 almgrin dr	agawam	ma	01001
35 mall ln	brimfield	ma	01010
460 fillir rd	chicopee	ma	01020
320 mimeraal dr ste 4	chicopee	ma	01020
4010 shiradan st	chicopee	ma	01022
5046 wistevir rd	chicopee	ma	01022
40 meple st	east longmeadow	ma	01028
242 biich st	holyoke	ma	01040

To fix the values in the Address field, you can use the `StrConv` function, which is a function that converts a string to a specified case. To use the `StrConv` function, you must provide two required arguments: the string to be converted and the conversion type.

```
StrConv(string to be converted, conversion type,)
```

The string to be converted is simply the text you're working with. In a query environment, you can use the name of a field to specify that you're converting all the row values of that field.

The conversion type tells Access whether you want to convert the specified text to all uppercase, all lowercase, or proper case. A set of constants identifies the conversion type:

- **Conversion type 1:** Converts the specified text to uppercase characters.
- **Conversion type 2:** Converts the specified text to lowercase characters.
- **Conversion type 3:** Converts the specified text to proper case. That is, the first letter of every word is uppercase.

For example:

`StrConv("My Text",1)` would be converted to "MY TEXT."

`StrConv("MY TEXT",2)` would be converted to "my text."

`StrConv("my text",3)` would be converted to "My Text."

The Update query shown in Figure 11.19 will convert the values of the Address field to proper case.

FIGURE 11.19

This query will convert addresses to proper case.

Field:	Address
Table:	LeadList
Update To:	StrConv([Address],3)
Criteria:	

> **NOTE**
> You can also use the `Ucase` and `Lcase` functions to convert your text to uppercase and lowercase text. These functions are highlighted in Appendix D of this book.

Removing leading and trailing spaces from a string

When you receive a dataset from a mainframe system, a data warehouse, or even a text file, it is not uncommon to have field values that contain leading and trailing spaces. These spaces can cause some abnormal results, especially when you're appending values with leading and trailing spaces to other values that are clean. To demonstrate this, look at the dataset in Figure 11.20.

This is intended to be an aggregate query that displays the sum of the dollar potential for California, New York, and Texas. However, the leading spaces are causing Access to group each state into two sets, preventing you from discerning the accurate totals.

FIGURE 11.20

The leading spaces are preventing an accurate aggregation.

State	SumOfDollarPotential
ca	$26,561,554.00
ny	$7,483,960.00
tx	$13,722,782.00
ca	$12,475,489.00
ny	$827,563.00
tx	$7,669,208.00

You can easily remove leading and trailing spaces by using the `Trim` function. Figure 11.21 demonstrates how you would update a field to remove the leading and trailing spaces by using an update query.

FIGURE 11.21

Simply pass the field name through the `Trim` function in an update query to remove the leading and trailing spaces.

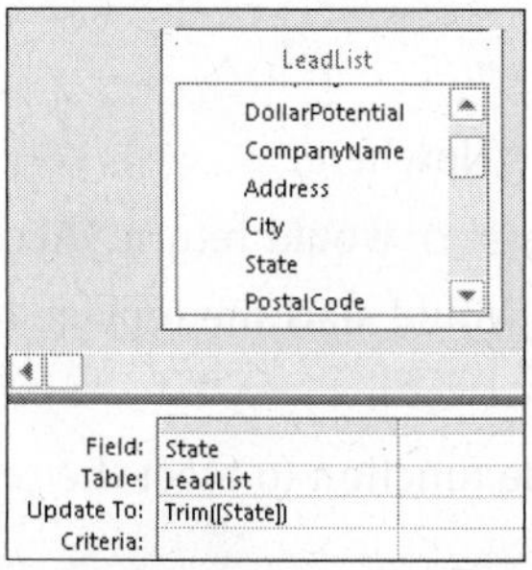

NOTE

Using the `Ltrim` function will remove only the leading spaces, while the `Rtrim` function will remove only the trailing spaces. These functions are highlighted in Appendix D of this book.

Finding and replacing specific text

Imagine that you work in a company called BLVD, Inc. One day, the president of your company informs you that the abbreviation "blvd" on all addresses is now deemed an infringement on your company's trademarked name and must be changed to "Boulevard" as soon as possible. How would you go about meeting this new requirement? Your first thought may be to use the built-in Find and Replace functionality that exists in all Office applications. However, when your data consists of hundreds of thousands of rows, the Find and Replace function will only be able to process a few thousand records at a time. This clearly would not be very efficient.

The `Replace` function is ideal in a situation like this:

```
Replace(Expression, Find, Replace[, Start[, Count[, Compare]]])
```

There are three required arguments in a `Replace` function and three optional arguments:

- **Expression (required):** This is the full string you're evaluating. In a query environment, you can use the name of a field to specify that you're evaluating all the row values of that field.
- **Find (required):** This is the substring you need to find and replace.

- **Replace (required):** This is the substring used as the replacement.
- **Start (optional):** The position within a substring to begin the search; the default is 1.
- **Count (optional):** The number of occurrences to replace; the default is all occurrences.
- **Compare (optional):** The kind of comparison to use; see Appendix D for details.

For example:

`Replace("Pear", "P", "B")` would return "Bear."

`Replace("Now Here", " H", "h")` would return "Nowhere."

`Replace("Microsoft Access", "Microsoft ", "")` would return "Access."

`Replace("Roadsign Road", "Road", "Rd",9)` would start the replace function at the ninth character, returning "Roadsign Rd"

Figure 11.22 demonstrates how you would use the Replace function to meet the requirements in this scenario.

FIGURE 11.22

This query finds all instances of "blvd" and replaces them with "Boulevard."

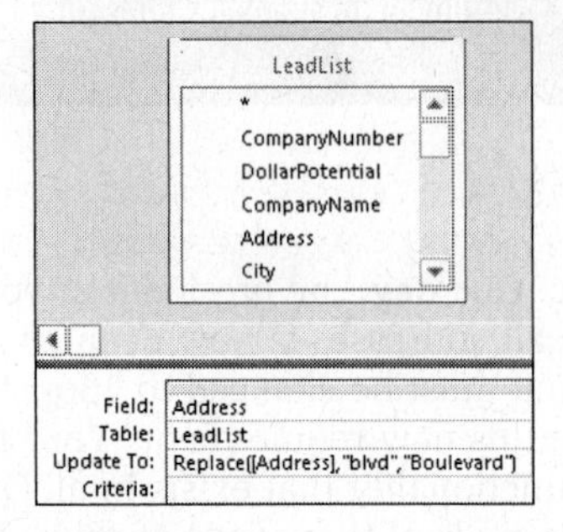

Adding your own text in key positions within a string

When transforming your data, you'll sometimes have to add your own text in key positions with a string. For example, in Figure 11.23, you'll see two fields. The Phone field is the raw phone number received from a mainframe report, while the MyTest field is the same phone number transformed into a standard format. As you can see, the two parentheses and the dash were added in the appropriate positions within the string to achieve the correct format.

11

FIGURE 11.23

The phone number has been transformed into a standard format by adding the appropriate characters to key positions with the string.

Phone	MyTest
6455364000	(645)536-4000
4545426660	(454)542-6660
4545420450	(454)542-0450
4545433000	(454)543-3000
5335656364	(533)565-6364
2051564000	(205)156-4000
2051453200	(205)145-3200
2051640400	(205)164-0400
2051432500	(205)143-2500
6452340665	(645)234-0665
2053513040	(205)351-3040

The edits demonstrated in Figure 11.23 were accomplished using the `Right` function, the `Left` function, and the `Mid` function in conjunction with each other. The `Right`, `Left`, and `Mid` functions allow you to extract portions of a string starting from different positions:

- The `Left` function returns a specified number of characters starting from the leftmost character of the string. The required arguments for the `Left` function are the text you're evaluating and the number of characters you want returned. For example, `Left("70056-3504", 5)` would return five characters starting from the leftmost character (`70056`).
- The `Right` function returns a specified number of characters starting from the rightmost character of the string. The required arguments for the `Right` function are the text you're evaluating and the number of characters you want returned. For example, `Right("Microsoft", 4)` would return four characters starting from the rightmost character (`soft`).
- The `Mid` function returns a specified number of characters starting from a specified character position. The required arguments for the `Mid` function are the text you're evaluating, the starting position, and the number of characters you want returned. For example, `Mid("Lonely", 2, 3)` would return three characters starting from the second character, or character number two in the string (`one`).

TIP

In a `Mid` function, if there are fewer characters in the text being used than the length argument, the entire text will be returned. For example, `Mid("go",1,10000)` will return `go`. As you'll see later in this chapter, this behavior comes in handy when you're working with nested functions.

Figure 11.24 demonstrates how the MyTest field was updated to the correctly formatted phone number.

FIGURE 11.24

This query will update the MyTest field with a properly formatted phone number.

LeadList
PostalCode
ContactName
ContactTitle
Phone
Fax
SicCode

Field:	MyTest
Table:	LeadList
Update To:	"(" & Left([Phone],3) & ")" & Mid([Phone],4,3) & "-" & Right([Phone],4)
Criteria:	

Take a moment to analyze the query breakdown:

- "(": This text will add an open parenthesis to the resulting string.
- **&:** The ampersand is a character operator that joins strings together.
- **Left([Phone],3):** This function will extract the left 3 characters of the [Phone] field.
- **&:** The ampersand is a character operator that joins strings together.
- ")": This text will add a close parenthesis to the resulting string.
- **&:** The ampersand is a character operator that joins strings together.
- **Mid([Phone],4,3):** This function will extract the three characters of the [Phone] field starting from character number four.
- **&:** The ampersand is a character operator that joins strings together.
- "-": This text will add a dash to the resulting string.
- **&:** The ampersand is a character operator that joins strings together.
- **Right([Phone],4):** This function will extract the right four characters of the [Phone] field.

Padding Strings to a Specific Number of Characters

You may encounter a situation where key fields are required to be a certain number of characters in order for your data to be able to interface with peripheral platforms such as ADP or SAP.

For example, imagine that the CompanyNumber field shown in the following figure must be ten characters long. Those that are not ten characters long must be padded with enough leading zeros to create a ten-character string.

NOTE

Number fields (fields with the Number data type) cannot have padded zeros, as Access will simply remove them. If you need a number string to have padded zeros, you will need to set the field to have a Text data type.

CompanyNumber
113
13792992
14280866
630
2298
3082
3128
19641288
3909
4758
13972608

The secret to this trick is to add ten zeros to every company number, regardless of the current length, and then pass them through a `Right` function that will extract only the right ten characters. For example, company number 29875764 would first be converted to 000000000029875764; then it would go into a `Right` function that extracted only the right ten characters: `Right("000000000029875764",10)`. This would leave you with 0029875764.

Although this is essentially two steps, you can accomplish the same thing with just one update query. The following figure demonstrates how this is done. This query first concatenates each company number with `0000000000`, and then passes that concatenated string through a `Right` function that extracts only the left ten characters.

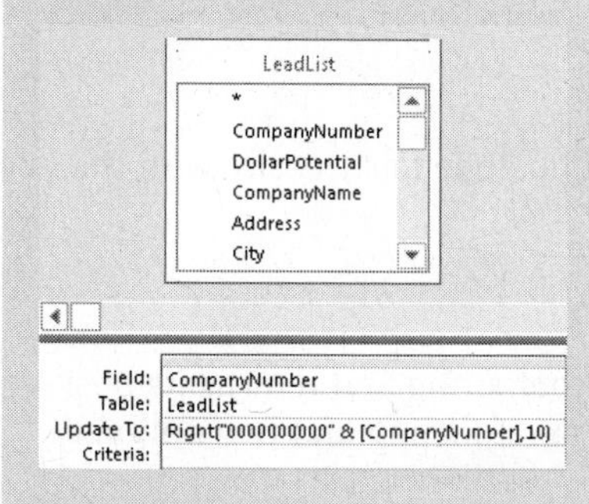

The following figure shows the results of this query. The CompanyNumber field now contains ten-character company numbers.

CompanyNumber
0000000113
0013792992
0014280866
0000000630
0000002298
0000003082
0000003128
0019641288
0000003909
0000004758
0013972608

Parsing strings using character markers

Have you ever gotten a dataset where two or more distinct pieces of data were jammed into one field and separated by commas? For example, in Figure 11.25, you can see that the values in the ContactName field are strings that represent "Last name, First name, Middle initial." You'll need to parse this string into three separate fields.

FIGURE 11.25

You need to parse the values in the ContactName field into three separate fields.

ContactName
DINBY, IRNIST, I.
MCGEVIRN, HIGH, B.
DATTCO, KATHY, R.
TAYIH, HANABAL, T.
LIMIK, CHRASTEPHIR, O.
WALLEIGHBY, FRANK, S.
KRIMSAIK, PIRRY, D.
SANTEN, MACHEIL, S.
MSWUINIY, RACHERD, T.
PHILEN, DALE, H.
JPERTIN, HANK, G.
PITIRS, JEE, P.
KIQJA, CANDY, D.
PERTIN, HANK, G.
CHESIN, JENATHAN, G.

Although this is not a straightforward undertaking, it can be done fairly easily with the help of the `InStr` function:

```
InStr(Start, String, Find, Compare)
```

The `InStr` function searches for a specified string in another string and returns its position number. There are two required arguments in an `InStr` function and two optional arguments.

- **Start (optional):** This is the character number with which to start the search; the default is 1.
- **String (required):** This is the string to be searched.
- **Find (required):** This is the string to search for.
- **Compare (optional):** This specifies the type of string comparison. If you specify a Compare argument, the Start argument becomes not optional.

For example:

`InStr("Alexander, Mike, H",",")` would return `10` because the first comma of the string is character number 10.

`InStr(11,"Alexander, Mike, H",",")` would return `16` because the first comma from character number 11 is character number 16.

If the `InStr` function only returns a number, how can it help you? Well, the idea is to use the `InStr` function with the `Left`, `Right`, or `Mid` functions in order to extract a string. For example, instead of using a hard-coded number in your `Left` function to pass it the required length argument, you can use a nested `InStr` function to return that number. For example, `Left("Alexander, Mike",9)` is the same as `Left("Alexander, Mike", Instr("Alexander, Mike", ",")-1)`.

NOTE

When you're nesting an `InStr` function inside a `Left`, `Right`, or `Mid` function, you may have to add or subtract a character, depending on what you want to accomplish. For example, `Left("Zey, Robert", InStr("Zey, Robert", ","))` would return `"Zey,"`. Why is the comma included in the returned result? The `InStr` function returns `4` because the first comma in the string is the fourth character. The `Left` function then uses this `4` as a length argument, effectively extracting the left four characters: "Zey,".

If you want a clean extract without the comma, you'll have to modify your function to read as follows:

```
Left("Zey, Robert", InStr("Zey, Robert", ",")-1)
```

Subtracting 1 from the `InStr` function would leave you with 3 instead of 4. The `Left` function then uses this `3` as the length argument, effectively extracting the left three characters: "Zey".

The easiest way to parse the contact name field, shown in Figure 11.26, is to use two Update queries.

CAUTION

This is a somewhat tricky process, so you'll want to create and work in test fields, giving yourself a way back from any mistakes you may make.

Query 1

The first query, shown in Figure 11.26, will parse out the last name in the ContactName field and update the Contact_LastName field. It will then update the Contact_FirstName field with the remaining string.

FIGURE 11.26

This query will update the Contact_LastName and Contact_FirstName fields.

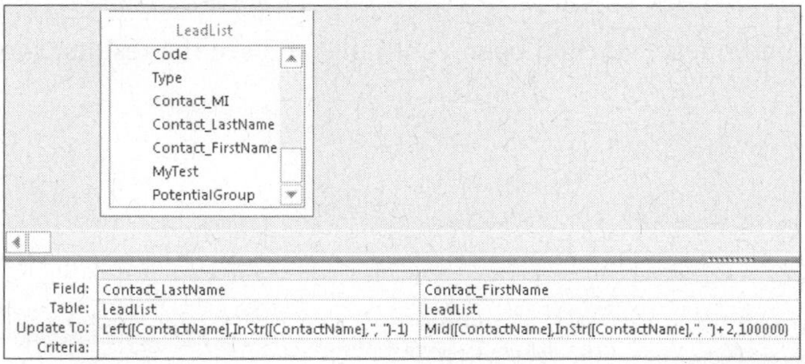

LeadList
Code
Type
Contact_MI
Contact_LastName
Contact_FirstName
MyTest
PotentialGroup

Field:	Contact_LastName	Contact_FirstName
Table:	LeadList	LeadList
Update To:	Left([ContactName],InStr([ContactName],", ")-1)	Mid([ContactName],InStr([ContactName],", ")+2,100000)
Criteria:		

If you open the LeadList table, you'll be able to see the impact of your first Update query. Figure 11.27 shows your progress so far.

FIGURE 11.27

Check your progress so far.

Contact_LastName	Contact_FirstName
DINBY	IRNIST, I.
MCGEVIRN	HIGH, B.
DATTCO	KATHY, R.
TAYIH	HANABAL, T.
LIMIK	CHRASTEPHIR, O.
WALLEIGHBY	FRANK, S.
KRIMSAIK	PIRRY, D.
SANTEN	MACHEIL, S.
MSWUINIY	RACHERD, T.
PHILEN	DALE, H.
JPERTIN	HANK, G.
PITIRS	JEE, P.
KIQJA	CANDY, D.
PERTIN	HANK, G.
CHESIN	JENATHAN, G.

Query 2

The second query, shown in Figure 11.28, will update the Contact_FirstName field and the Contact_MI.

FIGURE 11.28

This query parses out the first name and the middle initial from the Contact_FirstName field.

LeadList: Code, Type, Contact_MI, Contact_LastName, Contact_FirstName, MyTest, PotentialGroup

Field:	Contact_FirstName	Contact_MI
Table:	LeadList	LeadList
Update To:	Left([Contact_FirstName],InStr([Contact_FirstName],", ")-1)	Mid([Contact_FirstName],InStr([Contact_FirstName],", ")+2,100000)
Criteria:		

After you run your second query, you can open your table and see the results, shown in Figure 11.29.

FIGURE 11.29

With two queries, you've successfully parsed the ContactName field into three separate fields.

ContactName	Contact_LastName	Contact_FirstName	Contact_MI
DINBY, IRNIST, I.	DINBY	IRNIST	I.
MCGEVIRN, HIGH, B.	MCGEVIRN	HIGH	B.
DATTCO, KATHY, R.	DATTCO	KATHY	R.
TAYIH, HANABAL, T.	TAYIH	HANABAL	T.
LIMIK, CHRASTEPHIR, O.	LIMIK	CHRASTEPHIR	O.
WALLEIGHBY, FRANK, S.	WALLEIGHBY	FRANK	S.
KRIMSAIK, PIRRY, D.	KRIMSAIK	PIRRY	D.
SANTEN, MACHEIL, S.	SANTEN	MACHEIL	S.
MSWUINIY, RACHERD, T.	MSWUINIY	RACHERD	T.
PHILEN, DALE, H.	PHILEN	DALE	H.
JPERTIN, HANK, G.	JPERTIN	HANK	G.
PITIRS, JEE, P.	PITIRS	JEE	P.
KIQJA, CANDY, D.	KIQJA	CANDY	D.
PERTIN, HANK, G.	PERTIN	HANK	G.
CHESIN, JENATHAN, G.	CHESIN	JENATHAN	G.

CHAPTER 12

Working with Calculations and Dates

IN THIS CHAPTER

Using calculations in your analyses

Using dates in your analyses

The truth is that few organizations can analyze their raw data at face value. More often than not, some preliminary analysis with calculations and dates must be carried out before the big-picture analysis can be performed. Again, Excel is the preferred platform for working with calculations and dates. However, as you'll learn in this chapter, Access provides a wide array of tools and built-in functions that make working with calculations and dates possible.

ON THE WEB

The starting database for this walkthrough, `Chapter12.accdb`, can be downloaded from this book's website. When you use the sample database, you'll be able to open the queries shown in the figures. Some of the queries look a bit different from the screenshots shown here. Don't be alarmed — Access sometimes shuffles around criteria and expressions because of its built-in query optimizer. The query optimizer is charged with the task of structuring the query in the quickest, most cost-effective way possible.

Using Calculations in Your Analyses

If you're an Excel user trying to familiarize yourself with Access, one of the questions you undoubtedly have is, "Where do the formulas go?" In Excel, you have the flexibility to enter a calculation via a formula directly into the dataset you're analyzing. You can't do this in Access. So, the question is, "Where do you store calculations in Access?"

As you've already learned, things work differently in Access. A best practice when working in a database environment is to keep your data separate from your analysis. In this light, you won't be able to store a calculation (a formula) in your dataset. Now, it's true that you can store the calculated results in your tables, but using tables to store calculated results is problematic for several reasons:

- Stored calculations take up valuable storage space.
- Stored calculations require constant maintenance as the data in your table changes.
- Stored calculations generally tie your data to one analytical path.

Instead of storing the calculated results as hard data, it's a better practice to perform calculations in real time, at the precise moment when they're needed. This ensures the most current and accurate results and doesn't tie your data to one particular analysis.

Common calculation scenarios

In Access, calculations are performed using expressions. An *expression* is a combination of values, operators, or functions that are evaluated to return a separate value to be used in a subsequent process. For example, `2+2` is an expression that returns the integer `4`, which can be used in a subsequent analysis. Expressions can be used almost anywhere in Access to accomplish various tasks; in queries, forms, reports, data access pages, and even tables to a certain degree. In this section, you'll learn how to expand your analysis by building real-time calculations using expressions.

Using constants in calculations

Most calculations typically consist of hard-coded numbers or constants. A *constant* is a static value that doesn't change. For example, in the expression `[List_Price]*1.1`, `1.1` is a constant; the value of `1.1` will never change. Figure 12.1 demonstrates how a constant can be used in an expression within a query.

In this example, you're building a query that will analyze how the current price for each product compares to the same price with a 10 percent increase. The expression, entered under the alias "Increase" will multiply the List_Price field of each record with a constant value of 1.1, calculating a price that is 10 percent over the original value in the List_Price field.

FIGURE 12.1

In this query, you're using a constant to calculate a 10 percent price increase.

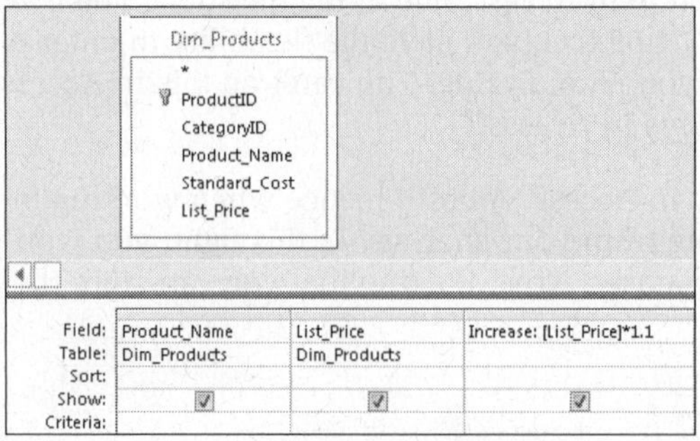

Dim_Products
*
ProductID
CategoryID
Product_Name
Standard_Cost
List_Price

Field:	Product_Name	List_Price	Increase: [List_Price]*1.1
Table:	Dim_Products	Dim_Products	
Sort:			
Show:	☑	☑	☑
Criteria:			

Using fields in calculations

Not all your calculations will require you to specify a constant. In fact, many of the mathematical operations you'll carry out will be performed on data that already resides in fields within your dataset. You can perform calculations using any fields formatted as number or currency.

For instance, in the query shown in Figure 12.2, you aren't using any constants. Instead, your calculation will be executed using the values in each record of the dataset. This is similar to referencing cell values in an Excel formula.

FIGURE 12.2

In this query, you're using two fields in a Dollar Variance calculation.

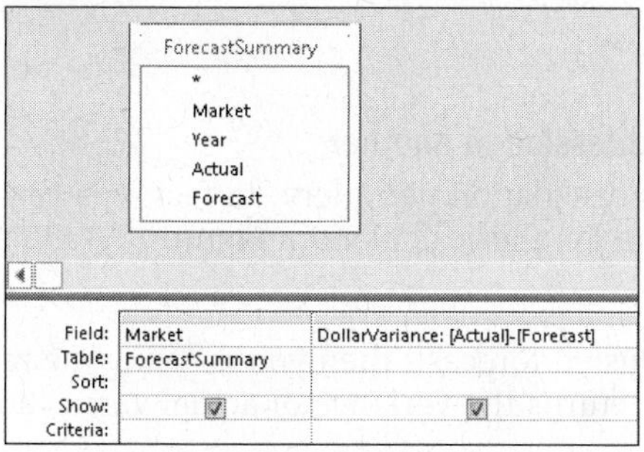

Using the results of aggregation in calculations

Using the result of an aggregation as an expression in a calculation allows you to perform multiple analytical steps in one query. In the example in Figure 12.3, you're running an aggregate query. This query will execute in the following order:

1. The query groups your records by market.
2. The query calculates the count of orders and the sum of revenue for each market.
3. The query assigns the aliases you've defined respectively (OrderCount and Rev).
4. The query uses the aggregation results for each branch as expressions in your AvgDollarPerOrder calculation.

FIGURE 12.3

In this query, you're using the aggregation results for each market as expressions in your calculation.

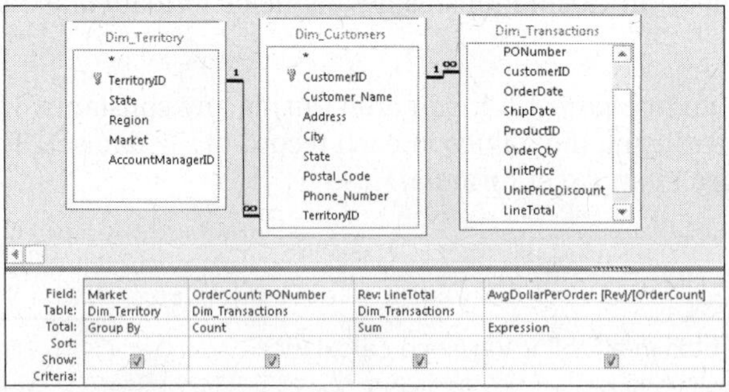

Field:	Market	OrderCount: PONumber	Rev: LineTotal	AvgDollarPerOrder: [Rev]/[OrderCount]
Table:	Dim_Territory	Dim_Transactions	Dim_Transactions	
Total:	Group By	Count	Sum	Expression
Sort:				
Show:	✓	✓	✓	✓
Criteria:				

Using the results of one calculation as an expression in another

Keep in mind that you aren't limited to one calculation per query. In fact, you can use the results of one calculation as an expression in another calculation. Figure 12.4 illustrates this concept.

In this query, you're first calculating an adjusted forecast; then you're using the results of that calculation in another calculation that returns the variance of actual versus adjusted forecast.

FIGURE 12.4

This query uses the results of one calculation as an expression in another.

Field:	Market	AdjustedForecast: [Forecast]*0.9	NewVariance: [Actual]-[AdjustedForecast]
Table:	ForecastSummary		
Sort:			
Show:	✓	✓	✓
Criteria:			

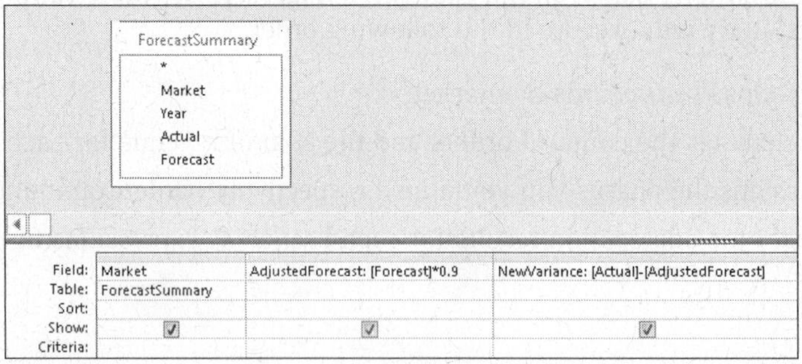

Using a calculation as an argument in a function

Look at the query in Figure 12.5. The calculation in this query will return a number with a fractional part. That is, it will return a number that contains a decimal point followed by many trailing digits. You would like to return a round number, however, making the resulting dataset easier to read.

FIGURE 12.5

The results of this calculation will be difficult to read because they'll all be fractional numbers that have many digits trailing a decimal point. Forcing the results into round numbers will make for easier reading.

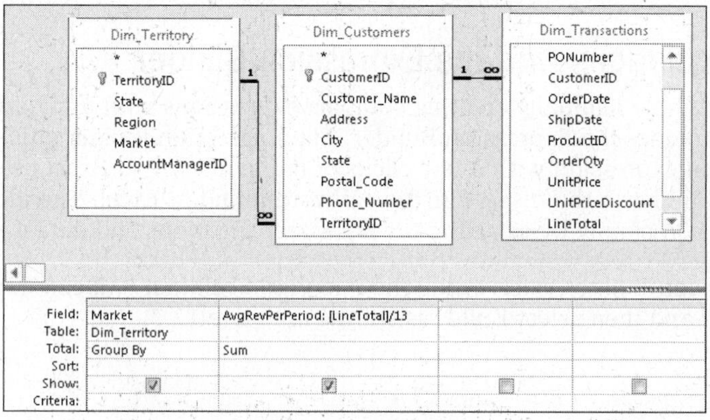

To force the results of your calculation into an integer, you can use the `Int` function. The `Int` function is a mathematical function that will remove the fractional part of a number and return the resulting integer. This function takes one argument, a number. However, instead of hard-coding a number into this function, you can use your calculation as the argument. Figure 12.6 demonstrates this concept.

FIGURE 12.6

You can use your calculation as the argument in the `Int` function, allowing you to remove the fractional part the resulting data.

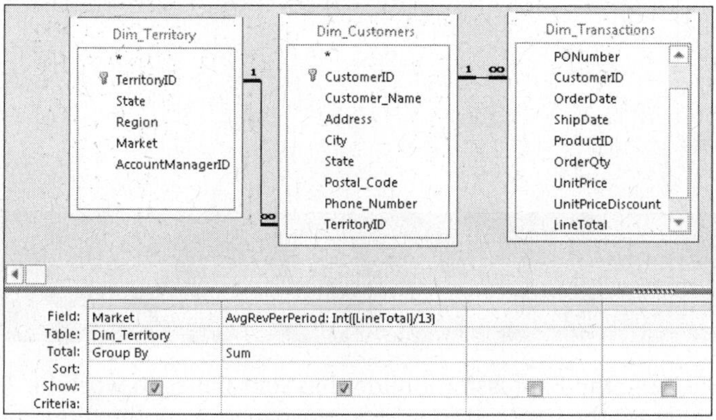

NOTE

You can use calculations that result in a numeric value in any function where a numeric value is accepted as an argument.

Constructing calculations with the Expression Builder

If you aren't yet comfortable manually creating complex expressions with functions and calculations, Access provides the Expression Builder. The Expression Builder guides you through constructing an expression with a few clicks of the mouse. Avid Excel users may relate the Expression Builder to the Insert Function Wizard found in Excel. The idea is that you build your expression simply by selecting the necessary functions and data fields.

To activate the Expression Builder, click inside the query grid cell that will contain your expression, right-click, and then select Build, as shown in Figure 12.7.

FIGURE 12.7

Activate the Expression Builder by right-clicking inside the Field row of the query grid and selecting Build.

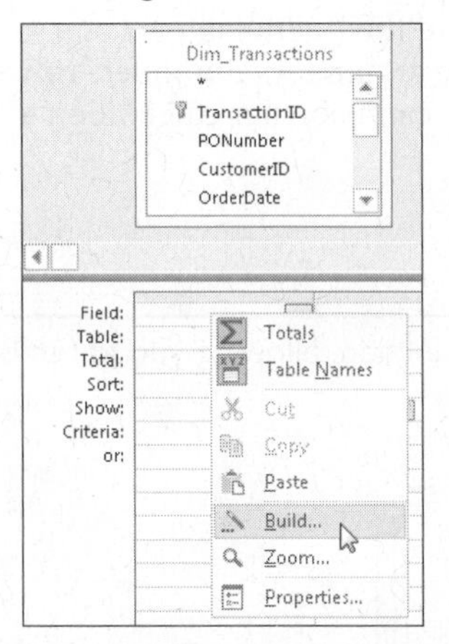

TIP

You can activate the Expression Builder by right-clicking anywhere you would write expressions, including control properties in forms, control properties in reports, and field properties in tables, as well as in the query design grid.

As you can see in Figure 12.8, the Expression Builder has four panes to work in. The upper pane is where you enter the expression. The lower panes show the different objects available to you. In the lower-left pane you can use the plus icons to expose the database objects that can be used to build out your expression.

FIGURE 12.8

The Expression Builder will display any database object you can use in your expression.

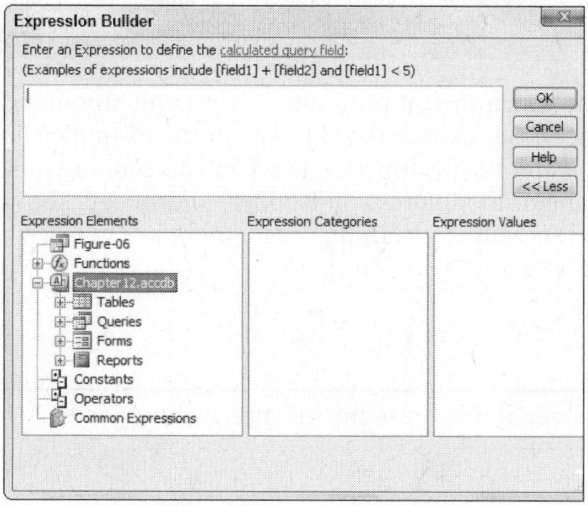

Double-click any of the database objects to drill down to the next level of objects. By double-clicking the `Functions` object, for example, you'll be able to drill into the `Built-In Functions` folder where you'll see all the functions available to you in Access. Figure 12.9 shows the Expression Builder set to display all the available math functions.

FIGURE 12.9

Similar to the Insert Function Wizard in Excel, the Expression Builder displays all the functions available to you.

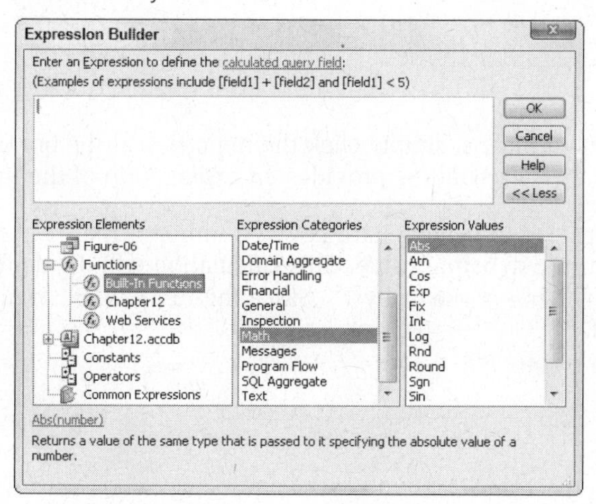

NOTE

If you're using a version of Access other than 2013, your Expression Builder will look slightly different from the one shown in Figure 12.9. However, the basic functionality remains the same.

The idea is that you double-click the function you need and Access will automatically enter the function in the upper pane of the Expression Builder. In the example shown in Figure 12.10, the selected function is the `Round` function. As you can see, the function is immediately placed in the upper pane of the Expression Builder, and Access shows you the arguments needed to make the function work. In this case, there are two arguments identified: a `Number` argument and a `Precision` argument.

FIGURE 12.10

Access tells you which arguments are needed to make the function work.

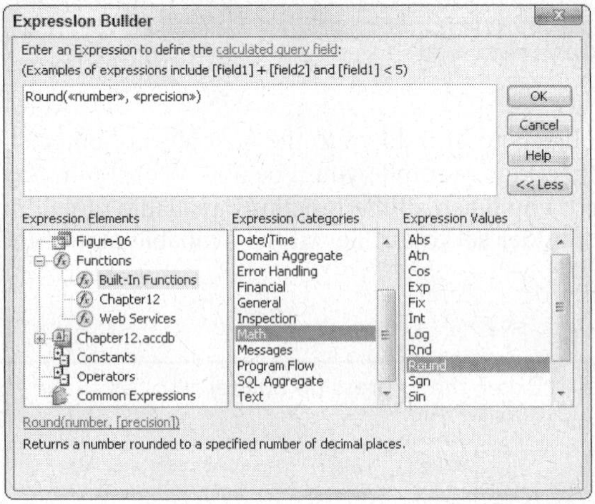

If you don't know what an argument means, simply click the hyperlink at the bottom of the dialog box (see Figure 12.11). A Help window provides an explanation of the function.

As you can see in Figure 12.12, instead of using a hard-coded number in the `Round` function, an expression is used to return a dynamic value. This calculation will divide the sum of `[Dim_TransactionMaster]![Line_Total]` by 13. Since the `Precision` argument is optional, that argument is left off.

FIGURE 12.11

Help files are available to explain each function in detail.

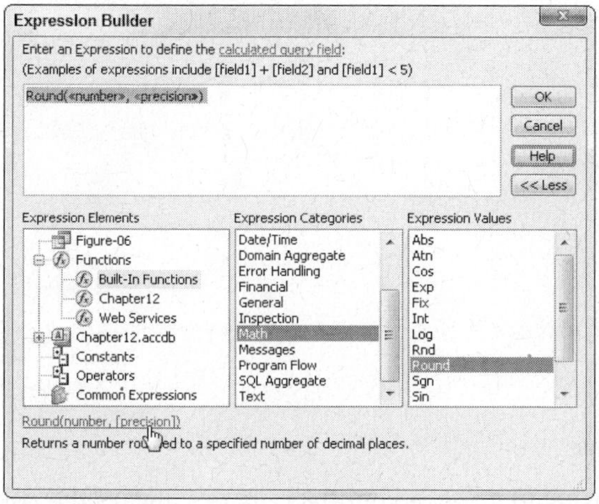

Expression Builder

Enter an Expression to define the calculated query field:
(Examples of expressions include [field1] + [field2] and [field1] < 5)

Round(«number», «precision»)

OK
Cancel
Help
<< Less

Expression Elements
Figure-06
Functions
Built-In Functions
Chapter12
Web Services
Chapter12.accdb
Constants
Operators
Common Expressions

Expression Categories
Date/Time
Domain Aggregate
Error Handling
Financial
General
Inspection
Math
Messages
Program Flow
SQL Aggregate
Text

Expression Values
Abs
Atn
Cos
Exp
Fix
Int
Log
Rnd
Round
Sgn
Sin

Round(number, [precision])
Returns a number rounded to a specified number of decimal places.

FIGURE 12.12

The function here will round the results of the calculation, `([Dim_TransactionMaster]![Line_Total])/13`.

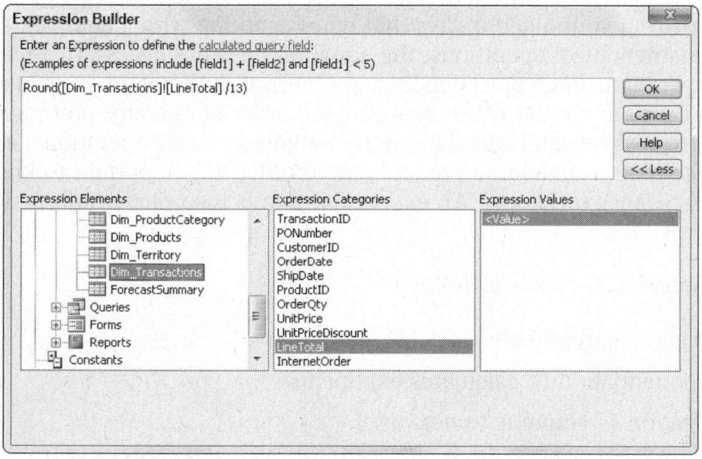

Expression Builder

Enter an Expression to define the calculated query field:
(Examples of expressions include [field1] + [field2] and [field1] < 5)

Round([Dim_Transactions]![LineTotal] /13)

OK
Cancel
Help
<< Less

Expression Elements
Dim_ProductCategory
Dim_Products
Dim_Territory
Dim_Transactions
ForecastSummary
Queries
Forms
Reports
Constants

Expression Categories
TransactionID
PONumber
CustomerID
OrderDate
ShipDate
ProductID
OrderQty
UnitPrice
UnitPriceDiscount
LineTotal
InternetOrder

Expression Values
<Value>

When you're satisfied with your newly created expression, click OK to insert it into the query grid. Figure 12.13 shows that the new expression has been added as a field. Note that the new field has a default alias of Expr1; you can rename this to something more meaningful.

FIGURE 12.13

Your newly created expression will give you the average revenue by period for all transactions.

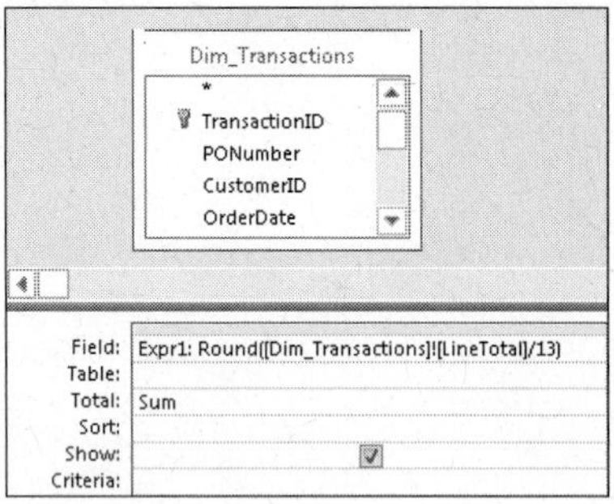

Common calculation errors

No matter what platform you're using to analyze your data, there's always the risk of errors when working with calculations. There is no magic function in Access that will help you prevent errors in your analysis. However, there are a few fundamental actions you can take to avoid some of the most common calculation errors.

Understanding the order of operator precedence

You might remember from your algebra days that when working with a complex equation, executing multiple mathematical operations, the equation does not necessarily evaluate left to right. Some operations have precedence over others and, therefore, must occur first. The Access environment has similar rules regarding the order of operator precedence. When you're using expressions and calculations that involve several operations, each operation is evaluated and resolved in a predetermined order. It's important to know the order of operator precedence in Access. An expression that is incorrectly built may cause errors on your analysis.

The order of operations for Access is as follows:

1. Evaluate items in parentheses.
2. Perform exponentiation (^ calculates exponents).
3. Perform negation (- converts to negative).
4. Perform multiplication (* multiplies) and division (/ divides) at equal precedence.
5. Perform addition (+ adds) and subtraction (- subtracts) at equal precedence.
6. Evaluate string concatenation (`&`).
7. Evaluate comparison and pattern matching operators (>, <, =, <>, >=, <=, `Like`, `Between`, `Is`) at equal precedence.
8. Evaluate logical operators in the following order: `Not`, `And`, `Or`.

NOTE
Operations that are equal in precedence are performed from left to right.

How can understanding the order of operations ensure that you avoid analytical errors? Consider this basic example: The correct answer to the calculation, `(20+30)*4`, is 200. However, if you leave off the parentheses — as in `20+30*4` — Access will perform the calculation like this: `30*4 = 120 + 20 = 140`. The order of operator precedence mandates that Access perform multiplication before subtraction. Therefore, entering `20+30*4` will give you the wrong answer. Because the order of operator precedence in Access mandates that all operations in parentheses be evaluated first, placing `20+30` inside parentheses ensures the correct answer.

Watching out for null values

A *null value* represents the absence of any value. When you see a data item in an Access table that is empty or has no information in it, it is considered null.

The concept of a null value causing errors in a calculation might initially seem strange to Excel power users. In Excel, if there is a null value within a column of numbers, the column can still be properly evaluated because Excel simply reads the null value as zero. This isn't the case in Access. If Access encounters a null value, it doesn't assume that the null value represents zero. Instead, it immediately returns a null value as the answer. To illustrate this behavior, build the query shown in Figure 12.14.

FIGURE 12.14

To demonstrate how null values can cause calculation errors, build this query in Design view.

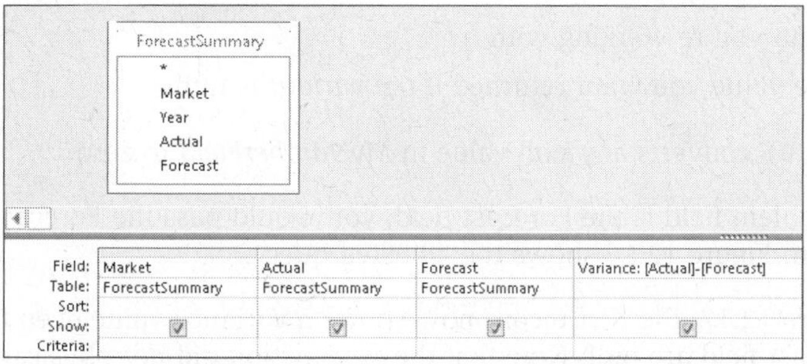

Run the query, and you'll see the results shown in Figure 12.15. Notice that the Variance calculation for the first record doesn't show the expected results; instead, it shows a null value. This is because the forecast value for that record is a null value.

FIGURE 12.15

As you can see, when any variable in your calculation is null, the resulting answer is a null value.

Market	Actual	Forecast	Variance
Baltimore	$8,571.00		
Buffalo	$2,103,749.00	$2,163,175.64	($59,426.64)
California	$3,970,922.40	$3,743,168.24	$227,754.16
CANADA	$1,300,568.10	$1,198,797.92	$101,770.18
Charlotte	$8,586,372.20	$7,969,278.04	$617,094.16
Chicago	$159,293.00	$140,286.23	$19,006.77
Dakotas	$149,198.70	$140,938.93	$8,259.77
Dallas	$2,130,941.40	$2,067,835.02	$63,106.38
Denver	$1,302,986.85	$1,221,948.00	$81,038.85
Florida	$36,117,372.05	$37,622,262.55	($1,504,890.50)
Great Lakes	$614,349.10	$573,346.94	$41,002.16
Kansas City	$950,374.15	$904,571.09	$45,803.06
Knoxville	$17,361.00	$16,564.09	$796.91
New England	$772,343.10	$731,248.87	$41,094.23
Omaha	$744,337.50	$687,854.12	$56,483.38
Phoenix	$1,703,992.80	$1,635,833.09	$68,159.71
Seattle	$156,448.00	$162,705.92	($6,257.92)
Tulsa	$987,686.75	$928,425.55	$59,261.20

Looking at Figure 12.15, you can imagine how a null calculation error can wreak havoc on your analysis, especially if you have an involved analytical process. Furthermore, null calculation errors can be difficult to identify and fix.

That being said, you can avoid null calculation errors by using the `Nz` function, which enables you to convert any null value that is encountered to a value you specify:

```
Nz(variant, valueifnull)
```

The `Nz` function takes two arguments:

- *variant*: The data you're working with
- *valueifnull*: The value you want returned if the *variant* is null

`Nz([`*MyNumberField*`],0)` converts any null value in *MyNumberField* to zero.

Armed Because the problem field is the Forecast field, you would pass the Forecast field through the `Nz` function. Figure 12.16 shows the adjusted query.

As you can see in Figure 12.17, the first record now shows a variance value even though the values in the Forecast field are null. Note that the `Nz` function did not physically place a zero in the null values. The `Nz` function merely told access to treat the nulls as zeros when calculating the Variance field.

FIGURE 12.16

Pass the Forecast field through the `Nz` function to convert null values to zero.

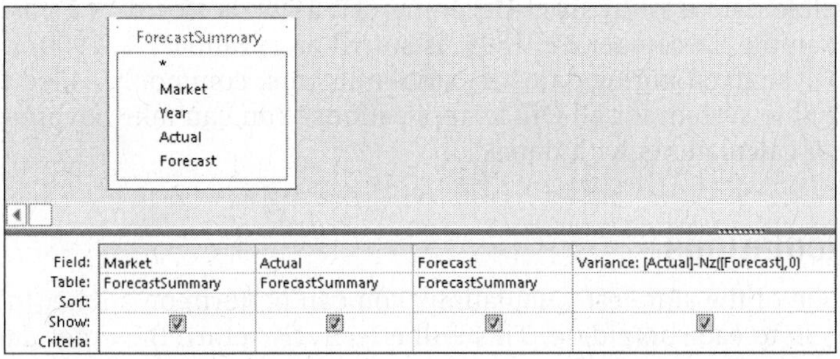

ForecastSummary
*
Market
Year
Actual
Forecast

Field:	Market	Actual	Forecast	Variance: [Actual]-Nz([Forecast],0)
Table:	ForecastSummary	ForecastSummary	ForecastSummary	
Sort:				
Show:	☑	☑	☑	☑
Criteria:				

FIGURE 12.17

The first record now shows a variance value.

Market	Actual	Forecast	Variance
Baltimore	$8,571.00		$8,571.00
Buffalo	$2,103,749.00	$2,163,175.64	($59,426.64)
California	$3,970,922.40	$3,743,168.24	$227,754.16
CANADA	$1,300,568.10	$1,198,797.92	$101,770.18
Charlotte	$8,586,372.20	$7,969,278.04	$617,094.16
Chicago	$159,293.00	$140,286.23	$19,006.77
Dakotas	$149,198.70	$140,938.93	$8,259.77
Dallas	$2,130,941.40	$2,067,835.02	$63,106.38
Denver	$1,302,986.85	$1,221,948.00	$81,038.85
Florida	$36,117,372.05	$37,622,262.55	($1,504,890.50)
Great Lakes	$614,349.10	$573,346.94	$41,002.16
Kansas City	$950,374.15	$904,571.09	$45,803.06
Knoxville	$17,361.00	$16,564.09	$796.91
New England	$772,343.10	$731,248.87	$41,094.23
Omaha	$744,337.50	$687,854.12	$56,483.38
Phoenix	$1,703,992.80	$1,635,833.09	$68,159.71
Seattle	$156,448.00	$162,705.92	($6,257.92)
Tulsa	$987,686.75	$928,425.55	$59,261.20

Watching the syntax in your expressions

Basic syntax mistakes in your calculation expressions can also lead to errors. Follow these basic guidelines to avoid slip-ups:

- If you're using fields in your calculations, enclose their names in square brackets (`[]`).
- Make sure you spell the names of the fields correctly.
- When assigning an alias to your calculated field, be sure you don't inadvertently use a field name from any of the tables being queried.
- Don't use illegal characters — period (`.`), exclamation point (`!`), square brackets (`[]`) or ampersand (`&`) — in your aliases.

Using Dates in Your Analyses

In Access, every possible date starting from December 31, 1899, is stored as a positive serial number. For example, December 31, 1899, is stored as 1; January 1, 1900, is stored as 2; and so on. This system of storing dates as serial numbers, commonly called the *1900 system,* is the default date system for all Office applications. You can take advantage of this system to perform calculations with dates.

Simple date calculations

Figure 12.18 shows one of the simplest calculations you can perform on a date. In this query, you're adding 30 to each ship date. This will effectively return the order date plus 30 days, giving you a new date.

FIGURE 12.18

You're adding 30 to each ship date, effectively creating a date that is equal to the ship date plus 30 days.

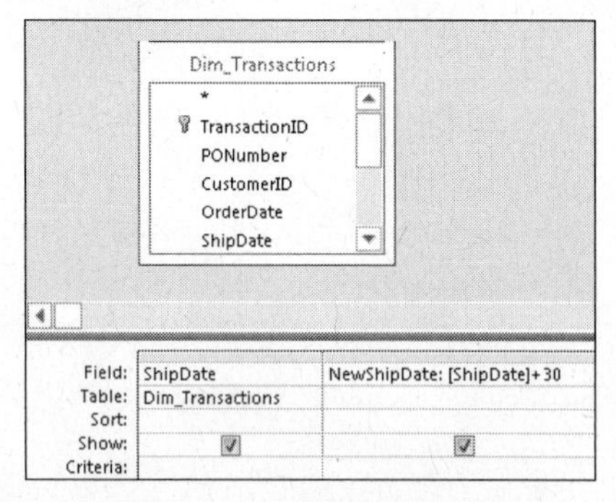

> **CAUTION**
> To be calculated correctly, dates must reside in a field that is formatted as a Date/Time field. If you enter a date into a Text field, the date will continue to look like a date, but Access will treat it like a string. The end result is that any calculation done on dates in this Text-formatted field will fail. Ensure that all dates are stored in fields that are formatted as Date/Time.

You can also calculate the number of days between two dates. The calculation in Figure 12.19, for example, essentially subtracts the serial number of one date from the serial number of another date, leaving you the number of days between the two dates.

FIGURE 12.19

In this query, you're calculating the number of days between two dates.

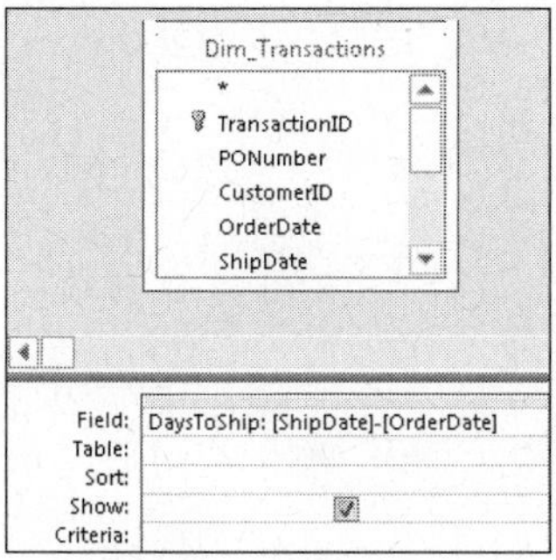

Advanced analysis using functions

As of Access 2013, 25 built-in Date/Time functions are available. Some of these are functions you'll very rarely encounter, whereas others you'll use routinely in your analyses. This section discusses a few of the basic Date/Time functions that will come in handy in your day-to-day analysis.

The Date function

The `Date` function is a built-in Access function that returns the current system date — in other words, today's date. With this versatile function, you never have to hard-code today's date in your calculations. That is to say, you can create dynamic calculations that use the current system date as a variable, giving you a different result every day. In this section, we look at some of the ways you can leverage the `Date` function to enhance your analysis.

Finding the number of days between today and a past date

Imagine that you have to calculate aged receivables. You need to know the current date to determine how overdue the receivables are. Of course, you could type in the current date by hand, but that can be cumbersome and prone to error.

To demonstrate how to use the `Date` function, create the query shown in Figure 12.20.

FIGURE 12.20

This query returns the number of days between today's date and each order date.

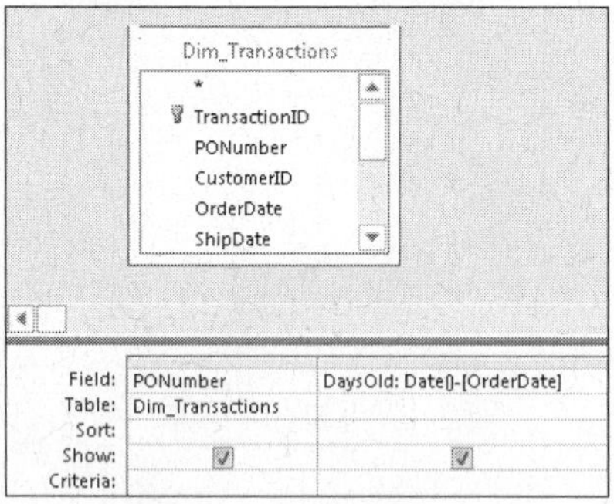

Using the Date function in a criteria expression

You can use the `Date` function to filter out records by including it in a criteria expression. For example, the query shown in Figure 12.21 will return all records with an order date older than 90 days.

FIGURE 12.21

No matter what day it is today, this query will return all orders older than 90 days.

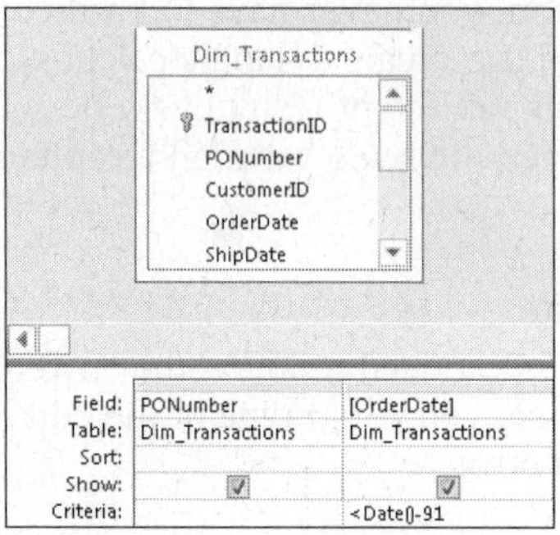

Calculating an age in years using the Date function

Imagine that you've been asked to provide a list of account managers along with the number of years they have been employed by the company. To accomplish this task, you have to calculate the difference between today's date and each manager's hire date.

The first step is to build the query shown in Figure 12.22.

FIGURE 12.22

You're calculating the difference between today's date and each manager's hire date.

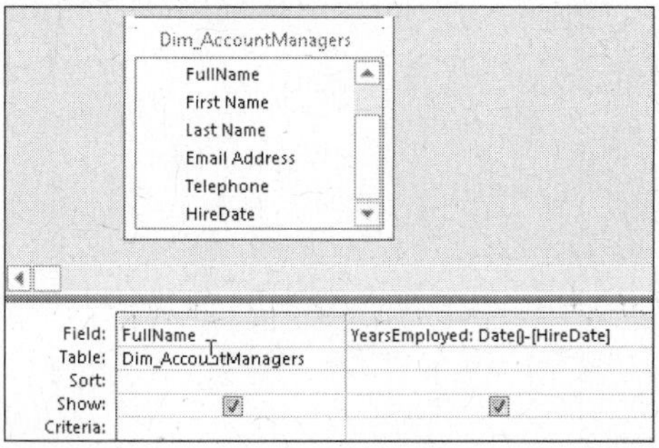

Dim_AccountManagers
FullName
First Name
Last Name
Email Address
Telephone
HireDate

Field:	FullName	YearsEmployed: Date()-[HireDate]
Table:	Dim_AccountManagers	
Sort:		
Show:	☑	☑
Criteria:		

When you look at the query results, shown in Figure 12.23, you'll realize that the calculation results in the number of *days* between the two dates, not the number of *years*.

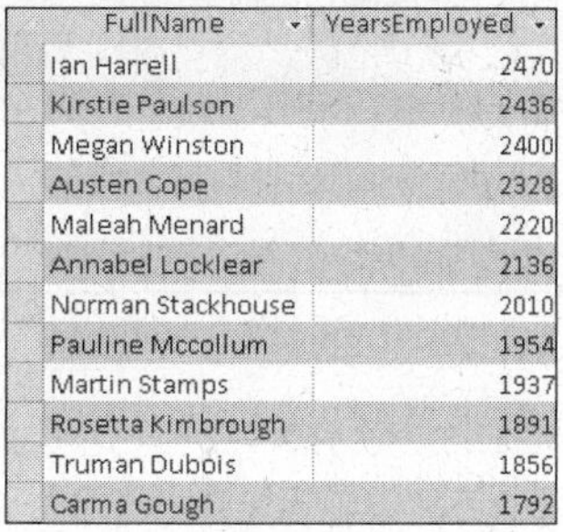

FIGURE 12.23

This dataset shows the number of days, not the number of years.

FullName	YearsEmployed
Ian Harrell	2470
Kirstie Paulson	2436
Megan Winston	2400
Austen Cope	2328
Maleah Menard	2220
Annabel Locklear	2136
Norman Stackhouse	2010
Pauline Mccollum	1954
Martin Stamps	1937
Rosetta Kimbrough	1891
Truman Dubois	1856
Carma Gough	1792

To fix this problem, switch back to Design view and divide your calculation by 365.25. Why 365.25? That's the average number of days in a year when you account for leap years. Figure 12.24 demonstrates this change. Note that your original calculation is now wrapped in parentheses to avoid errors due to order of operator precedence.

FIGURE 12.24

Divide your original calculation by 365.25 to convert the answer to years.

Dim_AccountManagers
FullName
First Name
Last Name
Email Address
Telephone
HireDate

Field:	FullName	YearsEmployed: (Date()-[HireDate])/365.25
Table:	Dim_AccountManagers	
Sort:		
Show:	✓	✓
Criteria:		

A look at the results, shown in Figure 12.25, proves that you're now returning the number of years. All that's left to do is to strip away the fractional portion of the date using the `Int` function. Why the `Int` function? The `Int` function doesn't round the year up or down; it merely converts the number to a readable integer.

TIP

Want to actually round the number of years? You can simply wrap your date calculation in the `Round` function. The `Round` function is highlighted in Appendix D of this book.

FIGURE 12.25

Your query is now returning years, but you have to strip away the fractional portion of your answer.

FullName	YearsEmployed
Ian Harrell	6.76249144421629
Kirstie Paulson	6.6694045174538
Megan Winston	6.57084188911704
Austen Cope	6.37371663244353
Maleah Menard	6.07802874743327
Annabel Locklear	5.84804928131417
Norman Stackhouse	5.50308008213552
Pauline Mccollum	5.34976043805613
Martin Stamps	5.30321697467488
Rosetta Kimbrough	5.1772758384668
Truman Dubois	5.08145106091718
Carma Gough	4.90622861054073

Wrapping your calculation in the `Int` function ensures that your answer will be a clean year without fractions (see Figure 12.26).

FIGURE 12.26

Running this query will return the number of years each employee has been with the company.

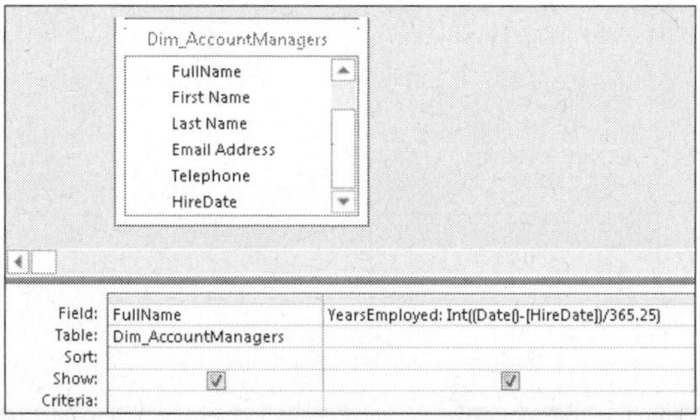

Dim_AccountManagers
FullName
First Name
Last Name
Email Address
Telephone
HireDate

Field:	FullName	YearsEmployed: Int((Date()-[HireDate])/365.25)
Table:	Dim_AccountManagers	
Sort:		
Show:	☑	☑
Criteria:		

TIP

You can calculate a person's age using the same method. Simply replace the hire date with the date of birth.

The Year, Month, Day, and Weekday functions

The `Year`, `Month`, `Day`, and `Weekday` functions are used to return an integer that represents their respective parts of a date. All these functions require a valid date as an argument. For example:

`Year(#12/31/1997#)` returns `1997`.

`Month(#12/31/1997#)` returns `12`.

`Day(#12/31/1997#)` returns `31`.

`Weekday(#12/31/1997#)` returns `4`.

NOTE

The `Weekday` function returns the day of the week from a date. In Access, weekdays are numbered from 1 to 7 starting with Sunday. Therefore, if the `Weekday` function returns `4`, then the day of the week represented is Wednesday. If Sunday is not the first day of the week in your part of the world, you can use the optional `FirstDayOfWeek` argument. This argument specifies which day you want to count as the first day of the week. Enter 1 in this argument to make the first day Sunday, 2 for Monday, 3 for Tuesday, and so on. If this argument is omitted, the first day is a Sunday by default.

Figure 12.27 demonstrates how you would use these functions in a query environment.

FIGURE 12.27

The `Year`, `Month`, `Day`, and `Weekday` functions enable you to parse out a part of a date.

Dim_Transactions: *, TransactionID, PONumber, CustomerID, OrderDate, ShipDate

Field:	Year: Year([OrderDate])	Month: Month([OrderDate])	Day: Day([OrderDate])	Weekday: Weekday([OrderDate])
Table:				
Sort:				
Show:	☑	☑	☑	☑
Criteria:				

An Easy Way to Query Only Workdays

Suppose that you've been asked to provide the total amount of revenue generated by product, but only revenue generated during workdays in calendar year 2008. Workdays are defined as days that are not weekends or holidays.

The first thing you need to accomplish this task is a table that lists all the company holidays in 2008. The following figure shows that a holidays table can be nothing more than one field listing all the dates that constitute a holiday.

Holidays
1/1/2008
1/19/2008
5/31/2008
7/5/2008
9/6/2008
11/25/2008
11/26/2008
12/23/2008
12/24/2008
12/31/2008

After you've established a table that contains all the company holidays, it's time to build the query. The following figure demonstrates how to build a query that filters out non-workdays.

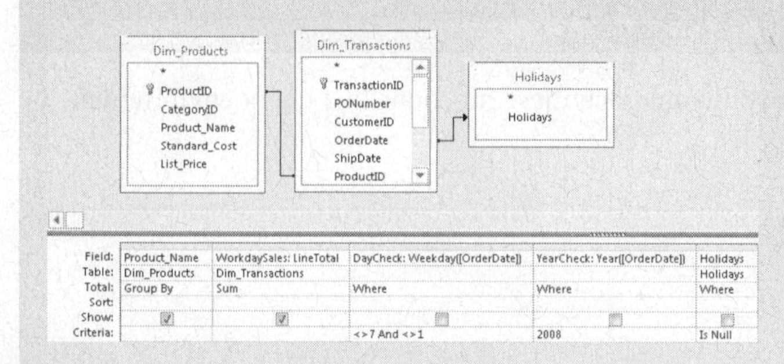

Take a moment to analyze what is going on in the preceding figure:

1. You create a left join from TransactionMaster to Holidays to tell Access that you want all the records from TransactionMaster.
2. You then use the Is Null criteria under Holidays. This limits the TransactionMaster to only those dates that do not match any of the holidays listed in the Holidays table.
3. You then create a field called Day Check where you're returning the weekday of every service date in the TransactionMaster.
4. You filter the newly created Day Check field to filter out those weekdays that represent Saturdays and Sundays (1 and 7).
5. Finally, you filter for only those records whose order dates fall in the year 2008.

The DateAdd function

A common analysis for many organizations is to determine on which date a certain benchmark will be reached. For example, most businesses want to know on what date an order will become 30 days past due. Furthermore, what date should a warning letter be sent to the customer? An easy way to perform these types of analyses is to use the `DateAdd` function, which returns a date to which a specified interval has been added:

```
DateAdd(interval, number, date)
```

The `DateAdd` function returns a date to which a specified interval has been added. There are three required arguments in the `DateAdd` function.

- ***interval* (required):** The interval of time want to use. The intervals available are as follows:
  - `"yyyy"`: Year
  - `"q"`: Quarter
  - `"m"`: Month
  - `"y"`: Day of year
  - `"d"`: Day
  - `"w"`: Weekday
  - `"ww"`: Week
  - `"h"`: Hour
  - `"n"`: Minute
  - `"s"`: Second
- ***number* (required):** The number of intervals to add. A positive number returns a date in the future, whereas a negative number returns a date in the past.
- ***date* (required):** The date value with which you're working.

For example:

`DateAdd("ww",1,#11/30/2008#)` returns 12/7/2008.

`DateAdd("m",2,#11/30/2008#)` returns 1/30/2008.

`DateAdd("yyyy",-1,#11/30/2008#)` returns 11/30/2007.

The query shown in Figure 12.28 illustrates how the `DateAdd` function can be used in determining the exact date a specific benchmark is reached. You're creating two new fields with this query: Warning and Overdue. The `DateAdd` function used in the Warning field will return the date that is three weeks from the original order date. The `DateAdd` function used in the Overdue field will return the date that is one month from the original order date.

FIGURE 12.28

This query will give you the original order date, the date you should send a warning letter, and the date on which the order will be 30 days overdue.

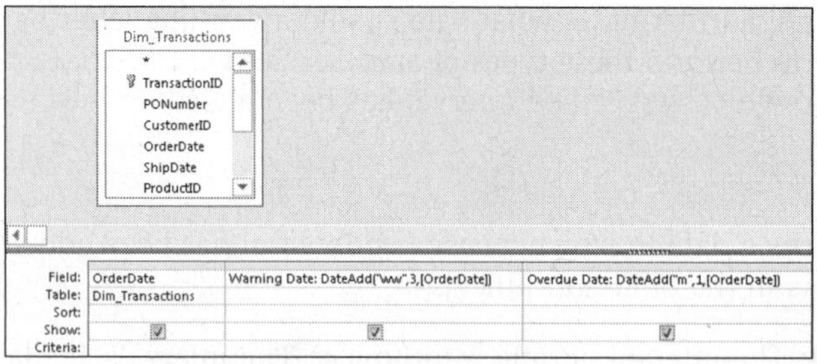

Grouping dates into quarters

Why would you need to group your dates into quarters? Most databases store dates rather than quarter designations. Therefore, if you wanted to analyze data on a quarter-over-quarter basis, you would have to convert dates into quarters. Surprisingly, there is no date/time function that allows you to group dates into quarters. There is, however, the `Format` function.

The `Format` function belongs to the Text category of functions and allows you to convert a variant into a string based on formatting instructions. From the perspective of analyzing dates, there are several valid instructions you can pass to a `Format` function:

`Format(#01/31/2004#, "yyyy")` returns `2004`.

`Format(#01/31/2004#, "yy")` returns `04`.

`Format(#01/31/2004#, "q")` returns `1`.

`Format(#01/31/2004#, "mmm")` returns `Jan`.

`Format(#01/31/2004#, "mm")` returns `01`.

`Format(#01/31/2004#, "d")` returns `31`.

`Format(#01/31/2004#, "w")` returns `7`.

`Format(#01/31/2004#, "ww")` returns `5`.

NOTE

Keep in mind that the value returned when passing a date through a `Format` function is a string that cannot be used in subsequent calculations.

The query in Figure 12.29 shows how you would group all the order dates into quarters and then group the quarters to get a sum of revenue for each quarter.

FIGURE 12.29

You can group dates into quarters by using the `Format` function.

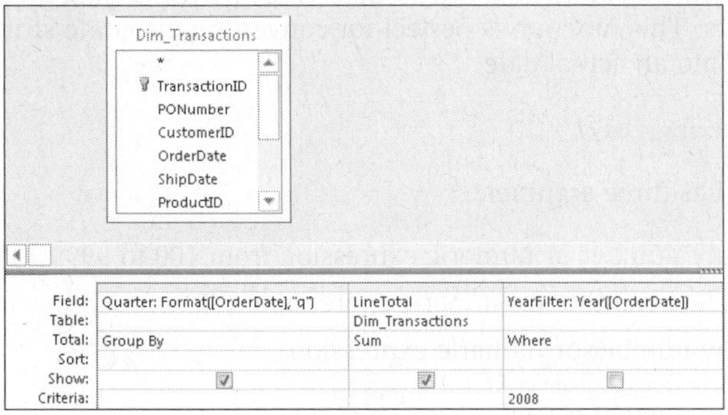

Dim_Transactions: *, TransactionID, PONumber, CustomerID, OrderDate, ShipDate, ProductID

Field:	Quarter: Format([OrderDate],"q")	LineTotal	YearFilter: Year([OrderDate])
Table:		Dim_Transactions	
Total:	Group By	Sum	Where
Sort:			
Show:	☑	☑	☐
Criteria:			2008

If you want to get fancy, you can insert the `Format` function in a crosstab query, using Quarter as the column (see Figure 12.30).

FIGURE 12.30

You can also use the `Format` function in a crosstab query.

Dim_Transactions: *, TransactionID, PONumber, CustomerID, OrderDate, ShipDate, ProductID

Dim_Products: *, ProductID, CategoryID, Product_Name, Standard_Cost, List_Price

Field:	Product_Name	Quarter: Format([OrderDate],"q")	LineTotal	YearFilter: Year([OrderDate])
Table:	Dim_Products		Dim_Transactions	
Total:	Group By	Group By	Sum	Where
Crosstab:	Row Heading	Column Heading	Value	
Sort:				
Criteria:				2008

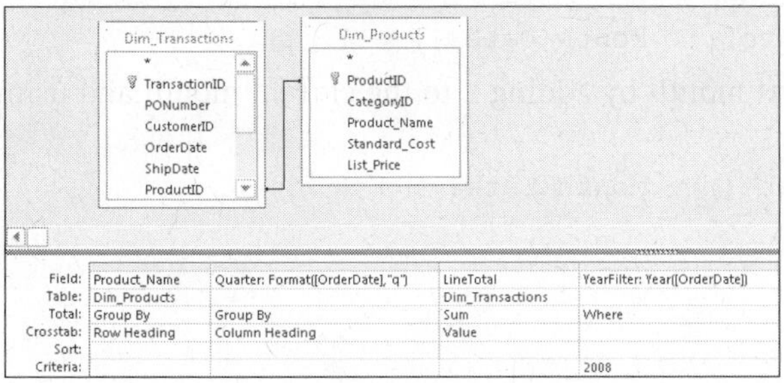

As you can see in Figure 12.31, the resulting dataset is a clean look at revenue by product by quarter.

FIGURE 12.31

You've successfully grouped your dates into quarters.

Product_Name	1	2	3	4
Filter Sheets 131/2" X 24"	$11,970.00	$22,548.75	$55,258.00	$29,307.25
Filter Sheets 14" X 22"	$28,284.60	$57,696.10	$190,679.15	$129,965.20
Filter Sheets 161/2" X 251/2"	$3,018.35	$3,402.60	$58,183.40	$63,390.65
Filter Sheets 163/8" X 243/8"	$49,286.10	$101,954.70	$106,431.90	$111,335.50
Food Warmer Pickup Stations 24"W		$7,901.60	$15,529.50	$9,389.10
Food Warmer Pickup Stations 72"W	$11,804.00	$18,532.80		

The DateSerial function

The `DateSerial` function allows you to construct a date value by combining given year, month, and day components. This function is perfect for converting disparate strings that, together, represent a date, into an actual date.

```
DateSerial(Year, Month, Day)
```

The `DateSerial` function has three arguments:

- **Year (required):** Any number or numeric expression from 100 to 9999
- **Month (required):** Any number or numeric expression
- **Day (required):** Any number or numeric expression

For example, the following statement would return `April 3, 2012`.

```
DateSerial(2012, 4, 3)
```

So, how is this helpful? Well, now you can put a few twists on this by performing calculations on the expressions within the `DateSerial` function. Consider some of the possibilities:

- Get the first day of last month by subtracting `1` from the current month and using `1` as the `Day` argument.

  ```
  DateSerial(Year(Date()), Month(Date()) - 1, 1)
  ```

- Get the first day of next month by adding `1` to the current month and using `1` as the `Day` argument.

  ```
  DateSerial(Year(Date()), Month(Date()) + 1, 1)
  ```

- Get the last day of this month by adding 1 to the current month and using `0` as the `Day` argument.

  ```
  DateSerial(Year(Date()), Month(Date())+1, 0)
  ```

- Get the last day of next month by adding `2` to the current month and using `0` as the `Day` argument.

  ```
  DateSerial(Year(Date()), Month(Date()) +2, 0)
  ```

TIP

Passing a `0` to the `Day` argument will automatically get you the last day of the month specified in the `DateSerial` function. It's worth mentioning that `DateSerial` is smart enough to work across years. `Month(Date()) - 1` will still work correctly in January, and `Month(Date()) + 1` will work correctly in December.

Performing Conditional Analyses

IN THIS CHAPTER

Using parameter queries

Using conditional functions

Comparing the IIf and Switch functions

Up until now, your analyses have been straightforward. You build a query, you add some criteria, you add a calculation, you save the query, then you run the query whenever you need to. What happens however, if the criteria that governs your analysis changes frequently, or if your analytical processes depend on certain conditions being met? In these situations, you would use a *conditional analysis*; an analysis whose outcome depends on a pre-defined set of conditions. Barring VBA and macros, there are several tools and functions that enable you to build conditional analyses; some of these are parameter queries, the `IIf` function, and the `Switch` function. In this chapter, you learn how these tools and functions can help you save time, organize your analytical processes, and enhance your analyses.

ON THE WEB

The starting database for this walkthrough, `Chapter13.accdb`, can be downloaded from this book's website.

Using Parameter Queries

You'll find that when building your analytical processes, anticipating every single combination of criteria that may be needed will often be difficult. This is where parameter queries can help.

A *parameter query* is an interactive query that prompts you for criteria before the query is run. A parameter query is useful when you need to ask a query different questions using different criteria each time it's run. To get a firm understanding of how a parameter query can help you, build the query shown in Figure 13.1. With this query, you want to see all the purchase orders logged during the 200705 system period.

FIGURE 13.1

This query has a hard-coded criterion for system period.

Field:	Period	PONumber	ProductID	LineTotal
Table:	Dim_Dates	Dim_Transactions	Dim_Transactions	Dim_Transactions
Sort:				
Show:	☑	☑	☑	☑
Criteria:	"200705"			

Although this query will give you what you need, the problem is that the criterion for system period is hard-coded as 200705. That means if you want to analyze revenue for a different period, you essentially have to rebuild the query. Using a parameter query will allow you to create a conditional analysis (that is, an analysis based on variables you specify each time you run the query). To create a parameter query, simply replace the hard-coded criteria with text that you've enclosed in square brackets ([]), as shown in Figure 13.2.

FIGURE 13.2

To create a parameter query, replace the hard-coded criteria with text enclosed in square brackets ([]).

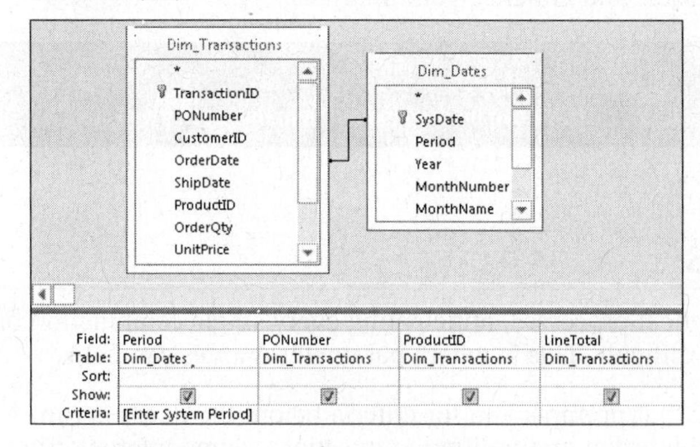

Running a parameter query forces the Enter Parameter Value dialog box to open and ask for a variable. Note that the text you typed inside the brackets of your parameter appears in the dialog box. At this point, you would simply enter your parameter, as shown in Figure 13.3.

FIGURE 13.3

Enter your criteria in the Enter Parameter Value dialog box and click OK.

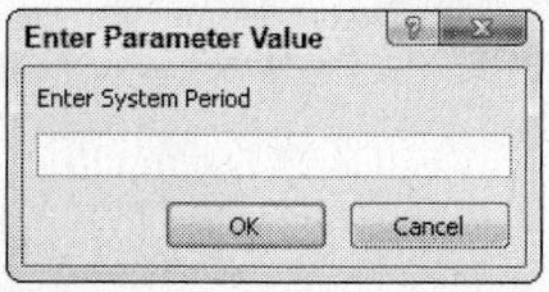

How parameter queries work

When you run a parameter query, Access attempts to convert any text to a literal string by wrapping the text in quotes. However, if you place square brackets ([]) around the text, Access thinks that it's a variable and tries to bind some value to the variable using the following series of tests:

1. Access checks to see if the variable is a field name. If Access identifies the variable as a field name, that field is used in the expression.
2. If the variable is not a field name, Access checks to see if the variable is a calculated field. If Access determines the expression is indeed a calculated field, it simply carries out the mathematical operation.
3. If the variable is not a calculated field, Access checks to see if the variable is referencing an object such as a control on an open form or open report.
4. If all else fails, the only remaining option is to ask the user what the variable is, so Access displays the Enter Parameter Value dialog box, showing the text you entered in the Criteria row.

Ground rules of parameter queries

As with other functionality in Access, parameter queries come with their own set of ground rules that you should follow in order to use them properly.

- You must place square brackets ([]) around your parameter. If you don't, Access will automatically convert your text into a literal string.
- You can't use the name of a field as a parameter. If you do, Access will simply replace your parameter with the current value of the field.

- You can't use a period (.), an exclamation point (!), square brackets ([ ]), or an ampersand (&) in your parameter's prompt text.
- You must limit the number of characters in your parameter's prompt text. Entering parameter prompt text that is too long may result in your prompt being cut off in the Enter Parameter Value dialog box. Moreover, you should make your prompts as clear and concise as possible.

TIP

If you really want to use a field name in your parameter's prompt, you can follow the field name with other characters. For example, instead of using `[System_Period]`, you could use `[System_Period: ?]`. As you read this, keep in mind that there is nothing magic about the colon (:) or the question mark (?). Any character will do. The idea is to allow Access to differentiate between your parameter and the field name while matching the original field name as closely as possible.

Working with parameter queries

The example shown in Figure 13.2 uses a parameter to define a single criterion. Although this is the most common way to use a parameter in a query, there are many ways to exploit this functionality. In fact, it's safe to say that the more innovative you get with your parameter queries, the more elegant and advanced your impromptu analysis will be. This section covers some of the different ways you can use parameters in your queries.

Working with multiple parameter conditions

You aren't in any way limited in the number of parameters you can use in your query. Figure 13.4, on the other hand, demonstrates how you can utilize more than one parameter in a query. When you run this query, you'll be prompted for both a system period and a product ID, allowing you to dynamically filter on two data points without ever having to rewrite your query.

FIGURE 13.4

You can employ more than one parameter in a query.

Field:	Period	PONumber	ProductID	LineTotal
Table:	Dim_Dates	Dim_Transactions	Dim_Transactions	Dim_Transactions
Sort:				
Show:	✓	✓	✓	✓
Criteria:	[Enter System Period]		[Enter Product ID]	

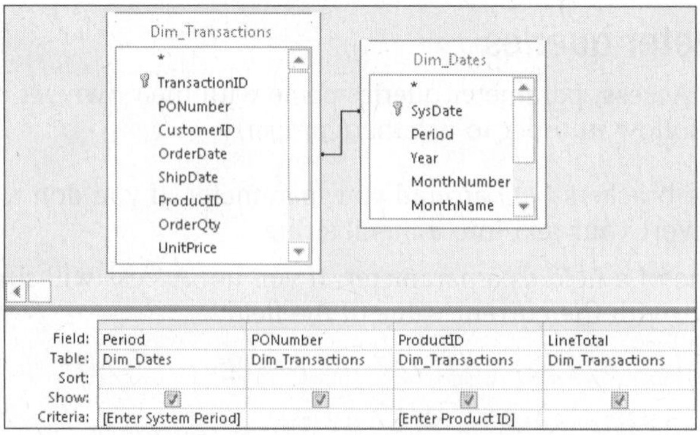

Combining parameters with operators

You can combine parameter prompts with any operator you would normally use in a query. Using parameters in conjunction with standard operators allows you to dynamically expand or contract the filters in your analysis without rebuilding your query. To demonstrate how this works, build the query shown in Figure 13.5.

This query uses the `BETWEEN...AND` operator and the > (greater than) operator to limit the results of the query based on the user-defined parameters. Since there are three parameter prompts built into this query, you'll be prompted for inputs three times: once for a starting period, once for an ending period, and once for a dollar amount. The number of records returned will depend on the parameters you input. For instance, if you input 200701 as the starting period, 200703 as the ending period, and 5000 as the dollar amount, you'll get 1,700 records.

FIGURE 13.5

This query combines standard operators with parameters in order to limit the results.

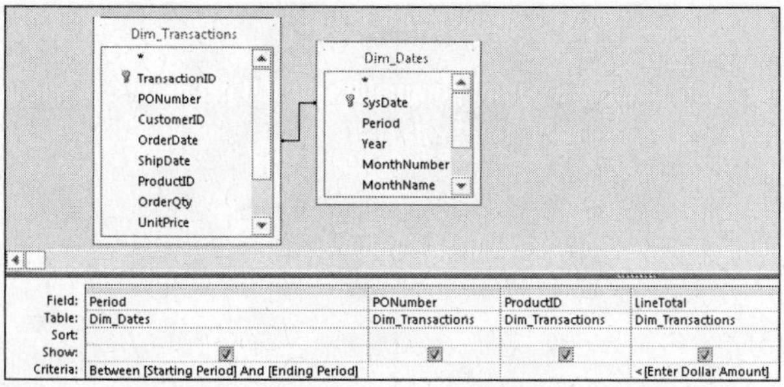

Combining parameters with wildcards

One of the problems with a parameter query is that if the parameter is ignored when the query is run, the query will return no records. One way to get around this problem is to combine your parameter with a wildcard so that if the parameter is ignored, all records will be returned.

To demonstrate how you can use a wildcard with a parameter, build the query shown in Figure 13.6. When you run this query, it'll prompt you for a period. Because you're using the wildcard, you have the option of filtering out a single period by entering a period designator into the parameter, or you can ignore the parameter to return all records.

FIGURE 13.6

If the parameter in this query is ignored, the query will return all records thanks to the wildcard (*).

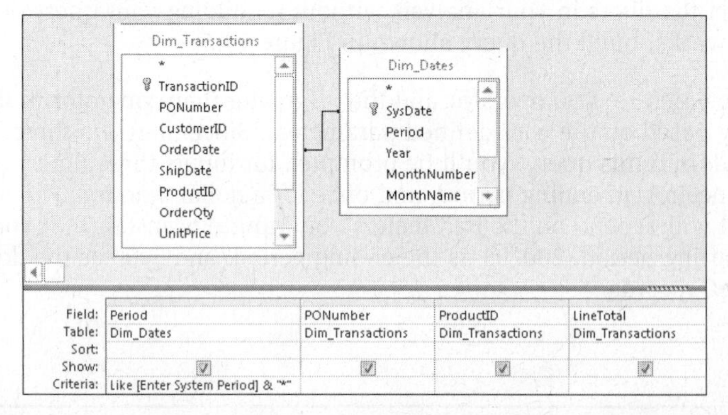

TIP

Using the wildcard with a parameter also allows users to enter a partial parameter and still get results. Suppose, for example, that the criteria in your parameter query is

```
Like [Enter Lastname] & "*"
```

Entering "A" as the parameter would return all last names that start with the letter *A*.

Or, suppose the criteria in your parameter query is

```
Like "*" & [Enter Lastname] & "*"
```

Entering "A" would return all last names that contain the letter *A*.

Note that this will only return all the records that have an actual value. This will not return records with a Null value in the field. To be able to have Null values also returned, you need to use the following:

```
Like "*" & [Enter Lastname] & "*" or IS NULL
```

Using parameters as calculation variables

You are not limited to using parameters as criteria for a query; you can use parameters anywhere you use a variable. In fact, a particularly useful way to use parameters is in calculations. For example, the query in Figure 13.7 enables you to analyze how a price increase will affect current prices based on the percent increase you enter. When you run this query, you'll be asked to enter a percentage by which you want to increase your prices. Once you pass your percentage, the parameter query uses it as a variable in the calculation.

FIGURE 13.7

You can use parameters in calculations, enabling you to change the calculations variables each time you run the query.

Dim_Products
*
ProductID
CategoryID
Product_Name
Standard_Cost
List_Price

Field:	List_Price	Price Increase: [List_Price]*(1+[Enter Percent Price Increase])
Table:	Dim_Products	
Sort:		
Show:	☑	☑
Criteria:		

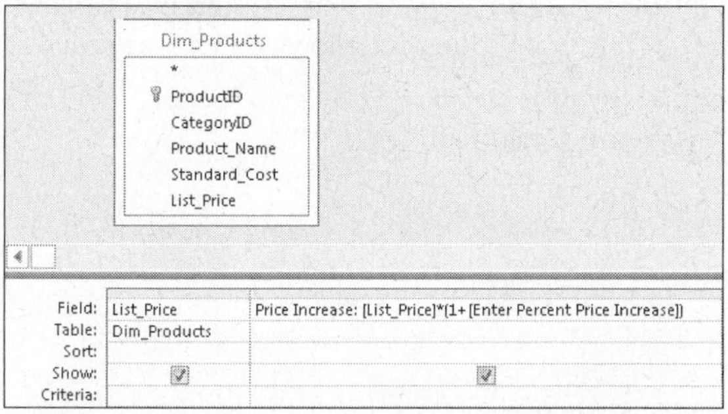

Using parameters as function arguments

You can also use parameters as arguments within functions. Figure 13.8 demonstrates the use of the `DateDiff` function using parameters instead of hard-coded dates. When this query is run, you'll be prompted for a start date and an end date. Those dates will then be used as arguments in the `DateDiff` function. Again, this allows you to specify new dates each time you run the query without ever having to rebuild the query.

FIGURE 13.8

You can use parameters as arguments in functions instead of hard-coded values.

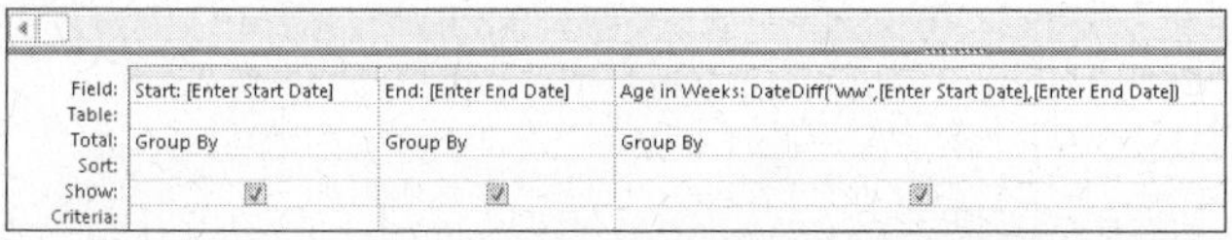

Field:	Start: [Enter Start Date]	End: [Enter End Date]	Age in Weeks: DateDiff("ww",[Enter Start Date],[Enter End Date])
Table:			
Total:	Group By	Group By	Group By
Sort:			
Show:	☑	☑	☑
Criteria:			

Caution

Be aware that values you enter into your parameters must fit into the data type required for the function's argument. For example, if you're using a parameter in a `DateDiff` function, the variable you assign that parameter must be a date or the function won't work.

Note

When you run the query in Figure 13.8, you'll only have to enter the start date and the end date one time, even though they're both used in two places in the query. This is because once you assign a variable to a parameter, the assignment persists to every future instance of that parameter.

If you are prompted more than once for a parameter used more than once in your query, odds are there's a slight variation in how the parameter names were typed. Consider copying your parameters to avoid this.

Creating a Parameter Prompt That Accepts Multiple Entries

The parameter query in the following figure enables you to dynamically filter results by a variable period that you specify within the parameter. However, this query does not allow you to see results for more than one period at a time.

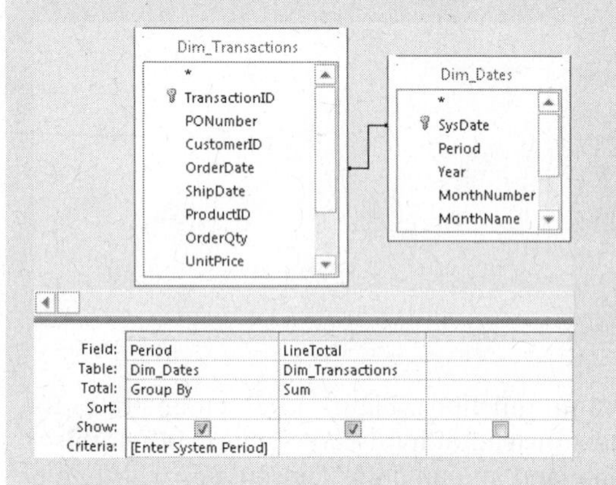

You could use more than one parameter, as shown in the following figure. Unlike the query in the preceding figure, this query allows you to include more than one period in your query results. However, you would still be limited to the number of parameters built into the query (in this case, three).

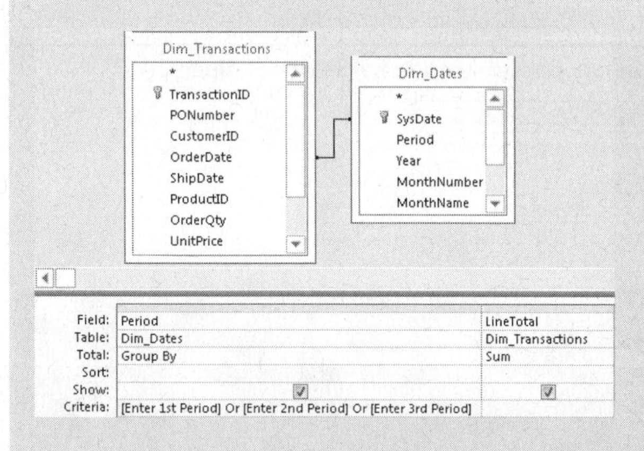

So, how do you allow for any number of parameter entries? The answer is relatively easy. You create a parameter that is passed through an `InStr` function to test for a position number. (Feel free to revisit Chapter 4 to get a refresher on the `InStr` function.)

The query shown in the following figure demonstrates how to do this.

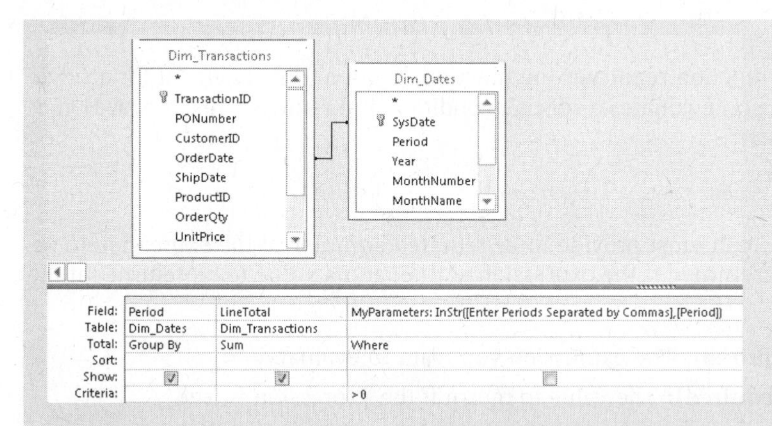

Notice that the parameter is not being used as criteria for the Period field. Instead, it is being used in an `InStr` function to test for the position number of the variable you enter into the parameter prompt, as follows:

```
InStr([Enter Periods separated by commas],[Period])
```

If the `InStr` function finds your variable, it returns a position number; if not, it returns zero. Therefore, you only want records that return a position number greater than zero (hence, the criteria for the parameter).

When you run this query, the Enter Parameter Value dialog box (shown in the following figure) appears. You can then type in as many variables as you want.

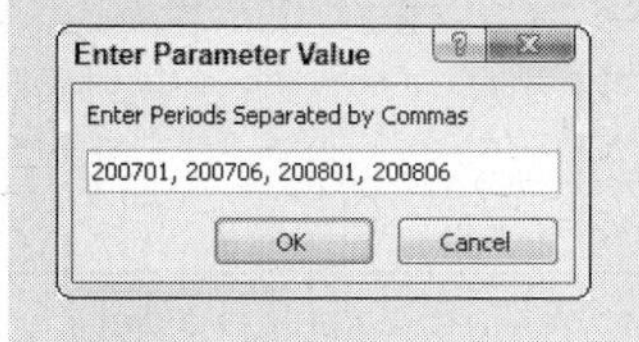

Using Conditional Functions

Parameter queries aren't the only tools in Access that allow for conditional analysis. Access also has built-in functions that facilitate value comparisons, data validation, and conditional evaluation. Two of these functions are the `IIf` function and the `Switch` function. These conditional functions (also called program flow functions) are designed to test for conditions and provide different outcomes based on the results of those tests. In this section, you'll learn how to control the flow of your analyses by utilizing the `IIf` and `Switch` functions.

The IIf function

The `IIf` (immediate if) function replicates the functionality of an `IF` statement for a single operation. The `IIf` function evaluates a specific condition and returns a result based on a true or false determination:

```
IIf(Expression, TrueAnswer, FalseAnswer)
```

To use the `IIf` function, you must provide three required arguments: the expression to be evaluated, a value to be returned if the expression is true, and a value to be returned if the expression is false.

- **Expression (required):** The expression you want to evaluate
- **TrueAnswer (required):** The value to return if the expression is true
- **FalseAnswer (required):** The value to return if the expression is false

TIP

Think of the commas in an `IIf` function as `THEN` and `ELSE` statements. Consider the following `IIf` function, for instance:

```
IIf(Babies = 2 , "Twins", "Not Twins")
```

This function literally translates to: If Babies equals 2, then Twins, else Not Twins.

Using IIf to avoid mathematical errors

To demonstrate a simple problem where the `IIf` function comes in handy, build the query shown in Figure 13.9.

FIGURE 13.9

This query will perform a calculation on the Actual and the Forecast fields to calculate a percent to forecast.

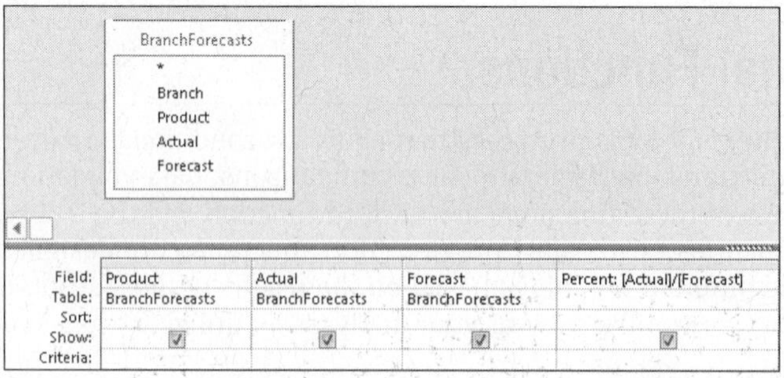

BranchForecasts
*
Branch
Product
Actual
Forecast

Field:	Product	Actual	Forecast	Percent: [Actual]/[Forecast]
Table:	BranchForecasts	BranchForecasts	BranchForecasts	
Sort:				
Show:	☑	☑	☑	☑
Criteria:				

When you run the query, you'll notice that not all the results are clean. As you can see in Figure 13.10, you're getting some errors due to division by zero. That is to say, you're dividing actual revenues by forecasts that are zero.

FIGURE 13.10

The errors shown in the results are due to the fact that some revenues are being divided by zeros.

Product	Actual	Forecast	Percent
90830	171	0	#Div/0!
90830	520	658	79.03%
90830	706	727	97.11%
90830	1,025	1,206	84.99%
90830	1,064	1,400	76.00%
90830	1,195	0	#Div/0!
90830	1,370	0	#Div/0!
90830	1,463	0	#Div/0!
90830	1,483	1,786	83.03%
90830	1,522	1,951	78.01%
90830	1,525	0	#Div/0!

Although this seems like a fairly benign issue, in a more complex, multilayered analytical process, these errors could compromise the integrity of your data analysis. To avoid these errors, you can perform a conditional analysis on your dataset using the `IIf` function, evaluating the Forecast field for each record before performing the calculation. If the forecast is zero, you'll bypass the calculation and simply return a value of zero. If the forecast is not zero, you'll perform the calculation to get the correct value. The `IIf` function would look like this:

```
IIf([Forecast]=0,0,[Actual]/[Forecast])
```

Figure 13.11 demonstrates how this `IIf` function is put into action.

FIGURE 13.11

This `IIf` function enables you to test for forecasts with a value of zero and bypass them when performing your calculation.

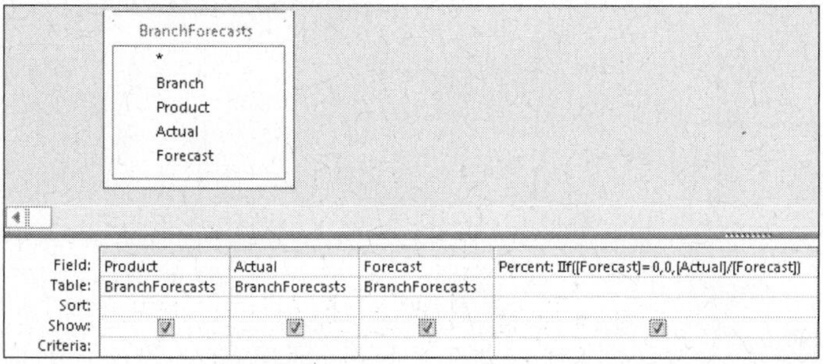

BranchForecasts

*
Branch
Product
Actual
Forecast

Field:	Product	Actual	Forecast	Percent: IIf([Forecast]=0,0,[Actual]/[Forecast])
Table:	BranchForecasts	BranchForecasts	BranchForecasts	
Sort:				
Show:	☑	☑	☑	☑
Criteria:				

As you can see in Figure 13.12, the errors have been avoided.

FIGURE 13.12

The `IIf` function helped you avoid the division by zero errors.

Product	Actual	Forecast	Percent
90830	171	0	0.00%
90830	520	658	79.03%
90830	706	727	97.11%
90830	1,025	1,206	84.99%
90830	1,064	1,400	76.00%
90830	1,195	0	0.00%
90830	1,370	0	0.00%
90830	1,463	0	0.00%
90830	1,483	1,786	83.03%
90830	1,522	1,951	78.01%
90830	1,525	0	0.00%

Saving time with IIf

You can also use the `IIf` function to save steps in your analytical processes and, ultimately, save time. For example, imagine that you need to tag customers in a lead list as either large customers or small customers, based on their dollar potential. You decide that you'll update the MyTest field in your dataset with "LARGE" or "SMALL" based on the revenue potential of the customer.

Without the `IIf` function, you would have to run the two update queries shown in Figures 13.13 and 13.14 to accomplish this task.

FIGURE 13.13

This query will update the MyTest field to tag all customers that have a revenue potential at or above $10,000 with the word "LARGE."

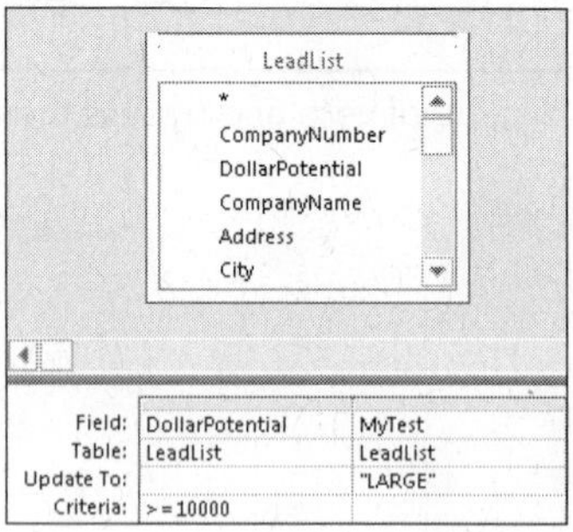

LeadList
*
CompanyNumber
DollarPotential
CompanyName
Address
City

Field:	DollarPotential	MyTest
Table:	LeadList	LeadList
Update To:		"LARGE"
Criteria:	>=10000	

FIGURE 13.14

This query will update the MyTest field to tag all customers that have a revenue potential less than $10,000 with the word "SMALL."

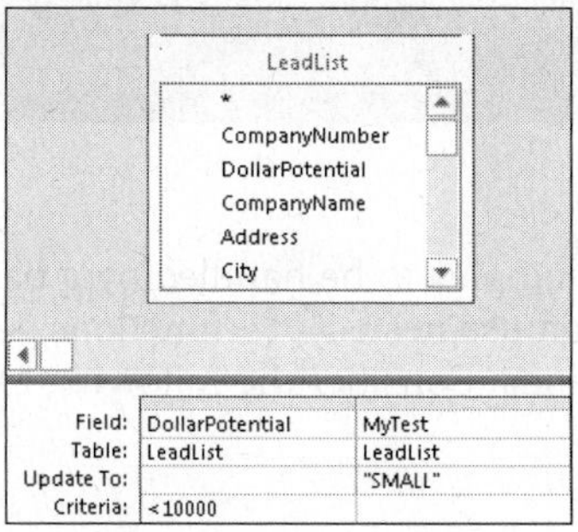

LeadList
*
CompanyNumber
DollarPotential
CompanyName
Address
City

Field:	DollarPotential	MyTest
Table:	LeadList	LeadList
Update To:		"SMALL"
Criteria:	<10000	

Will the queries in Figures 13.13 and 13.14 do the job? Yes. However, you could accomplish the same task with one query using the `IIf` function.

The update query shown in Figure 13.15 illustrates how you can use an `IIf` function as the update expression.

FIGURE 13.15

You can accomplish the same task in one query using the `IIf` function.

LeadList
*
CompanyNumber
DollarPotential
CompanyName
Address
City

Field:	MyTest
Table:	LeadList
Update To:	IIf([DollarPotential]>=10000,"LARGE","SMALL")
Criteria:	

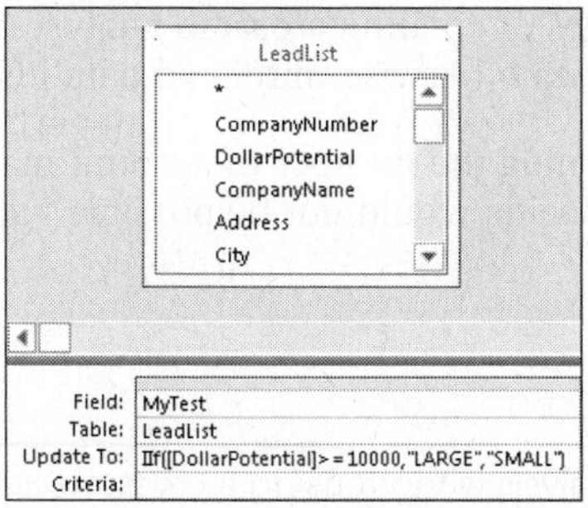

Take a moment and look at the `IIf` function being used as the update expression.

```
IIf([DollarPotential]>=10000,"LARGE","SMALL")
```

This function tells Access to evaluate the DollarPotential field of each record. If the DollarPotential field is greater than or equal to 10,000, use the word "LARGE" as the update value; if not, use the word "SMALL."

TIP

You can use conditional operators (AND, OR, BETWEEN) within your IIf functions to add a layer to your condition expression. For example, the following function tests for a dollar potential and segment to get a true or false value.

```
IIf([DollarPotential]>10000 And [Segment]="Metal Fabrication","True","False")
```

Nesting IIf functions for multiple conditions

Sometimes the condition you need to test for is too complex to be handled by a basic IF...THEN...ELSE structure. In such cases, you can use nested IIf functions — that is, IIf functions that are embedded in other IIf functions. Consider the following example:

```
IIf([VALUE]>100,"A",IIf([VALUE]<100,"C","B"))
```

This function will check to see if VALUE is greater than 100. If it is, then "A" is returned; if not (else), a second IIf function is triggered. The second IIf function will check to see if VALUE is less than 100. If yes, then "C" is returned; if not (else), "B" is returned.

The idea here is that because an IIf function results in a true or false answer, you can expand your condition by setting the false expression to another IIf function instead of to a hard-coded value. This triggers another evaluation. There is no limit to the number of nested IIf functions you can use.

Using IIf functions to create crosstab analyses

Many seasoned analysts use the IIf function to create custom crosstab analyses in lieu of using a crosstab query. Among the many advantages of creating crosstab analyses without a crosstab query is the ability to categorize and group otherwise unrelated data items.

In the example shown in Figure 13.16, you're returning the number of account managers hired before and after 2009. Categorizations this specific would not be possible with a crosstab query.

FIGURE 13.16

This query demonstrates how to create a crosstab analysis without using a crosstab query.

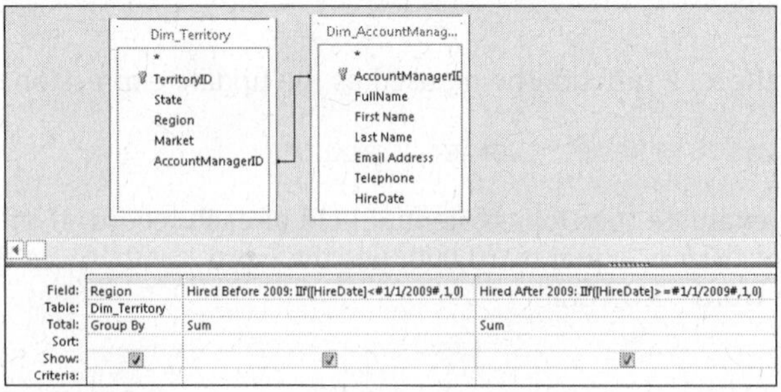

The result, shown in Figure 13.17, is every bit as clean and user-friendly as the results would be from a crosstab query.

FIGURE 13.17

The resulting dataset gives you a clean crosstab-style view of your data.

Region	Hired Before 2009	Hired After 2009
CANADA	0	5
Midwest	8	0
North	6	0
Northeast	14	0
South	6	0
Southeast	5	0
Southwest	6	0

Another advantage of creating crosstab analyses without a crosstab query is the ability to include more than one calculation in your crosstab report. For example, Figure 13.18 illustrates a query where the sum of units and revenue will be returned in crosstab format.

FIGURE 13.18

Creating crosstab-style reports using the `IIf` function allows you to calculate more than one value.

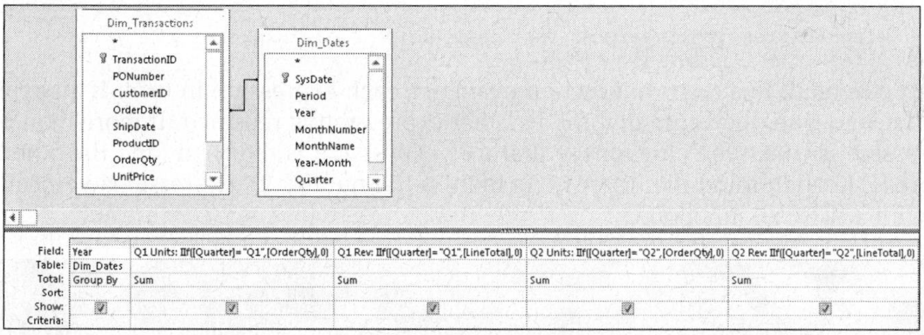

Field:	Year	Q1 Units: IIf([Quarter]="Q1",[OrderQty],0)	Q1 Rev: IIf([Quarter]="Q1",[LineTotal],0)	Q2 Units: IIf([Quarter]="Q2",[OrderQty],0)	Q2 Rev: IIf([Quarter]="Q2",[LineTotal],0)
Table:	Dim_Dates				
Total:	Group By	Sum	Sum	Sum	Sum
Sort:					
Show:	✓	✓	✓	✓	✓
Criteria:					

As you can see in Figure 13.19, the resulting dataset provides a great deal of information in an easy-to-read format. Because a standard crosstab query does not allow more than one value calculation (in this case, units and revenue are values), this particular view would not be possible with a standard crosstab query.

FIGURE 13.19

This analysis would be impossible to create in a standard crosstab query, where multiple calculations are not allowed.

Year	Q1 Units	Q1 Rev	Q2 Units	Q2 Rev
2006	0	$0.00	0	$0.00
2007	4517	$8,749,969.10	5865	$9,761,310.90
2008	12352	$9,262,135.00	18603	$12,554,344.60
2009	31540	$18,071,842.70	43700	$22,996,203.25

The Switch function

The `Switch` function enables you to evaluate a list of expressions and return the value associated with the expression determined to be true. To use the `Switch` function, you must provide a minimum of one expression and one value.

```
Switch(Expression, Value)
```

- **Expression (required):** The expression you want to evaluate.
- **Value (required):** The value to return if the expression is true.

The power of the `Switch` function comes in evaluating multiple expressions at one time and determining which one is true. To evaluate multiple expressions, simply add another `Expression` and `Value` to the function, as follows:

```
Switch(Expression1, Value1, Expression2, Value2, Expression3, Value3)
```

When executed, this `Switch` function evaluates each expression in turn. If an expression evaluates to true, the value that follows that expression is returned. If more than one expression is true, the value for the first true expression is returned (and the others are ignored). Keep in mind that there is no limit to the number of expressions you can evaluate with a `Switch` function.

CAUTION

If none of the expressions in your `Switch` function evaluate as true, the function will return a null value. For example, the following function evaluates `Count` and returns a value based on it.

```
Switch([Count] < 10, "Low", [Count] > 15, "High")
```

The problem with this function is that if `Count` comes in between 10 and 15, you will get a null value because none of the expressions include those numbers. This may indirectly cause errors in other parts of your analysis.

To avoid this scenario, you can add a "catch-all" expression and provide a value to return if none of your expressions is determined to be true.

```
Switch([Count] < 10, "Low", [Count] > 15, "High", True, "Middle")
```

Adding `True` as the last expression will force the value `"Middle"` to be returned instead of a null value if none of the other expressions evaluates as true.

Comparing the IIf and Switch functions

Although the `IIf` function is a versatile tool that can handle most conditional analyses, the fact is that the `IIf` function has a fixed number of arguments that limits it to a basic `IF...THEN...ELSE` structure. This limitation makes it difficult to evaluate complex conditions without using nested `IIf` functions. Although there is nothing wrong with nesting `IIf` functions, there are analyses in which the numbers of conditions that need to be evaluated make building a nested `IIf` impractical at best.

To illustrate this point, consider this scenario. It's common practice to classify customers into groups based on annual revenue or how much they spend with your company. Imagine that your organization has a policy of classifying customers into four groups: A, B, C, and D (see Table 13.1).

TABLE 13.1 Customer Classifications

Annual Revenue	Customer Classification
>= $10,000	A
>=5,000 but < $10,000	B
>=$1,000 but < $5,000	C
<$1,000	D

You've been asked to classify the customers in the TransactionMaster table, based on each customer's sales transactions. You can actually do this using either the `IIf` function or the `Switch` function.

The problem with using the `IIf` function is that this situation calls for some hefty nesting. That is, you'll have to use `IIf` expressions within other `IIf` expressions to handle the easy layer of possible conditions. Here's how the expression would look if you opted to use the `IIf` function:

```
IIf([REV]>=10000,"A",IIf([REV]>=5000 And [REV]<10000,"B",
IIf([REV]>1000 And [REV]<5000,"C","D")))
```

As you can see, not only is it difficult to determine what's going on here, but this is so convoluted, the chances of making a syntax or logic error are high.

In contrast to the preceding nested `IIf` function, the following `Switch` function is rather straightforward:

```
Switch([REV]<1000,"D",[REV]<5000,"C",[REV]<10000,"B",True,"A")
```

This function tells Access to return a value of `"D"` if `REV` is less than `1000`. If `REV` is less than `5000`, a value of `"C"` is returned. If `REV` is less than `10000, "B"` is returned. If all else fails, use `"A"`. Figure 13.20 demonstrates how you would use this function in a query.

FIGURE 13.20

Using the `Switch` function is sometimes more practical than using nested `IIf` functions. This query will classify customers by how much they spend.

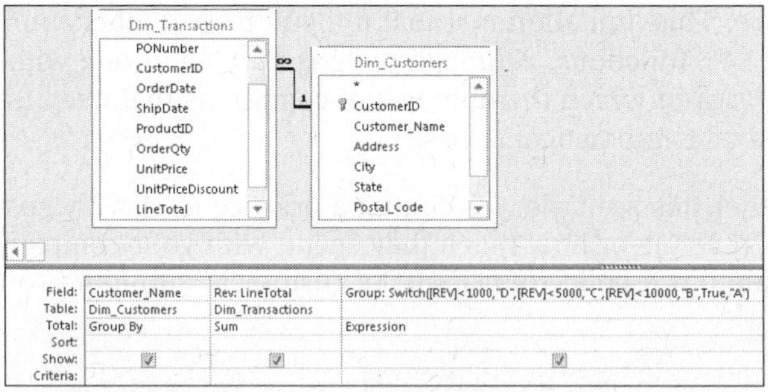

Dim_Transactions: PONumber, CustomerID, OrderDate, ShipDate, ProductID, OrderQty, UnitPrice, UnitPriceDiscount, LineTotal

Dim_Customers: *, CustomerID, Customer_Name, Address, City, State, Postal_Code

Field:	Customer_Name	Rev: LineTotal	Group: Switch([REV]<1000,"D",[REV]<5000,"C",[REV]<10000,"B",True,"A")
Table:	Dim_Customers	Dim_Transactions	
Total:	Group By	Sum	Expression
Sort:			
Show:	☑	☑	☑
Criteria:			

> **NOTE**
>
> You may shrewdly notice that those records that are less than 1,000 will also be less than 10,000. So why don't all the records get tagged with a value of B? Remember that the `Switch` function evaluates your expressions from left to right and only returns the value of the first expression that evaluates to true.
>
> In this light, you'll want to sort the expressions in your `Switch` function accordingly, using an order that is conducive to the logic of your analysis.

When you run the query, you'll see the resulting dataset shown in Figure 13.21.

FIGURE 13.21

Each customer is conditionally tagged with a group designation based on annual revenue.

Customer_Name	Rev	Group
ACASCO Corp.	$253.00	D
ACECUL Corp.	$14,771.00	A
ACEHUA Corp.	$9,095.00	B
ACOPUL Corp.	$10,190.00	A
ACORAR Corp.	$4,750.00	C
ACSBUR Corp.	$33.00	D
ADACEC Corp.	$395.00	D
ADADUL Corp.	$5,637.00	B
ADANAS Corp.	$8,573.00	B
ADCOMP Corp.	$4,206.00	C
ADDATI Corp.	$1,020.00	C
ADDOUS Corp.	$921.00	D

CHAPTER 14

Fundamentals of Using Access SQL

IN THIS CHAPTER

Understanding basic SQL

Getting fancy with advanced SQL

Using SQL specific queries

Structured Query Language (SQL) is the language that relational database management systems (such as Access) use to perform their various tasks. In order to tell Access to perform any kind of query, you have to convey your instructions in SQL. Don't panic — the truth is, you've already been building and using SQL statements, even if you didn't realize it.

In this chapter, you'll discover the role that SQL plays in your dealings with Access and learn how to understand the SQL statements generated when building queries. You'll also explore some of the advanced actions you can take with SQL statements, allowing you to accomplish actions that go beyond the Access user interface. The basics you learn here will lay the foundation for your ability to perform the advanced techniques you'll encounter throughout the rest of this book.

ON THE WEB

The starting database for this walkthrough, `Chapter14.accdb`, can be downloaded from this book's website.

Understanding Basic SQL

A major reason your exposure to SQL is limited is that Access is more user friendly than most people give it credit for being. The fact is, Access performs a majority of its actions in user-friendly environments that hide the real grunt work that goes on behind the scenes.

For a demonstration of this, build in Design view the query you see in Figure 14.1. In this relatively simple query, you're asking for the sum of revenue by period.

FIGURE 14.1

Build this relatively simple query in Design view.

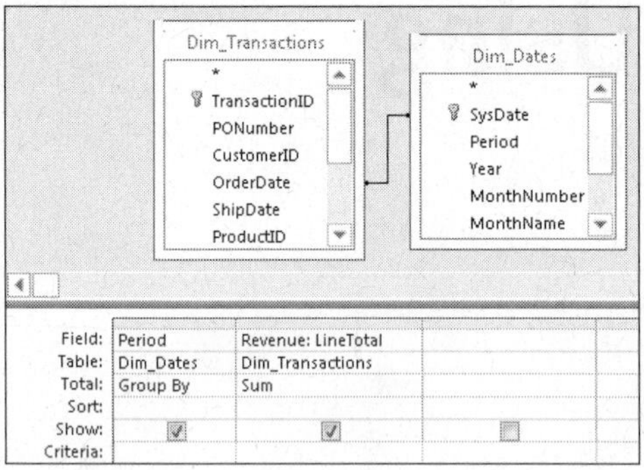

Dim_Transactions: *, TransactionID, PONumber, CustomerID, OrderDate, ShipDate, ProductID

Dim_Dates: *, SysDate, Period, Year, MonthNumber, MonthName

Field:	Period	Revenue: LineTotal	
Table:	Dim_Dates	Dim_Transactions	
Total:	Group By	Sum	
Sort:			
Show:	☑	☑	☐
Criteria:			

Next, select the Design tab on the Ribbon and choose View ➪ SQL View. Access switches from Design view to the view you see in Figure 14.2.

FIGURE 14.2

You can get to SQL view by selecting View ➪ SQL View.

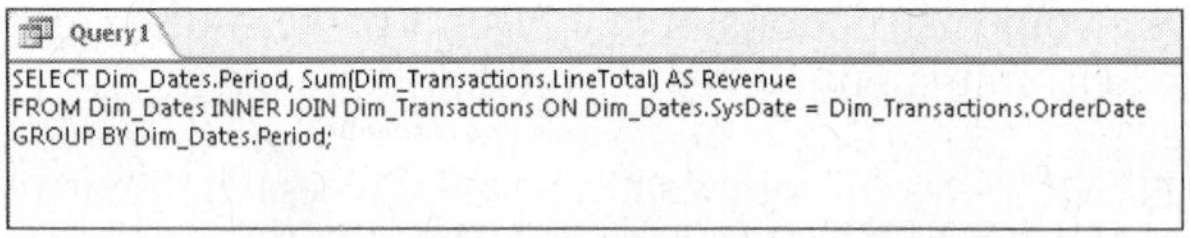

Query1

```
SELECT Dim_Dates.Period, Sum(Dim_Transactions.LineTotal) AS Revenue
FROM Dim_Dates INNER JOIN Dim_Transactions ON Dim_Dates.SysDate = Dim_Transactions.OrderDate
GROUP BY Dim_Dates.Period;
```

As you can see in Figure 14.2, while you were busy designing your query in Design view, Access was diligently creating the SQL statement that allows the query to run. This example shows that with the user-friendly interface provided by Access, you don't necessarily need to know the SQL behind each query. The question now becomes: If you can run queries just fine without knowing SQL, why bother to learn it?

Admittedly, the convenient query interface provided by Access does make it a bit tempting to go through life not really understanding SQL. However, if you want to harness the real power of data analysis with Access, you need to understand the fundamentals of SQL.

The SELECT statement

The `SELECT` statement, the cornerstone of SQL, enables you to retrieve records from a dataset. The basic syntax of a `SELECT` statement is as follows:

```
SELECT column_name(s)
FROM table_name
```

The SELECT statement is most often used with a FROM clause. The FROM clause identifies the table(s) that make up the source for the data.

Try this: Start a new query in Design view. Close the Show Table dialog box (if it's open), select the Design tab on the Ribbon, and choose View➪SQL View. In SQL view, type in the SELECT statement shown in Figure 14.3, and then run the query by selecting Run on the Design tab of the Ribbon.

FIGURE 14.3

A basic SELECT statement in SQL view.

```
Query1
SELECT FullName
FROM Dim_AccountManagers
```

Congratulations! You've just written your first query manually.

> **NOTE**
>
> You may notice that the SQL statement automatically created by Access in Figure 14.2 has a semicolon at the end of it. The semicolon is a standard way to end a SQL statement and is required by some database programs. However, it isn't necessary to end your SQL statements with a semicolon in Access, because Access will automatically add it when the query compiles.

Selecting specific columns

You can retrieve specific columns from your dataset by explicitly defining the columns in your SELECT statement, as follows:

```
SELECT AccountManagerID, FullName,[Email Address]
FROM Dim_AccountManagers
```


> **CAUTION**
>
> Any column in your database with a name that includes spaces or a non-alphanumeric character must be enclosed within brackets ([]) in your SQL statement. For example, the SQL statement selecting data from a column called Email Address would be referred to as [Email Address].

Selecting all columns

Using the wildcard (*) allows you to select all columns from a dataset without having to define every column explicitly.

```
SELECT * FROM Dim_AccountManagers
```

The WHERE clause

You can use the WHERE clause in a SELECT statement to filter your dataset and conditionally select specific records. The WHERE clause is always used in combination with an operator such as: = (equal), <> (not equal), > (greater than), < (less than), >= (greater than or equal to), <= (less than or equal to), or BETWEEN (within general range).

The following SQL statement retrieves only those employees whose last name is Winston:

```
SELECT AccountManagerID, [Last Name], [First Name]
FROM Dim_AccountManagers
WHERE [Last Name] = "Winston"
```

And this SQL statement retrieves only those employees whose hire data is later than May 16, 2007:

```
SELECT AccountManagerID, [Last Name], [First Name]
FROM Dim_AccountManagers
WHERE HireDate > #5/16/2007#
```

NOTE
Notice in the preceding two examples that the word *Winston* is wrapped in quotes (`"Winston"`) and the date 5/16/2007 is wrapped in pound signs (`#5/16/2007#`). When referring to a text value in a SQL statement, you must place quotes around the value; when referring to a date, pound signs must be used.

Making sense of joins

You'll often need to build queries that require that two or more related tables be joined to achieve the desired results. For example, you may want to join an employee table to a transaction table in order to create a report that contains both transaction details and information on the employees who logged those transactions. The type of join used will determine the records that will be output.

For a detailed review of joins, check out Chapter 8.

Inner joins

An *inner join* operation tells Access to select only those records from both tables that have matching values. Records with values in the joined field that do not appear in both tables are omitted from the query results.

The following SQL statement selects only those records in which the employee numbers in the AccountManagerID field are in both the Dim_AccountManagers table and the Dim_Territory table.

```
SELECT Region, Market, AccountManagerID, FullName
FROM Dim_AccountManagers INNER JOIN Dim_Territory
ON Dim_AccountManagers.AccountManagerID = Dim_Territory.AccountManagerID
```

Outer joins

An *outer join* operation tells Access to select all the records from one table and only the records from a second table with matching values in the joined field. There are two types of outer joins: left joins and right joins.

A *left join* operation (sometimes called an "outer left join") tells Access to select all the records from the first table regardless of matching *and* only those records from the second table that have matching values in the joined field.

This SQL statement selects all records from the Dim_AccountManagers table and only those records in the Dim_Territory table where values for the AccountManagerID field exist in the Dim_AccountManagers table.

```
SELECT Region, Market, AccountManagerID, FullName
FROM Dim_AccountManagers LEFT JOIN Dim_Territory
ON Dim_AccountManagers.AccountManagerID = Dim_Territory.AccountManagerID
```

A *right join* operation (sometimes called an "outer right join") tells Access to select all the records from the second table, regardless of matching, *and* only those records from the first table that have matching values in the joined field.

This SQL statement selects all records from the Dim_Territory table and only those records in the Dim_AccountManagers table where values for the AccountManagerID field exist in the Dim_Territory table.

```
SELECT Region, Market, AccountManagerID, FullName
FROM Dim_AccountManagers RIGHT JOIN Dim_Territory
ON Dim_AccountManagers.AccountManagerID = Dim_Territory.AccountManagerID
```


TIP

Notice that in the preceding join statements, table names are listed before each column name separated by a dot (for example, `Dim_AccountManager.AccountManagerID`). When you're building a SQL statement for a query that utilizes multiple tables, it's generally a good practice to refer to the table names as well as field names in order to avoid confusion and errors. Access does this for all queries automatically. You'll also need to use the square brackets if the table or field being referenced contains special characters such as spaces.

Getting Fancy with Advanced SQL Statements

You'll soon realize that the SQL language itself is quite versatile, allowing you to go far beyond basic `SELECT`, `FROM`, and `WHERE` statements. In this section, you'll explore some of the advanced actions you can accomplish with SQL.

Expanding your search with the Like operator

By itself, the Like operator is no different than the equal (=) operator. For instance, these two SQL statements will return the same number of records:

```
SELECT AccountManagerID, [Last Name], [First Name]
FROM Dim_AccountManagers
WHERE [Last Name] = "Winston"

SELECT AccountManagerID, [Last Name], [First Name]
FROM Dim_AccountManagers
WHERE [Last Name] Like "Winston"
```

The Like operator is typically used with wildcard characters to expand the scope of your search to include any record that matches a pattern. The wildcard characters that are valid in Access are as follows:

- *: The asterisk represents any number and type characters.
- ?: The question mark represents any single character.
- #: The pound sign represents any single digit.
- []: The brackets allow you to pass a single character or an array of characters to the Like operator. Any values matching the character values within the brackets will be included in the results.
- [!]: The brackets with an embedded exclamation point allow you to pass a single character or an array of characters to the Like operator. Any values matching the character values following the exclamation point will be excluded from the results.

Listed in Table 14.1 are some example SQL statements that use the Like operator to select different records from the same table column.

TABLE 14.1 Selection Methods Using the Like Operator

Wildcard Character(s) Used	SQL Statement Example	Result
*	SELECT Field1 FROM Table1 WHERE Field1 Like "A*"	Selects all records where Field1 starts with the letter *A*
*	SELECT Field1 FROM Table1 WHERE Field1 Like "*A*"	Selects all records where Field1 includes the letter *A*
?	SELECT Field1 FROM Table1 WHERE Field1 Like "???"	Selects all records where the length of Field1 is three characters long

Wildcard Character(s) Used	SQL Statement Example	Result
?	`SELECT Field1` `FROM Table1` `WHERE Field1 Like "B??"`	Selects all records where Field1 is a three-letter string that starts with *B*
#	`SELECT Field1` `FROM Table1` `WHERE Field1 Like "###"`	Selects all records where Field1 is a number that is exactly three digits long
#	`SELECT Field1` `FROM Table1` `WHERE Field1 Like "A#A"`	Selects all records where the value in Field1 is a three-character value that starts with *A*, contains one digit, and ends with *A*
#, *	`SELECT Field1` `FROM Table1` `WHERE Field1 Like "A#*"`	Selects all records where Field1 begins with *A* and any digit
[], *	`SELECT Field1` `FROM Table1` `WHERE Field1 Like "*[$%!*/]*"`	Selects all records where Field1 includes any one of the special characters shown in the SQL statement
[!], *	`SELECT Field1` `FROM Table1` `WHERE Field1 Like "*[!a-z]*"`	Selects all records where the value of Field1 is not a text value, but a number value or special character such as the @ symbol
[!], *	`SELECT Field1` `FROM Table1` `WHERE Field1 Like "*[!0-9]*"`	Selects all records where the value of Field1 is not a number value, but a text value or special character such as the @ symbol

14

Selecting unique values and rows without grouping

The `DISTINCT` predicate enables you to retrieve only unique values from the selected fields in your dataset. For example, the following SQL statement will select only unique job titles from the Dim_AccountManagers table, resulting in six records:

```
SELECT DISTINCT AccountManagerID
FROM Dim_AccountManagers
```

If your SQL statement selects more than one field, the combination of values from all fields must be unique for a given record to be included in the results.

If you require that the entire row be unique, you could use the DISTINCTROW predicate. The DISTINCTROW predicate enables you to retrieve only those records for which the entire row is unique. That is to say, the combination of all values in the selected fields does not match any other record in the returned dataset. You would use the DISTINCTROW predicate just as you would in a SELECT DISTINCT clause.

```
SELECT DISTINCTROW AccountManagerID
FROM Dim_AccountManagers
```

Grouping and aggregating with the GROUP BY clause

The GROUP BY clause makes it possible to aggregate records in your dataset by column values. When you create an aggregate query in Design view, you're essentially using the GROUP BY clause. The following SQL statement will group the Market field and give you the count of states in each market.

```
SELECT Market, Count(State)
FROM Dim_Territory
GROUP BY Market
```

When you're using the GROUP BY clause, any WHERE clause included in the query is evaluated before aggregation occurs. However, you may have scenarios when you need to apply a WHERE condition after the grouping is applied. In these cases, you can use the HAVING clause.

For instance, this SQL statement will group the records where the value in the Market field is Dallas, and then only return those records where the grouped average LineItem is less than 100. Again, the grouping is done before checking if the average LineItem is less than 100.

```
SELECT Market, Count(State)
FROM Dim_Territory
WHERE Market = "Dallas"
GROUP BY Market
HAVING Avg(LineItem) < 100
```

Setting sort order with the ORDER BY clause

The ORDER BY clause enables you to sort data by a specified field. The default sort order is ascending; therefore, sorting your fields in ascending order requires no explicit instruction. The following SQL statement will sort the resulting records by Last Name ascending and then First Name ascending:

```
SELECT AccountManagerID, [Last Name], [First Name]
FROM Dim_AccountManagers
ORDER BY [Last Name], [First Name]
```

To sort in descending order, you must use the `DESC` reserved word after each column you want sorted in descending order. The following SQL statement will sort the resulting records by Last Name descending and then First Name ascending:

```
SELECT AccountManagerID, [Last Name], [First Name]
FROM Dim_AccountManagers
ORDER BY [Last Name] DESC, [First Name]
```

Creating aliases with the AS clause

The `AS` clause enables you to assign aliases to your columns and tables. There are generally two reasons you would want to use aliases: Either you want to make column or table names shorter and easier to read, or you're working with multiple instances of the same table and you need a way to refer to one instance or the other.

Creating a column alias

The following SQL statement will group the Market field and give you the count of states in each market. In addition, the alias `State Count` has been given to the column containing the count of states by including the `AS` clause.

```
SELECT Market, Count(State) AS [State Count]
FROM Dim_Territory
GROUP BY Market
HAVING Market = "Dallas"
```

Creating a table alias

This SQL statement gives the Dim_AccountManagers the alias "MyTable."

```
SELECT AccountManagerID, [Last Name], [First Name]
FROM Dim_AccountManagers AS MyTable
```

Showing only the SELECT TOP or SELECT TOP PERCENT

When you run a `SELECT` query, you're retrieving all records that meet your definitions and criteria. When you run the `SELECT TOP` statement, or a top values query, you're telling Access to filter your returned dataset to show only a specific number of records.

Top values queries explained

To get a clear understanding of what the `SELECT TOP` statement does, build the aggregate query shown in Figure 14.4.

FIGURE 14.4

Build this aggregate query in Design view. Take note that the query is sorted descending on the Sum of LineTotal.

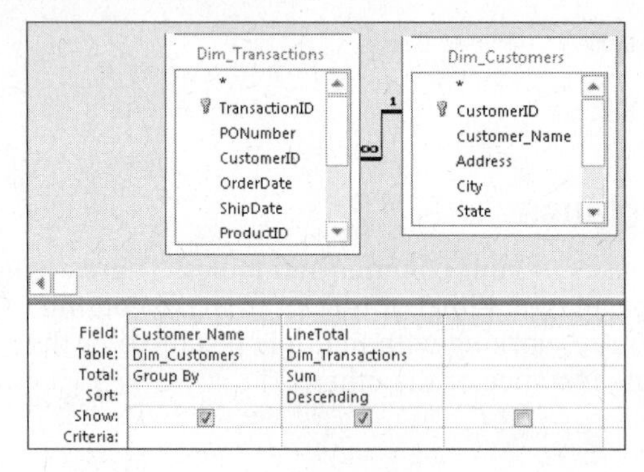

On the Query Tools Design tab, click the Property Sheet command. This will activate the Property Sheet dialog box shown in Figure 14.5. Alternatively, you can use the F4 key on your keyboard to activate the Property Sheet dialog box.

In the Property Sheet dialog box, change the Top Values property to 25.

FIGURE 14.5

Change the Top Values property to 25.

Property Sheet

Selection type: Query Properties

General

Description	
Default View	Datasheet
Output All Fields	No
Top Values	25
Unique Values	No
Unique Records	No

As you can see in Figure 14.6, after you run this query, only the customers that fall into the top 25 by sum of revenue are returned. If you want the bottom 25 customers, simply change the sort order of the LineTotal field to Ascending.

NOTE

Access does not break ties. If the 24th, 25th, and 26th customers all have the same total, you'll actually get 26 rows back.

FIGURE 14.6

Running the query will give you the top 25 customers by revenue.

Customer_Name	SumOfLineTotal
SUASHU Corp.	$2,738,933.20
GUPDYU Corp.	$2,062,418.05
CATYOF Corp.	$2,007,139.00
SCULOS Corp.	$1,374,781.70
WHATLU Corp.	$1,357,050.30
MADOSM Corp.	$1,282,750.00
USANGE Corp.	$1,226,356.55
CORULA Corp.	$1,201,995.95
RADASS Corp.	$1,198,185.00
SMEAS Corp.	$1,191,758.00
GRECUW Corp.	$1,187,312.80
AVAATA Corp.	$1,174,196.45
ZUQHYR Corp.	$1,173,088.50
ANATUD Corp.	$1,093,389.95
THEMOG Corp.	$1,087,385.00
BASHUQ Corp.	$1,081,070.55
ATLANT Corp.	$1,077,585.85
CUGGAN Corp.	$1,071,389.30
WORUTC Corp.	$1,068,895.55
EBANAU Corp.	$1,025,716.70
USLAND Corp.	$1,005,005.95
QAAKUY Corp.	$996,152.20
MUUZEO Corp.	$946,096.70
CUANTY Corp.	$937,880.00
SUASHF Corp.	$912,274.15

The SELECT TOP statement

The `SELECT TOP` statement is easy to spot. This is the same query used to run the results in Figure 14.6.

```
SELECT TOP 25 Customer_Name, Sum(LineTotal) AS SumOfLineTotal
FROM Dim_Customers INNER JOIN Dim_Transactions ON Dim_Customers.CustomerID =
   Dim_Transactions.CustomerID
GROUP BY Customer_Name
ORDER BY Sum(LineTotal) DESC
```

Bear in mind that you don't have to be working with totals or currency to use a top values query. In the following SQL statement, you're returning the ten account managers that have the earliest hire date in the company, effectively producing a seniority report:

```
SELECT Top 10 AccountManagerID, [Last Name], [First Name]
FROM Dim_AccountManagers
ORDER BY HireDate ASC
```

CAUTION

Note the use of the DESC and ASC clauses in the previous SQL statements. When you're using the `SELECT TOP`, it's important to specify the sort direction accurately because it can make the difference between select the biggest ten results or the smallest ten results.

The SELECT TOP PERCENT statement

The SELECT TOP PERCENT statement works in exactly the same way as SELECT TOP except the records returned in a SELECT TOP PERCENT statement represent the *n*th percent of total records rather than the *n*th number of records. For example, the following SQL statement will return the top 25 percent of records by revenue:

```
SELECT TOP 25 PERCENT Customer_Name, Sum(LineTotal) AS SumOfLineTotal
FROM Dim_Customers INNER JOIN Dim_Transactions ON Dim_Customers.CustomerID =
   Dim_Transactions.CustomerID
GROUP BY Customer_Name
ORDER BY Sum(LineTotal) DESC
```

NOTE

Keep in mind that SELECT TOP PERCENT statements only give you the top or bottom percent of the total number of records in the returned dataset, not the percent of the total value in your records. For example, the preceding SQL statement won't give you only those records that make up 25 percent of the total value in the LineTotal field. It will give you the top 25 percent of total records in the queried dataset. In other words, if you'd get 5,961 records using just SELECT, SELECT TOP 25 PERCENT will return 1,491 rows.

Performing action queries via SQL statements

You may not have thought about it before, but when you build an action query, you're building a SQL statement that is specific to that action. These SQL statements make it possible for you to go beyond just selecting records.

Make-table queries translated

Make-table queries use the SELECT...INTO statement to make a hard-coded table that contains the results of your query. The following example first selects account manager number, last name, and first name; then it creates a new table called Employees:

```
SELECT AccountManagerID, [Last Name], [First Name] INTO Employees
FROM Dim_AccountManagers
```

Append queries translated

Append queries use the INSERT INTO statement to insert new rows into a specified table. The following example will insert new rows into the Employees table from the Dim_AccountManagers table:

```
INSERT INTO Employees (AccountManagerID, [Last Name], [First Name])
SELECT AccountManagerID, [Last Name], [First Name]
FROM Dim_AccountManagers
```

Update queries translated

Update queries use the UPDATE statement in conjunction with SET in order to modify the data in a dataset. This example updates the List_Price field in the Dim_Products table to increase prices by 10 percent.

```
UPDATE Dim_Products SET List_Price = [List_Price]*1.1
```

Delete queries translated

Delete queries use the DELETE statement to delete rows in a dataset. In the example here, you're deleting all rows from the Employees table.

```
DELETE * FROM Employees
```

Creating crosstabs with the TRANSFORM statement

The TRANSFORM statement allows the creation of a Crosstab dataset that displays data in a compact view. The TRANSFORM statement requires three main components to work:

- The field to be aggregated
- The SELECT statement that determines the row content for the crosstab
- The field that will make up the column of the crosstab (the "pivot field")

The syntax is as follows:

```
TRANSFORM Aggregated_Field
SELECT Field1, Field2 FROM Table1 GROUP BY Select Field1, Field2
PIVOT Pivot_Field
```

For example, the following statement will create a crosstab that shows region and market on the rows and products on the columns, with revenue in the center of the crosstab.

```
TRANSFORM Sum(Revenue) AS SumOfRevenue
SELECT Region, Market
FROM PvTblFeed
GROUP BY Region, Market
PIVOT Product_Description
```


Using SQL Specific Queries

SQL specific queries are essentially action queries that cannot be run through the Access query grid. These queries must be run either in SQL view or via code (macro or VBA). There are several types of SQL specific queries, each performing a specific action. In this section, we introduce you to a few of these queries, focusing on those that can be used in Access to shape and configure data tables.

Merging datasets with the UNION operator

The UNION operator is used to merge two compatible SQL statements to produce one read-only dataset. For example, the following SELECT statement produces a dataset (see Figure 14.7) that shows revenue by region and market.

```
SELECT Region, Market, Sum(Revenue) AS [Sales]
FROM PvTblFeed
GROUP BY Region, Market
```

FIGURE 14.7

This dataset shows revenue by region and market.

Region	Market	Sales
MIDWEST	DENVER	$645,584.10
MIDWEST	KANSASCITY	$574,899.15
MIDWEST	TULSA	$628,407.41
NORTH	BUFFALO	$450,478.72
NORTH	CANADA	$776,247.78
NORTH	MICHIGAN	$678,708.11
NORTH	NEWYORK	$873,580.79
SOUTH	CHARLOTTE	$890,514.49
SOUTH	DALLAS	$467,086.11
SOUTH	FLORIDA	$1,450,397.76
SOUTH	NEWORLEANS	$333,452.80
WEST	CALIFORNIA	$2,254,751.64
WEST	PHOENIX	$570,254.17

A second SELECT statement produces a separate dataset (see Figure 14.8) that shows total revenue by region.

```
SELECT Region, "Total" AS [Market], Sum(Revenue) AS [Sales]
FROM PvTblFeed
GROUP BY Region
```

FIGURE 14.8

This dataset shows total revenue by region.

Region	Market	Sales
MIDWEST	Total	$1,848,890.66
NORTH	Total	$2,779,015.40
SOUTH	Total	$3,141,451.17
WEST	Total	$3,004,832.22

The idea is to bring these two datasets together to create an analysis that will show detail and totals all in one table. The UNION operator is ideal for this type of work, merging the results of the two SELECT statements. To use the UNION operator, simply start a new query in SQL view and enter the following syntax:

```
SELECT Region, Market, Sum(Revenue) AS [Sales]
FROM PvTblFeed
GROUP BY Region, Market
UNION
SELECT Region, "Total" AS [Market], Sum(Revenue) AS [Sales]
FROM PvTblFeed
GROUP BY Region
```

As you can see, the preceding statement is nothing more than the two SQL statements brought together with a UNION operator. When the two are merged (see Figure 14.9), the result is a dataset that shows both details and totals in one table!

FIGURE 14.9

The two datasets have now been combined to create a report that provides summary and detail data.

Region	Market	Sales
MIDWEST	DENVER	$645,584.10
MIDWEST	KANSASCITY	$574,899.15
MIDWEST	Total	$1,848,890.66
MIDWEST	TULSA	$628,407.41
NORTH	BUFFALO	$450,478.72
NORTH	CANADA	$776,247.78
NORTH	MICHIGAN	$678,708.11
NORTH	NEWYORK	$873,580.79
NORTH	Total	$2,779,015.40
SOUTH	CHARLOTTE	$890,514.49
SOUTH	DALLAS	$467,086.11
SOUTH	FLORIDA	$1,450,397.76
SOUTH	NEWORLEANS	$333,452.80
SOUTH	Total	$3,141,451.17
WEST	CALIFORNIA	$2,254,751.64
WEST	PHOENIX	$570,254.17
WEST	SEATTLE	$179,826.42
WEST	Total	$3,004,832.22

NOTE

When a union query is run, Access matches the columns from both datasets by their position in the SELECT statement. That means two things: Your SELECT statements must have the same number of columns, and the columns in both statements should, in most cases, be in the same order.

CAUTION

Note that the UNION operator effectively performs a SELECT DISTINCT on the resulting data sets. This means that the UNION statement could very well eliminate duplicate rows where all the values in every field are identical between the two data sets. If you find that you're missing records when running a UNION query, consider using the UNION ALL operator. UNION ALL performs the same function as UNION, except it does not apply the SELECT DISTINCT, thus does not eliminate duplicate rows.

Creating a table with the CREATE TABLE statement

Often in your analytical processes, you'll need to create a temporary table in order to group, manipulate, or simply hold data. The CREATE TABLE statement allows you to do just that with one SQL specific query.

Unlike a make-table query, the CREATE TABLE statement is designed to create only the structure or schema of a table. No records are ever returned with a CREATE TABLE statement. This statement allows you to strategically create an empty table at any point in your analytical process.

The basic syntax for a CREATE TABLE statement is as follows:

```
CREATE TABLE TableName
(<Field1Name> Type(<Field Size>), <Field2Name> Type(<Field Size>))
```

To use the CREATE TABLE statement, simply start a new query in SQL view and define the structure for your table.

In the following example, a new table called TempLog is created with three fields. The first field is a Text field that can accept 50 characters, the second field is a Text field that can accept 255 characters, and the third field is a Date field.

```
CREATE TABLE TempLog
([User] Text(50), [Description] Text, [LogDate] Date)
```

NOTE

Notice that in the preceding example, no field size is specified for the second text column. If the field size is omitted, Access will use the default field size specified for the database.

Manipulating columns with the ALTER TABLE statement

The ALTER TABLE statement provides some additional methods of altering the structure of a table behind the scenes. There are several clauses you can use with the ALTER TABLE statement, four of which are quite useful in Access data analysis: ADD, ALTER COLUMN, DROP COLUMN, and ADD CONSTRAINT.

NOTE

The ALTER TABLE statement along with its various clauses are used much less frequently than the SQL statements mentioned earlier in this chapter. However, the ALTER TABLE statement comes in handy when your analytical processes require to you change the structure of tables on the fly, helping you avoid any manual manipulations that may have to be done.

It should be noted that there is no way to undo any actions performed using an ALTER TABLE statement. This obviously calls for some caution when using these statements.

Adding a column with the ADD clause

As the name implies, the ADD clause enables you to add a column to an existing table. The basic syntax is as follows:

```
ALTER TABLE <TableName>
ADD <ColumnName> Type(<Field Size>)
```

To use the ADD statement, simply start a new query in SQL view and define the structure for your new column. For instance, running the example statement shown here will create a new column called SupervisorPhone that is being added to a table called TempLog.

```
ALTER TABLE TempLog
ADD SupervisorPhone Text(10)
```

Altering a column with the ALTER COLUMN clause

When using the ALTER COLUMN clause, you specify an existing column in an existing table. This clause is used primarily to change the data type and field size of a given column. The basic syntax is as follows:

```
ALTER TABLE <TableName>
ALTER COLUMN <ColumnName> Type(<Field Size>)
```

To use the ALTER COLUMN statement, simply start a new query in SQL view and define changes for the column in question. For instance, the example statement shown here will change the field size of the SupervisorPhone field.

```
ALTER TABLE TempLog
ALTER COLUMN SupervisorPhone Text(13)
```

Deleting a column with the DROP COLUMN clause

The DROP COLUMN clause enables you to delete a given column from an existing table. The basic syntax is as follows:

```
ALTER TABLE <TableName>
DROP COLUMN <ColumnName>
```

To use the DROP COLUMN statement, simply start a new query in SQL view and define the structure for your new column. For instance, running the example statement shown here will delete the column called SupervisorPhone from the TempLog table:

```
ALTER TABLE TempLog
DROP COLUMN SupervisorPhone
```

Dynamically adding primary keys with the ADD CONSTRAINT clause

For many analysts, Access serves as an easy to use extract, transform, load (ETL) tool. That is, Access allows you to extract data from many sources, and then reformat and cleanse that data into consolidated tables. Many analysts also automate ETL processes with the use of macros that fire a series of queries. This works quite well in most cases.

There are, however, instances in which an ETL process requires primary keys to be added to temporary tables in order to keep data normalized during processing. In these situations, most people do one of two things: They stop the macro in the middle of processing to manually add the required primary keys, or they create a permanent table solely for the purpose of holding a table where the primary keys are already set.

There is a third option, though: The ADD CONSTRAINT clause allows you to dynamically create the primary keys. The basic syntax is as follows:

```
ALTER TABLE <TableName>
ADD CONSTRAINT CONSTRAINTNAME PRIMARY KEY (<Field Name>)
```

To use the ADD CONSTRAINT clause, simply start a new query in SQL view and define the new primary key you're implementing. For instance, the example statement shown here will apply a compound key to three fields in the TempLog table.

```
ALTER TABLE TempLog
ADD CONSTRAINT CONSTRAINTNAME PRIMARY KEY (ID, Name, Email)
```

Creating pass-through queries

A pass-through query sends SQL commands directly to a database server (such as SQL Server, Oracle, and so on). Often these database servers are known as the back end of the system, with Access being the client tool or front end. You send the command by using the syntax required by the particular server.

The advantage of pass-through queries is that the parsing and processing is actually done on the back-end server, not in Access. This makes them much faster than queries that pull from linked tables, particularly if the linked table is a very large one.

Here are the steps for building a pass-through query:

1. **On the Create tab of the Ribbon, click the Query Design command.**
2. **Close the Show Table dialog box.**
3. **Click the Pass-Through command on the Query Tools Design tab.** The SQL design window appears.
4. **Type an SQL statement that is appropriate for the target database system.** Figure 14.10 demonstrates a simple SQL statement.
5. **On the Query Tools Design tab, click the Property Sheet command.** The Property Sheet dialog box (shown in Figure 14.11) appears.

FIGURE 14.10

To create a pass-through query, you must use the SQL window.

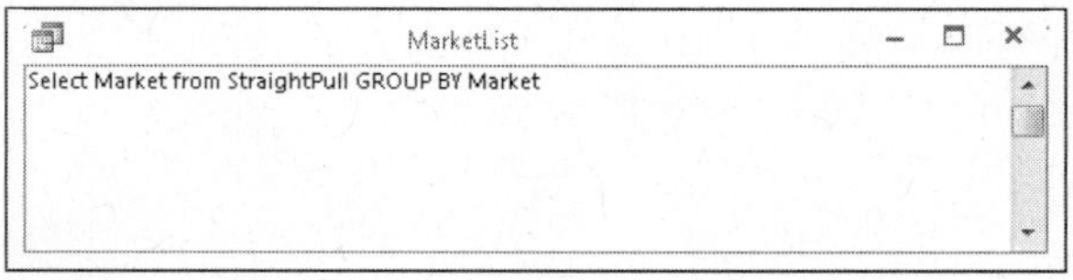

FIGURE 14.11

You must specify an ODBC connection string in the pass-through query's Property Sheet dialog box.

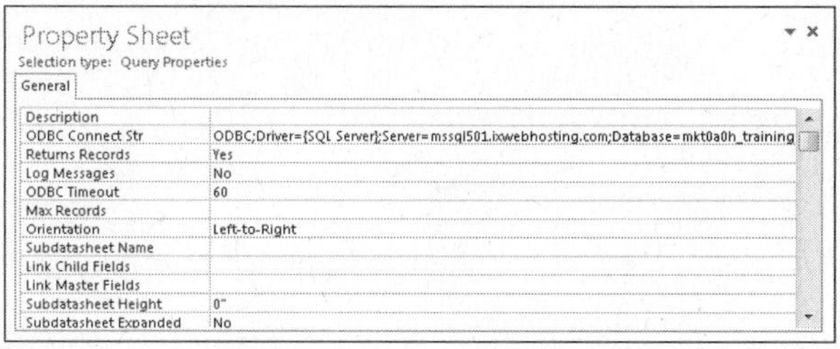

6. **Enter the appropriate connection string for your server.** This is typically the ODBC connection string you normally use to connect to your server.
7. **Click Run.**

There are a few things you should be aware of when choosing to go the pass-through query route:

- You'll have to build the SQL statements yourself. Access provides no help — you can't use the QBE to build your statement.
- If the connection string of your server changes, you'll have to go back into the properties of the pass-through query and edit the ODBC connection string property. Alternatively, if you are using an existing DSN, you can simply edit the DSN configuration.
- The results you get from a pass-through are read only. You can't update or edit the returned records.
- You can only write queries that select data. This means you can't write update, append, delete, or make-table queries.
- Because you're hard-coding the SQL statements that will be sent to the server, including dynamic parameters (like a parameter query) is impossible because there is no way to get your parameters to the server after the SQL statement is sent.

CHAPTER

15

Subqueries and Domain Aggregate Functions

IN THIS CHAPTER

Enhancing your analyses with subqueries

Using domain aggregate functions

Often, you'll carry out your analyses in layers, each layer of analysis using or building on the previous layer. This practice of building layers into analytical processes is actually very common. For instance, when you build a query using another query as the data source, you're layering your analysis. When you build a query based on a temporary table created by a make-table query, you're also layering your analysis.

All these conventional methods of layering analyses have two things in common:

- **They all add a step to your analytical processes.** Every query that has to be run in order to feed another query, or every temporary table that has to be created in order to advance your analysis, adds yet another task that must be completed before you get your final results.
- **They all require the creation of temporary tables or transitory queries, inundating your database with table and query objects that lead to a confusing analytical process, as well as a database that bloats easily.** This is where subqueries and domain aggregate functions can help.

Subqueries and domain aggregate functions allow you to build layers into your analyses within one query, eliminating the need for temporary tables or transitory queries.

The topic of subqueries and domain aggregate functions require an understanding of SQL. Most beginning Access users don't have the foundation in SQL. If you fall into this category, press the pause button here and review Chapter 14 of this book. There, you'll get enough of a primer on SQL to continue this chapter.

On the Web
The starting database for this walkthrough, `Chapter15.accdb`, can be downloaded from this book's website.

Enhancing Your Analyses with Subqueries

Subqueries (sometimes referred to as *subselect queries*) are select queries that are nested within other queries. The primary purpose of a subquery is to enable you to use the results of one query within the execution of another query. With subqueries, you can answer a multiple-part question, specify criteria for further selection, or define new fields to be used in your analysis.

The query shown in Figure 15.1 demonstrates how a subquery is used in the design grid. As you look at this, remember that this is one example of how a subquery can be used. Subqueries are not limited to being used as criteria.

FIGURE 15.1

To use a subquery in Query Design view, simply enter the SQL statement.

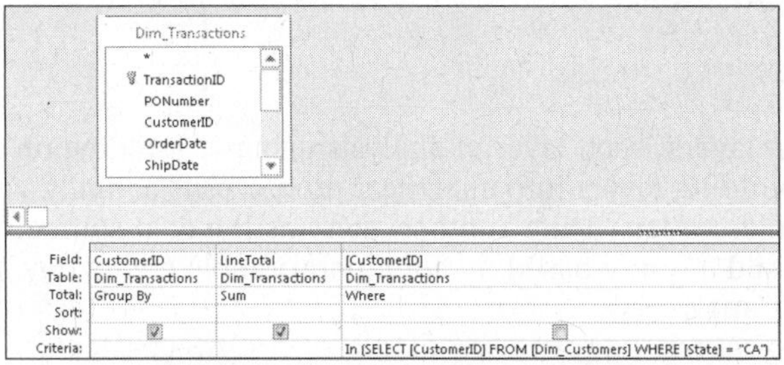

If you were to build the query in Figure 15.1 and switch to SQL view, you would see a SQL statement similar to this one. Can you pick out the subquery? Look for the second `SELECT` statement.

```
SELECT CustomerID, Sum(LineTotal) AS SumOfLineTotal
FROM Dim_Transactions
WHERE CustomerID IN
(SELECT [CustomerID] FROM [Dim_Customers] WHERE [State] = "CA")
GROUP BY CustomerID
```

NOTE

Subqueries must always be enclosed in parentheses.

The idea behind a subquery is that the subquery is executed first, and the results are used in the *outer query* (the query in which the subquery is embedded) as a criterion, an expression, a parameter, and so on. In the example shown in Figure 15.1, the subquery will first return a list of branches that belong to the Dallas market. Then the outer query will use that list as criteria to filter out any employee who does not belong to the Dallas market.

Why use subqueries?

Subqueries often run more slowly than a standard query using a join. This is because subqueries are either executed against an entire dataset or evaluated multiple times, one time per each row processed by the outer query. This makes them slow to execute, especially if you have a large dataset. So, why use them?

Many analyses require multistep processes that use temporary tables or transitory queries. Although there is nothing inherently wrong with temporary tables and queries, an excess amount of them in your analytical processes could lead to a confusing analytical process, as well as a database that bloats easily.

Even though using subqueries comes with a performance hit, it may be an acceptable trade for streamlined procedures and optimized analytical processes. You'll even find that as you become more comfortable with writing your own SQL statements, you'll use subqueries in on-the-fly queries to actually *save* time.

Subquery ground rules

There are a few rules and restrictions that you must be aware of when using subqueries:

- Your subquery must have, at a minimum, a `SELECT` statement and a `FROM` clause in its SQL string.
- You must enclose your subquery in parentheses.
- Theoretically, you can nest up to 31 subqueries within a query. This number, however, is based on your system's available memory and the complexity of your subqueries.
- You can use a subquery an expression as long as it returns a single value.
- You can use the `ORDER BY` clause in a subquery only if the subquery is a `SELECT TOP` or `SELECT TOP PERCENT` statement.
- You can't use the `DISTINCT` keyword in a subquery that includes the `GROUP BY` clause.
- You must implement table aliases in queries in which a table is used in both the outer query and the subquery.

Creating subqueries without typing SQL statements

You may have the tendency to shy away from subqueries because you feel uncomfortable writing your own SQL statements. Indeed, many of the SQL statements necessary to perform the smallest analysis can seem daunting.

Imagine, for example, that you've been asked to provide the number of account managers that have a time in service greater than the average time in service for all account managers. Sounds like a relatively simple analysis, and it *is* simple when you use a subquery.

But where do you start? Well, you could just write an SQL statement into the SQL view of a query and run it. But the truth is that not many Access users create SQL statements from scratch. The smart ones use the built-in functionalities of Access to save time and headaches. The trick is to split the analysis into manageable pieces:

1. **Find the average time in service for all account managers by creating the query shown in Figure 15.2.**

FIGURE 15.2

Create a query to find the average time in service for all account managers.

Dim_AccountManagers
*
AccountManagerID
FullName
First Name
Last Name
Email Address
Telephone
HireDate

Field: Avg_TIS_in_Months: Avg(DateDiff("m",[HireDate],Date()))
Table:
Total: Expression
Sort:
Show: ☑
Criteria:

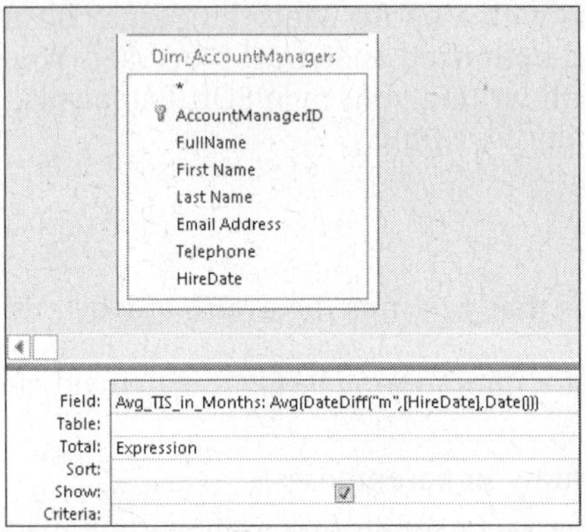

2. **Switch to SQL view (shown in Figure 15.3), and copy the SQL statement.**

FIGURE 15.3

Switch to SQL view and copy the SQL statement.

```
SELECT Avg(DateDiff("m",[HireDate],Date())) AS Avg_TIS_in_Months
FROM Dim_AccountManagers;
```

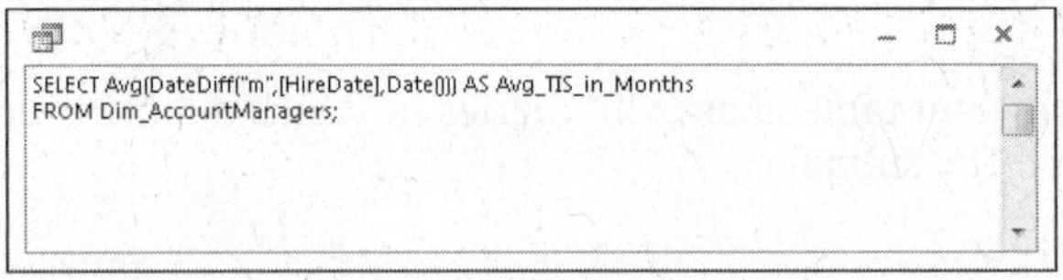

3. **Create a query that will count the number of account managers by time in service.** Figure 15.4 does just that.

FIGURE 15.4

Create a query to count the number of employees by time in service.

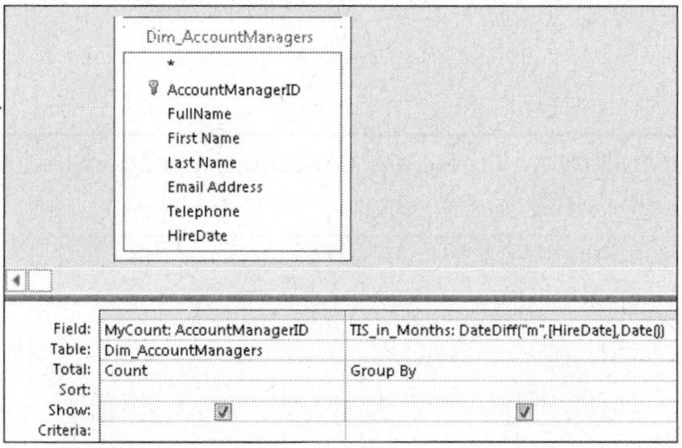

4. **Right-click in the Criteria row under the TIS_in_Months field and select Zoom.** The Zoom dialog box (shown in Figure 15.5) appears. The Zoom dialog does nothing more than help you more comfortably work with text that is too long to be easily seen at one time in the query grid.
5. **With the Zoom dialog box open, paste the SQL statement you copied previously into to the white input area.**

FIGURE 15.5

Paste the first SQL statement you copied into the Criteria row of the TIS_IN_MONTHS field.

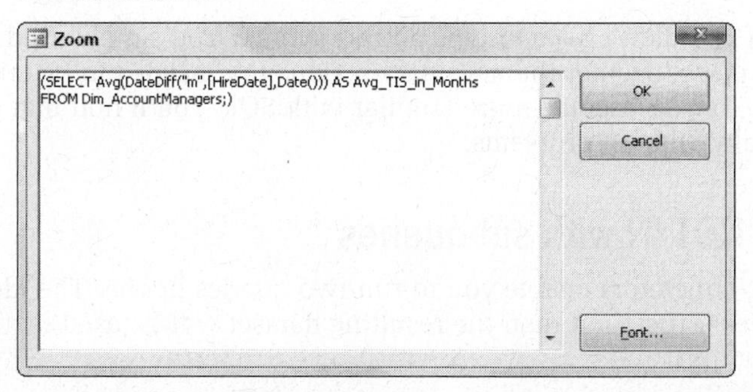

NOTE

Remember that subqueries must be enclosed in parentheses, so you'll want to enter parentheses around the SQL statement you just pasted. You'll also need to make sure you delete all carriage returns that were put in automatically by Access.

6. **Finish off the query by entering a greater than (>) symbol in front of your subquery and change the GROUP BY of the TIS_in_Months row to a WHERE clause.** At this point, your query should look like the one shown in Figure 15.6.

FIGURE 15.6

Running this query will tell you there are 12 account managers that have a time in service greater than the company average.

Now if you go to the SQL view of the query shown in Figure 15.6, you'll see the following SQL statement:

```
SELECT Count(AccountManagerID) AS MyCount
FROM Dim_AccountManagers
WHERE (((DateDiff("m",[HireDate],Date()))
>(SELECT Avg(DateDiff("m",[HireDate],Date())) AS Avg_TIS_in_Months FROM Dim_
   AccountManagers;)));
```

The beauty is that you didn't have to type all this syntax. You simply used your knowledge of Access to piece together the necessary actions that needed to be taken in order to get to the answer. As you become more familiar with SQL, you'll find that you can create subqueries manually with no problems.

Using IN and NOT IN with subqueries

The `IN` and `NOT IN` operators enable you to run two queries in one. The idea is that the subquery will execute first, and then the resulting dataset will be used by the outer query to filter the final output.

The example demonstrated in Figure 15.7 will first run a subquery that will select all customers based in California (CA). The outer query will then use the resulting dataset as a criteria to return the sum of LineTotal for only those customers that match the customer numbers returned in the subquery.

FIGURE 15.7

This query uses the IN operator with a subquery, allowing you to run two queries in one.

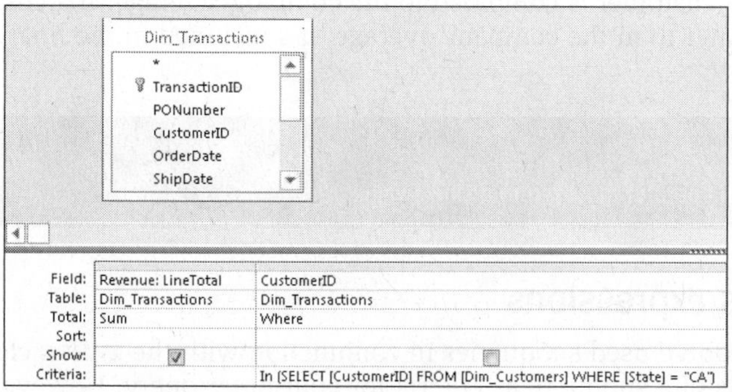

Dim_Transactions
*
TransactionID
PONumber
CustomerID
OrderDate
ShipDate

Field:	Revenue: LineTotal	CustomerID
Table:	Dim_Transactions	Dim_Transactions
Total:	Sum	Where
Sort:		
Show:	☑	☐
Criteria:		In (SELECT [CustomerID] FROM [Dim_Customers] WHERE [State] = "CA")

You would use `NOT IN` to go the opposite way and return the sum of LineTotal for those customers that don't match the customer numbers returned in the subquery.

Using subqueries with comparison operators

As its name implies, a comparison operator (=, <, >, <=, >=, <>, and so on) compares two items and returns `True` or `False`. When you use a subquery with a comparison operator, you're asking Access to compare the resulting dataset of your outer query to that of the subquery.

For example, to return all customers who have purchases greater than the average purchase for all customers, you can use the query shown in Figure 15.8.

FIGURE 15.8

Use comparison operators to compare the resulting dataset of your outer query to the results of the subquery.

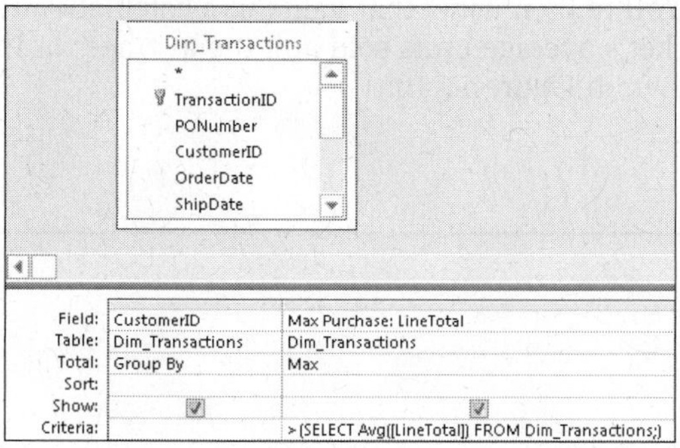

Dim_Transactions
*
TransactionID
PONumber
CustomerID
OrderDate
ShipDate

Field:	CustomerID	Max Purchase: LineTotal
Table:	Dim_Transactions	Dim_Transactions
Total:	Group By	Max
Sort:		
Show:	☑	☑
Criteria:		>(SELECT Avg([LineTotal]) FROM Dim_Transactions;)

The subquery runs first, giving you the average purchase for all customers. This is a single value that Access then uses to compare the outer query's resulting dataset. In other words, the max purchase for each customer is compared to the company average. If a customer's maximum purchase is greater than the company average, it's included in the final output; otherwise, it's excluded.

NOTE

A subquery that is used with a comparison operator must return a single value.

Using subqueries as expressions

In every example so far, you've used subqueries in conjunction with the `WHERE` clause, effectively using the results of a subquery as criteria for your outer query. However, you can also use a subquery as an expression, as long as the subquery returns a single value. The query shown in Figure 15.9 demonstrates how you can use a subquery as an expression in a calculation.

FIGURE 15.9

You're using a subquery as an expression in a calculation.

SalesByRegion
*
Market
SalesPeriod
Revenue
UnitsSold

Field:	Market	Market Avg: UnitsSold	Vs Company Avg: [Market Avg]-(SELECT Avg(UnitsSold) FROM SalesByRegion;)
Table:	SalesByRegion	SalesByRegion	
Total:	Group By	Avg	Expression
Sort:			
Show:	☑	☑	☑
Criteria:			

This example uses a subquery to get the average units sold for the entire company; that subquery will return a single value. You're then using that value in a calculation to determine the variance between each market's average units sold and the average for the company. The output of this query is shown in Figure 15.10.

FIGURE 15.10

Your query result.

Market	Market Avg	Vs Company Avg
Asia	1,142	-612
Australia	1,119	-635
Northern Europe	2,647	893
South America	1,165	-589
Southern Europe	1,800	46
United Kingdom	2,591	837
United States	1,814	60

Using correlated subqueries

A *correlated query* is essentially a subquery that refers back to a column that is in the outer query. What makes correlated subqueries unique is that whereas standard subqueries are evaluated one time to get a result, a correlated subquery has to be evaluated multiple times — once for each row processed by the outer query. To illustrate this point, consider the following two SQL statements.

Uncorrelated subqueries

This SQL statement is using an uncorrelated subquery. How can you tell? The subquery isn't referencing any column in the outer query. This subquery will be evaluated one time to give you the average revenue for the entire dataset.

```
SELECT MainSummary.Branch_Number,
     (SELECT Avg(Revenue)FROM MainSummary)
     FROM MainSummary
```

Correlated subqueries

This SQL statement is using a correlated subquery. The subquery is reaching back into the outer query and referencing the Branch_Number column, effectively forcing the subquery to be evaluated for every row that is processed by the outer query. The end result of this query will be a dataset that shows the average revenue for every branch in the company. Figure 15.11 demonstrates how this SQL statement looks in Design view.

```
SELECT MainSummary.Branch_Number,
     (SELECT Avg(Revenue)FROM MainSummary AS M2
     WHERE M2.Branch_Number = MainSummary.Branch_Number) AS AvgByBranch
FROM MainSummary
GROUP BY MainSummary.Branch_Number
```

FIGURE 15.11

A correlated subquery.

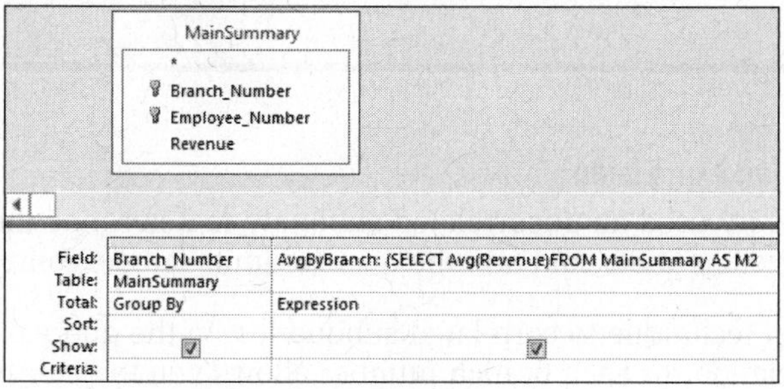

Using Aliases with Correlated Subqueries

Notice that in the correlated subquery, you're using the `AS` clause to establish a table alias of T2. The reason for this is that the subquery and the outer query are both utilizing the same table. By giving one of the tables an alias, you allow Access to distinguish exactly which table you're referring to in your SQL statement. Although the alias in this SQL statement is assigned to the subquery, you can just as easily assign an alias to the table in the outer query.

Note that the character T1 holds no significance. In fact, you can use any text string you like, as long as the alias and the table name combined do not exceed 255 characters.

To assign an alias to a table in Design view, simply right-click the field list and select Properties, as shown in the following figure.

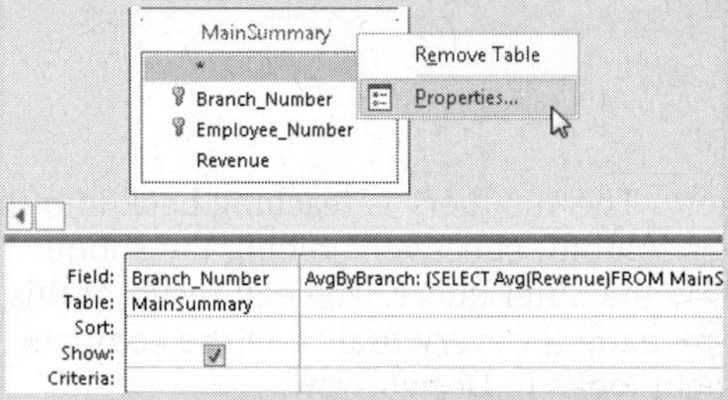

Next, edit the Alias property to the one you would like to use (see the following figure). You'll know that it took effect when the name on the Field List changes to your new alias.

Using a correlated subquery as an expression

The example shown in Figure 15.9 used an uncorrelated subquery to determine the variance between each market's average units sold and the average units for the company.

You can apply the same type of technique to correlated subqueries. In the query demonstrated in Figure 15.12, a correlation for each branch number allows you to determine the variance between each employee's annual revenue and the average revenue for that employee's branch.

FIGURE 15.12

You can use a correlated subquery as part of an expression.

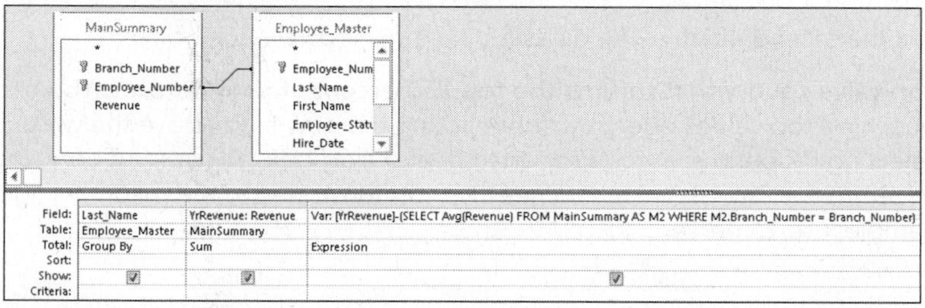

Using subqueries within action queries

Action queries can be fitted with subqueries just as easily as select queries can. Here are a few examples of how you would use a subquery in an action query.

A subquery in a make-table query

This example illustrates how to use a subquery within a make-table query:

```
SELECT E1.Employee_Number, E1.Last_Name, E1.First_Name
INTO OldSchoolEmployees
FROM Employee_Master as E1
WHERE E1.Employee_Number IN
     (SELECT E2.Employee_Number
     FROM Employee_Master AS E2
     WHERE E2.Hire_Date <#1/1/1995#)
```

A subquery in an append query

This example uses a subquery within an append query:

```
INSERT INTO CustomerMaster (Customer_Number, Customer_Name, State )
SELECT CompanyNumber,CompanyName,State
FROM LeadList
WHERE CompanyNumber Not In
     (SELECT Customer_Number from CustomerMaster)
```

A subquery in an update query

This example uses a subquery in an update query:

```
UPDATE PriceMaster SET Price = [Price]*1.1
WHERE Branch_Number In
     (SELECT Branch_Number from LocationMaster WHERE Region = "South")
```

Getting the Second Quartile of a Dataset with One Query

You can easily pull out the second quartile of a dataset by using a top values subquery:

1. **Create a top values query that returns the top 25 percent of your dataset.** You can specify that a query is a top values query by right-clicking the gray area above the white query grid and selecting Properties. In the Property Sheet dialog box, adjust the Top Values property to return the top *n*th value you need, as demonstrated in the following figure. For this example, use 25 percent.

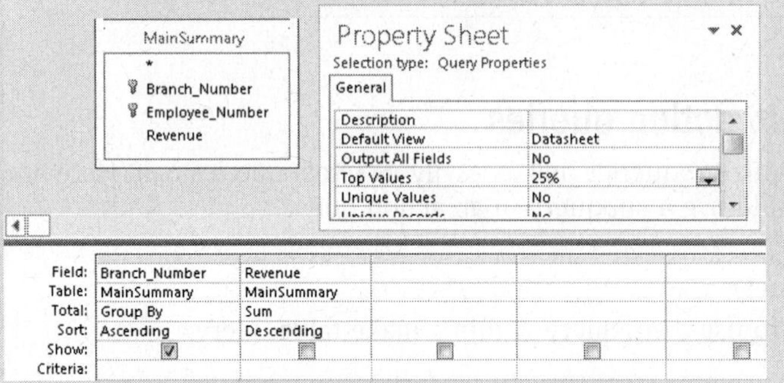

2. **Switch to SQL view (shown in the following figure), and copy the SQL string.**

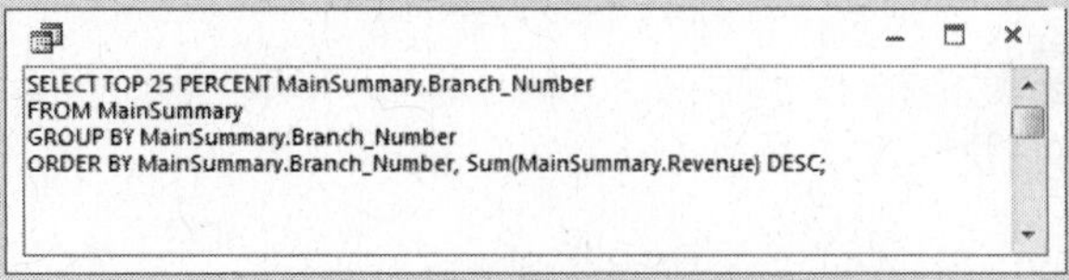

```
SELECT TOP 25 PERCENT MainSummary.Branch_Number
FROM MainSummary
GROUP BY MainSummary.Branch_Number
ORDER BY MainSummary.Branch_Number, Sum(MainSummary.Revenue) DESC;
```

3. **Switch back to Design view and paste the SQL statement you just copied into the Criteria row of the Branch_Number field.** To do this, right-click inside the Criteria row of the Branch_Number field and select Zoom. Then paste the SQL statement inside the Zoom dialog box, as shown in the following figure.

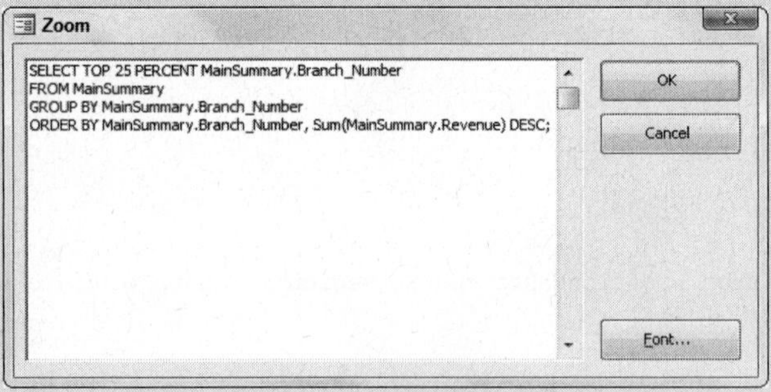

4. **This next part is a little tricky — you need to perform the following edits on the SQL statement in order to make it work for this situation:**
   - Because this subquery is a criteria for the Branch_Number field, you only need to select Branch_Number in the SQL statement; so, you can remove the line `Sum(MainSummary.Revenue) AS SumOfRevenue`.
   - Delete all carriage returns.
   - Place parentheses around the subquery and put the `NOT IN` operator in front of it all.

   At this point, your Zoom dialog box should look like the one shown in the following figure.

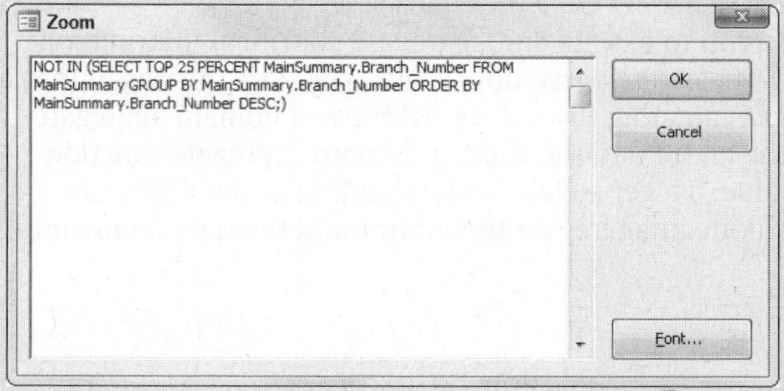

Zoom

NOT IN (SELECT TOP 25 PERCENT MainSummary.Branch_Number FROM MainSummary GROUP BY MainSummary.Branch_Number ORDER BY MainSummary.Branch_Number DESC;)

OK
Cancel
Font...

5. **Switch to Design view.** If all went well, you query should look similar to the following figure.

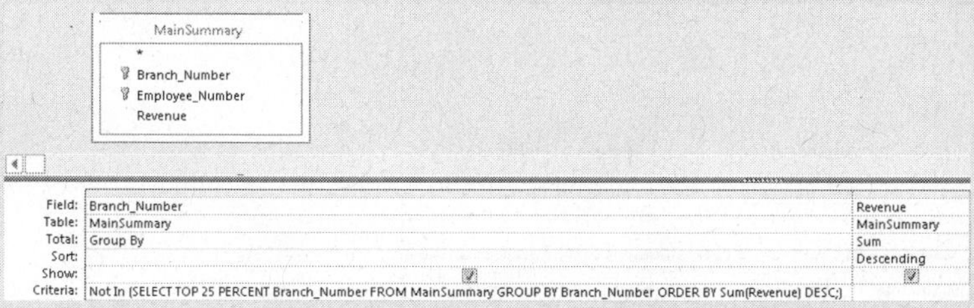

MainSummary
*
Branch_Number
Employee_Number
Revenue

Field:	Branch_Number	Revenue
Table:	MainSummary	MainSummary
Total:	Group By	Sum
Sort:		Descending
Show:	☑	☑
Criteria:	Not In (SELECT TOP 25 PERCENT Branch_Number FROM MainSummary GROUP BY Branch_Number ORDER BY Sum(Revenue) DESC;)	

There you have it. Running this query will return the second quartile in the dataset. To get the third quartile, simply replace `TOP 25 PERCENT` in the subquery with `TOP 50 PERCENT`; to get the fourth quartile, use `TOP 75 PERCENT`.

NOTE
Be sure to check this chapter's sample file to get the completed queries seen here.

A subquery in a delete query

This example uses a subquery in a delete query:

```
DELETE *
FROM LeadList
WHERE CompanyNumber In
     (SELECT Customer_Number from CustomerMaster)
```

Domain Aggregate Functions

Domain aggregate functions enable you to extract and aggregate statistical information from an entire dataset (a domain). These functions differ from aggregate queries in that an aggregate query groups data before evaluating the values, whereas a domain aggregate function evaluates the values for the entire dataset; thus, a domain aggregate function will never return more than one value. To get a clear understanding of the difference between an aggregate query and a domain aggregate function, build the query shown in Figure 15.13.

FIGURE 15.13

This query shows you the difference between an aggregate query and a domain aggregate function.

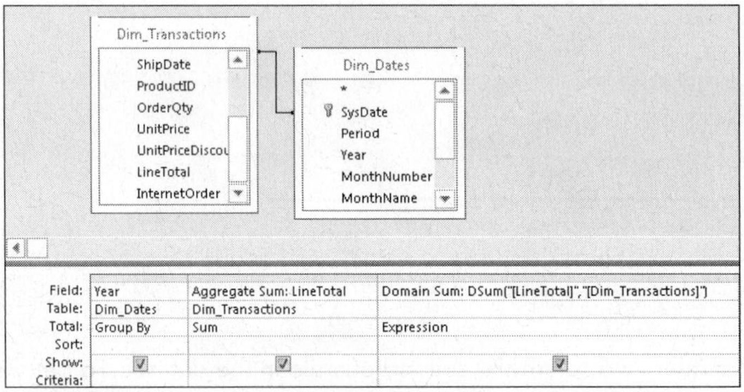

Run the query to get the results shown in Figure 15.14. You will notice that the Aggregate Sum column contains a different total for each year, whereas the Domain Sum column (the domain aggregate function) contains only one total (for the entire dataset).

The Anatomy of Domain Aggregate Functions

There are 12 different domain aggregate functions, but they all have the same anatomy:

```
FunctionName("[Field Name]","[Dataset Name]", "[Criteria]")
```

- FunctionName: This is the name of the domain aggregate function you're using.
- Field Name (required): This expression identifies the field containing the data with which you're working.
- Dataset Name (required): This expression identifies the table or query you're working with; also known as the domain.
- Criteria (optional): This expression is used to restrict the range of data on which the domain aggregate function is performed. If no criteria is specified, the domain aggregate function is performed against the entire dataset.

NOTE

You can't use a parameter query with a domain aggregate function.

FIGURE 15.14

You can clearly see the difference between an aggregate query and a domain aggregate function.

Year	Aggregate Sum	Domain Sum
2006	$16,402,703	164564683.25
2007	$45,317,067	164564683.25
2008	$61,776,867	164564683.25
2009	$41,068,046	164564683.25

NOTE

Although the examples in this chapter show domain aggregate functions being used in query expressions, keep in mind that you can use these functions in macros, modules, or the calculated controls of forms and reports.

Understanding the different domain aggregate functions

There are 12 different domain aggregate functions in Access, each one performing a different operation. In this section, we take a moment to review the purpose and utility of each function.

DSum

The `DSum` function returns the total sum value of a specified field in the domain. For example, `DSum("[LineTotal]", "[Dim_Transactions]")` would return the total sum of LineTotal in the Dim_Transactions table.

DAvg

The `DAvg` function returns the average value of a specified field in the domain. For example, `DAvg("[LineTotal]", "[Dim_Transactions]")` would return the average LineTotal in the Dim_Transactions table.

DCount

The `DCount` function returns the total number of records in the domain. `DCount("*", "[Dim_Transactions]")`, for example, would return the total number of records in the Dim_Transactions table.

DLookup

The `DLookup` function returns the first value of a specified field that matches the criteria you define within the `DLookup` function. If you don't supply a criteria, the `DLookup` function returns a random value in the domain. For example, `DLookUp("[Last_Name]", "[Employee_Master]","[Employee_Number]='42620' ")` would return the value in the Last_Name field of the record where the Employee_Number is 42620.

DMin and DMax

The `DMin` and `DMax` functions return the minimum and maximum values in the domain, respectively. `DMin("[LineTotal]", "[Dim_Transactions]")` would return the lowest LineTotal in the Dim_Transactions table, whereas `DMax("[LineTotal]", "[Dim_Transactions]")` would return the highest LineTotal.

DFirst and DLast

The `DFirst` and `DLast` functions return the first and last values in the domain, respectively. `DFirst("[LineTotal]", "[Dim_Transactions]")` would return the first LineTotal in the Dim_Transactions table, whereas `DLast("[LineTotal]", "[Dim_Transactions]")` would return the last.

DStDev, DStDevP, DVar, and DvarP

You can use the `DStDev` and `DStDevP` functions to return the standard deviation across a population sample and a population, respectively. Similarly, the `DVar` and the `DVarP` functions return the variance across a population sample and a population, respectively. `DStDev("[LineTotal]", "[Dim_Transactions]")` would return the standard deviation of all LineTotals in the Dim_Transactions table. `DVar ("[LineTotal]", "[Dim_Transactions]")` would return the variance of all LineTotals in the Dim_Transactions.

Examining the syntax of domain aggregate functions

Domain aggregate functions are unique in that the syntax required to make them work actually varies depending on the scenario. This has led to some very frustrated users who have given up on domain aggregate functions altogether. This section describes some general guidelines that will help you in building your domain aggregate functions.

Using no criteria

In this example, you're summing the values in the LineTotal field from the Dim_Transactions table (domain). Your field names and dataset names must always be wrapped in quotes.

```
DSum("[LineTotal]","[Dim_Transactions]")
```

TIP

Note the use of brackets. Although not always required, it's generally a good practice to use brackets when identifying a field, a table, or a query.

Using text criteria

In this example, you're summing the values in the Revenue field from the PvTblFeed table (domain) where the value in the Branch_Number field is 301316. Note that the Branch_Number field is formatted as text. When specifying criteria that is textual or a string, your criteria must be wrapped in single quotes. In addition, your entire criteria expression must be wrapped in double quotes.

```
DSum("[Revenue]", "[PvTblFeed]", "[Branch_Number] = '301316' ")
```

TIP

You can use any valid `WHERE` clause in the criteria expression of your domain aggregate functions. This adds a level of functionality to domain aggregate functions, because they can support the use of multiple columns and logical operators such as `AND`, `OR`, `NOT`, and so on. An example would be

```
DSum("[Field1]", "[Table]", "[Field2] = 'A' OR [Field2] = 'B' AND [Field3] = 2")
```

If you're referencing a control inside a form or report, the syntax will change a bit:

```
DSum("[Revenue]", "[PvTblFeed]", "[Branch_Number] = ' " & [MyTextControl] & " ' " )
```

Notice that you're using single quotes to convert the control's value to a string. In other words, if the value of the form control is 301316, then `" [System_Period] = ' " & [MyTextControl] & " ' "` is essentially translated to read `" [System_Period] = '301316' "`.

15

Using Number Criteria

In this example, you're summing the values in the LineTotal field from the Dim_Transactions table (domain) where the value in the LineTotal field is greater than 500. Notice that you aren't using the single quotes since the LineTotal field is an actual number field.

```
DSum("[LineTotal]", "[Dim_Transactions]", "[LineTotal] > 500 ")
```

If you're referencing a control inside a form or report, the syntax will change a bit:

```
DSum("[LineTotal]", "[Dim_Transactions]", "[LineTotal] >" [MyNumericControl])
```

Using Date Criteria

In this example, you're summing the values in the LineTotal field from the Dim_Transactions table (domain) where the value in the OrderDate field is 07/05/2008:

```
DSum("[LineTotal]", "[Dim_Transactions]", "[OrderDate] = #07/05/08# ")
```

If you're referencing a control inside a form or report, the syntax will change a bit:

```
DSum("[LineTotal]", "[Dim_Transactions]", "[OrderDate] = #" & [MydateControl] &
   "#")
```

Notice that you're using pound signs to convert the control's value to a date. In other words, if the value of the form control is `07/05/2008`, then `"[Service_Date] = #" & [MydateControl] & "#"` is essentially translated to read `"[Service_Date] = #07/05/2008# "`.

Using domain aggregate functions

Like subqueries, domain aggregate functions aren't very efficient when it comes to performing large-scale analyses and crunching very large datasets. These functions are better suited for use in specialty analyses with smaller subsets of data. Indeed, you'll most often find domain aggregate functions in environments where the dataset being evaluated is predictable and controlled (form example, functions, forms, and reports). This is not to say, however, that domain aggregate functions don't have their place in your day-to-day data analysis. This section walks through some examples of how you can use domain aggregate functions to accomplish some common tasks.

Calculating the percent of total

The query shown in Figure 15.15 will return products by group and the sum of LineTotal for each product category. This is a worthwhile analysis, but you could easily enhance it by adding a column that would give you the percent of total revenue for each product.

FIGURE 15.15

You want to add a column that shows the percent of total revenue for each product category.

Product_Category	Revenue
Bar Equipment	$1,806,137.90
Commercial Appliances	$8,634,337.05
Concession Equipment	$10,083,748.40
Fryers	$3,971,959.10
Ovens and Ranges	$58,399,471.75
Refrigerators and Coolers	$43,786,517.10
Warmers	$37,882,511.95

To get the percent of the total dollar value that each product makes up, you naturally would have to know the total dollar value of the entire dataset. This is where a `DSum` function can come in handy. The following `DSum` function will return the total value of the dataset:

```
DSum("[LineTotal]","[Dim_Transactions]")
```

Now you can use this function as an expression in the calculation that will return the percent of total for each product group. Figure 15.16 demonstrates how.

FIGURE 15.16

Use a `DSum` function as an expression in a calculation to get percent of total.

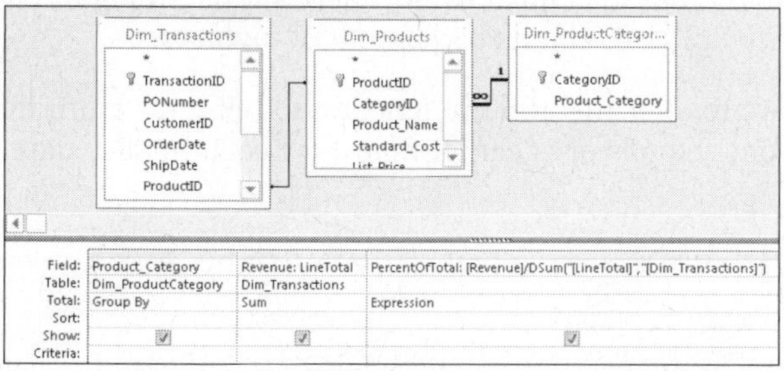

Field:	Product_Category	Revenue: LineTotal	PercentOfTotal: [Revenue]/DSum("[LineTotal]","[Dim_Transactions]")
Table:	Dim_ProductCategory	Dim_Transactions	
Total:	Group By	Sum	Expression
Sort:			
Show:	☑	☑	☑
Criteria:			

The result, shown in Figure 15.17, proves that this is a quick and easy way to get both total by group and percent of total with one query.

FIGURE 15.17

You retrieved both total by group and percent of total with one query.

Product_Category	Revenue	PercentOfTotal
Bar Equipment	$1,806,137.90	1.10%
Commercial Appliances	$8,634,337.05	5.25%
Concession Equipment	$10,083,748.40	6.13%
Fryers	$3,971,959.10	2.41%
Ovens and Ranges	$58,399,471.75	35.49%
Refrigerators and Coolers	$43,786,517.10	26.61%
Warmers	$37,882,511.95	23.02%

Creating a running count

The query in Figure 15.18 uses a `DCount` function as an expression to return the number of invoices processed on each specific invoice day.

FIGURE 15.18

This query will return all invoice dates and the number of invoices processed on each date.

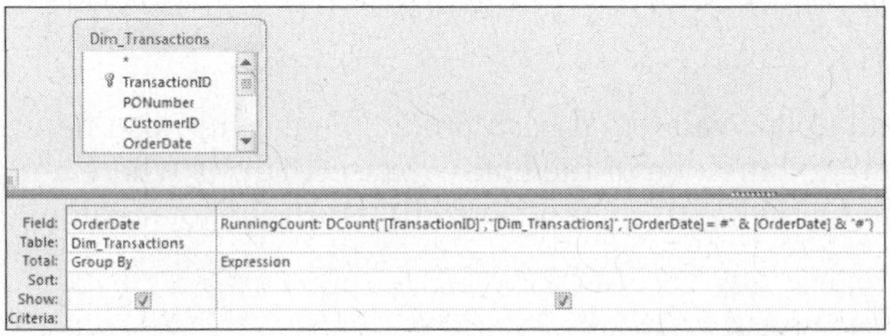

Take a moment to analyze what this `DCount` function is doing:

```
DCount("[TransactionID]","[Dim_Transactions]","[OrderDate]= #" & [OrderDate] &
   "#")
```

This `DCount` function will get the count of invoices where the invoice date equals (=) each invoice date returned by the query. So, in context of the query shown in Figure 15.18, the resulting dataset shows each invoice date and its own count of invoices.

What would happen if you were to alter the `DCount` function to tell it to return the count of invoices where the invoice date equals or is earlier than (<=) each invoice date returned by the query, as follows?

```
DCount("[TransactionID]","[Dim_Transactions]","[OrderDate]<= #" & [OrderDate] &
   "#")
```

The `DCount` function would return the count of invoices for each date *and* the count of invoices for any earlier date, thereby giving you a running count.

To put this into action, simply replace the = operator in the `DCount` function with the <= operator, as shown in Figure 15.19.

FIGURE 15.19

Use the <= operator in your `DCount` function to return the count of invoice dates that equals or is less than the date returned by the query.

Dim_Transactions
*
TransactionID
PONumber
CustomerID
OrderDate

Field:	OrderDate	RunningCount: DCount("[TransactionID]","[Dim_Transactions]","[OrderDate]<= #" & [OrderDate] & "#")
Table:	Dim_Transactions	
Total:	Group By	Expression
Sort:		
Show:	☑	☑
Criteria:		

Figure 15.20 shows the resulting running count.

FIGURE 15.20

You now have a running count in your analysis.

OrderDate	RunningCount
7/1/2006	279
7/2/2006	283
7/3/2006	288
7/4/2006	290
7/5/2006	295
7/6/2006	299
7/7/2006	302
7/8/2006	305
7/9/2006	311
7/10/2006	314
7/11/2006	318
7/12/2006	322
7/13/2006	324
7/14/2006	331

TIP

You can achieve a running sum instead of a running count by using the `DSum` function.

Using a value from the previous record

The query in Figure 15.21 uses a `DLookup` function to return the revenue value from the previous record. This value is placed into a new column called "Yesterday."

FIGURE 15.21

This query uses a DLookup to refer to the previous revenue value.

TimeSummary
*
Year
Month
OrderDate
Revenue

Field:	OrderDate	Revenue	Yesterday: DLookUp("[Revenue]","[TimeSummary]","[OrderDate] = #" & [OrderDate]-1 & "#")
Table:	TimeSummary	TimeSummary	
Sort:			
Show:	☑	☑	☑
Criteria:			

This method is similar to the one used when creating a running sum in that it revolves around manipulating a comparison operator in order to change the meaning of the domain aggregate function. In this case, the DLookup searches for the revenue value where the invoice date is equal to each invoice date returned by the query minus one (-1). If you subtract one from a date, you get yesterday's date!

```
DLookUp("[Revenue]","[TimeSummary]","[OrderDate] = #" & [OrderDate]-1 & "#")
```

TIP

If you add 1, you get the next record in the sequence. However, this trick won't work with textual fields. It only works with date and numeric fields. If you're working with a table that doesn't contain any numeric or date fields, create an autonumber field. This will give you a unique numeric identifier that you can use.

Running the query in Figure 15.21 will yield the results shown in Figure 15.22.

FIGURE 15.22

You can take this functionality a step further and perform a calculation for the previous day.

OrderDate	Revenue	Yesterday
1/5/2008	$1,218.87	
1/6/2008	$29,280.65	1218.8734
1/7/2008	$34,418.48	29280.6534
1/8/2008	$34,437.67	34418.4828
1/9/2008	$41,319.75	34437.6745
1/12/2008	$37,923.82	
1/13/2008	$37,900.75	37923.8214
1/14/2008	$33,318.55	37900.7498
1/15/2008	$44,478.61	33318.5515
1/16/2008	$31,350.05	44478.6144

You can enhance this analysis by adding a calculated field that gives you the dollar variance between today and yesterday. Create a new column and enter **[Revenue]-NZ([Yesterday],0)**, as shown in Figure 15.23. Note that the Yesterday field is wrapped in an NZ function in order to avoid errors caused by null fields.

FIGURE 15.23

Enhance your analysis by adding a variance between today and yesterday.

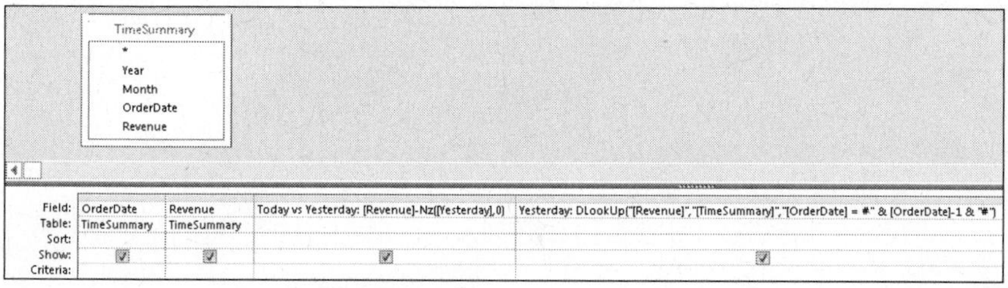

TimeSummary
*
Year
Month
OrderDate
Revenue

Field:	OrderDate	Revenue	Today vs Yesterday: [Revenue]-Nz([Yesterday],0)	Yesterday: DLookUp("[Revenue]","[TimeSummary]","[OrderDate] = #" & [OrderDate]-1 & "#")
Table:	TimeSummary	TimeSummary		
Sort:				
Show:	✓	✓	✓	✓
Criteria:				

Figure 15.24 shows the result.

FIGURE 15.24

Another task made possible by domain aggregate functions.

OrderDate	Revenue	Today vs Yesterday	Yesterday
1/5/2008	$1,218.87	$1,218.87	
1/6/2008	$29,280.65	$28,061.78	1218.8734
1/7/2008	$34,418.48	$5,137.83	29280.6534
1/8/2008	$34,437.67	$19.19	34418.4828
1/9/2008	$41,319.75	$6,882.07	34437.6745
1/12/2008	$37,923.82	$37,923.82	
1/13/2008	$37,900.75	($23.07)	37923.8214
1/14/2008	$33,318.55	($4,582.20)	37900.7498
1/15/2008	$44,478.61	$11,160.06	33318.5515
1/16/2008	$31,350.05	($13,128.57)	44478.6144

CHAPTER 16

Running Descriptive Statistics in Access

IN THIS CHAPTER

Determining rank, mode, and median

Pulling a random sampling from your dataset

Calculating percentile ranking

Determining the quartile standing of a record

Creating a frequency distribution

Descriptive statistics allow you to present large amounts of data in quantitative summaries that are simple to understand. When you sum data, count data, and average data, you're producing descriptive statistics. It's important to note that descriptive statistics are used only to profile a dataset and enable comparisons that can be used in other analyses. This is different from *inferential statistics,* in which you infer conclusions that extend beyond the scope of the data. To help solidify the difference between descriptive and inferential statistics, consider a customer survey. Descriptive statistics summarize the survey results for all customers and describe the data in understandable metrics, while inferential statistics infer conclusions such as customer loyalty based on the observed differences between groups of customers.

When it comes to inferential statistics, tools like Excel are better suited to handle these types of analyses than Access. Why? First, Excel comes with a plethora of built-in functions and tools that make it easy to perform inferential statistics — tools that Access simply does not have. Second, inferential statistics is usually performed on small subsets of data that can flexibly be analyzed and presented by Excel.

Running *descriptive statistics,* on the other hand, is quite practical in Access. In fact, running descriptive statistics in Access versus Excel is often the smartest option due to the structure and volume of the dataset.

ON THE WEB

The starting database for this walkthrough, `Chapter16.accdb`, can be downloaded from this book's website.

Basic Descriptive Statistics

This section discusses some of the basic tasks you can perform using descriptive statistics.

Running descriptive statistics with aggregate queries

At this point in the book, you have run many Access queries, some of which have been aggregate queries. Little did you know that when you ran those aggregate queries, you were actually creating descriptive statistics. It's true. The simplest descriptive statistics can be generated using an aggregate query. To demonstrate this point, build the query shown in Figure 16.1.

FIGURE 16.1

Running this aggregate query will provide a useful set of descriptive statistics.

RepSummary
*
Branch_Number
Employee_Number
Rev

Field:	Sum: Rev	Min: Rev	Max: Rev	Range: [Max]-[Min]	Avg: Rev	StDev: Rev	Var: Rev
Table:	RepSummary	RepSummary	RepSummary		RepSummary	RepSummary	RepSummary
Total:	Sum	Min	Max	Expression	Avg	StDev	Var
Sort:							
Show:	☑	☑	☑	☑	☑	☑	☑
Criteria:							

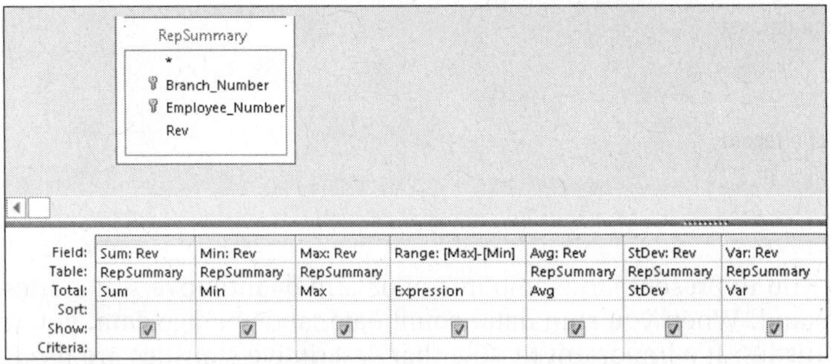

Similar to the descriptive statistics functionality found in Excel, the result of this query, shown in Figure 16.2, provides key statistical metrics for the entire dataset.

FIGURE 16.2

Key statistical metrics for the entire dataset.

Sum	Min	Max	Range	Avg	StDev	Var
$10,774,159	$86	$137,707	$137,621	$16,009	$21,059	$443,484,375

You can easily add layers to your descriptive statistics. In Figure 16.3, you're adding the Branch_Number field to your query. This will give you key statistical metrics for each branch.

FIGURE 16.3

Add the Branch_Number field to your query to add another dimension to your analysis.

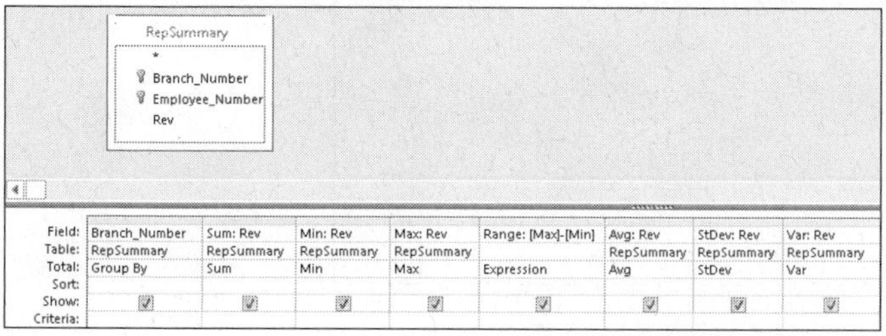

Field:	Branch_Number	Sum: Rev	Min: Rev	Max: Rev	Range: [Max]-[Min]	Avg: Rev	StDev: Rev	Var: Rev
Table:	RepSummary	RepSummary	RepSummary	RepSummary		RepSummary	RepSummary	RepSummary
Total:	Group By	Sum	Min	Max	Expression	Avg	StDev	Var
Sort:								
Show:	✓	✓	✓	✓	✓	✓	✓	✓
Criteria:								

As you can see in Figure 16.4, you can now compare the descriptive statistics across branches to measure how they perform against each other.

FIGURE 16.4

You have a one-shot view of the descriptive statistics for each branch.

Branch_Number	Sum	Min	Max	Range	Avg	StDev	Var
101313	$444,631	$124	$78,824	$78,700	$22,232	$29,111	$847,454,523
101419	$124,597	$99	$46,645	$46,546	$20,766	$19,027	$362,039,701
102516	$63,228	$678	$36,387	$35,709	$21,076	$18,390	$338,192,979
103516	$101,664	$151	$31,428	$31,277	$6,778	$9,338	$87,200,338
173901	$107,216	$402	$33,136	$32,734	$13,402	$13,371	$178,773,758
201605	$69,818	$624	$27,657	$27,033	$8,727	$9,496	$90,165,337
201709	$96,853	$184	$42,778	$42,593	$6,918	$12,375	$153,131,218
201714	$288,714	$145	$57,803	$57,658	$12,553	$15,901	$252,833,070
201717	$450,524	$169	$61,521	$61,352	$34,656	$25,160	$633,007,891
202600	$151,338	$277	$58,473	$58,196	$18,917	$25,557	$653,147,704

Determining rank, mode, and median

Ranking the records in your dataset, getting the mode of a dataset, and getting the median of a dataset are all tasks which a data analyst will need to perform from time to time. Unfortunately, Access doesn't provide built-in functionality to perform these tasks easily. This means you'll have to come up with a way to carry out these descriptive statistics. In this section, you'll learn some of the techniques you can use to determine rank, mode, and median.

Ranking the records in your dataset

You'll undoubtedly encounter scenarios in which you'll have to rank the records in your dataset based on a specific metric such as revenue. Not only is a record's rank useful in presenting data, but it's also a key variable when calculating advanced descriptive statistics such as median, percentile, and quartile.

The easiest way to determine a record's ranking within a dataset is by using a correlated subquery. The query shown in Figure 16.5 demonstrates how a rank is created using a subquery.

FIGURE 16.5

This query ranks employees by revenue.

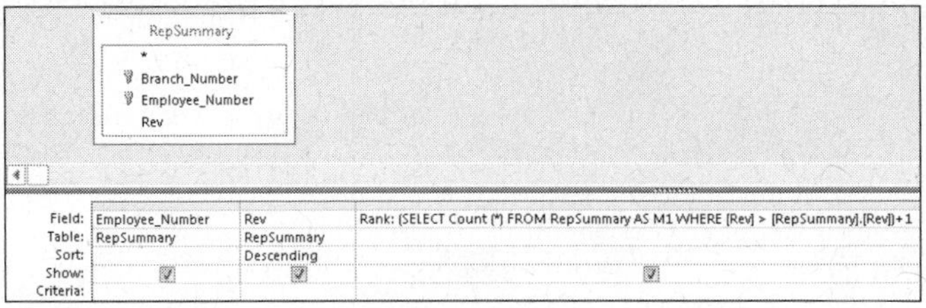

Field:	Employee_Number	Rev	Rank: (SELECT Count (*) FROM RepSummary AS M1 WHERE [Rev] > [RepSummary].[Rev])+1
Table:	RepSummary	RepSummary	
Sort:		Descending	
Show:	☑	☑	☑
Criteria:			

Take a moment to examine the subquery that generates the rank:

```
(SELECT Count(*)FROM RepSummary AS M1 WHERE [Rev]>[RepSummary].[Rev])+1
```

This correlated subquery returns the total count of records from the M1 table (this is the RepSummary table with an alias of M1), where the Rev field in the M1 table is greater than the Rev field in the RepSummary table. The value returned by the subquery is then increased by one. Why increase the value by one? If you don't, the record with the highest value will return `0` because zero records are greater than the record with the highest value. The result would be that your ranking starts with zero instead of one. Adding one effectively ensures that your ranking starts with one.

NOTE

Because this is a correlated subquery, this subquery is evaluated for every record in your dataset, thereby giving you a different rank value for each record.

Correlated subqueries are covered in detail in Chapter 15.

Figure 16.6 shows the result.

FIGURE 16.6

You've created a Rank column for your dataset.

Employee_Number	Rank	Rev
64621	1	$137,707.14
4136	2	$111,681.81
5060	3	$106,299.32
56422	4	$102,239.87
56405	5	$83,525.72
160034	6	$78,823.82
60425	7	$77,452.50
3466	8	$76,789.52
52635	9	$76,684.54
52404	10	$76,532.26

TIP

This technique is also useful when you want to create an AutoNumber field within a query.

Getting the mode of a dataset

The *mode* of a dataset is the number that appears the most often in a set of numbers. For instance, the mode for {4, 5, 5, 6, 7, 5, 3, 4} is 5.

Unlike Excel, Access doesn't have a built-in `Mode` function, so you have to create your own method of determining the mode of a dataset. Although there are various ways to get the mode of a dataset, one of the easiest is to use a query to count the occurrences of a certain data item, and then filter for the highest count. To demonstrate this method, follow these steps:

1. **Build the query shown in Figure 16.7.** The results, shown in Figure 16.8, don't seem very helpful, but if you turn this into a top values query, returning only the top record, you would effectively get the mode.

FIGURE 16.7

This query groups by the Rev field and then counts the occurrences of each number in the Rev field. The query is sorted in descending order by Rev.

RepSummary
*
Branch_Number
Employee_Number
Rev

Field:	Rev	Rev
Table:	RepSummary	RepSummary
Total:	Group By	Count
Sort:		Descending
Show:	☑	☑
Criteria:		

FIGURE 16.8

Almost there. Turn this into a top values query and you'll have your mode.

Rev	CountOfRev
$158.60	4
$145.02	3
$154.55	3
$185.27	3
$245.78	3
$151.03	3
$122.89	3
$309.11	3
$254.34	2

2. **Select the Query Tools Design tab and click the Property Sheet command.** The Property Sheet dialog box for the query appears.
3. **Change the Top Values property to 1, as shown in Figure 16.9.** You get one record with the highest count.

FIGURE 16.9

Set the Top Values property to 1.

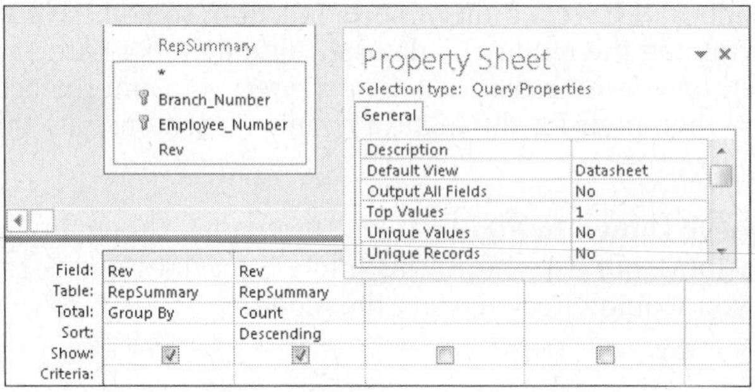

As you can see in Figure 16.10, you now have only one Rev figure — the one that occurs the most often. This is your mode.

FIGURE 16.10

This is your mode.

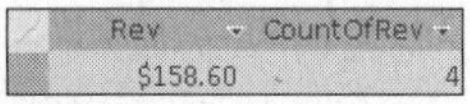

NOTE

Keep in mind that in the event of a tie, a top values query will show all records. This will effectively give you more than one mode. In this case, you'll have to make a manual determination which mode to use.

Getting the median of a dataset

The *median* of a dataset is the number that is the middle number in the dataset. In other words, half the numbers have values that are greater than the median, and half have values that are less than the median. For instance, the median number in {3, 4, 5, 6, 7, 8, 9} is 6 because 6 is the middle number of the dataset.

TIP

Why can't you just calculate an average and be done with it? Sometimes, calculating an average on a dataset that contains outliers can dramatically skew your analysis. For example, if you were to calculate an average on {32, 34, 35, 37, 89}, you would get an answer of 45.4. The problem is that 45.4 doesn't accurately represent the central tendency of this sampling of numbers. Using a median on this sample makes more sense. The median in this case would be 35, which is more representative of what's going on in this data.

Access doesn't have a built-in `Median` function, so you have to create your own method of determining the median of a dataset. An easy way to get the median is to build a query in two steps:

1. **Create a query that sorts and ranks your records.** The query shown in Figure 16.11 sorts and ranks the records in the RepSummary table.

FIGURE 16.11

The first step in finding the median of a dataset is to assign a rank to each record.

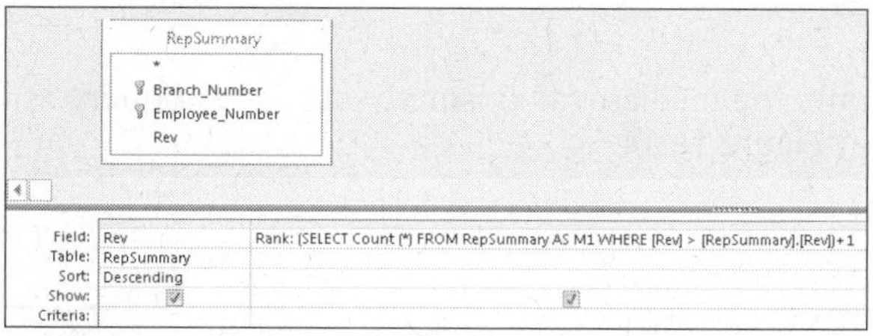

RepSummary
*
Branch_Number
Employee_Number
Rev

Field:	Rev	Rank: (SELECT Count (*) FROM RepSummary AS M1 WHERE [Rev] > [RepSummary].[Rev])+1
Table:	RepSummary	
Sort:	Descending	
Show:	✓	✓
Criteria:		

2. **Identify the middlemost record in your dataset by counting the total number of records in the dataset and then dividing that number by two.** This will give you a middle value. The idea is that because the records are now sorted and ranked, the record that has the same rank as the middle value will be the median. Figure 16.12 shows the subquery that will return a middle value for the dataset. Note that the value is wrapped in an `Int` function to strip out the fractional portion of the number.

FIGURE 16.12

The Middle Value subquery counts all the records in the dataset and then divides that number by 2.

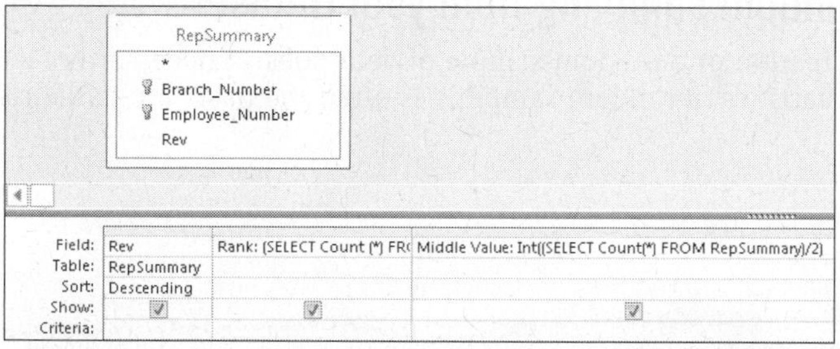

RepSummary
*
Branch_Number
Employee_Number
Rev

Field:	Rev	Rank: (SELECT Count (*) FR	Middle Value: Int((SELECT Count(*) FROM RepSummary)/2)
Table:	RepSummary		
Sort:	Descending		
Show:	✓	✓	✓
Criteria:			

As you can see in Figure 16.13, the middle value is 336. You can go down to record 336 to see the median.

FIGURE 16.13

Go down to record 336 to get the median value of the dataset.

Rev	Rank	Middle Value
$137,707.14	1	336
$111,681.81	2	336
$106,299.32	3	336
$102,239.87	4	336
$83,525.72	5	336
$78,823.82	6	336
$77,452.50	7	336
$76,789.52	8	336
$76,684.54	9	336
$76,532.26	10	336
$75,690.33	11	336
$75,489.77	12	336
$75,358.76	13	336
$74,653.99	14	336

If you want to return only the median value, simply use the subquery as a criterion for the Rank field, as shown in Figure 16.14.

FIGURE 16.14

Using the subquery as a criterion for the Rank field will ensure that only the median value is returned.

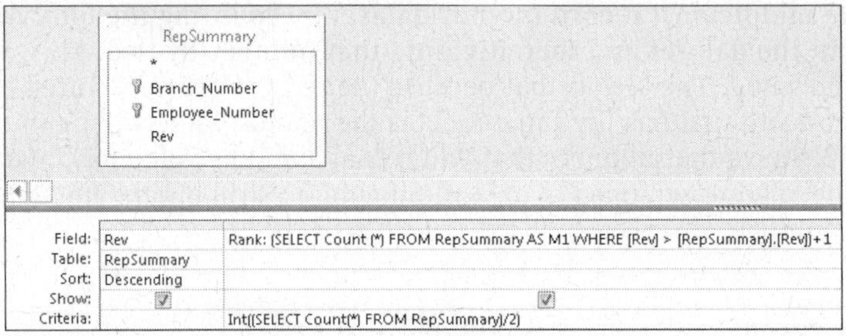

RepSummary

*

Branch_Number

Employee_Number

Rev

Field:	Rev	Rank: (SELECT Count (*) FROM RepSummary AS M1 WHERE [Rev] > [RepSummary].[Rev])+1
Table:	RepSummary	
Sort:	Descending	
Show:	✓	✓
Criteria:		Int((SELECT Count(*) FROM RepSummary)/2)

Pulling a random sampling from your dataset

Although the creation of a random sample of data doesn't necessarily fall into the category of descriptive statistics, a random sampling is often the basis for statistical analysis.

There are many ways to create a random sampling of data in Access, but one of the easiest is to use the `Rnd` function within a top values query. The `Rnd` function returns a random number based on an initial value. The idea is to build an expression that applies the `Rnd` function to a field that contains numbers, and then limit the records returned by setting the Top Values property of the query.

To demonstrate this method, follow these steps:

1. **Start a query in Design view on the TransactionMaster table.**
2. **Create a Random ID field, as shown in Figure 16.15, and then sort the field (either ascending or descending will work).**

FIGURE 16.15

Start by creating a Random ID field using the `Rnd` function with the Customer_Number field.

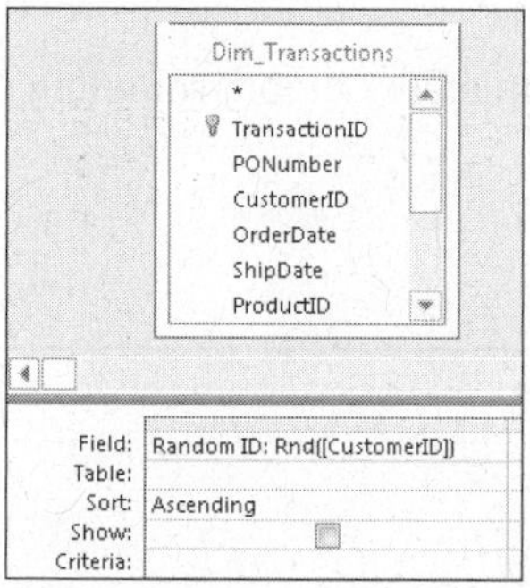

NOTE

The `Rnd` function won't work with fields that contain text or null values. Strangely enough, though, the `Rnd` function will work with fields that contain all numerical values even if the field is formatted as a Text field.

If your table is made up of fields that contain only text, you can add an AutoNumber field to use with the `Rnd` function. Another option is to pass the field containing text through the `Len` function, and then use that expression in your `Rnd` function — for example, `Rnd(Len([Mytext]))`.

3. **Select the Query Tools Design tab and click the Property Sheet command.** The Property Sheet dialog box for the query appears.
4. **Change the Top Values property to 1000, as shown in Figure 16.16.**

FIGURE 16.16

Limit the number of records returned by setting the Top Values property of the query.

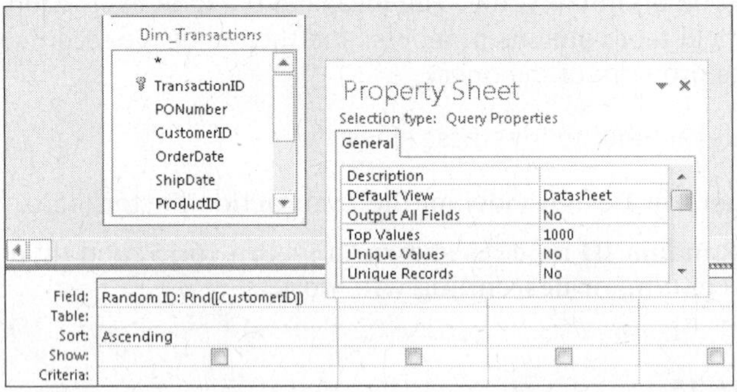

5. **Set the Show row for the Random ID field to false, and add the fields you will want to see in your dataset.**
6. **Run the query.** You'll will have a completely random sampling of data, as shown in Figure 16.17..

FIGURE 16.17

Running this query will produce a sample of 1,000 random records.

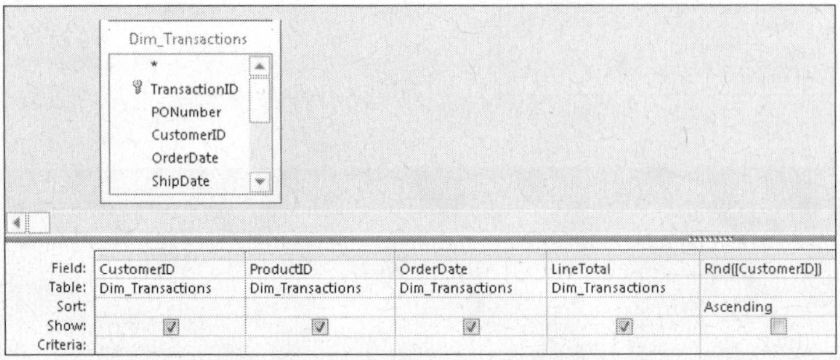

CAUTION

Rerunning the query, switching the view state, or sorting the dataset will result in a different set of random records. If you want to perform extensive analysis on an established set of random records that won't change, you'll need to run this query as a make-table query in order to create a hard table.

Advanced Descriptive Statistics

When working with descriptive statistics, a little knowledge goes a long way. Indeed, basics statistical analyses often leads to more advanced statistical analyses. In this section, you build on the fundamentals you've just learned to create advanced descriptive statistics.

Calculating percentile ranking

A *percentile rank* indicates the standing of a particular score relative to the normal group standard. Percentiles are most notably used in determining performance on standardized tests. If a child scores in the 90th percentile on a standardized test, her score is higher than 90 percent of the other children taking the test. Another way to look at it is to say that her score is in the top 10 percent of all the children taking the test. Percentiles often are used in data analysis as a method of measuring a subject's performance in relation to the group as a whole — for instance, determining the percentile ranking for each employee based on annual revenue.

Calculating a percentile ranking for a dataset is simply a mathematical operation. The formula for a percentile rank is (Record Count–Rank)/Record Count. The trick is getting all the variables needed for this mathematical operation.

Follow these steps:

1. **Build the query you see in Figure 16.18.** This query will start by ranking each employee by annual revenue. Be sure to give your new field an alias of "Rank."

FIGURE 16.18

Start with a query that ranks employees by revenue.

RepSummary
*
Branch_Number
Employee_Number
Rev

Field:	Employee_Number	Rev	Rank: (SELECT Count (*) FROM RepSummary AS M1 WHERE [Rev] > [RepSummary].[Rev])+1
Table:	RepSummary	RepSummary	
Sort:		Descending	
Show:	✓	✓	✓
Criteria:			

2. **Add a field that counts all the records in your dataset.** As you can see in Figure 16.19, you're using a subquery to do this. Be sure to give your new field an alias of "RCount."

FIGURE 16.19

Add a field that returns a total dataset count.

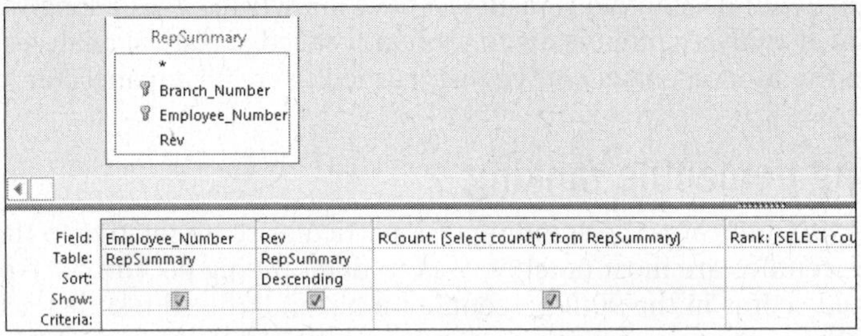

RepSummary
*
Branch_Number
Employee_Number
Rev

Field:	Employee_Number	Rev	RCount: (Select count(*) from RepSummary)	Rank: (SELECT Cou
Table:	RepSummary	RepSummary		
Sort:		Descending		
Show:	☑	☑	☑	
Criteria:				

3. **Create a calculated field with the expression (RCount–Rank)/RCount.** At this point, your query should look like the one shown in Figure 16.20.

FIGURE 16.20

The final step is to create a calculated field that will give you the percentile rank for each record.

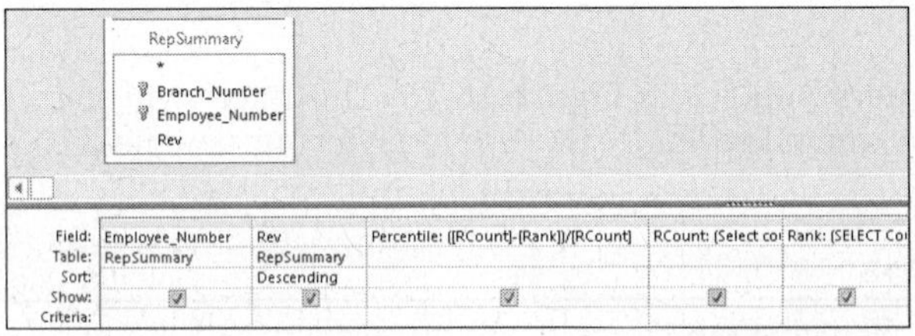

RepSummary
*
Branch_Number
Employee_Number
Rev

Field:	Employee_Number	Rev	Percentile: ([RCount]-[Rank])/[RCount]	RCount: (Select co	Rank: (SELECT Co
Table:	RepSummary	RepSummary			
Sort:		Descending			
Show:	☑	☑	☑	☑	☑
Criteria:					

4. **Run the query.** Sorting on the Rev field will produce the results shown in Figure 16.21.

FIGURE 16.21

You've successfully calculated the percentile rank for each employee.

Rank	Percentile	Employee_Number	Rev	RCount
1	99.85%	64621	$137,707.14	673
2	99.70%	4136	$111,681.81	673
3	99.55%	5060	$106,299.32	673
4	99.41%	56422	$102,239.87	673
5	99.26%	56405	$83,525.72	673
6	99.11%	160034	$78,823.82	673
7	98.96%	60425	$77,452.50	673
8	98.81%	3466	$76,789.52	673
9	98.66%	52635	$76,684.54	673
10	98.51%	52404	$76,532.26	673
11	98.37%	3660	$75,690.33	673
12	98.22%	1336	$75,489.77	673
13	98.07%	56416	$75,358.76	673
14	97.92%	55144	$74,653.99	673

Again, the resulting dataset enables you to measure each employee's performance in relation to the group as a whole. For example, the employee who is ranked 6th in the dataset is the 99th percentile, meaning that this employee earned more revenue than 99 percent of the other employees.

Determining the quartile standing of a record

A *quartile* is a statistical division of a dataset into four equal groups, with each group making up 25 percent of the dataset. The top 25 percent of a collection is considered to be the first quartile, whereas the bottom 25 percent is considered to be the fourth quartile. Quartile standings typically are used for the purposes of separating data into logical groupings that can be compared and analyzed individually. For example, if you want to establish a minimum performance standard around monthly revenue, you could set the minimum to equal the average revenue for employees in the second quartile. This ensures that you have a minimum performance standard that at least 50 percent of your employees have historically achieved or exceeded.

Establishing the quartile for each record in a dataset doesn't involve a mathematical operation; instead, it's a question of comparison. The idea is to compare each record's rank value to the quartile benchmarks for the dataset. What are quartile benchmarks? Imagine that your dataset contains 100 records. Dividing 100 by 4 would give you the first quartile benchmark (25). This means that any record with a rank of 25 or less is in the first quartile. To get the second quartile benchmark, you would calculate `100/4*2`. To get the third, you would calculate `100/4*3`, and so on.

Given that information, you know right away that you'll need to rank the records in your dataset and count the records in your dataset. Start by building the query shown in Figure 16.22. Build the Rank field the same way you did in Figure 16.18. Build the RCount field the same way you did in Figure 16.19.

FIGURE 16.22

Start by creating a field named Rank that ranks each employee by revenue and a field named RCount that counts the total records in the dataset.

RepSummary
*
Branch_Number
Employee_Number
Rev

Field:	Employee_Number	Rev	Rank: (SELECT Count (	RCount: (Select count
Table:	RepSummary	RepSummary		
Sort:		Descending		
Show:	✓	✓	✓	✓
Criteria:				

Once you've created the Rank and RCount fields in your query, you can use these fields in a `Switch` function that will tag each record with the appropriate quartile standing. Take a moment and look at the `Switch` function you'll be using:

```
Switch([Rank]<=[RCount]/4*1,"1st",[Rank]<=[RCount]/4*2,"2nd",
[Rank]<= [RCount]/4*3,"3rd",True,"4th")
```

This `Switch` function is going through four conditions, comparing each record's rank value to the quartile benchmarks for the dataset.

For more information on the `Switch` function, see Chapter 13.

Figure 16.23 demonstrates how this `Switch` function fits into the query. Note that you're using an alias of Quartile here.

FIGURE 16.23

Create the quartile tags using the `Switch` function.

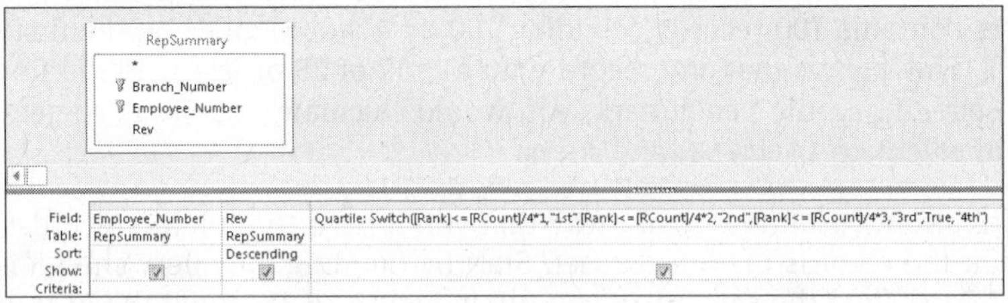

RepSummary
*
Branch_Number
Employee_Number
Rev

Field:	Employee_Number	Rev	Quartile: Switch([Rank]<=[RCount]/4*1,"1st",[Rank]<=[RCount]/4*2,"2nd",[Rank]<=[RCount]/4*3,"3rd",True,"4th")
Table:	RepSummary	RepSummary	
Sort:		Descending	
Show:	✓	✓	✓
Criteria:			

As you can see in Figure 16.24, you can sort the resulting dataset on any field without compromising your quartile standing tags.

FIGURE 16.24

Your final dataset can be sorted any way without the danger of losing your quartile tags.

Employee_Number	Rev	Rank	Quartile	RCount
104	$9,023.50	294	2nd	673
1044	$447.33	520	4th	673
1050	$179.74	614	4th	673
1054	$54,147.73	55	1st	673
106	$38,013.36	105	1st	673
113	$963.06	458	3rd	673
1130	$67,961.15	18	1st	673
1135	$1,477.21	429	3rd	673
1156	$192.07	602	4th	673
1245	$38,189.81	103	1st	673
1336	$75,489.77	12	1st	673
1344	$12,242.75	268	2nd	673
1416	$1,120.57	445	3rd	673
142	$1,622.30	421	3rd	673

Creating a frequency distribution

A *frequency distribution* is a special kind of analysis that categorizes data based on the count of occurrences where a variable assumes a specified value attribute. Figure 16.25 illustrates a frequency distribution created by using the `Partition` function.

FIGURE 16.25

This frequency distribution was created using the `Partition` function.

Employees	Dollars
158	: 499
183	500: 5499
49	5500: 10499
43	10500: 15499
31	15500: 20499
34	20500: 25499
36	25500: 30499
22	30500: 35499
23	35500: 40499
13	40500: 45499
19	45500: 50499
15	50500: 55499
17	55500: 60499
10	60500: 65499
5	65500: 70499
4	70500: 75499
6	75500: 80499
1	80500: 85499

With this frequency distribution, you're clustering employees by the range of revenue dollars they fall in. For instance, 183 employees fall into the 500: 5999 grouping, meaning that 183 employees earn between 500 and 5,999 revenue dollars per employee. Although there are several ways to get the results you see here, the easiest way to build a frequency distribution is to use the `Partition` function:

```
Partition(Number, Range Start, Range Stop, Interval)
```

The `Partition` function identifies the range that a specific number falls into, indicating where the number occurs in a calculated series of ranges. The `Partition` function requires the following four arguments:

- ***Number* (required):** The number you're evaluating. In a query environment, you typically use the name of a field to specify that you're evaluating all the row values of that field.
- ***Range Start* (required):** A whole number that is to be the start of the overall range of numbers. Note that this number cannot be less than zero.
- ***Range Stop* (required):** A whole number that is to be the end of the overall range of numbers. Note that this number cannot be equal to or less than the *Range Start*.
- ***Interval* (required):** A whole number that is to be the span of each range in the series from *Range Start* to *Range Stop*. Note that this number cannot be less than one.

To create the frequency distribution you saw in Figure 16.25, build the query shown in Figure 16.26. As you can see in this query, you're using a `Partition` function to specify that you want to evaluate the Revenue field, start the series range at 500, end the series range at 100,000, and set the range intervals to 5,000.

FIGURE 16.26

This simple query creates the frequency distribution you see in Figure 16.25.

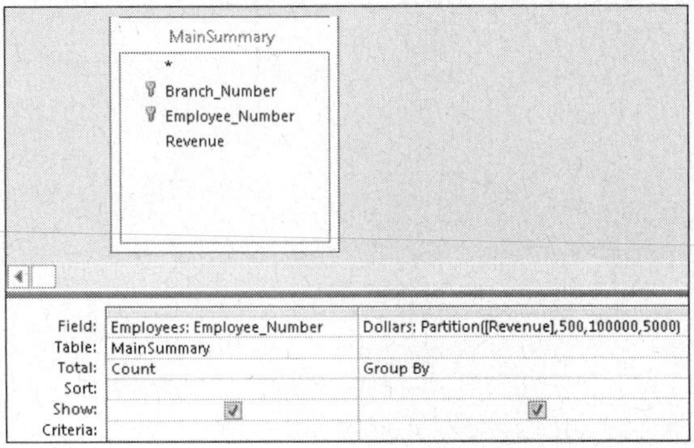

MainSummary
*
Branch_Number
Employee_Number
Revenue

Field:	Employees: Employee_Number	Dollars: Partition([Revenue],500,100000,5000)
Table:	MainSummary	
Total:	Count	Group By
Sort:		
Show:	☑	☑
Criteria:		

You can also create a frequency distribution by group by adding a Group By field to your query. Figure 16.27 demonstrates this by adding the Branch_Number field.

FIGURE 16.27

This query will create a separate frequency distribution for each branch number in your dataset.

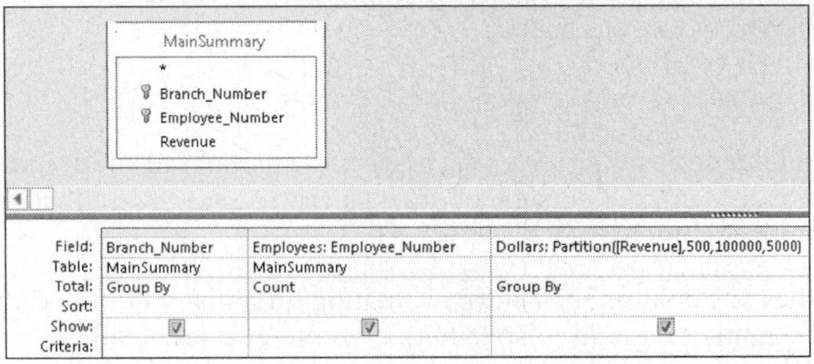

MainSummary
*
Branch_Number
Employee_Number
Revenue

Field:	Branch_Number	Employees: Employee_Number	Dollars: Partition([Revenue],500,100000,5000)
Table:	MainSummary	MainSummary	
Total:	Group By	Count	Group By
Sort:			
Show:	☑	☑	☑
Criteria:			

The result is a dataset (shown in Figure 16.28) that contains a separate frequency distribution for each branch, detailing the count of employees in each revenue distribution range.

FIGURE 16.28

You've successfully created multiple frequency distributions with one query.

Branch_Number	Employees	Dollars
101313	3	: 499
101313	7	500: 5499
101313	2	5500: 10499
101313	1	15500: 20499
101313	1	20500: 25499
101313	1	25500: 30499
101313	1	45500: 50499
101313	1	60500: 65499
101313	1	70500: 75499
101313	2	75500: 80499
101419	2	: 499
101419	1	10500: 15499
101419	1	25500: 30499
101419	1	30500: 35499
101419	1	45500: 50499

Part V

Working with Access Forms and Reports

Forms and reports are incredibly powerful components of the Access toolset.

Access forms enable you to build user interfaces on top of database tables, providing a robust rapid application development platform for many types of organizations. Access reports allow you to easily integrate your database analysis with polished PDF-style reporting functionality, complete with grouping, sorting, and conditional formatting.

The first three chapters in this part shows you everything you need to know in order to turn your simple database into a viable application with attractive interfaces that can be used for viewing, adding, editing, and deleting data.

The last two chapters in the part walk you through the steps for building Access reports, offering your users a flexible way of viewing summarized information in the desired level of detail, while enabling them to print their information in many different formats.

IN THIS PART

Creating Basic Access Forms

IN THIS CHAPTER

Creating different types of forms

Adding controls to a form

Working with the Property Sheet

Forms provide the most flexible way for viewing, adding, editing, and deleting your data. They're also used for *switchboards* (forms with buttons that provide navigation), for dialog boxes that control the flow of the system, and for messages. Controls are the objects on forms such as labels, text boxes, buttons, and many others. In this chapter, you learn how to create different types of forms. We also fill you in on the types of controls that are used on a form. This chapter also discusses form and control properties and how you determine the appearance and behavior of an Access interface through setting or changing property values.

The forms you add to an Access database are a critical aspect of the application you create. In most situations, users should not be permitted direct access to tables or query datasheets. It's far too easy for a user to delete valuable information or incorrectly input data into the table. Forms provide a useful tool for managing the integrity of a database's data. Because forms can contain VBA code or macros, a form can verify data entry or confirm deletions before they occur. Also, a properly designed form can reduce training requirements by helping the user understand what kind of data is required by displaying a message as the user tabs into a control. A form can provide default values or perform calculations based on data input by the user or retrieved from a database table.

ON THE WEB

In this chapter, you use `tblProducts`, `tblCustomers`, and other tables in `Chapter17.accdb`.

Formulating Forms

Use the Forms group on the Create tab of the Ribbon to add forms to your database. The commands in the Forms group — shown in Figure 17.1 — let you create the following different types of forms and ways to work with Access forms:

FIGURE 17.1

Use the Forms group on the Create tab of the Ribbon to add new forms to your database.

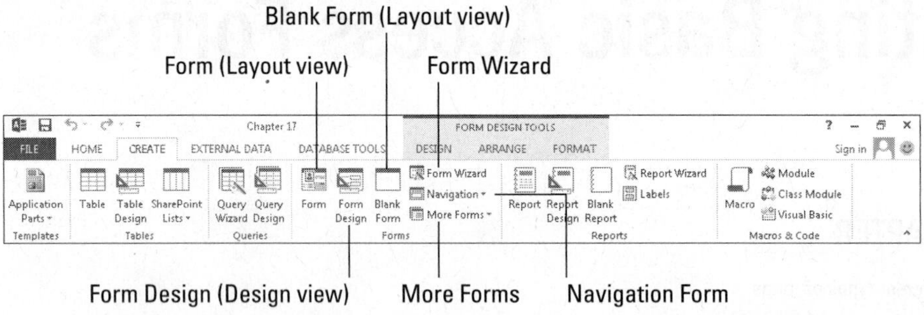

Blank Form (Layout view)
Form (Layout view)
Form Wizard
Form Design (Design view)
More Forms
Navigation Form

- **Form:** Creates a new form that lets you enter information for one record at a time. You must have a table, query, form, or report open or selected to use this command. When you click the Form button with a table or query highlighted in the Navigation pane, Access binds the new form to the data source and opens the form in Layout view.
- **Form Design:** Creates a new blank form and displays it in Design view. The form isn't bound to any data source. You must specify a data source (table or query) and build the form by adding controls from the data source's Field List.
- **Blank Form:** Instantly creates a blank form with no controls. Like Form Design, the new form is not bound to a data source, but it opens in Layout view.
- **Form Wizard:** Access features a simple wizard to help you get started building forms. The wizard asks for the data source, provides a screen for selecting fields to include on the form, and lets you choose from a number of very basic layouts for the new form.
- **Navigation Form:** The Access navigation form is a specialized form intended to provide user navigation through an application. Navigation forms are discussed in detail later in this chapter.
- **More Forms:** The More Forms button in the Forms group drops down a gallery containing a number of other form types.
  - **Multiple Items:** This is a simple tabular form that shows multiple records bound to the selected data source.
  - **Datasheet:** Creates a form that is displayed as a datasheet.

- **Split Form:** Creates a split form, which shows a datasheet in the upper, lower, left, or right area of the form, and a traditional form in the opposite section for entering information on the record selected in the datasheet.
- **Modal Dialog:** Provides a template for a modal dialog form. A modal dialog form (often called a *dialog box*) stays on the screen until the user provides information requested by the dialog or is dismissed by the user.

If any of the terminology in the preceding bullets is new to you, don't worry — each of these terms is discussed in detail in this chapter. Keep in mind that the Access Ribbon and its contents are very context dependent, so every item may not be available when you select the Create tab.

Creating a new form

Like many other aspects of Access development, Access provides multiple ways of adding new forms to your application. The easiest is to select a data source, such as a table, and click the Form command on the Create tab of the Ribbon. Another is to use the Form Wizard and allow the wizard to guide you through the process of specifying a data source and other details of the new form.

Using the Form command

Use the Form command in the Forms group of the Ribbon to automatically create a new form based on a table or query selected in the Navigation pane.

NOTE
This process was called *AutoForm* in previous versions of Access.

To create a form based on tblProducts, follow these steps:

1. **Select tblProducts in the Navigation pane.**
2. **Select the Create tab of the Ribbon.**
3. **Click the Form command in the Forms group.** Access creates a new form containing all the fields from tblProducts displayed in Layout view, shown in Figure 17.2. Layout view lets you see the form's data while changing the layout of controls on the form. (The form shown in Figure 17.2 is included in the `Chapter17.accdb` example database as frmProducts_AutoForm.)

FIGURE 17.2

Use the Form command to quickly create a new form with all the fields from a table or query.

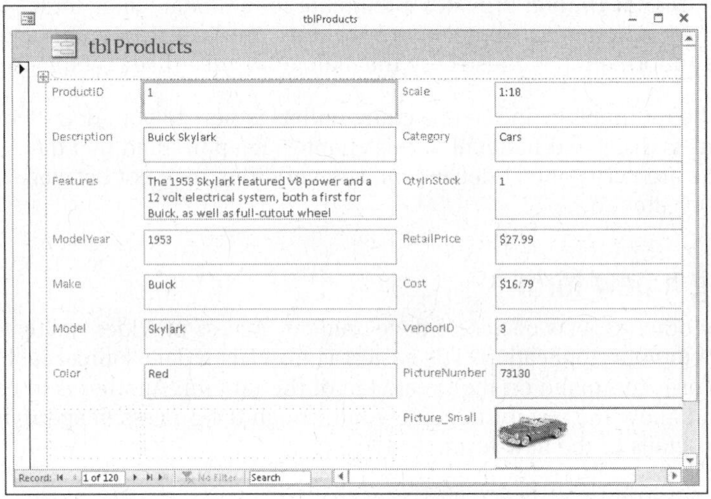

The new form is opened in Layout view, which is populated with controls, each of which is bound to a field in the underlying data source. Layout view gives you a good idea how the controls appear relative to one another, but it provides only limited ability to resize controls or move controls on the form. Right-click the form's title bar and select Design View to rearrange controls on the form.

The Form Design button in the Forms group does essentially the same thing as the Form button, except that no controls are added to the form's design surface and the form is opened in Design view. Form Design is most useful when you're creating a new form that might not use all the fields in the underlying data source, and you want more control over control placement from the start.

Similarly, the Blank Form option opens a new empty form, but this time in Layout view. You add controls to the form's surface from the Field List, but you have little control over control placement. The Blank Form option is most useful for quickly building a form with bound controls with little need for precise placement. A new blank form can be produced in less than a minute.

Using the Form Wizard

Use the Form Wizard command in the Forms group to create a form using a wizard. The Form Wizard visually walks you through a series of questions about the form that you want to create and then creates it for you automatically. The Form Wizard lets you select which fields you want on the form, the form layout (Columnar, Tabular, Datasheet, Justified), and the form title.

To start the Form Wizard based on tblCustomers, follow these steps:

1. **Select tblCustomers in the Navigation pane.**
2. **Select the Create tab of the Ribbon.**
3. **Click the Form Wizard button in the Forms group.** Access starts the Form Wizard, shown in Figure 17.3.

FIGURE 17.3

Use the Form Wizard to create a form with the fields you choose.

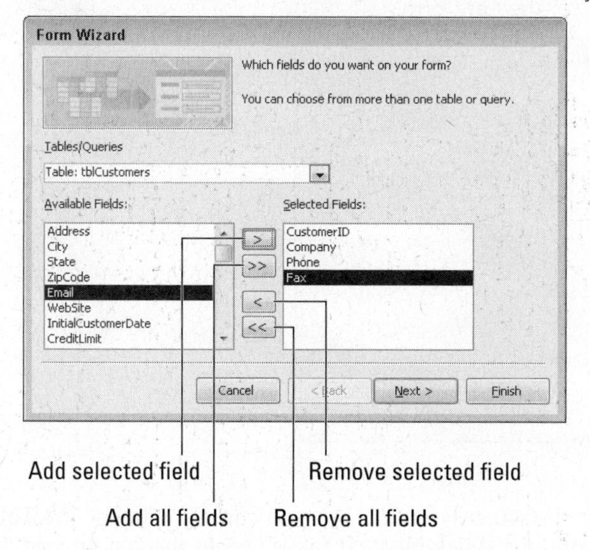

The wizard is initially populated with fields from tblCustomers, but you can choose another table or query with the Tables/Queries drop-down list above the field selection area. Use the buttons in the middle of the form to add and remove fields to the Available Fields and Selected Fields list boxes.

NOTE
You can also double-click any field in the Available Fields list box to add it to the Selected Fields list box.

The series of buttons at the bottom of the form let you navigate through the other steps of the wizard. The types of buttons available here are common to most wizard dialog boxes:

- **Cancel:** Cancel the wizard without creating a form.
- **Back:** Return to the preceding step of the wizard.
- **Next:** Go to the next step of the wizard.
- **Finish:** End the wizard using the current selections.

> **CAUTION**
> If you click Next or Finish without selecting any fields, Access tells you that you must select fields for the form before you can continue.

Clicking Next opens the second wizard dialog box (shown in Figure 17.4) where you specify the overall layout and appearance of the new form.

FIGURE 17.4

Select the overall layout for the new form.

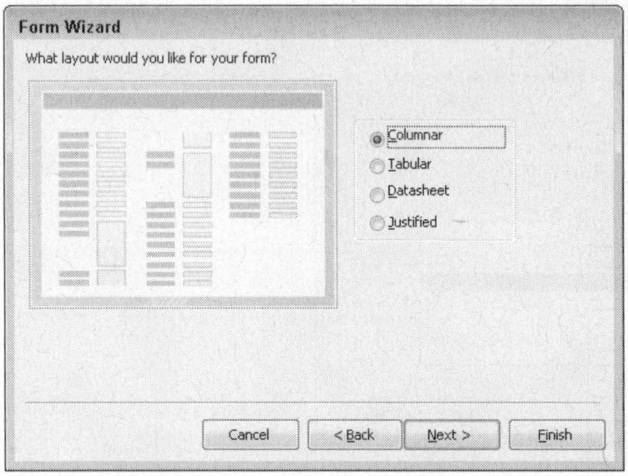

The Columnar layout is the wizard default, but you can also choose the Tabular, Datasheet, or Justified options. Clicking Next takes you to the last wizard dialog box (shown in Figure 17.5), where you provide a name for the new form.

FIGURE 17.5

Saving the new form.

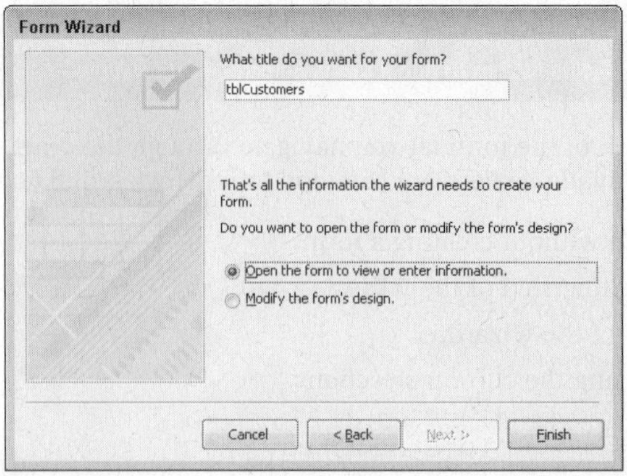

TIP

The main advantage of using the Form Wizard is that it binds the new form to a data source and adds controls for the selected fields. In most cases, however, you still have considerable work to do after the Form Wizard has finished.

Looking at special types of forms

When working with Access, the word *form* can mean any of several different things, depending on context. This section discusses several different ways that "forms" are used in Access and presents an example of each usage.

Navigation forms

Access 2010 introduced an entirely new form intended specifically as a navigation tool for users. Navigation forms include a number of tabs that provide instant access to any number of other forms in a form/subform arrangement. The Navigation button on the Ribbon offers a number of button placement options (shown in Figure 17.6). Horizontal Tabs is the default.

FIGURE 17.6

The Navigation button provides a number of tab placement options.

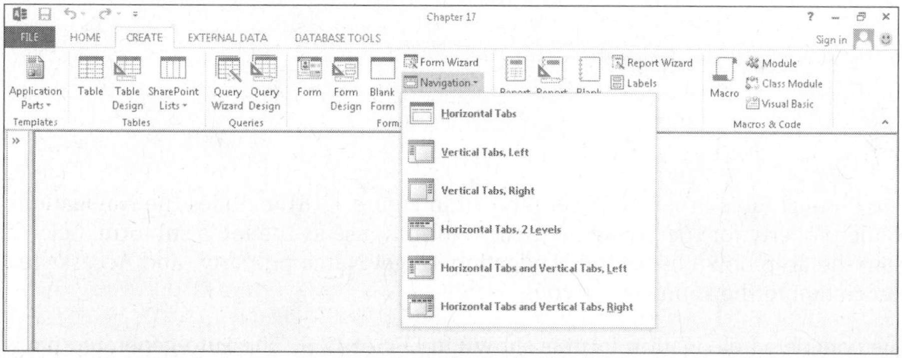

Selecting a tab placement in the Navigation drop-down list opens the new navigation form in Design view (see Figure 17.7). The new form includes a row of tabs along the top and a large area under the tabs for embedding subforms. You type the tab's label (like Products) directly into the tab, or add it through the tab's Caption property. As you complete the tab's label, Access adds a new, blank tab to the right of the current tab.

In Figure 17.7, the Horizontal Tabs option was selected when choosing a navigation form template and a tab was named Products, which generates a new Add New tab. The alternatives to Horizontal Tabs (Vertical Tabs, Left, Vertical Tabs, Right, and so on) are shown in Figure 17.6.

FIGURE 17.7

The Navigation form features a large area for embedding subforms.

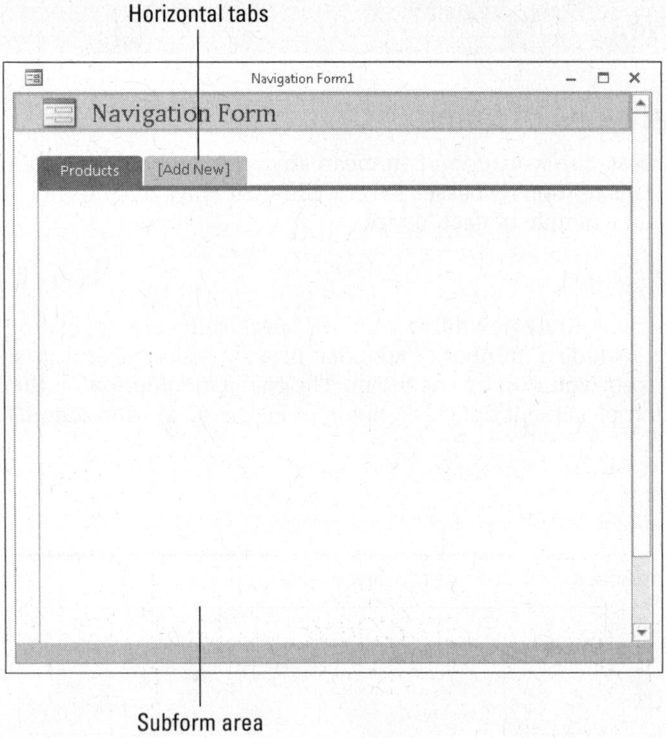

Horizontal tabs

Navigation Form1

Navigation Form

Products [Add New]

Subform area

The Product tab's Property Sheet (shown in Figure 17.8) includes the Navigation Target Name property for specifying the Access form to use as the tab's subform. Select a form from the drop-down list in the Navigation Target Name property, and Access creates the association to the subform for you.

The completed navigation form is shown in Figure 17.9. The auto-generated navigation form makes extravagant use of screen space. There are a number of things that could be done to enhance this form, such as removing the navigation form's header section and reducing the empty space surrounding the subform. frmProducts, shown in Figure 17.9, is included in the `Chapter17.accdb` example database.

FIGURE 17.8

Use the Navigation Target Name property to specify the tab's subform.

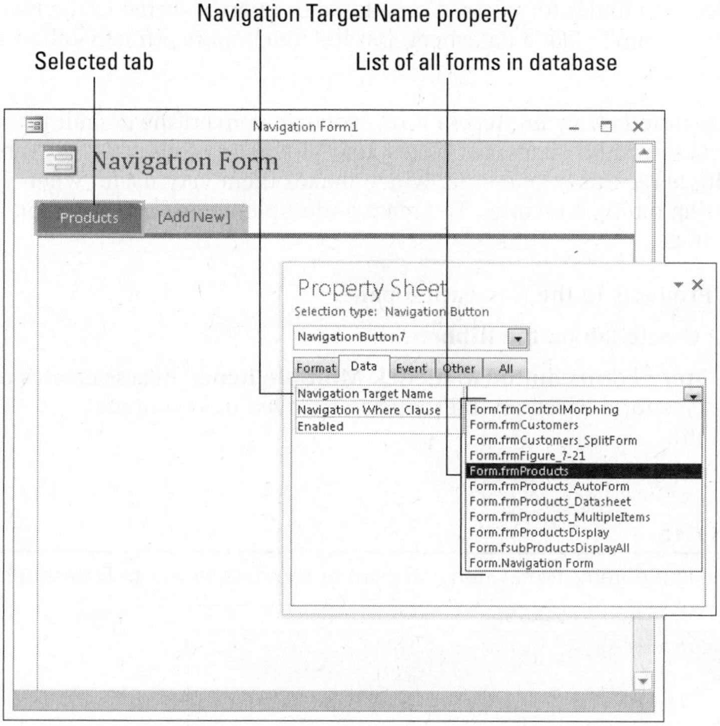

Navigation Target Name property

Selected tab

List of all forms in database

FIGURE 17.9

A navigation form is a quick and easy way to provide basic navigation features.

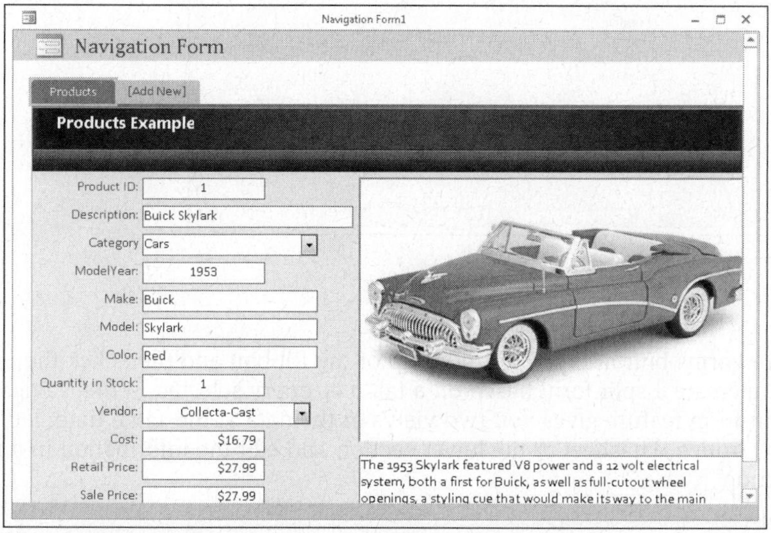

Multiple-items forms

Click the More Forms button in the Forms group of the Ribbon and then click the Multiple Items button to create a tabular form based on a table or query selected in the Navigation pane. A tabular form is much like a datasheet, but it's much more attractive than a plain datasheet.

Because the tabular form is truly an Access form, you can convert the default text box controls on the form to combo boxes, list boxes, and other advanced controls. Tabular forms display multiple records at one time, which makes them very useful when you're reviewing or updating multiple records. To create a multiple-items form based on tblProducts, follow these steps:

1. **Select tblProducts in the Navigation pane.**
2. **Select the Create tab on the Ribbon.**
3. **Click the More Forms button and click Multiple Items.** Access creates a new multiple-items form based on tblProducts displayed in Layout view (as shown in Figure 17.10).

FIGURE 17.10

Create a multiple-items form when you want to see data similar to Datasheet view.

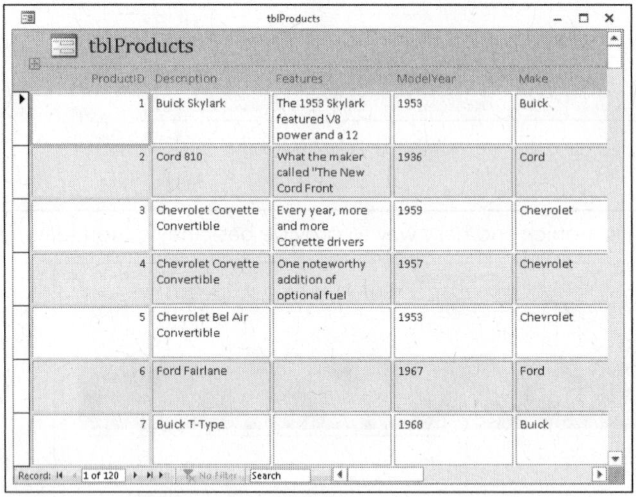

tblProducts

ProductID	Description	Features	ModelYear	Make
1	Buick Skylark	The 1953 Skylark featured V8 power and a 12	1953	Buick
2	Cord 810	What the maker called "The New Cord Front	1936	Cord
3	Chevrolet Corvette Convertible	Every year, more and more Corvette drivers	1959	Chevrolet
4	Chevrolet Corvette Convertible	One noteworthy addition of optional fuel	1957	Chevrolet
5	Chevrolet Bel Air Convertible		1953	Chevrolet
6	Ford Fairlane		1967	Ford
7	Buick T-Type		1968	Buick

Record: 1 of 120 No Filter Search

Split forms

Click the More Forms button in the Form group of the Ribbon and then click the Split Form button to create a split form based on a table or query selected in the Navigation pane. The split-form feature gives you two views of the data at the same time, letting you select a record from a datasheet in the lower section and edit the information in a form in the upper section.

To create a split form based on tblCustomers, follow these steps:

1. **Select tblCustomers in the Navigation pane.**
2. **Select the Create tab of the Ribbon.**
3. **Click the More Forms button and click Split Form.** Access creates a new split form based on tblCustomers displayed in Layout view (shown in Figure 17.11). Resize the form and use the splitter bar in the middle to make the lower section completely visible.

FIGURE 17.11

Create a split form when you want to select records from a list and edit them in a form. Use the splitter bar to resize the upper and lower sections of the form.

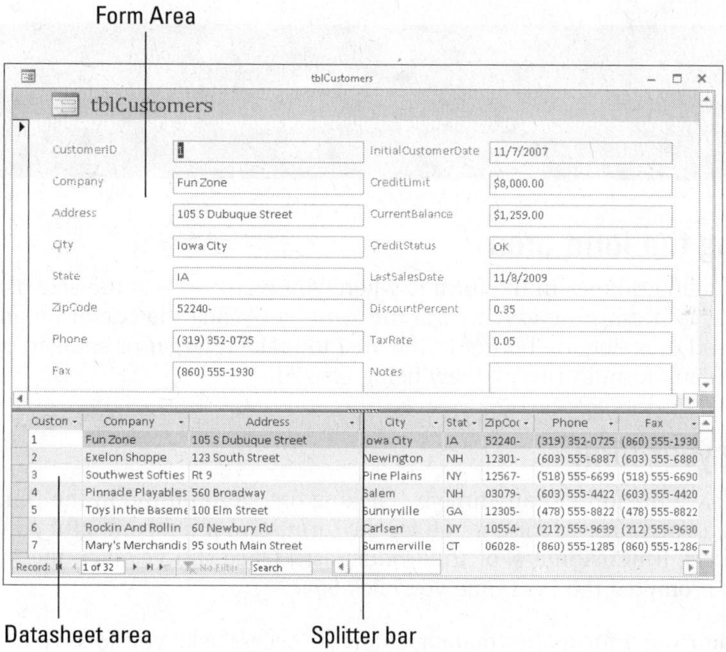

The Split Form Orientation property (on the Format tab of the form's Property Sheet) determines whether the datasheet is on the top, bottom, left, or right of the form area. The default is as shown in Figure 17.11, with the datasheet area on the bottom. frmCustomers_SplitForm (shown in Figure 17.11) is included in the `Chapter17.accdb` example database.

Datasheet forms

Click the More Forms button in the Forms group of the Ribbon and then click the Datasheet button to create a form that looks like a table or query's datasheet. A datasheet form is useful when you want to see the data in a row and column format, but you want to limit which fields are displayed and editable.

To create a datasheet form based on tblProducts, follow these steps:

1. **Select tblProducts in the Navigation pane.**
2. **Select the Create tab of the Ribbon.**
3. **Click the More Forms button in the Forms group and then click Datasheet.** You can view any form you create as a datasheet by selecting Datasheet View from the View drop-down menu on the Ribbon. A datasheet form appears in Datasheet View by default when you open it.

TIP

Some forms have their Allow Datasheet View property set to No by default. The View drop-down doesn't show a Datasheet View option for those forms. You'll learn more about form properties in the "Introducing Properties" section, later in this chapter.

Resizing the form area

The area with gridlines in the form is where you work. This is the size of the form when it's displayed. Resize the grid area of the form by placing the cursor on any of the area borders and dragging the border of the area to make it larger or smaller. Figure 17.12 shows a blank form in Design view being resized.

Saving your form

You can save the form at any time by clicking the `Save` button in the Quick Access toolbar. When you're asked for a name for the form, give it a meaningful name (for example, frmProducts, frmCustomers, or frmProductList.) Once you've given the form a name, you won't be prompted the next time you click Save.

When you close a form after making changes, Access asks you to save it. If you don't save a form, all changes since you opened the form (or since you last clicked Save) are lost. You should frequently save the form while you work if you're satisfied with the results.

TIP

If you're going to make extensive changes to a form, you might want to make a copy of the form. For example, if you want to work on the form frmProducts, you can copy and then paste the form in the Navigation pane, giving it a name like frmProductsOriginal. Later, when you've completed your changes and tested them, you can delete the original copy.

FIGURE 17.12

Design view of a blank form. Resize the form area by dragging the bottom-right corner.

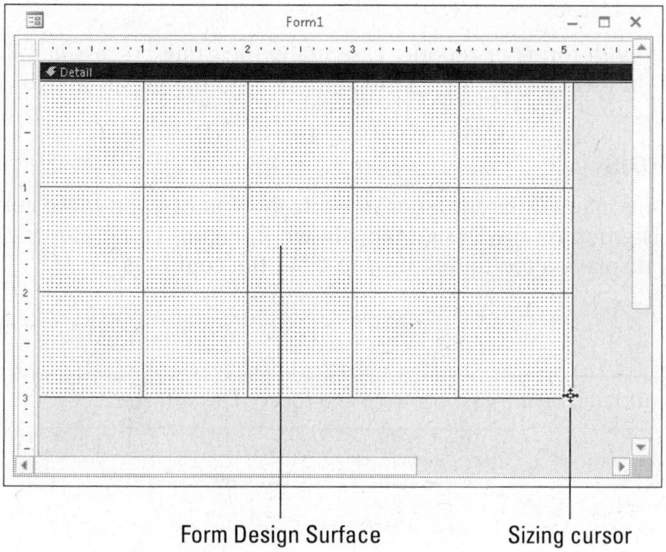

Form Design Surface

Sizing cursor

Working with Controls

Controls and properties form the basis of forms and reports. It's critical to understand the fundamental concepts of controls and properties before you begin to apply them to custom forms and reports.

NOTE

Although this chapter is about forms, you'll learn that forms and reports share many common characteristics, including controls and what you can do with them. As you learn about controls in this chapter, you'll be able to apply nearly everything you learn when you create reports.

The term *control* has many definitions in Access. Generally, a control is any object on a form or report, such as a label or text box. These are the same sort of controls used in any Windows application, such as Access, Excel, web-based HTML forms, or those that are used in any language, such as .NET, Visual Basic, C++, or C#. Although each language or product has different file formats and different properties, a text box in Access is similar to a text box in any other Windows product.

You enter data into controls and display data using controls. A control can be bound to a field in a table (when the value is entered in the control, it's also saved in some underlying table field), or data can be unbound and displayed in the form but not saved when the form is closed. A control can also be an object, such as a line or rectangle.

Some controls that aren't built into Access are developed separately — these are ActiveX controls. ActiveX controls extend the basic feature set of Access and are available from a variety of vendors.

Whether you're working with forms or reports, essentially the same process is followed to create and use controls. In this chapter, I explain controls from the perspective of a form.

Categorizing controls

Forms and reports contain many different types of controls. You can add these controls to forms using the Controls group on the Design tab, shown in Figure 17.13. Hovering the mouse over the control displays a tooltip telling you what the control is.

FIGURE 17.13

The Design tab lets you add and customize controls in a form's Design view.

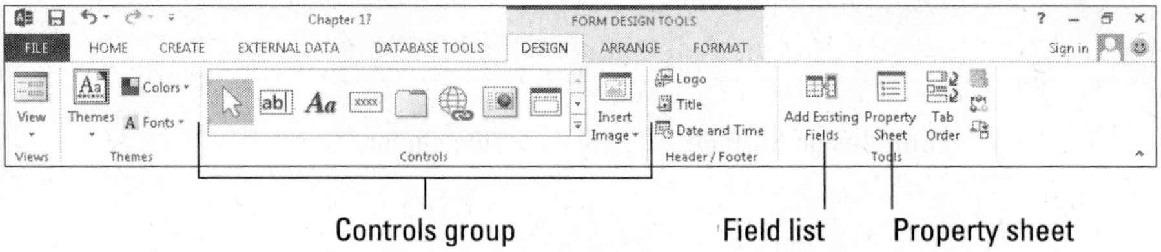

Table 17.1 briefly describes the basic Access controls.

TABLE 17.1 Controls in Access Forms

Control	What It Does
Text Box	Displays and allows users to edit data.
Label	Displays static text that typically doesn't change.
Button	Also called a command button. Runs macros or VBA code when clicked.
Combo Box	A drop-down list of values. Combo boxes include a text box at the top for inputting values that are not included in the drop-down list.
List Box	A list of values that is always displayed on the form or report.
Subform/Subreport	Displays another form or report within the main form or report.
Line	A graphical line of variable thickness and color, which is used for separation.
Rectangle	A rectangle can be any color or size or can be filled in or blank; the rectangle is used to group related controls visually.
Image	Displays a bitmap picture with very little overhead.

Control	What It Does
Option Group	Holds multiple option buttons, check boxes, or toggle buttons.
Check Box	A two-state control, shown as a square that contains a check mark if it's on and an empty square if it's off. Before a Check Box's value is set, it appears as a grayed-out square.
Option Button	Also called a radio button, this button is displayed as a circle with a dot when the option is on.
Toggle Button	This is a two-state button — up or down — which usually uses pictures or icons instead of text to display different states.
Tab Control	Displays multiple pages in a file folder type of interface.
Page	Adds a page on the form or report. Additional controls are added to the page, and multiple pages may exist on the same form
Chart	Displays data in a graphical format.
Unbound Object Frame	Holds an OLE object or embedded picture that isn't tied to a table field and can include graphs, pictures, sound files, and video.
Bound Object Frame	Holds an OLE object or embedded picture that is tied to a table field.
Page Break	Usually used for reports and indicates a physical page break.
Hyperlink	Creates a link to a web page, a picture, an e-mail address, or a program.
Attachment	Manages attachments for the Attachment data type. Attachment fields (see Chapter 3) provide a way to *attach* external files (such as music or video clips or Word documents) to Access tables.

The Use Control Wizards button, revealed by expanding the Controls group by clicking on the More button in the lower-right corner of the group, doesn't add a control to a form. Instead, the Use Control Wizards button determines whether a wizard is automatically activated when you add certain controls. The Option Group, Combo Box, List Box, Subform/Subreport, Bound and Unbound Object Frame, and Command Button controls all have wizards to help you when you add a new control. You can also use the ActiveX Controls button (also found at the bottom of the expanded Controls group) to display a list of ActiveX controls, which you can add to Access.

There are three basic categories of controls:

- **Bound controls:** These are controls that are bound to a field in the data source underlying the form. When you enter a value in a bound control, Access automatically updates the field in the current record. Most of the controls used for data entry can be bound. Controls can be bound to most data types, including Text, Date/Time, Number, Yes/No, OLE Object, and Memo fields.

- **Unbound controls:** Unbound controls retain the entered value, but they don't update any table fields. You can use these controls for text label display, for controls such as lines and rectangles, or for holding unbound OLE objects (such as bitmap pictures or your logo) that are stored not in a table but on the form itself. Very often, VBA code is used to work with data in unbound controls and directly update Access data sources.

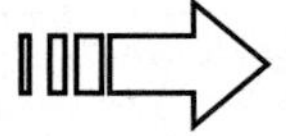

Turn to Chapters 28 for details on using VBA to manipulate forms and controls and to work with unbound data.

- **Calculated controls:** Calculated controls are based on expressions, such as functions or calculations. Calculated controls are unbound because they don't directly update table fields. An example of a calculated control is `=[SalePrice] - [Cost]`. This control calculates the total of two table fields for display on a form but is not bound to any table field. The value of an unbound calculated control may be referenced by other controls on the form, or used in an expression in another control on the form or in VBA in the form's module.

Adding a control

You add a control to a form in a number ways:

- **By clicking a button in the Controls group on the Design tab of the Ribbon and drawing a new unbound control on the form:** Use the control's ControlSource property to bind the new control to a field in the form's data source.
- **By dragging a field from the Field List to add a bound control to the form:** Access automatically chooses a control appropriate for the field's data type and binds the control to the selected field.
- **By double-clicking a field in the Field List to add a bound control to the form:** Double-clicking works just like dragging a field from the Field List to the form. The only difference is that, when you add a control by double-clicking a field, Access decides where to add the new control to the form. Usually the new control is added to the right of the most recently added control, and sometimes below it.
- **By right-clicking a field in the Field List and choosing Add Field to View:** Right-clicking places a bound control in the same location as if it were double-clicked.
- **By copying an existing control and pasting it to another location on the form:** Copying a control can be done in all the familiar ways: Click Copy on the Home tab of the Ribbon, right-click the control and choose Copy, or press Ctrl + C. Pasted controls are bound to the same field as the control that was copied.

Using the Controls group

When you use the buttons in the Controls group to add a control, you decide which type of control to use for each field. The control you add is *unbound* (not attached to the data in a table field) and has a default name such as Text21 or Combo11. After you create the control, you decide what table field to bind the control to, enter text for the label, and set any properties. You'll learn more about setting properties later in this chapter.

You can add one control at a time using the Controls group. To create three different unbound controls, perform these steps:

1. **With the form created earlier open in Design view, click the Text Box button in the Controls group.**
2. **Move the mouse pointer to the Form Design window, and click and drag the new control onto the form's surface in its initial size and position.**
3. **Click the Option button in the Controls group, and click and drag the new Option button onto the form's surface in its initial size and position.**
4. **Click the Check Box button in the Controls group and add it to the form as you added the other controls.** When you're done, your screen should resemble Figure 17.14.

FIGURE 17.14

Unbound controls added from the Controls group.

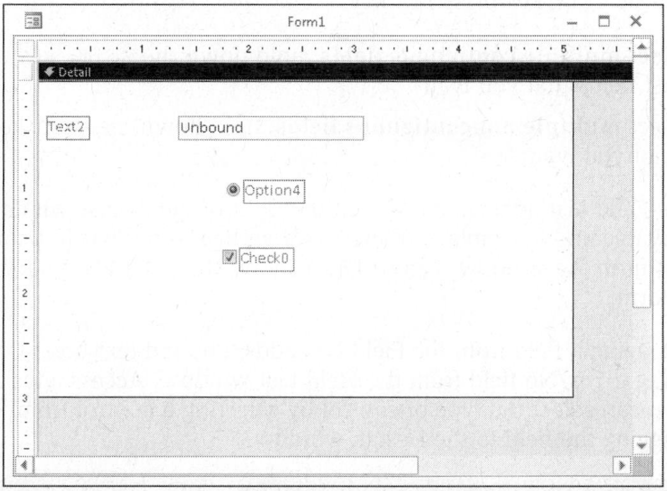

TIP

Clicking the Form Design window with a control selected creates a default-size control. If you want to add multiple controls of the same type, right-click the icon in the Controls group and choose Drop Multiple Controls, and then draw as many controls as you want on the form. Click the selector control (the arrow) to unlock the control and return to normal operation.

> **TIP**
> To remove the grid lines from the form's detail area, select Grid from the Size/Space control on the Arrange tab of the Ribbon while the form is in Design view. Most of the figures in this section don't show the grid so the edges of the controls are easier to see.

Using the Field List

The Field List displays a list of fields from the table or query the form is based on. Open the Field List by clicking the Add Existing Fields button in the Tools group on the Design tab of the Ribbon (refer to Figure 17.13).

If you created a form using a method that automatically binds the form to a table or query, the field list for that table or query will be displayed. For this example, we created a form using the Blank Form button, which does not automatically bind the form to a datasource. In this case, the Field List only shows a Show All Tables link. Click the Show All Tables link to get a list of tables. Then click the plus sign next to tblProducts to show the fields in that table.

Drag Model from the Field List and drop it onto the form to create a control bound to the Model field in tblProducts . You can select and drag fields one at a time or select multiple fields by using the `Ctrl` key or `Shift` key:

- **To select multiple contiguous fields,** hold down the `Shift` key and click the first and last fields that you want.
- **To select multiple noncontiguous fields,** hold down the `Ctrl` key and click each field that you want.

By default, the Field List appears docked on the right of the Access window. The Field List window is movable and resizable and displays a vertical scroll bar if it contains more fields than can fit in the window. Figure 17.15 shows the Field List undocked and moved on top of the form.

Most often, dragging a field from the Field List adds a bound text box to the Design window. If you drag a Yes/No field from the Field List window, Access adds a check box. Optionally, you can select the type of control by selecting a control from the Controls group and dragging the field to the Design window.

> **CAUTION**
> When you drag fields from the Field List window, the first control is placed where you release the mouse button. Make sure that you have enough space to the left of the control for the labels. If you don't have enough space, the labels slide under the controls.

FIGURE 17.15

Click `Add Existing Fields` in the Tools group to show the Field List.

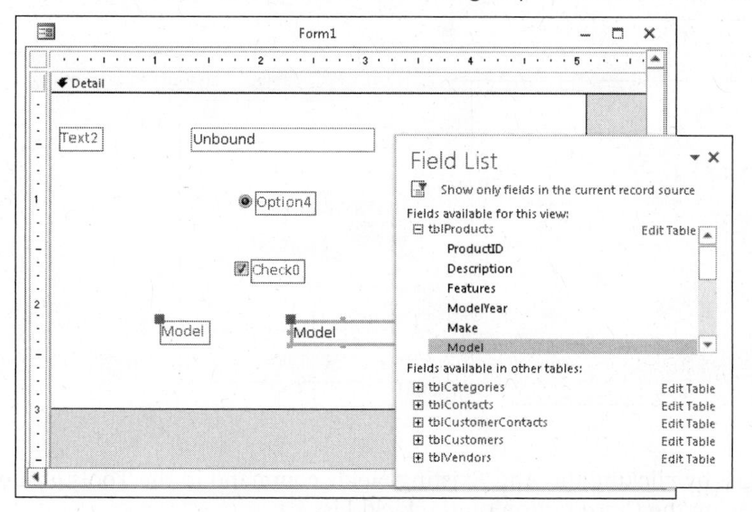

You gain several distinct advantages by dragging a field from the Field List window:

- The control is automatically bound to the field.
- Field properties inherit table-level formats, status bar text, and data validation rules and messages.
- The label control and label text are created with the field name as the caption.
- The label control is attached to the field control, so they move together.

Select and drag the Description, Category, RetailPrice, and Cost fields from the Field List window to the form, as shown in Figure 17.16. Double-clicking a field also adds it to the form.

You can see four new pairs of controls in the form's Design view — each pair consists of a Label control and a Text Box control (Access attaches the Label control to the Text Box automatically). You can work with these controls as a group or independently, and you can select, move, resize, or delete them. Notice that each control has a label with a caption matching the field name, and the Text Box control displays the bound field name used in the text box. If you want to resize just the control and not the label, you must work with the two controls (label and associated text box) separately. You'll learn about working with labels attached to controls later in this chapter.

FIGURE 17.16

Drag fields from the Field List to add bound controls to the form.

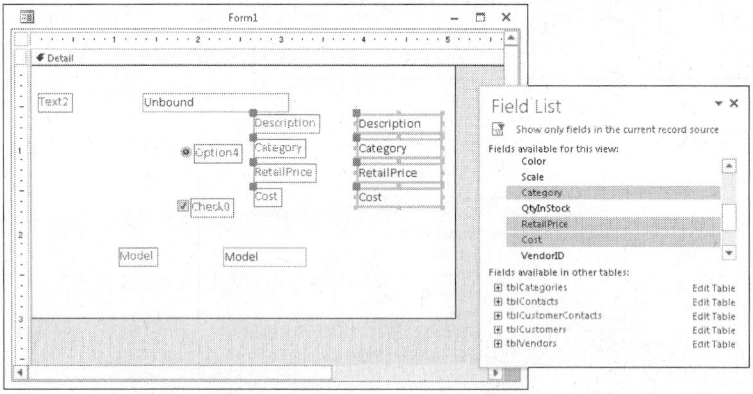

Close the Field List by clicking the Add Existing Fields command in the Tools group of the Ribbon or by clicking the Close button on the Field List.

TIP

In Access, you can change the type of control after you create it; then you can set all the properties for the control. For example, suppose that you add a field as a Text Box control and you want to change it to a List Box. Right-click the control and select Change To from the pop-up menu to change the control type. However, you can change only from some types of controls to others. You can change almost any type of control to a Text Box control, while Option Button controls, Toggle Button controls, and Check Box controls are interchangeable, as are List Box and Combo Box controls.

In the "Introducing Properties" section, later in this chapter, you learn how to change the control names, captions, and other properties. Using properties speeds the process of naming controls and binding them to specific fields. If you want to see the differences between bound and unbound controls, switch to Form view using the View command in the View group of the Ribbon. The Description, Category, RetailPrice, and Cost controls display data because they're bound to tblProducts. The other three controls don't display data because they aren't bound to any data source.

NOTE

As you add controls from the Field List, Access builds the form's RecordSource property as a SQL statement. The RecordSource after adding these four fields is

```
SELECT tblProducts.Model, tblProducts.Description, tblProducts.Category,
  tblProducts.RetailPrice, tblProducts.Cost FROM tblProducts;
```

If we had started with a form bound to a table or query, the RecordSource would have been set to the entire table or query and would not change as fields are added or removed.

Selecting and deselecting controls

After you add a control to a form, you can resize it, move it, or copy it. The first step is to select one or more controls. Depending on its size, a selected control might show from four to eight *handles* (small squares called *moving and sizing handles*) around the control — at the corners and midway along the sides. The move handle in the upper-left corner is larger than the other handles and you use it to move the control. You use the other handles to size the control. Figure 17.17 displays some selected controls and their moving and sizing handles.

FIGURE 17.17

Selected controls and their moving and sizing handles.

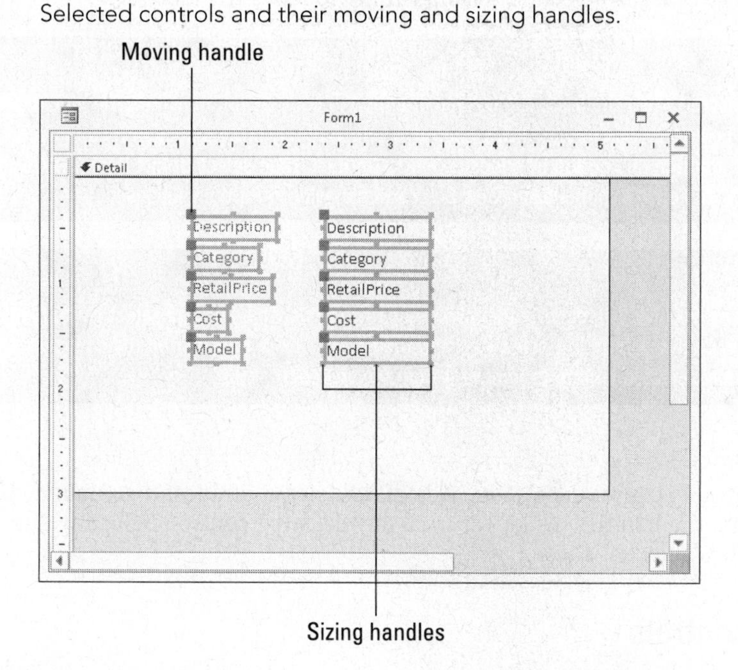

The Select command (which looks like an arrow) in the Controls group must be chosen in order for you to select a control. If you use the Controls group to create a single control, Access automatically reselects the pointer as the default.

Selecting a single control

Select any individual control by clicking anywhere on the control. When you click a control, the sizing handles appear. If the control has an attached label, the move handle for the label also appears in the upper-left corner of the control. If you select a label control that is associated with another control, all the handles for the label control are displayed, and only the move handle appears in the associated control.

Selecting multiple controls

You select multiple controls in these ways:

- By clicking each control while holding down the Shift key
- By dragging the pointer through or around the controls that you want to select
- By clicking and dragging in the ruler to select a range of controls

Figure 17.17 shows the result of selecting the multiple bound controls graphically. When you select multiple controls by dragging the mouse, a rectangle appears as you drag the mouse. Be careful to drag the rectangle only through the controls you want to select. Any control you touch with the rectangle or enclose within it is selected. If you want to select labels only, make sure that the selection rectangle only touches the labels.

TIP

If you find that controls are not selected when the rectangle passes through the control, you may have the global selection behavior property set to Fully Enclosed. This means that a control is selected only if the selection rectangle completely encloses the entire control. Change this option by choosing File ⇨ Options. Then select Object Designers in the Access Options dialog box and set the Form/Report Design view Selection behavior to Partially Enclosed.

TIP

By holding down the Shift or Ctrl key, you can select several noncontiguous controls. This lets you select controls on totally different parts of the screen. Click the form in Design view and then press Ctrl+A to select *all* the controls on the form. Press Shift or Ctrl and click any selected control to remove it from the selection.

Deselecting controls

Deselect a control by clicking an unselected area of the form that doesn't contain a control. When you do so, the handles disappear from any selected control. Selecting another control also deselects a selected control.

Manipulating controls

Creating a form is a multistep process. The next step is to make sure that your controls are properly sized and moved to their correct positions. The Arrange tab of the Ribbon (shown in Figure 17.18) contains commands used to assist you in manipulating controls.

FIGURE 17.18

The Arrange tab lets you work with moving and sizing controls, as well as manipulate the overall layout of the form.

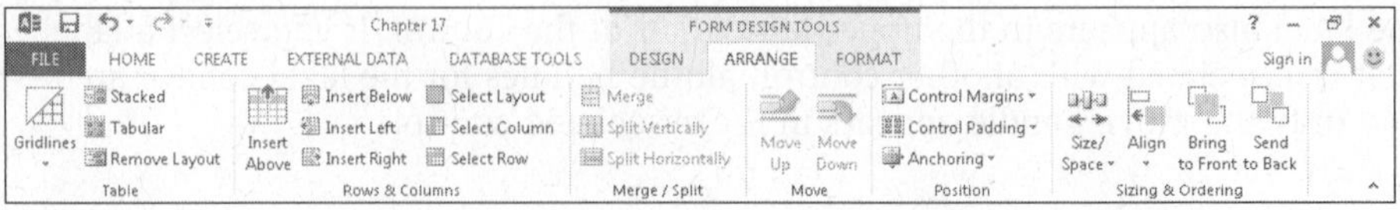

Resizing a control

You *resize* controls using any of the smaller handles in the upper, lower, and right edges of the control. The sizing handles in the control corners let you drag the control larger or smaller in both width and height — and at the same time. Use the handles in the middle of the control sides to size the control larger or smaller in one direction only. The top and bottom handles control the height of the control; the left and right handles change the control's width.

When the mouse pointer touches a corner sizing handle of a selected control, the pointer becomes a diagonal double arrow. You can then drag the sizing handle until the control is the desired size. If the mouse pointer touches a side handle in a selected control, the pointer changes to a horizontal or vertical double-headed arrow. Figure 17.19 shows the Description control after being resized. Notice the double-headed arrow in the corner of the Description control.

FIGURE 17.19

Resizing a control.

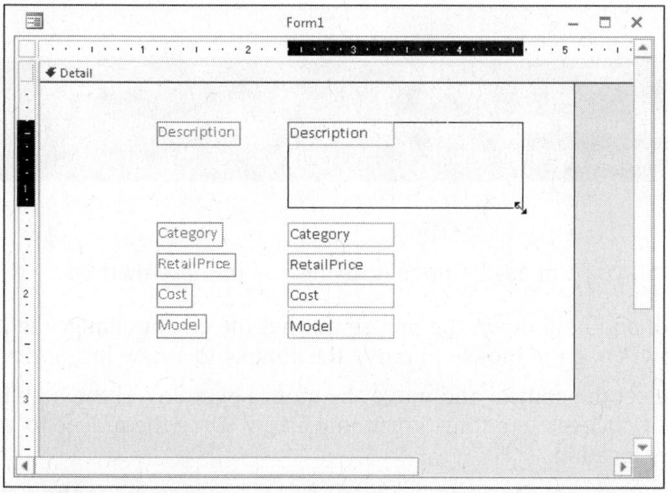

TIP

You can resize a control in very small increments by holding the Shift key while pressing the arrow keys (up, down, left, and right). This technique also works with multiple controls selected. Using this technique, a control changes by only 1 pixel at a time (or moves to the nearest grid line if Snap to Grid is selected in the Size/Space gallery of the Arrange tab of the Ribbon).

When you double-click on any of the sizing handles, Access resizes a control to a best fit the text contained in the control. This feature is especially handy if you increase the font size and then notice that the text is cut off either at the bottom or to the right. For label controls, note that this best-fit sizing adjusts the size vertically and horizontally, though text controls are resized only vertically. This is because when Access is in Form Design mode, it can't predict how much of a field to display — the field name and field contents can be radically different. Sometimes, Access doesn't correctly resize the label and you must manually change its size.

Sizing controls automatically

The Size/Space drop-down on the Size and Ordering group of the Arrange tab of the Ribbon has several commands that help the arrangement of controls:

- **To Fit:** Adjusts control height and width for the font of the text they contain
- **To Tallest:** Makes selected controls the height of the tallest selected control
- **To Shortest:** Makes selected controls the height of the shortest selected control
- **To Grid:** Moves all sides of selected controls in or out to meet the nearest points on the grid
- **To Widest:** Makes selected controls the width of the widest selected control
- **To Narrowest:** Makes selected controls the height of the narrowest selected control

TIP

You can access many commands by right-clicking after selecting multiple controls. When you right-click on multiple controls, a shortcut menu displays choices to size and align controls.

Moving a control

After you select a control, you can easily move it, using any of these methods:

- Click the control and hold down the mouse button; the cursor changes to a four-directional arrow. Drag the mouse to move the control to a new location.
- Click once to select the control and move the mouse over any of the highlighted edges; the cursor changes to a four-directional arrow. Drag the mouse to move the control to a new location.
- Select the control and use the arrow keys on the keyboard to move the control. Using this technique, a control changes by only 1 pixel at a time (or moves to the nearest grid line if Snap to Grid is selected in the Size/Space gallery on the Arrange tab of the Ribbon).

Figure 17.20 shows a Label control that has been separately moved to the top of the Text Box control.

FIGURE 17.20

Moving a control.

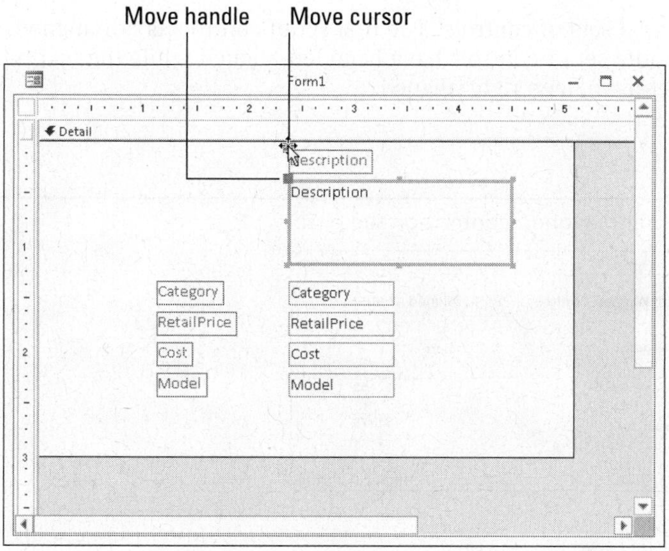

Press Esc before you release the mouse button to cancel a moving or a resizing operation. After a move or resizing operation is complete, click the Undo button on the Quick Access toolbar to undo the changes, if needed.

Aligning controls

You might want to move several controls so that they're all aligned. The Sizing and Ordering group's Align gallery on the Arrange tab of the Ribbon contains the following alignment commands:

- **To Grid:** Aligns the top-left corners of the selected controls to the nearest grid point
- **Left:** Aligns the left edge of the selected controls with the leftmost selected control
- **Right:** Aligns the right edge of the selected controls with the rightmost selected control
- **Top:** Aligns the top edge of the selected controls with the topmost selected control
- **Bottom:** Aligns the bottom edge of the selected controls with the bottommost selected control

You can align any number of selected controls by selecting an align command. When you choose one of the align commands, Access uses the control that's the closest to the desired selection as the model for the alignment. For example, suppose that you have three controls and you want to left-align them. They're aligned on the basis of the control farthest to the left in the group of the three controls.

Figure 17.21 shows several sets of controls. The first set of controls is not aligned. The label controls in the middle set of controls have been left-aligned while the text box controls in the right-side set have been right-aligned.

FIGURE 17.21

An example of unaligned and aligned controls on the grid.

Each type of alignment must be done separately. In this example, you can left-align all the labels or right-align all the text boxes at once.

By default, Access displays a series of small dots across the entire surface of a form while it's in Design view. The grid can assist you in aligning controls. Hide or display the grid by selecting the Grid command from the Size/Space gallery under the Sizing & Ordering group on the Arrange tab of the Ribbon. You can also hide or display the ruler using the Ruler command in the same gallery.

Use the Snap to Grid command in the Size/Space gallery to align controls to the grid as you draw or place them on a form. This also aligns existing controls to the grid when you move or resize them.

As you move or resize existing controls, Access lets you move only from grid point to grid point. When Snap to Grid is off, Access ignores the grid and lets you place a control anywhere on the form or report.

TIP

You can temporarily turn off Snap to Grid off by pressing the Ctrl key before you create a control (or while sizing or moving it). You can change the grid's *fineness* (number of dots) from form to form by using the Grid X and Grid Y form properties. (Higher numbers indicate greater fineness.)

You'll learn more about form properties in Chapter 18.

The Sizing & Ordering group on the Arrange tab of the Ribbon contains commands to adjust spacing between controls. The spacing commands adjust the distance between controls on the basis of the space between the first two selected controls. If the controls are across the screen, use horizontal spacing; if they're down the screen, use vertical spacing. The spacing commands are

- **Equal Horizontal:** Makes the horizontal space between selected controls equal. You must select three or more controls in order for this command to work.
- **Increase Horizontal:** Increases the horizontal space between selected controls by one grid unit.
- **Decrease Horizontal:** Decreases the horizontal space between selected controls by one grid unit.
- **Equal Vertical:** Makes the vertical space between selected controls equal. You must select three or more controls in order for this command to work properly.
- **Increase Vertical:** Increases the vertical space between selected controls by one grid unit.
- **Decrease Vertical:** Decreases the vertical space between selected controls by one grid unit.

TIP

Aligning controls aligns only the controls themselves. If you want to align the text within the controls (also known as *justifying the text*), you must use the Font group on the Format tab of the Ribbon and click the Left, Right, or Center buttons.

Modifying the appearance of a control

To modify the appearance of a control, select the control and click commands that modify that control, such as the options in the Font or Controls group. Follow these steps to change the text color and font of the Description label:

1. **Click the Description label on the form.**
2. **In the Font group on the Format tab of the Ribbon, change Font Size to 14, click the Bold button, and change Font Color to blue.**
3. **Resize the Description label so the larger text fits.** You can double-click any of the sizing handles to autosize the label.

To modify the appearance of multiple controls at once, select the controls and click commands to modify the controls, such as commands in the Font or Controls group. To change the text color and font of the Description, Category, and Cost labels and text boxes, follow these steps:

1. **Select the three labels and three text boxes by dragging a selection box through them (refer to Figure 17.11).**
2. **In the Font group on the Format tab of the Ribbon, change the Font Size to 14, click the Bold button, and change Font Color to blue.**

3. **Resize the labels and text boxes so the larger text fits.** You can double-click any of the sizing handles to autosize the controls. As you click the commands, the controls' appearances change to reflect the new selections (shown in Figure 17.22). The fonts in each control increase in size, become bold, and turn blue. Any changes you make apply to all selected controls.

FIGURE 17.22

Changing the appearance of multiple controls at the same time.

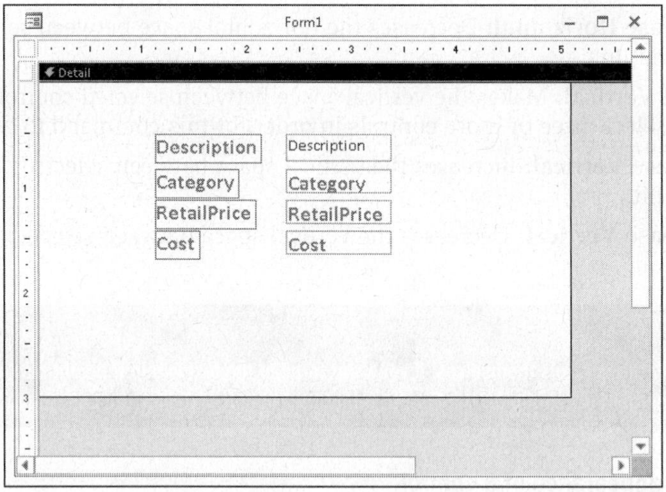

When multiple controls are selected, you can also move the selected controls together. When the cursor changes to the four-directional arrow, click and drag to move the selected controls. You can also change the size of all the controls at once by resizing one of the controls in the selection. All the selected controls increase or decrease by the same number of units.

Grouping controls

If you routinely change properties of multiple controls, you might want to group them together. To group controls together, select the controls by holding down the Shift key and clicking them or dragging the selection box through them. After the desired controls are selected, select the Group command from the Size/Space gallery on the Arrange tab of the Ribbon. When one control in a group is selected, all controls in that group are automatically selected, as shown in Figure 17.23.

FIGURE 17.23

Grouping multiple controls together.

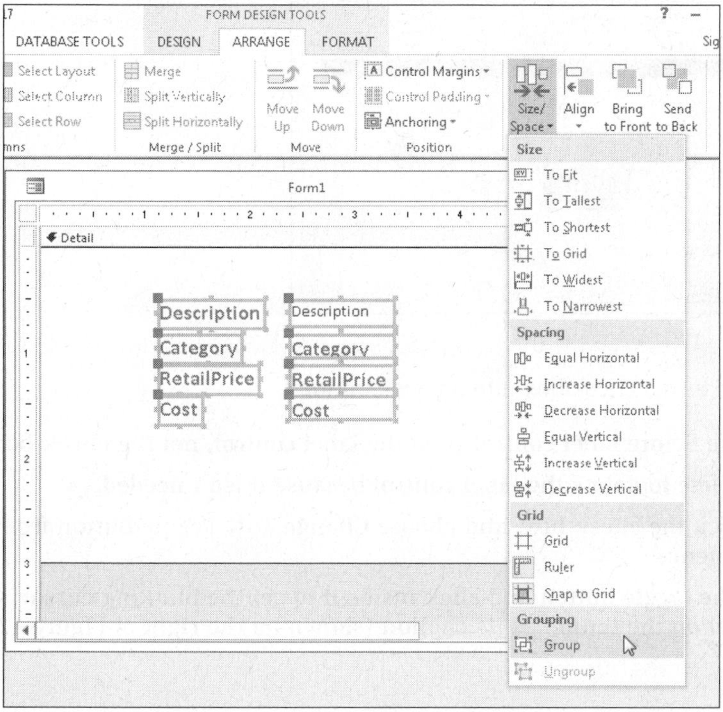

Double-click a control to select just one control in a group. After a single control in the group is selected, you can click any other control to select it.

To resize the entire group, put your mouse on the side you want to resize. After the double arrow appears, click and drag until you reach the desired size. Every control in the group changes in size. To move the entire group, click and drag the group to its new location. With grouped controls, you don't have to select all the controls every time you change something about them.

To remove a group, select the group by clicking any field inside the group, and then select the Ungroup command from the Size/Space gallery of the Arrange tab of the Ribbon.

Changing a control's type

Although there are times you may want to use a check box to display a Boolean (yes/no) data type, there are other ways to display the value, such as a toggle button, as shown in Figure 17.24. A toggle button is raised if it's true and depressed (or at least very unhappy) if it's false.

FIGURE 17.24

Turn a check box into a toggle button.

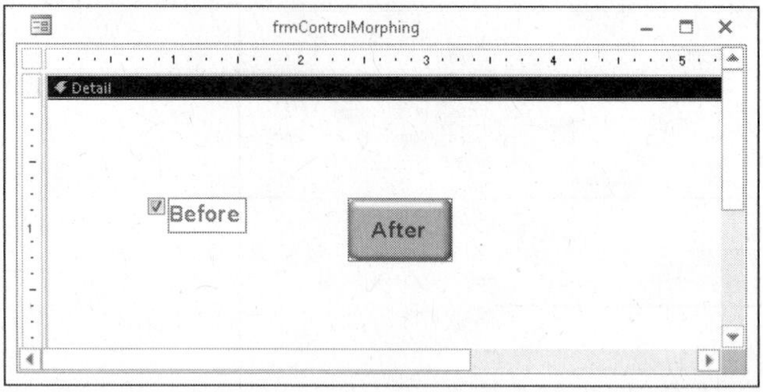

Use these steps to turn a check box into a toggle button:

1. **Select the Before label control (just the label control, not the check box).**
2. **Press Delete to delete the label control because it isn't needed.**
3. **Right-click the check box, and choose Change To➪Toggle Button from the pop-up menu.**
4. **Resize the toggle button and click inside it to get the blinking cursor; then type** After **on the button as its caption (shown on the right of Figure 17.24).**

Copying a control

You can create copies of any control by copying it to the Clipboard and then pasting the copies where you want them. If you have a control for which you've entered many properties or specified a certain format, you can copy it and revise only the properties (such as the control's name and bound field name) to make it a different control. This capability is useful with a multiple-page form when you want to display the same values on different pages and in different locations, or when copying a control from one form to another.

Deleting a control

You can delete a control by simply selecting it in the form's Design view and pressing the Delete key on your keyboard. The control and any attached labels will disappear. You can bring them back by immediately selecting Undo from the Quick Access toolbar. You can also select Cut from the Clipboard group on the Home tab of the Ribbon, or Delete from the Records group on the Home tab of the Ribbon.

You can delete more than one control at a time by selecting multiple controls and pressing Delete. You can delete an entire group of controls by selecting the group and pressing Delete. If you have a control with an attached label, you can delete only the label by clicking the label itself and then selecting one of the delete methods. If you select the control, both the control and the label are deleted.

To delete only the label of the Description control, follow the next set of steps (this example assumes that you have the Description text box control in your Form Design window):

1. **Select the Description label control only.**
2. **Press Delete to remove the label from the form.**

Reattaching a label to a control

If you accidentally delete a label from a control, you can reattach it. To create and then reattach a label to a control, follow these steps: Later in this chapter, in the "Naming control labels and their captions" section, you'll learn about the special relationship between a control and its label. By default, Access controls include a label when the control is added to a form; this label moves around with the control as you reposition the control on the form. The "Naming control labels and their captions" section describes these behaviors and how to work with control labels.

1. **Click the Label button on the Controls group.**
2. **Place the mouse pointer in the Form Design window.** The mouse pointer becomes a capital *A*.
3. **Click and hold down the mouse button where you want the control to begin; drag the mouse to size the control.**
4. **Type** Description: **and click outside the control.**
5. **Select the Description label control.**
6. **Select Cut from the Clipboard group on the Home tab of the Ribbon.**
7. **Select the Description text box control.**
8. **Select Paste from the Clipboard group on the Home tab of the Ribbon to attach the label control to the text-box control.**

Another way to attach a label to a control is to click the informational icon next to the label, shown in Figure 17.25. This informational icon lets you know that this label is unassociated with a control. Select the Associate Label with a Control command from the menu, and then select the control you want to associate the label with.

FIGURE 17.25

Associating a label with a control.

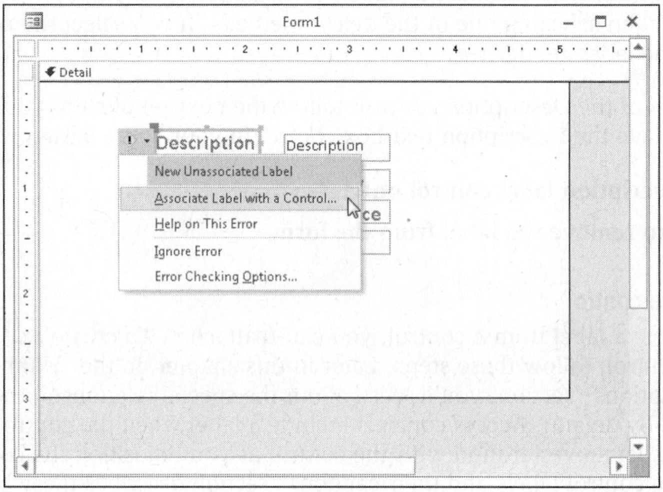

Introducing Properties

Properties are named attributes of controls, fields, or database objects that are used to modify the characteristics of a control, field, or object. Examples of these attributes are the size, color, appearance, or name of an object. A property can also modify the behavior of a control, determining, for example, whether the control is read-only or editable and visible or not visible.

Properties are used extensively in forms and reports to change the characteristics of controls. Each control on the form has properties. The form itself also has properties, as does each of its sections. The same is true for reports; the report itself has properties, as does each report section and individual control. The label control also has its own properties, even if it's attached to another control.

Everything that you do with the Ribbon commands — from moving and resizing controls to changing fonts and colors — can be done by setting properties. In fact, all these commands do is change properties of the selected controls.

Displaying the Property Sheet

Properties are displayed in a Property Sheet (sometimes called a Property window). To display the Property Sheet for the Description text box, follow these steps:

1. **Drag Description, Category, RetailPrice, and Cost from the Field List to the form's Design view.**
2. **Click the Description text box control to select it.**

3. **Click the Property Sheet command in the Tools group on the Design tab of the Ribbon, or press F4 to display the Property Sheet.** The screen should look like the one shown in Figure 17.26. In Figure 17.26, the Description text box control has been selected and the Format tab in the Property Sheet is being scrolled to find the margin properties associated with a text box.

FIGURE 17.26

Change an object's properties with the Property Sheet.

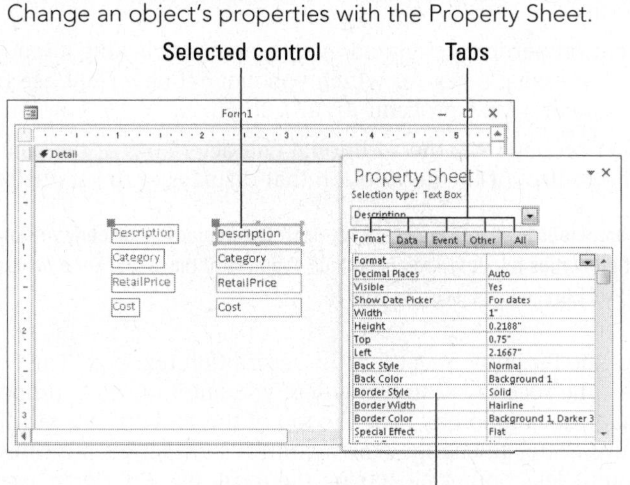

Because the Property Sheet is a window, it can be undocked, moved, and resized. It does not, however, have Maximize or Minimize buttons.

TIP

Double-click the title bar area of an undocked Property Sheet to return it to its most recent docked location.

There are several ways to display a control's Property Sheet if it isn't visible:

- Select a control and click the Property Sheet command in the Tools group on the Design tab of the Ribbon.
- Double-click the edge of any control.
- Right-click any control and select Properties from the pop-up menu.
- Press F4 while any control is selected.

Getting acquainted with the Property Sheet

With the Property Sheet displayed, click any control in Design view to display the properties for that control. Select multiple controls to display similar properties for the selected controls. The vertical scroll bar lets you move among various properties.

The Property Sheet has an All tab that lets you see all the properties for a control. Or you can choose another tab to limit the view to a specific group of properties. The specific tabs and groups of properties are as follows:

- **Format:** These properties determine how a label or value looks: font, size, color, special effects, borders, and scroll bars.
- **Data:** These properties affect how a value is displayed and the data source it's bound to: control source, input masks, validation, default value, and other data type properties.
- **Event:** Event properties are named events, such as clicking a mouse button, adding a record, pressing a key for which you can define a response (in the form of a call to a macro or a VBA procedure), and so on.
- **Other:** Other properties show additional characteristics of the control, such as the name of the control or the description that displays in the status bar.

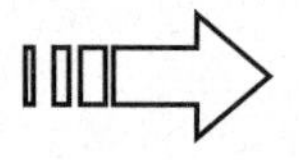

The number of properties available in Access has increased greatly since early versions of Access. The most important properties are described in various chapters of this book. For a discussion of Event properties and Event procedures, see Chapter 25.

Figure 17.26 shows the Property Sheet for the Description text box. The first column lists the property names; the second column is where you enter or select property settings or options. You can use the combo box near the top of the Property Sheet (displaying Description in Figure 17.26) to change which control's properties are shown. The combo box also allows you to select other objects on the form, like the Detail section, Form Header, or the Form itself.

Changing a control's property setting

There are many different methods for changing property settings, including the following:

- Enter or select the desired value in a Property Sheet.
- For some properties, double-clicking the property name in the Property Sheet cycles through all the acceptable values for the property.
- Change a property directly by changing the control itself, such as changing its size.
- Use inherited properties from the bound field or the control's default properties.
- Enter color selections for the control by using the Ribbon commands.
- Change label text style, size, color, and alignment by using the Ribbon commands.

You can change a control's properties by clicking a property and typing the desired value.

In Figure 17.27, you see a down arrow and a button with three dots to the right of the Control Source property entry area. Some properties display a drop-down arrow in the property entry area when you click in the area. The drop-down arrow tells you that Access has a list of values from which you can choose. If you click the down arrow in the Control Source property, you find that the drop-down list displays a list of all fields in the data source — tblProducts. Setting the Control Source property to a field in a table creates a bound control.

FIGURE 17.27

Setting a control's Control Source property.

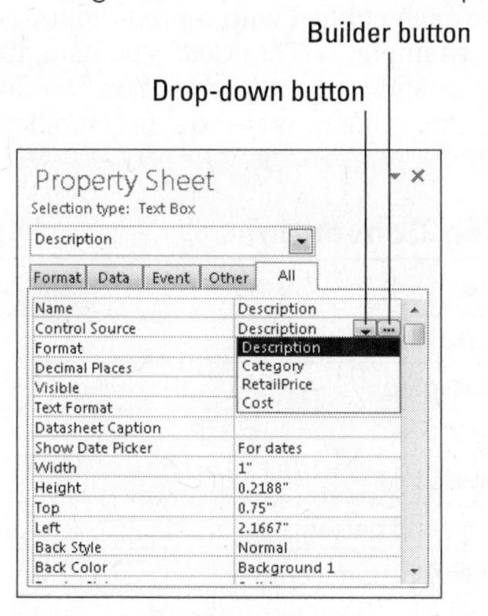

Some properties have a list of standard values such as Yes or No; others display varying lists of fields, forms, reports, or macros. The properties of each object are determined by the control itself and what the control is used for.

A nice feature in Access is the ability to cycle through property choices by repeatedly double-clicking the choice. For example, double-clicking the Display When property alternately selects Always, Print Only, and Screen Only.

The Builder button contains an ellipsis (...) and opens one of the many builders in Access — including the Macro Builder, the Expression Builder, and the Code Builder. When you open a builder and make some selections, the property is filled in for you. You'll learn about builders later in this book.

Each type of object has its own Property window and properties. These include the form itself, each of the form sections, and each of the form's controls. You display each of the Property windows by clicking the object first or by selecting the object from the Property Sheet's combo box. The Property window will instantly change to show the properties for the selected object.

Naming control labels and their captions

You might notice that each of the data fields has a label control and a text box control. Normally, the label's Caption property is the same as the text box's Name property. The text box's Name property is usually the same as the table's field name — shown in the Control Source property. Sometimes, the label's Caption is different because a value was entered into the Caption property for each field in the table.

When creating controls on a form, it's a good idea to use standard naming conventions when setting the control's Name property. Name each control with a prefix followed by a meaningful name that you'll recognize later (for example, txtTotalCost, cboState, lblTitle). Table 17.2 shows the naming conventions for form and report controls. You can find a very complete, well-established naming convention online at www.xoc.net/standards.

TABLE 17.2 Form/Report Control Naming Conventions

Prefix	Object
frb	Bound object frame
cht	Chart (graph)
chk	Check box
cbo	Combo box
cmd	Command button
ocx	ActiveX custom control
det	Detail (section)
gft[n]	Footer (group section)
fft	Form footer section
fhd	Form header section
ghd[n]	Header (group section)
hlk	Hyperlink
img	Image
lbl	Label
lin	Line
lst	List box
opt	Option button
grp	Option group
pge	Page (tab)
brk	Page break
pft	Page footer (section)
phd	Page header (section)

Prefix	Object
shp	Rectangle
rft	Report footer (section)
rhd	Report header (section)
sec	Section
sub	Subform/subreport
tab	Tab control
txt	Text box
tgl	Toggle button
fru	Unbound object frame

The properties displayed in Figure 17.27 are the specific properties for the Description text box. The first two properties, Name and Control Source, are set to Description.

The Name is simply the name of the field itself. When a control is bound to a field, Access automatically assigns the Name property to the bound field's name. Unbound controls are given names such as Field11 or Button13. However, you can give the control any name you want.

With bound controls, the Control Source property is the name of the table field to which the control is bound. In this example, Description refers to the field with the same name in tblProducts. An unbound control has no control source, whereas the control source of a calculated control is the actual expression for the calculation, as in the example `=[SalePrice] - [Cost]`.

Working with Data on Access Forms

IN THIS CHAPTER

Viewing and modifying data in Form view

Editing form data

Printing Access forms

Understanding form properties

Adding form headers and footers

Adjusting a form's layout

Adding calculated controls to a form

Converting a form to a report

In Chapter 17, you learned about the tools necessary to create and display a form — Design view, bound and unbound controls, the Field List, and the Controls group on the Ribbon. In this chapter, you learn how to work with data on the form, view and change the form's properties, and use Layout view.

An Access application's user interface is made up of forms. Forms display and change data, accept new data, and interact with the user. Forms convey a lot of the personality of an application, and a carefully designed user interface dramatically reduces the training required of new users.

Most often, the data displayed on Access forms is bound (either directly or indirectly) to Access tables. Changes made to a form's data affect the data stored in the underlying tables.

On the Web

In this chapter, you use tblProducts, tblSales, and tblContacts in the `Chapter18.accdb` database to provide the data necessary to create the examples.

Using Form View

Form view is where you actually view and modify data. The data in Form view is the same data shown in a table or query's Datasheet view, just presented a little differently. Form view presents the data in a user-friendly format, which you create and design.

For more information on working in Datasheet view, see Chapter 5.

To demonstrate the use of the Form view, follow these steps to create a new form based on tblProducts:

1. **Select tblProducts in the Navigation pane.**
2. **Select the Create tab on the Ribbon.**
3. **Click the Form command in the Form group.**
4. **Click the Form View button in the Views group of the Home tab to switch from Layout view to Form view.**

Figure 18.1 shows the Access window with the newly created form displayed in Form view. This view has many of the same elements as Datasheet view. At the top of the screen, you see the Access title bar, the Quick Access toolbar, and the Ribbon. The form in the center of the screen displays your data, one record at a time.

TIP

If the form contains more fields than can fit onscreen at one time, Access automatically displays a horizontal and/or vertical scroll bar that you can use to see the remainder of the data. You can also see the rest of the data by pressing the PgDn key. If you're at the bottom of a form, or the entire form fits on the screen without scrolling, and you press PgDn, you'll move to the next record.

The status bar at the bottom of the window displays the active field's Status Bar Text property that you defined when you created the table (or form). If no Status Bar Text exists for a field, Access displays "Form View" in the status bar. Generally, error messages and warnings appear in dialog boxes in the center of the screen (rather than in the status bar). The navigation controls and search box are found at the bottom of the form's window and the view shortcuts are found in the status bar. These features lets you move from record to record, quickly find data, or switch views.

FIGURE 18.1

A form in Form view.

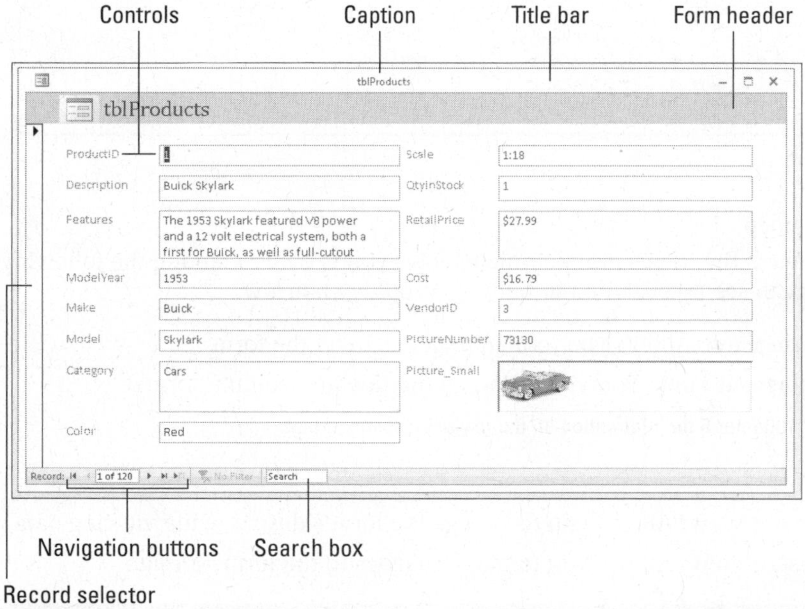

Controls
Caption
Title bar
Form header
Navigation buttons
Search box
Record selector

Looking at the Home tab of the Ribbon

The Home tab of the Ribbon tab (shown in Figure 18.2) provides a way to work with the data. The Home tab has some familiar objects on it, as well as some new ones. This section provides an overview of the Home tab. The individual commands are described in more detail later in this chapter.

NOTE

Keep in mind that the Ribbon and its controls are very context sensitive. Depending on your current task, one of more of the commands may be grayed out or not visible. Although this behavior can be confusing, Microsoft's intent is to simplify the Ribbon as much as possible to allow you to focus on the task at hand, and not have to deal with irrelevant commands as you work.

FIGURE 18.2

The Home tab of the Ribbon.

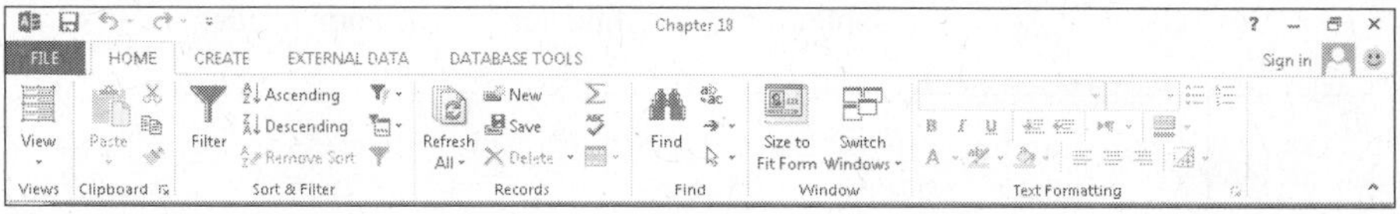

The Views group

At the far left is the Views group, which allows you to switch among the following views, which you can see by clicking the button's drop-down arrow.

- **Form view:** Allows you to manipulate data on the form
- **Datasheet view:** Shows the data in the row-and-column format

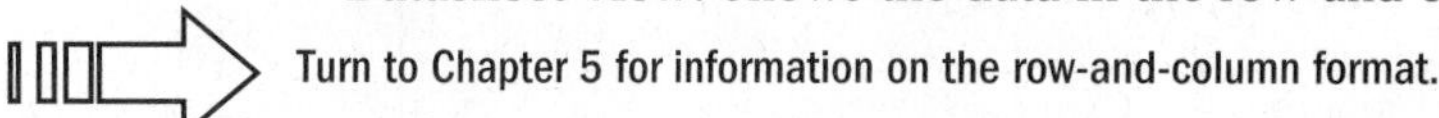

Turn to Chapter 5 for information on the row-and-column format.

- **Layout view:** Allows you to change the form's design while viewing data
- **Design view:** Allows you to make changes to the form's design

NOTE

All these commands may not be available on all forms. By setting the form's properties, you can limit which views are available. You'll learn more about form properties in the "Working with Form Properties" section, later in this chapter.

The Clipboard group

The Clipboard group contains the Cut, Copy, Paste, and Format Paint commands. These commands work like the same commands in other applications (like Word and Excel). The Clipboard is a resource provided by Windows and shared by virtually all Windows applications. Items you copy or cut from Excel, for example, can be pasted into Access if the context is appropriate. For example, you could copy a VBA procedure from an Excel worksheet and paste it into an Access VBA code module because the contexts are the same. But you can't copy an Excel spreadsheet and paste it into an Access form in Form view, because Form view has no way of working with an Excel spreadsheet.

TIP

Office has its own Clipboard that works with the Windows Clipboard by storing the copied content in additional, more Office-centric, formats. Copy an Excel range and the Office Clipboard will store that range in an Office format. Paste the range into a form in Design view, for instance, and an OLE control is automatically created.

The Paste command's drop-down arrow gives you three choices:

- **Paste:** Inserts whatever item has been copied to the Windows Clipboard into the current location in Access. Depending on the task you're working on, the pasted item might be plain text, a control, a table or form, or some other object.
- **Paste Special:** Gives you the option of pasting the contents of the Clipboard in different formats (text, CSV, records, and so on).
- **Paste Append:** Pastes the contents of the Clipboard as a new record — as long as a record with a similar structure was copied to the Clipboard. Obviously, Paste Append remains disabled for any operation that doesn't involve copying and pasting a database table record.

The other controls in the Clipboard group include

- **Cut:** Removes the item from its current place in the application and puts it onto the Windows Clipboard. The item is not destroyed by removing it from its current location, but it must be pasted before a second item is copied to the Clipboard — a cut or copied item overwrites whatever is on the Clipboard.
- **Copy:** Copies the item or object to the Clipboard. Copy can be applied to plain text, but it also applies to controls on a form or report (with the form or report in Design view, of course), database records, entire tables, queries, other database objects, and so on. The Windows Clipboard accepts virtually anything that is copied to it.
- **Format Painter:** The Format Painter (the icon that looks like a paint brush) is a special tool to use when working with Access forms and reports in Design view. The concept of Format Painter is quite simple: You copy the format of an item (such as its font settings) and paint the formatting onto another item or group of items.

TIP

The Format Painter is a huge timesaver when working with many controls on a form or report. Set a control (such as a text box) to look exactly the way you want all the text boxes to look, select the text box, and then click (or double-click) the Format Painter. Then, as you click on another text box, the first text box's formatting is applied to the second text box. Double-clicking the Format Painter "locks" it so that you can paint the format onto multiple items. (Click once on the Format Painter to unlock it.)

The Sort & Filter group

The Sort & Filter group lets you change the order of the records, and, based on your criteria, limit the records shown on the form.

The Records group

The Records group lets you save, delete, or add a new record to the form. It also contains commands to show totals, check spelling, freeze and hide columns, and change the row height and cell width while the form is displayed in Datasheet view.

The Find group

The Find group lets you find and replace data and go to specific records in the datasheet. Use the Select command to select a record or all records.

The Window group

The Window group contains two controls:

- **Size to Fit Form:** When you work with a form in Design view, Access "remembers" the size (height and width) of the form at the moment you save it. When working with the overlapping windows interface, a user may resize a form by dragging its borders to a new size and shape. The Size to Fit Form returns the form to the dimension set at design time.
- **Switch Windows:** Switch Windows provides a handy way to see all the objects (forms, reports, tables, and so on) that are currently open in the main Access windows. You can change to another object by selecting it from the drop-down list that appears when you click Switch Windows.

NOTE

When the current database's Document Window Options option is set to Tabbed Documents, the Home tab does not contain a Window group. With Tabbed Documents, all open Access objects are accessible through the tab interface, and the option to switch windows isn't necessary. To change the Document Window Options, choose File ⇨ Options and set the option in the Current Database area of the Access Options dialog box.

The Text Formatting group

The Text Formatting group lets you change the look of the datasheet in Datasheet view or Design view. Use these commands to change the font, size, bold, italic, color, and so on. Use the Align Left, Align Right, and Align Center commands to justify the data in the selected column. Click the Gridlines option to toggle gridlines on and off. Use Alternate Row Color to change the colors of alternating rows, or make them all the same. When modifying text in a Long Text field with the Text Format property set to Rich Text, you can use these commands to change the fonts, colors, and so on.

Navigating among fields

Navigating a form is nearly identical to moving around a datasheet. You can easily move around the form by clicking the control that you want and making changes or additions to your data. Because the form window displays only as many fields as can fit onscreen, you need to use various navigational aids to move within your form or between records.

Table 18.1 displays the navigational keys used to move between fields within a form.

TABLE 18.1 Navigating in a Form

Navigational Direction	Keystrokes
Next field	Tab, right-arrow (→) key, down-arrow (↓) key, or Enter
Previous field	Shift+Tab, left-arrow (←) key, or up-arrow (↑) key
First field of current record	Home
First field of first record	Ctrl+Home
Last field of current record	End
Last field of last record	Ctrl+End
Next page	PgDn or Next Record
Previous page	PgUp or Previous Record

Moving among records in a form

Although you generally use a form to display one record at a time, you still need to move between records. The easiest way to do this is to use the Navigation buttons, shown in Figure 18.3.

The Navigation buttons are the six controls located at the bottom-left corner of the Form window. The two leftmost controls move you to the first record and the previous record in the form. The three rightmost controls position you on the next record, last record, or new record in the form. If you know the record number (the row number of a specific record), you can click the Current Record box, enter a record number, and press Enter to go directly to that record.

FIGURE 18.3

The Navigation buttons of a form.

The record number displayed in the Navigation controls is just an indicator of the current record's position in the recordset and may change when you filter or sort the records. To the right of the record number is the total number of records in the current view. The record count may not be the same as the number of records in the underlying table or query. The record count changes when you filter the data on the form.

Changing Values in a Form

Earlier in this book, you learned datasheet techniques to add, change, and delete data within a table. These techniques are the same ones you use on an Access form. Table 18.2 summarizes these techniques.

TABLE 18.2 Editing Techniques

Editing Technique	Keystrokes
Move insertion point within a control	Press the right-arrow (→) and left-arrow (←) keys
Insert a value within a control	Select the insertion point and type new data
Select the entire contents of a control	Press F2
Replace an existing value with a new value	Select the entire field and enter a new value
Replace a value with value of the preceding field	Press Ctrl+' (single quotation mark)
Replace the current value with the default value	Press Ctrl+Alt+Spacebar
Insert the current date into a control	Press Ctrl+; (semicolon)
Insert the current time into a control	Press Ctrl+: (colon)
Insert a line break in a Text control	Press Ctrl+Enter
Insert a new record	Press Ctrl++ (plus sign)
Delete the current record	Press Ctrl+– (minus sign)
Save the current record	Press Shift+Enter or move to another record
Toggle values in a check box or option button	Spacebar
Undo a change to the current control	Press Esc or click the Undo button
Undo a change to the current record	Press Esc or click the Undo button a second time after you Undo the current control

NOTE

The right-arrow (→) and left-arrow (←) keys work differently in Navigation mode than they do in Edit mode. The F2 key switches between Navigation mode and Edit mode. The only visual cue for the mode that you're in is that the insertion point is displayed in Edit mode. The arrow keys navigate between controls in Navigation mode and are used to select text in Edit mode.

Knowing which controls you can't edit

Some controls, including the following, can't be edited:

- **Controls displaying AutoNumber fields:** Access maintains AutoNumber fields automatically, calculating the values as you create each new record.
- **Calculated controls:** Access may use calculated controls in forms or queries. Calculated values are not actually stored in your table.
- **Locked or disabled fields:** You can set certain form and control properties to prevent changes to the data.
- **Controls in multiuser locked records:** If another user locks the record, you can't edit any controls in that record.

Working with pictures and OLE objects

Object Linking and Embedding (OLE) objects are objects not part of an Access database. OLE objects commonly include pictures but may be any number of other data types, such as links to Word documents, Excel spreadsheets, and audio files. You can also include video files such as MPG or AVI files.

In Datasheet view, you can't view a picture or an OLE object without accessing the OLE server (such as Word, Excel, or the Windows Media Player). In Design view, however, you can size the OLE control area to be large enough to display a picture, chart, or other OLE objects in Form view. You can also size text-box controls on forms so that you can see the data within the field — you don't have to zoom in on the value, as you do with a datasheet field.

18

The Access OLE control supports many types of objects. As with a datasheet, you have two ways to enter OLE fields into a form:

- Copy the object (such as an MP3 file) to the Clipboard and paste it from the controls in the Clipboard group of the Ribbon.
- Right-click the OLE control and click Insert Object from the shortcut menu to display the Insert Object dialog box, shown in Figure 18.4. Use the Insert Object dialog box to add a new object to the OLE field, or add an object from an existing file. The Create from File option button adds a picture or other OLE object from an existing file.

When displaying a picture in an OLE control, set the Size Mode property to control how the image representing the OLE object is displayed. The settings for this property are

- **Clip:** Keeps the image at its original size and cuts off parts of the picture that don't fit in the control.
- **Zoom:** Fits the image in the control and keeps it in its original proportion, which may result in extra white space.
- **Stretch:** Sizes an image to fit exactly between the frame borders. The stretch setting may distort the picture.

FIGURE 18.4

The Insert Object dialog box.

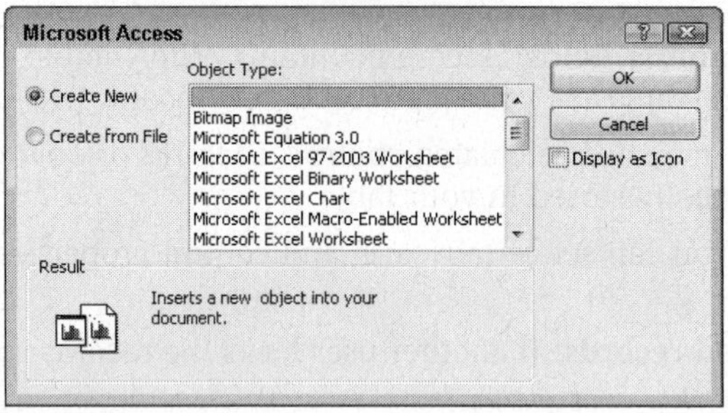

Entering data in the Long Text field

The Features field in the form shown in Figure 18.1 is a Long Text data type. This type of field contains up to 1GB of characters. The first three lines of data appear in the text box. When you click in this text box, a vertical scroll bar appears, allowing you to view all the data in the control.

Better yet, you can resize the control in the form's Design view if you want to make it larger to show more data. Another method for viewing more text in a Long Text field's text box, is to press Shift + F2 with the text box selected. A Zoom dialog box is displayed, as shown in Figure 18.5, allowing you to see more data. The text in the Zoom dialog box is fully editable. You can add new text or change text already in the control.

FIGURE 18.5

The Zoom dialog box.

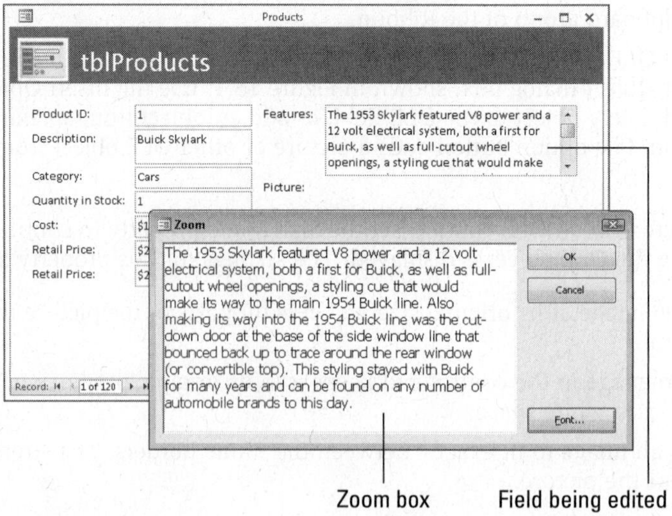

Entering data in the Date field

The SaleDate field in the frmSales_Layout form (shown in Figure 18.5) is a Date/Time data type. This field is formatted to accept and show date values. When you click in this text box, a Date Picker icon automatically appears next to it, as shown in Figure 18.6. Click the Date Picker to display a calendar from which you can choose a date.

FIGURE 18.6

Using the Date Picker control.

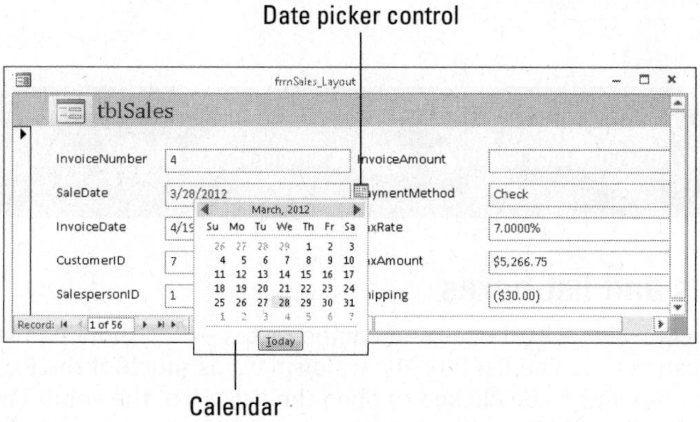

If the Date Picker doesn't appear, switch to Design view and change the control's Show Date Picker property to For Dates. Set the Show Date Picker property to Never if you don't want to use the Date Picker.

Using option groups

Option groups let you choose from a number of option buttons (sometimes called radio buttons). Option buttons let you select one value while deselecting all the other values. Option groups work best when you have a small number of mutually exclusive choices to select from. Figure 18.7 shows an option group next to the Follow-Up Date text box. Option groups also work with toggle buttons and check boxes.

The easiest and most efficient way to create option groups is with the Option Group Wizard. You can use it to create option groups with multiple option buttons, toggle buttons, or check boxes. When you're through, all your control's property settings are correctly set. To create an option group, switch to Design view and select the Option Group button from the Design tab's Controls group. Make sure the Use Control Wizards command is selected.

FIGURE 18.7

Using an option group to select a mutually exclusive value.

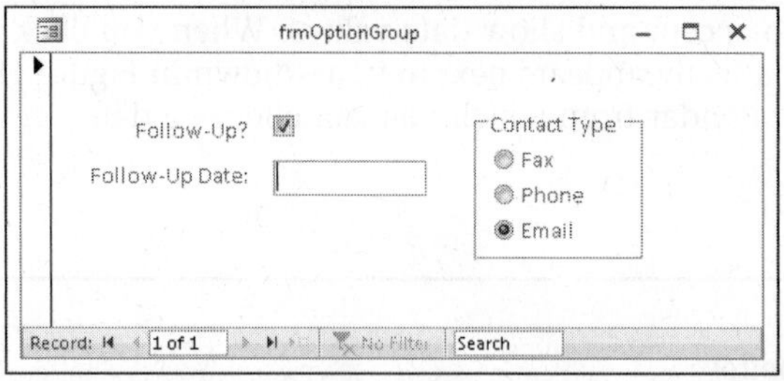

> **TIP**
>
> When creating an option group for a Yes/No field (which is actually stored as a number), set the Yes value to -1 and the No value to 0.

Using combo boxes and list boxes

Access has two types of controls — list boxes and combo boxes — for showing lists of data from which a user can select. The list box always displays as much of the list as possible, whereas the combo box has to be clicked to open the list. Also, the combo box enables you to enter a value that is not on the list and takes up less room on the form.

Because combo boxes are very efficient use of space on the surface of a form, you may want to use (for example) a combo box containing values from tblCustomers, as shown in Figure 18.8. The easiest way to do this is with the Combo Box Wizard. This wizard walks you through the steps of creating a combo box that looks up values in another table. To create a combo box, switch to Design view and select the Combo Box command from the Design tab's Controls group. Make sure the Use Control Wizards command is selected.

After you create the combo box, examine the Row Source Type, Row Source, Column Count, Column Heads, Column Widths, Bound Column, List Rows, and List Width properties. Once you become familiar with setting these properties, you can right-click a text box, choose Change To ⇨ Combo Box, and set the combo box's properties manually.

FIGURE 18.8

Using a combo box to select a value from a list.

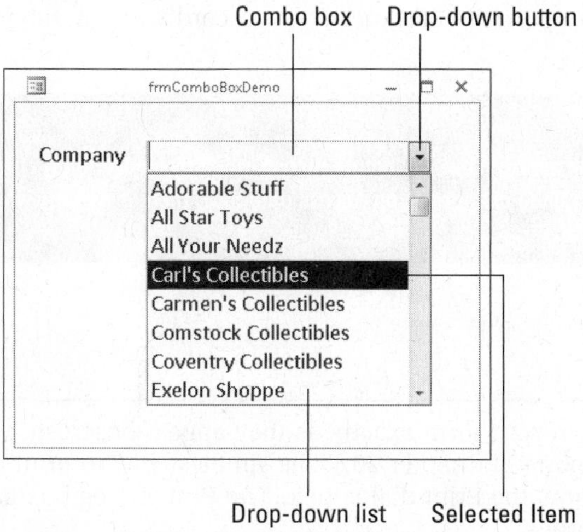

Combo box
Drop-down button
frmComboBoxDemo
Company
Adorable Stuff
All Star Toys
All Your Needz
Carl's Collectibles
Carmen's Collectibles
Comstock Collectibles
Coventry Collectibles
Exelon Shoppe
Drop-down list
Selected Item

Switching to Datasheet view

With a form open, switch to Datasheet view by using one of these methods:

- Click the Datasheet View command in the Home tab's Views group.
- Click the Datasheet View button in the View Shortcuts section at the bottom-right of the Access window.
- Right-click the form's title bar — or any blank area of the form — and choose Datasheet View from the pop-up menu.

The datasheet is displayed with the cursor on the same field and record that it occupied while in the form. Moving to another record and field and then redisplaying the form in Form view causes the form to appear with the cursor on the field occupied in Datasheet view.

To return to Form view — or any other view — select the desired view from the Views group, the View Shortcuts, or the pop-up menu.

NOTE

By default, a new form's Allow Datasheet View property is set to No. To be able to switch to Datasheet View, set this property to Yes.

Saving a record

Access automatically saves each record when you move off it. Pressing Shift + Enter or selecting Save from the Records group on the Ribbon saves a record without moving off it. Closing the form also saves a record.

CAUTION
Because Access automatically saves changes as soon as you move to another record, you may inadvertently change the data in the underlying tables. And, because you can't undo changes to an Access database, there is no easy way to revert to the record's previous state.

Printing a Form

You can print one or more records in your form exactly as they appear onscreen. (You learn how to produce formatted reports in Chapter 20.) The simplest way to print is to use the keyboard shortcut Ctrl + P to show the Print dialog box. The Print dialog box has several options to customize your printout.

- **Print Range:** Prints the entire form or only selected pages or records
- **Copies:** Determines the number of copies to be printed
- **Collate:** Determines whether copies are collated

You can also click the Properties button and set options for the selected printer or select a different printer. The Setup button allows you to set margins and print headings.

Printing a form is like printing anything else. Windows is a WYSIWYG ("What You See Is What You Get") environment, so what you see on the form is what you get in the printed hard copy. If you added page headers or page footers, they would be printed at the top or bottom of the page. The printout contains any formatting that you specified in the form (including lines, boxes, and shading) and converts colors to grayscale if you're using a black-and-white printer.

The printout includes as many pages as necessary to print all the data. If your form is wider than a single printer page, you need multiple pages to print your form. Access breaks up the printout as necessary to fit on each page.

The Print command under the File menu provides additional printing options:

- **Quick Print:** Prints the active form using the default printer with no opportunity to change any options
- **Print:** Shows the Print dialog box
- **Print Preview:** Shows what the printout will look like based on the current settings

TIP

In Print Preview mode, the Print Preview tab of the Ribbon is displayed (and all other tabs are hidden). Use the Ribbon commands to select different views, change print settings, and zoom in and out. Click Print to print the form to the printer. Click the Close Print Preview command on the right side of the Ribbon to return to the previous view.

Working with Form Properties

You use form properties to change the way the form is displayed and behaves. Property settings include the form's background color or picture, the form's width, and so on. Tables 18.3 through 18.5 cover some of the more important properties. Changing default properties is relatively easy: You select the property in the Property Sheet and type or select a new value.

ON THE WEB

The examples in this section use frmProducts from the `Chapter18.accdb` example database.

NOTE

The form selector is the area where the rulers meet while the form is in Design view. A small black square appears when the form is selected, as shown in Figure 18.9.

FIGURE 18.9

Using the form selector to display the form's Property Sheet.

Form selector

Property Sheet

To set a form's properties, you have to show the Property Sheet for the form. Switch to Design or Layout view and display the form's Property Sheet:

- Click the form selector so a small black square appears, and then click the Property Sheet button in the Design tab's Tools group.
- Click the Property Sheet command in the Design tab's Tools group, and then select Form from the drop-down at the top of the Property Sheet.
- Double-click the form selector.
- Right-click the form selector, either of the rulers, or in an empty area of the form and select Form Properties from the pop-up menu or by pressing F4 while the form is in Design or Layout view.

By default, the form's Property Sheet appears docked to the right side of the Access window. Because the Property Sheet is a window, it can be undocked, moved, and resized. In Figure 18.9, the Property Sheet has been undocked and dragged to a position overlying frmProducts. Notice that the Property Sheet window doesn't have Maximize or Minimize buttons, sorting capabilities, or searching capabilities.

Chapter 17 has more information on working with the Property Sheet.

Changing the title bar text with the Caption property

Normally, a form's title bar shows the name of the form after it's saved. The form's Caption property specifies the text displayed in the title bar when the form is in Form view. Follow these steps to change the title bar text:

1. **Click the form selector to make sure the form itself is selected.**
2. **Click the Property Sheet button in the Design tab's Tools group, or press F4 to open the Property Sheet.**
3. **Click the Caption property in the Property Sheet and enter** Products **in the property's text box, as shown in Figure 18.10.**
4. **Click any other property or press Enter to move off of the Caption property.**
5. **Switch to Form view to see the form's new title bar text.** The caption you enter in the form's properties overrides the name of the saved form.

NOTE

Obviously, using a property to change a form's caption is a trivial exercise. This exercise is designed simply to show you how easily you manipulate a form's appearance by changing its properties. As you work your way through this book, you'll encounter hundreds of examples of using the design tools provided by Access to enhance your application and make them more useful to your users.

FIGURE 18.10

Change the Caption property in the form's Property Sheet.

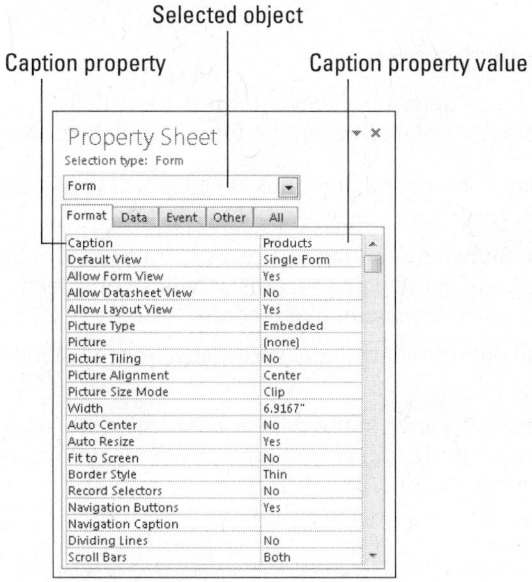

Selected object

Caption property

Caption property value

Property Sheet

Selection type: Form

Form

Format | Data | Event | Other | All

Caption	Products
Default View	Single Form
Allow Form View	Yes
Allow Datasheet View	No
Allow Layout View	Yes
Picture Type	Embedded
Picture	(none)
Picture Tiling	No
Picture Alignment	Center
Picture Size Mode	Clip
Width	6.9167"
Auto Center	No
Auto Resize	Yes
Fit to Screen	No
Border Style	Thin
Record Selectors	No
Navigation Buttons	Yes
Navigation Caption	
Dividing Lines	No
Scroll Bars	Both

18

Creating a bound form

A *bound form* is directly connected to a data source, such as a table or query. Bound forms usually automatically update data in the bound data source when the user moves to a new record in the form.

To create a bound form, you must specify a data source in the form's RecordSource property. In Figure 18.10, the Data tab of the Property Sheet contains the properties controlling what and how data is displayed on the form. Although not shown here, the Record Source property is at the very top of the Property Sheet's Data tab.

The data source can be one of three choices:

- **Table:** The name of a table in the current database file. The table can be a local table (stored in the database itself) or can be linked to another Access database or an external data source such as SQL Server.
- **Query:** The name of a query that selects data from one or more database tables.
- **SQL Statement:** A SQL `SELECT` statement that selects data from a table or query.

When a form is unbound — the Record Source property is blank and the data is obtained with VBA code — you can't have bound controls on the form. (Bound controls have their Control Source property set to a field in a table.)

For more information on adding bound controls with the Field List, see Chapter 17.

Specifying how to view the form

Access uses several properties to determine how a form is viewed. The Default View property determines how the data is displayed when the form is initially opened:

- **Single Form:** Displays one record at a time. Single Form is the default and displays one record per form page, regardless of the form's size.
- **Continuous Forms:** Shows more than one record at a time. Continuous Forms tells Access to display as many detail records as will fit onscreen. Figure 18.11 shows a continuous form displaying five records.
- **Datasheet:** Row and column view like a spreadsheet or the standard query Datasheet view.
- **Split Form:** Provides two views of the data at the same time, letting you select a record from a datasheet in the upper section and edit the information in the lower section of the split form.

FIGURE 18.11

The Continuous Forms setting of the Default view property shows multiple records at once.

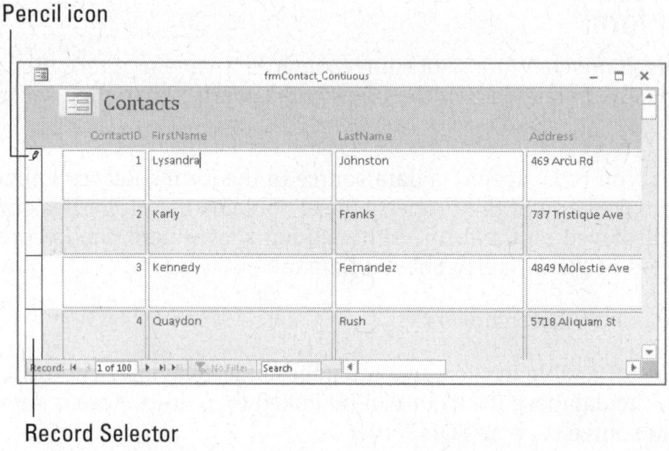

Pencil icon

Record Selector

There are three separate properties to allow the developer to determine if the user can change the default view. These include Allow Form View, Allow Datasheet View, and Allow Layout View. The default setting is Yes for Allow Form View and Allow Layout View and No for Allow Datasheet View. If you set the Allow Datasheet View property to Yes, the Datasheet view commands (in the Views group of the Ribbon, the form's View

Shortcuts, and right-click pop-up menu) will be available and the data can be viewed as a datasheet. If you set the Allow Form View property to No, the Form view commands won't be available.

Removing the Record Selector

The Record Selectors property determines whether the Record Selector (the vertical bar shown in Figure 18.11 on the left side of a form) is displayed. The Record Selector is important in multiple-record forms or datasheets because it points to the current record. A right arrow in the Record Selector indicates the current record, but changes to a pencil icon when the record is being edited. Though the Record Selector is important for datasheets, you probably won't want it for a single record form. To remove the Record Selector, change the form's Record Selectors property to No.

Looking at other form properties

Tables 18.3 through 18.5 list the most commonly used form properties and offers a brief description of each. You'll learn more about most of these properties when they're used in examples in this chapter and other chapters throughout this book.

TABLE 18.3 Form Format Properties

Property	Description	Options
Caption	Text that is displayed in the form's title bar	Up to 2,048 characters
Default View	Determines the initial view when the form is opened	Single Form: One record per page (default) Continuous Forms: As many records per page as will fit Datasheet: Row and column view Split Form: Displays a datasheet in the upper portion and a form in the lower portion
Allow Form View	Form view allowed	Yes/No
Allow Datasheet View	Datasheet view allowed	Yes/No
Allow Layout View	Layout view allowed	Yes/No

continued

TABLE 18.3 *(continued)*

Property	Description	Options
Scroll Bars	Determines whether any scroll bars are displayed	Neither: No scroll bars are displayed Horizontal Only: Displays only a horizontal scroll bar Vertical Only: Displays only a vertical scroll bar Both: Displays both horizontal and vertical scroll bars
Record Selectors	Determines whether the Record Selector is displayed	Yes/No
Navigation Buttons	Determines whether navigation buttons are visible	Yes/No
Dividing Lines	Determines whether lines between form sections are visible	Yes/No
Auto Resize	Automatically resizes form to display a complete record	Yes/No
Auto Center	Centers form onscreen when it's opened	Yes/No
Border Style	Determines the form's border style	None: No border or border elements (scroll bars, navigation buttons) Thin: Thin border, not resizable Sizable: Normal form settings Dialog: Thick border, title bar only, cannot be sized; use for dialog boxes
Control Box	Determines whether control menu (Restore, Move, and Size) is available	Yes/No
Min Max Buttons	Specifies whether the Min and Max buttons appear in the form's title bar	None: No buttons displayed in upper-right corner of form Min Enabled: Displays only Minimize button Max Enabled: Displays only Maximize button Both Enabled: Displays Minimize and Maximize buttons
Close Button	Determines whether to display Close button in upper-right corner and a close menu item on the control menu	Yes/No

Property	Description	Options
Width	Displays the value of the width of the form. Width can be entered or Access sets it as you adjust the width of the form.	A number from 0 to 22 inches (55.87 cm).
Picture	Displays the name of the file used as the background of the entire form	Any valid image file name.
Picture Type	Determines whether the form's picture is embedded or linked	Embedded: Picture is embedded in the form and becomes a part of the form Linked: Picture is linked to the form; Access stores the location of the picture and retrieves it every time the form is opened Shared: Picture is stored by Access and is available to other objects in the database
Picture Size Mode	Determines how the form's picture is displayed	Clip: Displays the picture at its actual size Stretch: Fits picture to form size (nonproportional) Zoom: Fits picture to form size (proportional), which may result in the picture not fitting in one dimension (height or width) Stretch Horizontal: Fits picture to width of form, ignoring height dimension Stretch Vertical: Fits picture to height of form, ignoring width dimension
Picture Alignment	Determines the form's picture alignment	Top Left: Displays the picture in the top-left corner of the form Top Right: Displays the picture in the top-right corner of the form Center (default): Centers the picture Bottom Left: Displays the picture in the bottom-left corner of the form Bottom Right: Displays the picture in the bottom-right corner of the form Form Center: Centers the picture horizontally and vertically
Picture Tiling	Used when you want to overlay multiple copies of a small bitmap (for example, a single brick can become a wall)	Yes/No

continued

TABLE 18.3 *(continued)*

Property	Description	Options
Grid X	Displays setting for number of points per inch when X grid is displayed	An number from 1 to 64
Grid Y	Displays setting for number of points per inch when Y grid is displayed	A number from 1 to 64
Layout for Print	Determines whether form uses screen fonts or printer fonts	Yes: Printer Fonts No: Screen Fonts
Sub-datasheet Height	Determines the height of a sub-datasheet when expanded	A number from 0 to 22 inches (55.87 cm).
Sub-datasheet Expanded	Determines the saved state of all sub-datasheets in a table or query	Yes: The saved state of sub-datasheets is expanded No: The saved state of sub-datasheets is closed
Palette Source	The palette for a form or report	(Default): Indicates the default Access color palette You can also specify other Windows palette files (PAL), ICO, BMP, DB, and WMF files.
Orientation	Determines view orientation	Right-to-Left: Appearance and functionality move from right to left Left-to-Right: Appearance and functionality move from left to right
Moveable	Determines whether the form can be moved	Yes/No
Split Form Orientation	Determines the look of a form in Split Form view	Datasheet on Top: Datasheet appears at the top of the form Datasheet on Bottom: Datasheet appears at the bottom of the form Datasheet on Left: Datasheet appears to the left of the form Datasheet on Right: Datasheet appears to the right of the form
Split Form Datasheet	Determines whether data can be edited in the data-sheet of a Split Form	Allow Edits: Edits are allowed Read Only: Data is read-only and cannot be changed

Property	Description	Options
Split Form Splitter Bar	Determines whether there's a splitter bar on a Split Form	Yes/No
Save Splitter Bar Position	Determines whether the position of the Splitter Bar should be saved	Yes/No
Split Form Size	Size of the form part of the Split Form	Auto to let Access size the form or a number to set the actual size
Split Form Printing	Determines which section of a Split Form to print	Form Only: Prints the form portion Datasheet Only: Prints the datasheet section
Navigation Caption	Overrides the word *Record* in the form's navigation buttons	Up to 255 characters

TABLE 18.4 Form Data Properties

Property	Description	Options
Record Source	Specifies the source of data displayed on the form	Unbound: Blank Bound: The name of a table, query, or a SQL statement
Filter	Used to specify a subset of records to be displayed when a filter is applied to a form; can be set in the form properties, with a macro, or through VBA	Any string that is a valid SQL `WHERE` clause without the `WHERE` keyword
Filter on Load	Applies filter at form/report startup	Yes/No
Order By	Specifies the field(s) used to order the data in the view	Any string that is a valid SQL `ORDER BY` clause with the `ORDER BY` keywords
Order By on Load	Applies sort at form/report startup	Yes/No
Allow Filters	Determines whether a user will be able to display a filtered form	Yes/No
Allow Edits	Determines whether a user will be able to edit data, making the form editable or read only	Yes/No
Allow Deletions	Determines whether a user will be able to delete records	Yes/No

continued

18

TABLE 18.4 *(continued)*

Property	Description	Options
Allow Additions	Determines whether a user will be able to add records	Yes/No
Data Entry	Determines whether form opens to a new blank record, not showing any saved records	Yes/No
Recordset Type	Used to determine whether multi-table forms can be updated	Dynaset: Only default table field controls can be edited Dynaset (Inconsistent Updates): All tables and fields are editable Snapshot: No fields are editable (same as read-only)
Record Locks	Used to determine default multiuser record locking on bound forms	No Locks: Locks record only as it's saved All Records: Locks entire form's records while using the form Edited Record: Locks only current record during an edit
Fetch Defaults	Determines whether default values should be retrieved.	Yes/No

TABLE 18.5 **Form "Other" Properties**

Property	Description	Option Definition
Pop Up	Form is a pop-up that floats above all other objects	Yes/No
Modal	User must close the form before doing anything else; disables other windows; when Pop Up set to Yes, Modal disables menus and toolbar, creating a dialog box	Yes/No
Cycle	Determines how Tab works in the last field of a record	All Records: Tabbing from the last field of a record moves to the next record Current Record: Tabbing from the last field of a record moves to the first field of that record Current Page: Tabbing from the last field of a record moves to the first field of the current page

Property	Description	Option Definition
Menu Bar	Used to specify an alternate menu bar	A valid menu bar name
Toolbar	Specifies the toolbar to use for the form	A valid toolbar name
Ribbon Name	Name of custom Ribbon to apply on open	A valid Ribbon name
Shortcut Menu	Determines whether shortcut (right-click) menus are available	Yes/No
Shortcut Menu Bar	Specifies the name of an alternate shortcut menu bar	A valid menu bar name
Fast Laser Printing	Prints rules instead of lines and rectangles	Yes/No
Help File	Name of compiled Help file to assign custom help to the form	N/A
Help Context Id	ID of context-sensitive entry point in the Help file to display	N/A
Tag	Allows you to store extra information about your form	N/A
Has Module	Allows you to show if your form has a class module; setting this property to `No` removes the VBA code module attached to the form	Yes/No
Use Default Paper Size	Uses the default paper size when printing	Yes/No

18

Adding a Form Header or Footer

Although the form's Detail section usually contains the majority of the controls that display data, there are other sections in a form that you can add:

- **Form header:** Displayed at the top of each page when viewed and at the top when the form is printed
- **Form footer:** Displayed at the bottom of each page when viewed and at the bottom of the form when the form is printed

The form header and footer remain on the screen, while any controls in the Detail section can scroll up and down.

You select the header and footer options in the Header/Footer group on the Design tab of the Ribbon (with the form open in Design view, of course).

Working with Section Properties

The Form properties discussed above apply to the entire form. Each section of the form has its own set of properties that effect the appearance and behavior of the section. The three form sections — Detail, Form Header, and Form Footer — share the same properties, with a few exceptions.

The Visible property

The Visible property is a Yes/No property that determines if the section is shown or hidden. All three sections' visible properties are set to Yes by default. The Detail section should remain visible in all but the strangest forms because that's where most of the controls will be. The Form Header and Form Footer sections may be hidden if they're not needed. Generally, the form header is used to display a title and possibly an image. Showing the form header on a continuous form helps the user stay oriented while using the form. The form footer is useful for showing summary or status information, like the current date and time.

The Height property

The Height property determines, in inches, how tall the section is. The most common way to change the Height property is to grab the edge of the section with your mouse and drag up or down to decrease or increase the height. With the Property Sheet visible, you can see the Height property value change when you drag the edge and release it in its new location. If you want a specific height, change the Height property value instead of dragging the edge of the section.

The Back Color property

The Back Color property determines the color of the background of the controls. You can change the Back Color property by using the drop-down control on the Property Sheet. Access give you many different built-in colors to choose from.

There's also a build button on the Property Sheet that displays the familiar color palette including Theme Colors and Standard Colors. The More Colors button at the bottom of the color palette allows you to specify any color you want.

Finally, you can type in the color you want. The Back Color property accepts a six-digit hexadecimal number. Hexadecimal consists of the numbers 0 through 9 and the letters A through F — 16 choices in all. You precede the hexadecimal number with a pound sign (#), such as #000000 for black and #FFFFFF for white. This method of setting Back Color is useful if you're trying to match a color and you already know that color's hexadecimal code.

Many developers prefer to keep the Back Color property of the Detail section to plain white. It's important that the color of the Detail section doesn't distract the user from the purpose of the form. However, a conservative Back Color can add depth to your form and provide a consistent brand across all your forms.

The Special Effect property

The Special Effect property can be set to Flat, Raised, or Sunken. Flat is the default value and Raised and Sunken provide a beveled effect at the edges of the section.

The Display When property

The Display When property can be set to Always, Screen Only, and Print Only. This allows you to hide or show a section when printing. You may want to show the Form Header and Form Footer sections on the screen, but only get the Detail section if the form is printed. You can achieve this by setting the Display When properties of the Form Header and Form Footer to Print Only and the by leaving the Detail section set to the default Always.

The printing properties

Most of the remaining section properties, such as Auto Height, Can Grow, and Can Shrink, are more applicable to reports than forms. They allow you to dynamically control the height of sections based on the data those sections contain. They have no effect on how your form displays on the screen and are rarely used.

Changing the Layout

In this section, you'll learn how to change a form's layout using Layout view. You'll add, move, and resize controls, as well as change a few other characteristics while viewing the form's data.

With a form open in Layout view, select the Arrange tab in the Form Design Tools area of the Ribbon. The Arrange tab includes controls for selecting a form's initial layout, including the default positions of controls on the form. The Arrange tab is highly context sensitive. The view you see in Figure 18.12 is the result of selecting a number of controls on the form. A somewhat different view may be seen if other controls or form sections (header, footer, and so on) are selected.

FIGURE 18.12

The Layout tab of the Ribbon for Layout view.

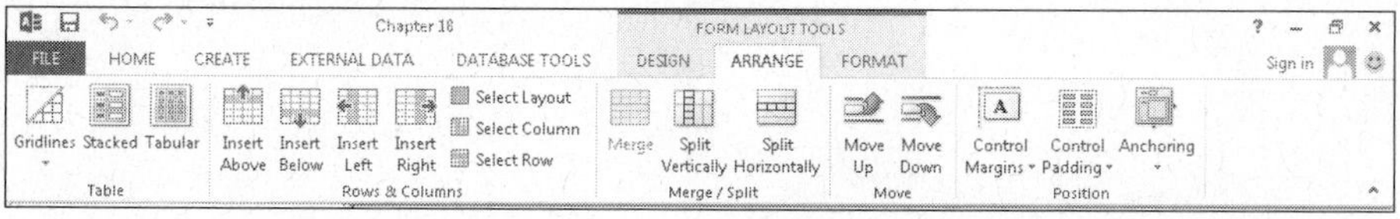

Changing a control's properties

In previous versions of Access, you had to make changes to the form in Design view. In Layout view, you can change these properties while looking at data instead of empty controls. Click the Property Sheet command in the Layout tab's Tools group to display the Property Sheet for the selected control.

For more information on changing control properties with the Property Sheet, see Chapter 17.

Setting the tab order

You may notice that when you use the Tab key to move from control to control, the cursor jumps around the screen. The route taken by the Tab key may seem strange, but that's the original order in which the controls were added to the form.

The tab order of the form is the order in which the focus moves from control to control as you press Tab. The form's default tab order is always the order in which the controls were added to the form. Moving controls around on the form means you'll need to change the form's tab order. Even though you may make heavy use of the mouse when designing your forms, most data-entry people use the keyboard, rather than the mouse, to move from control to control.

Select Tab Order from the Design tab's Tools group to display the Tab Order dialog box, shown in Figure 18.13. This dialog box shows the controls in the form arranged in the current tab order. Controls such as labels, lines, and other non-data controls don't appear in the Tab Order dialog box.

FIGURE 18.13

The Tab Order dialog box.

The Tab Order dialog box lets you select one or more rows at a time. Multiple contiguous rows are selected by clicking the first control and dragging to select multiple rows. After highlighting rows, the selected rows can be dragged to their new positions in the tab order.

The Tab Order dialog box has several buttons at the bottom. Auto Order places the controls in order from left to right and from top to bottom, according to their position in the form. This button is a good starting place when the tab order is very disorganized. The OK button applies the changes to the form, while the Cancel button closes the dialog box without changing the tab order.

Each control has two properties related to the Tab Order dialog box. The Tab Stop property determines whether pressing the Tab key lands you on the control. The default is Yes. Changing the Tab Stop property to No removes the control from the tab order. When you set the tab order, you're setting the Tab Index property values. Moving the fields around in the Tab Order dialog box changes the Tab Index properties of those (and other) controls.

Modifying the format of text in a control

To modify the formatting of text within a control, select the control by clicking it, and then select a formatting style to apply to the control. The Format tab of the Ribbon (shown in Figure 18.14) contains additional commands for changing the format of a control.

FIGURE 18.14

The Design tab of the Ribbon for Layout view.

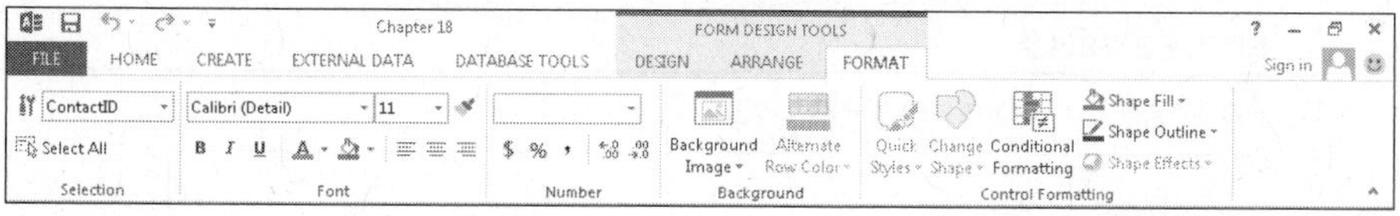

To change the fonts for the Category control, make sure you're in Layout view, and then follow these steps:

1. **Select the Category text box control by clicking on it.**
2. **Change the Font Size to 14, and then click the Bold button in the Format tab's Font group.** The control may not automatically resize when changing certain font properties. If you see only a portion of the text box, the control may require resizing to display all the text.

Using the Field List to add controls

The form's Field List displays a list of fields from the table or query on which the form is based. Use the Add Existing Fields button on the Design tab to open it if the Field List is not currently visible. Drag fields from the Field List to the form's surface to add bound controls to the form. Select and drag them one at a time, or select multiple fields by using the Ctrl key or Shift key. The Field List in Layout view works the same as the Field List in Design view, which is described in detail in Chapter 17.

Click the Add Existing Fields command in the Design tab's Controls group to display the Field List. By default, the Field List appears docked on the right of the Access window, shown in Figure 18.15. This window is movable and resizable and displays a vertical scroll bar if it contains more fields than can fit in the window.

Access adds a control that's appropriate for the data type of the bound field. For example, dragging a text field to the form's surface adds a text box, while an OLE data field adds a Bound OLE Object control.

To add fields from the Field List to a new form, follow these steps:

1. **Select tblProducts in the Navigation pane.**
2. **Select the Create tab on the Ribbon, and then select the Blank Form command in the Form group to open a new form in Layout view.** The new form is bound to tblProducts.
3. **If the Field List isn't displayed, select the Design tab of the Ribbon, and then select Add Existing Fields from the Tools group.**
4. **While holding down the Shift key, click the ProductID and Cost fields in the Field List.**
5. **Drag the selected fields to the form, as shown in Figure 18.15.**

FIGURE 18.15

Adding fields from the Field List in a form's Layout view.

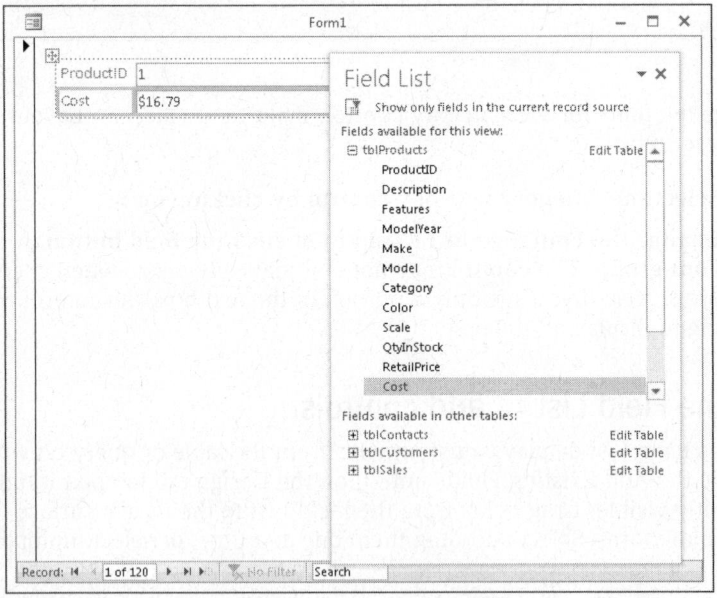

TIP

You can select noncontiguous fields in the list by clicking each field while holding down the Ctrl key. The selected fields can be dragged (as part of the group) to the form's design surface.

Converting a Form to a Report

To save a form as a report, open the form in Design view and choose File➪Save As. The entire form is saved as the report. If the form has headers or footers, these are used as the report's Header and Footer sections. If the form has page headers or page footers, these are used as the report's Page Header and Page Footer sections. You can now use the report in Design view, adding groups and other features without having to re-create general layout all over again. You'll learn more about reports in later chapters.

CHAPTER

19

Working with Form Controls

IN THIS CHAPTER

- Setting properties for Access forms and controls
- Creating a calculated control
- Using subforms in Access
- Reviewing basic techniques for designing forms
- Learning advanced Access forms techniques
- Working with tab controls in Access forms
- Collecting information with dialog boxes
- Creating a form from scratch

User interface is a term you hear frequently in discussions about computer software. In virtually all applications built with Microsoft Access, the user interface consists of a series of Access forms. If you intend to develop successful Access applications, you need to understand Access forms inside and out.

This chapter helps you improve your understanding of forms. First, we show you some common controls and their properties. These controls constitute the building blocks out of which forms are constructed. We also show you some powerful ways to take advantage of subforms. We devote one section of the chapter to presenting a grab bag of forms-related programming techniques that will help you create forms that elicit the best performance from Access and your computer. Then we present a step-by-step tutorial for creating a form from scratch.

On the Web

This chapter uses examples in the `Chapter19.accdb` database and other files available for download on this book's website.

Setting Control Properties

The building blocks of Access forms are known as *controls*. The Controls group on the Design tab of the Ribbon contains more than a dozen different types of controls from which you can build forms, including labels, text boxes, option groups, option buttons, toggle buttons, check boxes, combo boxes, list boxes, and other controls. This chapter doesn't discuss every type of Access form control in detail, but it does document the most commonly used controls found in Access applications.

Each control on an Access form has a set of properties that determines the control's appearance and behavior. In Design view, you manipulate a control's property settings through its Property Sheet. To display the Property Sheet, do one of the following:

- Right-click the object and select Properties from the pop-up menu.
- Select the object and click the Properties button on the Ribbon.
- Press F4 with the object selected.

Once the Property Sheet is open, clicking any other control in the form displays the selected control's property settings. Figure 19.1 shows the Property Sheet for the command button named cmdNew on the Customers form (frmCustomers) in the `Chapter19.accdb` application.

FIGURE 19.1

The Property Sheet for the cmdNew command button.

Property Sheet
Selection type: Command Button
cmdNew
Format | Data | Event | Other | All

Caption	&New
Picture Caption Arrangement	No Picture Caption
Visible	Yes
Picture Type	Embedded
Picture	(none)
Width	0.875"
Height	0.3333"
Top	0.1"
Left	4"
Back Style	Normal
Transparent	No
Use Theme	No
Back Color	#FFFFFF
Border Style	Transparent
Border Width	Hairline
Border Color	No Color
Hover Color	#FFFFFF
Pressed Color	#FFFFFF
Hover Fore Color	#FFFFFF
Pressed Fore Color	#FFFFFF
Font Name	Arial
Font Size	11
Alignment	Center
Font Weight	Bold
Font Underline	No
Font Italic	No
Fore Color	#000000

The form itself also has its own set of properties. If you display the Property Sheet in Design view before selecting a specific control, Access lists the form's properties in the Property Sheet, as indicated by the caption "Form" in the Property Sheet's title bar (see Figure 19.2). To display the form's properties in the Property Sheet after first displaying a control's properties, click a completely blank area in the form design window (outside the form's defined border).

FIGURE 19.2

The Property Sheet for the Customers form.

Property Sheet
Selection type: Form

Form

Format | Data | Event | Other | All

Caption	Customers
Default View	Single Form
Allow Form View	Yes
Allow Datasheet View	Yes
Allow Layout View	No
Picture Type	Embedded
Picture	(none)
Picture Tiling	No
Picture Alignment	Center
Picture Size Mode	Clip
Width	6.4375"
Auto Center	Yes
Auto Resize	Yes
Fit to Screen	No
Border Style	Thin
Record Selectors	No
Navigation Buttons	Yes
Navigation Caption	
Dividing Lines	No
Scroll Bars	Neither
Control Box	Yes
Close Button	Yes
Min Max Buttons	Both Enabled
Moveable	Yes
Split Form Size	Auto
Split Form Orientation	Datasheet on Top
Split Form Splitter Bar	Yes

19

Customizing default properties

Whenever you create a control from the Ribbon, the control is created with a default set of property values. This may seem obvious, but what you may not know is that you can set many of these default values yourself. For example, if you want all list boxes in your form to be flat rather than sunken, it's more efficient to change the default SpecialEffect property to Flat before you design the form, instead of changing the SpecialEffect property for every list box individually.

To set control defaults, select a tool in the toolbox and then set properties in the Property Sheet without adding the control to the form. Notice that the title in the Property Sheet is "Selection type: Default <ControlType>." As you set the control's properties, you're actually setting the default properties for that type of control for the current form. Instead of adding the control to the form, select another control (such as the Select control in the upper-right corner of the Controls group) to "lock down" the default settings. Then, when you reselect the control you want, you'll see that the control's default properties have been set the way you wanted. When you save the form, the property defaults you've set for the form's controls are saved along with the form.

In addition to saving you time while designing a form, customizing default properties can speed the saving and loading of forms. If most controls on the form use the default property settings, the saved form takes less space, saves faster, and subsequently loads faster when your application uses it (but doesn't save memory).

Looking at common controls and properties

In this section, we describe the most common controls needed to build an Access application and the properties that control their appearance and behavior. We don't list every control or property. But the controls and properties described here will give you a solid understanding of form development, and many of the properties are shared by other controls. Many properties work together to achieve a specific result and the Property Sheet lists these related properties together.

The Text Box control

The Text Box control is the workhorse of the controls when it comes to displaying data. The data in this control is always a String data type, even when it looks like a number or a date. The most important properties of the Text Box control determine how data is entered and displayed.

The Format property

The Format property determines the format of the data displayed. The choices available under Format are determined by the data type of the underlying field. For instance, Text Boxes bound to date fields show date formats and Text Boxes bound to numeric fields show numeric formats. Unbound Text Boxes show all available formats.

When an appropriate Format is set, the Decimal Places property controls how many digits are displayed to the right of the decimal point.

Properties that control appearance

The Back Style and Back Color properties control how the background of the Text Box is displayed. Setting Back Style to Transparent allows anything underneath the control to show through. A Back Style of Normal colors the background according to the Back Color property.

The Border Style, Border Width, and Special Effect properties control how the edges of the Text Box appear. Set Border Style to Transparent to show no border, or choose one of the other combinations of solid lines, dashes, and dots. When Border Style is set to something other than Transparent, the Border Width property controls the thickness of the border. There are several options for Special Effect that give your Text Boxes a more polished appearance.

Properties that control data appearance

Font Name and Font Size control the font of the data in the Text Box. While these properties can be set in the Property Sheet, they're more often set using the Format tab of the Ribbon.

The Text Align property can be set to General, Left, Center, Right, or Distribute. The General setting determines the most appropriate alignment for the data type displayed. Distribute attempts to fill the entire width of the Text Box with the data by increasing the spacing between characters.

The Font Underline and Font Italic properties are Yes/No options that determine if the data is shown with an underline or in an italicized font, respectively. Bold is the most common setting for the Font Weight property, but several other options allow a great deal of control of the boldness of the data.

The Fore Color property controls the color of the font. It's not simply a color name, however. It's actually a number that represents the value of the text color in the control. The easiest way to set this property is to use the Font Color command on the Format tab of the Ribbon.

Data entry properties

The Text Format property can be set to Plain Text or Rich Text. Rich Text is a format that allows you to apply formatting to the characters during data entry. When you enter data in a Text Box whose Text Format property is set to Rich Text, certain controls on the Ribbon are enabled that are disabled for Plan Text. The data is stored with HTML tags that define the formatting that is applied.

The Input Mask property can be set to limit how data is entered. There are several built-in input masks, such as Phone Number and Social Security Number, that can be used to encourage the user to enter data correctly. You can also create your own input masks — for instance, if your company uses part numbers that are in a well-defined format.

The Default Value property is used to populate a Text Box with a defined value when a new record is created. In addition to hard-coded values, calculations can be used to create a different Default Value depending on the values of other controls.

The Validation Rule and Validation Text properties can be used to ensure that the user has entered data that is appropriate for the Text Box. For instance, you may want to limit the entry of a date into a text box to only a certain range of dates. The Validation Rule property can be set to show a message when data falls outside a range. If a rule is broken, Validation Text is used to give the user more information about what is expected in the Text Box.

The Command Button control

Just as the Text Box control is the workhorse of data entry, the Command Button control is the go-to control for user actions. Command Buttons are primarily used to run macros or VBA code. Common actions associated with the Command Button are showing another form, navigating to another record, or automating another Office application.

Properties that control appearance

The Command Button control has many of the same appearance-related properties as the Text Box. And they work in much the same way. In addition, the Command Button has the Picture Type and Picture properties that allow you to specify an image to be shown as a button.

The Hover Color, Hover Fore Color, Pressed Color, and Pressed Fore Color properties control the appearance of the Command Button when the user hovers over it or when the user clicks it. They can be used to provide a visual indicator of where the user's mouse is and give the user confidence that the correct button was pressed.

Default action properties

The Default property is a Yes/No property. When set to Yes, the user can press Enter anywhere on the form and get the same effect as clicking the Command Button. A Command Button with the Default property set to Yes is a useful to tool to speed data entry on a form.

The Cancel property is also a Yes/No property and is closely related to the Default property. When set to Yes, the user can press Esc anywhere on the form and get the same effect as clicking the Command Button. Generally, a Command Button designated as Cancel should perform an action consistent with cancelling the current operation or closing the form.

TIP

Only one Command Button can be designated as Default. Similarly, only one Command Button can be designated as Cancel. Setting either of these properties to Yes will set the property for all other Command Buttons on the form to No.

The Combo Box and List Box controls

The Combo Box and List Box controls are used to display a list to the user to aid in data entry. The List Box control shows as many items as the size of the control will allow while the Combo Box must be clicked to display the list. The Combo Box gets its name because it is intended to be a combination of a Text Box and a List Box. The user can either enter text directly into the Text Box part of a Combo Box or select an item from the List Box portion. Properties unique to Combo Boxes and List Boxes control how the data is displayed and what actions the user can take with the list.

List content properties

The Row Source property determines what data is displayed in the list. The list data generally comes from a Table, Query, or SQL statement. It can also be a list of values typed directly into Row Source at design time or assigned at run time. The Row Source Type property determines what options are available for the Row Source property. When Row Source Type is set to Value List, the form designer can type a list of values into Row Source. When Row Source Type is set to Table/Query, Row Source can be a table name, query name, or SQL statement. The third option for Row Source Type is Field List. When Row Source Type is set to Field List, Row Source can be a table name, query name, or

SQL statement, just like when it's set to Table/Query. The difference is that the control will display a list of the field names rather than the values.

The Bound Column property determines the "value" of the control. List Boxes and Combo Boxes can show more than one column of data in the list. When two or more columns are shown, Bound Column determines which column's data will be stored in the field for bound controls or saved for later use in unbound controls.

List display properties

The Column Count property determines how many columns are displayed in the list. If this property's value does not equal the number of columns in the data (defined by the Row Source property) some data may not be shown or blank columns may be shown. The Column Widths property holds a semicolon-delimited list of values that represent the width of each column. If the property is left blank or if fewer column widths are entered than specified in Column Count, Access guesses how wide to make the unspecified columns. The Column Heads property is a Yes/No property that determines if column headings are displayed at the top of the list.

The List Rows property is a number that specifies how many list items to show. If there are more list items than specified in List Rows, a vertical scroll bar appears for the user to scroll down to see more list items. The List Width property determines how wide the list is. You can use a wide list with a relatively narrow Combo Box as a very efficient use of space on your form. List Rows and List Width are not properties associated with the List Box control. The List Box control shows as many rows as will fit and is as wide as the control itself.

List selection properties

For Combo Boxes, the Validation Rule, Validation Text, and Input mask properties work the same as they do for Text Boxes. List Boxes do not have these properties because the user is restricted to selecting items in the list.

The Limit to List property of the Combo Box control is a Yes/No property. A setting of Yes forces the user to type or select only values that are in the list, making the Combo Box work the same as a List Box. A setting of No allows the user to either select an item from the list or type an unlisted value in the Combo Box.

The Multi Select property that applies to List Boxes determines how the user can select multiple items in the List Box. A value of None means that multiple selection is not allowed. A value of Simple means that items are selected or deselected one at a time by clicking on them. A value of Extended means that items can be selected one at a time by holding down CTRL and clicking the time or in blocks by holding down SHIFT and clicking the last item in the block.

The Check Box and Toggle Button controls

The Check Box and Toggle Button controls are most commonly bound to Yes/No fields. A check mark in a Check Box control and a depressed Toggle Button are Yes values. An empty Check Box and a raised Toggle Button are No values. The Triple State property is unique to these two controls. When Triple State is set to Yes, the Check Box or Toggle Button can represent three values: Yes, No, and Null. Triple State is useful when you want to track whether the user has positively set the field to Yes or No.

The Option Group control

An Option Group isn't really a control at all. In fact, it's a group of separate, but related, controls. The group contains a Frame control and one or more Option Button controls. When you create an Option Group, you also have the option of using Check Box controls or Toggle Button controls instead of Option Buttons. Check Boxes and Toggle Buttons that are part of an Option Group behave differently than the same controls that are not part of an Option Group. Controls that are part of an Option Group are mutually exclusive; that is, selecting one of the controls automatically deselects the others in the group.

The Frame Control determines the value that is stored in the database. It has a Control Source property that identifies which field it's bound to. It also has a Default Value property that works the same as the Default Value property in other types of controls. The option controls within the Frame don't have these properties.

The option controls have an Option Value property. This property determines the actual value that is inherited by the Frame control and eventually stored in a field or saved for future use. By default, Access assigns the numbers 1, 2, 3, and so on to the option controls in the order in which they appear in the Frame.

TIP

You can change the Option Value property, but be careful not to assign the same number to two different controls.

The Web Browser control

The Web Browser control is a mini web browser on your form. You can use it to display data that the user completing the form might find useful, like weather or stock prices. The key property of the Web Browser control is the Control Source property. Control Source takes a formula of sorts. A proper Control Source value is an equal sign followed by the URL of a website enclosed in double quotes. For example, `="http://www.wiley.com"` will display that web page in the Web Browser control. Generally, the Control Source property is changed with VBA based on other data entered in the form.

Creating a Calculated Control

Unbound controls may use an expression as their Control Source property. As the form loads, Access evaluates the expression and populates the control with the value returned by the expression. The following example demonstrates creating an unbound calculated control:

1. **Select tblProducts in the Navigation pane.**
2. **Select the Create tab of the Ribbon, and then click the Blank Form command in the Form group.** A new form appears in Layout view.
3. **Drag Cost and RetailPrice from the Field List onto the form's surface.**
4. **Switch the form to Design view.**
5. **Click Text Box in the Controls group, and draw a new text box on the form.**
6. **Set the Name property to txtCalculatedProfit and set its Control Source property to: = [RetailPrice]-[Cost].**
7. **Change the Format property to Currency and its Decimal Places to Auto.**
8. **Change the label's Caption property to Net Profit:.**
9. **Switch to Form view to test the expression.** Your screen should look like Figure 19.3. txtCalculatedProfit shows the difference between the RetailPrice and Cost.

FIGURE 19.3

Creating a calculated control.

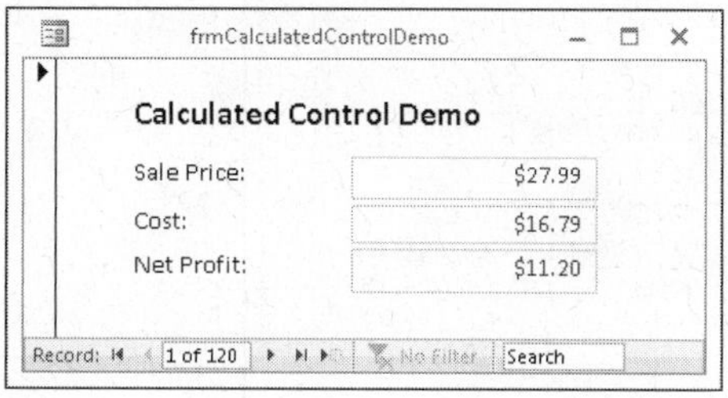

Working with Subforms

Subforms are indispensable for displaying information from two different tables or queries on the screen together. Typically, subforms are used where the main form's record source has a one-to-many relationship with the subform's record source. Many records in the subform are associated with one record in the main form.

Access uses the LinkMasterFields and LinkChildFields properties of the subform control to choose the records in the subform that are related to each record in the main form. Whenever a value in the main form's link field changes, Access automatically requeries the subform.

When creating a subform, you might want to display subform aggregate information in the master form. For example, you might want to display the count of the records in the subform somewhere on your main form. For an example of this technique, see the txtItemCount control in frmCustomerSales in `Chapter19.accdb`. In this case, the Control Source expression in the txtItemCount control is

```
="(" & [subfPurchases].[Form]![txtItemCount] & " items)"
```

(Note that the equal sign needs to be included.) The result of this expression is shown in Figure 19.4.

FIGURE 19.4

Aggregate data from a subform can be displayed on the main form.

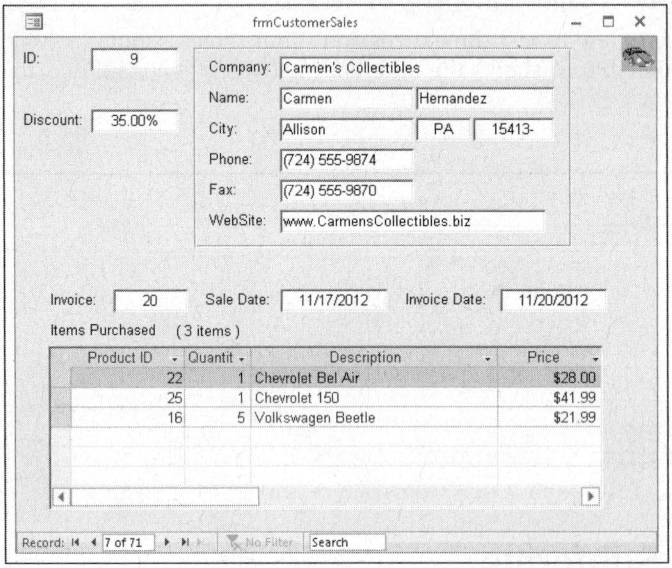

Before you can put aggregate data in the master form, its value must be found in the subform. Place a text box wherever you want in the subform, and set its Visible property to No (False) so that it's hidden. Put an aggregate expression, such as = Count([ProductID]), into the Control Source property of the hidden control.

In the main form, insert a new text box with Control Source set to the following value:

```
=[Subform1].Form![Name-of-Aggregate-Control]
```

where *Subform1* is the name of the control on the main form that contains the embedded subform and *Name-of-Aggregate-Control* is the name of the control on the subform that contains the aggregate data. The name of the control, Subform1 in this example, is not necessarily the name of the Form object that the control contains. When you add `.Form` to the name of the control, you refer to the underlying form and you don't need to know its object name.

The control on the main form updates each time you change its value in the subform.

Form Design Tips

Following is a grab bag of form design tips that you might find handy. We hope they inspire you to come up with many more on your own!

Using the Tab Stop property

From time to time, you might place a control on a form that is intended to trigger a fairly drastic result, such as deleting a record, or printing a long report. If you want to reduce the risk that the user might activate this control by accident, you might want to make use of the Tab Stop property, which specifies whether you can use the Tab key to move the focus to the control.

For example, suppose you've placed a command button named cmdDelete on a form that deletes the current record. You don't want the user to click this button by mistake. Modify the Tab Stop property of cmdDelete to No to remove the button from the form's tab order (the default is Yes). A user will have to explicitly click the button to activate it, and the user won't be able to accidentally choose it while entering data.

Tallying check boxes

If you ever need to count the number of True values in a Check Box control, consider using the following expression:

```
Sum(Abs([CheckBoxControl]))
```

`Abs` converts every -1 to `1`, and the `Sum` function adds them up. To count False values, use the following expression:

```
Sum([CheckBoxControl] + 1)
```

Each True value (`-1`) is converted to `0` and each False value (`0`) is converted to `1` before being summed.

Using SQL for a faster refresh

You can generate faster combo box refreshes on a form by making the control's row source a SQL statement instead of a query name. Complete the following steps:

1. **Select the combo box and show the Property Sheet.**
2. **Click the build button next to the control's Row Source property.**

3. **Use the query builder to construct the query for the combo box's rows.**
4. **Select Datasheet from the View drop-down to make sure the proper data is returned**

When you close the query builder, the SQL statement from the query you just build is inserted into the Row Source property.

Setting up combo boxes and list boxes

Combo boxes and list boxes are powerful tools in your form-building toolbox, but they can be complicated to set up. When you build combo boxes and list boxes, it's important to keep in mind the distinction between Control Source (the table or query field to and from which the control saves and loads data) and Row Source (the source of the data displayed in the list). Because combo and list boxes support multiple columns, they allow you to easily relate data from another table without basing your form on a query that joins the tables. This technique, which involves a bound Combo Box or List Box control that stores an ID number but displays names in a list, is used in the Organization combo box in the form named frmContacts_Northwind in `Chapter19.accdb`, as well as in several of the forms found in the Northwind sample database.

For example, suppose you're creating a form to display information about your clients and customers (your "contacts"), and you want to identify the organization with which these contacts are associated. In a well-designed database, you store only an organization ID number with each contact record, while you store the organization's name and other information in a separate table. You want your form to include a combo box that displays organization names and addresses in the list but stores organization ID numbers in the field. (For an example of this technique, see frmContacts_Northwind in `Chapter19.accdb`.)

To accomplish your design goal, create a multiple-column combo box. Set the Control Source to the OrgID field (the field in the Contacts table that contains the organization ID number for each contact person). Set the Row Source Type property of the combo box to Table/Query. You could base the list on a table, but you want the list of names to be sorted; instead, set the Row Source property to a query that includes OrgID numbers in the first field, and organization names sorted ascending in the second field. The best way to do this is using the Query Builder for the Row Source property to create a SQL statement; alternatively, you can create and save a query to provide the list. In frmContacts_Northwind example (the Organization combo box), the Row Source query is as follows:

```
SELECT Organizations.OrgID, Organizations.Name,
Organizations.AddressLine1, Organizations.AddressLine2,
Organizations.City, Organizations.State,
Organizations.ZipCode, Organizations.Country
FROM Organizations ORDER BY Organizations.Name
```

Because you're interested in seeing all this data listed in the combo box, set the ColumnCount property to 8. You hide the OrgID column in a minute, but you need it in the combo box Row Source because it contains the data that's saved by the control when a row is selected by the user. This column is identified by the combo box's BoundColumn property (set to 1 by default). The bound column containing ID numbers doesn't have to be visible to the user. The ColumnWidths property contains a semicolon-separated list of visible column widths for the columns in the drop-down list. Access uses default algorithms to determine the widths of any columns for which you don't explicitly choose a width. If you choose a width of 0 for any column, that column is effectively hidden from the user on the screen, but it isn't hidden from the rest of your forms, VBA code, or macros. In this case, you set the property to the following:

```
0";1.4";1.2";0.7";0.7";0.3;0.5";0.3"
```

This indicates to Access that you want the first column to be invisible and sets explicit column widths for the other columns.

The second column — in this case, the organization name — is the one against which the user's text input is matched. The first visible column in the combo box is always used for this purpose. Figure 19.5 shows the resulting drop-down list. Although this is a rather extreme example of loading a combo box with data, it effectively illustrates the power of the Access Combo Box control.

FIGURE 19.5

The drop-down list for the Organizations combo box.

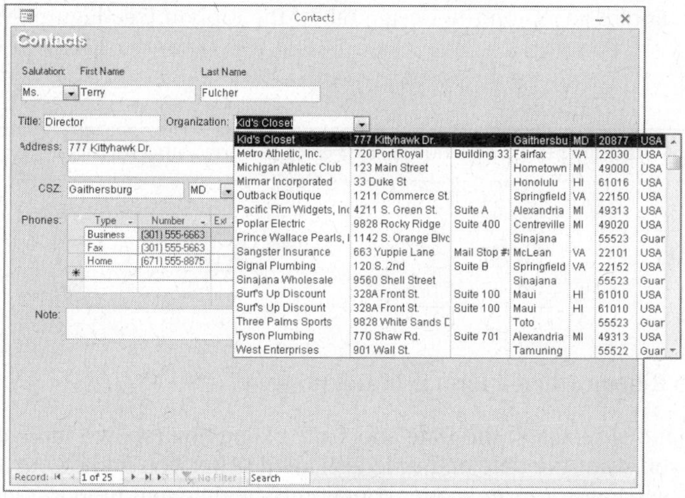

When working with combo boxes, if you set the Limit to List property to Yes, the user is required to choose from only the entries in the drop-down list. You can then construct an event procedure for the control's NotInList event to handle what should happen if a user enters a value not in the list. You might want to open a form into which the user can enter new information; or perhaps you want to display a message box that instructs the user what procedure to follow to add data.

The NotInList event is discussed in more detail in Chapter 25.

Tackling Advanced Forms Techniques

Access contains many powerful and exciting features in its forms design and user interface capabilities. As you well know, the forms in your applications are the main component of the user interface. To a large extent, a user's perception of an application's ease of use and strength is determined by the attractiveness and effectiveness of its user interface. You'll be pleased to know that Microsoft has provided Access forms with significant capabilities to control the user interface. Many of these features have been in Access for a very long time but haven't been discovered by many developers.

Using the Page Number and Date/Time controls

Very often, forms include the current date and time. Many developers add this information to a form or report with an unbound text box, and `Date()` function to return this information to the unbound text box. Access simplifies this process with the Date and Time commands on the Header/Footer group on the Design tab of the Ribbon (see Figure 19.6).

FIGURE 19.6

These commands simplify adding the page number or date to forms and reports.

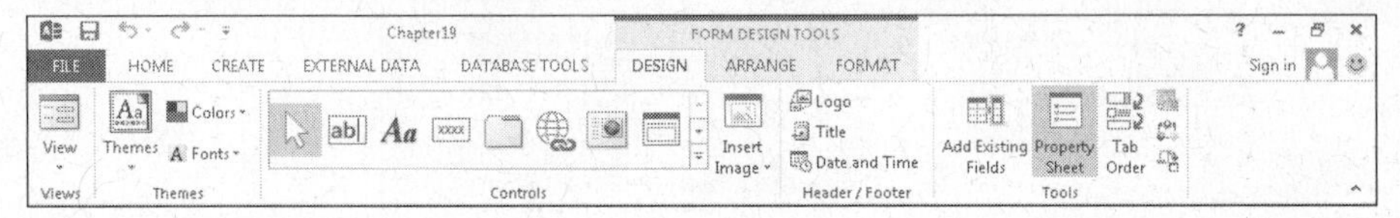

Figure 19.6 shows the Ribbon when a form is in Design view.

When the date command is selected, the Date and Time dialog box (shown in Figure 19.7) appears, asking how you want the date and time formatted. After you make your selections and click OK, Access adds a form header containing the date and time formatted as you requested. The date and time shown in the header reflects when the form was opened, not the necessarily the current time.

FIGURE 19.7

Tell Access how you want the date to appear.

The Header/Footer group includes other commands for adding a logo (virtually any image file) and a title to the form header area. Using the Header/Footer controls in an application gives all the forms a consistent appearance (see Figure 19.8, which is frmDialog in the sample database).

FIGURE 19.8

The header and footer controls provide a consistent look to your Access forms.

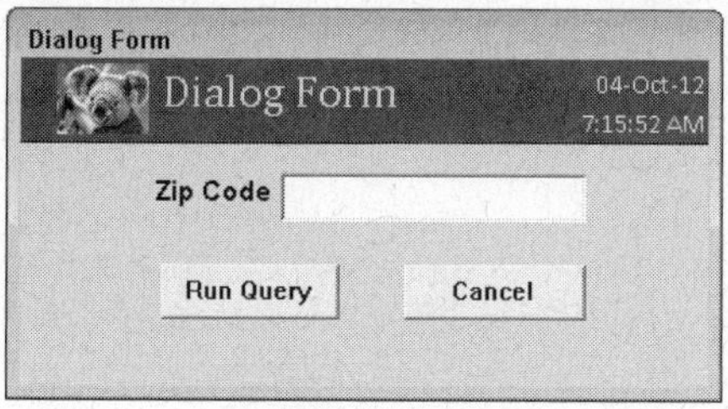

Using the Image control

A subtle and often overlooked performance issue in Access applications occurs when static images are added to forms. Images are often added to Access forms as OLE objects, which means that a certain amount of memory and disk space is required to maintain the image's connection to its parent application. This overhead is used even when the image is a company logo or other graphic that will not be changed or edited at runtime.

Access simplifies this process and provides a great deal more flexibility with the Image control. The Image control places an image frame onto a form or report but doesn't burden the image object with the overhead associated with OLE objects. The Image control accepts virtually any type of image data type recognized by Windows (BMP, PCX, ICO, DIB, GIF, WMF, JPG, PNG, TIF, and so on), and enables you to specify the path to the image file at runtime in its Picture property. The Image control also accepts image data stored in an Access table, although it doesn't provide the flexibility of in-place editing.

Morphing a control

Surely one of the most frustrating problems when building Access forms is the need to specify the control type as a control is added to a form. For example, consider the issues involved when you add a list box to an Access form, specify the Control Source, Row Source Type, Row Source, and other properties and then discover there's not enough room on the form for the list box. In this case, it seems the only solution is to remove the list box, add a combo box, and reset all the properties, even though the properties for the combo box are identical for the list box you just removed.

In Access, you can change a control to any other compatible type (a process sometimes called *morphing* the control). For example, a text box can be changed to a label, list box, or combo box. Simply right-click the control and select the Change To command from the shortcut menu to see the options. Figure 19.9 shows the options for changing a Text Box control.

FIGURE 19.9

Access lets you change the type of a control without losing the properties you've already set.

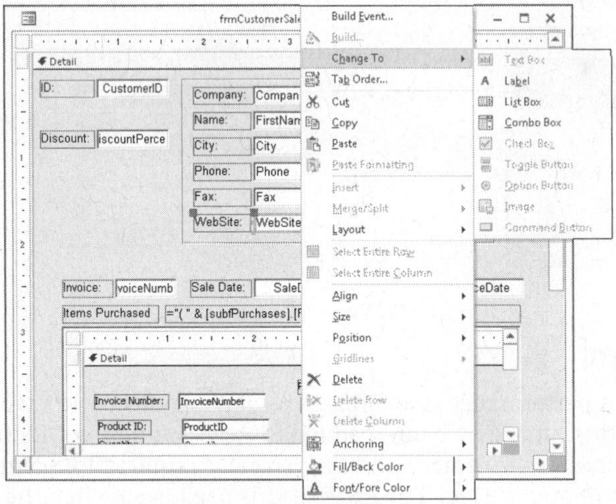

The choices you see in the shortcut menu are specific for the type of control you're changing. For example, an option button can be changed to a check box or toggle button, but not to a text box.

Using the Format Painter

Access includes a Format Painter that functions much like the same feature in Word. When creating a form, you set the appearance of a control (its border, font, special effects, like sunken or raised) and then click the Format Painter button on the Font group on the Design tab of the Ribbon to copy the properties to a special internal buffer. When you click another control of the same type, the appearance characteristics of the selected control are transferred to the second control. In Figure 19.10, the format properties of one text box are about to be "painted" onto the City text box. (The little paint brush adjacent to the mouse pointer tells you that you're in Paint mode.)

FIGURE 19.10

The Format Painter makes it easy to "paint" the appearance of a control onto other controls on a form.

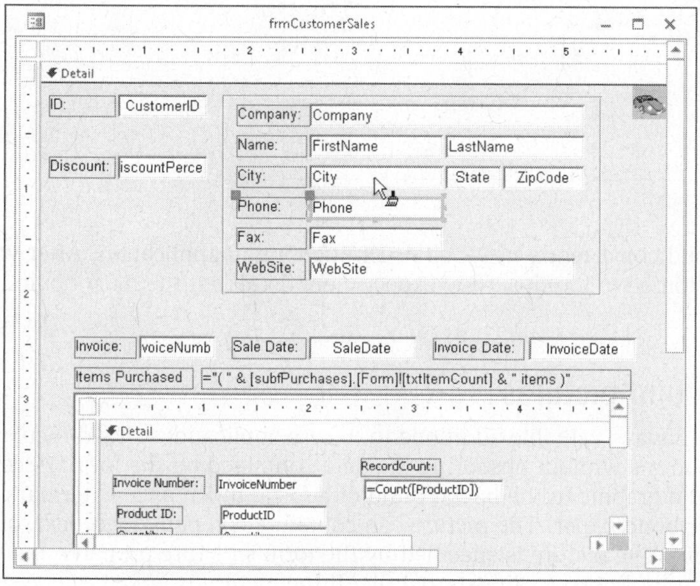

You can lock the Format Painter by double-clicking its button on the Ribbon. Note that not all properties are painted onto the second control. The size, position, and data properties of the control are not affected by the Format Painter. Only the most basic text properties are influenced by the Format Painter.

Offering more end-user help

Beginning with Office 4.x all Microsoft products have featured tooltip help — those little notes that appear when you hold the mouse cursor over a control or button. (Microsoft calls these prompts *control tip help*.)

You add tooltips to Access forms by adding the help text to the control's ControlTip Text property (see Figure 19.11). By default, the text in a tooltip doesn't wrap, but you can add a new line character by pressing Ctrl + Enter in the ControlTip Text property wherever you want the break to appear.

FIGURE 19.11

Tooltips help make your applications easier to use.

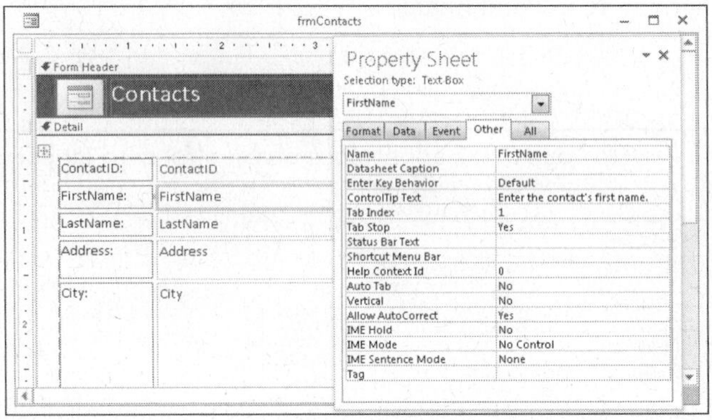

In general, you should consistently use tooltips throughout an application. After your users become accustomed to tooltips, they expect them on all but the most obvious controls.

Adding background pictures

Attractive forms are always valuable additions to Access applications. It's difficult to add color or graphics to forms without obscuring the data contained on the form. Access makes it easy to add a graphic to the background of a form, much as a watermark might appear on expensive bond paper. The picture can contain a company logo, text, or any other graphic element. The picture is specified by the form's Picture property and can be embedded in the form or linked to an external file. If the picture is linked, the graphic displayed on the form changes anytime the external file is edited.

The picture can also be positioned at any of the form's four corners or centered in the middle of the form. Although the picture can be clipped, stretched, or zoomed to fit the dimensions of the form, you can't modify the picture to make it smaller (other than editing the image file, of course). Figure 19.12 shows a small background picture of an automobile positioned in the upper-right corner of frmCustomerSales.

You can even make controls on a form transparent so that the form's background picture shows through the controls (see Figure 19.13). In this case (frmEmployees_Background), the Back Style property of each label control is set to Transparent, letting the form's background picture show through.

FIGURE 19.12

A small BMP file has been added to frmCustomerSales as the Picture property.

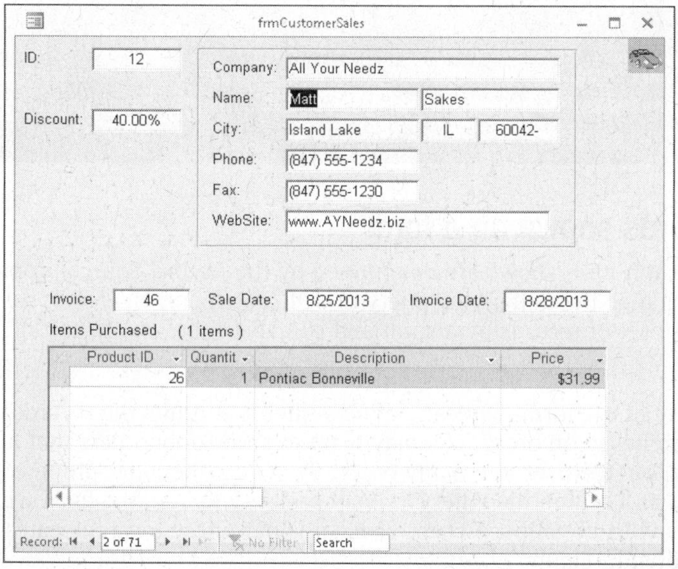

frmCustomerSales

ID: 12

Discount: 40.00%

Company: All Your Needz

Name: Matt Sakes

City: Island Lake IL 60042-

Phone: (847) 555-1234

Fax: (847) 555-1230

WebSite: www.AYNeedz.biz

Invoice: 46 Sale Date: 8/25/2013 Invoice Date: 8/28/2013

Items Purchased (1 items)

Product ID	Quantit	Description	Price
26	1	Pontiac Bonneville	$31.99

Record: 2 of 71 No Filter Search

FIGURE 19.13

Transparent controls allow the background picture to show through.

Employees

Employees

ID: Title: First Name: Middle Name: Last Name: Nickname:

1 Account Executi Samuel S. Pate Sam

Address: 411 S. Green St. Suite A

City: Alexandria

State: MI ZipCode: 49313

Country: USA

HireDate: 9/30/2011 Salary: $45,900.00

Phones: (3 numbers)

Type	Number	Ext	DialCode
Business	(616) 249-3344		1
Fax	(616) 531-1625		1
Home	(616) 534-4998		1

Note: Sam is the senior sales representative in the region.
His territory includes all northeastern states from New York to Maine, as well as Ohio and

Record: 1 of 5 No Filter Search

It's easy to overdo the background picture added to Access forms, but, when carefully used, background pictures can make forms easier for users to understand.

CAUTION

Background pictures added to a form noticeably slow down the form's appearance on the screen. Generally speaking, you should use a background picture only when the benefit provided by the picture outweighs the unavoidable performance degradation caused by the picture's presence.

Limiting the records shown on a form

Usually, the records that a form shows are determined by the Record Source property. To show fewer records, change the underlying query or SQL statement. However, sometimes you want to show a subset of records by default and still allow the user to see all the records if she chooses.

With the Filter property of the form, you can define a filter that limits the records shown. For example, on a form based on order, you may want to show only orders that haven't shipped yet, but still allow the user to see any order. By setting the Filter property to [Shipped Date] Is Null and setting the Filter On Load property to Yes, the form will open filtered only to records with no Shipped Date. The status bar of the form indicates that a filter is applied, as shown in Figure 19.14.

FIGURE 19.14

The status bar indicates that the form has a filter applied.

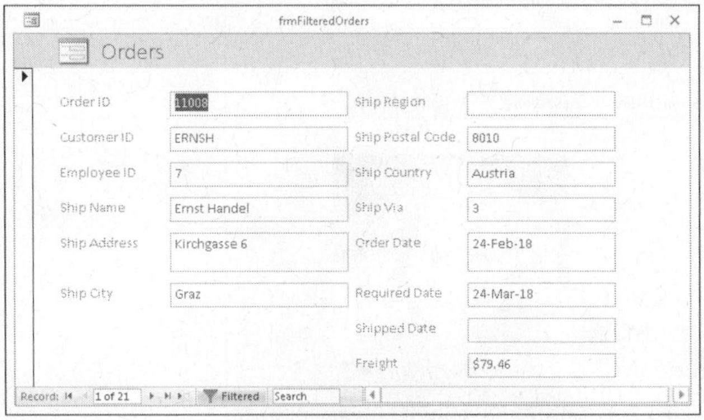

The user can click the Filtered button on the status bar to remove the filter and see all records. The button caption will change to Unfiltered. Another click of the button reapplies the filter.

Using the Tab Control

A tab control provides several pages, each accessed through a tab at the top, bottom, or side of the dialog box. Figure 19.15 shows frmCustomers, a perfect example of a tabbed Access form. frmCustomers contains a tab control with three pages, allowing the form to contain many more controls than possible without the tab control. Each of the tabs along the top of the form reveals a different page of the form's data. Each page contains many controls. Figure 19.15 shows buttons, labels, and text boxes. Each control on the page behaves independently of all other controls on the form and can be accessed through Access VBA code as an independent unit.

FIGURE 19.15

The tab control allows a form to host a large amount of data.

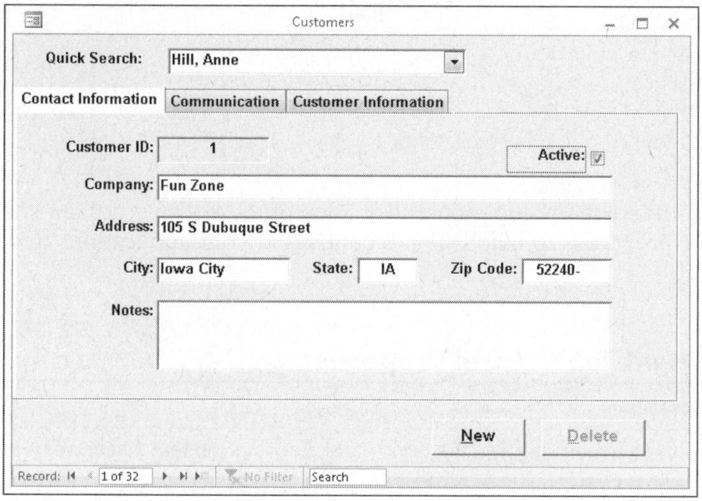

As you might guess, the tab control is fairly complex. It includes its own properties, events, methods, and object collections. You have to know and understand these items before you can effectively use the tab control in your applications.

NOTE

Developers often use the term *tab* when referring to the pages of a tabbed dialog box. In this chapter, the terms *page* and *tab* are used interchangeably.

A tab control consists of a number of tabs. From the user interface, the quickest and easiest way to add or delete a page is to right-click the control and select the appropriate command from the shortcut menu (see Figure 19.16).

FIGURE 19.16

The tab control's shortcut menu contains relevant commands.

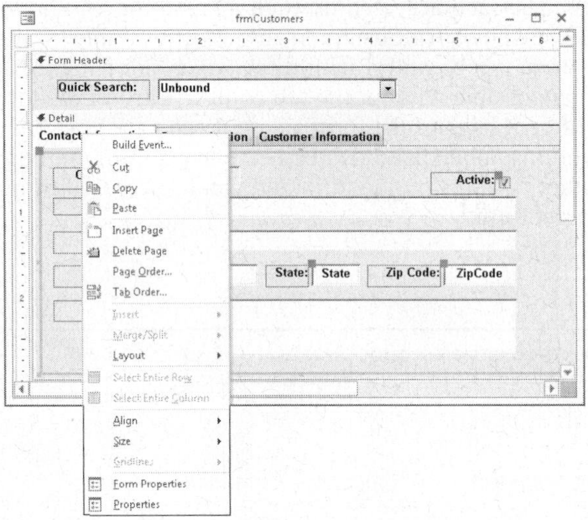

The tab control contains some unique properties. Some of these properties are shown in Table 19.1. Use these properties to tailor the tab controls in your applications to suit the needs of your users.

TABLE 19.1 Important Tab Control Properties

Property	Description
Caption	Applies to each page in the tab control. Provides the text that appears on the tab.
MultiRow	Applies to the tab control. Determines whether the tabs appear as a single row or as multiple rows. You can't specify how many tabs appear in each row. Instead, Access adds as many rows as necessary to display all tabs, given their respective widths.
Style	By default, tabs appear as tabs. The alternative (Buttons) forces the tabs to appear as command buttons.
TabFixedHeight	This value determines the height (in inches or centimeters, depending on the units of measurement settings in the Windows Control Panel) of the tabs on the control. When the TabFixedHeight is set to 0, the tab height is determined by the size of the font specified for the tab control.
TabFixedWidth	This value determines the width (in inches or centimeters) of the tabs on the control. Text that is too wide to fit on the tab when the TabFixedWidth value is set is truncated. When the TabFixedWidth is set to 0, the width of the tab is determined by the font size selected for the tab control and the text specified in the tab's Caption property.
Picture	Applies to each page on the tab control. The Picture property specifies an image (BMP, ICO, or built-in picture) to display on the tab.

A tab control can contain virtually any type of control, including text boxes, combo and list boxes, option buttons, check boxes, and OLE objects. A tab control can even include other tab controls! Although a form can contain multiple tab controls, it's probably not a good idea to overload the user by putting more than one tab control on a form. After all, the reason you use tab controls in an application is to simplify the form by fitting multiple pages of controls within a single control. In most cases, there is no point in challenging the user with more than one tab control on a form.

Using Dialog Boxes to Collect Information

The dialog box is one of the most valuable user-interface components in Windows applications. When properly implemented, dialog boxes provide a way to extend the available screen space on the computer. Instead of having to place every text box, option button, and other user input control on the main form, dialog boxes provide a handy way to move some of these controls to a convenient pop-up device that is on the screen only when needed.

Dialog boxes usually collect a certain type of information, such as font attributes or hard-copy parameters. Dialog boxes are a valuable way to prefilter or qualify user input without cluttering the main form. Or use a dialog box to allow the user to enter query criteria before running a query that populates a form or report, or to gather information that is added to a report's header or footer area.

Although they are forms, dialog boxes should not look like or behave as other forms in the application do. Dialog boxes often pop up over the user's work. When properly implemented, dialog boxes also provide a means to simply cancel the query without breaking anything on the user's workspace.

A simple query form implemented as a dialog box is shown in Figure 19.8. This simple form asks for a zip code that is used to query the database for contact information.

The relevant properties of this dialog box are outlined in Table 19.2.

TABLE 19.2 Property Settings for Dialog Forms

Property	Setting	Purpose
ScrollBars	Neither	Not needed.
NavigationButtons	No	Not needed.
PopUp	Yes	Keeps the form on top of other forms in the application.
Modal	Yes	Prevents the user from working with another part of the application until the dialog box is removed.
RecordSelectors	No	Not needed.
BorderStyle	Dialog	Specifies wide borders that can't be resized. Also removes Minimize and Maximize buttons.
ShortcutMenu	No	Not needed.

After these changes have been made, you have a form that's always on top of the user's work and won't leave the screen until the user clicks the Run Query or Cancel button.

There are a couple rules you should follow when constructing dialog boxes. These rules ensure that your dialog boxes conform to the generally accepted behavior for Windows dialog boxes.

Designing the query

When the user clicks Run Query, Access runs a query named qryDialog. The qryDialog query has a special criterion that uses the value in the form's only text box to limit the records shown. Here's the SQL statement for qryDialog:

```
SELECT Contacts.FirstName, Contacts.LastName Contacts.City, Contacts.State,
    Contacts.ZipCode FROM Contacts WHERE (((Contacts.ZipCode)=[Forms]![frmDialog]
    ![tbxZipCode]));
```

The `WHERE` clause references tbxZipCode. As long as the form is open, the query can retrieve that value and insert it as criteria for the query.

Setting up the command buttons

When a command button is added to a form, Access presents a wizard to help you define the actions for the button. The Run Query action was selected for the Run Query button, as shown in Figure 19.17.

FIGURE 19.17

Assigning an action to a command button.

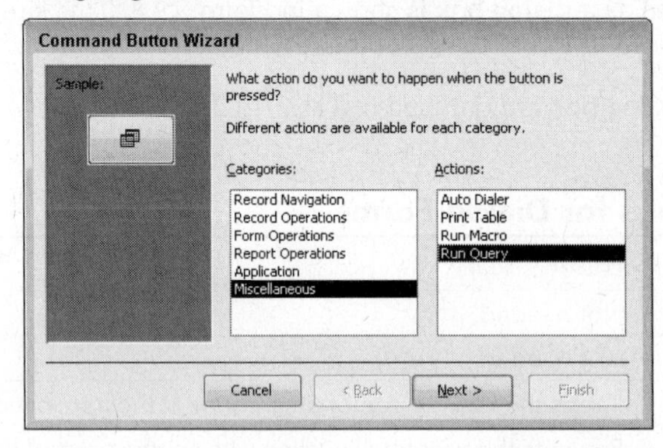

On the next screen of the wizard, qryDialog was selected as the query to run. Now when the button is pressed, that query will execute and use the form's text box as a criterion.

The Cancel button was similarly set up, except that Close Form was selected from the Form Operations category on the wizard.

Adding a default button

There should be a button on the form that's automatically selected if the user presses the Enter key while the dialog box is open. The default button doesn't have to be selected by the user to be triggered; Access automatically fires the default button's `Click` event as the user presses the Enter key.

For example, the user enters 22152 in the Zip Code text box and presses Enter. Unless a default button is specified, the input cursor simply moves to the next control. If you've designated the Run Query button as the dialog box's default, Access interprets the Enter key press as a `Click` event for the Run Query button.

Set the Run Query's Default property to Yes to make it the default for this dialog box. Only one button on a form can have its Default property set to Yes — if you move to the Cancel button and set its Default property to Yes, Access silently changes the Run Query's Default property to No.

Normally, the designated default button is on the left of the form. If you've arranged the command buttons vertically on a form, the top button should be the default.

You should select a button that won't cause trouble if accidentally triggered as the default for a form. For example, to avoid the risk of losing data, it's probably not a good idea to set a button that performs a delete action query as the default. In this case, you might decide to make the Cancel button the default.

Setting a Cancel button

The Cancel button on a form is automatically selected if the user presses the Esc key while the form is open. In most cases, you simply want the dialog box to disappear if the user hits the Esc key while the dialog box is open.

Set a button's Cancel property to designate it as the form's Cancel button. In this example, cmdCancel has been designated as the dialog box's Cancel button. As with the default button, only one button on a form can be the Cancel button. Access triggers the Cancel button's `On Click` event whenever the user presses the Esc key.

Removing the control menu

After you've designated default and Cancel buttons, you have no need for the control menu button in the upper-left corner of the form. Set the form's Control Box property to No to hide the control menu button. When the control menu box is removed, the user will have to use the Cancel or Run Query buttons to remove the form from the screen.

Designing a Form from Scratch

In this section, you'll create an invoice entry form from scratch and apply much of what you learned from this chapter and previous chapters. The main focus of this form will be to record sales, so tblSales will provide many of the fields you use.

Creating the basic form

To create the form, follow these steps:

1. **On the Create tab of the Ribbon, click Form Design.**
2. **On the Form Design Tools Design tab, click Add Existing Fields.** The Field List dialog box appears.
3. **From tblSales, double-click InvoiceNumber, SaleDate, InvoiceDate, CustomerID, SalespersonID, PaymentMethod, and TaxRate to add them to the form.** Don't worry about the placement of these controls just yet. At this point, your form should look similar to Figure 19.18. You can close the Field List dialog box to get it out of your way.

FIGURE 19.18

Placing controls on a new form.

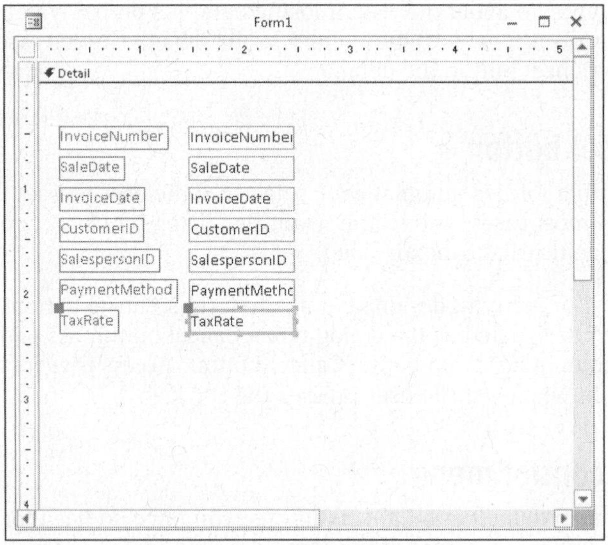

4. **Save the form as frmInvoiceEntry.**

Your new form, frmInvoiceEntry, is a working form that's bound to tblSales. You can view the form in Form view and cycle through all the records in tblSales. It's nice to get something working so quickly, but you have some work to do to make it user friendly. The most glaring omission is that there's no way to identify the product being sold. Also, entering CustomerID and SalespersonID would require the user to have an outstanding memory (or very few customers and salespeople). Note that the frmInvoiceEntry form included in `Chapter19.accdb` is the final version of the form and has a few more features than the form at this stage.

Creating a subform

Next, you'll add a subform so the user can enter products and quantities. The best way to add a subform is to create the subform on its own prior to adding it to the main form. To create the subform, follow these steps:

1. **From the Create tab on the Ribbon, click Form Design to create a new form.**
2. **From the tblSalesLineItems table, add the SalesLineItemID, InvoiceNumber, ProductID, Quantity, DiscountPercent, and Selling Price fields to the subform.** This subform will be displayed as a datasheet on the main form, so it's not important that this form look pretty. It is important that the fields are in the order you want them to appear in the datasheet.
3. **Right click on the ProductID text box and choose Combo Box from the Change To menu.** This converts the ProductID control to a combo box so the user can select a product more easily.
4. **Change the Row Source property of ProductID to the following SQL statement:**

```
SELECT ProductID, Description FROM tblProducts ORDER BY
   Descripton;
```

5. **Change the Column Count property to 2, the Column Widths property to 0";1", and the Bound Column property to 1.** The Column Widths property determines how wide the columns are in the drop-drown list. By setting the first column width to zero, the first column is hidden. The Bound Column property determines which field is stored in the table. In this case, the first field (ProductID) is stored in the table. This is a very typical way to select values on a form. The user sees the user-friendly Description field, but the database-friendly ProductID field is stored.
6. **Change the label from ProductID to Product.**
7. **Change the Default View property of the Form to Datasheet.** That's the view you'll want when you display the subform on the main form.
8. **Save the form as sfrmInvoiceEntryLines, and compare what you have to Figure 19.19.**

FIGURE 19.19

A subform for invoice lines.

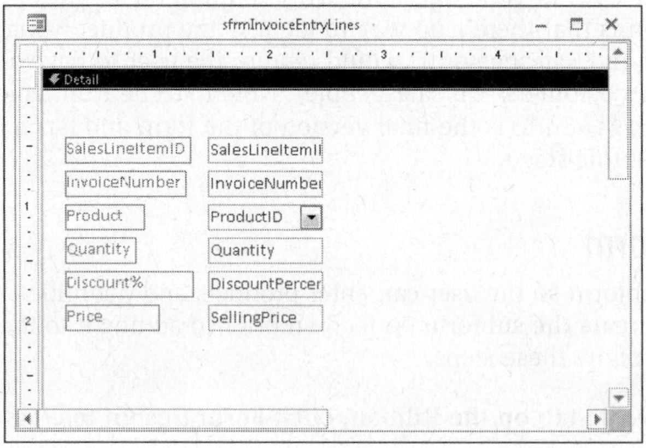

FIGURE 19.20

Selecting an existing form as a subform.

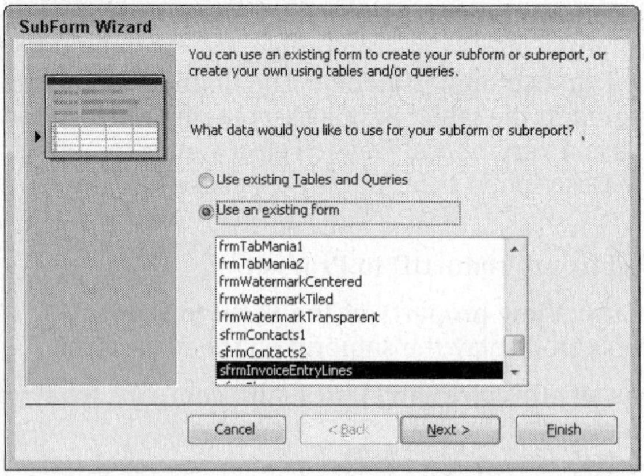

Adding the subform

To add the subform to the main form, follow these steps:

1. **Open frmInvoiceEntry in Design view.**
2. **Draw a Subform/Subreport control across the bottom of the form.** The SubForm Wizard will appear as shown in Figure 19.20.

3. **Choose Use an Existing Form and select sfrmInvoiceEntryLines; then click Next.**
4. **On the next screen of the SubForm, choose the first option for linking the forms as shown in Figure 19.21.**

FIGURE 19.21

Linking a subform to a main form.

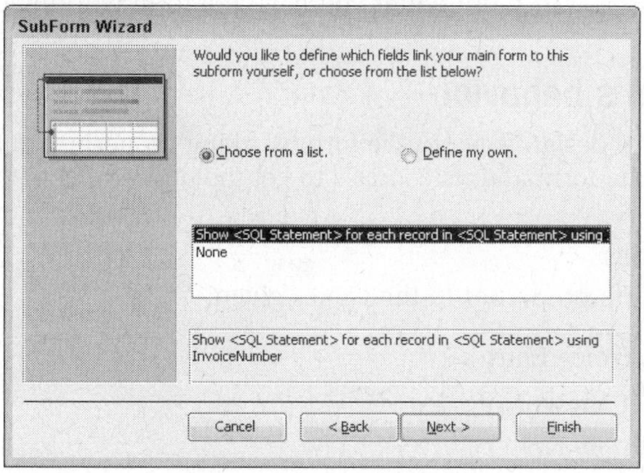

5. **Keep the default name on the final screen of the wizard and click Finish.**
6. **Delete the label that was automatically created for the subform.**

NOTE

When you add a subform, Access does a good job of guessing how the main form and subform are linked. In the fourth step and in Figure 19.21, you accepted the guess that Access made for the link. That step of the wizard actually sets two properties of the subform: Link Master Fields and Link Child Fields.

The Link Master Fields property contains the name of the field on the main form that links to the subform. Similarly, the Link Child Fields property contains the name of the field on the subform. In the example in this section, both properties contain the field InvoiceNumber. InvoiceNumber is a field on both the main form and the subform that ties the two together.

If Access guesses wrong, you can easily change these properties by typing in the proper field names or by clicking the build button next to one of properties and selecting the proper fields from a list.

Now that you've added a subform to your main form, you have a pretty messy-looking form. Don't worry — we're going to spruce it up. The subform displays inside the main form in Design view even though we'll be displaying it in Datasheet view when we show the main form. The subform is fully editable while inside the main form.

In general, the best way to create a form in Access is to follow three steps:

1. **Add all the controls and subforms you want to the form.**
2. **Set the form and control properties that affect the behavior of the form.**
3. **Position the controls on the form and set the properties that affect the appearance of the form.**

You can do the second two steps in the opposite order, but you'll find it easier to save fine-tuning the form's appearance until after you have the form working correctly.

Changing the form's behavior

The next step in the form design is to get the form working properly. You need to change the some properties of the form and its controls to get the desired behavior.

Setting the form properties

Change the following form properties to the values given:

- **Caption:** New Invoice Entry
- **Allow Datasheet View:** No
- **Allow Layout View:** No
- **Record Selectors:** No
- **Navigation Buttons:** No
- **Control Box:** No
- **Data Entry:** Yes
- **Cycle:** Current Record

These are typical property settings for a data entry form. The purpose of the form is to enter a new invoice, so hiding the record navigation aspects of the form makes sense. The Data Entry property ensures that the form shows a new record when it's opened. Setting the Cycle property to Current Record disables the default behavior of moving to the next record when the user leaves the last field. By disabling that behavior, you can control when the record is saved.

Looking up values during data entry

On the subform, we converted the ProductID text box to a combo boxes so the user would be selecting from a list of descriptions rather than a list of numbers. On the main form, there are more fields where we can use the same technique: CustomerID, SalespersonID, PaymentMethod, and TaxRate. In these cases, it'll be easier for the user entering the invoice to select from a name or other description rather than an ID. To convert the CustomerID text box into a combo box, follow these steps:

1. **Right click on the CustomerID text box and choose Combo Box from the Change To menu.**
2. **Change the Row Source property to SELECT CustomerID, Company FROM tblCustomers ORDER BY Company;.**
3. **Change the Limit To List property to Yes.**
4. **Change the Column Count property to 2 and the Column Widths property to 0";1".**

Change the properties of the other controls similarly. The Row Source property of each control is shown in Table 19.3. Be sure to change the Column Count property based on the number of fields returned in the SQL statement.

TABLE 19.3 Row Source Properties

Control Name	Row Source Property
Customer ID	SELECT CustomerID, Company FROM tblCustomers ORDER BY Company;
SalespersonID	SELECT SalespersonID, SalespersonName FROM tblSalesperson ORDER BY SalespersonName;
Payment Method	SELECT PaymentType FROM tblPaymentType;
Tax Rate	SELECT TaxLocation, TaxRate from tblTaxRates ORDER BY TaxRate DESC;

The CustomerID and SalespersonID fields store a foreign key from another table just as ProductID did on the subform. The PaymentMethod and TaxRate fields are a little different. For example, the PaymentMethod control doesn't store a foreign key to tblPaymentType. Instead, it stores text, and tblPaymentType simply stores common payment types. Similarly, tblTaxRates stores some common tax rates to choose from. For both PaymentMethod and TaxRate, change the Limit to List property to No so the user can enter whatever value is appropriate.

Note also that the value from tblTaxRates that we want to store in the tblSales table is from the second column. To store the proper value, change the Bound Column property of TaxRate to 2. Since the PaymentMethod only has one column and you want to show both columns for TaxRate, leave the ColumnWidths property blank for both controls. When ColumnWidths is blank, Access displays all columns and chooses a width that's best for the data.

Saving the record

The last area of form behavior is saving the record. Earlier, you set the Cycle property to Current Record to prevent the record from changing when the user leaves the last field. You can control the flow of the form through command buttons. To create a command button to save the record, follow these steps:

1. **From the Controls group of the Design tab of the Ribbon, select the Button control and place it on the form.**
2. **On the Command Button Wizard's first screen, select Record Navigation and Go to Next Record; then click Next.**
3. **On the next screen of the wizard, check the Show All Pictures check box and choose the Save Record picture; then click Next.**
4. **On the last screen of the wizard, name the button cmdSave and click Finish.**

Using a Command Button to go to the next record automatically saves the current record. It provides a more familiar interface to saving than simply leaving the last field. It also displays a new, empty record ready for more data entry.

You should also provide a way for the user to cancel entering the invoice. Add another command button to the form and choose Undo Record from the Record Operations group in the wizard. Choose the default picture for Undo and name the button cmdCancel.

Finally, you'll need to add a button that allows the user to close the form. You set the Control Box property to No, so the X at the top right of the form is hidden. Add a button to the form that uses the Close Form action from the Form Operations category. Name the button cmdClose.

Changing the form's appearance

The last step is to make the form pretty. On the main form, change the width and placement of the controls and position the command buttons near the bottom right. On the subform, make the width of the SalesLineItemID and InvoiceNumber columns zero by dragging the right border of each column all the way to the left. To drag the border of these columns, you'll need to view the form in Form view or Layout view. Figure 19.22 shows the placement of the controls.

Finally, change the tab order of the controls on the form. Click the Tab Order control on the Design tab of the Ribbon to show the Tab Order dialog box, as shown in Figure 19.23. Once the tab order is set, change the Tab Stop property of the InvoiceNumber control to No. The invoice number is an AutoNumber field, so the user has no business in there.

FIGURE 19.22

Controls placed on a form.

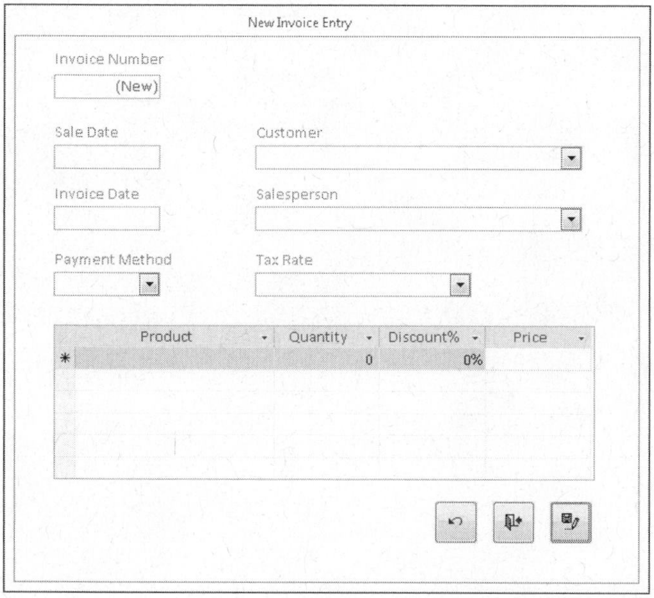

FIGURE 19.23

Setting the tab order of controls.

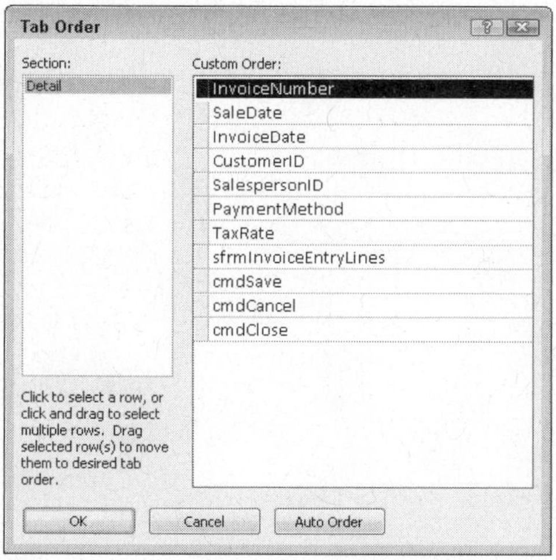

Presenting Data with Access Reports

IN THIS CHAPTER

- Looking at the different types of Access reports
- Creating reports with a Report Wizard
- Creating a report from scratch
- Improving the form's appearance

It's hard to underestimate the importance of reports in database applications. Many people who never work with an Access application in person use reports created by Access. A lot of maintenance work on database projects involves creating new and enhancing existing reports. Access is well known and respected for its powerful reporting features.

Reports provide the most flexible way of viewing and printing summarized information. They display information with the desired level of detail, while enabling you to view or print your information in many different formats. You can add multilevel totals, statistical comparisons, and pictures and graphics to a report.

In this chapter, you learn to use the Report Wizard as a starting point. You also learn how to create reports and what types of reports you can create with Access.

On the Web

In this chapter, you create new reports using the Report Wizard and by creating a blank report without using a wizard. You use tables created in previous chapters. The `Chapter20.accdb` database file on the book's website contains the completed reports described in this chapter.

Introducing Reports

Reports present a customized view of your data. Report output is viewed onscreen or printed to provide a hard copy of the data. Very often, reports provide summaries of the information contained in the database. Data can be grouped and sorted in any order and can be used to create totals that perform statistical operations on data. Reports can include pictures and other graphics as well as memo fields in a report. If you can think of a report you want, Access probably supports it.

Identifying the different types of reports

Three basic types of reports are used by most businesses:

- **Tabular reports:** Print data in rows and columns with groupings and totals. Variations include summary and group/total reports.
- **Columnar reports:** Print data and can include totals and graphs.
- **Mailing label reports:** Create multicolumn labels or snaked-column reports.

Tabular reports

Tabular reports are similar to a table displaying data in rows and columns. Figure 20.1 is a typical tabular report (rptProductsSummary) displayed in Print Preview.

Unlike forms or datasheets, tabular reports often group data by one or more fields. Often, tabular reports calculate and display subtotals or statistical information for numeric fields in each group. Some reports include page totals and grand totals. You can even have multiple snaked columns so that you can create directories (such as telephone books). These types of reports often use page numbers, report dates, or lines and boxes to separate information. Reports may have color and shading and display pictures, business graphs, and memo fields. A special type of summary tabular report can have all the features of a detail tabular report but omit record details.

Columnar reports

Columnar reports generally display one or more records per page, but they do so vertically. Columnar reports display data very much as a data entry form does, but they're used strictly for viewing data and not for entering it. Figure 20.2 shows part of a columnar report (rptProducts) in Print Preview.

FIGURE 20.1

A tabular report (rptProductsSummary) displayed in Print Preview.

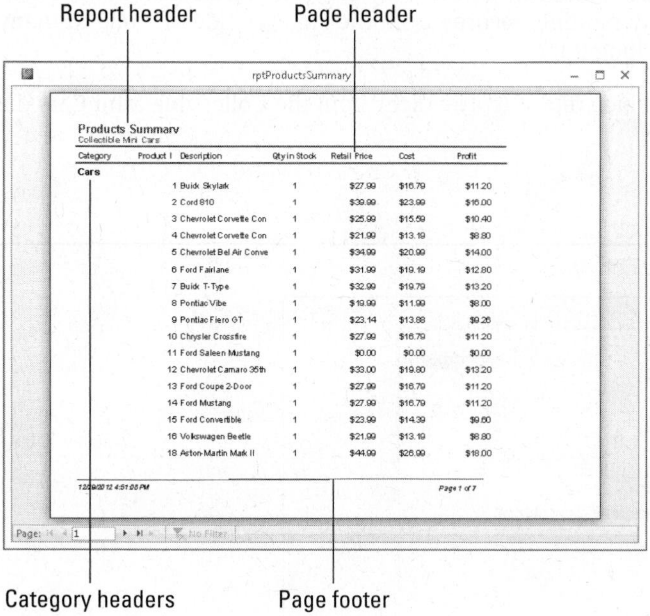

Report header

Page header

rptProductsSummary

Products Summary

Collectible Mini Cars

Category	Product I	Description	Qty in Stock	Retail Price	Cost	Profit
Cars						
	1	Buick Skylark	1	$27.99	$16.79	$11.20
	2	Cord 810	1	$39.99	$23.99	$16.00
	3	Chevrolet Corvette Con	1	$25.99	$15.59	$10.40
	4	Chevrolet Corvette Con	1	$21.99	$13.19	$8.80
	5	Chevrolet Bel Air Conve	1	$34.99	$20.99	$14.00
	6	Ford Fairlane	1	$31.99	$19.19	$12.80
	7	Buick T-Type	1	$32.99	$19.79	$13.20
	8	Pontiac Vibe	1	$19.99	$11.99	$8.00
	9	Pontiac Fiero GT	1	$23.14	$13.88	$9.26
	10	Chrysler Crossfire	1	$27.99	$16.79	$11.20
	11	Ford Saleen Mustang	1	$0.00	$0.00	$0.00
	12	Chevrolet Camaro 35th	1	$33.00	$19.80	$13.20
	13	Ford Coupe 2-Door	1	$27.99	$16.79	$11.20
	14	Ford Mustang	1	$27.99	$16.79	$11.20
	15	Ford Convertible	1	$23.99	$14.39	$9.60
	16	Volkswagen Beetle	1	$21.99	$13.19	$8.80
	18	Aston-Martin Mark II	1	$44.99	$26.99	$18.00

12/29/2012 4:51:05 PM

Page 1 of 7

Page: 1 No Filter

Category headers

Page footer

FIGURE 20.2

A columnar report showing report controls distributed throughout the entire page.

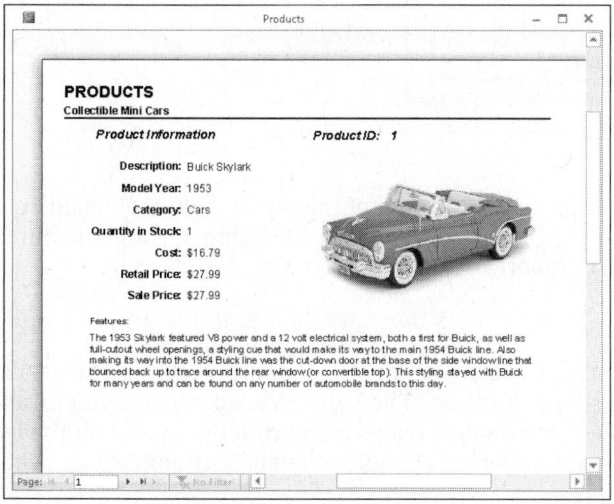

Products

PRODUCTS

Collectible Mini Cars

Product Information

Product ID: 1

Description: Buick Skylark

Model Year: 1953

Category: Cars

Quantity in Stock: 1

Cost: $16.79

Retail Price: $27.99

Sale Price: $27.99

Features:

The 1953 Skylark featured V8 power and a 12 volt electrical system, both a first for Buick, as well as full-cutout wheel openings, a styling cue that would make its way to the main 1954 Buick line. Also making its way into the 1954 Buick line was the cut-down door at the base of the side window line that bounced back up to trace around the rear window (or convertible top). This styling stayed with Buick for many years and can be found on any number of automobile brands to this day.

Page: 1 No Filter

Another type of columnar report displays one main record per page (like a business form) but can show many records within embedded subreports. An invoice is a typical example. This type of report can have sections that display only one record and at the same time have sections that display multiple records from the "many" side of a one-to-many relationship — and even include totals.

Figure 20.3 shows an invoice report (rptInvoice) from the Collectible Mini Cars database system in Report view.

FIGURE 20.3

An invoice report (rptInvoice).

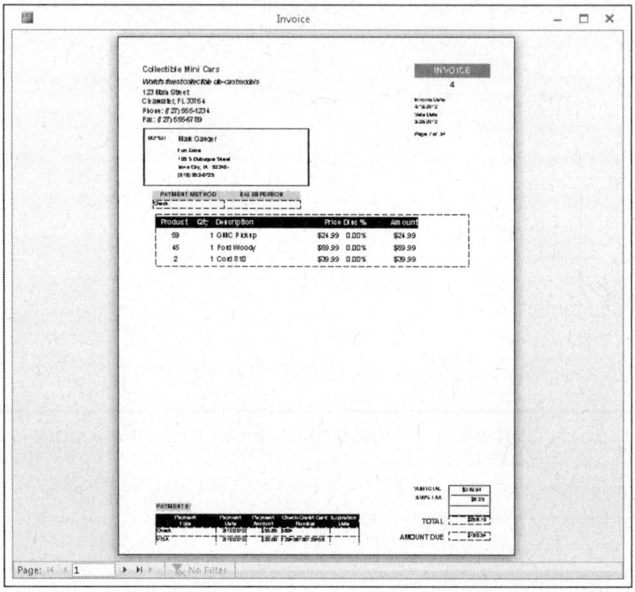

In Figure 20.3, the information in the top portion of the report is on the "main" part of the report, whereas the product details near the bottom of the figure are contained in a subreport embedded within the main report.

Mailing label reports

Mailing labels (shown in Figure 20.4) are also a type of report. Access includes a Label Wizard to help you create this type of report. The Label Wizard enables you to select from a long list of label styles. Access accurately creates a report design based on the label style you select. You can then open the report in Design mode and customize it as needed.

FIGURE 20.4

rptCustomerMailingLabels, a typical mailing label report.

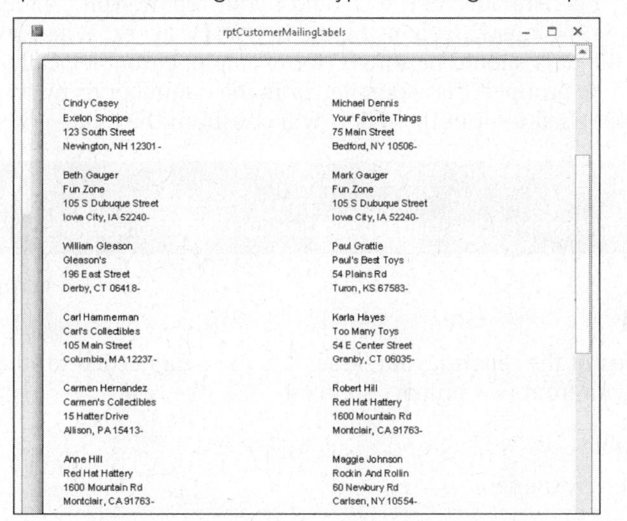

Distinguishing between reports and forms

The main difference between reports and forms is the intended output. Whereas forms are primarily for data entry and interaction with the users, reports are for viewing data (either onscreen or in hard-copy form). Calculated fields can be used with forms to display an amount based on other fields in the record. With reports, you typically perform calculations on groups of records, a page of records, or all the records included in the report. Anything you can do with a form — except input data — can be duplicated by a report. In fact, you can save a form as a report and then refine it in the Report Design window.

Creating a Report, from Beginning to End

The report process begins with your desire to view data, but in a way that differs from a form or datasheet display. The purpose of the report is to transform raw data into a meaningful set of information. The process of creating a report involves several steps:

1. Defining the report layout
2. Assembling the data
3. Creating the report with the Access Report Wizard
4. Printing or viewing the report
5. Saving the report

Defining the report layout

You should begin by having a general idea of the layout of your report. You can define the layout in your mind, on paper, or interactively using the Report Designer. When laying out a report, consider how the data should be sorted (for example, chronologically or by name), how the data should be grouped (for example, by invoice number or by week), and how the size of the paper used to print the report will constrain the data.

TIP

Very often, an Access report is expected to duplicate an existing paper report or form used by the application's consumers.

Assembling the data

After you have a general idea of the report layout, assemble the data needed for the report. Access reports use data from two primary sources:

- A single database table
- A recordset produced by a query

You can join many tables in a query and use the query's recordset as the record source for your report. A query's recordset appears to an Access report as if it were a single table.

As you learned in Chapter 8, you use queries to specify the fields, records, and sort order of the records stored in tables. Access treats a recordset data as if it were a single table (for processing purposes) in datasheets, forms, and reports. When the report is run, Access matches data from the recordset or table against the fields specified in the report and uses the data available at that moment to produce the report.

NOTE

Reports don't follow the sort order specified in an underlying query. Reports are sorted at the report level, either in the detail section or in a group section. It's a waste of time to sort data in a query that is used solely to populate a report because the data is re-sorted and rearranged by the report itself.

In the following example, you use data from tblProducts to create a relatively simple tabular report.

Creating a report with the Report Wizard

Access enables you to create virtually any type of report. Some reports, however, are easier to create than others, especially when a Report Wizard is used as a starting point. Like form wizards, the Report Wizard gives you a basic layout for your report, which you can then customize.

The Report Wizard simplifies laying out controls by stepping you through a series of questions about the report that you want to create. In this chapter, you use the Report Wizard to create tabular and columnar reports.

Creating a new report

The Ribbon contains several commands for creating new reports for your applications. The Create tab of the Ribbon includes the Reports group, which contains several options such as Report, Labels, and Report Wizard. For this exercise, click the Report Wizard button. The first screen of the Report Wizard (shown in Figure 20.5) appears.

FIGURE 20.5

The first screen of the Report Wizard after selecting a data source and fields.

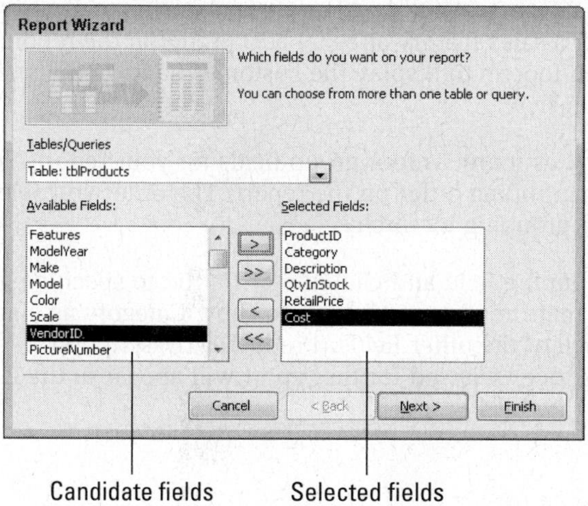

Candidate fields   Selected fields

In Figure 20.5, tblProducts has been selected as the data source for the new report. Under the Tables/Queries drop-down list is a list of available fields. When you click a field in this list and click the right-pointing arrow, the field moves from the Available Fields list to the report's Selected Fields list. For this exercise, select Product ID, Category, Description, QtyInStock, RetailPrice, and Cost.

TIP

Double-clicking any field in the Available Fields list adds it to the Selected Fields list. You can also double-click any field in the Selected Fields list to remove it from the box.

You're limited to selecting fields from the original record source you started with. You can select fields from other tables or queries by using the Tables/Queries drop-down list in the Report Wizard. As long as you've specified valid relationships so that Access properly links the data, these fields are added to your original selection and you use them on the report. If you choose fields from unrelated tables, a dialog box asks you to edit the relationship and join the tables. Or you can return to the Report Wizard and remove the fields.

After you've selected your data, click Next to go to the next wizard dialog box.

Selecting the grouping levels

The next dialog box enables you to choose which field(s) to use for grouping data. Figure 20.6 shows the Category field selected as the data grouping field for the report. The field selected for grouping determines how data appears on the report, and the grouping fields appear as group headers and footers in the report.

Groups are most often used to combine data that are logically related. One example is grouping all products by product category. Another example is choosing to group on CustomerID so that each customer's sales history appears as a group on the report. You use the report's group headers and footers to display the customer name and any other information specific to each customer.

The Report Wizard lets you specify as many as four group fields for your report. You use the Priority buttons to change the grouping order on the report. The order you select for the group fields is the order of the grouping hierarchy.

Select the Category field as the grouping field and click the > button to specify a grouping based on category values. Notice that the picture changes to show Category as a grouping field, as shown in Figure 20.6. Each of the other fields (ProductID, Description, QtyInStock, RetailPrice, and SalesPrice) selected for the report will appear in the Category group's details section.

FIGURE 20.6

Specifying the report's grouping.

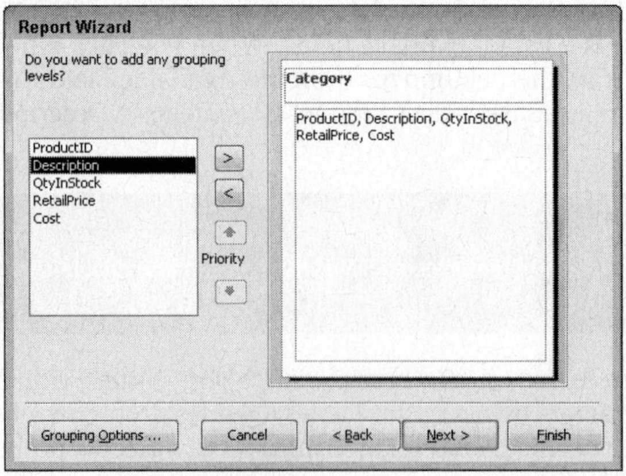

Defining the group data

After you select the group field(s), click the Grouping Options button at the bottom of the dialog box to display the Grouping Options dialog box, which enables you to further define how you want groups displayed on the report.

For example, you can choose to group by only the first character of the grouping field. This means that all records with the same first character in the grouping field are grouped. If you group a customers table on CustomerName, and then specify grouping by the first character of the CustomerName field, a group header and footer appears for all customers whose name begins with the same character. This specification groups all customer names beginning with the letter *A*, another group for all records with customer name beginning with *B*, and so on.

The Grouping Options dialog box enables you to further define the grouping. This selection can vary in importance, depending on the data type.

The Grouping Intervals list box displays different values for various data types:

- **Text:** Normal, 1st Letter, 2 Initial Letters, 3 Initial Letters, 4 Initial Letters, 5 Initial Letters
- **Numeric:** Normal, 10s, 50s, 100s, 500s, 1000s, 5000s, 10000s, 50000s, 100000s
- **Date:** Normal, Year, Quarter, Month, Week, Day, Hour, Minute

Normal means that the grouping is on the entire field. In this example, use the entire Category field.

Notice that the grouping options simplify creating reports grouped by calendar months, quarters, years, and so on. This means that you can easily produce reports showing sales, payroll, or other financial information needed for business reporting.

If you displayed the Grouping Options dialog box, click the OK button to return to the Grouping Levels dialog box, and then click the Next button to move to the Sort Order dialog box.

Selecting the sort order

By default, Access automatically sorts grouped records in an order meaningful to the grouping field(s). For example, after you've chosen to group by Category, Access arranges the groups in alphabetical order by Category. However, you can't be sure of the order of the records within the group, so it's a good idea to specify a sort within each group. As an example, your users might want to see the product records sorted by Retail Price in descending order so that the most expensive products appear near the top for each category group.

In this example, Access sorts data by the Category field. As Figure 20.7 shows, the data is also sorted by Description within each group.

FIGURE 20.7

Selecting the field sorting order.

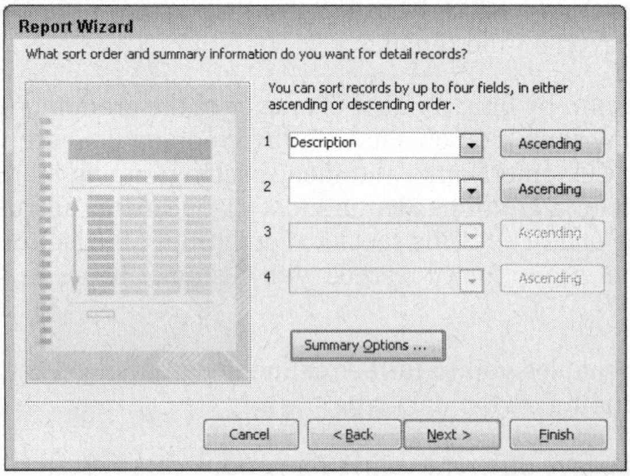

Sort fields are selected by the same method you use for selecting grouping fields. You can select sorting fields that haven't been chosen for grouping. The fields chosen in this dialog box affect only the sorting order in the data displayed in the report's Detail section. Select ascending or descending sort by clicking the button to the right of each sort field.

Selecting summary options

Near the bottom of the sorting screen of the Report Wizard is a Summary Options button. Clicking this button displays the Summary Options dialog box (shown in Figure 20.8), which provides additional display options for numeric fields. All the numeric and currency fields selected for the report are displayed and may be summed. Additionally, you can display averages, minimums, and maximums.

FIGURE 20.8

Selecting the summary options.

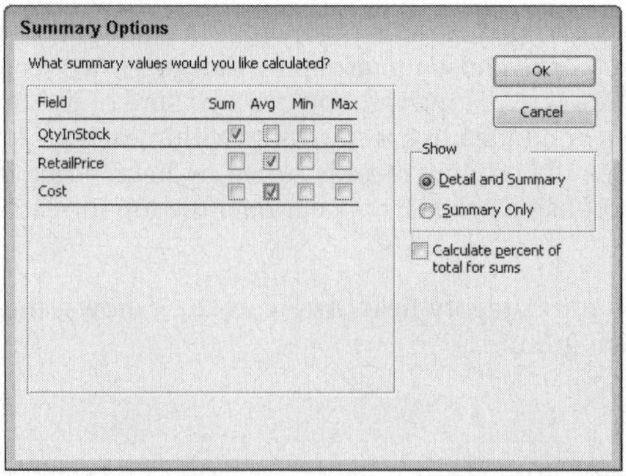

You can also decide whether to show or hide the data in the report's Detail section. If you select Detail and Summary, the report shows the detail data, whereas selecting Summary Only hides the Detail section and shows only totals in the report.

Finally, checking the Calculate Percent of Total for Sums box adds the percentage of the entire report that the total represents below the total in the group footer. If, for example, you have three products and their totals are 15, 25, and 10, respectively, 30%, 50%, and 20% shows below their total (that is, 50) — indicating the percentage of the total sum (100%) represented by their sum.

Clicking the OK button in this dialog box returns you to the sorting screen of the Report Wizard. There you can click the Next button to move to the next wizard screen.

Selecting the layout

The next step in the Report Wizard affects the look of your report. The Layout area enables you to determine the basic layout of the data. The Layout area provides three layout choices that tell Access whether to repeat the column headers, indent each grouping, and add lines or boxes between the detail lines. As you select each option, the picture on the left changes to show how the choice affects the report's appearance.

You choose between Portrait (up-and-down) and Landscape (across-the-page) layout for the report in the Orientation area. Finally, the Adjust the Field Width So All Fields Fit on a Page check box enables you to cram a lot of data into a little area. (A magnifying glass may be necessary!)

For this example, choose Stepped and Portrait, as shown in Figure 20.9. Then click the Next button to move to the next dialog box.

FIGURE 20.9

Selecting the page layout.

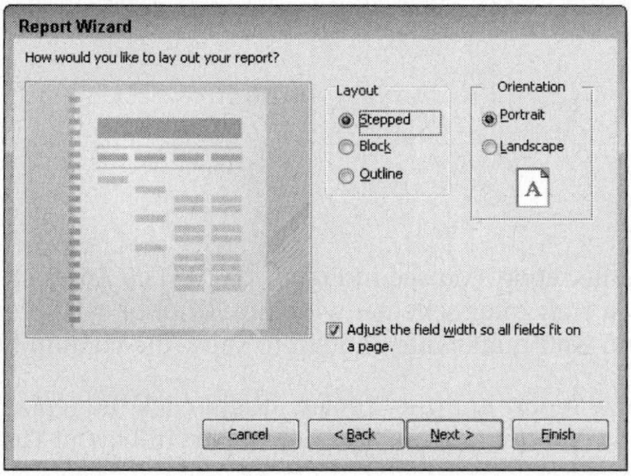

Opening the report design

The final Report Wizard screen contains an area for you to enter a title for the report. This title appears only once, at the very beginning of the report, not at the top of each page. The report title also serves as the new report's name. The default title is the name of the table or query you initially specified as the report's data source. The report just created in the `Chapter20.accdb` example is named rptProducts_Wizard.

Next, choose one of the option buttons at the bottom of the dialog box:

- Preview the report
- Modify the report's design

For this example, leave the default selection intact to preview the report. Click Finish and the report displays in Print Preview (see Figure 20.10).

FIGURE 20.10

rptProducts_Wizard displayed in Print Preview.

Category	Description	ProductID	QtyInStock	RetailPrice
Cars				
	Alfa-Romeo GT Coupe	76	0	$29.99
	Aston-Martin Mark II	18	1	$44.99
	BMW Z4	72	0	$29.99
	Buick Electra 225	55	0	$39.99
	Buick Roadmaster	108	0	$19.99
	Buick Skylark	1	1	$27.99
	Buick Skylark	93	0	$29.99
	Buick T-Type	7	1	$32.99
	Cadillac Biarritz	97	0	$29.99
	Cadillac Convertible	50	0	$29.99
	Cadillac DeVille Convertible	64	0	$39.99
	Cadillac Deville Limo	41	1	$49.99
	Cadillac Fleetwood	113	0	$49.99
	Cadillac Town Car	99	0	$19.99
	Chevrolet 150	25	2	$41.99
	Chevrolet Bel Air	22	1	$28.00
	Chevrolet Bel Air	24	1	$27.99
	Chevrolet Bel Air Convertible	5	1	$34.99
	Chevrolet Camaro 35th Anniversary	12	1	$33.00
	Chevrolet Corvette Convertible	3	1	$25.99
	Chevrolet Corvette Convertible	4	1	$21.99
	Chevrolet Impala	28	1	$26.99
	Chevrolet Z-28	40	1	$29.99
	Chevy Bel Air	57	0	$29.99

Adjusting the report's layout

There are a few small issues with the report you see in Figure 20.10. The Access Report Wizard has chosen the fonts and overall color scheme, which may not be what you had in mind. Also, the Retail Price column isn't quite wide enough to show the column heading.

The Report Wizard displays the new report in Print Preview. Right-click the report's title bar and select Layout View from the shortcut menu. The new report in Layout view is shown in Figure 20.11.

FIGURE 20.11

Layout view is useful for resizing controls in a columnar report.

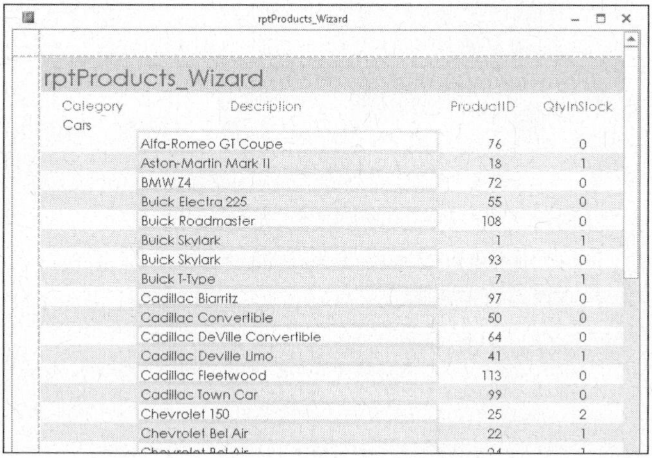

rptProducts_Wizard

rptProducts_Wizard

Category	Description	ProductID	QtyInStock
Cars			
	Alfa-Romeo GT Coupe	76	0
	Aston-Martin Mark II	18	1
	BMW Z4	72	0
	Buick Electra 225	55	0
	Buick Roadmaster	108	0
	Buick Skylark	1	1
	Buick Skylark	93	0
	Buick T-Type	7	1
	Cadillac Biarritz	97	0
	Cadillac Convertible	50	0
	Cadillac DeVille Convertible	64	0
	Cadillac Deville Limo	41	1
	Cadillac Fleetwood	113	0
	Cadillac Town Car	99	0
	Chevrolet 150	25	2
	Chevrolet Bel Air	22	1

In Figure 20.11, the Category column has been shrunk to eliminate some wasted space, the Description column has been widened to the left to fill that space, and the remaining columns have been separated so that the column headings show and aren't all pushed together. Working with controls in Layout view for a report is identical to working with them in Layout view for a form. To shrink a column, for example, drag the right edge of the control to the left.

Choosing a theme

After you adjust the layout, you can use controls in the Themes group on the Design tab of the Ribbon to change the report's colors, fonts, and overall appearance. The Themes button opens a gallery containing several dozen themes (see Figure 20.12).

Themes are an important concept in Access 2013. A theme sets the color scheme, selected font face, font colors, and font sizes for Access 2013 forms and reports. As you hover the mouse over the theme icons in the gallery, the report open in Layout view behind the gallery instantly changes to show you how the report would look with the selected theme.

Each theme has a name, like Office, Facet, Organic, and Slice. Theme names are useful when you want to refer to a particular theme in the application's documentation or in an e-mail or other correspondence. Themes are stored in a file with a THMX extension, in the `Program Files\Microsoft Office\Document Themes 15` folder. Themes apply to all the Office 2013 documents (Word, Excel, and Access), making it easy to determine a style to apply to all of a company's Office output.

FIGURE 20.12

Choosing a theme for the report.

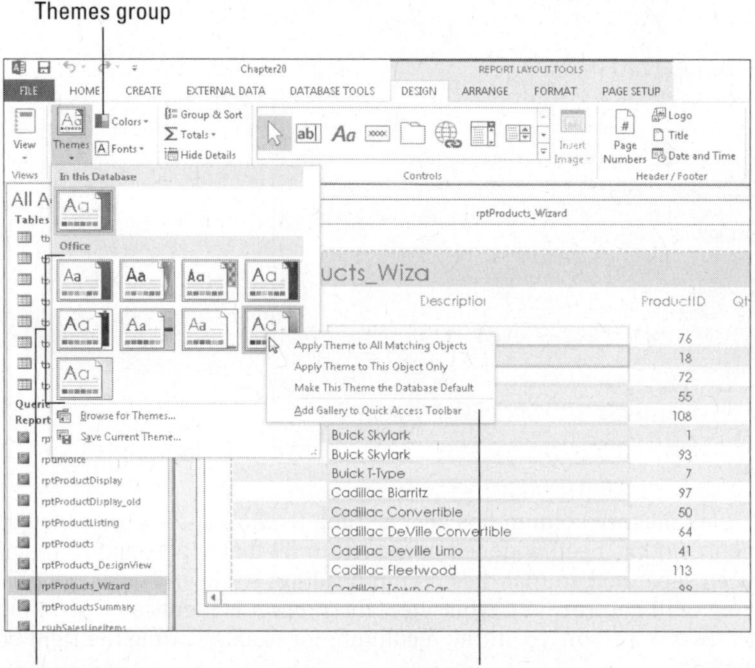

> **NOTE**
>
> Access 2007 users may be wondering what happened to the AutoFormat feature. For a number of reasons, Microsoft decided to replace AutoFormat with themes in later versions of Office. AutoFormat applied to individual controls, which meant a lot of work when building a complicated form or report. AutoFormat also tended to be all or nothing, making it difficult to apply an AutoFormat and then alter the colors and fonts to controls on a form or report. Themes are much more flexible. They even allow you to save a completed form or report as a new theme (see the Save Current Theme option at the bottom of the theme gallery in Figure 20.12). There was no way to create a custom AutoFormat in Access 2007.

As the right-click menu in Figure 20.12 indicates, you can apply the selected theme just to the current report (Apply Theme to this Object Only), all reports (Apply Theme to All Matching Objects), or all forms *and* reports in the application (Make This Theme the Database Default). There's even an option to add the theme as a button to the Quick Access toolbar, an extremely useful option for selectively applying the theme to other objects in the database.

TIP

It's very tempting to try out every reporting style and option when building Access forms and reports. Unfortunately, when carried too far, your Access application may end up looking like a scrapbook of design ideas rather than being a valuable business tool. Professional database developers tend to use a minimum of form and report styles and use them consistently throughout an application. Be considerate of your users and try not to overwhelm them with a lot of different colors, fonts, and other user interface and reporting styles.

For the purposes of this exercise, the Whisp theme was selected for the new products report.

Creating new theme color schemes

Access 2013 provides several default themes, with each theme consisting of a set of complementary colors, fonts, and font characteristics. In addition, you can set up entirely new color and font themes and apply them to your forms and reports. Creating a custom color theme is a great way to apply a company's corporate color scheme to the forms and reports in an application.

With a form or report open in Design view, follow these steps:

1. **Click the Colors button in the Themes group on the Design tab of the Ribbon.** The color theme list opens.
2. **Select the Customize Colors command at the very bottom of the list of color themes.** The Create New Theme Colors dialog box (shown in Figure 20.13) appears, showing the currently selected color theme.

FIGURE 20.13

Setting up a custom color theme.

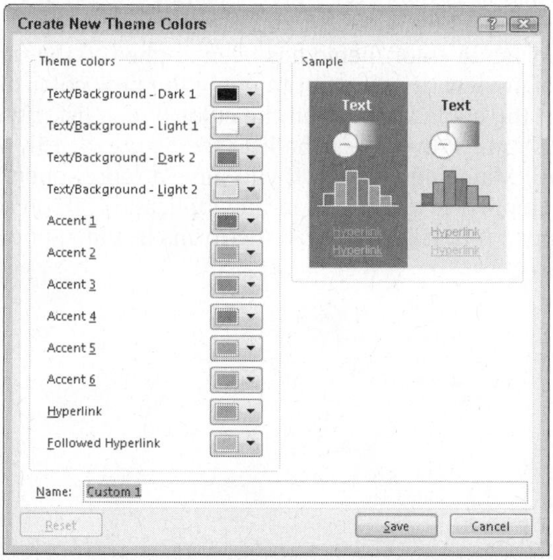

Modifying a color theme requires a considerable amount of work. As you can see from Figure 20.13, each color theme includes 12 different colors. Each of the 12 buttons on the Create New Theme Colors dialog box opens a color palette (shown in Figure 20.14) where you select a theme element's color, such as the color for the Text/Background - Light 2 element.

FIGURE 20.14

Selecting a theme element's color.

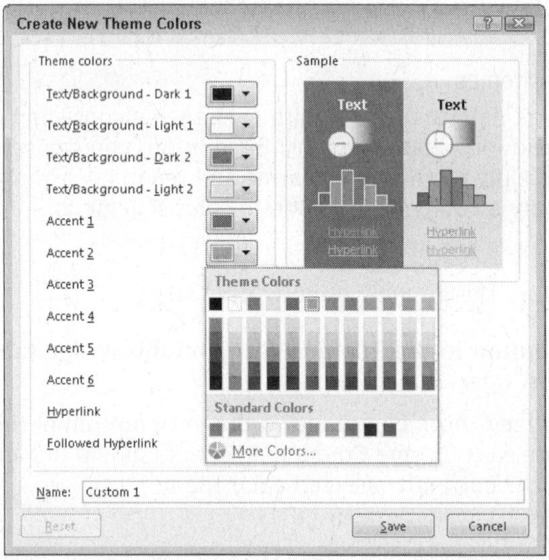

3. **When the color customization is complete, assign a name for the custom color theme and click Save.** When you close the Create New Theme Colors dialog box, you'll see that the custom color theme has been applied to the form or report currently open in Design view. If you want to apply the new color theme to all the forms or reports in the application, open the color theme list, right-click the name of a custom color theme at the top of the list (see Figure 20.15), and select Apply Color Scheme to All Matching Objects. If you have a report open in Design view, the theme will be applied to all reports in the application. If, on the other hand, you have a form open in Design view, all the forms in the application receive the new color theme.

FIGURE 20.15

Applying a color theme to all matching objects in an application.

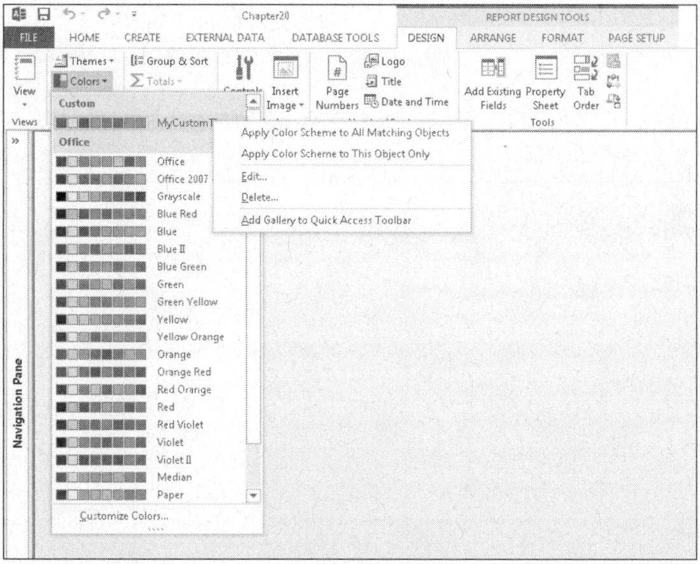

Even after applying a color theme, you can adjust the colors of individual items on a report (or form, for that matter). Open the report in Design view, select the item to change, and choose its new color(s) in the Property Sheet.

Although not described or shown here, a similar dialog box is available (Create New Theme Fonts) in the Fonts drop-down list in the Themes group on the Design tab. The Create New Theme Fonts dialog box enables you to set up a custom font theme (heading and body fonts, and so on) to apply to forms and reports. Creating custom fonts themes works just like adding your own color themes to an application. Save the theme with a name you'll recognize, and apply the font theme to forms and reports as needed.

Using the Print Preview window

Figure 20.16 shows the Print Preview window in a zoomed view of rptProducts_Wizard. This view displays your report with the actual fonts, shading, lines, boxes, and data that will be used on the report when printed to the default Windows printer. Clicking the left mouse button on the report's surface changes the view to a page preview that shows the entire page.

FIGURE 20.16

Displaying rptProducts_Wizard in the zoomed preview mode.

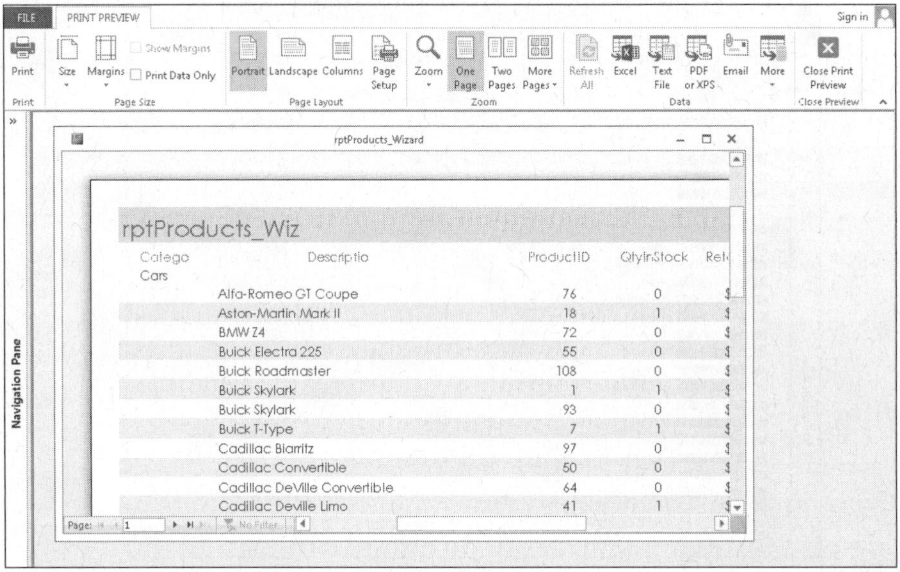

The Ribbon transforms to display controls relevant to viewing and printing the report. The Print Preview tab of the Ribbon includes controls for adjusting the size, margins, page orientation (Portrait or Landscape), and other printing options. The print options are stored with the report when you save the report's design. The Print Preview tab also includes a Print button for printing the report, and another button for closing Print Preview and returning to the report's previous view (Design, Layout, or Report view).

You can move around the page by using the horizontal and vertical scroll bars, or use the Page controls (at the bottom-left corner of the window) to move from page to page. The Page controls include DVD-like navigation buttons to move from page to page or to the first or last page of the report. You can also go to a specific page of the report by entering a value in the text box between the Previous and Next controls.

Right-clicking the report and selecting the Multiple Pages option, or using the controls in the Zoom group on the Print Preview tab of the Ribbon, lets you view more than one page of the report in a single view. Figure 20.17 shows a view of the report in the Print Preview's two-page mode. Use the navigation buttons (in the lower-left section of the Print Preview window) to move between pages, just as you would to move between records in a datasheet. The Print Preview window has a toolbar with commonly used printing commands.

FIGURE 20.17

Displaying multiple pages of a report in Print Preview's page preview mode.

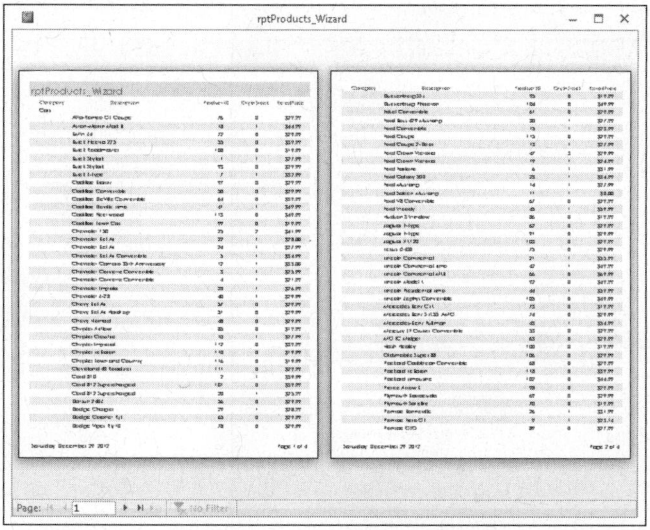

If, after examining the preview, you're satisfied with the report, click the Print button on the toolbar to print the report. If you're dissatisfied with the design, select the Close button to switch to the Report Design window and make further changes.

Publishing in alternate formats

An important feature of the Print Preview tab is the ability to output the Access report in a number of common business formats, including PDF, XPS (XML Paper Specification), HTML, and other formats.

Clicking the PDF or XPS button in the Data group on the Print Preview tab of the Ribbon opens the Publish as PDF or XPS dialog box (shown in Figure 20.18). This dialog box provides options for outputting in standard PDF format or in a condensed version (for use in a web context). You also specify the destination folder for the exported file.

The PDF or XPS view of an Access report is indistinguishable from the report when viewed in Access. Either format is common in many business environments these days.

FIGURE 20.18

Access 2013 provides powerful options for publishing reports.

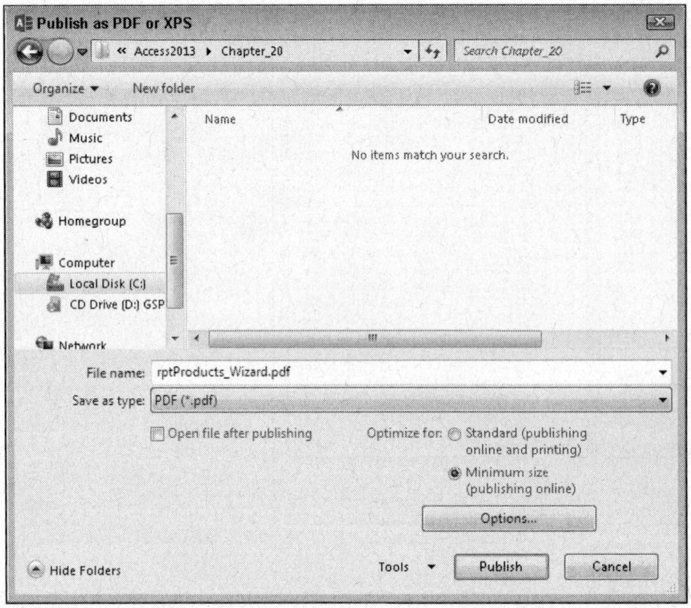

Viewing the Report Design window

Right-clicking the report's title bar and selecting Design View opens the Access Report Designer on the report. As shown in Figure 20.19, the report design reflects the choices you made using the Report Wizard.

FIGURE 20.19

The Report Design window.

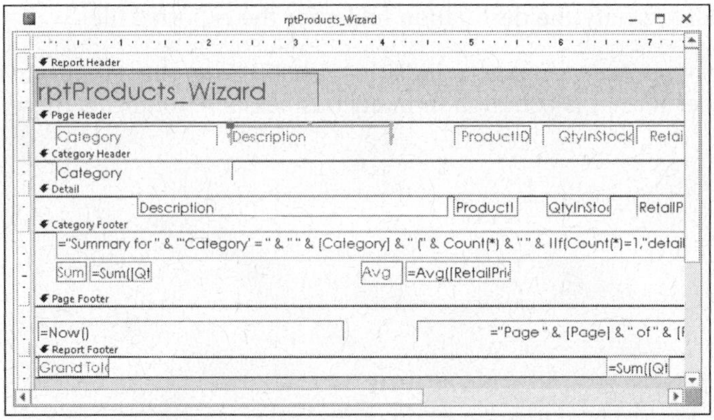

Return to the Print Preview mode by clicking the Print Preview button on the Report Design toolbar or by choosing Print Preview in the Views group.

Printing or viewing the report

The final step in the process of creating a report is printing or viewing it.

Printing the report

There are several ways to print your report:

- **Choose File⇨Print in the main Access window (with a report highlighted in the Navigation pane).** The standard Print dialog box appears. You use this dialog box to select the print range, number of copies, and print properties.
- **Click the Print button on the Print Preview tab of the Ribbon.** The report is immediately sent to the default printer without displaying a Print dialog box.

Viewing the report

You can view a report in four different views: Design, Report, Layout, and Print Preview. (Layout view is described in the next section.) You can also print a report to the default Windows printer. You've already seen various preview windows in previous chapters. This chapter focuses on the Report Design window.

The Report Design window is one of two places where you create and modify reports. You began working with a new report by selecting a table or query to serve as the new report's data source. Click the Blank Report button on the Create tab of the Ribbon. By default, the new report appears in Layout view, as shown in Figure 20.20.

FIGURE 20.20

Layout view of a new report based on tblProducts.

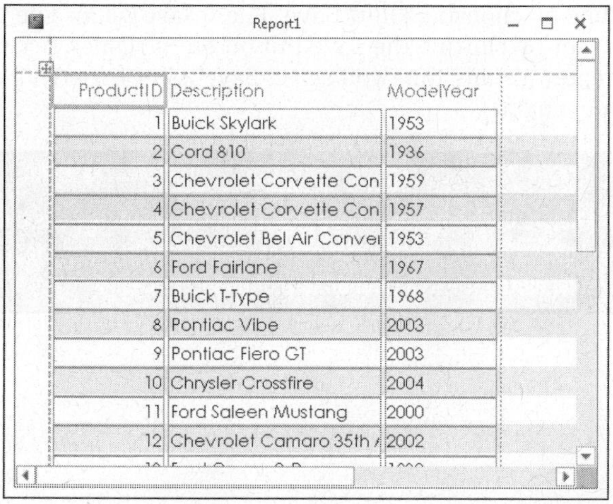

Layout view enables you to see the relative positions of the controls on the report's surface, as well as the margins, page headers and footers, and other report details.

The main constraint of Layout view is that you can't make fine adjustments to a report's design unless you put the report in Design view. Layout view is primarily intended to allow you to adjust the relative positions of controls on the report and is not meant for moving individual controls around on the report.

While in Layout view, you can also right-click any control and select Properties from the shortcut menu. The Property Sheet allows you to modify the default settings for the selected control.

Figure 20.21 shows the Ribbon while a report is open in Layout view. Not surprisingly, the options on the Ribbon are mostly involved with adjusting the appearance of the controls on the report.

FIGURE 20.21

The Ribbon while a report is open in Layout view.

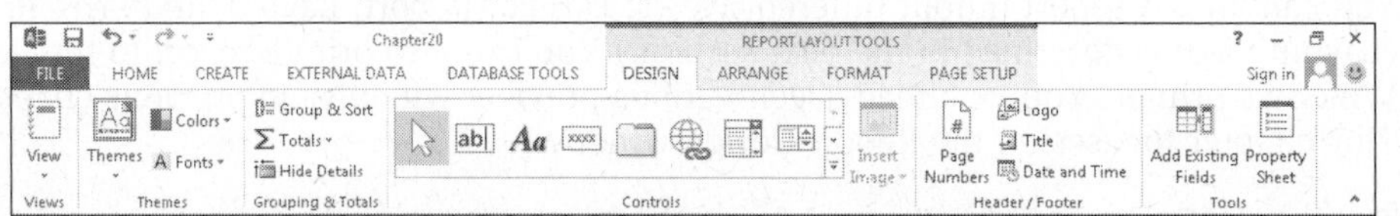

> **NOTE**
>
> Layout view first became available in Access 2007. Versions earlier than 2007 do not support Layout view.

Saving the report

Save the report design at any time by choosing File➪Save, File➪Save As, or File➪Export from the Report Design window, or by clicking the Save button on the Quick Access toolbar. The first time you save a report (or any time you select Save As or Export), a dialog box enables you to select or type a name.

> **TIP**
>
> You might find it useful to save a copy of a report before beginning maintenance work on the report. Reports tend to be pretty complicated, and it's easy to make a mistake on a report's design and not remember how to return the report to its previous state. A backup provides a valuable safeguard against accidental loss of a report's design.

Banded Report Design Concepts

Access reports support a "banded" approach to design. The banded report design is an important concept and must be mastered by Access developers. In an Access report, data is processed one record at a time. Individual fields may be placed in different places on a report and can even appear more than once in a report, if needed.

Many first-time Access developers are confused by a report's appearance in Design view. Some people expect to see a "page" that is decorated by adding fields in a large design surface, much like how forms are built. However, because Access processes report data one record at a time, Design view is meant to help you specify how each row is laid out on the printed page. In addition, Design view shows you elements such as a page's header and footer, as well as areas occupied by group headers and footers. Each area occupied by controls plays a vital role in the report's appearance when printed.

Reports are divided into *sections,* known as *bands* in most report-writing software packages. (In Access, these are simply called *sections.*) Access processes each record in the underlying data set, processing each section in order and deciding (for each record) whether to process fields or text in that section. For example, the report footer section is processed only after the last record is processed in the recordset.

In Figure 20.22, rptProductsSummary is shown in Print Preview. Notice that the data on the report is grouped by Category (Cars, Trucks, and so on). Each group has a *group header* containing the category name. Each group also has a footer displaying summary information for the category. The *page header* contains column descriptions (Product ID, Description, and so on). The group footer that ends each group contains summary data for several columns in each group.

The following Access sections are available:

- **Report header:** Prints only at the beginning of the report; used for the title page
- **Page header:** Prints at the top of each page
- **Group header:** Prints before the first record of a group is processed
- **Detail:** Prints each record in the table or recordset
- **Group footer:** Prints after the last record of a group is processed
- **Page footer:** Prints at the bottom of each page
- **Report footer:** Prints only at the end of a report after all records are processed

Figure 20.23 shows rptProductSummary open in Design view. As you can see, the report is divided into as many as seven sections. The group section displays data grouped by categories, so you see the sections Category Header and Category Footer. Each of the other sections is also named based on where it displays on the report.

FIGURE 20.22

A portion of rptProductsSummary, a grouped report containing summary data.

Group header
Page header

rptProductsSummary

Category	Product I	Description	Qty in Stock	Retail Price	Cost	Profit
	119	Harley Davidson FLHR	0	$19.99	$11.99	$8.00
	121	Ducati Monster	0	$49.99	$29.99	$20.00
		Category Motorcycles Total:	2	$219.95	$131.97	$87.98
Special Interest						
	34	Porsche 935	2	$47.99	$28.79	$19.20
	35	Honda F1 RA272	2	$149.99	$89.99	$60.00
	36	Watson Roadster	1	$98.99	$59.39	$39.60
	37	Kurtis Kraft #99 Art Cro	1	$98.99	$59.39	$39.60
	38	Eagle #6 Bobby Unser	1	$119.99	$71.99	$48.00
	39	AAR Eagle	1	$119.99	$71.99	$48.00
	77	Ford GT40 Concept Ca	0	$69.99	$41.99	$28.00
	79	Chrysler ME Four-Twel	0	$29.99	$17.99	$12.00
		Category Special Interest Total:	8	$735.92	$441.55	$294.37
SUVs						
	94	Jeep Grand Cherokee	0	$27.99	$16.79	$11.20
		Category SUVs Total:	0	$27.99	$16.79	$11.20

Page: 6 No Filter

Group footer
Category totals
Page number

FIGURE 20.23

rptProductSummary in Design view.

Detail section
Group header
Page header
Report header

rptProductsSummary

Report Header
Products Summary
Collectible Mini Cars
Page Header
Category | Product ID | Description | Qty in Stock | Retail Price | Cost
Category Header
Category
Detail
ProductID | Description | QtyInStock | RetailPrice | Cost
Category Footer
="Category " & [Category] & " Total:" | m([QtyInSto | =Sum([RetailPri | =Sum([Cost])
Page Footer
=Now() | ="Page " & [Page] & "
Report Footer
="Grand Total:" | =Sum([Qtyl | =Sum([RetailPrice]) | =Sum([Cost])

Page footer
Report footer
Group footer

You can place any type of text or text-box controls in any section, but Access processes the data one record at a time. It also takes certain actions (based on the values of the group fields or current section of the page being processed) to make the bands or sections active. The example in Figure 20.23 is typical of a report with multiple sections. As you learned, each section in the report has a different purpose and different triggers.

NOTE
Page and report headers and footers are added as pairs. To add one without the other, remove any controls in the section you don't want and resize the section to a height of 0 or set its Visible property to No.

CAUTION
If you remove a header or footer section, you also lose the controls in those sections.

The Report Header section

Controls in the Report Header section are printed only once, at the beginning of the report. A common use of a Report Header section is as a cover page or a cover letter or for information that needs to be communicated only once to the user of the report.

You can also have controls in the Report Header section print on a page that is separate from the rest of the report, which enables you to create a title page and include a graphic or picture in the Report Header. The Force New Page property in the Report Header section can be set to After Section to place the information in the report header in a separate page.

NOTE
Only data from the first record can be placed in a report header.

The Page Header section

Controls in the Page Header section normally print at the top of every page. If a report header on the first page is not on a page of its own, the information in the Page Header section prints just below the report header information. Typically, page headers contain column headers in group/total reports. Page headers often contain a title for the report that appears on every page.

The Page Header section shown in Figure 20.23 contains a horizontal line below the label controls. Each label control can be moved or sized individually. You can also change special effects (such as color, shading, borders, line thickness, font type, and font size) for each control.

Both the Page Header and Page Footer sections can be set to one of four settings (found in the Report's properties, not the section properties):

- **All Pages:** The section (either page header or page footer) prints on every page.
- **Not with Rpt Hdr:** The section does not print on the page with the report header.
- **Not with Rpt Ftr:** The report footer is forced onto its own page when either Page Header or Page Footer is set to Not with Rpt Ftr. The section with this setting does not print on that page.
- **Not with Report Header/Footer:** The report footer is forced onto its own page. The section does not print on that page, nor does it print on the page with the report header.

The Group Header section

A Group Header section normally displays the name of the group, such as Trucks or Motorcycles. Access knows that all the records in a group have been displayed in a Detail section when the group name changes. In this example, the detail records are all about individual products. The Category control in the Category Header tells you that the products within the group belong to the indicated category (Trucks or Motorcycles). Group Header sections immediately precede Detail sections.

You can have multiple levels of group headers and footers. In this report, for example, the data is only for categories. However, in some reports you might have groups of information with date values. You could group your sections by year or by month and year, and within those sections by another group such as category.

NOTE
To set group-level properties such as Group On, Group Interval, Keep Together, or something other than the default, you must first set the Group Header and Group Footer property (or both) to Yes for the selected field or expression. You learn about these later in the chapter.

The Detail section

The Detail section processes *every* record in the data and is where each value is printed. The Detail section frequently contains calculated fields such as profit that is the result of a mathematical expression. In this example, the Detail section simply displays information from the tblProduct table except for the last control. The profit is calculated by subtracting the cost from the RetailPrice.

TIP
You can tell Access whether you want to display a section in the report by changing the section's Visible property in the Report Design window. Turning off the display of the Detail section (or excluding selected group sections) displays a summary report with no detail or with only certain groups displayed.

The Group Footer section

You use the Group Footer section to calculate summaries for all the detail records in a group. In the Products Summary report, the expression `= Sum([RetailPrice] - [Cost])` adds a value calculated from all the records within a category. The value of this text-box control is automatically reset to 0 every time the group changes.

You learn more about expressions and summary text boxes in Chapters 9 and 21.

TIP

You can change the way summaries are calculated by changing the Running Sum property of the text box in the Report Design window. A Running Sum of No will only show the value of the current record and is the default setting. A value of Over Group will accumulate the amounts for that control over every record in the group. A value of Over All accumulates the values for that control over every record in the report.

The Page Footer section

The Page Footer section usually contains page numbers or control totals. In very large reports, such as when you have multiple pages of detail records with no summaries, you might want page totals, as well as group totals. For the Products Summary Report, the page number is printed by combining some literal text and the built-in page number controls. These controls show Page *x* of *y* where *x* is the current page number and *y* is the total number of pages in the report. A text-box control with the following expression in the Control Source property can be used to display page-number information that keeps track of the page number in the report:

```
="Page: " & [Page] & " of " & [Pages]
```

You can also print the date and the time printed. You can see the page number text box in the Page Footer section in Figure 20.23. The Page Footer in rptProductsSummary also contains the current date and time at the left side of the Page Footer section.

The Report Footer section

The Report Footer section is printed once at the end of the report after all the detail records and group footer sections are printed. Report footers typically display grand totals or other statistics (such as averages or percentages) for the entire report. The report footer for the Products Summary report uses the expression `= Sum` with each of the numeric fields to sum the amounts.

NOTE

When there is a report footer, the Page Footer section is printed after the report footer.

The Report Writer in Access is a two-pass report writer, capable of preprocessing all records to calculate the totals (such as percentages) needed for statistical reporting. This capability enables you to create expressions that calculate percentages as Access processes those records that require foreknowledge of the grand total.

Creating a Report from Scratch

Fundamental to all reports is the concept that a report is another way to view records in one or more tables. It's important to understand that a report is bound to either a single table or a query that brings together data from one or more tables. When you create a report, you must select which fields from the query or table you want to see in your report. Unless you want to view all the records from a single table, bind your report to a query. Even if you're accessing data from a single table, using a query lets you create your report on the basis of a particular search criterion and sorting order. If you want to access data from multiple tables, you have almost no choice but to bind your report to a query. In the examples in this chapter, all the reports are bound to queries (even though it's possible to bind a report to a table).

It may be obvious, but it bears mentioning that the data in a printed report is static and only reflects the state of data in the database at the moment the report is printed. For this reason, every report should have a "printed" date and time somewhere on the report (often in the report header or footer area) to document exactly when the report was printed.

NOTE

Access lets you create a report without first binding it to a table or query, but you'll have no bound controls on the report. This capability can be used to work out page templates with common text headers or footers such as page numbering or the date and time, which can serve as models for other reports. You can add controls later by changing the underlying control source of the report.

Throughout the rest of this chapter, you learn the tasks necessary to create the Product Display Report (a part of a page is shown in Figure 20.24). In these sections, you design the basic report, assemble the data, and place the data in the proper positions.

TIP

As with almost every task in Access, there are many ways to create a report without wizards. It is important, however, to follow some type of methodology, because creating a good report involves a fairly consistent approach. You should create a checklist that is a set of tasks that will result in a good report every time. As you complete each task, check it off your list. When you're done, you'll have a great-looking report. The following section outlines this approach.

FIGURE 20.24

The Product Display report.

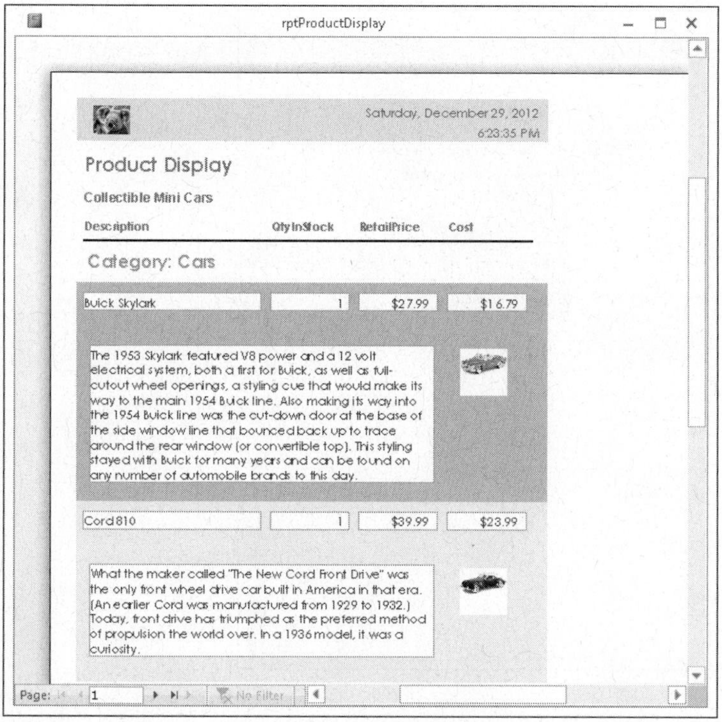

Creating a new report and binding it to a query

The first step is to create a new, empty report and bind it to tblProducts. Creating a blank report is quite easy:

1. **Select the Create tab of the Ribbon.**
2. **Click the Blank Report button in the Reports group.** Access opens a blank report in Layout view, and either positions a Field List dialog box on top of the new report (see Figure 20.25) or docks the Field List on the right side of the application window.

   At this point, you have two different paths for adding controls to the report: continue working in Layout view, or switch to Design view. Each of these techniques has advantages, but for the purposes of this exercise, I'll use Design view because it better demonstrates the process of building Access reports.

FIGURE 20.25

A blank report in Layout view.

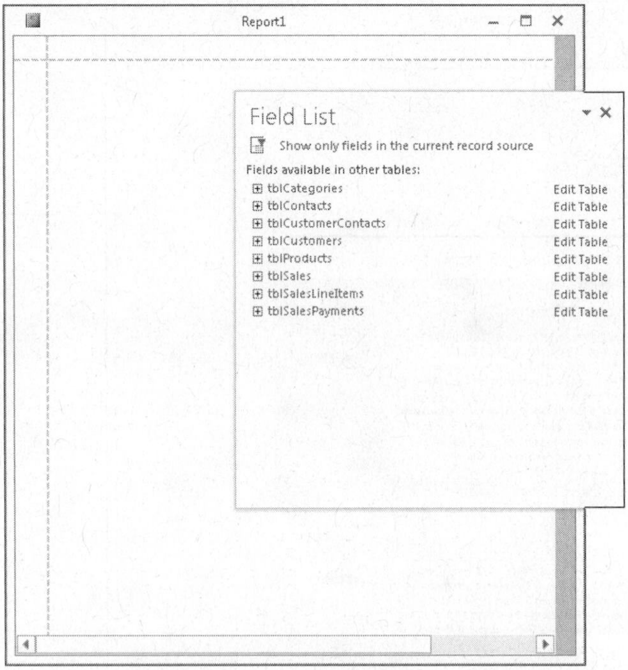

3. **Right-click the report's title bar, and select Design view from the shortcut menu.** The Report window transforms to the traditional Access banded Report Designer, as shown in Figure 20.26. This figure also shows the Field List open on tblProducts, allowing you to add fields from the list to the appropriate section on the new report.

   In Figure 20.26, the Description field has been dragged onto the Detail section of the report.

FIGURE 20.26

Building the new report in Design view.

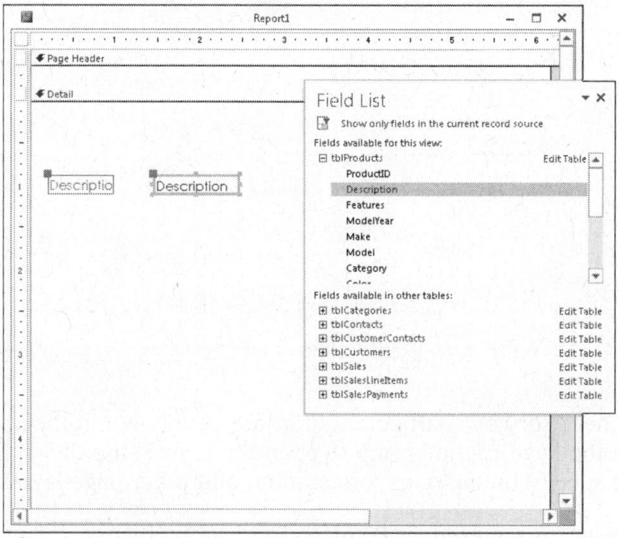

Defining the report page size and layout

As you plan your report, consider the page-layout characteristics, as well as the kind of paper and printer you want to use for the output. As you make these decisions, you use several dialog boxes and properties to make adjustments. These specifications work together to create the desired output.

Select the Page Setup tab of the Ribbon to select the report's margins, orientation, and other overall characteristics. Figure 20.27 shows a portion of the Access screen with the Page Setup tab selected and the Margins option open.

Notice that the Page Setup tab includes options for setting the paper size, the report's orientation (Portrait or Landscape), its margins, and other details. Dropping down either the Size or Margins option reveals a gallery containing common settings for each of these options.

rptProductDisplay is to be a portrait report, which is taller than it is wide. You want to print on letter size paper ($8^1/_2$ x 11 inches), and you want the left, right, top, and bottom margins all set to 0.25 inch. In Figure 9.27 notice that the Narrow margins option is selected, which specifies exactly 0.25 inch for all four margin settings.

FIGURE 20.27

Setting a report's margins.

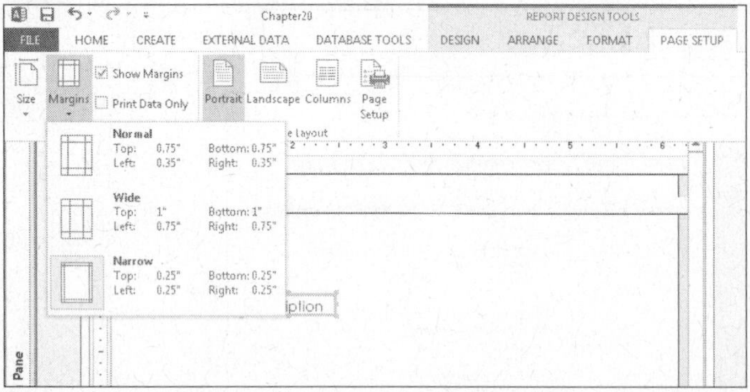

If the margins you need for your particular report are not shown in the Margins options, click Page Setup in the Page Layout group to open the Page Setup dialog box. This dialog box enables you to specify the margins, orientation, and other page-layout specifications.

To set the right border for the Product Display report to 7½ inches, follow these steps:

1. **Click the right edge of the report body (where the white page meets the gray background).** The mouse pointer changes to a double-headed arrow.
2. **Drag the edge to the 7½-inch mark.**

NOTE

Your units of measure may be different, depending on the regional settings in the Control Panel.

If the ruler isn't displayed in the Report Designer, click Ruler from the Size/Space drop down on the Arrange tab.

NOTE

You can also change the Width property in the Property window for the report.

TIP

If you run your report and every other page is blank, it's a sign that the width of your report exceeds the width of your page. To fix this problem, decrease the left and right margin size or reduce the report's width. Sometimes, when you move controls around, you accidentally make the report width larger than you originally intended. For example, in a portrait report, if your left margin plus report width plus right margin is greater than 8½ inches, you'll see blank pages.

Placing controls on the report

Access takes full advantage of drag-and-drop capabilities of Windows. The method for placing controls on a report is no exception:

1. **Click the Add Existing Fields button in the Tools group on the Design tab of the Ribbon.** The Field List window appears.
2. **Choose a control in the Toolbox if you want to use something other than the default control types for the fields.**
3. **Select each field that you want on your report and then drag them to the appropriate section of the Report Design window.** Select multiple fields by holding down the Ctrl key as you click fields in the Field List. Depending on whether you choose one or several fields, the mouse pointer changes shape to represent your selection as you drag fields onto the report.

   The fields appear in the detail section of the report, as shown in Figure 20.28. Notice that for each field you dragged onto the report, there are two controls. When you use the drag-and-drop method of placing fields, Access automatically creates a label control with the field name attached to the Text Box control to which the field is bound.

FIGURE 20.28

The report with several fields added.

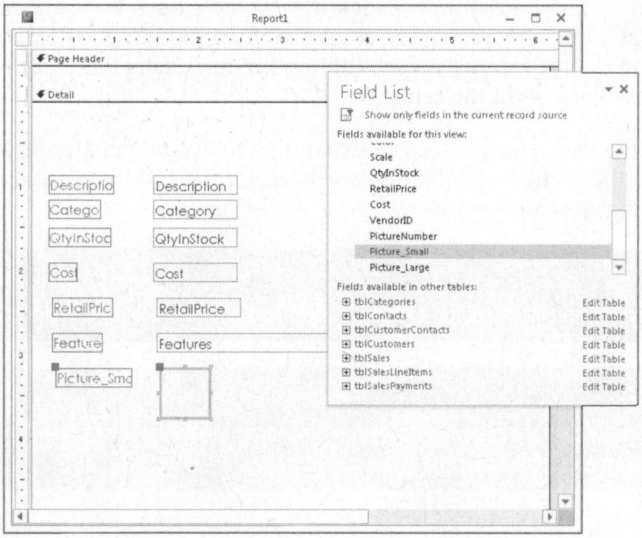

NOTE
Access always creates a Bound Object Frame control for an OLE-type object found in a table, such as for the Picture_Small field in Figure 20.28. Also notice that the Detail section automatically resizes itself to fit all the controls. Above the Bound Object Frame control is the control for the Long Text field Features.

Controls are needed for the customer information in the page header section. Before you do this, however, you must resize the page header to leave room for a title you'll add later.

Resizing a section

To make room on the report for the title information in the page header, you must resize it. You resize by using the mouse to drag the bottom of the section you want to resize. The mouse pointer turns into a vertical double-headed arrow as it's positioned over the bottom of a report section. Drag the section border up or down to make the section smaller or larger.

Resize the Page Header section to make it about ¾ inch high by dragging the bottom margin of the page header downward. Use the Controls group on the Design tab of the Ribbon to drag labels to the report. Add two labels to the Page Header section, and enter **Product Display** as the Caption property of one label, and **Collectible Mini Cars** for the other.

The labels you just added are unattached; they aren't related to any other controls on the report. When you drag a field from the Field List, Access adds not only a text box to contain the field's data, but also a label to provide an identifier for the text box. Labels that you drag from the Controls group on the Ribbon are unattached and not related to text boxes or any other control on the report.

You may notice the Page Header section expanding to accommodate the label controls that you dragged into the section. All the fields needed for the Product Display report are now placed in their appropriate sections.

TIP
To create a multiple-line label entry, press Ctrl+Enter to force a line break where you want it in the control.

TIP
If you enter a caption that is longer than the space in the Property window, the contents scroll as you type. Otherwise, open a Zoom box that gives you more space to type by pressing Shift+F2.

Modifying the appearance of text in a control

To modify the appearance of the text in a control, select the control by clicking its border (not in the control itself). You can then select a formatting style to apply to the label by clicking the appropriate button on the Format tab.

To make the titles stand out, follow these steps to modify the appearance of label text:

1. **Click the newly created report heading Product Display label in the Report Header section.**
2. **Select the Format tab of the Ribbon, and click the Bold button in the Font group.**
3. **From the Font Size drop-down list, select 18.**
4. **Repeat for the Collectible Mini Cars label, using a 12 pt Arial font and Bold.** The size of the labels may not fit their displayed text. To tighten the display or to display all the text when a label isn't big enough, double-click any of the sizing handles, and Access chooses an appropriate size for the label.

   Figure 20.29 shows these labels added, resized, and formatted in the report's Page Header section.

FIGURE 20.29

Adding unbound labels to the report.

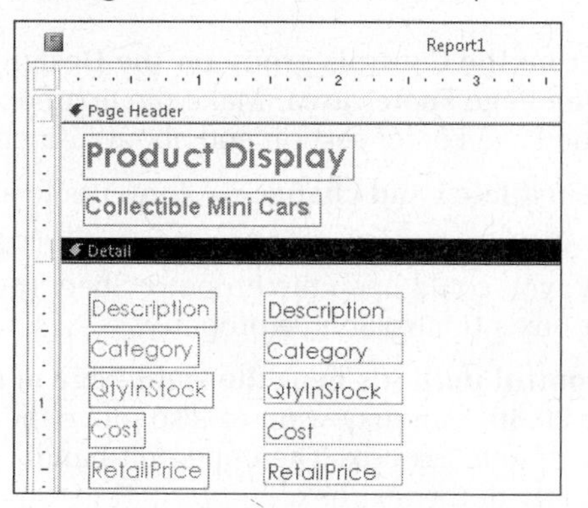

Working with text boxes

So far, you added controls bound to fields in the tables and unbound label controls used to display titles in your report. There is another type of Text Box control that is typically added to a report: unbound text boxes that are used to hold expressions such as page numbers, dates, or a calculation.

Adding and using Text Box controls

In reports, Text Box controls serve two purposes:

- They enable you to display stored data from a particular field in a query or table.
- They display the result of an expression.

Expressions can be calculations that use other controls as their operands, calculations that use Access functions (either built in or user defined), or a combination of the two.

Entering an expression in a text control

Expressions enable you to create a value that is not already in a table or query. They can range from simple functions (such as a page number) to complex mathematical computations.

Chapter 9 discusses expressions in greater detail.

A function is a small program that, when run, returns a single value. The function can be one of many built-in Access functions or it can be user defined.

The following steps show you how to use an unbound text box to add a page number to your report:

1. **Click in the middle of the Page Footer section, and resize the page footer so that it's ½ inch in height.**
2. **Drag a Text Box control from the Controls group on the Design tab of the Ribbon and drop it into the Page Footer area.** Make the text box about three-quarters of the height of the Page Footer section and about ½ inch wide.
3. **Select the text box's attached label and change its contents to say** Page:.
4. **Select the Text Box control (it says "Unbound") and enter** = Page **directly into the text box.** Alternatively, you could open the Property Sheet (press F4) and enter = **[Page]** as the text box's ControlSource property.
5. **Drag the new Text Box control until it's near the right edge of the report's page, as shown in Figure 20.30.** You may want to also move the text box's label so that it's positioned close to the text box. The upper-left handle on the label moves the label independently of the text box.

FIGURE 20.30

Adding a page-number expression in a Text Box control.

TIP
You can always check your result by clicking the Print Preview button on the toolbar and zooming in on the Page Footer section to check the page number.

Sizing a Text Box control or Label control

You select a control by clicking it. Depending on the size of the control, from three to seven sizing handles appear — one on each corner except the upper-left corner and one on each side. Moving the mouse pointer over one of the sizing handles changes the mouse pointer to a double-headed arrow. When the pointer changes, click the control and drag it to the size you want. Notice that, as you drag, an outline appears indicating the size the label control will be when you release the mouse button.

If you double-click any of the sizing handles, Access resizes a control to best fit for text in the control. This feature is especially handy if you increase the font size and then notice that the text no longer fits the control.

Note that, for label controls, the *best-fit sizing* resizes both vertically and horizontally, although text controls resize only vertically. The reason for this difference is that in Report Design mode, Access doesn't know how much of a field's data you want to display. Later on, the field's name and contents might be radically different. Sometimes label controls are not resized correctly, however, and have to be adjusted manually.

TIP
You can also choose Arrange ➪ Size/Space ➪ To Fit to change the size of the label control text automatically.

Before continuing, you should check how the report is progressing. You should also save the report frequently as you make changes to it. You could send a single page to the printer, but it's probably easier to view the report in Print Preview. Right-click the report's title bar, and select Print Preview from the shortcut menu. Figure 20.31 shows a print preview of the report's current appearance. The page header information is at the very top of the page, and the first product record appears below the header.

As you move the mouse over the print preview, the cursor changes to a magnifying glass. Click any portion of the view to zoom in so that you can closely examine the report's layout. Only one record per page appears on the report because of the vertical layout. In the next section, you move the controls around and create a more horizontal layout.

FIGURE 20.31

A print preview of the report so far.

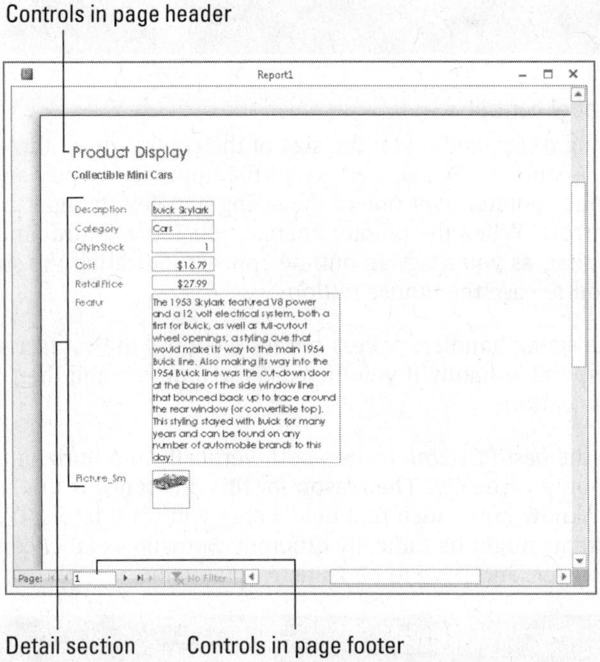

Controls in page header

Detail section

Controls in page footer

Deleting and cutting attached labels from text controls

To create a more horizontal report, you must move the text-box labels from the Detail section to the Page Header section and reposition the Text Boxes to a tabular layout. Once moved, these controls appear as headings above each column of data and are repeated on each page of the report.

You can easily delete one or more attached controls in a report. Simply select the desired controls and press Delete. However, if you want to *move* the label to the Page Header section (instead of simply deleting it), you can cut the label instead of deleting it. When removing attached controls, there are three choices:

- Delete only the Label control.
- Cut the Label control to the Clipboard.
- Delete or cut the Label control and the Text Box control.

Oddly enough, you can't simply drag a label from the Detail section to the page header. Dragging an attached label from the Detail section drags its text box along with it. You must cut the label from the Detail section and paste it into the Page Header section.

If you select the Label control and cut it by pressing Ctrl + X, only the Label control is removed. If you select the Text Box control and cut or delete it, the Label and Text Box controls are removed. To cut an attached label control (in this case, the label attached to the Description text box), follow these steps:

1. **Click the Close Print Preview button on the Ribbon to exit Print Preview mode.**
2. **Select the Description label in the Detail section.**
3. **Press Ctrl + X (Cut).** After you've cut the label, you may want to place it somewhere else. In this example, place it in the Page Header section.

Pasting labels into a report section

It's as easy to cut labels from controls placed in the Detail section and paste them into the page header as it is to delete the labels and create new ones in the page header. Regardless, you now paste the label you cut in the previous steps:

1. **Click anywhere in or on the Page Header section.**
2. **Press Ctrl + V (Paste).** The Description label appears in the page header.
3. **Repeat for the Quantity in Stock, Retail Price, and Cost labels.** If you accidentally selected the data Text Box control and both controls are cut or deleted, click the Undo toolbar button, or press Ctrl + Z, to undo the action.

TIP

If you want to delete only the Text Box control and keep the attached Label control, right-click the Label control and select Copy from the shortcut menu. Next, to delete the Text Box control and the Label control, select the Text Box control and press the Delete key. Finally, right-click anywhere on the form and select Paste from the shortcut menu to paste only the copied Label control to the report.

Moving Label and Text Box controls

Before discussing how to move Label and Text Box controls, it's important to review a few differences between attached and unattached controls. When an attached label is created automatically with a Text Box control, it's called a *compound control*. In a compound control, whenever one control in the set is moved, the other control moves along with it. This means that moving either the label or the text box also moves the related control.

To move both controls in a compound control, select either of the pair of controls with the mouse. As you move the mouse pointer over either of the objects, the pointer turns into a hand. Click the controls and drag them to their new location. As you drag, an outline for the compound control moves with your pointer.

To move only one of the controls in a compound control, drag the desired control by its moving handle (the large square in the upper-left corner of the control). When you click a compound control, it looks like both controls are selected, but if you look closely, you see that only one of the two controls (Text Box or Label) is selected (as indicated by the presence of both moving and sizing handles). The unselected control displays only a moving handle. A pointing finger indicates that you've selected the move handles and can now move one control independently of the other. To move either control individually, select the control's move handle and drag it to its new location.

TIP

To move a label that isn't attached, simply click any border (except where there is a handle) and drag it.

To make a group selection, click with the mouse pointer anywhere outside a starting point and drag the pointer through (or around) the controls you want to select. A gray, outlined rectangle appears, showing the extent of the selection. When you release the mouse button, all controls the rectangle surrounds are selected. You can then drag the group of controls to a new location.

TIP

The Select Behavior option (choose File ➪ Options ➪ Object Designers ➪ Form/Report design view ➪ Selection Behavior) determines how controls are selected with the mouse. You can enclose them fully (the rectangle must completely surround the selection) or partially (the rectangle must touch only the control), which is the default.

Make sure you also resize all the controls as shown in the figure. Change the size and shape of the Features Long Text field and the OLE picture field Picture. The OLE picture field displays as a rectangle with no field name in Design view. (It's the bottommost control above the footer in Figure 20.32.)

Place all the controls in their proper position to complete the report layout. Figure 20.32 shows one possible layout of the controls. You make a series of group moves by selecting several controls and positioning them close to where you want them. Then, if needed, you can fine-tune their position by dragging individual controls.

Use Figure 20.32 as a guide to placing controls on the report.

At this point, you're about halfway done. The screen should look something like Figure 20.32. Remember that these screenshots are taken with the Windows screen resolution set to 1,024 x 768. If you're using a lower resolution, or you have large fonts turned on in the Windows Display Properties (in the Control Panel), you have to scroll the screen to see the entire report.

These steps complete the rough design for this report. There are still properties, fonts, and sizes to change. When you make these changes, you have to move controls around again. Use the designs in Figure 20.32 only as a guideline. How it looks to *you*, as you refine the look of the report in the Report window, determines the final design.

FIGURE 20.32

Rearranging the controls on the report.

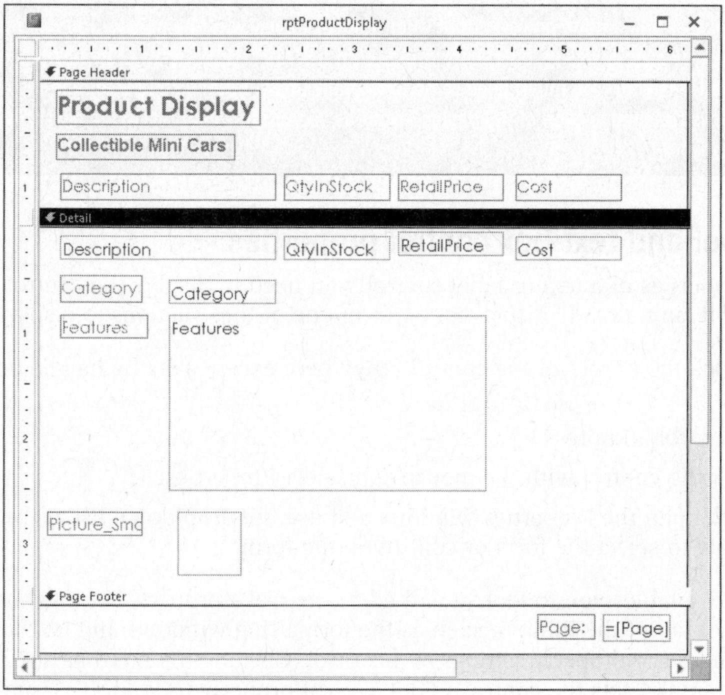

Modifying the appearance of multiple controls

The next step is to apply bold formatting to all the label controls in the Page Header section directly above the section separator. The following steps guide you through modifying the appearance of text in multiple label controls:

1. **Select all label controls in the bottom of the Page Header section by clicking them one at a time while holding down the Shift key.** Alternatively, click in the vertical ruler immediately to the left of the labels in the Page Header. Access selects all controls to the right of where you clicked in the vertical ruler. There are four label controls to select (refer to Figure 20.32).

   Alternatively, you can drag a bounding box around the label controls in the page header.

2. **Click the Bold button on the toolbar.** After you make the final modifications, you're finished, except for fixing the picture control. To do this, you need to change properties, which you do in the next section.

NOTE
This may seem to be an enormous number of steps because the procedures were designed to show you how laying out a report design can be a slow process. Remember, however, that when you click away with the mouse, you don't realize how many steps you're doing as you visually design the report layout. With a WYSIWYG (What You See Is What You Get) layout tool like the Access Report Designer, you might need to perform many tasks, but it's still easier and faster than programming. Figure 20.32 shows the final version of the design layout as seen in this chapter. In the next chapter, you continue to improve this report layout.

Changing label and text-box control properties

To change the properties of a text or label control, you need to display the control's Property Sheet. If it isn't already displayed, perform one of these actions to display it:

- Double-click the border of the control (anywhere except a sizing handle or move handle).
- Select a control and press F4.
- Right-click the control with the mouse and select Properties.
- Press F4 to open the Properties window, and use the drop-down list at the top of the window to select the form or control on the form.

The Property Sheet enables you to look at and edit a control's property settings. Using tools on the Format tab of the Ribbon, such as the formatting windows and text-formatting buttons, also changes the property settings of a control. Clicking the `Bold` button in the Format tab, for example, sets the control's Font Weight property to Bold. It's usually easier and more intuitive to use the controls on the Format tab of the Ribbon, but many properties are not accessible through the Ribbon. Plus, objects often have more options available through the Property Sheet.

The Size Mode property of an OLE object (bound object frame), with its options of Clip, Stretch, and Zoom, is a good example of a property that is available only through the Property Sheet.

The image control, which is a bound object frame, presently has its Size Mode property set to Zoom, which is the default. With Size Mode set to Clip, the picture is displayed in its original size and Access either cuts off the picture at the edge of its control or shows extra space around the image. With Size Mode set to Stretch, the image will fit the control frame but may be distorted if the control frame has a different aspect ratio than the image. A Size Mode of Zoom keeps the image's aspect ratio and fits the image inside the control frame. You may find that extra space is shown around the image, but it's usually a good trade-off so the image isn't distorted.

You might consider changing the Border Style property to Transparent. When set to Transparent, no boxes are drawn around the picture and the picture blends into the report's surface. Finally, delete the label bound to the picture control.

The labels for Features and Pictures aren't needed because a user will surely know what data is being presented without them. Select each label and press the Delete key to remove them. Next, reposition the picture control to the right of the Feature control.

These steps complete the changes to your report so far. A print preview of the first few records appears in Figure 20.33. If you look at the pictures, notice how the picture is properly displayed and the product's Features text box now appears across the bottom of each Detail section.

FIGURE 20.33

The report displayed in Print Preview.

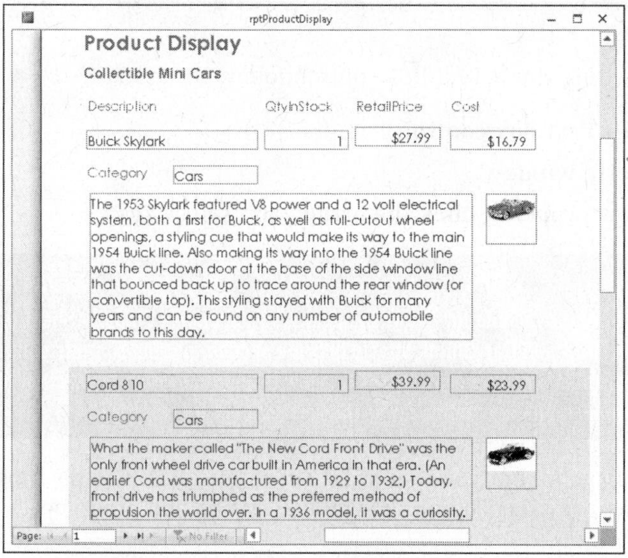

Growing and shrinking Text Box controls

When you print or print-preview controls that can have variable text lengths, Access provides options for enabling a control to grow or shrink vertically, depending on the exact contents of a record. The Can Grow and Can Shrink properties determine whether a text control resizes its vertical dimension to accommodate the amount of text contained in its bound field. Although these properties are usable for any text control, they're especially helpful for Text Box controls.

Table 20.1 explains the acceptable values for these two properties.

TABLE 20.1 Text Box Control Values for Can Grow and Can Shrink

Property	Value	Description
Can Grow	Yes	If the data in a record uses more lines than the control is defined to display, the control resizes to accommodate additional lines.
Can Grow	No	If the data in a record uses more lines than the control is defined to display, the control does not resize. Rather, it truncates the data in the control.
Can Shrink	Yes	If the data in a record uses fewer lines than the control is defined to display, the control resizes to eliminate blank space. The Can Shrink property of all controls in the section must be set to Yes before the section can shrink.
Can Shrink	No	If the data in a record uses fewer lines than the control is defined to display, the control does not resize to eliminate blank space.

To change the Can Grow settings for a Text Box control, follow these steps:

1. **Select the Features Text Box control.**
2. **Display the Property window.**
3. **Click the Can Grow property, click the arrow, and select Yes.**

NOTE

The Can Grow and Can Shrink properties are also available for report sections. Use a section's Property Sheet to modify these values. Setting a report section's Can Grow and Can Shrink affects only the section, not the controls contained within the section. However, you must set the section's Can Grow to Yes to allow the control within the section to grow. If the section's Can Grow is not set, the control can only expand as far as the section's border permits.

The report is starting to look good, but you may want to see groups of like data together and determine specific orders of data. To do this, you use sorting and grouping.

Sorting and grouping data

You can often make the data on the report more useful to users by grouping the data in informative ways. Suppose that you want to list your products first by category and then by description within each category. To do this, you use the Category and Description fields to group and sort the data.

Creating a group header or footer

Grouping on a field in the report's data adds two new sections — Group Header and Group Footer — to the report. In the following steps, you use the group header to display the name of the product category above each group of records. You won't use the Category group footer in this example because there are no totals by category or other reasons to use a group footer.

Follow these steps to create a Category group header:

1. **Click the Group & Sort button in the Grouping & Totals group on the Design tab of the Ribbon.** The Group, Sort, and Total pane appears at the bottom of the screen.
2. **Click the Add a Group button in the Group, Sort, and Total area.**
3. **Select Category from the field list.** Access adds Group on Category with A on top of the Group, Sort, and Total area. Access adds Category Header and Category Footer sections to the report's design as soon as you select the Category field for grouping. The Category Header section appears between the Page Header and Detail sections. If you define a group footer, it appears below the Detail section, and above the Page Footer area. If a report has multiple groupings, each subsequent group becomes the one closest to the Detail section. The groups defined first are farthest from the Detail section.

The Group Properties pane (displayed when you click the More button on the group) displays a sentence with each option separated by a comma. The options are drop-down lists or clickable text for setting the property. The options sentence for the Category group contains these choices:

- **Group on Category:** Determines the field on which to group. You can change this field even after you've set the group field by selecting a different field from the drop down.
- **With A on top:** Determines the sort order. In this case it's alphabetical. Select With Z on top to reverse the sort.
- **By entire value:** Groups are separated based on the value in the field. You can also group on the first character of the field, the first two characters of the field, or any number of characters that you type into the Characters box in the drop down.
- **With no totals:** Determines what totals are displayed in the group header or footer. You can select which field to total and the type of total to display.
- **With title:** Allows you to specify a title for the group.
- **With a header section:** Displays the group header section. Choose "without a header section" to hide the header.
- **Without a footer section:** Hides the group footer section. Choose "with a footer section" to display the footer.
- **Do not keep together on one page:** Allows the group to be continued on the next page if there is too much information for the current page. Choose "keep whole group together on one page" to start a new page when there is too much information for the current page. Choose "keep header and first record together on one page" to start a new page only when there isn't enough room for the first record.

Click the Less button to hide these options once set. The options above are shown for a grouping on the Category field, which is a text field. Other field types have some of the same options and some different options. Date fields show these options:

- **From oldest to newest:** Instead of "with A on top" as with text fields, date fields are sorted from oldest to newest. Choose "from newest to oldest" to reverse the sort.
- **By quarter:** Allows you to group by the entire date, by day, by week, by month, by quarter, by year, or by a custom date or time increment.

The other date field options are the same as for text fields and are not repeated. Numeric fields show these options:

- **From smallest to largest:** Determines the numeric sort. Choose "from largest to smallest" to reverse the order.
- **By entire value:** Group by each numeric value individually or by 5s, 10s, 100s, 1,000s, or by a custom interval.

Sorting data within groups

Sorting enables you to determine the order in which the records are viewed on the report, based on the values in one or more controls. This order is important when you want to view the data in your tables in a sequence other than that of your input. For example, new products are added to tblProducts as they're needed on an invoice. The physical order of the database reflects the date and time a product is added. Yet, when you think of the product list, you probably expect it to be in alphabetical order by Product ID, and you want to sort it by Description or the cost of the product. By sorting in the report itself, you don't have to worry about the order of the data. Although you can sort the data in the table by the primary key or in a query by any field you want, there are good reasons to do it in the report. This way, if you change the query or table, the report is still in the correct order.

In the case of the products report, you want to display the records in each category group sorted by description. Follow these steps to define a sort order based on the Description field within the Category grouping:

1. **Click the Grouping button on the Design tab of the Ribbon to display the Group, Sort, and Total area, if it isn't already open.** You should see that the Category group already exists in the report.
2. **Click the Add a Sort button in the Group, Sort, and Total area.**
3. **Select Description in the Field List.** Notice that Sort by defaults to "with A on top."
4. **Close the Group, Sort, and Total area by clicking the X in the upper-right corner.** The Group, Sort, and Total section should now look like Figure 20.34.

FIGURE 20.34

The Group, Sort, and Total area completed.

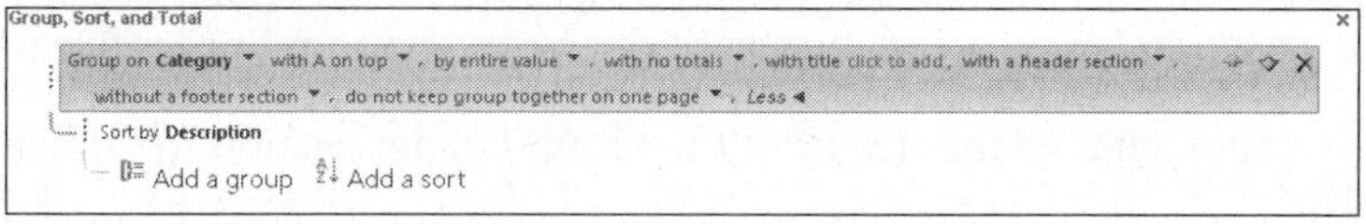

Group, Sort, and Total

Group on **Category** with A on top, by entire value, with no totals, with title click to add, with a header section, without a footer section, do not keep group together on one page, Less

Sort by **Description**

Add a group Add a sort

Although in this example you used a field, you can also sort (and group) with an expression. To enter an expression, click the Add a Sort or Add a Group button in the Group, Sort, and Total area and click the Expression button at the bottom of the field list. The Expression Builder dialog box opens, enabling you to enter any valid Access expression, such as in `= [RetailPrice]-[Cost]`.

To change the sort order for fields in the Field/Expression column, simply click the drop-down arrow to the right of the With A on Top button (see Figure 20.34) to display the Sort Order list. Select "with Z on top" from the sort options that appear.

Removing a group

To remove a group, display the Group, Sort, and Total area; select the group or sort specifier to delete; and press the Delete key. Any controls in the group header or footer will be removed.

Hiding a section

Access also enables you to hide headers and footers so that you can break data into groups without having to view information about the group itself. You can also hide the Detail section so that you see only a summary report. To hide a section, follow these steps:

1. **Click the section you want to hide.**
2. **Display the section's Property Sheet.**
3. **Click the Visible property and select No from the drop-down list in the property's text box.**

NOTE

Sections are not the only objects in a report that can be hidden; controls also have a Visible property. This property can be useful for expressions that trigger other expressions.

20

Sizing a section

Now that you've created the group header, you might want to put some controls in the section, move some controls around, or even move controls between sections. Before you start manipulating controls within a section, you should make sure the section is the proper height.

To modify the height of a section, drag the top border of the section below it. If, for example, you have a report with a page header, Detail section, and page footer, change the height of the Detail section by dragging the top of the Page Footer section's border. You can make a section larger or smaller by dragging the bottom border of the section.

For this example, change the height of the group header section to 3/8 inch by following these steps:

1. **Move your mouse pointer to the bottom of the Category Header section.** The pointer changes to a horizontal line split by two vertical arrows.
2. **Select the top of the Detail section (which is also the bottom of the Category Header section).**
3. **Drag the selected band lower until three dots appear in the vertical ruler (3/8") and release the mouse button when you have the band positioned.** The gray line indicates where the top of the border will be when you release the mouse button.

Moving controls between sections

You now want to move the Category control from the Detail section to the Category Header section. You can move one or more controls between sections simply by dragging the control with your mouse from one section to another or by cutting it from one section and pasting it to another section:

1. **Select the Category control in the Detail section and drag it up to the Category Header section, as shown in Figure 20.35.** You should now perform the following steps to complete the report design.
2. **Delete the Category label from the group header.**
3. **Set the Border Style property of the Category control and all of the controls in the Page Header to Transparent.**
4. **Change the font size, bold, and font color of the Category control to visually distinguish it from the records below it.** Figure 20.35 shows the placement of the controls on the completed report design.

TIP

Access names the group header and footer sections automatically. To change this name, select the group header in the Property Sheet and change the Name property to something more appropriate. For example, change the Name property from GroupHeader0 to CategoryHeader so that it's easier to identify.

FIGURE 20.35

Completing the Group Header section.

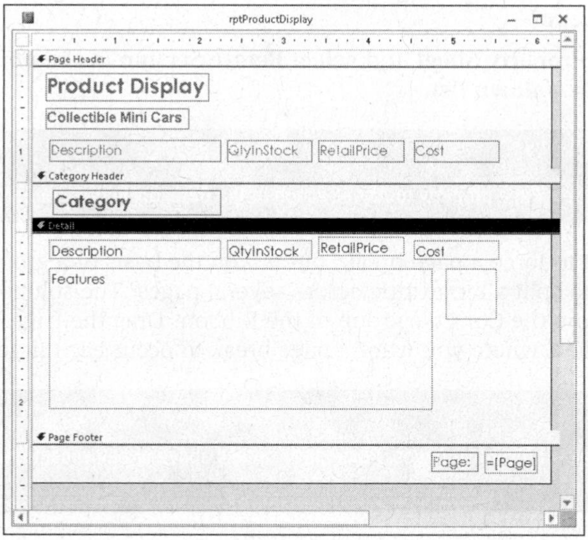

Adding page breaks

Access enables you to force page breaks based on groups. You can also insert forced breaks within sections, except in Page Header and Page Footer sections.

In some report designs, it's best to have each new group begin on a different page. You can achieve this effect easily by using the Force New Page property of a group section, which enables you to force a page break every time the group value changes.

The four Force New Page property settings are

- **None:** No forced page break (the default)
- **Before Section:** Starts printing the current section at the top of a new page every time there is a new group
- **After Section:** Starts printing the next section at the top of a new page every time there is a new group
- **Before & After:** Combines the effects of Before Section and After Section

To force a page break before the Category group:

1. **Click anywhere in the Category header, or click the Category Header bar above the section.**
2. **Display the Property Sheet and select Before Section in the Force New Page property's drop-down list.**

TIP

Alternatively, you can set the Force New Page property to After Section in the Category Footer section.

Sometimes, you want to force a page break, but not on the basis of a grouping. For example, you might want to split a report title across several pages. The solution is to use the Page Break control from the Controls group of the Ribbon. Drag the Page Break control and drop it on the report where you want a page break to occur each time the page prints.

NOTE

Be careful not to split control and show it over two pages. Place page breaks above or below controls without overlapping them.

Improving the Report's Appearance

As you near completion of testing your report design, you should also test the printing of your report. Figure 20.36 shows the first page of the Product Display report. There are a number of things still to do to complete the report.

The report is pretty boring and plain. If your goal is to just look at the data, this report is done. However, you need to do more before you're really done.

Although the report has good, well-organized data, it isn't of professional quality. To make a report more visually appealing, you generally add a few graphic elements like lines and rectangles, and possibly some special effects such as shadows or sunken areas. You want to make sure sections have distinct areas separate from each other using lines or colors. Make sure controls aren't touching each other (because text might eventually touch if a value is long enough). Make sure text is aligned with other text above or below and to the right or left.

In Figure 20.36, you can see opportunities for improvements.

FIGURE 20.36

The report is pretty plain and uninteresting at this point.

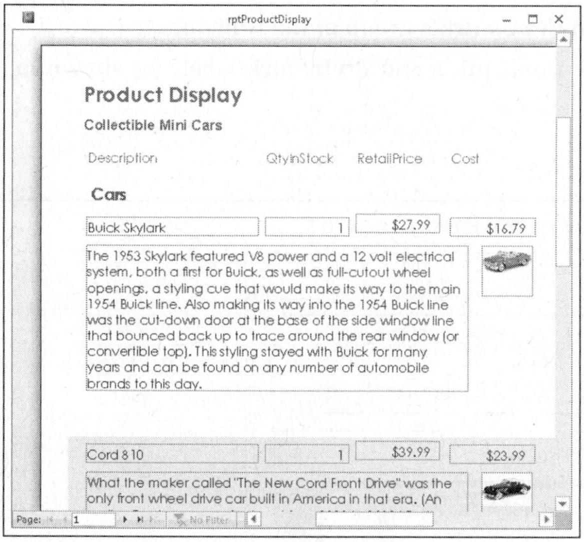

Adjusting the page header

The page header contains several large labels positioned far apart from each other. The column headers are small and just hanging there. They could be made one font size larger. The entire page header should be separated from the Detail section by a horizontal line.

If you wanted to add some color to your report, you could make the report name a different color. Be careful not to use too many colors unless you have a specific theme in mind, though. Most serious business reports use one or two colors, and rarely more than three with the exception of graphs and charts. Furthermore, colors are not much use when printed on most laser printers. Color laser printers are just becoming widely available, so adding a lot of color to your Access reports may not be appreciated by your users.

Figure 20.37 shows these changes. The Product Display label has been changed to a blue background color with white foreground text. This is done by first selecting the control and then selecting Blue for the background. They've also been placed under each other and left aligned. The rectangle around each of the controls was also properly sized by double-clicking each control's sizing handles.

The next step is to add a nice thick line separating the Page Header section from the Category Group Header section:

1. **Select the Line tool in the Controls group of the Ribbon.**
2. **Drag a line below the Description and QtyInStock labels, as shown in Figure 20.37.**

FIGURE 20.37

Adjusting controls in the page header.

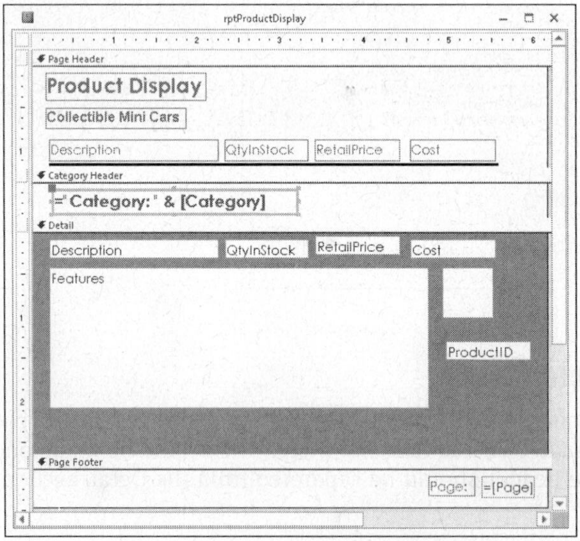

3. **Select the line and change the Border Width property to 2 pt on the line's property window.**

Creating an expression in the group header

Figure 20.37 also shows that the Category field has been replaced by an expression. If you place the value of the category in the Group Header section, it looks out of place and may not be readily identifiable. Most data values should have some type of label to identify what they are.

The expression `="Category: " & [Category]` displays `Category:` followed by a space and the value of the `Category` field (such as `Category: Cars`) in the text box. The `&` symbol (the concatenation operator) joins strings. Make sure you leave a space after the colon or the value won't be separated from the label. The text control has been bolded and underlined, and the font point size has been increased as well.

You may find that Access complains about a circular reference on the Category text box after you change the control's ControlSource. This happens because the name of the control is Category, and the text box is bound to a field named Category. Access doesn't understand that `[Category]` in the expression you entered as the ControlSource actually refers to the field, not the text box. (A text box's value can't be based on the text box's contents — that's the definition of *circular reference.*) The solution is to rename the text box to txtCategory to distinguish it from its bound field.

CAUTION

When you create a bound control, it uses the name of the data field as the default control name. Using the control in an expression without changing the name of your control, causes circular references. You must manually rename the control to something other than the original field name. This is another reason why a simple naming convention, such as prefixing text boxes with txt, is such a good idea. You'll avoid a lot of nagging problems by adopting a naming convention for the controls on your Access reports.

Follow these steps to complete the expression and rename the control:

1. **Select the Category control in the Category Group Header section and display the property window for the control.**
2. **Change the ControlSource property to = "Category: " & [Category].**
3. **Change the Name property to txtCategory.**

The final formatting step for the Category Header is to change the Border Style property of the txtCategory control to Transparent. You have visually distinguished this control by changing the font, and a border is unnecessary.

Creating a report header

The Report Header section is printed only once for the entire report. The report header is the logical place to put things such as the report's title, a logo, and the print date and time. Having this information in the report header makes it easy for any user of the report to know exactly what's in the report and when the report was printed.

With the report open in Design view, the ribbon includes a Design tab. Within the Header/Footer group on the Design tab are a number of controls that help you add important features to the report's header and footer.

For example, click the Logo button, and Access opens the Insert Picture dialog box (shown in Figure 20.38) for browsing to an image file to insert as the report's logo. Virtually any image file (JPG, GIF, BMP, and so on) is a candidate for inclusion as the report's logo.

FIGURE 20.38

Browsing to an image file to use as the report's logo.

The Title button in the Header/Footer group adds the report's name as the report header's title, and positions the edit cursor within the title label to make it easy for you to adjust the report's title.

Finally, the Date and Time button opens the Date and Time dialog box (shown in Figure 20.39). Specify the date and time format you'd like to use for the date control by selecting the Date and Time control in the Header/Footer group on the Design tab of the Ribbon.

FIGURE 20.39

Specifying the date and time format.

The completed report in Print Preview is shown in Figure 20.40. The report header in this figure was created in less than a minute using the tools built into Access 2013.

FIGURE 20.40

The completed report in Print Preview.

rptProductDisplay_final

Saturday, December 29, 2012
7:06:49 PM

Product Display

Collectible Mini Cars

Description	QtyInStock	RetailPrice	Cost

Category: Cars

Buick Skylark	1	$27.99	$16.79

The 1953 Skylark featured V8 power and a 12 volt electrical system, both a first for Buick, as well as full-cutout wheel openings, a styling cue that would make its way to the main 1954 Buick line. Also making its way into the 1954 Buick line was the cut-down door at the base of the side window line that bounced back up to trace around the rear window (or convertible top). This styling stayed with Buick for many years and can be found on any number of automobile brands to this day.

Cord 810	1	$39.99	$23.99

What the maker called "The New Cord Front Drive" was the only front wheel drive car built in America in that era. (An earlier Cord was manufactured from 1929 to 1932.) Today, front drive has triumphed as the preferred method

Page: 1 No Filter

As you close the report, Access will prompt you for the report's name.

20

CHAPTER 21

Advanced Access Report Techniques

IN THIS CHAPTER

Organizing reports to present the data in a logical manner

Producing more attractive reports

Providing additional information about the report

Learning other approaches to enhance your presentation

Back in the bad old days, most computer-generated reports were printed on pulpy, green-bar paper in strict *tabular* (row-and-column) format. The user was expected to further process the data to suit his particular needs — often, a time-consuming process that involved manually summarizing or graphing the data.

Things have changed. Visually oriented businesspeople want useful, informative reports produced directly from their databases. No one wants to spend time graphing data printed in simple tabular format anymore. Today, users want the software to do much of the work for them. This means that reporting tools such as Access must be able to produce the high-quality, highly readable reports that users demand.

Because Access is a Windows application, you have all the Windows facilities at your disposal: TrueType fonts, graphics, and a graphical interface for report design and preview. In addition, Access reports feature properties and an event model (although with fewer events than you saw on forms) for customizing report behavior. You can use the Visual Basic language to add refinement and automation to the reports you build in Access.

In this chapter, we provide some general principles and design techniques to keep in mind as you build Access reports. These principles will help make your reports more readable and informative.

This chapter does not discuss the basic process of building Access reports (see Chapter 20 for those details). Instead, this chapter describes a number of design techniques you can apply to Access reports using the skills described in Chapter 9.

On the Web

All of the examples presented in this chapter can be found in the `Chapter21.accdb` sample database on this book's website. Please note that many of the figures in this chapter appear with the report Design view grid turned off to make the report design details easier to see.

Note

This chapter uses data from the Northwind Traders example database. The Northwind data is ideally suited for the example report described in this chapter and is a good model for most Access databases. The techniques described in the following sections should be adaptable to any well-designed database without too much trouble.

Grouping and Sorting Data

To be most useful, the data on a report should be well organized. Grouping data that's similar can reduce the amount of data presented, which makes it easier to find specific data. As you'll see in this section, the Access Report Builder offers a fair degree of flexibility in this regard.

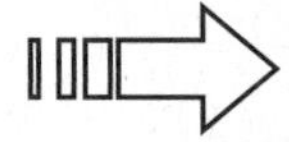

Grouping and sorting was introduced in Chapter 20. This section expands on that information and provides more examples.

Grouping data alphabetically

Data is often displayed with too much granularity to be useful. A report displaying every sale made by every employee arranged in a tabular format can be difficult to read. Anything you do to reduce the overload of tabular reports can make the data more meaningful.

The Group, Sort, and Total dialog box (which is opened by clicking the Group & Sort button in the Grouping & Totals group on the Design tab) controls how data is grouped on Access reports. Sorting alphabetically arranges the records in alphabetical order based on the first character of the company name, while grouping by company name creates a separate group for each company.

Clicking the Add a Group button below the Sorting and Grouping area opens a list from which you choose a field to use for grouping data on the report. In Figure 21.1, both CompanyName and OrderDate have been selected, with CompanyName being grouped first and then OrderDate sorted within the company groups.

FIGURE 21.1

Alphabetical grouping is easy!

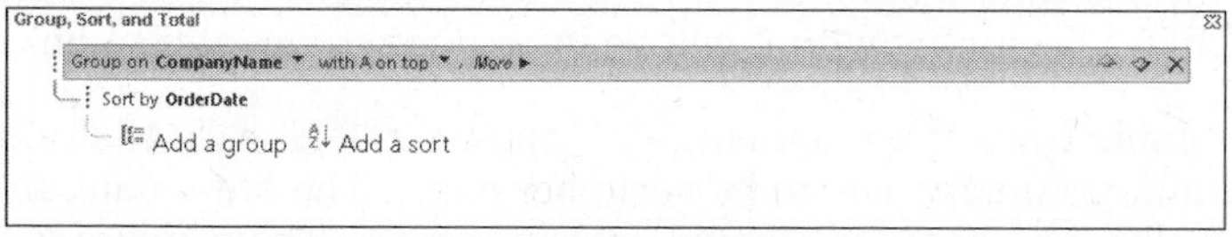

Group, Sort, and Total
Group on CompanyName ▾ with A on top ▾ , More ▸
Sort by OrderDate
Add a group
Add a sort

Typically, data is grouped on the entire contents of a field or combination of fields. Simple grouping on the CompanyName field means that all records for Bottom Dollar Markets appear together as a group and all the records for Ernst Handel appear together as another group. You can, however, override the default and group based on *prefix characters* by changing the Group On property in the Group, Sort, and Total dialog box.

Notice the More button in the CompanyName sorting bar in Figure 21.1. Clicking the More button reveals the sorting details you want to apply to the CompanyName field (see Figure 21.2). By default, text fields such as CompanyName are sorted alphabetically by the field's entire contents. You can change this behavior to alter how Access applies grouping to the field's data (see Figure 21.3).

FIGURE 21.2

Many options are available to you for grouping and sorting.

Group, Sort, and Total
Group on CompanyName ▾ with A on top ▾ , by entire value ▾ , with no totals ▾ , with title click to add ,
with a header section ▾ , with a footer section ▾ , do not keep group together on one page ▾ , Less ◂
Sort by OrderDate
Add a group
Add a sort

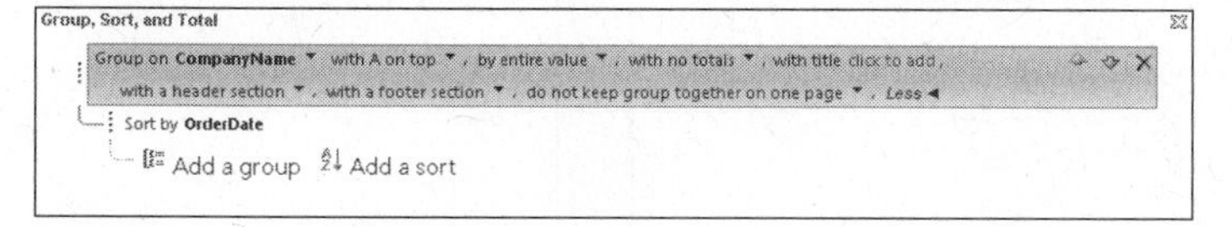

FIGURE 21.3

Modifying a text-base grouping.

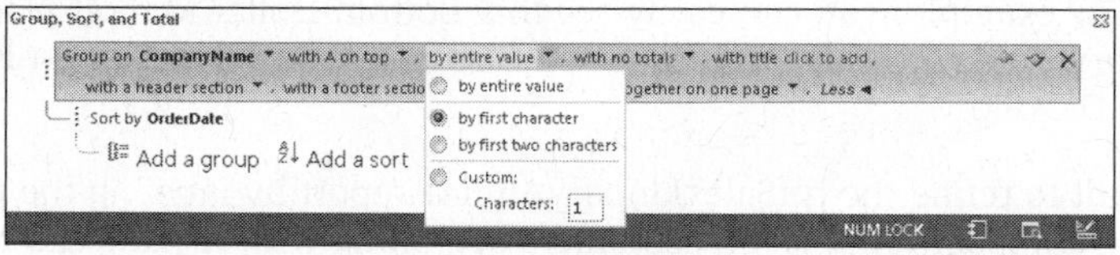

Group, Sort, and Total
Group on CompanyName ▾ with A on top ▾ , by entire value ▾ , with no totals ▾ , with title click to add ,
with a header section ▾ , with a footer sectio
ogether on one page ▾ , Less ◂
by entire value
by first character
by first two characters
Custom:
Characters: 1
Sort by OrderDate
Add a group
Add a sort
NUM LOCK

When you select by first character, the GroupInterval property tells Access how many characters to consider when grouping on prefix characters. In this case, the grouping interval is set to 1, meaning, "Consider only the *first* character when grouping." You could choose to group by the first character, the first two characters, or any number of characters in the field, depending on your requirements.

Notice also that the CompanyName field is set to ascending sort (with *A* on top), which causes alphabetic grouping starting at names beginning with *A* and progressing to names beginning with *Z*. With this combination of properties, all companies starting with *A* will be grouped together, those beginning with *B* will be in another group, and so on.

The report for this example (rptSalesJanuarayAlpha1, shown in Figure 21.4) shows purchases during the month of January, sorted by customer name. The order date, the order ID, and the employee filling the order are shown across the page. The result of the sorting and grouping specification in Figure 21.1 is shown in Figure 21.4.

FIGURE 21.4

A rearrangement of the data shown in Figure 21.13, later in this chapter.

Northwind Sales: January

Northwind Sales: January

Company Name	Order Date	Order ID	Sales Person
Antonio Moreno Taquería	24-Jan-12	10365	Janet Leverling
Around the Horn	12-Jan-12	10355	Michael Suyama
Blondel père et fils	19-Jan-12	10360	Margaret Peacock
Bon app'	22-Jan-12	10362	Janet Leverling
Bottom-Dollar Markets	17-Jan-12	10358	Steven Buchanan
	25-Jan-12	10367	Robert King
	30-Jan-12	10371	Nancy Davolio
Chop-suey Chinese	30-Jan-12	10370	Michael Suyama
Die Wandernde Kuh	04-Jan-12	10348	Margaret Peacock
	15-Jan-12	10356	Michael Suyama
Drachenblut Delikatessen	23-Jan-12	10363	Margaret Peacock
Eastern Connection	23-Jan-12	10364	Nancy Davolio
Ernst Handel	08-Jan-12	10351	Nancy Davolio
	26-Jan-12	10368	Andrew Fuller

It's important to note that the data shown in Figure 21.4 is identical to the data shown in Figure 21.13. In fact, the same record source (qrySalesJanuary, shown in Figure 21.11, later in this chapter) is used for both of these reports. Often, a data rearrangement yields useful information. For example, you can easily see that Bottom-Dollar Market placed three orders in January, one with salesperson Steven Buchanan, one with Robert King, and one with Nancy Davolio.

Let's assume you want to refine the rptSalesJanuaryAlpha1 report by labeling the groups with the letters of the alphabet. That is, all customers beginning with *A* (Antonio Moreno Tagueria and Around the Horn) are in one group, all customers beginning with *B* (Blondel père et fils, Bon app', and Bottom-Dollar Market) are in one group, and so on. Within each group, the company names are sorted in alphabetical order. The sales to each customer are further sorted by order date.

To emphasize the alphabetical grouping, a text box containing the first character for each group has been added to the report (see rptSalesJanuaryAlpha2 in Figure 21.5). Although the data set in this example is rather small, in large reports such headings can be useful.

FIGURE 21.5

An alphabetic heading for each customer group makes the rptSalesJanuaryAlpha2 report easier to read.

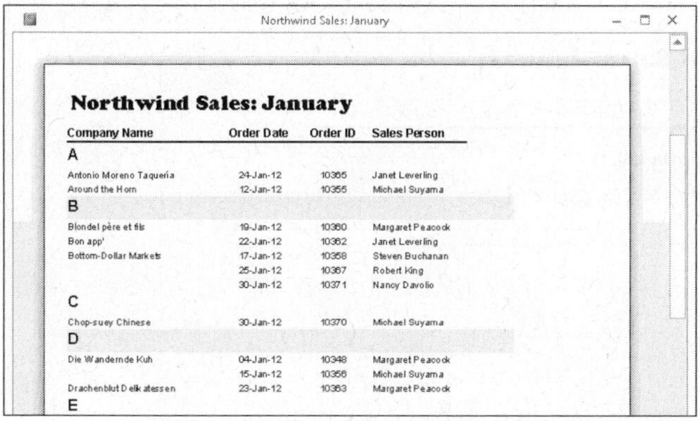

Adding the text box containing the alphabetic character is easy:

1. **Right click the report's title bar and choose Design View.**
2. **Choose Group & Sort from the Design tab of the Ribbon.** The Group, Sort, and Total task pane appears.
3. **Add a Group for CompanyName.**
4. **Click More, and ensure that With a Header Section is selected.** This action adds a band for a group based on the CompanyName information (see Figure 21.6).
5. **Select By First Character instead of the default By Entire Value.**
6. **Expand the CompanyName group header and add an unbound text box to the CompanyName group header.**
7. **Set the text box's Control Source property to the following expression:**

   ```
   =Left$([CompanyName],1)
   ```
8. **Set the other text box properties (Font, Font Size, and so on) appropriately.**
9. **While you're grouping on the first character of the company name, you still need to ensure that company names are sorted correctly. Click Add a Sort and select the CompanyName field again. Click More to ensure that the entire field is going to be sorted, and that no header section will be added.**

10. **Finally, add a sort for OrderDate so that multiple orders for the same company are in order.** When you're done, the report in Design view should appear as shown in Figure 21.6.

FIGURE 21.6

rptSalesJanuaryAlpha2 in Design view.

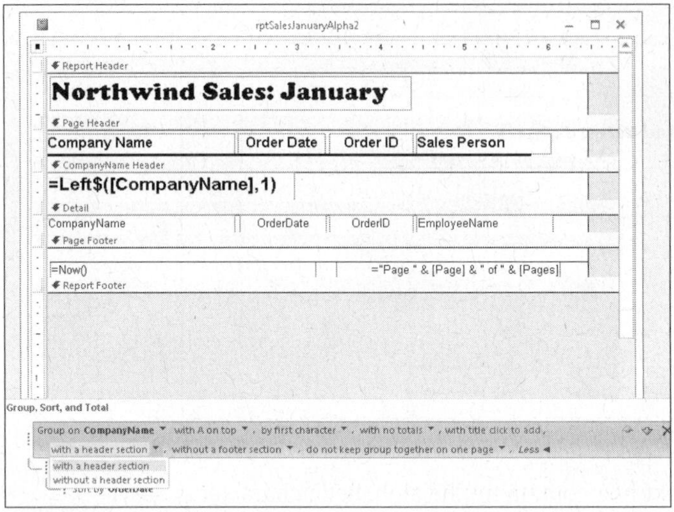

Notice the CompanyName group header that was added by the Group Header setting in the Group, Sort, and Total dialog box. The Property Sheet for the unbound text box is shown so you can see the expression used to fill the text box.

This little trick works because all the rows within a CompanyName group have the first character in common. Using the `Left$()` function to peel off the first character and use it as the text in the text box in the group header provides an attractive, useful heading for the CompanyName groups.

Grouping on date intervals

Many reports require grouping on dates or date intervals (day, week, or month). For example, Northwind Traders may want a report of January sales grouped on a weekly basis so that week-to-week patterns emerge.

Fortunately, the Access report engine includes just such a feature. An option in the Group, Sort, and Total task pane enables you to quickly and easily group report data based on dates or date intervals. Just as I grouped data based on prefix characters in an earlier example, I can group on dates using the group's GroupOn property. Figure 21.7 shows the January sales report grouped by each week during the month. This report is named rpt-SalesJanuaryByWeek.

FIGURE 21.7

The January sales data grouped by each week during the month.

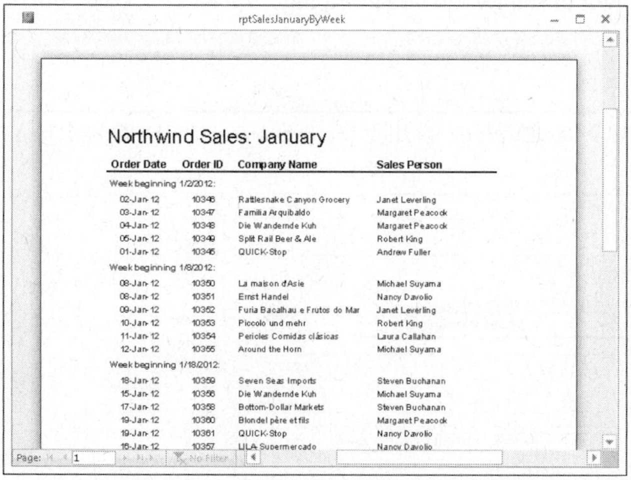

This report is easy to set up. Open the Group, Sort, and Total dialog box again and establish a group for the OrderDate field. Set the OrderDate GroupHeader option to Yes and select the the Group On drop-down list (shown in Figure 21.8). Notice that Access is smart enough to present Group On options (Year, Quarter, Month, Week, and so on) that make sense for Date/Time fields like OrderDate. Selecting Week from this list instructs Access to sort the data on the OrderDate, grouped on a week-by-week basis. Note, though, that you still need to sort by the entire value of the OrderDate to ensure that they're in sequential order within the week.

FIGURE 21.8

OrderDate is a Date/Time field, so the grouping options are relevant for date and time data.

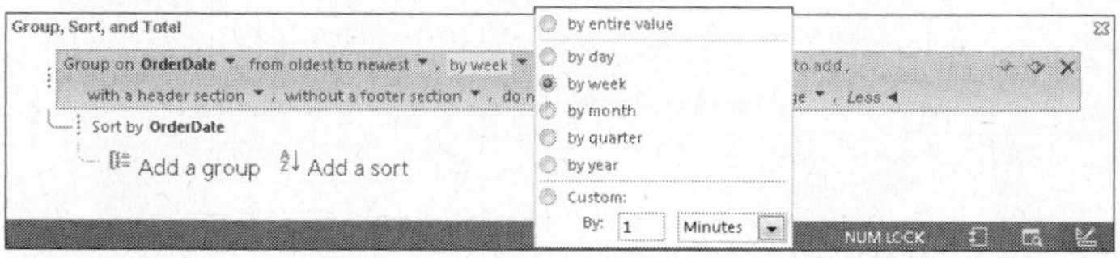

The label at the top of the group identifying the week (the first one reads `Week beginning 1/1/12:`) is the product of the following expression in an unbound text box in the `OrderDate` group header:

```
="Week beginning " & [OrderDate] & ":"
```

See the Design view of rptSalesJanuaryByWeek in Figure 21.9. Notice the unbound text box in the OrderDate group header. This text box contains the value of the order date that Access used to group the data in the OrderDate grouping.

FIGURE 21.9

The Design view of rptSalesJanuaryByWeek. Notice the expression in the OrderDate group header.

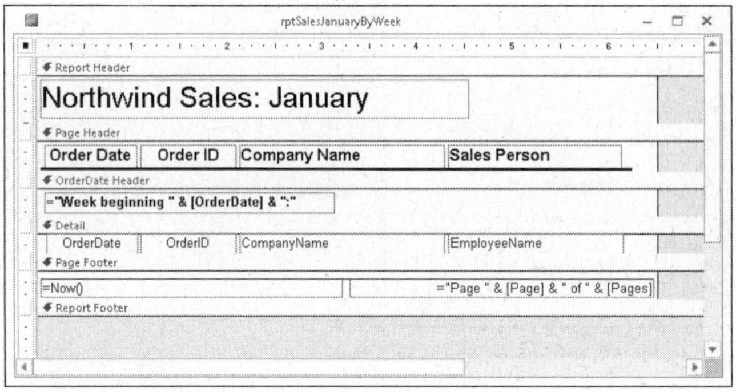
rptSalesJanuaryByWeek
Report Header
Northwind Sales: January
Page Header
Order Date
Order ID
Company Name
Sales Person
OrderDate Header
="Week beginning " & [OrderDate] & ":"
Detail
OrderDate
OrderID
CompanyName
EmployeeName
Page Footer
=Now()
="Page " & [Page] & " of " & [Pages]
Report Footer

Hiding repeating information

An easy improvement to tabular reports is to reduce the amount of repeated information on the report. Figure 21.10 shows a typical tabular report (rptTabularBad) produced by Access, based on a simple query of the Northwind Traders data.

FIGURE 21.10

Simple tabular reports can be confusing and boring.

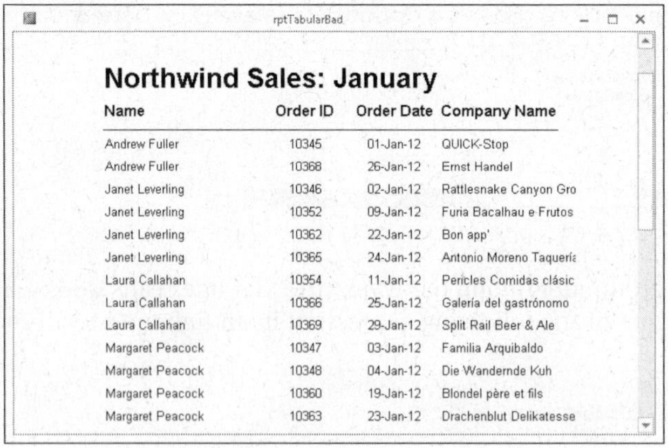
rptTabularBad
Northwind Sales: January
Name
Order ID
Order Date
Company Name
Andrew Fuller 10345 01-Jan-12 QUICK-Stop
Andrew Fuller 10368 26-Jan-12 Ernst Handel
Janet Leverling 10346 02-Jan-12 Rattlesnake Canyon Gro
Janet Leverling 10352 09-Jan-12 Furia Bacalhau e Frutos
Janet Leverling 10362 22-Jan-12 Bon app'
Janet Leverling 10365 24-Jan-12 Antonio Moreno Taquería
Laura Callahan 10354 11-Jan-12 Pericles Comidas clásic
Laura Callahan 10366 25-Jan-12 Galería del gastrónomo
Laura Callahan 10369 29-Jan-12 Split Rail Beer & Ale
Margaret Peacock 10347 03-Jan-12 Familia Arquibaldo
Margaret Peacock 10348 04-Jan-12 Die Wandernde Kuh
Margaret Peacock 10360 19-Jan-12 Blondel père et fils
Margaret Peacock 10363 23-Jan-12 Drachenblut Delikatesse

The report in Figure 21.10 was produced with the Access Report Wizard, selecting the tabular report format and all defaults. The query underlying this report selects data from the Customers, Orders, and Employees tables in `Chapter21.accdb` and is shown in Figure 21.11. Notice that the data returned by this query is restricted to the month of January 2012. Also, the first and last names of employees are concatenated as the Name field.

FIGURE 21.11

The simple query underlying rptTabularBad.

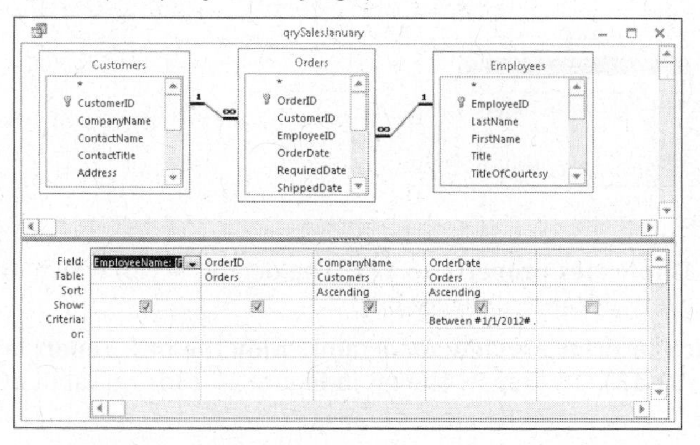

The query in Figure 21.11 (qrySalesJanuary) is used as the basis of several examples in this chapter.

You can significantly improve the report in Figure 21.10 simply by hiding repeated information in the Detail section. As soon as Andrew Fuller's name is given, there's no need to repeat it for every sale that Andrew made in January 2012. The way the data is arranged on rptTabularBad, you have to search for where one employee's sales data ends and another employee's data begins.

Making the change to hide the repeated values is very easy:

1. **Open the report in Design view.**
2. **In the Detail section, select the EmployeeName field containing the employee's first and last names.**
3. **Open the property sheet for the Name field (see Figure 21.12).**

FIGURE 21.12

The default property values sometimes lead to unsatisfactory results.

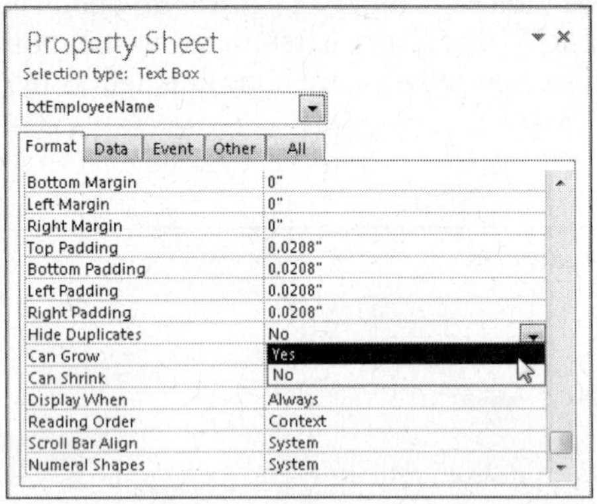

Property Sheet

Selection type: Text Box

txtEmployeeName

Format | Data | Event | Other | All

Property	Value
Bottom Margin	0"
Left Margin	0"
Right Margin	0"
Top Padding	0.0208"
Bottom Padding	0.0208"
Left Padding	0.0208"
Right Padding	0.0208"
Hide Duplicates	No
Can Grow	Yes
Can Shrink	No
Display When	Always
Reading Order	Context
Scroll Bar Align	System
Numeral Shapes	System

4. **Change the Hide Duplicates property to Yes.** The default is No, which directs Access to display every instance of every field.
5. **Put the report back to Print Preview mode and enjoy the new report layout (shown in Figure 21.13).** The report shown in Figure 21.13 is rptTabularGood.

FIGURE 21.13

Much better! Hide that repeating information.

rptTabularGood

Northwind Sales: January

Name	Order ID	Order Date	Company Name
Andrew Fuller	10345	01-Jan-12	QUICK-Stop
	10368	26-Jan-12	Ernst Handel
Janet Leverling	10346	02-Jan-12	Rattlesnake Canyon Gro
	10352	09-Jan-12	Furia Bacalhau e Frutos
	10362	22-Jan-12	Bon app'
	10365	24-Jan-12	Antonio Moreno Taquerí
Laura Callahan	10354	11-Jan-12	Pericles Comidas clásic
	10366	25-Jan-12	Galería del gastrónomo
	10369	29-Jan-12	Split Rail Beer & Ale
Margaret Peacock	10347	03-Jan-12	Familia Arquibaldo
	10348	04-Jan-12	Die Wandernde Kuh
	10360	19-Jan-12	Blondel père et fils
	10363	23-Jan-12	Drachenblut Delikatesse
Michael Suyama	10350	08-Jan-12	La maison d'Asie

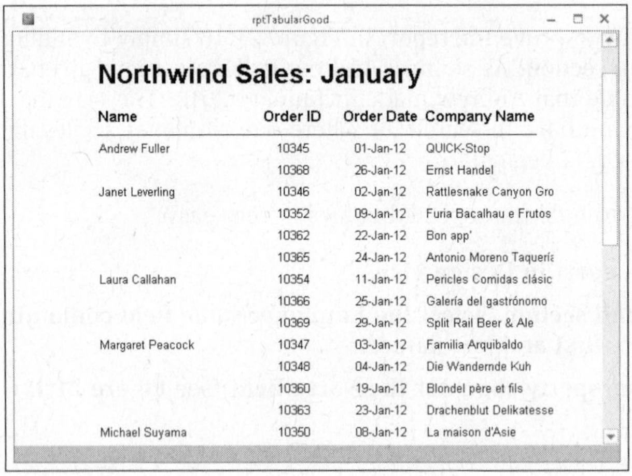

Distinguishing the sales figures for individual employees in Figure 21.13 is much easier than it is when the repeating information is printed on the report. Notice that no fancy programming or report design was required. A simple property-value change resulted in a much more readable and useful report. (Mainframe report designers working with traditional report writers would *kill* for a report as good looking as the one shown in Figure 21.13!)

The Hide Duplicates property only applies to records that appear sequentially on the report. As soon as Access has placed a particular Name value on the report, the name won't be repeated in records immediately following the current record. In Figure 21.13, the records are sorted by the EmployeeName field, so all records for an employee appear sequentially as a group. If the report were sorted by another field (for example, OrderID or OrderDate), the Hide Duplicates property set on the Name field would apply only to those instances where the employee's name coincidentally appeared sequentially in multiple records on the report.

The Hide Duplicates property can be applied to multiple controls within a report. As long as you understand that Hide Duplicates only hides subsequent duplicate values within a detail section, you should be able to achieve the results you expect. (Note, though, that you may occasionally run into unexpected results if only one of the multiple fields changes.)

Hiding a page header

Sometimes you need to display a page header or footer on just the first page of a report. An example is a terms and conditions clause in the header of the first page of an invoice. You want the terms and conditions to appear only on the first page of the invoice but not on subsequent pages.

Some of the examples in this chapter use Visual Basic for Applications (VBA). VBA is discussed more fully in Chapters 23-28.

Add an unbound Text Box control to the report with its ControlSource property set to the expression `=HideHeader()`. Delete the text box's label. The `HideHeader()` function returns a null string making the textbox invisible.

NOTE
You can't actually set the control's Visible property to No; if you did, the control wouldn't be able to respond to events.

The `HideHeader()` function is as follows:

```
Function HideHeader() As String

  'Set the visible property of the header
  Me.Section("PageHeader0").Visible = False
  HideHeader = vbNullString

End Function
```

The invisible text box can be placed virtually anywhere on the first page but is most logically located in the page footer. The assumption is that, because the page header is the first item printed on the page, you'll always get the first page header. Once the page footer containing the invisible text box has been processed, the page header's Visible property will be set to False, and the page header will not be seen on any other pages in the report.

Starting a new page number for each group

Sometimes a report will contain a number of pages for each group of data. You might want to reset page numbering to 1 as each group prints, so that each group's printout will have its own page-numbering sequence. For example, assume you're preparing a report with sales data grouped by region. Each region's sales may require many pages to print, and you're using the ForceNewPage property to ensure that grouped data doesn't overlap on any page. But how do you get the page numbering within each group to start at 1?

The report's Page property, which you use to print the page number on each page of a report, is a read/write property. This means that you can reset Page at any time as the report prints. Use the group header's `Format` event to reset the report's Page property to 1. Every time a group is formatted, Page will be reset to 1 by the following code:

```
Private Sub GroupHeader0_Format(Cancel As Integer, FormatCount As Integer)
  Me.Page = 1
End Sub
```

Use the Page property to display the current page number in the page header or footer as usual. For example, include the following expression in an unbound text box in the page footer:

```
= "Page " & [Page]
```

The report named rptResetPageEachGroup is included in Chapter21.accdb and shows this technique. Unfortunately, it's not nearly as easy to count the pages within a group so that you could put a "Page *x* of *y*" in the page footer, where *y* is the number of pages within the group.

Formatting Data

In addition to sorting and grouping data, you can make reports more useful by formatting them to highlight specific information. Numbering the entries or using bullets can make things stand out, as can using lines or spaces to separate parts of the report. Ensuring that the elements on the report are positioned in a consistent manner is important as well — you might have all the necessary data in a report, but poor presentation can leave a very negative impression on the users. The techniques discussed in this section will help you produce reports that are more professional looking.

Creating numbered lists

By default, the items contained on an Access report are not numbered. They simply appear in the order dictated by the settings in the Group, Sort, and Total task pane.

Sometimes it would be useful to have a number assigned to each entry on a report or within a group on a report. You might need a number to count the items in a list or uniquely identify items in the list. For example, an order details report might contain an item number for each item ordered, plus a field for items ordered, showing how many things were ordered.

The Access Running Sum feature provides a way to assign a number to each item in a list on an Access report. For example, the Northwind Traders sales management has asked for a report showing the sum of all purchases by each customer during the month of January, sorted in descending order so that the top purchaser appears at the top. Oh, yes — and they want a number assigned to each line in the report to provide a ranking for the Northwind customers.

What an assignment! The query to implement this request is shown in Figure 21.14 (qry-CustomerPurchasesJanuary). This query sums the purchases by each customer for the month beginning 1/1/12 and ending 1/31/12. Because the Purchases column is sorted in descending order, the customers buying the most product will appear at the top of the query results set. The OrderDate field is not included in the query results and is used only as the query's selection criterion (notice the *Where* in the Total row).

FIGURE 21.14

An interesting query that sums data and sorts the query results in descending order of the sum.

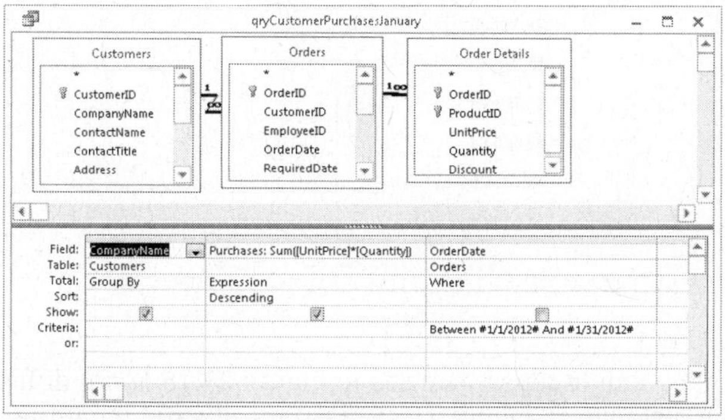

Although you could do much of this work at runtime using VBA to programmatically sum the values returned by the query or a SQL statement in the report's RecordSource property, you should always let the Access query engine perform aggregate functions. All Access queries are optimized when you save the query. You're guaranteed that the query will run as fast as possible — much faster than a filter based on a SQL statement in a report's RecordSource property.

> **TIP**
>
> The Access Query Builder's aggregate functions perform flawlessly. Furthermore, ACE will perform the aggregate function exactly the same way every time the query is run. There is no reason you should be tempted to manually sum data when the query will do it for you.

The basic report (rptUnNumberedList) prepared from the data provided by qryCustomer-PurchasesJanuary is shown in Figure 21.15. All sorting options have been removed from the Group, Sort, and Total dialog box to permit the records to arrange themselves as determined by the query.

FIGURE 21.15

A straightforward report (rptUnNumberedList) produced with data from qryCustomerPurchasesJanuary.

rptUnNumberedList

Northwind Sales: January

Company Name	Purchases
Queen Cozinha	$12,281.20
Piccolo und mehr	$10,741.60
Ernst Handel	$7,511.80
Blondel père et fils	$7,390.20
QUICK-Stop	$5,198.40
Seven Seas Imports	$3,654.40
Split Rail Beer & Ale	$2,668.80
Rattlesnake Canyon Grocery	$1,731.20
Bon app'	$1,549.60

Page: 1 No Filter

Adding a Ranking column to the simple report you see in Figure 21.15 is not difficult. Although the information that's shown in Figure 21.15 is useful, it's not what the user asked for.

To add a Ranking column to the report, use the RunningSum property of an unbound text box to sum its own value over each item in the report. When the RunningSum property is set to Over Group, Access adds 1 to the value in this text box for each record displayed in the Detail section of the report (RunningSum can also be used within a group header or footer). The alternate setting (Over All) instructs Access to add 1 each time the text box appears in the entire report. Add an unbound text box to the left of the CompanyName text box on the report, with an appropriate header in the Page Header area. Set the RecordSource property for the text box to =1 and the RunningSum property to Over All. Figure 21.16 shows how the Rank text box is set up on rptNumberedList.

Chapter 20 discuss how to move labels from the Detail section to another section.

FIGURE 21.16

The value in the unbound text box named txtRank will be incremented by 1 for each record in the report.

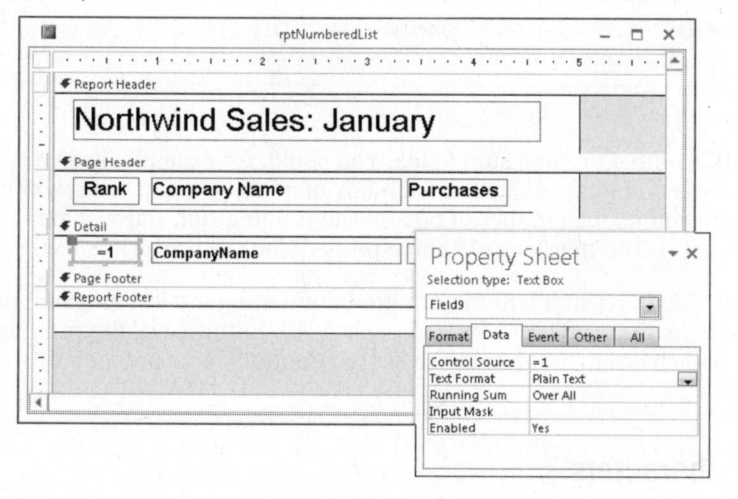

When this report (rptNumberedList) is run, the Rank column is filled with the running sum calculated by Access (see Figure 21.17). Once again, the data in this report is the same as in other report examples. The main difference is the amount of manipulation done by the query before the data arrives at the report and the additional information provided by the running sum.

FIGURE 21.17

The Running Sum column provides a ranking for each customer in order of purchases during January.

rptNumberedList

Northwind Sales: January

Rank	Company Name	Purchases
1	Queen Cozinha	$12,281.20
2	Piccolo und mehr	$10,741.60
3	Ernst Handel	$7,511.80
4	Blondel père et fils	$7,390.20
5	QUICK-Stop	$5,198.40
6	Seven Seas Imports	$3,654.40
7	Split Rail Beer & Ale	$2,668.80
8	Rattlesnake Canyon Grocery	$1,731.20
9	Bon app'	$1,549.60

Page: 1 No Filter

Reports can contain multiple running sum fields. You could, for example, keep a running sum to show the number of items packed in each box of a multiple-box order while another running sum counts the number of boxes. The running sum starts at zero, hence the need to initialize it to 1 in the Control Source property on the Property Sheet.

You can also assign a running sum within each group by setting the RunningSum property of the unbound text box to Over Group instead of Over All. In this case, the running sum will start at zero for each group. So, be sure to set the ControlSource property of a group's running sum to 1.

Adding bullet characters

You can add bullet characters to a list instead of numbers, if you want. Instead of using a separate field for containing the bullet, however, you can simply concatenate the bullet character to the control's RecordSource property — a much easier solution. Access will "glue" the bullet character to the data as it's displayed on the report, eliminating alignment problems that might occur with a separate unbound text box.

The design of rptBullets is shown in Figure 21.18. Notice the bullet character in the txt-CompanyName text box as well as in the Property Sheet for this text box.

FIGURE 21.18

The bullet character is added to the ControlSource property of the txtCompanyName text box.

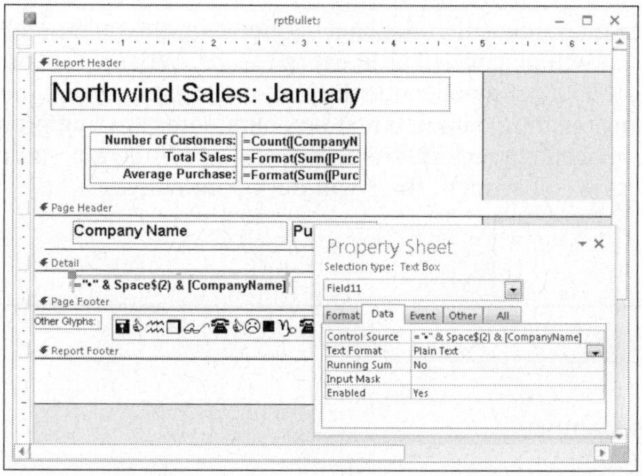

The bullet is added by exploiting a Windows feature. Position the text insertion character in the RecordSource property for the CompanyName field, hold down the Alt key, and type **0149**. Windows inserts the standard Windows bullet character, which you see in the property sheet. Looking at Figure 21.18, you can see that the bullet character is inserted correctly into the text box on the report. The expression you use in the ControlSource property is the following:

```
= "•" & Space$(2) & [CompanyName]
```

where the bullet is inserted by the Alt + 0149 trick.

You can produce the same effect by using the following expression in the text box:

```
= Chr(149) & Space$(2) & [CompanyName]
```

This expression concatenates the bullet character — returned by `Chr(149)` — with the data in the CompanyName field.

NOTE

This particular trick only works if the character set (such as Arial) assigned to the control (label or text box) includes a bullet character as the 149th ASCII character. Not all fonts accessible by Access applications include a bullet character, but popular typefaces such as Arial do tend to include this character.

The report now appears as shown in Figure 21.19. You can increase the number in the `Space$()` function to pad the white space between the bullet and the text. Because the bullet character and CompanyName field have been concatenated together in the text box, they'll be displayed in the same typeface. Also, adding the bullet character to the text box containing the company name guarantees that the spacing between the bullet and first character of the company name will be consistent in every record. When using proportionally spaced fonts such as Arial, it can sometimes be difficult to get precise alignment between report elements. Concatenating data in a text box eliminates spacing problems introduced by proportionally spaced characters. Note, though, that if the amount of text in the text box exceeds a single row, subsequent rows will not be indented.

FIGURE 21.19

Use a Windows feature to insert the bullet in front of the CompanyName field.

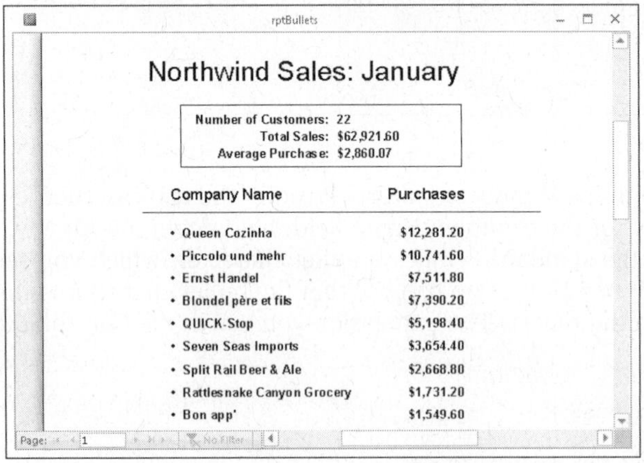

rptBullets

Northwind Sales: January

Number of Customers: 22
Total Sales: $62,921.60
Average Purchase: $2,860.07

Company Name	Purchases
• Queen Cozinha	$12,281.20
• Piccolo und mehr	$10,741.60
• Ernst Handel	$7,511.80
• Blondel père et fils	$7,390.20
• QUICK-Stop	$5,198.40
• Seven Seas Imports	$3,654.40
• Split Rail Beer & Ale	$2,668.80
• Rattlesnake Canyon Grocery	$1,731.20
• Bon app'	$1,549.60

You might want to add other special characters to the control. For a complete display of the characters available in the font you've chosen for the Text Box control, run `Charmap.exe`, the Windows Character Map application (see Figure 21.20). Be sure to select the font you've chosen for the Text Box control. The only constraint on the characters you use on an Access report is that the font used in the text boxes on the report must contain the specified characters. Not all Windows TrueType character sets include all the special characters, like bullets.

Charmap is quite easy to use. Select a font from the drop-down list at the top of the dialog box, and the main area fills with the font's default character set. Some character sets are incredibly large. For example, the Arial Unicode MS font includes more than 53,000 different characters, including traditional and simplified Chinese, Japanese Kanji, and Korean Hangul character sets.

FIGURE 21.20

Charmap is a useful tool for exploring Windows font sets.

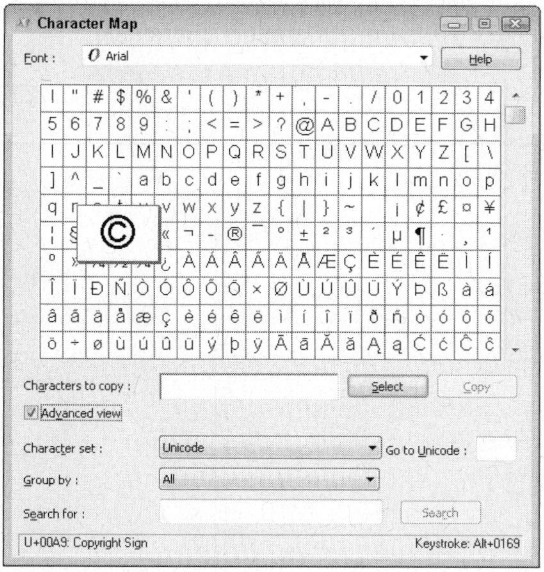

Most characters in a Windows font are accessible through the `Chr$()` function. The page footer of rptBullets includes a text box filled with characters specified by the `Chr$()` function. For example, the smiley face character in the Wingdings font is specified with `Chr$(74)`. Some of the characters displayed by Charmap are identified only by their hexidecimal values. If the decimal value is not given, the hexidecimal value can be used with `Chr$()` by using the `CLng()` function to convert the hex value to integer: `Chr$(CLng("&H00A9"))` displays the familiar copyright symbol (©) when used to set the contents of a control set to the Arial font.

Adding emphasis at runtime

You might add a number of hidden controls to your reports to reduce the amount of clutter and unnecessary information. You can hide and show controls based on the value of another control. You hide a control, of course, by setting its Visible property to False (or No) at design time. Only when the information contained in the control is needed do you reset the Visible property to True.

An example might be a message to the Northwind Traders customers that a certain item has been discontinued and inventory is shrinking. It's silly to show this message for every item in the Northwind catalog; including the number of units in stock, in conjunction with a message that a particular item has been discounted, might encourage buyers to stock up on the item.

Figure 21.21 shows rptPriceList in Print Preview mode. (You may have to right-click on the report name and select Print Preview from the context menu.) Notice that the Guarana Fantastica beverage product appears in italics, the price is bold italics, and the `Only 20 units in stock!` message appears to the right of the product information.

FIGURE 21.21

Can you tell Guarana Fantastica is on sale?

rptPriceList

Beverages

Product Name	Unit Price	
Ipoh Coffee	$46.00	
Chai	$18.00	
Lakkalikööri	$18.00	
Rhönbräu Klosterbier	$7.75	
Laughing Lumberjack L	$14.00	
Chartreuse verte	$18.00	
Côte de Blaye	$263.50	
Steeleye Stout	$18.00	
Sasquatch Ale	$14.00	
Guaraná Fantástica	***$2.25***	Only 20 units in stock!
Chang	$19.00	
Outback Lager	$15.00	

Condiments

Product Name	Unit Price
Gula Malacca	$19.45

Page: 1 No Filter

Figure 21.22 reveals part of the secret behind this technique. The visible unit price text box is actually unbound. This is the text box used to display the unit price to the user. Another text box is bound to the UnitPrice field in the underlying recordset, but it's hidden by setting its Visible property to No. Just to the left of the hidden UnitPrice field is a hidden check box representing the Discontinued field. txtMessage, which contains the `Only x units in stock!` Message, is also hidden.

Use the Detail section's Format event to switch the Visible property of txtMessage to True whenever txtDiscontinued contains a true value. The code is quite simple:

```
Private Sub Detail1_Format(Cancel As Integer, _
  FormatCount As Integer)

    Me.txtProductName.FontItalic = Me.Discontinued.Value
    Me.txtPrice.FontItalic = Me.Discontinued.Value
    Me.txtPrice.FontBold = Me.Discontinued.Value

    'Cut price in half for discontinued
```

```
        Me.txtPrice = Me.UnitPrice * IIf(Me.Discontinued.Value, 0.5, 1)
        Me.txtMessage.Visible = Me.Discontinued.Value

    End Sub
```

FIGURE 21.22

rptPriceList in Design view reveals how this effect is implemented.

In this procedure, `Me` is a shortcut reference to the report. You must explicitly turn the italics, bold, and other font characteristics off when the product is not discontinued. Otherwise, once a discontinued product has been printed, all products following the discontinued product will print with the special font attributes. The font characteristics you set in a control's Property Sheet are just the initial settings for the control. If you change any of those properties at runtime, they stay changed until modified again. Similarly, txtMessage must be hidden after it's been displayed by setting its Visible property to False, or in this case the value of Discontinued.

Avoiding empty reports

If Access fails to find valid records to insert into the Detail section of a report, all you'll see is a blank Detail section when the report is printed. To avoid this problem, attach code to the report's `NoData` event that displays a message and cancels the print event if no records are found.

The `NoData` event is triggered when Access tries to build a report and finds no data in the report's underlying recordset. Using `NoData` is easy:

```
Private Sub Report_NoData(Cancel As Integer)

    MsgBox "There are no records for this report."
    Cancel = True

End Sub
```

The `Cancel = True` statement instructs Access to stop trying to show the report. The user will see the dialog box shown in Figure 21.23 and will avoid getting a report that can't be printed. (Open rptEmpty in `Chapter21.accdb` for this example.)

FIGURE 21.23

Inform the user that there are no records to print.

Microsoft Access

There are no records for this report.

OK

Because the `NoData` event is tied to the report itself, don't look for it in any of the report's sections. Simply add this code as the report's `NoData` event procedure, and your users will never wonder why they're looking at a blank report.

Inserting vertical lines between columns

You can easily add a vertical line to a report section whose height is fixed (like a group header or footer). Adding a vertical line to a section that can grow in height (like a Detail section on a grouped report) is more difficult. It's really difficult to get a vertical line between columns of a report (see rptVerticalLines in Figure 21.24). If you simply add a vertical line to the right side of a section of a snaking columns report, the line will appear to the right of the rightmost column on the page. You have to be able to specify where vertical lines will appear on the printed page.

Reports using snaking columns are discussed in the "Trying More Techniques" section, later in this chapter.

Although you add most controls at design time, sometimes you have to explicitly draw a control as the report is prepared for printing. The easiest approach in this case is to use the report's `Line` method to add the vertical line at runtime. The following subroutine, triggered by the Detail section's `Format` event, draws a vertical line 3½ inches from the left printable margin of the report:

```
Private Sub Detail_Format(Cancel As Integer, FormatCount As Integer)
  Dim X1 as Single
  X1 = 3.5 * 1440
  Me.Line (X1, 0)-(X1, 32767)
End Sub
```

FIGURE 21.24

Vertical lines in rptVerticalLines help segregate data.

rptVerticalLines

Northwind Sales: January

Name	Order Date	Order ID	Company Name
Andrew Fuller	10345	01-Jan-12	QUICK-Stop
Andrew Fuller	10368	26-Jan-12	Ernst Handel
Janet Leverling	10346	02-Jan-12	Rattlesnake Canyon Gr
Janet Leverling	10352	09-Jan-12	Furia Bacalhau e Frutos
Janet Leverling	10362	22-Jan-12	Bon app'
Janet Leverling	10365	24-Jan-12	Antonio Moreno Taquer
Laura Callahan	10354	11-Jan-12	Pericles Comidas clásic
Laura Callahan	10366	25-Jan-12	Galería del gastrónomo
Laura Callahan	10369	29-Jan-12	Split Rail Beer & Ale
Margaret Peacock	10347	03-Jan-12	Familia Arquibaldo
Margaret Peacock	10348	04-Jan-12	Die Wandernde Kuh
Margaret Peacock	10360	19-Jan-12	Blondel père et fils
Margaret Peacock	10363	23-Jan-12	Drachenblut Delikatess

Page: 1 No Filter

The syntax of the `Line` method is as follows:

```
object.Line (X1, Y1) - (X2, Y2)
```

The `Line` method requires four arguments. These arguments (`X1`, `X2`, `Y1`, and `Y2`) specify the top and bottom (or left and right, depending on your perspective) coordinates of the line. Notice that all calculated measurements on a report must be specified in twips (there are 1,440 twips per inch or 567 twips per centimeter). In this case, `X1` and `X2` are the same value and we're forcing the line to start at the very top of the Detail section (`0`) and to extend downward for 32,767 twips.

You might wonder why we're using 32,767 as the `Y2` coordinate for the end of the line. Access will automatically "clip" the line to the height of the Detail section. Because the line control doesn't contain data, Access won't expand the Detail section to accommodate the line you've drawn in code. Instead, Access draws as much of the 32,767-twip line as needed to fill the Detail section, and then it stops. The maximum value for `Y2` is 32,767.

The same procedure could be used to draw horizontal lines for each section on the report. In the report example (rptVerticalLines) in the database accompanying this chapter (`Chapter21.accdb`), we've added line controls to the report instead. Using the `Line` control when the height of the report section is fixed (for example, in the group header and footer) is simply faster than drawing the line for each of these sections.

NOTE
When a report is double-clicked in the Object Navigation pane, it opens in Report view by default. To see certain techniques, like the vertical line technique, you must switch to Print Preview view.

Adding a blank line every *n* records

Detail sections chock-full of dozens or hundreds of records can be difficult to read. It's easy to lose your place when reading across columns of figures and when the rows are crowded together on the page. Wouldn't it be nice to insert a blank row every fourth or fifth record in a Detail section? It's much easier to read a single row of data in a report (rptGapsEvery5th in `Chapter21.accdb`) where the records have been separated by white space every fifth record (see Figure 21.25).

FIGURE 21.25

Using white space to break up tabular data can make it easier to read.

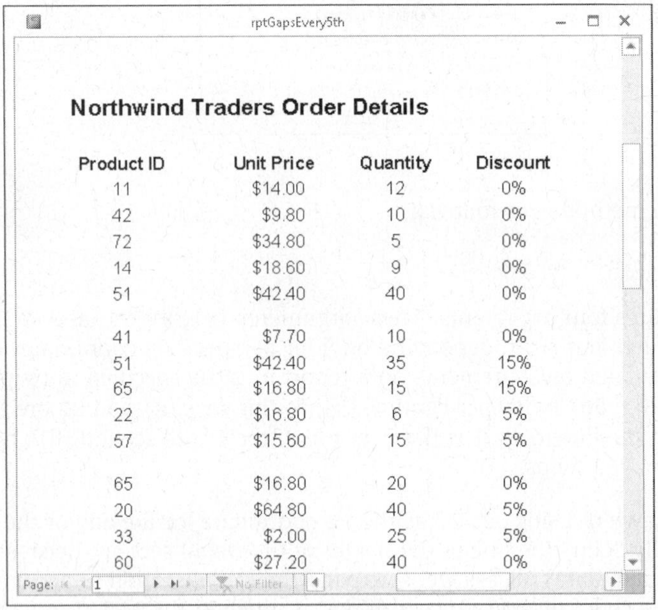

rptGapsEvery5th

Northwind Traders Order Details

Product ID	Unit Price	Quantity	Discount
11	$14.00	12	0%
42	$9.80	10	0%
72	$34.80	5	0%
14	$18.60	9	0%
51	$42.40	40	0%
41	$7.70	10	0%
51	$42.40	35	15%
65	$16.80	15	15%
22	$16.80	6	5%
57	$15.60	15	5%
65	$16.80	20	0%
20	$64.80	40	5%
33	$2.00	25	5%
60	$27.20	40	0%

Page: 1 No Filter

Access provides no way to insert a blank row in the middle of a Detail section. You can, however, trick Access into inserting white space in the Detail section now and then with a little bit of programming and a couple of hidden controls.

Figure 21.26 reveals the trick behind the arrangement you see in Figure 21.25. An empty, unbound text box named txtSpacer is placed below the fields containing data in the Detail section. To the left of txtSpacer is another unbound text box named txtCounter.

FIGURE 21.26

This report trick uses hidden unbound text boxes in the Detail section.

Set the properties in Table 21.1 for txtSpacer, txtCounter, and the Detail section.

TABLE 21.1 Properties for the "Blank Line" Example

Control	Property	Value
txtSpacer	Visible	Yes
	CanShrink	Yes
txtCounter	Visible	No
	RunningSum	Over All
	ControlSource	=1
Detail1	CanShrink	Yes

These properties effectively hide the unbound txtSpacer and txtCounter controls, and permit these controls and the Detail section to shrink as necessary when the txtSpacer Text Box control is empty. Even though txtSpacer is visible to the user, Access shrinks it to 0 height if it contains no data. The txtCounter control never needs any space because its Visible property is set to No, hiding it from the user.

The last step is to enter the following code as the Detail section's `Format` event procedure:

```
Private Sub Detail1_Format(Cancel As Integer, _
  FormatCount As Integer)

  If Me.txtCounter.Value Mod 5 = 0 Then
    Me.txtSpacer.Value = Space$(1)
  Else
    Me.txtSpacer.Value = Null
  End If

End Sub
```

The `Format` event occurs as Access begins to format the controls within the Detail section. The value in txtCounter is incremented each time a record is added to the Detail section. The `Mod` operator returns whatever number is left over when the value in txtCounter is divided by 5. When txtCounter is evenly divisible by 5, the result of the `txtCounter Mod 5` expression is 0, which causes a space character to be assigned to txtSpacer. In this situation, because txtSpacer is no longer empty, Access increases the height of the Detail section to accommodate txtSpacer, causing the "empty" space every fifth record to be printed in the Detail section. You never actually see txtSpacer because all it contains is an empty space character.

txtCounter can be placed anywhere within the Detail section of the report. Make txtSpacer as tall as you want the blank space to be when it's revealed on the printout.

Even-odd page printing

If you've ever prepared a report for two-sided printing, you may have encountered the need for knowing whether the data is being printed on the even side of the page or the odd side of the page. Most users prefer the page number to be located near the outermost edge of the paper. On the odd-numbered page, the page number should appear on the right edge of the page, while on the even-numbered side, the page number must appear on the left side of the page. How, then, do you move the page number from side to side?

Assuming the page number appears in the Page Footer section of the report, you can use the page footer's `Format` event to determine whether the current page is even or odd, and align the text to the left or right side of the text box accordingly.

The basic design of rptEvenOdd is shown in Figure 21.27. Notice that the Width property of txtPageNumber is set to the same as the report header. Also, the TextAlign property is set to Right. The `Format` event will determine whether the text is aligned to the right or left, so setting TextAlign to Right is a bit arbitrary.

FIGURE 21.27

txtPageNumber is the same width as the report.

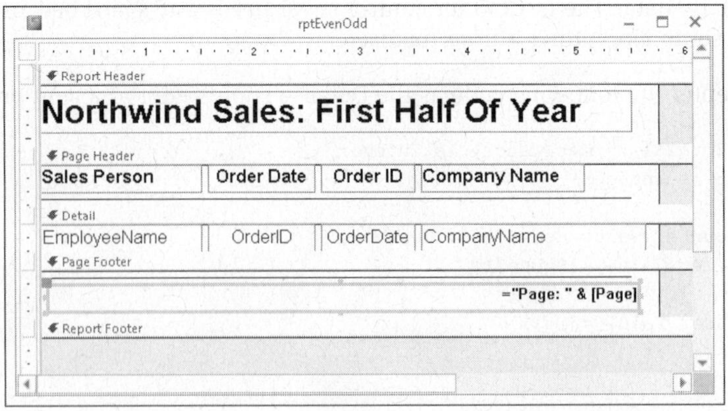

The Page Footer `Format` event procedure is a bit more involved than the `IsEven` function shown earlier. You have to adjust the TextAlign property of txtPageNumber to shift the page number all the way to the left or right side of the text box depending on whether the page is even or odd.

```
Private Sub PageFooter1_Format(Cancel As Integer, _
    FormatCount As Integer)

    Const byALIGN_LEFT As Byte = 1
    Const byALIGN_RIGHT As Byte = 3

    If Me.Page Mod 2 = 0 Then
      Me.txtPageNumber.TextAlign = byALIGN_LEFT
    Else
      Me.txtPageNumber.TextAlign = byALIGN_RIGHT
    End If

End Sub
```

In this event procedure, any time the expression `Me.Page Mod 2` is zero (meaning, the page number is even) the TextAlign property is set to Left. On odd-numbered pages, TextAlign is set to Right.

Like magic, this event procedure causes the Page Number text to move from the right side on odd-numbered pages to the left side on even-numbered pages (see Figure 21.28).

FIGURE 21.28

txtPageNumber jumps from right to left.

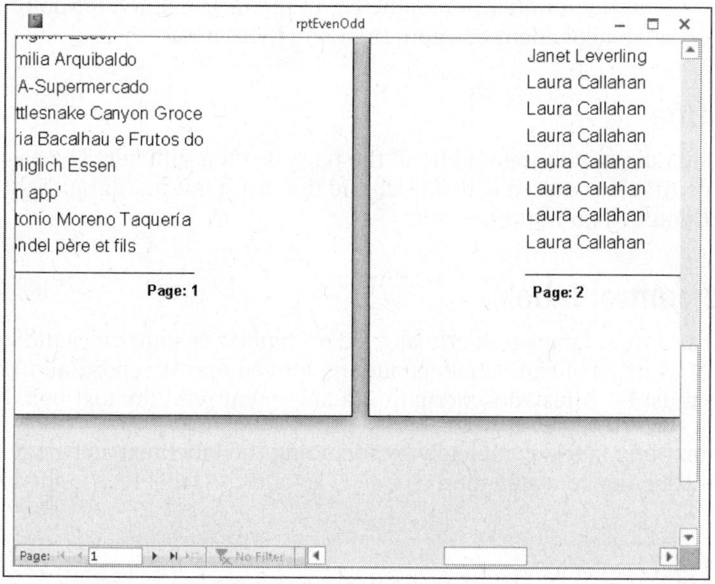

Using different formats in the same text box

On some reports, you may want the format of certain fields in a record to change according to the values in other fields on the report. A good example is a journal voucher report in a multicurrency financial system in which the voucher detail debit or credit amount format varies according to the number of decimal places used to display the currency value.

Unfortunately, a control in a Detail section of a report can have but a single format specified in its Property Sheet. Use the following trick to flexibly set the format property at run time. The `FlexFormat()` function uses the `lDecimals` argument to return a string specifying the desired format:

```
Public Function FlexFormat(lDecimals As Long) As String

    FlexFormat = "#,##0." & String(lDecimals, "0")

End Function
```

The `String` function returns text that has `lDecimal` number of characters and all the characters are 0. If `lDecimals` is 2, for example, FlexFormat returns `"#,##0.00"`.

Assume that the field to be dynamically formatted has its ControlSource set to [Amount]. The format of the Amount text box should vary depending on the value of the CurrDecPlaces field in the same record. CurrDecPlaces is a Long Integer data type. To use FlexFormat, change the ControlSource property of the Amount text box to the following:

```
=Format([Amount],FlexFormat([CurrDecPlaces]))
```

The Amount text box will be dynamically formatted according to the value contained in the CurrDecPlaces text box. This trick may be generalized to format fields other than currency fields. By increasing the number of parameters of the user-defined formatting function, the formatting can be dependent on more than one field, if necessary.

Centering the title

Centering a report title directly in the middle of the page is often difficult. The easiest way to guarantee that the title is centered is to stretch the title from left margin to right margin, and then click the Center Align button.

Easily aligning control labels

Keeping text boxes and their labels properly aligned on reports is sometimes difficult. Because a text box and its label can be independently moved on the report, all too often the label's position must be adjusted to bring it into alignment with the text box.

You can eliminate text-box labels completely by including the label text as part of the text box's record source. Use the concatenation character to add the label text to the text box's control source:

```
= "Product: " & [ProductName]
```

Now, whenever you move the text box, both the label and the bound record source move as a unit. The only drawback to this technique is that you must use the same format for the text box and its label.

Micro-adjusting controls

The easiest way to adjust the size or position of controls on a report in tiny increments is to hold down either the Shift or Control key and press the arrow key corresponding to Table 21.2.

TABLE 21.2 Micro-Adjustment Keystroke Combinations

Shift Combination	Adjustment
Control+Left Arrow	Move left
Control+Right Arrow	Move right
Control+Up Arrow	Move up
Control+Down Arrow	Move down
Shift+Left Arrow	Reduce width
Shift+Right Arrow	Increase width
Shift+Up Arrow	Reduce height
Shift+Down Arrow	Increase height

Another resizing technique is to position the cursor over any of the sizing handles on a selected control and double-click. The control automatically "sizes to fit" the text contained within the control. This quick method can also be used to align not only labels but also text boxes to the grid.

Adding Data

When you're looking at data through forms, you can usually assume that the data is current. However, with printed reports, you don't always know if the data is old. Adding little touches like when the report was printed can help increase the usefulness of a report. In this section, I show you some techniques that will let you add additional information to the report to let the users know something of its origin.

Adding more information to a report

You probably know that the following expression in an unbound text box prints the current page and the number of pages contained in the report:

```
="Page " & [Page] & " of " & [Pages]
```

Both Page and Pages are report properties that are available at runtime and can be included on the report.

But consider the value of adding other report properties on the report. Most of the report properties can be added to unbound text boxes as long as the property is enclosed in square brackets. For the most part, these properties are only of value to you as the developer, but they may also be useful to your users.

For example, the report's Name, RecordSource, and other properties are easily added the same way. Figure 21.29 demonstrates how unbound text boxes can deliver this information to a report footer or some other place on the report.

FIGURE 21.29

rptMoreInfo demonstrates how to add more information to your reports.

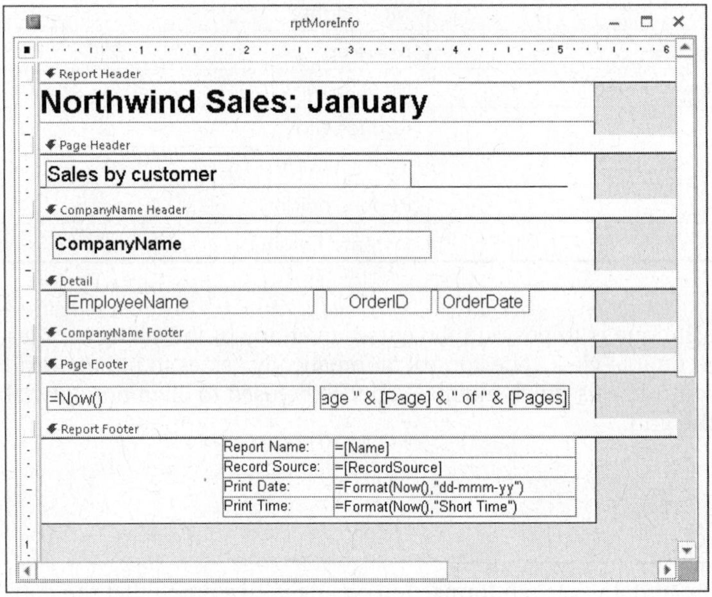

The inset in the lower-right part of Figure 21.29 shows the information provided by adding the four text boxes to this report. Very often, the user is not even aware of the name of a report — the only text the user sees associated with reports is the text that appears in the title bar (in other words, the report's Caption property). If a user is having problems with a report, it might be helpful to display the information you see in Figure 21.29 in the report footer.

Adding the user's name to a bound report

An unbound text box with its ControlSource set to an unresolved reference will cause Access to pop up a dialog box requesting the information necessary to complete the text box. For example, an unbound text box with its RecordSource set to the following displays the dialog box you see in the middle of Figure 21.30 when the report is run:

```
=[What is your name?]
```

Access displays a similar Parameter dialog box for each parameter in a parameter query. The text entered into the text box is then displayed on the report. (rptUserName in `Chapter21.accdb` on this book's companion website demonstrates this technique.)

FIGURE 21.30

Use an unbound text box to capture useful information.

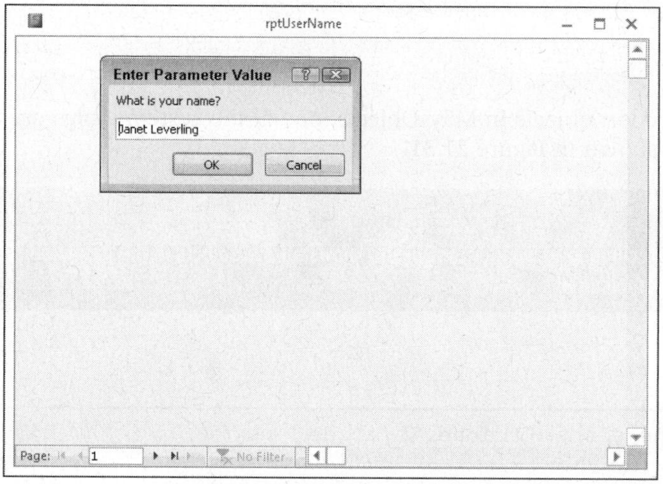

The unbound text box on the report can be referenced by other controls on the report. The Parameter dialog box appears before the report is prepared for printing, which means that the data you enter into the dialog box can be used in expressions, calculations, or the VBA code behind the report.

> **TIP**
>
> VBA includes the function `ENVIRON()` that can be used to get the user's name automatically. Use `ENVIRON("USERNAME")` in a VBA function and refer to that function a text box's ControlSource to display the user's name without prompting for it. The username returned by ENVIRON() is easily changed by the user, so don't use it where identity is critical.

Trying More Techniques

As you've probably discovered by now, reporting in Access is a very large topic. We've included a few additional techniques that will help you make your reports even more flexible to users.

Displaying all reports in a combo box

The names of all the top-level database objects are stored in the MSysObjects system table. You can run queries against MSysObjects just as you can run queries against any other table in the database. It's easy to fill a combo box or list box with a list of the report objects in an Access database.

Choose Table/Query as the RowSource Type for the list box and put this SQL statement in the RowSource of your list box to fill the box with a list of all reports in the database:

```
SELECT DISTINCTROW [Name] FROM MSysObjects
WHERE [Type] = -32764
ORDER BY [Name];
```

The `-32764` identifies report objects in MSysObjects, one of the system tables used by Access. The results are shown in Figure 21.31.

> **NOTE**
> Reports don't have to be open for this technique to work. MSysObjects knows all the objects in the database, so no reports will escape detection using this technique.

FIGURE 21.31

frmAllReports displays the reports in `Chapter21.accdb`.

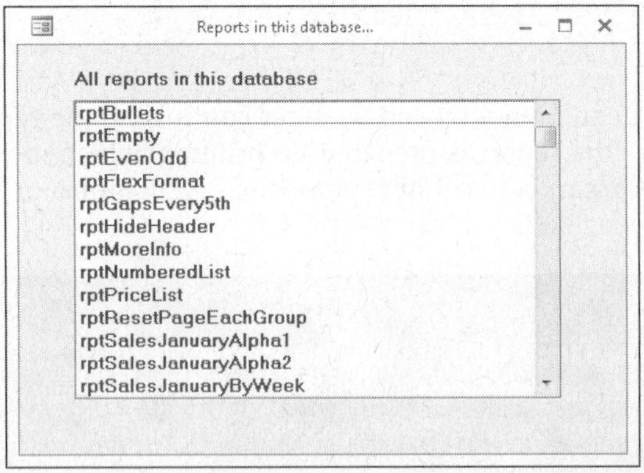

If you're using a naming convention for your database objects, use a prefix to show only the reports you want. The following code returns only those reports that begin with tmp:

```
SELECT DISTINCTROW [Name] FROM MSysObjects
WHERE [Type] = -32764 AND Left([Name], 3) = "tmp"
ORDER BY [Name];
```

Because MSysObjects stores the names of all database objects, you can return the names of the other top-level database objects as well. Just substitute the `-32764` as the type value in the preceding SQL statement with the Table 21.3 values to return different database object types.

TABLE 21.3 Access Object Types and Values

Object	Type Value
Local Tables	1
Linked tables (except tables linked using ODBC)	6
Linked tables using ODBC	4
Forms	–32768
Modules	–32761
Macros	–32766
Queries	5

To view the MSysObjects table, set the Show System Objects setting to Yes in the Navigation Options dialog box (which you can get to by right-clicking on the Navigation pane's title bar, and selecting Navigation Options from the shortcut menu). MSysObjects does *not* have to be visible for this trick to work.

NOTE

Although Microsoft says that MSysObjects and the type values are not supported and are, therefore, prone to change at any time, Access has used the same type values for many, many years. It's unlikely Microsoft will drop the MSysObjects table or change the type values, but this trick is not guaranteed to work indefinitely.

Fast printing from queried data

A report that is based on a query can take a long time to print. Because reports and forms can't share the same recordset, once a user has found the correct record on a form, it's a shame to have to run the query over again to print the record on a query. A way to "cache" the information on the form is to create a table (we'll call it tblCache) containing all the fields that are eventually printed on the report. Then, when the user has found the correct record on the form, copy the data from the form to tblCache, and open the report. The report, of course, is based on tblCache.

The query is run only once to populate the form. Copying the data from the form to tblCache is a very fast operation, and multiple records can be added to tblCache as needed. Because the report is now based on a table, it opens quickly and is ready to print as soon as the report opens.

Using snaking columns in a report

When the data displayed on a report doesn't require the full width of the page, you may be able to conserve the number of pages by printing the data as snaking columns, as in a dictionary or phone book. Less space is wasted and fewer pages need to be printed, speeding the overall response of the report. More information is available at a glance and many people find snaking columns more aesthetically pleasing than simple blocks of data.

For the examples in this section, we need a query that returns more data than we've been using up to this point. Figure 21.32 shows the query used to prepare the sample reports in this section.

FIGURE 21.32

This query returns more detailed information than we've been using.

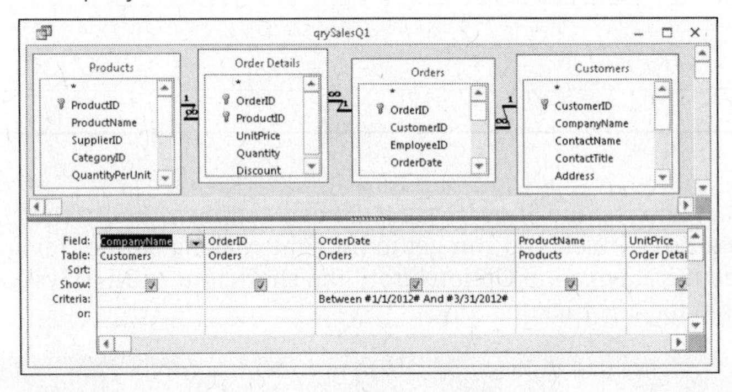

This query returns the following information: CompanyName, OrderID, OrderDate, ProductName, UnitPrice, and Quantity for the period from January 1, 2012, to March 31, 2012.

The initial report design to contain this data is shown in Design view in Figure 21.33. This rather complex report includes a group based on the order ID for each order placed by the company, as well as a group based on the company itself. This design enables us to summarize data for each order during the quarter, as well as for the company for the entire quarter.

FIGURE 21.33

Notice how narrow the records in this report are.

The same report in Print Preview mode is shown in Figure 21.34. Notice that the report really doesn't make good use of the page width available to it. In fact, each record of this report is only 3¼ inches wide.

FIGURE 21.34

The report makes poor use of the available page width.

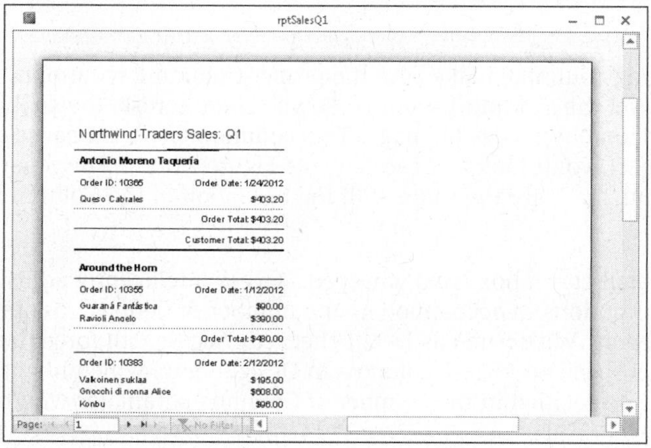

Setting a report to print as snaking columns is actually part of the print setup for the report, not an attribute of the report itself. With the report in Design view, click on the Columns button on the Report Design Tools Page Setup tab of the Ribbon to open the Page Setup dialog box (shown in Figure 21.35) with the Columns tab selected. Change the Number of Columns property to 2. As you change Number of Columns from 1 to 2, the Column Layout area near the bottom of the Layout tab becomes active, showing you that Access has selected the Across, Then Down option to print items across the page first, and then down the page. Although this printing direction is appropriate for mailing labels, it's not what we want for our report. Select the Down, Then Across option to direct Access to print the report as snaking columns (see Figure 21.35).

FIGURE 21.35

Only a few changes are needed to produce snaking columns.

When working with snaking columns, make sure the proper Column Layout option is selected. If you neglect to set the Column Layout to Down, Then Across, the snaking columns will be laid out horizontally across the page. This common error can cause a lot of confusion because the report won't look as expected (see Figure 21.36). The reports shown in Figures 21.36 and 21.37 are the same with the exception of the Column Layout setting.

As long as the Same as Detail check box is *not* checked, Access intelligently adjusts the Column Spacing and other options to accommodate the number of items across that you've specified for the report. With Same as Detail checked, Access will force the columns to whatever width is specified for the columns in Design view, which might mean that the number of columns specified in the Number of Columns parameter won't fit on the page.

FIGURE 21.36

The wrong Column Layout setting can be very confusing!

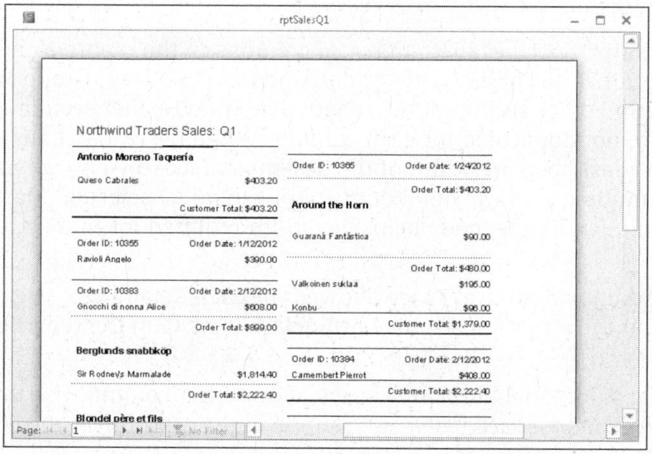

Figure 21.37 clearly demonstrates the effect of changing the report to a snaking two-column layout. Before the change, this report required 17 pages to print all the data. After this change, only nine pages are required.

FIGURE 21.37

Snaking multiple columns conserve page space and provide more information at a glance.

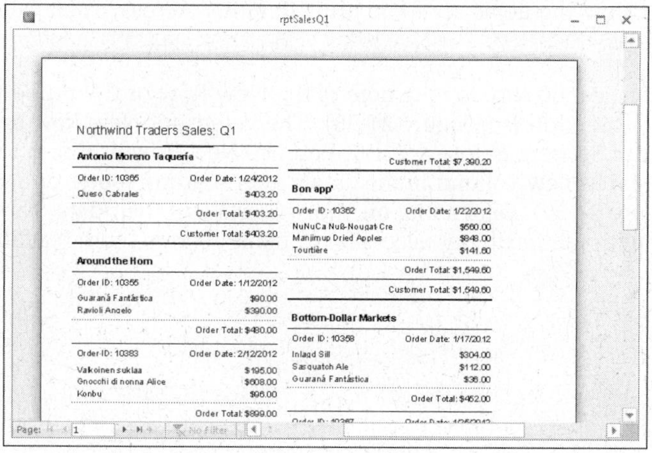

You may be wondering about the other print options in the Page Setup dialog box (refer to Figure 21.35). Here is a short description of each of the relevant settings in the Layout tab of the Page Setup dialog box:

- **Number of Columns:** Specifies the number of columns in the report. You should be aware that Number of Columns affects only the Detail section, Group Header section, and Group Footer section of the report. The Page Header section and Page Footer section are not duplicated for each column. When designing a multi-column report, you must keep the width of the design area narrow enough to fit on the page when multiplied by the number of columns you've selected. Most often, printing a report in landscape mode helps the width required for more than one column in a report.
- **Row Spacing:** Additional vertical space allowed for each detail item. Use this setting if you need to force more space between detail items than the report's design allows.
- **Column Spacing:** Additional horizontal space allowed per column. Use this setting if you need to force more space between columns in the report than the design allows.
- **Column Size – Same as Detail:** The column width and detail height will be the same as on the report in Design view. This property is useful when you need to fine-tune the column placement on a report (for example, when printing the data onto preprinted forms). Making adjustments to the report's design will directly influence how the columns print on paper.
- **Column Size – Width and Height:** The width and height of a column. These options are handy when printing onto preprinted forms to ensure that the data falls where you want it to.
- **Column Layout:** How the items are to be printed: either Across, Then Down or Down, Then Across.

In addition to these properties, be sure to take note of the New Row or Col property for the CompanyName Header section (see Figure 21.38). The values for New Row or Col are None, Before Section, After Section, Before & After. You use New Row or Col to force Access to, for example, start a new column immediately after a group footer or detail section has printed (see Figure 21.39). Depending on your reports and their data, New Row or Col may provide you with the flexibility necessary to make reports more readable.

FIGURE 21.38

Headers (and footers) have properties that can be used to control actions when the grouping value changes.

FIGURE 21.39

New Row or Col forces Access to start a column before or after a section.

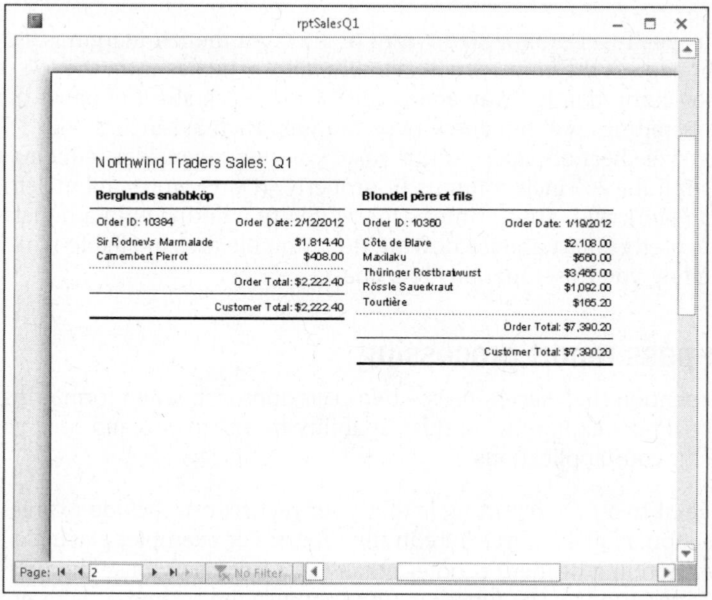

Keep in mind that the measurement units you see on the Page Setup tab of the Ribbon are determined by the Windows international settings. For example, in Germany or Japan where the metric system is used, the units of measure will be centimeters instead of inches. Also, you must allow for the margin widths set in the Margins gallery, accessed from the Page Setup tab of the Ribbon (see Figure 21.40).

FIGURE 21.40

All report page settings must consider the margin widths.

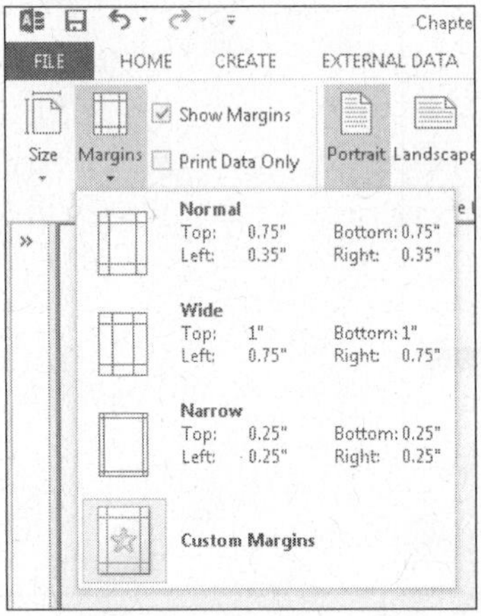

For example, if you specify a Column Size Width of 3.5" and the left margin is set to 1", this means the right edge of the column will actually fall 4½ inches from the left physical edge of the paper, or more than halfway across an 8½-x-11-inch sheet of paper printed in portrait mode. These settings will not allow two columns, each 3½ inches wide, to print on a standard letter-size sheet of paper. In this case, you might consider reducing the left and right margins until the 3½-inch columns fit properly. (Don't worry about setting the margins too small to work with your printer. Unless you're working with a nonstandard printer, Windows is pretty smart about knowing the printable area available with your printer and won't allow you to set margins too small.)

Exploiting two-pass report processing

In Chapter 20, we mention that Access uses a two-pass approach when formatting and printing reports. We'll now explore what this capability means to you and how you can exploit both passes in your applications.

The main advantage of two-pass reporting is that your reports can include expressions that rely on information available anywhere in the report. For example, placing a control with the `Sum()` function in a header or footer means that Access will use the first pass to accumulate the data required by the function, and then use the second pass to process the values in that section before printing them.

Another obvious example is putting an unbound text box in the footer of a report containing the following expression:

```
="Page " & [Page] & " of " & [Pages]
```

The built-in `Pages` variable (which contains the total number of pages in the report) isn't determined until Access has completed the first pass through the report. On the second pass, Access has a valid number to use in place of the `Pages` variable.

The biggest advantage of two-pass reporting is that you're free to use aggregate functions that depend on the report's underlying record source. Group headers and footers can include information that can't be known until the entire record source is processed.

There are many situations where aggregate information provides valuable insight into data analysis. Consider a report that must contain each salesperson's performance over the last year measured against the total sales for the sales organization, or a region's sales figures against sales for the entire sales area. A bookstore might want to know what portion of its inventory is devoted to each book category.

Figure 21.41 shows such a report. The Number of Customers, Total Sales, and Average Purchase information at the top of this report (rptSummary) are all part of the report header. In a one-pass report writer, the data needed to perform these calculations would not appear until the bottom of the page, after all the records have been processed and laid out.

FIGURE 21.41

The summary information is part of the report's header.

rptSummary

Northwind Sales: January

Number of Customers:	22
Total Sales:	$62,921.60
Average Purchase:	$2,860.07

Company Name	Purchases
• Queen Cozinha	$12,281.20
• Piccolo und mehr	$10,741.60
• Ernst Handel	$7,511.80
• Blondel père et fils	$7,390.20
• QUICK-Stop	$5,198.40
• Seven Seas Imports	$3,654.40
• Split Rail Beer & Ale	$2,668.80
• Rattlesnake Canyon Grocery	$1,731.20
• Bon app'	$1,549.60
• Die Wandernde Kuh	$1,502.40
• Bottom-Dollar Markets	$1,377.40
• LILA-Supermercado	$1,360.00
• Chop-suey Chinese	$1,174.00
• Eastern Connection	$950.00
• Familia Arquibaldo	$928.00

Page: 1 No Filter

A glance at rptSummary in Design view (see Figure 21.42) reveals that the text boxes in the report header are populated with data derived from these mathematical expressions:

```
Number of Customers: =Count([CompanyName])
Total Sales: =Format(Sum([Purchases]),"Currency")
Average Purchase: =Format(Sum([Purchases])/ _
    Count([CompanyName]), "Currency")
```

The `Count()` and `Sum()` functions both require information that isn't available until the entire report has been processed in the first pass. As long as Access can find the arguments provided to these functions (`CompanyName` and `Purchases`) in the underlying recordset, the calculations proceed without any action by the user.

FIGURE 21.42

rptSummary in Design view.

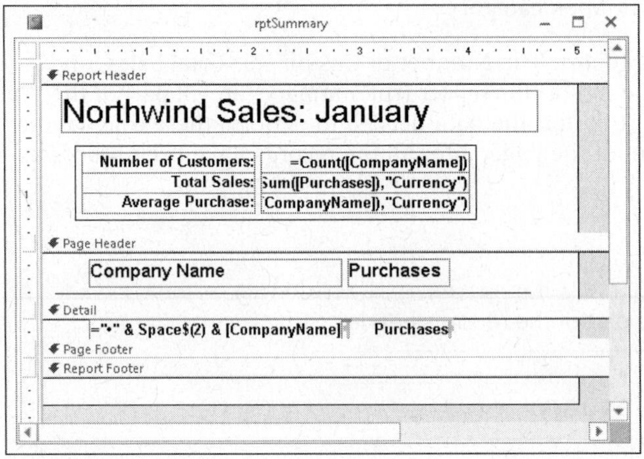

Assigning unique names to controls

If you use the Report Wizard or drag fields from the Field List when designing your reports, Access assigns the new text boxes the same names as the fields in the recordset underlying the report. For example, if you drag a field named Discount from the field list, both the Name and ControlSource properties of the text box are set to Discount.

If another control on the report references the text box, or if you change the ControlSource of the text box to a calculated field, such as

```
=IIf([Discount]=0,"N/A",[Discount])
```

you'll see `#Error` when you view the report. This happens because Access can't distinguish between the control named Discount and the field in the underlying recordset named Discount.

You must change the Name property of the control to something like txtDiscount so that Access can tell the difference between the control's name and the underlying field.

Part VI

Access Programming Fundamentals

Part VI introduces macro programming and explains the art and science of Visual Basic for Applications (VBA). Very few professional-quality Access applications have been written without liberal use of either the VBA programming language or macros, or a combination of both.

With Access 2007, Microsoft began a significant effort to enhance macros as a valuable contributor to Access development. Long maligned as weaker or inferior to VBA, macros were often relegated to second-class citizenship in many Access developer toolkits. However, as you'll read in Chapter 22, Microsoft introduced *embedded macros,* a very efficient technique for automating many tasks in forms and reports.

Starting with Chapter 23, Part VI turns your attention to automation with VBA. VBA provides functionality that goes far beyond simply opening forms and reports and controlling the user interface. You'll use VBA code to validate data, as well as to transform and combine data in new and interesting ways. VBA code is used to import and export data, respond to user input, and handle the mistakes inevitably made by users.

IN THIS PART

Using Access Macros

IN THIS CHAPTER

- Getting acquainted with macros
- Understanding macro security
- Working with multi-action macros
- Using submacros for actions that are frequently required
- Making decisions with conditions
- Using temporary variables
- Handling errors and debugging your macros
- Understanding embedded macros
- Comparing macros to VBA

Macros have been a part of Access since the beginning. As Access evolved as a development tool, the Visual Basic for Applications (VBA) programming language became the standard in automating Access database applications. Macros in previous versions of Access lacked variables and error handling, which caused many developers to abandon macros altogether. Access 2013 has these capabilities (added in Access 2007), which make macros a better alternative to VBA than in previous versions. If you're creating a database to be used on the web, or if you aren't a VBA guru but you still want to customize the actions that your application executes, then building structured macros is the answer.

On the Web

This chapter uses a database named `Chapter22.accdb`. If you haven't already downloaded it from this book's website, you'll need to do so now. This database contains the tables, forms, reports, and macros used in this chapter.

An Introduction to Macros

A *macro* is a tool that allows you to automate tasks in Access. It's different from Word's Macro Recorder, which lets you record a series of actions and play them back later. (It's also different from Word in that Word macros are actually VBA code, whereas Access macros are something very different.) Access macros let you perform defined actions and add functionality to your forms and reports. Think of macros as a simplified, step-wise programming language. You build a macro as a list of actions to perform, and you decide when you want those actions to occur.

Building macros consists of selecting actions from a drop-down list, and then filling in the action's *arguments* (values that provide information to the action). Macros let you choose actions without writing a single line of VBA code. The macro actions are a subset of commands VBA provides. Most people find it easier to build a macro than writing VBA code. If you're not familiar with VBA, building macros is a great stepping-stone to learning some of the commands available to you while providing added value to your Access applications.

Suppose you want to build a main form with buttons that open the other forms in your application. You can add a button to the form, build a macro that opens another form in your application, and then assign this macro to the button's `Click` event. The macro can be a stand-alone item — which appears in the Navigation pane — or an embedded object that is part of the event itself (see the "Embedded Macros" section).

Creating a macro

A simple way to demonstrate how to create macros is to build one that displays a message box that says `Hello World!` To create a new stand-alone macro, click the Macro button on the Macros & Code group on the Create tab of the Ribbon (shown in Figure 22.1).

FIGURE 22.1

Use the Create tab to build a new stand-alone macro.

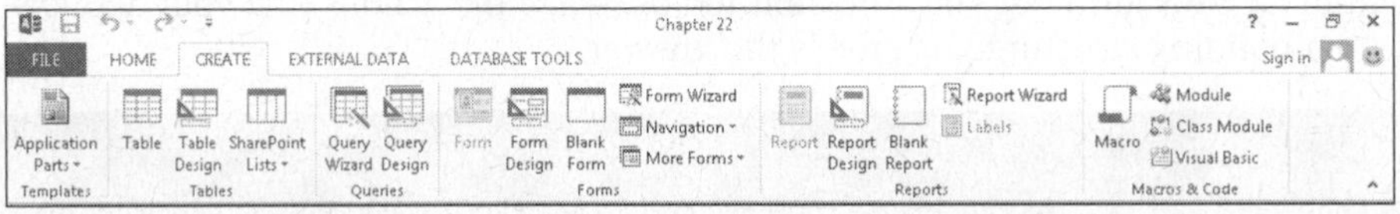

Clicking the Macro button opens the macro design window (shown in Figure 22.2). Initially, the macro design window is almost featureless. The only thing in the Macro window is a drop-down list of macro actions.

FIGURE 22.2

The macro design window displaying the Macro window and Action Catalog.

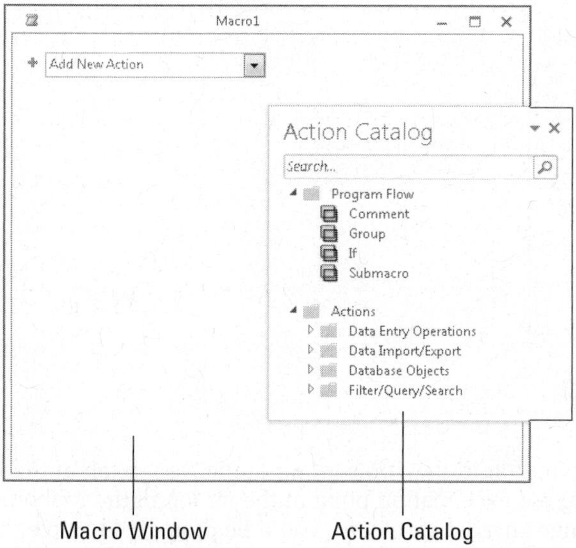

Macro Window

Action Catalog

To the right of the Macro window you may see the Action Catalog. There are dozens of different macro actions, and knowing which action to use for a particular task can be an issue. The Action Catalog provides a tree view of all available macro actions and helps you know which action is needed to perform a particular task. I'll give you a closer look at the Action Catalog later in this chapter.

Select `MessageBox` from the drop-down list in the macro window. The macro window changes to display an area where you input the arguments (`Message`, `Beep`, `Type`, and `Title`) associated with the `MessageBox` action.

Set the arguments as follows:

- **Message:** Hello World!
- **Beep:** No
- **Type:** None
- **Title:** A Simple Macro

Your screen should look similar to Figure 22.3. The `Message` argument defines the text that appears in the message box and is the only argument that is required and has no default. The `Beep` argument determines whether a beep is heard when the message box appears. The `Type` argument sets which icon appears in the message box: None, Critical, Warning?, Warning!, or Information. The `Title` argument defines the text that appears in the message box's title bar.

FIGURE 22.3

The Hello World macro uses the MessageBox action to display a message.

Macro action Message

mcrHelloWorld

MessageBox

Message Hello World!

Beep No

Type None

Title A Simple Macro

Add New Action

Title bar caption

To run the macro, click the Run button in the Tools group of the Design tab of the Ribbon. (The Run button looks like a big red exclamation point at the far left of the Ribbon.) When you create a new macro or change an existing macro, you'll be prompted to save the macro. In fact, you must save the macro before Access runs it for you. When prompted, click Yes to save it, provide a name such as `mcrHelloWorld`, and click OK. The macro runs and displays a message box with the arguments you specified (shown in Figure 22.4).

FIGURE 22.4

Running the Hello World macro displays a message box.

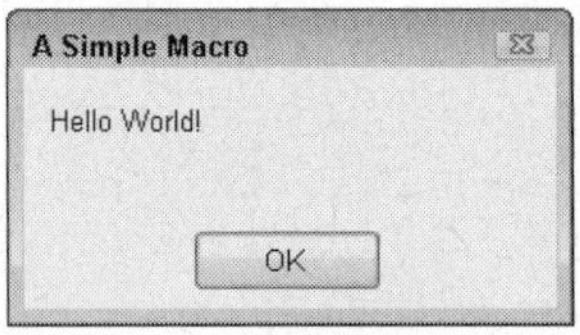

A Simple Macro

Hello World!

OK

You can also run the macro from the Navigation pane. Close the macro design window and display the Macros group in the Navigation pane. Double-click the `mcrHelloWorld` macro to run it. You'll see the same message box that displayed when you ran the macro from the design window.

Notice that the message box always appears right in the middle of the screen and blocks you from working with Access until you click OK. These are built-in behaviors of the message box object and are identical in every regard to a message box displayed from VBA code.

When you're satisfied with the Hello World macro, click the close button in the upper-right corner of the macro window to return to the main Access window.

Assigning a macro to an event

When you're creating macros, you probably don't want end-users using the Navigation pane to run them — or worse, running them from the macro design window. Macros are intended for you to automate your application without writing VBA code. In order to make an application easy to use, assign your macros to an object's event.

The most common event to which you might assign a macro is a button's `Click` event. Follow these steps to create a simple form with a button that runs `mcrHelloWorld`:

1. **Select the Create tab on the Ribbon, and then click the Form Design button in the Forms group.**
2. **On the Form Design Tools Design tab of the Ribbon, deselect the Use Control Wizards option in the Controls group.** For this example, you don't want to use a wizard to decide what this button does.
3. **Click the Button control and draw a button on the form.**
4. **Set the button's Name property to cmdHelloWorld.** `Press F4 to open the button's Property Sheet if it isn't visible on the screen.`
5. **Set the button's Caption property to Hello World!.**
6. **Click the drop-down list in the button's On Click event property, and select mcrHelloWorld from the list (shown in Figure 22.5).**

FIGURE 22.5

Set any object's event property to the macro to trigger that macro when that event occurs.

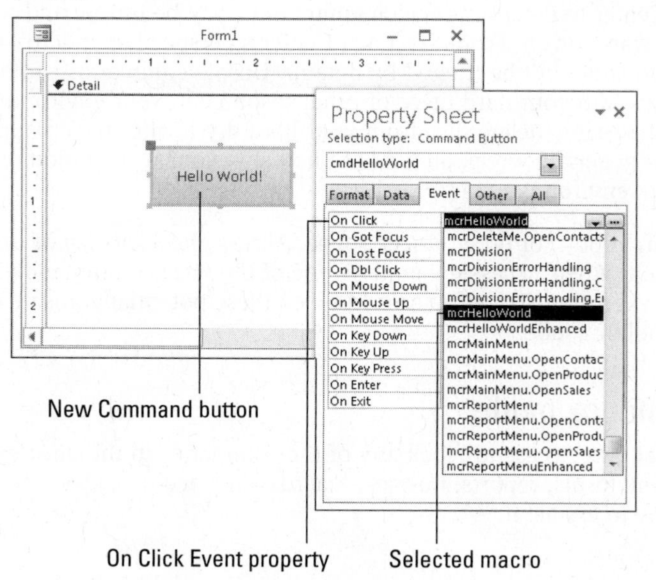

That's all there is to creating and running a macro. Just select the action, set the action arguments, and assign the macro to an event property.

TIP

You aren't limited to the button's `Click` event. If you want a macro to run every time a form loads, set the `On Load` event property of the form to the macro's name. Select the Event tab on any object's Property Sheet to see the available events.

NOTE

Historically, there has been quite a bit of confusion about the names of events and their associated event properties. An event is always an action, such as `Click`, while its event property is `OnClick` or `On Click`. Conceptually, they're almost the same thing, but in technical terms, an event (like `Click` or `Open`) is an action supported by an Access object (like a form or command button), and an event procedure (`OnClick` or `OnOpen`) is how the event is attached or bound to the object.

Understanding Macro Security

The Hello World macro we built in the last section is as harmless as they come. But not all macros are harmless. You can do almost anything in a macro that you can do in the Access user interface. Some of those things, like running a delete query, can cause data loss. Access has built-in a security environment that helps you prevent unwanted, harmful macros from being run.

When you run forms, reports, queries, macros, and VBA code in your application, Access uses the Trust Center to determine which commands may be unsafe and which unsafe commands you want to run. From the Trust Center's perspective, macros and VBA code are "macros" and shouldn't be trusted by default. Unsafe commands could allow a malicious user to hack into your hard drive or other resource in your environment. A malicious user could possibly delete files from your hard drive, alter the computer's configuration, or generally wreak all kinds of havoc in your workstation or even throughout your network environment.

Each time a form, report, or other object opens, Access checks its list of unsafe commands. By default, when Access encounters one of the unsafe commands, it blocks the command from execution. To tell Access to block these potentially unsafe commands, you must enable sandbox mode.

Enabling sandbox mode

Sandbox mode allows Access to block any of the commands in the unsafe list it encounters when running forms, reports, queries, macros, data access pages, and Visual Basic code. Here's how to enable it:

1. **Open Access, click the File button, and select Options.** The Access Options dialog box appears.
2. **Select the Trust Center tab, and then click Trust Center Settings.** The Trust Center dialog box appears.
3. **Select the Macro Settings tab (shown in Figure 22.6).**
4. **Select either Disable All Macros without Notification or Disable All Macros with Notification.**

FIGURE 22.6

Enabling sandbox mode.

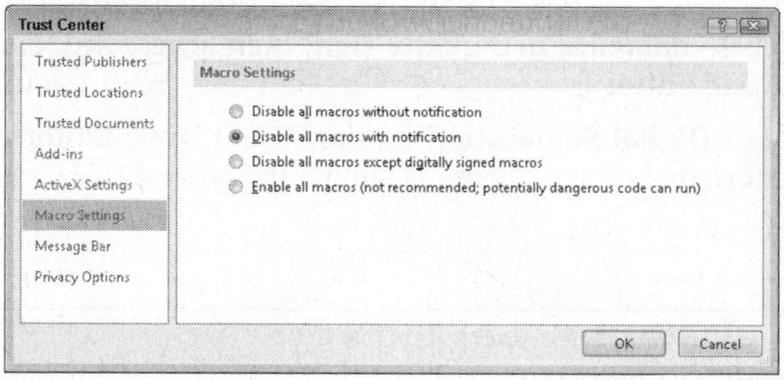

5. **Restart Access to apply the security change.**

The Macro Settings tab provides four levels of macro security:

- **Disable All Macros without Notification:** All macros and VBA code are disabled and the user isn't prompted to enable them.
- **Disable All Macros with Notification:** All macros and VBA code are disabled and the user is prompted to enable them.
- **Disable All Macros Except Digitally Signed Macros:** The status of the macro's digital signature is validated for digitally signed macros. For unsigned macros, a prompt displays advising the user to enable the macro or to cancel opening the database.
- **Enable All Macros (Not Recommended; Potentially Dangerous Code Can Be Run):** Macros and VBA code are not checked for digital signatures and no warning displays for unsigned macros.

A *digital signature* (contained within a *digital certificate*) is an encrypted secure file that accompanies a macro or document. It confirms that the author is a trusted source for the macro or document. Digital signatures are generally implemented within large organizations that are willing to fund the expense of purchasing and maintaining digital signatures. You, or your organization's IT department, can obtain a digital certificate through a commercial certification authority, like VeriSign, Inc., or Thawte. Search http://msdn.microsoft.com for "Microsoft Root Certificate Program Members" to obtain information on how to obtain a digital certificate.

The default, and generally the best choice, is Disable All Macros with Notification. During the development and maintenance cycles, you'll want all the code and macros in the application to execute without interrupting you with permissions dialog boxes. The next section describes Trusted Locations. You can put your development database in a trusted location to avoid having to enable unsigned code, but still be protected from other databases you may open.

If you or your organization has acquired a digital certificate, you can use it to sign your Access projects:

1. **Open the Access database to digitally sign; then access any module to open the Visual Basic Editor.**
2. **Choose Tools ⇨ Digital Signature from the Visual Basic Editor menu.** The Digital Signature dialog box opens, as shown in Figure 22.7.

FIGURE 22.7

Digitally signing an Access project.

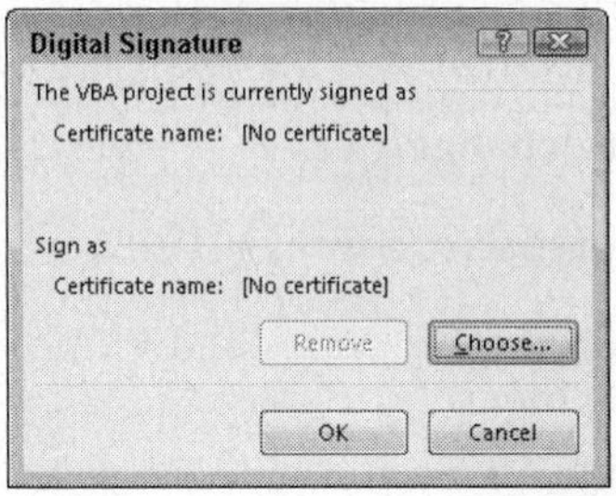

3. **Click Choose to display the Select Certificate dialog box and select a certificate from the list, as shown in Figure 22.8.**
4. **Select the certificate to add to the Access project.**
5. **Click OK to close the Select Certificate dialog box, and click OK again to close the Digital Signature dialog box and save the security setting.**

FIGURE 22.8

Choosing a digital certificate.

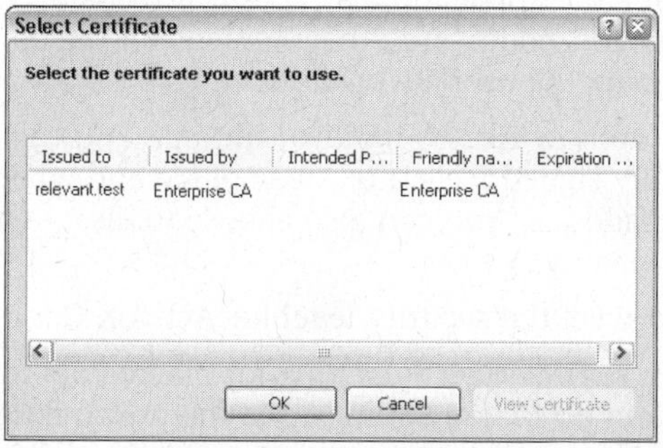

NOTE
Don't sign your Access project until the application has been thoroughly tested and you don't expect to make any further changes to it. Modifying any of the code in the project invalidates the digital signature.

TIP
To prevent users from making unauthorized changes to the code in your project, be sure to lock the project and apply a project password.

The Trust Center

The Trust Center is where you can find security and privacy settings for Access. (It replaces the Security dialog box in previous versions of Access.) To display the Trust Center, click the File button and click Options to open the Access Options dialog box. Select the Trust Center tab, and then click Trust Center Settings.

Here's a description of each section and what it controls:

- **Trusted Publishers:** Displays a list of trusted publishers — publishers where you clicked Trust All Documents from This Publisher when encountering a potentially unsafe macro — for Office. To remove a publisher from this list, select the publisher and click Remove. Trusted publishers must have a valid digital signature that hasn't expired.
- **Trusted Locations:** Displays the list of trusted locations on your computer or network. From this section, you can add, remove, or modify folders on your computer that will always contain trusted files. Any file in a trusted location can be opened without being checked by the Trust Center. You can also choose not to allow network locations and to disable all Trusted Locations and accept signed files.

- **Trusted Documents:** When Trusted Documents is selected, the name of the Access application is added to a special area in the system registry on the user's computer. Then, each time the application is used, it is recognized as a *trusted document,* and all the macros, code, and other elements of the application are enabled without interrupting the user's workflow.
- **Add-ins:** Lets you to set up how Access handles add-ins. You can choose whether add-ins need to be digitally signed from a trusted source and whether to display a notification for unsigned add-ins. You can also choose to disable all add-ins, which may impair functionality.
- **ActiveX Settings:** Lets you set the security level for ActiveX Controls.
- **Macro Settings:** Lets you set the security setting for macros not in a trusted location. (For more information on Macro Settings, see the previous section on sandbox mode.)
- **Message Bar:** Lets you set whether to display the message bar that warns you about blocked content, or to never show information about blocked content.
- **Privacy Options:** Lets you choose how Microsoft Office Online communicates with your computer. You can set options to use Microsoft Office Online for help, show featured links at startup, download files to determine system problems, and sign up for the Customer Experience Improvement Program.

Multi-Action Macros

The true power of macros comes from performing multiple actions at the click of a button. Creating a macro that runs a series of action queries is better than double-clicking each action query in the Navigation pane — you may forget to run one or you may run them out of proper sequence.

For this next example, the `Chapter22.accdb` contains two delete queries that remove data from two different tables — tblContacts_Backup and tblProducts_Backup. `Chapter22.accdb` also includes two append queries that copy records from tblContacts and tblProducts to the backup tables. Table 22.1 shows the macro actions and action arguments for `mcrBackupContactsAndProducts` (a portion of which is shown in Figure 22.9).

NOTE

If all the actions don't appear in the Action drop-down list, click the Show All Actions command in the Show/Hide group on the Macro Tools Design tab of the Ribbon. Some macro actions require a trusted database or enabling macros through your security settings. Also, some macro actions are considered unsafe because they modify data in the database or perform actions that may cause damage to the application if used incorrectly. Macro actions that are considered unsafe are indicated by a warning icon (which looks like an inverted yellow triangle containing an exclamation point) in the macro designer. By default, Access only displays trusted macro actions that run regardless of the security settings.

TABLE 22.1 mcrBackupContactsAndProducts

Action	Action Argument	Action Argument Setting
DisplayHourglassPointer	Hourglass On	Yes
SetWarnings	Warnings On	No
Echo	Echo On	No
	Status Bar Text	Step 1: Deleting Data
OpenQuery	Query Name	qryDeleteContactsBackup
	View	Datasheet
	Data Mode	Edit
OpenQuery	Query Name	qryDeleteProductsBackup
	View	Datasheet
	Data Mode	Edit
Echo	Echo On	No
	Status Bar Text	Step 2: Appending Data
OpenQuery	Query Name	qryAppendContactsBackup
	View	Datasheet
	Data Mode	Edit
OpenQuery	Query Name	qryAppendProductsBackup
	View	Datasheet
	Data Mode	Edit
Echo	Echo On	Yes
	Status Bar Text	<Leave Blank>
SetWarnings	Warnings On	Yes
DisplayHourglassPointer	Hourglass On	No
MessageBox	Message	Contacts and Products have been archived.
	Beep	Yes
	Type	Information
	Title	Finished Archiving

FIGURE 22.9

`mcrBackupContactsAndProducts` archives data from the live tables into the backup tables.

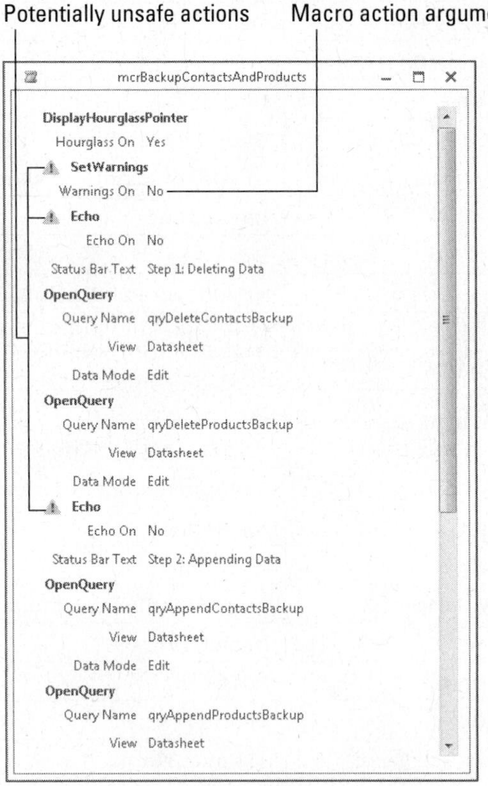

Potentially unsafe actions

Macro action argument

mcrBackupContactsAndProducts

DisplayHourglassPointer
Hourglass On Yes
SetWarnings
Warnings On No
Echo
Echo On No
Status Bar Text Step 1: Deleting Data
OpenQuery
Query Name qryDeleteContactsBackup
View Datasheet
Data Mode Edit
OpenQuery
Query Name qryDeleteProductsBackup
View Datasheet
Data Mode Edit
Echo
Echo On No
Status Bar Text Step 2: Appending Data
OpenQuery
Query Name qryAppendContactsBackup
View Datasheet
Data Mode Edit
OpenQuery
Query Name qryAppendProductsBackup
View Datasheet

Here's a look at the actions this macro performs:

- `DisplayHourglassPointer`: This action changes the cursor to an hourglass or a pointer using the `Hourglass On` argument. For macros that may take a while to run, set this argument to `Yes` at the beginning of the macro and to `No` at the end of the macro. Be sure not to forget to set `Hourglass` off at the conclusion of the macro. Otherwise, the hourglass cursor stays on indefinitely.
- `SetWarnings`: This action turns the system messages on or off using the `Warnings On` argument. When running action queries, you'll be prompted to make sure you want to run the action query, asked whether it's okay to delete these 58 records, and then asked again for the next action query. Set `Warnings On` to No at the beginning of the macro to turn these messages off. Setting `Warnings On` to No has the effect of automatically clicking the default button of the warning (usually OK or Yes). Set it back to Yes at the end of the macro.

Don't forget to turn warnings back on at the conclusion of the macro. Once warnings are turned off, the user won't get confirmation messages from Access on important actions like record deletions until warnings are re-enabled.

- `Echo`: This action shows or hides the results of a macro while it runs using the `Echo On` argument. Set it to No to hide the results of the macro or Yes to show the results. Set the `Status Bar Text` argument to give the user an indication of what's happening. This is useful in longer-running macros to know where in the process the macro is.

  The `Echo` command "freezes" the screen so that the user isn't aware of activities performed by the macro. `Echo` is much like `DisplayHourglassPointer` and `SetWarnings` — be sure to restore the `Echo On` status to Yes so that Access resumes its normal appearance. If `Echo On` is not set back to Yes, the user may think the application has "locked up" because of a problem.

- `OpenQuery`: This action is the heart of the `mcrBackupContactsAndProducts` macro. `OpenQuery` opens a select or crosstab query or runs an action query. The `Query Name` argument contains the name of the query to open or run. The `View` argument lets you pick the view — Datasheet, Design, Print Preview, PivotTable, or PivotChart — for a select or crosstab query. The `Data Mode` argument lets you choose from Add, Edit, or Read Only to limit what users can do in a select query. The `View` and `Data Mode` arguments are ignored for action queries.

The heart of the macro is the four `OpenQuery` actions that run the four action queries. qryDeleteContactsBackup and qryDeleteProductsBackup clear the contents of tblContacts_Backup and tblProducts_Backup, so the current data can be copied into them. qryAppendContactsBackup and qryAppendProductsBackup append data from tblContacts and tblProducts into the backup tables.

You could easily build this macro just using the four `OpenQuery` actions, but running it would be cumbersome, especially if one of the queries took a few minutes — or hours — to run. Use the `DisplayHourglassPointer`, `SetWarnings`, `Echo`, and `MessageBox` actions to eliminate the need for user interaction and to let the user know what's happening and when the macro has completed its activity.

Submacros

When automating your application with macros, you might easily get carried away filling the Navigation pane with a bunch of little macros for opening every form and every report. If you have a series of actions that are performed in a number of places, ideally you only want one copy, so that you need to make changes only in one place. *Submacros* give you that capability: You define the series of actions in one place as a submacro, and then invoke that submacro wherever it's needed. Only the submacro object appears in the Navigation pane, rather than multiple smaller macros.

The macro action drop-down list contains Submacro as an entry. While working on a macro, selecting Submacro from the action list adds an area to the macro where you can input the actions associated with the submacro.

Without using submacros, you'd have to create three separate macros to automate a main menu form with three buttons that open frmContacts, frmProducts, and frmSales. Using submacros, just create a single top-level macro that contains three submacros. Each of the submacros opens one form. Only the top-level macro appears in the Navigation pane. Table 22.2 shows the submacro names, the actions, and submacro actions for `mcrMainMenu`.

TABLE 22.2 mcrMainMenu

Submacro	Action	Action Argument	Action Argument Setting
OpenContacts	OpenForm	Form Name	frmContacts
		View	Form
		Filter Name	<Leave Blank>
		Where Condition	<Leave Blank>
		Data Mode	<Leave Blank>
		Window Mode	Normal
OpenProducts	OpenForm	Form Name	frmProducts
		View	Form
		Filter Name	<Leave Blank>
		Where Condition	[ProductID]=3
		Data Mode	Read Only
		Window Mode	Dialog
OpenSales	OpenForm	Form Name	frmSales
		View	Layout
		Filter Name	qrySales2008
		Where Condition	<Leave Blank>
		Data Mode	Edit
		Window Mode	Icon

Figure 22.10 shows the creation of mcrMainMenu in progress. The developer has selected `Submacro` from the `Add New Action` list, provided a name (`OpenContacts`) for the submacro, and filled in its properties.

TIP

The Add New Action drop-down displays a list of available actions sorted alphabetically. However, the first four items — Comment, Group, If, and Submacro — are shown at the top of the list rather than in their proper place. These four items are really program flow elements and are separated from the items considered actions.

Next, the developer selected Submacro a second time from the Add New Action list, and provided `OpenProduct` as its name. None of the arguments for the second submacro has been filled in.

FIGURE 22.10

Adding a second submacro to a macro.

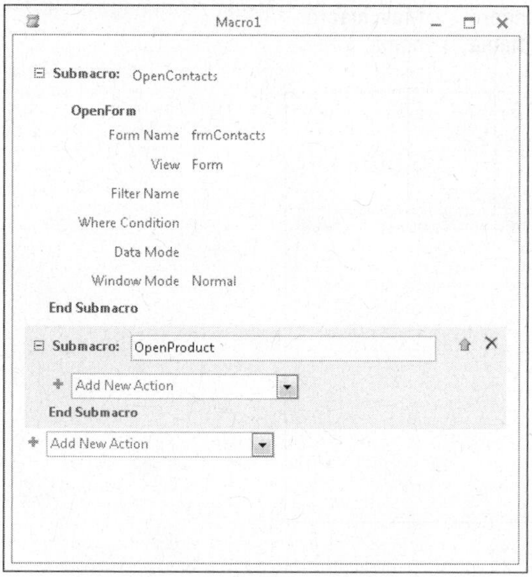

The confusing thing about submacros is that you see two Add New Action lists in Figure 22.10. One is at the very bottom of the main macro, while the second is inside the second submacro. The submacro that is currently being developed (`OpenProducts`) is enclosed in a lightly shaded box, while the completed submacro (`OpenContacts`) at the top of the main macro is not contained in a box.

NOTE

In Figure 22.10, notice the small minus sign to the left of `Submacro` in the first line of the macro. The minus sign is there to show you that the submacro is currently expanded so that you can see all the steps in the submacro. Clicking the minus sign collapses the macro to a single line, which lets you view more of the macro and its actions in a single glance. Several figures in this chapter show macros with portions collapsed (identifiable by the small plus sign to the left), so don't be confused if portions of a macro illustrated in a figure appear to be missing.

To implement a macro using submacros, create a form (frmMainMenu) with three buttons — in this case, cmdContacts, cmdProducts, and cmdSales. Then set the `On Click` event properties of these buttons as follows (see Figure 22.11):

Button Name	On Click Event Property
cmdContacts	mcrMainMenu.OpenContacts
cmdProducts	mcrMainMenu.OpenProducts
cmdSales	mcrMainMenu.OpenSales

FIGURE 22.11

The submacro names appear after the macro object in the event property drop-down list.

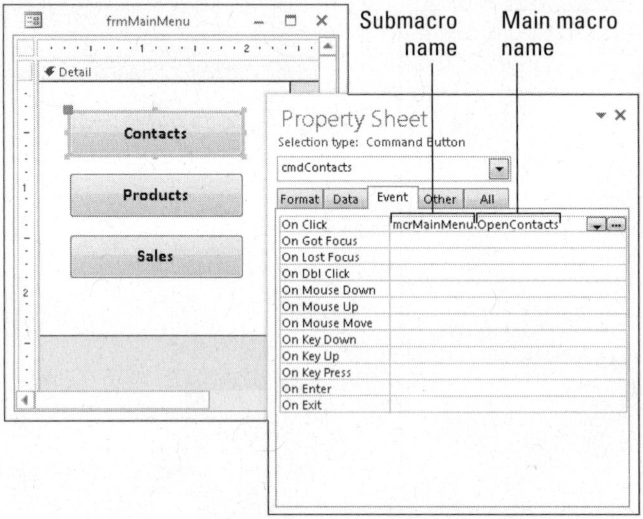

Open frmMainMenu in Form view and click the Contacts button; frmContacts opens and displays all the records. Click the Products button to display frmProducts, which only displays one record. Click the Sales button to display frmSales in a minimized state, which displays the sales made in 2012.

To see why these forms open differently, take a look at the action arguments for the `OpenForm` action:

- `Form Name`: This argument is the name of the form you want the macro to open.
- `View`: This argument lets you select which view to open the form in: Form, Design, Print Preview, Datasheet, PivotTable, PivotChart, or Layout. For this example, frmContacts and frmProducts open in Form view, while frmSales opens in Layout view.

- `Filter Name`: This argument lets you select a query or a filter saved as a query to restrict and/or sort the records for the form. For this example, this argument is set to qrySales2012 for the `OpenSales` macro. qrySales2012 is a query that outputs all the fields in the table and only displays sales between 1/1/2012 and 12/31/2012. This query also sorts the records by `SaleDate`.
- `Where Condition`: This argument lets you enter a SQL `Where` clause or expression that selects records for the form from its underlying table or query. For this example, this argument is set to `[ProductID]=3` for the `OpenProducts` submacro, which only shows one record when you open frmProducts.
- `Data Mode`: This argument lets you choose the data-entry mode for the form. Select Add to only allow users to add new records, Edit to allow adding and editing of records, or Read Only to allow only viewing of records. This setting only applies to forms opened in Form view or Datasheet view, and overrides settings of the form's AllowEdits, AllowDeletions, AllowAdditions, and DataEntry properties. To use the form's setting for these properties, leave this argument blank. For this example, frmProducts opens in read-only mode, while frmContacts and frmSales allow editing.
- `Window Mode`: This argument lets you choose the window mode for the form. Select Normal to use the form's properties. Select Hidden to open the form with its Visible property set to No. Select Icon to open the form minimized. Select Dialog to open the form with its Modal and PopUp properties set to Yes and Border Style property set to Dialog. For this example, frmContacts opens normally, frmProducts opens as a dialog box, and frmSales opens minimized.

For more information on form properties, see Chapter 17.

NOTE

When you run a macro with submacros from the Navigation pane, only the first submacro executes.

If you're careful in planning your macros, you can create one top-level macro object for each form or report and use submacros for each action you want to perform in the form or report. Submacros let you limit the number of macros that appear in the Navigation pane and make managing numerous macros much easier.

Conditions

Submacros let you put multiple groups of actions in a single macro object, but a *condition* specifies certain criteria that must be met before the macro performs the action. In Access 2007 and prior versions, macros had a Conditions column in which you could enter any expression that evaluates to True or False. Beginning in Access 2010, the `If` macro action was introduced to replace Conditions. The `If` macro action also takes a Boolean expression. If the expression evaluates to False, No, or 0, the action will not execute. If the expression evaluates to any other value, the action is performed.

Opening reports using conditions

To demonstrate conditions and the `If` macro action, `frmReportMenu` (shown in Figure 22.12), contains three buttons and a frame control (`fraView`) with two option buttons: Print and Print Preview. Clicking Print sets the frame's value to 1; clicking Print Preview sets the frame's value to 2.

FIGURE 22.12

`frmReportMenu` uses a frame to select the view in which to open the Contacts, Products, and Sales reports.

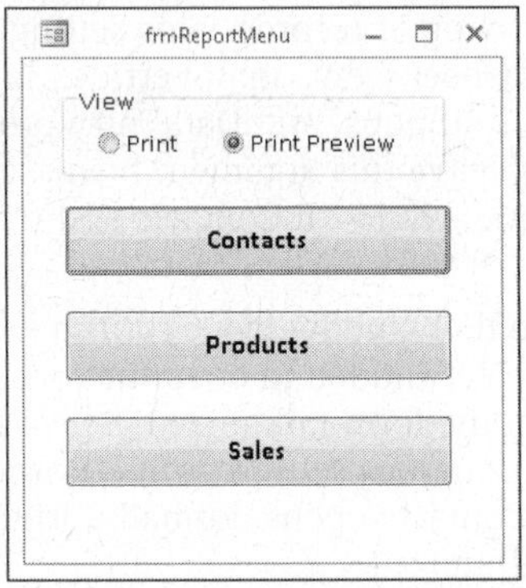

The macro that opens the reports uses submacros, as well as the `If` macro action. Table 22.3 shows the submacro names, conditions, actions, and action arguments for `mcrReportMenu` (a portion of which is shown in Figure 22.13), which opens one of three reports. The `Filter Name` and `Where Condition` arguments are blank for each `OpenReport` action.

TABLE 22.3 mcrReportMenu

Submacro Name	If Macro Action Condition	Action	Action Argument	Action Argument Setting
`OpenContacts`	`[Forms]![frmReportMenu]![fraView]=1`	`OpenReport`	`Report Name`	`rptContacts_Landscape`
			`View`	`Print`
			`Window Mode`	`Normal`

Submacro Name	If Macro Action Condition	Action	Action Argument	Action Argument Setting
	[Forms]![frm ReportMenu]![fraView]=2	OpenReport	Report Name	rptContacts_Landscape
			View	Print Preview
			Window Mode	Normal
OpenProducts	[Forms]![frm ReportMenu]![fraView]=1	OpenReport	Report Name	rptProducts
			View	Print
			Window Mode	Normal
	[Forms]![frm ReportMenu]![fraView]=2	OpenReport	Report Name	rptProducts
			View	Print Preview
			Window Mode	Normal
OpenSales	[Forms]![frm ReportMenu]![fraView]=1	OpenReport	Report Name	rptSales_Portrait
			View	Print
			Window Mode	Normal
	[Forms]![frm ReportMenu]![fraView]=2	OpenReport	Report Name	rptSales_Portrait
			View	Print Preview
			Window Mode	Normal

FIGURE 22.13

`mcrReportMenu` uses an `If` action to open reports in Print or Print Preview view.

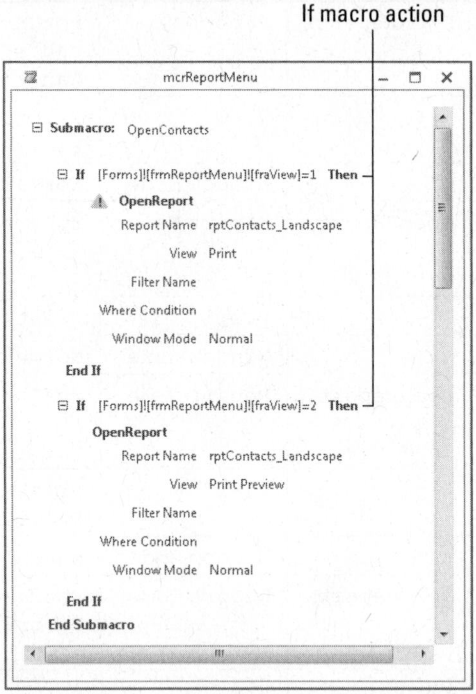

If macro action

```
mcrReportMenu

Submacro: OpenContacts

  If [Forms]![frmReportMenu]![fraView]=1 Then
    OpenReport
          Report Name  rptContacts_Landscape
                 View  Print
          Filter Name
      Where Condition
          Window Mode  Normal
  End If

  If [Forms]![frmReportMenu]![fraView]=2 Then
    OpenReport
          Report Name  rptContacts_Landscape
                 View  Print Preview
          Filter Name
      Where Condition
          Window Mode  Normal
  End If
End Submacro
```

To implement this macro, set the `On Click` event properties of the buttons (cmdContacts, cmdProducts, and cmdSales) on `frmReportMenu` as follows:

Button Name	On Click Event Property
cmdContacts	mcrReportMenu.OpenContacts
cmdProducts	mcrReportMenu.OpenProducts
cmdSales	mcrReportMenu.OpenSales

The `If` macro action in `mcrReportMenu` has two expressions that look at `fraView` on `frmReportMenu` to determine whether Print or Print Preview is selected:

- `[Forms]![frmReportMenu]![fraView]=1`: Print view selected
- `[Forms]![frmReportMenu]![fraView]=2`: Print Preview view selected

If Print is selected on `frmReportMenu`, the `OpenReport` action with the `View` arguments set to Print executes. If Print Preview is selected on `frmReportMenu`, the `OpenReport` action with the `View` arguments set to Print Preview executes. This structure is set up for each submacro in `mcrReportMenu`.

Multiple actions in conditions

If you want to run multiple actions based on a condition, add multiple actions within the `If` and `End If` actions. Figure 22.14 illustrates this concept.

FIGURE 22.14

Multiple actions within `If` and `End If` actions execute as a group.

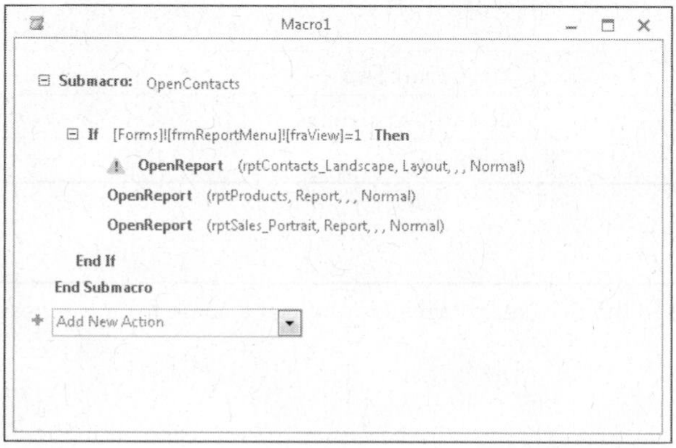

Macro1

Submacro: OpenContacts

If [Forms]![frmReportMenu]![fraView]=1 Then

OpenReport (rptContacts_Landscape, Layout, , , Normal)

OpenReport (rptProducts, Report, , , Normal)

OpenReport (rptSales_Portrait, Report, , , Normal)

End If

End Submacro

Add New Action

The `If` macro action lets you selectively run actions based on other values in your application. Use the `If` macro action to reference controls on forms or reports and other objects and determine which actions to execute.

Temporary Variables

In previous versions of Access, you could use variables only in VBA code. Macros were limited to performing a series of actions without carrying anything forward from a previous action. Beginning with Access 2007, three new macro actions — `SetTempVar`, `RemoveTempVar`, and `RemoveAllTempVars` — let you create and use temporary variables in your macros. You can use these variables in conditional expressions to control which actions execute, or to pass data to and from forms or reports. You can even access these variables in VBA to communicate data to and from modules.

Enhancing a macro you've already created

A simple way to demonstrate how to use variables in macros is to enhance the Hello World example created earlier in this chapter (see "Creating a macro"). Table 22.4 shows the macro actions and action arguments for `mcrHelloWorldEnhanced` (shown in Figure 22.15).

TABLE 22.4 mcrHelloWorldEnhanced

Action	Action Argument	Action Argument Setting
SetTempVar	Name	MyName
	Expression	InputBox("Enter your name.")
MessageBox	Message	="Hello " & [TempVars]![MyName] & "."
	Beep	Yes
	Type	Information
	Title	Using Variables
RemoveTempVar	Name	MyName

FIGURE 22.15

`mcrHelloWorldEnhanced` uses the `SetTempVar` action to get a value from the user and display it in a message box.

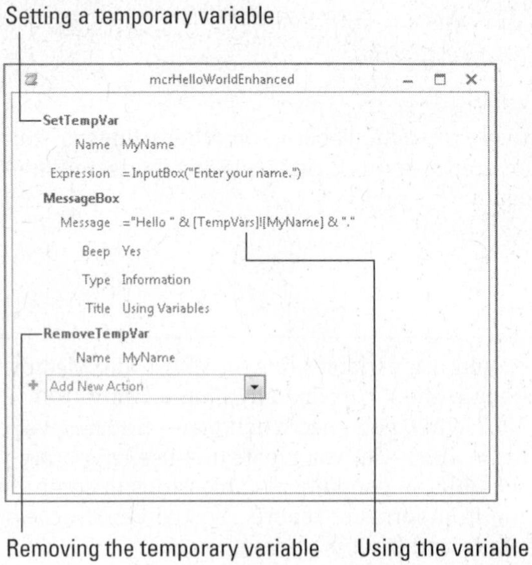

Setting a temporary variable

Removing the temporary variable

Using the variable

The SetTempVar action has two arguments: Name and Expression. The Name argument (MyName in this example) is simply the name of the temporary variable. The Expression argument is what you want the value of the variable to be. In this example, the InputBox() function prompts the user for his name.

The MessageBox action's Message argument contains the following expression:

```
="Hello " & [TempVars]![MyName] & "."
```

This expression concatenates the word Hello with the temporary variable MyName, created in the SetTempVar action of the macro. When referring to a temporary variable created with the SetTempVar action, use the following syntax:

```
[TempVars]![VariableName]
```


For more information on string concatenation using the ampersand (&), see Chapter 9.

The RemoveTempVar action removes a single temporary variable from memory — in this example, MyName. You can have only 255 temporary variables defined at one time. These variables stay in memory until you close the database, unless you remove them with RemoveTempVar or RemoveAllTempVars. It's a good practice to remove temporary variables when you're done using them.

CAUTION
Using the RemoveAllTempVars action removes all temporary variables created with the SetTempVar action. Unless you're sure you want to do this, use the RemoveTempVar action instead.

Temporary variables are global. Once you create a temporary variable, you can use it in VBA procedures, queries, macros, or object properties. For example, if you remove the RemoveTempVar action from mcrHelloWorldEnhanced, you can create a text box on a form and set its Control Source property as follows to display the name the user entered:

```
=[TempVars]![MyName]
```

Using temporary variables to simplify macros

Using temporary variables, you can sometimes eliminate steps from a macro. You can get the form or report name from another control on a form. With a temporary variable, you eliminate the need for creating a structure of multiple OpenForm or OpenReport actions. You can also use more than one variable in a macro.

For this example, use frmReportMenuEnhanced (shown in Figure 22.16), which contains the same fraView shown in Figure 22.12, but adds a combo box (cboReport), which contains a list of reports to run. The Run Command button executes mcrReportMenu Enhanced, which doesn't use submacros to decide which report to open.

FIGURE 22.16

frmReportMenuEnhanced uses a combo box to select which report to open.

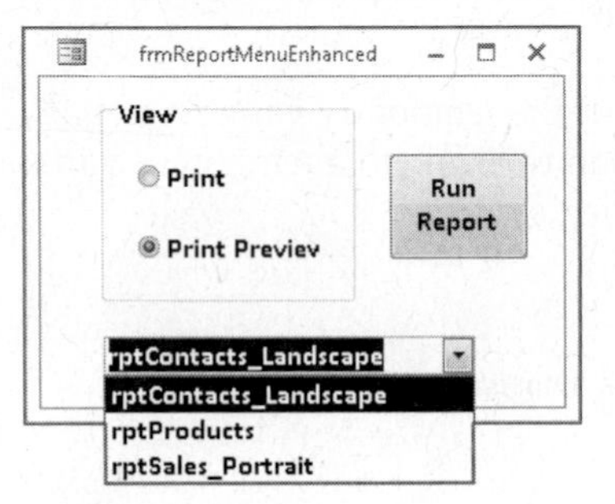

Table 22.5 shows the conditions, actions, and action arguments for mcrReportMenu Enhanced (shown in Figure 22.17), which opens one of three reports.

TABLE 22.5 mcrReportMenuEnhanced

Condition	Action	Action Argument	Action Argument Setting
	SetTempVar	Name	ReportName
		Expression	[Forms]![frmReport MenuEnhanced]![cboReport]
	SetTempVar	Name	ReportView
		Expression	[Forms]![frmReport MenuEnhanced]![fraView]
[TempVars]![ReportView]=1	OpenReport	Report Name	=[TempVars]![ReportName]
		View	Print
		Window Mode	Normal
[TempVars]![ReportView]=2	OpenReport	Report Name	=[TempVars]![ReportName]
		View	Print Preview
		Window Mode	Normal
	RemoveTempVar	Name	ReportName
	RemoveTempVar	Name	ReportView

FIGURE 22.17

mcrReportMenuEnhanced uses temporary variables to open the report in Print or Print Preview view.

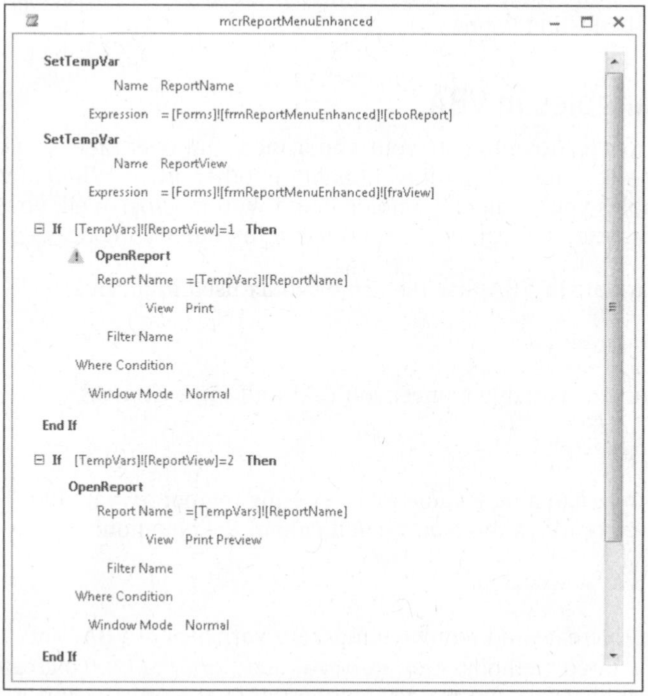

```
mcrReportMenuEnhanced

SetTempVar
        Name  ReportName
  Expression  = [Forms]![frmReportMenuEnhanced]![cboReport]
SetTempVar
        Name  ReportView
  Expression  = [Forms]![frmReportMenuEnhanced]![fraView]
If [TempVars]![ReportView]=1 Then
    OpenReport
      Report Name  =[TempVars]![ReportName]
             View  Print
      Filter Name
  Where Condition
      Window Mode  Normal
End If
If [TempVars]![ReportView]=2 Then
    OpenReport
      Report Name  =[TempVars]![ReportName]
             View  Print Preview
      Filter Name
  Where Condition
      Window Mode  Normal
End If
```

The first two SetTempVar actions in mcrReportMenuEnhanced set the values of the temporary variables — ReportName and ReportView — from cboReport and fraView on frmReportMenuEnhanced. The OpenReport actions use the temporary variables in the Condition column and for the ReportName argument. When using temporary variables as a setting for an argument, you must use an equal (=) sign in front of the expression:

```
=[TempVars]![ReportName]
```

There are still two OpenReport actions in this macro. Certain arguments — such as View — don't allow the use of temporary variables in expressions. Because one of your variables is a setting for the report's view, you still have to use the Condition column to decide which view to open the report in.

The last two RemoveTempVar lines remove the temporary variables — ReportName and ReportView — from memory. Because these variables probably won't be used later on in the application, it's important to remove them.

Using temporary variables in macros gives you far more flexibility in Access 2013 than in versions prior to Access 2007. You can use these variables to store values to use later on in the macro, or anywhere in the application. Just remember that you have only 255 temporary variables to use, so don't forget to clean up after yourself by removing them from memory once you're finished using them.

Using temporary variables in VBA

You may start out using macros to automate your application, but over time, you may begin using VBA code to automate and add functionality to other areas. What do you do with the temporary variables you've already implemented with macros? Well, you don't have to abandon them; instead, you can use them directly in your VBA code.

To access a temporary variable in VBA, use the same syntax used in macros:

```
X = [TempVars]![VariableName]
```

If you don't use spaces in your variable names, you can omit the brackets:

```
X = TempVars!VariableName
```

Use the previous syntax to assign a new value to an existing temporary variable. The only difference is to put the temporary variable on the left side of the equation:

```
TempVars!VariableName = NewValue
```

Use the `TempVars` object to create and remove temporary variables in VBA. The `TempVars` object contains three methods: `Add`, `Remove`, and `RemoveAll`. To create a new temporary variable and set its value, use the `Add` method of the `TempVars` object as follows:

```
TempVars.Add "VariableName", Value
```

Use the `Remove` method of the `TempVars` object to remove a single temporary variable from memory:

```
TempVars.Remove "VariableName"
```

TIP

When adding or removing temporary variables in VBA, remember to put the temporary variable's name in quotation marks.

To remove all the temporary variables from memory, use the `RemoveAll` method of the `TempVars` object as follows:

```
TempVars.RemoveAll
```

Any VBA variables you create are available to use in your macros, and vice versa. Any variables you remove in VBA are no longer available to use in your macros, and vice versa. Using temporary variables, your macros and VBA code no longer have to be independent from each other.

Error Handling and Macro Debugging

In previous versions of Access, if an error occurred in a macro, the macro stopped execution, and your users saw an ugly dialog box (shown in Figure 22.18) that didn't really explain what was going on. If he was unfamiliar with Access, he quickly became disgruntled using the application. The lack of error handing in macros is one main reason many developers use VBA instead of macros to automate their applications.

FIGURE 22.18

Errors in macros cause the macro to cease operation.

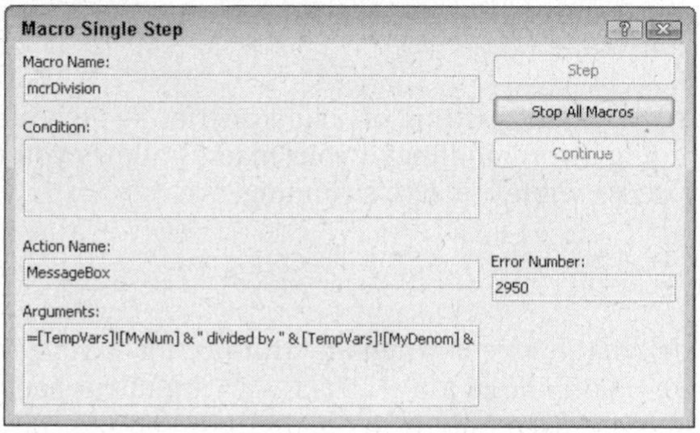

A common error that's easy to demonstrate is the divide-by-zero error. For the next example, `mcrDivision` (shown in Figure 22.19) contains two temporary variables — `MyNum` and `MyDenom` — set with the `InputBox()` function asking for a numerator and denominator. The `MessageBox` action shows the result — `[TempVars]![MyNum]/[TempVars]![MyDenom]` — in a message box and the `RemoveTempVar` actions remove the variables from memory.

Run the macro and enter **1** for the numerator and **2** for the denominator; the macro runs and displays a message box saying `1 divided by 2 is 0.5`. Run the macro again and enter **0** in the denominator; a divide-by-zero error occurs and the macro stops running. Without error handling, the two `RemoveTempVar` actions won't run and won't remove the temporary variables from memory.

FIGURE 22.19

`mcrDivision` divides the numerator by the denominator and generates an error when the denominator is zero.

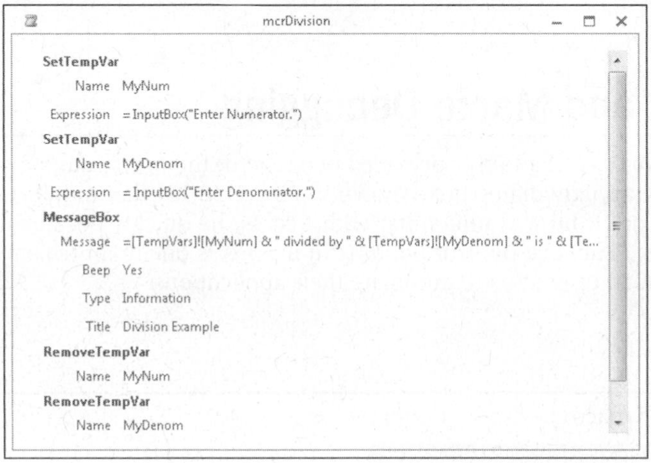

```
mcrDivision
SetTempVar
    Name  MyNum
    Expression  =InputBox("Enter Numerator.")
SetTempVar
    Name  MyDenom
    Expression  =InputBox("Enter Denominator.")
MessageBox
    Message  =[TempVars]![MyNum] & " divided by " & [TempVars]![MyDenom] & " is " & [Te...
    Beep  Yes
    Type  Information
    Title  Division Example
RemoveTempVar
    Name  MyNum
RemoveTempVar
    Name  MyDenom
```

If an error occurs in another macro — such as a string of action queries — any queries after an error occurs won't run. Adding error handling to your macros allows you to choose what to do when an error occurs while a macro's running.

The OnError action

The `OnError` action lets you decide what happens when an error occurs in your macro. This action has two arguments: `Go to` and `Macro Name`. The `Go to` argument has three settings and the `Macro Name` argument is used only with one of these settings, described as follows:

- **Next:** This setting records the details of the error in the `MacroError` object but does not stop the macro. The macro continues with the next action.
- **Macro Name:** This setting stops the current macro and runs the macro in the `Macro Name` argument of the `OnError` action.
- **Fail:** This setting stops the current macro and displays an error message. This is the same as not having error handling in the macro.

The VBA equivalents of these settings are as follows:

```
On Error Resume Next        'Next
On Error GoTo LABELNAME     'Macro Name
On Error GoTo 0            'Fail
```

The simplest way to add error handling to a macro is to make `OnError` the first action and set the `Go to` argument to `Next`. This will cause your macro to run without stopping, but you won't have any clue which actions ran and which ones didn't.

Instead, create an error-handling structure. Table 22.6 shows the macro names, actions, and action arguments for `mcrDivisionErrorHandling` (shown in Figure 22.20).

TABLE 22.6 mcrDivisionErrorHandling

Submacro Name	Action	Action Argument	Action Argument Setting
	OnError	Go to	Macro Name
		Macro Name	ErrorHandler
	SetTempVar	Name	MyNum
		Expression	InputBox("Enter Numerator.")
	SetTempVar	Name	MyDenom
		Expression	InputBox("Enter Denominator.")
	MessageBox	Message	=[TempVars]![MyNum] & " divided by " & [TempVars]![MyDenom] & " is " & [TempVars]![MyNum]/ [TempVars]![MyDenom]
		Beep	Yes
		Type	Information
		Title	Division Example
	RunMacro	Macro Name	mcrDivisionError Handling.Cleanup
ErrorHandler	MessageBox	Message	="The following error occurred: " & [MacroError]. [Description]
		Beep	Yes
		Type	Warning?
		Title	="Error Number: " & [MacroError].[Number]
	ClearMacroError		
	RunMacro	Macro Name	mcrDivisionError Handling.Cleanup
Cleanup	RemoveTempVar	Name	MyNum
	RemoveTempVar	Name	MyDenom

FIGURE 22.20

mcrDivisionErrorHandling uses the OnError action to display a user-friendly error message and remove the temporary variables.

Setting up an error handler

Error handler name

Error handler submacro

Collapsed macro actions

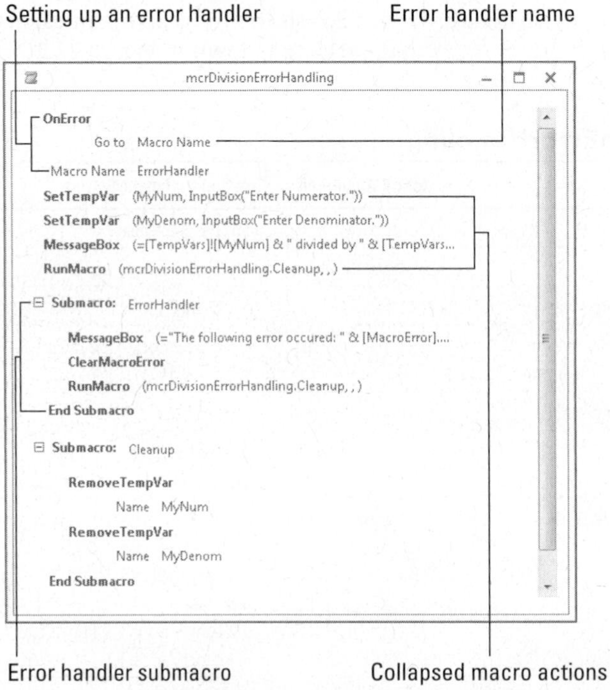

The first OnError action in the macro lets Access know to move to the submacro ErrorHandler when an error occurs. If an error occurs (by entering 0 as the denominator), the macro stops and moves to the ErrorHandler submacro. The ErrorHandler submacro displays a message box — using the MacroError object (described in the next section) to display the error's description in the Message and the error's number in the Title, using the following expressions:

```
[MacroError].[Description]
[MacroError].[Number]
```

After the error handler's message box, the ClearMacroError action clears the MacroError object. The RunMacro action moves execution to the macro's Cleanup submacro. The Cleanup section of the macro removes the temporary variables.

NOTE

There's no Resume functionality in macro error handling. If you want to run additional code after the error-handling actions, you must use the RunMacro action in the error-handling submacro to run another macro, or place the actions in the error handler.

The `RunMacro` action also appears after the `MessageBox` action in the main section of the macro. Because you're using submacros, the macro stops after it reaches the `ErrorHandler` submacro. In order to force the cleanup of the temporary variables, use the `RunMacro` action to run the `Cleanup` submacro. Otherwise, you'd have to put the `RemoveTempVar` actions in the main section and in the `ErrorHandler` section of the macro.

The MacroError object

The `MacroError` object contains information about the last macro error that occurred. It retains this information until a new error occurs or you clear it with the `ClearMacroError` action. This object contains a number of read-only properties you can access from the macro itself or from VBA. These properties are as follows:

- `ActionName`: This is the name of the macro action that was running when the error occurred.
- `Arguments`: The arguments for the macro action that was running when the error occurred.
- `Condition`: This property contains the condition for the macro action that was running when the error occurred.
- `Description`: The text representing the current error message — for example, Divide by Zero or Type Mismatch.
- `MacroName`: Contains the name of the macro that was running when the error occurred.
- `Number`: This property contains the current error number — for example, 11 or 13.

Use the `MacroError` object as a debugging tool or to display messages to the user, who can then relay that information to you. You can even write these properties to a table to track the errors that occur in your macros. Use this object within an `If` action to customize what actions execute based on the error that occurs. When used in combination with the `OnError` action, it gives you additional functionality by handling errors, displaying useful messages, and providing information to you and the user.

Debugging macros

Trying to figure out what's going on in a macro can be difficult. The `OnError` action and `MacroError` object make debugging Access macros easier than in previous versions. There are other tools and techniques that are useful when debugging macros. Use the following list as a guideline for troubleshooting macros.

- **Single Step:** Click the Single Step button in the Tools group on the Macro Tools Design tab of the Ribbon to turn on Single Step mode. The Macro Single Step dialog box (shown in Figure 22.21) lets you see the macro name, condition, action name, arguments, and error number of a macro action before the action executes.

From this dialog box, click Step to execute the action, Stop All Macros to stop the macro from running, or Continue to finish the macro with Single Step mode turned off.

FIGURE 22.21

Use the Macro Single Step dialog box to step through a macro.

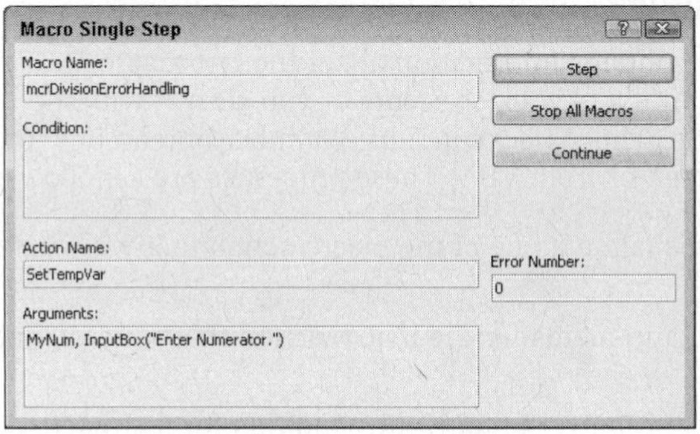

- `MessageBox`: Use the `MessageBox` macro action to display values of variables, error messages, control settings, or whatever else you want to see while the macro is running. To see the value of a combo box on a form, set the `Message` argument as follows:

```
[Forms]![frmReportMenuEnhanced]![cboReport]
```

- `StopMacro`: Use the `StopMacro` action to stop the macro from executing. Insert this action at any point in the macro to stop it at that point. Use this in conjunction with the debug window to check values.
- Debug window: Use the debug window to look at any values, temporary variables, or properties of the `MacroError` object after you stop the macro. Press Ctrl + G to display the code window after you stop the macro. Just type a question mark (?) and the name of the variable or expression you want to check the value of, and press Enter. Here are some examples of expressions to display in the Debug window:

```
? TempVars!MyNum
? MacroError!Description
? [Forms]![frmReportMenuEnhanced]![cboReport]
```

These techniques are similar to ones you'd use when debugging VBA code. You can step through sections of code, pause the code and look at values in the debug window, and display message boxes to display variables or errors that occur. Granted, you don't have all the tools available — such as watching variables and `Debug.Print` — but at least you have the new `MacroError` object to provide the information you need to figure out what's going wrong.

For more information on error handling and debugging VBA code see Chapter 26.

Embedded Macros

An *embedded macro* is stored in an event property and is part of the object to which it belongs. When you modify an embedded macro, you don't have to worry about other controls that might use the macro because each embedded macro is independent. Embedded macros aren't visible in the Navigation pane and are only accessible from the object's Property Sheet.

As an example, let's say you want to add a command button to a form that opens a report. You could use a global macro (one that's in the Navigation pane) to open the report, or you could add an embedded macro to the command button.

Embedded macros are trusted. They run even if your security settings prevent the running of code. Using embedded macros allows you to distribute your application as a trusted application because embedded macros are automatically prevented from performing unsafe operations.

One big change since Access 2003 is that when you use a wizard to create a button, it no longer creates an event procedure — it creates an embedded macro. So, if you're used to running a wizard and using the wizard's VBA code for another purpose, you'll have to abandon that technique. Using embedded macros instead of code accomplishes two things:

- It allows you to quickly create a distributable application.
- It allows users not familiar with VBA code to customize buttons created with wizards.

Follow these steps to create an embedded macro that opens `frmContacts`:

1. **Select the Create tab on the Ribbon, and then click the Form Design button in the Forms group.**
2. **On the Form Design Tools Design tab of the Ribbon, deselect the Use Control Wizards option in the Controls group.** For this example, you don't want to use a wizard to decide what this button does.
3. **Click the Button control and draw a new button on the form.**
4. **Set the button's Name property to cmdContacts and the Caption property to Contacts.**

5. **Display the Property Sheet for cmdContacts, select the Event tab, and then click the On Click event property.**
6. **Click the builder button — the button with the ellipsis (...).** The Choose Builder dialog box (shown in Figure 22.22) appears.

FIGURE 22.22

Use the builder button in the event property to display the Choose Builder dialog box to create an embedded macro.

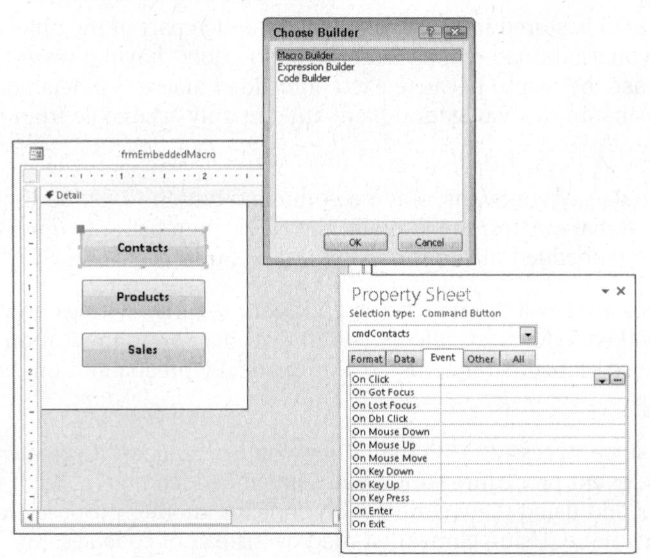

7. **Choose Macro Builder and click OK to display the macro window (shown in Figure 22.23).**
8. **Add the OpenForm action to the macro, and then set the Form Name argument to frmContacts.**
9. **Close the embedded macro, and click OK when you're prompted to save the changes and update the property.** The `On Click` event property of `cmdContacts` now displays `[Embedded Macro]`.

FIGURE 22.23

An embedded macro doesn't have a name. The title bar displays the control and the event in which the macro is embedded.

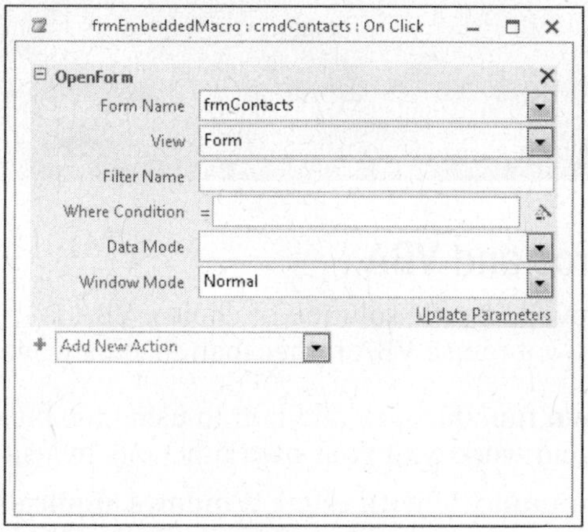

Using an embedded macro has some advantages over using an event procedure containing VBA code. If you copy the button and paste it on another form, the embedded macro goes with it. You don't have to copy the code and paste it as a separate operation. Similarly, if you cut and paste the button on the same form (for example, moving it onto a Tab control), you don't have to reattach the code to the button.

Embedded macros offer another improvement to macros in previous versions. If you automate your application with embedded macros and import a form or report into another database (or just copy the control within the same database), you don't have to worry about importing or copying the associated macros. By using embedded macros, all the automation moves with the form or report. This makes maintaining and building applications easier.

Macros versus VBA Statements

In Access, macros often offer an ideal way to take care of many details, such as running reports and forms. You can develop applications and assign actions faster using a macro because the arguments for the macro actions are displayed with the macro (in the bottom portion of the macro window). You don't have to remember complex or difficult syntax.

Several actions you can accomplish with VBA statements are better suited for macros. The following actions tend to be more efficient when they're run from macros:

- Using macros against an entire set of records with action queries — for example, to manipulate multiple records in a table or across tables (such as updating field values or deleting records)

- Opening and closing forms
- Running reports

> **NOTE**
> The VBA language supplies a `DoCmd` object that accomplishes many macro actions. Under the surface, `DoCmd` runs a macro task to accomplish the same result provided by a macro action. You could, for example, specify `DoCmd.Close` to run the `Close` macro action and close the currently active form.

Choosing between macros and VBA

Although macros sometimes prove to be the solution of choice, VBA is the tool of choice at other times. You'll probably want to use VBA rather than macros when you want to

- **Create and use your own functions.** In addition to using the built-in functions in Access, you can create and work with your own functions by using VBA code.
- **Use Automation to communicate with other Windows applications or to run system-level actions.** You can write code to see whether a file exists before you take some action, or you can communicate with another Windows application (such as a spreadsheet), passing data back and forth.
- **Use existing functions in external Windows Dynamic Link Libraries (DLLs).** Macros don't enable you to call functions in other Windows DLLs.
- **Work with records one at a time.** If you need to step through records or move values from a record to variables for manipulation, code is the answer.
- **Create or manipulate objects.** In most cases, you'll find that creating and modifying an object is easiest in that object's Design view. In some situations, however, you may want to manipulate the definition of an object in code. With a few VBA statements, you can manipulate virtually any and all objects in a database, including the database itself.
- **Display a progress meter on the status bar.** If you need to display a progress meter to communicate progress to the user, VBA code is the answer.

> **NOTE**
> Access 2013 supports a type of database that is used only in SharePoint. These "web-enabled" databases require the use of macros instead of VBA for all their forms and reports.

Converting existing macros to VBA

After you become comfortable with writing VBA code, you may want to rewrite some of your application macros as VBA procedures. As you begin this process, you quickly realize how mentally challenging the effort can be as you review every macro in your various macro libraries. You can't merely cut the macro from the macro window and paste it into a module window. For each condition, action, and action argument for a macro, you must analyze the task it accomplishes and then write the equivalent statements of VBA code in your procedure.

Fortunately, Access provides a feature that converts macros to VBA code automatically. On the Tools group of the Design tab of the Ribbon, there is a Convert Macro to Visual Basic button. This option enables you to convert a macro to a module in seconds.

NOTE

Only macros that appear in the Navigation pane can be converted to VBA. Macros that are embedded in a form or report must be converted manually.

To try the conversion process, convert the `mcrHelloWorldEnhanced` macro used earlier in this chapter. Follow these steps to run the conversion process:

1. **Click the Macros group in the Navigation pane.**
2. **Open mcrHelloWorldEnhanced in Design view.**
3. **Click the Convert Macros to Visual Basic button on the Design tab.** The Convert Macro dialog box (shown in Figure 22.24) appears.

FIGURE 22.24

The Convert Macro dialog box.

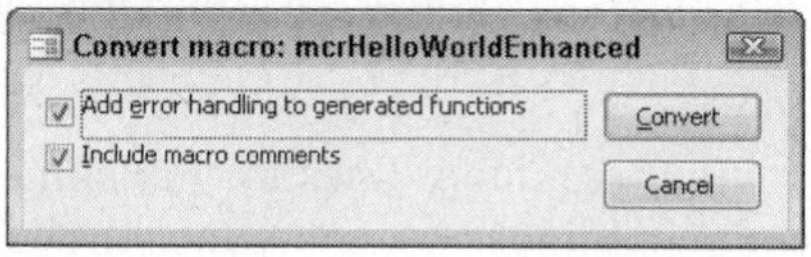

4. **Select the options that include error handling and macro comments, and click Convert.** When the conversion process completes, the Visual Basic Editor (VBE) is displayed and the `Conversion Finished!` message box appears.
5. **Click OK to dismiss the message box.**
6. **In the VBE, open the Project Explorer from the View menu (Ctrl + R) and double-click the module named Converted Macro- mcrHelloWorldEnhanced.** The code and Project Explorer are shown in Figure 22.25.

FIGURE 22.25

The newly converted module.

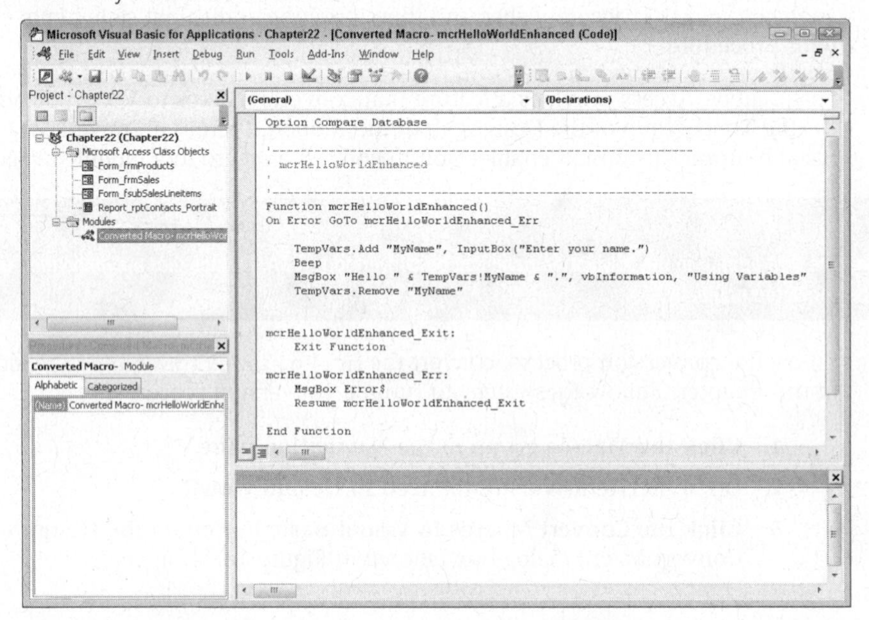

When you open the VBE for the new module, you can view the procedure created from the macro. Figure 22.25 shows the `mcrHelloWorldEnhanced` function that Access created from the `mcrHelloWorldEnhanced` macro.

At the top of the function, Access inserts four comment lines for the name of the function. The `Function` statement follows the comment lines. Access names the function, using the macro library's name (`mcrHelloWorldEnhanced`).

When you specify that you want Access to include error processing for the conversion, Access automatically inserts the `On Error` statement as the first command in the procedure. The `On Error` statement tells Access to branch to other statements that display an appropriate message and then exit the function.

The statement beginning with `TempVars.Add` is the actual code that Access created from the macro. Each line of the macro is converted into a line of VBA code including the TempVars object, the Beep method, and the MsgBox function.

If you're new to VBA and want to learn code, a good starting point is converting your macros to modules. Just save your macros and modules, and then look at the VBA code to become familiar with the syntax. The macro features in Access 2013 make it harder to decide whether to use macros or VBA.

CHAPTER

23

Getting Started with Access VBA

IN THIS CHAPTER

Working with VBA

Reviewing VBA terminology

Understanding VBA code basics

Creating your first procedure

Adding branching constructs

Learning looping constructs

Understanding objects and collections

Exploring the Visual Basic Editor

Most Access developers use macros now and then. Although macros provide a quick and easy way to automate an application, writing Visual Basic for Applications (VBA) modules is the best way to create applications. VBA provides data access, looping and branching, and other features that macros simply don't support — or at least not with the flexibility most developers want. In this chapter, you learn how to use VBA to extend the power and usefulness of your applications.

On the Web

Download the database file `Chapter23.accdb` from this book's website.

The Limitations of Macros

For a number of reasons, this book doesn't extensively cover Access macro creation. To begin with, there are so many important topics that we had to choose which topics to cover in detail. Plus, macros are pretty easy to learn on your own, and they're well documented in the Access online help. There are, however, two areas where macros can't be beat: data macros in tables and embedded macros on forms and controls. The ability to embed macros in tables and forms make macros much more attractive than in versions prior to Access 2007.

But, by far, the biggest reason we don't document macros is that macros are guaranteed to be non-portable to other applications. You can't use an Access macro anywhere other than in Access. VBA code, on the other hand, is very portable to Word, Excel, Outlook, Visio, and even Visual Studio .NET (with changes).

It's impossible to tell where an Access application might end up. Very often, Access apps are upsized and upgraded to SQL Server and Visual Studio .NET. The VBA code in your Access applications is readily converted to Visual Basic .NET, and many Access procedures can be used (perhaps with a few changes) in Word or Excel. VBA is a very portable, useful language, and VBA skills are applicable in many situations other than building Access applications.

I don't mean to imply that macros have no place in Access applications, or that macros are necessarily inferior to VBA code. Microsoft has issues related to previous versions of Access macros. In particular, macros in Access 2013 include variables and simple error handling (mostly jumping to a named location when an error occurs). These updates to the Access macro engine are significant, but, in the opinion of many Access developers, they aren't enough to justify using macros instead of VBA in professional applications.

Introducing Visual Basic for Applications

Visual Basic for Applications (VBA) is the programming language built into Microsoft Access. VBA is shared among all the Office applications, including Word, Excel, Outlook, PowerPoint, and even Visio. If you aren't already a VBA programmer, learning the VBA syntax and how to hook VBA into the Access event model is a definite career builder.

VBA is a key element in most professional Access applications. Microsoft provides VBA in Access because VBA provides significant flexibility and power to Access database applications. Without a full-fledged programming language like VBA, Access applications would have to rely on the somewhat limited set of actions offered by Access macros. Although macro programming also adds flexibility to Access applications, VBA is much easier to work with when you're programming complex data-management features or sophisticated user-interface requirements.

If you want more information on macros, including converting macros to VBA code, turn to Chapter 22.

What's in a Name?

The name Visual Basic is a source of endless confusion for people working with Microsoft products. Microsoft has applied the name Visual Basic to a number of different products and technologies. For more than a decade, Microsoft marketed a stand-alone product named Visual Basic that was, in many ways, comparable to and competitive with Access. Visual Basic was folded into Visual Studio in its very first version. In 1995, Microsoft added the Visual Basic for Applications (VBA) programming language to Access, Word, and Excel in Microsoft Office (although it was called Access Basic until Access 2000). The name Visual Basic for Applications was chosen because the VBA syntax is identical in Access, Word, and Excel.

Although the VBA language used in Access is very similar to Visual Basic .NET, they aren't exactly the same. You can do some things with VB .NET that can't be done with Access VBA, and vice versa.

In this book, the expressions *VBA* and *Visual Basic* refer to the programming language built into Access and should not be confused with the Microsoft VB .NET product.

If you're new to programming, try not to become frustrated or overwhelmed by the seeming complexity of the VBA language. As with any new skill, you're much better off approaching VBA programming by taking it one step at a time. You need to learn exactly what VBA can do for you and your applications, along with the general syntax, statement structure, and how to compose procedures using the VBA language.

This book is chock-full of examples showing you how to use the VBA language to accomplish useful tasks. Each of the procedures you see in this book has been tested and verified to work correctly. If you find that a bit of code in this book doesn't work as expected, take the time to ensure that you've used the example code exactly as presented in this book. Very often, the most difficult problems implementing any programming technique stem from simple errors, such as misspelling or forgetting to include a comma or parentheses where required.

Note

A programming language is much like a human language. Just as humans use words, sentences, and paragraphs to communicate with one another, a computer language uses words, statements, and procedures to tell the computer what you expect it to do. The primary difference between human and computer languages is that a computer language follows a very strict format. Every word and sentence must be precisely composed because a computer doesn't understand context or nuance. Every task must be carefully defined for the computer, using the syntax supported by the programming language.

Understanding VBA Terminology

Before you plunge into our VBA coverage, here's a review of some basic VBA terminology:

- **Keyword:** A word that has special meaning in VBA. For example, in the English language, the word *now* simply indicates a point in time. In VBA, `Now` is the name of a built-in VBA function that returns the current date and time.
- **Statement:** A single VBA word or combination of words that constitutes an instruction to be performed by the VBA engine.
- **Procedure:** A collection of VBA statements that are grouped together to perform a certain task. You might, for example, write a complex procedure that extracts data from a table, combines the data in a particular way, and then displays the data on a form. Or, you might write three smaller procedures, each of which performs a single step of the overall process.

  There are two types of VBA procedures: *subs* (subroutines) and *functions:*

  - **Subroutines** perform a task or tasks and then just go away.
  - **Functions** perform a task and then return a value, such as the result of a calculation.

  The example described earlier, where the procedure extracts data from a table, is actually a subroutine. It performs a specific task; then, when it ends, the procedure just goes away.

  The example where the operation is split into three smaller procedures includes a function. In this case, the first procedure that opens the database and extracts data most likely returns the data as a recordset, and the recordset is passed to the other procedures that perform the data combination and data display.
- **Module:** Procedures live in *modules.* If statements are like sentences and procedures are like paragraphs, modules are the chapters or documents of the VBA language. A module consists of one or more procedures and other elements combined as a single entity within the application.
- **Variable:** Variables are sometimes tricky to understand. Because Access is a database development tool, it makes sense that VBA code has to have some way of managing the data involved in the application. A variable is nothing more than a name applied to represent a data value. In virtually all VBA programs, you create and use variables to hold values such as customer names, dates, and numeric values manipulated by the VBA code.

VBA is appropriately defined as a *language.* And, just as with any human language, VBA consists of a number of words, sentences, and paragraphs, all arranged in a specific fashion. Each VBA sentence is a *statement.* Statements are aggregated as *procedures,* and procedures live within *modules.* A *function* is a specific type of procedure — one that returns a value when it's run. For example, `Now()` is a built-in VBA function that returns the current date and time, down to the second. You use the `Now()` function in your application whenever you need to capture the current date and time, such as when assigning a timestamp value to a record.

Starting with VBA Code Basics

Each statement in a procedure is an instruction you want Access to perform.

There are, literally, an infinite number of different VBA programming statements that could appear in an Access application. Generally speaking, however, VBA statements are fairly easy to read and understand. Most often, you'll be able to understand the purpose of a VBA statement based on the keywords (such as `DoCmd.OpenForm`) and references to database objects in the statement.

Each VBA statement is an instruction that is processed and executed by the VBA language engine built into Access. Here's an example of a typical VBA statement that opens a form:

```
DoCmd.OpenForm "frmMyForm", acNormal
```

Notice that this statement consists of an action (`OpenForm`) and a noun (`frmMyForm`). Most VBA statements follow a similar pattern of action and a reference either to the object performing the action or to the object that's the target of the action.

`DoCmd` is a built-in Access object that performs numerous tasks for you. Think of `DoCmd` as a little robot that can perform many different jobs. The `OpenForm` that follows `DoCmd` is the task you want `DoCmd` to run, and `frmMyForm` is the name of the form to open. Finally, `acNormal` is a modifier that tells `DoCmd` that you want the form opened in its "normal" view. The implication is that there are other view modes that may be applied to opening a form; these modes include Design (`acDesign`) or Datasheet (`acFormDS`) view, and Print Preview (`acPreview`, when applied to reports).

23

NOTE

Although this and the following chapters provide only the fundamentals of VBA programming, you'll learn more than enough to be able to add advanced features to your Access applications. You'll also have a good basis for deciding whether you want to continue studying this important programming language.

Creating VBA Programs

Access has a wide variety of tools that enable you to work with tables, queries, forms, and reports without ever having to write a single line of code. At some point, you might begin building more sophisticated applications. You might want to "bulletproof" your applications by providing more intensive data-entry validation or implementing better error handling.

Some operations can't be accomplished through the user interface, even with macros. You might find yourself saying, "I wish I had a way to . . ." or "There just has to be a function that will let me. . . ." At other times, you find that you're continually putting the same formula or expression in a query or filter. You might find yourself saying, "I'm tired of typing this formula into . . ." or "Doggone it, I typed the wrong formula in this. . . ."

For situations such as these, you need the horsepower of a high-level programming language such as VBA. VBA is a modern, structured programming language offering many of the programming structures available in most programming languages. VBA is *extensible* (capable of calling Windows API routines) and can interact through ActiveX Data Objects (ADO), through Data Access Objects (DAO), and with any Access or VBA data type.

Getting started with VBA programming in Access requires an understanding of its event-driven environment.

Modules and procedures

In this section, you'll create a very simple procedure. First, we'll take you through the steps to create the procedure including creating a module, inputting the statements, and running the procedure. Then, we'll describe each of the elements of the procedure in greater detail. The procedure you'll create in this section displays the result of squaring a number.

To create the SquareIt procedure, follow these steps:

1. **Select the Create tab of the Ribbon, and click the Module button.** The Visual Basic Editor (VBE) will open with a blank *code pane,* as shown in Figure 23.1

FIGURE 23.1

Creating a module presents a blank code pane.

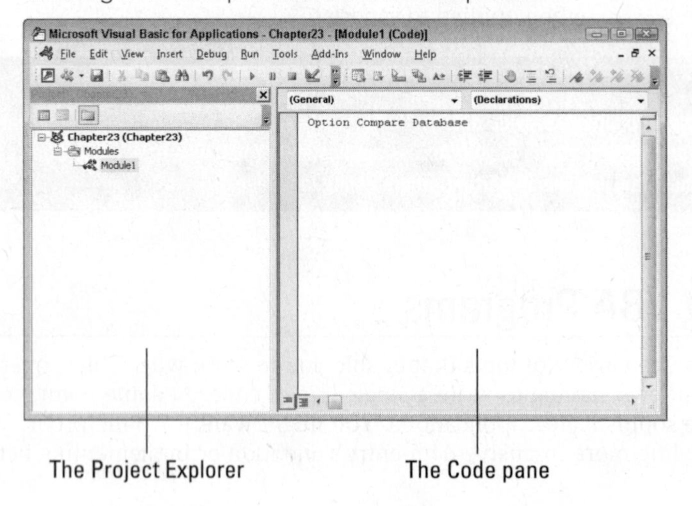

2. **In the code pane, type the following statements:**

```
Sub SquareIt()

    Dim lNumber As Long

    lNumber = 2

    MsgBox lNumber & " squared is " & lNumber ^ 2

End Sub
```

3. **Place your cursor anywhere inside the code you just typed and choose Run Sub/Userform from the Run menu.** You should see a message box similar to Figure 23.2.

FIGURE 23.2

Running the code displays a message box.

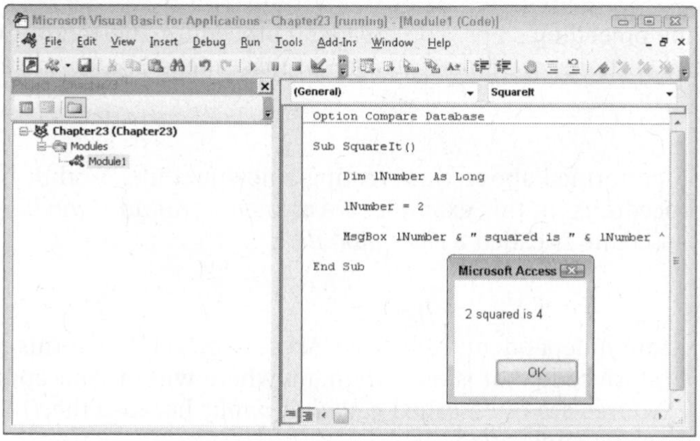

4. **Click OK to dismiss the message box and return to the VBE.**
5. **Choose File ⇨ Save and name the module when prompted (see Figure 23.3).**

FIGURE 23.3

Saving the database prompts you to save any unsaved modules.

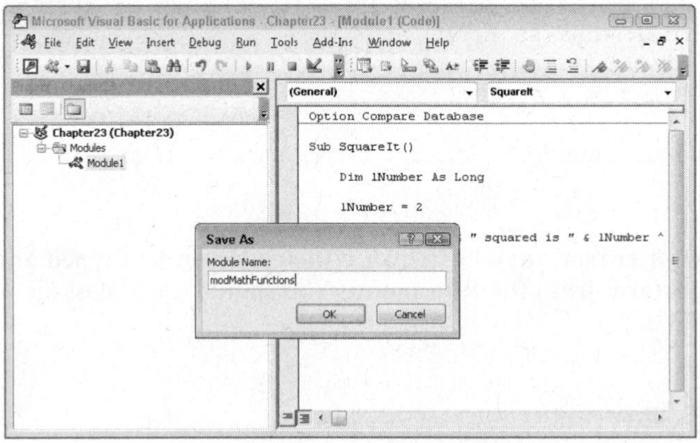

If you followed the preceding steps, you created a procedure and ran it. Congratulations! In the next several sections, we'll discuss each of these steps in more detail.

Modules

The first step you performed above was creating a new module. Modules are containers that hold your procedures. In this example, we created a *standard module*. The other type of module you can create is called a *class module*.

Standard modules

Standard modules are independent from other Access objects, like forms and reports. Standard modules store code that is used from anywhere within your application. By default, these procedures are often called *global* or *public* because they're accessible to all elements of your Access application.

Use public procedures throughout your application in expressions, macros, event procedures, and other VBA code. To use a public procedure, you simply reference it from VBA code in event procedures or any other procedure in your application.

TIP

Procedures *run;* modules *contain.* Procedures are executed and perform actions. Modules, on the other hand, are simple containers, grouping procedures and declarations together. A module can't be run; instead, you run the procedures contained *within* the module.

Standard modules are stored in the Module section of the Navigation pane. Form and report modules (see the next section) are attached to their hosts and are accessed through the Form Property Sheet or Report Property Sheet.

TIP

Generally speaking, you should group related procedures into modules, such as putting all of an application's data conversion routines into a single module. Logically grouping procedures make maintenance much easier because there is a single place in the application for all the procedures supporting a particular activity. Plus, most modules contain procedures that are related in some way.

NOTE Separating related procedures into modules can also help to speed up your application. Appendix B discusses organizing modules to optimize speed and memory use.

Class modules

The other type of module is called a *class module.* A *class* defines how an *object* behaves. You can create your own classes, called *custom classes,* but the most common class module you'll use is a class module that's bound to a form or report.

In the above example, you created a standard module using the Ribbon. For class modules that are bound to a form or report, the module is created automatically by Access whenever you add VBA code to the form or report.

The most important difference between standard modules and class modules is that class modules support events. Events respond to user actions and run VBA code that's contained within the event procedure.

NOTE The Access event module and event procedures are discussed in Chapter 25.

Module sections

You may have noticed that when you created the module, there was already code in it. Depending on the options you have set for your environment, Access will insert code into new modules automatically.

The area above the first procedure in a module is called the declaration section. The declaration section is used to store options and variables that will apply to every procedure in the module. Two common option declarations are `Option Compare Database` and `Option Explicit`. `Option Compare Database` determines how two strings are compared to each other and directs VBA to use the same comparison method that the database uses. The other options for comparing strings are `Option Compare Text` and `Option Compare Binary`. Basically, `Option Compare Text` doesn't care whether the letters are uppercase or lowercase and `Option Compare Binary` does care. It's a little more complicated than that, but `Option Compare Database` is usually the best option.

`Option Explicit` directs VBA to warn you if you have undeclared variables. By setting this option, you're telling VBA that you intend to explicitly declare any variables that you'll use. You'll learn more about declaring variables later.

Everything below the declarations section is known as the procedure section or code section. This section contains the subprocedures and function of the module. It's important to understand the differences between these two sections because you can't put statements that belong in the declaration section into the code section, nor can you put code in the declaration section. If you do, the VBE will let you know that it's not allowed.

Procedures and functions

The next step you completed after creating a module to hold your procedure was to create the procedure itself. It's a very simple procedure that does some simple math and displays the result. Each statement is structured according to the language's *syntax,* meaning that the spelling of keywords and the order of the words in the statement is important.

Subprocedures

A subprocedure (or *sub*) is the simplest type of procedure in a VBA project. A subprocedure is nothing more than a container for VBA statements that typically perform a task such as opening a form or report or running a query.

Subprocedures have two required statements: `Sub procname` and `End Sub`. If those were the only two statements you had, it would be a pretty uninteresting sub, but it would be legal. In our example, the procedure is started with the `Sub SquareIt()` statement. The procedure ends with the `End Sub` statement.

When determining the name of your procedure, there are a few rules that you must follow. The most important rules to remember are that the name must begin with a letter, can't contain most punctuation, and can't be more than 255 characters long. Rules aside, you should pick names for your procedures that describe what they do in a way that will be obvious to you when you read them later. Procedure names like `GetData()` will likely be hard to understand later, but `ReadDataFromEmployeeTable()` will be crystal clear. You probably don't want to push the 255-character limit on procedure names, but don't be afraid to make long, descriptive names.

Variable declaration

The first statement in our simple subprocedure is a *variable declaration statement.* It starts with the `Dim` keyword, which is short for dimension. The variable's name, `lNumber`, comes next. Variable names follow the same rules as procedure names, described in the previous section. The `As` keyword follows the name, which is followed by the data type. In this case, `lNumber` was declared as a Long Integer data type.

Variables and data types are discussed extensively in Chapter 24.

Variables hold data that you can use later in your procedure. When you declare a variable with the `Dim` keyword, you're telling VBA to reserve a spot in the computer's memory to store that data. The amount of memory that VBA will reserve depends on the data type. In this example, you told VBA to hold enough memory to store a Long Integer, or 32 bits of memory.

The `As datatype` portion of the variable declaration statement is optional. You could declare `lNumber` with the statement:

```
Dim lNumber
```

When you omit the data type, VBA will determine an appropriate data type when you assign a value to the variable. That may seem like a handy service VBA is providing, but it's not a very good practice. VBA will assign a data type to the variable based on the first time you use it, but it doesn't know all the plans you have in mind for that variable. It may end up assigning a data type that's too small for what you need. Having VBA assign data types is also slower than if you assign them as you write the code.

TIP

If you're new to VBA, don't get too hung up on which data type to use for your variables. Use `String` for text, `Long` for numbers without decimals, `Double` for numbers with decimals, and `Boolean` for true/false values. You can get a lot done with just those four data types. As your VBA skills improve, you'll have plenty of opportunities to learn about the other data types.

Variable assignment

By declaring a variable with the `Dim` statement, you've reserved a place in memory where you can store data for later use. The next line in the procedure stores the number `2` in the variable `lNumber`. Here's what that line looks like in the procedure:

```
lNumber = 2
```


Assigning values to variables is easy. There are really only two things you need to remember:

- **You must assign a value that is appropriate for the variable's data type.** In this case, you're storing a number without a decimal in a variable declared as `Long`. If you tried to store data that isn't appropriate for the variable's data type, VBA would do its best to convert the value into the appropriate data type. If you tried to store the value `8.26`, for example, in a `Long` variable, VBA would convert it to `8` by truncating the number to remove the decimals. If VBA were unable to convert the data, you'd get an error.
- **The variable name goes on the left of the equal sign, and the value goes on the right.** Everything on the right of the equal sign is evaluated before it's assigned to the variable. For this example, there's not much to evaluate because it's simply the number `2`. Consider the following statement, which computes the product of two numbers and assigns it to a variable.

  ```
  dProduct = 3 * 6.1
  ```

  In that statement, `3` is multiplied by `6.1` and the result, `18.3`, is assigned to the variable. That's still pretty straightforward, but consider yet another example.

  ```
  bIsEqual = dProduct = 18.3
  ```

In this statement, bIsEqual is a variable declared as Boolean, and dProduct is a variable declared as Double. But there are two equal signs. The first equal sign is the assignment operator — setting a variable equal to a value. Any other equal signs (there's only one other, in this case) are comparison operators. Comparison operators return True or False. If dProduct were equal to 18.3, then bIsEqual would get the value True. Everything to the right of the first equal sign (the assignment operator) is evaluated first, and the result is assigned to the variable.

Functions

A function is very similar to a subprocedure with one major exception: A function returns a value when it ends. A simple example is the built-in VBA Now() function, which returns the current date and time. Now() can be used virtually anywhere your application needs to use or display the current date and time. An example is including Now() in a report header or footer so that the user knows exactly when the report was printed.

Now() is just one of several hundred built-in VBA functions. As you'll see throughout this book, the built-in VBA functions provide useful and very powerful features to your Access applications.

In addition to built-in functions, you might add custom functions that perform tasks required by your applications. An example is a data transformation routine that performs a mathematical operation (such as currency conversion or calculating shipping costs) on an input value. It doesn't matter where the input value comes from (table, form, query, and so on). The function always returns exactly the correct calculated value, no matter where the function is used.

Within the body of a function, you specify the function's return value by assigning a value to the function's name (and, yes, it does look pretty strange to include the function's name within the function's body). You then can use the returned value as part of a larger expression. The following function calculates the square footage of a room:

```
Function SquareFeet(dHeight As Double, _
   dWidth As Double) As Double

  'Assign this function's value:
  SquareFeet = dHeight * dWidth

End Function
```

This function receives two parameters: dHeight and dWidth. Notice that the function's name, SquareFeet, is assigned a value within the body of the function. The function is declared as a Double data type, so the return value is recognized by the VBA interpreter as a Double.

The main thing to keep in mind about functions is that they return values. The returned value is often assigned to a variable or control on a form or report:

```
dAnswer = SquareFeet(dHeight, dWidth)
Me!txtAnswer = SquareFeet(dHeight, dWidth)
```

If the function (or subroutine, for that matter) requires information (such as the `Height` and `Width` in the case of the `SquareFeet` function), the information is passed as arguments within the parentheses in the function's declaration.

Arguments (also called parameters) are discussed in more detail in Chapter 24.

Working in the code window

Unlike designing a table or dropping controls in the sections of a report, a module's code pane is a very unstructured place to work. VBA code is simply text, and there aren't a lot of visual cues to tell you how to write the code or where to put particular pieces of the code. In this section, we'll describe some features of the code window and some techniques to keep your code organized and readable.

White space

In the code already presented in this chapter, you may have noticed some indentation and some blank lines. In the programming world, this is known as white space. White space consists of spaces, tabs, and blank lines. With very few exceptions, VBA ignores white space. The following two procedures are identical as far as the VBA compiler is concerned.

```
Function BMI(dPounds As Double, lHeight As Long) As Double

    BMI = dPounds / (lHeight ^ 2) * 703

End Function

Function BMI(dPounds As Double, lHeight As Long) As Double
BMI = dPounds / (lHeight ^ 2) * 703
End Function
```

In the first function, a blank line was inserted after the `Function` statement, and another blank line was inserted before the `End Function` statement. Also, a tab was inserted before the single statement within the procedure. All the whitespace elements were removed in the second function. Despite the difference in appearance, the VBA compiler reads the two functions identically, and the two functions return the same result.

In some programming languages, white space is important and meaningful. As we've seen, that isn't the case for VBA. The purpose of white space is to make your code more readable. Different programmers format their code with white space in different ways. Whatever formatting conventions you choose to use, the most important thing is to be consistent. Consistency in formatting will help you read and understand your code more easily, even if you're reading months or years later.

Line continuation

The VBE window can expand to be as wide as your screen. Sometimes your statements are so long that they extend beyond the window even when it's as wide as it can be. VBA provides a way to continue the current line onto the next line. When used with long statements, this can help make your code more readable. The line continuation characters are a space followed by an underscore. When the VBA compiler sees a space and an underscore at the end of the line, it knows that the next line is a continuation of the current one. Figure 23.4 shows a simple procedure with one very long statement. The statement extends beyond the code pane window, and you must scroll to read it.

FIGURE 23.4

A long statement extends beyond the code window.

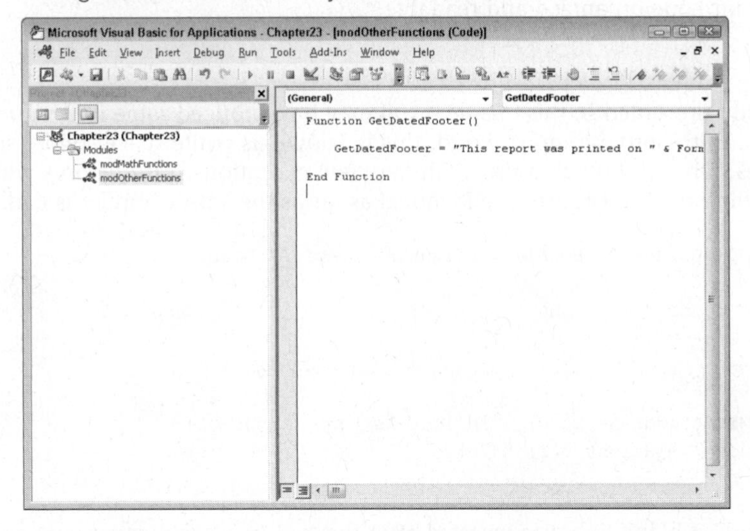

Use the line continuation characters to break the long statement into multiple lines. This will allow you to see the whole statement. The statement in Figure 23.4 could be rewritten as the statement below:

```
Function GetDatedFooter() As String

    GetDatedFooter = "This report was printed on " _
        & Format(Now, "dd-mmm-yyyy") & _
        " and changes made to the data after that " & _
        "date won't be reflected."

End Function
```

The underscore is typically referred to as the line continuation character, but the space that comes before it is equally important. You need both characters, space and underscore, to continue a line. The line continuation character can't be used in the middle of a string. Notice in the above example that the long string is broken up into four smaller strings and concatenated together with ampersands. To spread a long string over multiple lines, it must be broken up so that the line continuation character can be used.

Multi-statement lines

Another way to improve the readability of your code is by putting two or more statements on one line. VBA uses the colon to separate statements on the same line. If you have a lot of short statements that are taking up a lot of vertical space in the code pane, you can put a few of them on the same line to clean up the code. In the following example, many similar statements are grouped together.

```
i = 12: j = 45: k = 32
l = 87: m = 77: n = 2
o = 89: p = 64: q = 52
```

Those nine statements are assigning numbers to nine different variables. If they were written out one after the other, they would eat up a lot of the code window. By putting three statements on each line, less space is wasted. This technique is useful when you have small statements that are all doing roughly the same operation. If your statements are long or diverse, it actually hinders the readability of the code and should be avoided.

IntelliSense

Suppose that you know you want to use a specific command, but you can't remember the exact syntax. Access features four types of IntelliSense to help you create each line of code:

- **Complete Word:** Any time you're typing a keyword, you can press Ctrl + Space to get a list of keywords. The list automatically scrolls to the keyword that matches what you've already typed. If there is only one match, you don't see the list and the word is simply completed for you. Figure 23.5 shows what happens when you type "do" and press Ctrl + Space.

FIGURE 23.5

Complete Word shows a list of keywords.

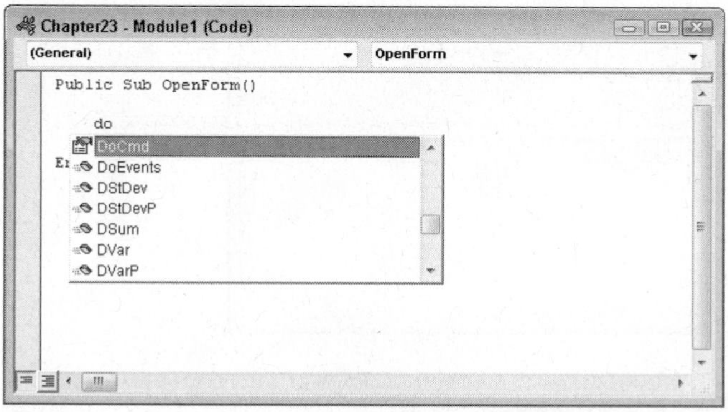

If you were to type "doc" instead of just "do," the keyword `DoCmd` would be completed rather than a list because there is only one keyword that starts with `doc`.

- **Auto List Members:** Auto List Members is a drop-down list that is automatically displayed when you type the beginning of a keyword that has associated objects, properties, or methods. For example, if you enter `DoCmd.Open`, a list of the possible options displays, as shown in Figure 23.6. Scroll through the list box and press Enter to select the option you want.

FIGURE 23.6

Access Auto List Members help in a module.

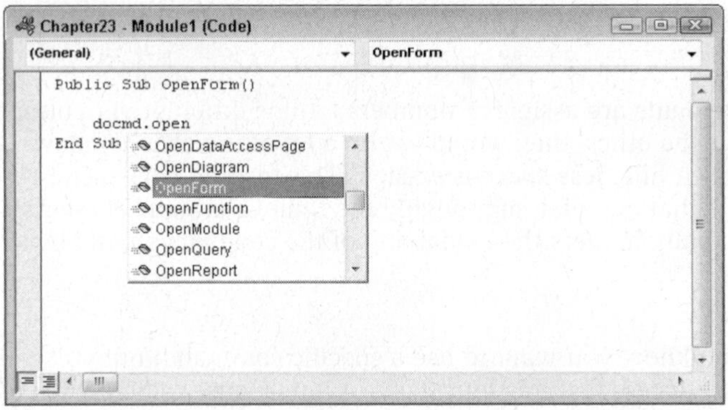

In this example, the `OpenForm` method is selected (actions associated with an object are called *methods*). After choosing an item in the list, more Auto List Members help is displayed. Or, if parameters are associated with the keyword, the other type of module help, Auto Quick Info (see the next bullet), is displayed, as shown in Figure 23.7.

FIGURE 23.7

Access Auto Quick Info help in a module.

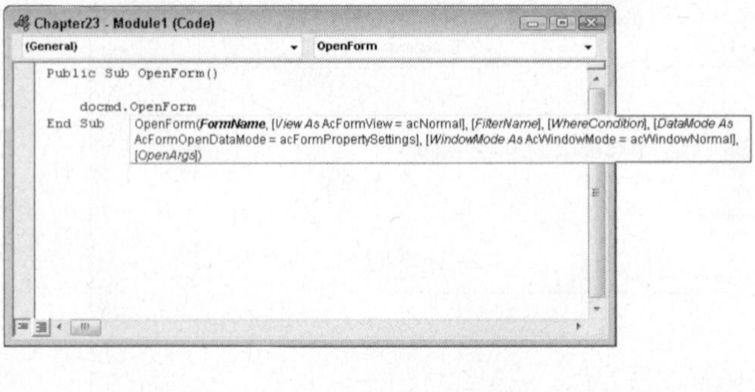

- **Auto Quick Info:** Auto Quick Info guides you through all the options (called *parameters*) for the specific item. The bold word (`FormName`) is the next parameter available for the `DoCmd` object. Figure 23.7 shows that there are many parameters available for the `OpenForm` command. The parameters are separated by commas. As each parameter is entered, the next parameter is highlighted in bold. The position of parameters is significant; they can't be rearranged without causing problems. Press the Esc key to hide Auto List Members help.

  Not every parameter is required for every VBA command. Parameters surrounded by square brackets (such as `View` in Figure 23.7) are optional. Access provides reasonable defaults for all optional arguments that are omitted from the statement using the command.

- **Auto Constants:** Auto Constants is a drop-down list that displays when you're on a parameter that requires a built-in constant. In Figure 23.7, the Auto Quick Info shows that the second parameter is `View` and is described as `[View As acFormView = acNormal]`. The brackets around the parameter indicate that it's an optional parameter. `acFormView` is a family of built-in constants that you can use for this parameter. The default constant, `acNormal`, is used if you omit this parameter. Figure 23.8 shows the list of `acFormView` constants available. Simply select the one you want and type a comma. The constant and the comma are inserted into the statement and you're ready for the next parameter.

23

FIGURE 23.8

Access Auto Constants help in a module.

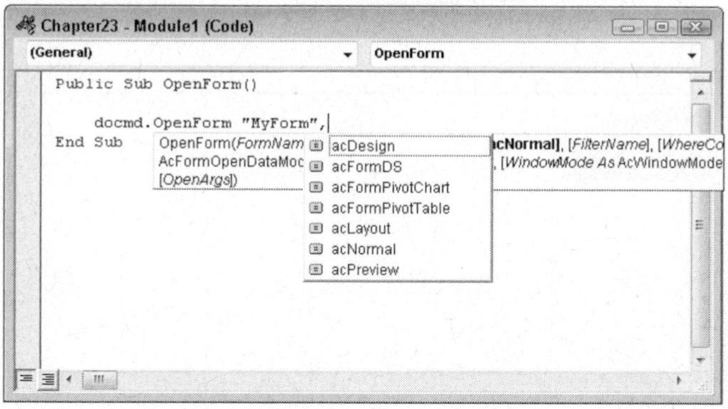

TIP

You can split the code window into two independent edit panes by dragging down the splitter bar (the little horizontal bar at the very top of the vertical scroll bar at the right edge of the code window). Splitting the window enables simultaneous editing of two sections of code. Each section of a split VBA code window scrolls independently, and changes you make in one pane of a split window show up in the other pane. Double-click the splitter bar to return the window to its former state, or grab the splitter bar with the mouse and drag it to the top of the code editor window to close the second edit pane. (Word and Excel feature a similar splitter button, making it very easy to edit different parts of the same Word document or Excel worksheet.)

Compiling procedures

After code has been written, you should compile it to complete the development process.

The compilation step converts the English-like VBA syntax to a binary format that is easily executed at runtime. Also, during compilation, all your code is checked for incorrect syntax and other errors that will cause problems when the user works with the application.

If you don't compile your Access applications during the development cycle, Access compiles the code whenever a user opens the application and begins using it. In this case, errors in your code might prevent the user from using the application, causing a great deal of inconvenience to everyone involved.

Compile your applications by choosing Debug⇨Compile from the code window. An error window appears if the compilation is not successful. Figure 23.9 shows the result of an unsuccessful compile due to a misspelling of a variable name.

FIGURE 23.9

The compiler reports errors.

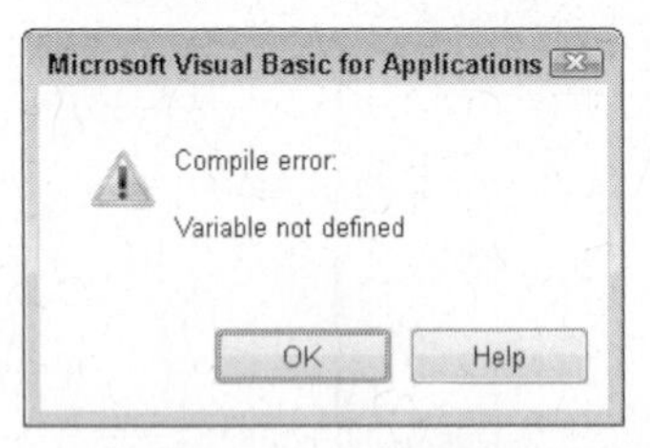

NOTE

Access compiles all procedures in the module, and all modules in the Access database, not just the current procedure and module.

Saving a module

Modules differ from other Access objects in that there isn't an explicit way to save a module. New modules that are created don't display in the Navigation pane until they're saved, and the modules that are displayed there open in the VBE when double-clicked.

Modules are saved by saving the database and responding to the prompts that Access displays. In the VBE, choose File ⇨ Save to save the database. You'll be prompted to save all unsaved modules and other unsaved objects. You aren't prompted to save modules that have already been saved, even if they've been changed. Those modules are simply saved with the name you provided previously.

Class modules that are attached to a form or report are saved when the form or report is saved.

Understanding VBA Branching Constructs

The real power of any programming language is its capability to make a decision based on a condition that might be different each time the user works with the application. VBA provides two ways for a procedure to execute code conditionally: branching and looping.

Branching

Often, a program performs different tasks based on some value. If the condition is true, the code performs one action. If the condition is false, the code performs a different action. An application's capability to look at a value and, based on that value, decide which code to run is known as *branching* (or conditional processing).

The procedure is similar to walking down a road and coming to a fork in the road; you can go to the left or to the right. If a sign at the fork points left for home and right for work, you can decide which way to go. If you need to go to work, you go to the right; if you need to go home, you go to the left. In the same way, a program looks at the value of some variable and decides which set of code should be processed.

VBA offers two sets of conditional processing statements:

- `If...Then...Else...End If`
- `Select Case...End Select`

The If keyword

The `If` keyword and its many forms check a condition and, based on the evaluation, perform an action. The condition must evaluate to a Boolean value (true or false). If the condition is true, the program moves to the line following the `If` statement. If the condition is false, the program skips to the statement following the `Else` statement, if present, or the `End If` statement if there is no `Else` clause.

The If...Then construct

An `If` statement can take a few different forms. The first form is the `If...Then` construct. It is a one line statement where the condition and the action are all in the same statement. In the following example, the `sState` variable is set if the `sCity` variable contains certain data.

```
If sCity = "Dallas" Then sState = "Texas"
```

VBA first evaluates `sCity = "Dallas"` and determines if the conditional is true or false. If it's true (that is, if `sCity` has been assigned the value `Dallas`), the portion of the statement after the `Then` keyword is executed. In this case, the `sState` variable is assigned the value `Texas`. If the conditional is false, the program moves on to the next line in the procedure and the `sState` variable doesn't change.

The If...End If construct

The next form is the `If...End If` construct. This construct, and the ones that follow, are commonly known as *If blocks* because they can contain more than one line of code (a block of code), unlike the `If...Then` construct that can only execute one line. The previous example can be rewritten as an `If...End If`.

```
If sCity = "Dallas" Then
   sState = "Texas"
End If
```

This example is exactly the same as the one before it. If the conditional statement is true, the single line in the `If` block is executed. The difference is when the conditional is false. In that case, the program braches to the line immediately following the `End If` statement and program execution continues.

The benefit of the `If...End If` construct is that you can execute multiple statements when a conditional is true. In the next example, two variables are assigned values when the conditional is true.

```
If sCity = "Dallas" Then
  sState = "Texas"
  dTaxRate = 0.075
End If
```

If the conditional is true, both statements are executed. Otherwise, the program branches to the line just below `End If` and continues executing.

The If...Else...End If construct

In the previous examples, one or more statements are executed when the conditional is true and nothing happens when the conditional is false. The `Else` keyword can be included in an `If` block to identify statements that should run when the conditional is false.

```
If sCity = "Dallas" Then
    sState = "Texas"
    dTaxRate = 0.075
Else
    sState = "Michigan"
    dTaxRate = 0.05
End If
```

When the conditional is true, the first two statements are executed (setting `sState` to `Texas` and `dTaxRate` to `0.075`). Then the program braches to the line below `End If` and continues executing. The two statements between `Else` and `End If` aren't executed.

If the conditional is false, however, the program braches to the statement below the `Else` statement and skips the first two. It's very common to see a construct like this that executes certain lines of code when a condition is met and certain other lines when it's not.

You must use an `If` block to use an `Else` statement. `Else` statements do not work with the first construct (the `If...Then` construct).

The If...ElseIf...End If construct

The final `If` construct is yet another `If` block type of construct. Instead of only one conditional, there are multiple conditionals. The `ElseIf` statement defines as many other conditionals as you need.


```
If sCity = "Dallas" Then
    sState = "Texas"
    dTaxRate = 0.075
ElseIf sCity = "Detroit" Then
    sState = "Michigan"
    dTaxRate = 0.05
Else
    sState = "Oregon"
    dTaxRate = 0.0625
End If
```

The program flows through an `If...ElseIf...EndIf` construct much like it does through the others. If the first conditional is true, the statements in the first section are executed and the program branches to the line just below the `End If`. If the first conditional is false, the program branches to the second conditional (the first `ElseIf`) and tests that conditional. If none of the conditionals is true, the statements in the `Else` section are executed. The `Else` statement is optional when using `ElseIf`. If you omit the `Else` statement and none of the conditionals is true, no statements in the `If` block are executed.

Nested If statements

Nesting statements refers to putting statements inside a block of other statements. In the case of `If`, nesting means that one `If` block is inside another `If` block.

```
If sState = "Michigan" Then
    If sCity = "Detrioit" Then
        dTaxRate = 0.05
    ElseIf sCity = "Kalamazoo" Then
        dTaxRate = 0.045
    Else
        dTaxRate = 0
    End If
End If
```

The outer `If` block tests the `sState` variable. If that condition is true, the inner `If` block is executed and the `sCity` variable is tested. If the conditional in the outer `If` block is false, the program branches to the line below the `End If` statement that matches up the `If` statement being evaluated. Proper indenting, though not required, is helpful to see which `Else` and `End If` statements go with which `If` statements.

Boolean values and conditionals

`If` statements are wonderful, and you'll see them in almost every piece of code you write. But there are two situations in which they're misused. Consider this code fragment:

```
If bIsBuyer = True Then
    bIsInPurchasing = True
Else
    bIsInPurchasing = False
End If
```

This is a simple `If...Else...End If` construct where the conditional checks to see if the Boolean variable `bIsBuyer` is true. Based on the result of that conditional, another Boolean variable is set to true or false. There's nothing wrong with the code — it will compile and run just fine — but there is a way to simplify the code and make it more readable. First, comparing a Boolean variable to true or false is unnecessary because the variable already is true or false. The first line can be simplified to

```
If bIsBuyer Then
```

Assuming `bIsBuyer` is `True`, then in the first example, the compiler evaluates `bIsBuyer = True`, which reduces to `True = True`, and of course that returns `True`. In the simpler example, `bIsBuyer` is evaluated and returns `True`. Because `bIsBuyer` is a Boolean variable, comparing it to a Boolean value is redundant.

The second simplification step is to remove the `If` statement altogether. Whenever your setting a Boolean value in an `If` block, you should consider whether the Boolean value can be set directly.

```
bIsInPurchasing = bIsBuyer
```

This one line of code does the same things as the five lines we started with. If `bIsBuyer` is true, `bIsInPurchasing` will also be true. If `bIsBuyer` is false, `bIsInPurchasing` will also be false. There may be situations in which you need to set one variable to the opposite of the other. VBA provides the `Not` keyword to convert Booleans from true to false and vice versa.

```
bIsInPurchasing = Not bIsTruckDriver
```

The variable `bIsTruckDriver` is evaluated as either true or false and the `Not` keyword returns the opposite. If `bIsTruckDriver` is true, `bIsInPurchasing` will be assigned the value `False`.

When you have many conditions to test, the `If...Then...ElseIf...Else` conditions can get rather unwieldy. A better approach is to use the `Select Case...End Select` construct.

The Select Case...End Select statement

VBA offers the `Select Case` statement to check for multiple conditions. Following is the general syntax of the `Select Case` statement:

```
Select Case Expression

    Case Value1
        [Action to take when Expression = Value1]

    Case Value2
        [Action to take when Expression = Value2]

    Case ...

    Case Else
       [Default action when no value matches Expression]

End Select
```

Notice that the syntax is similar to that of the `If...Then` statement. Instead of a Boolean condition, the `Select Case` statement uses an expression at the very top. Then, each `Case` clause tests its value against the expression's value. When a `Case` value matches the expression, the program executes the block of code until it reaches another `Case` statement or the `End Select` statement. VBA executes the code for only one matching `Case` statement.

NOTE

If more than one `Case` statement matches the value of the test expression, only the code for the first match executes. If other matching `Case` statements appear after the first match, VBA ignores them.

Figure 23.10 shows `Select...Case` used by frmDialogContactPrint to decide which of several reports to open.

FIGURE 23.10

Using the `Select Case` statement.

```
Select Case Me![grpTypeOfPrint]
    Case 1
        DoCmd.OpenReport "rptContacts", lReportDest, , _
            "[ContactID]=[Forms]![frmContacts]![txtContactID]"

    Case 2
        DoCmd.OpenReport "rptContacts", lReportDest

    Case 3
        DoCmd.OpenReport "rptContactListing", lReportDest

End Select
```

The code in Figure 23.10 shows the expression in the `Select Case` is `Me![grpTypeOfPrint]`. This expression represents a group of option buttons on the form. When evaluated, it returns a 1, 2 or 3 depending on which option button is selected. The value in each `Case` statement is then compared to the expression's value and, if there is a match, any statements between the matching `Case` statement and the next `Case` statement (or the `End Select` statement) are executed.

Using the `Case Else` statement is optional, but it's always a good idea. The `Case Else` clause is always the last `Case` statement of `Select Case` and is executed when none of the `Case` values matches the expression at the top of the `Select Case` statement.

The `Case` statement can be inequality comparisons by incorporating the `Is` keyword.

```
Select Case dTaxRate
    Case Is < 0.03
        MsgBox "Low taxes"
    Case Is > 0.07
        MsgBox "High taxes"
    Case Else
        MsgBox "Average taxes"
End Select
```

By including the `Is` keyword, you can make a comparison in the `Case` statement. In this example, the `dTaxRate` variable is evaluated in the `Select Case` statement. In the first `Case` statement, the value is compared to `0.03` and if it's lower, the code under that `Case` statement is executed. If `dTaxRate` is in between `0.03` and `0.07`, the `Case Else` statement will be executed because neither of the first two `Case` statements would be true.

The `Case` statement also accepts multiple values. You can separate multiple values in the same `Case` statement with a comma. You can also specify a range of values using the `To` keyword. The following example shows both of these techniques.

```
Select Case dSalesAmt
  Case 0.99, 1.99
    dCommissionPct = 0.1
  Case 2 To 4.99
    dCommissionPct = 0.15
  Case Is >= 5
    dCommissionPct = 0.17
End Select
```

In some procedures, you might want to execute a group of statements more than one time. VBA provides some constructs for repeating a group of statements.

Looping

Another very powerful process that VBA offers is *looping*, the capability to execute a single statement or a group of statements over and over. The statement or group of statements is repeated until some condition is met.

VBA offers two types of looping constructs:

- `Do...Loop`
- `For...Next`

`Do...Loop` constructs are used when you need to repeat a statement or group of statements and you don't know how many times you need to repeat them. `For...Next` constructs are used when you already know how many times to repeat the statements.

Loops are commonly used to process records within a recordset, change the appearance of controls on forms, and a number of other tasks that require repeating the same VBA statements multiple times.

The Do...Loop statement

`Do...Loop` is used to repeat a group of statements *while* a condition is true or *until* a condition is true. This statement is one of the most commonly used VBA looping constructs:

```
Do [While | Until Condition]
    [VBA statements]
    [Exit Do]
    [VBA statements]
Loop
```

Alternatively, the `While` (or `Until`) may appear at the bottom of the construct:

```
Do
    [VBA statements]
    [Exit Do]
    [VBA statements]
Loop [While | Until Condition]
```

Notice that `Do...Loop` has several options. The `While` clause causes the VBA statements within the `Do...Loop` to execute as long as the condition is true. Execution drops out of the `Do...Loop` as soon as the condition evaluates to false.

The `Until` clause works in just the opposite way. The code within the `Do...Loop` executes only as long as the condition is false.

Placing the `While` or `Until` clause at the top of the `Do...Loop` means that the loop never executes if the condition is not met. Placing the `While` or `Until` at the bottom of the loop means that the loop executes at least once because the condition is not evaluated until after the statements within the loop has executed the first time.

`Exit Do` immediately terminates the `Do...Loop`. Use `Exit Do` as part of a test within the loop:

```
Do While Condition1
   [VBA statements]
   If Condition2 Then Exit Do
   [VBA statements]
Loop
```

`Exit Do` is often used to prevent endless loops. An endless loop occurs when the condition's state (true or false) never changes within the loop.

In case you're wondering, *Condition1* and *Condition2* in this example may be the same. There is no requirement that the second condition be different from the condition used at the top of the `Do...Loop`.

Figure 23.11 illustrates how a `Do` loop may be used. In this particular example, a recordset has been opened and each record is processed within the `Do` loop. In this example, the company's name is printed in the Immediate window, but the data is not modified or used in any way.

FIGURE 23.11

Using the `Do...Loop` statement.

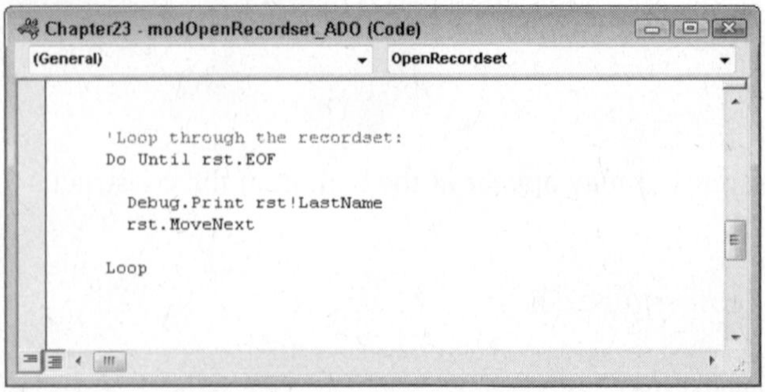

The `While` and `Until` clauses provide powerful flexibility for processing a `Do...Loop` in your code.

The For...Next statement

Use `For...Next` to repeat a statement block a set number of times. The general format of `For...Next` is

```
For CounterVariable = Start To End
    [VBA Statements]
    [Exit For]
    [VBA Statements]
Next CounterVariable
```

The following procedure uses the built-in `Beep` function to emit a sound a set number of times. The `For...Next` loop determines the number of beeps.

```
Sub BeepWarning()

    Dim lBeep As Long
    Dim lBeepCount As Long

    lBeepCount = 5

    For lBeep = 1 To lBeepCount
        Beep
    Next lBeep

End Sub
```

In this procedure, `lBeep` is the counter variable, `1` is the start, and `lBeepCount` is the end. When the program reaches the `For` line, `lBeep` is set to `1`. As long as `lBeep` is less than or equal to `lBeepCount`, the statements inside the `For...Next` block are executed. When the `Next` line is reached, `lBeep` is increased by one and again compared to `lBeepCount`. If `lBeep` is still less than or equal to `lBeepCount`, the loop is executed again. When `lBeep` becomes greater than `lBeepCount`, the loop is complete and the remaining code in the procedure is executed.

`For Each...Next` is a special implementation of `For...Next` for looping through collections. `For Each...Next` is discussed in the "Working with Objects and Collections" section, later in this chapter.

An alternate form of `For...Next` is

```
For CounterVariable = Start To End Step StepValue
    [Statement block]
Next CounterVariable
```

The only difference here is that the `StepValue` is added to the first statement. The `Step` keyword followed by an increment causes the counter variable to be incremented by the step value each time the loop executes. For example, if *Start* is `10` and *End* is `100` and *StepValue* is `10`, the counter variable starts at 10 and increments by 10 each time the loop executes. As you saw in the previous example, when `Step` is omitted, the default is to increment *CounterVariable* by 1.

Most of the time, a `For...Next` loop counts upward, starting at an initial value and incrementing the counter variable by the amount specified by the step value. In some cases, however, you might need a loop that starts at a high start value and steps downward to an end value. In this case, use a negative number as the step value. The `Step` keyword is required when looping backward. If you omit it, the `For` statement will see that *CounterVariable* is greater than `End` and the loop won't be executed.

Up until this point, you've been working with simple variables such as Booleans, Longs, and Strings. The following section explains the special syntax to use when working with objects instead of simple variables.

Working with Objects and Collections

Very often, you have to work with objects such as the controls on a form or a recordset object containing data extracted from the database. VBA provides several constructs specifically designed to work with objects and collections of objects.

An object primer

Although Access is not object oriented, it's often referred to as *object based*. Many of the things you work with in Access are objects and not just simple numbers and character strings. Generally speaking, an *object* is a complex entity that performs some kind of job within an Access application. Access uses *collections* to aggregate similar objects as a single group.

For example, when you build an Access form, you're actually creating a `Form` object. As you add controls to the form, you're adding them to the form's `Controls` collection. Even though you might add different types of controls (such as buttons and text boxes) to the form, the form's `Controls` collection contains all the controls you've added to the form.

You'll see many, many examples of working with individual objects and collections of objects in this book. Understanding how objects differ from simple variables is an important step to becoming a proficient Access developer.

Each type of Access object includes its own properties and methods, and shares many other properties (such as `Name`) and methods with many other Access objects.

Collections are usually named by taking the name of the objects they contain and making it plural. The `Forms` collection contains the `Form` object. The `Reports` collection contains the `Report` object. There are exceptions, however, such as the `Controls` collection. While the `Controls` collection does contain `Control` objects, each `Control` object is also another type of object. A `Control` object can be a `Textbox` object, a `Combobox` object, or any one of several more specific object types. Collections have just a few properties. These are the two most important properties associated with Access collections:

- `Count`: The number of items contained with the collection. A collection with a `Count` of `0` is empty. Collections can contain virtually any number of items, but performance degrades when the `Count` becomes very large (in excess of 50,000 objects).
- `Item`: Once you have objects stored in a collection, you need a way to reference individual objects in the collection. The `Item` property points to a single item within a collection.

The following example demonstrates setting a property on just one item in a collection:

```
MyCollection.Item(9).SomeProperty = Value
```

or:

```
MyCollection.Item("ItemName").SomeProperty = Value
```

where *MyCollection* is the name assigned to the collection, *SomeProperty* is the name of a property associated with the item, and *Value* is the value assigned to the property.

NOTE

The Forms and Reports collections are a little unusual in that they only contain Form and Report objects that are currently open. By contrast, the `TableDefs` collection contains all the tables in the database regardless of whether they are open.

This small example demonstrates a few important concepts regarding collections:

- **There are different ways to reference the items stored in a collection.** In most cases, each item stored in a collection (such as a form's `Controls` collection) has a name and can be referenced using its name:

  ```
  MyForm.Controls("txtLastName").FontBold = True
  ```

  As a consequence, each object's name within a collection must be unique. You can't, for example, have two controls with the same name on an Access form.

  The alternate way to reference an object in a collection is with a number that indicates the item's ordinal position within the collection. The first item added to a collection is item 0 (zero), the second is item 1, and so on.
- **Collections have default properties.** You may have noticed that the last code fragment didn't use the `Item` property to get at the `txtLastName` control. The

`Item` property is the default property for most collections and is often omitted. The following two lines of code are the same.

```
MyForm.Controls.Item(1).Text = "Name"
MyForm.Controls(1).Text = "Name"
```

- **A collection might contain many thousands of objects.** Although performance suffers when a collection contains tens of thousands of objects, a collection is a handy way to store an arbitrary number of items as an application runs. You'll see several examples of using collections as storage devices in this book.

> **NOTE**
> The period that exists between an object and its properties or methods is commonly known as the *dot operator*. The dot operator gives you access to an object's properties and methods.

Properties and methods

Objects have properties and methods. They also have events, and we'll discuss events thoroughly in Chapter 25.

Properties

Properties let you read and change simple values that are the characteristics of the object. The `Label` object has a `Caption` property. The `Caption` property is the string that is displayed in the label. The `Label` object also has `Height` and `Width` properties that hold numbers determining the object's size. These are examples of properties that hold simple values.

Properties can also return other objects. As you've seen, the `Form` object has a `Controls` property. But isn't `Controls` a collection object? Yes, it is. And for each collection object, there is a property that returns it. When you write `MyForm.Controls.Count`, you're using the `Controls` property of `MyForm` to get access to the `Controls` collection object. Fortunately, the Access object model is so well designed that you don't have to worry about what is a simple property and what is a property returning an object. When you see two dot operators in a single statement, you can be sure you're accessing another object. Typing a dot operator after a simple value property won't give you any options.

Methods

You can also access an object's methods through the dot operator. Methods differ from properties because they don't return a value. Methods can generally be put into two categories: Methods that change more than one property at once and methods that perform an action external to the object.

The first type of method changes two or more properties at once. The `Commandbutton` object has a method called `SizeToFit`. The `SizeToFit` property changes the `Height` property, the `Width` property, or both so that all the text in the `Caption` property can be displayed.

The second type of method performs some action outside its parent object. It usually changes a few properties on the way. The Form object has an Undo method. The Undo method has to go outside of the form and read the undo stack from Access to determine what the last action was. When this method is called after a text box is changed, the text box's Text property is changed back to its previous value.

The With statement

The With statement enables you to access an object's properties and methods without typing the object's name over and over. Any properties or methods used between With and End With automatically refer to the object specified in the With statement. Any number of statements can appear between the With and End With statements, and With statements can be nested. Properties and methods will refer to the object in the innermost With block that contains them.

As an example, consider the code using the following For...Next looping construct. This code loops through all members of a form's Controls collection, examining each control. If the control is a command button, the button's font is set to 10 point, Bold, Times New Roman:

```
Private Sub cmdOld_Click()
  Dim i As Integer
  Dim MyControl As Control

  For i = 0 To Me.Controls.Count - 1
    Set MyControl = Me.Controls(i) 'Grab a control
    If TypeOf MyControl Is CommandButton Then
      'Set a few properties of the control:
      MyControl.FontName = "Times New Roman"
      MyControl.FontBold = True
      MyControl.FontSize = 12
    End If
  Next
End Sub
```

Don't be confused by the different expressions you see in this example. The heart of this procedure is the For...Next loop. The loop begins at zero (the start value) and executes until the i variable reaches the number of controls on the form minus one. (The controls on an Access form are numbered beginning with zero. The Count property tells you how many controls are on the form.) Within the loop, a variable named MyControl is pointed at the control indicated by the i variable. The If TypeOf statement evaluates the exact type of control referenced by the MyControl variable.

Within the body of the If...Then block, the control's properties (FontName, FontBold, and FontSize) are adjusted. You'll frequently see code such as this when it's necessary to manipulate all the members of a collection.

Notice that the control variable is referenced in each of the assignment statements. Referencing control properties one at a time is a fairly slow process. If the form contains many controls, this code executes relatively slowly.

An improvement on this code uses the `With` statement to isolate one member of the `Controls` collection and apply a number of statements to that control. The following code uses the `With` statement to apply a number of font settings to a single control.

```
Private Sub cmdWith_Click()
  Dim i As Integer
  Dim MyControl As Control

  For i = 0 To Me.Controls.Count - 1
    Set MyControl = Me.Controls(i)  'Grab a control
    If TypeOf MyControl Is CommandButton Then
      With MyControl
        'Set a few properties of the control:
        .FontName = "Arial"
        .FontBold = True
        .FontSize = 8
      End With
    End If
  Next
End Sub
```

The code in this example (`cmdWith_Click`) executes somewhat faster than the previous example (`cmdOld_Click`). Once Access has a handle on the control (`With MyControl`), it's able to apply all the statements in the body of the `With` without having to fetch the control from the controls on the form as in `cmdOld_Click`.

In practical terms, however, it's highly unlikely that you'll notice any difference in execution times when using the `With` construct as shown in this example. However, when working with massive sets of data, the `With` statement might contribute to overall performance. In any case, the `With` statement reduces the wordiness of the subroutine, and makes the code much easier to read and understand. It also saves tons of typing when you're changing a lot of properties of an object.

Think of the `With` statement as if you're handing Access a particular item and saying "Here, apply all these properties to *this* item." The previous example said, "Go get the item named *x* and apply this property to it" over and over again. The speed difference in these commands is considerable.

The For Each statement

The code in `cmdWith_Click` is further improved by using the `For Each` statement to traverse the `Controls` collection. `For Each` walks through each member of a collection, making it available for examination or manipulation. The following code shows how `For Each` simplifies the example.

```
Private Sub cmdForEach_Click()
  Dim MyControl As Control

  For Each MyControl In Me.Controls
    If TypeOf MyControl Is CommandButton Then
      With MyControl
        .FontName = "MS Sans Serif"
        .FontBold = False
        .FontSize = 8
      End With
    End If
  Next
End Sub
```

The improvement goes beyond using fewer lines to get the same amount of work done. Notice that you no longer need an integer variable to count through the `Controls` collection. You also don't have to call on the `Controls` collection's `Count` property to determine when to end the `For` loop. All this overhead is handled silently and automatically for you by the VBA programming language.

The code in this listing is easier to understand than in either of the previous procedures. The purpose of each level of nesting is obvious and clear. You don't have to keep track of the index to see what's happening, and you don't have to worry about whether to start the `For` loop at `0` or `1`. The code in the `For...Each` example is marginally faster than the `With...End With` example because no time is spent incrementing the integer value used to count through the loop and Access doesn't have to evaluate which control in the collection to work on.

On the Web

The `Chapter23.accdb` example database includes frmWithDemo (see Figure 23.12), which contains all the code discussed in this section. Each of the three command buttons along the bottom of this form uses different code to loop through the `Controls` collections on this form, changing the font characteristics of the controls.

FIGURE 23.12

frmWithDemo is included in `Chapter23.accdb`.

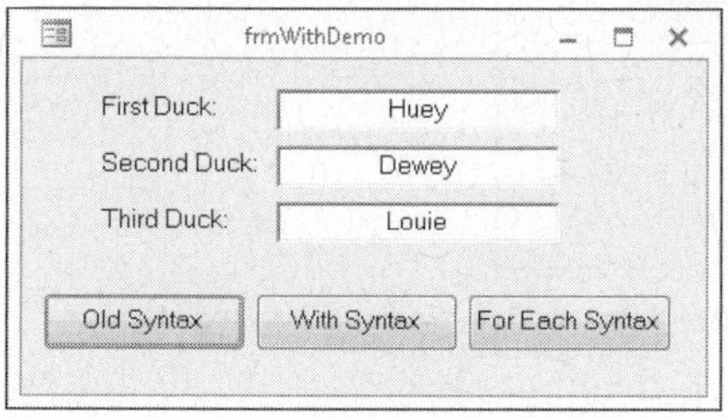

Exploring the Visual Basic Editor

To be a productive Access developer, you need to know your way around the Visual Basic Editor (VBE). This section explores the features of the VBE and how to use them.

The Immediate window

When you write code for a procedure, you might want to try the procedure while you're in the module, or you might need to check the results of an expression. The Immediate window (shown in Figure 23.13) enables you to try your procedures without leaving the module. You can run the module and check variables.

Press Ctrl + G to view the Immediate window, or choose View ➪ Immediate Window in the VBA code editor.

NOTE

Notice that the VBE window doesn't use the Ribbon. Instead, the code window appears much as it has in every version of Access since Access 2000. Therefore, in this book, you'll see references to the code window's toolbar and menu whenever we describe working with Access VBA modules. Don't confuse references to the code editor's toolbar with the main Access window's Ribbon.

FIGURE 23.13

The Immediate window.

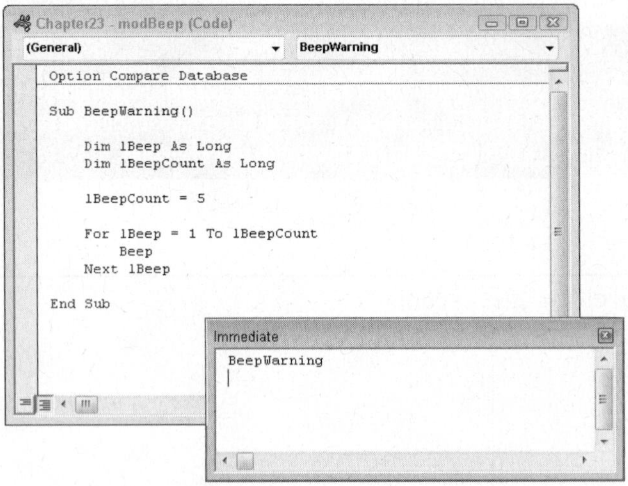

```
Chapter23 - modBeep (Code)
(General)    BeepWarning

Option Compare Database

Sub BeepWarning()

    Dim lBeep As Long
    Dim lBeepCount As Long

    lBeepCount = 5

    For lBeep = 1 To lBeepCount
        Beep
    Next lBeep

End Sub
```

```
Immediate
BeepWarning
```

Running the `BeepWarning` procedure is easy. Simply type **BeepWarning** into the Immediate window and press Enter. You might hear five beeps or only a continuous beep because the interval between beeps is short.

The Immediate Window is an excellent debugging tool. Debugging VBA code is discussed in Chapter 26.

The Project Explorer

The Project Explorer is a window within the VBE that displays all the modules in your project, both standard modules and form and report modules. It provides an easy way to move between modules without going back to the main Access application.

To view the Project Explorer, press Ctrl+R or choose View➪Project Explorer from the VBE's menu. By default, the Project Explorer is docked to the left side of the VBE window, as shown in Figure 23.14.

FIGURE 23.14

The Project Explorer shows all the modules in your database.

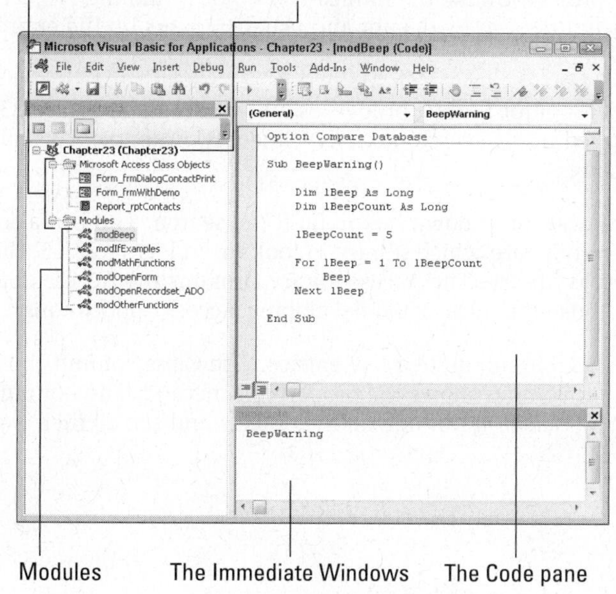

The Project Explorer shows your project at the top of a collapsible list. The project name is the same as the database name without the ACCDB extension. Beneath the project name is one or more folders. In Figure 23.14, you can see that our project has a folder for Access

Class Objects and one for Modules. The `Class Objects` folder holds class modules that are associated with a form or report, while the `Modules` folder holds standard modules.

There are three icons at the top of the Project Explorer:

- **View Code:** Clicking View Code will put the focus into the code pane — the large area where you write and edit VBA code. It offers little advantage over just moving your mouse and clicking in the code pane.
- **View Object:** Clicking View Object will display the object associated with the module. If you're in a module associated with a form or report, that form or report will be displayed. It's a handy shortcut for moving back to the main Access window. This button has no effect on standard modules.
- **Toggle Folders:** Modules are displayed in folders by default. To remove the folders and display all the modules as one list, click Toggle Folders. Click it again to return to folder view. With proper naming conventions, showing folders in the Project Explorer is unnecessary. If you prefix all your standard modules with *mod,* they'll all be grouped together in either view.

The Object Browser

The Object Browser is a window in the VBE that lets you see all the objects, properties, methods, and events in your project. Unlike the Immediate window and the Project Explorer, the Object Browser not docked by default and usually covers up the entire code pane.

The Object Browser is a useful tool for finding properties and methods. In Figure 23.15, the search term *font* was entered in the search box. The Object Browser displays all the elements that contain that string.

The Object Browser has a Libraries drop-down box to limit the search. You can also search "All Libraries" if you're not sure which library to look in. In Figure 23.15, the search was limited to the Access library. The Access library contains the Access object model and is the library you'll use the most when developing Access applications.

The search shown in Figure 23.15 found quite a few entries. The Class column shows the object's name, and the Member column shows the property or method. The bottom section of the Object Browser lets you scroll through all the objects and see all their properties and methods.

FIGURE 23.15

Search the Object Browser to find properties and methods.

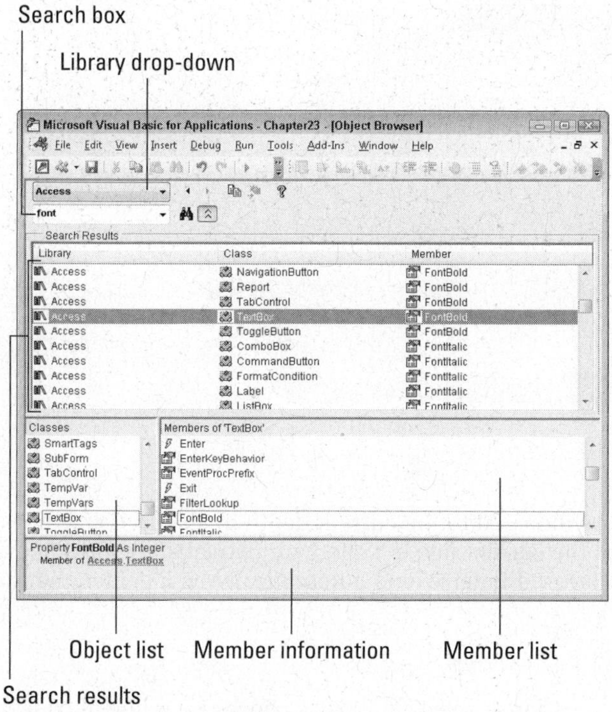

VBE options

Many of the most important features in Access affect only developers. These features are hidden from end-users and benefit only the person building the application. Spend some time exploring these features so that you fully understand their benefits. You'll soon settle on option settings that suit the way you work and the kind of assistance you want as you write your VBA code.

The Editor tab of the Options dialog box

The Options dialog box contains several important settings that greatly influence how you interact with Access as you add code to your applications. These options are accessed by choosing Tools⇨Options from the VBE menu. Figure 23.16 shows the Editor tab of the Options dialog box.

FIGURE 23.16

The Editor tab of the Options dialog box.

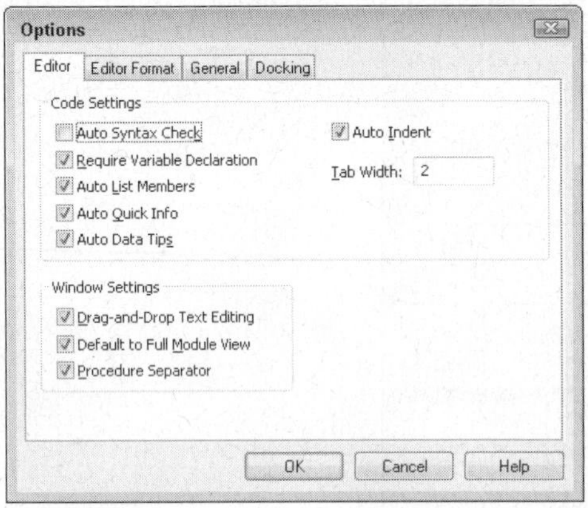

Auto Indent

Auto Indent causes code to be indented to the current depth in all successive lines of code. For example, if you indented the current line of code with two tabs, the next line of code that you created when your pressed Enter would automatically be indented the same amount.

Auto Syntax Check

When the Auto Syntax Check option is selected, Access checks each line of code for syntax errors as you enter it in the code editor and displays a message box when it finds one. Many experienced developers find this behavior intrusive and prefer to keep this option disabled. With Auto Syntax Check disabled, lines with syntax errors are colored red, but no message box is displayed. The benefit of the message box is that it gives you a little more information about the error it found, although often these messages are hard to understand.

Require Variable Declaration

This setting automatically inserts `the Option Explicit` directive into all new VBA modules in your Access application. This option is *not* selected by default. It's almost universally accepted that `Option Explicit` should be used and this option should be enabled. Any modules created before this option is set will not be updated to include `Option Explicit`. The good news is, you can simply type the directive into those modules.

TIP

When you get used to having `Option Explicit` set on every module (including global and class modules), the instances of rogue and unexplained variables (which, in reality, are almost always misspellings of declared variables) disappear. With `Option Explicit` set in every module, your code is more self-explanatory and easier to debug and maintain because the compiler catches every single misspelled variable.

Auto List Members

This option pops up a list box containing the members of an object's hierarchy in the code window. In Figure 23.6, the list of the `DoCmd` object's members appeared as soon as we typed as the period following `DoCmd` in the VBA statement. You select an item from the list by continuing to type it in or scrolling the list and pressing the spacebar.

Auto Quick Info

When Auto Quick Info has been selected, Access pops up syntax help (refer to Figure 23.7) when you enter the name of a procedure (function, subroutine, or method) followed by a period, space, or opening parenthesis. The procedure can be a built-in function or subroutine or one that you've written yourself in Access VBA.

Auto Data Tips

The Auto Data Tips option displays the value of variables when you hold the mouse cursor over a variable with the module in break mode. Auto Data Tips is an alternative to setting a watch on the variable and flipping to the Debug window when Access reaches the break point.

Debugging Access VBA is described in Chapter 26.

The Project Properties dialog box

All the code components in an Access application, including all the modules, procedures, variables, and other elements are aggregated as the application's VBA project. The VBA language engine accesses modules and procedures as members of the project. Access manages the code in your application by keeping track of all the code objects that are included in the project, which is different and separate from the code added into the application as runtime libraries and wizards.

Each Access project includes a number of important options. The Project Properties dialog box (shown in Figure 23.17) contains a number of settings that are important for developers. Open the Project Properties dialog box by choosing Tools➪*Project Name* Properties (where *Project Name* is the name of your database's project).

FIGURE 23.17

The Project Properties dialog box contains a number of interesting options.

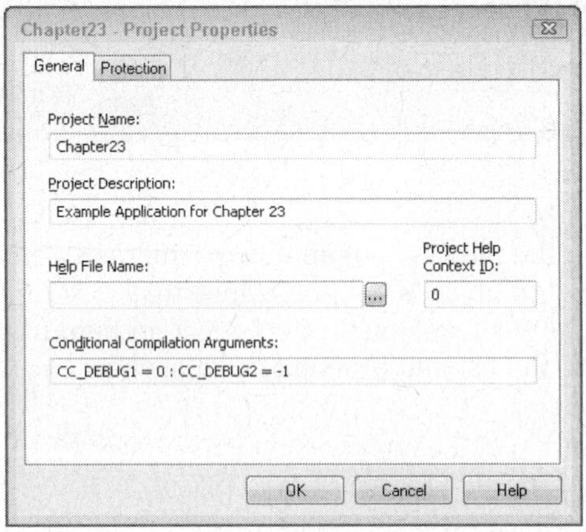

Project name

Certain changes in an application's structure require Access to recompile the code in the application. For example, changing the code in a global module affects all statements in other modules using that code, so Access must recompile all the code in the application. Until the code is recompiled, Access "decompiles" the application by reverting to the plain-text version of the code stored in the ACCDB file and ignoring the compiled code in the ACCDB. This means that each line of the code must be interpreted at runtime, dramatically slowing the application.

Sometimes insignificant modifications, such as changing the name of the project itself, are sufficient to cause decompilation. This happens because of the hierarchical nature of Access VBA. Because all objects are "owned" by some other object, changing the name of a high-level object might change the dependencies and ownerships of all objects below it in the object hierarchy.

Access maintains a separate, independent project name for the code and executable objects in the application. Simply changing the name of the ACCDB file is not enough to decompile the code in an Access application. By default, the project name is the same as the name of the ACCDB, but it's not dependent on it. You can assign a unique name to the project with the Project Name text box in the General tab of the Project Properties dialog box.

Project description

The project description is, as its name implies, a description for the project. Because this area is so small, it isn't possible to add anything of significance that might be helpful to another developer.

Conditional compilation arguments

Compiler directives instruct the Access VBA compiler to include or exclude portions of code, depending on the value of a constant established in the module's declarations section. Code lines that begin with # are conditionally compiled.

One of the limitations of using compiler directives is that the constant declaration is local to the module. This means that you have to use the `#Const` compiler directive to set up the constant in every module that includes the `#If` directive. This limitation can make it difficult to remove all the `#Const` compiler directives to modify the code at the conclusion of development.

For example, consider a situation in which you want to use conditional compilation to include certain debugging statements and functions during the development cycle. Just before shipping the application to its users, you want to remove the compiler directives from the code so that your users won't see the message boxes, status bar messages, and other debugging information. If your application consists of dozens of forms and modules, you have to make sure you find every single instance of the `#Const` directive to make sure you successfully deactivated the debugging code. (This is why it's such a good idea to apply a naming convention to the identifiers you use with the `#Const` directive.)

Fortunately, Access provides a way for you to set up "global" conditional compilation arguments. The General tab of the Project Properties dialog box contains the Conditional Compilation Arguments text box, where you can enter arguments to be evaluated by the conditional compilation directives in your code.

As an example, assume you've set up the following sort of statements in all the modules in your application:

```
#If CC_DEBUG2 Then
  MsgBox "Now in ProcessRecords()"
#End If
```

Instead of adding the constant directive (`#Const CC_DEBUG2 = True`) to every module in the application, you might enter the following text into the Conditional Compilation Arguments text box:

```
CC_DEBUG2 = -1
```

This directive sets the value of `CC_DEBUG2` to `-1` (true) for all modules (global and form and report class modules) in the application. You need to change only this one entry to `CC_DEBUG2=0` to disable the debugging statements in all modules in the application.

NOTE

You don't use the words *true* or *false* when setting compiler constants in the Project Properties dialog box, even though you do use these values within a VBA code module. You must use `-1` for true and `0` for false in the Project Properties dialog box.

Separate multiple arguments with colons — for example: `CC_DEBUG1=0 : CC_DEBUG2=-1`.

CHAPTER 24

Mastering VBA Data Types and Procedures

IN THIS CHAPTER

- Naming and declaring variables
- Looking at the VBA data types
- Understanding the scope and lifetime of variables
- Using constants
- Looking at arrays
- Working with subs and functions
- Building functions

All VBA applications require *variables* to hold data while the program executes. Variables are like a white board where important information can be temporarily written and read later on by the program. For example, when a user inputs a value on a form, you'll most often use a variable to temporarily hold the value until it can be permanently stored in the database or printed on a report. Simply put, a variable is the name you've assigned to a particular bit of data in your application. In more technical terms, a variable is a named area in memory used to store values during program execution.

Variables are transient and do not persist after an application stops running. And, as you'll read in the "Understanding variable scope and lifetime" section, later in this chapter, a variable may last a very short time as the program executes or may exist as long as the application is running.

In most cases, you assign a specific data type to each of the variables in your applications. For example, you may create a string variable to hold text data such as names or descriptions. A currency variable, on the other hand, is meant to contain values representing monetary amounts. You shouldn't try to assign a text value to a currency variable because a runtime error may occur as a result.

The variables you use have a dramatic effect on your applications. You have many options when it comes to establishing and using variables in your Access programs. Inappropriately using a variable can slow an application's execution or potentially cause data loss.

This chapter contains everything you need to know about creating and using VBA variables. The information in this chapter helps you use the most efficient and effective data types for your variables while avoiding the most common problems related to VBA variables.

Using Variables

One of the most powerful concepts in programming is the variable. A *variable* is a temporary storage location for some value and is given a name. You can use a variable to store the result of a calculation, hold a value entered by the user, or read from a table, or you can create a variable to make a control's value available to another procedure.

To refer to the result of an expression, you use a variable's name to store the result. To assign an expression's result to a variable, you use the = operator. Here are some examples of expressions that assign values to variables:

```
counter = 1

counter = counter + 1

today = Date()
```

Figure 24.1 shows a simple procedure using several different variables. Although this is a very simple example of using variables, it effectively demonstrates the basics of using VBA variables:

- The `Dim` keyword establishes the new variables — `sFormName` and `sCriteria` — within a procedure.
- You provide a meaningful name for the variable as part of the `Dim` statement. In Figure 24.1, the variable names are `sFormName` and `sCriteria`, indicating how the variables are used by the procedure.
- The `Dim` statement includes the data type of the new variable. In Figure 24.1, both variables are declared as the `String` data type.
- Different techniques can be used to assign a value to a variable. Figure 24.1 uses the = operator to assign a literal value — `frmContactLog` — to `sFormName`. Notice that `frmContactLog` is surrounded by quotation marks, making it a *literal* value. A value pulled from the `txtContactID` text box on the form's surface is combined with a literal string — `"[ContactID]="` — and assigned to the `sCriteria` variable. The data assigned to variables should always be appropriate for the variable's data type.

- Variables are manipulated with a variety of operators. Figure 24.1 uses the VBA concatenation operator (`&`) to combine `[ContactID]=` and the value in `txtContactID`.

FIGURE 24.1

Variable declarations appear at the top of VBA procedures.

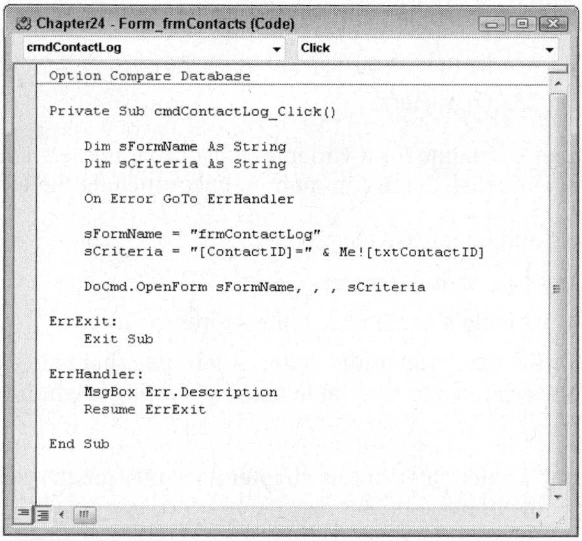

Chapter24 - Form_frmContacts (Code)

cmdContactLog | Click

```
Option Compare Database

Private Sub cmdContactLog_Click()

    Dim sFormName As String
    Dim sCriteria As String

    On Error GoTo ErrHandler

    sFormName = "frmContactLog"
    sCriteria = "[ContactID]=" & Me![txtContactID]

    DoCmd.OpenForm sFormName, , , sCriteria

ErrExit:
    Exit Sub

ErrHandler:
    MsgBox Err.Description
    Resume ErrExit

End Sub
```

There are a number of ways to perform each of the tasks you see in Figure 24.1. For example, as you'll read in the "Declaring variables" section, later in this chapter, the `Dim` statement is not the only way to establish a variable. And, as you'll see throughout this book, the = operator is not the only way to assign a value to a variable. Also, you don't need to use a variable like `sCriteria` to temporarily hold the value generated by combining two values. The two values can just as easily be combined on the fly within the `DoCmd.OpenForm` statement:

```
DoCmd.OpenForm "frmContactLog", _
    "[ContactID] = " & Me![txtContactID]
```

There are very few rules governing how you declare and use your variables. You should always strive for readability in your VBA code. In the small example shown in Figure 24.1, you can easily see that `sFormName` holds the name of a form, especially because it's used as part of the `DoCmd.OpenForm` statement.

Naming variables

Every programming language has its own rules for naming variables. In VBA, a variable name must meet the following conditions:

- It must begin with an alphabetical character.
- It must have a unique name. The variable's name cannot be used elsewhere in the procedure or in modules that use the variables.
- It must not contain spaces or punctuation characters (except underscore).
- It must not be a reserved word, such as `Sub`, `Module`, or `Form`.
- It must be no longer than 255 characters.

Although you can make up almost any name for a variable, most programmers adopt a standard convention for naming variables. Some common practices include the following:

- Using a mix of uppercase and lowercase characters, as in `TotalCost`.
- Using all lowercase characters, as in `counter`.
- Separating the parts of a variable's name with underscores, as in `Total_Cost`.
- Preceding the name with the data type of the value. A variable that stores a number might be called `iCounter`, while a variable holding a string might be named `sLastName`.

The "Using a naming convention" section later in this chapter goes into greater detail about the benefits of a naming convention.

NOTE

One source of endless confusion to Access developers is the fact that Access object names (tables, queries, forms, and so on) may contain spaces, while variable names never include spaces. One reason not to use spaces in Access object names is to eliminate confusion when mixing different naming conventions within a single application. You're really better off being consistent in how you apply names to your Access objects, variables, procedures, and other application entities.

TIP

When creating variables, you can use uppercase, lowercase, or both to specify the variable or call it later. VBA variables are not case sensitive. This means that you can use the `TodayIs` variable later without having to worry about the case that you used for the name when you created it; `TODAYIS`, `todayis`, and `tOdAyIs` all refer to the same variable. VBA automatically changes any explicitly declared variables to the case that was used in the declaration statement (the `Dim` statement).

When you need to see or use the contents of a variable, you simply reference its name. When you specify the variable's name, the computer program goes into memory, finds the variable, and gets its contents for you. This process means, of course, that you need to be able to remember and correctly reference the name of the variable.

Declaring variables

There are two principle ways to add variables to your applications. The first method — called *implicit declaration* — is to let VBA automatically create the variables for you. As with most things that are not carefully controlled, you'll find that letting VBA prepare your variables for you is not a particularly good idea and can lead to performance issues in, and problems debugging, your programs (see the "Comparing implicit and explicit variables" section, later in this chapter).

Implicit declaration means that VBA automatically creates an Empty variable for each identifier it recognizes as a variable in an application. In the following, there are two implicitly declared variables — `sFirstName` and `sLastName`. In this example, two variables (`sFirstName` and `sLastName`) are assigned the text contained in two text boxes (`txtFirstName` and `txtLastName`), and a third variable (`sFullName`) is assigned the combination of `sFirstName` and `sLastName`, with a space between them.

```
Private Sub Combine_Implicit()

  sFirstName = Me.txtFirstName.Text
  sLastName = Me.txtLastName.Text
  sFullName = sFirstName & Space(1) & sLastName

End Sub
```

The second approach is to *explicitly* declare them with one of the following keywords: `Dim`, `Static`, `Private`, or `Public` (or `Global`). The choice of keyword has a profound effect on the variable's scope within the application and determines where the variable can be used in the program. (Variable scope is discussed in the "Understanding variable scope and lifetime" section, later in this chapter.)

TIP

To force explicit variable declaration, type the directive Option Explicit at the top of each module. Better yet, check Require Variable Declarations in the VBE Options dialog box, and all new modules will automatically include the Option Explicit directive.

24

The syntax for explicitly declaring a variable is quite simple:

```
Dim VariableName As DataType
Static VariableName As DataType
Private VariableName As DataType
Public VariableName As DataType
```

In each case, the name of the variable and its data type are provided as part of the declaration. VBA reserves the amount of memory required to hold the variable as soon as the declaration statement is executed. Once a variable is declared, you can't change its data type, although you can easily convert the value of a variable and assign the converted value to another variable.

The following example shows the `Combine_Implicit` sub rewritten to use explicitly declared variables:

```
Private Sub Combine_Explicit()

  Dim sFirstName As String
  Dim sLastName As String
  Dim sFullName As String

  sFirstName = Me.txtFirstName.Text
  sLastName = Me.txtLastName.Text
  sFullName = sFirstName & Space(1) & sLastName

End Sub
```

So, if there's often very little difference between using implicit and explicit variables, why bother declaring variables at all? The following code demonstrates the importance of using explicitly declared variables in your applications:

```
Private Sub Form_Load()

  sDepartment = "Manufacturing"
  sSupervisor = "Joe Jones"
  sTitle = "Senior Engineer"

  'Dozens of lines of code go here

  Me.txtDepartment = sDepartment
  Me.txtSupervisor = sSuperviser
  Me.txtTitle = sTitle

End Sub
```

In this example code, the `txtSupervisor` text box on the form is always empty and is never assigned a value. A line near the bottom of this procedure assigns the value of an implicitly declared variable named `Superviser` to the `txtSupervisor` text box. Notice that the name of the variable (`Superviser`) is a misspelling of the intended variable (`Supervisor`). Because the source of the assignment appears to be a variable, VBA simply creates a new variant named `Superviser` and assigns its value (which is, literally, `nothing`) to the `txtSupervisor` text box. And, because the new `Superviser` variable has never been assigned a value, the text box always ends up empty. Misspellings such as this are very common and easy to overlook in long or complex procedures.

Furthermore, the code shown in this example runs fine and causes no problem. Because this procedure uses implicit variable declaration, Access doesn't raise an error because of the misspelling, and the problem isn't detected until someone notices the text box is always empty. Imagine the problems you'd encounter in a payroll or billing application if variables went missing because of simple spelling errors!

When you declare a variable, Access sets up a location in the computer's memory for storing a value for the variable ahead of time. The amount of storage allocated for the variable depends on the data type you assign to the variable. More space is allocated for a variable that will hold a currency amount (such as $1,000,000) than for a variable that will never hold a value greater than, say, 255. This is because a variable declared with the Currency data type requires more storage than another variable declared as a Byte data type. (Data types are discussed later in this chapter, in the "Working with Data Types" section.)

Even though VBA doesn't require you to declare your variables before using them, it does provide various declaration commands. Getting into the habit of declaring variables is good practice. A variable's declaration assures that you can assign only a certain type of data to it — always a numeric value or only characters, for example. In addition, you attain real performance gains by pre-declaring variables.

TIP
A programming best practice is to explicitly declare all variables at the top of the procedure; this makes the program easier for other programmers to work with later on.

The Dim keyword

To declare a variable, you use the `Dim` keyword. (*Dim* is an abbreviation of the archaic *Dimension* programming term — because you're specifying the dimension of the variable.) When you use the `Dim` keyword, you must supply the variable name that you assign to the variable. Here's the format for a `Dim` statement:

```
Dim [VariableName] [As DataType]
```

The following statement declares the variable `iBeeps` as an integer data type:

```
Dim iBeeps As Integer
```

Notice that the variable name follows the `Dim` statement. In addition to naming the variable, use `As` *Data Type* to specify a data type for the variable. The data type is the kind of information that will be stored in the variable — String, Integer, Currency, and so on. The default data type is Variant; it can hold any type of data.

24

Table 24.1 in the next section lists all the data types available.

When you use the `Dim` statement to declare a variable in a procedure, you can refer to that variable only within that procedure. Other procedures, even if they're stored in the same module, don't know anything about the variable declared within a procedure. Such a variable is often described as *local* because it's declared *locally* within a procedure and is known only by the procedure that owns it. (You can read more about variable scope in the "Understanding variable scope and lifetime" section, later in this chapter.)

Variables also can be declared in the declarations section of a module. Then all the procedures in the module can access the variable. Procedures *outside* the module in which you declared the variable, however, can't read or use the variable.

CAUTION

You can declare multiple variables in one `Dim` statement, but you must supply the data type for each variable. If you don't supply a data type, the variable is created as a Variant. The statement `Dim sString1, sString2 As String` results in `sString1` (a Variant) and `sString2` (a String). The proper statement, `Dim sString1 As String, sString2 As String`, results in both variables being Strings.

The Public keyword

To make a variable available to all modules in the application, use the Public keyword when you declare the variable. Figure 24.2 illustrates declaring a public variable.

FIGURE 24.2

Declaring a public variable.

Chapter24 - Module1 (Code)

(General) | test

```
Option Compare Database
Option Explicit

Public gsUserName As String

Private mlCounter As Long
Private mdtStart As Date
```

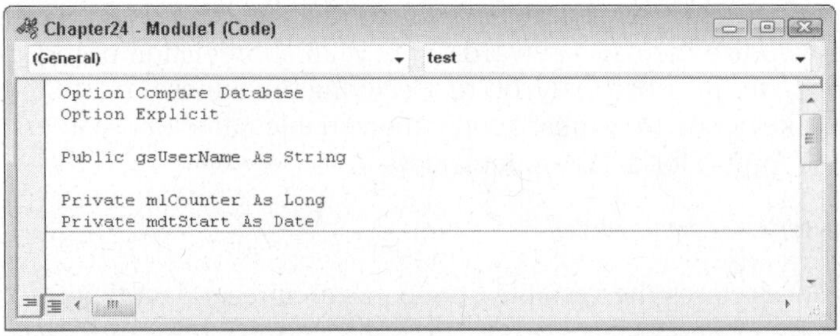

CAUTION

You can't declare a public variable within a procedure. It must be declared in the declarations section of a module. If you try to declare a variable public within a procedure, you get an error message.

Although you can declare a public variable in any module, the best practice for declaring public variables is to declare them all in a single standard module that's used only to store public variables. Public variables, while necessary in some cases, should be limited. Because any procedure in your project can change a public variable's value, it can be difficult to find which procedure is making an unwanted change. With all the publically declared variables in one place, it's easy to locate them and it's easy to see if you're using too many and may need to rethink your code structure.

TIP

You can declare public variables in the code module attached to a form or report. Referencing these public variables from another module is a little bit different than referencing public variables declared in standard modules. To reference the value of a public variable declared behind a form or report from another module, you must qualify the variable reference, using the name of the form or report object. `frmMainForm.MyVariable`, for example, accesses a form named `frmMainForm` and obtains the value of the public variable `MyVariable` declared in the form's code module. Public variables declared within a form or report's module cannot be referenced unless the form or report is open.

The Private keyword

The declarations section in Figure 24.2 shows the use of the `Private` keyword to declare variables. Technically, there is no difference between `Private` and `Dim` when used in the declarations section of a module, but using `Private` at the module level to declare variables that are available to only that module's procedures is a good idea. The `Private` keyword ensures that all procedures in the module can access the variable, but all procedures in other modules cannot. Declaring private variables contrasts with

- `Dim`, which *must* be used at the procedure level, distinguishing where the variable is declared and its scope (`Module` versus `Procedure`).
- `Public`, the other method of declaring variables in modules, making understanding your code easier.

TIP

You can quickly go to the declarations section of a module while you're working on code in a form's module by selecting `(General)` in the Object drop-down list in the code editor. The Procedure drop-down list will change to `(Declarations)`. (Refer to the Module window combo boxes in Figure 24.2.) The Declarations item is not available when a control, or the form, is selected in the Object drop-down list.

When you declare a variable, you use the `AS` clause to specify a data type for the new variable. Because Access is a database development system, it's not surprising that variable data types are similar to field data types in an Access database table.

Working with Data Types

When you declare a variable, you also specify the data type for the variable. Each variable has a data type. The data type of a variable determines what kind of information can be stored in the variable.

A string variable — a variable with a data type of String — can hold any character that you can type on a keyboard, plus a few others. Once created, a string variable can be used in many ways: comparing its contents with another string, pulling parts of information out of the string, and so on. If you have a variable defined as a String, however, you cannot use it to do mathematical calculations.

Table 24.1 describes the 12 fundamental data types supported by VBA.

TABLE 24.1 VBA Data Types

Data Type	Range	Description
`Boolean`	True or false	2 bytes
`Byte`	0 to 255	1-byte binary data
`Currency`	–922,337,203,685,477,5808 to 922,337,203,685,477,5807	8-byte number with fixed decimal point
`Decimal`	+/–79,228,162,514,264,337,593,543,950,335 with no decimal point +/–7.9228162514264337593543950335 with 28 places to the right of the decimal; smallest nonzero number is +/–0.0000000000000000000000000001	14 bytes
`Date`	01 Jan 100 00:00:00 to 31 Dec 9999 23:59:59	8-byte date/time value
`Double`	–1.79769313486231E308 to –4.94065645841247E–324 for negative values and 4.94065645841246544E–324 through 1.79769313486231570E+308 for positive values	8-byte floating-point number
`Integer`	–32,768 to 32,767	2-byte integer
`Long`	–2,147,483,648 to 2,147,483,647	4-byte integer
`Object`	Any object reference	4 bytes
`Single`	–3.402823E38 to –1.401298E–45 for negative values and 1.401298E–45 to 3.402823E38 for positive values	4-byte floating-point number
`String` (fixed length)	1 to approximately 65,400	Length of string
`String` (variable length)	0 to approximately 2,000,000,000	10 bytes plus length of string
`Variant` (with characters)	0 to approximately 2,000,000,000	22 bytes plus length of string
`Variant` (with numbers)	Any numeric value up to the range of the `Double` data type (see earlier in this table)	16 bytes

Most of the time, you use the String, Date, Long, and Currency or Double data types. If a variable always contains whole numbers between –32,768 and 32,767, you can save bytes of memory and gain a little speed in arithmetic operations if you declare the variable an Integer data type.

NOTE

How big is a string variable? As shown in Table 24.1, string variables can contain quite a bit of data. How much text data could be stored in a single VBA string? The *Oxford English Dictionary* (OED) is widely accepted as the definitive reference of the English language. Although not the world's largest dictionary (the Dutch *Woordenboek de Nederlandsche Taal* is considerably longer), the OED is quite impressive. Containing more than 301,000 main entries, 22,000 pages, and 59,000,000 individual words, the OED is available as a 20-volume printed edition. As large as it is, the OED is only 540MB of data. A single VBA string variable, therefore, could contain almost four complete copies of the OED!

When you want to assign the value of an Access field to a variable, you need to make sure that the type of the variable can hold the data type of the field. Table 24.2 shows the corresponding VBA data types for Access field types.

TABLE 24.2 Access and VBA Data Types

Access Field Data Type	VBA Data Type
Attachment	—
AutoNumber (Long Integer)	Long
AutoNumber (Replication ID)	—
Currency	Currency
Calculated	—
Date/Time	Date
Long Text	String
Number (Byte)	Byte
Number (Integer)	Integer
Number (Long Integer)	Long
Number (Single)	Single
Number (Double)	Double
Number (Replication ID)	—
OLE object	String
Short Text	String
Hyperlink	String
Yes/No	Boolean

Now that you understand variables and their data types, you're ready to learn how to use them when writing procedures.

Comparing implicit and explicit variables

The default data type for VBA variables is Variant. This means that, unless you specify otherwise, every variable in your application will be a Variant. As you read earlier in this chapter, although useful, the Variant data type is not very efficient. Its data storage requirements are greater than the equivalent simple data type (a String, for instance), and the computer spends more time keeping track of the data type contained in a Variant than for other data types.

Here's an example of how you might test for the speed difference when using implicitly declared Variant variables and explicitly declared variables. This code is found behind `frmImplicitTest` in `Chapter24.accdb`:

```
'Use a Windows API call to get the exact time:
Private Declare Function GetTickCount _
    Lib "kernel32" () As Long

Private Sub cmdGo_Click()

  Dim i As Integer
  Dim j As Integer
  Dim snExplicit As Single

  Me.txtImplicitStart.Value = GetTickCount()

  For o = 1 To 10000
    For p = 1 To 10000
      q = i / 0.33333
    Next p
  Next o

  Me.txtImplicitEnd.Value = GetTickCount()

  Me.txtImplicitElapsed.Value = _
  Me.txtImplicitEnd.Value - Me.txtImplicitStart.Value

  DoEvents 'Force Access to complete pending operations

  Me.txtExplicitStart.Value = GetTickCount()

  For i = 1 To 10000
    For j = 1 To 10000
      snExplicit = i / 0.33333
    Next j
```

```
    Next i

    Me.txtExplicitEnd.Value = GetTickCount()

    Me.txtExplicitElapsed.Value = _
      Me.txtExplicitEnd.Value - Me.txtExplicitStart.Value
    DoEvents

End Sub
```

In this small test, the loop using implicitly declared variables required approximately 2.7 seconds to run while the loop with the explicitly declared variables required only 2.5 seconds. This is a performance enhancement of approximately 10 percent just by using explicitly declared variables.

The actual execution time of this — or any — VBA procedure depends largely on the relative speed of the computer and the tasks the computer is executing at the time the procedure is run. Desktop computers vary a great deal in CPU, memory, and other resources, making it quite impossible to predict how long a particular bit of code should take to execute.

Forcing explicit declaration

Access provides a simple *compiler directive* that forces you to always declare the variables in your applications. The `Option Explicit` statement, when inserted at the top of a module, instructs VBA to require explicit declaration of all variables in the module. If, for example, you're working with an application containing a number of implicitly declared variables, inserting `Option Explicit` at the top of each module results in a check of all variable declarations the next time the application is compiled.

Because explicit declaration is such a good idea, it may not come as a surprise that Access provides a way to automatically ensure that every module in your application uses explicit declaration. The Editor tab of the Options dialog box (shown in Figure 24.3) includes a Require Variable Declaration check box. This option automatically inserts the `Option Explicit` directive at the top of every module created from this point in time onward.

The Require Variable Declaration option doesn't affect modules already written. This option applies only to modules created *after* this option is selected, so you'll have to insert the `Option Explicit` statement in existing modules. Require Variable Declaration is not set by default in current versions of Access. You must set this option yourself to take advantage of having Access add `Option Explicit` to all your modules.

FIGURE 24.3

Requiring variable declaration is a good idea in most Access applications.

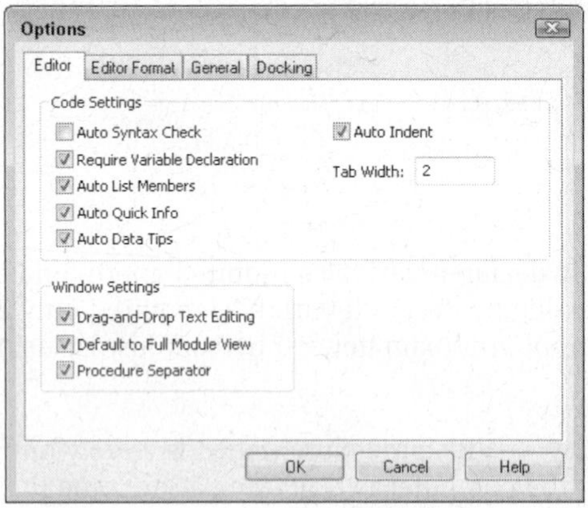

Using a naming convention

Like most programming languages, applications written in VBA tend to be quite long and complex, often occupying many thousands of lines of code. Even simple VBA programs may require hundreds of different variables. VBA forms often have dozens of different controls on them, including text boxes, command buttons, option groups, and other controls. Keeping track of the variables, procedures, forms, and controls in even a moderately complicated VBA application is a daunting task.

One way to ease the burden of managing the code and objects in an application is through the use of a naming convention. A *naming convention* applies a standardized method of supplying names to the objects and variables in an application.

The most common naming convention used in Access applications uses a one- to four-character prefix (a *tag*) attached to the base name of the objects and variables in a VBA application. The tag is generally based on the type of control for controls and the type of data the variable holds or the scope for variables. For example, a text box containing a person's last name might be named `txtLastName`, while a command button that closes a form would be named `cmdClose` or `cmdCloseForm`.

The names for variables follow a similar pattern. The string variable holding a customer name might be named `sCustomer`, and a Boolean variable indicating whether the customer is currently active would be `bActive`.

Using a naming convention is not difficult. Most of the code in this book uses one-character prefixes for variables and three-character prefixes for control names. The actual naming convention you use is not important. The important point is that you use the convention consistently. As you write more VBA code, the right convention for you will become obvious. Table 24.3 shows one naming convention.

TABLE 24.3 A Sample Naming Convention

Control/Data Type	Prefix	Example
Control: Text Box	txt	txtFirstName
Control: Label	lbl	lblFirstName
Control: Command Button	cmd	cmdClose
Control: Frame	frm	frmOptions
Control: Combo Box	cbx	cbxCustomers
Control: List Box	lbx	lbxProducts
Control: Check Box	chk	chkActive
Control: Option Button	opt	optFemale
Type: Byte	bt	btCounter
Type: Boolean	b	bActive
Type: Integer	i	iCounter
Type: Long	l	lCustomerID
Type: Single	sn	snTaxRate
Type: Double	d	dGrossPay
Type: Currency	c	cNetSales
Type: Date	dt	dtHired
Type: Object	o	oControl
Type: String	s	sLastName
Type: Variant	v	vCompany
Scope: Local	None	sState
Scope: Private	m	msState
Scope: Public	g	gsState

One benefit to using shorter prefixes for variables and longer prefixes for controls is that it becomes easy to tell them apart when you're reading your code. Also note that more commonly used data types get the one-character prefixes. You'll typically use Booleans more often than Bytes, so a shorter prefix for Booleans saves typing.

Some developers don't use any prefixes for variables. There's nothing wrong with that. There are some advantages to using prefixes, however. The first advantage is that you can identify the data type at the point you're using the variable. It's easy to see that a statement like `sCustomer = chkActive` may cause a problem. You know `sCustomer` is a String data type and `chkActive`, being a Check Box control, returns a Boolean value. Another advantage is variable name uniqueness. Recall that the variable naming rules state that all variable names must be unique and that you can't use reserved keywords for variable names. That means that you can't have a Boolean variable named `Print` that determines whether to print a report. By using a prefix, `bPrint` does not violate any rules.

Including an additional prefix for the scope conveys similar advantages. Knowing the scope of the variable in the portion of code you're working helps debug the code when things go wrong. It also allows you to use similar variables with different scopes. For example, you could have a private module-level variable `mbIsEnabled` that applies to all the code in your module and still have a local procedure-level variable `bIsEnabled` for use in only that procedure.

One final advantage to a naming convention that uses a mix of uppercase and lowercase letters is that you can detect spelling errors in your variable names very quickly. VBA will change the case of the variable name to match the case you use when you declare it. If you declare a variable using `Dim sFirstName As String` and later type `sfirstname = "Larry"` (all lowercase), as soon as you complete that line of code, your variable will change to `sFirstName = "Larry"`. That immediate feedback will help you catch spelling errors before they become problems.

Understanding variable scope and lifetime

A variable is more than just a simple data repository. Every variable is a dynamic part of the application and may be used at different times during the program's execution. The declaration of a variable establishes more than just the name and data type of the variable. Depending on the keyword used to declare the variable and the placement of the variable's declaration in the program's code, the variable may be visible to large portions of the application's code. Alternatively, a different placement may severely limit where the variable can be referenced in the procedures within the application.

Examining scope

The visibility of a variable or procedure is called its *scope*. A variable that can be seen and used by any procedure in the application is said to have *public scope*. A variable that is available to any procedure in one module is scoped *private* to that module. A variable that is usable by a single procedure is said to have scope that is *local* to that procedure.

There are many analogies for public and private scope. For example, a company is likely to have a phone number that is quite public (the main switchboard number) and is listed in the phone book and on the company's website; each office or room within the company might have its own extension number that is private within the company. A large office building has a public street address that is known by anyone passing by the building; each office or suite within that building will have a number that is private within that building.

Variables declared within a procedure are local to that procedure and can't be used or referenced outside that procedure. Most of the listings in this chapter have included a number of variables declared within the procedures in the listings. In each case, the `Dim` keyword was used to define the variable. `Dim` is an instruction to VBA to allocate enough memory to contain the variable that follows the `Dim` keyword. Therefore, `Dim iMyInt As Integer` allocates less memory (2 bytes) than `Dim dMyDouble As Double` (8 bytes).

The `Public` (or `Global`) keyword makes a variable visible throughout an application. `Public` can be used only at the module level and can't be used within a procedure. Most often, the `Public` keyword is used only in standard (stand-alone) modules that are not part of a form. Figure 24.4 illustrates variables declared with three very different scopes.

FIGURE 24.4

Variable scope is determined by the variable's declaration.

Available to all procedures in this module

Available to all procedures in all modules

Chapter24 - modScope (Code)

(General) | CreateMessage

```
Option Compare Database
Option Explicit

Public gsAppName As String
Private mbIsComplete As Boolean

Sub CreateMessage()

  Dim sMessage As String

  gsAppName = "Order Processor"

  sMessage = "Processing is " & IIf(mbIsComplete, _
    "Done", "Not done") & "."

  MsgBox sMessage, vbOKOnly, gsAppName

End Sub
```

Available only within this procedure

Uses local, module, and global variables

Every variable declared in the declarations section of a standard module is private to that module unless the `Public` keyword is used. `Private` restricts the visibility of a variable to the module in which the variable is declared. In Figure 24.4, the `gsAppName` variable declared with `Public` scope at the top of the module will be seen everywhere in the application while the `mbIsComplete` variable declared in the next statement is accessible only within the module. The `sMessage` variable is declared inside a procedure, so only that procedure can see it.

Misunderstanding variable scope is a major cause of serious bugs in many Access applications. It's entirely possible to have two same-named variables with different scopes in an Access VBA project. When ambiguity exists, Access always uses the "closest" declared variable.

Consider two variables named `MyVariable`. One of these variables is global (`public`) in scope, while the other is a module-level variable declared with the `Private` keyword. In any procedure Access uses one or the other of these variables. In a module where `MyVariable` is *not* declared, Access uses the public variable. The private variable is used only within the module containing its declaration.

The problem comes when multiple procedures use a variable with the same name as the multiply-declared `MyVariable`. Unless the developer working on one of these procedures has diligently determined which variable is being used, a serious error may occur. All too easily, a procedure might change the value of a public variable that is used in dozens of places within an application. If even one of those procedures changes the public variable instead of a more local variable, a very difficult-to-resolve bug occurs.

Determining a variable's lifetime

Variables are not necessarily permanent citizens of an application. Just as their visibility is determined by the location of their declaration, their *lifetime* is determined by their declaration as well. A variable's lifetime determines when it's accessible to the application.

By default, local variables exist only while the procedure is executing. As soon as the procedure ends, the variable is removed from memory and is no longer accessible. As already discussed, the scope of procedure-level variables is limited to the procedure and cannot be expanded beyond the procedure's boundaries.

A variable declared in the declarations section of a form's module exists as long as the form is open regardless of how it's declared (Public, Private, Dim, and so on). All the procedures within the form's module can use the module-level variables as often as they need, and they all share the value assigned to the variable. When the form is closed and removed from memory, all its variables are removed as well.

The greatest variable lifetime is experienced by the variables declared as `Public` in standard modules. These variables are available as soon as the VBA application starts up, and they persist until the program is shut down and removed from memory. Therefore, public variables retain their values throughout the application and are accessible to any of the procedures within the program. Private variables (declared with the `Private` keyword) declared at the top of standard modules endure throughout the application, but following the rules of variable scope, they're accessible only from within the module.

There is one major exception to the general rule that procedure-level variables persist only as long as the procedure is running. The `Static` keyword makes a procedure-level variable persist between calls to the procedure. Once a value has been assigned to a static variable, the variable retains its value until it's changed in another call to the procedure.

An alternative to using static variables is to declare a global or module-level variable and use it each time a particular procedure is called. The problem with this approach is that a global or module-level variable is accessible to other procedures that are also able to modify its value. You can experience undesirable side-effect bugs by unwittingly changing the value of a widely-scoped variable without realizing what has happened. Because of their procedure-limited scope, static variables are one way to avoid side-effect bugs.

Incidentally, declaring a procedure with the `Static` keyword makes all variables in the procedure static as well. In the following listing, both variables — `iStatic` and `iLocal` — in the `StaticTest` sub are static, in spite of their local declarations within the procedure. The `Static` keyword used in the procedure's heading makes both variables static in nature.

```
Private Static Sub StaticTest()

  'Both variables are static because of the
  ' 'Static' keyword in the procedure declaration
  Static lStatic As Long
  Dim lLocal As Long

  lStatic = lStatic + 1
  lLocal = lLocal + 1

  Me.txtLocal.Value = lLocal
  Me.txtStatic.Value = lStatic

End Sub
```

Deciding on a variable's scope

Now that you know how declaring a variable affects its scope and lifetime, you may be wondering how you decide what scope to make a particular variable. The answer is easy: Always limit the scope of your variables as much as possible. That means that most of your variables will be at the procedure level and declared with the `Dim` keyword. If you find that you need to retain the value of a variable for the next time you call the procedure, change the `Dim` to `Static`. By doing that, you'll increase the lifetime but not the scope. Limiting the scope reduces the number of places that a variable can change, which makes it easier to track down problems when they occur.

24

If another procedure in the same module needs to use a variable, pass that variable to the other procedure as a parameter. Parameters are discussed later in this chapter. When passed as a parameter, the variable is local to the procedure it's declared in and local to the procedure it's passed to, but no other procedures can see it. If the value of your variable changes unexpectedly, you have only two procedures to debug to find out why.

Sometimes you find yourself passing variables from procedure to procedure within the same module. When more than a few procedures in a module have the same variable passed to them, it may be time to declare that variable as `Private` to the module.

The next level of variable scope is when a procedure outside the module needs to use a variable. It's tempting to make the variable global with the `Public` keyword at this point, but in trying to follow the rule to keep the variable's scope as limited as possible, there are a couple other considerations. First, consider whether that other procedure belongs in the module with the variable. Modules should be designed to contain related procedures, and it's possible this "outsider" procedure should be moved. If that's not the case, consider passing the variable to the other procedure as a parameter. If you were to pass a module-level variable to a procedure outside the module, the variable would be available to any procedure in its own module and only the one other procedure it was passed to. The scope of such a variable is starting to grow but is still as limited as you can make it.

Global variables, declared in standard module with the `Public` keyword, should be kept to a minimum. However, almost all projects have at least one global variable. The name of your application, your application's version, and a Boolean flag that determines if the current user of the application has special permissions are all good examples of data to store in global variables.

Using constants

Constants differ from variables in one major respect: A constant's value never changes. The value is assigned to the constant when it's declared, and attempts to change that value in code will result in an error.

Declaring constants

Constants are declared with the `Const` keyword. The format of a constant declaration is as follows:

```
[Public | Private] Const constname [As type] = constvalue
```

Using constants improves the readability of your code. Constants can also aid in error-proofing your code if you use the same value in more than one place. Figure 24.5 shows a procedure that uses a constant.

If the procedure in Figure 24.5 did not use a constant for the discount rate, it might contain a line that looks like this:

```
dFinalPrice = dFullPrice * (1 - 0.15)
```

Because of the variable names, you might be able to decipher that `0.15` is a discount rate. By using a constant like `dDISCOUNT`, its purpose is obvious to anyone reading the code.

The scope and lifetime of a constant are very similar to variables. Constants declared inside a procedure are available only within that procedure. Constants declared with the `Private` keyword in a module are available to all the procedures in that module and none of the procedures in other modules. Global constants, declared with the `Public` keyword, are available throughout the project. The values of constants never change, so the `Static` keyword is not available, and unnecessary, when declaring constants.

FIGURE 24.5

Constants are declared with the `Const` keyword.

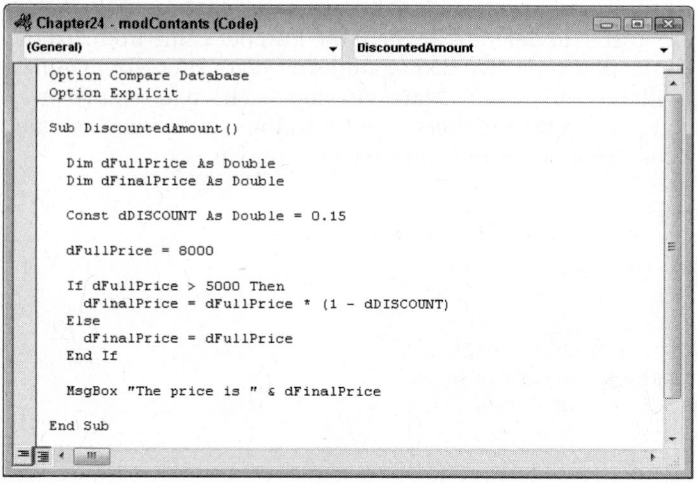

Chapter24 - modContants (Code)

(General) DiscountedAmount

```
Option Compare Database
Option Explicit

Sub DiscountedAmount()

  Dim dFullPrice As Double
  Dim dFinalPrice As Double

  Const dDISCOUNT As Double = 0.15

  dFullPrice = 8000

  If dFullPrice > 5000 Then
    dFinalPrice = dFullPrice * (1 - dDISCOUNT)
  Else
    dFinalPrice = dFullPrice
  End If

  MsgBox "The price is " & dFinalPrice

End Sub
```

Using a naming convention with constants

It's a good practice to use the same naming convention for constants that you use with variables. Prefixing a constant's name with a `g` for public constants and an `m` for private constants allows you to know the scope of the constant at the point of use. Also including a prefix identifying the data type of the constant helps keep your constant names unique and prevents errors, such as using a String constant in a mathematical operation.

In Figure 24.5, the constant name is all uppercase except for the prefix. There is no requirement to use uppercase with constants. Constants can be declared with any combination of uppercase and lowercase letters. The rules regarding naming variables and procedures also apply to constants. However, the all-uppercase convention is used by many developers.

```
dFinalPrice = dFullPrice * (1 - dDISCOUNT)
```

In the line above, it's easy to see what's a variable and what's a constant by using a proper-case naming scheme for variables and an uppercase naming scheme for constants.

Unlike variables, using global constants poses no risk to the maintainability of your code. Constant values never change, so there's no need to track down which procedures use them. Like variables, it's a good practice to put all globally scoped constants in a single module used only for global variables and constants. If you see a module named `modGlobals` in a project, it's a good bet the developer is using that convention.

Eliminating hard-coded values

Numbers used in a procedure are sometimes referred to as *magic numbers*. The term doesn't imply that the numbers have any special powers, but that another developer reading your code may not be able to determine where the number came from. To the other developer — or to you reading your own code months or years later — the numbers seem to appear *magically*, without explanation. Many developers strive to remove any magic numbers from their code except the numbers 0 and 1 and numbers being assigned to variables. This keeps the code well organized and easy to maintain.

```
Sub DiscountedAmount2()

  Dim dFullPrice As Double
  Dim dFinalPrice As Double

  Const dDISCOUNT As Double = 0.15
  Const dDISCTHRESHOLD As Double = 5000
  Const sPROMPT As String = "The price is "

  dFullPrice = 8000

  If dFullPrice > dDISCTHRESHOLD Then
    dFinalPrice = dFullPrice * (1 - dDISCOUNT)
  Else
    dFinalPrice = dFullPrice
  End If

  MsgBox sPROMPT & dFinalPrice

End Sub
```

In this rewrite of the procedure in Figure 24.5, the magic numbers have been removed. If you want to change the message that's displayed, the discount rate, or the discount threshold, you don't have to look through the code to find where those values are used. All the important values used in the procedure can be found in the declarations section's `Const` statements. Changing the values in the `Const` statements changes them anywhere they're used in the procedure. The line `If dFullPrice > dDISCTHRESHOLD Then` is easily understood as a comparison of the full price to a discount threshold. You can get carried away removing magic numbers from your code. The best practice is to use a constant for any number that's used more than once and to read your code as if you're reading it for the first time and deciding if a descriptive comment name is a better choice over a magic number.

Working with arrays

Arrays are a special type of variable. One array variable actually holds multiple pieces of data. Instead of reserving one block of memory, like a variable, an array reserves several blocks of memory. The size of an array can be fixed or dynamic. With dynamic arrays, you can increase or decrease the size in a procedure.

Fixed arrays

When you declare a fixed array, you specify the size in the `Dim` statement, and that size cannot be changed later. The simplest way to declare a fixed array is by putting the upper bound index in parentheses after the variable name.

```
Dim aCustomers(10) as Long
```

In this example, `aCustomers` is an array that can hold 11 long integers, perhaps from a CustomerID field. Why 11? By default, the lower bound of arrays declared in this way is zero. That means a value can be stored at `aCustomers(0)`, `aCustomers(1)`, all the way up to `aCustomers(10)`.

Another way to declare a fixed array is to specify both the lower and upper bound indices. It's a good practice to include the lower bound in the declaration statement even if you intend to use the default. Use the `To` keyword to specify the lower and upper bound indices of an array.

```
Dim aCustomers(1 to 10) as Long
```

Unlike the previous example, this array has only enough room to hold ten long integers. Long integers use 8 bytes of memory, and declaring this array reserves 80 bytes to hold all ten values. The memory is used when the array is declared, so even if you never assign any values to the array, nothing else can access that memory. If you're having performance problems or your application is using a lot of memory, one place you can look is your arrays to make sure they're not larger than you need. However, with modern computers, 80 bytes here and there probably isn't an issue.

Assigning values to an array is just like assigning them to any other variable except that you must specify in which index you want the variable. The following procedure assigns long integers to an array in a loop:

```
Sub ArrayAssignment()

  Dim aCustomers(1 To 5) As Double

  aCustomers(1) = 0.2
  aCustomers(2) = 24.6
  aCustomers(3) = 7.1
  aCustomers(4) = 99.9
  aCustomers(5) = 14.7

End Sub
```

Just as with a variable, the array name goes on the left of the equal sign and the value goes on the right. Unlike variables, however, each assignment includes the index of the array that is being assigned the value.

TIP

VBA includes a directive for setting the default lower bound for arrays where the lower bound is not specified. The `Option Base` directive determines the default lower bound. Including `Option Base 1` at the top of the module forces the lower bound to `1`. Arrays declared with both a lower and upper bound ignore the `Option Base` directive. The `Option Base` directive applies only to the module in which it's declared.

Reading values from an array will look very familiar. Like reading values from variables, you simply use the variable name. With arrays, you always must include the index you want to read. The following procedure stores five random numbers in an array, multiplies those numbers by 10, and finally prints the numbers to the Immediate window.

```
Sub ArrayRandom()

  Dim aRandom(1 To 5) As Double
  Dim i As Long

  For i = 1 To 5
    aRandom(i) = Rnd
  Next i

  For i = 1 To 5
    aRandom(i) = aRandom(i) * 10
  Next i

  For i = 1 To 5
    Debug.Print aRandom(i)
  Next i

End Sub
```

Because array indexes increase by one, `For...Next` loops are a common way to access all the elements in an array.

The arrays we've looked at so far are known as one-dimensional arrays. One-dimensional arrays are like lists — they have many rows, but only one column. You can also have two-dimensional arrays. Two-dimensional arrays are like tables — they have many rows and columns. Declare a two-dimensional array using a comma to separate the bounds of the first dimension from the bounds of the second dimension.

```
Dim aContact(1 to 10, 1 to 3) As String
```

The `aContact` array has 30 places to store data. This array might be used to store three pieces of data for ten contacts. Reading and writing to a two-dimensional array requires that you specify the index for both dimensions.

```
Sub TwoDArray()

  Dim aPotus(1 To 2, 1 To 3)
```

```
  Dim i As Long

  aPotus(1, 1) = "George"
  aPotus(1, 2) = "Washington"
  aPotus(1, 3) = "1789-1797"
  aPotus(2, 1) = "John"
  aPotus(2, 2) = "Adams"
  aPotus(2, 3) = "1797-1801"

  For i = 1 To 2
    Debug.Print aPotus(i, 1) & Space(1) & aPotus(i, 2) & Space(1) & _
      "was President in the years" & Space(1) & aPotus(i, 3)
  Next i

End Sub
```

NOTE

You can specify dimensions beyond two, but those arrays can get very difficult to manage. If you need to store that much data, consider a user-defined type or a custom class module.

Dynamic arrays

Dynamic arrays are declared without any indices and can be resized later in the procedure. Other than the lack of index numbers, they're declared in the same way as fixed arrays.

```
Dim aProductIDs() as Long
```

With a dynamic array declaration, no memory is allocated until the array is initialized by providing dimensions. You can't assign values to this array until it's initialized. To initialize a dynamic array, use the `ReDim` keyword.

```
ReDim aProductIDs(1 to 100)
```


Note that the data type is not included in the `ReDim` statement. The data type is set when the array is declared and cannot be changed. Use a dynamic array when you don't know the size of array you'll need until run time. In this example, all the open forms' names in a database are put into an array. Since you can't know which forms will be open, declare a dynamic and resize it when the procedure executes.

```
Sub FormArray()

  Dim aForms() As String
  Dim frm As Form
  Dim lFrmCnt As Long
  Dim i As Long

  ReDim aForms(1 To Application.Forms.Count)

  For Each frm In Application.Forms
```

```
    lFrmCnt = lFrmCnt + 1
    aForms(lFrmCnt) = frm.Name
  Next frm

  For i = LBound(aForms) To UBound(aForms)
    Debug.Print aForms(i) & " is open."
  Next i

End Sub
```

The `Forms.Count` property is used to size the dynamic array. Then a `For...Each` loop puts each open form's name into a different index in the array. Finally, the procedure loops through the array and prints each form's name to the Immediate window.

If you know the size of the array at design time, it's best to create a fixed array. If you must use a dynamic array, you'll get the best performance by determining the array size you need and issuing a `ReDim` statement to resize the array. There are times, however, where you don't know how many elements you'll need until you start filling the array. VBA provides the `Preserve` keyword to resize a dynamic array without losing any of the data that's already in the array. Using `ReDim` without `Preserve` resizes the array, as you've seen, but the array is re-initialized and any existing data is lost.

```
ReDim Preserve aCustomerIDs(1 to x) As Long
```

The `Preserve` keyword makes a new array of the new size and then copies all the data from the old array to the new one. Even for moderately sized arrays, this can be a performance killer. Only use Preserve when there is no other option.

Array functions

VBA provides several useful functions to use with arrays. We don't have room to cover all of them, but we'll cover the most used and most interesting.

Boundary functions

VBA provides two functions, `LBound` and `UBound`, to determine the size of an array. `LBound` returns the lower bound, and `UBound` returns the upper bound. These functions are most useful when used to loop through all the elements of an array.

```
For i = LBound(aContacts) To UBound(aContacts)
  Debug.Print aContacts(i)
Next i
```

If `aContacts` is declared as `Dim aContacts(1 to 5) As String`, the `LBound` will return `1` and `UBound` will return `5`. The real benefit comes when you revise the code to `Dim aContacts(1 to 6) As String`. If you had hardcoded the boundaries in the `For...Next` loop, you would've needed to change the upper bound in two places. By using `LBound` and `UBound`, you only have to make the change in the `Dim` statement.

For two-dimensional arrays, LBound and UBound require a second argument for the dimension. The following example is a typical method for looping through all the elements of a two-dimensional array.

```
For i = LBound(aBounds, 1) To UBound(aBounds, 1)
  For j = LBound(aBounds, 2) To UBound(aBounds, 2)
    Debug.Print aBounds(i, j)
  Next j
Next i
```

The Array function

The Array function allows you to create an array by supplying all the values for the array in one statement. The array returned by the Array function is known as a *variant array* — a Variant data type holding an array. To return the results of the Array function to a variable, that variable must be declared as a Variant. The arguments of the Array function are separated by commas, with each argument becoming an element of the array.

```
Sub ArrayFunction()

  Dim vaRates As Variant
  Dim i As Long

  vaRates = Array(0.05, 0.055, 0.06, 0.065, 0.07)

  For i = LBound(vaRates) To UBound(vaRates)
    Debug.Print vaRates(i)
  Next i

End Sub
```

In the preceding example, the vaRates variable is a Variant containing an array with five elements (the five numbers from the Array function). Since the variable is a Variant, you don't specify the size of the array beforehand. The number of arguments in the Array function determines the size. Because of this, the lower and upper bounds are determined by VBA. The default lower bound is zero, and the default upper bound is one less than the number of arguments in the Array function. For vaRates in the above example, the bounds would be 0 to 4. The lower bound of an array returned by the Array function is determined by the Option Base directive, if one exists, at the top of the module.

NOTE

The Array function returns a variant array – a Variant containing an array. You can also declare an array of Variants. An array of Variants is a fixed or dynamic array whose data type is Variant. A variant array and an array of Variants are two different types of arrays.

The Split function

The `Split` function converts text into a Variant array. VBA can't know the size of the array the `Split` function will return, so the variable holding the array must be declared as a Variant. The `Split` syntax is as follows:

```
Split(string_expression, [delimiter],[limit],[compare])
```

The first argument is the string you want to split into an array. The delimiter argument tells the `Split` function on which characters to split the string. The limit argument determines how large the resulting array is. Once the array reaches the limit defined, `Split` stops splitting the string even if more delimiters are present.

```
Sub TheSplitFunction()

  Dim vaWords As Variant
  Dim i As Long

  vaWords = Split("Now is the time.", Space(1))

  For i = LBound(vaWords) To UBound(vaWords)
    Debug.Print vaWords(i)
  Next i

End Sub
```

The `vaWords` variable will be a variant array containing four elements: `Now`, `is`, `the`, and `time.` The delimiter — in this case, a single space — is not included in the elements. The period at the end *is* included, making the last element `time.` (with a period) rather than `time` (without a period).

The Join function

The `Join` function is the opposite of `Split`. `Join` takes an array and returns a string. The syntax for `Join` is:

```
Join(source_array, [delimiter])
```

The first argument is the one-dimensional array to be converted into a String. The source array can be any data type that VBA can convert into a String, even numbers and dates. The delimiter is the character or characters to be inserted between the elements of the array.

```
Sub TheJoinFunction()

  Dim sResult As String
  Dim aWords(1 To 5) As String

  aWords(1) = "The"
  aWords(2) = "quick"
```

```
    aWords(3) = "brown"
    aWords(4) = "fox"
    aWords(5) = "jumped"

    sResult = Join(aWords, Space(1))

    Debug.Print sResult

End Sub
```

The `sResult` variable will contain the String `The quick brown fox jumped`. Each element of the array is concatenated together with the delimiter inserted between them.

Understanding Subs and Functions

The code in a VBA application lives in containers called *modules*. As you learned in Chapter 23, modules exist behind the forms and reports in an Access application, as well as in stand-alone modules. The modules themselves contain many procedures, variable and constant declarations, and other directives to the VBA engine.

The code within the modules is composed of procedures. There are two main types of procedures in VBA: *subroutines* or *subprocedures* (often called *subs*) and *functions*.

The general rules for procedures include the following:

- **You must give the procedure a unique name within its *scope* (see "Understanding variable scope and lifetime," earlier in this chapter).** Although it isn't a good idea — because of the chance of confusing the VBA engine or another person working with your code — it is possible to have more than one procedure with the same name, as long as the name is unique within each procedure's scope.
- **The name you assign to a procedure can't be the same as a VBA keyword.**
- **A procedure and a module cannot have the same name.** This is one place where a naming convention can be very useful. If you always prefix module names with `bas` or `mod`, you don't run the risk of an error occurring from having a procedure and module with the same name.
- **A procedure can't contain other procedures within it.** A procedure can, however, call another procedure and execute the code in the other procedure at any time.

Because of the rules governing procedure scope, you can't have two public procedures both named `MyProcedure`, although you can have two private procedures, both named `MyProcedure`, or one public procedure named `MyProcedure` and one private procedure named `MyProcedure`, but not in the same module. The reason it's a bad idea to use the same procedure name for multiple procedures, even when the procedures have different scopes, should be obvious.

The following sections cover some of the specifics regarding VBA procedures. Planning and composing the procedures in your modules is the most time-consuming part of working with VBA, so it's important to understand how procedures fit into the overall scheme of application development.

Subroutines and functions both contain lines of code that you can run. When you run a subroutine or function, you *call* it. *Calling, running,* and *invoking* are all terms meaning *to execute* (or run) the statements (or lines of code) within the procedure or function. All these terms can be used interchangeably (and they will be, by different developers). No matter how you invoke a VBA procedure — using the `Call` keyword, referencing the procedure by its name, or running it from the Immediate window — they all do the same thing, which is to cause lines of code to be processed, run, executed, or whatever you want to call it.

The only real difference between a procedure and a function is that, when it's called, a function returns a value — in other words, it generates a value when it runs, and makes the value available to the code that called it. You can use a Boolean function to return a `True` or `False` value indicating, for example, where the operation the procedure performed was successful. You can see if a file exists, if a value was greater than another value, or anything you choose. Functions return dates, numbers, or strings; functions can even return complex data types such as recordsets.

A subprocedure does not return a value. However, although a function directly returns a value to a variable created as part of the function call, there are other ways for functions and subprocedures to exchange data with form controls or declared variables in memory.

Understanding where to create a procedure

You create procedures in one of two places:

- **In a standard VBA module:** You create a subprocedure or function in a standard module when the procedure will be shared by code in more than one form or report or by an object other than a form or report. For example, queries can use functions to handle very complex criteria.
- **Behind a form or report:** If the code you're creating will be called only by a single procedure or form, the subprocedure or function should be created in the form or report's module.

NOTE
A *module* is a container for multiple subprocedures and functions.

Calling VBA procedures

VBA procedures are called in a variety of ways and from a variety of places. They can be called from events behind forms and reports, or they can be placed in module objects and called simply by using their name or by using the `Call` statement. Here are some examples:

```
SomeSubRoutineName
Call SomeSubRoutineName
Somevalue = SomeFunctionName
```

Only functions return values that may be assigned to variables. Subprocedures are simply called, do their work, and end. Although functions return a single value, both subprocedures and functions can place values in tables, in form controls, or even in public variables available to any part of your program. You can see several examples of different ways to use subprocedures and functions throughout this chapter.

The syntax used for calling subprocedures with parameters changes depending on how you call the procedure. For example, when using the `Call` keyword to call a subprocedure that includes arguments, the arguments must be enclosed in parentheses:

```
Call SomeSubRoutineName(arg1, arg2)
```

However, when the same procedure is called without the `Call` keyword it requires no parentheses:

```
SomeSubRoutineName arg1, arg2
```

Also, using the `Call` keyword with a function tells Access your code is not capturing the function's return value:

```
Call SomeFunctionName
```

Or, when arguments are required:

```
Call SomeFunctionName(arg1, arg2)
```

In this case, the function is treated as if it is a subroutine.

24

TIP

The `Call` keyword has been in the BASIC programming language since the beginning. There's no advantage to using `Call`, and most developers have stopped using it altogether.

Creating subs

Conceptually, subroutines are easy to understand. A *subroutine* (usually called a *sub* and sometimes called a *subprocedure*) is a set of programming statements that is executed as a unit by the VBA engine. VBA procedures can become complex, so this elementary description of subroutines is quickly overwhelmed by the actual subroutines you'll compose in your Access applications.

Figure 24.6 shows a typical subroutine. Notice the `Sub` keyword that begins the routine, followed by the name of the subroutine. The declaration of this particular subroutine includes the `Private` keyword, which restricts the availability of this subroutine to the module containing the subroutine.

FIGURE 24.6

A typical subroutine in an Access application.

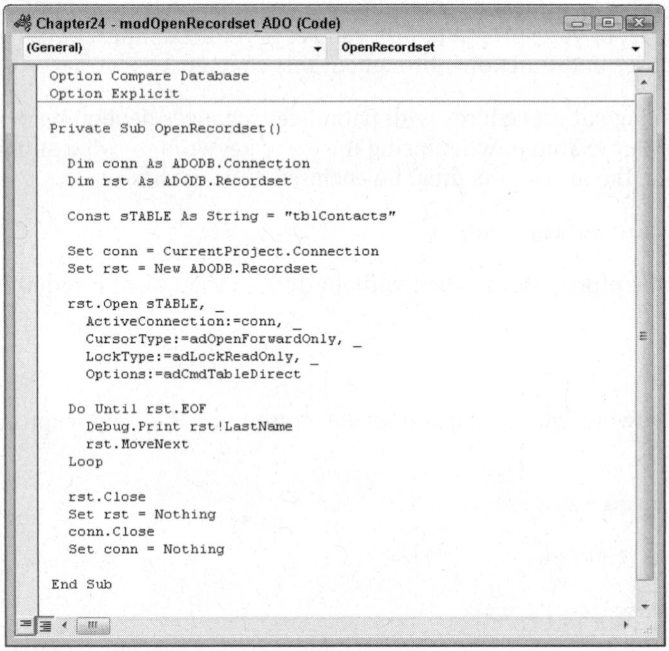

Chapter24 - modOpenRecordset_ADO (Code)

(General) | OpenRecordset

```
Option Compare Database
Option Explicit

Private Sub OpenRecordset()

  Dim conn As ADODB.Connection
  Dim rst As ADODB.Recordset

  Const sTABLE As String = "tblContacts"

  Set conn = CurrentProject.Connection
  Set rst = New ADODB.Recordset

  rst.Open sTABLE, _
    ActiveConnection:=conn, _
    CursorType:=adOpenForwardOnly, _
    LockType:=adLockReadOnly, _
    Options:=adCmdTableDirect

  Do Until rst.EOF
    Debug.Print rst!LastName
    rst.MoveNext
  Loop

  rst.Close
  Set rst = Nothing
  conn.Close
  Set conn = Nothing

End Sub
```

The subroutine you see in Figure 24.6 contains most of the components you'll see in almost every VBA sub or function:

- **Declaration:** All procedures must be *declared* so that VBA knows where to find them. The name assigned to the procedure must be unique within the VBA project. The `Sub` keyword identifies this procedure as a subroutine.
- **Terminator:** All procedures must be terminated with the `End` keyword followed by the type of procedure that is ending. In Figure 24.6, the terminator is `End Sub`. Functions are terminated with `End Function`.
- **Declarations area:** Although variables and constants can be declared anywhere in the body of the procedure (as long as it's before they're used), good programming conventions require variables and constants to be declared near the top of the procedure where they'll be easy to find.

- **Statements:** A VBA procedure can contain many statements. Usually, however, you'll want to keep your VBA procedures small to make debugging as painless as possible. Very large subroutines can be difficult to work with, and you'll avoid problems if you keep them small. Instead of adding too many features and operations in a single procedure, place operations in separate procedures, and call those procedures when those operations are needed.

At the conclusion of a subroutine, program flow returns to the code or action that originally called the sub. The subroutine shown in Figure 24.6 may be called from a form's `Load` event, so control is returned to that event.

As an example of a useful VBA subroutine, the next several paragraphs describe building an event procedure for a control on an Access form. This procedure retrieves a value from one of the `cboCustomerID` combo box columns and uses it to find a record. The `RowSource` of the `cboCustomerID` combo box is a SQL statement that returns the CustomerID and the Company fields. The SQL statement is shown below.

```
SELECT DISTINCT tblCustomers.CustomerID, tblCustomers.Company FROM tblCustomers
   INNER JOIN tblSales ON tblCustomers.CustomerID = tblSales.CustomerID ORDER BY
   tblCustomers.Company;
```

The `tblCustomers` table is inner-joined with the `tblSales` table so only those customers with an invoice are displayed in the combo box. The `DISTINCT` keyword is used so that each customer is only returned once.

Chapter 14 covers SQL syntax in detail.

The objective of this exercise is to learn about procedures, but it also serves to teach you some additional VBA commands. The code is added to the form as `cboCustomerID_AfterUpdate` event.

To create an event procedure in a form, follow these steps:

1. **Select the cboCustomerID control in frmSales Design view.**
2. **Press F4 to display the Property window for the control.**
3. **Click in the After Update event property in the Event tab of the Property Sheet and select [Event Procedure] from the event's drop-down list.**
4. **Press the builder button (...) to open the VBA code editor.**
5. **Enter the following code into the cboCustomerID_AfterUpdate event procedure, as shown in Figure 24.7. The following code goes between Private Sub cboCustomerID_AfterUpdate() and End Sub in the VBA code editor.**

```
Me.txtCustomerID.SetFocus

If Not IsNull(Me.cboCustomerID.Value) Then
    DoCmd.FindRecord Me.cboCustomerID.Value
```

```
        End If

        Me.txtInvoiceDate.SetFocus
```

6. **Select Compile Chapter24 from the Debug menu in the code editor to check your syntax.**
7. **Close the VBA window and return to the frmSales form.**

The code first moves the focus to the txtCustomerID text box to make that field the current field. The `Me.` refers to the current form and substitutes in this example for `Forms!frmSales!`.

The first `If` statement checks to make sure a Customer ID was selected by making sure the current value of the combo box's bound column — `CustomerID` — is not null.

The heart of the procedure is the `FindRecord` method of the `DoCmd` object. `FindRecord` searches through the recordset and returns a record that matches the arguments. There are several arguments to `FindRecord`, but we supply only the first, `FindWhat`. The `FindWhat` argument is what `FindRecord` searches for through the records. In this case, it's searching for `Me.cboCustomerID.Value`. The other arguments to `FindRecord` are optional, and we have accepted the defaults. By setting the focus to `Me.txtCustomerID`, we made that field the current field. By default, `FindRecord` only searches in the current field, and setting the current field before calling `FindRecord` achieves our aims.

The final line of code sets the focus to the `txtInvoiceDate` text box. When the user locates a record, it's a good practice to set the focus to a good starting point for navigating through the record. While not required, it provides a good user experience.

Figure 24.7 shows the procedure created in the code editor after entering the procedure described earlier. After you finish entering these statements, press the Save button on the toolbar to save your code before closing the VBA window.

FIGURE 24.7

The `frmSales cboCustomerID_AfterUpdate` event procedure in the VBA code window.

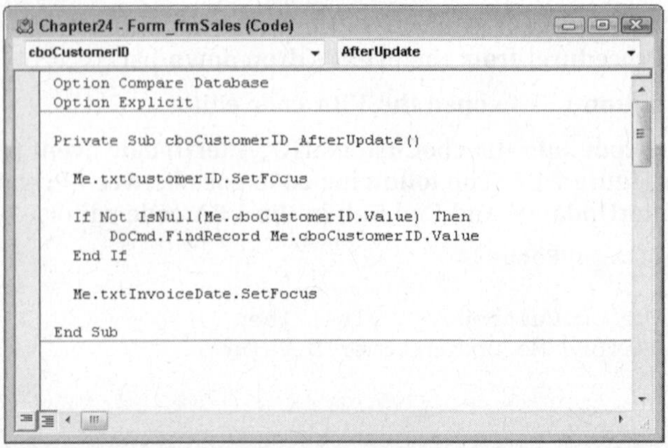

Chapter24 - Form_frmSales (Code)

cboCustomerID | AfterUpdate

```
Option Compare Database
Option Explicit

Private Sub cboCustomerID_AfterUpdate()

  Me.txtCustomerID.SetFocus

  If Not IsNull(Me.cboCustomerID.Value) Then
      DoCmd.FindRecord Me.cboCustomerID.Value
  End If

  Me.txtInvoiceDate.SetFocus

End Sub
```

The procedure behind this form runs each time the user selects a different customer in cboCustomerID. This code shows the first invoice for that customer.

Creating Functions

Functions differ from subprocedures in that functions return a value. In the examples in this section, you'll see functions that calculate the extended price (quantity × price) for a line item, create a function to calculate the total of all the taxable line items, and then apply the current tax rate to the total.

Although functions can be created behind individual forms or reports, usually they're created in standard modules. This first function will be created in a new module that you'll name modSalesFunctions. Putting this function in a standard module makes it available to all parts of the applications. To do this, follow these steps:

1. **Select the Modules tab in the Navigation pane.**
2. **Right-click the modSalesFunctions module and select Design view from the context menu.** The VBA window is displayed with the title modSalesFunctions (Code) in the title bar.
3. **Move to the bottom of the module, and enter the following code:**

```
Public Function CalcExtendedPrice( _
    lQuantity As Long, _
    cPrice As Currency, _
    dDiscount As Double _
    ) As Currency

    Dim cExtendedPrice As Currency

    cExtendedPrice = lQuantity * cPrice

    CalcExtendedPrice = cExtendedPrice * (1 - dDiscount)

End Function
```

The first statement declares the variable cExtendedPrice as the Currency data type. cExtendedPrice is used in an intermediate step in the function. The next line of code performs a calculation assigning the product of two variables, lQuantity and cPrice, to the cExtendedPrice variable. You might notice that the lQuantity and cPrice variables are not declared within the function; these variables are explained in the next section, "Handling parameters."

Finally, the last line of code performs one more calculation to apply any discount to cExtendedPrice. The function's name is treated as if it were a variable and is assigned the value of the calculation. This is how a function gets the value that it returns to the calling program.

Handling parameters

Now, the question you should be asking is: Where did the lQuantity, cPrice, and dDiscount variables come from? The answer is simple. They're the parameters passed from another procedure, as you may have already guessed.

Parameters (often called *arguments*) passed to a procedure are treated like any other variable by the procedure. Parameters have a name and a data type and are used as a way to send information to a procedure. Parameters are often used to get information back from a procedure, as well.

The following table shows the names and data types of the arguments used in the CalcExtendedPrice function.

Parameter Name	Data Type
lQuantity	Long
cPrice	Currency
dDiscount	Double

These parameter names can be anything you want them to be. Think of them as variables you would normally declare. All that's missing is the Dim statement. They don't have to be the same name as the variables used in the call to the function. Very often, you'll pass the names of fields in a table or controls on a form or variables created in the calling procedure as parameters to a procedure.

The completed CalcExtendedPrice function is shown in Figure 24.8. Notice how this function's parameters are defined in the function's declaration statement. The parameters are separated by continuation characters (a space followed by an underscore) to make the code easier to read.

FIGURE 24.8

The completed CalcExtendedPrice function.

Chapter24 - modSalesFunctions (Code)

(General) CalcExtendedPrice

```
Public Function CalcExtendedPrice( _
    lQuantity As Long, _
    cPrice As Currency, _
    dDiscount As Double _
    ) As Currency

    Dim cExtendedPrice As Currency

    cExtendedPrice = lQuantity * cPrice

    CalcExtendedPrice = cExtendedPrice * (1 - dDiscount)

End Function
```

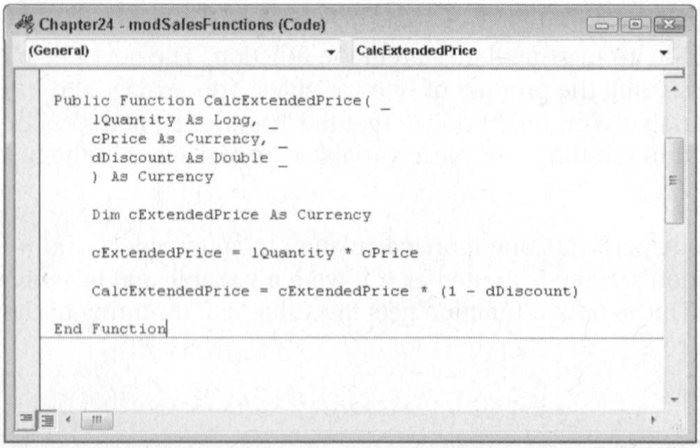

Calling a function and passing parameters

Now that you've completed the function, it's time to test it.

Normally, a function call comes from a form or report event or from another procedure, and the call passes information as parameters. The parameters passed to a procedure are often variables or data taken from a form's controls. You can test this function by going to the Immediate window and using hand-entered values as the parameters.

Follow these steps to test the function:

1. **Press Ctrl + G to display the Immediate window.**
2. **Enter** ? CalcExtendedPrice(5, 3.50, .05)**.** This statement passes the values as 5, 3.50, and .05 (5 percent) to the `lQuantity`, `dPrice`, and `dDiscount` parameters, respectively. `CalcExtendedPrice` returns `16.625` using those values, as shown in Figure 24.9.

FIGURE 24.9

Testing the `CalcExtendedPrice` function in the Immediate window.

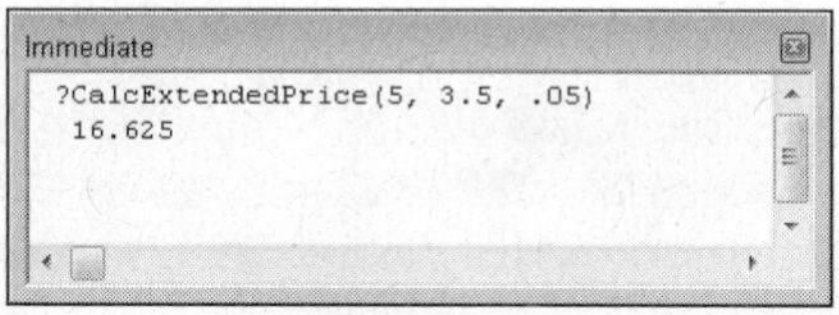

```
Immediate
?CalcExtendedPrice(5, 3.5, .05)
 16.625
```

3. **Close the Immediate window and the VBA window and return to the Database window.**

The next task is to use the function to calculate the extended price (price multiplied by quantity) of each item included in a sales invoice. You can add a call to the function from the Amount box on `fsubSalesLineItems`. This is a subform embedded on `frmSales`. Follow these steps:

1. **Display the frmSales form in Design view.**
2. **Click into the fsubSalesLineitems subform.**
3. **Click into the txtAmount control in the subform.**
4. **Display the Property window and enter the following into the Control Source property, as shown in Figure 24.10:** =CalcExtendedPrice (Nz(txtQuantity,0),Nz (txtPrice,0),Nz(txtDiscountPercent,0)). This expression passes the values from three controls — `txtQuantity`, `txtPrice`, and `txtDiscountPercent` — in the subform to the `CalcExtendedPrice` function in the module and returns the value back to the control source of the `txtAmount` control each time the line is recalculated or any of the parameters change. The references to `txtQuantity`, `txtPrice`, and `txtDiscountPercent` are enclosed in calls to the `Nz` function, which converts null values to zero. This is one way to avoid `Invalid use of null` errors that would otherwise occur.

FIGURE 24.10

Adding a function call to the Control Source of a control.

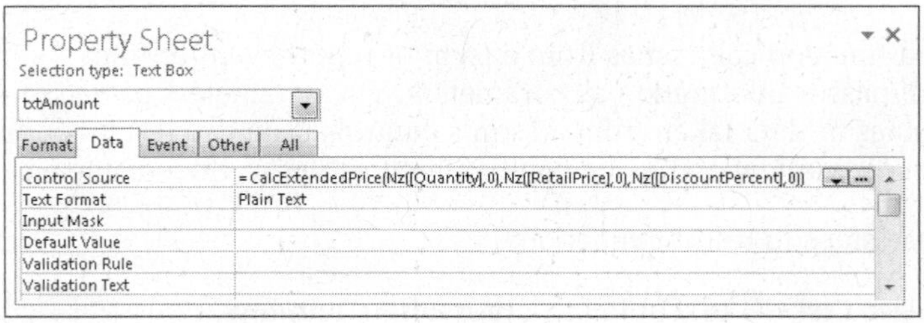

Property Sheet	
Selection type: Text Box	
txtAmount	
Format, Data, Event, Other, All	
Control Source	=CalcExtendedPrice(Nz([Quantity],0),Nz([RetailPrice],0),Nz([DiscountPercent],0))
Text Format	Plain Text
Input Mask	
Default Value	
Validation Rule	
Validation Text	

The sales form (`frmSales`) enforces a business rule that the extended price is recalculated any time the user changes the quantity, price, or discount on the sales form.

In Figure 24.10, notice that the `Control Source` property for `txtAmount` simply calls the `CalcExtendedPrice` function. The call does not specify the module that contains the function. Because `CalcExtendedPrice` was declared with the `Public` keyword, Access easily finds it and passes the required arguments to it.

TIP

The `CalcExtendedPrice` example illustrates an important aspect of Access development: Add a public function in a single location anywhere in the application's code and use the function anywhere it's needed. The ability to reuse a procedure in multiple places reduces maintenance. Changing the single instance of the function is reflected everywhere the public procedure is used.

Creating a function to calculate sales tax

In the Collectible Mini Cars application, whenever you add a line item to a sales invoice, you specify whether the item is taxable. The sales form adds up the extended prices for all the taxable line items to determine the sales tax for the sale. This total can then be multiplied by the tax rate to determine the tax.

The Collectable Mini Cars sales form (`frmSales`) includes a Text Box control for the tax amount. You can simply create an expression for the control's value such as:

```
=fSubSalesLineitems.Form!txtTaxableTotal * txtTaxRate
```

This expression references `txtTaxableTotal` in the subform (`fSubSalesLineitems`) and multiplies it by the tax rate (`txtTaxRate`) from the main form (`frmSales`).

However, although this expression displays the tax amount, the expression entered into the `txtTaxAmount` control would make the `txtTaxAmount` control read-only because it contains an expression. You wouldn't be able to override the calculated amount if you wanted to. The tax applied to a sale is one of the fields that needs to be changed once in a while for specific business purposes.

Better than using a hard-coded expression is creating a function to calculate a value and then place the value of the calculation in the control. This way, you can simply type over the calculated value if needed.

You can enter the following lines of code to the `AfterUpdate` events behind the `txtQuantity`, `txtPrice`, `txtDiscountPercent`, and `chkTaxable` controls. This way, each time one of those controls' values is changed, the tax is recalculated after the contact's tax rate is retrieved on the `frmSales` form.

```
txtTaxAmount = _
  fSubSalesLineitems.Form!txtTaxableTotal * txtTaxRate
```

Actually, better would be to place this statement in the `AfterUpdate` event of `fsub SalesLineitems`. This way, the tax is recalculated each time a value is updated in any record of this form. Because `fsubSalesLineitems` is displayed as a datasheet, the `AfterUpdate` event fires as soon as the user moves to another line in `fsubSales Lineitems`.

Although you can use a simple expression that references controls on forms and subforms, this technique works only behind the form containing the code. Suppose you also need to calculate tax in other forms or in reports. There's a better way than relying on a form.

This is an old developer's expression: "Forms and reports lie; tables never lie." This means that the controls of a form or report often contain expressions, formats, and VBA code that may make a value seem to be one thing when the table actually contains a completely different value. The table containing the data is where the real values are stored, and it's where calculations and reports should retrieve data from.

You can easily use VBA code to extract data from a table, use the data in a complex calculation, and return the result to a control on a form, on a report, or to another section of code.

Figure 24.11 shows the completed `CalcTax` function.

The function is called from the `AfterUpdate` event behind the `frmSalesLineitems` subform. The `CalcTax` function calculates the sum of the taxable line items from the `tblSalesItems` table. The `SQLstatement` is combined with a bit of ADO code to determine the total. The calculated total amount is then multiplied by the `dTaxPercent` parameter to calculate the tax. The tax is set to the `cReturn` variable, which is set to `CalcTax` (the name of the expression) at the end of the function.

FIGURE 24.11

The `CalcTax` function.

Chapter24 - modSalesFunctions (Code)

(General) CalcTax

```
Public Function CalcTax( _
  dTaxPercent As Double, _
  lInvoiceNum As Long) As Currency

  Dim rs As New ADODB.Recordset
  Dim sSql As String
  Dim cReturn As Currency

  Const sFLDNAME As String = "TaxableAmount"

  sSql = "SELECT" _
    & " Sum(CalcExtendedPrice(Nz([Quantity],0)," _
    & " Nz([RetailPrice],0), Nz([DiscountPercent],0)))" _
    & " AS " & sFLDNAME _
    & " FROM tblSalesLineItems" _
    & " WHERE [InvoiceNumber] = " & lInvoiceNum

  rs.Open sSql, CurrentProject.Connection, _
    adOpenForwardOnly, adLockReadOnly

  If Not rs.EOF Then
    cReturn = rs.Fields(sFLDNAME).Value * dTaxPercent
  Else
    cReturn = 0
  End If

  rs.Close
  Set rs = Nothing

  CalcTax = cReturn

End Function
```

An important feature of this example code is that it combines data extracted from a database table (`Quantity`, `RetailPrice`, `DiscountPercent`) with data passed as parameters (`dTaxPercent`, `lInvoiceNum`). All the extraction and calculations are automatically performed by the code, and the user is never aware of how the tax amount is determined.

TIP

Functions and subprocedures are important to the concept of reusable code within an application. You should try to use functions and subprocedures and pass them parameters whenever possible. A good rule is this: The first time you find yourself copying a group of code, it's time to create a procedure or function.

Simplifying Code with Named Arguments

Another significant feature of Access VBA is the use of named arguments for procedures. Without named arguments, the arguments passed to procedures must appear in the correct left-to-right order. With named arguments, you provide the name of each parameter passed to a subroutine or function, and the subroutine or function uses the argument based on its *name* rather than on its *position* in the argument list.

Also, because every parameter passed to a procedure is explicitly named, you can omit an unused parameter without causing an error. Named arguments are a great way to clean up your code while making it much easier to read and understand.

Assume your application includes the function shown here:

```
Function PrepareOutput(sStr1 As String, sStr2 As String, _
    sStr3 As String) As String

  PrepareOutput = sStr1 & Space(1) & sStr2 & Space(2) & sStr3

End Function
```

This function, of course, does nothing more than concatenate `sStr1`, `sStr2`, and `sStr3` and return it to the calling routine. The next example shows how this function may be called from another procedure:

```
Private Sub cmdForward_Click()

  Me.txtOutput.Value = PrepareOutput( _
    Me.txtFirstName.Value, _
    Me.txtLastName.Value, _
    Me.txtHireDate.Value)

End Sub
```

The arguments required by `PrepareOutput()` must be passed in the same order they're listed in the procedure declaration. The results of this function are shown in Figure 24.12. The text in the Function Output text box on this form shows the arguments in the order in which they appear in the text boxes on the left side of this form.

FIGURE 24.12

`frmNamedArguments` demonstrates the value of using named arguments in VBA procedures.

Each argument can be specified by its name as you pass it to functions. Naming arguments makes them position independent.

Examine the code in the following listing to see how named arguments work:

```
Private Sub cmdBackward_Click()

  Me.txtOutput.Value = PrepareOutput( _
    sStr2:=Me.txtLastName.Value, _
    sStr3:=Me.txtFirstName.Value, _
    sStr1:=Me.txtHireDate.Value)

End Sub
```

The thing to notice in `cmdBackward_Click` is that the arguments are not passed to `PrepareOutput()` in the order specified by the procedure's argument list. As long as the name used for an argument matches an argument in the `PrepareOutputs` argument list, Access VBA correctly uses the arguments in `PrepareOutput()`.

ON THE WEB

The `Chapter24.accdb` example database includes the `frmNamedArguments` you see in Figure 24.12 and Figure 24.13. The two buttons below the Function Output text box pass the text from the First Name, Last Name, and Hire Date text boxes to the `PrepareOutput()` function using positional and named arguments.

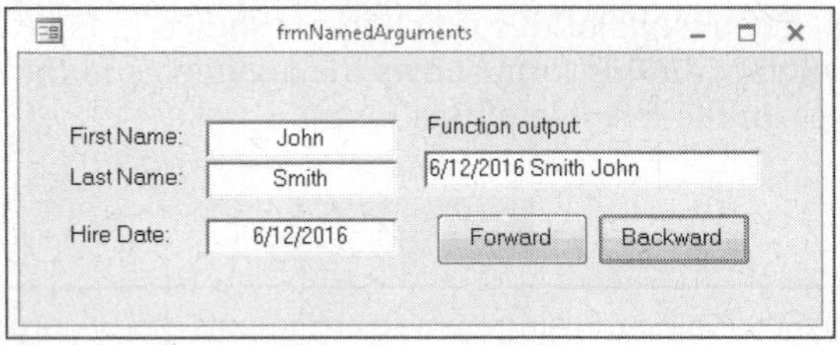

FIGURE 24.13

`PrepareOutput()` is able to use arguments submitted in any order as long as they're named.

CHAPTER

25

Understanding the Access Event Model

IN THIS CHAPTER

Mastering Access event programming

Reviewing common events

Understanding event sequences

When working with a database system, the same tasks may be performed repeatedly. Instead of doing the same steps each time, you can automate the process with VBA or macros.

Database management systems continually grow as you add records in a form, build new queries, and create new reports. As the system grows, many of the database objects are saved for later use — for a weekly report or monthly update query, for example. You tend to create and perform many tasks repetitively. Every time you add contact records, you open the same form. Likewise, you print the same form letter for contacts that have purchased a vehicle in the past month.

You can add VBA code throughout your application to automate these tasks. The VBA language offers a full array of powerful commands for manipulating records in a table, controls on a form, or just about anything else. This chapter continues the previous chapters' discussions of working with procedures in forms, reports, and standard modules.

On the Web

In this chapter, you'll use the database file `Chapter25.accdb`. Download this database file from the book's website if you want to follow along with the examples presented in this chapter.

This chapter focuses on the Access event model, a vitally important aspect of Access development. As you'll see in this chapter, Access provides a wide variety of events to trigger your code in response to user actions.

Programming Events

An Access event is the result or consequence of some user action. An Access event occurs when a user moves from one record to another in a form, closes a report, or clicks a command button on a form. Even moving the mouse generates a continuous stream of events.

Access applications are event driven, and Access objects respond to many types of events. Access events are hooked into specific object properties. For example, checking or unchecking a check box triggers a `MouseDown`, a `MouseUp`, and a `Click` event. These events are hooked into the check box through the `OnMouseDown`, `OnMouseUp`, and `OnClick` properties, respectively. You use VBA to compose event procedures that run whenever the user clicks the check box.

Access events can be categorized into seven groups:

- **Windows (form, report) events:** Opening, closing, and resizing
- **Keyboard events:** Pressing or releasing a key
- **Mouse events:** Clicking or pressing a mouse button
- **Focus events:** Activating, entering, and exiting
- **Data events:** Changing the current row, deleting, inserting, or updating
- **Print events:** Formatting and printing
- **Error and timing events:** Happening after an error has occurred or some time has passed

In all, Access supports more than 50 different events that can be harnessed through VBA event procedures.

Of these types of events, by far the most common are the keyboard and mouse events on forms. As you'll see in the following sections, forms and most controls recognize keyboard and mouse events. In fact, exactly the same keyboard and mouse events are recognized by forms and controls. The code you write for a mouse-click event on a command button is exactly the same sort of code that you might write for the mouse-click on a form.

In addition, most Access object types have their own unique events. The following sections discuss the most commonly programmed events, but Microsoft has a habit of introducing new event capabilities with each new version of Access. Also, many ActiveX controls you might use in your Access applications may have their own unique and special events. When using an unfamiliar control or a new type of object in your Access applications, be sure to check out what events and properties are supported by the control or object.

Understanding how events trigger VBA code

You can create an event procedure that runs when a user performs any one of the many different events that Access recognizes. Access responds to events through special form and control properties. Reports have a similar set of events, tailored to the special needs and requirements of reports.

Figure 25.1 shows the Property Sheet for frmProducts. This form has many event properties. Each form section (page header, form header, detail, page footer, form footer) and every control on the form (labels, text boxes, check boxes, and option buttons, for example) has its own set of events.

FIGURE 25.1

The Property Sheet for frmProducts with the Events tab open.

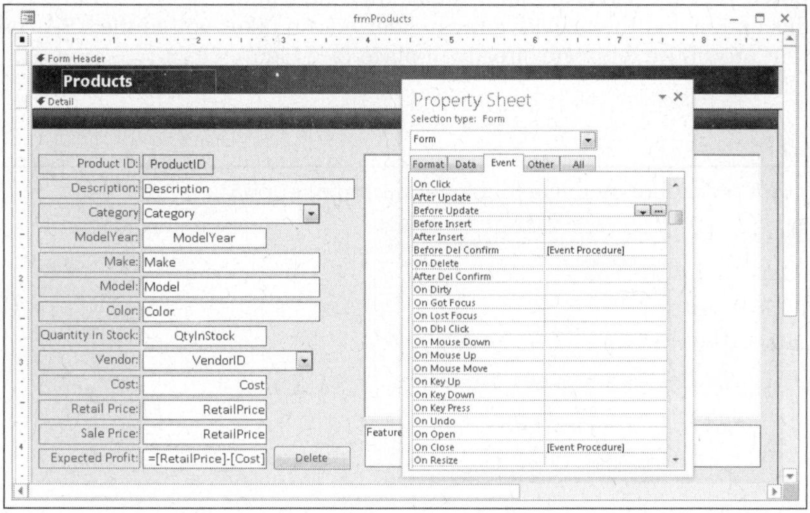

In Figure 25.1, notice that the Property Sheet is open on the Event tab. Access forms include more than 50 events, and each form section includes a number of events, as well as each control on the form. As you select a form section or a control on the form, the Event tab in the Property Sheet changes to show you the events for that object.

In Figure 25.1, all the events with existing event procedures contain `[Event Procedure]`, which indicates that the property has associated VBA code that executes whenever this event is triggered. The events may also contain `[Embedded Macro]`, the name of a non-embedded macro, or the name of a function.

Creating event procedures

In Access, you execute event procedures through an object's event properties.

Access provides event properties you use to tie VBA code to an object's events. For example, the On Open property is associated with a form or report opening on the screen.

> **NOTE**
> Access event procedures, as seen in the Property Sheet, often contain spaces. For instance, the `Open` event appears as the `On Open` event procedure. The event itself, of course, is `Open`. Many, but not all, event property names begin with On.

You add an event procedure to a form or report by selecting the event property (Before Update, for this example) in the object's Property Sheet. If no event procedure currently exists for the property, a drop-down arrow and builder button appear in the property's box, as shown in the Before Update event property in Figure 25.1.

The drop-down list exposes a list that contains the single item `[Event Procedure]`. Selecting this option and then clicking the builder button takes you to the VBA code editor with an event procedure template already in place (see Figure 25.2).

FIGURE 25.2

An empty event procedure template for the form's `BeforeUpdate` event.

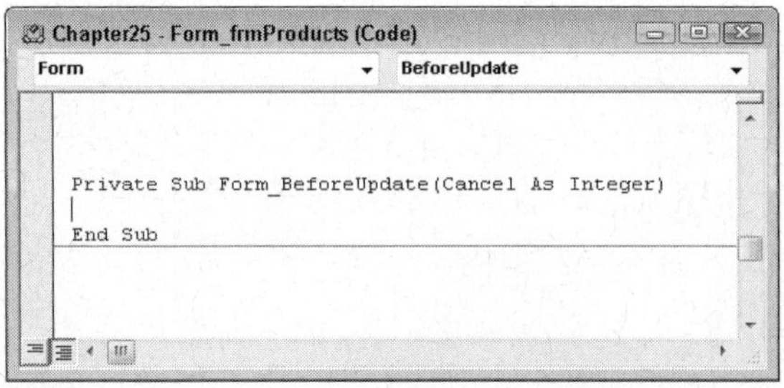

Notice the general format of the event procedure's declaration:

```
Private Sub Object_Event()
```

The *Object* portion of the procedure's name is, of course, the name of the object raising the event, while the *Event* portion is the specific event raised by the object. In Figure 25.2, the object is `Form` and the event is `BeforeUpdate`. Some events support arguments, which appear within the parentheses at the end of the declaration.

In case you're wondering, you can't change the name, or the arguments, of an event procedure and expect it to continue working. Access VBA relies on the `Object_Event` naming convention to tie a procedure to an object's event.

Identifying Common Events

Certain events are raised by many different Access objects. Microsoft has taken great care that these events behave exactly the same way, regardless of the object raising them. Table 25.1 lists several of the events most commonly used by Access developers. Most of these events apply to forms and all the different controls you might add to an Access form.

TABLE 25.1 Events Common to Multiple Object Types

Event	Event Type	When the Event Is Triggered
Click	Mouse event	When the user presses and releases (clicks) the left mouse button on an object
DblClick	Mouse event	When the user presses and releases (clicks) the left mouse button twice on an object
MouseDown	Mouse event	When the user presses the mouse button while the pointer is on an object
MouseMove	Mouse event	When the user moves the mouse pointer over an object
MouseUp	Mouse event	When the user releases a pressed mouse button while the pointer is on an object
MouseWheel	Mouse event	When the user spins the mouse wheel
KeyDown	Keyboard event	When the user presses any key on the keyboard when the object has focus or when the user uses a `SendKeys` macro action
KeyUp	Keyboard event	When the user releases a pressed key or immediately after the user uses a `SendKeys` macro action
KeyPress	Keyboard event	When the user presses and releases a key on an object that has the focus or when the user uses a `SendKeys` macro action

Not surprisingly, these events are all associated with the mouse and the keyboard because these are the user's primary means of inputting information and giving directions to an application. Not every object responds to every one of these events, but when an object responds to any of these events, the event exhibits exactly the same behavior.

TIP

Many developers simply copy and paste VBA code from one event procedure to the same event procedure on another object. For example, you might want to do some fancy formatting on a text box when the user clicks into the box. You can copy the code performing the fancy formatting into another control's `Click` event procedure to get the same effect without having to retype the code. Even though you'll have to fix up the pasted code with the second text box's name, it's much less work than retyping the entire procedure.

Access supports many, many different events. In fact, one of Access's fundamental strengths is the wide variety of events available to developers. You can control virtually every aspect of an Access application's behavior and data management through event procedures. Although Microsoft makes no formal distinction between types of events, the following sections categorize events and event procedures into groups based on the type of object (forms, reports, and so on) that raise the events within the group.

TIP

Access supports a very, very rich event model. Not many Access developers master every Access event, nor is there need to. Virtually every Access developer learns and uses the events that are important for the applications he's building and then learns other events as he goes. You don't need to worry about memorizing all these events – instead, just be aware that Access supports many different types of events and that they're there when you need them.

Form event procedures

When you work with forms, you can create event procedures based on events at the form level, the section level, or the control level. If you attach an event procedure to a form-level event, whenever the event occurs, the action takes effect against the form as a whole (such as when you move to another record or leave the form).

To have your form respond to an event, you write an event procedure and attach it to the event property in the form that recognizes the event. Many properties can be used to trigger event procedures at the form level.

NOTE

When we refer to *form events,* we're talking about events that happen to the form as a whole – not about an event that can be triggered by a specific control on a form. Form events execute when moving from one record to another or when a form is being opened or closed. We cover control events in the "Control event procedures" section, later in this chapter.

Essential form events

Access forms respond to many, many events. You'll never write code for most of these events because of their specialized nature. There are, however, some events that you'll program over and over again in your Access applications. Table 25.2 lists some of the most fundamental and important Access form events. Not coincidentally, these are also the most commonly programmed Access form events.

In Table 25.2, notice how many events are related to data (`Current`, `BeforeInsert`, and so on). Because Access forms are usually involved in working with data (adding new data, editing, and so on), Access forms include these events to provide you with a high level of control over data management.

TABLE 25.2 Essential Form Events

Event	When the Event Is Triggered
Open	When a form is opened, but the first record is not yet displayed.
Load	When a form is loaded into memory but not yet opened.
Resize	When the size of a form changes.
Unload	When a form is closed and the records unload, and before the form is removed from the screen.
Close	When a form is closed and removed from the screen.
Activate	When an open form receives the focus, becoming the active window.
Deactivate	When a different window becomes the active window, but before it loses focus.
GotFocus	When a form with no active or enabled controls receives the focus.
LostFocus	When a form loses the focus.
Timer	When a specified time interval passes. The interval (in milliseconds) is specified by the TimerInterval property.
BeforeScreenTip	When a screen tip is activated.

Form mouse and keyboard events

Access forms also respond to a number of mouse and keyboard events, as shown in Table 25.3.

TABLE 25.3 Form Mouse and Keyboard Events

Event	When the Event Is Triggered
Click	When the user presses and releases (clicks) the left mouse button
DblClick	When the user presses and releases (clicks) the left mouse button twice on a form
MouseDown	When the user presses the mouse button while the pointer is on a form
MouseMove	When the user moves the mouse pointer over an area of a form
MouseUp	When the user releases a pressed mouse button while the pointer is on a form
MouseWheel	When the user spins the mouse wheel
KeyDown	When the user presses any key on the keyboard when a form has focus or when the user uses a `SendKeys` macro action
KeyUp	When the user releases a pressed key or immediately after the user uses a `SendKeys` macro action
KeyPress	When the user presses and releases a key on a form that has the focus or when the user uses a `SendKeys` macro

In addition, the KeyPreview property is closely related to form keyboard events. This property (which is found only in forms) instructs Access to allow the form to see keyboard events before the controls on the form. By default, the controls on an Access form receive events before the form. For example, when you click a button on a form, the button — not the form — sees the click, even though the form supports a `Click` event. This means that a form's controls mask key events from the form, and the form can never respond to those events. You must set the KeyPreview property to Yes (true) before the form responds to any of the key events (`KeyDown`, `KeyUp`, and so on).

Form data events

The primary purpose of Access forms is to display data. Not surprisingly then, Access forms have a number of events that are directly related to a form's data management. You'll see these events programmed over and over again in this book, and you'll encounter event procedures written for these events virtually every time you work on an Access application. These events are summarized in Table 25.4.

TABLE 25.4 Form Data Events

Event	When the Event Is Triggered
Current	When you move to a different record and make it the current record
BeforeInsert	After data is first entered into a new record, but before the record is actually created
AfterInsert	After the new record is added to the table
BeforeUpdate	Before changed data is updated in a record
AfterUpdate	After changed data is updated in a record
Dirty	When a record is modified
Undo	When a user has returned a form to clean state (the record has been set back to an unmodified state); the opposite of OnDirty
Delete	When a record is deleted, but before the deletion takes place
BeforeDelConfirm	Just before Access displays the Delete Confirm dialog box
AfterDelConfirm	After the Delete Confirm dialog box closes and confirmation has happened
Error	When a runtime error is produced
Filter	When a filter has been specified, but before it is applied
ApplyFilter	After a filter is applied to a form

The `Current` event fires just after the data on a form is refreshed. Most often this occurs as the user moves the form to a different record in the recordset underlying the form. The `Current` event is often used to perform calculations based on the form's data or to format controls. For example, if a certain numeric or date value is outside an expected range, the `Current` event can be used to change the text box's BackColor property so the user notices the issue.

The BeforeInsert and AfterInsert events are related to transferring a new record from the form to an underlying data source. BeforeInsert fires as Access is about to transfer the data, and AfterInsert is triggered after the record is committed to the data source. For example, you could use these events to perform a logging operation that keeps track of additions to a table.

The BeforeUpdate and AfterUpdate events are frequently used to validate data before it's sent to the underlying data source. As you'll see later in this chapter, many form controls also support BeforeUpdate and AfterUpdate. A control's update is triggered as soon as the data in the control is changed.

TIP

A form's Update event fires much later than the BeforeInsert or AfterInsert events. The Update event occurs just as the form prepares to move to another record. Many developers use the form's BeforeUpdate event to scan all the controls on the form to ensure that all the data in the form's controls is valid. A form's BeforeUpdate event includes a Cancel parameter that, when set to True, causes the BeforeUpdate event to terminate. Canceling an update event is an effective way to protect the integrity of the data behind an Access application.

TIP

Users often want to be notified of pending updates before they move off a record to another record. By default, Access forms automatically update a form's underlying data source as the user moves to another record or closes the form. The Dirty event fires whenever the user changes any of the data on a form. You can use the Dirty event to set a module-level Boolean (true/false) variable (let's call it bDirty) so that other controls on the form (such as a close button) know that pending changes exist on the form. If bDirty is True when the close button is clicked or when the BeforeUpdate event fires, you can display an Are you sure? message box to confirm the user's intention to commit the changes to the database.

Control event procedures

Controls also raise events. Control events are often used to manipulate the control's appearance or to validate data as the user makes changes to the control's contents. Control events also influence how the mouse and keyboard behave while the user works with the control. A control's BeforeUpdate event fires as soon as focus leaves the control (more precisely, BeforeUpdate fires just before data is transferred from the control to the recordset underlying the form, enabling you to cancel the event if data validation fails), whereas a form's BeforeUpdate does not fire until you move the form to another record. (The form's BeforeUpdate commits the entire record to the form's data source.)

This means that a *control's* BeforeUpdate is good for validating a single control while the *form's* BeforeUpdate is good for validating multiple controls on the form. The form's BeforeUpdate would be a good place to validate that values in two different controls are in agreement with each other (such as a zip code in one text box and the city in another text box), instead of relying on the BeforeUpdate in each of the controls.

You create event procedures for control events in exactly the same way you create procedures for form events. You select `[Event Procedure]` in the Property Sheet for the event, and then add VBA code to the event procedure attached to the event. Table 25.5 shows each control event property, the event it recognizes, and how it works. As you review the information in Table 25.5, keep in mind that not every control supports every type of event.

TABLE 25.5 Control Events

Event	When the Event Is Triggered
BeforeUpdate	Before changed data in the control is updated to the underlying recordset
AfterUpdate	After changed data is transferred to the form's recordset
Dirty	When the contents of a control change
Undo	When the form is returned to a clean state
Change	When the contents of a text box change or a combo box's text changes
Updated	When an ActiveX object's data has been modified
NotInList	When a value that isn't in the list is entered into a combo box
Enter	Before a control receives the focus from another control
Exit	Just before the control loses focus to another control
GotFocus	When a nonactive or enabled control receives the focus
LostFocus	When a control loses the focus
Click	When the left mouse button is pressed and released (clicked) on a control
DblClick	When the left mouse button is pressed and released (clicked) twice on a control or label
MouseDown	When a mouse button is pressed while the pointer is on a control
MouseMove	When the mouse pointer is moved over a control
MouseUp	When a pressed mouse button is released while the pointer is on a control
KeyDown	When any key on the keyboard is pressed when a control has the focus or when a `SendKeys` macro action is used
KeyPress	When a key is pressed and released on a control that has the focus or when a `SendKeys` macro action is used
KeyUp	When a pressed key is released or immediately after a `SendKeys` macro is used

Report event procedures

Just as with forms, reports also use event procedures to respond to specific events. Access reports support events for the overall report itself and for each section in the report. Individual controls on Access reports do not raise events.

Attaching an event procedure to the report runs code whenever the report opens, closes, or prints. Each section in a report (header, footer, and so on) also includes events that run as the report is formatted or printed.

Several overall report event properties are available. Table 25.6 shows the Access report events. As you can see, the list of report events is much shorter than the form event list.

TABLE 25.6 Report Events

Event Property	When the Event Is Triggered
Open	When the report opens but before printing
Close	When the report closes and is removed from the screen
Activate	When the report receives the focus and becomes the active window
Deactivate	When a different window becomes active
NoData	When no data is passed to the report as it opens
Page	When the report changes pages
Error	When a runtime error is produced in Access

Even though users do not interact with reports as they do with forms, events still play a vital role in report design. Opening a report containing no data generally yields erroneous results. The report may display a title and no detail information. Or, it may display `#error` values for missing information. This situation can be a little scary for the user. Use the `NoData` event to inform the user that the report contains no data. `NoData` fires as a report opens and there is no data available in the report's RecordSource. Use the `NoData` event procedure to display a message box describing the situation to the user and then cancel the report's opening. Figure 25.3 shows a typical `NoData` event procedure.

FIGURE 25.3

Running a `NoData` event procedure when there is no data for a report.

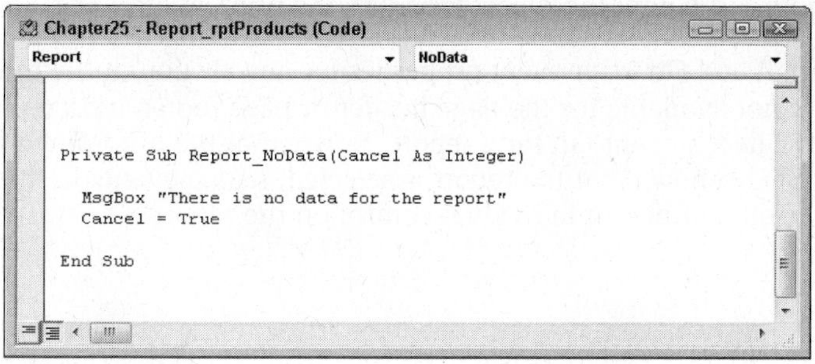

Chapter25 - Report_rptProducts (Code)

Report | NoData

```
Private Sub Report_NoData(Cancel As Integer)

  MsgBox "There is no data for the report"
  Cancel = True

End Sub
```

25

The Report_NoData event illustrated in Figure 25.3 first displays a message box to advise the user that the report contains no data. Then the event procedure cancels the report's opening by setting the Cancel parameter to True. Because the Cancel parameter is set to True, the report never appears on the screen and is not sent to the printer.

Many Access events are accompanied by parameters, such as the Cancel parameter you see in Figure 25.3. In this case, setting Cancel to True instructs Access to simply ignore the process that triggered the event. Because NoData was triggered as part of the report's opening process, setting Cancel to True prevents the report from being sent to the printer or being displayed on the screen. You'll see many examples of event property procedure parameters throughout this book.

Report section event procedures

In addition to the event properties for the form itself, Access offers three specialized event properties to use with report sections. Table 25.7 shows each property, the event it recognizes, and how it works.

TABLE 25.7 Report Section Events

Event	When the Event Is Triggered
Format	When the section is pre-formatted in memory before being sent to the printer. This is your opportunity to apply special formatting to controls within the section.
Print	As the section is sent to the printer. It is too late to format controls in a report section when the Print event fires.
Retreat	After the Format event but before the Print event. Occurs when Access has to back up past other sections on a page to perform multiple formatting passes. Retreat is included in all sections except headers and footers.

Use the Format event to apply special formatting to controls within a section before the section is printed. Format is useful, for example, to hide controls you don't want to print because of some condition in the report's data. The event procedure runs as Access lays out the section in memory but before the report is sent to the printer.

You can set the On Format and On Print event properties for any section of the report. However, OnRetreat is not available for the page header or page footer sections. Figure 25.4 shows the Property Sheet's event tab for a report. Notice that the drop-down list at the top of the Property Sheet shows that the report is selected, so the events in the Event tab relate to the report itself and not an individual control on the report.

FIGURE 25.4

Specifying an event procedure for a report's On No Data event.

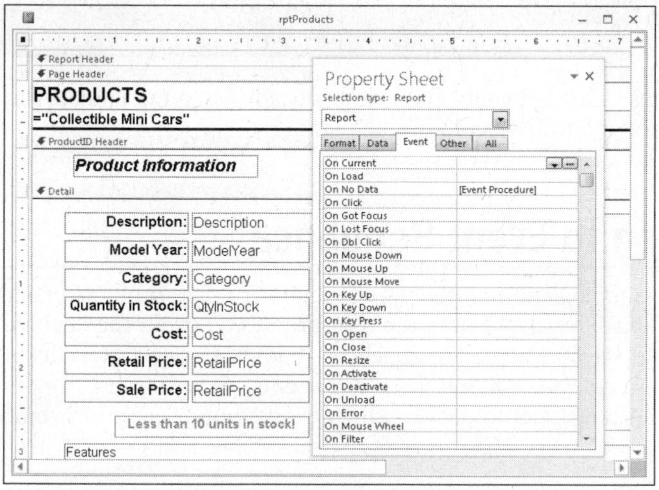

In addition to the NoData event, other report events are frequently programmed. Figure 25.5 shows how to add code to a report section's Format event to control the visibility of controls on the report.

FIGURE 25.5

Running an event procedure to display or hide a control on a report.

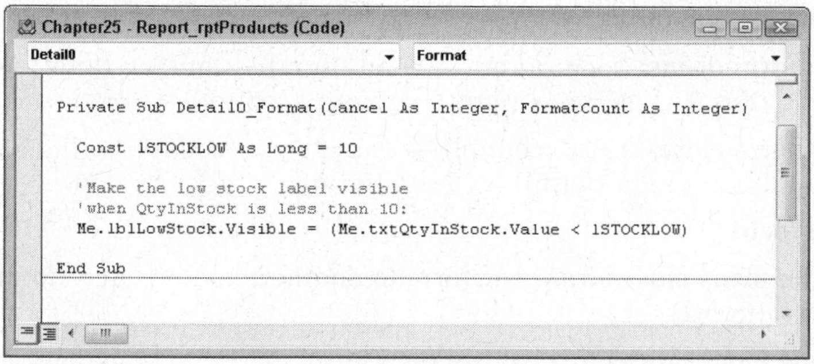

```
Private Sub Detail0_Format(Cancel As Integer, FormatCount As Integer)

  Const lSTOCKLOW As Long = 10

  'Make the low stock label visible
  'when QtyInStock is less than 10:
  Me.lblLowStock.Visible = (Me.txtQtyInStock.Value < lSTOCKLOW)

End Sub
```

The Detail0_Format event procedure illustrated in Figure 25.5 first checks the value of the txtQtyInStock control. If the value of txtQtyInStock is less than 10, lblLowStock is displayed; otherwise, the warning control is hidden.

TIP
Access names the sections of reports by appending a digit to the type of section, such as Detail0. You can rename these sections by changing the Name property of the section.

You'll see many examples of using events and event procedures to manipulate forms, reports, and controls throughout this book.

Paying Attention to Event Sequence

Sometimes even a fairly simple action on the part of the user raises multiple events in rapid succession. As an example, every time the user presses a key on the keyboard, the `KeyDown`, `KeyPress`, and `KeyUp` events are raised, in that order. Similarly, clicking the left mouse button fires the `MouseDown` and `MouseUp` events, as well as a `Click` event. It's your prerogative as a VBA developer to decide which events you program in your Access applications.

Events don't occur randomly. Events actually fire in a predictable fashion, depending on which control is raising the events. Sometimes the trickiest aspect of working with events is keeping track of the order in which events occur. It may not be intuitive, for example, that the `Enter` event occurs before the `GotFocus` event (see Table 25.2) or that the `KeyDown` event occurs before the `KeyPress` event (see Table 25.3).

Looking at common event sequences

Here are the sequences of events for the most frequently encountered form scenarios:

- **Opening and closing forms**
  - **When a form opens:** `Open` (form) → `Load` (form) → `Resize` (form) → `Activate` (form) → `Current` (form) → `Enter` (control) → `GotFocus` (control)
  - **When a form closes:** `Exit` (control) → `LostFocus` (control) → `Unload` (form) → `Deactivate` (form) → `Close` (form)
- **Changes in focus**
  - **When the focus moves from one form to another:** `Deactivate` (form1) → `Activate` (form2)
  - **When the focus moves to a control on a form:** `Enter` → `GotFocus`
  - **When the focus leaves a form control:** `Exit` → `LostFocus`
  - **When the focus moves from control1 to control2:** `Exit` (control1) → `LostFocus` (control1) → `Enter` (control2) → `GotFocus` (control2)

- **When the focus leaves the record in which data has changed, but before entering the next record:** `BeforeUpdate` (form) → `AfterUpdate` (form) → `Exit` (control) → `LostFocus` (control) → `Current` (form)
- **When the focus moves to an existing record in Form view:** `BeforeUpdate` (form) → `AfterUpdate` (form) → `Current` (form)

- **Changes to data**
  - **When data is entered or changed in a form control and the focus is moved to another control:** `BeforeUpdate` → `AfterUpdate` → `Exit` → `LostFocus`
  - **When the user presses and releases a key while a form control has the focus:** `KeyDown` → `KeyPress` → `KeyUp`
  - **When text changes in a text box or in the text-box portion of a combo box:** `KeyDown` → `KeyPress` → `Change` → `KeyUp`
  - **When a value that is not present in the drop-down list is entered into a combo box's text area:** `KeyDown` → `KeyPress` → `Change` → `KeyUp` → `NotInList` → `Error`
  - **When data in a control is changed and the user presses Tab to move to the next control:**

    Control1: `KeyDown` → `BeforeUpdate` → `AfterUpdate` → `Exit` → `LostFocus`

    Control2: `Enter` → `GotFocus` → `KeyPress` → `KeyUp`
  - **When a form opens and data in a control changes:** `Current` (form) → `Enter` (control) → `GotFocus` (control) → `BeforeUpdate` (control) → `AfterUpdate` (control)
  - **When a record is deleted:** `Delete` → `BeforeDelConfirm` → `AfterDelConfirm`
  - **When the focus moves to a new blank record on a form and a new record is created when the user types in a control:** `Current` (form) → `Enter` (control) → `GotFocus` (control) → `BeforeInsert` (form) → `AfterInsert` (form)

- **Mouse events**
  - **When the user presses and releases (clicks) a mouse button while the mouse pointer is on a form control:** `MouseDown` → `MouseUp` → `Click`
  - **When the user moves the focus from one control to another by clicking the second control:**

    Control1: `Exit` → `LostFocus`

    Control2: `Enter` → `GotFocus` → `MouseDown` → `MouseUp` → `Click`
  - **When the user double-clicks a control other than a command button:** `MouseDown` → `MouseUp` → `Click` → `DblClick` → `MouseUp`

Writing simple form and control event procedures

Writing simple procedures to verify a form or control's event sequence is quite easy. Use the preceding information to determine which event should be harnessed in your application. Very often unexpected behavior can be traced to an event procedure attached to an event that occurs too late — or too early! — to capture the information that is needed by the application.

The `Chapter25.accdb` example database includes a form named frmEventLogger that prints every event for a command button, a text box, and a toggle button in the Debug window. The form is not bound to a recordset, so the list of events will be slightly different than for a bound form. It is provided to demonstrate just how many Access events are triggered by minor actions. For example, clicking the command button one time, and then tabbing to the text box and pressing one key on the keyboard fires the following events:

- `cmdButton_MouseDown`
- `cmdButton_MouseUp`
- `cmdButton_Click`
- `cmdButton_KeyDown`
- `cmdButton_Exit`
- `cmdButton_LostFocus`
- `txtText1_Enter`
- `txtText1_GotFocus`
- `txtText1_KeyPress`
- `txtText1_KeyPress`
- `txtText1_KeyUp`
- `txtText1_KeyDown`
- `txtText1_KeyPress`
- `txtText1_Change`
- `txtText1_KeyUp`

You'll have to open the code editor and display the Immediate window to see these events displayed. From anywhere in the Access environment, press Ctrl + G and the code editor instantly opens with the Immediate window displayed. Then, Alt + Tab back to the main Access screen, open the form, and click on the various controls and type something into the text box. You'll see a long list of event messages when you use Ctrl + G to return to the Immediate window.

Obviously, this is far more events than you'll ever want to program. Notice that, on the command button, both the `MouseDown` and `MouseUp` events fire before the `Click` event.

Also, a KeyDown event occurs as the Tab key is pushed, and then the command button's Exit event fires before its LostFocus event. (The focus, of course, moves off the command button to the text box as the Tab key is pressed.)

Also, notice that the text box raises more than one KeyPress event. The first is the KeyPress from the Tab key, and the second is the KeyPress that occurs as a character on the keyboard is pressed. Although it may seem strange that the Tab key's KeyPress event is caught by a text box and not by the command button, it makes sense when you consider what is happening under the surface. The Tab key is a directive to move the focus to the next control in the tab sequence. Access actually moves the focus before passing the KeyPress event to the controls on the form. This means that the focus moves to the text box, and the text box receives the KeyPress raised by the Tab key.

Keep in mind that you write code only for events that are meaningful to your application. Any event that does not contain code is ignored by Access and has no effect on the application.

Also, it's entirely likely that you'll occasionally program the wrong event for a particular task. You may, for example, be tempted to change the control's appearance by adding code to a control's Enter event. (Many developers change a control's BackColor or ForeColor to make it easy for the user to see which control has the focus.) You'll soon discover that the Enter event is an unreliable indicator of when a control has gained focus. The GotFocus and LostFocus events are specifically provided for the purpose of controlling the user interface, while the Enter and Exit events are more "conceptual" in nature and are not often programmed in Access applications.

This small example helps explain, perhaps, why Access supports so many different events. Microsoft has carefully designed Access to handle different *categories* of events, such as data or user-interface tasks. These events provide you with a rich programming environment. You'll almost always find exactly the right control, event, or programming trick to get Access to do what you need.

Opening a form with an event procedure

Most applications require multiple forms and reports to accomplish the application's business functions. Instead of requiring the users of the application to browse the database container to determine which forms and reports accomplish which tasks, an application generally provides a switchboard form to assist users in navigating throughout the application. The switchboard provides a set of command buttons labeled appropriately to suggest the purpose of the form or report it opens. Figure 25.6 shows the switchboard for the Collectible Mini Cars application.

FIGURE 25.6

Using a switchboard to navigate through the forms and reports of an application.

Main Switchboard

Collectible Mini Cars

Customers

Sales

Products

Reports

Company Setup

EXIT

(Quit Access)

Version 14.07

Handle Navigation Pane

Hide

UnHide

Collapse

The Collectible Mini Cars switchboard includes five command buttons. Each command button runs an event procedure when the button is clicked. The Products button (cmd-Products), for example, runs the event procedure that opens frmProducts. Figure 25.7 shows the Properties window for cmdProducts. Figure 25.8 shows the VBA code for the `Click` event of cmdProducts.

FIGURE 25.7

Specifying an event procedure for a control event.

FIGURE 25.8

Using an event procedure to open a form.

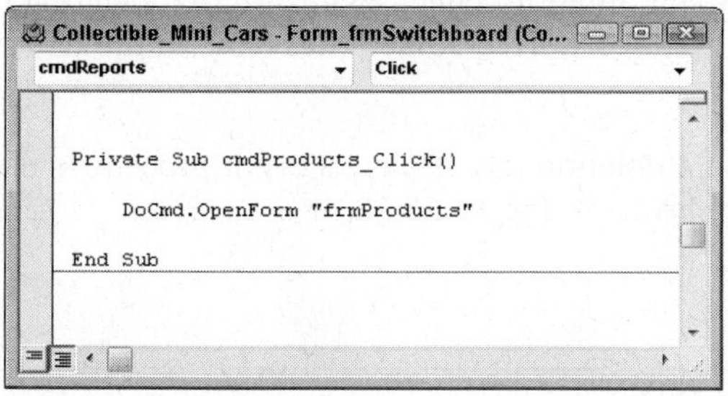

```
Collectible_Mini_Cars - Form_frmSwitchboard (Co...
cmdReports                Click

Private Sub cmdProducts_Click()

    DoCmd.OpenForm "frmProducts"

End Sub
```

Running an event procedure when closing a form

Sometimes, you'll want to perform some action when you close or leave a form. For example, you might want Access to keep a log of everyone using the form, or you might want to close the form's Print dialog box every time a user closes the main form.

To automatically close frmDialogProductPrint every time frmProducts is closed, create an event procedure for the frmProducts `Close` event. Figure 25.9 shows this event procedure.

FIGURE 25.9

Running an event procedure when a form closes.

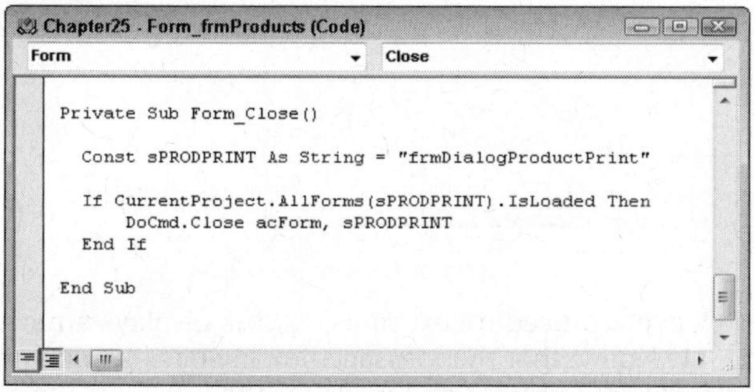

```
Chapter25 - Form_frmProducts (Code)
Form                      Close

Private Sub Form_Close()

  Const sPRODPRINT As String = "frmDialogProductPrint"

  If CurrentProject.AllForms(sPRODPRINT).IsLoaded Then
      DoCmd.Close acForm, sPRODPRINT
  End If

End Sub
```

The `Form_Close` event illustrated in Figure 25.9 first checks to see if frmDialogProduct-Print is open. If it is open, the statement to close it executes. Although trying to close a form that isn't currently open doesn't cause an error, it's a good idea to check to see if an object is available before performing an operation on the object.

25

Using an event procedure to confirm record deletion

Although you can use the Delete button on the Records group of the Home tab of the Ribbon to delete a record in a form, a better practice is to provide a Delete button on the form. A Delete button is more user-friendly because it provides a visual cue to the user as to how to delete a record. Plus, a command button affords more control over the delete process because you can include code to verify the deletion before it's actually processed. Or you might need to perform a referential integrity check to ensure that deleting the record doesn't cause a connection to the record from some other table in the database to be lost.

Use the `MsgBox()` function to confirm a deletion. cmdDelete's event procedure uses `MsgBox()` to confirm the deletion, as shown in Figure 25.10.

FIGURE 25.10

Using the `MsgBox()` function to confirm a deletion.

Chapter25 - Form_frmProducts (Code)

(General) (Declarations)

```
Private Sub cmdDelete_Click()

  Dim lResponse As Long
  Dim sPrompt As String

  On Error GoTo ErrHandler

  sPrompt = "Are you sure you want to delete this product?"

  lResponse = MsgBox(sPrompt, vbQuestion + vbYesNo, "DeleteProduct")

  If lResponse = vbYes Then
      DoCmd.RunCommand acCmdSelectRecord
      DoCmd.RunCommand acCmdDeleteRecord
  End If

ErrExit:
  Exit Sub

ErrHandler:
  MsgBox "Error is " & Err.Description
  Resume ErrExit

End Sub
```

When the `cmdDelete_Click()` event procedure executes, Access displays a message box prompt, as shown in Figure 25.11. Notice that the message box includes two command buttons: Yes and No. Access displays the prompt and waits for the user to make a selection. The record is deleted only when the user confirms the deletion by clicking the Yes button.

FIGURE 25.11

A confirmation dialog box before deleting a record.

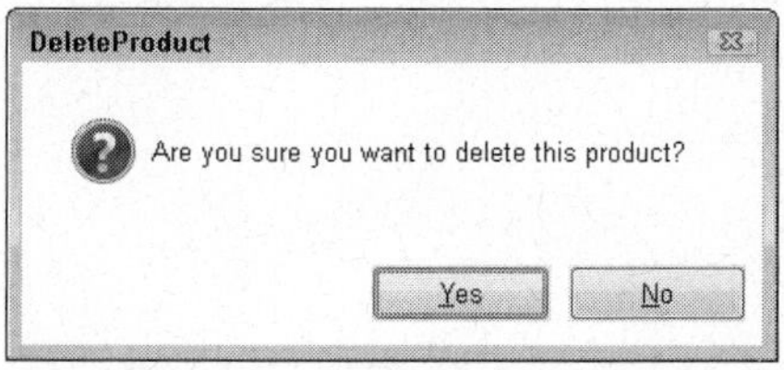

CAUTION

Before the `RunCommand acCmdDeleteRecord` statement executes, it automatically checks to see if deleting the record violates referential integrity rules that you've set up in the Relationships diagram. If a violation occurs, an Access error message displays and the deletion is canceled.

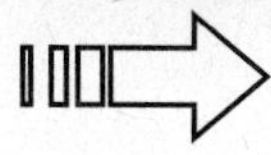

See Chapter 4 for more information on setting up referential integrity in a database.

CHAPTER

26

Debugging Your Access Applications

IN THIS CHAPTER

Organizing VBA code

Testing an application

Debugging the traditional way, with `MsgBox` and `Debug.Print`

Taking advantage of the debugging tools available in Access

Trapping unexpected errors

Many Access applications rely on significant amounts of VBA code in forms and reports, and as stand-alone modules. Because of its power and flexibility, VBA is used for all aspects of application development, from communicating with the user to massaging and transforming data on its way from tables and queries to forms and reports.

Because VBA code is often complicated (or at least, seems complicated!) debugging an error or problem in an application can be difficult and time-consuming. Depending on how well organized the code is, and whether simple conventions, such as providing descriptive names for variables and procedures, were followed, tracking down even a small coding bug can be a frustrating experience.

Fortunately, Access provides a full complement of debugging tools to make your life easier. These tools not only save time by helping you pinpoint where a coding error occurs, but can help you better understand how the code is organized and how execution passes from procedure to procedure.

NOTE

This chapter largely ignores the errors caused by poor design — misrepresentation of data caused by ill-designed queries, update and insert anomalies caused by inappropriate application of referential integrity rules, and so on. For the most part, these problems occur because of issues such as failing to conform to proper design disciplines, misunderstanding Access query design, and so on. What we can help you with, however, are the bugs that creep into your VBA code, particularly those bugs that cause noticeable problems with the data or user interface in your applications.

NOTE
This chapter assumes that you're comfortable designing and implementing the data structures in your applications and that the tables, queries, and other structural components of your databases are not a source of problems.

ON THE WEB
This chapter is a departure from the other example files you've used in the book. The sample database file (`Chapter26.accdb`) contains the basic example code shown throughout this chapter. The code in `Chapter26.accdb` does not necessarily do anything useful. It's provided mostly as a "test bench" for practicing with the Access debugging tools rather than as a good example of practical VBA code.

Many of the statements in the examples have been commented out because they contain syntax errors and other types of problems. You may have to remove the single quotes in front of some of the example statements to experience the error or view the assistance already built into Access.

Organizing VBA Code

The first step in debugging your code is to avoid coding errors in the first place. It shouldn't come as any surprise that your coding habits have a lot to do with the type and amount of errors you encounter in your applications. Very often, the adoption of simple coding conventions eliminates all but the toughest syntactical and logical errors in VBA code. Some of these conventions are described elsewhere in this book but are repeated here as a helpful reminder.

- **Use a naming convention.** Naming conventions for procedures, variables, and constants don't have to be complicated. But a consistently applied naming convention can help you spot errors that might otherwise slip through the cracks. Trying to assign a value to a constant, using a `String` variable in a mathematical operation, and passing improperly typed arguments to a function are examples of problems that a naming convention can help you avoid.
- **Limit scopes for variables.** Your variables should have the smallest scope possible that still allows your program to work efficiently and effectively. Create your variables at the procedure level by default and only increase the scope when the logic of your code requires it. Keep your globally scoped variables in their own module. When the list of global variables starts to get too big, consider refactoring your code.
- **Use constants.** Constants are a great way to add readability to your code and prevent errors. When you use a constant like `dDISCOUNT_THRESHOLD`, your intent is immensely more obvious than when you have a magic number like `5000`. Try to remove all magic numbers from your code and put them in descriptively named constants. Even if you don't succeed in getting all of them, your code will be more robust and error-proof than if you spread numbers around liberally.

- **Keep your procedures short.** In general, a procedure should do one thing. If you find your procedures are getting too long to fit on one screen, consider breaking the procedure into multiple procedures and calling each of them from the main procedure. There are certainly cases in which procedures will do more than one thing. However, you'll find your code much easier to manage when you have many simple procedures as opposed to a few giant ones.
- **Keep your modules clean.** There is virtually no limit to the number of modules you can have in your project. All the procedures in a module should be related in some way. Modules behind forms and reports will contain event procedures for their parent object but should only contain other procedures that support those event procedures. Keeping only related procedures in a module will also give you more confidence that private variables in that module won't be misused.
- **Use comments when necessary.** Comments can be an important part of the code in your project. If you have too many comments, however, nobody will ever read them and they'll quickly become out of date as your code changes. Use well-named procedures, variables, and constants to make your code self-documenting. Use comments when you've coded something a little out of the ordinary or to explain why you took one approach to a problem over another. Comments should not describe what the code does, but why the code does it.
- **Don't repeat yourself.** Much of the code you write will seem repetitive, particularly when you're coding the events on a form with a lot of controls. If it seems like you're writing the same code over and over, consider moving the code to separate procedures and passing in arguments from the event procedure. If a change is required, you'll only have to change the code in one place, saving you time and preventing errors.
- **Compile often.** Compile your project after you've written or changed several lines of code. Don't wait until the entire module or project is written to compile. Catching syntax errors while you're writing code enables you to fix those errors easily. You'll have a lot of the information about what your procedure does and where it's used when you're writing it, which makes it the best time to catch errors.

Testing Your Applications

Testing Access applications is an ongoing process. Each time you switch a form or report from Design view to Normal view, or leave the VBA Editor to run a bit of code, you're testing your application. Every time you write a line of code and move to another line, the VBA syntax parser checks the code you just wrote. Each time you change a property in a form or report and move your cursor to another property or another control, you're testing the property you've changed.

Testing is the time to see if your application runs the way you intend, or even if it runs at all. When you run an application and it doesn't work, you've found a bug. Fixing problems is most often referred to as *debugging*.

NOTE

This term dates back to the earliest electro-mechanical computers. Legend has it that a moth shorted out an electrical circuit. The late Admiral Grace Hopper, an early pioneer in computing, coined the term *debugging* to describe the process of removing the moth.

When you run a report and no data appears, you've had to check the report's RecordSource property to ensure that the report is pulling the correct data. You may have viewed the data in a query or table to see if the data source is the problem. If you run a form and you see `#Name` or `#Error` in individual controls, you've learned to check the control's ControlSource property. Perhaps you have an incorrect reference to a table field or you spelled something wrong and Access is unable to evaluate the reference.

Maybe you have too many parentheses in an expression, or you've used a control name in a formula that conflicts with an Access keyword. Each time you had this problem, you may have asked someone with more experience than you what the problem was, or perhaps you looked it up online or in a book, or you researched the syntax of the formula.

Most problems with query, form, and report design are pretty obvious. You know you have a problem when a query returns the wrong data, or a form or report fails to open or displays an error message as it opens. Behind the scenes, Access does a great deal to help you notice and rectify problems with your application's design. When you run forms and reports, Access often reports an error if it finds something seriously and obviously wrong.

It's much more difficult for Access to help you with incorrectly written code. Very often, a problem in VBA code exists for months or even years before a user notices it. Even poorly written code can run without throwing errors or exhibiting obvious problems. However, determining exactly where a bug exists in VBA code — and figuring out what to do to repair the bug — can be very challenging. When you create VBA code, you're pretty much on your own when it comes to detecting and resolving problems. Fortunately, a wide variety of tools have been built into the editor to help you.

TIP

Testing and debugging takes quite a bit of time. Many good developers easily spend a third of their time designing a program, another third writing code, and another third testing and debugging. Having someone other than the developer test a program's operation is often a good idea. A person who is unfamiliar with an application is more likely to do something the developer never expected, leading to new and surprising bugs and instability issues.

Testing functions

Functions return values, and that makes them easier to test than other types of procedures. A good developer will write a separate procedure to test each function to make sure the output is what's expected. Testing your function when it's written will expose any problems at a time when the problem is easiest to fix. If a function contains an error and that error propagates to a control on a form, it may be harder to track down. Writing tests also forces you to think through the logic of your functions from different angles.

VBA provides the `Assert` method of the `Debug` object to aid in writing tests. The following example procedure computes a discount on an invoice. There are several factors that determine whether a discount is given. See if you can identify them as you read the code.

```
Function InvoiceDiscountAmount( _
  sCustomerID As String, _
  cInvoiceTotal As Currency, _
  dtInvoice As Date _
  ) As Currency

  Dim cReturn As Currency

  Const dDISCOUNT_THRESHOLD As Double = 10000
  Const dDEFAULT_DISCOUNT As Double = 0.1

  cReturn = 0

  If cInvoiceTotal >= dDISCOUNT_THRESHOLD Then
    cReturn = cInvoiceTotal * dDEFAULT_DISCOUNT
  ElseIf IsDiscountCustomer(sCustomerID) Then
    cReturn = cInvoiceTotal * dDEFAULT_DISCOUNT
  ElseIf IsLastDayOfMonth(dtInvoice) Then
    cReturn = cInvoiceTotal * dDEFAULT_DISCOUNT
  End If

  InvoiceDiscountAmount = cReturn

End Function
```

There are three situations that will result in a discount. If the invoice is over a certain amount, if the customer is flagged as getting a discount, or if it's the last day of the month, the default discount is applied to the invoice. Comparing the invoice total to the threshold is fairly straightforward. In order to make the code clean and readable, the other two conditions were moved to their own function. Those functions are shown here:

```
Private Function IsDiscountCustomer(sCustomerID As String) As Boolean

  Dim rsCustomer As ADODB.Recordset
  Dim conn As ADODB.Connection
  Dim sSql As String

  Set conn = CurrentProject.Connection
  sSql = "SELECT GetsDiscount FROM Customers " & _
    "WHERE CustomerID = '" & sCustomerID & "'"

  Set rsCustomer = conn.Execute(sSql)

  If Not rsCustomer.EOF Then
    IsDiscountCustomer = rsCustomer.Fields(0).Value
```

```
  End If

End Function

Private Function IsLastDayOfMonth(dtDate As Date) As Boolean

  'The zeroth day of the next month is the last
  'day of the current month
  IsLastDayOfMonth = (dtDate = DateSerial(Year(dtDate), Month(dtDate), 0))

End Function
```

Now that the functions are written, we can write a test procedure to see if it works as expected. We know the three conditions that should result in a discount, and we'll test the combinations of those. The `Debug.Assert` method will halt the code if a test doesn't pass. For illustration purposes, there is an error in the `IsLastDayOfMonth` function. We'll fix that error shortly. Figure 26.1 shows the test procedure after it has been run.

FIGURE 26.1

`Debug.Assert` halts code when a test fails.

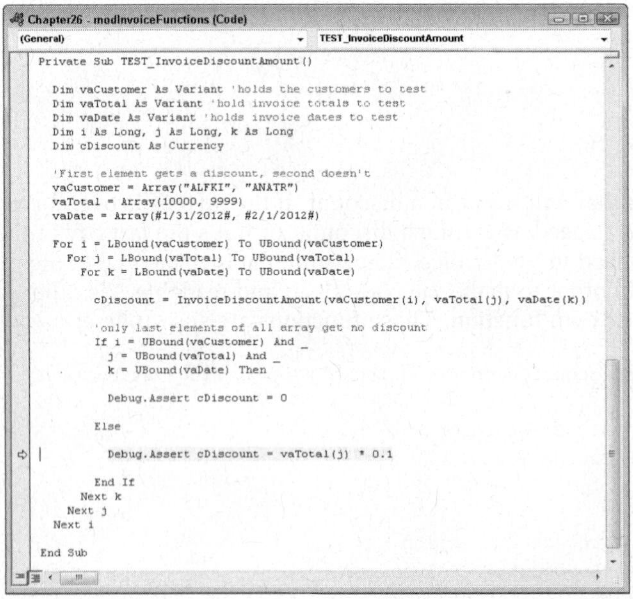

Chapter26 - modInvoiceFunctions (Code)

(General) | TEST_InvoiceDiscountAmount

```
Private Sub TEST_InvoiceDiscountAmount()

  Dim vaCustomer As Variant 'holds the customers to test
  Dim vaTotal As Variant 'hold invoice totals to test
  Dim vaDate As Variant 'holds invoice dates to test
  Dim i As Long, j As Long, k As Long
  Dim cDiscount As Currency

  'First element gets a discount, second doesn't
  vaCustomer = Array("ALFKI", "ANATR")
  vaTotal = Array(10000, 9999)
  vaDate = Array(#1/31/2012#, #2/1/2012#)

  For i = LBound(vaCustomer) To UBound(vaCustomer)
    For j = LBound(vaTotal) To UBound(vaTotal)
      For k = LBound(vaDate) To UBound(vaDate)

        cDiscount = InvoiceDiscountAmount(vaCustomer(i), vaTotal(j), vaDate(k))

        'only last elements of all array get no discount
        If i = UBound(vaCustomer) And _
          j = UBound(vaTotal) And _
          k = UBound(vaDate) Then

          Debug.Assert cDiscount = 0

        Else

          Debug.Assert cDiscount = vaTotal(j) * 0.1

        End If
      Next k
    Next j
  Next i

End Sub
```

To test the function, three arrays were created containing information to pass to the function. The `vaCustomer` array contains one customer that gets a discount and one customer that doesn't. These customers were selected by inspecting the Customers table. The vaTotal array contains an invoice total amount that gets a discount and one that doesn't. The first value is the amount of the threshold (and should pass), and the second value is one less than the threshold (and should fail). Picking values around the value that defines pass/fail is called picking *edge cases*. The last array contains a date that should pass (because it's the last day of the month) and a date that shouldn't.

The procedure contains three nested loops so that all eight combinations of data are passed to the function. Only when the last element of each array is the current element should there be no discount (that is, when ANATR, 9999, and #2/1/2012# are passed to the function). The If statement checks to see if each loop is referencing the last element. If they are, Debug.Assert compares the calculated discount to zero. If any loop is not referencing the last element, then Debug.Assert compares the calculated discount to 10 percent of the invoice total.

Running the test procedure caused execution to stop on the Debug.Assert line. Checking the values of i, j, and k, we can see that the combination of "ANATR", 9999, and #1/31/2012# resulted in a calculated discount of zero, but our test says it should have been 999.9. We know there is a problem in our function — now we just have to find it.

Upon closer inspection of the IsLastDayOfMonth function, we see that it should have read:

```
IsLastDayOfMonth = (dtDate = DateSerial(Year(dtDate), Month(dtDate) + 1, 0))
```

We forgot to include the +1 to advance the month to the next month. After correcting the error and rerunning TEST_InvoiceDiscountAmount, the code runs without error. Debug.Assert only stops the code when a test doesn't pass. If everything is fine, nothing happens. You may want to include a MsgBox or Debug.Print statement at the end of your tests to give you a visual cue that the test procedure completed.

In this example, it took almost as long to write the test as it did to write the three functions. However, if we hadn't caught the error, it could have caused many worse problems in the form where the function was used. The erroneous procedure would have returned no discount when one was warranted. It's easy to imagine that the user would not notice the error, and the result would be an unhappy customer. Another benefit of testing functions in this way is that any changes to the function can be tested using the same test procedure. If the tests pass, we know our changes haven't violated the business rules of our application.

Compiling VBA code

After you create a subprocedure or function and want to make sure that all your syntax is correct, you should compile your procedures by choosing Debug➪Compile *Project Name* from the VBA code editor window menu (where *Project Name* is the name of the project set in the Project dialog box, accessed from the Tools menu). Figure 26.2 shows the Debug menu opened in the editor window.

FIGURE 26.2

The Debug menu in the VBA code editor window contains valuable debugging tools.

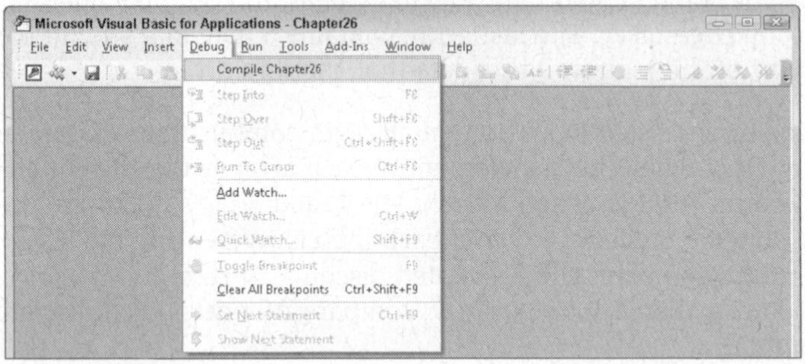

The compile action checks your code for errors and also converts the programs to a form that your computer can understand. If the compile operation is not successful, an error window appears, as shown in Figure 26.3.

This level of checking is more stringent than the single-line syntax checker. Variables are checked for proper references and type. Each statement is checked for all proper parameters. All text strings are checked for proper delimiters, such as the quotation marks surrounding `text string`. Figure 26.3 illustrates a typical compile-time error. In this case, the name of a method (`GetOption`) has been misspelled, and the compiler is unable to resolve the misspelled reference.

FIGURE 26.3

Viewing a compile error.

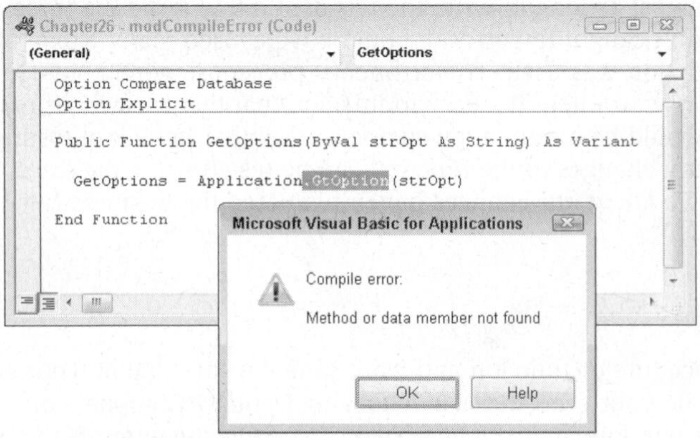

Access compiles all currently uncompiled procedures, not just the one you're currently viewing. If you receive a compilation error, immediately modify the code to rectify the problem. Then try to compile the procedure again. If there are further compile errors, you'll see the next error.

NOTE
Unfortunately, the VBA compiler reports compilation errors one at a time. Most other compilers (such as the compilers in Visual Studio .NET) show you as many errors as they find during compilation.

TIP
After compiling your application, you can't choose Debug➪Compile (it's grayed out). Before implementing an application, you should make sure that your application is compiled.

Your database is named with a standard Windows name, such as `Chapter26.accdb`, but Access uses an internal project name to reference the VBA code in your application. You'll see this name when you compile your database. When the database file is first created, the project name and the Windows filename will be the same. The project name isn't changed when you change the Windows filename of the ACCDB file. You can change the project name by choosing Tools➪*Project Name* Properties (where *Project Name* is the current internal project name).

Compiling your database only makes sure that you have no syntax errors. The compiler can check only for language problems by first recognizing the VBA statement and then checking to see that you specify the correct number of options and in the right order. The VBA compiler can't detect logical errors in your code, and it certainly can't help with runtime problems.

TIP
After you compile your program, be sure to compact your database. Every time you make a change to your program, Access stores both the changes and the original version. When you compile your program, it may double in size as the compiled and uncompiled versions of your code are stored. Compacting the database can reduce the size of the database by as much as 80 percent to 90 percent, because it eliminates all previous versions internally.

Traditional Debugging Techniques

Two widely used debugging techniques have been available since Access 1.0. The first is to insert `MsgBox` statements to display the value of variables, procedure names, and so on. The second common technique is to insert `Debug.Print` statements to output messages to the Immediate window.

Using MsgBox

Figure 26.4 shows an example of a message box displaying a long SQL statement to enable the developer to verify that the statement was properly composed by the application. The example in Figure 26.4 is found in the `modUsingMsgBox` module in the `Chapter26.accdb` example database.

FIGURE 26.4

The `MsgBox` statement makes a satisfactory debugging tool (with some limitations).

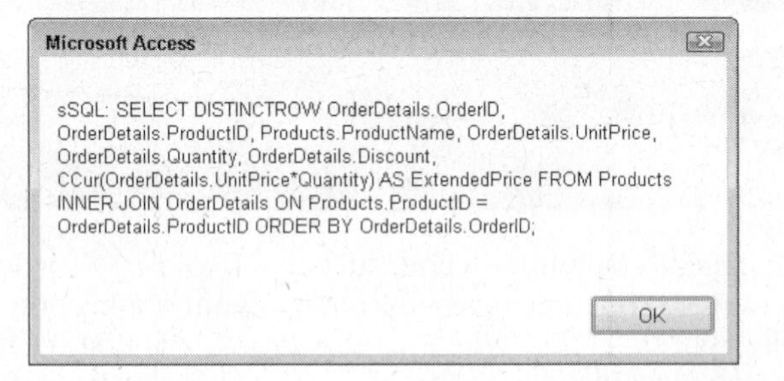

Here are the advantages of using the `MsgBox` statement:

- The `MsgBox` statement is simple and easy to use and only occupies a single line of code.
- The `MsgBox` statement can output many types of data.
- The message box itself pops up right on the user interface, and you don't have to have the Immediate window open or flip to the Immediate window to view the message box.
- `MsgBox` halts code execution, and because you know where you've put the `MsgBox` statements, you know exactly where the code is executing.

There are also some problems associated with `MsgBox` statements:

- There is nothing about the `MsgBox` statement to prevent it from popping up in front of an end-user, causing all kinds of confusion and other problems.

CAUTION

Never, ever forget to remove all debugging statements from your code before shipping to end-users. Search your code for MsgBox and Debug.Print to make sure all debugging statements have been removed.

- Message boxes are modal, which means you can't flip to the code editor window or Immediate window (discussed in the "Running code with the Immediate window" section, later in this chapter) to examine the value of variables or examine the code underlying the application. Using the `MsgBox` statement is an all-or-nothing proposition (with the one exception described in the "Compiler Directives" sidebar).
- It's difficult to get the text out of a message box. You can't copy the text or select parts of it. Other than reading the text in a message box, about the only other action you can do is print the screen.

Compiler Directives

A refinement of the `MsgBox` technique is to use compiler directives to suppress the `MsgBox` statements, unless a special type of constant has been set in the code or within the Access environment. Examine the code in the following figure. Notice the `#Const` compiler directive above the `MsgBox` statement and the `#If` and `#End If` directives surrounding the `MsgBox` statement.

Chapter26 - modCompilerDirective (Code)

(General) FillRecordset2

```
#Const DEBUG1 = False

Public Function FillRecordset2()
  Dim db As DAO.Database
  Dim rs As DAO.Recordset
  Dim rs1 As DAO.Recordset
  Dim sSQL As String

  Set db = DBEngine.Workspaces(0).Databases(0)

  sSQL = "SELECT DISTINCTROW OrderDetails.OrderID, " _
    & "OrderDetails.ProductID, " _
    & "Products.ProductName, " _
    & "OrderDetails.UnitPrice, " _
    & "OrderDetails.Quantity, " _
    & "OrderDetails.Discount, " _
    & "CCur(OrderDetails.UnitPrice*Quantity) AS ExtendedPrice " _
    & "FROM Products INNER JOIN OrderDetails " _
    & "ON Products.ProductID = OrderDetails.ProductID " _
    & "ORDER BY OrderDetails.OrderID;"


  #If DEBUG1 Then
    MsgBox "sSQL: " & sSQL
  #End If

  Set rs = db.OpenRecordset(sSQL, dbOpenDynaset)

End Function
```

All the keywords beginning with the pound sign (#) are seen only by the VBA compiler. These keywords (`#Const`, `#If`, `#Else`, and `#End If`) constitute directives to the VBA compiler to include (or exclude) certain statements in the compiled version of your project.

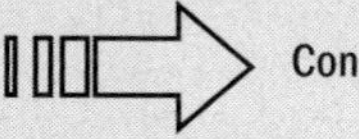

Conditional compilation using compiler directives is introduced in Chapter 23.

The `#Const` directive you see in the preceding figure can appear anywhere in the module as long as it's placed above the `#If` directive. The logical place for the `#Const` is in the module's declaration section, since `#Const` values are global to the module. In the figure, the compiler constant is set to `False`, which means the statements between `#If` and `#End If` won't be compiled into the application's VBA project. In this case, the `MsgBox` statement isn't processed and doesn't appear in the user interface. Setting the `#Const` directive's value to `True` displays the `MsgBox` statement when the code is run.

continued

continued

Compiler directives also can be used for statements other than `MsgBox`. You could, for example, use compiler directives to conditionally compile features, additional help, or other capabilities into an application. Compiler directives are particularly effective for suppressing `MsgBox` statements that are used for debugging purposes and must be squelched before giving the application to users. You can easily reactivate `MsgBox` statements by setting the `#Const` statement to `True`.

Perhaps the biggest impediment to using compiler constants is that the `#Const` statement is module-level in scope. A compiler constant declared in one module is not seen by other modules in the application. This means that you must add compiler constants to every module in which you want to employ conditional compilation.

Access provides the Conditional Compilation Arguments text box in the General tab of the application's Project Properties dialog box (Tools *Application Name* Properties) to get around this constraint. As shown in the following figure, you use the Conditional Compilation Arguments text box to specify any number of compiler constants that apply to the entire application. These settings make it very easy to toggle conditional compilation from a single location in the application, instead of changing the `#Const` statements in every module.

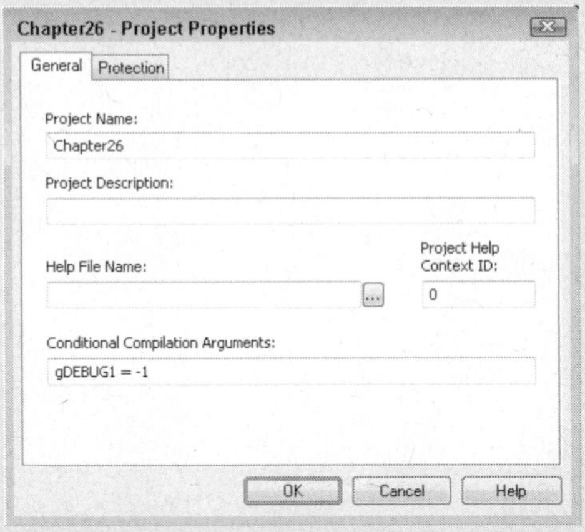

Conditional Compilation Arguments and other settings set in the Project Properties dialog box are relevant only to the current application. Unlike the options you set in the Options dialog box (accessible from the Tools menu), the Project Properties settings are not shared among multiple Access applications.

TIP

In the preceding figure, notice that the value assigned to the Conditional Compilation Argument is numeric. Assigning zero to a Conditional Compilation Argument sets the argument's logical value to False; any nonzero value is interpreted as `True`. You can't use the words True and False in the Conditional Compilation Arguments text box. Setting the value to 0 (false) means that you can leave all the conditional compilation directives in your code. Setting the value to false effectively disables them, allowing your code to execute as if they don't exist.

If you're confused about the conflicting terminologies applied to the VBA conditional compilation feature, you're not alone. In a VBA code module, you assign conditional compilation constants using the `#Const` keyword, yet in the Project Properties dialog box, you set Conditional Compilation Arguments. Also, you assign the `True` and `False` keywords to conditional compilation constants in a VBA module, but use `-1` and `0` to assign True and False, respectively, to Conditional Compilation Arguments. This is one place where the terminology and syntax used for the same purpose are quite different in different parts of an Access VBA project.

In case you're wondering, the name you apply to a compiler constant is anything you want it to be. The example in this section uses `gDEBUG1` merely as a convenience, but it could have been `MyComplierConstant`, `Betty`, `DooDah`, or any other valid constant name.

Using Debug.Print

The second commonly used debugging technique is using `Debug.Print` to output messages to the Immediate window. (`Print` is actually a method of the `Debug` object.) Figure 26.5 shows how the `sSQL` variable appears in the Immediate window.

FIGURE 26.5

Use `Debug.Print` to output messages to the Immediate window.

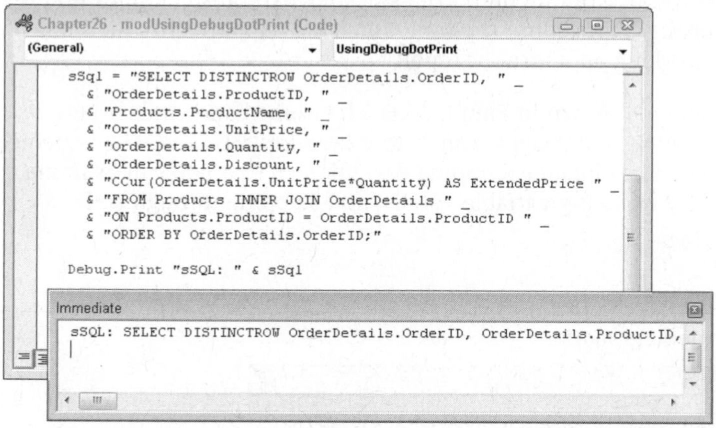
Chapter26 - modUsingDebugDotPrint (Code)
(General)
UsingDebugDotPrint
sSql = "SELECT DISTINCTROW OrderDetails.OrderID, " _
& "OrderDetails.ProductID, " _
& "Products.ProductName, " _
& "OrderDetails.UnitPrice, " _
& "OrderDetails.Quantity, " _
& "OrderDetails.Discount, " _
& "CCur(OrderDetails.UnitPrice*Quantity) AS ExtendedPrice " _
& "FROM Products INNER JOIN OrderDetails " _
& "ON Products.ProductID = OrderDetails.ProductID " _
& "ORDER BY OrderDetails.OrderID;"
Debug.Print "sSQL: " & sSql
Immediate
sSQL: SELECT DISTINCTROW OrderDetails.OrderID, OrderDetails.ProductID,

Unlike the `MsgBox` statement, you don't have to do anything special to suppress the `Debug.Print` output from the user interface. The output of `Debug.Print` only goes to the Immediate window, and because end-users never see the Immediate window, you don't have to worry about a user encountering debug messages.

The problems with `Debug.Print` are obvious from Figure 26.5. Long strings don't wrap in the Immediate window. Also, the Immediate window must be visible in order for you to view its output. But these limitations are relatively harmless and you'll frequently use `Debug.Print` in your applications.

NOTE

Some people have reported that excessive numbers of `Debug.Print` statements can slow an application. Even though the Immediate window is not visible, Access executes the `Debug.Print` statements that it finds in its code. You may want to consider surrounding each `Debug.Print` statement with the compiler directives described in the "Compiler Directives" sidebar to remove them from the end-user's copy of the application.

Using the Access Debugging Tools

Access features a full complement of debugging tools and other capabilities. You use these tools to monitor the execution of your VBA code, halt code execution on a statement so that you can examine the value of variables at that moment in time, and perform other debugging tasks.

Running code with the Immediate window

Open the Immediate window (also called the Debug window) by choosing View➪Immediate or by pressing Ctrl+G. You can open the Immediate window any time (for example, while you're working on a form's design). You'll sometimes find it useful to test a line of code or run a procedure (both of which are supported by the Immediate window) while you're working on a form or report.

The Immediate window is shown in Figure 26.6. The Immediate window permits certain interactivity with the code and provides an output area for `Debug.Print` statements. The basic debugging procedures include stopping execution so that you can examine code and variables, dynamically watching variable values, and stepping through code.

FIGURE 26.6

Get to know the Immediate window! You'll use it a lot in Access.

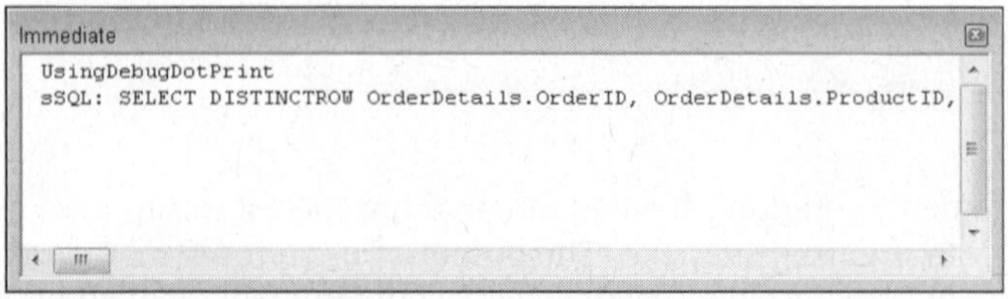

```
Immediate
UsingDebugDotPrint
sSQL: SELECT DISTINCTROW OrderDetails.OrderID, OrderDetails.ProductID,
```

One of the most basic uses of the Immediate window is to run code, such as built-in functions, or subroutines and functions that you've written. Figure 26.7 shows several examples that have been run in the Immediate window.

FIGURE 26.7

Running code from the Immediate window is a common practice.

```
Immediate
UsingDebugDotPrint
sSQL: SELECT DISTINCTROW OrderDetails.OrderID, OrderDetails.ProductID,

?Now
11/5/2012 7:29:07 AM

SomeProcedureName
```

The first example in Figure 26.7 shows the same convention used to run a function (UsingDebugDotPrint) that's been added to the VBA project. You see the result of the function's execution (a long SQL statement), as long as the function is declared with the `Public` keyword, and any arguments required by the function are provided. This function includes a `Debug.Print` statement, and that output is displayed just below where the function is called.

The `Now()` function has been run from the Immediate window, returning the current date and time. The question mark (`?`) in front of the `Now()` function name is a shortcut for the Print keyword. Instead of typing **?Now**, you can type **Print Now**. Both the question mark and the Print keyword are a directive to the Immediate window to display (or print) the value returned by the `Now()` function.

The third example in Figure 26.7 (SomeProcedureName) shows calling a subroutine from the Immediate window. Because subroutines don't return values, the question mark is not used. The `SomeProcedureName` procedure doesn't include any `Debug.Print` statements, so no additional information is displayed in the Immediate window.

Suspending execution with breakpoints

You suspend execution by setting a *breakpoint* in the code. When Access encounters a breakpoint, execution immediately stops, allowing you to switch to the Immediate window to set or examine the value of variables.

Setting a breakpoint is easy. Open the code window and click the gray Margin Indicator bar to the left of the statement on which you want execution to stop (see Figure 26.8). Alternatively, position the cursor on the line and click the Breakpoint toolbar button. The breakpoint itself appears as a large brown dot in the gray bar along the left edge of the code window and as a brown highlight behind the code. The text of the breakpoint statement appears in a bold font.

TIP

You can change all these colors and font characteristics in the Editor Format tab of the Options dialog box.

Removing a breakpoint involves nothing more than clicking the breakpoint indicator in the Margin Indicator bar. Breakpoints are also automatically removed when you close the application.

FIGURE 26.8

Setting a breakpoint is easy.

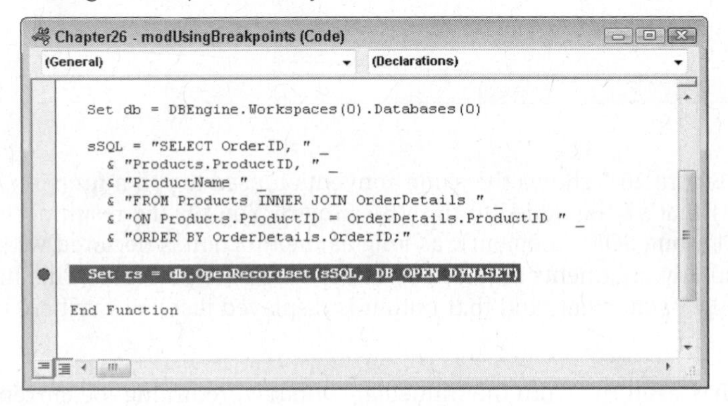

When execution reaches the breakpoint, Access halts execution and opens the module at the breakpoint (see Figure 26.9). You now use the Immediate window (see the preceding section) to examine the values of variables and perform other operations, or use any of the other debugging tools described in this section. Neither the code window nor the Immediate window are modal, so you still have full access to the development environment.

FIGURE 26.9

Execution stops on the breakpoint.

Chapter26 - modUsingBreakpoints (Code)

(General) UsingBreakpoints

```
    Set db = DBEngine.Workspaces(0).Databases(0)

    sSQL = "SELECT OrderID, " _
      & "Products.ProductID, " _
      & "ProductName " _
      & "FROM Products INNER JOIN OrderDetails " _
      & "ON Products.ProductID = OrderDetails.ProductID " _
      & "ORDER BY OrderDetails.OrderID;"

    Set rs = db.OpenRecordset(sSQL, DB_OPEN_DYNASET)

End Function
```

Figure 26.10 illustrates two techniques for viewing the values of variables while execution is stopped at a breakpoint. The Locals window contains the names and current values of all the variables in the current procedure. You open the Locals window by choosing Locals Window from the View menu. If you want to see the value of a variable in a slightly different format, use the print command (?) in the Immediate window to display the variable's value.

FIGURE 26.10

Variables are in scope when in break mode.

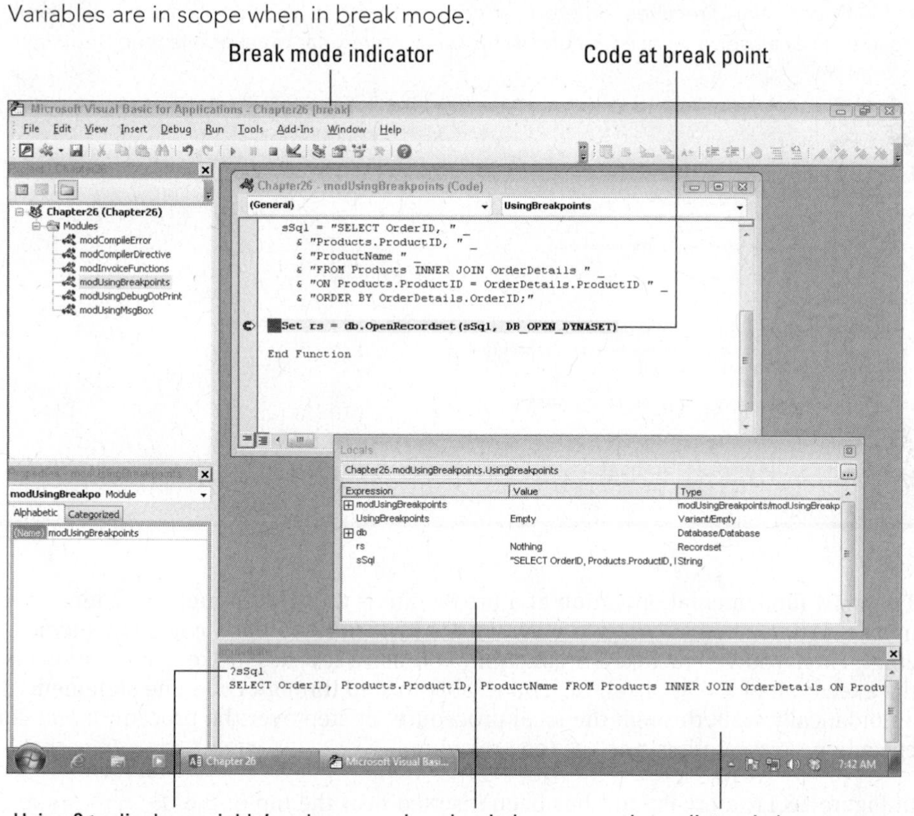

Using Stop Statements instead of Setting Breakpoints

An alternative to setting breakpoints is to use `Stop` statements. The `Stop` statement halts execution but is more permanent than a breakpoint. A `Stop` statement, like any other VBA statement, persists from session to session until explicitly removed. You can, however, surround the `Stop` statement with conditional compilation expressions and toggle their action by changing the value assigned to a conditional compilation constant. The following figure illustrates using the `Stop` statement.

Using `Stop` is a bit dangerous, however. Because `Stop` is an executable statement, unless it's carefully controlled with compiler directives, deleted, or commented out, your application will, literally, *stop executing* in front of a user. You're probably better off using regular breakpoints than `Stop` statements in most situations.

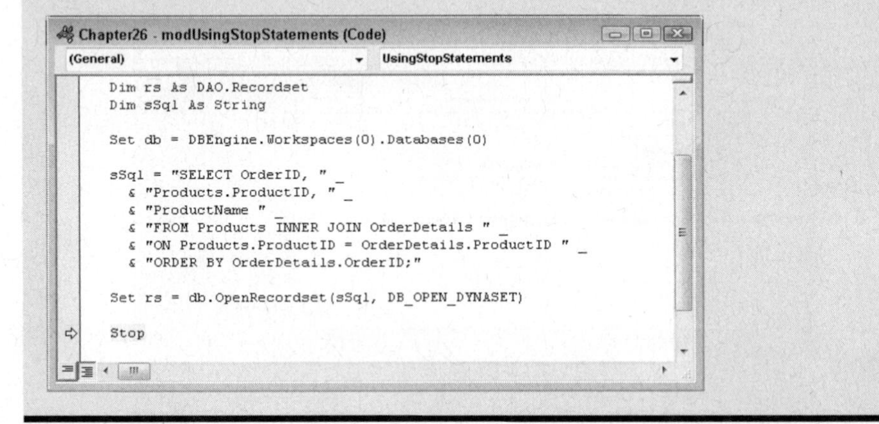

The most fundamental operation at a breakpoint is to walk through the code, one statement at a time, enabling you to view what's happening to the application's logic and variables. After you've reached a breakpoint, you use a few keystroke combinations to control the execution of the application. You're able to step through code one statement at a time, automatically walk through the local procedure, or step over the procedure and continue execution on the "other side" of the procedure.

In Figure 26.11, a breakpoint has been inserted near the top of the `UsingBreakpoints()` function. When execution reaches this statement a breakpoint asserts itself, allowing you to take control of program execution.

FIGURE 26.11

Insert a breakpoint near the location of the code you want to step through.

```
Chapter26 - modUsingBreakpoints (Code)
(General)                         UsingBreakpoints

    Dim sSql As String

    Set db = DBEngine.Workspaces(0).Databases(0)

    sSql = "SELECT OrderID, " _
      & "Products.ProductID, " _
      & "ProductName " _
      & "FROM Products INNER JOIN OrderDetails " _
      & "ON Products.ProductID = OrderDetails.ProductID " _
      & "ORDER BY OrderDetails.OrderID;"

    Set rs = db.OpenRecordset(sSql, DB_OPEN_DYNASET)
```

In Figure 26.12, the break has occurred and we've clicked the Step Into button (or pressed F8). The Step Into button executes the current statement and moves to the next statement in the program's flow of execution. In this case, the `db` variable is set and the current line becomes the statement that sets the `sSql` variable (indicated by a yellow highlight and an arrow in the left margin). At this point, the `sSql` assignment statement has not been executed and the value of `sSql` is an empty string. Press F8 again to execute the `sSql` assignment statement and move the current line to the next line. After `sSql` is set, you can see the value of `sSql` in the Immediate window by using `?sSql` or by opening the Locals window (described in the "Looking at variables with the Locals window" section, later in this chapter).

FIGURE 26.12

Step Into executes one line at a time.

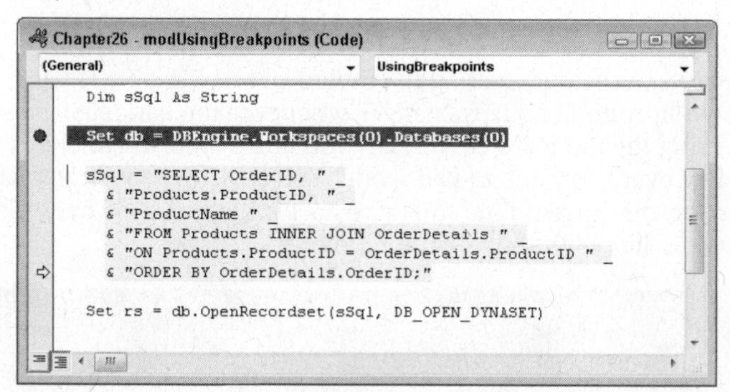

Consecutive clicks on the Step Into button (or pressing F8) walks through the code one statement at a time. If a statement includes a call to a child procedure, you'll be taken to that procedure and walked through it. If you want, you can use the Step Over button (or press Shift + F8) to step "through" the child routine. If you've previously debugged the child routine and you're sure it contains no errors, there is no reason to walk through its code. The code in the called routine is actually executed when you click the Step Over button, changing any variables involved.

When you're satisfied that you don't need to continue walking through the code in the child procedure, click the Step Out button (or press Ctrl + F8) to complete the procedure. The Step Out button is handy if you've stepped into a called routine and you're sure there's nothing interesting going on in it.

One very nice feature in the Access VBA window is the Auto Data Tips option in the Editor tab in the Options dialog box. With this option selected, you're able to view the value of any variable in a tooltip-like window by hovering the mouse pointer over the variable's name in the module window (see Figure 26.13).

FIGURE 26.13

Auto Data Tips are a powerful tool for debugging.

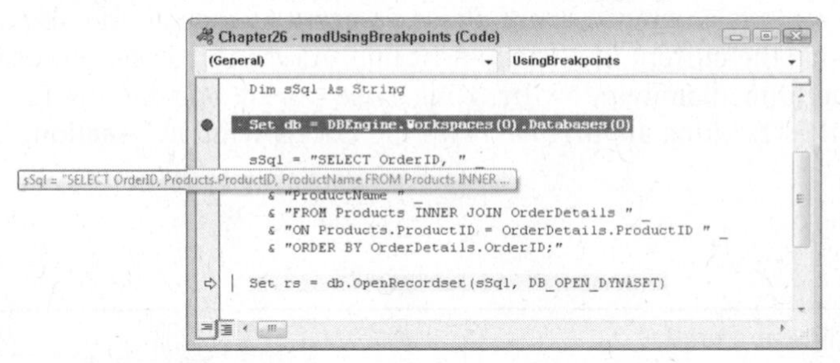

The Auto Data Tips display you see by hovering the mouse over a variable is very dynamic. The value shown in Auto Data Tips changes whenever the variable is assigned a new value. Because hovering the mouse is easy to do, you don't have to use the Immediate window to view every variable in your code. You can hover over any variable in the procedure, not just on the current line. In Figure 26.13, the mouse is over the `sSql` variable in the line above the line with the execution pointer.

NOTE

The Auto Data Tips option must be selected in the Editor tab in order for the data tip you see in Figure 26.13 to appear.

TIP

Figure 26.13 shows an Auto Data Tip for a variable with a very long string. You can't see the whole value using this method. You can, however, see the last part of the screen by holding down the Ctrl key while you hover over a variable.

One very nice feature of breakpoints is that the execution pointer (the yellow arrow in the left margin) is movable. You can use the mouse to reposition the pointer to another statement within the current procedure. For example, you can drag the pointer to a position above its current location to re-execute several lines of code.

You can easily reposition the execution pointer in such a way that your code's execution is invalid, such as moving it into the body of an `If...Then...Else` statement, or into the middle of a loop. Also, moving the pointer to a position *lower* in the code may mean that variables aren't set correctly or an important bit of code is ignored. Overall, though, the ability to easily re-execute a few lines of code is a valuable debugging aid.

Looking at variables with the Locals window

The Locals window (View ➪ Locals Window) shows all variables that are currently in scope, saving you from having to examine each variable one at a time. The variable's name, its data type, and its current value are displayed.

Notice the items in the Locals window in Figure 26.14. Any line in the Locals window that begins with a plus sign will unfold to reveal more information. For example, you can set a breakpoint on the `End Function` statement at the bottom of the function to halt execution so that you can examine the results of the `rs` assignment statement. Unfolding the `rs` entry in the Locals window reveals all the properties of the `rs` object and its contents (see Figure 26.14).

FIGURE 26.14

Use the Locals window to examine the values of complex objects.

Locals

Chapter26.modUsingBreakpoints.UsingBreakpoints

Expression	Value	Type
db		Database/Database
rs		Recordset/Recordset2
AbsolutePosition	0	Long
BatchCollisionCount	<Operation is not supported for this type of (	Long
BatchCollisions	<Operation is not supported for this type of (	Variant
BatchSize	<Operation is not supported for this type of (	Long
BOF	False	Boolean
Bookmark		Byte(0 to 3)
Bookmarkable	True	Boolean
CacheSize	0	Long
CacheStart		Byte()
Connection	<Operation is not supported for this type of (	Connection
DateCreated	<Operation is not supported for this type of (	Variant
EditMode	0	Integer
EOF	False	Boolean
Fields		Fields/Fields
Count	3	Integer
Item 1		Variant/Object/Field2
AllowZeroLength	False	Boolean
AppendOnly	False	Boolean
Attributes	33	Long
CollatingOrder	1033	Long
CollectionIndex	0	Integer
ComplexType	<Invalid operation.>	ComplexType
DataUpdatable	True	Boolean
DefaultValue	""	Variant/String
Expression	""	String

One powerful feature of the Locals window is that you can set the values of simple variables (numeric, string, and so on) by clicking on the Value column in a variable's row and typing in a new value for the variable. This makes it very easy to test how various combinations of variable values affect your application.

In the preceding section, we tell you how to move the execution point within a procedure by dragging the yellow arrow with the mouse. By changing the value of a variable and moving the execution point to different places in the procedure, you can verify that the code executes as expected. Directly manipulating variables is much easier than other methods of testing the effect of outliers and unexpected values.

NOTE
The Locals window shows module-level variables under the name of the module. Globally scoped variables are not shown in the Locals window. You have to use the Immediate window or the Auto Data Tips to inspect global variables.

Setting watches with the Watches window

The Locals window can be overrun with variables in a large application or in an application with many variables in scope. The Watches window enables you to specify just which variables you want to monitor as you single-step through your code. The value of a watched variable changes dynamically as the code runs. (You need to be at some kind of breakpoint, of course, to actually see the values.) The advantage of using the Watches window is that the variables displayed don't have to be from the local procedure. In fact, the variables in the Watch window can be from any part of the application.

Setting a watch is more complicated than using the Locals window or setting a breakpoint:

1. **Choose View⇨Watch Window to display the Watches window.**
2. **Right-click anywhere in the Watches window and select Add Watch from the shortcut menu.** The Add Watch dialog box (see Figure 26.15) appears.
3. **Enter the name of the variable or any other expression in the Expression text box.**

FIGURE 26.15

The Add Watch dialog box includes some powerful options.

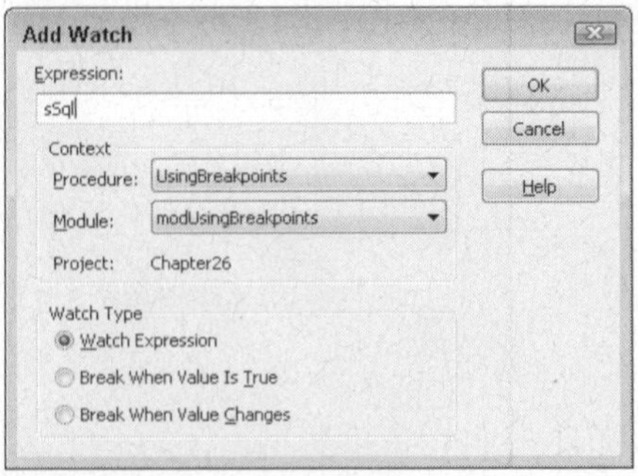

The Add Watch dialog box includes some important options. In addition to the name of a variable or expression (an expression might be something like `Len(sSql) = 0`), there are options for specifying the module and procedure within the module to watch. In Figure 26.16, the Add Watch dialog box is set up to watch the `sSql` variable, but only with the `UsingBreakpoints` procedure in the `modUsingBreakpoints` module. If an `sSql` variable exists in any other procedure or any other module, you can't see it here.

At the bottom of the Add Watch dialog box are the following options:

- **Watch Expression:** The variable's value will dynamically change in the Watch window. You must use an explicit breakpoint or `Stop` statement in order to observe the value of the watched variable.
- **Break When Value Is True:** This option asserts a break whenever the value of the watched variable or expression becomes `True`. If you set the expression to `Len(sSql) = 0`, a breakpoint occurs whenever the value of the `sSql` variable changes to an empty string.
- **Break When Value Changes:** This directive causes Access to halt execution whenever the value of the variable or expression changes. Obviously, this setting can generate a *lot* of breakpoints, but it can be useful if a variable is changing unexpectedly and you can't figure out where.

CAUTION

Use watches wisely. You don't want to be breaking into program execution too frequently, or you'll never get through the code. On the other hand, you don't want to overlook some important change in the value of a variable because you didn't set a watch appropriately.

Figure 26.16 shows the Watches window in action. This watch window contains the `rs` variable that is expandable and the `sSql` variable showing the string assigned.

FIGURE 26.16

The Watches window reveals all of a variable's details.

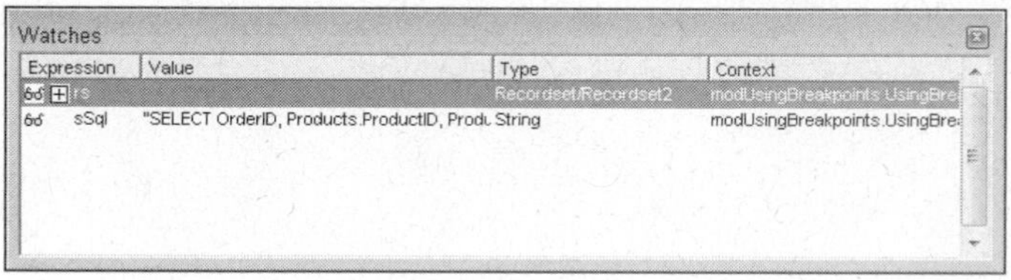

TIP

The Watches window can "float" or be docked at any side of the VBA editor window. If you don't like the Watches window's current position, use its title bar to drag it to another location. As you drag the window to a docking position, a gray rectangle appears where Access thinks you want to dock the window. Just release the mouse button when you have the window positioned in its new location, and Access will either dock the window or leave it floating freely, as you directed. The Watches window will be in the same position the next time you open the VBA editor window.

If you don't like the "docking" behavior, right-click anywhere within the body of the Watches window and deselect the Dockable option.

Using conditional watches

Although watching variables in the Locals window or Watches window can be entertaining, you can spend a lot of unproductive time hoping to see something unexpected happen. You'll probably find it much more efficient to set a *conditional watch* on a variable, and instruct the VBA engine to break when the condition you've established is met.

The Add Watch dialog box (see Figure 26.17) accepts a Boolean (true or false) expression, such as `rs.Fields("OrderID").Value=10251` in the text box near the top. You specify where in the application (which procedures and which modules) the expression is applied, and you tell Access what you want the VBA engine to do when the expression is evaluated. For our purposes, we want execution to break when the loop reaches a record whose OrderID field is equal to 10251 — that is, when the above expression is True.

FIGURE 26.17

A conditional watch halts execution when the expression `rs.Fields("OrderID").Value=10251` is true.

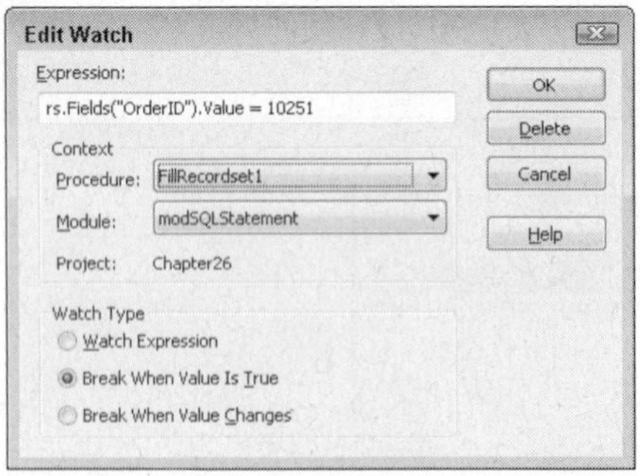

Running the `FillRecordset1` procedure in the `modSQLStatement` module with this watch set will cause the code to stop on the `Loop` statement. At this point, you can inspect the other values in the recordset via the Locals window or write some statements in the Immediate window to investigate a problem.

The conditional watches you set up through the Add Watch dialog box are added to the Watches window. The watch expression appears in the Watches window's Expression column.

You can use conditional watches in other ways, too, such as using compound conditions (`X = True And Y = False`), and forcing a break whenever a value changes from the value set in the Expression text box. The small example illustrated in Figure 26.17 only hints at the capabilities possible with conditional watches.

TIP

The Watches window is more than a static display. If needed, you can click on an item in the Expression column and change a watched expression. For example, let's say you set up a watch containing an expression as `TotalSale > 100` and directed the watch to assert a breakpoint as soon as this expression becomes true. You may find that the breakpoint occurs much too often for your testing purposes. Instead of deleting the watch expression and starting over, you can easily modify the expression, replacing 100 with 200 or any other value you'd like to try.

You can have as many watches as you want, but, as with all other debugging tools, the watches are removed when you exit Access.

TIP

If, while working with conditional watches, you find a particular expression useful, you may want to write it down for future use.

Using the Call Stack window

The last debugging tool I'll examine is a bit more difficult to understand because it involves "multiple dimensions" of execution. In many Access applications, you'll have procedures that call other procedures that call still other procedures. To my knowledge, there is no practical limit on the number of procedures that can be sequentially called in a VBA project. This means you may have a "tree" of procedures many levels deep, one level of which is causing problems in your application. This situation is particularly true in the case of an application that has been modified many times, or when little thought was given to optimizing how the code in the application is used.

Even so, some very carefully designed applications end up with deeply nested code, making it difficult to understand how all the code ties together.

Imagine a function that performs a common operation (such as calculating shipping costs) in an application. As a general rule, rather than include this function in every module in the application, you'll put the function into a single module, declare it with the `Public` keyword so that it's recognized and used by the entire application, and then call it from whichever procedure needs a shipping costs calculation.

Furthermore, imagine that this application has many such functions and subroutines, each calling the other, depending on the application's logic at that moment. Finally, imagine that users report that the shipping fee appears to be incorrectly calculated under some conditions but not others.

You could single-step through all the code in the application, hoping to discover the cause of the erroneous shipping fee. However, this approach wouldn't be efficient. You'd be much better off setting a conditional watch on an important variable within the shipping fee function, forcing the code to break when the condition is True. Then open the Call Stack window (see Figure 26.18) to view the path that the VBA engine has taken to reach this particular point in the code.

FIGURE 26.18

The Call Stack window shows you how the execution point reached its current position.

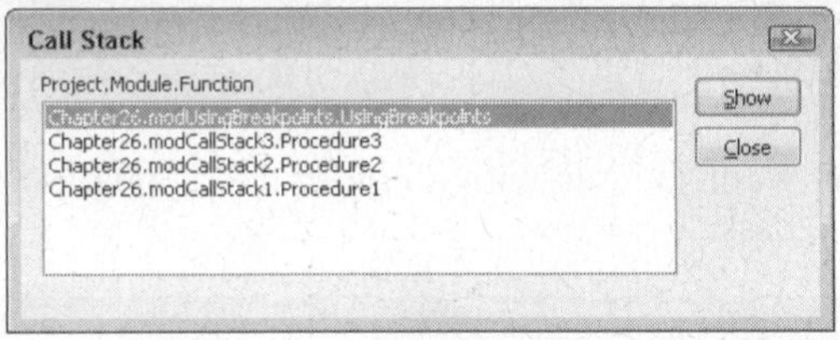

The bottom entry in the Call Stack window (`Chapter26.modCallStack1.Procedure1`) indicates that `Procedure1` (contained in module `modCallStack1`) was the first function called. The entry above it (`Chapter26.modCallStack2.Procedure2`) indicates that `Procedure1` called `Procedure2` (contained in `modCallStack2`) and so on. You can quite easily trace the path that the VBA code has taken to reach the current breakpoint.

Double-click any of the items listed in the Call Stack to be taken to the statement that sent execution to the next procedure. Using the Call Stack window in conjunction with conditional watches enables you to stop code wherever relevant, and to diagnose how code has executed up to the breakpoint.

Trapping Errors in Your Code

You can test and debug your code to your heart's content, but you still won't find every possible bug. All projects of a significant size contain bugs that the developers were not able to uncover during the testing and debugging phase of development. As a developer, it's your job to ensure that your program handles unexpected problems gracefully.

Understanding error trapping

When VBA encounters an error in your code, it *raises an error.* A number of things happen when an error is raised, most notably the VBA engine looks for an `On Error` statement and the `Err` object is created. You include the On Error keywords in your code when you want VBA to act in a certain way when an error occurs.

On Error Resume Next

An `On Error Resume Next` statement instructs VBA to ignore any errors in the statements that follow it and continue executing as if the error never happened. This can be a very dangerous statement. If statements in your code rely on prior statements being executed successfully, the errors will pile up and can cause a mess. Used judiciously, however, `On Error Resume Next` can be very useful.

VBA contains an object called a `Collection` that can hold multiple items. When items are added to a collection, the key associated with that item must be unique. If you try to add a key that already exists, an error will occur. You can use this feature of the `Collection` object with `On Error Resume Next` to get a unique list of items.

```
Sub IgnoringErrors()

  Dim colUnique As Collection
  Dim vaFruit As Variant
  Dim i As Long

  vaFruit = Array("Apple", "Pear", "Orange", "Apple", "Grape", "Pear")
  Set colUnique = New Collection

  For i = LBound(vaFruit) To UBound(vaFruit)
    On Error Resume Next
      colUnique.Add vaFruit(i), vaFruit(i)
    On Error GoTo 0
  Next i

  For i = 1 To colUnique.Count
    Debug.Print colUnique.Item(i)
  Next i

End Sub
```

In the above procedure, there is an array that contains duplicates. To get a list of items in the arrays without the duplicates, each item is added to a collection and that item's name is also used as the key (the second argument to the `Add` method). When VBA encounters the `colUnique.Add` statement for an item that already exists in the collection, it raises an error. The `On Error Resume Next` statement above that line instructs VBA to ignore the error and continue processing. The duplicate item does not get added and only unique items end up in the collection.

This procedure demonstrates how a known error can be suppressed to your advantage. The very next line after the line that will generate an error instructs VBA to treat errors normally. Resetting the error handler in this way ensures that you don't suppress errors unintentionally. It's also a good practice to indent any statements between the `On Error` statements to provide a visual cue about which errors should be suppressed.

CAUTION
`On Error Resume Next` suppresses all errors that would otherwise cause the code to stop. While it can be useful to suppress particular errors, it doesn't know the difference between the error that you want to ignore and the error that you unintentionally coded. Be sure to carefully debug the statements covered by `On Error Resume Next`.

On Error Goto 0

As demonstrated above, the `On Error Goto 0` statement resets the error handler to the default. If no `On Error` statement were included in the code, VBA would break on any error and display a message. The `On Error Goto 0` statement does the same thing. Typically, it's used with `On Error Resume Next` to return the error handler back to the default state after intentionally suppressing a particular error.

On Error Goto Label

The most common use of `On Error` is to direct the program flow to a label in your procedure. Labels are special statements that provide anchors in your code. Labels are text followed by a colon and cannot be indented. When VBA raises an error after `On Error Goto Label`, the program branches to the line just below the label and continues executing.

```
Sub BranchError()

  Dim x As Long

  On Error GoTo ErrHandler

  x = 1 / 0

  Debug.Print x

ErrHandler:
  MsgBox "An error occurred"

End Sub
```

In this simple example, an error is generated by attempting to divide by zero. When the error is raised, VBA braches to the line below `ErrHandler:`, displays a message box, and continues on to the `End Sub` statement. The `Debug.Print` statement is never executed.

The Resume keyword

We've seen how `Resume Next` can be used with `On Error` to ignore certain errors. `Resume` can also be used on its own. Used alone, `Resume` branches the program back to the line that caused the error and the error is re-raised. This is useful when you want to handle errors but have the option of inspecting the line that caused the error, but it can cause an infinite loop of raising errors and resuming if you're not careful.

Resume can also be used with a label to branch program execution elsewhere. Generally, Resume Label branches to a part of the code that performs clean-up duty and exits the procedure. A label is a special line in VBA code that ends with a colon (:). Labels are like bookmarks or anchors in your code — they're places that you can jump to, such as when using a Resume statement.


```
Sub ErrorResumeOptions()

  Dim x As Long
  Dim lResp As Long

  On Error GoTo ErrHandler

  x = 1 / 0

  Debug.Print x

ErrExit:
  Exit Sub

ErrHandler:
  lResp = MsgBox("Do you want to inspect the error?", vbYesNo)
  If lResp = vbYes Then
      Stop
      Resume
  Else
      Resume ErrExit
  End If

End Sub
```

Like the previous example, this code intentionally raises an error by attempting to divide by zero. The error handler is called and the program is branched to ErrHandler:. Inside the error handler, the user is asked whether he would like to inspect the error. Clicking No on the message box executes the Resume ErrExit statement, and execution is branched to that label where Exit Sub is executed. Clicking Yes first executes a Stop statement. Without the Stop statement, Resume would send program execution back to the line that caused the error, the error would be raised again, and the program would head back to the error handler. Stop allows the developer to step through the code line-by-line, first executing Resume to see what line caused the error, and then inspecting variables to diagnose the problem.

The Err object

In addition to raising an error and branching based on On Error, VBA also creates an Err object that contains information about the error. In fact, the Err object is always present, even when no error has been raised. When VBA encounters an error, regardless of whether there is error handling in place, the `Number` property of the `Err` object is set to the number of the error that occurred. When no error has been encountered, `Number` is zero.

The `Err` object also has a Description property. The error number may not be meaningful to you, but the Description property generally helps you identify the error.

Including error handling in your procedures

Some procedures are so trivial that error handling is not needed. For all other procedures, you should include some error handling to avoid having your users thrust into the VB Editor when an unexpected error occurs.

Your error handling technique should include an `On Error Goto Label` statement near the top of the procedure, suspension of the error handling in the code when needed, an exit label that cleans up any in-process variables, and an error handling label that displays the error and controls program flow.

A typical procedure with error handling is shown below:

```
Sub ATypicalErrorHandler()

  Dim statements

  On Error GoTo ErrHandler

  Multiple statements

  On Error Resume Next
    Intentional errors to ignore
  On Error GoTo ErrHandler

Multiple statements

ErrExit:
  Clean up code
  Exit Sub

ErrHandler:
  MsgBox Err.Description, vbOKOnly
  If gbDebugMode Then
    Stop
    Resume
  Else
    Resume ErrExit
  End If

End Sub
```

The procedure starts with `On Error Goto ErrHandler`, which directs the program to the `ErrHandler` label if an unexpected error occurs. In the middle of the procedure is an example of stopping the error handler using `On Error Resume Next` to trap an intentional error. The error handler is restarted after the statements with the intentional errors. Above the error handling section, the clean-up and exiting statements are executed. If there are no errors, this code will be run and the procedure will complete without running the error handling code.

The error handling section displays a message using the `Description` property of the `Err` object. There is a global variable, `gbDebugMode`, that the developer can set to `True` during debugging and `False` when the application is sent to the users. If `gbDebugMode` is `True`, the program stops and the developer can step through the code to investigate the error. Otherwise, the `ErrExit` portion of the code is executed and the user sees only the message box.

Part VII

Advanced Access Programming Techniques

The chapters in this part cover issues that concern professional database developers, including customization of the Access Ribbon interface, accessing external data with VBA, integrating with SQL Server databases, and distributing Access application.

Many developers may never need to use the capabilities described in this part. However, it's important not to overlook the capabilities provided by a system like Access.

Each version of Access has extended previous capabilities as an enterprise development platform while introducing new features geared to true professional client-server applications. Part VII takes you on a tour of some of the high-end features provided by Access so that you not only know they're there, but also have a blueprint for using these capabilities in your own applications.

IN THIS PART

CHAPTER 27

Accessing Data with VBA Code

IN THIS CHAPTER

- Working with Access data
- Examining the ADO object model
- Looking at DAO objects
- Updating a table with VBA code

Data access and data management are at the core of any database application. Although you can do a fine job building applications with bound forms, using Visual Basic for Applications (VBA) code to access and manipulate data directly provides far greater flexibility than a bound application can. Anything that can be done with bound forms and controls can be done with a bit of VBA code using ActiveX data objects (ADO) or data access objects (DAO) to retrieve and work with data.

The VBA language offers a full array of powerful commands for manipulating records in a table, providing data for controls on a form, or just about anything else. This chapter provides some in-depth examples of working with procedures that use SQL and ADO to manipulate database data.

ON THE WEB

In the `Chapter27.accdb` database, you'll find a number of forms to use as a starting point and other completed forms to compare to the forms you change in this example.

Working with Data

The first thing to note when discussing data access objects is that the DAO and ADO object models are separate from the Access object model. DAO and ADO represent the objects managed and "owned" by the Access database engines (ACE or Jet), which are software components installed along with Office. In the past, Excel (with the MSQuery add-on) and Visual Basic (the stand-alone application development product) could directly use the Jet database engine or access it through open database connectivity (ODBC) or Microsoft Query.

Using Access VBA enables you to manipulate your database objects behind the scenes, giving you a great amount of flexibility within your applications. Access provides two different object models for working with data: ADO and DAO.

ADO is the newer of the two syntaxes. It's based on Microsoft's ActiveX technology, which provides the basis for independent objects that perform complex tasks without input from their hosts. When applied to ADO, the ActiveX objects are able to perform a wide variety of data access tasks without hampering Access in any way. Because ADO objects are quite powerful, the ADO object model (meaning, the ADO object hierarchy) is fairly sparse. Only a few objects are needed to perform virtually all data access tasks in Access applications.

The older data access object model supported by Access is DAO. Unlike ADO, DAO objects are simple and direct, and they are part of a more complex hierarchy of objects. DAO is widely used and was the only data access methodology in Access for many years.

The distinction between Access and DAO is important because Access's user interface tends to blur the line between objects belonging to Access and those belonging to the database engine. There are some features available in code that you may *think* are data access objects but are really features of Access, and vice versa. In code, you'll have to develop with this distinction in mind. For example, ADO and DAO objects have many built-in properties and methods; other properties are added by Access.

In any case, working with ADO and DAO in VBA procedures provides you with much greater flexibility than dealing strictly with forms and reports bound to queries and tables. As you'll see in the rest of this chapter, relatively few lines of ADO or DAO code perform complex operations on data, such as updating or deleting existing records, or adding new records to tables. Using VBA code means that an application can respond to current conditions on a form, such as missing or incorrect values. It's quite easy to perform ad hoc queries against data that would otherwise require complex queries with many parameters.

Entire books — *big* books — have been written on the topics covered in this chapter. All we can do in this chapter is provide you with some fundamental examples of using ADO and DAO in Access applications, and, coupled with the material in the other chapters in this book, you should be well prepared to incorporate VBA-based data management in your Access applications.

NOTE

ADO and DAO are not equivalent in every regard. Both syntaxes enable you to add to or modify the data in tables, build recordsets, work with data in recordsets, and populate forms with data. However, ADO has a distinct edge when it comes to working with external data sources. As you'll soon see, ADO requires a provider that defines the data source used by the ADO objects in an application. ADO providers are specific to the data source, such as SQL Server or Access. The provider endows the ADO objects with special abilities (such as the ability to test the connection to the data source), depending on the underlying data sources. DAO, on the other hand, is a more generic data access syntax and is not specific to any one data source. ADO is the logical choice where advanced data access tasks must be performed, while DAO is very good at routine querying, updating, and other data tasks.

The following sections describe each of these objects and explain how each object adds to the ADO data access capabilities.

Although Access is not strictly object oriented, it is most certainly object *based*. The remainder of this chapter describes the *object models* you use in VBA code to perform data-management tasks in your Access applications. An object model is simply the arrangement of the objects that perform the data-management tasks. A sound understanding of the ADO and DAO object models is an essential requirement when using VBA code to manage Access data.

Many of the objects described in this chapter contain a *collection* of zero or more objects. A collection is a container holding all the members of a certain type of object. (A collection is, itself, an object.)

A collection is like a stack of baseball cards. Each card in the stack is different from all the other cards, but all baseball cards have certain characteristics (like size, the statistics printed on the back, and so on) in common. In Access, a *recordset* object (either ADO or DAO) contains a collection of *field* objects. Every recordset object shares certain characteristics with all other recordset objects, and every field object is similar to all other fields in certain ways.

The name of a collection is almost always the plural of the object type within the collection. Therefore, a `Fields` collection contains a number of different `Field` objects.

NOTE

It's important to know when a term applies to an object of the same name or is just the name of a general category of database items. In this book, a capitalized word like *Field* refers to a `Field` object, in contrast to *field* (lowercase), which is a generic reference to any field in any table. Similarly, *Fields* means a `Fields` collection, while *fields* refers to a number of different fields.

Each ADO or DAO object comes with a collection of properties and methods. Each property or method provides you with a way to define the object, or represents an action you use to direct the object to perform its job.

An object's `Properties` collection is made up of a number of `Property` objects. Each `Property` object has its *own* set of properties. Properties can be referenced directly, created through the Access interface, or created by a user and added to the `Properties` collection. You generally refer to a property in this way: *ObjectName.PropertyName*. For example, to refer to the `Name` property of a field, the syntax would be as follows:

```
MyField.Name
```

Methods are a little different. A method is an *action* an object can perform, or is an action performed *on* an object. The purpose of a data access object is to manipulate or display data in a database; therefore, each object must have some way to act upon that data. You can't add or delete methods in the ADO or DAO objects. (This is one of the several ways that Access is not truly object oriented.) You can only invoke the method on the object.

For example, the following code places the record pointer of the recordset `MyRecordset` at the next record:

```
MyRecordset.MoveNext
```

Like properties, every ADO and DAO object has a set of methods applicable to that object.

If you ever need to know more about an ADO or DAO object, use the Object Browser (shown in Figure 27.1). Open the Object Browser from within the VBA Editor by pressing F2 or choosing View⇨Object Browser from the menu in the VBA editor window. The Object Browser lets you examine each object's methods and properties and the arguments you can expect when using them. The Object Browser is used by all Microsoft applications that feature VBA as their language engine.

FIGURE 27.1

The Object Browser provides a view into an object's properties and methods.

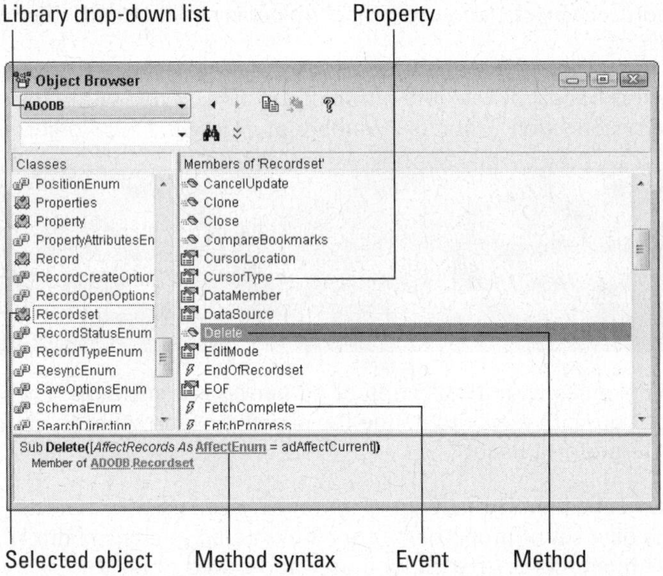

Library drop-down list

Property

Selected object

Method syntax

Event

Method

The Object Browser is easy to use. Select a library (ADODB, for example) from the drop-down list in the upper-left corner; then scroll through the object list on the left side of the browser to find an object of interest. Selecting an object fills the right-side list with the object's properties, methods, and events (if applicable). Clicking a property, method, or event reveals the item's syntax in the area below the lists.

Although the Object Browser doesn't show specific code examples, very often seeing the syntax associated with the property, method, or event may be enough to get you started writing VBA code, or to clarify the object's details.

Understanding ADO Objects

We'll begin our explanation of the ActiveX Data Objects by examining the ADO object model and describing the purpose of each object. Then we'll look at a number of code examples that use the ADO objects to perform common database tasks.

The ADO object model is shown in Figure 27.2. As you can see, the ADO object model is quite simple and includes only a few types of objects. Notice that the ADO object model is not hierarchical. Each object stands alone and is not subordinate to another object in the model.

FIGURE 27.2

The ADO object model.

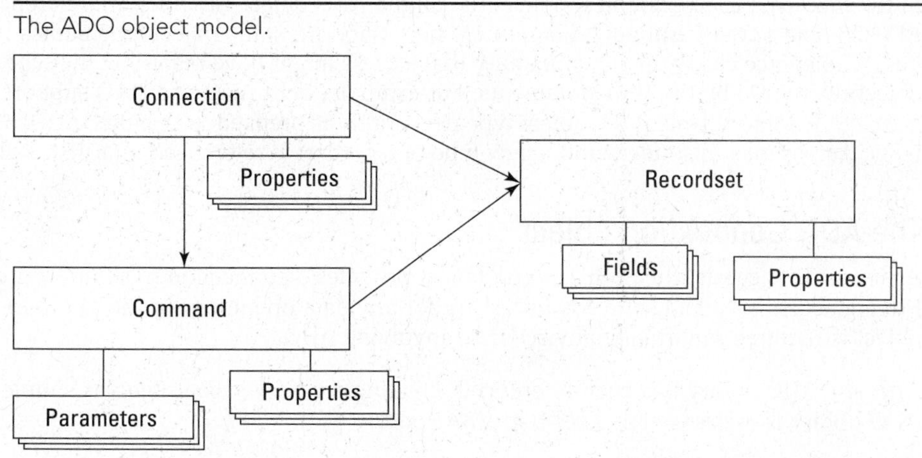

Using ADO objects requires a reference to the ADO library. Figure 27.3 shows the References dialog box (opened by choosing Tools➪References in the VBA editor window) with the ADO library (Microsoft ActiveX Data Objects) selected. The exact version of the ADO library installed on your machine may vary, and, in fact, there may be more than one ADO library in the References dialog box. Select the highest-numbered library if you want to use the latest version available to Access. You may want to select a lower-numbered library to maintain compatibility with an existing system.

FIGURE 27.3

Referencing the ADO library.

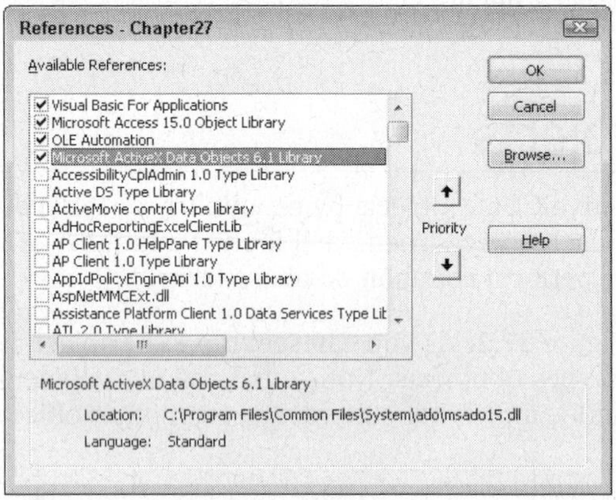

In the following code examples, notice that all the ADO object variables are referenced as ADODB object types. Although not entirely necessary, prefixing object type names with a library reference clears up any ambiguity that Access might have regarding the type of object referenced by the VBA statements. For example, both ADO and DAO support a `Recordset` object. Unless the object type declaration is prefixed with either ADODB or DAO, Access may misunderstand *which* type of recordset is referenced in a VBA statement.

The ADO Connection object

As its name suggests, the `Connection` object provides a connection to a data source. Having access to a data source is necessary for any data operation, so the `Connection` object is required in virtually any scenario involving ADO.

After the ADO library has been referenced, creating a `Connection` object is simple (the ADO library is referenced as `ADODB` in VBA code):

```
Dim adConn as ADODB.Connection
Set adConn = New ADODB.Connection
```

These two statements are typical of VBA's approach to object-oriented programming. In the first statement, an object variable (`adConn`) is established as an `ADODB.Connection` object type. This means that VBA recognizes `adConn` as a `Connection`, with all the properties and methods associated with `Connection` objects, as defined by the ADO library. However, at this point, `adConn` is just a placeholder — it doesn't yet exist in memory.

The second statement instantiates the `adConn` object variable. As this statement executes, VBA creates a `Connection` object in the computer's memory, points the `adConn` variable to the object in memory, and prepares it for use.

The `Connection` must be opened before it can be used. The following statement is the easiest way to open an ADO `Connection`:

```
adConn.Open CurrentProject.Connection
```

In this case, the `Connection` connects to the current database. As you'll soon see, a `Connection` object requires a number of properties to be set before it can successfully open, but opening a `Connection` on the current database's `Connection` property provides all those settings. `CurrentProject.Connection` is actually a long string (specifically, a *connection string*) that includes all the information needed about the current database. A typical `Connection` property setting is as follows:


```
Provider=Microsoft.ACE.OLEDB.12.0;User ID=Admin;
Data Source=C:\Access2013\Chapter_27\Chapter27.accdb;
Mode=Share Deny None;Extended Properties="";
Jet OLEDB:System database=C:\...\Access\System.mdw;
Jet OLEDB:Registry Path=...\Access Connectivity Engine;
Jet OLEDB:Database Password="";
Jet OLEDB:Engine Type=6;
Jet OLEDB:Database Locking Mode=1;
Jet OLEDB:Global Partial Bulk Ops=2;
Jet OLEDB:Global Bulk Transactions=1;
Jet OLEDB:New Database Password="";
Jet OLEDB:Create System Database=False;
Jet OLEDB:Encrypt Database=False;
Jet OLEDB:Don't Copy Locale on Compact=False;
Jet OLEDB:Compact Without Replica Repair=False;
Jet OLEDB:SFP=False;
Jet OLEDB:Support Complex Data=True
```

NOTE

Line breaks have been added above for clarity, and some lines have been shortened.

This is actually considerably more than the `Connection` object actually needs, but Microsoft wanted to make sure nothing was missing.

Notice the `Data Source` portion of the `ConnectionString` property. This is the part that points to a specific ACCDB file. Changing this path means the `Connection` object can open virtually any Access database as long as the path is valid and terminates at an ACCDB file.

The following procedure opens a `Connection` against the current database, prints the `Connection` object's `Provider` property, and then closes and discards the `Connection` object:

```
Public Sub OpenConnection()

    Dim adConn As ADODB.Connection

    Set adConn = New ADODB.Connection
```

```
        adConn.Open CurrentProject.Connection

        ' Connection is open
        Debug.Print adConn.Provider

        adConn.Close
        Set adConn = Nothing

    End Sub
```

When working with ADO, it's very important to close an object (if the object supports a `Close` method) and set it to `Nothing` when your code is done with the object. ADO objects tend to stay in memory once they've been opened, and must be explicitly closed and discarded (set to `Nothing`) to clear them from memory. If an ADO object is not properly terminated, it may remain in memory causing problems for users.

A `Connection` object requires the provider information and the data source. The provider specifies which ADO provider (essentially a driver) to attach to the `Connection` object. For example, there are providers for SQL Server databases: one for the Jet database engine, and another for the ACE database engine. Each provider knows how to connect to a different type of data and endows the `Connection` object with features specific to the data source.

The downside to the `Connection` object, and one that causes a lot of problems for Access developers, is the correct syntax to use for the `Connection` object's `ConnectionString` property. The `ConnectionString` must be properly composed and must reference a provider that is installed on the local machine.

There is a little trick to discovering the `ConnectionString` to use against an ADO provider. Start by creating an empty text file, and change its extension from TXT to UDL (universal data link). Next, double-click the empty file, and Windows opens the Data Link Properties dialog box (shown in Figure 27.4). Use this dialog box to select a provider (on the Provider tab) and a data source (on the Connection tab); then close the dialog box.

FIGURE 27.4

Use the Data Link Properties dialog box to set up a connection string.

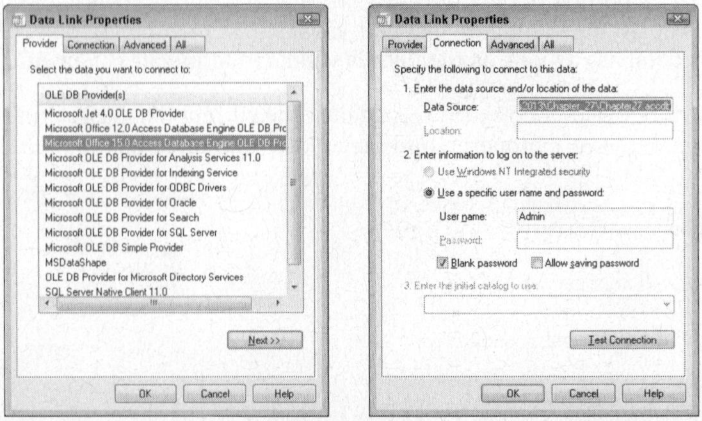

Finally, open the UDL file in Notepad, copy the connection string from the file's contents, and paste the connection string into your VBA program. The connection string in the following procedure was generated using this trick:

```
Public Sub OpenConnection()

    Dim adConn As ADODB.Connection
    Dim sConn As String

    Set adConn = New ADODB.Connection

    'Be sure to use the path to Chapter27.accdb on your
    'computer, which may be different than used here
    sConn = "Provider=Microsoft.ACE.OLEDB.15.0;" & _
"Data Source=C:\Access2013\Chapter_27\Chapter27.accdb;" & _
      "Persist Security Info=False"

    adConn.ConnectionString = sConn

    adConn.Open

    ' Connection is open
    Debug.Print adConn.Provider

    adConn.Close
    Set adConn = Nothing

End Sub
```

The reason this trick works is that a UDL file is recognized by Windows as a container for an ADO connection string. Double-clicking the file opens the Data Link Properties dialog box, which is the default editor for UDL files. You specify all the attributes needed in an ADO connection string through the Data Link Properties dialog box, and those attributes are added to the UDL file.

The Provider tab in the Data Link Properties dialog box shows all the providers currently installed on the local machine. ADO is a local process, so the provider must be installed locally for ADO to work. The ADO providers you see in Figure 27.4 were installed either along with Windows or as part of Office 2013.

The ADO Command object

The second major ADO topic is the `Command` object. As its name implies, a `Command` object executes a command against the data source opened through a `Connection`. The command can be as simple as the name of an Access query, or as complex as a long SQL statement that selects dozens of fields and includes `WHERE` and `ORDER BY` clauses. In fact, the `Command` object is the most common way to execute SQL Server stored procedures from Access applications.

As you'll see later in this chapter, the output from executing a `Command` object can be directed into a recordset. The data in the recordset can then be used to populate a form or controls such as text boxes, combo boxes, and list boxes.

There are many, many ways to use `Command` objects. The following procedure is just one example of using a `Command` object. In this case, the `Command` object populates a recordset with data taken directly from `tblCustomers`. (Recordsets are discussed in the next section.) The following procedure (`ExecuteCommand`) is included in `basADO_Commands` in the `Chapter 13.accdb` example database.

```
Public Sub ExecuteCommand()

    Dim adRs As ADODB.Recordset
    Dim adCmd As ADODB.Command

    Const sTABLE As String = "tblCustomers"

    Set adRs = New ADODB.Recordset
    Set adCmd = New ADODB.Command

    adCmd.ActiveConnection = CurrentProject.Connection
    adCmd.CommandText = sTABLE

    Set adRs = adCmd.Execute

    Debug.Print adRs.GetString

    adRs.Close
    Set adRs = Nothing
    Set adCmd = Nothing

End Sub
```

Notice the following actions in this procedure:

- A `Recordset` and a `Command` object are both declared and instantiated.
- The `Command` object's `ActiveConnection` property is set to the current project's `Connection` property.
- The `Command` object's `CommandText` property is set to the name of a table in the database.
- The recordset is populated by setting it to the value returned when the `Command` object is executed.

Notice the use of the recordset's `GetString` method. `GetString` is a handy way to output everything that's in the recordset. Figure 27.5 shows the output from `ExecuteCommand` in the Immediate window.

The Immediate window is thoroughly discussed in Chapter 26.

FIGURE 27.5

GetString is a convenient way to see what's in a recordset.

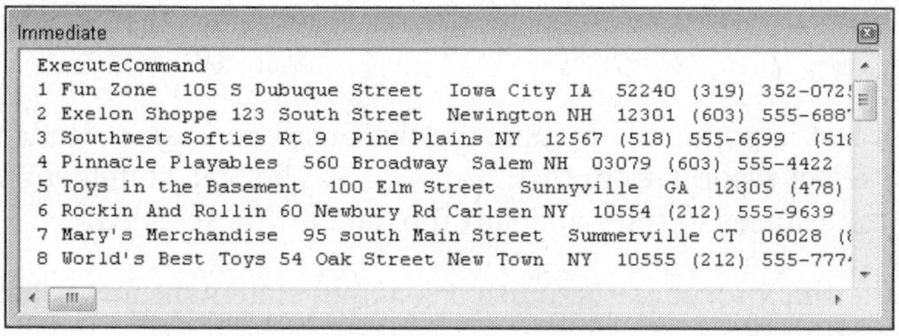

```
Immediate
ExecuteCommand
1 Fun Zone  105 S Dubuque Street  Iowa City IA  52240 (319) 352-072
2 Exelon Shoppe 123 South Street  Newington NH  12301 (603) 555-688
3 Southwest Softies Rt 9  Pine Plains NY  12567 (518) 555-6699  (51
4 Pinnacle Playables  560 Broadway  Salem NH  03079 (603) 555-4422
5 Toys in the Basement  100 Elm Street  Sunnyville  GA  12305 (478)
6 Rockin And Rollin 60 Newbury Rd Carlsen NY  10554 (212) 555-9639
7 Mary's Merchandise  95 south Main Street  Summerville CT  06028 (
8 World's Best Toys 54 Oak Street New Town  NY  10555 (212) 555-777
```

This little example illustrates the basics of what you need to know about ADO Command objects. A Command object must be attached to an available Connection through its ActiveConnection property. The ActiveConnection can be a connection string or an open Connection object. It doesn't make any difference where the Connection is pointing — an Access or SQL Server database, Oracle or any other data source. The Command object uses the Connection's special knowledge of the data source to get at the data.

Command objects are most valuable when working with parameterized queries. Each Command object includes a Parameters collection containing, naturally, Parameter objects. Each parameter corresponds to a parameter required by the query or stored procedure referenced by the Command's CommandText property.

Very often the CommandText property is set to a SQL statement that includes parameters:

```
SELECT * FROM tblCustomers
WHERE State = 'NY' OR State = 'NJ';
```

You'll see many examples of using the ADO Command object to populate recordsets and perform actions on data throughout this book.

The ADO Recordset object

The ADO Recordset is a very versatile object. Most often, it's populated by executing a Command, or directly through its Open method. Open_ADO_Recordset illustrates how easily the Recordset object opens an Access table (Open_ADO_Recordset is included in modADO_Recordsets in the Chapter27.accdb example database):

```
Public Sub Open_ADO_Recordset()

    Dim adRs As ADODB.Recordset

    Set adRs = New ADODB.Recordset
```

```
    adRs.Open "SELECT * FROM tblCustomers;", _
      CurrentProject.Connection

    Debug.Print adRs.GetString

    adRs.Close
    Set adRs = Nothing

End Sub
```

In this example, the recordset is populated by opening the Customers table. Notice that a SQL statement is used to select records from `tblCustomers`. The SQL statement could include `WHERE` or `ORDER BY` clauses to filter and sort the data as it's selected.

An alternative way to write this procedure is to use a separate statement for assigning the `ActiveConnection` property:

```
Public Sub Open_ADO_Rs_Connection()

  Dim adRs As ADODB.Recordset

  Set adRs = New ADODB.Recordset
  adRs.ActiveConnection = CurrentProject.Connection

  adRs.Open "SELECT * FROM tblCustomers;"

  Debug.Print adRs.GetString

  adRs.Close
  Set adRs = Nothing

End Sub
```

The `Open_ADO_Rs_Connection` procedure is included in `modADO_Recordsets` in the `Chapter27.accdb` example database.

Many developers prefer the approach in `Open_ADO_Rs_Connection` because it's easier to see exactly what's happening to the `Recordset` object and where its properties are being set. Although these very small procedures are easily understood, in larger code segments finding all the references to an object like `adRs` can be challenging, especially when the VBA statements become long and complex.

As with the other ADO objects, a `Recordset` object must be declared and instantiated. Like the `Command` object, if the `Open` method is used to populate a `Recordset` object, an open connection must be provided as an argument to the `Open` method.

`Recordset` objects are used in many different places in this book. Depending on context, the most commonly used `Recordset` methods include `Open`, `Close`, `MoveFirst`, `MoveNext`, `MovePrevious`, and `MoveLast`.

Navigating recordsets

Recordsets wouldn't be much use if all you could do is open and close them, or if the `GetString` method were the only way to use the data in a recordset. Depending on context, the word *recordset* means several different things:

- The rows of data returned by a query
- The data bound to an Access form
- The object filled with data as the result of an ADO operation

In all cases, however, a recordset is a data structure containing rows and columns of data. The rows, of course, are *records,* while the columns are *fields.*

It makes sense that Access provides ways to *navigate* through a recordset. When viewing a table or query results as a datasheet, you can use the vertical and horizontal scroll bars or arrow keys to move up and down, left and right, through the Datasheet view of the recordset. It's not surprising, then, that ADO `Recordset` objects support methods for moving through the records contained in a recordset.

The following procedure demonstrates the fundamental ADO recordset navigation methods. (As you'll see in the "Understanding DAO Objects" section, later in this chapter, DAO recordsets support identically named methods.)

```
Public Sub RecordsetNavigation()

    Dim adRs As ADODB.Recordset

    Set adRs = New ADODB.Recordset
    adRs.ActiveConnection = CurrentProject.Connection

    adRs.CursorType = adOpenStatic
    adRs.Open "SELECT * FROM tblCustomers;"

    Debug.Print adRs!CustomerID, adRs!Company

    adRs.MoveNext
    Debug.Print adRs!CustomerID, adRs!Company

    adRs.MoveLast
    Debug.Print adRs!CustomerID, adRs!Company

    adRs.MovePrevious
    Debug.Print adRs!CustomerID, adRs!Company

    adRs.MoveFirst
    Debug.Print adRs.Fields("CustomerID").Value, _
      adRs.Fields("Company").Value

    adRs.Close
```

```
        Set adRs = Nothing

    End Sub
```

This procedure begins by opening a `Recordset` object populated with data from `tblCustomers`. It immediately displays the `CustomerID` and `Company` from the very first record; then it moves around the recordset a few rows at a time, displaying the `CustomerID` and `Company` for each record along the way. It ends by returning to the first record and displaying its data. The output produced by `RecordsetNavigation` is shown in Figure 27.6.

FIGURE 27.6

Demonstrating recordset navigation.

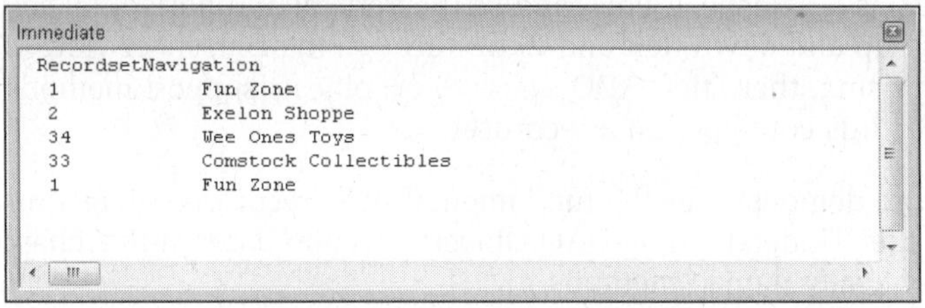

```
Immediate
RecordsetNavigation
1             Fun Zone
2             Exelon Shoppe
34            Wee Ones Toys
33            Comstock Collectibles
1             Fun Zone
```

Obviously, this is a trivial example meant to demonstrate how easily ADO recordsets can be navigated. As a developer, you're free to work with any record in the recordset, moving up and down the rows as needed.

Access recordsets support the concept of a *current record pointer*. Only one record at a time within a recordset is *current*. When you make changes to a recordset or navigate through its rows, your code affects only the current record.

The `RecordsetNavigation` procedure also demonstrates two methods for referencing individual fields within a record: using the bang operator (`!`) and the `Fields` collection. After moving to a row, individual fields are referenced as members of the recordset. Access works on just one record at a time, so any reference to a field evaluates to the field within the current record.

Understanding CursorType

In the `RecordsetNavigation` procedure, notice the recordset's `CursorType` property. In this example, it's set to `adOpenStatic`. There are several settings for `CursorType`; `adOpenStatic` means to open the recordset with a static type cursor. Access uses a cursor to keep track of the current record in a recordset. A static cursor means that the data in the recordset is static, and new records can't be added to the recordset. Static cursors are ideal when the purpose of the recordset is to review data in the underlying tables and adding new records is not necessary.

Table 27.1 shows the permissible values for `CursorType`.

TABLE 27.1 CursorType Values

Value	Effect of CursorType
`adOpenDynamic`	A dynamic cursor supports all navigation methods, and the recordset is completely editable. New records can be added and existing records can be edited. Changes made by other users are reflected in the recordset currently in memory.
`adOpenForwardOnly`	The recordset is opened as a static copy of the underlying data, and new records can't be added. The recordset also won't reflect changes made to the underlying tables by other users. Most important, only the `MoveNext` and `MoveLast` methods are valid against a forward-only recordset.
`adOpenKeyset`	Supports full navigation and records are editable. However, records added or deleted by other users are not seen.
`adOpenStatic`	Opens a static recordset that does not show changes made to the underlying tables by other users. Similar to a forward-only cursor, except that all navigation methods are valid.

Each type of cursor has a specific effect on the data contained in a recordset. For example, you wouldn't want to use a forward-only cursor on data where the user expects to be able to move forward and backward through the data. A forward-only recordset is most often used for updating records as a bulk operation, such as updating area codes or tax rates in a number of records.

On the other hand, it doesn't make sense to use a dynamic cursor (`adOpenDynamic`) for simple tasks such as scanning a recordset for updates. A dynamic cursor keeps track of changes by the current user and changes in the underlying tables. A dynamic cursor is, therefore, slower and requires more memory and CPU cycles than a simpler forward-only cursor.

Detecting the recordset end or beginning

The `MovePrevious` and `MoveNext` methods move the current record pointer one row through the recordset. If the pointer is at the very first or very last record, these methods move the pointer off the beginning or end of the recordset without raising an error. When you're navigating a recordset, you need to be sure the current record pointer is resting on a valid record before referencing data or executing an action on the record.

The ADO `Recordset` object supports two Boolean properties, `EOF` and `BOF`, that indicate when the current record pointer is at the end or beginning (respectively) of the recordset. (*EOF* and *BOF* are acronyms for *end of file* and *beginning of file.*) `EOF` and `BOF` are both `False` when the record pointer is on a valid record. `EOF` is `True` only when the record pointer is off the end of the recordset, and `BOF` is `True` only when the pointer is off the beginning of the recordset. `EOF` and `BOF` are both `True` *only* when the recordset contains no records at all.

The `Use_EOF_BOF` procedure illustrates using `EOF` and `BOF` in an ADO `Recordset`:

```
Public Sub Use_EOF_BOF()

    Dim adRs As ADODB.Recordset

    Set adRs = New ADODB.Recordset
    adRs.ActiveConnection = CurrentProject.Connection
    adRs.CursorType = adOpenStatic

    adRs.Open "SELECT * FROM tblCustomers " _
        & "WHERE State = 'NY' " _
        & "ORDER BY Company;"

    Debug.Print "RecordCount: " & adRs.RecordCount

    If adRs.BOF And adRs.EOF Then
        Debug.Print "No records to process"
        Exit Sub
    End If

    Do Until adRs.EOF
        Debug.Print adRs!Company
        adRs.MoveNext
    Loop

    adRs.MoveLast

    Do Until adRs.BOF
        Debug.Print adRs!Company
        adRs.MovePrevious
    Loop

    adRs.Close
    Set adRs = Nothing

End Sub
```

Previous examples in this chapter have included code like this. The main differences are checking `EOF` and `BOF` state before executing the `MoveLast` and `MovePrevious` methods. Notice that these properties change to `True` only *after* these methods have executed. When moving toward the end of the recordset, the `EOF` value is checked after `MoveNext` has executed (at the top of the `Do Until` loop).

Counting records

It's often very useful to know how many records are in a recordset before beginning operations that may take a long time. Otherwise, a user may unwisely select criteria that return too many records to handle efficiently. Fortunately, ADO `Recordset` objects provide a `RecordCount` property that tells you exactly how many records are present in the recordset:

```
Public Sub UseRecordCount()

  Dim adRs As ADODB.Recordset
  Dim lCnt As Long

  Set adRs = New ADODB.Recordset
  adRs.ActiveConnection = CurrentProject.Connection
  adRs.CursorType = adOpenStatic

  adRs.Open "SELECT * FROM tblCustomers;"

  Do While Not adRs.EOF
    lCnt = lCnt + 1
    Debug.Print "Record " & lCnt & " of " & adRs.RecordCount
    adRs.MoveNext
  Loop

  adRs.Close
  Set adRs = Nothing

End Sub
```


The `RecordCount` property is not valid for forward-only recordsets. Notice that the `CursorType` is set to `adOpenStatic` in this code. If it's set to `adOpenForwardOnly`, the `RecordCount` property is set to `-1` and does not change while the recordset is in memory.

`RecordCount` is a convenient way to determine whether a recordset contains any records at all. The only issue with `RecordCount` is that, on large recordsets, `RecordCount` penalizes performance. The `Recordset` object actually counts the number of records it contains, halting execution until the count is complete.

A much faster way to detect an empty recordset is determining whether `EOF` and `BOF` are both `True`:

```
If adRs.BOF And rs.EOF Then
    Debug.Print "No records to process"
    Exit Sub
End If
```

If `BOF` and `EOF` are both `True`, the cursor is both before the first record and after the last record at the same time. That only can happen when there are no records.

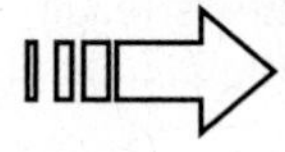

ADO `Recordset` objects include many capabilities not covered in this chapter. Many of the remaining recordset features are covered in Chapter 28, while others are documented in various other chapters of this book. The ADO `Recordset` object is a powerful tool for Access developers and deserves careful study in a variety of contexts.

Understanding DAO Objects

DAO is the older Access data access object model. DAO has been included in Access since the very beginning, and, although not the focus of this book, it's frequently used in Access applications.

Unlike ADO, DAO objects are arranged in a hierarchical fashion. Certain objects are subordinate to other objects, and they can't exist without an instance of the superior object. The top-level DAO object is `DBEngine`, and all other DAO objects are descendants of `DBEngine` (see Figure 27.7).

FIGURE 27.7

The DAO object model.

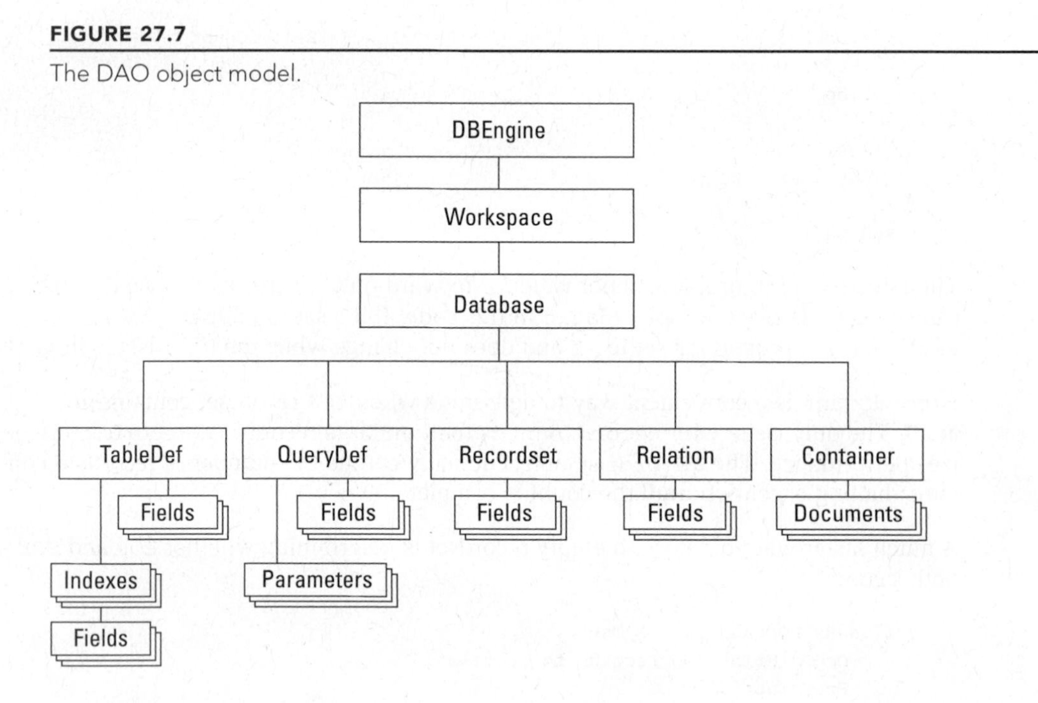

Each of the most frequently used DAO objects is described later in this section.

Generally speaking, the DAO hierarchy closely follows the arrangement of Access database objects. For example, an Access table (which is a `TableDef` object) contains fields (each of which is a `Field` object). A field has a set of properties you use to specify the details of its data type, the default value, validation rules, and so on.

NOTE

For clarity's sake, the set of properties associated with each DAO object is left out of Figure 27.7. But you can safely assume that every object in Figure 27.7 includes an attached set of property objects.

Each DAO object also has a collection of properties appropriate for its object type. A `TableDef` object may have some properties in common with a `QueryDef`, but each object has properties that are unique to its object type. A `QueryDef` has a `Name` property, as does a `TableDef`, but a `QueryDef` has a `SQL` property and a `TableDef` does not. The same is true of methods. Each DAO object has actions that only it can perform. For example, an action query defined by a `QueryDef` has an `Execute` method but a `TableDef` does not. Learning which properties and methods apply to each DAO object is perhaps the biggest challenge facing Access developers.

NOTE

As you read through the following sections, you'll notice that details have been omitted from the discussions of each type of data access object. Because of the numerous properties and methods associated with each DAO object, and the many ways these objects are used in Access applications, it's not possible to present a detailed description of the entire DAO object model in a single chapter. Instead, examples of specific ways to use DAO (and ADO) are given throughout this book. Please refer to the index to find the chapters and sections in this book discussing particular data access objects.

NOTE

Access 2007 introduced ACE (Microsoft Access Engine), a new database engine for the Office products. ACE is why Access 2007 through 2013 support advanced features such as attachment and multi-value fields. Because of the new data types, ACE required an updated version of DAO (called ACEDAO) to support the new capabilities. The biggest differences between DAO and ACEDAO are the introduction of the `Recordset2` and `Field2` objects and new properties and methods required to support the features introduced with Access 2007. Access 2013 continues to support DAO 3.6, the most recent version of "traditional" DAO. Although this section describes traditional DAO, all the explanations and examples in this section apply equally to ACEDAO as well. The Access 2003 MDB format only supports DAO 3.6, not ACEDAO.

The DAO DBEngine object

The `DBEngine` object, the object representing the ACE engine, is at the very top of the DAO hierarchy. It isn't a member of any collection, and all collections are children of `DBEngine`. There is only one instance of this object, and it's one of the few data access objects that you can't create yourself. You open the `DBEngine` object when you start Access and issue a DAO operation. It has relatively few properties and methods. For property changes to take effect, they must be issued *before* a data access object operation has been performed; otherwise, you'll receive an error. Because `DBEngine` is at the top of the hierarchy, you almost always begin a DAO code sequence with `DBEngine`.

The DAO Workspace object

A `Workspace` object represents an open, active session for each user working with Access. All databases are opened within a workspace, either as a default database session or one that has been created using the `CreateWorkspace` method of the `DBEngine` object.

TIP

If you choose to use transaction tracking (`BeginTrans...EndTrans`) within your application, these statements include all recordsets opened within the current workspace. If you don't want to use transactions with a particular recordset, create a new workspace and open the recordset within the new `Workspace` object.

Security is also implemented from `Workspace` objects (but, only for the MDB file format). The security methods available to `Workspace` objects allow you to create your own security interfaces and routines. If necessary, you can create users or groups using the `CreateUser` or `CreateGroup` methods of the `Workspace` object.

The DAO Database object

A `Database` object represents a data source and is analogous to an ADO `Connection` object. Access is able to directly open a number of different database formats. When working directly with the ACE or Jet database engines, a database could be any number of sources: a dBASE file, a FoxPro file, another MDB, or even an ODBC data source. The distinguishing feature is how you set your database object variables.

The following code refers to the currently open Access database:

```
Dim daDb As DAO.Database
Set daDb = CurrentDb
```

`CurrentDb` is a method of the Access `Application` object, which represents the entire Access environment and all its objects. `CurrentDb` is a fast, easy way to open the database that the user is currently working with.

It's also possible to open an Access database *outside* the current database:

```
Dim daDb As DAO.Database
Set daDb = OpenDatabase("C:\Northwind.mdb")
```

Notice that the `OpenDatabase` method accepts the path to an existing MDB or ACCDB file. The `OpenDatabase` method may fail, depending on whether the external Access database is available, or whether its current state prevents opening from another Access application.

As with ADO objects, be sure to prefix DAO object type declarations with DAO so that Access is clear as to which library to use when setting up the object.

NOTE

ACEDAO objects use DAO as the prefix, just as DAO 3.6 objects do.

The DAO TableDef object

The DAO `TableDef` object represents a table in an Access database. The table may be local or linked to the current database. The following procedure (which is included in the `Chapter27.accdb` example database) creates a new table named MyTempTable, adds three text fields to it, and adds the table to the current database's `TableDefs` collection.

```
Public Sub CreateNewTableDef()

  Dim daDb As DAO.Database
  Dim daTdf As DAO.TableDef

  Const sTABLENAME As String = "MyTempTable"

  Set daDb = Application.CurrentDb

 'Delete an existing table, but ignore the error
 'if table doesn't exist
  On Error Resume Next
    daDb.TableDefs.Delete sTABLENAME
  On Error GoTo 0

  ' Create a new TableDef object:
  Set daTdf = daDb.CreateTableDef(sTABLENAME)

  With daTdf
      ' Create fields and append them to the TableDef
      .Fields.Append .CreateField("FirstName", dbText)
      .Fields.Append .CreateField("LastName", dbText)
      .Fields.Append .CreateField("Phone", dbText)
  End With

  ' Append the new TableDef object to the current database:
  daDb.TableDefs.Append daTdf

  daDb.Close
  Set daDb = Nothing

End Sub
```

Running this code in the `Chapter27.accdb` database creates a new table named `MyTempTable`, a permanent addition to the database. Notice that the `CreateNewTableDef` procedure deletes this table if it exists, before creating it as a new `TableDef`. Access won't be able to append the new `TableDef` object to its `TableDefs` collection if a table with the same name already exists in the database.

TIP
If a newly created `TableDef` (or other object) doesn't appear in the Navigation pane, press F5 to refresh it.

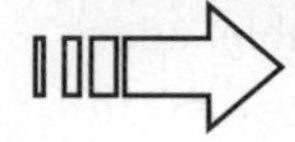

The CreateNewTableDef procedure includes two statements that control how Access handles errors in this code. Chapter 26 discusses the VBA error handling statements, and explains why you'd use On Error Resume Next and On Error GoTo 0 in a procedure such as this.

`TableDef` objects are stored in the `TableDefs` collection. The following procedure displays the names of all `TableDef` objects (including hidden and system tables) in the current database:

```
Public Sub DisplayAllTableDefs()

  Dim daDb As DAO.Database
  Dim daTdf As DAO.TableDef

  Set daDb = CurrentDb

  With daDb
    Debug.Print .TableDefs.Count & _
      " TableDefs in " & .Name

    For Each daTdf In .TableDefs
       Debug.Print , daTdf.Name
    Next daTdf
  End With

  daDb.Close
  Set daDb = Nothing

End Sub
```

The DAO QueryDef object

A `QueryDef` object represents a saved query in an Access database. Using VBA code, you can point a `QueryDef` object variable at an existing query (or create a new query), and change the query's SQL statement, populate parameters used by the query, and execute the query. The query could be a select query that returns a recordset, or an action query that modifies code in the tables underlying the query.

Creating a `QueryDef` in code is similar to creating a `TableDef` except that the new `QueryDef` doesn't have to be explicitly appended to the database's `QueryDefs` collection:

```
Public Sub CreateNewQueryDef()

  Dim daDb As DAO.Database
```

```
    Dim daQdf As DAO.QueryDef

    Const sQRYNAME As String = "MyQueryDef"

    Set daDb = CurrentDb

    Set daQdf = daDb.CreateQueryDef(sQRYNAME, _
      "SELECT * FROM tblCustomers;")

    daDb.Close
    Set daDb = Nothing

  End Sub
```


In fact, as soon at the `CreateQueryDef` method is executed, Access adds the new `QueryDef` to the database. You must explicitly delete the `QueryDef` if you don't want it to appear in the Navigation pane:

```
CurrentDb.TableDefs.Delete "QueryDefName"
```

You could, if desired, create a `QueryDef` without a name. In this case, the new `QueryDef` is not saved and does not show up in the Navigation pane. This technique might be useful, for instance, if you're filling a combo box or list box with data and you don't want to create a permanent `QueryDef` because the criteria changes every time the code is executed.

One time-honored advanced Access technique is dynamically changing an existing `QueryDef` object's SQL statement. Once the SQL property has been changed, the query returns the recordset specified by the new SQL statement:

```
Public Sub ChangeQueryDefSQL()

  CurrentDb.QueryDefs("MyQueryDef").SQL = _
    "SELECT * FROM tblProducts;"

End Sub
```

Notice that the `ChangeQueryDefSQL` procedure doesn't declare any object variables, such as `daDb` or `daQdf`, to refer to the `Database` or `QueryDef`. Instead, the procedure uses `CurrentDb` to refer to the `Database` and accesses the `SQL` property directly on the object returned by the `QueryDefs` property. It is advisable to use object variables for longer procedures, but for short procedures like this one, using `CurrentDb` directly is easier and can actually improve readability.

It's very easy to populate a DAO `Recordset` object directly from a `QueryDef` (see the next section for more on the `Recordset` object). Notice how much simpler this procedure is than the equivalent ADO process:

```
Public Function GetRecordset() As DAO.Recordset

  Dim daRs As DAO.Recordset
  Dim daQdf As DAO.QueryDef

  Set daQdf = CurrentDb.QueryDefs("MyQueryDef")

  'Open Recordset from QueryDef.
  Set daRs = daQdf.OpenRecordset(dbOpenSnapshot)

  daRs.MoveLast
  Debug.Print "Number of records = " & daRs.RecordCount

  Set GetRecordset = daRs

End Sub
```

Notice that the locally declared `Recordset` object (`daRs`) is assigned to the function just before the function ends. This is one way for a procedure to build recordsets without having to duplicate the code setting up the recordset and running the `QueryDef` every place a recordset is needed by an application.

The DAO Recordset object

`Recordset` objects are declared and set to a particular table, query, or ODBC data source within your application. Using a `Recordset` object's methods you can update, edit, and delete records, move forward and backward within the recordset, or locate specific records using the `Find` and `Seek` methods.

A `Recordset` object can be a `Table`, a `Dynaset`, or a `Snapshot` type; the type you specify depends on your needs. For example, suppose you only wanted to scan through a table to search for a particular value of a field. A `Snapshot`, which is a read-only view of your data, would probably be a good choice. Or maybe you'd like to query a table on the fly, but the query depends on user input. In this case, you might build a SQL statement based on an input value, and use the SQL statement to build a `Dynaset`-type recordset.

You specify the type of recordset using the `dbOpenTable`, `dbOpenDynaset`, and `dbOpenSnapshot` constants as arguments of the `OpenRecordset` method of a `Database` object. The following example shows how to open a `Snapshot`-type recordset based on a SQL string.

```
Dim daDb As DAO.Database
Dim daRs As DAO.Recordset
Dim sSql As String
```

```
sSql = "SELECT * FROM tblCustomers;"
Set daDb = CurrentDb
Set daRs = daDb.OpenRecordset(sSql, dbOpenSnapshot)
```

If you don't explicitly choose a type of `Recordset`, Access uses what it believes to be the most efficient method. You can't open an ODBC data source using the `dbOpenTable` option. Instead, you must use the `dbOpenDynaset` and `dbOpenSnapshot` constants.

As you'll see in many different places in this book, there are a number of different ways to open DAO recordsets. The following procedure illustrates just one of these techniques. In this particular example, the recordset is created directly against `tblCustomers`, and each field in every row in the table is displayed in the debug window (the `Field` object and `Fields` collection are discussed in the next section):


```
Public Sub OpenDAORecordset()

  Dim daDb As DAO.Database
  Dim daRs As DAO.Recordset
  Dim i As Long

  Set daDb = CurrentDb

  'Open recordset directly against a table:
  Set daRs = daDb.OpenRecordset("tblCustomers")

  Debug.Print "Table-type recordset: " & daRs.Name

  ' Enumerate records.
  Do While Not daRs.EOF
    For i = 0 To daRs.Fields.Count - 1
        Debug.Print daRs.Fields(i).Name & ": " & daRs.Fields(i).Value
    Next i

    Debug.Print

    daRs.MoveNext
  Loop

  daRs.Close
  Set daRs = Nothing
  Set daDb = Nothing

End Sub
```

The DAO Field objects (recordsets)

`Field` objects within recordsets represent a column of data from a table or returned by a query. Recordset `Field` objects differ from their `TableDef` and `QueryDef` counterparts in that they actually contain a data value. Each `TableDef` object contains a `Fields` collection containing the data held within the table represented by the `TableDef`.

You'll see many, many references to DAO (and ADO) fields in this book, so there isn't much to discuss at this point. In the meantime, it's enough to know that the DAO `Field` object supports many more properties than are visible in the Access Table Designer. The `Chapter27.accdb` example database includes the following procedure that enumerates all the "valid" properties of the `Company` field in `tblCustomers`:

```
Public Sub DisplayFieldProperties()

  Dim daDb As DAO.Database
  Dim daTdf As DAO.TableDef
  Dim daFld As DAO.Field
  Dim daProp As DAO.Property

  Set daDb = CurrentDb
  Set daTdf = daDb.TableDefs("tblCustomers")

  Set daFld = daTdf.Fields("Company")

  Debug.Print "Properties in Company field:"

  For Each daProp In daFld.Properties
    On Error Resume Next
      Debug.Print Space(2) & daProp.Name & " = " & daProp.Value
    On Error GoTo 0
  Next daProp

  daDb.Close

End Sub
```

Not every property associated with a `Field` object is *valid* at a particular time. Some properties are set only after the field contains data, or when the field is involved in an index. For example, the `Value` property of the `Field` object cannot be referenced directly from code. Instead, you set or get the value of a field only through the field's membership in a `Recordset` object. The On Error Resume Next statement allows this code to run, in spite of invalid properties. The errors that may occur when invalid properties are referenced by this code are ignored.

Deciding between ADO and DAO

Given the obvious similarities between ADO and DAO, you might be confused as to which syntax to choose for new Access applications. (We're assuming that existing Access applications already specify either ADO or DAO.) After all, Microsoft continues to support ADO and DAO, and it has introduced ACEDAO for more recent versions of Access. So, which is best for *your* applications?

As with everything else in database development, the answer depends on your specific situation. In spite of its more complex object model, DAO is somewhat faster and easier for certain tasks. Because DAO doesn't require a connection string, DAO code tends to be simple and easy to write. Very often a successful DAO procedure can be written strictly from memory, without having to look up the syntax in a book or online. DAO is also somewhat faster than ADO, especially when working with small data sets.

ADO, on the other hand, excels when connecting to external databases, whether the data source is another Access application or a SQL Server database. Depending on the referenced provider, ADO connections include properties that tell you the connection's state (open, connecting, disconnected, and so on). This information can be extremely valuable in some situations.

TIP

There is no problem including both ADO and DAO code in the same application — but you can't use DAO and ACEDAO in the same project. Just be sure to prefix object references with DAO (or ACEDAO), or ADODB, depending on the object syntax you're using.

In many cases, the decision to use DAO or ADO depends on the example code you might find to use in your application. There are, literally, thousands of VBA code examples available using either DAO or ADO. From a purely technical standpoint, there is no compelling reason to use either DAO or ADO. The only exception is when working with SQL Server data. Because Microsoft provides a native ADO provider for SQL Server, ADO is clearly the better choice when working with SQL Server. Once a connection is established to the SQL Server database, the ADO `Command` object is the ideal way to invoke a stored procedure or run an ad hoc query against SQL Server tables. In a SQL Server context, ADO will almost always be faster and more efficient than DAO because DAO's access to SQL Server is limited to using an OLEDB data source pointing to the SQL Server database.

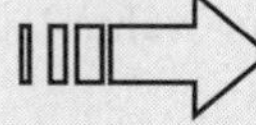

OLEDB is covered in Chapter 29.

In case you're wondering, ACEDAO is the default data access library in Access 2013. Every new Access 2013 database is created with a reference set to the Microsoft Office 15.0 Access Database Engine Object Library (ACEDAO) already in place. If you want to use ADO in your Access 2013 applications, you'll have to manually add a reference to the Microsoft ActiveX Data Objects 6.1 Library.

Writing VBA Code to Update a Table

Updating data in a table by using a form is easy. You simply place controls on the form for the fields of the table that you want to update. For example, Figure 27.8 shows `frmSales`. The controls on `frmSales` update data in `tblSales`, `tblSalesLineitems`, and `tblSalesPayments` because these fields are directly bound to controls on `frmSales`.

FIGURE 27.8

Using a form to update data in tables.

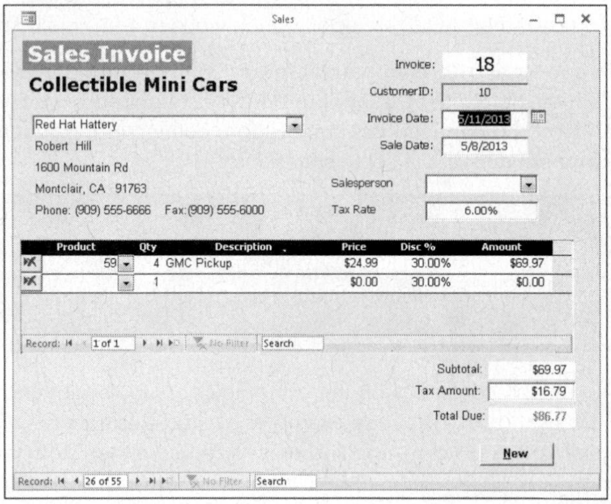

Sometimes, however, you want to update a field in a table that isn't displayed on the form. When information is entered in `frmSales`, for example, the field for the last sales date (`LastSalesDate`) in `tblCustomers` should be updated to reflect the most recent date on which the contact purchased a product. When you enter a new sale, the value for the `LastSalesDate` field is the value of the `txtSaleDate` control on `frmSales`.

Because the contact's last sales date refers to the `txtSaleDate` control on `frmSales`, you don't want the user to have to enter it twice. Theoretically, you could place the `LastSalesDate` field as a calculated field that is updated after the user enters the `Sale Date`, but displaying this field would be confusing and is irrelevant to the items for the current sale.

The best way to handle updating the `LastSalesDate` field in `tblCustomers` is to use a VBA procedure. You can use VBA code to update individual fields in a record, add new records, or delete records.

Updating fields in a record using ADO

Use the `AfterUpdate` event procedure to update `LastSalesDate` (see Figure 27.9). This procedure uses ADO syntax to operate directly on `tblCustomers`.

FIGURE 27.9

Using ADO to update a table.

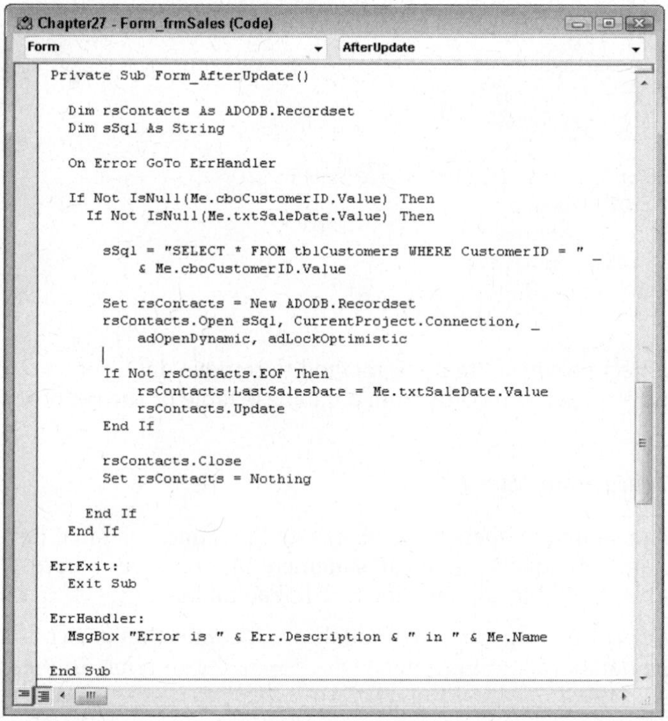

```
Chapter27 - Form_frmSales (Code)
Form                                  AfterUpdate

Private Sub Form_AfterUpdate()

  Dim rsContacts As ADODB.Recordset
  Dim sSql As String

  On Error GoTo ErrHandler

  If Not IsNull(Me.cboCustomerID.Value) Then
    If Not IsNull(Me.txtSaleDate.Value) Then

      sSql = "SELECT * FROM tblCustomers WHERE CustomerID = " _
          & Me.cboCustomerID.Value

      Set rsContacts = New ADODB.Recordset
      rsContacts.Open sSql, CurrentProject.Connection, _
          adOpenDynamic, adLockOptimistic

      If Not rsContacts.EOF Then
          rsContacts!LastSalesDate = Me.txtSaleDate.Value
          rsContacts.Update
      End If

      rsContacts.Close
      Set rsContacts = Nothing

    End If
  End If

ErrExit:
  Exit Sub

ErrHandler:
  MsgBox "Error is " & Err.Description & " in " & Me.Name

End Sub
```

The programming syntax used to access and manipulate the data in an Access database is ADO. ADO defines a number of different objects, each with a set of properties and methods for performing a variety of data-oriented operations.

ADO is not a programming language. Instead, it's a VBA syntax specifically designed for data access. *Syntax* simply refers to the words and phrases you use in your VBA code to accomplish a particular task.

ADO is a versatile means of accessing data from various locations. The examples you've seen so far show you how to use Access to update data in a local Access database. All tables, queries, forms, and reports are stored in a single Access database file located either in a folder on your desktop or on a file server. But Access, as a generic database development tool, can interact with all kinds of databases. You can develop forms and reports in one Access database that get their data from another Access database that may be on your local desktop or on a remote file server. You can even link to non-Access server databases, like Oracle and SQL Server, just as easily as you can link to an Access database.

As a data access interface, ADO allows you to write programs to manipulate data in local or remote databases. Using ADO, you can perform database functions including querying, updating, data-type conversion, indexing, locking, validation, and transaction management.

Here is a fragment of a procedure showing how to use the ADO `Recordset` object to open a table:

```
Dim adRs As ADODB.Recordset

Set adRs = New ADODB.Recordset

adRs.ActiveConnection = CurrentProject.Connection
adRs.Source = "tblCustomers"
adRs.CursorType = adOpenDynamic
adRs.LockType = adLockOptimistic

adRs.Open
```

The ADO `Recordset` object provides the `Open` method to retrieve data from a table or query. A recordset is simply a set of records from a database table or the set of records returned by a query.

The `Open` method has four parameters:

- `Source`: The data source to open. `Source` can be the name of a table (as in this example), the name of a query, or a SQL statement that retrieves records. When referencing a table, the table can be a local or linked table.
- `ActiveConnection`: A connection to a database. A connection is a communication line into the database. `CurrentProject.Connection` refers to the current Access database.
- `CursorType`: A *cursor* is a pointer, or set of pointers, to records. Think of a cursor the way ADO keeps track of records. Depending on the property settings used to retrieve data, ADO cursors can move only *forward* through records (`adOpenForwardOnly`) or permit forward and backward movement (`adOpenDynamic`). A dynamic cursor (`adOpenDynamic`) allows movement in both directions, while `adOpenForwardOnly` permits only forward movement. (The `CursorType` property is explained in detail in the "Understanding `CursorType`" section, earlier in this chapter.)
- `LockType`: Determines how ADO locks records when updating. `adLockOptimistic` allows other users to work with a record that is locked by the ADO code, while `adLockPessimistic` completely locks other users out of the record while changes are made to the record's data.

This same ADO statement can be rewritten in a somewhat more condensed fashion:

```
Dim adRs As ADODB.Recordset

Set adRs = New ADODB.Recordset

adRs.Open "tblCustomers", CurrentProject.Connection, _
  adOpenDynamic, adLockOptimistic
```

In this example, the recordset properties are set as part of the `Open` statement. Either syntax is correct; it's completely the choice of the developer. Also, because we are directly accessing the table, there is no way to specify an `ORDER BY` for the data. The data is likely to be returned in an unpredictable order.

Here is another example extracting a single record, based on a `CustomerID`:

```
Dim adRs As ADODB.Recordset

Set arRs = New ADODB.Recordset

adRs.ActiveConnection = CurrentProject.Connection
adRs.Source = _
  "SELECT * FROM tblCustomers WHERE CustomerID = 17"
adRs.CursorType = adOpenDynamic
adRs.LockType = adLockOptimistic

adRs.Open
```

Notice that, in Figure 27.9 rather than specifying a table, the `Source` property is a SQL `SELECT` statement. The SQL statement used to extract records returns a single record, based on the `CustomerID`. In this case, because the `LockType` property is set to `adLock-Optimistic`, the data in the record can be changed by the user.

Both `CursorType` and `LockType` are optional. If you don't specify a `CursorType` or `LockType`, ADO creates the recordset as an `adOpenForwardOnly/adLockReadOnly` type of recordset by default. This type of recordset is not updatable. If you need to make changes to the data in the recordset, you need an understanding of the various `Cursor Type` and `LockType` combinations and how they affect the capabilities of a recordset.

When you use ActiveX Data objects, you interact with data almost entirely through `Recordset` objects. Recordsets are composed of rows containing fields, just like database tables. Once a recordset has been opened, you can begin working with the values in its rows and fields.

You've seen recordsets many times in this book. The records returned by a query are delivered as a recordset. Actually, when you open an Access table, Access arranges the table's records as a recordset and presents it in Datasheet view. You never really "see" an Access table — you see only a representation of the table's data as a recordset displayed in Datasheet view.

When you open an updatable recordset — by using the `adOpenDynamic` or `adOpenKeySet` cursor type and specifying the `adLockOptimistic` lock type — the recordset opens in edit mode.

One major difference between a table open in Datasheet view and an ADO recordset is that a recordset provides no visual representation of the data it contains. A datasheet provides you with rows and columns of data, and even includes column headings so you know the names of the fields in the underlying table.

An ADO (or DAO, for that matter) recordset exists only in memory. There is no easy way to visualize the data in a recordset. As a developer you must always be aware of the field names, row count, and other data attributes that are important to your application.

When working with datasheets and recordsets only one record is active. In a datasheet the active record is indicated by a color difference in the row. Recordsets have no such visual aid, so you must always be aware of which record is current in a recordset.

Fortunately, both ADO and DAO provide a number of ways to keep track of records in a recordset, and different techniques for moving around within a recordset. It's also quite easy to learn the field names in a recordset and to modify the data within each field.

This chapter, and many of the chapters in this book, demonstrate many of the data management techniques available through the VBA language. As an Access developer, you'll almost certainly learn new and more effective ways to work with data every time you work on an Access application.

Before you change data in any of the recordset's fields, however, you need to make sure that you're in the record you want to edit. When a recordset opens, the current record is the first record in the set. If the recordset contains no records, the recordset's `EOF` property is `True`.

CAUTION

A runtime error occurs if you try to manipulate data in a recordset that contains no records. Be sure to check the value of the `EOF` property immediately after opening a recordset:

```
Set adRs = New ADODB.Recordset
adRs.Open "tblCustomers".... etc.
If Not adRs.EOF Then
    'Okay to process records
End If
```

Errors will occur if the code moves past either `EOF` (`MoveNext`) or `BOF` (`MovePrevious`). Your code should always check the `EOF` and `BOF` property after executing a move method.

To update a field in the current record of the recordset, in an ADO recordset, you simply assign a new value to the field. When using DAO, you must execute the `Recordset` object's `Edit` method before assigning a new value. In the `Form_AfterUpdate` procedure in Figure 27.9, you assign the value of `txtSaleDate` on the `frmSales` form to the recordset's `LastSaleDate` field.

After you change the record, use the recordset's `Update` method to commit the record to the database. The `Update` method copies the data from the memory buffer to the recordset, overwriting the original record. The entire record is replaced, not just the updated field(s). Other records in the recordset, of course, are not affected by the update.

Changes to an ADO recordset are automatically saved when you move to another record or close the recordset. In addition, the edited record is also saved if you close a recordset or end the procedure that declares the recordset or the parent database. However, you should use the `Update` method for better code readability and maintainability.

Use the record's `CancelUpdate` method to cancel pending changes to an ADO recordset. If it's important to undo changes to a record, you must issue the `CancelUpdate` method before moving to another record in an ADO recordset because moving off of a record commits the change and an undo is no longer available.

The `rsContacts.Close` statement near the end of the `Form_AfterUpdate` procedure closes the recordset. Closing recordsets when you're done with them is good practice. In Figure 27.9, notice also that the `Recordset` object is explicitly set to nothing (`Set rsContacts = Nothing`) to clear the recordset from memory. Omitting this important step can lead to "memory leaks" because ADO objects tend to persist in memory unless they're explicitly set to `Nothing` and discarded.

Updating a calculated control

In the `frmSales` example, the `txtTaxAmount` control displays the tax to collect at the time of the sale. The tax amount's value is not a simple calculation. The tax amount is determined by the following items:

- The sum of the item amounts purchased that are taxable
- The customer's tax rate in effect on the sale date
- The value in `txtOtherAmount` and whether the `txtOtherAmount` is a taxable item

When the user changes information for the current sale, any one or all three of these factors can change the tax amount. The tax amount must be recalculated whenever any of the following events occur in the form:

- Adding or updating a line item
- Deleting a line item
- Changing the buyer to another customer
- Changing `txtTaxLocation`
- Changing `txtOtherAmount`

You use VBA procedures to recalculate the tax amount when any of these events occurs.

Recalculating a control when updating or adding a record

Figure 27.10 shows the code for adding or updating a line item on `frmSales`.

FIGURE 27.10

Recalculating a field after a form is updated.

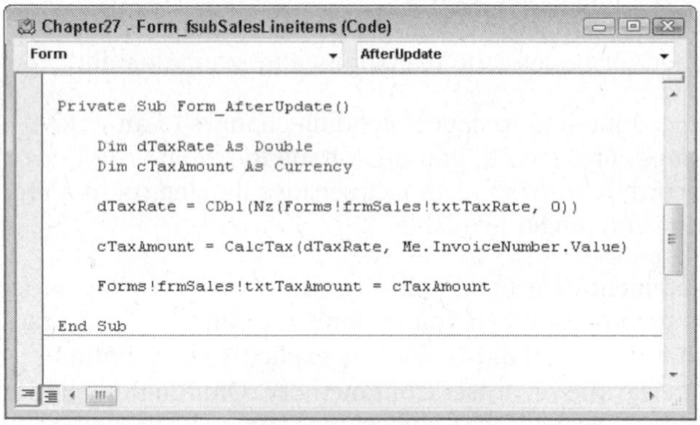

Chapter27 - Form_fsubSalesLineitems (Code)

Form | AfterUpdate

```
Private Sub Form_AfterUpdate()

    Dim dTaxRate As Double
    Dim cTaxAmount As Currency

    dTaxRate = CDbl(Nz(Forms!frmSales!txtTaxRate, 0))

    cTaxAmount = CalcTax(dTaxRate, Me.InvoiceNumber.Value)

    Forms!frmSales!txtTaxAmount = cTaxAmount

End Sub
```

A single event can handle recalculating the tax amount when new line items are added or when a line item is changed — when an item's price or quantity is changed, for example. In any case, you can use the subform's `AfterUpdate` event to update the sales tax. `AfterUpdate` occurs when a new record is entered or when any value is changed for an existing record.

The `Form_AfterUpdate` procedure for `fsubSalesLineItems` executes when a line item is added to the subform, or when any information is changed in a line item. The `Form_AfterUpdate` procedure recalculates the tax amount control (`txtTaxAmount`) on `frmSales`. The `dTaxRate` variable holds the customer's tax rate (the value of `txtTaxRate` on `frmSales`) and `cTaxAmount` stores the value returned by the `CalcTax()` function. `CalcTax()` calculates the actual tax amount. When the `After_Update` procedure calls `CalcTax()`, it passes two parameters: the value of `dTaxRate` and the current line item's invoice number (`Me.InvoiceNumber`). Figure 27.11 shows the `CalcTax()` function.

`CalcTax()` uses ADO syntax to create a recordset that sums the quantities and prices for the taxable items in `tblSalesLineItems` for the current sale. The function receives two parameters: the tax rate (`dTaxPercent`) and the invoice number (`lInvoiceNum`). The ADO code checks to see whether the recordset returned a record. If the recordset is at the end of the field (`EOF`), the recordset did not find any line items for the current sale — and `CalcTax` returns `0`. If the recordset does contain a record, the return value for `CalcTax` is set to the recordset's `Subtotal` field times the tax rate (`dTaxPercent`).

FIGURE 27.11

`CalcTax()` uses ADO to determine sales tax.

Chapter27 - modSalesFunctions (Code)

(General) | CalcTax

```
Public Function CalcTax(dTaxPercent As Double, lInvoiceNum As Long) As Currency

    Dim adCn As ADODB.Connection
    Dim adRs As ADODB.Recordset
    Dim sSQL As String

    sSQL = "SELECT Sum(CalcExtendedPrice(Nz([Quantity],0), " _
        & "Nz([RetailPrice],0), Nz([DiscountPercent],0))) AS SubTotal " _
        & "FROM tblSalesLineItems " _
        & "WHERE [InvoiceNumber] = " & lInvoiceNum

    Set adCn = CurrentProject.Connection
    Set adRs = New ADODB.Recordset

    adRs.Open sSQL, adCn, adOpenForwardOnly

    If Not adRs.EOF Then
        CalcTax = adRs!subtotal * dTaxPercent
    End If

    adRs.Close
    Set adRs = Nothing

End Function
```

At the end of the procedure that calls `CalcTax`, shown in Figure 27.12, `txtTaxAmount` is set to the `cTaxAmount` value.

When the Buyer, Tax Location, or Tax Rate controls are changed in `frmSales`, you use the `AfterUpdate` event for the individual control to recalculate the tax amount. Figure 27.12 shows the code for the `txtTaxRate_AfterUpdate` event.

FIGURE 27.12

Recalculating a control after a control is updated.

Chapter27 - Form_frmSales (Code)

txtTaxRate | AfterUpdate

```
Private Sub txtTaxRate_AfterUpdate()

  Dim dTaxRate As Double
  Dim cTaxAmount As Currency

  dTaxRate = CDbl(Nz(Me.txtTaxRate.Value, 0))

  cTaxAmount = CalcTax(dTaxRate, Me.InvoiceNumber.Value)

  Me.txtTaxAmount.Value = cTaxAmount

End Sub
```

The logic implemented in `txtTaxRate_AfterUpdate` is identical to the logic in `fsubSalesLineItems_AfterUpdate`. In fact, you can use the same code for the Buyer and

Tax Location controls as well. The only difference between the code in Figure 27.10 and the code in Figure 27.12 is that the procedure in Figure 27.10 runs whenever a change occurs in the sales line items subform, while the code in Figure 27.12 runs whenever a change is made to `txtTaxRate` on the main form.

Checking the status of a record deletion

Use the form's `AfterDelConfirm` event to recalculate the `txtTaxAmount` control when deleting a line item. The form's `AfterDelConfirm` event (shown in Figure 27.13) is similar to the code for the subform's `AfterUpdate` event. Notice however, that `txtTax Amount` on the main sales form is set by this procedure, even though this code runs in `fsubSalesLineItems` subform embedded on `frmSales`.

FIGURE 27.13

Recalculating a control after a record is deleted.

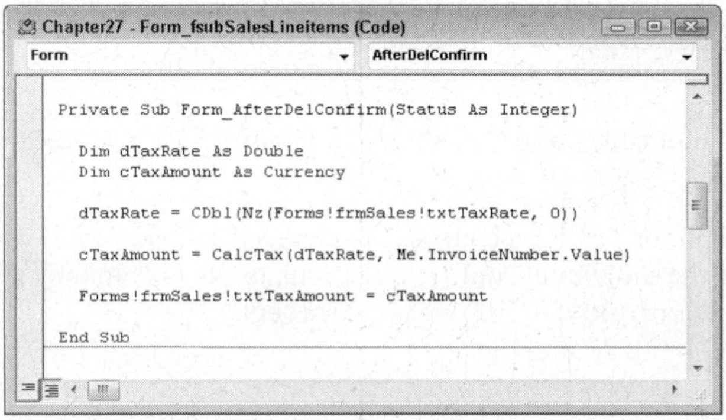

Chapter27 - Form_fsubSalesLineitems (Code)

Form | AfterDelConfirm

```
Private Sub Form_AfterDelConfirm(Status As Integer)

  Dim dTaxRate As Double
  Dim cTaxAmount As Currency

  dTaxRate = CDbl(Nz(Forms!frmSales!txtTaxRate, 0))

  cTaxAmount = CalcTax(dTaxRate, Me.InvoiceNumber.Value)

  Forms!frmSales!txtTaxAmount = cTaxAmount

End Sub
```

Access always confirms deletions initiated by the user. Access displays a message box asking the user to confirm the deletion. If the user affirms the deletion, the current record is removed from the form's recordset and temporarily stored in memory so that the deletion can be undone if necessary. The `AfterDelConfirm` event occurs after the user confirms or cancels the deletion. If the `BeforeDelConfirm` event isn't canceled, the `AfterDel Confirm` event occurs after the delete confirmation dialog box is displayed. The `AfterDelConfirm` event occurs even if the `BeforeDelConfirm` event is canceled.

The `AfterDelConfirm` event procedure returns status information about the deletion. Table 27.2 describes the deletion status values.

TABLE 27.2 Deletion Status Values

Status value	Description
acDeleteOK	Deletion occurred normally
acDeleteCancel	Deletion canceled programmatically
acDeleteUserCancel	User canceled deletion

The `Status` argument for the `AfterDelConfirm` event procedure can be set to any of these values within the procedure. For example, if the code in the `AfterDelConfirm` event procedure determines that deleting the record may cause problems in the application, the `Status` argument should be set to `acDeleteCancel`:

```
If <Condition_Indicates_a_Problem> Then
  Status = acDeleteCancel
  Exit Sub
Else
  Status = acDeleteOK
End If
```

The `Status` argument is provided to enable your VBA code to override the user's decision to delete a record if conditions warrant such an override. In the case that `Status` is set to `acDeleteCancel`, the copy of the record stored in the temporary buffer is restored to the recordset, and the delete process is terminated. If, on the other hand, `Status` is set to `acDeleteOK`, the deletion proceeds and the temporary buffer is cleared after the user moves to another record in the recordset.

Eliminating repetitive code

The examples in this section result in three procedures containing nearly identical code. If the code needs to be modified, you will have to modify it in the `Form_AfterDelConfirm` and `Form_AfterUpdate` events of the subform and the `txtTaxRate_AfterUpdate` event of the main form. If your modifications are not identical or if you simply forget to modify the code in one of the procedures, you can introduce errors into the project.

When you find yourself writing the same, or very similar, code in multiple event procedures, the best practice is to move the code to a standard module and call it from the event procedures. We can't simply copy the code to a standard module because, while very similar, the code isn't exactly the same. The differences in the code, for example how `txtTaxRate` is referenced, need to be handled in parameters to the new procedure.

```
Public Sub UpdateTaxRate(frmMain As Form, _
  dTaxRate As Double, _
  lInvoiceNumber As Long)

  Dim cTaxAmount As Currency
```

```
    cTaxAmount = CalcTax(dTaxRate, lInvoiceNumber)

    frmMain.txtTaxAmount.Value = cTaxAmount

End Sub
```

This procedure is placed in the `modSalesFunctions` module. Instead of having similar code in three event procedures, each of those event procedures calls this procedure. If any changes are necessary, only this procedure needs to be updated. The code below shows how to call this procedure from the subform's `Form_AfterUpdate` event and the main form's `txtTaxRate_AfterUpdate` event.

```
Private Sub txtTaxRate_AfterUpdate()

  UpdateTaxRate Me, CDbl(Nz(Me.txtTaxRate.Value, 0)), _
    Me.InvoiceNumber.Value

End Sub

Private Sub Form_AfterUpdate()

  UpdateTaxRate Me.Parent, _
    CDbl(Nz(Me.Parent.txtTaxRate.Value, 0)), _
    Me.InvoiceNumber.Value

End Sub
```

From the main form, the `Me` keyword is passed (referring to the form itself) and the other parameters are taken from controls on the form. From the subform, `Me.Parent` is used to refer to the main form to retrieve the necessary values.

Adding a new record

You can use ADO to add a record to a table just as easily as updating a record. Use the `AddNew` method to add a new record to a table. The following shows an ADO procedure for adding a new customer to `tblCustomerContacts`:

```
Public Sub AddNewContact(sFirstName As String, sLastName As String)

    Dim adRs As ADODB.Recordset
    Set adRs = New ADODB.Recordset

    adRs.Open "tblCustomerContacts", CurrentProject.Connection, _
        adOpenDynamic, adLockOptimistic

    With adRs
        .AddNew  'Add new record

        'Add data:
```

```
        .Fields("LastName").Value = sLastName
        .Fields("FirstName").Value = sFirstName

        .Update  'Commit changes
    End With

    adRs.Close
    Set adRs = Nothing

End Sub
```

As you see in this example, using the AddNew method is similar to using ADO to edit recordset data. AddNew creates a buffer for a new record. After executing AddNew, you assign values to fields in the new record. The Update method adds the new record to the end of the recordset, and then to the underlying table.

Deleting a record

To remove a record from a table, you use the ADO method Delete. The following code shows an ADO procedure for deleting a record from tblCustomerContacts.

```
Public Sub DeleteContact(ContactID As Long)

    Dim adRs As ADODB.Recordset
    Dim sSQL As String

    Set adRs = New ADODB.Recordset

    sSQL = "SELECT * FROM tblCustomerContacts " _
        & "WHERE ID = " & ContactID & ";"

    adRs.Open sSQL, CurrentProject.Connection, _
        adOpenDynamic, adLockOptimistic

    With adRs
        If Not .EOF Then
            .Delete  'Delete the record
        End If
    End With

    adRs.Close
    Set adRs = Nothing

End Sub
```

NOTE

Notice that you don't follow the Delete method with Update. As soon as the Delete method executes, the record is permanently removed from the recordset.

Deleting records using ADO doesn't trigger the deletion confirmation dialog box. Generally speaking, changes made to data with ADO code are not confirmed because confirmation would interrupt the user's workflow. This means that, as the developer, you're responsible for making sure that deletions are appropriate before proceeding. Once the record is deleted, there is no way to undo the change to the underlying table. Access does, however, still enforce referential integrity. If you attempt to delete a record that violates referential integrity, you'll get an error.

Deleting related records in multiple tables

When you write ADO code to delete records, you need to be aware of the application's relationships. The table containing the record that you're deleting may be participating in a one-to-many relationship with another table.

Take a look at the relationships diagram (see Figure 27.14) for the tables used in the `frmSales` example. `tblSales` has two dependent tables associated with it: `tblSalesLineItems` and `tblSalesPayments`.

FIGURE 27.14

Examining the tables of a one-to-many relationship.

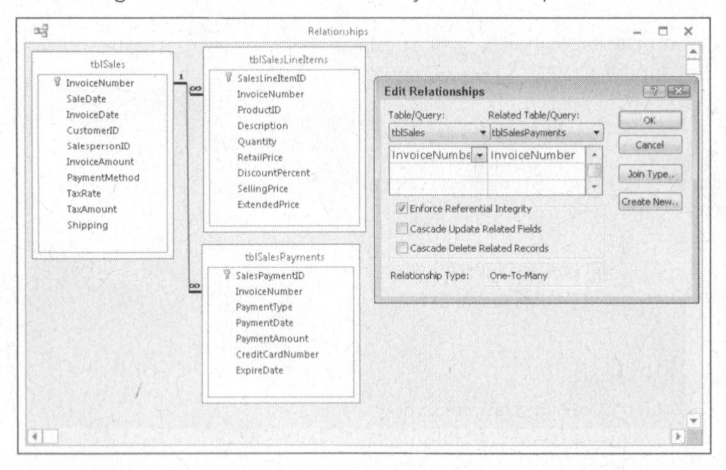

The Edit Relationships dialog box shows how the relationship is set up between `tblSales` and `tblSalesLineItems`. The relationship type is a one-to-many (1:M) and referential integrity is enforced. A one-to-many relationship means that each record in the parent table (`tblSales`) may have one or more records in the child table (`tblSalesLineItems`). Each record in the parent table must be unique — you can't have two sales records with exactly the same `InvoiceNumber`, `SalesDate`, and other information.

Relationships between tables are discussed in Chapter 4.

In a one-to-many relationship each child record (in `tblSalesLineItems`) *must* be related to one record (and *only* one record) in the parent table (`tblSales`). But each sales record in `tblSales` may be related to more than one record in `tblSalesLineItem`.

When you enforce referential integrity on a one-to-many relationship, you're telling Access that a record in `tblSales` *can't* be deleted if records with the same invoice number value exist in `tblSalesLineItems`. If Access encounters a delete request that violates referential integrity, Access displays an error message and the delete will be canceled, unless cascading deletes have been enabled in the Edit Relationships dialog box (refer to Figure 27.14).

As you'll recall from Chapter 4, you have the option of setting Cascade Update Related Fields and Cascade Delete Related Fields in the Edit Relationships dialog box. By default, these options are not enabled — and for good reason. If cascading deletes is turned on, when you use VBA code to delete a sales record, all the related records in `tblSalesLineItems` and `tblSalesPayments` are also deleted. Depending on the situation, this may or may not be a good thing. In the case of a canceled sales order, there is probably no harm done by deleting the unsold sales line items. However, when working on a canceled order where payment has been made, deleting the customer's payment history may be an issue. Surely, they'll expect a refund of payments made on the order, but Access just deleted the payment records.

In most cases, you're far better off using an `Active` field (`Yes/No` data type) to indicate a parent record's status. The `Active` field is set to `Yes` when the order is placed, and only set to `No` when the order has been canceled or completed. You might also consider adding a `CancellationDate` field to `tblSales`, and set it to the date on which an order is canceled. If `CancellationDate` is null, the order has not been canceled.

When you write ADO code to delete a record, you need to first check to see whether there are any one-to-many relationships between the table containing the record to delete and any other tables in the database. If there are dependent tables, the records in the dependent tables need to be deleted before Access allows you to delete the record in the parent table.

Fortunately, you can write a single procedure using ADO code to delete records in both the dependent table(s) and the parent table. Figure 27.15 shows the code for the `cmdDelete` command button in `frmSales`.

The `cmdDelete_Click` event procedure deletes records in `tblSalesPayments`, `tblSalesLineItems`, and `tblSales` that have an invoice number matching the current invoice number.

The first statement in `cmdDelete_Click` (`If Me.NewRecord Then`) uses the `NewRecord` property to see whether the current sales record is new. If the record is new, `Me.Undo` rolls back changes to the record. If the current record is not new, the procedure displays a message box to confirm that the user really wants to delete the record. If the user clicks the Yes button, the procedure deletes the record from the tables.

FIGURE 27.15

Using ADO code to delete multiple records.

Chapter27 - Form_frmSales (Code)

(General) cmdDelete_Click

```
Private Sub cmdDelete_Click()

  Dim lAnswer As Long

  Const sSQL_DELPMTS As String = _
    "DELETE * FROM tblSalesPayments WHERE InvoiceNumber = "
  Const sSQL_DELLINE As String = _
    "DELETE * FROM tblSalesLineitems WHERE InvoiceNumber = "

  If Me.NewRecord Then
    Me.Undo
  Else

    lAnswer = MsgBox("Are you sure you want to delete this Invoice?", _
      vbQuestion + vbYesNo, "Delete Invoice")

    If lAnswer = vbYes Then

      'Delete all payments for this invoice
      CurrentDb.Execute sSQL_DELPMTS & Me.InvoiceNumber.Value & ";"

      'Delete all line items for this invoice
      CurrentDb.Execute sSQL_DELLINE & Me.InvoiceNumber.Value & ";"

      'Now delete the invoice record
      DoCmd.RunCommand acCmdSelectRecord
      DoCmd.RunCommand acCmdDeleteRecord

    End If

  End If

End Sub
```

Two constants, `sSQL_DELPMTS` and `sSQL_DELLINE`, hold the SQL statements for locating and deleting records in `tblSalesPayments` and `tblSalesLineItems`, respectively, with an invoice number that matches the invoice number on `frmSales`. The invoice number is concatenated to the end of the constants, and they're passed as a parameter to the `Execute` method of `CurrentDb`. You can pass either the name of a query or a SQL statement as a parameter to the `Execute` method. The `Execute` method simply runs the specified query or SQL statement.

NOTE

If the query or SQL statement contains a `WHERE` clause and the `Execute` method does not find any records that meet the `WHERE` condition, no error occurs. If the query or SQL statement contains invalid syntax or an invalid field or table name, however, the `Execute` method fails and an error is raised.

After the `tblSalesPayments` and `tblSalesLineItems` records are deleted, the `tblSales` record can then be deleted.

CHAPTER

28

Advanced Data Access with VBA

IN THIS CHAPTER

Using a combo box to find a record on a form

Using the form's filter options

Using parameter queries to filter a form

In the previous few chapters, you learned the basics of Access programming, reviewed some built-in VBA functions, and experienced the various VBA logical constructs. You learned about DAO and ADO and how to access data in tables and queries through SQL recordsets. You also learned a lot about forms and queries.

In this chapter, you use all this knowledge and learn how to display selected data in forms or reports using a combination of techniques involving forms, Visual Basic code, and queries.

ON THE WEB

In the `Chapter28.accdb` database, you'll find several forms to use as a starting point, and other completed forms to compare to the forms you change in this example. All the examples use a modified version of frmProducts and tblProducts.

Adding an Unbound Combo Box to a Form to Find Data

When viewing an Access form, you often have to page through hundreds or even thousands of records to find the record or set of records you want to work with. You can teach your users how to use the Access "find" features, what to do to see other records, and so on, but this defeats the purpose of a programmed application. If you build an application, you want to make it easier for your users to be productive with your system, not teach them how to use the tools built into Access.

Figure 28.1 shows frmProducts with an additional control at the top — a combo box that is not bound to any data in the form. The unbound combo box is used to directly look up a record in tblProducts and then display the record in the form using a bit of code. This chapter shows several ways to build this combo box and use it as a quick way to find records in the form.

FIGURE 28.1

The frmProductsExample1 form with an unbound combo box.

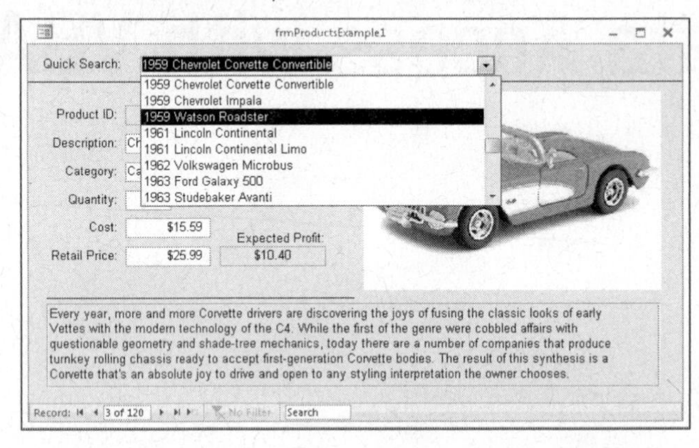

The design for the combo box is shown in Figure 28.2. Notice that the Control Source property is empty. This indicates that the combo box is not bound to any field in a table and is used only by the form, not to change data in the underlying database.

FIGURE 28.2

The Property Sheet for the unbound combo box control.

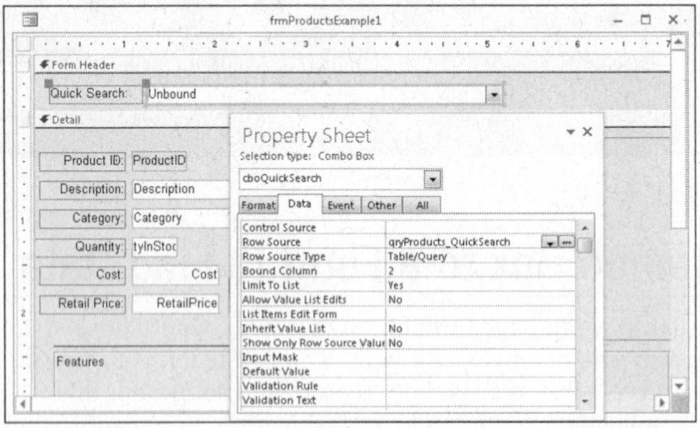

The combo box contains two columns selected by the query shown in Figure 28.3. The first column, LongDescription, concatenates ModelYear and Description from tblProducts. The second column is the ProductID field in tblProducts. The ProductID column serves as the bound column for the combo box and is the value returned by the combo box when a row is selected in the combo box. The second column's width is 0, which hides the column when the combo box list is pulled down.

NOTE

In the code examples that follow, you'll see references to cboQuickSearch.Value. Keep in mind that the value of the combo box comes from the Bound Column and in this case is the Product ID of the item selected in the combo box.

FIGURE 28.3

The query behind the Row Source property of cboQuickSearch.

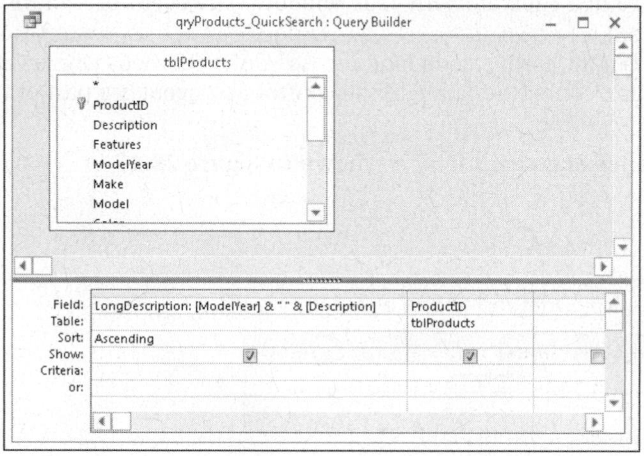

This combo box is used for several of the examples in this chapter. Next, you see how to find records in a variety of ways using the combo box and the code behind it.

Using the FindRecord method

Let's take a look how the quick search combo box on frmProductsExample1 works. Selecting a product from cboQuickSearch fires the `AfterUpdate` event. Code in the `AfterUpdate` event procedure performs the search on the form, and the form instantly displays the selected record.

The `FindRecord` method locates a record in the form's bound recordset. This is equivalent to using the binoculars on the Ribbon to find a record in a datasheet.

When performing a search on a datasheet, you begin by clicking the column you want to search, perhaps LastName. Next, you click the binoculars on the Ribbon to open the Find and Replace dialog box, and enter the name you want to find in the recordset. Access knows to use the LastName field because that's the column you selected in the datasheet. When you enter **Smith** as the search criteria, Access moves the datasheet record pointer to the first row that contains Smith in the LastName field.

When you use code to search through the contents of a bound Access form, you actually perform these same steps using VBA statements.

Follow these steps to create an AfterUpdate event procedure behind the combo box:

1. **Display frmProductsExample1 in Design view, click cboQuickSearch, and press F4 to display the Property Sheet.**
2. **Select the Event tab and select the AfterUpdate event.**
3. **Click the combo box arrow in the AfterUpdate event property and select Event Procedure.**
4. **Click the Builder button that appears in the right side of the property.** The procedure appears in a separate VBA code window. The event procedure template (`Private Sub cboQuickSearch_AfterUpdate()...End Sub`) is automatically created in the form's code module. As you've learned, whenever you create an event procedure, the name of the control and event are part of the subprocedure.
5. **Enter the four lines of code exactly as shown in Figure 28.4.**

FIGURE 28.4

Using the `FindRecord` method to find a record.

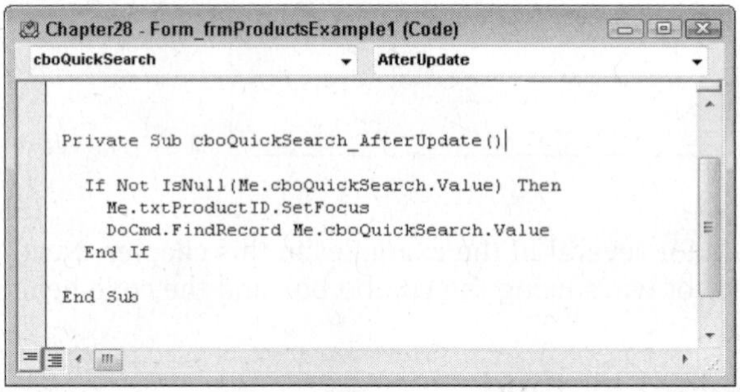

```
Chapter28 - Form_frmProductsExample1 (Code)
cboQuickSearch                    AfterUpdate

Private Sub cboQuickSearch_AfterUpdate()

  If Not IsNull(Me.cboQuickSearch.Value) Then
    Me.txtProductID.SetFocus
    DoCmd.FindRecord Me.cboQuickSearch.Value
  End If

End Sub
```

The first line checks to make sure that cboQuickSearch contains a value (is not null). If cboQuickSearch is null, the program flows to the `End If` statement and no search takes place. If cbQuickSearch has a value, the code inside the `If` block is executed, starting with this statement:

```
Me.txtProductID.SetFocus
```

This statement moves the cursor to the txtProductID control. Just as you need to manually move the cursor to a column in a datasheet in order to use the Find icon on the Ribbon, you must place the cursor in the bound control you want to use as the search's target. In this case, you're moving the cursor to the control containing the ProductID value because the search will look for a particular ProductID in the form's bound recordset.

The next statement in the If block is

```
DoCmd.FindRecord Me.cboQuickSearch.Value
```

In this statement, the FindRecord method uses the combo box's value (which is the selected item's Product ID) to search for the selected product's record. Access matches the value in cboQuickSearch with the ProductID in the recordset bound to the form.

The first value found by the FindRecord method is determined by a series of parameters, including whether the case is matched and whether the search is forward, backward, or the first record found. Enter **DoCmd.FindRecord** in the code window and press the spacebar, to see all available options. The FindRecord method finds only one record at a time, while allowing all other records to be viewed.

Using a bookmark

The FindRecord method is a good way to search when the control you want to use to find a record is displayed on the form. It's also a good way if the value being searched for is a single value. However, many times multiple values are used as lookup criteria. A *bookmark* is another way of finding a record.

frmProductsExample2 contains the code for this example.

Figure 28.5 shows the combo box's AfterUpdate event procedure. This code uses a bookmark to locate the record in the form's recordset matching the search criteria.

28

FIGURE 28.5

Using a RecordsetClone bookmark to find a record.

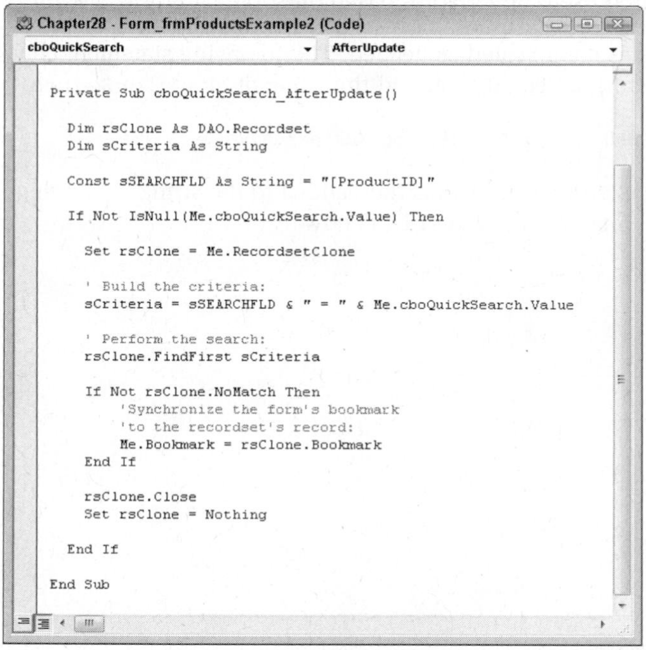

Chapter28 - Form_frmProductsExample2 (Code)

cboQuickSearch | AfterUpdate

```
Private Sub cboQuickSearch_AfterUpdate()

  Dim rsClone As DAO.Recordset
  Dim sCriteria As String

  Const sSEARCHFLD As String = "[ProductID]"

  If Not IsNull(Me.cboQuickSearch.Value) Then

    Set rsClone = Me.RecordsetClone

    ' Build the criteria:
    sCriteria = sSEARCHFLD & " = " & Me.cboQuickSearch.Value

    ' Perform the search:
    rsClone.FindFirst sCriteria

    If Not rsClone.NoMatch Then
        'Synchronize the form's bookmark
        'to the recordset's record:
        Me.Bookmark = rsClone.Bookmark
    End If

    rsClone.Close
    Set rsClone = Nothing

  End If

End Sub
```

The first several lines are

```
Dim rsClone As DAO.Recordset
Dim sCriteria As String

Const sSEARCHFLD As String = "[ProductID]"

If Not IsNull(Me.cboQuickSearch.Value) Then

    Set rsClone = Me.RecordsetClone
```

The first three lines declare a recordset named `rsClone`, a string named `sCriteria`, and a constant named `sSEARCHFLD` that is set to the name of the field to search. These will be used later in the code. Next, the procedure checks whether `cboQuickSearch` has a value, which means the user selected something in the combo box. The following line sets the recordset to a copy of the form's bound recordset (the `RecordsetClone`).

A `RecordsetClone` is exactly what its name implies: an in-memory clone of the form's recordset that you can use when searching for records. If you used the form's bound recordset instead, your search will move the current record away from the record displayed in the form. If the search target is not found in the form's bound recordset, the form ends up positioned at the last record in the bound recordset, which is sure to confuse users.

The `Recordset` object's `FindFirst` method requires a search string containing criteria to look up in the recordset. (Yes, that's correct — you're actually asking the `RecordsetClone` to search itself for a record, based on some criteria.)

The criteria string can be as complicated as needed. The following statement concatenates `[ProductID]` (our constant), an equal sign, and the value of `cboQuickSearch`:

```
sCriteria = sSEARCHFLD & " = " & Me.cboQuickSearch.Value
```

The value of `Me.cboQuickSearch.Value` is then added to the string. Assuming the value of `cboQuickSearch` is 17, `strCriteria` is now

```
[ProductID] = 17
```

NOTE

The criteria string works only because ProductID is a numeric field. If it were text, quotes would be required around the value, as in

```
sCriteria = sSEARCHFLD & " = '" & Me.cboQuickSearch.Value & "'"
```

so that the criteria would actually be

```
[ProductID] = '17'
```

In this example, we have a lot of control over the criteria string because we're using a combo box's value. In other cases, we may get parts of the criteria string from a text box where a user could type virtually anything he wants. If, for instance, he included an apostrophe in a text box that was used in a criteria string, we would have a situation known as an *embedded quote* (a quote inside a quoted string).

Fortunately, embedded quotes are easy to avoid. If you need a quote inside a quoted string, you simply use two quotes. For example, if you search for the name O'Mally, it would look like this:

```
sCriteria = [LastName] = 'O''Mally'
```

Note the two quotes in `O''Mally` that get converted to one quote when the criteria string is processed. To accomplish this with a text box, use the `Replace` function to replace one quote with two quotes.

```
sCriteria = "[LastName] = " & Replace(Me.txtLastName, String(1, "'"), String(2,
  "'"))
```

28

TIP

Creating criteria in code is sometimes a complicated process. The objective is to build a string that could be copied into a query SQL window and run as is. Often, the best way to create a criteria string is to build a query, switch to SQL view, and copy the SQL into a VBA code window. Then, break the code's `WHERE` clause into field names and control values, inserting concatenation operators and delimiters as needed around string and date values.

After the criteria string is completed, use the recordset's `FindFirst` method to search for the record in the `RecordsetClone`. The following line uses the `FindFirst` method of the recordset, passing the criteria string as the argument:

```
rsClone.FindFirst sCriteria
```

NOTE

You don't have to create an `sCriteria` variable and then set the criteria string to it. You can simply place the criteria after the `rsClone.FindFirst` method, like this:

```
rsClone.FindFirst "ProductID = " & Me.cboQuickSearch.Value
```

However, when you have complex criteria, it may be easier to create the criteria separately from the command that uses the criteria string so you can debug the string separately in the query editor.

The next lines are used to determine whether the record pointer in the form should be moved. Notice the `Bookmark` property referenced in the following code block. A *bookmark* is a stationary pointer to a record in a recordset. The `FindFirst` method positions the recordset's bookmark on the found record.

```
If Not rsClone.NoMatch Then
  Me.Bookmark = rsClone.Bookmark
End If
```

If no record was found, the recordset's `NoMatch` property is True. Because you want to set the bookmark if a record *is* found, you need the computer equivalent of a double negative. Essentially, it says if there is "not no record found," and then the bookmark is valid. Why Microsoft chose `NoMatch` instead of `Match` (which would reduce the logic to `If rsClone.Match Then...`) is a mystery to everyone.

If a matching record is found, the form's bookmark (`Me.Bookmark`) is set to the found recordset's bookmark (`rsClone.Bookmark`) and the form repositions itself to the bookmarked record. This doesn't filter the records — it merely positions the form's bookmark on the first record matching the criteria. All other records are still visible in the form.

The last lines of code simply close the recordset and remove it from memory.

NOTE
Criteria can be as complex as you need them to be, even involving multiple fields of different data types. Remember that strings must be delimited by single quotes (not double quotes, because double quotes surround the entire string), dates are delimited by pound signs (#), and numeric values are not delimited.

Using the `FindFirst` or `Bookmark` method is preferable to using `FindRecord` because it allows for more complex criteria and doesn't require the control being searched to be visible. You don't have to preposition the cursor on a control to use the recordset's `FindFirst` method.

NOTE
In case you're wondering, the recordset created from the form's `RecordsetClone` property is a DAO-type recordset. Only DAO recordsets support the `FindFirst`, `FindLast`, `FindNext`, and `FindPrevious` methods. There is no reason for Microsoft to re-architect Access forms (and reports, for that matter) to use ADO-type recordsets. The DAO model works very well when working with bound forms and reports.

Filtering a Form

Although using the `FindRecord` or `FindFirst` methods allow you to quickly locate a record meeting the criteria you want, it still shows all the other records in a table or query recordset and doesn't necessarily keep all the records together. Filtering a form lets you view only the record or set of records you want, hiding all non-matching records.

Filters are good when you have large recordsets and want to view only the subset of records matching your needs.

You can filter a form with code or with a query. I cover both approaches in this section.

With code

Figure 28.6 shows the two lines of code necessary to create and apply a filter to a form's recordset. Each form contains a `Filter` property that specifies how the bound records are filtered. By default, the `Filter` property is blank and the form shows all the records in the underlying recordset.

FIGURE 28.6

Code for filtering and clearing a filter behind a form.

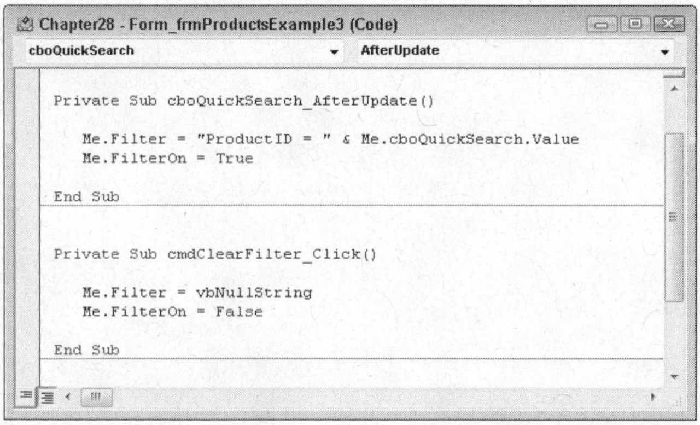

```
Chapter28 - Form_frmProductsExample3 (Code)
cboQuickSearch                AfterUpdate

Private Sub cboQuickSearch_AfterUpdate()

   Me.Filter = "ProductID = " & Me.cboQuickSearch.Value
   Me.FilterOn = True

End Sub

Private Sub cmdClearFilter_Click()

   Me.Filter = vbNullString
   Me.FilterOn = False

End Sub
```


The first line of code sets the form's `Filter` property:

```
Me.Filter = "ProductID = " & Me.cboQuickSearch.Value
```

Notice that this is exactly the same string used as the criteria passed to the recordset's `FindFirst` property.

The second line of code (`Me.FilterOn = True`) turns on the filter. You can put all the criteria that you want in a filter property, but unless you explicitly set the `FilterOn` property to True, the filter is never applied to the form's recordset. The filter hides all the records that do not meet the criteria, showing only the records meeting the filter's value.

```
Me.FilterOn = True
```

Whenever you turn on a filter, it's useful to provide a way to turn off the filter. There is a small button (`cmdClearFilter`) next to the combo box on frmProductsExample3. This button turns off the filter and sets the form's `Filter` property to an empty string (vbNullString). The second procedure shown in Figure 28.6 is the button's Click event procedure:

```
Private Sub cmdClearFilter_Click()

  Me.Filter = vbNullString
  Me.FilterOn = False
  Me.cboQuickSearch.Value = Null
End Sub
```

CAUTION

If you create a form filter and then save the form design with the filter set, the filter is saved with the form. The next time the form is opened, the filter is active. It's a good practice to set the form's Filter property to an empty string as the form closes. The following code uses the form's Close event procedure to clear the filer:

```
Private Sub Form_Close()

    Me.Filter = vbNullString
    Me.FilterOn = False

End Sub
```

Other than the line to clear the combo box, this code is identical to the code in cmdClearFilter_Click. In order to have a cleaner code base, it's a good idea to move the repetitive code into its own procedure. The two event procedures and the new procedure with the repetitive code are shown below:

```
Private Sub cmdClearFilter_Click()

  ResetFilter
  Me.cboQuickSearch.Value = Null

End Sub


Private Sub Form_Close()

  ResetFilter

End Sub

Private Sub ResetFilter()

  Me.Filter = vbNullString
  Me.FilterOn = False

End Sub
```

Instead of duplicate code, both event procedures call ResetFilter.

With a query

You might want to have one form control another. Or you might want a recordset to display selected data based on ad hoc criteria entered by the user. For example, each time a report is run, a dialog box is displayed and the user enters a set of dates or selects a product or customer. One way to do this is to use a parameter query.

Creating a parameter query

A parameter query is any query that contains criteria based on a reference to a variable, a function, or a control on a form. Normally, you enter a value such as **SMITH**, **26**, or **6/15/12** in a criteria entry area. You can also enter a prompt such as **[Enter the Last Name]** or a reference to a control on a form such as **Forms!frmProducts![cboQuickFind]**.

The `Chapter28.accdb` database contains a parameter query named `qryProductParameterQuery`.

The simplest way to create a parameter query is to create a select query, specify the query's criteria, and run the query to make sure it works. Then change the criteria to the following:

```
Like [<some prompt>] & "*"
```

or:

```
Like "*" & [<some prompt>] & "*"
```

where <*some prompt*> is the question you want to ask the user. Figure 28.7 shows a parameter query that prompts the user whenever the query is run to enter the Product Category.

FIGURE 28.7

Creating a simple parameter query.

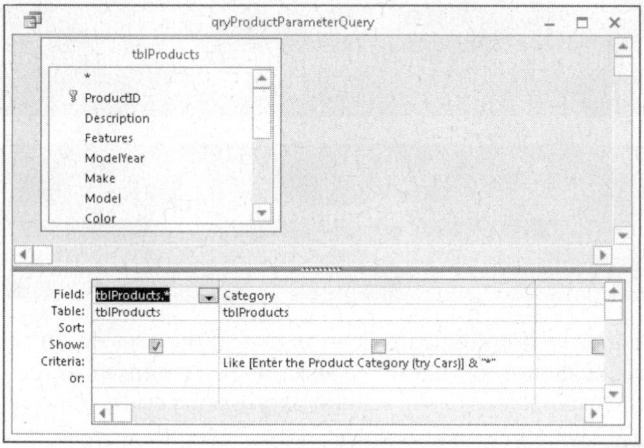

Anytime the query is run, even if it's used as the record source for a form or report or the row source for a list or combo box, the parameter dialog box is displayed — and depending on what's entered, the query criteria filters the query results. Figure 28.8 shows the parameter dialog box open, asking for the product category value required by the query.

FIGURE 28.8

Running the parameter query.

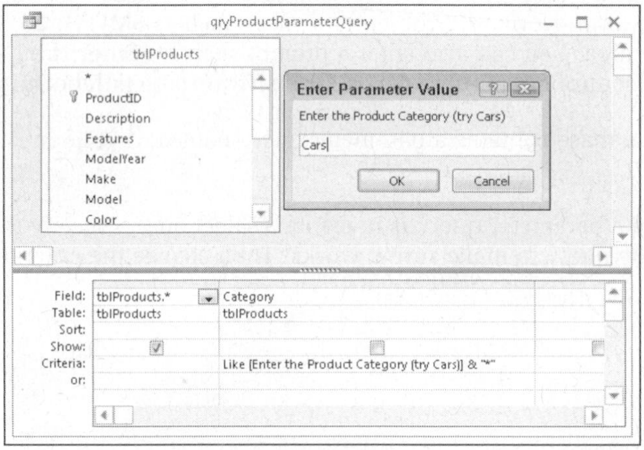

You may remember learning that the `Like` operator allows for wildcard searches. For example, if you want to filter the query records for any product category that starts with "car" (or "CAR"), you enter **CAR** in the parameter dialog box. Without the parameter, you would have to enter **Like "CAR*"** in the criteria area of the query. Also, because the wildcard (*) is included as part of the parameter, users don't have to include the wildcard when they respond to the parameter dialog box.

TIP

You can use the wildcards `*` (anything after this position) and `?` (one character in this position) with a `Like` operator in any query or SQL string.

NOTE

If SQL Server Compatible Syntax (ANSI 92) is selected (choose File ⇨ Options, then select the Object Designers tab), or if ADO is being used to run the SQL statement, the wildcards are `%` (anything in this position) and _ (one character in this position).

A consequence of adding the asterisk to the parameter is that, if the user doesn't enter a parameter value, the criteria evaluates to `"LIKE *"`, and the query returns all records except the nulls. Leaving the asterisk out of the criteria expression results in no returned records if the user fails to provide a product category.

Figure 28.9 shows the Query Parameters dialog box (opened by right-clicking the query's upper area and selecting Parameters from the shortcut menu). You use the Query Parameters dialog box to specify parameters that require special consideration, such as date/time entries or specially formatted numbers. One text entry has been entered in the Query Parameters dialog box to show how it works. You enter the parameter text and choose the parameter's data type.

FIGURE 28.9

The Query Parameters dialog box.

Query Parameters

Parameter	Data Type
[Enter the Product Category (try Cars)]	Short Text

OK

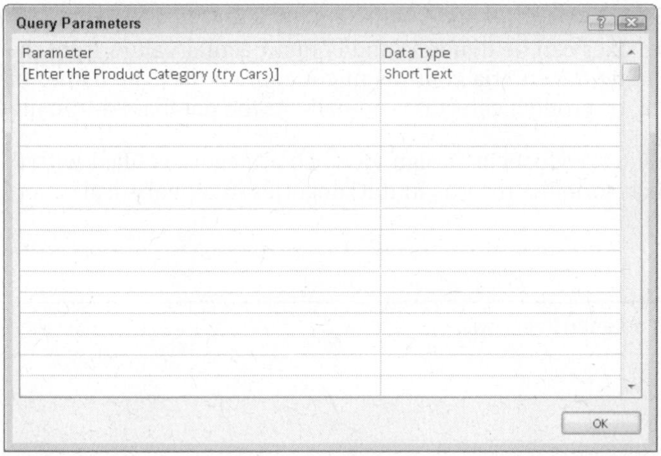

TIP

If you want to add more-complex parameters, such as a range of dates, use an expression such as Between [Enter the Start Date] and [Enter the End Date] as a criterion in a date field. This would display two separate parameter dialog boxes and then filter the date value appropriately.

Unfortunately, Access parameter queries don't provide a way to supply default values for parameters. Your best bet is to always include the asterisk in your criteria expression so that, if the user closes the parameter dialog box without entering a value, the query will return all records because the criteria expression will resolve to `Like "*"`.

CAUTION

You can only use `Like "*"` with text fields. For numeric fields, you can set the criteria to `[My Prompt] OR ([My Prompt] IS NULL)`. Just be certain that both occurrences of `My Prompt` are typed identically. (Copy-and-paste is a good idea.) You can also use this technique with text fields if you want to return all the records including those with null values.

Creating an interactive filter dialog box

The problem with parameter queries is that they're only suitable for simple parameters. The users have to know exactly what to type into the parameter dialog box, and if they enter the parameter incorrectly, they won't see the results they expect. Also, using parameter queries for entering complex criteria is fairly difficult.

A better technique is to create a simple form, place controls on the form, and reference the controls from a query as parameters. In other words, the query uses the form's controls to get its parameter values. This is a huge advantage to the users because the controls can help the user select the criteria by presenting lists or drop-down menus of the acceptable parameter values. Plus, code can be added to each control's `AfterUpdate` event to validate the user's input to ensure that the query will actually run. The content of controls like combo boxes or list boxes can be dynamic and contain actual values from the underlying tables. This means that the criteria controls might contain only the names of customers who've placed orders, or product categories actually in the database at the moment.

Figure 28.10 shows frmFilterProducts in Design view. cboCategory is filled with the data from qryCategories, which sorts the records in tblCategories in alphabetical order.

FIGURE 28.10

Creating a dialog box for selecting records.

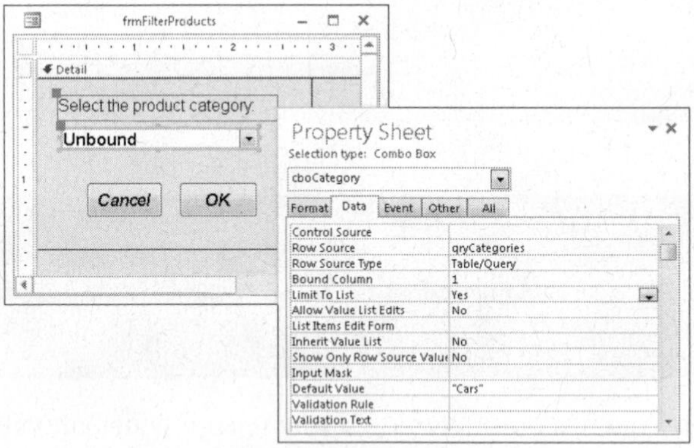

cboCategory's `DefaultValue` property is set to Cars because this is the most commonly used criteria for the Products form. In this case, LimitToList is set to Yes because we want to force users to select only from the categories actually in tblCategories.

Figure 28.11 shows qryProducts_FormParameter. This query selects all fields in tblProducts based on the category retrieved from cboCategory on frmFilterProducts. Notice the criteria expression in the Category column:

```
= [Forms]![frmFilterProducts]![cboCategory]
```

As the query runs, it automatically retrieves the criteria value from cboCategory. The combo box returns Cars, unless the user has choosen a different category.

FIGURE 28.11

Creating a query that references a form control.

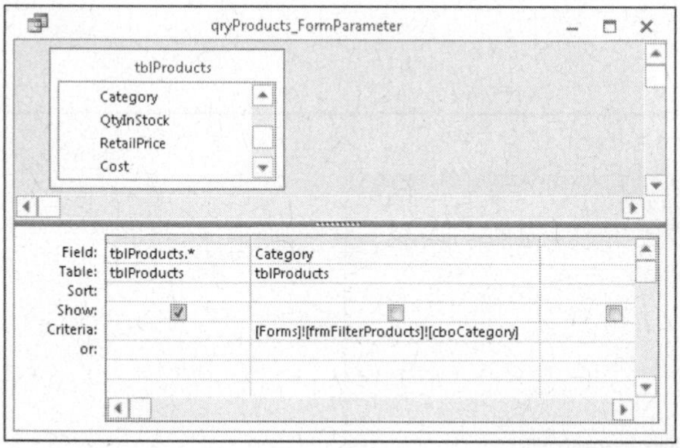

In normal operation, the user selects a product category from frmFilterProducts and clicks OK. Code behind the button opens frmProductsExample4, which is bound to qryProducts_FormParameter. The criteria for the Category field in qryProducts_FormParameter looks up the selected value in cboCategory on frmFilterProducts, and magically frmProductsExample4 opens with just the selected product category loaded.

The only issue facing developers working with tightly integrated database objects like this (in this case, frmFilterProducts, qryProducts_FormParameter, and frmProductsExample4) is that it may not be obvious that the objects work together. Removing or modifying any of these objects might break the workflow or cause problems for the users.

You might choose to use a naming convention that implies the relationship between the two forms and the query, such as giving each item the same name, but with different prefixes. Or, you could use the custom groups in the Navigation pane, and add the objects to a single group. Very often things that are obvious to you — the original designer and developer — may not be as clear to someone else, so it pays to take advantage of simple techniques that help document your applications.

CAUTION

Running qryProducts_FormParameter when frmFilterProducts is not open will result in the query prompting the user to enter a value. When frmFilterProducts is not open, Access can't figure out what the criteria `[Forms]![frmFilterProducts]![cbCategory]` means because there is not a form named frmFilterProducts loaded. In this situation, Access assumes the parameter is a prompt and displays an input box.

Linking the dialog box to another form

The frmFilterProducts dialog box (you saw this back in Figure 28.10) does more than just create a value that can be referenced from a query. It also contains code to open frmProductsExample4.

Figure 28.12 shows the `cmdCancel_Click` and `cmdOK_Click` event procedures behind the Cancel and OK buttons found on frmFilterProducts.

FIGURE 28.12

Creating a dialog box that opens a form.

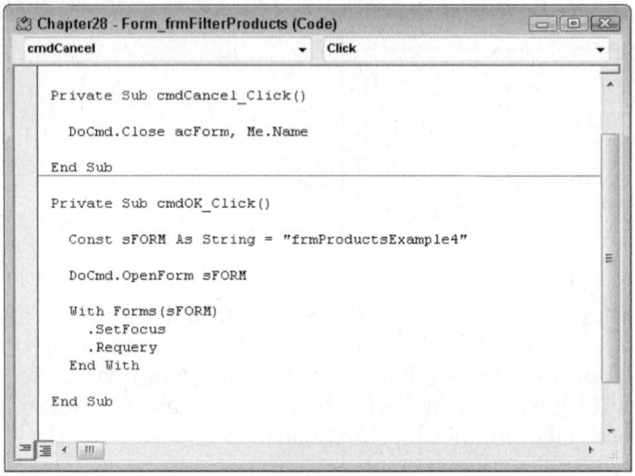

Chapter28 - Form_frmFilterProducts (Code)

cmdCancel | Click

```
Private Sub cmdCancel_Click()

  DoCmd.Close acForm, Me.Name

End Sub

Private Sub cmdOK_Click()

  Const sFORM As String = "frmProductsExample4"

  DoCmd.OpenForm sFORM

  With Forms(sFORM)
    .SetFocus
    .Requery
  End With

End Sub
```

The `cmdOK_Click` event procedure code opens frmProductsExample4, sets the focus on it, and then re-queries the form to make sure that the latest selection is used on the form. The `SetFocus` method is necessary to move focus to the form that is opened. The `Requery` method isn't strictly required, because a form automatically re-queries its record source the first time it's opened. However, if the form is already opened — for example, if you use the dialog box a second time to search for another record — the `Requery` method ensures that the form displays fresh data.

Although not implemented in frmFilterProducts, the `cmdOK_Click` event procedure could also contain a `DoCmd.Close` statement to close the dialog box after it has opened frmProductExample4. Or, you may elect to keep the dialog box open to make it easy for users to select another product category to view.

Using the With Keyword

The `With` keyword is used to save execution time by not referencing the controls on the form explicitly (that is, directly) — for example, `Forms!frmProductsExample4.SetFocus`. This syntax requires Access to search alphabetically through the list of forms in the database container. If there were 500 forms (and some large systems have this many or more) and the form name started with *z*, this would take a considerable amount of time. Because there is more than one reference to the form, this process would have to take place multiple times. The `With` command sets up an internal pointer to the form so that all subsequent references to controls, properties, or methods (like `Requery` or `SetFocus`) of the form are much faster.

When you use the `With` keyword and reference the form name, you simply use a dot (`.`) or an exclamation point (`!`) to reference a control, property, or method just like the `Forms!FormName` was first. You can see this in Figure 28.12.

For each `With`, you must have an `End With`.

Integrating Access and SQL Server

IN THIS CHAPTER

Understanding data types in SQL Server

Installing SQL Server Express

Linking SQL Server tables

Accessing SQL Server with ADO

Understanding SQL Server database objects

Microsoft has increasingly positioned Access as a gateway to SQL Server data. SQL Server, of course, is Microsoft's flagship enterprise database engine, and it's frequently used to drive mission-critical applications for tens of thousands of companies around the world. Because of its excellent scalability, fault tolerance, transaction logging, and other features, SQL Server is often used as the data store behind large websites for data warehousing and for business intelligence purposes.

Depending on installation specifics, SQL Server is able to serve many thousands of users simultaneously. From SQL Server's perspective, an Access application making requests for data is just another user — and it's treated no differently from any other client.

ON THE WEB

This chapter uses a database named `Chapter29.accdb`. If you haven't already downloaded it from this book's website, you'll need to do so now. The linked tables in `Chapter29.accdb` won't work unless you happen to have the exact same setup used in this chapter.

Databases that contain linked tables generally don't work when used on a different computer. Chapter 7 discusses linked tables in detail and how to handle linked tables when a database has moved.

NOTE
SQL Server Express is a free download from Microsoft. (www.microsoft.com/sqlserver/en/us/editions/2012-editions/express.aspx). You can use it as a development and deployment database server for your Access applications if you don't have access to a SQL Server Enterprise installation.

Before beginning this chapter, keep in mind that the architecture discussed in the following sections uses SQL Server to store data and Access to build the user interface, the application's reports, and the logic controlling the application's behavior and features.

This chapter examines a number of different ways to use SQL Server data in Access applications. Although there are no SQL Server object designers (tables, stored procedures, views, and so on) in the ACCDB file format, you can use Open Database Connectivity (ODBC) to link to SQL Server data objects.

Downloading SQL Server Express

Microsoft is vitally interested in developers learning and using SQL Server. But the truth is that acquiring and installing the "full" versions of SQL Server can be a daunting process. As a server application, SQL Server is relatively expensive to license, and its hardware requirements are rather extensive. Not to worry! Microsoft has a wonderful gift available to you, free for the downloading.

SQL Server Express is a somewhat stripped-down version of SQL Server intended to be used as a database engine for smallish workgroup applications, and as a test platform for developers working on SQL Server front-end applications. You may freely download and install SQL Server Express, to use on your computer, and even bundle it with applications you distribute to users.

SQL Server Express works and behaves exactly like SQL Server Enterprise, its much bigger brother. SQL Server Express supports all the data types, stored procedures, triggers, and other database objects used in SQL Server Enterprise. In fact, migrating a SQL Server Express database to SQL Server Enterprise involves nothing more than disconnecting from SQL Server Express and connecting the database files to SQL Server Enterprise.

The primary differences between the standard editions of SQL Server and SQL Server Express is that SQL Server Express databases are limited to 4GB in size (twice that of Access!), and SQL Server Express doesn't support some of the more advanced features of SQL Server Standard and Enterprise editions. Otherwise, the database engines in all editions of SQL Server are identical.

You really owe it to yourself and your users to take a look at SQL Server Express. At the time of publication, the official home of SQL Server Express is www.microsoft.com/sqlserver/en/us/editions/2012-editions/express.aspx, or do a web search for "SQL Server Express download."

Introducing SQL Server Express

SQL Server is Microsoft's premier database engine for enterprise, web, and large database systems. SQL Server is just an engine, with a minimal interface necessary to create and maintain databases and database objects. There is no provision for building user interfaces or reporting features in SQL Server.

Because SQL Server is scalable — from tiny individual desktop list managers to multi-terabyte databases serving thousands of simultaneous users — it's the database engine of choice for many small and large companies. Large SQL Server installations can be *clustered,* allowing multiple servers to work together as a single, huge computer system. There is no practical limit on the number of tables, stored procedures, and other objects in a SQL Server database, and each table can have a virtually unlimited number of records.

SQL Server also provides significant security for its databases. The SQL Server security system directly incorporates with Windows Active Directory, which means that (depending on configuration) SQL Server may recognize a user by virtue of his Windows login and membership in Active Directory groups, or it may require each user to log in each time a SQL Server database is accessed from an application. Because the physical SQL Server database resides only on an application server, there is little chance an unauthorized user is able to access data stored in SQL Server or abscond with an entire SQL Server database.

For all these reasons, SQL Server is the natural destination for Access databases that have outgrown the practical limits of a file-based database, or databases that must be shared with more users than is practical using the Access database engines.

Microsoft provides SQL Server Express as a practical server-based database engine for moderate-size databases. Because SQL Server Express is binary-compatible with full SQL Server, no conversion is necessary to move a SQL Server Express database to full SQL Server. All you have to do is detach the database files from the Express edition and attach the file to the full edition.

SQL Server Express contains exactly the same core code as all SQL Server editions and works with exactly the same format database files as SQL Server Enterprise. The data file format, Transact-SQL syntax, security architecture, and other specifications are the same in SQL Server Express and SQL Server Enterprise. The primary difference between these database engines is that SQL Server Express does not include several of the more-advanced features (such as full text searches) that SQL Server Enterprise includes. Also, SQL Server Express supports databases up to 4GB in size; SQL Server Enterprise supports databases in excess of 500,000TB.

SQL Server Express includes SQL Server Management Studio and SQL Server Reporting Services. Furthermore, unlike the Microsoft Database Engine (MSDE) that preceded SQL Server Express, the Express edition does not contain the performance throttle that inhibited more than a few connections to MSDE. Consult the SQL Server Express pages (www.microsoft.com/sqlserver/en/us/editions/2012-editions/express.aspx) on the Microsoft website for more details.

SQL Server Express is the ideal database engine for small workgroups and individuals wanting to make the leap into client-server architecture. And the price is definitely right! SQL Server Express is a free download from the MSDN site.

Understanding Data Types in SQL Server

SQL Server uses different data type names than Access. If you'll be working in SQL Server, you'll need to learn these data types and how they relate to the data types in Access. Table 29.1 shows the data types available in Access 2013.

TABLE 29.1 The Details of Access and SQL Server Data Types

Access Data Type	SQL Server Data Type	Used to Store	Limitations/Restrictions
Short Text	char(10), varchar(50), varchar(n), varchar(MAX): ASCII (8-bit) character set string variables. nchar(10), nvarchar(50), nvarchar(n), nvarchar(MAX): Unicode (16-bit) character set string variables. char: Fixed-length string, usually short and known sizes, where string is padded up to fixed length regardless of value. varchar(50-n): Variable-length strings where no padding is added for shorter strings. MAX: Used for extremely large values	Alphanumeric data (text and numbers)	Stores up to 255 characters.
Long Text	text and ntext: Large variable text strings stored in binary form. ntext stores unicode character set.	Alphanumeric data (text and numbers)	Stores up to 2GB of data (the size limit for all Access databases), if you fill the field programmatically. Remember that adding 2GB of data causes your database to operate slowly. If you enter data manually, you can enter and view a maximum of 65,535 characters in the table field and in any controls that you bind to the field. When you create databases in the Access file format, Long Text fields also support rich-text editing.

Access Data Type	SQL Server Data Type	Used to Store	Limitations/Restrictions
Number	tinyint, smallint, int, bigint: Very small integers up to very large integers. Smaller data types use less bytes and occupy less physical space. real, float: Real numbers and floating point numbers are the same thing. decimal[(18,0)]: A decimal defaults to 2 decimal places but can be sized up to 18 bytes with no decimals. numeric[(18,0)]: Can be a specified length as for decimal.	Numeric data	Uses a Field Size setting that controls the size of the value that the field can contain. You can set the field size to 1, 2, 4, 8, or 16 bytes.
Date/Time	datetime, smalldatetime, timestamp	Dates and times	Stores all dates as 8-byte double-precision integers.
Currency	money, smallmoney	Monetary data	Stores data as 8-byte numbers with precision to four decimal places. Use this data type to store financial data and when you don't want Access to round values.
AutoNumber	int (with identity property defined)	Unique values created by Access when you create a new record	Stores data as 4-byte values; typically used in primary keys.
Yes/No	Bit	Boolean (true or false) data	Uses –1 for all Yes values and 0 for all No values.

continued

29

TABLE 29.1 *(continued)*

Access Data Type	SQL Server Data Type	Used to Store	Limitations/Restrictions
OLE Object	Image: Intended specifically for storing images in binary form	Images, documents, graphs, and other objects from Office- and Windows-based programs	Stores up to 2GB of data (the size limit for all Access databases). Remember that adding 2GB of data causes your database to operate slowly. OLE Object fields create bitmap images of the original document or other object, and then display that bitmap in the table fields and form or report controls in your database. For Access to render those images, you must have an OLE server (a program that supports that file type) registered on the computer that runs your database. If you don't have an OLE server registered for a given file type, Access displays a broken image icon. This is a known problem for some image types, most notably JPG images. As a rule, you should use Attachment fields for your ACCDB files instead of OLE Object fields. Attachment fields use storage space more efficiently and are not limited by a lack of registered OLE servers.
Hyperlink	No equivalent	Web addresses	Stores up to 1GB of data. You can store links to websites, sites, or files on an intranet or local area network (LAN), and sites or files on your computer.

Access Data Type	SQL Server Data Type	Used to Store	Limitations/Restrictions
Attachment	No equivalent	Any supported type of file	New to Access ACCDB files. You can attach images, spreadsheet files, documents, charts, and other types of supported files to the records in your database, much like you attach files to e-mail messages. You can also view and edit attached files, depending on how the database designer sets up the Attachment field. Attachment fields provide greater flexibility than OLE Object fields, and they use storage space more efficiently because they don't create a bitmap image of the original file.
No equivalent	binary(50), varbinary, varbinary(50), varbinary(MAX)	No Access equivalent	No Access equivalent
No equivalent	uniqueidentifier	No Access equivalent	No Access equivalent
No equivalent	xml: XML data type for storing both content and functionality of XML documents.	No Access equivalent	No Access equivalent
No equivalent	sql_variant: A variable data type, except it does not allow text, ntext, image, or timestamp.	No Access equivalent	No Access equivalent

Installing SQL Server Express

The examples in this chapter use SQL Server Express 2012 with Tools. If you already have SQL Server Enterprise available, you may choose to use it or you may want to use a SQL Server Express instance to keep example data out of your primary SQL Server installation. If you install a different version of SQL Server Express 2012 (such as Database Only or Advanced Services), you may have more or less options than shown here.

Installing the database engine

To install SQL Server Express, follow these steps:

1. **Download the installation file from the Microsoft website.** Download the x86 or x64 version, depending on which version of Windows you're running. To determine which version of Windows you have, display the Charms menu, click on the Settings charm, and choose PC Info. Look for the `system type` property that reads either `32-bit Operating System` or `64-bit Operating System`.
2. **Right-click the downloaded installation file and choose Run as Administrator to begin installation.**

> **NOTE**
> Depending on your system, SQL Server Express can take some time to extract files and install.

3. **Choose to install a New SQL Server stand-alone installation, as shown in Figure 29.1.**

FIGURE 29.1

Install a New SQL Server stand-alone installation.

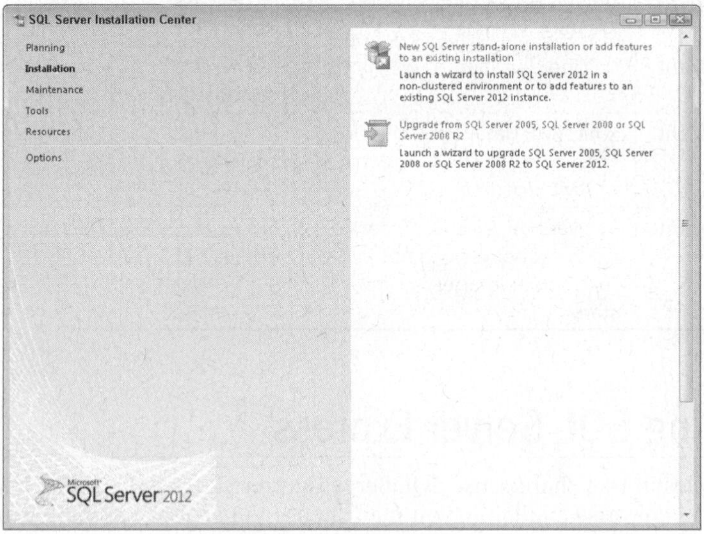

4. **Accept the license terms and click Next.**
5. **On the Feature Selection screen, choose Select All to install all the available features, as shown in Figure 29.2.**

FIGURE 29.2

Select which features to install.

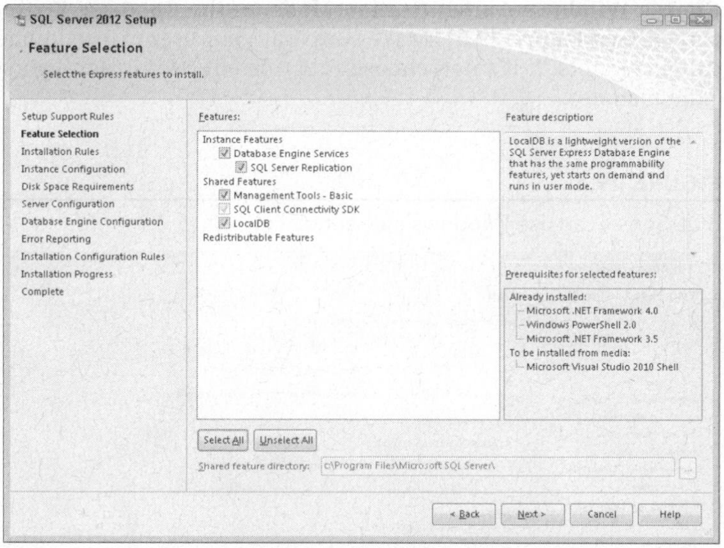

SQL Server 2012 Setup

Feature Selection

Select the Express features to install.

Setup Support Rules
Feature Selection
Installation Rules
Instance Configuration
Disk Space Requirements
Server Configuration
Database Engine Configuration
Error Reporting
Installation Configuration Rules
Installation Progress
Complete

Features:

Instance Features
Database Engine Services
SQL Server Replication
Shared Features
Management Tools - Basic
SQL Client Connectivity SDK
LocalDB
Redistributable Features

Feature description:

LocalDB is a lightweight version of the SQL Server Express Database Engine that has the same programmability features, yet starts on demand and runs in user mode.

Prerequisites for selected features:

Already installed:
Microsoft .NET Framework 4.0
Windows PowerShell 2.0
Microsoft .NET Framework 3.5
To be installed from media:
Microsoft Visual Studio 2010 Shell

Select All | Unselect All

Shared feature directory: c:\Program Files\Microsoft SQL Server\

< Back | Next > | Cancel | Help

6. **On the Instance Configuration screen, choose Named Instance and choose a name or accept the default (see Figure 29.3).**

FIGURE 29.3

Name your SQL Server Express instance.

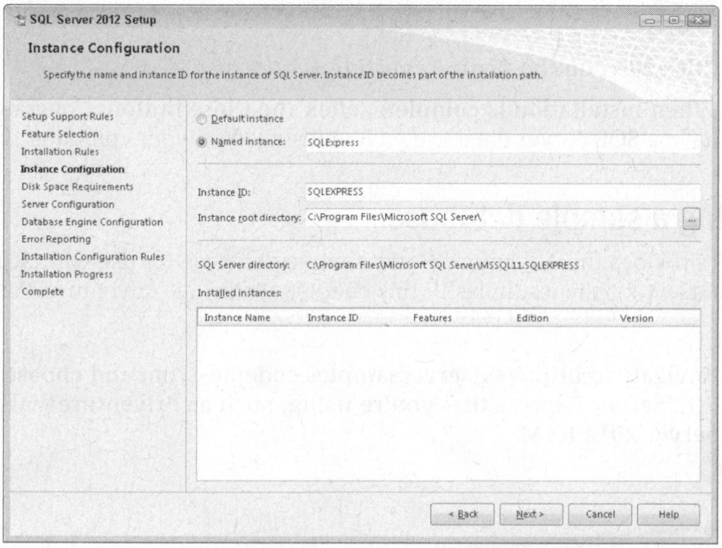

SQL Server 2012 Setup

Instance Configuration

Specify the name and instance ID for the instance of SQL Server. Instance ID becomes part of the installation path.

Setup Support Rules
Feature Selection
Installation Rules
Instance Configuration
Disk Space Requirements
Server Configuration
Database Engine Configuration
Error Reporting
Installation Configuration Rules
Installation Progress
Complete

Default instance

Named instance: SQLExpress

Instance ID: SQLEXPRESS

Instance root directory: C:\Program Files\Microsoft SQL Server\

SQL Server directory: C:\Program Files\Microsoft SQL Server\MSSQL11.SQLEXPRESS

Installed instances:

Instance Name	Instance ID	Features	Edition	Version

< Back | Next > | Cancel | Help

7. **On the Server Configuration screen, accept the default options to start the SQL Server Database Engine automatically by clicking Next.**
8. **Choose Windows Authentication Mode on the Database Engine Configuration screen (see Figure 29.4).** Make sure that your user is listed under Server Administrators. If it's not, choose Add Current User to add yourself as an Administrator.

FIGURE 29.4

SQL Server can use Windows authentication.

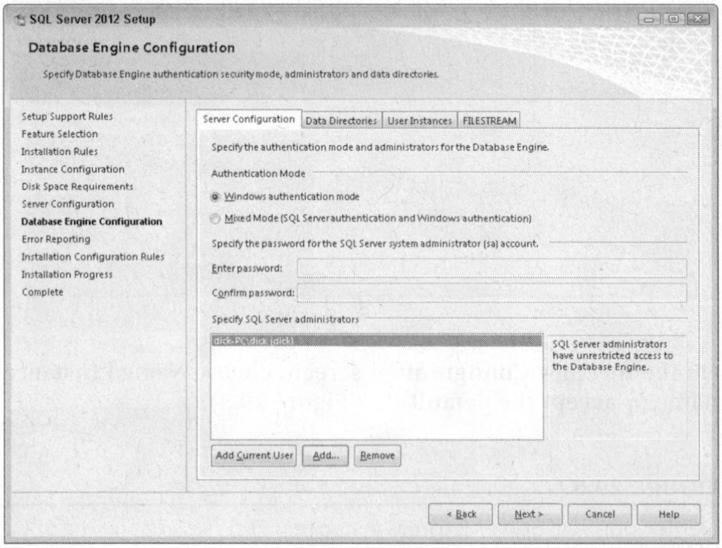

9. **Click Next on the Error Reporting screen.**
10. **When installation is complete, click the Close button.** Congratulations! You have a SQL Server database engine installed on your computer.

Installing a sample database

Microsoft provides the AdventureWorks sample database for use with SQL Server Express, and we'll use it for the examples in this chapter. To install AdventureWorks, follow these steps:

1. **Navigate to http://sqlserversamples.codeplex.com and choose the version of SQL Server Express that you're using, such as AdventureWorks for SQL Server 2012 RTM.**

2. **Locate the link for AdventureWorksLT2012_Data.** The "LT" sample database is a lightweight version of the `AdventureWorks2012_Data` file. It's considerably smaller, but it has everything we'll need to demonstrate integrating SQL Server with Access. Click the link to download the database.

3. **Copy the MDF file that you downloaded to a folder on your computer.** Do not attempt to open the MDF file directly, or Windows will complain that it's a system file.

4. **Start the SQL Server Management Studio as an Administrator.** Click the Windows Start button, open the Microsoft SQL Server 2012 folder, right click SQL Server Management Studio, and choose Run as Administrator. This will ensure that SQL Server Management Studio has the proper permissions to access the MDF file. Figure 29.5 shows the right-click menu.

FIGURE 29.5

Run SQL Server Management Studio as an Administrator.

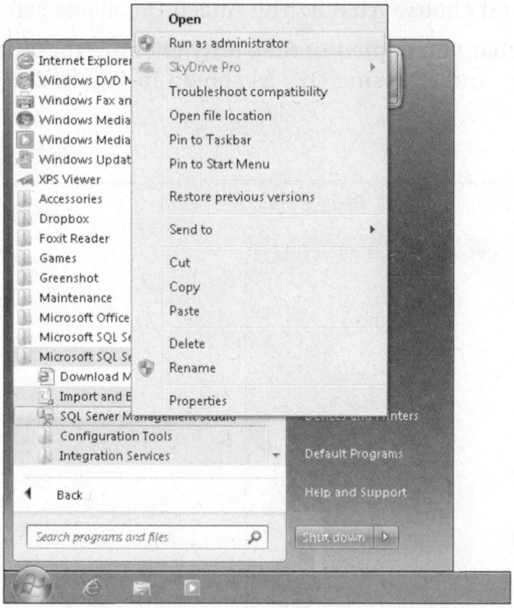

5. **Connect to SQL Server by choosing the server name and the authentication to use.** If you've just installed SQL Server, you only have one server to choose. The authentication should be Windows Authentication if you installed SQL Server Express following the steps in the previous section. Figure 29.6 shows the Connect to Server dialog box.

FIGURE 29.6

Connect to a server in SQL Server 2012.

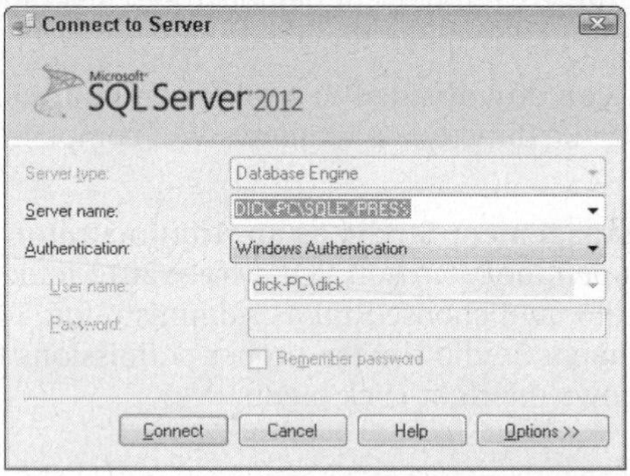

6. **In the Object Explorer pane on the left side of the screen, right-click the Databases folder and choose Attach.** The Attach Databases screen appears.
7. **Add the MDF file that you copied in Step 3 by clicking the Add button, browsing to the MDF file, and choosing OK, as shown in Figure 29.7.**

FIGURE 29.7

Select the AdventureWorks MDF file to attach.

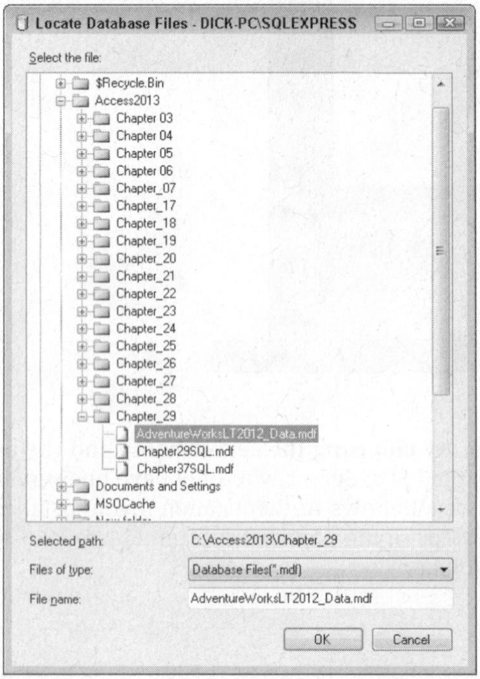

The Attach Databases screen should look similar to Figure 29.8. When you attach an MDF file, SQL Server attempts to attach an LDF file (a log file) with the same name. Because this is a new database, there is no log file.

8. **Select the LDF file from the bottom box and click Remove; click OK when the LDF file has been removed.**

FIGURE 29.8

Remove the LDF file when attaching a new database.

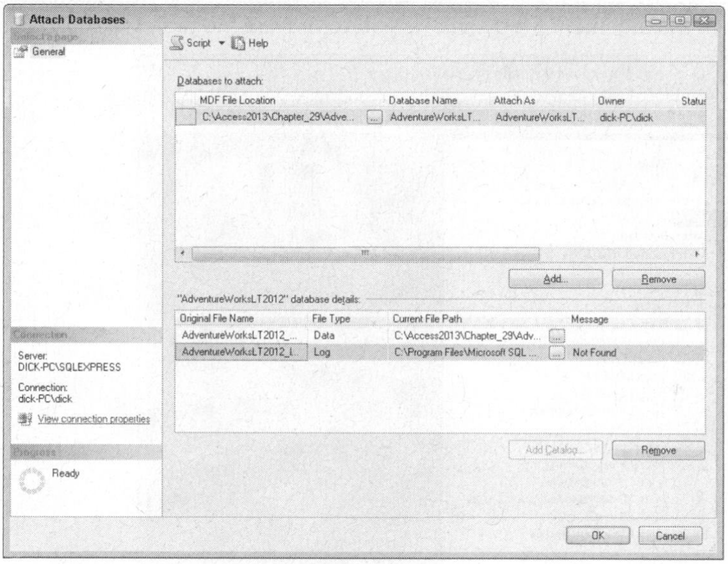

9. **In the Object Explorer, expand the Database folder.** You should see an entry named AdventureWorksLT2012.

Getting to know Management Studio

Working in SQL Server is well beyond the scope of this book. Nevertheless, a quick look at the SQL Server Management Studio will be helpful in understanding how Access and SQL Server work together.

In the last section, you attached the AdventureWorks database to SQL Server. In the Management Studio, there is an Object Explorer pane for navigating the objects on the server. If the Object Explorer is not visible, you can show it by choosing View ➪ Object Explorer.

The top-level object is the server instance that you connected to when you started the Management Studio. If there are no folders below the server instance object, click the plus sign next to its name to expand the child objects. The first folder is `Databases`, which houses the AdventureWorks database you attached in the previous section.

Beneath the AdventureWorks object are folders for all the SQL Server objects in a database. We discuss most of these objects in more detail later in the chapter. One of the objects is the `Table` object. Figure 29.9 shows the `Tables` folder expanded to show all the tables in the database.

FIGURE 29.9

SQL Server Management Studio allows you to browse the tables in a database.

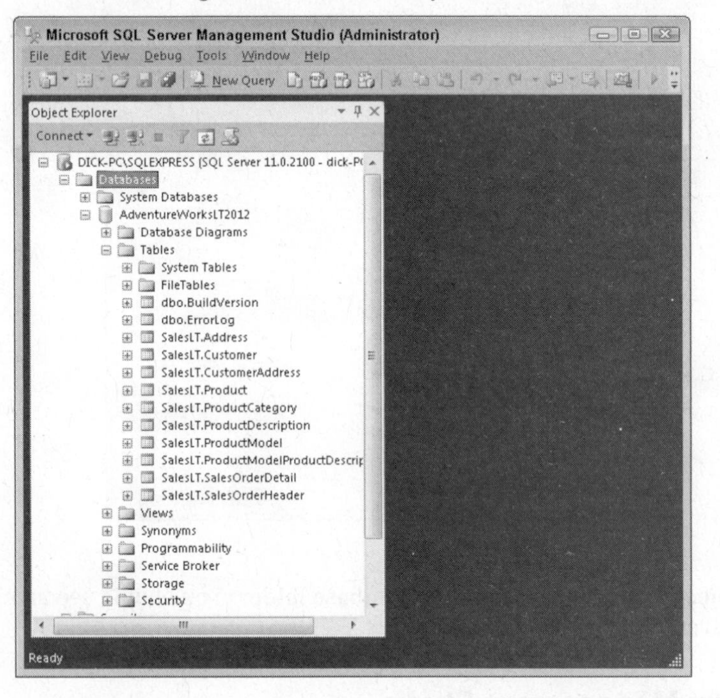

If you locate the `SalesLT.Product` table and expand it by clicking the plus sign next to its name, you'll see a number of folders containing properties of the table. In Figure 29.10, the `Columns` folder is expanded and the `ProductNumber` field is selected.

From the listing shown in Figure 29.10, you can already see some properties of the `ProductNumber` field. The list entry shows the name of the field, and following that, `(nvarchar(25), not null)`. The `nvarchar(25)` portion of the entry shows that `ProductNumber` is a string with a maximum length of 25 characters (`nvarchar` is similar to the `Short Text` data type in Access). The `not null` portion means that the `Allow Nulls` property has been set to `False`. Double-clicking the field name opens the Column Properties dialog box, which lists all the properties of the field, as shown in Figure 29.11.

FIGURE 29.10

The Object Explorer is a hierarchical list of objects on the server.

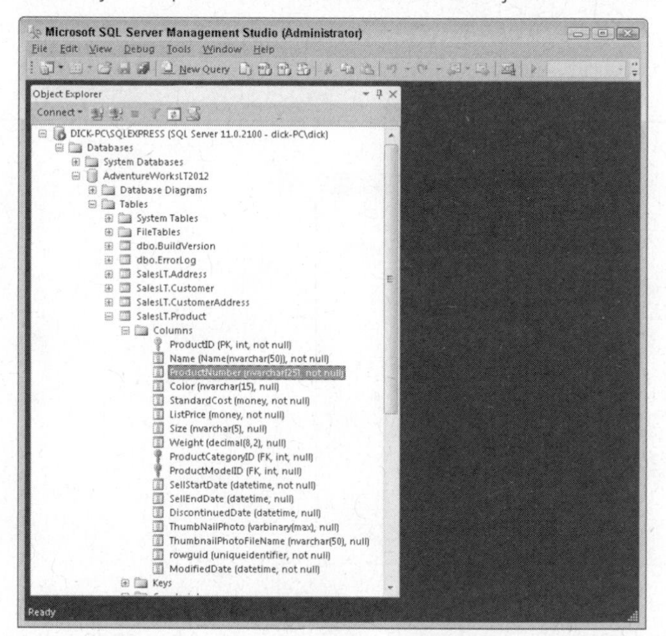

FIGURE 29.11

The Column Properties dialog box for the `ProductNumber` field.

Column Properties - ProductNumber

Select a page: General; Extended Properties

Script ▾ Help

Name	ProductNumber
Data Type	nvarchar
System Type	nvarchar
Primary Key	False
Allow Nulls	False
Is Computed	False
Computed text	
Identity	False
Identity Seed	0
Identity Increment	0
Default Binding	
Default Schema	
Rule	
Rule Schema	
Length	25
Collation	SQL_Latin1_General_CP1_CI_AS
Numeric Precision	0
Numeric Scale	0
XML Schema Namespace	
XML Schema Namespace schema	
Is Sparse	False
Is Column Set	False
Statistical Semantics	False
Not For Replication	False
ANSI Padding Status	True

Name
The column's name.

Connection
Server: DICK-PC\SQLEXPRESS
Connection: dick-PC\dick
View connection properties

Progress
Ready

OK Cancel

Another folder under the `SalesLT.Product` table is named `Constraints`. Constraints are roughly equivalent to Validation in Access. Figure 29.12 shows the Check Constraints dialog box.

FIGURE 29.12

Constraints are like Validation in Access.

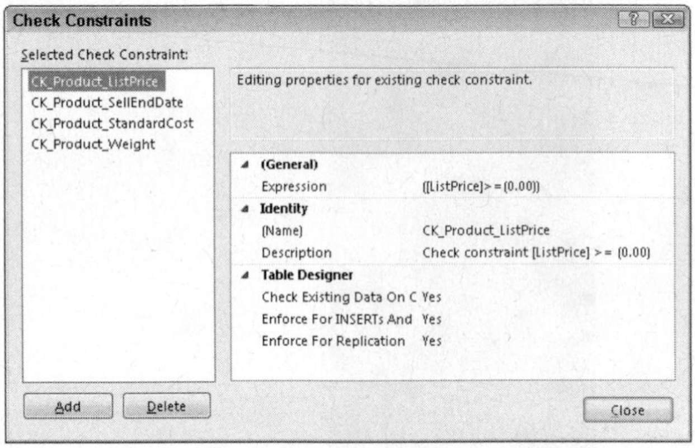

The constraint selected in Figure 29.12, `CK_Product_ListPrice`, has an `Expression` of `([ListPrice]>=(0.00)`. If you were to try to assign a negative list price to a product, it would violate this constraint and SQL Server would complain.

The final area of the Management Studio we'll look at is the Query window. SQL Server doesn't have a Datasheet view like Access, but you can browse the data by writing queries. You get to the Query window by clicking the New Query button on the toolbar. Figure 29.13 shows an executed query on the `SalesLT.Product` table.

Using the command line

SQL Server provides a command line utility called SQLCMD for accessing your data. The SQLCMD utility is useful for quick queries or for running a batch file on a schedule. From a command prompt, you can type `sqlcmd -?` to get a list of options for SQLCMD. Figure 29.14 shows a simple query run as a command line.

At the command prompt, `sqlcmd -s SQLEXPRESS` was used to open the command line utility attached to at SQL Server instance named SQLEXPRESS. The resulting prompt, `>1`, is where SQL statements and SQLCMD commands are typed.

FIGURE 29.13

Running queries in SQL Server.

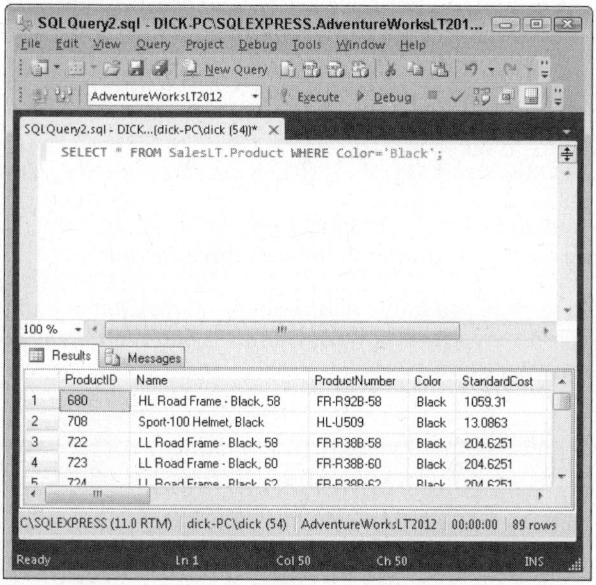

FIGURE 29.14

Using the SQLCMD command-line utility.

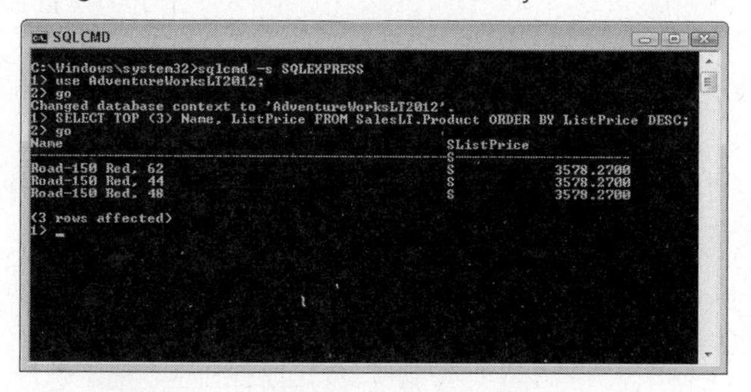

29

The first command, `use AdventureWorksLT2012`, instructs SQLCMD which database to use for future commands. The SQLCMD command `go` runs the previous statement. SQLCMD replies that it `Changed database context to 'AdventureWorksLT2012'` and is ready to accept SQL statements. A new `>1` prompt is presented.

The next command shown in Figure 29.14 is a `SELECT` query run against the `SalesLT.Product` table.

```
SELECT TOP (3) Name, ListPrice FROM SalesLT.Product ORDER BY ListPrice DESC;
```

The statement pulls the `Name` and `ListPrice` columns from the `Product` table, sorts the table with the highest list prices on top, and returns the first three records.

The command-line utility works well if you know all the server names, table names, and column names for your query. You may find it easier to simply open the Management Studio and execute your queries from there.

Named Pipes Error

For some users, SQLCMD requires more configuration to work properly. You may receive the following error when starting SQLCMD.

```
Sqlcmd: Error: Microsoft SQL Server Native Client 11.0 : Named Pipes Provider:
  Could not open a connection to SQL Server [2].
```

To avoid this error, complete the following steps:

1. **Open the SQL Server Configuration Manager.**
2. **Expand the SQL Server Network Configuration folder and select Protocols for SQLEXPRESS.**

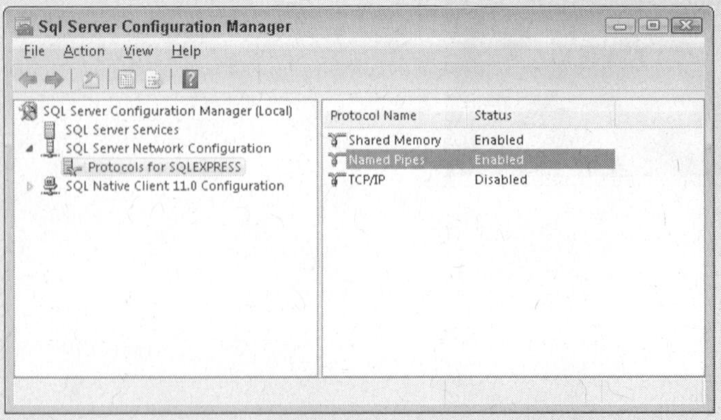

3. Double click Named Pipes to open the Named Pipes Properties dialog box.
4. Change the Pipe Name to \\.\pipe\sql\query.

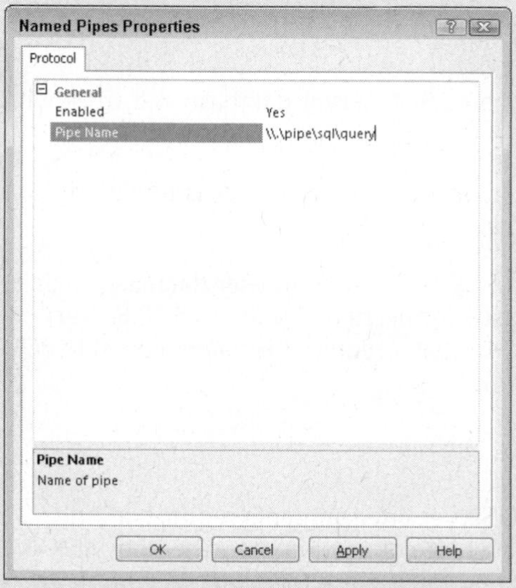

5. Click OK to close the dialog box and dismiss any messages about restarting the service.
6. Select SQL Server Services in the Configuration Manager.
7. Right-click SQL Server (SQLEXPRESS) and choose Restart to restart SQL Server.

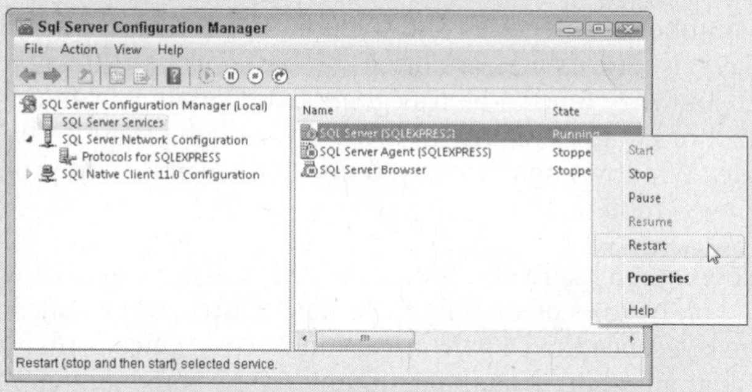

8. Close the SQL Server Configuration Manager.

Connecting to SQL Server

There are two ways for Access to use SQL Server data:

- Linking to SQL Server tables and using them as if they were tables linked to another Access database
- Using ADO code to programmatically open a SQL Server database and work with its data

As you'll soon see, working with SQL Server data through linked tables is no different than using tables linked to any other data source.

One of the most fundamental operations with any large-scale multiuser database engine, such as SQL Server, is connecting to the database. Connecting directly to SQL Server, using SQL Server front-end tools, is quite easy. All that's required is a connection to SQL Server, and Access does the rest.

Creating a data source

Creating a connection between Access and SQL Server environments requires a little something extra, as opposed to just a simple database connection, because both Access and SQL Server are autonomous environments that must work together. As with many relational databases running under Windows, drivers are used to allow tools such as SQL Server and Access to communicate. As is common with many Microsoft software tools, special drivers are created to facilitate communication between different software products. These drivers can be used to connect tools such as Excel and Access to an Oracle or DB2 database or, in this case, an Access database connected to SQL Server.

The drivers in question fall into a number of categories and include ODBC, Object Linked Embedding (OLE), and native drivers. Native drivers are often the best and fastest way to connect to server database engines, but they tend to be less generic and adaptable and usually apply to one specific product or database. Many of these drivers are produced by Microsoft because they all run under Windows operating systems. Some vendors do produce their own ODBC and OLE drivers, though.

Let's focus on the ODBC driver allowing Access to communicate with a SQL Server. How do you deal with an ODBC driver? You have to create an ODBC data source, often called a *Data Source Name* (DSN), and then reference the DSN from within Access. Once configured, a DSN remains on the local computer and is available to any ODBC-compliant application, such as Access. The DSN contains enough information about the ODBC data source that the Access database engine (Jet or ACE) is able to use the ODBC driver to communicate with SQL Server.

Create a data source as follows:

1. **Right-click on the Windows Start screen and choose All Apps. Click the Control Panel tile to open the Control Panel.**

2. **In the Control Panel, double-click the Administrative Tools option, and select Data Sources (ODBC).** The three ODBC configuration options are
   - **User DSN:** A User DSN applies to a specific user on the client computer on which the User DSN is created.
   - **System DSN:** A System DSN is similar to a User DSN, except it applies over a network (to a certain extent).
   - **File DSN:** A File DSN creates a connection configuration (a connection string), for a database, into a file on your client computer.

TIP

Of these three options, the File DSN is the best choice in most situations. Because the connection information is stored in a file (the default location for DSN files is your `Documents` folder), you can easily share a DSN configuration with other users.

3. **Select the File DSN tab and click the Add button to create a new data source.**
4. **On the first screen of the Create New Data Source Wizard, scroll down and select the SQL Server driver, as shown in Figure 29.15; click Next to continue.**

FIGURE 29.15

Selecting the driver for a new data source.

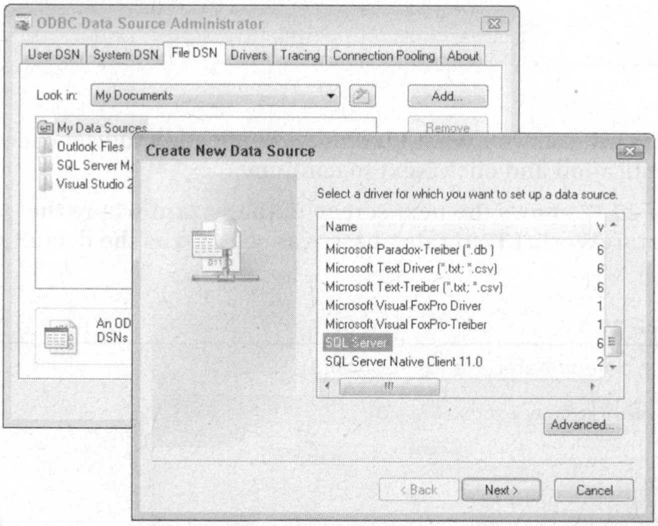

NOTE

The drivers you see on your computer may be different from the list shown here.

5. **In the next step, name the file data source.** The name is entirely up to you, but should be descriptive so you'll know what it refers to later. For this example, you might name the data source `AdventureWorks` because it will be connecting to the AdventureWorksLT2012 database.
6. **When you've completed the Create New Data Source Wizard, the SQL Server driver presents a wizard of its own.** Figure 29.16 shows the first screen of the wizard where you can type a description and identify which server to use.

FIGURE 29.16

The SQL Server driver has its own wizard.

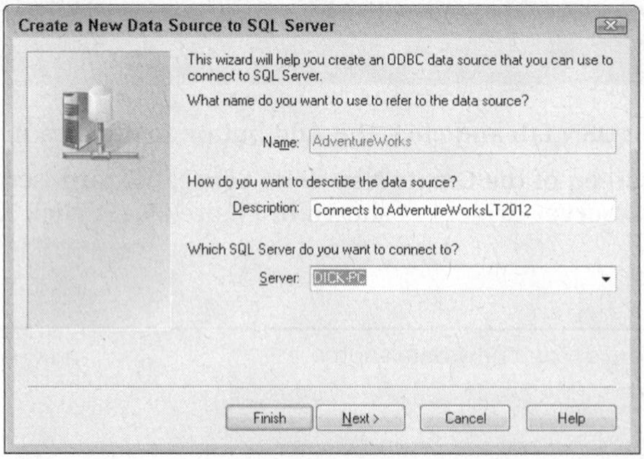

7. **The wizard asks you what kind of authentication to use; choose Windows authentication and click Next to continue.**
8. **Figure 29.17 shows the next screen of the wizard where the AdventureWorksLT2012 database was selected as the default database.**

FIGURE 29.17

Select a default database for your data source.

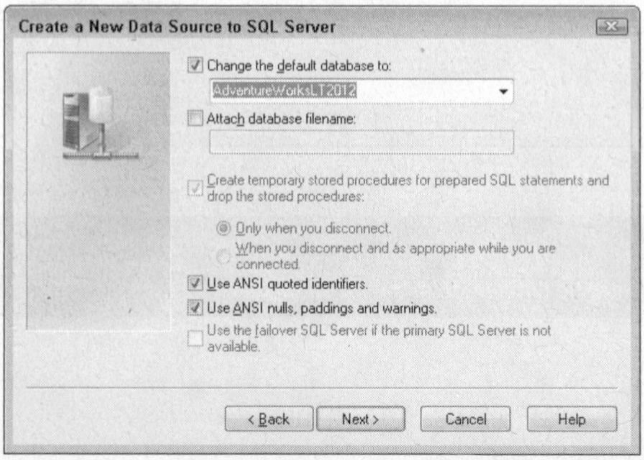

9. **Accept the defaults on the final screen of the wizard and click Finish.** The driver shows a message box with the options you've selected and allows you to test the connection.
10. **Click Test Data Source to make sure everything is working.** If you've set it up correctly, you'll receive a notification similar to Figure 29.18.

FIGURE 29.18

The SQL Server driver reports a successful connection.

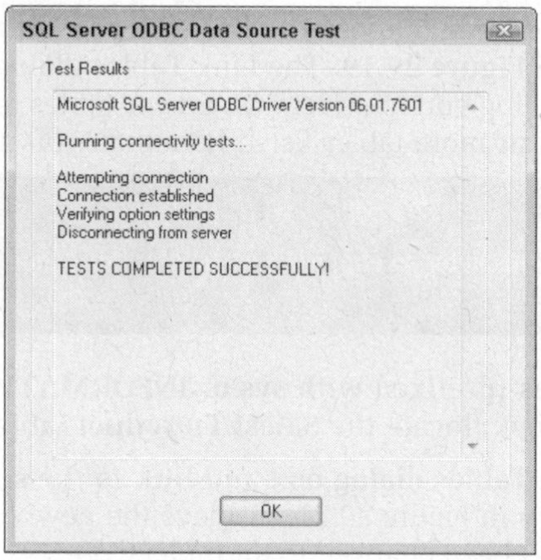

The Data Sources list will now show a new DSN file for the data source you just created. You'll use this file to link SQL Server tables in Access.

Sharing a File DSN is easy: Simply locate the DSN on your machine and attach it to an e-mail, or move it to a common location on the network. User DSNs and System DSNs are actually stored in the computer's Registry, and must be manually set up on each computer needing access to an ODBC data source.

TIP

SQL Server is rather fussy about its name. Prior to SQL Server 2000, SQL Server assumed the same name as its host computer because only one instance of SQL Server could be installed on a computer. However, beginning with SQL Server 2000, a single computer can host multiple SQL Server installations, so the name you use to reference a SQL Server instance is a bit more complex. The syntax used to reference a SQL Server instance is MyComputer\MySQLServerInstance, where MyComputer is the name of the host computer, and MySQLServerInstance is the instance you want to reference.

If only a single SQL Server instance is installed on the local computer, you may be able to specify `(local)` as the name of the server. Otherwise, you'll have to provide the name of the computer and the SQL Server instance name as described in the preceding paragraph.

Linking SQL Server to Access

After creating, configuring, and testing the new DSN, you can use that DSN to create a link between SQL Server and your Access database.

To link the `SalesLT.Product` table, follow these steps:

1. **On the External Data tab on the Ribbon, click ODBC Database.**
2. **Select the Link to the data source by creating a linked table option and click OK.**
3. **On the Select Data Source screen, choose the DSN file you created in the previous section, as shown in Figure 29.19.** The Link Tables dialog box (shown in Figure 29.20) appears, enabling you to select SQL Server tables to link to your Access database. There are far more tables listed here than you might expect.

NOTE

If the Link Tables dialog box doesn't appear, or if you encounter an error while waiting for this dialog box, there may be a problem with the DSN.

4. **Ignore all the system tables (prefixed with sys or INFORMATION_SCHEMA) in the Link Tables dialog box; locate the SalesLT.Product table and select it.**
5. **Click OK to close the Link Tables dialog box and link to the selected table.** The Navigation pane, shown in Figure 29.21, displays the newly linked table. The period in the table name has been changed to an underscore.

FIGURE 29.19

Select the `AdventureWorks.dsn` File Data Source.

FIGURE 29.20

Selecting tables from a SQL Server database.

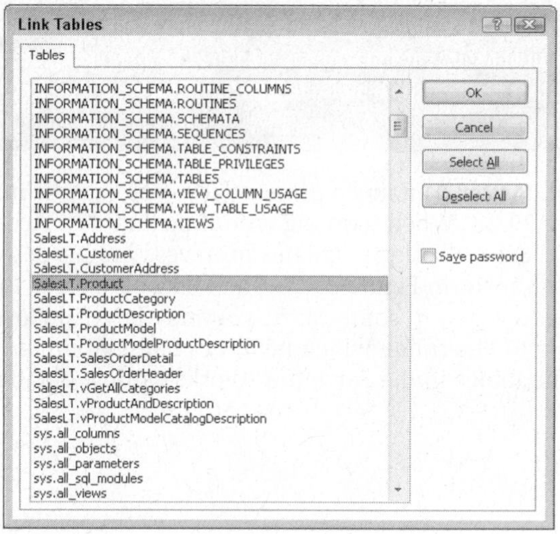

Link Tables

Tables

INFORMATION_SCHEMA.ROUTINE_COLUMNS
INFORMATION_SCHEMA.ROUTINES
INFORMATION_SCHEMA.SCHEMATA
INFORMATION_SCHEMA.SEQUENCES
INFORMATION_SCHEMA.TABLE_CONSTRAINTS
INFORMATION_SCHEMA.TABLE_PRIVILEGES
INFORMATION_SCHEMA.TABLES
INFORMATION_SCHEMA.VIEW_COLUMN_USAGE
INFORMATION_SCHEMA.VIEW_TABLE_USAGE
INFORMATION_SCHEMA.VIEWS
SalesLT.Address
SalesLT.Customer
SalesLT.CustomerAddress
SalesLT.Product
SalesLT.ProductCategory
SalesLT.ProductDescription
SalesLT.ProductModel
SalesLT.ProductModelProductDescription
SalesLT.SalesOrderDetail
SalesLT.SalesOrderHeader
SalesLT.vGetAllCategories
SalesLT.vProductAndDescription
SalesLT.vProductModelCatalogDescription
sys.all_columns
sys.all_objects
sys.all_parameters
sys.all_sql_modules
sys.all_views

OK
Cancel
Select All
Deselect All
Save password

FIGURE 29.21

Linked tables have a globe icon.

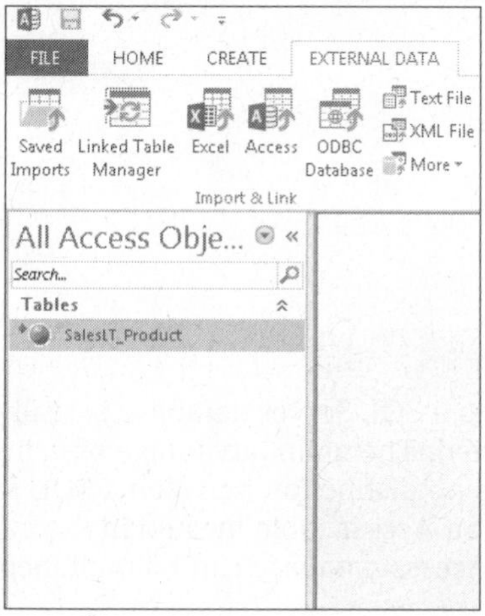

FILE HOME CREATE EXTERNAL DATA

Saved Imports
Linked Table Manager
Excel
Access
ODBC Database
Text File
XML File
More
Import & Link

All Access Obje...
Search...
Tables
SalesLT_Product

NOTE
`dbo` is shorthand for *database owner* and is the default prefix for all objects you create within a SQL Server database. A full explanation of SQL Server authentication, security, and ownership is beyond the scope of this chapter. For now, just keep in mind that SQL Server supports multiple users, each of whom is identified by a name. When a user creates a SQL Server object, he creates the object with either his own name prefix, or with the default `dbo` prefix, depending on how SQL Server security is configured.

Depending on whether SQL Server contains a primary key, you may or may not see the dialog box shown in Figure 29.22. When working with linked tables, Access needs a unique identifier in the SQL Server table so updates in Access are properly performed in SQL Server. In the example shown in Figure 29.22, the logical choice is to use the `ContactID` as the unique identifier. In some cases, you may have to closely examine the data in the SQL Server table to determine which field, or combination of fields, to use as the unique identifier. All the tables in the AdventureWorks sample database contain primary keys.

FIGURE 29.22

Selecting a unique identifier in the SQL Server table.

Select Unique Record Identifier
Fields in table 'dbo_SalesLT_Contact':
ContactID
FirstName
LastName
To ensure data integrity and to update records, you must choose a field or fields that uniquely identify each record. Select up to ten fields.
OK Cancel

As you can see, connecting from Access to a SQL Server database is really quite simple, even though a number of steps are involved. The main advantage of using ODBC to link to SQL Server tables is that Access makes no distinction between a SQL Server table located on a remote database server and an Access table located in the current database. Furthermore, there is no reason why an Access database can't simultaneously connect to multiple data sources.

The ability to link to many different data sources is a fundamental advantage of using Access over other desktop database systems. Access and SQL Server integrate particularly well, and users are seldom aware that they're using data hosted in a remote database in a properly maintained Access application.

Using ADO with SQL Server

Linked tables are a great way to work with SQL Server data. If you already know how to work with Access tables, linked tables are a breeze. If, however, your project only needs data from SQL Server occasionally, you might prefer to use ADO in VBA to get the data. That way, you won't have a bunch of linked tables cluttering your Navigation pane for the few times you need them.

ADO is discussed in Chapters 27 and 28.

Creating a connection string

The first bit of information you'll need to use ADO is a connection string. In Chapter 27, you used the `CurrentProject.Connection` property to get an OLEDB connection string for the current project. Since the data we want is in SQL Server, we'll need a different connection string. One option is use the UDL file technique introduced in Chapter 27. If you have a linked table, or if you can create one, there are two other options that you may find easier.

Finding a connection string using table properties

The first option is to inspect the properties of the linked table. If you open a linked table in Design view, Access will warn you about certain restrictions, such as the inability to modify the design. Figure 29.23 shows the warning if you open `SalesLT.Product` in Design view.

FIGURE 29.23

Access shows a warning when opening linked tables in Design view.

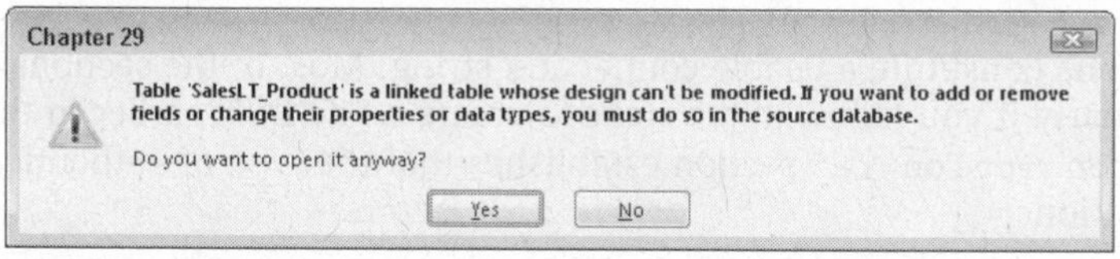

Chapter 29

Table 'SalesLT_Product' is a linked table whose design can't be modified. If you want to add or remove fields or change their properties or data types, you must do so in the source database.

Do you want to open it anyway?

Yes No

Click Yes to open the linked table anyway, and you'll see the familiar table design window. You can't make any changes to the table; you must use SQL Server to modify the table. Open the Property Sheet for the table's properties by clicking on Property Sheet on the Table Tools Design tab of the Ribbon. The `Description` property contains the information you need to build a connection string, as shown in Figure 29.24.

FIGURE 29.24

The table properties `Description` property.

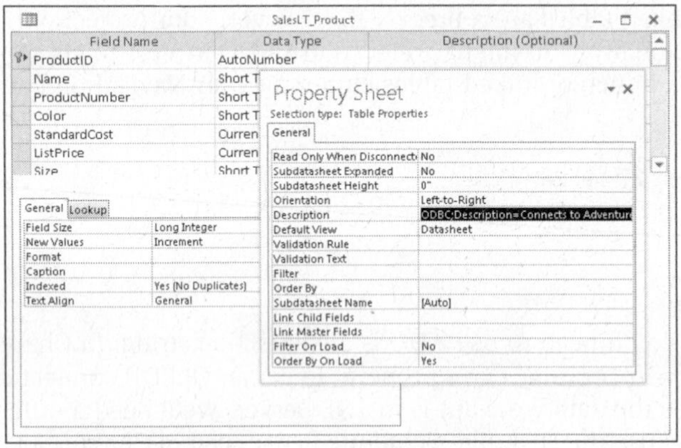

The `Description` property for the `SalesLT.Product` table you linked to in the last section is shown below.

```
ODBC;Description=Connects to AdventureWorksLT2012;DRIVER=SQL Server;SERVER=DICK-
   PC;Trusted_Connection=Yes;APP=Microsoft® Windows® Operating System;DATABASE=A
   dventureWorksLT2012;TABLE=SalesLT.Product
```

Of course, the `Description` property for your database will be slightly different. The `Description` property provides more information than you need for a connection string. The first section, `ODBC;`, is an identifier that tells Access the type of connection and is not needed for the connection string. Also not needed is the last section, `TABLE=SalesLT.Product`, because the ADO connection connects to a database, not a specific table.

The remaining sections constitute a usable connection string. Most of the sections are self-explanatory, particularly if you followed the steps to create a File DSN earlier in this chapter. The `Trusted_Connection=Yes` section establishes that the type of authentication is Windows authentication.

You can copy the `Description` property and paste it into your code. After deleting the sections you don't need, you'll be ready to make an ADO connection to your SQL Server database. We'll show you an example of how to do that later in this chapter.

Finding a connection string using VBA

Another way to find a connection string is using the `Connect` property of the `TableDef` object. Even though the `SalesLT_Product` table is a linked table, it's included in the `TableDefs` collection object. You can use the Immediate window to inspect the properties of a `TableDef` object. Figure 29.25 shows the command executed in the Immediate window that reveals the `Connect` property.

FIGURE 29.25

Using the Immediate window to find a connection string.

```
Immediate
?CurrentDb.TableDefs("SalesLT_Product").Connect
ODBC;Description=Connects to AdventureWorksLT2012;DRIVER=SQL Server;SERVER
```

As usual, the Immediate window doesn't wrap long text, so Figure 29.25 only shows the first part of the string. The full `Connection` property output is shown below:

```
ODBC;Description=Connects to AdventureWorksLT2012;DRIVER=SQL Server;SERVER=DICK-
   PC;Trusted_Connection=Yes;APP=Microsoft® Windows® Operating System;DATABASE=A
   dventureWorksLT2012
```

You'll note that it's exactly the same as the `Description` property you saw in the table properties except that no table name is specified. To use this connection string, you still have to remove the `ODBC;` section from the beginning of the string.

Querying SQL Server with ADO

Once you have a connection string, getting the data out of SQL Server is as easy as writing a SQL statement. In the following example, all the products whose `Color` field is `Black` are returned in a recordset and that recordset is printed to the Immediate window.

```
Sub GetSQLServerDataWithADO()

  Dim adCn As ADODB.Connection
  Dim adRs As ADODB.Recordset
  Dim sConn As String
  Dim sSql As String

  sConn = "Description=Connects to AdventureWorksLT2012;"
  sConn = sConn & "DRIVER=SQL Server;SERVER=DICK-PC;"
  sConn = sConn & "Trusted_Connection=Yes;"
  sConn = sConn & "APP=Microsoft® Windows® Operating System;"
  sConn = sConn & "DATABASE=AdventureWorksLT2012"

  sSql = "SELECT Name, Color, ListPrice FROM SalesLT.Product "
  sSql = sSql & "WHERE Color = 'Black';"

  Set adCn = New ADODB.Connection
  adCn.Open sConn

  Set adRs = adCn.Execute(sSql)
```

```
    Debug.Print adRs.GetString

    adRs.Close
    adCn.Close
    Set adRs = Nothing
    Set adCn = Nothing

End Sub
```

Two variables, `sConn` and `sSQL`, are used to build the connection string and SQL statement, respectively. A portion of the output is shown in Figure 29.26.

FIGURE 29.26

An ADO recordset output to the Immediate window.

```
Immediate
HL Road 4Frame - Black, 58 Black 1431.5
Sport-100 Helmet, Black Black 34.99
LL Road Frame - Black, 58 Black 337.22
LL Road Frame - Black, 60 Black 337.22
LL Road Frame - Black, 62 Black 337.22
LL Road Frame - Black, 44 Black 337.22
LL Road Frame - Black, 48 Black 337.22
LL Road Frame - Black, 52 Black 337.22
HL Mountain Frame - Black, 42 Black 1349.6
HL Mountain Frame - Black, 44 Black 1349.6
HL Mountain Frame - Black, 48 Black 1349.6
HL Mountain Frame - Black, 46 Black 1349.6
```

You can also write a function in VBA that will return a value. For a function, you generally structure your SQL Statement to return only one value. In the following example, the largest `ListPrice` in the `SalesLT.Product` table is returned. The function can be used anywhere in VBA or on forms and reports. Figure 29.27 shows the results of the function in the Immediate window.

```
Public Function GetMaxListPrice()

    Dim adCn As ADODB.Connection
    Dim adRs As ADODB.Recordset
    Dim sConn As String
    Dim sSql As String

    sConn = "Description=Connects to AdventureWorksLT2012;"
    sConn = sConn & "DRIVER=SQL Server;SERVER=DICK-PC;"
    sConn = sConn & "Trusted_Connection=Yes;"
    sConn = sConn & "APP=Microsoft® Windows® Operating System;"
    sConn = sConn & "DATABASE=AdventureWorksLT2012"

    sSql = "SELECT TOP (1) ListPrice FROM SalesLT.Product "
```

```
    sSql = sSql & "ORDER BY ListPrice DESC;"

    Set adCn = New ADODB.Connection
    adCn.Open sConn

    Set adRs = adCn.Execute(sSql)

    GetMaxListPrice = adRs.Fields(0).Value

    adRs.Close
    adCn.Close
    Set adRs = Nothing
    Set adCn = Nothing

End Function
```

FIGURE 29.27

A VBA function called in the Immediate window.

The function above uses the `SELECT TOP (1)` SQL keywords to return only one record. The `ORDER BY` clause sorts the records in descending order by `ListPrice`, ensuring the record with the largest `ListPrice` is at the top. Only one field is returned in the SQL statement, so `adRs.Fields(0).Value` will return the only value in the recordset.

You might find that retrieving data from SQL Server via ADO degrades the performance of your project, particularly if you're making several calls to the server. One way to speed up the process is to keep the connection open for as long as you need it, instead of closing it at the end of each procedure.

You can make the `ADODB.Connection` object variable a module-level variable and only open the connection if it hasn't already been opened. The `Connection` object has a `State` property that can be checked to determine if the connection is open. A `State` value of `1` means the connection is open and a value of `0` means that it's closed. Figure 29.28 shows the `GetSQLServerDataWithADO` procedure from earlier in this section modified to use a module-level `Connection` variable. It also replaces the output with a simple method for timing the procedure.

FIGURE 29.28

Using a module-level `Connection` variable.

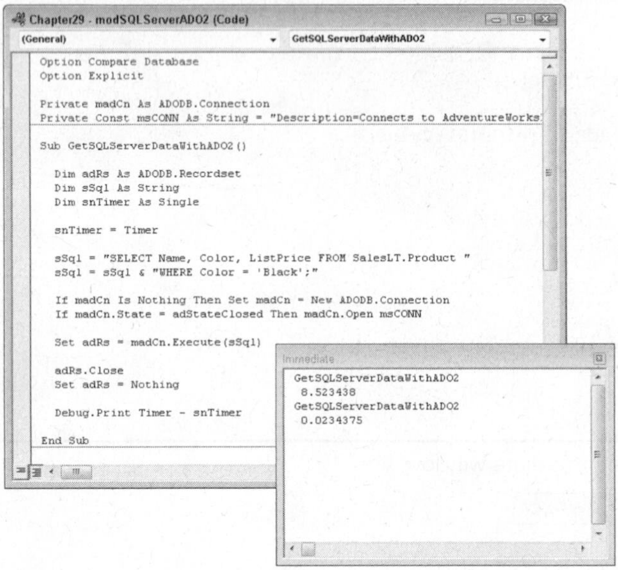

Chapter29 - modSQLServerADO2 (Code)

(General) GetSQLServerDataWithADO2

```
Option Compare Database
Option Explicit

Private madCn As ADODB.Connection
Private Const msCONN As String = "Description=Connects to AdventureWorks

Sub GetSQLServerDataWithADO2()

  Dim adRs As ADODB.Recordset
  Dim sSql As String
  Dim snTimer As Single

  snTimer = Timer

  sSql = "SELECT Name, Color, ListPrice FROM SalesLT.Product "
  sSql = sSql & "WHERE Color = 'Black';"

  If madCn Is Nothing Then Set madCn = New ADODB.Connection
  If madCn.State = adStateClosed Then madCn.Open msCONN

  Set adRs = madCn.Execute(sSql)

  adRs.Close
  Set adRs = Nothing

  Debug.Print Timer - snTimer

End Sub
```

Immediate

```
GetSQLServerDataWithADO2
 8.523438
GetSQLServerDataWithADO2
 0.0234375
```

The Immediate window shown in Figure 29.28 displays the time it took to run the procedure twice. The first run, when the connection was closed, took over 4 seconds to run. The second time the procedure was run, the connection was still open from the previous call to the procedure. This time, the procedure runs so fast that it doesn't even register using VBA's `Timer` function. Keeping a connection open will use more memory, so you need to balance between speed and memory as your project dictates.

NOTE

Prior to Access 2013, Access supported Access Data Projects (ADP files). These files connected directly to SQL Server. Access even provided a utility to upsize your database for use in SQL Server. While existing ADPs still work in Access, the current version provides no way to create them. Further, only SQL Server version 2008 and earlier support ADPs. Microsoft encourages developers to use SharePoint Services as a replacement for ADPs.

Working with SQL Server Objects

SQL Server contains many types of objects that are not supported in Access.

SQL Server supports database objects such as stored procedures, functions, and triggers. So far in this chapter, we've only covered using Access tables linked to SQL Server tables, but most SQL Server databases include more than just tables.

There are two approaches to sharing SQL Server data at the table level:

- **Import SQL Server tables into Access.** Any changes to the Access copy of the table won't be reflected in SQL Server. Any changes to the same tables in SQL Server will require a refresh in Access, which means a complete re-import of the table. It may be possible to use VBA code to create an automatic update process, but such a scheme may not perform well when you're working with large sets of data.
- **Link to tables that remain within SQL Server.** Linked Access tables can update SQL Server data because the table and data actually reside in SQL Server, not in Access. In fact, the interaction between an Access table linked to SQL Server is so seamless that most users are unaware that they're working with remote data.

Using SQL Server tables from Access

In the Linking SQL Server to Access section earlier in this chapter, we discussed creating a table in Access that's linked to SQL Server. In this section, we'll focus on importing SQL Server data and the differences between linking and importing.

To import the `SalesLT.Customer` table from the AdventureWorksLT2012 database, follow these steps:

1. **Click ODBC Databases on the External Data tab of the Ribbon.** The Get External Data – ODBC Database dialog appears.
2. **Choose the Import option, as shown in Figure 29.29, and click OK.**

FIGURE 29.29

Choose Import on the Get External Data – ODBC Database dialog box.

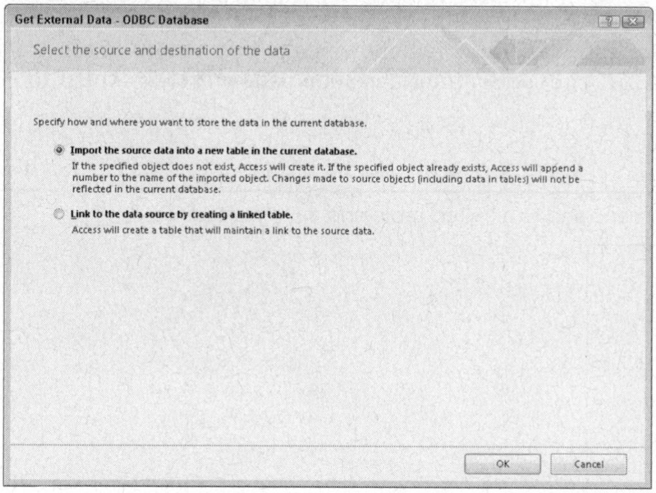

3. **In the Select Data Source dialog box, choose the AdventureWorks.dsn file that you created earlier in this chapter and click OK.** The Import Object dialog box appears and shows all of the objects in the AdventureWorks database.
4. **Select SalesLT.Customer from the list and click OK.** Figure 29.30 shows the Import Objects dialog box with the table selected.

FIGURE 29.30

Select an object to import.

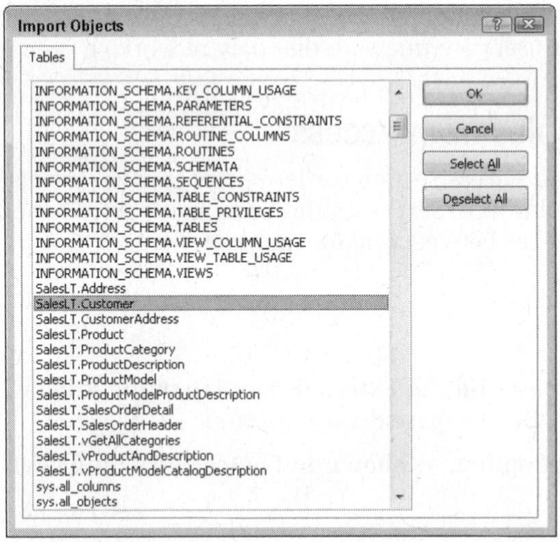

5. **Click Close in the Save Import Step dialog box to complete the process.**

If you linked `SalesLT.Product` by following the instructions in the previous section and imported `SalesLT.Customer`, the Navigation pane will look similar to Figure 29.31.

FIGURE 29.31

The Navigation pane shows a linked table and an imported table.

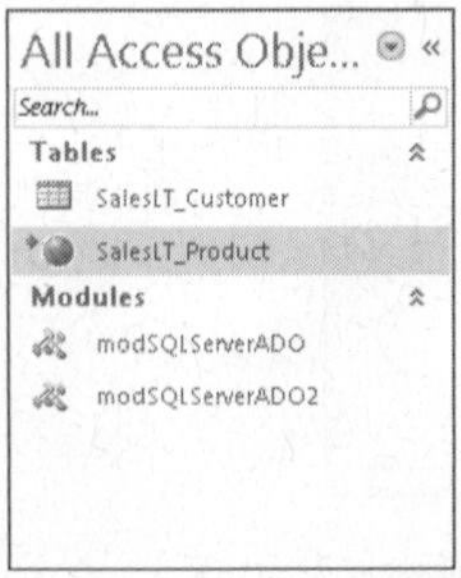

In Figure 29.31, the linked table's icon is a globe and the imported table's icon is exactly the same icon as a native Access table. The icon is the same, because `SalesLT_Customer` *is* a native Access table. The only difference between `SalesLT_Customer` and a table you create from scratch is how the table is created.

NOTE

If you attempt to link a table that has the same name as an existing table, Access will append an integer to the end of the name to ensure it's unique. Importing or linking `SalesLT_Product` more than once, will result in a table name like `SalesLT_Product1`.

Figure 29.32 shows a new record being added to `SalesLT_Customer`.

FIGURE 29.32

Adding a new record to an imported table.

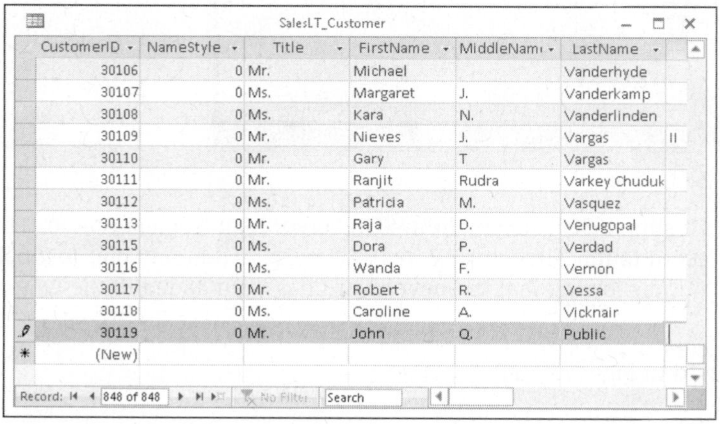

SalesLT_Customer

	CustomerID	NameStyle	Title	FirstName	MiddleName	LastName
	30106	0	Mr.	Michael		Vanderhyde
	30107	0	Ms.	Margaret	J.	Vanderkamp
	30108	0	Ms.	Kara	N.	Vanderlinden
	30109	0	Mr.	Nieves	J.	Vargas
	30110	0	Mr.	Gary	T	Vargas
	30111	0	Mr.	Ranjit	Rudra	Varkey Chuduk
	30112	0	Ms.	Patricia	M.	Vasquez
	30113	0	Mr.	Raja	D.	Venugopal
	30115	0	Ms.	Dora	P.	Verdad
	30116	0	Ms.	Wanda	F.	Vernon
	30117	0	Mr.	Robert	R.	Vessa
	30118	0	Ms.	Caroline	A.	Vicknair
✎	30119	0	Mr.	John	Q.	Public
*	(New)					

Record: 848 of 848 No Filter Search

The `CustomerID` of the new customer added in Figure 29.32 is `30119`. Executing a query in SQL Server Management Studio, shown in Figure 29.33, demonstrates that the new record is not present in SQL Server. This is the fundamental difference between linked tables and imported tables. Making changes to an imported table does not make the change in SQL Server. Similarly, any changes made to the SQL Server data won't be reflected in Access.

There is no automatic refresh for *imported* tables in either direction. Linked data, on the other hand, is (more or less) constantly synchronized between the two databases. Keeping the data synchronized is a rather expensive process. The Access database engine has to monitor SQL Server for changes, and when the user indicates a need to see the freshest data, the database engine retrieves the most recent set of data from SQL Server.

FIGURE 29.33

Changes made to an imported table aren't made in SQL Server.

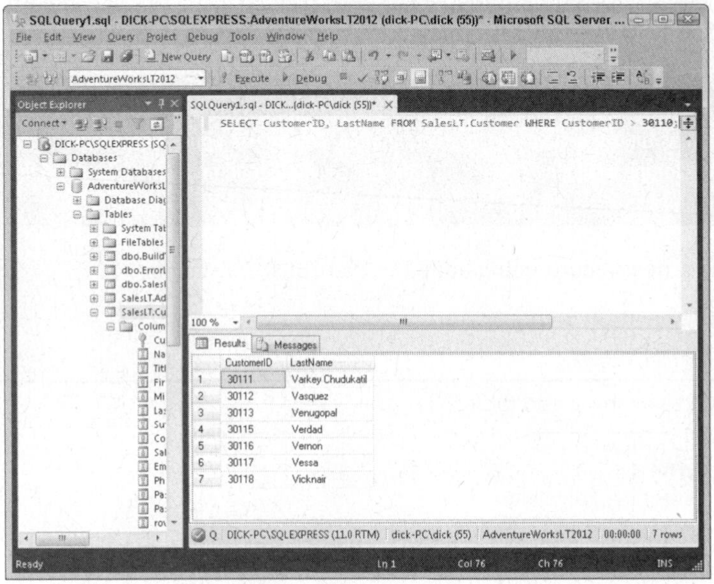

Figure 29.34 shows a simple SQL statement in SQL Server Management Studio. This statement adds a new record to the AdventureWorks `SalesLT.Product` table. Just below the SQL editor area is a grid showing that the new record has been added to the `SalesLT.Product` table.

This is the script used in Figure 29.34:

```
INSERT INTO SalesLT.Product
(Name, ProductNumber, StandardCost,
ListPrice, SellStartDate)
VALUES
('New Bike', 'NN-1234', 99, 299, 2012-01-01)

SELECT * FROM SalesLT.Product
WHERE ProductID > 995;
```

After running this short SQL script in SQL Server and opening the linked table, `SalesLT_Product`, in Access (or pressing F5 to refresh the table if it's already open), `SalesLT_Product` now shows the record just added in SQL Server (see Figure 29.35).

FIGURE 29.34

Making changes directly to SQL Server tables.

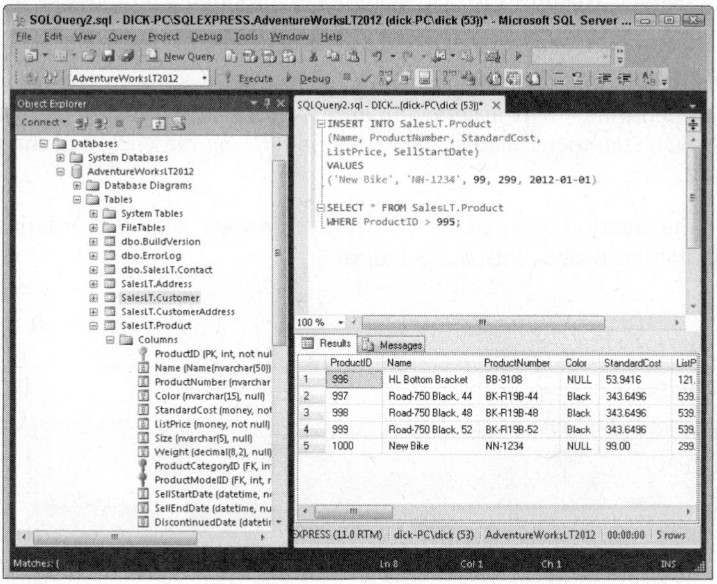

FIGURE 29.35

SQL Server changes are automatically reflected in linked Access tables.

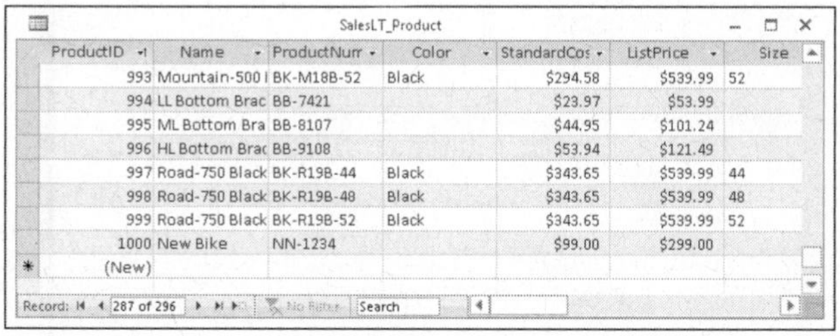

The syncing between linked tables works both ways. In this example, we added a record in SQL Server and it appeared in the linked table in Access. If we had added the record in Access, it would have similarly appeared in SQL Server.

Views

Another object used in SQL Server databases is called a *view*. A view is really a stored query that joins tables and sorts and filters data. Essentially, when you create a form in Access, you're creating a query behind that form. A SQL Server view object creates a table-like object based on a SQL statement that may join tables, sort the data, and perform other fundamental operations on the data as it's selected. When a client application references the view, SQL Server executes the SQL statements, producing a table-like dataset of the data.

The result is that an Access query can be executed against a SQL Server view, as if the view were a table. When the view is accessed in an Access `SELECT` command, SQL Server executes the view's SQL statement against the tables underlying the view and the records returned to the client.

Figure 29.36 shows the creation of a SQL Server view. This view joins the Orders and Customers tables limited to orders with a `Status` of `5`.

FIGURE 29.36

Creating a view in SQL Server.

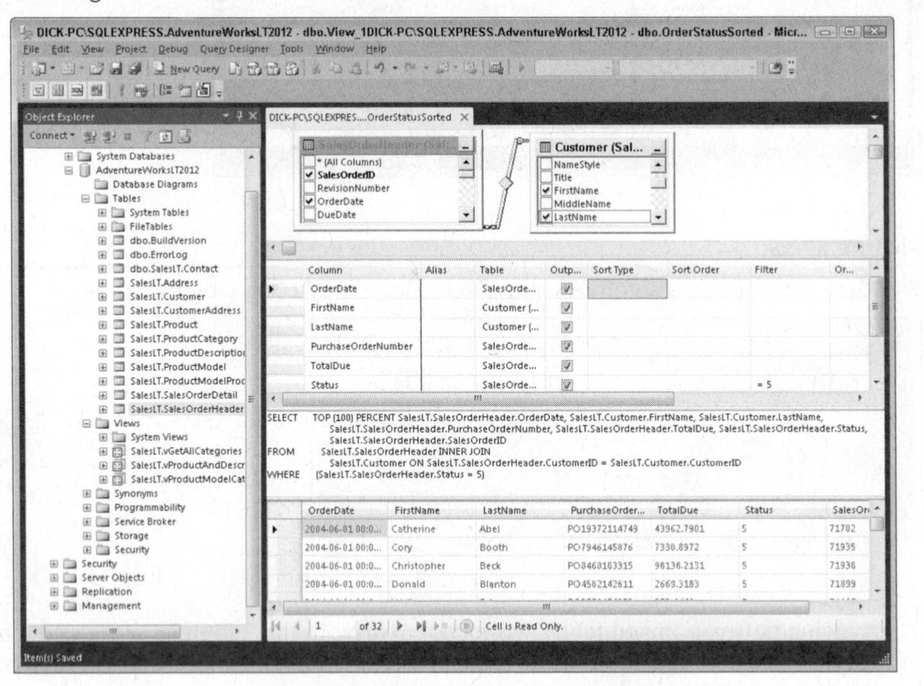

From Access's perspective, this view is just another SQL Server table. This view can be linked just like a native SQL Server table, as shown in Figure 29.37.

FIGURE 29.37

A view is the same as an Access table or datasheet.

dbo_OrderStatusSorted

OrderDate	FirstName	LastName	PurchaseOrc	TotalDue	Status	SalesOrderI
6/1/2004	vid	Hodgson	PO348186287	$972.79	5	71774
6/1/2004	Andrea	Thomsen	PO1995219205	$87.09	5	71776
6/1/2004	Raja	Venugopal	PO1960417323	$42,452.65	5	71780
6/1/2004	Catherine	Abel	PO1937211474	$43,962.79	5	71782
6/1/2004	Kevin	Liu	PO1934311360	$92,663.56	5	71783
6/1/2004	Terry	Eminhizer	PO1928513591	$119,960.82	5	71784
6/1/2004	Anthony	Chor	PO1705215966	$63,686.27	5	71796
6/1/2004	Jon	Grande	PO1650113488	$86,222.81	5	71797
6/1/2004	Michael John	Troyer	PO1302115578	$1,261.44	5	71815
6/1/2004	Joseph	Mitzner	PO1299218044	$3,754.97	5	71816
6/1/2004	Matthew	Miller	PO1029511108	$2,228.06	5	71831
6/1/2004	Pamala	Kotc	PO1035314075	$39,531.61	5	71832
6/1/2004	Frank	Campbell	PO2697119362	$45,992.37	5	71845
6/1/2004	Roger	Van Houten	PO2378131604	$2,711.41	5	71846
6/1/2004	Vassar	Stern	PO1653017764	$665.43	5	71856
6/1/2004	Pei	Chow	PO1615311227	$15,275.20	5	71858

Record: 1 of 32 No Filter Search

In this particular case, during the linking process the `SalesOrderID` was chosen to uniquely identify each row. The unique identifier is needed so that, when data in the view is changed in Access, Access can tell SQL Server which row has been updated. Without a unique identifier, it would be impossible for Access to reliably update SQL Server data.

Stored procedures

Although superficially similar to Access queries, SQL Server stored procedures often perform significant data processing at the database-engine level. SQL Server's SQL dialect is capable of looping, using variables and temporary tables, calling any of hundreds of different built-in SQL Server functions (such as returning the current date and time), and performing many other tasks.

NOTE

Stored procedures, functions, and triggers are not queries. A stored procedure is a block of SQL statements that are executed as a single entity.

One use of stored procedures is as handy container for storing the SQL statements used throughout an application. Instead of writing SQL statements in your application code, you can store them in the database as stored procedures, calling them from your code in much the same way that you call a VBA function. Here are some of the many benefits of stored procedures:

- They can contain multiple SQL statements.
- They can call another stored procedure.
- They can receive parameters and return a value or a result set.

- They're stored in a semi-compiled, interpretive state on the database server, so they execute faster than if they were embedded in your code. In other words, stored procedures are typically not compiled into a relational database as binary code, but they're usually pre-parsed, and partially pre-executed, making for faster execution.
- They're stored in a common container in your application so that others can maintain them more easily because there is less database access code.
- After a stored procedure has been added to a SQL Server database, it's accessible to any client application using that database. This means that an Access desktop database application will execute the exact same logic as a web application written with Visual Studio .NET, if they both use the same stored procedure to access data.

Here are some of the disadvantages of stored procedures:

- Overuse of stored procedures tends to place too much business logic into a database. This can sometimes make number-crunching-type business logic execute in a database very slowly. Some types of processing are best left to application coding, which is often much better suited to intense calculations.
- Overuse of stored procedures for data access can sometimes cause serious issues with network performance.

SQL Server stored procedures are usually executed through ADO code. Here is a small example of calling a SQL Server stored procedure:

```
Public Sub StoredProcTest()

  Dim adCn As ADODB.Connection
  Dim adCmd As ADODB.Command
  Dim adRs As ADODB.Recordset
  Dim sConn As String

  Const sPROCNAME = "dbo.uspGetProductModel"

  sConn = "driver={sql server};" _
    & "server=DICK-PC\SQLEXPRESS;" _
    & "Database=AdventureWorksLT2012;" _
    & "UID=;PWD=;"

  Set adCn = New ADODB.Connection
  adCn.Open sConn

  Set adCmd = New ADODB.Command
  adCmd.ActiveConnection = adCn
  adCmd.CommandText = sPROCNAME
  adCmd.CommandType = adCmdStoredProc
  adCmd.Parameters.Refresh
  adCmd.Parameters(1).Value = 10
```

```
    Set adRs = adCmd.Execute

    Debug.Print adRs.GetString

    adRs.Close
    adCn.Close
    Set adRs = Nothing
    Set adCmd = Nothing
    Set adCn = Nothing

End Sub
```

This code is intended simply to show how ADO is able to run a SQL Server stored procedure, retrieve the procedure's return value as a recordset, and then use the recordset in Access. In this particular case, the connection to SQL Server is made through the ADO provider, and not through ODBC. Here's the stored procedure in SQL server:

```
CREATE PROCEDURE uspGetProductModel
   @pm_id     int
AS
BEGIN
   SELECT * FROM SalesLT.ProductModel WHERE
      SalesLT.ProductModel.ProductModelID = @pm_id
END
```

Triggers

A *trigger* is a bit of SQL code that executes when some action occurs on a table in a database. You don't interact with triggers directly; instead, triggers are listening for changes and execute when a change is detected. Typically, triggers execute as "before" (`FOR` in SQL Server), "after" (`AFTER` in SQL Server), and "instead of" (`INSTEAD OF` in SQL Server) triggers. As the name implies, a "before" trigger fires *before* data is changed in the table, while an "after" trigger files *after* the data has changed.

The biggest danger with triggers is that they can be recursive, calling themselves over and over, resulting in serious performance problems. For example, consider an `AFTER` trigger that changes data in a table. If the change invokes the trigger a second time, an endless recursive loop may occur.

Creating a trigger is very similar to creating a procedure or a function. This example creates an entry in a log file every time a new product is added:

```
USE test

CREATE TRIGGER LogEntries ON Products
    FOR INSERT
        INSERT INTO LogFile(id,event)
        VALUES(<autocounter>,'New product added');
```

CHAPTER

30

Customizing the Ribbon

IN THIS CHAPTER

Working with the default Ribbon

Examining Ribbon architecture

Studying Ribbon controls

Learning the XML necessary to construct Ribbons

Adding VBA callbacks

Unless you're upgrading from Access 2003, the Ribbon will already be familiar to you. The Ribbon was introduced in Office 2007 and replaced the toolbar and menu system that ruled the computing world for decades. The toolbars and menus were an effective user interface when working with a variety of tasks and operations, but the CommandBars model used in versions of Access prior to 2007 was quite complex, and sometimes difficult to program. The Ribbon introduced an entirely new way of working with user-interface components.

The Ribbon is quite unlike traditional toolbars or menus and supports features not possible with toolbars and menus. As you'll soon see, customizing the Ribbon is a very different process than using CommandBars to compose toolbars and menus in previous versions of Access.

ON THE WEB

In the `Chapter30.accdb` database, you can't see the `USysRibbons` table until you right-click the Navigation pane, select Navigation Options, and select the Show System Objects check box in the Navigation Options dialog box. Included with the database are several XML files that are used in this chapter.

The Ribbon Hierarchy

The Ribbon itself is a fairly complex structure and is hierarchical in nature. At the top level are the tabs you see along the top of the ribbon. Each tab contains one or more groups, each containing one or more controls. The Ribbon is highly adaptable to your current tasks, so the description that follows may not be exactly the same as you see on your screen:

- **Tabs:** The top object in the Ribbon hierarchy. You use tabs to separate the most fundamental operations into logical groups. For instance, the default Ribbon contains four tabs: Home, Create, External Data, and Database Tools. The file menu, which looks like a tab, acts quite differently. It opens a backstage area with typical file operations.
- **Groups:** The second highest object in the Ribbon hierarchy. Groups contain any of the number of different types of controls and are used to logically separate operations supported by a Ribbon tab. In Figure 30.1, the Home tab contains seven groups: Views, Clipboard, Sort & Filter, Records, Find, Window, and Text Formatting.
- **Controls:** In Figure 30.1, notice the variety of controls within each group on the Home tab. The Views group contains a single control, while the Text Formatting group contains 18 different controls. Normally, the controls within a group are related to one another, but this is not a hard-and-fast rule.

FIGURE 30.1

The default Ribbon.

As you design your custom Ribbons, you should keep the basic Ribbon hierarchy in mind. Microsoft has spent a great deal of time experimenting with and testing the Ribbon paradigm, and it works well for a wide variety of applications.

The maximum number of tabs you can add to a custom Ribbon is 100. That's a very high limit. The other objects have similarly high limits. Obviously, too many tabs or too many groups can become a real problem for your users. Generally speaking, you should design your Ribbons in a conservative manner, including only the items at each level that your users actually need. Microsoft recommends four or five tabs and never more than seven.

Controls for Access Ribbons

The Ribbon supports many more types of controls than the older command bars. In previous versions of Access, the type and variety of controls you could add to menus and toolbars were severely limited. Most toolbars included buttons, and a few other types of controls like drop-down lists, but there were very few options for adding complex or sophisticated controls to command bars.

Ribbons can contain buttons, text boxes, labels, separators, check boxes, toggle buttons, edit boxes, and even controls nested within other controls. This chapter has only enough room to explore a few of these controls, but you can find examples showing how to use every type of ribbon control in Access on the Microsoft Office website (http://office.microsoft.com).

Access features some very interesting controls to use on your custom Ribbons. These controls are used in the default Ribbon and are accessible to the custom Ribbons you add to your applications. These controls have no analogues in older versions of Access and are completely new to Access.

SplitButton

The SplitButton is similar to a traditional button in an Access interface. What makes the SplitButton different is that it is, quite literally, split vertically or horizontally into two different controls. The left or top side of the control works as any other button and responds to a single click. The right or bottom side of the button includes an arrow that, when clicked, reveals a selection list of single-select options.

An example of a SplitButton (shown in Figure 30.2) is the View button on the Home tab.

FIGURE 30.2

The SplitButton is a powerful Ribbon control.

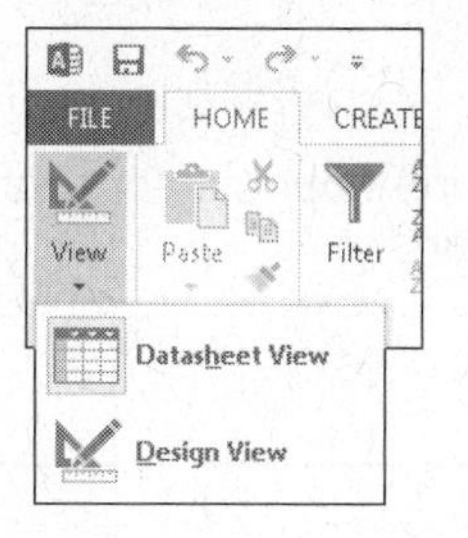

The top portion of the View button can be clicked to switch to Design view. Or the arrow on the View button can be clicked to reveal a list of other options. Only one option in the SplitButton list can be selected. As soon as an item in the list is selected, the SplitButton closes, and the action selected by the user is performed.

The button portion of the SplitButton control is independently programmable.

Menu

The Menu control is shown in Figure 30.3. Although the Menu looks very much like a ComboBox or DropDown, they are not the same type of object. Notice that the items in the drop-down list in Figure 30.3 include not only text (Clear All Filters, Filter By Form, and so on), but also an image and tooltip help (not shown in Figure 30.3) associated with each item.

Only one item in the list can be selected at a time, providing an easy-to-understand interface for your users, when a limited number of options exist.

FIGURE 30.3

The Menu control simplifies a user's selections.

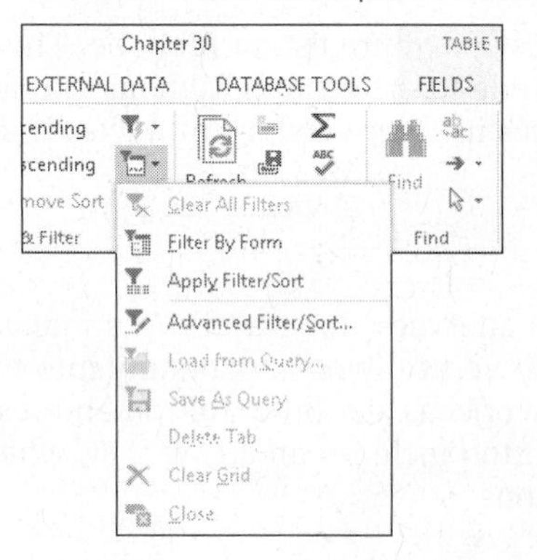

The SplitButton and Menu are very similar in many ways. They both expose a list when clicked and present a list of single-select items. The main difference is that a SplitButton is, literally, split into two portions (horizontal or vertical), whereas the Menu simply drops down the list when clicked.

Gallery

The Gallery presents the user with an abbreviated view of different options for formatting and other tasks. Figure 30.4 shows the Themes Gallery for reports.

FIGURE 30.4

The Gallery provides the user with a preview of the options.

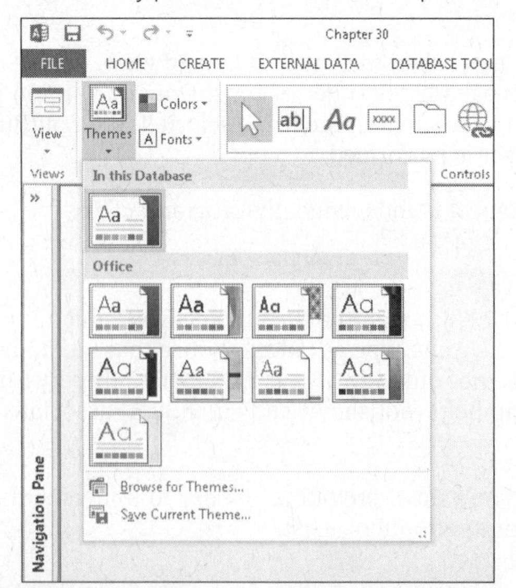

Gallery controls are used extensively in Access for displaying options such as ForeColor, BackColor, and font selections.

Button

The Button is a familiar control from the CommandBar user-interface in older versions. A button can be clicked to perform an action. It does not provide options like a Menu or Gallery, but it can open a dialog box that contains additional options. The Copy button in the Clipboard group of the Home tab is an example of a button. Clicking Copy copies the current selection onto the Clipboard, but it doesn't provide any other options or perform any other actions.

ToggleButton

A special type of button control, called a ToggleButton, is used to set a state or condition of the application. ToggleButtons have two states: on and off. When a ToggleButton is in the off state, it appears like a normal button on the Ribbon. When a ToggleButton is clicked to set the on state, its background color changes to indicate its state and its tooltip caption may change. Figure 30.5 shows the Apply Filter ToggleButton in its on state. The change in appearance is an indicator that a filter has been applied. Its tooltip changed from Apply Filter to Remove Filter.

FIGURE 30.5

A ToggleButton changes appearance to indicate state.

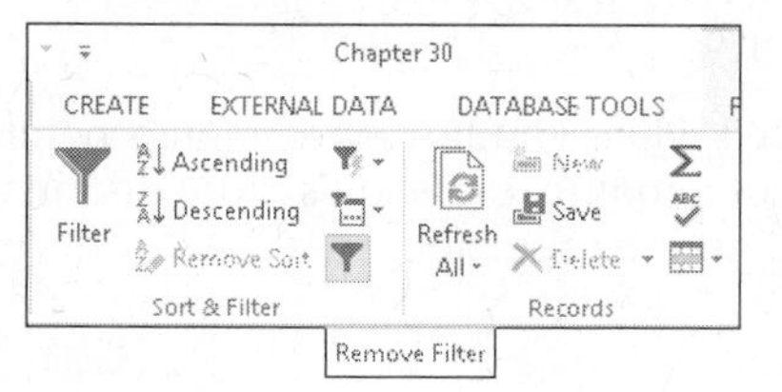

ComboBox

A ComboBox on the Ribbon is very similar to the Combo Box control on a form. It is a combination of a text box and a list box in that you can type directly into a ComboBox or click the down arrow portion of the control to display a list of options. The Font control on the Text Formatting group of the Home tab is an example of a ComboBox control.

CheckBox

A CheckBox control is another control that may seem familiar. It looks and acts just like a check box you put on a form. When a CheckBox has been clicked, a check mark appears in the box. Otherwise, the box appears empty. The Required control on the Field Validation group of the Table Tools tab is an example of a CheckBox control.

Special Ribbon features

The Ribbon contains two other special features that are worth noting. Some controls have SuperTips that can expand the amount of information shown in a tooltip. Also, the ribbon can be hidden to increase the screen space available.

SuperTips

The SuperTip is very similar to the tooltip used in previous versions of Access. A SuperTip is relatively large and contains text that you specify, helping the user understand the purpose of a control. The SuperTip, shown in Figure 30.6, appears as the user hovers the mouse over a control on the Ribbon.

FIGURE 30.6

The SuperTip provides helpful information to the user.

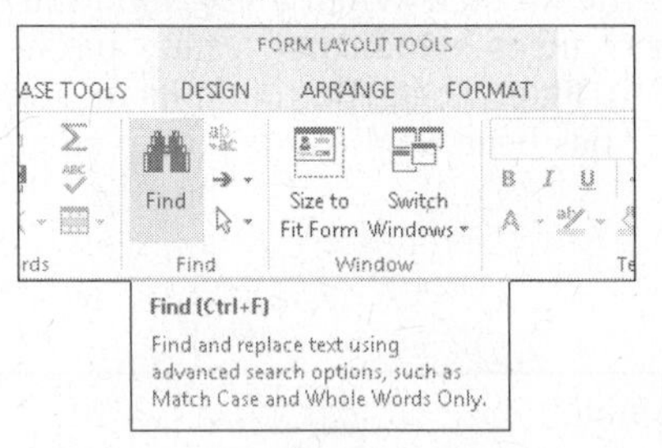

The SuperTip example in Figure 30.6 is displayed when you hover the mouse pointer over the Find button on the Home tab. It's larger than a tooltip and shows more information, such as the shortcut key and a longer explanation of its function.

Collapsing the Ribbon

By default, the Ribbon is always open on the screen. However, the Ribbon, with all its controls and tabs, is quite large and may be in the way while users work with an application. There are several ways to collapse the Ribbon. The easiest methods are to press Ctrl + F1 or to double-click any tab. Pressing Ctrl + F1 again expands the Ribbon and keeps it visible. Single-clicking any tab brings the Ribbon back again, but only temporarily; the Ribbon will "auto-collapse" until you double-click a tab to restore the Ribbon to its pinned state.

The Ribbon contains a Collapse/Pin button in the lower-right corner. When the Ribbon is pinned (expanded) the button is a small up arrow. When the Ribbon is collapsed, the button shows a push pin. Figure 30.7 shows the Collapse/Pin button in both states.

Any forms or reports that are open as the Ribbon is collapsed and expanded are moved up or down so that their positions (relative to the Ribbon) remain the same. For example, a form that is open right below the Ribbon moves upward to occupy the same distance between the top of the form and the bottom of the Ribbon area.

FIGURE 30.7

The Ribbon can be collapsed or pinned.

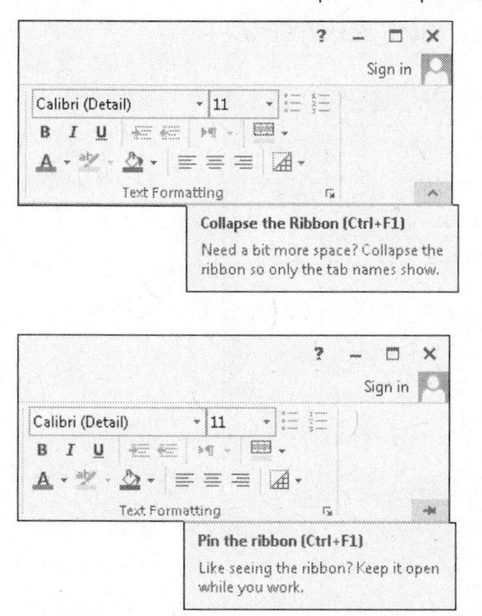

Editing the Default Ribbon

A feature that was added in Access 2010 is the ability to edit the default Ribbon. Changes made to the Ribbon stay with Access on the machine where the changes were made, but an option to export modifications is available in the Ribbon Designer.

The Customize the Ribbon window (see Figure 30.8) uses the "two list" paradigm where one list contains available commands and the other contains selected commands. You select the category of Ribbon you want to modify (File Tabs, Main Tabs, Macros, All Commands, Popular Commands, and so on) from the drop-down above the list on the left side, and then you use the Add and Remove buttons between the lists to add or remove items from the Ribbon.

From the perspective of Access, there is just one Ribbon, but it has a number of Main tabs on it: Print Preview, Home, Create, External Data, Database Tools, Source Control, and Add-Ins. Within a Main tab are a number of groups such as Views, Clipboard, and Sort & Filter. You cannot add or remove tabs or commands from the default Ribbon, but you can remove individual groups.

You can take away entire built-in groups, but you can't remove individual commands within a group. You can use the buttons below the right list to add new custom tabs or to add new groups within existing Ribbon tabs, and then add commands to the custom group. Using a new custom tab or group is the only way to add commands from the left list to the Ribbon definition on the right side.

FIGURE 30.8

The Ribbon Designer allows ribbon customization.

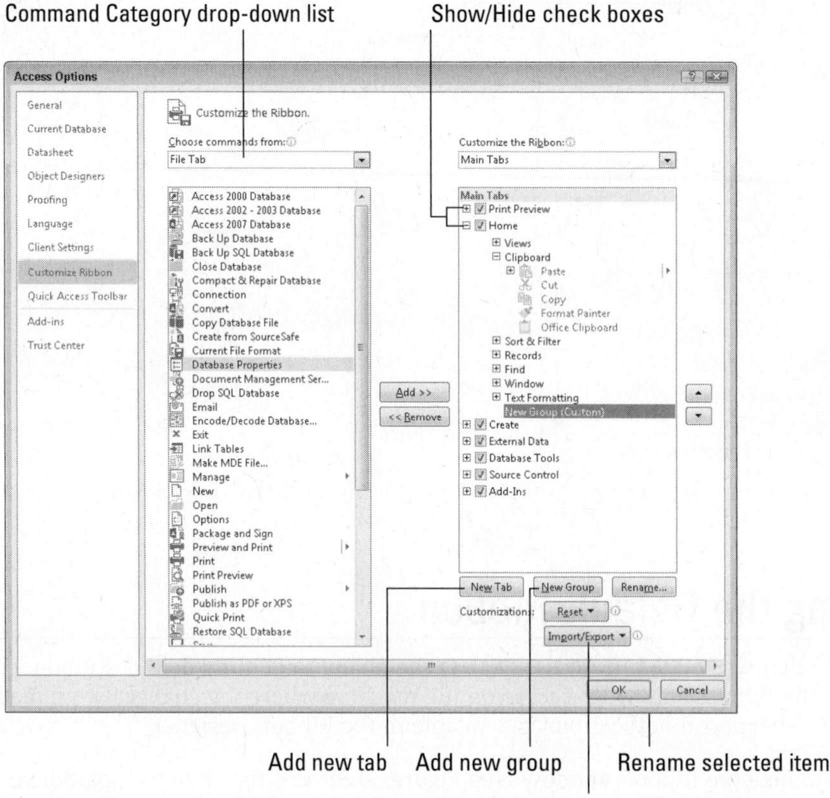

You can't add commands directly to tabs. Commands must reside within groups on a tab. It's easy to add a command to a group: Select the command from the list on the left, select the custom group to receive the command in the list on the right, and click the right-pointing arrow between the lists.

If your objective is to take "dangerous" commands away from your users, you have to remove the built-in group containing the bad command, add a custom group, move it to the appropriate tab, and then add only the commands you want your users to have in the group. Right-click the new group and select Rename from the shortcut menu, or select the new group and click the Rename button under the Customize the Ribbon list. The Rename dialog box appears (see Figure 30.9). Use this dialog box to assign a new name to the group and select the group's icon.

FIGURE 30.9

Renaming a custom group and setting the group's icon.

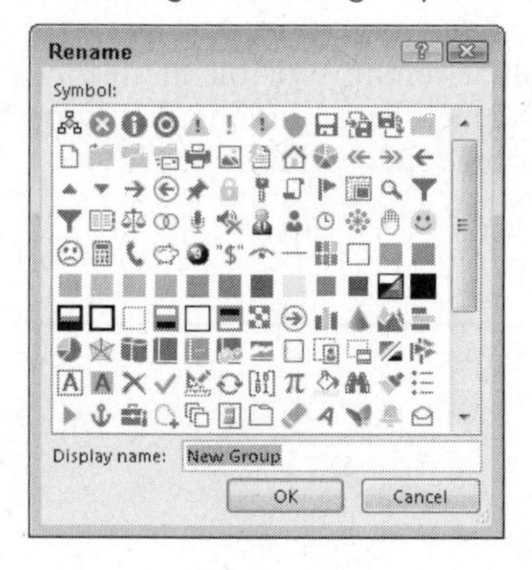

You can hide built-in Ribbon tabs if you prefer. Notice the check boxes next to the items in the list on the right side of Figure 30.8. Deselecting a box next to a tab hides the tab from the user. If the tab contains commands the user must have, you can add a custom tab (with the New Tab button under the Customize the Ribbon list on the right side of Figure 30.8), and then add custom groups as needed. Finally, add the necessary commands to the custom groups.

In many cases, simply hiding tabs is probably easier than removing them from the Ribbon. If they're hidden, you can easily restore their visibility later on, if you need to.

The Ribbon Designer includes up and down arrows at the far right side for repositioning tabs and groups within tabs. You could, for instance, add a custom group (or use an existing group) and move the most commonly used commands into it with the up- and down-arrow keys.

If the changes you've made don't work out as expected, click the Reset button below the Customize the Ribbon list to return the built-in Ribbon to its original state. The Reset button (notice its drop-down arrow in Figure 30.8) lets you reset the entire Ribbon or just the selected tab.

Click the Import/Export button below the Customize the Ribbon list to export the customizations you've made to the Ribbon as an external file. Alternatively, the list that appears when you click the Import/Export button includes a command to import a customization file and apply it to your Ribbon. Not surprisingly, the customization file is in XML format and is shared by all of the Office 2013 applications.

Using a customization file makes it easy to apply custom Ribbon changes to all users working with an Access 2013 application. It's also a great way to back up the changes you've made if you need to reapply the changes later on. You could, for instance, set up the Ribbon exactly as you want your users to see it, export the customization, and then reset the Ribbon to its original state so that you have access to all Ribbon features during your development cycle.

Working with the Quick Access Toolbar

The Quick Access toolbar is in the upper-left corner of the main Access screen (see Figure 30.10) just above the File tab. The Quick Access toolbar remains visible at all times in Access and provides a handy way to give your users quick access to commonly performed tasks such as opening a database file or sending an object to a printer.

FIGURE 30.10

The Quick Access toolbar remains on the screen at all times.

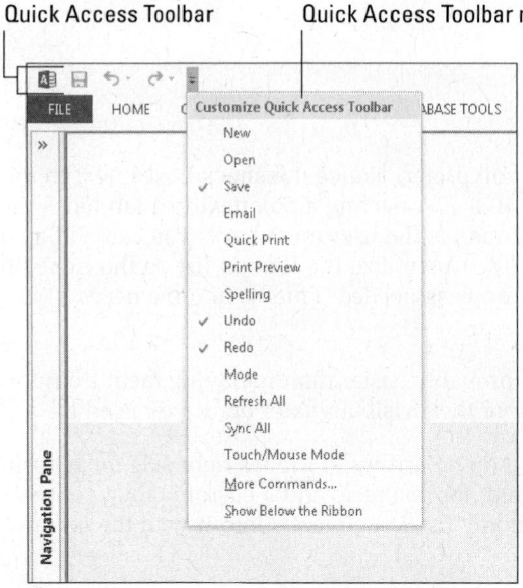

Quick Access Toolbar

Quick Access Toolbar menu

The Quick Access toolbar is fully customizable. It comes with a list of default controls, some of which are hidden, that you can hide or unhide with the Quick Access Toolbar menu (see Figure 30.10). You can quickly and easily add any of a large number of operations to the Quick Access toolbar. Also, the controls you add are applicable either to the current database, or to all Access databases.

The easiest way to add a command to the Quick Access toolbar is to locate the command on the Ribbon, right-click it, and select Add to Quick Access Toolbar from the shortcut menu that appears. Access adds the selected item to the rightmost position in the Quick Access toolbar.

A more flexible approach to modifying the Quick Access toolbar is to open the Quick Access Toolbar customization screen by selecting the File tab in the upper-left corner of the main Access screen and clicking the Options button near the bottom of the Backstage. Then select the Quick Access Toolbar item from the Access Options list to open the Customize the Quick Access Toolbar screen (see Figure 30.11).

FIGURE 30.11

You can easily add new commands to the Quick Access toolbar.

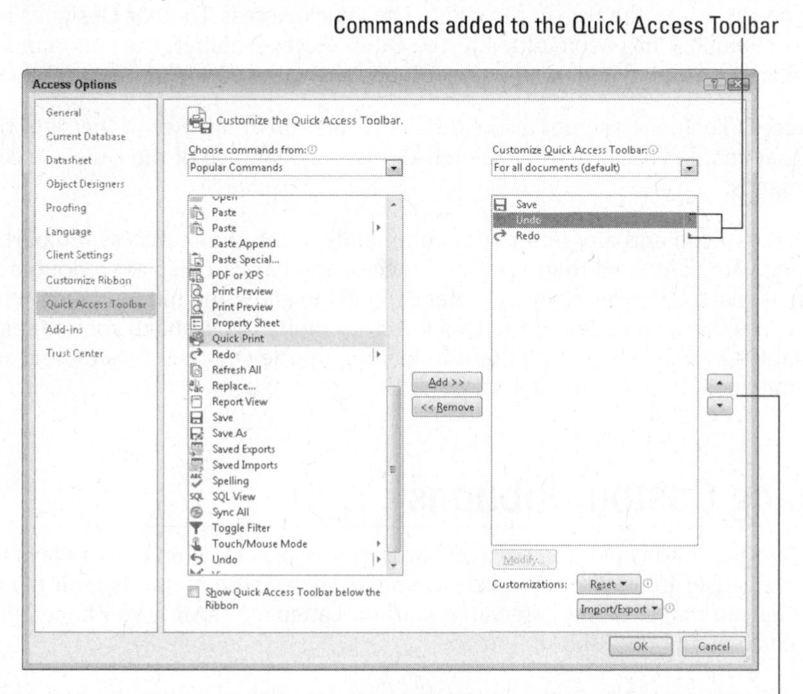

Like the Ribbon Designer, the Quick Access Toolbar Designer uses a list of available commands and a list of selected commands. The list on the left side of the screen contains items representing every command available in Access, categorized as Popular Commands, Commands Not in the Ribbon, All Commands, and Macros. You select the command category from the drop-down control above the list. The category list also contains entries for all the Ribbon tabs in Access (File, Home, External Data, and so on). Selecting an item from this drop-down list reveals the commands within that category.

The Quick Access toolbar provides a handy way for you to control which commands the users access as they work with your Access applications. The tasks available to the Quick Access toolbar include operations such as backing up the current database, converting the current database to another Access data format, viewing database properties, and linking tables.

Because the Quick Access toolbar is visible to all users, be sure not to include commands (such as Design View) that may be confusing to users or harmful to your applications. Because the Quick Access toolbar is easy to customize, it's not difficult to add the commands you need at the time you need them, instead of leaving them visible to all users all the time.

Use the Add and Remove buttons in the Quick Access Toolbar Designer to move an item from the list on the left to the list on the right. The Quick Access Toolbar Designer is quite smart. After a command has been added to the Quick Access toolbar, the command is no longer available to be added again, so you can't add the same command more than once.

The Quick Access Toolbar Designer also contains up and down arrows to the right of the selected list that enable you to reorder the left-to-right appearance of the Quick Access toolbar commands.

Be warned that you can add any number of commands to the Quick Access toolbar. When more commands are contained than the Quick Access toolbar can display, a double-right-arrow button appears at the far right side that expands to show the hidden commands. However, because the whole idea of the Quick Access toolbar is to make commands quickly available to users, there is no point in loading up the Quick Access toolbar with dozens of commands that only make it more difficult for the user.

Developing Custom Ribbons

The Ribbon Designer and Quick Access Toolbar Designer provide convenient ways to customize the Access user interface. However, as you've seen, these methods limit the customizations you can make. Using Extensible Markup Language (XML), you have a lot of flexibility in customizing the Ribbon.

Ribbons are not represented by a programmable object model in Access. Ribbon customizations are defined by XML statements contained in a special table named `USysRibbons`. Access uses the information it finds in the XML to compose and render the Ribbon on the screen.

The Ribbon creation process

Briefly, creating custom Ribbons is a five-step process:

1. **Design the Ribbon and compose the XML that defines the Ribbon.**
2. **Write VBA callback routines (described in the following section) that support the Ribbon's operations.**
3. **Create the USysRibbons table.**

4. **Provide a Ribbon name and add the custom Ribbon's XML to the USysRibbons table.**
5. **Specify the custom Ribbon's name in the Access options screen.**

None of these steps is particularly intuitive, especially when it comes to composing the XML and writing callback routines. Your best bet is to find an example that is reasonably close to what you want and customize its XML to suit your purposes.

Using VBA callbacks

A *callback* is code that is passed to another entity for processing. Each procedure you write to support operations on a Ribbon is passed to the "Ribbon processor" in Access that actually performs the Ribbon's actions. This is very unlike the event-driven code you've been working with in Access. Clicking a button on a form *directly* triggers the code in the button's `Click` event procedure. A Ribbon's callback procedure is linked to the Ribbon but is internally processed by Access and does not directly run in response to the click on the Ribbon.

To fully understand this process, imagine that Access contains a process that constantly monitors activity on the Ribbon. As soon as the user clicks a Ribbon control, the Ribbon processor springs into action, retrieving the callback procedure associated with the control and performing the actions specified in the callback.

This means that there are no `Click`, `DblClick`, or `GotFocus` events associated with the Ribbon in Access. Instead, you bind a callback to a Ribbon control through the XML that defines the Ribbon. Each Ribbon control includes a number of action attributes that can be attached to callbacks, and the Ribbon processor takes over when the user invokes a control's action.

Here is an example. The following XML statements define a button control on a Ribbon:

```
<button id="ViewProducts"
    label="All Products"
    size="large"
    imageMso="FindDialog"
    onAction="OpenProductsForm"
    tag="frmProductsDisplay"/>
```

NOTE
These lines are a single XML statement. Line breaks have been added for readability.

Notice the `onAction` attribute in this XML code. Notice also that the `onAction` attribute is set to `OpenProductsForm`. The `onAction` attribute is similar to the events associated with a form's controls. Each interactive Ribbon control (buttons, SplitButtons, and so on) includes the `onAction` attribute. The callback procedure (`OpenProductsForm`, in this example) assigned to the `onAction` attribute is passed to the Ribbon processor when the control's action occurs.

A control's attributes may appear in any order within the control's XML, but they must be spelled correctly. XML is case sensitive, so attributes must be entered exactly as you see in the examples in this chapter and in the `Chapter30.accdb` example database. And, attribute values (like `"FindDialog"`) must be surrounded by double or single quote characters.

Notice that the button control does not contain a click event. Instead, each interactive control's `onAction` attribute handles whatever action is expected by the control. In the case of a button, the action is a user clicking the button, whereas for a text box, the action is the user typing into the text box. Both of these controls include the `onAction` attribute, but `onAction` means something different for each control.

NOTE

Be aware than `onAction` is not an event. It is just an XML attribute that points to the callback procedure tied to the Ribbon control. The callback procedure runs whenever the user interacts with the control. In this case, the ViewProducts button's callback procedure is invoked when the user clicks the button.

Ribbon controls have several other important attributes, such as `imageMso`, `screentip`, and `supertip`. These attributes are described in the "Adding Ribbon Controls" section, later in this chapter.

TIP

You probably want to see any errors generated by your custom Ribbon during development. By default, Ribbon error reporting is disabled, and you must enable it before you see error messages thrown by the Ribbon. Select the File tab in the upper-left corner of the main Access screen and choose the Options button at the bottom. Next, select the Client Settings tab in the Options dialog box and scroll down to the General section. Make sure the Show Add-In User Interface Errors check box is selected; click OK at the bottom of the dialog box. The error messages generated by the Ribbon are invaluable debugging aids (see Figure 30.12). Without these messages, you have no idea what has failed in your custom Ribbons.

FIGURE 30.12

An error message thrown by a custom Ribbon.

Creating a Custom Ribbon

As mentioned before, creating and customizing Ribbons is very different from working with CommandBars in earlier versions of Access. Creating Access Ribbons is, at minimum, a five-step process. Each of these steps is described in detail in the following sections. Later you'll see many more examples of these steps.

Step 1: Design the Ribbon and build the XML

As with most database objects, the first step to creating a new Access Ribbon is to design it carefully on paper. If you're converting an existing toolbar or menu to an Access Ribbon, you have a pretty good idea of the controls and other items to add to the Ribbon.

The XML document you create for your Ribbon mirrors the design you've laid out. Perhaps the most challenging aspect of composing the Ribbons XML is visualizing how the Ribbon will look, based on the XML behind it. There are no visual cues in a Ribbon XML document that hint at the Ribbon's appearance when rendered in Access. Experience will be your best guide as you work with Ribbon customization, and sometimes trial and error is the only way to achieve a desired objective.

As a final point, Access is extremely fussy about the XML used to compose Ribbons. There is no "parser" in Access that validates the XML as a Ribbon is rendered. If an error exists in the XML document, Access refuses to render the Ribbon, or the Ribbon will be missing elements defined in the XML. This is one reason that using a good XML editor to compose your XML is important. Most often, the only way you know that an error exists in your Ribbon XML code is that Access loads the default Ribbon instead of your custom Ribbon.

Inevitably, Ribbon development in Access requires a number of back-and-forth cycles in which you modify the XML, transfer it to Access, and view the results. You have no real way of really knowing how well your XML will work as a Ribbon specification until Access renders the Ribbon on the screen.

The "Basic Ribbon XML" section, later in this chapter, describes the fundamental XML statements required by Access Ribbons.

For this example, we'll create a new tab on the default Ribbon. The new tab will be named "Messages" and will contain one control that opens a form. First, design a form with one label control on it containing a message to be displayed. Figure 30.13 shows the form `frmMessage` that can be found in the `Chapter30.accdb` database.

FIGURE 30.13

A simple form that displays a message.

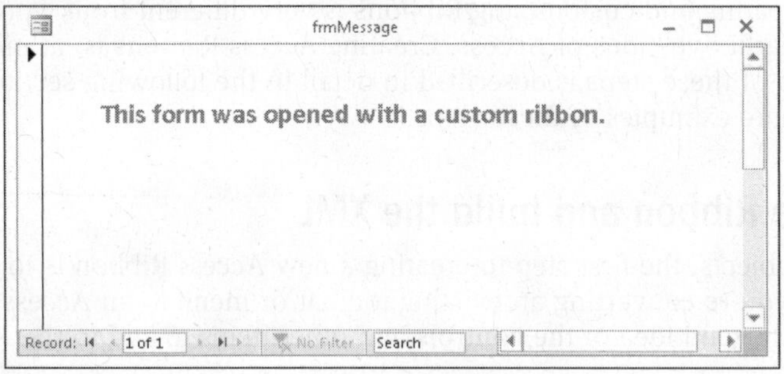

To create the XML that will define the new Ribbon elements, open your favorite XML editor. The examples in this chapter use the XML Notepad application that is available for free from Microsoft.com (www.microsoft.com/en-us/download/details.aspx?id = 7973). Figure 30.14 shows the XML in XML Notepad.

FIGURE 30.14

XML Notepad can be used to write XML.

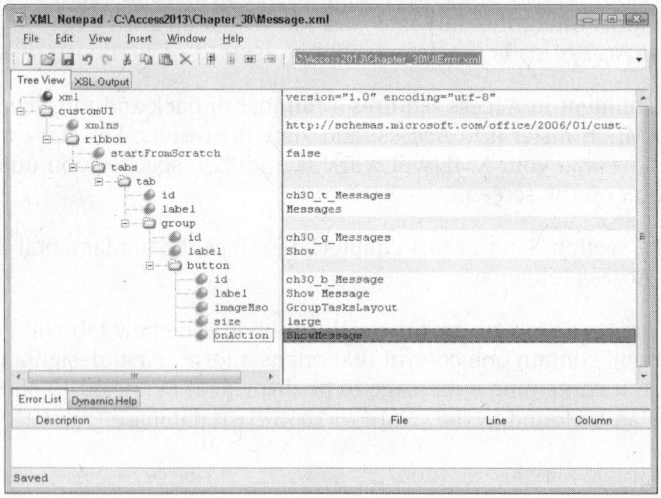

In XML Notepad, you can choose Source from the View file to see the XML that is generated. Here's the XML for `Message.xml`:

```
<?xml version="1.0" encoding="utf-8"?>
<customUI xmlns="http://schemas.microsoft.com/office/2006/01/customui">
  <ribbon startFromScratch="false">
    <tabs>
      <tab id="ch30_t_Messages" label="Messages">
        <group id="ch30_g_Messages" label="Show">
          <button id="ch30_b_Message" label="Show Message"
  imageMso="GroupTasksLayout" size="large" onAction="ShowMessage" />
        </group>
      </tab>
    </tabs>
  </ribbon>
</customUI>
```

We'll discuss each of the parts of this XML file later in the chapter. For now, note that this XML creates a button labeled Show Messages on a Group labeled Show on a tab labeled Messages. The `onAction` attribute is named `ShowMessage` and we'll need that name for the next step.

Step 2: Write the callback routines

Before writing any callback code for Ribbon controls, you must reference the Microsoft Office 15.0 Object Library in the References dialog box (choose Tools➪References, and select the check box next to Microsoft Office 15.0 Object Library). Otherwise, the VBA interpreter will have no idea how to handle references to Ribbon controls.

As we described earlier in this chapter, callback routines are similar to event procedures, but they don't directly respond to control events. Each type of callback routine has a specific "signature" that must be followed in order for the Ribbon processor to locate and use the callback. For instance, the prototype `onAction` callback signature for a button control is

```
Public Sub OnAction(control as IRibbonControl)
```

The prototype `onAction` callback for a check box is

```
Public Sub OnAction(control As IRibbonControl, _
    pressed As Boolean)
```

Even though these callbacks support the same `onAction` control attribute, because the controls are different, the signatures are different. Clicking a button is just that — click once, and the action is done. In the case of a check box, a click either selects (`pressed = True`) or deselects (`pressed = False`) the control. Therefore, an additional parameter is required for check boxes.

These procedures are just prototypes and do not apply to any particular control on a Ribbon. In practice, the callback procedure for a control is usually named after the control to distinguish it from callback procedures for other controls. For this example, write the following code in a standard module:

```
Public Sub ShowMessage(control As IRibbonControl)

  'Called from Messages > Show > Show Message
  DoCmd.OpenForm "frmMessage"

End Sub
```

Notice that this procedure's declaration matches the prototype for a button control's `onAction` callback procedure. Although not required, this procedure even contains a comment that identifies the Ribbon control that calls the routine.

Callback routines must be declared with the `Public` attribute in a standard module, or they can't be seen by the Ribbon process.

The name you apply to callback routines is entirely your choice, as long as the procedure's declaration matches the control's `onAction` signature. Obviously, the procedure's name must match the value you assign to the control's `onAction` attribute, and documenting the procedure's relationship to a Ribbon control is very helpful when it comes time to modify the Ribbon or the callback.

Notice that the callback procedure above doesn't reference the control by name. This means that you have to write a uniquely named callback for each control, or use a single callback for multiple similar controls.

Step 3: Create the USysRibbons table

Access looks for a table named `USysRibbons` to see whether there are any custom Ribbons in the current database application. This table does not exist by default, and, if present, it contains the XML that defines the custom Ribbons in the application.

Note

`USysRibbons` is hidden in the Navigation pane by virtue of the `USys` prefix in its name (any database object with `USys` as the first four characters of its name is automatically hidden in the Navigation pane). If you want to see `USysRibbons` in the Navigation pane, you must enable Show System Objects in the Navigation Options: Right-click the Navigation pane title bar, select Navigation Options, and select Show System Objects in the lower-left corner of the Navigation Options dialog box.

`USysRibbons` is very simple, and contains only three fields, shown in Table 30.1.

TABLE 30.1 The USysRibbons Table Design

Field	Data Type
ID	AutoNumber
RibbonName	Short Text 255
RibbonXML	Long Text

The `ID` field just keeps track of the Ribbons in the table. The `RibbonName` is used to specify which Ribbon Access should load at startup (described in Step 5, later in this chapter), whereas `RibbonXML` is a Long Text field containing the XML that defines the Ribbon.

Because `USysRibbons` is a table, your Access database may actually include the definitions of many different custom Ribbons. However, only one custom Ribbon can be active at a time. Later in this chapter, we cover how to invalidate an existing Ribbon and load a new Ribbon in its place.

You might find good reasons to add additional fields to `USysRibbons`, if necessary. For instance, you could add a `Notes` or `Comments` field that helps another developer understand how the Ribbon should be used. You could also add a modification date and other fields that help track changes to your custom Ribbons. If you modify `USysRibbons`, be sure not to remove or rename the three required fields (`ID`, `RibbonName`, and `RibbonXML`). These three fields must exist in `USysRibbons` and must be named correctly for your custom Ribbons to work.

Step 4: Add XML to USysRibbons

Now you're ready to store your XML in the `USysRibbons` table. Open the `USysRibbons` table in Datasheet view. In the `RibbonName` field, enter **rbnMessages** and move the cursor to the `RibbonXml` field.

Copy the XML that you created in Step 1 and paste it into the `RibbonXml` field of `USysRibbons`. If you're using XML Notepad, open the XML file in XML Notepad and choose View⇨Source to output the XML to Windows Notepad. Then copy the XML from there to paste into `USysRibbons`. Figure 30.15 show `USysRibbons` with the fields completed.

The XML that was pasted into the `RibbonXml` field contains a lot of white space. Don't worry about the tabs and line breaks in the XML. Be sure, however, that if you replace existing data in the `RibbonXml` field you replace all the existing data. With tabs and line breaks, it can be difficult to know if you've left any remnants from the previous data.

FIGURE 30.15

Copy the XML into `USysRibbons`.

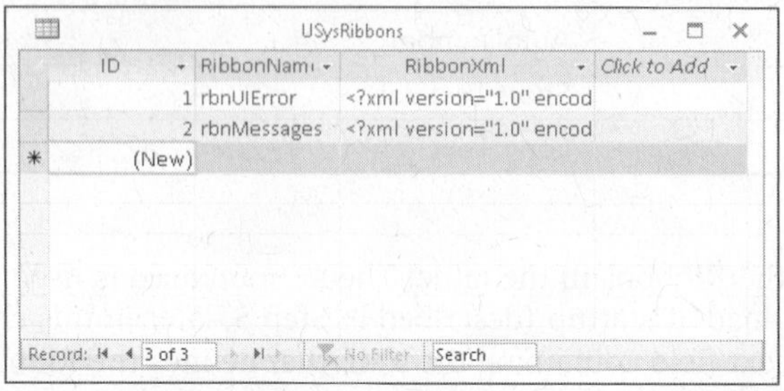

ID	RibbonName	RibbonXml	Click to Add
1	rbnUIError	<?xml version="1.0" encod	
2	rbnMessages	<?xml version="1.0" encod	
(New)			

FIGURE 30.16

`frmRibbons` displays the information stored in the `USysRibbons` table.

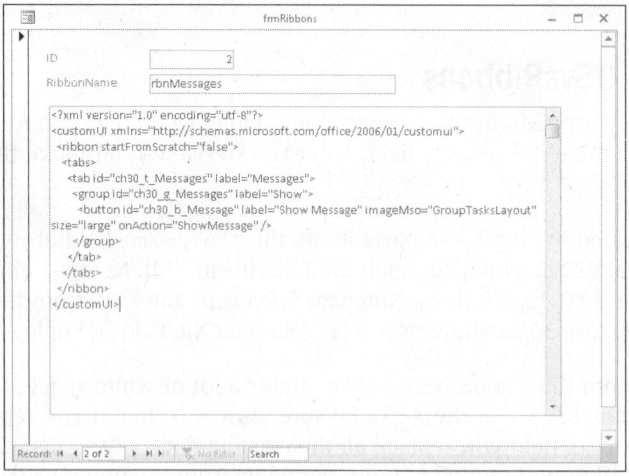

ID: 2

RibbonName: rbnMessages

```
<?xml version="1.0" encoding="utf-8"?>
<customUI xmlns="http://schemas.microsoft.com/office/2006/01/customui">
  <ribbon startFromScratch="false">
    <tabs>
      <tab id="ch30_t_Messages" label="Messages">
        <group id="ch30_g_Messages" label="Show">
          <button id="ch30_b_Message" label="Show Message" imageMso="GroupTasksLayout"
size="large" onAction="ShowMessage" />
        </group>
      </tab>
    </tabs>
  </ribbon>
</customUI>
```

TIP

Because it's difficult to read long XML strings in Datasheet view, you may want to create a form with a large enough text box to display more of the string. Figure 30.16 shows a form named `frmRibbons` from the `Chapter30.accdb` that shows the contents of the `USysRibbons` table.

Step 5: Specify the custom Ribbon property

The last step, before restarting the application, is to open the Current Database properties (choose File ➪ Options ➪ Current Database), scroll to the Ribbons and Toolbar Options section, and select the name of the new Ribbon from the `RibbonName` combo box (see Figure 30.17). The combo box's list contains only the names of custom Ribbons in `USysRibbons` that were in the table as Access started (apparently Access only reads `USysRibbons` one time as Access opens a database), so it does not contain the name of the new Ribbon. You have to type the Ribbon's name into the combo box, or restart the application and let Access find the new Ribbon in `USysRibbons`.

FIGURE 30.17

Specifying the new custom Ribbon in the Current Database options dialog box.

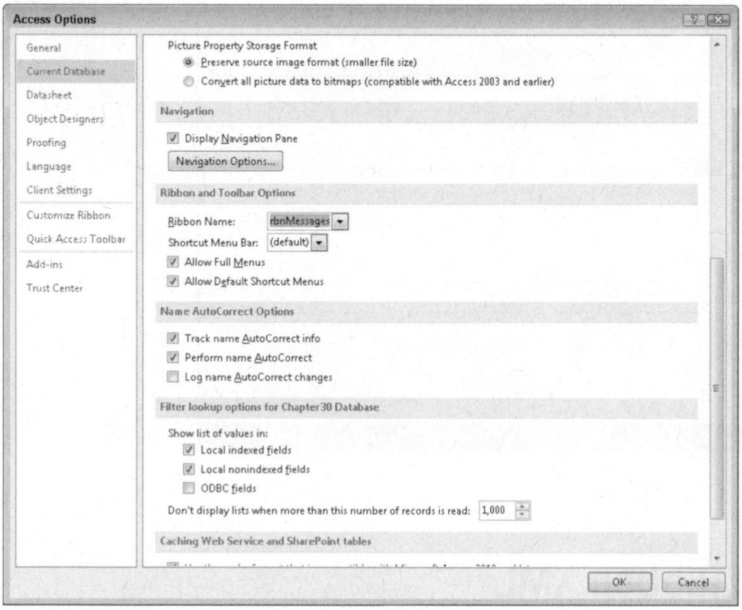

When you close the Options dialog box after selecting a new `Ribbon Name`, Access displays a message that you must close and reopen the database for the changes to take effect. Figure 30.18 shows the message displayed.

FIGURE 30.18

Changes to the `Ribbon Name` property require a restart of the application.

Once Access is restarted, the new tab shows on the default Ribbon. Figure 30.19 shows the new tab, the Show group on that tab, the lone Show Message button, and the form that is opened when the button is pushed.

FIGURE 30.19

The XML produces new Ribbon elements that open a form.

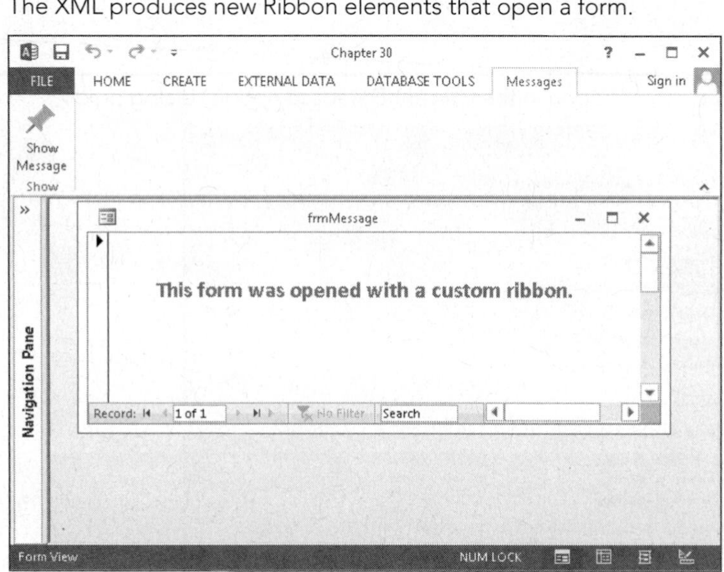

The Basic Ribbon XML

Take a closer look at the basic XML required by Ribbons. The following XML represents a prototype Ribbon (line numbers have been added to make the discussion following this XML easier to understand):

```
1 <?xml version="1.0" encoding="utf-8"?>
2 <!-- This is a comment in the ribbon's XML -->
3 <customUI xmlns="http://schemas.microsoft.com/office
    /2006/01/customui" onLoad="onRibbonLoad">
4   <ribbon startFromScratch="true">
5     <tabs>
6       <tab id="tab1" ...
7         <group id="group1" ... >
8          ... Controls go here ...
9         </group>
10      </tab>
```

```
11        <tab id="tab2" ...
12          <group id="group2" ... >
13           ... Controls go here ...
14          </group>
15          ... Repeat Groups ...
16        </tab>
17        ... Repeat Tabs ...
18      </tabs>
19    </ribbon>
20 </customUI>
```

The first statement (`<?xml version="1.0" encoding="utf-8"?>`), is not required by and does not affect Access Ribbons. It's completely your choice whether to keep this line or not in the `USysRibbons` table. Well-formed XML includes the version line and it helps other programs to render the file, so it's a good practice to include it. Line 2 shows how to add a comment to a Ribbon's XML code. The `<!--` and `-->` are standard commenting tags for XML documents.

Line 3 (beginning with `<customUI...`) specifies an XML *namespace* (`xmlns`), an XML document that predefines acceptable tags for the XML statements that follow. The Office namespace defines the Office Ribbon constructs, such as tabs, groups, controls, and so on. Every Ribbon defined in the `RibbonXML` field in `USysRibbons` must start with this statement, so be sure it's included.

NOTE

Beginning with Office 2010, you have another option for the `CustomUI` tag. The tag you see in the preceding code applies to Ribbons intended to be used in Access 2007 through 2013. If you're building a Ribbon and you know (for sure!) that it will only be used with Access 2010 or Access 2013 (perhaps to take advantage of new features in those versions), you can use the following `CustomUI` statement:

```
<customUI xmlns="http://schemas.microsoft.com/office/2009/07/customui">
```

The statement in line 4 is rather important. The `startFromScratch` directive determines whether we're building an entire Ribbon from scratch or modifying the default Ribbon by adding or taking things away. Depending on your situation, the majority of your custom Ribbons may be built from scratch because the default Ribbon knows nothing about the forms, reports, and other objects and operations in your database. Also, the default Ribbon contains commands that may be dangerous to your application's integrity. For instance, a user could open a form, report, or table in Design view and make changes without your being aware of it. Removing these commands from the user interface is a first line of defense for your applications.

When `startFromScratch` is set to `false`, your custom Ribbon definition is added to the default Ribbon to the right of the built-in tabs. Because Access only includes four tabs by default, you may have enough room for your additional tabs without overcrowding the Ribbon. When `startFromScratch` is set to `true`, none of the default tabs, groups, or controls is shown on the Ribbon. Only what you include in the XML will be displayed.

Most of the tags in an XML file have a corresponding closing tag that defines the end of the section that relates to that tag. All the statements between the opening and closing tags are children of that tag. Lines 19 and 20 are the closing tags for the `Ribbon` and `CustomUI` elements, respectively.

The `<tabs>` (line 5) and `</tabs>` (line 18) tags indicate the beginning and end of the tabs on the Ribbon. Ribbons are hierarchical, with tabs containing groups, which contain controls. The tabs, therefore, are the highest-level objects within a Ribbon and enclose all other Ribbon objects.

Line 6 defines the leftmost tab on the Ribbon. In this example, the tab's name is `tab1`. The other attributes for this tab are not shown but are implied by the ellipsis (`...`). The ending tag for `tab1` is located on line 10.

Line 7 begins the definition of the first group on `tab1` and line 9 ends this group. Within the group are the controls displayed by the group.

The rest of this prototype Ribbon is simple repetition of the first few items.

NOTE

XML is case sensitive. Be careful to use exactly the same case and spelling for all references in your XML as well as in the callback code driving the Ribbon.

Adding Ribbon Controls

The previous section presented a simple prototype Ribbon. In this example, the controls were indicated by `... Controls go here ....` on lines 8 and 13. In this section, you'll see the XML and the callback procedures for several controls. Many XML attributes are common to more than one control. We won't discuss every attribute for every control, but we'll look at the most-used attributes.

Specifying imageMso

Most, but not all, Ribbon controls include an `imageMso` attribute that specifies the picture attached to the control. You can't provide simple references to image files; instead, you must use an `imageMso` identifier for this purpose. Every Ribbon control in the Office 2013 applications has an associated `imageMso` value. You use these values on your custom Access Ribbon controls and provide a label that tells your users the exact purpose of the control.

To find the `imageMso` for a particular Ribbon control, use the Customize the Ribbon window to open a particular Ribbon. Then use the drop-down in the upper left of the designer to select the Ribbon category containing the Ribbon command and hover the mouse over the command's entry in the list (see Figure 30.20).

FIGURE 30.20

Using the Ribbon Designer to obtain a Ribbon command's `imageMso` attribute.

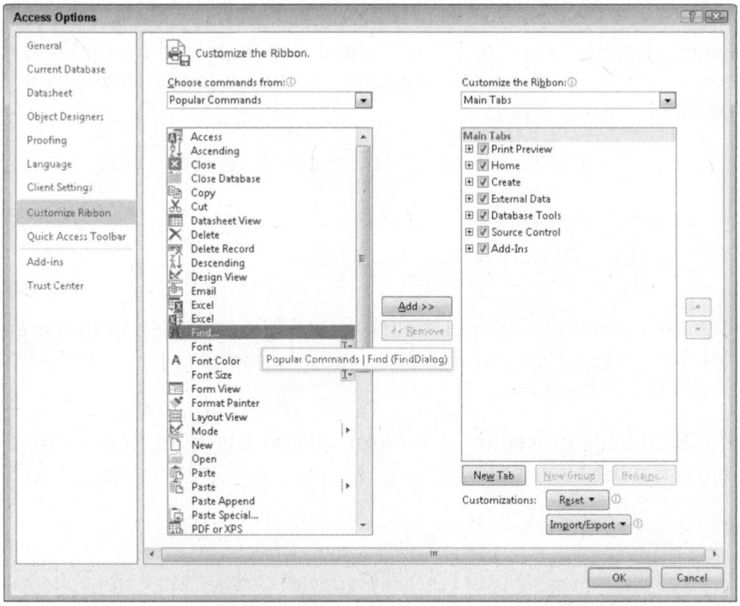

The `imageMso` for the Find command (`FindDialog`) is shown in parentheses in the tooltip that appears near the selected command.

The Label control

The `Label` control is, by far, the simplest and easiest to add to a Ribbon. A Ribbon label is completely analogous to a label you add to an Access form. It contains either hard-coded text or text that is generated by a callback procedure.

Here is a sample label definition:

```
<group id="ch30_g_Settings" label="Settings">
  <labelControl id="lbl1" label="Font Things" />
  <separator id="s1"/>
  <labelControl id="lbl2" label="Choose Font Settings" />
  <checkBox id="chk1" label="Bold" onAction="SetBold"/>
  <checkBox id="chk2" label="Italics" onAction="SetItalics"/>
</group>
```

This XML contains two labels, a separator, and two check boxes. The text in each of these labels is hard coded, rather than returned by a callback procedure. You can set the label's caption at runtime using a callback procedure and the `getLabel` attribute.

```
<group id="ch30_g_Label" label="Labels">
  <labelControl id="lbl3" getLabel="lbl3_getLabel" />
</group>
```

The above XML code uses `getLabel` to identify the callback procedure that will determine what the label displays. In a standard module, the following procedure will show the current date in the label.

```
Public Sub lbl3_getLabel(control As IRibbonControl, ByRef label)

  label = FormatDateTime(Date, vbLongDate)

End Sub
```

The `label` argument is passed `ByRef` and whatever string is assigned to that argument is displayed in the `labelControl`. In this example, the `FormatDateTime` function is used to create a string with the current date.

You can also use one callback procedure to control several labels. In this example, three labels use the same `getLabel` attribute.

```
<group id="ch30_g_Label" label="Labels">
  <labelControl id="lbl3" getLabel="lbl3_getLabel" />
  <labelControl id="lbl4" getLabel="lbl456_getLabel" />
  <labelControl id="lbl5" getLabel="lbl456_getLabel" />
  <labelControl id="lbl6" getLabel="lbl456_getLabel" />
</group>
```

The `lbl456_getLabel` callback procedure uses the control's `id` property to determine which control is calling the procedure.

```
Public Sub lbl456_getLabel(control As IRibbonControl, ByRef label)

  Select Case control.Id
    Case "lbl4"
      label = "This is Label 4"
    Case "lbl5"
      label = "This is Label 5"
    Case "lbl6"
      label = "This is Label 6"
  End Select

End Sub
```

NOTE

Most attributes have both a static form and a dynamic form. By prefixing the attribute's name with get, you transform it from an attribute whose value is set in the XML to an attribute whose value is determined by a callback procedure. For example, the `labelControl` has a label attribute and a `getLabel` attribute. Use `label` when you want to set the value in the XML and `getLabel` when you want to set the value dynamically in a VBA callback procedure. An attributes and its `getAttribute` cousin are mutually exclusive. Only specify one or the other in the XML.

The Button control

The Button control is, perhaps, the most useful and fundamental of all of the Ribbon controls. A button is very simple. A button has a label, an `imageMso` attribute for setting the button's image, and an `onAction` attribute that names the callback routine. An example of a button XML is

```
<button id="btn1" size="large"
  label="Browse"
  imageMso="OutlookGlobe"
  onAction="btn1_onAction" />
```

The `btn1_onAction` callback procedure, shown below, uses the `FollowHyperlink` method of the `Application` object to launch a web browser. The Button Ribbon control does not support double-click actions, so tying a button to a callback procedure is very simple.

```
Public Sub btn1_onAction(control As IRibbonControl)

  Application.FollowHyperlink "http://www.wiley.com"

End Sub
```

Another attribute that you can use with the Button control is the `keytip` attribute. Access assigns key tips to most controls that you add to the ribbon. Key tips are shown when the Alt key is pressed; they allow you to navigate the Ribbon from the keyboard. You can specify your own key tip with the `keytip` attribute. The XML for the above button with a `keytip` attribute look like this:

```
<button id="btn1" size="large"
label="Browse" keytip="B"
imageMso="OutlookGlobe"
onAction="btn1_onAction" />
```

Figure 30.21 shows the new button with a *B* for the key tip allowing the user to access the button with an easy-to-remember keyboard shortcut.

FIGURE 30.21

You can specify a custom key tip for controls.

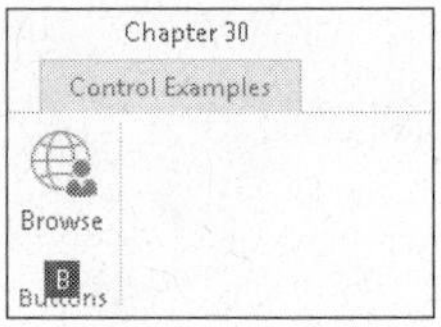

Separators

A separator is a graphical element that divides items in a group, as shown in Figure 30.22. Separators contain no text and appear as a vertical line within a group. By themselves, they're not very interesting, but they graphically separate controls that would otherwise be too close within a group.

FIGURE 30.22

Separators provide a way to divide controls within a group.

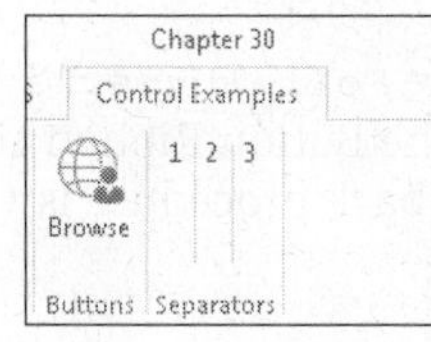

The XML code for the separators in Figure 30.22 is

```
<group id="ch30_g_Separator" label="Separators">
  <labelControl id="lbl7" label="1" />
  <separator id="s2" />
  <labelControl id="lbl8" label="2" />
  <separator id="s3" />
  <labelControl id="lbl9" label="3" />
</group>
```

The only requirement for separators is that each be assigned a unique ID value.

Check boxes

Check boxes are effective for allowing the user to select any of a number of different options. Check boxes are not mutually exclusive, so the user can choose any of the check boxes within a group without affecting other selections.

Check boxes are established much like any other Ribbon control:

```
<tab id="ch30_t_Outdoor" label="Outdoor">
  <group id="ch30_g_Sports" label="Sports">
    <checkBox id="chkBaseball" label="Baseball" ...
    <checkBox id="chkBasketball" label="Basketball" ...
    <separator id="outdoor_Sep1"/>
    <checkBox id="chkTennis" label="Tennis" ...
    <checkBox id="chkWaterPolo" label="Water Polo" ...
  </group>
  <group id="ch30_g_Camping" label="Camping Supplies">
    <checkBox id="chkTent" label="Tent" ...
```

```
        <checkBox id="chkGranola" label="Granola" ...
        <checkBox id="chkLantern" label="Lantern" ...
        <separator id="camping_Sep1"/>
        <button id="btnCamping" imageMso="StartTimer"
          size="large" label="A Big Button" />
      </group>
    </tab>
```

NOTE

We removed some XML and replaced it with ellipsis characters to improve clarity of this example XML.

The tab produced by this XML code is shown in Figure 30.23 and is included in the `ControlExamples.xml` example Ribbon in the `Chapter30.accdb` database.

FIGURE 30.23

Check boxes are a good choice when the user needs to be able to select among a number of options.

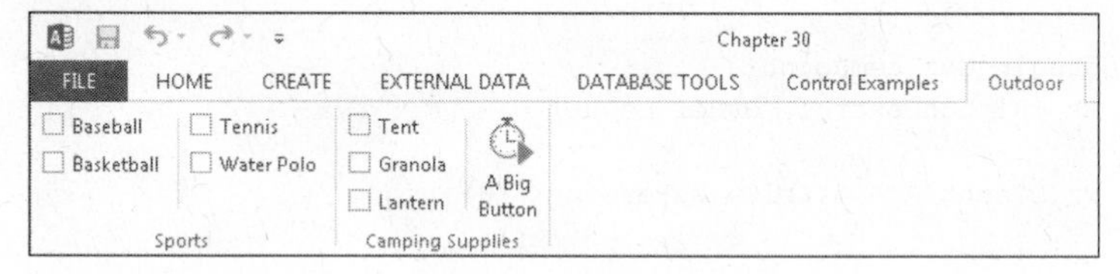

The Ribbon check boxes you see in Figure 30.23 work exactly as you would expect. The check boxes may be selected individually, or in any combination. Check boxes are not mutually exclusive, and each check box can have its own `onAction` attribute, or multiple check boxes can share a callback procedure.

The DropDown control

The DropDown control is more complex than the label, button, and check box examples we've covered. It includes a list of items for the user to choose from. Therefore, a DropDown has a number of attributes that define its appearance, as well as callbacks that populate its list:

```
<dropDown
  id="ddLogin"
  label="Login" supertip="Select your employee name...
  screentip="Login Name"
  getItemCount="ddLogin_getItemCount"
  getItemLabel="ddLogin_getItemLabel"
  onAction="ddLogin_onAction" />
```

The id, label, screentip, and supertip attributes define the DropDown control's appearance. The getItemCount and getItemLabel populate the DropDown's list. onAction specifies the callback that handles the control's action. Figure 30.24 shows the DropDown created in this section.

FIGURE 30.24

A DropDown control lists users' names.

The VBA callbacks for a typical DropDown are shown in the following code. Two primary callbacks are required for a DropDown. The first sets the count of items to appear in the list, and the second actually populates the list.

```
Public Sub ddLogin_GetItemCount( _
    control As IRibbonControl, ByRef count)

    count = Nz(DCount("*", "tblSalesPerson"), 0)

End Sub

Public Sub ddLogin_getItemLabel( _
    control As IRibbonControl, index As Integer, ByRef label)

    Dim sName As String

    sName = Nz(DLookup("SalespersonName", _
        "tblSalesPerson", "SalesPersonID = " & index + 1), _
        vbNullString)

    label = sName

End Sub
```

The first callback (ddLogin_getItemCount) gets the count of items to be placed on the DropDown's list. Notice the ByRef count parameter. This parameter tells the DropDown how many items to accommodate on its list.

The second procedure (ddLogin_getItemLabel) actually retrieves the items for the list. In this case, the procedure pulls the SalesPerson name field from tblSalesPerson using DLookup. ddLogin_getItemLabel is called by the DropDown multiple times; the exact number of calls is determined by the count value established by ddLogin_getItemCount.

An accurate count of values to add to the DropDown is important. The DropDown has no way, other than the count parameter, to know how many items to expect. Setting a count too low means that not all items will be added, whereas setting the count too high means that list contains blank spaces. If, for instance, you set the count to ten items, but only five are available, the DropDown's list contains the five items, but also five blank spaces.

The `ddLogin_getItemLabel` routine cheats a little bit to supply this information. Notice the index parameter passed to this routine. Index tells the procedure which slot on the drop-down list is being filled when the procedure is called. The `DLookup` adds 1 to this value and extracts the name of the salesperson whose ID matches this value. This means that the `SalesPersonID` values have to be sequential, starting with 1, or this procedure will fail.

Extracting data with nonsequential ID values, or where the ID value is non-numeric, requires a bit more work. In the following code, `ddLogin_getItemLabel` has been rewritten to use an ADO recordset rather than the `DLookup` function. The `ddLogin_onAction` procedure uses a recordset in the same way.

```
Private Const msSQLSALESPERSON As String = _
  "SELECT SalespersonName FROM tblSalesPerson ORDER BY
   SalesPersonName;"

Public Sub ddLogin_getItemLabel( _
  control As IRibbonControl, index As Integer, ByRef label)

  Dim adRs As ADODB.Recordset

  Set adRs = CurrentProject.Connection.Execute(msSQLSALESPERSON)
  adRs.Move index

  label = adRs.Fields(0).Value

End Sub

Public Sub ddLogin_onAction( _
  control As IRibbonControl, id As String, index As Integer)

  Dim adRs As ADODB.Recordset

  Set adRs = CurrentProject.Connection.Execute(msSQLSALESPERSON)
  adRs.Move index

  MsgBox "You are logged in as " & _
    adRs.Fields(0).Value & ".", _
    vbOKOnly, "Logged In"

End Sub
```

Both procedures use the same module-level constant, `msSQLSALESPERSON`. This ensures that the records are sorted in exactly the same order. The `Move` method moves to the record specified by `index`, and if the records were in a different order from one procedure to the next, the wrong name would be returned. The name of the salesperson is retrieved using the `adRs.Fields(0).Value` statement. By controlling the SQL statement in a module-level constant, you can be sure that the first field (`.Fields(0)`) will contain the proper information.

NOTE

The Ribbon includes three controls that appear quite similar. The DropDown control discussed in this section shares many visual characteristics with the Menu control (see Figure 30.3) and the ComboBox control (the Font combo box in the Text Formatting group on the Home tab is an example). The DropDown and ComboBox controls use the `getItemCount` and `getItemLabel` callbacks to populate their lists, while the Menu control contains Button elements directly in the XML. You should understand the differences among these controls so you can choose the best one for your application.

The DropDown control forces the user to select an item on the list and displays the selected item in the control. While the DropDown control looks like a ComboBox control, the user can't edit the value directly.

The ComboBox control works just like a DropDown except that the user can edit the value directly in the control and is not limited to the items in the list. DropDown controls and CombBox controls are analogous to List Boxes and Combo Boxes that you might use on a form.

The simplest of the three controls, the Menu control, is a list of buttons that perform an action. The value of the selection is not displayed in the control, and the buttons cannot be created dynamically.

The SplitButton Control

The SplitButton control is very useful in situations where the user may select from a number of different options, but one option is used more frequently than the others. An example might be a number of reports, one of which is commonly printed and the others of which are printed less often. The View SplitButton that's on the Home tab when you're designing a table is a good example (refer to Figure 30.2). The button portion of the View SplitButton changes, depending on the context. If the user is already in Datasheet view, the button changes to Design view, and vice versa.

The items on a SplitButton's list are contained within `<menu>` and `</menu>` tags. Whatever controls (within reason, of course) that appear within these tags show up in the SplitButton's list. The definition of the default button portion of a SplitButton lies outside the `<menu>` and `</menu>` tags. In the following code fragment, `spbtn1_btn1` is the default button, whereas the other buttons (`spbtn1_btn2`, `spbtn1_btn3`, and so on) occupy the SplitButton's list.

```
<group id="ch30_g_Splits" label="Split Button">
  <splitButton id="spbtn1" size="large">
    <button id="spbtn1_btn1"
      imageMso="ModuleInsert"
```

```
          label="Button1"
          onAction="spbtn1_onAction" />
        <menu id="spbtn1_menu" itemSize="large">
          <button id="spbtn1_btn2"
            imageMso="OutlookGlobe"
            label="Button2"
            onAction="spbtn1_onAction" />
          <button id="spbtn1_btn3"
            imageMso="OutlookGears"
            label="Button3"
            onAction="spbtn1_onAction" />
          <button id="spbtn1_btn4"
            imageMso="Organizer"
            label="Button4"
            onAction="spbtn1_onAction" />
        </menu>
      </splitButton>
    </group>
```

This Ribbon XML example produces the SplitButton shown in Figure 30.25. This example is contained in the `rbnControls` example in the `Chapter30.accdb` database.

FIGURE 30.25

SplitButtons are a very useful Ribbon control.

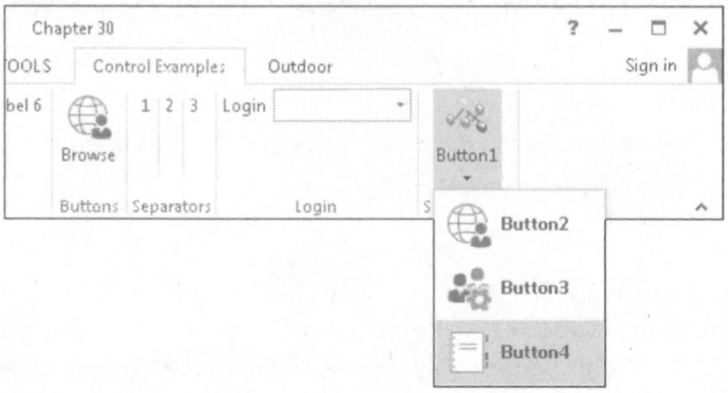

Attaching Ribbons to Forms and Reports

The Ribbon elements that we've created so far are always visible. Often, you'll want the Buttons, DropDowns, and Menus that you place on the Ribbon to be available all the time. However, you may have certain Ribbon elements that you want to display only in certain situations. Fortunately, Access provides a simple way to display Ribbons when a form or report is active.

Forms and Reports have a RibbonName property that you can set in the Property Sheet or with VBA. The RibbonName property in the Property Sheet provides a drop-down for all the Ribbons in the USysRibbons table. Figure 30.26 shows a Ribbon being attached to a form.

FIGURE 30.26

Setting a form's RibbonName property.

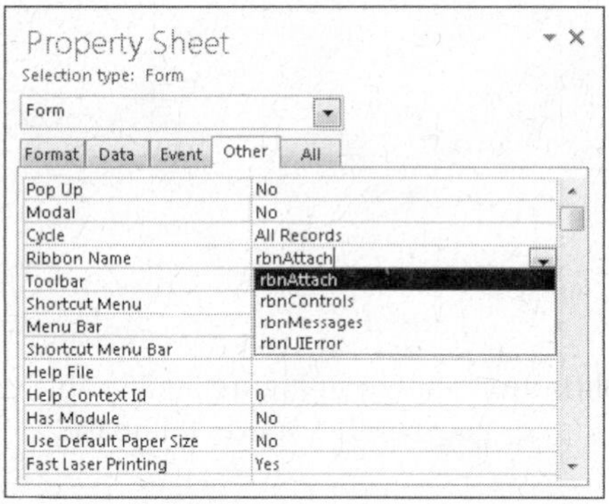

The rbnAttach XML code is in the FormAttach.xml file included with the sample files for this chapter and is in the USysRibbons table in the Chapter30.accdb example database. Here's the XML:

```
<?xml version="1.0" encoding="utf-8"?>
<customUI xmlns="http://schemas.microsoft.com/office/2006/01/customui"
   onLoad="onRibbonLoad">
  <ribbon startFromScratch="false">
    <tabs>
      <tab id="ch30_t_Attach" label="My Form">
        <group id="ch30_g_Attach" label="My Form">
          <button id="ch30_b_Attach" label="My Form" imageMso="GroupTasksLayout"
   size="large" />
        </group>
      </tab>
    </tabs>
  </ribbon>
</customUI>
```

The button doesn't have an onAction attribute, so the Ribbon doesn't actually do anything. It's just an example to show how the Ribbon changes when attached to the form. The startFromScratch attribute is set to false so that the tab is added to the default Ribbon instead of replacing it. Figure 30.27 shows the new tab that is displayed when the form is opened.

FIGURE 30.27

Opening a form opens its Ribbon.

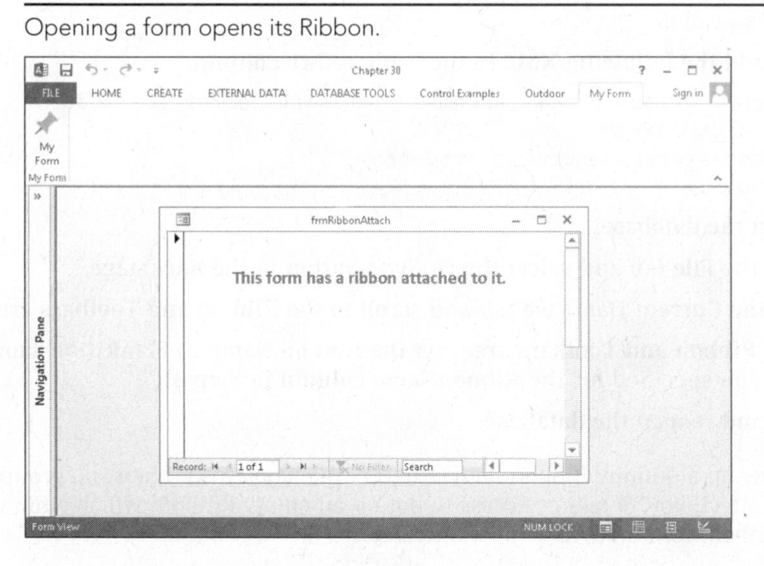

The My Form tab with its associated controls is available while the form is open. Closing the form causes the new tab to disappear. The list of Ribbons in the Property Sheet acts like the list in the Options sheet. That is, it doesn't update whenever you add a new Ribbon to `USysRibbons`. You have to close and reopen your application to update the list.

TIP

Choosing Compact and Repair from File ➪ Info automatically closes and reopens your database. It's a one-click method for updating the loaded Ribbons list. It has the added benefit of keeping your database compacted.

Completely Removing the Ribbon

Assume, for a moment, that there are perfectly legitimate reasons why you don't want to use the Ribbon in your applications. Perhaps you've developed a set of effective switchboard forms, or you've mimicked the old-style toolbars and menus with borderless forms. Or, your applications are entirely forms-driven and don't need the flexibility provided by toolbars and Ribbons.

Here's how you can completely remove the Ribbon from the Access interface:

1. **Create a new table called USysRibbons, if you haven't already done so.**
2. **If creating the USysRibbons table for the first time, add three fields, ID (AutoNumber), RibbonName (Text) and RibbonXML (Memo).**

30

3. **Create a new record with the RibbonName set to Blank.** It doesn't really matter what you call it.
4. **Then add the following XML to the RibbonXML column:**

```
<CustomUI xmlns="http://schemas.microsoft.com/office/2006
/01/CustomUI">
 <Ribbon startFromScratch="true"/>
</CustomUI>
```

5. **Restart the database.**
6. **Select the File tab and select the Options button in the Backstage.**
7. **Click the Current Database tab and scroll to the Ribbon and Toolbars area.**
8. **In the Ribbon and Toolbars area, set the Ribbon Name to Blank (the same name you specified for the RibbonName column in Step 3).**
9. **Close and reopen the database.**

This process sets up a dummy Ribbon named `Blank` that contains no tabs, no groups, and no controls. In effect, you're telling Access to put up an empty Ribbon, which simply removes the Ribbon from the Access user interface.

CHAPTER

31

Preparing Your Access Application for Distribution

IN THIS CHAPTER

Setting options for your current database

Developing your application

Putting the finishing touches on your application

Hardening your application

Securing the Access environment

You're lucky if you have the luxury of developing only single-user, in-house applications and you never have to worry about distributing an application within a company or across the country. Most developers have to prepare an Access application for distribution sooner or later. You don't even have to develop commercial software to deal with distribution — when you develop an application to be run on a dozen workstations in one organization, you need to distribute your application in some form or other.

This chapter covers the issues relevant to distributing Access applications. However, because some of these items — such as error handling and splitting tables — are covered in detail elsewhere in this book, this chapter focuses primarily on setting database options when preparing your application for distribution.

You need to be concerned with many issues when preparing an Access application for distribution. Distributing your application properly not only makes installing and using the application easier for the end-user, but also makes updating and maintaining the application easier for you, the application's developer. In addition, the support required for an application is greatly decreased by properly preparing and packaging the database and associated files for distribution.

ON THE WEB

This chapter uses the `Chapter31.accdb` database. If you haven't already copied it onto your machine from the CD, you'll need to do so now.

TIP

Most of the techniques described in this chapter have been applied to the sample database. In order to open it so that you can see the options, open Access first, and then hold down the Shift key while you click the name of the database to open. Don't release the Shift key until the database has opened. The database has a custom icon as described in this chapter. The icon file won't be in the same place on your computer and you'll have to adjust the settings for it to show properly.

Defining the Current Database Options

Access databases have a number of options that simplify the distribution process. You can access these database options by choosing File⇨Options, and then selecting the Current Database tab (shown in Figure 31.1). You can still use an Autoexec macro to execute initialization code, but the Current Database options enable you to set up certain aspects of your application, thus reducing the amount of startup code that you have to write. It's very important to correctly structure these options before you distribute an Access application.

FIGURE 31.1

The Current Database options enable you to take control of your application from the moment a user starts it.

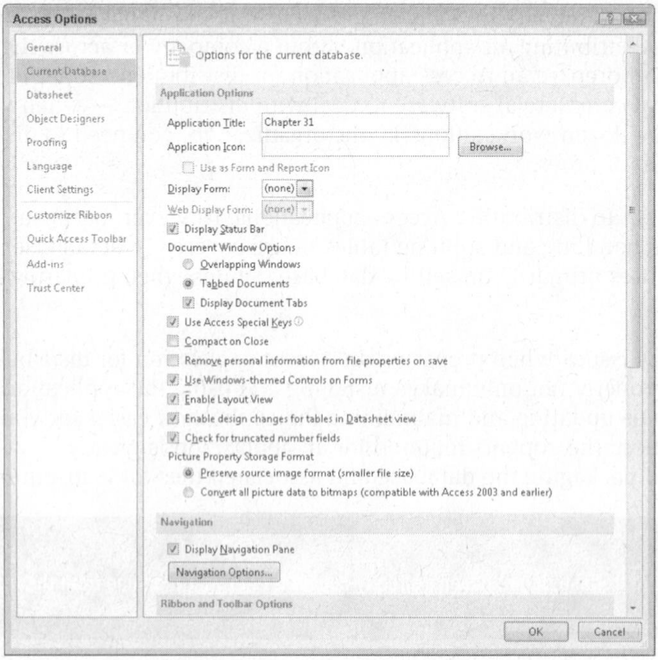

NOTE
The Current Database options replace the Startup dialog box from previous versions of Access.

TIP
Setting the Current Database options saves you many lines of code that you would ordinarily need in order to perform the same functions and enables you to control your application's interface from the moment the user starts it. Always verify the Current Database options before distributing your application.

Application options

The settings in the Application Options section let you define parameters for your database as an application.

Application Title

The text that you provide in the Application Title field displays on the main Access window's title bar. The Application Title is also the text that's displayed in the Windows task bar when the application is open and running.

TIP
You should always specify an application title for your distributed applications. If you don't, the database name and "Access" appear on the title bar of your application.

Application Icon

The icon that you specify in the Application Icon field displays on the title bar of your application and in the task switcher (Alt + Tab) of Windows. If you check the Use as Form and Report Icon box, this icon is also displayed when a form or report is minimized.

If you don't specify your own icon, Access just displays the default Access icon, so you might want to provide an application-specific icon for your application. Using special program icons helps your users distinguish between different Access applications.

TIP
You can create small bitmaps in Windows Paint and use a conversion tool to convert a BMP file to the ICO file format. You can also create icons using other graphics programs or search for application icons online.

Display Form

The form you select in the Display Form drop-down list automatically opens when Access starts the application. When the form loads, the `Form Load` event of the display form fires (if it contains any code), reducing the need to use an Autoexec macro.

TIP

Consider using a splash screen (see the "A splash screen" section, later in this chapter) as your startup display form.

Display Status Bar

Deselect the Display Status Bar check box to remove the status bar from the bottom of the Access screen. (This option is selected by default.)

TIP

The status bar is an informative and easy-to-use tool because it automatically displays key states (such as Caps Lock and Scroll Lock), as well as the Status Bar Text property for the active control. Instead of hiding the status bar, you should make full use of it and disable it only it if you have a very good reason to do so.

Document Window Options

Under Document Window Options, you can choose how the forms and reports look in your distributed application. Your options are

- **Overlapping Windows:** Overlapping Windows retains the look of previous versions of Access, letting you look at multiple forms at once.
- **Tabbed Documents:** Tabbed Documents uses a single-document interface (shown in Figure 31.2) similar to recent versions of Internet Explorer.

FIGURE 31.2

A database with the Tabbed Documents option selected. The tabs let you select which Access object to work with.

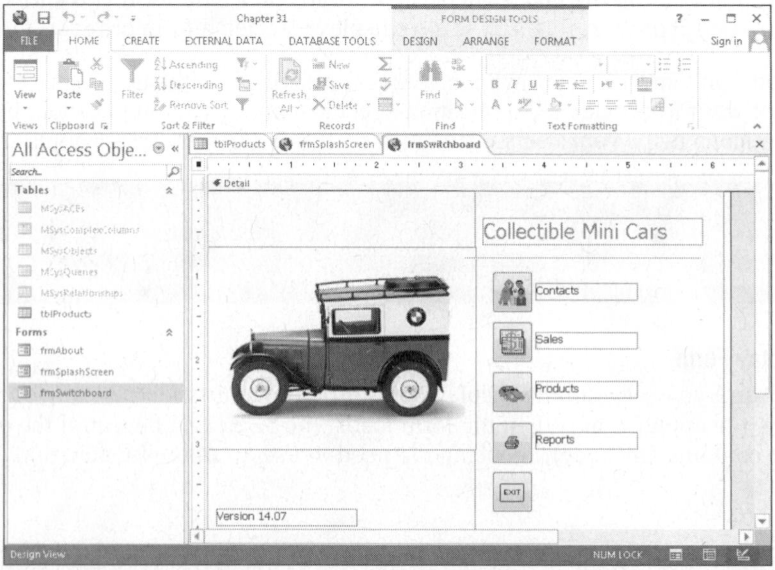

You must close and reopen the current database for the changes to take effect.

The Display Document Tabs check box is only available when you select Tabbed Documents; it turns on or off the tabs that appear at the top of any open database object. This setting turns off only the tabs and does not close tabbed objects themselves.

Use Access Special Keys

If you select this option, users of your application can use accelerator keys that are specific to the Access environment in order to circumvent some security measures, such as unhiding the Navigation pane. If you deselect this option, the following keys are disabled:

- **F11:** Press to show the Navigation pane (if hidden).
- **Ctrl + G:** Press to open the Immediate window in the Visual Basic Editor.
- **Ctrl + Break:** In Access projects, press to interrupt Access while retrieving records from the server database.
- **Alt + F11:** Press to start the VBA Editor.

TIP

It's a good idea to deselect the Access Special Keys check box when distributing the application, in order to prevent users from circumventing the options you select. Otherwise, users might inadvertently reveal the Navigation pane or VBA code edition, leading to confusion and other problems.

TIP

When using the Access Special Keys property to disable Access's default accelerator keys, you can still use an AutoKeys macro to set your application's shortcut keys.

Compact on Close

Checking the Compact on Close check box tells Access to automatically compact and repair your database when you close it. Some Access developers use Compact on Close as a way to perform this maintenance process each time a user works with a database, while others find it unnecessary. We're in the latter camp, but you can decide for yourself based on the level of activity in your database. You must close and reopen the current database in order for this change to take effect.

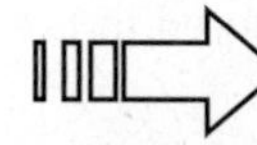

For more information on the benefits of compacting and repairing a database, see Appendix B.

CAUTION

Keep in mind that compacting a large database might take a considerable amount of time. Plus, Compact on Close only affects the front-end database. Unless your application uses the front end for temporary tables or other operations that cause the front end to bloat, the Compact and Repair option may be of minimal benefit to your users.

Remove Personal Information from File Properties on Save

Checking this box automatically removes the personal information from the file properties when you save the file. You must close and reopen the current database for this change to take effect.

Use Windows-Themed Controls on Forms

Checking this box uses your system's Windows theme on the form/report controls. This setting only applies when you use a Windows theme other than the standard theme.

Enable Layout View

The Enable Layout View check box shows or hides the Layout View button on the Access status bar and in the shortcut menus that appear when you right-click on an object tab.

NOTE

Remember that you can disable the Layout view for individual objects, so even when you enable this option, Layout view may not be available for certain forms and reports.

Enable Design Changes for Tables in Datasheet View

The Enable Design Changes for Tables in Datasheet View check box allows you to make structural changes to your tables in Datasheet view, as opposed to having to be in Design view. In most well-designed Access applications, the users never see the tables in either Design view or Datasheet view, instead interacting with data via forms. If your application allows viewing tables in Datasheet view, you should uncheck this option to prevent unwanted changes to your tables' designs.

Check for Truncated Number Fields

Checking this option makes numbers appear as ##### when the column is too narrow to display the entire value. (This behavior has been in Excel for a long time.) Unchecking this box truncates values that are too wide to be displayed in the datasheet, which means that users see only a part of the column's value when the column is too narrow and might misinterpret the column's contents.

Picture Property Storage Format

Under Picture Property Storage Format, you can choose how graphic files are stored in the database. Your options are

- **Preserve Source Image Format (Smaller File Size):** Choose this option if you want to store the image in the original format, which also reduces the database size.
- **Convert All Picture Data to Bitmaps (Compatible with Access 2003 and Earlier):** Choose this option if you want to store all images as bitmaps, which increases the database size but keeps it compatible with previous versions of Access (Access 2003 and earlier).

Earlier versions of Access always stored images twice within the database. The first copy was the original format of the image file (such as JPG), while the second copy was a bitmap used only to display the image on Access forms and reports. Because images were stored twice, early Access databases were prone to severe bloating when a lot of image data was stored in the MDB.

You have the option to Preserve Source Image Format to conserve disk space by reducing the database file's size. (This option is only available in the ACCDB file format.) When using this option, Access only stores one copy of an image (in its original format) and dynamically generates a bitmap when the image is displayed on a form or report.

Navigation options

The settings in the Navigation section let you define parameters when navigating your database as an application.

The Display Navigation Pane check box

With most distributed applications, you might never want your users to have direct access to any of your tables, queries, forms, or other database objects. It's far too tempting for a user to try to "improve" a form or report, or to make some minor modification to a table or query. Rarely are users really qualified to make such changes to an Access database. Deselecting the Display Navigation Pane option hides the Navigation pane from the user at startup.

Note

Unless you also deselect the Use Access Special Keys option (described earlier in this chapter), users can press F11 to unhide the Navigation pane.

You must close and reopen the current database for this change to take effect.

The Navigation Options button

One nice addition to recent versions of Access is the ability to select which database options are exposed to users when the Navigation pane is visible at startup. Clicking the Navigation Options button opens the Navigation Options dialog box (shown in Figure 31.3), which you use to change the categories and groups that appear in the Navigation pane.

In the Grouping Options section, click a category on the left side of the dialog box to change the category display order or to add groups to the right side of the dialog box. Click the Object Type category to disable viewing of certain Access objects (tables, queries, forms, reports, macros, or modules).

FIGURE 31.3

The Navigation Options dialog box.

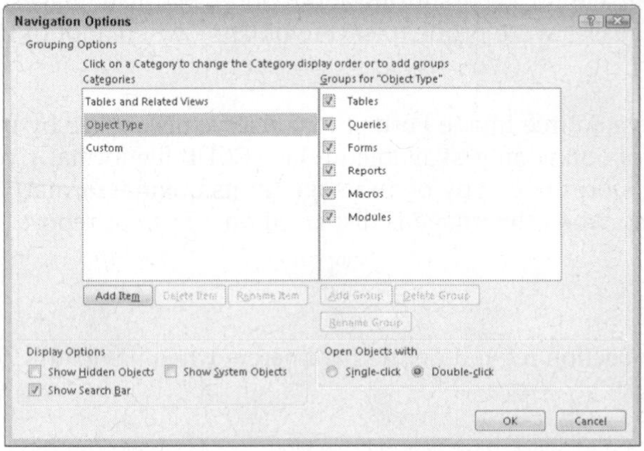

In the Display Options section, you can select the Show Hidden Objects, Show System Objects, and Show Search Bar check boxes.

TIP

It's usually a good idea to hide the hidden and system objects, which you normally don't want to modify. (They're hidden for a reason!)

The Search Bar (shown in Figure 31.4), on the other hand, is useful in the Navigation pane when you have a lot of objects and want to narrow the list to avoid excessive scrolling, so you should select the Show Search Bar check box. For example, if you wanted to see the forms that had the word Product in them, you'd type Prod in the Search Bar to limit the tables shown in the Navigation pane.

FIGURE 31.4

The Search Bar appears at the top of the Navigation pane.

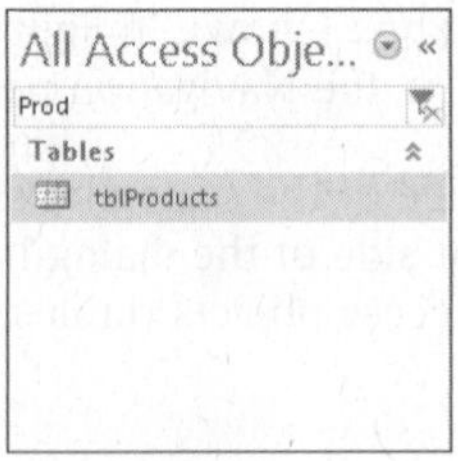

In the Open Objects With section, select Single-Click or Double-Click to choose how you open a database object. Double-Click is the default option and is most likely familiar to all your users.

Ribbon and toolbar options

The settings in the Ribbon and Toolbar Options section let you define custom Ribbons and toolbars when using your database as an application. All the options in this section require you to close and reopen the current database for the change to take effect.

Custom Ribbon creation is explained in Chapter 30.

Ribbon Name

The Ribbon Name option lets you specify a customized (usually trimmed-down) version of the Ribbon. If you don't supply a Ribbon name, Access uses its built-in Ribbon, which might be inappropriate for your application. The default Ribbon contains many controls for modifying database objects, which might lead to problems with your users.

Shortcut Menu Bar

Setting the Shortcut Menu Bar changes the default menu for shortcut menus (right-click menus) to a menu bar that you specify. Using custom shortcut menus that have functionality specific to your application is always preferable.

Allow Full Menus

Checking the Allow Full Menus box determines whether Access displays all the commands in its menus or just the frequently used commands. If you supply custom menus for all your forms and reports and set the Menu Bar property to a custom menu bar, this setting has no effect.

Allow Default Shortcut Menus

The Allow Default Shortcut Menus setting determines whether Access displays its own default shortcut menus when a user right-clicks an object in the Navigation pane or a control on a form or report.

Name AutoCorrect Options

Several chapters in this book mention the problems associated with changing the names of fundamental database objects such as tables and fields within tables. For example, if you change the name of a table, everywhere you refer to that table (a query, a control's `ControlSource` property, VBA code, a macro, and so on) becomes invalid, causing the application to malfunction.

Microsoft added the Name AutoCorrect feature to Access 2000 as a way of mitigating the problems that inevitably occur when database objects are renamed. Unfortunately, this feature has never worked quite as well as Microsoft had hoped. Primarily, Name AutoCorrect is a major drag on performance. Because Access must constantly monitor activity while Access is used, a database with this option selected runs noticeably slower than it does when the option is turned off. Plus, there are far too many places where an object's name may appear for an AutoCorrect feature to effectively capture every instance when the object is renamed. This is especially true of object names appearing in VBA code; many applications contain hundreds of thousands of lines of VBA code, making it virtually impossible to find and update every object reference.

TIP

The Name AutoCorrect option is turned on by default in Access applications. Unless you find this option useful in your projects, you should consider turning it off, as it has been in the `Chapter31.accdb` example accompanying this chapter.

Developing the Application

Developing an application generally consists of defining the requirements, building the database objects and writing the code, creating the documentation, and testing the application. If you're developing an application for your own use, the requirements are probably in your head. You also may be so familiar with the problem that you're trying to solve that you don't feel a need to formalize the requirements. Consider writing them down anyway as a way to clarify your thoughts and identify any problems early in the development process.

Building to a specification

All databases are meant to solve some problem experienced by users. The problem might be inefficiency in their current methods or the inability to view or retrieve data in a format they need. Or you may simply be converting an obsolete database to a more modern equivalent. The effectiveness of the solution you build will be judged by how well it resolves the problem the users are having. Your best guarantee of success is to carefully plan the application before building any table, query, or form. Only by working to a plan will you know how well the application will solve the user's problem.

Most Access development projects follow this general sequence of events:

1. **Define the problem.** Something is wrong or inadequate with the current methods — a better system is needed and Access appears to be a good candidate to produce the new system.
2. **Determine the requirements.** Interviews with the users yield a description of the basic features the program should provide. The product of these discussions is the *design specification,* a written document that outlines and details the application.
3. **Finalize the specifications.** Review the design specifications with the users to ensure accuracy and completeness.
4. **Design the application.** The developer uses the initial design specification to design the basic structure of the database and its user interface.

5. **Develop the application.** This is where most developers spend most of their time. You spend a great deal of time building the tables, queries, forms, and other database objects needed to meet the specification produced in Step 2.
6. **Test.** The developer and client exercise the application to verify that it performs as expected. The application is tested against the requirements defined in the design specification, and discrepancies are noted and corrected for Step 7.
7. **Distribute and roll out.** After the application's performance has been verified, it's distributed to its users. If necessary, users are trained in the application's use and instructed on how to report problems or make suggestions for future versions.

Many Access developers dive right into development without adequately defining the application's objectives or designing the database's structure. Unless the application is incredibly simple, a developer who doesn't work to a specification will surely end up with a buggy, unreliable, and trouble-prone database.

Another major error is allowing the database to stray too far from the initial design specification. Adding lots of bells and whistles to an otherwise simple and straightforward database is all too tempting. If implementation digresses too far from the design specification, the project may fail because too much time is spent on features that don't directly address the users' problems. This is one of the reasons for the third step (finalize the specifications). The developer and the user are essentially entering into a contract at that point, and you might want to include a process to be followed in order for either party to make changes to the specification once it's been agreed upon.

Before any work begins, most professional application developers expect the client to submit a written document describing the intended application and specifying what the program is expected to do. A well-written design specification includes the following information:

- **Expected inputs:** What kind of data (text, numeric, binary) will the database have to handle? Will the data be shared with other applications like Excel or another database system? Does the data exist in a format that is easily imported into an Access database, or will the data have to be re-keyed at runtime? Will all the data always be available? Is there a chance that the type might vary? For example, birth dates are obviously dates, but what happens if you know the year of birth but not the month or day?
- **User interface:** Will the users be comfortable with simple forms, or will they need custom menus and Ribbons and other user-interface components? Is context-sensitive online Help required?
- **Expected outputs:** What kinds of reports are needed by the user? Will simple select queries be adequate to produce the desired results, or are totals, crosstabs, and other advanced queries necessary as well?

The whole point of a design specification is to avoid adding unplanned features that decrease the database's reliability without contributing to its utility. Writing a design specification before beginning the actual implementation will consistently yield the following benefits:

- **A guide to development effort:** Without some kind of design specification, how can you possibly know whether you're building an application that truly meets the client's expectations? As you work through the development phase, you can avoid adding features that don't contribute to the application's objectives and concentrate on those items that the client has identified as having priority.
- **Verification that the application meets expectations:** All aspects of the application must be tested to verify its operation. The best way to conduct testing is to confirm that all design objectives have been met and that no unexpected behavior is observed during the testing phase.
- **Minimization of design changes during implementation:** Many problems can be avoided by sticking to the specification. One of the easiest ways to break an application is to add new features not included in the original design. If the application was properly planned, the specified features will have been designed to work together. Introducing new features after development has begun most likely will result in a less reliable system.

Overall, a well-written design specification provides the basis for creating tight, bulletproof applications that fulfill the user's requirements. At the conclusion of the project, the finished database can be compared to the design specification, and its effectiveness in addressing the original problem can be objectively evaluated. Without a design specification written at the beginning of a project, you have no valid measure of how well the application resolves the problem that inspired the project in the first place.

Creating documentation

Even the best-written Access application will fail if users don't fully understand how to use it. And it's not just the user interface that needs to be understood: the logic of what happens when the user clicks a particular button needs to be understood both by at least some of the users as well as by any technical support staff who might be involved with the application.

While many developers dislike writing documentation, leaving it as a last step that they hopefully won't have time for because they've moved onto another project, documentation really is a "necessary evil."

Documenting the code you write

Over time, changes or additions might be required to the application. Even if you're the one making those changes, the passage of time since you originally wrote the code might mean that even *you* have problems understanding exactly what the code does. Imagine how much harder it'll be if someone else has to figure it out!

Write self-documenting code by using consistent naming conventions for your variables, constants, and procedures. Provide logical names for your procedures that describe simply and clearly what the procedure does. If you can't come up with a reasonable name for a procedure, it may be that you're tying to do too much in one procedure and you should consider breaking it up. Use comments when necessary, but don't overuse them or they'll never be read and will be quickly out-of-date. Create a comment when you make an important design decision that you want to document or when you use a non-intuitive programming technique that would be otherwise difficult to understand.

Figure 31.5 shows a short procedure that is mostly self-documenting. The procedure, variables, and constants are well named and a comment is included to explain an unusual line of code.

FIGURE 31.5

Produce self-documenting code when possible.

Chapter31 - modComments (Code)

(General) | LoanProduct

```
Option Compare Database
Option Explicit

Sub LoanProduct(clsProduct As CProduct, dtLoaned As Date)

  Dim dtDueBack As Date

  Const sALREADYLOANED As String = _
    "Product is already loaned.  You must receive it back before loaning again."

  If clsProduct.IsOnLoan Then
    MsgBox sALREADYLOANED, vbOKOnly
  Else
    'Loaners due back at the end of the next month
    'The 0th day of a month is the last day of the previous month
    dtDueBack = DateSerial(Year(dtLoaned), Month(dtLoaned) + 2, 0)
    clsProduct.LoanedDate = dtLoaned
    clsProduct.IsOnLoan = True
    clsProduct.DueBack = dtDueBack
  End If

End Sub
```

Name your database objects and controls and don't accept the default names that Access provides for database objects such as forms and controls. The default names are simply a convenience for simple applications and shouldn't be used in professional-quality work.

Documenting the application

The applications you deliver to end-users should be accompanied by documentation that explains how the applications are meant to be used. End-user documentation doesn't have to include descriptions of the internal structure or logic behind the user interface. It should, however, explain how the forms and reports work, describe things the users should avoid (for example, changing existing data), and include printouts of sample reports. Use screenshots to illustrate the documentation.

TIP

Be sure the documentation includes the exact version number in the title or footer so that users can verify that the documentation is the right version for the software they're using.

The users of your applications will benefit from the online Help you build into the database. Online Help, of course, means everything from the tooltips you attach to the controls on a form to status-bar text, to sophisticated context-sensitive and "What's this?" help you see in many Microsoft products.

TIP

It's often useful to have a user write the actual user documentation (in conjunction with the developer, of course). In this way, you can ensure that it's written in language that the users understand.

Testing the application before distribution

As you design your application, consider how you'll test the various aspects of it. Planning your tests during the design phase is the best time because the functions of a form or report will be fresh in your mind. Don't wait until you're completely done developing to start thinking about testing, or you'll have a hard time remembering all the important features that you should test. Write out a test plan during, or shortly after, designing an object in your application (such as a table or form). Don't worry if the test plan isn't perfect, you'll be able to change it before you distribute the application.

Execute your test plans as soon as it's practical to do so. Then execute them again when the whole project is complete and you're ready to distribute it. The first time you execute them assures that you designed the object as you intended. Executing them at the end ensures that future changes didn't introduce bugs. You may find that your tests are no longer valid because of changes you made to the design. Design changes happen all the time during development and when tests become invalid you can simply remove them or change them to test the new functionality.

TIP

Distributing an application that is 100 percent bug-free is almost impossible. The nature of the software development beast is that, if you write a program, someone can — and will — find an unanticipated way to break it. Certain individuals seem to have a black cloud above their heads and can break an application (in other words, hit a critical bug) within minutes of using it. If you know of such people, hire them! They can be great assets when you're testing an application.

While working through the debugging process of an application, categorize your bugs into one of three categories:

- **Category 1: Catastrophic bugs:** These bugs are absolutely unacceptable — for example, numbers in an accounting application that don't add up the way they should or a routine that consistently causes the application to terminate unexpectedly. If you ship an application with known Category 1 bugs, prepare for your users to revolt!
- **Category 2: Major bugs that have a workaround:** Category 2 bugs are fairly major bugs, but they don't stop users from performing their tasks because some workaround exists in the application. For example, a button that doesn't call a procedure correctly is a bug. If the button is the only way to run the procedure, this bug is a Category 1 bug. But if a corresponding Ribbon command calls the

procedure correctly, the bug is a Category 2 bug. Shipping an application with a Category 2 bug is sometimes necessary. Although shipping a bug is officially a no-no, deadlines sometimes dictate that exceptions need to be made. Category 2 bugs will annoy users, but shouldn't send them into fits.

TIP

If you ship an application with known Category 2 bugs, document them! Some developers have a don't-say-anything-and-act-surprised attitude regarding Category 2 bugs. This attitude can frustrate users and waste their time by forcing them to discover not only the problem, but also the solution. For example, if you were to ship an application with the Category 2 bug just described, you should include a statement in your application's `README` file that reads something like this: "The button on the XYZ form does not correctly call feature such-and-such. Please use the corresponding command such-and-such found on the Ribbon. A patch will be made available as soon as possible."

- **Category 3: Small bugs and cosmetic problems:** Category 3 bugs are small issues that don't affect the operation of your application. They may be caption or label misspellings or incorrect text-box colors. Category 3 bugs should be fixed soon, but they shouldn't take precedence over Category 1 bugs. They should take precedence over Category 2 bugs only when they're so extreme that the application looks completely unacceptable or when they cause enough trouble for users that a fix is quickly needed.

Categorizing bugs, and approaching them systematically, helps you create a program that looks and behaves the way its users think it should. Sometimes you may feel like you'll never finish your Category 1 list, but you will. You'll be smiling the day you check your bug sheet and realize that you're down to a few Category 2s and a dozen or so Category 3s! Although you might be tempted to skip this beta-testing phase of development, don't. You'll only pay for it in the long run.

TIP

Not all Access features are available when an application is run within the Access runtime environment. You can operate in the runtime environment and use the full version of Access to test for problems with your code and with the runtime environment by using the `/Runtime` command-line option when starting your Access application. From the Charms menu, select the App charm and then the Run app or create a shortcut.

Polishing Your Application

When your application has been thoroughly tested and appears ready for distribution, spend some time polishing your application.

Giving your application a consistent look and feel

First and foremost, decide on some visual design standards and apply them to your application. This step is incredibly important if you want a professional look and feel to your applications. Figure 31.6 shows a form with samples of different styles of controls.

FIGURE 31.6

You can decide on any interface style that you like for your application. But after you decide on a style, use it consistently.

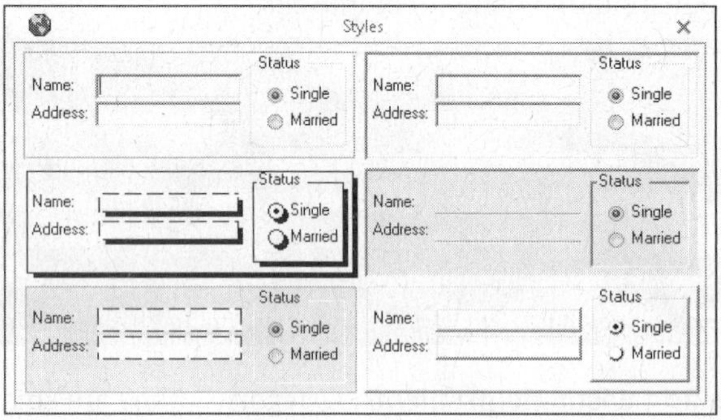

Your design decisions may include the following:

- Will text boxes be sunken, flat with a border, flat without a border, chiseled, or raised?
- What back color should text boxes be?
- What color will the forms be?
- Will you use chiseled borders to separate related items or select a sunken or raised border?
- What size will buttons on forms be?
- For forms that have similar buttons, such as Close and Help, in what order will the buttons appear?
- Which accelerator keys will you use on commonly used buttons, such as Close and Help?
- Which control will have focus when the form opens?
- How will the tab order be set?
- What will your Enter key property be for text boxes?
- Will you add some visual indication for when list boxes are multi-select and when they aren't?
- Will you add some visual indication for when combo boxes have their Limit to List property set?

TIP

Making your application look and work in a consistent manner is the single most important way to make it appear professional. For ideas on design standards to implement in your applications, spend some time working with some of your favorite programs and see what standards they use.

CAUTION

In the area of look and feel, copying from another developer is generally not considered plagiarism but is instead often looked upon as a compliment. Copying does *not* extend, however, to making use of another application's icons or directly copying the look and feel of a competitor's product; this is a very bad practice.

Adding common professional components

Most professional applications have some similar components. The most common components are the splash screen, an application switchboard, and an About box. These may seem like trivial features, but they can greatly enhance your application's appeal. They don't take much time to implement and should be included in all your distributed applications.

A splash screen

The splash screen (see Figure 31.7 for an example) not only aids in increasing perceived speed of an application but also gives the application a polished, professional appearance from the moment a user runs the program.

FIGURE 31.7

A splash screen not only increases perceived speed of your application, but it also gives your application a professional appearance.

ON THE WEB

Figure 31.7 shows the design window for a splash screen template that you can use when building your own applications. This form is included in the `Chapter31.accdb` database. It's named `frmSplashScreen`. Import this form into your application and use it as a template for creating your own splash screen.

Most splash screens contain information such as the following:

- The application's title
- The application's version number
- Your company information
- A copyright notice (© Copyright)

In addition, you might want to include the licensee information and/or a picture on the splash screen. If you use a picture on your splash screen, make it relevant to your application's function. For example, some coins and an image of a check could be used for a check-writing application. If you want, you can also use clip art for your splash screen — just be sure that the picture is clear and concise and doesn't interfere with the text information presented on your splash screen.

To implement the splash screen, have your application load the splash form before it does anything else. (Consider making your splash screen the Display Form in the Application Options, described earlier in this chapter.) When your application finishes all its initialization procedures, close the form. Make the splash form a light form and convert any bitmaps that you place on your splash screen to pictures in order to decrease the splash form's load time.

An application switchboard

An application switchboard is essentially a steering wheel for users to find their way through the functions and forms that are available in the application. Use the switchboard itself as a navigation form, using buttons to display other forms, as shown in the switchboard example in Figure 31.8. This is the switchboard named `frmSwitchboard` created for the Collectible Mini Cars database in this book.

FIGURE 31.8

The switchboard provides a handy way to navigate throughout the application.

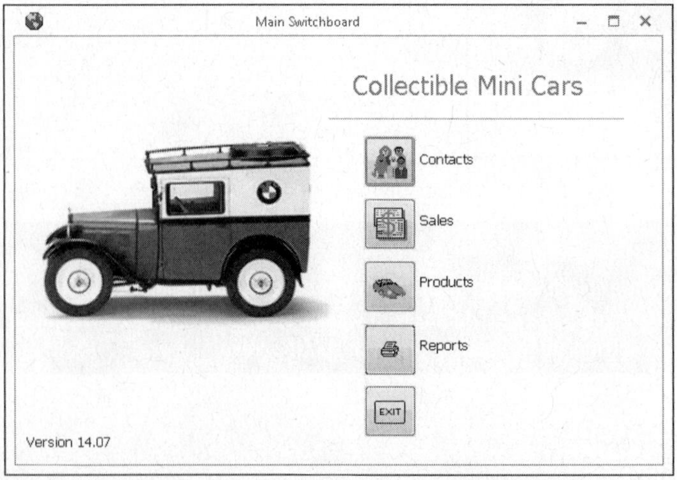

The switchboard provides a familiar place where users can be assured that they won't get lost in the application.

TIP

Make sure that the switchboard redisplays whenever the user closes a form.

An About box

The About box (like the one shown in Figure 31.9) contains your company and copyright information, as well as the application name and current version. Including your application's licensee information (if you keep such information) in the About box is also a good idea.

The About box serves as legal notice of ownership and makes your application easier to support by giving your users easy access to the version information. Some advanced About boxes call other forms that display system information. You can make the About box as fancy as you want, but usually a simple one works just fine.

FIGURE 31.9

An About box provides useful information to the user and protects your legal interests.

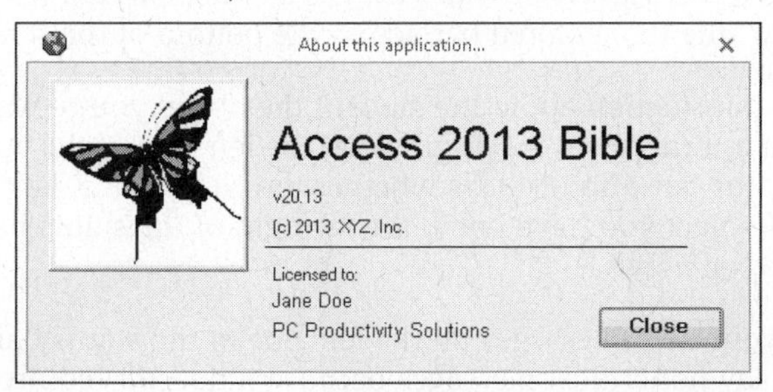

ON THE WEB

Figure 31.9 shows an About box template form that you can use when building your own applications. This form is included in the `Chapter31.accdb` database. It's named `frmAbout`. Import this form into your application and use it as a template for creating your own About box.

The About box should be accessible from a Help menu or from a button on your switchboard form.

Making the Most of Pictures

Most users love pictures, and most developers love to use pictures on buttons. Studies have shown that clear and concise pictures are more intuitive and are more easily recognized than textual captions. Most developers, however, are not graphic artists, and they usually slap together buttons made from any clip-art images that are handy. These ugly buttons make an application look clumsy and unprofessional. In addition, pictures that don't clearly show the function of the button make the application harder to use.

Select or create pictures that end-users will easily recognize. Avoid abstract pictures or pictures that require specific knowledge to understand them. If your budget permits, consider hiring a professional design firm to create your button pictures. A number of professional image galleries and tools to create and edit buttons are available.

Picture buttons that are well thought out can really make your application look outstanding, as well as make it easier to use.

The status bar

Keeping your users informed about what's happening with your application is an important part of building a good user experience. Access provides a `SysCmd` function that let's you display messages in the status bar (the thin colored bar across the bottom of the screen).

By default, the status bar shows information about the state of the object you're working on. For example, when you have a form open in Design view, the left side of the status bar reads "Design View." The status bar also displays whether the NUM LOCK key is active. Depending on the type of object you have open, the far right of the status bar provides a quick way to switch between views.

Using `SysCmd`, you can display your own messages on the left side of the status bar. The status bar is a great place to display noncritical messages because it doesn't require any user interaction (other than reading it, of course).

To show a message in the status bar, use the `acSysCmdSetStatus` parameter as shown in the following code:

```
Private Sub cmdHelpText_Click()

  Const sMSG As String = "Hello, World!"

  SysCmd acSysCmdSetStatus, sMSG

End Sub
```

This code displays `"Hello, World!"` in the status bar, and you can display any string you'd like. However, if the string is longer than Access has space to show, nothing will display. The status bar can also be used to show the user what's happening during a long process. In the following code, the status bar is updated while looping through a large recordset.

```
Private Sub cmdLoop_Click()

  Dim rs As ADODB.Recordset
  Dim sSql As String
  Dim lCnt As Long

  sSql = "SELECT * FROM tblLarge;"
  Set rs = New ADODB.Recordset
  rs.Open sSql, CurrentProject.Connection, _
    adOpenKeyset, adLockReadOnly

  Do While Not rs.EOF
    lCnt = lCnt + 1
    If lCnt Mod 10 = 0 Then
      SysCmd acSysCmdSetStatus, _
        "Processing record " & lCnt & " of " & rs.RecordCount
      DoEvents
    End If
    rs.MoveNext
  Loop

  SysCmd acSysCmdClearStatus

  rs.Close
  Set rs = Nothing

End Sub
```

When processing a lot of records, it's useful to display a counter like in the code above. This code updates the status bar every tenth record. If it were updated for every record, it would move so fast the user would barely be able to see it. Also, overuse of the status bar can degrade performance, so updating it only as needed helps speed up the process. The `Mod` function returns the remainder when the first number is divided by the second. When the remainder is zero, the counter is a multiple of 10 and the status bar is updated. Find a multiple that works for your data. The status bar should update frequently enough that the user doesn't think the program has stopped, but not so frequently that the text is a blur or the performance of the process is affected.

There are a couple other aspects of the above code that are worth mentioning. The recordset was opened with a cursor type of `adOpenKeyset`. Opening a recordset with this cursor type allows you to use the `RecordCount` property to return the total number of records. Inside the loop, the `DoEvents` keyword is used. While the code is running, it can use all the Windows resources; certain activities, like refreshing the screen, are put on hold until the code stops. That's not very helpful when you're trying to display text in the status bar. `DoEvents` is a command that briefly gives control to Windows so it can complete any tasks in its events queue.

Figure 31.10 shows the status bar being updated.

FIGURE 31.10

Use the status bar to provide feedback on a long process.

Processing record 5710 of 10000

Near the end of the procedure, the `acSysCmdClearStatus` parameter is used to return control of the status bar back to Access.

TIP

If you don't want to display a status bar message, but you don't want Access to display one either, you can use `SysCmd` to put a single space in the status bar. The code `SysCmd acSysCmdSetStatus, Space(1)` will keep the status bar blank until you're ready to use it.

A progress meter

Access provides a built-in progress meter in the status bar at the bottom of the main Access window. This progress meter is a rectangle that grows horizontally as a long-running process is executed by Access.

Setting up and using a progress meter requires an initializing step, and then setting the meter to its next value. As your code progresses, you don't just increment a counter that is managed by `SysCmd`. You must explicitly set the meter's value to a value between `0` and the maximum you set at initialization.

ON THE WEB

The following code and demonstration is contained in a form named `frmSysCmdDemo` in the `Chapter31.accdb` database.

Use the `acSysCmdInitMeter` constant to initialize the meter. You must pass some text that is used to label the meter, as well as the meter's maximum value:

```
Private Sub cmdInitMeter_Click()

  Const sSTATUSTEXT As String = "Reading Data"

  mlMeterMax = 100
  mlMeterIncrement = 0

  SysCmd acSysCmdInitMeter, sSTATUSTEXT, mlMeterMax

End Sub
```

This procedure sets the max to 100 and initializes the `mlMeterIncrement` variable to zero. When this procedure is run, the Access status bar appears, as shown in Figure 31.11.

FIGURE 31.11

The progress meter after initialization.

Custom status bar label

READING DATA NUM LOCK

Status bar progress meter

Incrementing the meter is a little tricky. In the following subroutine, the module-level variable `mlMeterIncrement` is incremented by 10 and the meter's position is set to the value of `mlMeterIncrement`.

```
Private Sub cmdIncrementMeter_Click()

  mlMeterIncrement = mlMeterIncrement + 10

  If mlMeterIncrement > mlMeterMax Then
    mlMeterIncrement = 0
  End If

  SysCmd acSysCmdUpdateMeter, mlMeterIncrement

End Sub
```

This procedure also checks to see if the value of `mlMeterIncrement` exceeds the maximum set in the initialization routine. If it does, it starts back at zero. That's interesting for a demonstration, but in real-world situations it's best to set the maximum to an appropriate value that won't be exceeded. Figure 31.12 shows the progress meter after five increments. It's easy to see that the meter has moved a distance proportional to the value of `mlMeterIncrement` after being incremented five times.

FIGURE 31.12

The progress meter midway in its movement.

READING DATA NUM LOCK

You'll have to choose values for the progress meter's maximum and increment settings in your application. Also, be sure to update the progress meter at appropriate intervals, such as every time one-tenth of a process has run (assuming, of course, that you know ahead of time how many items will be processed or how long an operation may take).

A meter is a valuable way of keeping the user informed of the progress of a lengthy process. Because you control its initial value and the rate at which it increments, you're able to fairly precisely report the application's progress to its users.

The only issue with the default Access progress meter is that it appears at the very bottom of the screen and is easily overlooked by users. Also, if the status bar is hidden through the Display Status Bar option on the Current Database tab of the Access Options dialog box (refer to Figure 31.1), the progress meter can't be seen at all.

If you prefer to keep the status bar hidden and show a progress meter that the users are sure to see, you can create your own progress meter with a form and a couple of label controls. Figure 31.13 shows just such a progress meter. It starts with an unbound form and two label controls. One label is on top of the other and they have the same `Top`, `Left`, `Height`, and `Width` properties. The label underneath has a lighter `BackColor` than the label on top.

FIGURE 31.13

A homemade progress meter.

Progress

As the program progresses, the top label's `Width` property is increased, giving the illusion that a darker color is filling a box. The form has certain properties set to give it the look and feel of a progress meter. Table 31.1 shows some of the properties of the form.

TABLE 31.1 Form Properties for a Progress Meter

Property	Value	Description
Pop Up	Yes	Along with Modal, ensures that the form is always on top and other forms can't be selected.
Modal	Yes	Along with Pop Up, ensures that the form is always on top and other forms can't be selected.
Caption	Progress	You can change this property to customize your progress meter.
Allow Datasheet View	No	Progress meters should only be shown in Form view.
Allow Layout View	No	Progress meters should only be shown in Form view.
Auto Center	Yes	Puts the progress meter in the middle of the screen.
Record Selectors	No	Hides the record selectors.
Navigation Buttons	No	Hides the navigation buttons.
Control Box	No	Hides the control box.
Close Button	No	Hides the close button.
Min Max Buttons	No	Hides the minimize and maximize buttons.
Border Style	Dialog	Makes the progress meter appear as a dialog box.

ON THE WEB

In the `Chapter 31.accdb` database, the `frmSysCmdDemo` form calls the `frmProgress` form and includes all the code in this section.

To create the progress meter in Figure 31.13, start by adding two custom properties to `frmProgress`. In addition to the form properties built-in to Access, you can add properties unique to your application. Add a `Max` property to set the maximum length of the progress bar and a `Progress` property to set how far along the process is.

```
Private mlMax As Long
Private mdProgress As Double

Public Property Get Max() As Long
  Max = mlMax
End Property

Public Property Let Max(lMax As Long)
  mlMax = lMax
End Property

Public Property Get Progress() As Double
  Progress = mdProgress
End Property

Public Property Let Progress(dProgress As Double)
  mdProgress = dProgress
End Property
```

The `Property` keyword in VBA is used to define the custom properties. Declare a module-level variable to hold the property's value, like `mlMax`. Then create `Property Get` and `Property Let` procedures to read and write the property, respectively. You can also omit either the `Get` or `Let` property statement if you want to make the property read-only or write-only.

Use the `Form_Load` event to initialize the width of the top label, `lblPmFront`. The underneath label, `lblPmBack`, always stays the same width.

```
Private Sub Form_Load()

  Me.lblPmFront.Width = 0

End Sub
```

The last piece of code behind `frmProgress` is a custom method to update the progress bar. A custom method is simply a sub-procedure declared with the `Public` keyword.

```
Public Sub UpdateProgress(lProgress As Long)

  If lProgress >= Me.Max Then
```

```
    Me.Progress = 1
  Else
    Me.Progress = lProgress / Me.Max
  End If

  Me.lblPmFront.Width = Me.lblPmBack.Width * Me.Progress

End Sub
```

The first part of the custom method determines if the `lProgress` argument is greater than the maximum. If it is, `Progress` is set to `1`, or 100%. This way, the progress meter will never go above 100%. If `lProgress` is less than the max, `Progress` is set to the ratio of `lProgress` to the maximum. Finally, the width of `lblPmFront` is increased by that proportion.

The procedure in the `frmSysCmdDemo` form that uses this progress meter is shown below. It is very similar to the code used earlier in this chapter to update the status bar when looping through a large recordset.

```
Private Sub cmdLoopProgress_Click()

  Dim rs As ADODB.Recordset
  Dim sSql As String
  Dim lCnt As Long

  Const sFORMPROGRESS As String = "frmProgress"

  sSql = "SELECT * FROM tblLarge;"
  Set rs = New ADODB.Recordset
  rs.Open sSql, CurrentProject.Connection, _
    adOpenKeyset, adLockReadOnly

  DoCmd.OpenForm sFORMPROGRESS
  Set frmProgress = Forms(sFORMPROGRESS)
  frmProgress.Max = rs.RecordCount

  Do While Not rs.EOF
    lCnt = lCnt + 1
    If lCnt Mod 10 = 0 Then
      frmProgress.UpdateProgress lCnt
      DoEvents
    End If
    rs.MoveNext
  Loop

  DoCmd.Close acForm, sFORMPROGRESS

End Sub
```

In this procedure, the `frmProgress` form is opened and assigned to a variable that allows access to the `Max` property and the `UpdateProgress` method. The `Max` property is set to `rs.RecordCount` and the `UpdateProgress` method is called within the loop, passing the `lCnt` variable. Finally, the progress form is closed at the end of the procedure.

Making the application easy to start

You shouldn't expect users to locate the Access data file (ACCDB or MDB) or to choose File⇨Open in Access to invoke the application. Pinning items to the Windows Start screen isn't difficult. When properly implemented, a program icon creates the impression that the application exists as an entity separate from Access, and endows it with a status equivalent to Word, Excel, or other task-oriented programs.

Creating a program icon isn't difficult. Many freeware and shareware versions of icon editors are available online, enabling you to create entirely new icons. The `Chapter31.accdb` example database comes with its own program icon (`Earth.ico`) for you to experiment with. You designate the program icon in the Access startup options (see the "Application options" section earlier in this chapter) or by setting a program icon in Windows Explorer.

Follow these steps to establish a Windows shortcut for an Access database application:

1. **In the Microsoft Office program folder (usually C:\Program Files\Microsoft Office\Office15) locate MSACCESS.EXE.**
2. **Right-click MSACCESS.EXE and select Create Shortcut.**
3. **Press F2 while the shortcut is highlighted and enter a new caption for the icon.**
4. **Right-click the icon and select Properties.** The icon's Properties dialog box appears.
5. **Select the Shortcut tab and add a complete path reference to the application's ACCDB or MDB file to the Target text box.**

Caution

Be sure not to delete or alter the path to the Access executable file.

In Figure 31.14 the application database's path is `C:\Access2013\Chapter31.accdb`. Notice that the Target text box contains the path to the Access executable followed by the path to the ACCDB file.

Note

If the path to the database includes spaces, you need to put double quotes around the full path.

FIGURE 31.14

It's easy to get Access to automatically open a database from a shortcut icon.

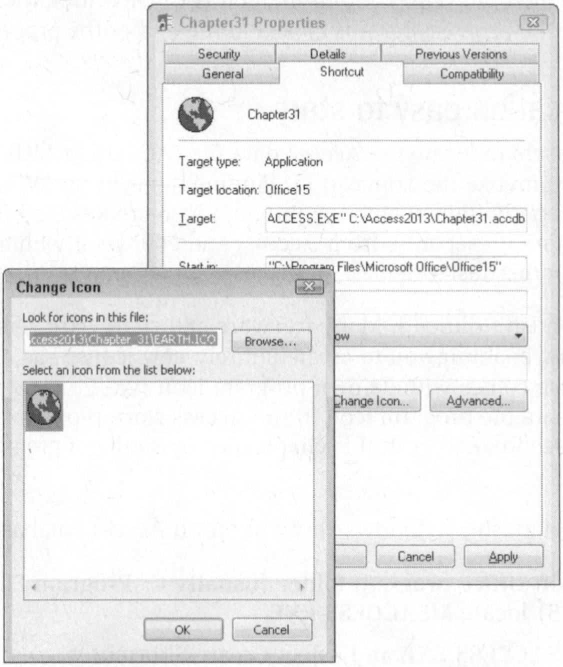

6. **Click the Change Icon button.** The Change Icon dialog box appears.
7. **Click the Browse button and navigate to the icon file (with an ICO extension) you want to use (see Figure 31.15).**

FIGURE 31.15

A colorful icon can make an application easy to find in a crowded folder or desktop.

8. **Drag the shortcut to the computer's desktop or Quick Launch toolbar to provide a convenient way to start the Access application.**

TIP

Windows 7 adds the ability to *pin* an application to the taskbar at the bottom of the window. Right-click an application icon and select Pin to Taskbar. Pinning an application icon to the taskbar is a convenient way to make an application available at all times.

Bulletproofing an Application

Bulletproofing (or hardening) an application is the process of making the application more stable and less prone to problems caused by unskilled users. Bulletproofing involves trapping errors that can be caused by users, such as invalid data entry, attempting to run a function when the application is not ready to run the function, and allowing users to click a Calculate button before all necessary data has been entered. Bulletproofing your application is an additional stage that should be completed in parallel with debugging and should be performed again after the application is working and debugged.

Chapter 26 discusses error trapping in VBA.

Using error trapping on all Visual Basic procedures

An error-handling routine gives you a chance to display a friendly message to the user, rather than some unintuitive default message box. Figure 31.16 shows a message box with a runtime error "2102," which is unintuitive; however, it also shows a more-detailed message of a form missing or misspelled. The user won't know the name of the form or if it's misspelled or missing. An error-handling routine is needed to provide the user with a more informative and meaningful error message than what's shown in Figure 31.16.

FIGURE 31.16

An error message resulting from a procedure with no error-handling routine.

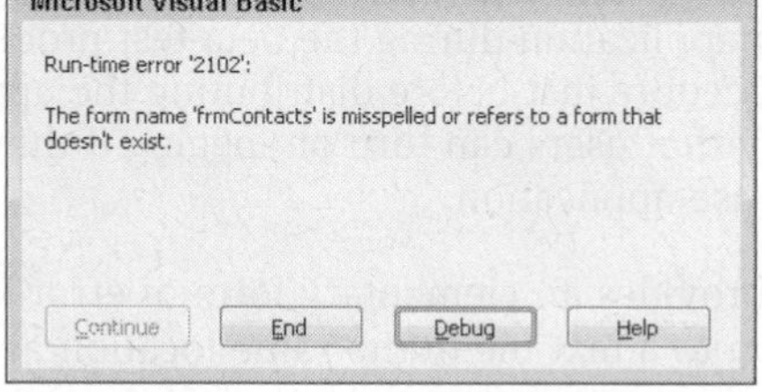

One of the most important elements of bulletproofing an application is making sure that the application never *crashes* (ceases operation completely and unexpectedly). Although

Access provides built-in error processing for most data-entry errors (for example, characters entered into a currency field), automatic processing doesn't exist for VBA code errors. You should include error-handling routines in every VBA procedure, as described in Chapter 26.

When running an application at runtime, any untrapped error encountered in your code causes the program to terminate completely. Your users can't recover from such a crash, and serious data loss might occur. Your users have to restart the application after such an application error.

Maintaining usage logs

Usage logs capture information such as the user's name or ID, the date, and the time. They provide valuable information, especially if an error occurs. Although you can easily record too much information, a properly designed usage log will permit you to pinpoint whether a certain type of error always seems to occur when a particular user is working with the system or when a certain query is run.

The logging information you add to a database might include updating a time stamp on records in a table when changes are made. Be aware, however, that the more logging you do, the slower the application becomes. The log information will cause the database to grow as well, unless the log information is stored in another location.

You can even tailor the level of logging to suit individual users or groups of users. Using the information captured on a login form, the application can determine at startup what level of logging to impose during the session. To make reviewing the logs much easier, you can even log to a table located in an external database in a different location on the network.

Usage logs can also provide an excellent way to perform a postmortem on an application that doesn't operate properly. If you have logging in each subroutine and function that might fail at runtime, you can see exactly what happened at the time an error occurred, instead of relying on the user's description of the error.

Logging can produce undesirable results when errors occur. For example, an error that causes an endless loop can easily consume all available disk space on the user's computer if each iteration of the loop adds a message to an error log. Use logging wisely. You may want to add logging to *every* procedure in an application during the beta-test process, and reduce the number of calls to the logging procedure just before distributing the application to its users. You may even provide some way that users can turn on logging if they encounter a reproducible problem in a database application.

The function shown in the following listing provides an elementary form of error logging. `LogError()` writes the following information to a text file in the same location as the database:

- The current date and time
- The procedure name that produced the error

- The error number
- The error description
- The form that was active at the time the error occurred (may be null if no form is open)
- The name of the control that was active at the time the error occurred (may be null if no control is selected)

Using a text file as a log instead of writing to the database keeps the database smaller and improves performance.

```
Public Sub LogError(ProcName As String, _
     ErrNum As Integer, ErrDescription As String)

  Dim sFile As String, lFile As Long
  Dim aLogEntry(1 To 6) As String

  Const sLOGFILE = "Error.log"
  Const sLOGDELIM = "|"

  On Error Resume Next

  sFile = CurrentProject.Path & "\" & sLOGFILE
  lFile = FreeFile

  aLogEntry(1) = Format(Now, "yyyy-mm-dd hh:mm:ss") 'Date stamp
  aLogEntry(2) = ErrNum
  aLogEntry(3) = ErrDescription
  aLogEntry(4) = ProcName
  'The following may be NULL
  aLogEntry(5) = Screen.ActiveForm.Name
  aLogEntry(6) = Screen.ActiveControl.Name

  Open sFile For Append As lFile
  Print #lFile, Join(aLogEntry, sLOGDELIM)
  Close lFile

End Sub
```

This simple subroutine adds to or creates a text file named `Error.log` in the same directory as the database. Each error encountered is one line in the text file and each piece of information is separated by a pipe delimiter.

The most critical items in the error log are the date and time, the error number, and the error description. The procedure name is useful, but it has to be hard-coded for each procedure (subroutine or function) you log with `LogError()`.

The following procedure intentionally generates an error to test the `LogError` procedure. A button on the `frmError` form runs this procedure. After the button has been clicked a few times, the `Error.log` file might look like Figure 31.17.

```
Private Sub cmdError_Click()

  Dim x As Long

  On Error GoTo ErrHandler

  x = 1 / 0

ErrExit:
  Exit Sub

ErrHandler:
  LogError "cmdError_Click", Err.Number, Err.Description
  Resume ErrExit

End Sub
```

FIGURE 31.17

A text file can be used to log errors.

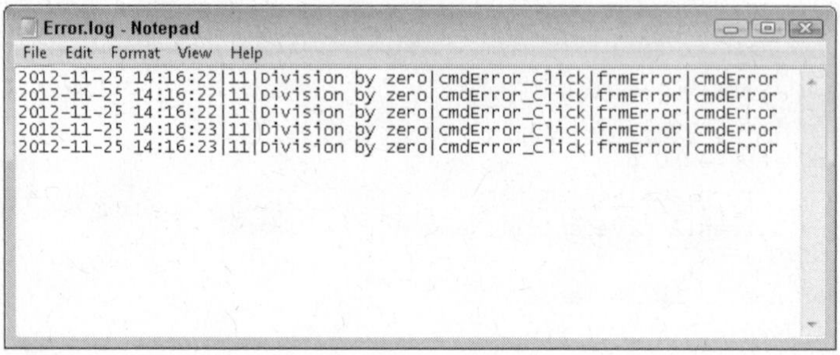

```
Error.log - Notepad
File  Edit  Format  View  Help
2012-11-25 14:16:22|11|Division by zero|cmdError_Click|frmError|cmdError
2012-11-25 14:16:22|11|Division by zero|cmdError_Click|frmError|cmdError
2012-11-25 14:16:22|11|Division by zero|cmdError_Click|frmError|cmdError
2012-11-25 14:16:23|11|Division by zero|cmdError_Click|frmError|cmdError
2012-11-25 14:16:23|11|Division by zero|cmdError_Click|frmError|cmdError
```

When it's time to review the errors, you can open the text file to see what's happened. You can also import the text file into an Access table to allow you to sort and filter the entries. Figure 31.18 shows `Error.log` imported into a table.

Once the data has been analyzed, the Error table can be deleted to keep the database small. Importing an error log is a good candidate for saving the import steps so that it can be easily imported the next time you want to review the data.

See Chapter 6 for more information on importing text files.

FIGURE 31.18

The error log can be imported into a table.

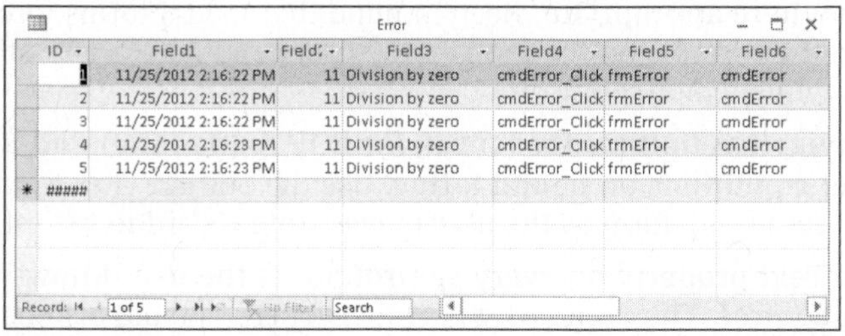

Error

ID	Field1	Field2	Field3	Field4	Field5	Field6
1	11/25/2012 2:16:22 PM	11	Division by zero	cmdError_Click	frmError	cmdError
2	11/25/2012 2:16:22 PM	11	Division by zero	cmdError_Click	frmError	cmdError
3	11/25/2012 2:16:22 PM	11	Division by zero	cmdError_Click	frmError	cmdError
4	11/25/2012 2:16:23 PM	11	Division by zero	cmdError_Click	frmError	cmdError
5	11/25/2012 2:16:23 PM	11	Division by zero	cmdError_Click	frmError	cmdError
* #####						

Record: 1 of 5 No Filter Search

Separating tables from the rest of the application

You should separate your code objects (forms, reports, queries, modules, and macros) from your table objects. Many benefits are gained from distributing these objects in separate ACCDB files:

- Network users benefit from speed increases by running the code ACCDB (the database containing the queries, forms, macros, reports, and modules) locally and accessing only the shared data on the network.
- Updates can easily be distributed to users.
- Data can be backed up more efficiently because disk space and time aren't used to continuously back up the code objects.

All professionally distributed applications — especially those intended for network use — should have separate code and data database files.

Chapter 7 has more information on separating tables from the rest of the database, called *splitting a database*.

Building bulletproof forms

You can take several steps to make each form in an application virtually bulletproof:

- **Consider removing the Control Box, Min, Max, and Close buttons from the form at design time.** Your users will be forced to use the navigation aids you've built into the application to close the form, ensuring that your application is able to test and verify the user's input. When using the tabbed documents interface, the Min and Max buttons don't apply. The Close button is represented by an X at the far right of the tab above the form's body. Removing the Close button from a tabbed form disables the X in the tab but doesn't actually remove it.
- **Always put a Close or Return button on forms to return the user to a previous or next form in the application.** The buttons should appear in the same general location on every form and should be consistently labeled. Don't use Close on one form, Return on another, and Exit on a third.

- **Set the ViewsAllowed property of the form to Form at design time.** This setting prevents the user from ever seeing a form as a datasheet.
- **Use modal forms where appropriate.** Keep in mind that modal forms force the user to respond to the controls on the form — the user can't access any other part of the application while a modal form is open.
- **Use your own navigation buttons that check for EOF (end of file) and BOF (beginning of file) conditions on bound forms.** Use the `OnCurrent` event to verify information or set up the form as the user moves from record to record.
- **Use the StatusBarText property on every control, to let the user know what's expected in each control.** The `Control TipText` property should also be set on all relevant controls.

> **NOTE**
> In order for the `StatusBarText` to be used, the status bar must be displayed (see Figure 31.1).

Validating user input

One of the most important bulletproofing techniques is to simply validate everything the user enters into the database. Capturing erroneous data input during data entry is an important safeguard that you can build into your applications. In many cases, you can use the table-level validation (determined by each field's `ValidationRule` and `ValidationText` properties), but in many other cases you'll want more control over the message the user receives or the actions taken by the database in response to erroneous input.

One of the major problems with the `ValidationRule` property is that it isn't checked until the user actually tabs to the next control, making it impossible to capture bad data entry. You're much better off in many cases validating entries in code. Very often you'll want to validate all controls on a form from the form's `BeforeUpdate` event instead of individually checking each and every control on the form.

Using the /runtime option

If you're not concerned with protecting your application, and you just want to prevent users from mistakenly breaking your application by modifying or deleting objects, you can force your application to be run in Access's *runtime mode.* When a database is opened in Access's runtime mode, all the interface elements that allow changes to objects are hidden from the user. In fact, while in runtime mode, it's impossible for a user to access the Navigation pane.

When using the runtime option, you must ensure that your application has a startup form that gives users access to any objects you want them to access. Normally, this is the main menu or main switchboard of your application.

TIP

To assign a form as a startup form, open the database that you want to use, select the File tab, select Options, and select the Current Database tab. Under Application Options, set the Display Form drop-down list to the form you want to be the startup form for the application. Startup forms are covered in more depth in the "Polishing Your Application" section, earlier in this chapter.

Earlier in this chapter, in the "Making the application easy to start" section, you read how to create a Windows shortcut that launches an Access application. Forcing runtime behavior in Access is quite easy. Simply add the `/runtime` switch after the reference to the database file in the shortcut properties, as shown in Figure 31.19.

FIGURE 31.19

Adding the `/runtime` switch to a shortcut.

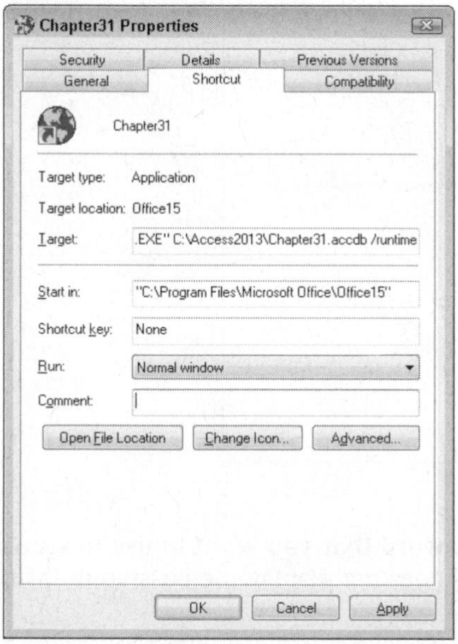

TIP

If your database has a password associated with it, the user will still be prompted to enter the password prior to opening the database.

NEW FEATURE

Access contains a new data file extension — ACCDR — that automatically opens your Access database in runtime mode when it's opened. Change your database file's extension from ACCDB to ACCDR to create a locked-down version of your Access database. Change the extension back to ACCDB to restore full functionality.

Encrypting or encoding a database

When security is of utmost importance, one final step that you need to take is to encrypt or encode the database. Access uses strong encryption, based on the RC4 and large key values, to secure the data and contents of Access databases.

Follow these steps to encrypt an Access ACCDB database:

1. **Open an existing ACCDB database (Chapter31.accdb) exclusively.**
2. **Click the File button in the upper-left corner of the screen, and select the Encrypt with Password command on the Info tab (see Figure 31.20).**

FIGURE 31.20

Choosing to encrypt an Access database.

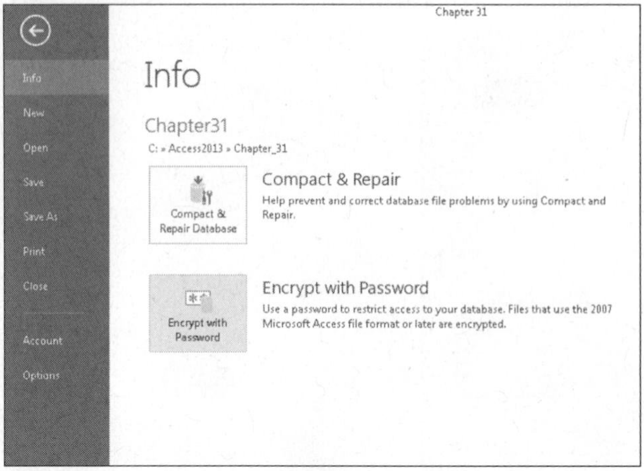

3. **In the Password field, type the password that you want to use to secure the database (see Figure 31.21).** Access does *not* display the password; instead, it shows an asterisk (*) for each letter.
4. **Retype the same password in the Verify field and click OK.**

FIGURE 31.21

Providing a password to encrypt an Access database.

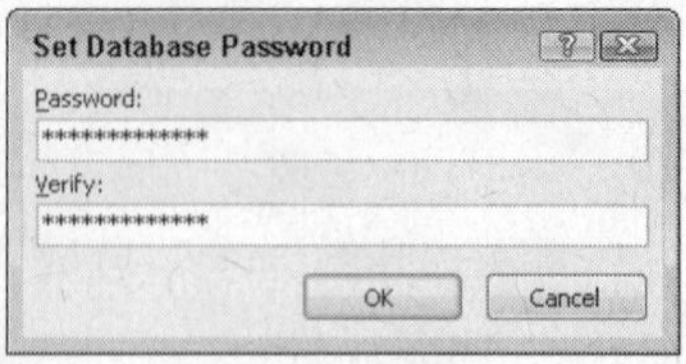

An encrypted database looks like any other Access application to its users. There is no outward difference in the appearance of the application's forms or reports after encryption. The only difference is that the user is required to provide the password each time the database is opened.

When encrypting a database, however, be aware of the following drawbacks:

- **Encrypted databases don't compress from their original size when used with compression programs, such as WinZip or sending it to a compressed (zipped) folder.** Encryption modifies the way that the data is stored on the hard drive so compression utilities have little or no effect.
- **Encrypted databases suffer some performance degradation (up to 15 percent).** Depending on the size of your database and the speed of your computer, this degradation may be imperceptible.

Also, be aware that encrypting a database makes it impossible to access the data or database objects without the proper password. Always maintain an unencrypted backup copy of the database in a secure location in the event that the password is lost or accidentally changed. There is no "universal" password for decrypting an encrypted Access database, and because Access uses strong encryption, there is no way to decrypt the database without the proper password.

Removing a database password

Follow these steps to remove the password from an encrypted database, and restore it to its previous, unencrypted state.

1. **Open the encrypted ACCDB database (for example, Chapter31.accdb) exclusively.**
2. **Click the File button in the upper-left corner of the screen, and select the Decrypt Database command on the Info tab (see Figure 31.22).** The Unset Database Password dialog box appears (see Figure 31.23).

FIGURE 31.22

Choosing to remove a password from an encrypted Access database.

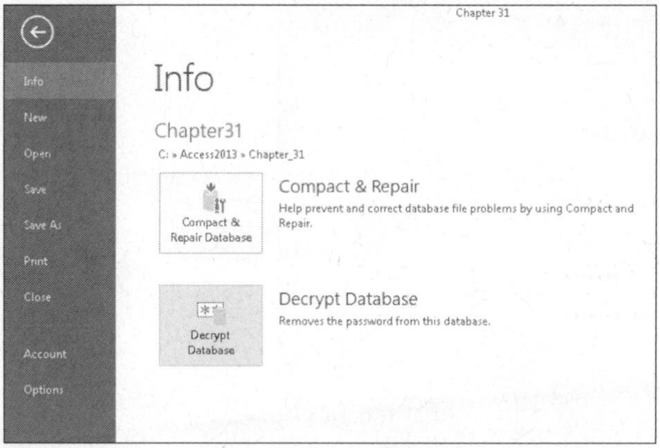

FIGURE 31.23

Providing a password to remove a password from an encrypted Access database.

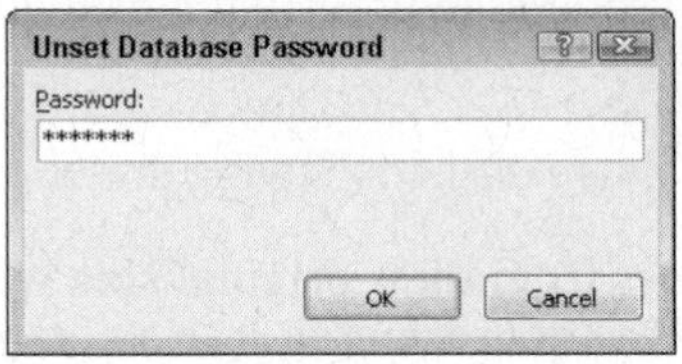

3. **Enter the database password and click OK.**

Protecting Visual Basic code

You control access to the VBA code in your application by creating a password for the Visual Basic project that you want to protect. When you set a database password for a project, users are prompted to enter the password each time they try to view the Visual Basic code in the database.

NOTE

A Visual Basic project refers to the set of standard and class modules (the code behind forms and reports) that are part of your Access database.

1. **Open the Visual Basic Editor by pressing Alt + F11.**
2. **In the Visual Basic Editor, choose Tools➪Chapter31 Properties.** The Project Properties dialog box appears.
3. **Select the Protection tab (shown in Figure 31.24).**

FIGURE 31.24

Creating a project password restricts users from viewing the application's Visual Basic code.

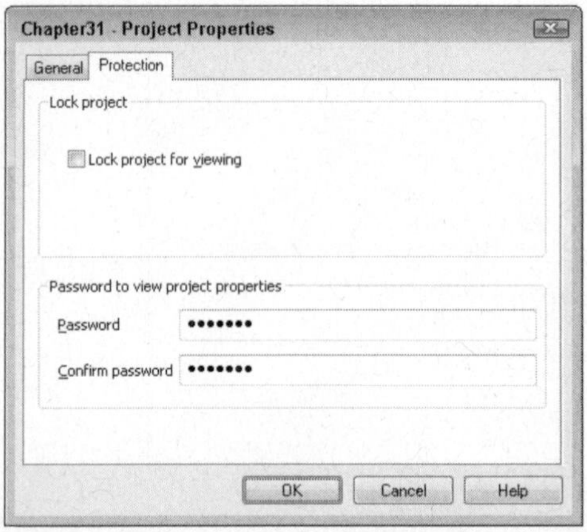

4. **Select the Lock Project for Viewing check box.**
5. **Enter a password in the Password text box.** Access does *not* display the password; instead, it shows an asterisk (*) for each letter.
6. **Type the password again in the Confirm Password text box and click OK.** This security measure ensures that you don't mistype the password (because you can't see the characters that you type) and mistakenly prevent everyone, including yourself, from accessing the database.

After you save and close the project, users attempting to view the application's code must enter the password. Access prompts for the project password only once per session.

A more secure method of securing your application's code, forms, and reports is to distribute your database as an ACCDE file. When you save your database as an ACCDE file, Access compiles all code modules (including form modules), removes all editable source code, and compacts the database. The new ACCDE file contains no source code but continues to work because it contains a compiled copy of all your code. Not only is this a great way to secure your source code, but it also enables you to distribute databases that are smaller (because they contain no source code) and always keep their modules in a compiled state.

To create an ACCDE file, choose Save As from the File tab, Save Database As, and Make ACCDE, as shown in Figure 31.25.

FIGURE 31.25

Create an ACCDE file to protect your database.

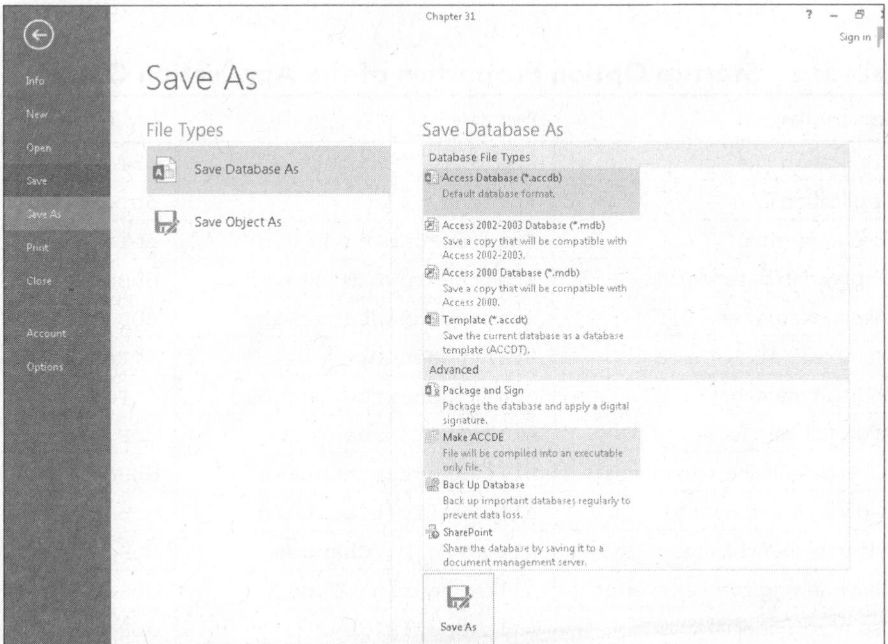

Securing the Environment

A serious Access application must be secured from unauthorized users. The built-in user-level security system (enforced by the ACE database engine, not by Access) provides multiple levels of security. You can, for example, secure a single database object (form, table, report) from individuals, groups, or individuals within groups. A user can even have multiple levels of security (provided the user has been assigned multiple login names). All the Access security objects, their properties, and methods are accessible throughout Access Visual Basic code.

User-level security is only available in the MDB database format. The ACCDB format provides other types of data protection, such as password-protected strong encryption, that is not available in the MDB format. As a developer, you'll have to decide whether user-level security or strong encryption is needed to protect the data in your Access applications.

Setting startup options in code

The options you set on the Current Database tab of the Access Options dialog box (refer to Figure 31.1) apply globally to every user who logs into the database. There are times when you want to control these options through startup code instead of allowing the global settings to control the application. For example, a database administrator should have access to more of the database controls (menus, the Navigation pane) than a data-entry clerk has.

Almost every option you see on the Options screen can be set through code. As you'll see in the "Setting property values" section, you can use Access VBA to control the setting of the current database properties listed in Table 31.2.

TABLE 31.2 Startup Option Properties of the Application Object

Startup Option	Property to Set	Data Type
Application title	AppTitle	dbText
Application icon	AppIcon	dbText
Display form	StartupForm	dbText
Display database window	StartupShowDBWindow	dbBoolean
Display status bar	StartupShowStatusBar	dbBoolean
Menu bar	StartupMenuBar	dbText
Shortcut menu bar	StartupShortcutMenuBar	dbText
Allow full menus	AllowFullMenus	dbBoolean
Allow default shortcut menus	AllowShortcutMenus	dbBoolean
Allow built-in toolbars	AllowBuiltInToolbars	dbBoolean
Allow toolbar changes	AllowToolbarChanges	dbBoolean
Allow viewing code after error	AllowBreakIntoCode	dbBoolean
Use Access special keys	AllowSpecialKeys	dbBoolean

Depending on the username (and password) provided on the login form, you can use VBA code on the splash screen or switchboard form to set or reset any of these properties. Clearly, these properties have a lot to do with controlling the Access environment at startup.

Be aware that many of the database options in Table 31.2, such as `AppIcon`, require restarting the Access database before they take effect.

Disabling startup bypass

In old versions of Access, developers used the `AutoExec` macro to do things like hide the database container, open a startup form, and execute some startup code. The problem was that any user could easily bypass the `AutoExec` macro by holding down the Shift key while opening the database.

The Access startup properties provide some relief from reliance on startup macros and other routines. Unfortunately, the user is still able to bypass your carefully designed startup options by holding down the Shift key as the application starts. Bypassing your startup routines, of course, will reveal the application's design and objects that you've hidden behind the user interface.

Fortunately, the Access designers anticipated the need for bulletproofing an application's startup by providing a database property named `AllowBypassKey`. This property, which accepts `True` or `False` values, disables (or enables) the Shift key bypass at application startup.

NOTE

Because `AllowBypassKey` is a developer-only property, it isn't built into Access databases. You must create, append, and set this property sometime during the development process. Once appended to the database's Properties collection, you can set and reset it as needed.

Here's the code you need to implement the `AllowBypassKey` property:

```
Public Sub SetBypass(bFlag As Boolean)

  Dim db As DAO.Database
  Dim pBypass As DAO.Property
  Const sKEYNAME As String = "AllowBypassKey"

  Set db = CurrentDb
  On Error Resume Next
    Set pBypass = db.Properties(sKEYNAME)
  On Error GoTo 0

  If pBypass Is Nothing Then
    Set pBypass = db.CreateProperty(sKEYNAME, dbBoolean, bFlag)
    db.Properties.Append pBypass
```

```
    Else
      pBypass.Value = bFlag
    End If

  End Sub
```

This procedure first tries to point a variable (`pBypass`) to the `AllowBypassKey` property. If the variable is `Nothing`, then the `AllowBypassKey` property doesn't exist and it is created and appended to the database. If it does already exist, its `Value` property is set to `bFlag` (the value passed into the procedure).

Setting property values

You use the `CurrentDb` object's `CreateProperty` and `Properties.Append` methods to add each of these properties. In most cases, unless the property has already been set in the Access Options dialog box, the property hasn't been appended to the database's Properties collection. You must make sure the property exists before trying to set its value in code. The following function sets the value of a startup property, creating and appending the property to the Properties collection if the property doesn't exist:

```
Public Function SetStartupProperty(sPropName As String, _
  ePropType As DAO.DataTypeEnum, vPropValue As Variant) As Boolean

  Dim db As DAO.Database
  Dim prp As DAO.Property
  Dim bReturn As Boolean

  Set db = CurrentDb
  On Error Resume Next
    Set prp = db.Properties(sPropName)

    If prp Is Nothing Then
      Set prp = db.CreateProperty(sPropName, ePropType, vPropValue)

      If prp Is Nothing Then
        bReturn = False
      Else
        db.Properties.Append prp
        bReturn = True
      End If
    Else
      prp.Value = vPropValue
      bReturn = True
    End If

    SetStartupProperty = bReturn

End Function
```

Using `SetStartupProperty()` is quite easy. You must know the exact property name and data type of the property before invoking `SetStartupProperty()`. The following subroutine demonstrates how to set a startup property with `SetStartupProperty()`:

```
Sub ChangeAppTitle()

  Dim bSuccess As Boolean

  bSuccess = SetStartupProperty("AppTitle", dbText, "My Application")

  If bSuccess Then
    MsgBox "Application title has been changed."
  Else
    MsgBox "Application title has not been changed."
  End If

End Sub
```

Notice that the `AppTitle` property is a string data type (`dbText`).

TIP

Use the `RefreshTitleBar` method to see the changes made by setting either the `AppTitle` or `AppIcon` property. The syntax of `RefreshTitleBar` is simple:

```
Application.RefreshTitleBar
```

Getting property values

Getting the value of a property is much easier than setting a property's value. The `Properties` collection returns the property, and the `Value` property returns the value. The syntax to get the value of the `AppTitle` property is as follows:

```
On Error Resume Next
GetAppTitle = CurrentDb.Properties("AppTitle").Value
```

where `GetAppTitle` is a string variable. The `On Error Resume Next` statement is necessary in case the property has not been set.

Part VIII

Access and Windows SharePoint Services

Access continues to grow as an integral part of enterprise data management. Important capabilities have been added with each new release of the application. Even though Access is not a strong tool for creating or driving websites, Access 2013 includes outstanding capabilities for publishing Access data and application objects on SharePoint servers.

The chapters in Part VIII position SharePoint as an enterprise-collaborative platform and explain the process of integrating Access with SharePoint. Starting with simple data sharing, the chapters in this part progress to publishing Access applications to SharePoint.

We conclude the part with a look at data macros, which enable you to perform important data management tasks at the table level. This means that the same tasks (very often, business rules) are enforced even when the table's data is used in an Access web application.

IN THIS PART

CHAPTER 32

Understanding Windows SharePoint Services

IN THIS CHAPTER

Getting familiar with SharePoint

Understanding SharePoint Lists

Considering the concept behind Access and SharePoint integration

Throughout this book you've read about the many new features that Microsoft has added to Access 2013. As exciting and interesting as these new capabilities are, they pale in comparison to the ability to upsize Access applications to Windows SharePoint Server. Each recent version of Access has demonstrated greater and greater ability to integrate with SharePoint. The most exciting aspect of this new paradigm is the ability to actually run your Access application as a SharePoint website.

In the next few chapters, we'll explore the various techniques that will allow you to upsize your Access databases to SharePoint. But first, this chapter gives you a base understanding of what SharePoint is and how it helps organizations share and collaborate data.

Introducing SharePoint

SharePoint is Microsoft's collaborative server environment, providing tools for sharing documents and data across various organizations within your company network.

SharePoint is typically deployed on a company's network as a series of SharePoint *sites*. A SharePoint site is configured as an intranet site, giving various departments the ability to control their own security, workgroups, documents, and data. These sites can be nested within other sites in a hierarchical fashion.

As with any other website, a SharePoint site, or an individual page within the site, is accessible through a URL that the user can access via a standard web browser.

NOTE
SharePoint is commonly used for intranet applications running on local area networks (LANs), rather than across the Internet. SharePoint provides many features that aren't needed in a pure web context, such as sorting lists and searching for keywords. Also, SharePoint pages have too many constraints on them to make SharePoint a general-purpose web development tool. For example, by default, SharePoint pages have a navigation panel along the left side, a menu bar across the top, and a large area to the right of the navigation panel for the page's main content. Although SharePoint pages can be coerced into almost any layout, the effort required to customize a SharePoint page is considerably larger than a traditional ASP.NET page.

Reviewing Various Types of SharePoint Sites

Although SharePoint is most frequently used for sharing documents, data tables, and other content management tasks, SharePoint is frequently applied to many other applications. In fact, Microsoft provides a wide variety of application templates that can be modified to suit specific implementation requirements.

Here's a partial list of the available SharePoint templates:

- Business Performance Reporting
- Classroom Management
- Clinical Trial Initiation and Management
- Competitive Analysis Site
- Discussion Database
- Disputed Invoice Management
- Employee Activities Site
- Employee Self-Service Benefits
- Employee Training Scheduling and Materials
- Integrated Marketing Campaign Tracking
- Manufacturing Process Management
- New Store Opening
- Product and Marketing Requirements Planning
- Request for Proposal
- Sports League
- Team Work Site
- Timecard Management

SharePoint is frequently used, for example, to handle the documentation required for product development. A SharePoint site devoted to a development project easily handles the project initiation, tracking, and progress reporting tasks. Because SharePoint easily handles virtually any type of document, project drawings, videos, schematics, photographs, and so on can be added to the project's SharePoint site for review and comment by project members.

Companies often use SharePoint for distributing human resource and policy documents. Because SharePoint provides user- and group-level security, it's quite easy to grant a particular department access to a SharePoint page while denying other users access to the same site.

SharePoint also logs changes to documents and supports a check-in/check-out paradigm for controlling who is eligible to make changes to existing documents and who is allowed to post new documents and files.

Some of the most common SharePoint deployments are storing of version-controlled documents, such as Word documents and Excel spreadsheets. In many environments, e-mail is used for passing documents back and forth between users. The potential for mixing up different versions of the same document is considerable. Also, storing multiple copies of the same document takes up a lot of disk space. Because SharePoint provides a single source for storing, viewing, and updating documents, many of these issues are eliminated entirely.

Looking at a SharePoint Website

Before going into the detail of describing how Access integrates with SharePoint technology, it's helpful to picture a typical SharePoint website. In the next section, you'll get a brief understanding of the two most common aspects of a SharePoint site: documents and lists.

Note

The topic of SharePoint is vast and is worthy of its own book. In that light, we won't be discussing how to create and manage SharePoint lists or document libraries. In this book, we'll assume that your organization has a SharePoint site ready for consumption via Access. If you want to immerse yourself in SharePoint setup and administration, consider picking up the book *Beginning SharePoint 2013: Building Business Solutions with SharePoint,* by Amanda Perran, Shane Perran, Jennifer Mason, and Laura Rogers (published by Wiley).

Understanding SharePoint documents

Perhaps the most common use of SharePoint is storing shared documents and other files. SharePoint keeps track of files from the moment they're added to a list until they're removed or deleted. Anyone with write-access to a SharePoint site can upload a document for sharing. Figure 32.1 shows a short list of several different types of files uploaded to a SharePoint document library.

FIGURE 32.1

A SharePoint document library.

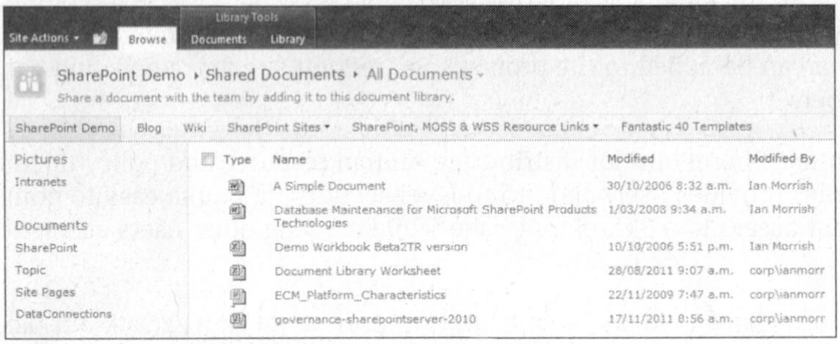

In Figure 32.1, notice that the library contains several different types of documents. Each row in the document list includes an icon indicating the document's type, the document's name, the size of the document, and the name of the person who added the document to the list. The library also includes tracking information ("In progress," "Approved") for each item.

SharePoint document libraries support a check-in/check-out paradigm. Only one person at a time is able to check out a document for changes. Although not shown in Figure 32.1, SharePoint records when a document is checked in or out and keeps track of the individuals making changes. SharePoint can even be instructed to roll back document changes to an earlier version, if necessary.

Again, this document sharing paradigm is most commonly used to share information across organizations, allowing for collaboration between the users of the SharePoint site.

Understanding SharePoint lists

In addition to storing and tracking entire documents, SharePoint users can store and share data via SharePoint lists. SharePoint lists are conceptually similar to database tables in that each list consists of rows and columns of data. Each column holds a particular type of data such as text, a date, or an object (such as a photo). From this simplistic perspective, SharePoint lists are analogous to Access tables.

Figure 32.2 illustrates a typical SharePoint list. As you can see, the relevant information is presented in a single screen. You add a new item, edit an existing item, or delete an item through this same screen.

SharePoint can manage virtually any type of data you want to share with other people. Although the site shown in Figure 32.2 is designed for a specific purpose, SharePoint is suitable for many other scenarios. For example, an HR department could use a SharePoint list for sharing and tracking required training courses. An IT department could maintain a list of assets, including status and locations. Even smaller organizations like a local bowling club can share and maintain tournament schedules and player rankings as SharePoint lists.

FIGURE 32.2

A SharePoint list allows for the storage and tracking of data in a table format.

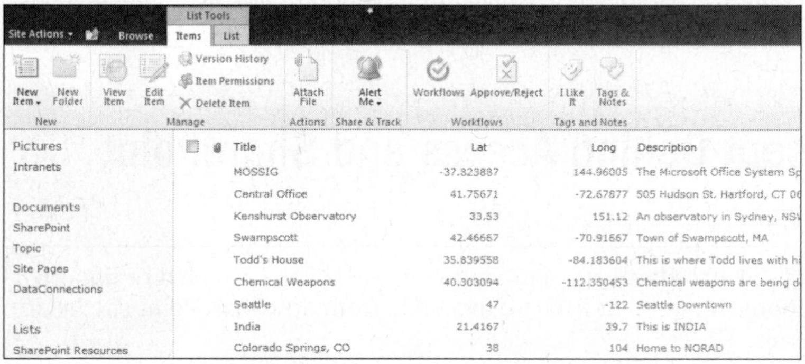

SharePoint easily supports multiple lists, allowing an organization to add as many lists as needed. Figure 32.3 shows all the lists available on this particular SharePoint site.

FIGURE 32.3

The lists on a particular SharePoint site.

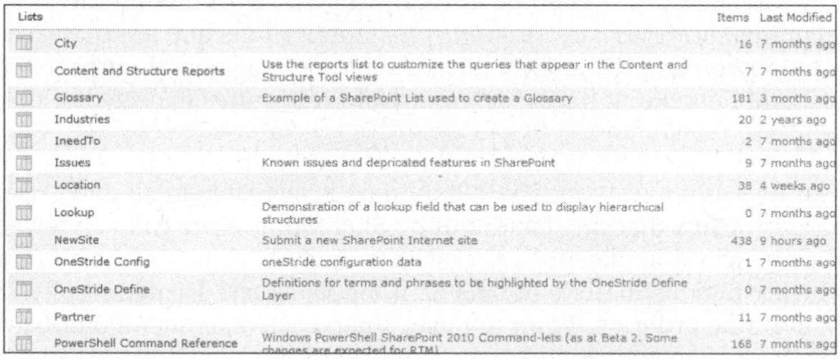

Unlike Access tables, SharePoint lists are not relational. There is no way to directly relate data in two different SharePoint lists or to query multiple SharePoint lists to find related data. Also, you can't add validation rules to individual SharePoint list columns or to the list as a whole. You can, however, restrict values in list columns to ensure that a list contains valid data.

When linking SharePoint data (see Chapter 33), you're somewhat limited in your use of the SharePoint data in an Access application. Because the data is not relational, and because there are no primary keys in SharePoint lists, you can't easily create meaningful relationships between linked SharePoint lists and Access tables.

However, as you'll see in Chapter 33, there is still plenty you can do with SharePoint data. Common uses of SharePoint data in Access are to populate reports or to combine SharePoint data with Access data. Because of the ability to create ad hoc joins in Access queries, you can create reports with data from both sources.

The Concept Behind Access and SharePoint Integration

SharePoint data are stored as lists, and SharePoint lists can be linked or imported into Access applications. SharePoint lists are available from any SharePoint site, sharing data across the Internet.

Linking to SharePoint lists makes data stored on a SharePoint website appear as linked tables in Access. From a data perspective, linking to a SharePoint list is no different from linking to a SQL Server database table or other remote data source. The only difference (from the user's perspective) may be a slight delay as data is transferred from a remote SharePoint site to Access and back.

Essentially, SharePoint is a way of sharing data over the Internet. Quite literally, SharePoint represents an Internet address from which data can be shared between multiple applications. Those applications can be virtually anywhere on the Internet. Most SharePoint installations, however, are strict *intranet* applications and are only accessed from within a company on its private LAN. SharePoint is not a general-purpose tool for building websites, and SharePoint pages lack many of the features expected of public websites.

When linked to an Access application, SharePoint data is available to all other users of that application. This means that the data input by SharePoint users can be viewed and utilized through your Access application. Access essentially becomes a feature-rich front-end application, using remote SharePoint data as if the data were located locally. The user notices nothing out of the ordinary. From the user's perspective, a SharePoint-hosted Access application looks like any other Access application and contains the same data-entry screens and reports as any other Access database.

NOTE

Many IT organizations today have already implemented a SharePoint environment. It is likely that your organization already has SharePoint running on your network. No one user can simply stand up a SharePoint site. If you're interested in using SharePoint, you'll need to contact your IT department to inquire about getting access to a SharePoint site.

Integrating Access with SharePoint

IN THIS CHAPTER

Linking to SharePoint lists

Importing SharePoint lists

Exporting Access tables to SharePoint

Upsizing Access databases to SharePoint

Using SharePoint list templates

Several of the previous chapters of this book have touched on different data sources for Access. You've seen how Access supports importing, linking, and exporting data. Access has no equal when it comes to sharing data with other applications.

SharePoint data linked to an Access application is live and reflects changes made by users almost instantly. In reality, SharePoint integration is one of the big stories (from Microsoft's perspective) in Access and Office 2013. Microsoft is busily enhancing the ability of Access and SharePoint to cooperate and share data. SharePoint services can be both local to a specific company or rented/leased from service providers. When a user opens an Access report, at least a portion of the data may be hosted on a SharePoint site many thousands of miles away.

This chapter demonstrates the power and flexibility of using SharePoint data within Access applications.

ON THE WEB

The starting database for this walkthrough, `Chapter33.accdb`, can be downloaded from this book's website.

NOTE

You'll need access to a SharePoint server to experiment with the data sharing techniques described in this chapter. If you're interested in using SharePoint, you'll need to contact your IT department to inquire about getting access to a SharePoint site. You can also find a commercial site, or perhaps even a free demonstration service, to experiment with. This chapter uses a demo site located here: www.wssdemo.com.

Sharing Access Data with SharePoint

Building Access interfaces with SharePoint simply means going into an Access application, linking to SharePoint lists, and then writing forms and reports based on those linked tables. A linked SharePoint list appears (to Access) as any other linked data source.

Turn to Chapter 7 for more on linking to external data.

In addition, Access 2013 enables you to import SharePoint data directly into local Access tables. Although imported data is no longer connected to the SharePoint site, and is therefore "stale" compared to data remaining on the site, a snapshot of data from a SharePoint site may be useful in some situations.

Linking to SharePoint lists

The most fundamental data sharing between Access and SharePoint is for Access to link to a SharePoint list and use the data as with any other linked data source. The only difference is that because SharePoint doesn't support a wide variety of data types, the linked SharePoint lists are somewhat less flexible than links to, for instance, SQL Server tables.

Linking to a SharePoint list is much like linking to any other data source:

1. **Click the More drop-down button in the Import & Link group on the External Data tab.** The list of more advanced import and linking options (see Figure 33.1) appears.

FIGURE 33.1

Preparing to link to a SharePoint list.

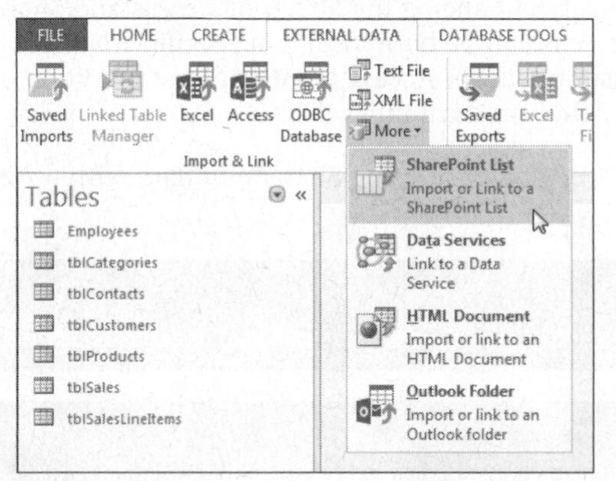

2. **Select SharePoint List from the list of import and linking options.** The Get External Data – SharePoint Site dialog box (see Figure 33.2) appears. The top portion of this dialog box shows a list of recently visited SharePoint sites, and just below this list is a text box for entering the destination SharePoint site's URL. As you may recall from Chapter 32, a SharePoint site is accessible through a URL and actually resides on a web server, most often located on a LAN.

FIGURE 33.2

The Get External Data – SharePoint Site dialog box.

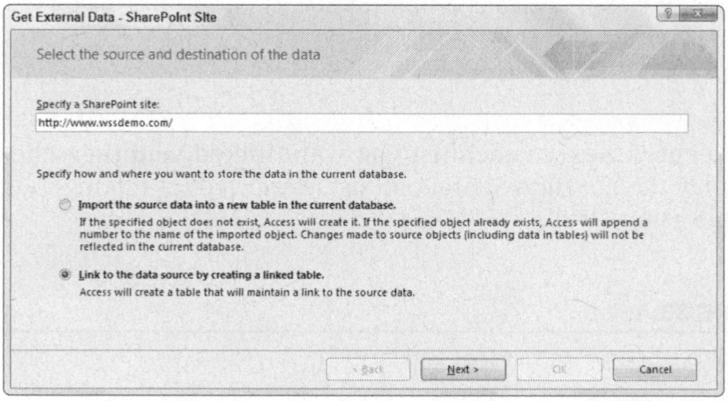

You must have appropriate permissions to link to a SharePoint list. In fact, without proper permissions, Access can't even display a list of SharePoint lists on the designated site. Figure 33.3 shows the standard SharePoint login dialog box, asking for the user's credentials. SharePoint users are recognized by their membership in Windows Active Directory services and their inclusion in designated SharePoint groups. These topics are beyond the scope of this book, but you should be aware that access to SharePoint sites and SharePoint data is protected by processes similar to any other Windows application.

3. **Enter your username and password.** If you're following along using the demo site www.spsdemo.com, you can use corp\demouser as the username and pass@word1 as the password. You're presented with a list of SharePoint lists in the designated SharePoint site. Each item in the list is accompanied by a check box.

FIGURE 33.3

The SharePoint login dialog box.

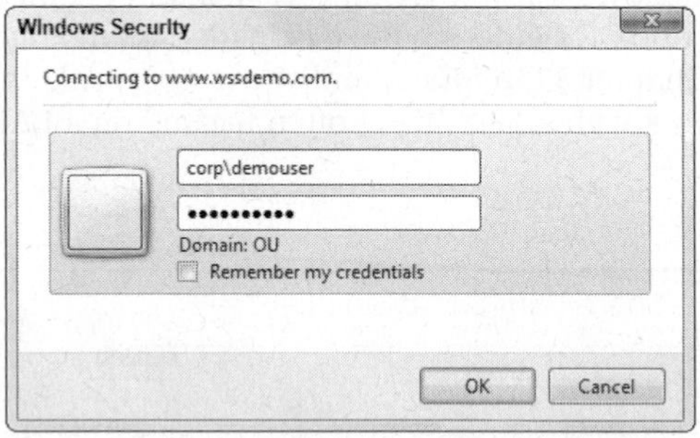

Windows Security

Connecting to www.wssdemo.com.

corp\demouser

••••••••••

Domain: OU

Remember my credentials

OK Cancel

4. **Place a check next to each list you want linked, and then click OK.** In Figure 33.4, only the Location SharePoint list is selected for linking, but you can select multiple lists as well.

FIGURE 33.4

Selecting a SharePoint list for Linking.

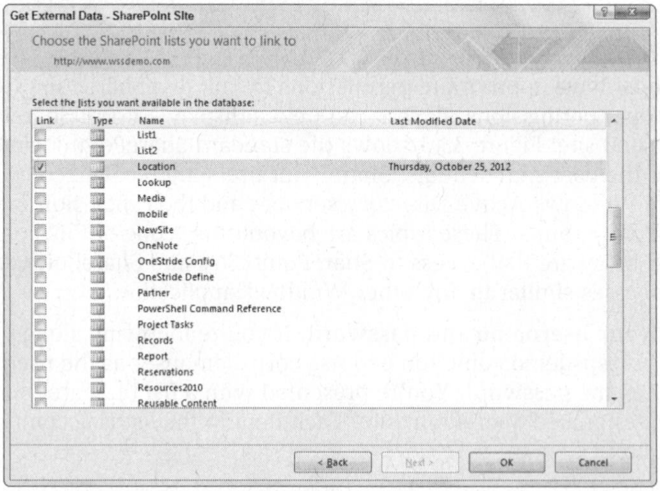

Get External Data - SharePoint Site

Choose the SharePoint lists you want to link to

http://www.wssdemo.com

Select the lists you want available in the database:

Link	Type	Name	Last Modified Date
		List1	
		List2	
✓		Location	Thursday, October 25, 2012
		Lookup	
		Media	
		mobile	
		NewSite	
		OneNote	
		OneStride Config	
		OneStride Define	
		Partner	
		PowerShell Command Reference	
		Project Tasks	
		Records	
		Report	
		Reservations	
		Resources2010	
		Reusable Content	

< Back Next > OK Cancel

Figure 33.5 shows the linked SharePoint list. The icons indicating linked SharePoint lists look very much like Access table icons. Each linked list is accompanied by an arrow, and the color of the icon has changed to a yellowish-orange color.

The data in the linked table is compatible with Access, and you can build queries, forms, and reports against this data if needed. It's important to note that the data in the linked list is read-only, meaning you can't update the data in the SharePoint list via Access 2013.

FIGURE 33.5

A linked SharePoint list appears much like any other Access table.

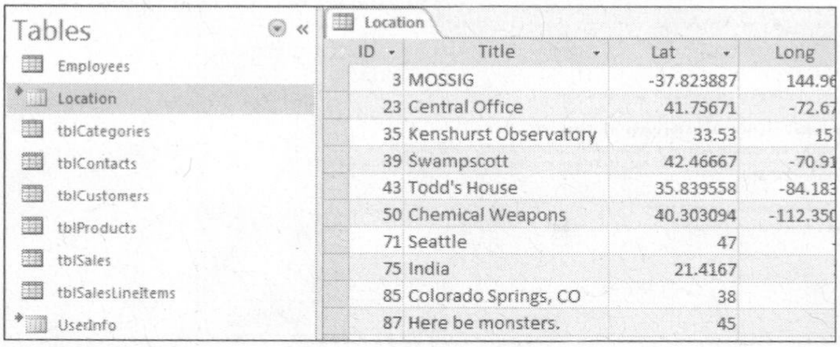

Tables

- Employees
- Location
- tblCategories
- tblContacts
- tblCustomers
- tblProducts
- tblSales
- tblSalesLineItems
- UserInfo

Location

ID	Title	Lat	Long
3	MOSSIG	-37.823887	144.96
23	Central Office	41.75671	-72.67
35	Kenshurst Observatory	33.53	15
39	Swampscott	42.46667	-70.91
43	Todd's House	35.839558	-84.183
50	Chemical Weapons	40.303094	-112.350
71	Seattle	47	
75	India	21.4167	
85	Colorado Springs, CO	38	
87	Here be monsters.	45	

NOTE

Instead of requiring the user to log in each and every time she uses SharePoint data, after a user's SharePoint credentials have been established, Access creates a UserInfo table containing information about the user and her role in SharePoint. Although the user has to provide a password to initially access SharePoint, the UserInfo table is a repository of additional information about the user. The UserInfo table resides within Access, which means that it's available before the user logs in to SharePoint. This enables Access to provide SharePoint with the user information as the user logs in to SharePoint.

Importing SharePoint lists

Instead of having a live link to SharePoint lists, you may want to import a list. Importing a SharePoint list allows you to simply take a snapshot of the list and bring the data into Access as a stand-alone disconnected table. Unlike a linked SharePoint list, an imported list will not be automatically updated with new SharePoint data.

The steps for importing a SharePoint list are similar to those for linking:

1. **Click the More drop-down button in the Import & Link group on the External Data tab.** The list of more advanced import and linking options appears.
2. **Select SharePoint List from the list of import and linking options.** The Get External Data – SharePoint Site dialog box appears.
3. **In the top portion of this dialog box, either select a recently visited SharePoint site or enter a new destination SharePoint URL; then select the Import option as shown in Figure 33.6.**

FIGURE 33.6

Selecting a SharePoint list for importing.

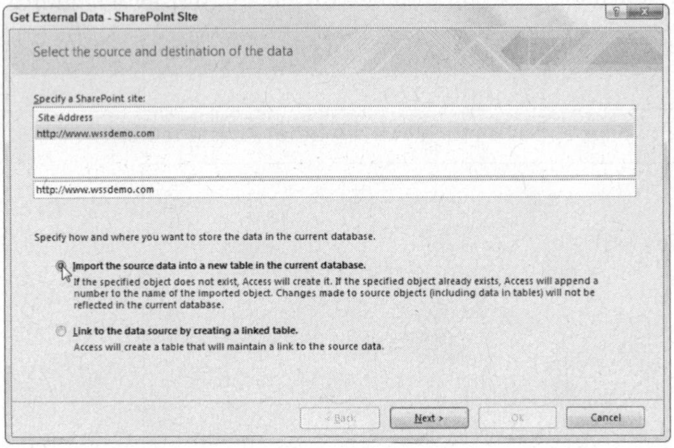

4. **Enter the appropriate permissions to link to a SharePoint list.** You're presented with a list of SharePoint lists in the designated SharePoint site. Each item in the list is accompanied by a check box.
5. **Place a check next to each list you want imported, and then click OK.** Access imports your chosen lists into a table that can be viewed and utilized like any other standard table through the Navigation pane.

Exporting Access tables to SharePoint

Sometimes you need to transfer data from Access to SharePoint so that SharePoint users have access to the same data as Access users. The first example exports a table from Access to SharePoint:

1. **Open the Chapter33.accdb example database.**
2. **Open the tblCustomers table, or just highlight tblCustomers in the Navigation pane.** When you open the table, a few more controls are added to the Ribbon.
3. **Select the More drop-down list in the Export group on the External Data tab of the Ribbon, and click SharePoint List (shown in Figure 33.7).** The SharePoint Site Wizard starts.
4. **Enter or select the SharePoint site URL (see Figure 33.8).** The objective is to create a SharePoint list for the selected table in your Access database.

FIGURE 33.7

Selecting SharePoint as the export destination.

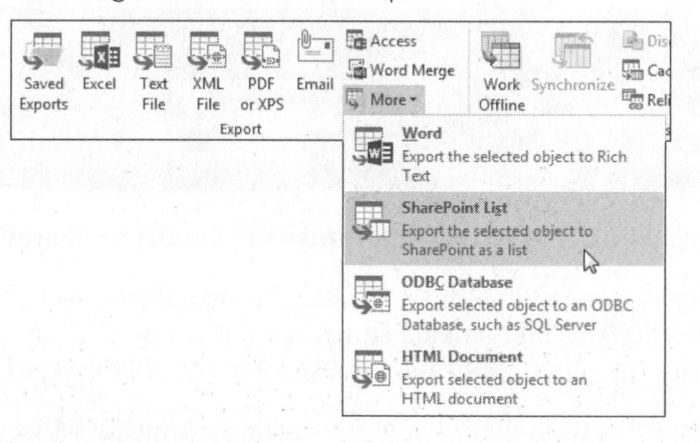

FIGURE 33.8

Selecting the destination SharePoint site.

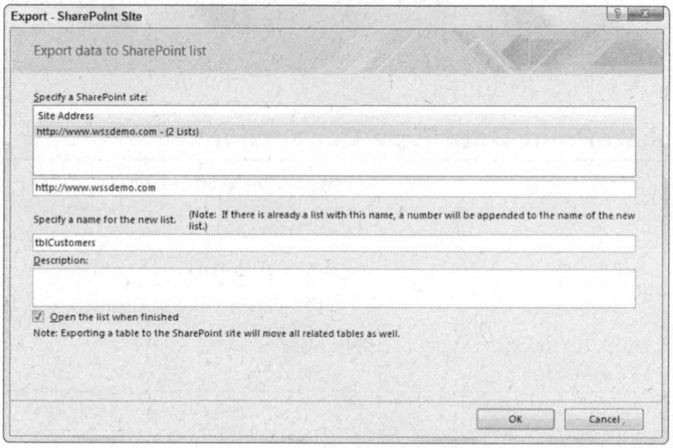

5. **Click OK.**
6. **If you're prompted for a login, enter a valid SharePoint username and password.** The SharePoint login dialog box will be similar to the dialog box shown in Figure 33.3. The difference is that this dialog box will require only the user's password because the username was previously cached.

   As the wizard progresses, you see a small dialog box indicating the progress of the conversion process. The dialog box means that the Access table design is being copied to SharePoint and a new SharePoint list is being created. When the conversion is complete, the new SharePoint list is displayed in your default web browser.

7. **If you get any errors or warnings, check the Show Details box in the wizard's dialog box, and read the information displayed.**

NOTE

If you're following along using the demo SharePoint site www.wssdemo.com, you won't be able to create a new list on that site. This is understandable, as the kind folks who provide that service don't want hundreds of unknown new lists being created. You'll have to gain access to a SharePoint site that allows you to "write" permissions.

8. **Click the Close button in Access to dismiss the Export to SharePoint dialog box.**

When the export process is complete, the data exists in two places: in the original Access table and as a SharePoint list. The two data stores are not connected, so if changes are made in either location, the other application doesn't see the change.

Certain fields don't export well to SharePoint. For instance, an OLE Object field is simply left empty on the SharePoint side and contains no data. But most other field data types are properly translated into compatible SharePoint columns and populated with data from the Access table. Table 33.1 shows how Access data types are translated to compatible column types in SharePoint. Notice that far fewer types of data are available in SharePoint lists than in Access tables. The data types in Table 33.1 are applied any time an Access table is exported to SharePoint.

TABLE 33.1 SharePoint Data Type Conversion

Access Data Type	Converted Type in SharePoint
AutoNumber	Number
Text	Single line of text
Memo	Multiple lines of text, limited to 8,192 characters
All Number Types (Byte, Integer, Long Integer, Single, Double, Decimal)	Number
Date/Time	Date and Time
Currency	Currency
Yes/No	YesNo
OLE Object	Single line of text
Calculated	Calculated
Hyperlink	Hyperlink or Picture

Moving Access tables to SharePoint

Instead of simply exporting Access tables to SharePoint, another approach to data sharing is to move all the tables in an Access application to SharePoint as a single export operation and link the new SharePoint lists back to the Access application. All of the tables in the Access database are moved to SharePoint and linked back to Access in a single process.

The advantage of moving Access tables to SharePoint is that you can build out your data model in Access, using all convenient tools for table creation, and then upsize the data model to SharePoint. Once the data is in SharePoint, any changes made in SharePoint will be immediately seen in Access.

This level of integration allows SharePoint to be used as the data collaboration and tracking portal, while giving users the benefit of Access's superior user reporting tools.

Moving Access tables to SharePoint is not one of the import/export features of Access 2013. Instead, the commands necessary to move the entire set of Access tables to SharePoint are on the Database Tools tab of the Ribbon (see Figure 33.9).

FIGURE 33.9

The Move Data group on the Ribbon contains the wizard to upsize to SharePoint.

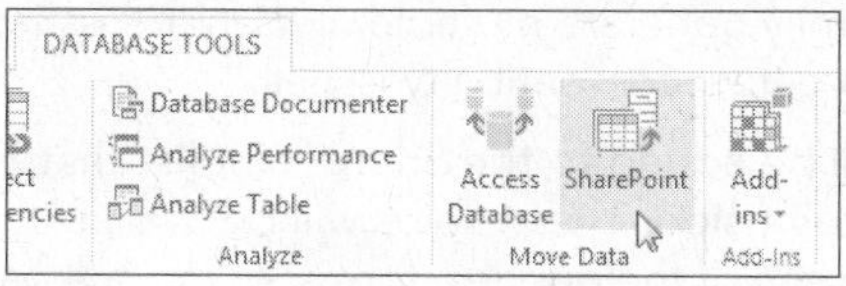

DATABASE TOOLS
Database Documenter
Analyze Performance
Analyze Table
Analyze
Access Database
SharePoint
Add-ins
Move Data
Add-Ins

Clicking the SharePoint command in the Move Data group on the Ribbon opens the Export Tables to SharePoint Wizard dialog box (shown in Figure 33.10). The only information that you need is the URL of the destination SharePoint site. Access handles the rest.

FIGURE 33.10

The Export Tables to SharePoint Wizard dialog box specifies the destination SharePoint site.

Export Tables to SharePoint Wizard
Where do you want to move your data?
This wizard moves all your data to a SharePoint site by creating a SharePoint list for each table and then linking each list back to your existing database.
What SharePoint site do you want to use?
http://www.wssdemo.com
http://www.wssdemo.com
< Back
Next >
Cancel

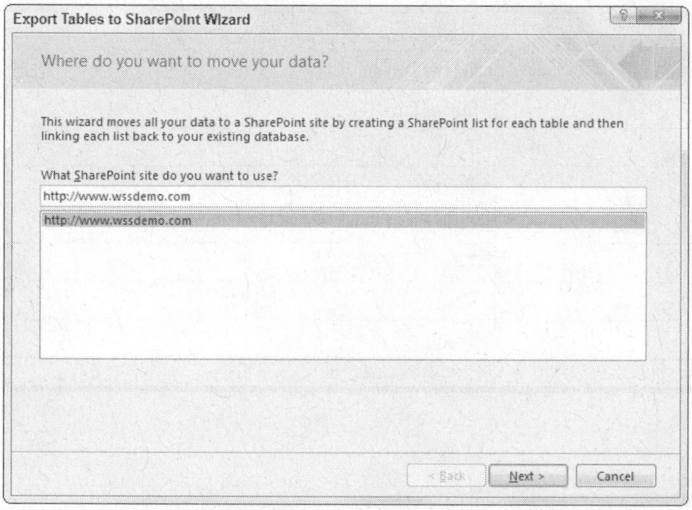

Things to Be Aware of before Moving Access Tables to SharePoint

Before attempting to upsize your Access tables to SharePoint, keep in mind the following:

- **The export might fail if an Access table name does not conform to SharePoint naming rules.** For example, Access table names may contain spaces and limited punctuation characters, while SharePoint tables are plain text with no spaces. If the export fails, it's likely to be caused by a list-naming violation.
- **All the queries, forms, and reports that are based on the linked tables should function as before, with a few exceptions.** Because of incompatibilities between Access and SharePoint data, not every Access data type migrates to SharePoint. The incompatible fields are created in the SharePoint list, but they're added to the SharePoint list as text columns and are left empty.
- **Export issues are reported in a table named Move to SharePoint Site Issues, with one row for each problem.** A single Access field may generate multiple rows in the issues table. Most export problems are traceable to data incompatibility issues.
- **During the export process, several fields will be added to the SharePoint list that are required for list management on the SharePoint side.** These fields will be available in the linked table in Access but are not included in any of the queries, forms, or reports based on the table before it was exported to SharePoint. These additional fields are listed in the following table. It's possible that you may be able to make use of at least some of these columns, but by and large, they serve no purpose in an Access application.

SharePoint Field Name	Data Type
_OldId	Number (Double)
Content Type	Text
Workflow Instance ID	Text
File Type	Text
Modified	Date/Time
Created	Date/Time
Created By	Text
Modified By	Text
URL Path	Text
Path	Text
Item Type	Text
Encoded Absolute URL	Text

The Next button initiates the export process, which may take more than a few minutes, depending on the number of tables in the Access database, the volume of data in each record, and the efficiency of the SharePoint server hardware and software. You may also be asked for your SharePoint username and password because SharePoint must verify that you have the proper permissions to create objects in the destination SharePoint site.

NOTE

Again, if you're following along using the demo SharePoint site www.wssdemo.com, you won't have the permission to create new lists on that site. This is understandable, as the kind folks who provide that service don't want hundreds of unknown new lists being created. You'll have to gain access to a SharePoint site that allows you to "write" permissions.

The newly created SharePoint lists are given the same name. At the conclusion of the process, all the tables in the Access database have been moved to SharePoint and linked back to the Access application. The tables and their data are now stored and managed by SharePoint Services. All that's left in the Access database are logical links to the SharePoint website. The tables and data are no longer stored in the Access database.

Just as with other export processes, you can save the export steps for future use. Access also makes a backup of the Access database file prior to the export process so that you can revert to the prior state, if necessary.

Using SharePoint Templates

In this chapter, we examine the options available when an Access database already exists and users require the same data on a SharePoint website. In its attempt to solidify the connection between Access and SharePoint, Microsoft has provided yet another approach to integrating Access applications with SharePoint.

Instead of exporting existing Access tables to SharePoint or linking to SharePoint lists, this alternative technique involves building entirely new SharePoint lists within the Access environment. Access 2013 provides SharePoint list *templates,* which contain all the details necessary to build SharePoint lists, including column names and data types and other list properties. This is essentially meant to be a time-saver for anyone who wants to quickly stand up a new list on SharePoint.

The SharePoint templates in Access 2013 cover a number of important business functions: Contacts, Tasks, Issues, and Events, as shown in Figure 33.11. In addition, the Custom list template (near the bottom of the list) allows adding virtually any combination of SharePoint-compatible columns to an otherwise blank list. The last item in the drop-down list (Existing SharePoint List) provides the same linking capability discussed in the "Linking to SharePoint lists" section, earlier in this chapter.

FIGURE 33.11

SharePoint list templates available in Access.

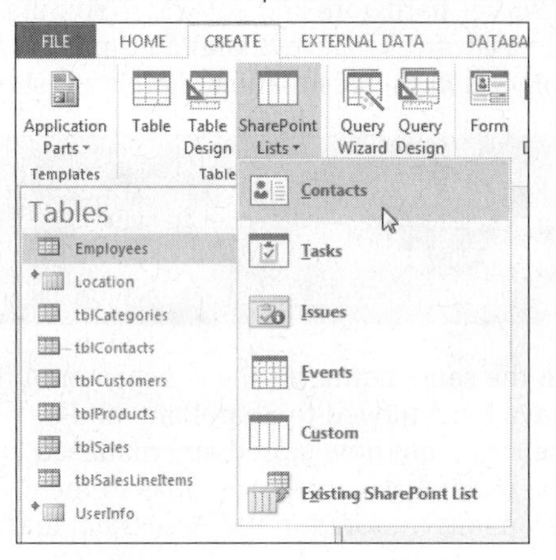

Selecting an item from the list of SharePoint list templates opens the Create New List dialog box (shown in Figure 33.12). You'll have to provide a SharePoint URL and a name for the new list.

Notice that you don't have an option to modify the template before you create it in SharePoint. This means, of course, that the list will include a predetermined set of columns, each set to a particular data type required for the list's operations.

FIGURE 33.12

The Create New List dialog box when creating a new SharePoint list from an Access template.

Create New List

Contacts

Create a contacts list when you want to manage information about people that your team works with such as customers or partners. You can share information between your contacts list and Microsoft SharePoint Foundation-compatible contacts programs.

Specify a SharePoint site:

Site Address

http://www.wssdemo.com - (2 Lists)

http://www.wssdemo.com

Specify a name for the new list.

MyContacts

Description:

Open the list when finished

Note: Exporting a table to the SharePoint site will move all related tables as well.

OK Cancel

You may be asked to provide SharePoint credentials as the new list is created. You need administrative rights to add lists to a SharePoint site, so even if you can link to a SharePoint list, you may not be entitled to create an entirely new list.

The newly created list will be automatically added to Access as a linked table that behaves like any other linked SharePoint list.

In the future, other SharePoint list templates — potential tracking application templates, projects and project management, marketing, sales channels and pipelines, student management, school and college student management, and others — may become available.

CHAPTER 34

Understanding Access Services

IN THIS CHAPTER

Understanding managed applications

Introducing Access's web publishing features

Looking at Access Services in SharePoint 2013

Explaining the limits of Access web applications

Over the last decade, Microsoft has been emphasizing and promoting SharePoint as a platform for collaborative development. Chapters 32 and 33 explore some of the long-standing capabilities built into Access that enable Access users to seamlessly share data with SharePoint users.

With the release of Access 2010 and SharePoint 2010, Microsoft took the next step with SharePoint and Access Services. Access Services is a SharePoint implementation that allows Access applications to run directly in the browser via SharePoint. This meant that for the first time, SharePoint offered Access developers the ability to bring their applications to the web.

SharePoint 2013 continues to improve on the integration between SharePoint and Access with new architecture and the ability to store Access data in SQL Server tables.

In this chapter, you get an understanding of Access Services and how it can help you create Access 2013 applications with a credible web presence.

Explaining Managed Applications

Access has long been relegated to a role as a workgroup and departmental database development system. In spite of its outstanding user interface and report tools, Access's reliance on a database file that can be corrupted or lost due to hardware failure or accidentally (or deliberately) deleted has made Access a hard sell in many environments.

A Word about SharePoint Requirements and Office 365

In order to take advantage of the functionality afforded by Access Services, you must have permissions to publish to a SharePoint site that is running Access Services. Access Services is a SharePoint implementation that is available only with SharePoint 2010 or 2013, so you'll want to ensure your SharePoint site is one of those two versions.

Most people work within companies that already have a SharePoint 2010 or 2013 environment. However, if you don't have access to an already existing SharePoint environment, hundreds of service providers offer subscription-based SharePoint services. Many of these providers provide volume-based pricing on a subscription model.

In fact, Microsoft has an offering called Office 365. Office 365 is a cloud-based Microsoft environment that offers subscribers a line of collaborative Microsoft Office–like tools that can be accessed through the web. Similar to Google Docs or Google Spreadsheets, Microsoft offers Word, Excel, and PowerPoint in Office 365. It also offers Access Services with connections to SQL Azure (the cloud-based version of SQL Server). This means you can use Office 365 to publish and host your Access web applications.

Subscribing to a commercial SharePoint service provider may be the fastest and most affordable way to host Access applications on SharePoint. Again, the only caveat is that the commercial service provider you choose must offer either SharePoint 2010 or 2013 with Access Services implemented.

Traditionally, IT departments are charged with maintaining a company's mission-critical database systems. These systems — whether implemented as SQL Server, Oracle, DB2, or another server database — require professional management, including careful design, periodic backups, and maintaining user and group permissions. The objectives of large-scale database systems are to ensure the availability and integrity of the data.

The objectives of departments and business units (even small businesses), on the other hand, are flexibility and access to data. Time is money, and waiting for an IT department to develop a user interface or a new report in a development tool such as SQL Server Reporting Services can be costly. Many business units prefer using Access because of its ability to quickly turn user requirements into bona fide, completed applications.

The problem comes when a business unit wants to store mission-critical data in an Access data file on a file server or (worse) on a user's desktop or laptop computer. Without proper management, it's easy to lose data due to a hard disk crash or a stolen laptop.

Furthermore, without careful data synchronization, different copies of a database can exist in multiple locations. As a result, Access reports can't be trusted because no one is sure whether a report reflects the state of the company's data.

There is a trade-off between an expensive, large, carefully managed application such as a .NET web form application running on top of SQL Server and a smaller, lighter, and more agile application built with Access. Even when an Access application is built around data stored in SQL Server, providing access to the data through a web browser is difficult at best. In most cases, users must work with SQL Server data through a LAN and depend on SQL Server database administrators (DBAs) to provide permissions to the data and other support to the Access front ends as needed.

Managed applications (such as server-based database systems) offer many advantages to businesses and organizations. However, these same businesses and organizations also benefit from the flexibility and agility of unmanaged applications written with Access.

Looking at Web Publishing in Access

Ideally, users would have fast, simple access to their data, without the constraints of large database systems such as SQL Server. Although linking to SQL Server database tables from Access applications removes the problems caused by multiple copies of the database on different computers and provides a high degree of database security, users often depend on database administrators for simple tasks such as developing stored procedures to sort or filter data in various ways.

Microsoft's solution to the conflicting needs of business users and IT departments is to provide tools in Access 2013 that allow Access developers to *publish* Access applications on SharePoint sites. When you publish a properly prepared Access application to SharePoint, users instantly gain the ability to view and work with web-based Access forms via a SharePoint site.

Access developers also benefit from the Access Services paradigm. First of all, there is no need to learn a web-development language; SharePoint and Access Services do all the work to translate the Access application to a website. Secondly, there is only a single point of maintenance. Versioning issues go away with the ability to republish your Access application any time changes are needed. Once the application is republished, all users receive the updates the next time they use the web application.

In Access 2010, publishing web applications to SharePoint created SharePoint lists that housed the application. With Access 2013, Microsoft improved the architecture by provisioning SQL tables for your application. When you publish an Access 2013 web application to SharePoint, new SQL Server 2012 tables will be created to store the data. If the application is served up through Office 365, new SQL Azure tables are used. This new architecture allows for greater scalability because SQL tables can handle larger, more complex sets of data than SharePoint lists. Also, because the data coming from your Access application is already in a SQL Server environment, SQL developers can more easily integrate and work with the data.

The data is secure because users must be granted permission to use SharePoint, but after they provide their username and password, the SharePoint data is accessible through any web browser.

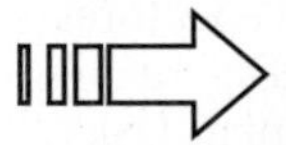

Chapter 35 covers this process in detail and explains the changes required in an Access application to make Access objects compatible with SharePoint.

> **NOTE**
> Users utilizing your published Access web application don't need Access installed on their machine. However, you must have Access installed in order to make any changes to the database structure.

Why SharePoint?

Many developers question why Microsoft chose to make Access web development reliant on SharePoint Services. If the intent is to make Access a bona-fide web development tool, doesn't it make sense to incorporate true web development capabilities into Access, like Microsoft did with Visual Studio, many years ago?

When Microsoft examined the issues involved, it quickly became clear that adding credible web development capabilities to Access wasn't practical. Many people forget that a website is far more than just HTML pages. Security, performance, and data integrity issues must be considered.

For instance, Jet (or ACE, for that matter) is unsuitable as a web database system. You cannot coerce the multiuser, stability, and capacity requirements of a public website into an ACCDB database. The architecture is wrong, and making it right would require rewriting ACE for the web environment.

Leveraging SharePoint features

Microsoft chose SharePoint as the platform for Access web publishing because of the significant features built into SharePoint, including the following:

- **Security:** SharePoint supports users and groups of users. Users and groups may be granted or denied access to various parts of a SharePoint website, and designated users may be granted permission to add, delete, or modify the site.
- **Versioning:** SharePoint automatically maintains a version history of objects and data. Changes can be rolled back to an earlier state at virtually any time. The ability to roll back changes can be granted to individual users, and DBA support is not required.
- **Recycle bin:** Deleted data and objects are held in a recycle bin so that they may be recovered. Unlike Access, in which every deletion or change is permanent, SharePoint supports an undo feature for its data.
- **Alerts:** Users and groups can be e-mailed when specific data in a SharePoint list is added, deleted, or changed. If granted the proper permissions, users can manage their own alerts.
- **End-user maintenance:** SharePoint sites are meant to be maintained by their users, without the intervention of IT departments. Although SharePoint pages are not as flexible as typical web pages, a SharePoint developer can add or remove features from pages; change fonts, headings, colors, and other attributes of pages; create subsites and lists; and perform many other maintenance and enhancement tasks.
- **Other features:** Every SharePoint site includes a number of features — such as a calendar, a task list, and announcements — that users may turn off or remove.

The ability of users to maintain a SharePoint site is a major difference between a SharePoint site and a website built with a tool such as ASP.NET. The web pages in a .NET website are tightly bound to the compiled code that manages the site. A user can't change an ASPX page because it's stored on a web server, and (in most cases) the code behind the page must be recompiled when changes are made to the page's interface.

Understanding Access Services

Earlier in this chapter, you read that SharePoint Server 2010 is the first version of SharePoint to support Access Services, the server-side support necessary for hosting Access applications in SharePoint.

Access applications are built in Access, of course, using essentially the same tools as in previous versions of Access. When the application is published to SharePoint, Access Services renders the ASPX pages necessary to display the Access application in a web browser. In other words, Access Services is the driving force behind SharePoint-hosted Access applications.

Access Services compiles and executes the queries in the Access web application and directs the queries against the SharePoint lists containing the data. Access Services also synchronizes updates between versions of the Access application on a developer's desktop and the version stored in SharePoint.

These steps are described in detail in Chapter 35.

Perhaps the most important role played by Access Services is maintaining the relational nature of the tables exported to SharePoint when an Access application is published to SharePoint. SharePoint itself can't recognize the relational nature of your data. Access Services provides the logic required to join list data and maintain referential integrity between lists, as long as the relationships between tables are defined before the Access application is published to SharePoint.

As described in Chapter 35, Access is used as the database designer to make updates to the application's schema and resynchronize the changes with the database previously published to SharePoint.

Access Services in SharePoint also provides data caching. Instead of relying on the native ability of SharePoint to locate and deliver data, Access Services provides a middle-tier caching service that stores data that is likely to be consumed by the application and delivers the data much more quickly than SharePoint alone. The caching is transparent to users and developers, and no configuration options exist for setting up the cache or modifying its parameters.

The Access Services layer filters data in a query before adding it to the cache. This means that queries that include a `WHERE` clause are guaranteed to run more quickly and make better use of Access Services caching than a query that selects all rows from the underlying table(s). As with any database application, you should plan on using query predicates (the WHERE clause) when possible to minimize the amount of data that moves between the data store (in this case, SharePoint lists) and the user interface.

Examining Access Web Application Limits

Access web applications are not the best solution for public-facing websites — they're better suited for departmental or workgroup environments. Certain limitations mean that the Access/SharePoint web option is targeted for specific situations.

The limitations of Access web applications are determined more by SharePoint than anything in Access itself. For instance, SharePoint doesn't support anonymous access to SharePoint sites. Users are expected to log on to a SharePoint site, using a valid username and password. (SharePoint uses Windows Active Directory services to identify users.)

Although workarounds exist for this limitation, it can be difficult to restrict users to certain portions of a SharePoint application. In general, after a user is authenticated by SharePoint's security system, the user is able to access the lists, calendars, and other features supported by the SharePoint site. Restricting users means determining which features should be allowed for which sets of users, and individually setting permissions for those features throughout the SharePoint site. Most web applications, on the other hand, present only the features the developer has specified.

SharePoint was never meant to be a general-purpose web development tool; instead, it was designed and built primarily as a collaborative platform for sharing data and documents. This means that SharePoint pages are built from templates, rather than from free-form HTML. As a result, all SharePoint pages share certain appearance features.

In most cases, the similarities between pages hosted on different SharePoint sites are an asset, not a hindrance. After a user is familiar with SharePoint and SharePoint pages, no further instruction is needed, so users are productive more quickly than with applications where each page is different. Common tasks such as adding a new item to a list or editing an existing item are the same in every SharePoint page.

You can customize colors, fonts, and some other appearance attributes of a SharePoint page. The basic layout, however, with the Navigation pane at the left, a Ribbon and "breadcrumbs" at the top, and an items list to the right of the Navigation pane, are common to all SharePoint pages.

If absolutely necessary, you can create a custom page template from scratch, or from an existing template, and use it on a SharePoint site. But because most SharePoint sites are used on an intranet for a specialized audience, the default page layout usually works quite well.

Limitations of Access Services

As with other Microsoft technologies, Access Services comes with its own set of limitations (see Table 34.1). It's important to be aware of these before deciding whether to publish your Access applications to SharePoint.

You'll note a default value for each of these limitations. These default values represent the standard value when Access Services is installed on the SharePoint site. In order to utilize the maximum values, your SharePoint administrator will have to explicitly configure each attribute to the maximum allowable.

TABLE 34.1 Access Services Limits

Type of Query or Field	Comments
Maximum records per table	The maximum number of records that a table in an application can contain. Maximum: No limit Default: 500,000
Maximum columns per query	The maximum number of columns that can be referenced in a query. Note that some columns may automatically be referenced by the query engine and will be included in this limit. Maximum: 255 Default: 40
Maximum rows per query	The maximum number of rows that the output of the query can have. Maximum: 200,000 Default: 25,000
Maximum sources per query	The maximum number of lists that may be used as input to one query. Maximum: 20 Default: 12
Maximum calculated columns per query	The maximum number of inline calculated columns that can be included in a query, either in the query itself or in any subquery on which it is based. Maximum: 32 Default: 10
Maximum Order By clauses per query	The maximum number of fields referenced in the Order By clause in a query. Maximum: 8 Default: 4
Maximum request duration (request time-out setting)	The maximum duration (in seconds) allowed for a request from an application. Maximum: No limit Default: 30
Memory utilization	The maximum number of private bytes (in MB) allocated by the Access Database Service process. Maximum: 50% of physical memory on the client computer Default: 50% of physical memory on the client computer

After looking at these limitations, it should be clear that not all Access applications are good candidates for a web application. In the past, Microsoft has been blunt in suggesting that applications with more than 40,000 rows in one table are not good candidates for SharePoint-hosted Access applications. This, however, is a blanket suggestion to help you avoid performance issues after publishing your applications to the web.

The fact is that the performance of your Access web application depends on many factors — the number of records, number of tables, complexity of queries, the number of data calls to the server, and so on. It really depends on your situation.

If your Access application exceeds any of the limits shown in Table 34.1, you'll need to consider a more traditional web development path, using tools such as ASP.NET and SQL Server. These development platforms are geared toward large-scale, high-performance, data-driven websites.

Transactional limitations

A SharePoint-hosted Access web application is not a great platform for environments where hundreds of users are constantly adding to or updating data. Although SharePoint uses SQL Server as its underlying database, database updates are considerably slower than when working directly with SQL Server tables through linked Access tables or stored procedures.

In other words, a SharePoint-hosted Access database should not be used for applications requiring high-volume data entry features. Instead, the SharePoint-hosted Access application would be used ideally for moderate database updates and reporting.

CHAPTER

35

Deploying Access Applications to SharePoint

IN THIS CHAPTER

Building a starting data model

Initializing a web application

Editing tables and default views

Creating validation rules and events

Creating your own views

Managing your web applications

Access 2013 provides significant features for developers working on applications that must be shared among many users. In particular, Microsoft is exploiting the features provided by SharePoint and Access Services to extend the reach of Access 2013 to the web.

The good news for Access developers is that you don't have to become a SharePoint expert to use these techniques. All you need is the URL to a SharePoint server and proper permissions to create SharePoint sites on the server. All the development work is performed in Access 2013; SharePoint and Access Services do the rest.

NOTE

You'll need access to a SharePoint Server to experiment with the data sharing techniques described in this chapter. If you're interested in using SharePoint, you'll need to contact your IT department to inquire about getting access to a SharePoint site. If you don't have access to an already existing SharePoint environment, Microsoft has an offering called Office 365. Office 365 is a cloud-based Microsoft environment that offers subscribers a line of collaborative Microsoft Office–like tools that can be accessed through the web. Similar to Google Docs or Google Spreadsheets, Microsoft offers Word, Excel, and PowerPoint in Office 365. It also offers Access Services with connections to SQL Azure, the cloud-based version of SQL Server. This means you can use Office 365 to publish and host your Access web applications.

Publishing a Custom Access Application to SharePoint

In the following example, an entire Access 2013 application is *published* to SharePoint. Specifically, the Access application is published to Access Services running within SharePoint. The user works with the Access application from within SharePoint. The tables, queries, and underlying elements are hidden from the user and are handled by Access Services in SharePoint. All forms are expressed as web pages. Any user (with proper SharePoint credentials) can access the application through a web browser, and the Access runtime is not needed on the user's desktop.

The publishing to SharePoint technique is different from the deployment techniques used in previous versions of Access and, frankly, requires some adjustment.

Preparing the Access data model

In this example, we'll create a sales opportunity web application. With this web application, sales reps will be able to enter new sales opportunities via a SharePoint web page. Managers will also be able to run reports from our new web application.

When starting an Access web application, you'll need to begin with a basic Access data model. Because Access Services can't accept complex logic and VBA procedures, your starting data model will have to be fairly simple.

NOTE

SharePoint and Access Services won't be able to accept Access applications that include VBA because Access forms and VBA can't be converted to the JavaScript used by SharePoint. Also, advanced features such as ActiveX controls may not have .NET analogs, so Access Services can't create an appropriate substitute. This may seem disappointing to experienced Access developers, but as you'll see later in this chapter, you can substitute much of the necessary VBA logic with validation rules and data macros.

We'll start with a set of base tables (see Figure 35.1). These tables are found in a standard ACCDB database.

FIGURE 35.1

Start with a set of base tables.

All Access Objects
Search...
Tables
Categories
Customers
Employees
Opportunities

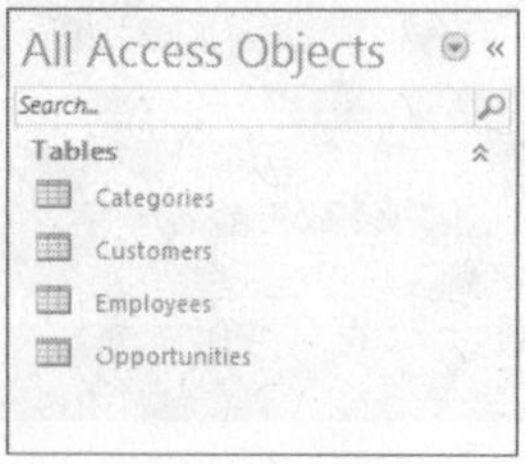

On the Web

The starting database for this walkthrough, `SalesApplication.accdb`, can be downloaded with the sample files for this book.

You'll want to establish defined relationships between each table via the Relationships tool in the Database Tools dialog box. These relationships will ensure that Access Services properly handles the interactivity between each table in your model. Figure 35.2 illustrates the Relationships screen for our starting data model.

FIGURE 35.2

Be sure to establish Relationships between the tables in your data model.

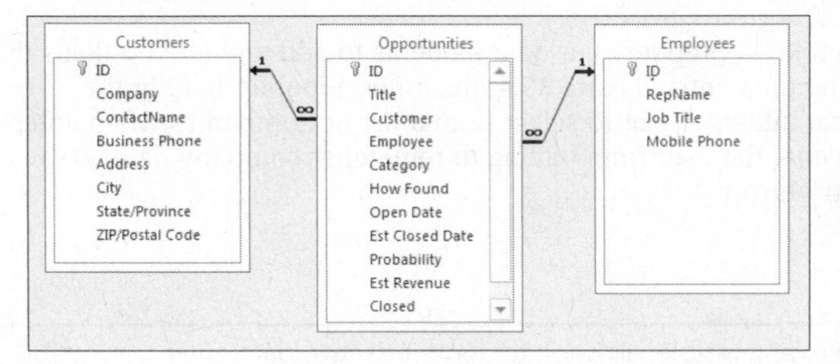

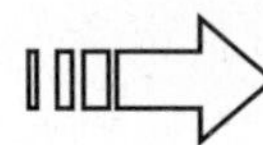

Need a refresher on the topic of table relationships? Feel free to peruse Chapter 4 of this book.

In Figure 35.2, notice that each table contains a primary key. It's important to note that Access Services does not effectively handle many-to-many relationships, so you'll need to ensure that each table in your starting data model has a single-field primary key that serves as a unique identifier for the rows within the table. The best way to achieve this is to create an AutoNumber field in each table that serves as the primary key. To do this, simply go into the Design view of each table and add a field called "ID" (see Figure 35.3). Then set the Data Type for the field to AutoNumber. Once that's done, set it as the primary key.

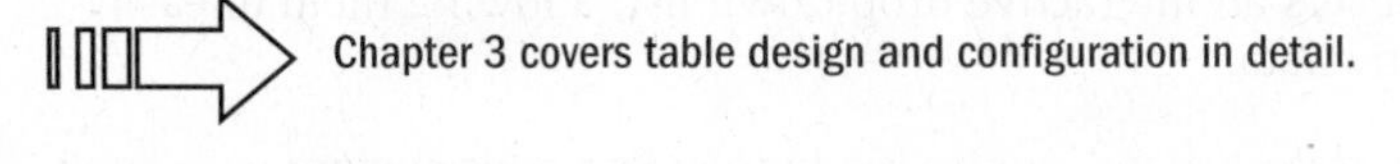

Chapter 3 covers table design and configuration in detail.

35

FIGURE 35.3

Create an AutoNumber field for each table; then set the AutoNumber field as the primary key.

Opportunities

Field Name	Data Type
ID	AutoNumber
Title	Short Text
Customer	Number
Employee	Number
Category	Short Text
How Found	Short Text
Open Date	Date/Time
Est Closed Date	Date/Time
Probability	Number
Est Revenue	Currency
Closed	Yes/No
Comments	Long Text

Another step you can take to prepare your data model is to add any lookup fields that will assist your users during data entry. Figure 35.4 illustrates a lookup field in the Opportunities table that allows a user to select from a list of Companies when entering a new record. This prevents the user from having to remember company names, saving time and avoiding data entry errors.

FIGURE 35.4

Add lookup fields wherever possible, allowing for more effective data entry.

Opportunities

Title	Customer	Employe
r Order for January	DataPig Technologies	Dick Kusleika
rs for New Facility	Azep Corp.	Geoff Clark
ers Purchase	DataPig Technologies	Dick Kusleika
rs for April Opening	PalPoint Inc.	Earl Pierce

Azep Corp.	Duke M. Good
DataPig Technologies	Mike Alexander
PalPoint Inc.	Joey Dough

Chapter 3 of this book covers lookup fields in detail, but as a refresher, look at Figure 35.5. A lookup field is set in the Design view of the table. In this example, the Company field has a lookup that returns the ID, Company, and ContactName from the Customers table. Again, this gives your users an interactive drop-down list, allowing them to easily select and tag correct company data.

Once you've taken these preparatory steps, you're ready to create your custom web application. Now, notice that we haven't created any queries or forms in this starting data model. The data model truly consists of base tables with some rudimentary logic. Access 2013 web applications simply will not accept any more than that initially. However, as you'll see in the next section, you'll be able to add queries, nuanced logic, and other configurations once the web application has been created.

FIGURE 35.5

You can set lookup fields in the Design view of your tables.

Opportunities

Field Name	Data Type	
ID	AutoNumber	
Title	Short Text	
Customer	Number	
Employee	Number	

General | Lookup

Display Control	Combo Box
Row Source Type	Table/Query
Row Source	SELECT ID, Company, ContactName FROM Customers ORDER BY Company;
Bound Column	1
Column Count	3
Column Heads	No
Column Widths	0";1.5";1.5"
List Rows	16
List Width	1"

Initializing and configuring the custom web application

Now that you have a starting data model, it's time to create the custom web application:

1. **Open Access 2013 via the Windows Start button (Start⇨Programs⇨Access 2013).** You'll see the default welcome screen shown in Figure 35.6.
2. **Click the Custom Web App button.** The Custom Web App dialog box appears.

FIGURE 35.6

Start Access 2013 via the Windows Start button, and press the Custom Web App button.

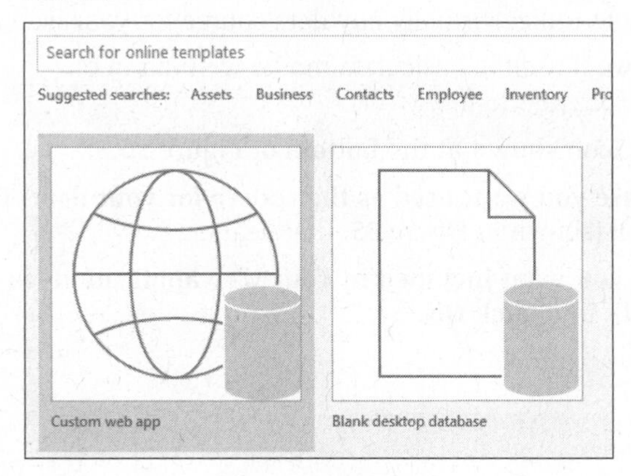

3. **Enter a name for your application and the URL for the target SharePoint site (see Figure 35.7), and click Create.**

4. **When prompted, enter your username and password.** Access caches this information for future use and doesn't ask for them again unless they change.

FIGURE 35.7

Enter a name for your application and the URL for the target SharePoint site.

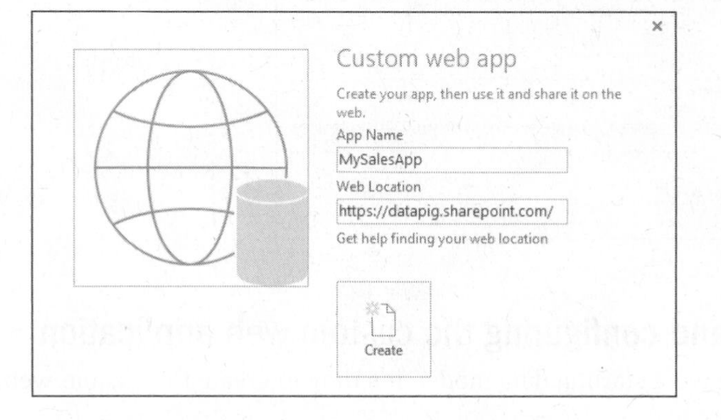

After a bit of gyrating, SharePoint creates an empty web application on the SharePoint site. In Access, you see a new web database similar to the one shown in Figure 35.8.

5. **Here, you need to tell Access which tables you want to use for your web application.** Take a moment to look at the bottom of Figure 35.8. Notice that you have the option of pulling tables in from all kinds of sources: Access, Excel, SQL Server, Other ODBC connections, text files, and even SharePoint lists. This gives you the flexibility to utilize virtually any data source for your web application.

   In this example, we'll use the basic data model we built in our `SalesApplication.accdb` file.

6. **Click the Access icon shown at the bottom of Figure 35.8.**
7. **Select the database you want used as the source for your data.** The Import Objects dialog box (shown in Figure 35.9) appears.
8. **Select the tables you want included in your web application (in this case, choose Select All), and click OK.**

FIGURE 35.8

Click the Access icon to pull data from the data model in the `SalesApplication.accdb` file.

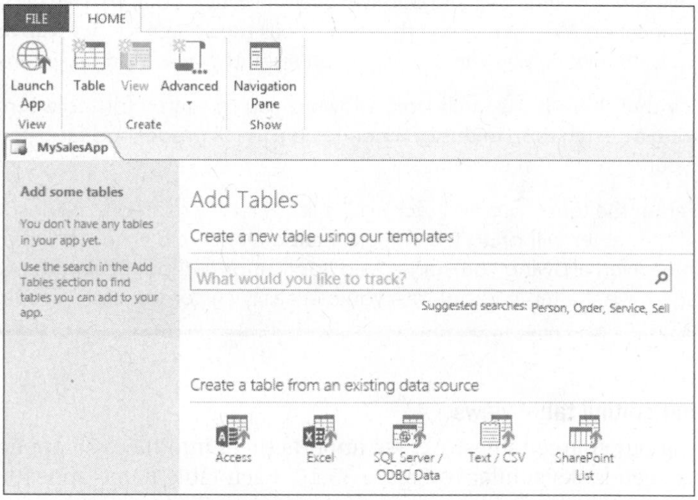

FIGURE 35.9

Select all the tables you want included in your web application.

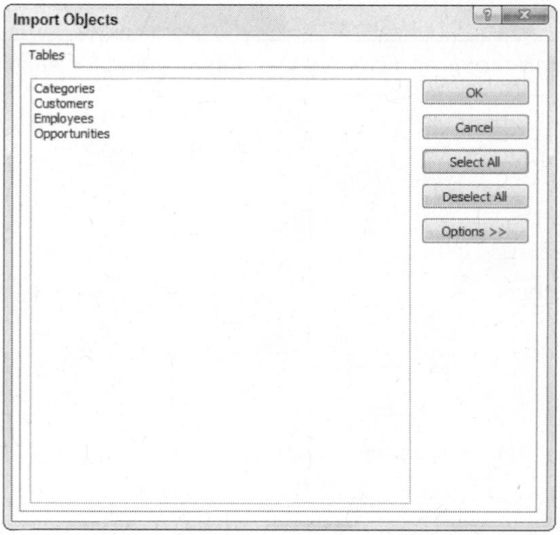

A Word about Table Templates

In this walkthrough, we took the time to build our own custom data model, which includes the tables we need for our sales application. We then chose those tables as the source for our web application. But if you don't want to do all that work, you can use Microsoft's set of predefined table templates.

In Figure 35.8, notice that there is a search box, allowing you to search for table templates from the Microsoft site. Entering a search term in this box brings up a list of predefined table templates that you can use in place of your own custom data model.

For example, if you enter the term "project tracking," a list of tables related to project tracking will pop up. Selecting one of the tables will bring the selected table along with other tables related to project tracking. This is a time-saver, allowing you start a web application without having to build out your own data model. Once you have the table templates, you can easily customize them to suit your needs.

Reviewing and editing table views

After selecting our source tables, Access imports them into the web application. At this point, your screen looks similar to Figure 35.10. Each table name appears on the left of the screen with a set of views in the middle of the screen. Clicking the Navigation Pane button on the Ribbon will activate the familiar-looking Navigation pane you're used to seeing in a standard Access database.

FIGURE 35.10

Access imports all the selected tables and creates two default views for each table.

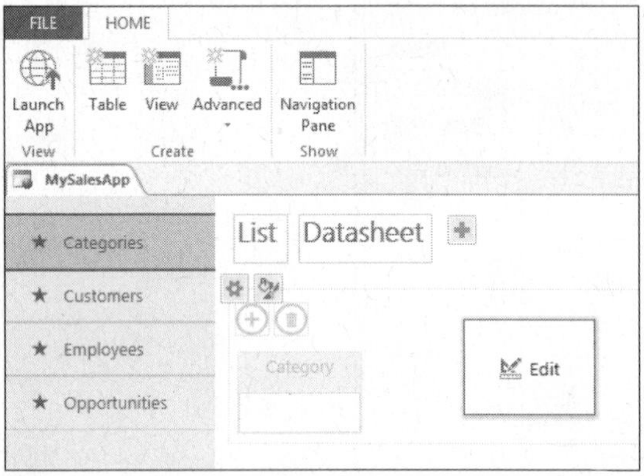

Each table will have two default views associated with it: a List view and a Datasheet view. Clicking the List view for a table allows you to view and edit each field in the table in a form (see Figure 35.11). That's right — Access automatically created a form for each table. In fact, you'll find the design and layout of the automatically created forms to be surprisingly good. Nevertheless, you can edit the form if you want.

Clicking the Datasheet view for a table allows you to view and edit each field in a datasheet format. Again, you can edit the view to add or remove fields as needed.

FIGURE 35.11

Access automatically creates a form for each table in a List view.

Some of the tables in your data model are there simply as reference tables, not to be shown to the public. In Figure 35.12, the Categories table is not something we want the users of our application to see. In this case, we can hide that table by selecting the table and selecting the gear icon to reveal the Hide command. This ensures that our users are not able to view or edit this table.

FIGURE 35.12

You can hide tables you don't want to be viewed or edited by your users.

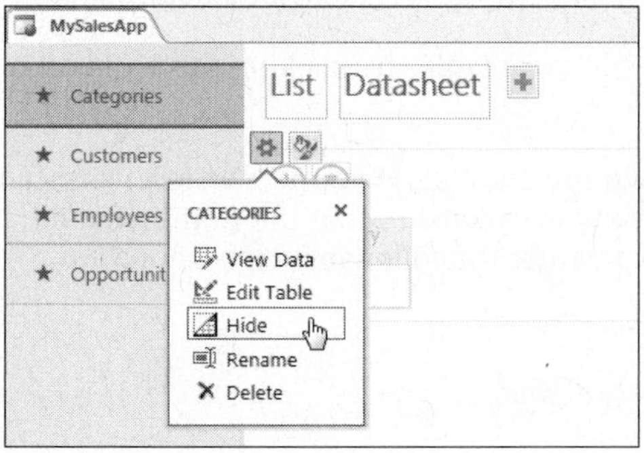

After a table is set to be hidden, it will have a perforated border around it and it will be given a lighter, subdued color. This way, you can tell it's hidden from the public.

Adding a validation rule to a table

At this point, you'll want to add any rules or logic to make your application more than just a few simple tables. To do so, you'll need to edit each table individually. Select the target table and click the gear icon to reveal the Edit Table option (see Figure 35.13).

FIGURE 35.13

Choose to edit the Customers table.

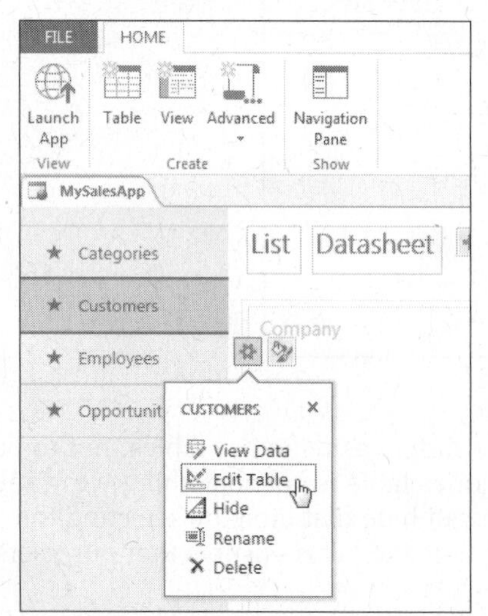

In Figure 35.14, you'll see the Customers table in Design View. When users enter a new customer into the Customers form, we want to ensure that they can't save the record without entering values in the Company field and the ContactName field.

Access allows you to add validation rules to your tables by clicking the Validation Rule command on the Ribbon.

The Expression Builder dialog box (shown in Figure 35.15) appears. Here, you can enter any expression you want. In this case, we want to ensure that the Company and ContactName fields are not null, so we can enter the following expression:

```
Coalesce([Company], [ContactName]) IS NOT NULL
```

FIGURE 35.14

Add a new validation rule to the Customers table.

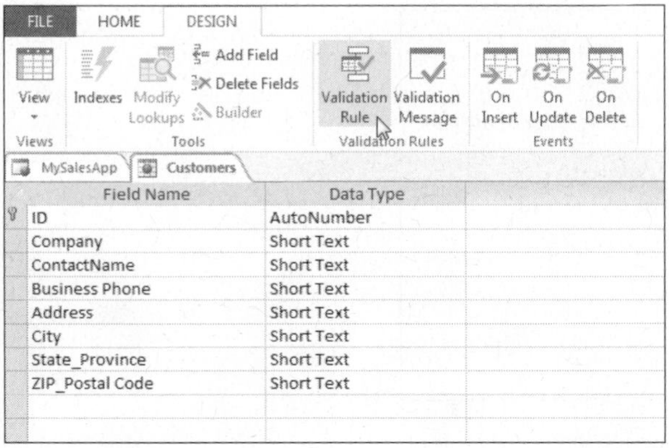

FIGURE 35.15

Enter the desired validation rule in the form of an expression. This expression ensures that the Company and ContactName fields are not left blank.

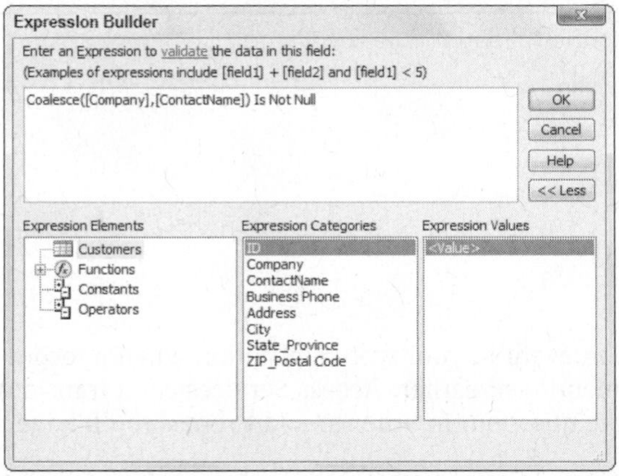

> **NOTE**
>
> The Coalesce function is a SQL function that returns the first non-null expression among its arguments. We are using it here to validate that neither the CustomerName nor the Company field is blank.

Once we confirm the expression, we can click the Validation Message command (shown in Figure 35.16) to enter a message to our users.

FIGURE 35.16

Click the Validation Message command.

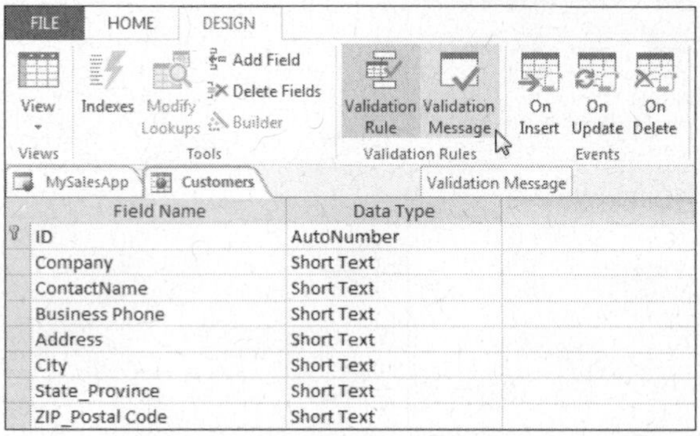

In the Enter Validation Message dialog box (shown in Figure 35.17), we want to enter the message that the users will see when they violate our newly created validation rule.

FIGURE 35.17

Enter a message that will show when the validation rule is violated.

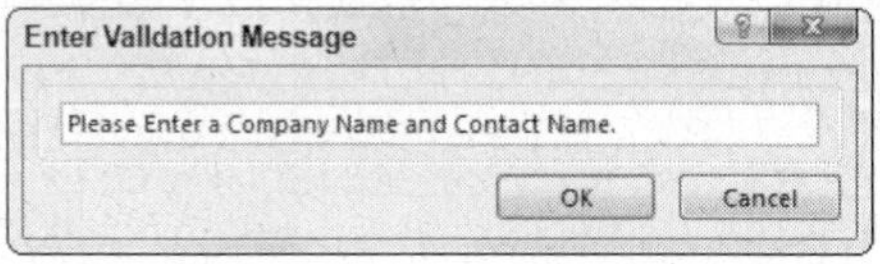

Adding events to a table

Sometimes, you'll want to trigger an event in your web application when a record is inserted, updated, or deleted. As mentioned earlier, Access Services can't translate VBA into JavaScript, so VBA is out of the question. In order to add events, you'll have to use data macros.

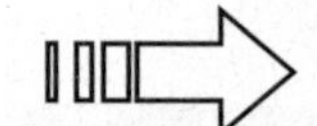

The topic of how to create and configure data macros is discussed in Chapter 22 of this book.

To illustrate how to utilize events, let's add an event to our Opportunities table.

In our custom web application, we have a table where users can enter new sales opportunities. When entering a new sales opportunity, users will have to provide an estimated revenue value and a probability percent. We'll want to fire an event when either of those fields doesn't conform to what the application needs.

First select the Opportunities table and click the gear icon to reveal the Edit Table option. After clicking Edit Table, you see the Opportunities table in Design view (see Figure 35.18). Here, click the On Insert command in the Events group.

FIGURE 35.18

The Events group shown while in Design view allows you to add data macros that fire On Insert, On Update, and On Delete.

Field Name	Data Type
ID	AutoNumber
Title	Short Text
Customer	Lookup
Employee	Lookup
Category	Short Text
How Found	Lookup
Open Date	Date/Time
Est Closed Date	Date/Time
Probability	Number
Est Revenue	Currency
Closed	Yes/No
Comments	Long Text

Access activates the Macros window, where you can build the inner workings of your data macro. As you can see in Figure 35.19, we'll trigger an error message if the Est Event field is less than 0 or if the Probability field is not between 0 and 1.

FIGURE 35.19

Use the Macros window to add the logic for your event.

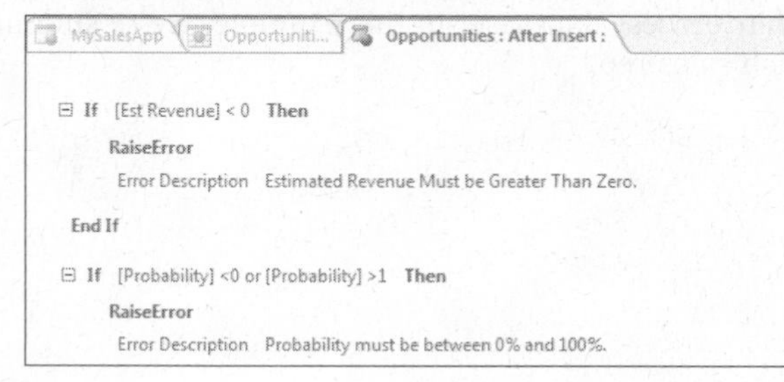

Creating your own queries and views

As mentioned before, Access will start you off with two default views for each table in your web application: a List view and a Datasheet view. You can extend the functionality of your application by adding your own views based on custom queries.

Start by selecting the Advanced drop-down list and selecting Query (see Figure 35.20).

FIGURE 35.20

Select the Advanced drop-down list, and select Query.

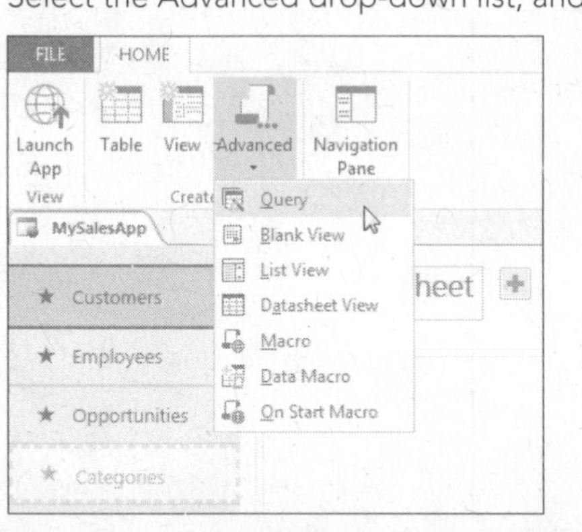

NOTE

Note that in Figure 35.20 you can choose to create your own List view, Datasheet view, or even Blank view. When you choose any one of these options, Access presents you with a list of fields you can add to your new view. Simply choose the fields you want included and start building.

When you choose Query from the Advanced drop-down list, Access activates the familiar Query Builder. As you can see in Figure 35.21, building a query in a web application is similar to building one in a standard Access database. In this example, we're summarizing the open opportunity sales for each sales rep.

FIGURE 35.21

Build your query in the same fashion you would in a standard Access database.

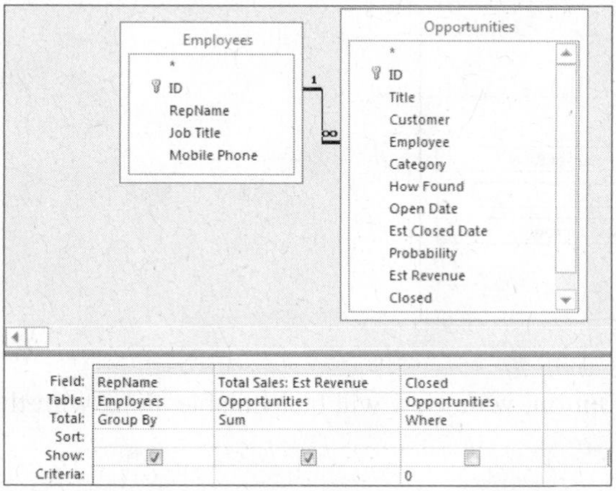

After you save your query with a name (SalesSummary in this case), Access shows you the results (see Figure 35.22).

FIGURE 35.22

Save your query with a name and view the results.

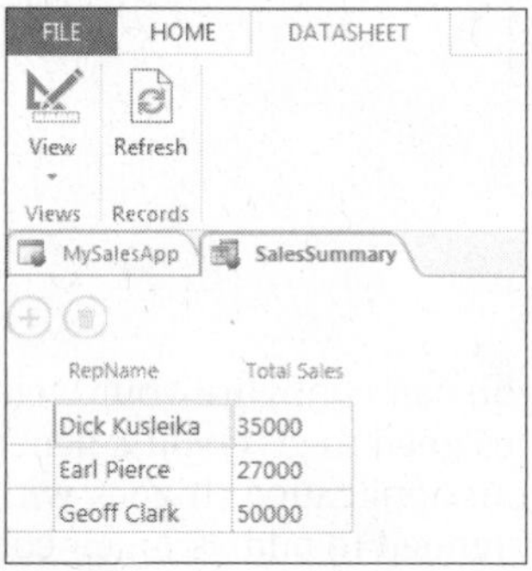

Now it's time to create a new view from the query. Select any table used in the query, and then click the plus icon. The dialog box shown in Figure 35.23 appears. Here, provide a name for your new view, select a view type (List or Datasheet), and then choose your query as the data source for the view.

FIGURE 35.23

Start a new view by clicking the plus icon and fill in the required attributes.

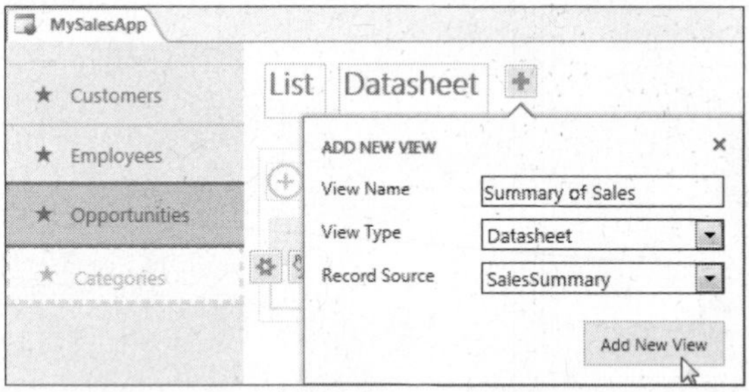

After clicking the Add New View button, your view will be available along with the default views (see Figure 35.24).

FIGURE 35.24

Any new views will show next to the default views.

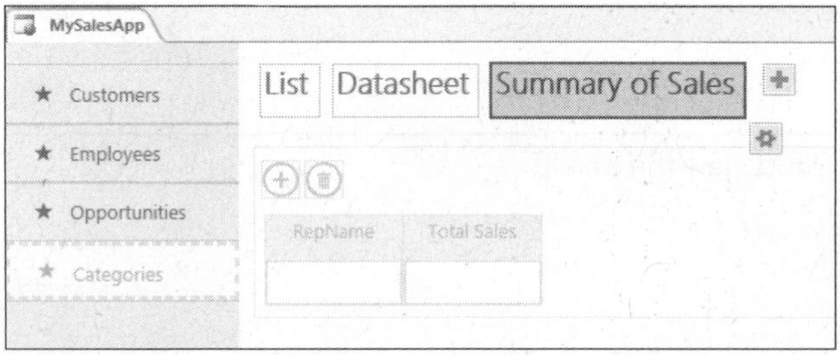

A final word on configuring your web application

In this section, we quickly looked at the various ways you can configure your web application. Obviously, the basic scenarios shown here are designed to give you a general overview of the tools Access has provided for configuring your application. It goes without saying that these fundamental building blocks can be extended to add as much complexity as you need to your web application.

The key concept you should take away is that configuration of an Access 2013 web application is done after a web application has been created. Many Access developers approach web applications with the notion that they can take their existing database and simply make it web-enabled. Unfortunately, it doesn't work that way in Access 2013.

You start a web application with nothing more than tables that have a basic relationship schema. All the logic, rules, and events are built within the web application environment.

Launching and managing your web application

Once you've completed the configuration of your web application, you can click the Launch App command (as shown in Figure 35.25). Enter your username and password if asked to do so.

FIGURE 35.25

Launch your web application.

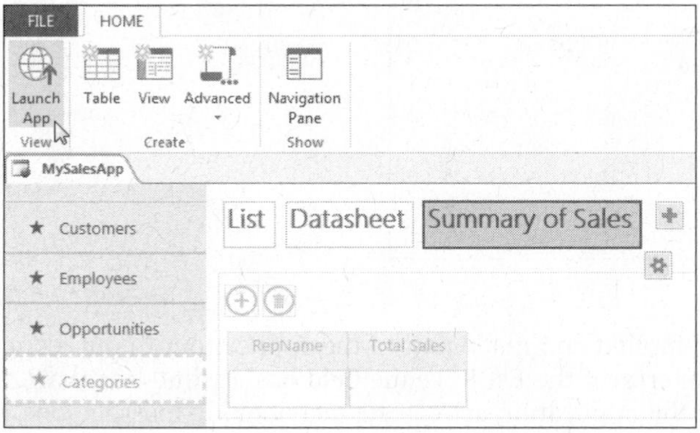

Your web application will show through a SharePoint screen, with easy navigation and filtering options built in (see Figure 35.26).

FIGURE 35.26

Your web application will be displayed via a SharePoint portal.

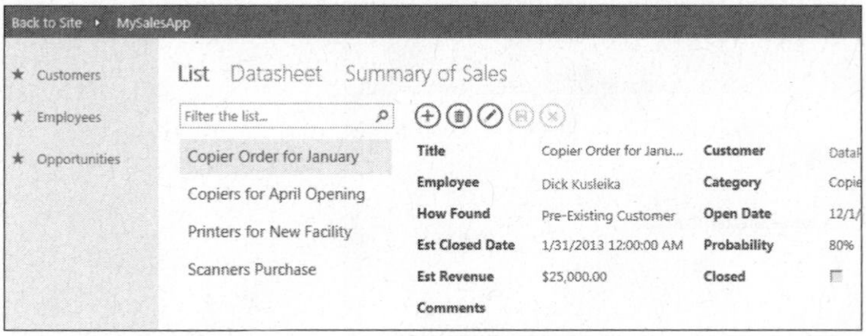

SharePoint and Access Services do a nice job of making your web application look professional. For example, in Figure 35.27, you can see that any date field comes with a visually appealing calendar selector.

FIGURE 35.27

SharePoint and Access Services automatically add nice touches to your web application.

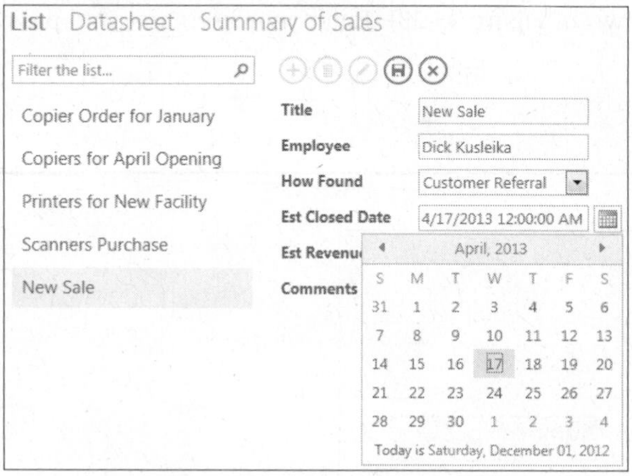

FIGURE 35.28

Any events you added are compiled and made part of the application. In our example, we added an event that raises an error if the Est Revenue field has a value less than zero. As you can see in Figure 35.28, the application activates a nice-looking message box based on our event.

FIGURE 35.28

Any event built into the web application is triggered as designed.

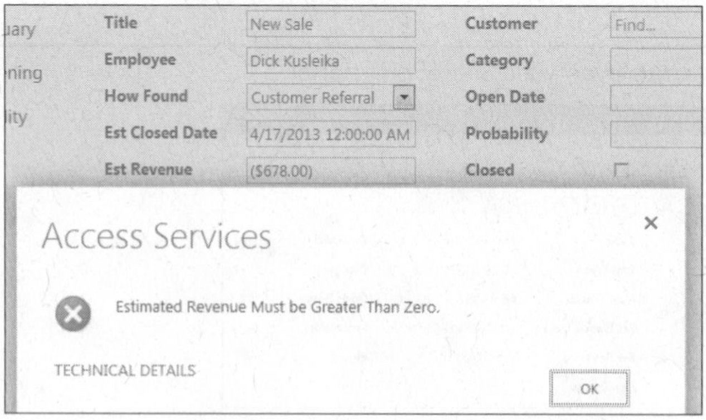

And because we created our application with properly formed table relationships, Access services is able to automatically add useful hierarchical views for our users. In Figure 35.29, you can see that when DataPig Technologies is selected from the Customers table, a list of existing opportunities from the Opportunities table is also shown.

FIGURE 35.29

Useful hierarchical views are automatically created based on table relationships.

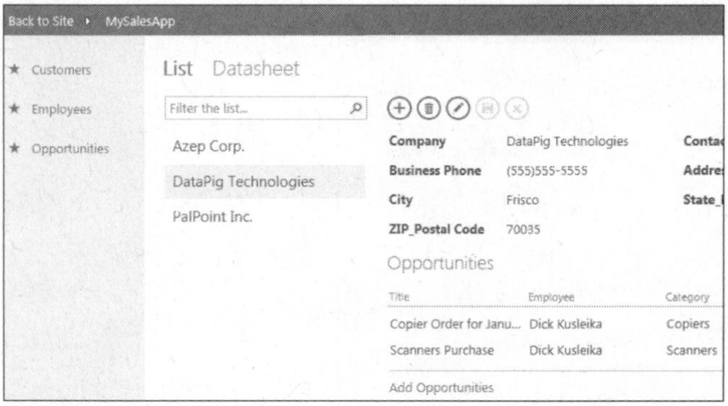

Our custom-made view is also available, automatically including any new data that has been entered (see Figure 35.30).

FIGURE 35.30

Custom-made views dynamically keep up with the data in the web application.

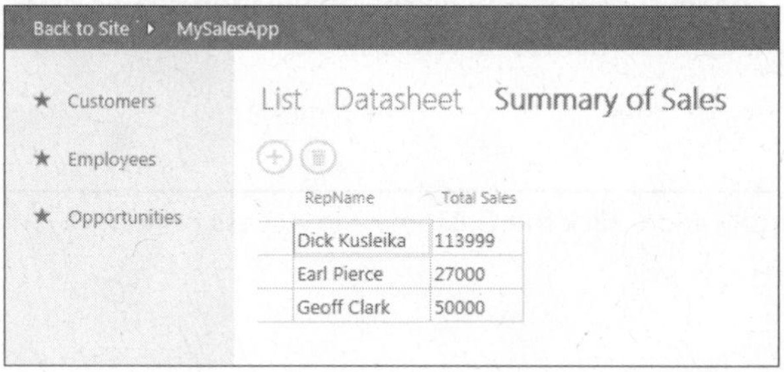

Right-clicking any Datasheet view through SharePoint portal allows the user to export the table to a local Excel spreadsheet (see Figure 35.31).

FIGURE 35.31

Exporting data to Excel is as easy as right-clicking any Datasheet view.

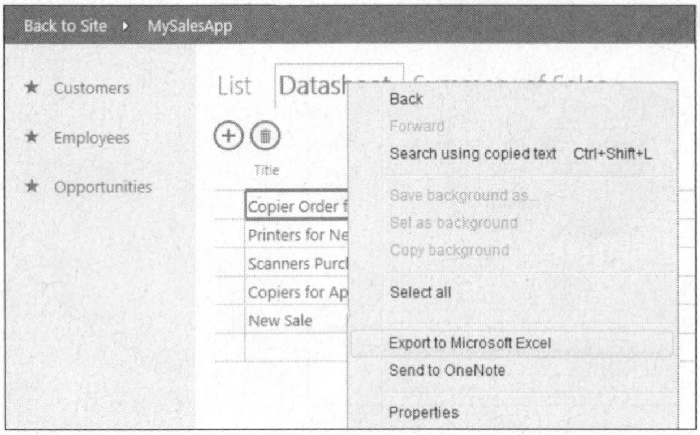

If you need to make changes to your web application, simply click the gear icon located at the top right of your application. Then click the Customize in Access option shown in Figure 35.32. An ACCDW database file, which can be opened and edited with Access 2013, is downloaded. Note that not all users will see the gear icon. You must have publishing permissions (set by the SharePoint Administrator) to choose this action.

Once you make the necessary changes, simply launch the application again. Users will seamlessly get any changes you make to the ACCDW database.

FIGURE 35.32

To make changes to the web application, click the Customize in Access option.

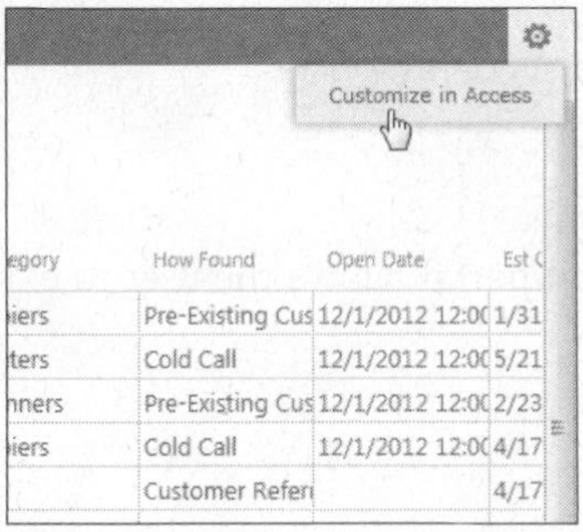

You can view and manage all your web applications via SharePoint. Clicking the three dots next to each application will activate a dialog box (shown in Figure 35.33) that gives you the ability to view usage logs, manage permissions for your application, and remove the application.

FIGURE 35.33

SharePoint allows administrators and publishers to view all the applications on the site, view logs, manage permissions, and remove applications.

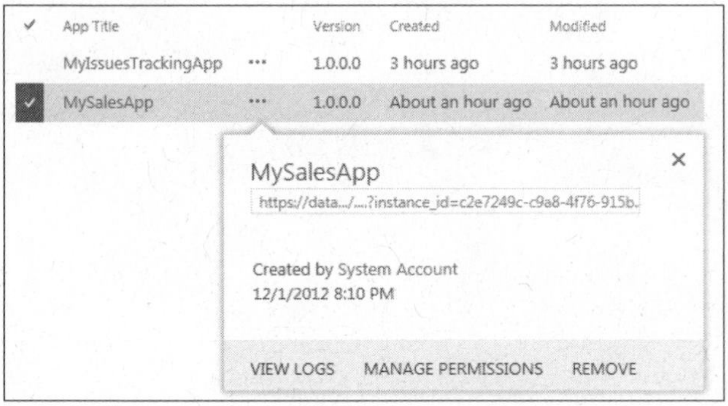

CHAPTER 36

Using Access Data Macros

IN THIS CHAPTER

Creating data macros

Understanding table events

Building data macros

Understanding data macro limitations

Beginning with Access 2007, macros have played a more significant role in many Access applications. For a very long time, macros were considered the poor cousins of VBA statements. Although in many ways VBA and macros were equivalent in their capabilities, macros have always been considered inferior to VBA for handling an application's logic.

The problems with traditional Access macros were considerable:

- **Macros existed as separate database objects, so keeping track of the macros in effect on a particular form was often difficult.** Because there was no direct connection between a form (or a report, for that matter) and a macro, it was easy to break the macro by deleting or renaming it. VBA code encapsulated within the form's code module never had this problem.
- **There was no way to trap or handle errors in macros.** In versions of Access prior to 2007, macros would simply stop running and display an error dialog box if something unexpected happened. These interruptions were not welcomed by users, particularly because there was, most often, nothing a user could do to correct the problem or prevent it from happening again. VBA code has always featured strong error handling and could often provide a default value or instruct the user what to do in the event of a problem.
- **Macros were unable to work with code.** There was no way for a macro to loop through a recordset, for example, to sum field values or detect out-of-range data. VBA code is well-suited for data management tasks and includes all the looping constructs necessary to iterate over recordsets.

In Access 2013, those concerns are all but a distant memory. Macros now offer error handling and temporary variables during a macro's execution. Access 2013 also offers embedded macros. As discussed in Chapter 22, embedded macros eliminate the objection that macros were always external to the form or report they serviced. Chapter 22 also demonstrates that macros in Access 2013 allow for looping and trapping errors.

This chapter specifically covers data macros, which add yet another reason macros in Access 2013 are a more attractive option than ever before.

On the Web

The starting database for this walkthrough, `Chapter36.accdb`, can be downloaded from this book's website.

If you haven't done so, you'll want to explore Chapter 22. There, you'll get the foundation needed to better understand the terms and features you'll see in this chapter.

Introducing Data Macros

A data macro is logic you attach to a table to enforce business rules at the table level. In some ways, a data macro is similar to a validation rule, except that a validation rule is rather unintelligent. Validation rules can't modify data or determine whether corrective action is needed. Data macros are specifically provided to allow you to manage data-oriented activity at the table level.

Most often, data macros are used to enforce business rules — such as a value can't be less than some threshold — or to perform data transformation during data entry. The real value of data macros is that they're in effect wherever a table's data is used, even in web applications that run on SharePoint. That's right, data macros work in both desktop and web applications.

Because data macros work in SharePoint environments, they're especially useful in Access web applications. For example, if a data macro is attached to a sales table in your web application, anytime the sales data is displayed on a web form the data macro is at work, watching for changes to the data and automatically controlling what happens to the table's data.

Data macros are intended to make it easier to ensure consistent data handling throughout your application, even when your application is running on the web. Because data macros are applied at the table level, the exact same action happens each time the table's data is updated. Although the subset of actions available to data macros is considerably smaller than standard macros, when carefully crafted and implemented, data macros are a powerful addition to Access applications.

Note

Data macros are especially handy in split database applications (applications where the tables live in a separate Access file from the forms and reports). Because the macros are attached to the tables, they continue to work even if someone links to the tables in some other way than the designed front-end application.

Understanding Table Events

There are five different macro-programmable table events: `BeforeChange`, `BeforeDelete`, `AfterInsert`, `AfterUpdate`, and `AfterDelete`.

To see these events in the Ribbon, start up the `Chapter36.accdb` database and open tblProducts in Datasheet view. On the Ribbon, you'll see a Table tab. Select that tab and you'll see the events shown in Figure 36.1: `BeforeChange`, `BeforeDelete`, `AfterInsert`, `AfterUpdate`, and `AfterDelete`.

FIGURE 36.1

Every Access table includes five data-oriented events that can be selected when in Datasheet view.

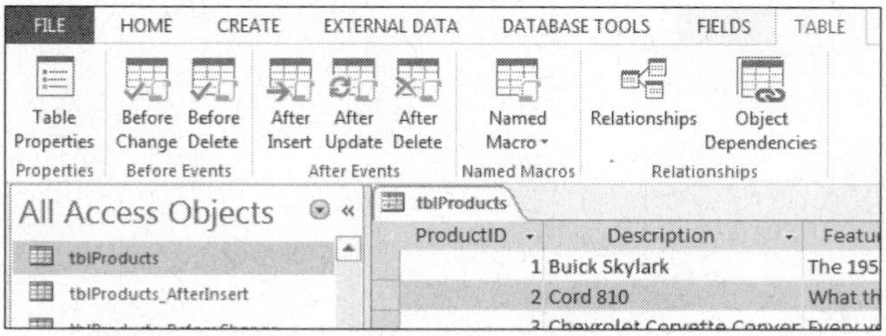

ON THE WEB

The starting database for this chapter, appropriately named `Chapter36.accdb`, can be downloaded from this book's website.

These events are designated as "before" and "after" events. The "before" events occur before changes are made to the table's data, while the "after" events indicate that successful changes have been made.

"Before" events

The "before" events (`BeforeChange` and `BeforeDelete`) are very simple and support only a few macro actions. They support the program flow constructs (`Comment`, `Group`, and `If`) and just the `LookupRecord` data block. The only macro data actions they provide are `ClearMacroError`, `OnError`, `RaiseError`, `SetLocalVar`, and `StopMacro`.

The `BeforeChange` event is similar to the `BeforeUpdate` event attached to forms, reports, and controls. As its name implies, `BeforeChange` fires just before the data in a table is changed by the user, a query, or VBA code.

BeforeChange gives you a chance to look at new values in the current record and make changes if needed. By default, references to a field within a BeforeChange or BeforeDelete data macro automatically refer to the current record.

BeforeChange is an excellent opportunity to validate user input before committing values to a table. A simple example is shown in Figure 36.2. In this case, the default value of the Description field in tblProducts_BeforeChange is set to Description. If the user fails to change the Description field while adding a new record to the table, the BeforeChange event updates the field to "Please provide description."

FIGURE 36.2

Using BeforeChange to update a field.

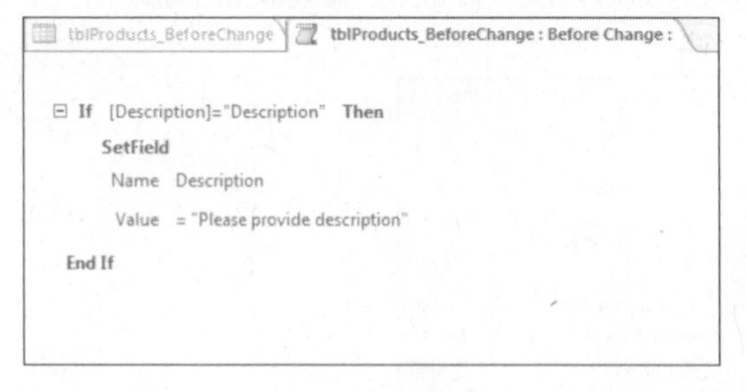

The BeforeChange event can't interrupt the user with a message box or stop the record from updating in the underlying table. All BeforeChange can do is set a field's value or set a local macro variable's value before the record is added or updated in the table.

BeforeChange fires for both updates to existing records and new record insertions into the table. Access provides the IsInsert property that tells the macro whether the current change is the result of inserting a new record or is because a record is being updated.

Figure 36.3 illustrates how IsInsert can be used within an If block to ensure the BeforeChange fired as the result of a new record inserted into the table.

FIGURE 36.3

Using IsInsert to determine if BeforeChange fired as the result of adding a new record.

```
tblProducts_BeforeChange | tblProducts_BeforeChange : Before Change :

If [IsInsert] Then
    If [Description]="Description" Then
        SetField
          Name Description
          Value = "Please provide description"
    End If
End If
```

Figure 36.3 also illustrates that program-flow blocks (like `If`) can be nested. The outer `If` block checks the value of `IsInsert`, while the inner `If` conditionally sets the Description field value.

The `BeforeDelete` event is parallel in almost every regard to `BeforeChange`, so no examples are given here. Use `BeforeDelete` to verify that conditions are appropriate for deletion. As with `BeforeChange`, the `BeforeDelete` event can't prevent a record's deletion, but it can set a local variable or raise an error if conditions warrant.

"After" events

The "after" events (`AfterChange`, `AfterInsert`, and `AfterDelete`) are more robust than their "before" counterparts. Each of these events supports the entire family of data macro actions (`DeleteRecord`, `SetField`, `SendEmail`, and so on), so it's likely that you'll frequently use these events as the basis of your data macros.

Figure 36.4 shows a typical use of the `AfterInsert` event. The `AfterInsert` event fires whenever a new record is added to a table. The new record has already been committed to the table, and `AfterInsert` is used to update a table name tblProductActivityLog.

FIGURE 36.4

Using `AfterInsert` to add a record to tblProductActivityLog.

```
tblProducts_AfterInsert | tblProducts_AfterInsert : After Insert :

⊟ Create a Record In  tblProductActivityLog
    SetField
        Name   tblProductActivityLog.ProductActivity
        Value  = "Insert"
  ⊟ SetField
        Name   tblProductActivityLog.ProductID
        Value  = [tblProducts_AfterInsert].[ProductID]
    SetField
        Name   tblProductActivityLog.ProductDescription
        Value  = [tblProducts_AfterInsert].[Description]
```

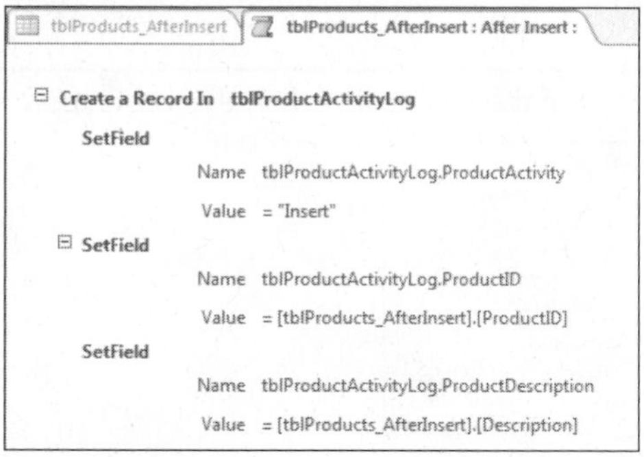

In Figure 36.4, notice that three fields (ProductActivity, ProductID, and ProductDescription) in tblProductActivityLog are being updated as part of a `CreateRecord` data block. The ProductID is an AutoNumber field in tblProducts_AfterInsert. The `CreateRecord` block has already added the record to the table, so the new record's ProductID value is available to this data macro. Therefore, when the `SetField` macro action updates the ProductID field in tblProductActivityLog, the new product record's ID is successfully added to the log table.

The `AfterInsert` data macro runs whenever a record is added to the table. Similar data macros can be added to the table's `AfterUpdate` and `AfterDelete` to log other changes to the table.

The most useful aspect of the "after" events is that they can use the `ForEachRecord` macro block to iterate over recordsets provided by tables or queries. This ability makes these events ideal for scanning a table for consistency, adding a record to a log table, or performing some other compute-intensive updates.

Using the Macro Designer for Data Macros

Data macros use the same macro editor used to create embedded and user interface macros. Once you master the macro editor, you'll use it for all macro development and macro management. The primary difference is that the action catalog (described later in this section) contains different actions, depending on the context.

Adding data macros to a table is quite easy. In fact, an Access table doesn't even have to be in Design view — you can add data macros to a table displayed as a datasheet, if you like. The data macros you construct for a table are in effect immediately, so you can easily work on a macro and observe how well the macro works without compiling or switching between Design view and Datasheet view.

In the `Chapter36.accdb` database, start by opening tblProducts in Datasheet view. On the Ribbon, you'll see a Table tab. Selecting that tab will expose the events seen in Figure 36.5.

FIGURE 36.5

To open the Macro Designer, double-click any of the events listed on the Table tab.

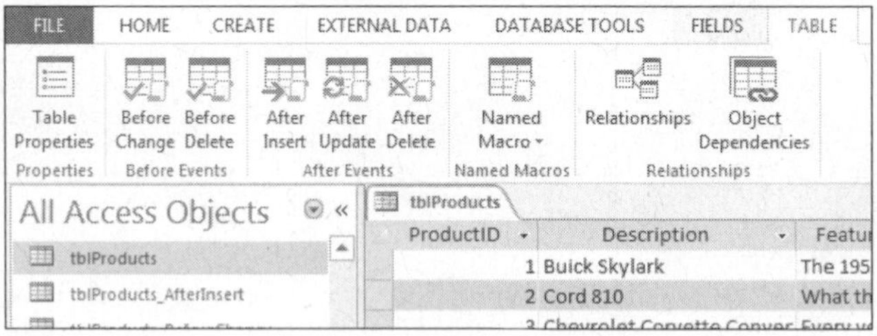

Double-click the After Update command to open the Macro Designer (shown in Figure 36.6). Initially, at least, there's not much to look at.

The large blank area to the left is the macro design area. This is where you place macro actions. On the right side is the Action Catalog, a hierarchical list of all macro actions currently available. The only indication of which table event is being programmed is in the main Access window caption and in the tab above the macro design area.

FIGURE 36.6

The Macro Designer for the table's AfterUpdate event.

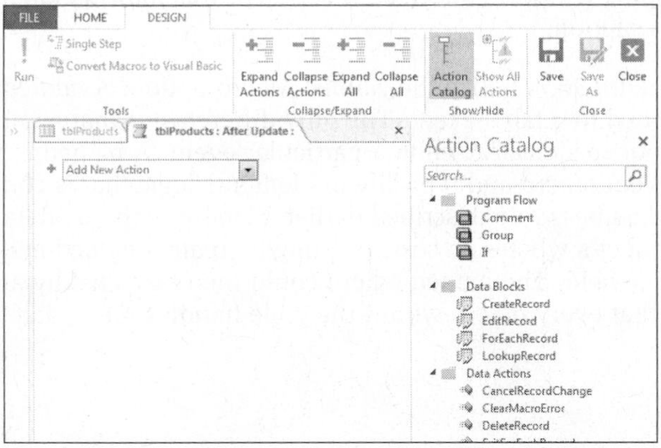

With a macro open in the design area, the Ribbon contains several tools you use when working with the macro. Notice that you can collapse or expand macro sections, save the macro currently under construction, and close the Macro Designer.

You'll notice that the Ribbon you see in Figure 36.6 is exactly the same seen when working with embedded or standard macros. However, some options are not available to you. All the items in the Tools group, for example, are grayed out. This is because data macros don't provide the option of single-stepping through macro actions or converting to VBA code. Data macros are intended to be relatively simple, short, and to the point, rather than large and complex.

Incidentally, if your table is in Design view, you can get to the data macro designer by selecting the Create Data Macros command from the Design tab (see Figure 36.7).

FIGURE 36.7

Selecting a table event when a table is in Design view.

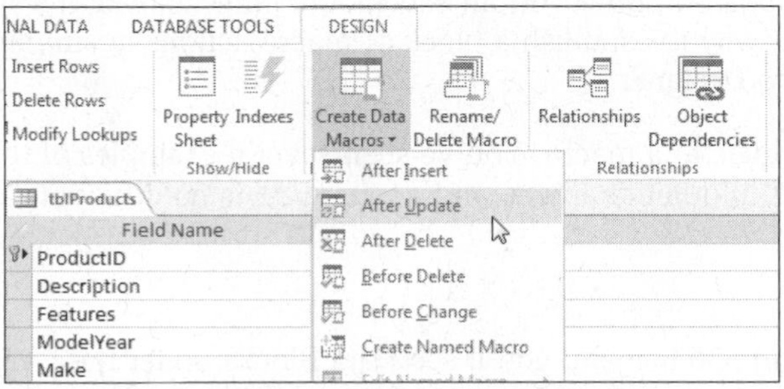

In either case, the Macro Designer opens as shown in Figure 36.6. When the Access tabbed interface is used, the table's name and selected event appear in the Macro Designer's tab. If the overlapping windows interface is selected, this information appears in the Access main window's caption.

In Figure 36.5 and again in Figure 36.7, notice the Named Macro option. A *named macro* is just like a data macro attached to a table event. The only difference is that a named macro is "free floating" and not specifically tied to a particular event. A named macro is meant to be called from an event macro and typically implements logic that is common to a table's fields. Consider the business rule described earlier. If more than one data macro in a table might change a product's wholesale cost, you might create a named macro to handle updating the RetailPrice field. The named macro could then be called by any of the table's other data macros so that every macro within the table handles the update in the same way.

Understanding the Action Catalog

The Action Catalog on the right side of the Macro Designer serves as the repository of macro actions you add to your data macros. The contents of the Action Catalog depend entirely on which table event has been selected, so its appearance varies considerably while you work with Access macros.

Program flow

At the top of the Action Catalog in Figure 36.6 are certain program flow constructs you apply to your macros. When working with data macros, the only program flow constructs available are comments, groups, and `If` blocks.

Comments help document your macros and should be used if the macro's logic is not easily understood. Macro comments are not executable — they're there simply to provide some text describing the goings-on in the macro.

A group (also called a *macro group*) provides a way to wrap a number of macro actions as a named entity. The group can be independently collapsed, copied, and moved around within a macro. A macro group is not, however, an executable unit. Instead, it's simply meant to provide a convenient way to establish a block of macro actions to simplify your view of the macro in the Macro Designer.

The `If` block adds branching logic to a macro. You've seen several examples of the VBA `If...Then...Else` construct in other chapters, and a macro `If` is no different.

Data blocks

If you go back and look at Figure 36.6 again, you'll see Data Blocks under the Program Flow constructs. Each of the data block constructs includes an area for adding one or more macro actions. A data block construct performs all the macro actions as part of its operation. In other words, you typically set up the data block you want to perform (for example, `EditRecord`) and then add the actions you want to execute as part of the block.

Data blocks may also be nested. You could, for example, set up a `ForEachRecord` and then run the `CreateRecord` block, adding records to another table with data contained in the records returned by the `ForEachRecord`.

The data blocks macro actions are:

- `CreateRecord`: The `CreateRecord` action provides a way to add a record to the current table (which is rarely done) or to another table (which is more typical). An example of using `CreateRecord` is building a log of all changes to the Products table (similar to Figure 36.4). The `CreateRecord` macro action can add a new record to a table, populating fields in the record with data passed from the current table. The reason `CreateRecord` is not often used to add a record to the current table is that recursion can occur. Adding a new record to the current table triggers events such as `AfterInsert` (described in the "'After' events" section, earlier in this chapter), which may run the `CreateRecord` action again and again.
- `EditRecord`: As its name implies, `EditRecord` provides a way to change the content of an existing record in the current, or another, table. `EditRecord` is ideal for situations such as adjusting inventory levels when a product is sold or returned or calculating sales tax or shipping costs when the quantity field has been provided.
- `ForEachRecord`: The `ForEachRecord` action is a looping construct. Given the name of a table or query, `ForEachRecord` can perform an operation on every record in the recordset. The action can be an update using the `SetField` action (described in the next section), can copy data, or can perform a mathematical operation on the data in the recordset. The `ForEachRecord` block has a macro action included within the block to make it easy to specify the action you want this block to perform. And you can stack multiple macro actions within the `ForEachBlock` to perform more-complex operations.
- `LookupRecord`: The `LookupRecord` action is quite simple and easy to understand. `LookupRecord` returns a record found in a table and provides a macro action area for specifying the actions you want to perform on the returned record.

NOTE

The `CreateRecord`, `EditRecord`, and `ForEachRecord` blocks will only be available when you're building "after" macro events. This means they'll only be available when creating `AfterInsert`, `AfterUpdate`, and `AfterDelete` data macros. The "before" events are meant to be very fast and lightweight, so they don't provide for CPU-intensive operations such as adding or editing new records.

Data actions

The next group of actions in the Action Catalog is the Data actions; these are the *actions* a data macro can take. You've already read that a data macro consists of one or more actions that are executed as a single unit in response to a table event. You need a good understanding of the variety of macro actions available to data macros.

Here are the data macro actions:

> **NOTE**
>
> **Not all these actions are available to every table event. `BeforeChange` and `BeforeDelete` (described in the "'Before' events" section, earlier in this chapter) support only a subset of these actions because many actions are computationally intensive (such as updating or adding records), and the "before" events are meant to be very fast and lightweight.**

- `DeleteRecord`: As its name implies, `DeleteRecord` deletes a record in a table (without confirmation from the user). Obviously, `DeleteRecord` must be used carefully to prevent deleting valuable data from the application. A typical use of `DeleteRecord` would be as part of an archiving operation, where data in a table is copied into another table (perhaps a linked SQL Server table) and then deleted from the current table.
- `CancelRecordChange`: `EditRecord` and `CreateRecord` both make irrevocable changes to a record. `CancelRecordChange`, in conjunction with an `If` block, allows a data macro to cancel the changes made by `EditRecord` and `CreateRecord` before the changes are committed to the database.
- `ExitForEachRecord`: The `ForEachRecord` loops through a recordset returned from a table or query, enabling the data macro to make changes to the recordset's data or scan the data for "interesting" values. There are many situations where a data macro may need to escape from a `ForEachRecord` loop before it has run to the end of its recordset. For example, consider a data macro that searches for a certain value in a table, and once the value is found, there is no need to continue the loop. The `ExitForEachRecord` is typically executed as part of an `If` block (also discussed in the next section) and is executed only when a certain condition is true.
- `LogEvent`: Every Access 2013 application includes a hidden USysApplicationLog table (this table is hidden by virtue of the USys prefix in its name). USysApplicationLog is used to record data macro errors and can be used to log other information as well. The `LogEvent` macro action is specifically designed to add a record to USysApplicationLog anytime you want from a data macro. The only field in USysApplicationLog that can be written using `LogEvent` is Description, a memo type field. The other fields in USysApplicationLog (Category, Context, DataMacroInstanceID, ErrorNumber, ObjectType, and SourceObject) are provided by the macro itself.

- SendEmail: This macro action, obviously, sends an e-mail using the default Windows e-mailer (usually Outlook). The arguments for SendEmail are To, CC, BCC, Subject, and Body. SendEmail is quite useful in certain situations, such as automatically dispatching an e-mail when an error condition occurs, or when a product's inventory level falls below some threshold.
- SetField: The SetField action updates the value of a field in a table. The arguments to SetField include the table and field names and the new value to assign to the field. SetField is not available to BeforeChange and BeforeDelete table events.
- SetLocalVar: Access 2013 macros are able to use local variables for passing values from one part of a macro to another. For example, you might have a macro that looks up a value in a table and passes the value as a variable to the next macro action. SetLocalVar is an all-purpose variable declaration and assignment action that creates a variable and assigns a value to it.
- StopMacro: The StopMacro action interrupts the currently executing macro, causing it to terminate and exit. Most often used in conjunction with an If data block, or in the destination of an OnError macro action, there are no arguments to StopMacro.
- StopAllMacros: This macro action is parallel to StopMacro, except that it applies to all currently executing macros. Macros may run asynchronously because table events might launch multiple macros at one time, or a macro might call a named macro as part of its execution.
- RunDataMacro: This macro action is very simple. Its only argument is the name of some other data macro that Access runs. RunDataMacro is useful in situations where a certain data macro performs some task that another data macro finds useful. Instead of duplicating the macro's actions, it's simpler just to call the macro and allow it to perform its actions as a single operation.
- OnError: The OnError macro action is the heart of Access macro error handling. OnError is a directive that tells Access what to do in the event an error occurs during a macro's execution. The first argument (GoTo) is required and is set to either Next, Macro Name, or Fail. Next directs Access to simply ignore the error and continue execution at the macro action following the action that caused the error.

  Unless another OnError is positioned within the data macro, OnError GoTo Next tells Access to ignore all errors in the data macro and continue execution regardless of whatever errors occur. The Macro Name directive names a macro you want to jump to in the event of an error. The destination of Macro Name is a named macro, which is just a collection of macro actions not attached to a table event. The Macro Name destination could be a named macro within the current table or in another table.

- `RaiseError`: The `RaiseError` macro action passes an error up to the user interface layer. An example is using `RaiseError` on a `BeforeChange` event to validate data before it's committed to the database. `RaiseError` passes an error number and description to the application, adding the error details to `USysApplicationLog`.
- `ClearMacroError`: Once an error has been handled by running the `RaiseError` macro action or redirecting execution to a named macro, `ClearMacroError` resets `MacroError`, the macro error object, and prepares Access for the next error.

Creating Your First Data Macro

Now that you have some orientation on the macro designer and the action catalog, it's time to create your first data macro.

For this walk-through, let's assume that your company uses a standard markup of 66.66 percent on its products. This means that a product's wholesale cost is multiplied by 1.6666 to yield the default selling price of an item. Your company has found that a 66.66 percent markup provides the margin necessary for you to offer volume discounts, special sales, and significant discounts to selected buyers while remaining profitable.

The problem to be solved with a data macro is updating the retail price of a product anytime the product's cost is changed. Although this could be done quite easily with code or a macro behind Access forms, consider the issue if there were dozens of different forms where the product's cost might be changed. The same code or macro would have to be added in many different places, contributing to development and maintenance costs. Also, there is always the chance that one or more forms would not be updated should your company ever decide on a different approach for setting the default retail price of its products.

Using a data macro attached directly to the Products table, for example, simplifies development and maintenance of the application's forms and reports. Because the business rule (multiplying cost by 1.6666) is enforced at the data layer, every form, report, and query using the Products data benefits from the data macro.

On the Web

If you haven't done so already, open the database for this walkthrough, `Chapter36.accdb`, which can be downloaded from this book's website.

1. **Open the tblProducts table in Datasheet view.**
2. **Select the Table tab on the Ribbon, and choose the BeforeChange event.** At this point, Access will activate the macro designer.

3. **Double-click or drag the Group program flow action onto the macro's design surface.** Here, you're creating a new macro group. Give the macro group a name as shown in Figure 36.8.

FIGURE 36.8

Add a Group to the macro and give it a name.

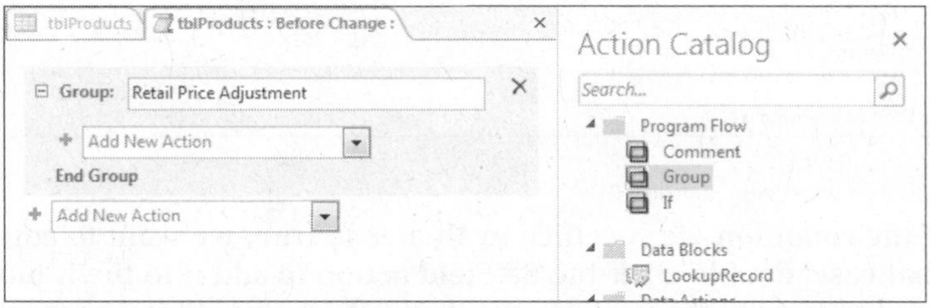

4. **While in the newly created group, double-click the Comment program flow action to place a comment onto the macro's design surface.** With this comment, enter some friendly text describing what you're doing here (see Figure 36.9).

FIGURE 36.9

Add a Comment describing the actions taken in this macro.

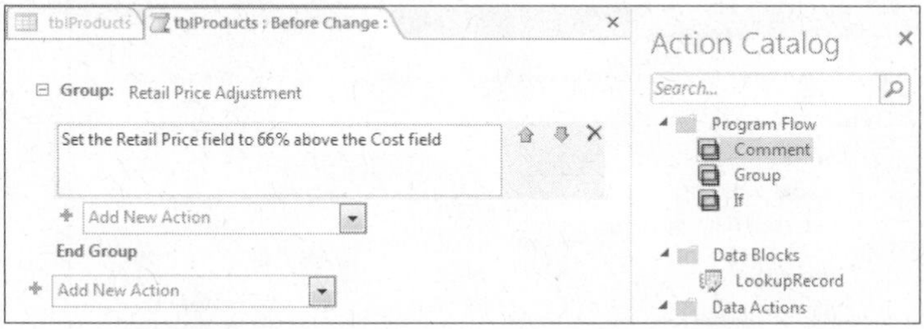

5. **Now double-click the If program flow action to place a new logic check onto the macro's design surface.** As you can see in Figure 36.10, you're evaluating the Cost field to ensure the value is greater than zero. This check will ensure the rest of the macro only triggers if the conditions you specified are met.

NOTE

You'll notice that in the lower-right corner of the `If` block there are options to add an `Else` or an `Else If` to the `If` block. You can use these options to extend the `If` block to include other conditions you want to check as part of the same `If` block.

FIGURE 36.10

The `If` block conditionally executes macro actions based on logic you provide.

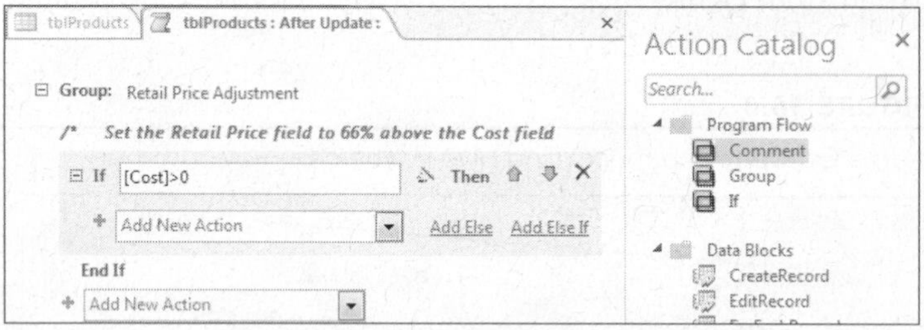

6. **If the condition we specified evaluates to true, we want to edit the record. In that case, double-click the SetField action to add it to the If block.** Here, you need to identify the field you want edited and the value you want to use. Figure 36.11 illustrates that we want to set the [RetailPrice] field to the value returned by [Cost]*1.66.

FIGURE 36.11

Adding the `SetField` action tell Access to change the record if the condition specified is true.

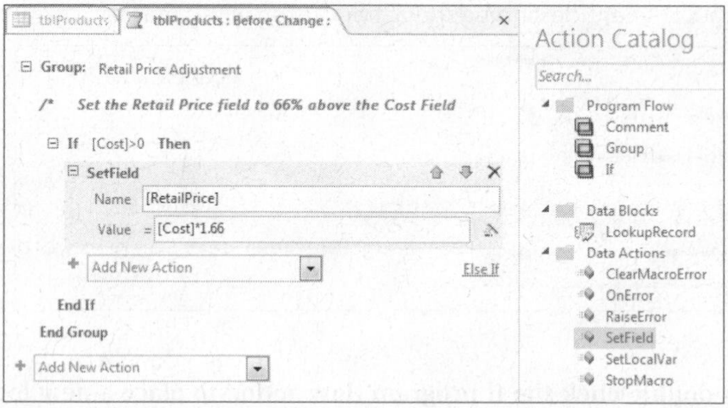

7. **At this point, the logic for our macro is complete. The last step is to click the Save command to finalize your data macro (see Figure 36.12).**

FIGURE 36.12

Clicking Save will finalize the macro and have it take effect.

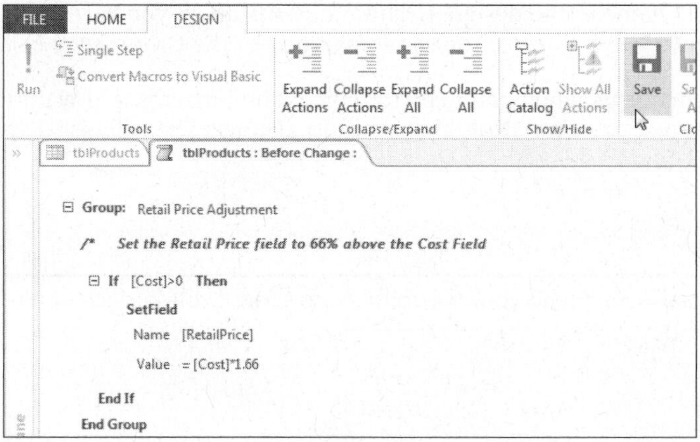

```
Group: Retail Price Adjustment
  /* Set the Retail Price field to 66% above the Cost Field
  If [Cost]>0 Then
      SetField
        Name [RetailPrice]
        Value = [Cost]*1.66
  End If
End Group
```

To test the macro, simply open tblProducts and enter a positive value in the Cost field of any record (as demonstrated in Figure 36.13). The RetailPrice field will automatically calculate per the actions provided by the BeforeChange data macro you just created.

FIGURE 36.13

Entering a positive cost will now automatically update the RetailPrice field.

RetailPrice	Cost	VendorID	PictureNumb
$19.99	$11.99	3	92508
$23.14	$13.88	4	92588
$27.99	$16.79	6	73121
$166.00	$100.00	9	73150
$33.00	$19.80	12	61029
$27.99	$16.79	5	92248
$27.99	$16.79	7	73164

Again, this data macro will be in full effect even when edits are made via an Access form in a desktop database or an Access web application.

Managing Macro Objects

At this point, you should have a solid sense of how the Macro Designer works. In this section, let's dig deeper and explore some of the options for managing macro objects once they're added to a macro's design.

Collapsing and expanding macro items

Notice in Figure 36.12 that each macro item is accompanied by a collapse/expand button to the left of its name in the designer. These buttons allow you to view or hide parts of the macro. In Figure 36.14, you see the same macro with the Group level collapsed.

Collapsing items helps when you need to review large macros and want to see only a subset of the macro at one time. Note that you can also use the Collapse/Expand commands found in the Ribbon.

FIGURE 36.14

You can collapse and expand your macro items to simplify the surface of the Macro Designer.

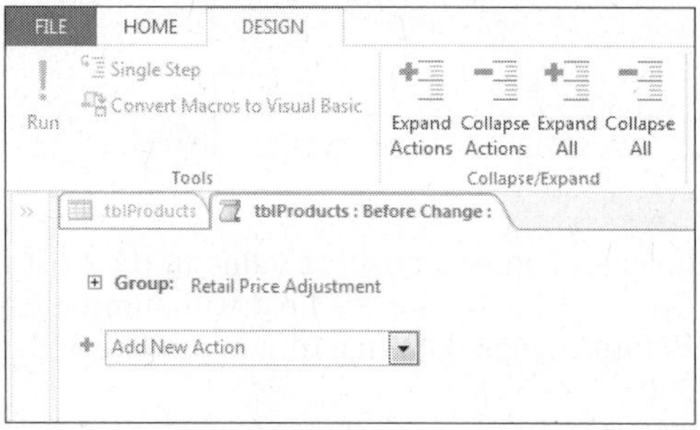

Moving macro items

You may find it necessary to change the order of the actions you place in your macro. Access provides several methods for adjusting the items within the macro designer.

Macro items (blocks, actions, and so on) can be copied and pasted within the macro. Simply click any given macro item and press Ctrl + C or Ctrl + X to copy or cut the item respectively, then place your cursor in another location within the macro designer and press Ctrl + V.

Alternatively, macro items can be dragged into a new position with the mouse. This process is a little tricky because it's very easy to drag the wrong item away from its proper position. Carefully position the mouse pointer near the top of the target item, click with the mouse, and drag the item to its new location.

Access also provides the convenient up and down arrows (see Figure 36.15) that allow you to quickly move any macro item where you need it.

FIGURE 36.15

The order of macro items can be changed by using the up and down arrows next to the target item, by clicking and dragging items, or by copying and pasting.

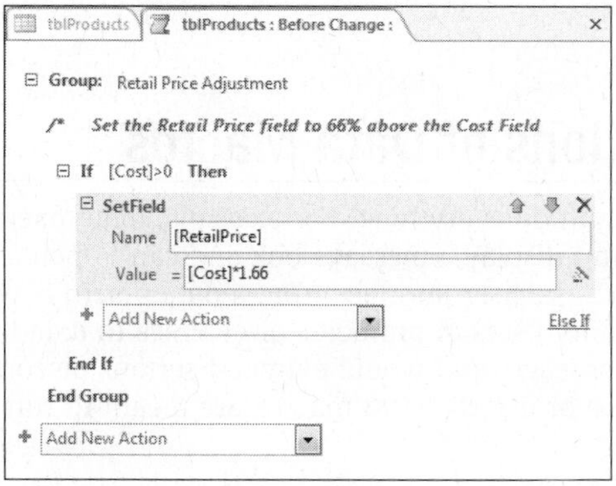

Saving a macro as XML

A completely hidden feature of Access data macros is the ability to copy them from the Macro Designer and paste them into a text editor as XML. Access internally stores macros as XML, and copying a macro actually means copying its XML representation.

There are a couple reasons you may want to save a macro as XML:

- **To e-mail the macro to someone else.**
- **To archive it as a backup.** Because each table contains only one copy of each event macro (`AfterUpdate`, for example) there's no easy way to set aside a copy of the macro before embarking on changes to the macro's logic.

Figure 36.16 shows the XML of the same macro you see in Figure 36.15 pasted into Windows Notepad. To get the XML, simply copy the macro in the Navigation pane, and then you can paste into an e-mail message, Notepad, or some other text editor.

FIGURE 36.16

Saving a macro as XML.

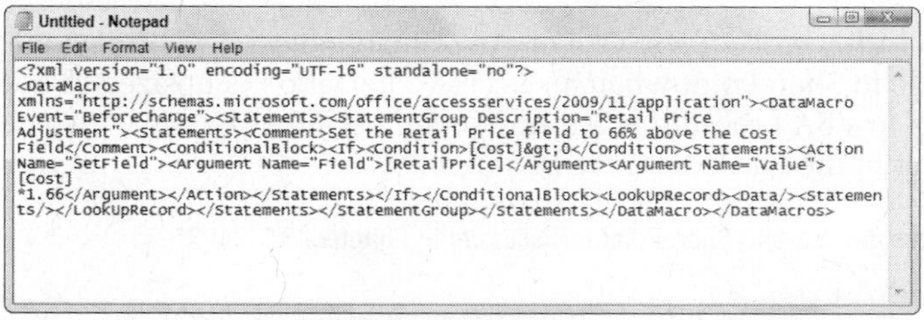

```
<?xml version="1.0" encoding="UTF-16" standalone="no"?>
<DataMacros
xmlns="http://schemas.microsoft.com/office/accessservices/2009/11/application"><DataMacro
Event="BeforeChange"><Statements><StatementGroup Description="Retail Price
Adjustment"><Statements><Comment>Set the Retail Price field to 66% above the Cost
Field</Comment><ConditionalBlock><If><Condition>[Cost]&gt;0</Condition><Statements><Action
Name="SetField"><Argument Name="Field">[RetailPrice]</Argument><Argument Name="Value">
[Cost]
*1.66</Argument></Action></Statements></If></ConditionalBlock><LookUpRecord><Data/><Statemen
ts/></LookUpRecord></Statements></StatementGroup></Statements></DataMacro></DataMacros>
```

The XML saved in a text file can be pasted right into the Macro Designer surface, and Access will display it as usual. The paste action works exactly as it does in Word or a plain text editor. The pasted macro actions appear exactly where the cursor is when the paste is initiated.

Recognizing the Limitations of Data Macros

As powerful as they are, data macros can't do everything. For example, data macros have no user interface at all. Data macros can't display a message box and can't open a form or report. Your ability to communicate with the user interface from a data macro is very limited, so data macros can't be used to notify users of problems or changes to data in tables. Displaying a user interface (such as a message box) would extract a serious performance penalty, particularly during bulk updates or inserts. Data macros are meant to run invisibly, with the highest possible performance.

Data macros are attached directly to Access tables and not to individual fields. If you have a situation where more than a few fields must be monitored or updated, the macro may become quite complex. Using the `If` block construct is a good way to conditionally execute blocks of macro statements.

The Macro Designer supports only one macro at a time. You must come to a stopping point on the current macro before closing it and opening another data macro.

Similarly, the Macro Designer is modal. You can't leave the Macro Editor without closing and saving (or not saving) the current macro. This restriction makes it difficult to view a table's data when working on a data macro's logic. As always, careful planning is a good idea when considering adding a data macro to a table.

Data macro execution doesn't occur on the back end in a spiit-database paradigm. Although the data macro resides in the table in the back-end database, the data macro is only executed in the front end.

Data macros can't work on multi-value or attachment fields. If it's important to use logic to control these data types, you must use traditional user-interface macros or VBA.

Access 2013 data macros are not supported on linked tables. If the table in an Access database is linked to SQL Server, you can't write data macros for the table. You must use traditional user-interface macros or VBA code for this purpose.

Data macros can't call VBA procedures. One of the primary objectives for data macros is to make them portable to SharePoint when an Access application is upsized to a web application. Any calls to VBA procedures are sure to fail because there is no way to convert VBA to JavaScript in the SharePoint environment.

Publishing an Access database to SharePoint is discussed in Chapters 34 and 35.

Data macros don't support transactions. Every field and record update is executed immediately, and there's no way to roll back multiple table changes.

Finally, data macros are not compatible with versions of Access earlier than 2007. Access 2007 application (with Service Pack 1 installed) can read, but not write to, Access 2010 or 2013 tables containing data macros.

Part IX

Appendixes

This book concludes with several appendixes to serve as reference material as you work with Access 2013.

Appendix A covers the Access 2013 specifications and includes information such as the limits (database size, number of database objects, maximum number of rows in an Access table, and so on) of Access objects. Appendix B offers some best practices to keeping your Access applications running optimally. Appendix C provides ideas on how to avoid performance and corruption issues when working with Access databases. Appendix D details some of the most commonly used built-in Access functions available to data analysts.

IN THIS PART

APPENDIX

A

Access 2013 Specifications

IN THIS APPENDIX

Identifying the Access 2013 specifications and limits

Looking at limits for Access 2013 tables, queries, forms, and reports

Reviewing limits for SQL Server Express Edition

This appendix shows the limits of Access 2013 database files, tables, queries, forms, reports, and macros. Be aware that the values given in this appendix are subject to change. Refer to www.microsoft.com for the latest information on these specifications.

The maximum database size, number of columns, and other limits of Access databases are more than adequate for the vast majority of Access applications. That being said, the database size limit is one that many Access developers find themselves frequently bumping up against. The size limit for an Access database is currently 2GB. You may find that, due to sheer volume of data, your database easily hits that limit.

Generally speaking, if you have a database that contains more than 2GB of data and you can't split your database into multiple Access databases, it's probably time to consider upsizing to SQL Server Express. Because its database size is 10GB, SQL Server Express might help with the initial move. SQL Server Express is a free download and may be freely distributed with your Access applications.

TIP

Simply enter *SQL Server Express 2008 R2* into your favorite search engine to find the free download.

Always keep in mind that Access is a file-based database system. The Access database file, whether it's an ACCDB, an MDB, or any other type, is just a Windows file. Access databases don't support logging, rollbacks, archiving, or other administrative tasks intended to protect a database's data. There is a point at which it really doesn't make good business sense to continue storing vast amounts of mission-critical data in a file-based database system. Server database systems (like SQL Server Express) provide all the tools necessary to properly administer and protect very large amounts of data.

Access Database Specifications

Tables A.1 through A.5 include the specifications for Access database files. Each table outlines the specifications of the component parts of an Access database.

TABLE A.1 Databases

Attribute	Maximum
ACCDB or MDB file size, including all database objects and data	2GB, minus space needed for system objects*
Total number of objects in a database (tables, queries, forms, reports, and so on)	32,768
Number of modules, including modules attached to forms and reports	1,000
Number of characters in object names	64
Number of characters in a database password	14
Number of characters in a username or group name	20
Number of concurrent users	255

* Because your database can include attached tables in multiple files, its total size is limited only by available storage capacity.

TABLE A.2 Tables

Attribute	Maximum
Number of characters in a table name	64
Number of characters in a field name	64
Number of fields in a record or table	255
Number of open tables	2,048, including system tables opened by Access internally, as well as linked tables
Table size	2GB, minus space needed for system objects*
Number of characters in a Text field	255
Number of characters in a Memo field	65,535 when entering data through the user interface; 1GB when entering data programmatically
Size of OLE Object field	1GB
Number of indexes in a record or table (including composite indexes, primary key indexes, and other indexes)	32, including single-field and composite indexes, and indexes created internally for maintaining table relationships
Number of fields in an index or primary key	10

Attribute	Maximum
Number of characters in a validation message	255
Number of characters in a validation rule (including punctuation and operators)	2,048
Number of characters in a table or field description	255
Number of characters in a record	4,000, excluding Memo and OLE Object fields
Number of characters in a field property setting	255

* There is no set limit on the number of rows in an Access table.

TABLE A.3 Queries

Attribute	Maximum
Number of tables in a query	32
Number of enforced relationships	32 per table, minus indexes that are on the table for the fields or combinations of fields that are not involved in the relationship
Number of fields in a recordset	255
Maximum recordset size	1GB
Sort limit	255 characters in one or more fields
Number of levels of nested queries	50
Number of characters in a cell of the design grid	1,024
Number of characters in a parameter name for a parameterized query	255
Number of `AND`s in a `WHERE` or `HAVING` clause	99
Number of characters in a SQL statement	Approximately 64,000

TABLE A.4 Forms and Reports

Attribute	Maximum
Number of characters in a label	2,048
Number of characters in a text box	65,535
Form or report width	22.75 inches (57.79 centimeters)
Section height	22.75 inches (57.79 centimeters)
Height of all sections plus section headers in Design view	200 inches (508 centimeters)

continued

TABLE A.4 *(continued)*

Attribute	Maximum
Number of levels of nested forms or reports	7 (form-subform-subform)
Number of fields/expressions you can sort or group on (reports only)	10
Number of headers and footers in a report	1 report header/footer, 1 page header/footer, 10 group headers/footers
Number of printed pages in a report	65,536
Number of characters in a SQL statement that is the `RecordSource` or `RowSource` property of a form, report, or control (both MDB and ADP)	32,750
Number of controls or sections you can add over the lifetime of the form or report	754
Number of characters in a SQL statement that serves as either the `RowSource` property of a form or report or the `ControlSource` property of a control	32,750

TABLE A.5 **Macros**

Attribute	Maximum
Number of actions in a macro	999
Number of characters in a condition	255
Number of characters in a comment	255
Number of characters in an action argument	255

SQL Server Express Specifications

Table A.6 includes the specifications for SQL Server 2008 R2 Express Edition only. Other versions of SQL Server Express editions are available. They're all similar in most regards, with the exception of maximum database size; for instance, SQL Server 2005 Express has a database limit of 4GB.

TABLE A.6 SQL Sever 2008 Express Capacities

SQL Server Database Engine Object	Maximum Size or Number
CPU core utilization	1*
Maximum memory utilization	1GB
Batch size	65,536 × network packet size
Bytes per short string column	8,000
Bytes per GROUP BY, ORDER BY	8,060
Bytes per index key	900
Bytes per foreign key	900
Bytes per primary key	900
Bytes per row	8,060
Bytes in source text of a stored procedure	Lesser of batch size or 250MB
Bytes per varchar(max), varbinary(max), xml, text, or image column	1,073,741,823
Characters per ntext or nvarchar(max) column	536,870,910
Clustered indexes per table	1
Columns in GROUP BY, ORDER BY	Limited only by number of bytes
Columns or expressions in a GROUP BY WITH CUBE or WITH ROLLUP statement	10
Columns per index key	16
Columns per foreign key	16
Columns per primary key	16
Columns per base table	1,024
Columns per SELECT statement	4,096
Columns per INSERT statement	1,024
Connections per client	Maximum value of configured connections
Database size	10GB
Databases per instance of SQL Server	32,767
File groups per database	32,767
Files per database	32,767

continued

TABLE A.6 *(continued)*

SQL Server Database Engine Object	Maximum Size or Number
File size (data)	4GB, not including log file size
File size (log)	2TB
Foreign key table references per table	253
Identifier length (in characters)	128
Instances per computer	16
Length of a string containing SQL statements (batch size)	65,536 × network packet size
Locks per connection	Maximum locks per server
Locks per instance of SQL Server	Up to 2,147,483,647
Nested stored procedure levels	32
Nested subqueries	32
Nested trigger levels	32
Nonclustered indexes per table	999
Parameters per stored procedure	2,100
Parameters per user-defined function	2,100
`REFERENCES` per table	253
Rows per table	Limited by available storage
Tables per database	Limited by number of objects in a database
Partitions per partitioned table or index	1,000
Statistics on nonindexed columns	30,000
Tables per `SELECT` statement	256
Triggers per table	Limited by number of objects in a database
User connections	32,767
XML indexes	249

* SQL Server Express doesn't utilize more than one CPU core on multicore machines.

APPENDIX

B

Optimizing Access Applications

IN THIS APPENDIX

Taking advantage of VBA's Load on Demand functionality

Achieving better performance through compilation

Increasing the speed of your application

Using special techniques with large databases

When Microsoft introduced 32-bit Access, the new features and functions raised a number of new performance concerns. Microsoft continues to make a conscious effort to enhance the performance of the Access database engine, as well as compilation techniques and features such as the formerly undocumented Decompile command. The end result is that Microsoft has helped to *ease* your burden, but in no way has it completely eliminated that burden.

TIP

The published minimum RAM requirement for a computer to run Access on Windows XP (SP2 or later), Windows Server 2003 (or higher), Windows Vista, or Windows 7 is 256MB — with an emphasis on *minimum.* If you plan to do serious development with Access, you should have at least 512MB to 1GB of RAM (preferably, 2GB or more).

With today's computers and memory prices, this amount of memory is a valuable investment. In fact, simply adding more memory will increase speed much more than changing your processor speed because Access must use the hard drive as a virtual memory area if it doesn't have enough memory. Hard drives are slow, and big hard drives are even slower — regardless of the processor speed.

Understanding Module Load on Demand

One of the great features of Visual Basic for Applications (VBA), the core language of Access, is its Load on Demand functionality. Using Load on Demand, Access loads code modules only as they're needed or referenced. In early versions of Access, on-demand loading of modules wasn't fully realized because referencing a procedure in a module loaded the entire module's potential *call tree* (all the modules containing procedures that *might* be called by the procedure). With Access, the Load on Demand feature truly does help reduce the amount of RAM needed and helps your program run faster.

TIP
Because Access doesn't unload code after it has been loaded into memory, you should periodically close your application while you develop. When developing, most of us have a tendency to open and work with many different procedures in many different modules. These modules stay in memory until Access is closed, which can lead to performance degradation.

Organizing your modules

When any procedure or variable is referenced in your application, the entire module that contains the procedure or variable is loaded into memory. To minimize the number of modules loaded into memory, you need to organize your procedures and variables into logical modules. For example, it's a good idea to place all global variables in the same module. If only one global variable is declared in a module, the entire module is loaded into memory. By the same token, you should put only procedures that are always used by your application (such as startup procedures) into the module containing the global variables.

Pruning the call tree

NOTE
In the discussion that follows, the term *procedure* is used to mean either a function or a sub.

The call tree for a procedure contains any additional procedures that the current procedure has referenced within it, as well as those referenced by the newly loaded procedures, and so on. Because a procedure may reference numerous additional procedures stored in different modules, based on the action taken by the procedure, this loading of all potentially called procedures takes a lot of time and memory.

Remember that when a procedure is called, the entire module in which that procedure is stored is placed in memory.

Therefore, a potential call tree consists of all the procedures that *could* be called by the current procedure that you're calling. In addition, all the procedures that could be called from *those* procedures and so forth are part of the potential call tree. For example:

1. **If you call procedure A, the entire module containing procedure A is loaded.**
2. **Modules containing variable declarations used by procedure A are loaded.**
3. **Procedure A has lines of code that call procedures B and C; the modules containing procedure B and procedure C are loaded.** Even if the call statements are in conditional loops and are never executed, they're still loaded because they could *potentially* be called.

4. **Any procedures that could be called by procedure B and procedure C are loaded, as well as the entire modules containing those potential procedures.**
5. **And so on and so on. . . .**

Fortunately for all Access developers, this complete loading of a potential call tree is addressed by compiling modules on demand, instead of loading the entire potential call tree.

NOTE
You can turn off the Compile on Demand option if you prefer, making Access compile all modules at one time. You do this in the VBA program rather than in Access. (Access links directly to VBA's development environment for working with VB code.)

To check the status of the Compile on Demand option, follow these steps:

1. **In the VBA Editor window, choose Tools⇨Options.** The Options dialog box appears.
2. **Select the General tab, and either check or uncheck the Compile on Demand check box.**
3. **Click OK.**

With the Compile on Demand option selected, Access loads only the portion of the call tree required by the executed procedure. For example, if you call procedure A in module A, any modules that contain procedures referenced in procedure A are loaded and compiled. However, Access doesn't take into consideration procedures that may be called from other procedures in module A, and it doesn't look at the potential call tree of the modules loaded because one of their procedures is referenced in procedure A. Because Access loads modules one level deep from the executed procedure's immediate call tree— and *not* the module's call tree — your applications should load and execute somewhat faster than they did in previous versions.

Even though Access has made a significant improvement in the way modules are loaded and compiled, you can still reduce the number of modules loaded and compiled. For example, never place infrequently called procedures in a module with procedures that are called often. Be aware, though, that organizing your procedures like this might make your modules less logical and harder to conceptualize.

For example, you might have a dozen functions that perform various manipulations to contact information in your application. Ordinarily, you might make one module called modContacts and place all the contact-related procedures and variables into this one module. Because Access loads the entire module when one procedure or variable in it is called, you might want to separate the contact-related procedures into separate modules — one for procedures that are frequently called and one for procedures that are rarely called.

TIP

Keep in mind that all modules with procedures that are referenced from a different module are loaded when the procedure is called. In your application, if any of your common procedures reference a procedure that isn't frequently called, place the infrequently called procedure in the same module as the common procedures to prevent a different module (containing the uncommon procedure) from being loaded and compiled. You may even decide to use more than two modules if you have very large amounts of code in multiple procedures that are rarely called. Although breaking related procedures into separate modules may make your code a bit harder to understand, it can greatly improve the performance of your application.

Distributing ACCDE Files

One way to ensure that your application's code is always compiled is to distribute your database as an ACCDE file. When you save your database as an ACCDE file, Access compiles all code modules (including form and report modules), removes all editable source code, and compacts the database. The new ACCDE file contains no source code but continues to work because it does contain a compiled copy of all your code. Not only is using an ACCDE file a great way to secure your source code, but it also allows you to distribute databases that are smaller (because they contain no source code) and always keep their modules in a compiled state. Because the code is always in a compiled state, less memory is used by the application, and you suffer no performance penalty for code being compiled at runtime.

In addition to not being able to view existing code because it's all compiled, the following restrictions apply:

- You can't view, modify, or create forms, reports, or modules in Design view. You can, however, create and modify tables and queries in an ACCDE file.
- You can't add, delete, or change references to object libraries or databases.
- You can't change your database's VBA project name by using the Options dialog box.
- You can't import or export forms, reports, or modules. Note, however, that tables, queries, and macros can be imported from or exported to non-ACCDE databases.

Because of these restrictions, it may not be possible to distribute your application as an ACCDE file. For example, if your application creates forms at runtime, you wouldn't be able to distribute the database as an ACCDE file.

TIP

If you want to create a demo of your application — and if you don't want the users to be able to see your code or form and report designs — you should create an ACCDE file. Because the designs of your forms, reports, and all code modules are simply not present (they're stored in a compiled version only), you don't have to worry about someone stealing or even modifying your designs and code. An ACCDE file is also good for distributing your work in environments where you don't want the user to change your designs.

CAUTION
You have no way to convert an ACCDE file back into a normal database file, so always save and keep a copy of the original database! When you need to make changes to the application, you must open the normal database and then create a new ACCDE file before distribution. If you delete your original database, you won't be able to access any of your objects in Design view.

To create an ACCDE file, follow these steps:

1. **Save and close all the database objects.** If you don't close these objects, Access tries to close them for you, prompting you to save changes where applicable. When working with a shared database, all users must close the database; Access needs exclusive rights to work with the database.

TIP
Since Access can't convert an application into an ACCDE if it can't compile it, you may want to compile your application first.

2. **Choose File⇨Save As⇨Make ACCDE.** The Save As dialog box appears.
3. **Specify a name, drive, and folder for the database.** Don't try to save the ACCDE file with the same filename (including the filename extension) as the original database.

CAUTION
Don't delete or overwrite your original database! You can't convert an ACCDE file to a normal database, and you can't edit any objects in an ACCDE file. If you delete or otherwise lose your original database, you'll never again be able to access any of the objects in the design environment.

NOTE
You can create an ACCDE file only if you first convert the database into the Access ACCDB format. If the file is in an Access 2002-2003 format, you can create an MDE file — the Access 2002-2003 equivalent of an ACCDE file.

Understanding the Compiled State

Understanding how Access performs Compile on Demand is critical to achieving maximum performance from your Access application. However, it's also paramount that you understand what compilation is and what it means for an application to be in a compiled state.

Access has two types of code — code that you write and code that Access understands and executes. Before a VBA procedure is executed, the code must be run through a *compiler* to generate code in a form that Access understands — called *compiled code*.

Access lacks a true compiler; instead, it uses partially compiled code and an interpreter. A true compiler converts source code to machine-level instructions, which are executed by your computer's CPU. Access converts your source code to an intermediate state that it can rapidly interpret and execute. The code in the converted form (compiled code) is known as being in a *compiled state.*

If a procedure is called that isn't in a compiled state, the procedure must be compiled and the compiled code passed to the interpreter for execution. In reality, as previously stated, this doesn't happen at the procedure level but at the module level. When you call a procedure, the module containing the procedure and all modules that have procedures referenced by the called procedure are loaded and compiled. You can manually compile your code, or you can let Access compile it for you on the fly. It takes time to compile the code, however, so the performance of your application suffers if you let Access compile it on the fly.

In addition to the time required for Access to compile your code at runtime, uncompiled programs use considerably more memory than compiled code does. When your application is completely compiled, only the compiled code is loaded into memory when a procedure is called. If you run an application that is in a decompiled state, Access loads the decompiled code and generates the compiled code as needed. Access doesn't unload the decompiled code as it compiles, so you're left with two versions of the same code in memory.

Even on computers with large amounts of installed memory, loading both the compiled and uncompiled versions of modules takes more time than loading compiled modules alone.

There is one drawback to compiled applications: They use a bit more hard drive space than their decompiled versions because both the compiled and decompiled versions of the code are stored on the hard drive as part of the database.

Hard drive space shouldn't often be a problem, but if you have an application with an enormous amount of code, you can save hard drive space by keeping it in a decompiled state. Remember that a trade-off is made between hard drive space used and the performance of your database. Most often, when given the choice, a user would rather give up a few megabytes of hard drive space in exchange for faster applications.

TIP

You can use this space-saving technique to your advantage if you need to distribute a large application and your recipients have a full development version of Access. By distributing the uncompiled versions, you need much less hard drive space to distribute the application, and the end- users can compile it again at their location. If you're going to do this, you should put the entire application into a decompiled state. We cover fully decompiling an application in the "The Six Steps to Large Database Success" sidebar, later in this appendix.

Putting your application's code into a compiled state

You have only one way to put your entire application into a compiled state: In the VBA Editor window, on the Modules toolbar, choose Debug➪Compile *Database Name.*

You must have a module open to access the Debug menu. Generally, you should always use the Compile *Database Name* command to ensure that all the code is saved in a compiled state. Complex applications may take a long time to compile, and, in general, you may choose to compile your Access projects only before distributing to end-users or before performing benchmark tests.

NOTE

When you choose Debug ➪ Compile *Database Name*, you see the name of your project. This is the name that you used to save your database file the first time that it was created or saved. If you later rename the database file, the project name doesn't change. You can change it by choosing Tools ➪ Properties in the module window; the database Properties dialog box contains the database name setting.

Losing the compiled state

In the past, one of the greatest roadblocks to optimizing Access applications has been the fact that an application could be uncompiled very easily. When the Access application was in an uncompiled state, Access had to constantly compile code as it was called. In fact, losing the compiled state was so easy to do in previous versions of Access that it would often happen without developers even realizing that they'd done it.

In Access 2013, only portions of code affected by certain changes are put into an uncompiled state — not the entire application.

The following actions cause portions of your code to be uncompiled:

- Saving a modified form, report, control, or module. (If you don't save the modified object, your application is preserved in its previous state.)
- Adding a new form, report, control, or module, including adding new code behind an existing form or report.
- Deleting or renaming a form, report, control, or module.
- Adding or removing a reference to an object library or database by using the References command on the Tools menu.

Okay, so you think that you have a handle on code that loses its compiled state? Well, here are a couple of gotchas to consider:

- If you make structural changes to objects — such as reports or forms — at runtime through VBA code, portions of your application are put into an uncompiled state when the objects are modified. (Wizards often do this.)
- If your application creates objects like reports or forms on the fly, portions of your application are put into an uncompiled state when the objects are created. (Wizards often do this as well.)

CAUTION
When you change a project name (but not the filename), the entire application loses its compiled state. Because of this, you should change the project name only if absolutely necessary, and you should compile your database immediately after making the change.

Improving Speed

When discussing an application's performance, the word *performance* is usually synonymous with speed. Speed is how quickly your application performs a function, such as running a certain query. Among the most important steps for increasing absolute speed are the following:

- **Keeping your application in a compiled state:** As was discussed in the "Distributing ACCDE Files" section, converting your ACCDB file to an ACCDE file is a good way to ensure that the code is always in a compiled state.
- **Organizing your procedures into "smart" modules:** As was discussed in the "Understanding Module Load on Demand" section, separating procedures into modules based on how frequently they'll be used is a good approach.
- **Compacting databases regularly:** An often-overlooked way of maximizing a database's performance is to routinely compact the database. When records are deleted from an Access database, the hard drive space that held the deleted data is not recovered until a compact is performed. In addition, a database becomes fragmented as data is modified in the database. Compacting a database defragments the database and recovers hard drive space.

All the preceding methods are excellent (and necessary) ways to help keep your applications running at their optimum performance level, but these aren't the only tasks that you can perform to increase the absolute speed of your application. Almost every area of development, from forms to modules, can be optimized to give your application maximum absolute speed.

Tuning your system

One important aspect of performance has nothing to do with the actual application design — that is, the computer on which the application is running. Even though it's impossible to account for all the various configurations your clients may have, you can do some things for your computer and recommend that end-users do them for theirs:

- **Equip the computer with as much memory as possible.** This step often becomes an issue related to the cost of purchasing and installing the computer memory. However, as memory prices continue to decrease, one of the most effective methods of increasing the speed of Access applications is to add additional memory to the user's computer.

- **Close all applications that aren't being used.** Windows makes it very handy to keep as many applications loaded as you want — on the odd chance that you may need to use one of them. Although Windows XP, Windows Vista, and Windows 7 are very good at handling memory for multiple applications, each application still uses computer resources.
- **Make sure that your Windows swap file is on a fast drive with plenty of free space.** If possible, you should also set the minimum hard drive space available for virtual memory to at least twice the physical RAM installed and make it a permanent swap file.
- **Defragment the hard drive often.** Defragmenting a hard drive allows data to be retrieved in larger sections, thus causing fewer reads and less repositioning of the read heads.

Getting the most from your tables

The preceding sections document many technical issues that should be reviewed to improve application speed, but sometimes it's advantageous to get back to the basics when designing your applications. Tools like Access enable novices to create relational databases quickly and easily, but they don't teach good database design techniques in the process. (An exception to this statement is the Table Analyzer Wizard. Select the ribbon's Database Tools tab, and then click the Analyze Table command in the Analyze group to start the Table Analyzer Wizard.)

B

CAUTION
Even though the Table Analyzer Wizard offers suggestions that are often helpful in learning good design technique, its recommendations should never be taken as gospel. The Table Analyzer has been proven to be wrong on many occasions.

Entire volumes of text have been devoted to the subject of database theory. Teaching database theory is certainly beyond the scope of this appendix (or even this book). However, you should be familiar with many basics of good database design.

Creating efficient indexes

Indexes help Access find and sort records faster and more efficiently. To find data, Access looks up the location of the data in the index and then retrieves the data from its location. You can create indexes based on a single field or on multiple fields. Multiple-field indexes enable you to distinguish between records in which the first field may have the same value. If they're defined properly, multiple-field indexes improve the performance of queries. This is because Microsoft's Rushmore query optimization (the technology that ACE uses to optimize the speed at which queries execute) knows how to use multiple-field indexes.

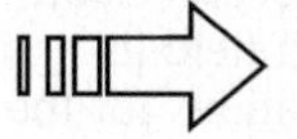
For more on indexes, turn to Chapters 3 and 4.

Deciding which fields to index

People new to database development typically make two mistakes: First, not using indexes and, second, using too many indexes (sometimes putting an index on every field in a table). Both of these mistakes are serious. Sometimes a table with too many indexes may give *slower* performance than a table with no indexes. Why? When a record is saved, Access must check every index in the table, taking time and using a considerable amount of disk space. The time used is rarely noticed with a few indexes, but with numerous indexes updates can require a huge amount of time.

In addition, indexes can slow some action queries (such as append queries) because the indexes for updated fields need to be updated while performing the query's operations.

When you create a primary key for a table, the field(s) used to define the key are automatically indexed. You can index any field unless the field's data type is Memo or OLE Object. You should consider indexing a field if any of the following rules apply:

- The field's data type is Text, Number, or Date/Time.
- You anticipate searching for values stored in the field.
- You anticipate sorting records based on the values in the field.
- You'll join the field to fields in other tables in queries.
- You anticipate storing many different values in the field. (If many of the values in the field are the same, the index may not significantly speed up searches or sorting.)

When defining an index, you have the option of creating an ascending or descending index. Ascending indexes are the default. But a descending index can be valuable in the case of fields such as dates, where the field may be sorted in descending order so that more recent dates appear at the top of the query's results.

Using multiple-field indexes

When frequently searching or sorting by multiple fields at the same time, you can create an index on the combined fields. For example, if you often set criteria for LastName and FirstName fields in the same query, it makes sense to create a multiple-field index on both fields.

When sorting a table by a multiple-field index, Access first sorts by the first field defined for the index. If the first field contains records with duplicate values, Access then sorts by the second field defined for the index, and so on. This creates a drill-down effect. For a multiple-field index to work, a search criterion *must* be defined for the first field in the index, but not for additional fields in the index. In the preceding example, if you wanted to search for someone with the last name Jones, but you didn't specify a first name to use in the search, the multi-field index wouldn't be used. If you need to perform searches on individual fields in a multiple-field index, you should create an index for each field in addition to the multiple-field index. It's not necessary to create an additional index for the first field in the multi-field index. For example, if you already have an index on LastName and FirstName, there is no need to create a new index to cover LastName only.

Getting the most from your queries

The performance problems of many Access applications result from query design. Database applications are all about looking at and working with data, and queries are the heart of determining what data to look at or work with. Queries are used to bind the data in tables to forms and reports, fill list boxes and combo boxes, make new tables, and perform many other functions within an Access application. Because they're so widely used, optimize your queries is extremely important.

A query that is properly designed can provide results minutes to hours faster than a poorly designed query that returns the same result set. Consider the following:

- When designing queries and tables, you should create indexes for all fields that are used in sorts, joins, and criteria fields. Indexes enable ACE to quickly sort and search through your database.
- When possible, use a primary key in place of a regular index when creating joins. Primary keys don't allow nulls, and they give the query optimizer more ways to use the joins.
- Limit the columns of data returned in a select query to only those you need. If you don't need the information from a field, don't return it in the query. Queries run much faster when returning less information.

TIP
If you need to use a field for a query condition and it isn't necessary to display the field in the results table, deselect the View check box to suppress displaying the field and its contents.

- When you need to return a count of the records returned by an SQL statement, use `Count(*)` instead of `Count([FieldName])` because `Count(*)` is considerably faster. `Count(*)` counts records that contain null fields; `Count([FieldName])` checks for nulls and disqualifies them from the count. This means that `Count` doesn't count records that have a null in the specified field.

TIP
You may also replace `FieldName` with an expression in the `Count` function, but this slows down the function even further.

- Avoid using calculated fields in nested queries. A calculated field in a subordinate query considerably slows down the top-level query. You should use calculated fields only in top-level queries, and even then, only when necessary.
- When you need to group records by the values of a field used in a join, specify the `Group By` for the field that is in the same table that you're totaling. You can drag the joined field from either table, but using `Group By` on the field from the table that you're totaling yields faster results.
- Domain aggregate functions (such as `DLookup` or `DCount`) that are used as expressions considerably slow down queries. Instead, you should add the table to the query or use a subquery to return the needed information.

- As with VBA code modules, queries are compiled. To compile a query, the query optimizer evaluates the query to determine the fastest way to execute the query. If a query is saved in a compiled state, it runs at its fastest speed the first time that you execute it. If it isn't compiled, it takes longer the first time because it must be compiled, but then it runs faster in succeeding executions. To compile a query, run the query by opening it in Datasheet view and then close the query without saving it. If you make changes to the query definition, run the query again after saving your changes, and then close it without saving it.
- If you really want to squeeze the most out of your queries, experiment by creating your queries in different ways (such as specifying different types of joins). You'll be surprised at the varying results.

Getting the most from your forms and reports

Forms and reports can slow an application by taking a long time to load or process information. You can perform a number of tasks to increase the performance of forms and reports.

Minimizing form and report complexity and size

One of the key elements to achieving better performance from your forms and reports is reducing complexity and size, which you can accomplish by

- **Minimizing the number of objects on a form or report:** The fewer objects used, the fewer resources needed to display and process the form or report.
- **Reducing the use of subforms:** When a subform is loaded, two forms are in memory — the parent form and the subform. Use a list box or a combo box in place of a subform whenever possible.
- **Using labels instead of text boxes for hidden fields because text boxes use more resources than labels do.** Hidden fields are often used as an alternative to creating variables to store information. (Remember, though, that you cannot use labels as parameters for queries.)

TIP

You can't write a value directly to a label like you can to a text box, but you can write to the labels caption property using VBA like this: `Label1.Caption = "MyValue"`..

- **Moving some code from a form's module into a standard module:** This enables the form to load faster because the code doesn't need to be loaded into memory. If the procedures that you move to a normal module are referenced by any procedures executed upon loading a form (such as in the form load event), moving the procedures won't help because they're loaded anyway as part of the potential call tree of the executed procedure.
- **Not overlapping controls on a form or report.**

- **Placing related groups of controls on form pages:** If only one page is shown at a time, Access doesn't need to generate all the controls at the same time.
- **Using a query that returns a limited result set for a form or report's RecordSource rather than using a table or underlying query that uses tables:** The less data returned in the `RecordSource`, the faster the form or report loads. In addition, you should return only those fields actually used by the form or report. Don't use a query that gathers fields that won't be displayed on the form or report (except for a conditional check).

Speeding up list boxes and combo boxes

It's important to pay attention to list boxes and combo boxes when optimizing your application. You can take a number of steps to make your combo boxes and list boxes run faster:

- When using multipage or tabbed forms containing list boxes or combo boxes on more than one page, don't set the `RowSource` of the list boxes or combo boxes until the actual page containing the control is displayed.
- Index the first field displayed in a list box or combo box. This enables Access to find entries that match text entered by the user much faster.
- Although it's not always practical, try to refrain from hiding a combo box's Bound column. Hiding the Bound column causes the control's searching features to slow down.
- If you don't need the search capabilities of AutoExpand, set the AutoExpand property of a combo box to No. Access is then relieved of constantly searching the list for entries matching text entered in the text portion of the combo box.
- When possible, make the first nonhidden column in a combo or list box a text data type, and not a numeric one. To find a match in the list of a combo box or list box, Access must convert a numeric value to text to do the character-by-character match. If the data type is text, Access can skip the conversion step.
- Often overlooked is the performance gain achieved by using saved queries for `RecordSource` and `RowSource` properties of list boxes and combo boxes. A saved query gives much better performance than an SQL `SELECT` statement because an SQL query is optimized on the fly.

B

Getting the most from your modules

An area where you'll often be able to use smart optimization techniques is in your modules. For example, in code behind forms, use the `Me` keyword when referencing controls. This approach takes advantage of the capabilities of Access. Using `Me` is faster than creating a form variable and referencing the form in the variable. Other optimization techniques are simply smart coding practices that have been around for many years. Try to use the optimum coding technique at all times. When in doubt, try different methods to accomplish a task and see which one is fastest.

TIP

Consider reducing the number of modules and procedures in your application by consolidating them whenever possible. A small memory overhead is incurred for each module and procedure that you use, so consolidation may free up some memory. When doing this, though, keep in mind the discussion in the "Understanding Module Load on Demand" section.

Using appropriate data types

You should always explicitly declare variables using the `Dim` function instead of arbitrarily assigning values to variables that haven't been dimmed. To make sure that all variables in your application are explicitly declared, choose Tools⇨Options in the VBA Editor window, select the Editor tab, and then set the Require Variable Declarations option on the tab.

NOTE

If you forgot to set the Require Variable Declarations option before you started coding, you'll need to add the line of code `Option Explicit` to the top of each existing module.

TIP

Use integers and long integers rather than singles and doubles when possible. Integers and long integers use less memory, and they take less time to process than singles and doubles do. Table B.1 shows the relative speed of the different data types available in Access.

TABLE B.1 Data Types and Their Mathematical Processing Speed

Data Type	Relative Processing Speed
Integer/Long	Fastest
Single/Double	Next to fastest
Currency	Next to slowest
Variant	Slowest

In addition to using integers and long integers whenever possible, you should also use integer math rather than precision math when applicable. For example, to divide one long integer by another long integer, you can use the following statement:

```
x = Long1 / Long2
```

This statement is a standard math function that uses floating-point math. You can perform the same function by using integer math (the backward slash specifies integer division):

```
x = Long1 \ Long2
```

Of course, integer math isn't always applicable. It is, however, commonly applied when returning a percentage. For example, the following expression returns a percentage:

```
x = Total / Value
```

However, you can perform the same function using integer division by first multiplying the Total by 100 and then using integer division like this:

```
x = (Total * 100) \ Value
```

You should also use string functions (`$`) where applicable. When you're manipulating string variables, use the string functions (for example, `Str$()`) as opposed to their variant counterparts (`Str()`). If you're working with variants, use the non-`$` functions. Using string functions when working with strings is faster because Access doesn't need to p erform type conversions on the variables.

When you need to return a substring by using `Mid$()`, you can omit the third parameter to have the entire length of the string returned. For example, to return a substring that starts at the second character of a string and returns all remaining characters, use a statement like this:

```
strReturn = Mid$(strMyString, 2)
```

When using arrays, use dynamic arrays with the `Erase` and `ReDim` statements to reclaim memory. By dynamically adjusting the size of the arrays, you can ensure that only the amount of memory needed for the array is allocated.

TIP

In addition to using optimized variables, consider using constants when applicable. Constants can make your code easier to read and won't slow your application.

Writing faster routines

You can make your procedures faster by optimizing the routines that they contain in a number of ways. By keeping performance issues in mind as you develop, you'll find and take advantage of situations like the ones discussed here.

Some Access functions perform similar processes but vary greatly in execution time. You probably use one or more of these regularly, and knowing the most efficient way to perform these routines can greatly affect your application's speed:

- The `IIF()` function is much slower than `If...Then...Else`.
- The `With` and `For Each` functions accelerate manipulating multiple objects and their properties.
- Change a variable with `Not` instead of using an `If...Then` statement. (For example, use `x = Not(y)` instead of `If y = True then x= False`.)

- Instead of comparing a variable to the value `True`, use the value of the variable. (For example, instead of `If x = True then...`, use `If x then...`)
- Use the `Requery` method instead of the `Requery` action. The method is significantly faster than the action. For instance, the action `Docmd.Requery "TxtField"` is slower than method `Me.TxtField.Requery`.

Using control variables

When referencing controls on a form in code, there are some very slow and some very fast ways to use references to controls. The slowest possible way is to reference each control explicitly, requiring Access to sequentially search for the control on the form. For example:

```
Forms![frmSales]![SaleDate] = something
Forms![frmSales]![InvoiceDate] = something
Forms![frmSales]![SalespersonID] = something
```

If the code is in the code module behind frmSales, you can use the `Me` reference. The `Me` reference substitutes for `Forms![formname]` and is much faster because it can go right to the form:

```
Me![SaleDate] = something
Me![InvoiceDate] = something
Me![SalespersonID] = something
```

If your code is not stored behind the form but is in a module procedure, you can use a control variable like the following:

```
Dim frm as Form
set frm = Forms![frmSales]
frm![SaleDate] = something
frm![InvoiceDate] = something
frm![SalespersonID] = something
```

This way, the form name is looked up only once.

An even faster way is to use the `With` construct:

```
With Forms![frmSales]
  ![SaleDate] = something
  ![InvoiceDate] = something
  ![SalespersonID] = something
End With
```

You can also use the `Me` pointer for a bit more efficiency:

```
With Me
  ![SaleDate] = something
  ![InvoiceDate] = something
  ![SalespersonID] = something
End With
```

Using field variables

The preceding technique also applies to manipulating field data when working with a recordset in VBA code. For example, a typical loop looks something like this:

```
...
Do Until tbl.EOF
  MyTotal = MyTotal + tbl![OrderTotal]
  tbl.MoveNext
Loop
```

If this routine loops through many records, you should use the following code snippet instead:

```
Dim MyField as Field
...
Set MyField = tbl![OrderTotal]
Do Until tbl.EOF
  MyTotal = MyTotal + MyField
  tbl.MoveNext
Loop
```

This code executes much faster than explicitly referencing the field in every iteration of the loop.

Increasing the speed of finding data in code

Use the `FindRecord` and `FindNext` methods on indexed fields. These methods are much more efficient when used on indexed fields. Also, take advantage of bookmarks when you can. Returning to a bookmark is much faster than performing a `Find` to locate the data.

Listing B.1 is an example of using a bookmark. Bookmark variables must be dimmed as variants, and you can create multiple bookmarks by dimming multiple variant variables. The following code opens tblCustomers, moves to the first record in the database, sets the bookmark, moves to the last record, and finally repositions back to the bookmarked record. For each step, the `debug.print` command shows the relative position in the database.

LISTING B.1 Using a Bookmark to Mark a Record

```
Public Sub BookmarkExample()

  Dim rs As DAO.Recordset
  Dim bk As Variant

  Set rs = Workspaces(0).Databases(0).OpenRecordset( _
    "tblContacts", dbOpenTable)

  'Move to the first record in the database:
  rs.MoveFirst
```

continued

LISTING B.1 *(continued)*

```
    'Print the position in the database:
    Debug.Print rs.PercentPosition

    'Set the bookmark to the current record:
    bk = rs.Bookmark

    'Move to the last record in the database:
    rs.MoveLast

    'Print the position in the database:
    Debug.Print rs.PercentPosition

    'Move to the bookmarked record:
    rs.Bookmark = bk

    'Print the position in the database:
    Debug.Print rs.PercentPosition

    rs.Close
    Set rs = Nothing
End Sub
```

Eliminating dead code and unused variables

Before distributing your application, remove any *dead code* (code that isn't used at all) from your application. You'll often find entire procedures or even modules that once served a purpose but are no longer called. Also, it's quite common to forget to remove variable declarations after removing code using the variables. By eliminating dead code and unused variables, you reduce the memory your application uses and the time required to compile code at runtime.

Other things that you can do to increase the speed of your modules include opening any add-ins that your application uses for read-only access and replacing procedure calls within loops with in-line code. Also, don't forget one of the most important items: delivering your applications with the modules compiled.

Increasing network performance

The single most important action that you can take to make sure that your networked databases run at peak performance is to run Access and the application database on the user's computer and link tables to the shared network database. Running Access over the network is much slower than running it locally.

When using ACE as the database engine, an Access application can run only so fast. With ACE, each time you open a table, run a query, or perform an operation on data, all the data referenced by the process or query must be moved from the data database (assuming that you've split your program and data database files) to the computer running the program. This may mean moving a lot of data across the network. In contrast, an Access project using the SQL Server or SQL Server Express Edition can use stored procedures to minimize network traffic, drastically speeding up most Access applications.

TIP
If you're working with large amounts of data, consider using SQL Server as your back-end database file.

Working with Large Access Databases

When someone mentions large databases in Access, he's generally thinking about a database containing tables holding hundreds of thousands of records. Although this is a large database, another definition is a database containing hundreds or thousands of objects — tables, queries, forms, reports, and lots of VBA modules. Although you can sometimes solve data performance problems by using SQL Server as the database engine, you'll probably have a much more complex problem dealing with applications containing many queries, forms, reports, and modules.

If your database has hundreds of objects, especially forms and reports, you may have run into problems that cause your database to exhibit strange behavior, including

- Not staying compiled
- Growing and growing, even after compiling and compacting
- Running more slowly over time
- Displaying the wrong record in linked subforms
- Displaying compile errors when you know that the code is correct
- Frequent database corruption

Compacting your database doesn't always work as advertised. Compiling and saving all modules takes a long time. After you compact and open the database, the database is uncompiled again. If you work with large databases, chances are, you've had these experiences. This section shows how to solve these problems and get your databases up and running fast again.

Understanding how databases grow in size

Many things can cause a database to grow. Each time that you add an object to an Access database (ACCDB) file, it gets larger. And why shouldn't it? You're certainly using more space to define the properties and methods of the object. Reports and forms take up a lot of space because of the properties associated with forms and reports and their controls. Table attachments (links) and queries take up very little space, but VBA code grows proportionally with the number of forms and reports. Storing data in a program database (rather than in a linked back-end database) also takes up space.

Many other things cause a database to grow: Each time you add another new form or report, more space is used. Each time you add a new control and define some properties, even more space is used. When you define any event in a form or report that contains even a single line of VBA code, more overhead is used, because the form or report is no longer a lightweight object. This requires more space and resources than a form or report containing no VBA code. Embedded images in forms and reports also use space. Embedded OLE data, such as pictures or sound, use more space than unbound objects or images.

Every time you make a change to any object — even a simple one — a duplicate copy of the object remains in the database file until you compact the database. Within a few hours of work, Access databases can begin to grow larger and larger. If the database contains thousands of lines of VBA code, the database can grow to two or three times its original size very quickly, especially when it's compiled and before it's compacted.

Recognizing that compiling and compacting may not be enough

As you add, delete, and modify objects, Access doesn't always clean up after itself. You've probably learned that after you make changes to your objects, especially VBA code, you should open any module and choose Debug➪Compile *Database Name,* save the module, and close the VBA Editor window. After you do this, click the Microsoft Office button, select the Info tab, and click the Compact and Repair This Database button. This action compacts the database with the same name and reopens the database.

Compiling and compacting may not be enough to solve some of the problems mentioned in the preceding section. Databases have been known to grow in size after compiling and compacting — even without adding new objects, code, or data. Sometimes, strange things happen to databases without a good explanation. The database might not compile code properly if the database is too large, or you might see compile errors on perfectly written code. The database might run slowly even if there's nothing wrong. There are a few more techniques to use, even when you think you're out of options.

Rebooting to get a clean memory map

Strange behavior in any program often gets better when you reboot your computer. Access applications are particularly prone to *memory leaks* (situations that arise when the application is unable to release memory it's acquired so that the operating system can use it for other purposes), especially if you're going in and out of form, report, and module design and using a lot of data objects (mostly recordsets).

TIP

If you don't want to reboot, at least close your database and exit Access as a first step in resolving a problem.

Fixing a corrupt form by removing the record source

Sometimes, you may have a form that doesn't run properly. Try opening the form in Design view and removing its record source. Then close and save the form, reopen it in Design view, and restore the record source. When the record source of an Access form or report is changed, it forces various pieces of internal code behind the form to be rebuilt and may help resolve the issue.

Creating a new database and importing all objects

Having your database as clean as possible is important. Although we aren't sure if gremlins crawl into some obscure portion of the database file, we *are* sure that you can't import or export resident gremlins. A technique that often proves successful is to create a new database and import all the objects from the original database. Access makes it easy to import all of a database's objects:

1. **Open a new empty database.**
2. **Select the External Data ribbon tab.**
3. **Click the Access option on the Import group.**
4. **Select the database you're having problems with.**
5. **Ensure that the Import Tables, Queries, Forms, Reports, Macros, and Modules into the Current Database option is selected.**
6. **Click OK.**
7. **Click on Select All for each of the relevant object types.**
8. **Click OK.**

If you have any custom menus and toolbars, import/export specifications, or Navigation Pane groups, remember to select the appropriate items in the Import Objects dialog box. If the old database contains custom database properties, you have to create them again because they can't be imported. You'll also need to repoint to any Reference Libraries used by the VBA code.

B

The Six Steps to Large Database Success

If you're ready to release your application for a real test by the users, follow these steps to insure a clean-running system:

1. Reboot your computer to clean up memory.
2. Create a new Access database and import all the objects.
3. Restart Access by using the /decompile option while holding down the Shift key. Close Access after the database window is displayed.
4. Restart Access normally while holding down the Shift key.
5. Compile the database.
6. Compact and repair the database.

If you release a clean, fully compiled and compacted system, your application will run faster and have fewer technical or maintenance problems.

Making small changes to large databases

When you're making lots of changes to a database, you're constantly opening and closing objects. Work with a copy of the database, and then when you have the changes just the way you want, export the changed objects to the production database. (An exported object with the same name as an object in the production database is exported with a 1 at the end of its name.) You can then delete the original object in the production database, and rename the exported objects. New objects are exported with their names intact.

The fewer changes to a large database, the better off you are. By following the tips and techniques in this section, you'll have fewer problems and be more productive.

APPENDIX

C

Understanding Query Performance and Database Corruption

IN THIS APPENDIX

Optimizing query performance

Handling database corruption

One of the most important aspects of working with Access is keeping your database healthy. In this appendix, you'll learn some of the best practices around building and maintaining your database, ensuring that it runs efficiently and error free.

Optimizing Query Performance

When you're analyzing a few thousand records, query performance is not an issue. Analytical processes run quickly and smoothly with few problems. However, when you're moving and crunching hundreds of thousands of records, performance becomes a huge issue. There is no getting around the fact that the larger the volume of data, the slower your queries will run. That said, there are steps you can take to optimize query performance and reduce the time it takes to run your large analytical processes.

Normalizing your database design

Many users who are new to Access build one large, flat table and call it a database. This structure seems attractive because you don't have to deal with joins and you only have to reference one table when you build your queries. However, as the volume of data grows in a structure such as this one, query performance will take a nose dive.

Understanding the Access Query Optimizer

Most relational database programs have a built-in optimizer to ensure efficient performance, even in the face of large volumes of data. Access also has a built-in query optimizer. Have you ever noticed that when you build a query, close it, and then open it again, Access sometimes shuffles your criteria and expressions around? This is because of its built-in query optimizer.

The query optimizer is charged with the task of establishing a query execution strategy. The query execution strategy is a set of instructions given to the Access database engine (ACE) that tells it how to run the query in the quickest, most cost-effective way possible. Access's query optimizer bases its query execution strategy on the following factors:

- The size of the tables used in the query
- Whether indexes exist in the tables used in the query
- The number of tables and joins used in the query
- The presence and scope of any criteria or expressions used in the query

This execution strategy is created when the query is first run, and it's recompiled each time you save a query or compact your database. Once a query execution strategy has been established, the ACE database engine simply refers to it each time the query is run, effectively optimizing the execution of the query.

You've heard the term "garbage in, garbage out," referring to the fact that the results you get out of a database are only as good as the data you put in. This concept also applies to Access's query optimizer. Since Access's optimization functionality largely depends on the makeup and utility of your tables and queries, poorly designed tables and queries can limit the effectiveness of Access's query optimizer.

When you normalize your database to take on a relational structure, you break up your data into several smaller tables. This has two effects:

- You inherently remove redundant data, giving your query less data to scan.
- You can query only the tables that contain the information you need, preventing you from scanning your entire database each time you run a query.

Using indexes on appropriate fields

Imagine that you have a file cabinet that contains 1,000 records that aren't alphabetized. How long do you think it would take you to pull out all the records that start with *S*? You would definitely have an easier time pulling out records in an alphabetized filing system. Indexing fields in an Access table is analogous to alphabetizing records in a file cabinet.

When you run a query in which you're sorting and filtering on a field that hasn't been indexed, Access has to scan and read the entire dataset before returning any results. As you can imagine, on large datasets this can take a very long time. By contrast, queries that sort and filter on fields that have been indexed run much more quickly because Access uses the index to check positions and restrictions.

You can create an index on a field in a table by going into the table's Design view and adjusting the Indexed property.

Turn to Chapter 3 for a refresher on indexes.

Now, before you go out and start creating an index on every field in your database, there is one caveat to indexing: Although indexes do speed up Select queries dramatically, they significantly slow down action queries such as Update, Delete, and Append. This is because when you run an action query on indexed fields, Access has to update each index in addition to changing the actual table. To that end, it's important that you limit the fields that you index.

A best practice is to limit your indexes to the following types of fields:

- Fields in which you'll routinely filter values using criteria
- Fields that you anticipate using as joins on other tables
- Fields in which you anticipate sorting values regularly

Optimizing by improving query design

You'd be surprised how a few simple choices in query design can improve the performance of your queries. Take a moment to review some of the actions you can take to speed up your queries and optimize your analytical processes:

- Avoid sorting or filtering fields that aren't indexed.
- Avoid building queries that select * from a table. For example, `SELECT * FROM MyTable` forces Access to look up the field names from the system tables every time the query is run.
- When creating a totals query, include only the fields needed to achieve the query's goal. The more fields you include in the `GROUP BY` clause, the longer the query will take to execute.
- Sometimes you need to include fields in your query design only to set criteria against them. Fields that aren't needed in the final results should be set to "not shown." In other words, remove the check from the check box in the Show row of the query design grid.
- Avoid using open-ended ranges such as > or <. Instead, use the `Between...And` statement.
- Use smaller temporary tables in your analytical processes instead of your large core tables. For example, instead of joining two large tables together, consider creating smaller temporary tables that are limited to only the relevant records and

then joining those two. You'll often find that your processes will run faster even with the extra steps of creating and deleting temporary tables.

- Use fixed column headings in Crosstab queries whenever possible. This way, Access doesn't have to take the extra step of establishing column headings in your Crosstab queries.
- Avoid using calculated fields in subqueries or domain aggregate functions. Subqueries and domain aggregate functions already come with an inherent performance hit. Using calculated fields in them compounds your query's performance loss considerably.

Subqueries and domain aggregate queries are discussed in detail in Chapter 15.

Compacting and repairing your database regularly

Over time, your database will change due to the rigors of daily operation. The number of tables may have increased or decreased, you may have added and removed several temporary tables and queries, you may have abnormally closed the database once or twice, and the list goes on. All this action may change your table statistics, leaving your previously compiled queries with inaccurate query execution plans.

When you compact and repair your database, you force Access to regenerate table statistics and re-optimize your queries so that they'll be recompiled the next time the query is executed. This ensures that Access will run your queries using the most accurate and efficient query execution plans. To compact and repair your database, simply select the Database Tools tab on the Ribbon and choose the Compact and Repair Database command.

You can set your database to automatically compact and repair each time you close it by doing the following:

1. **On the Ribbon, select File.**
2. **Click Options.** The Access Options dialog box appears.
3. **Select Current Database to display the configuration settings for the current database.**
4. **Place a check mark next to Compact on Close and click OK to confirm the change.**

Handling Database Corruption

Corruption is a state in which an error occurs in your Access database and causes unpredictable behavior or, in worst-case scenarios, renders your database unusable. To understand why corruption happens, you need to understand how the ACE database engine manages data.

ACE administers your data in a series of blocks. When you see a table in a database, you see it as a solid object, but it's actually made up of blocks of data. Depending on the size of the table, a table can be made of one block of data or many blocks that point to each other. Most corruption is caused by errors that occur when writing to one or more of these blocks. In fact, small-scale corruption happens all the time; you just don't know it because ACE usually resolves these corruption issues during the course of reading and writing data. However, sometimes ACE can't resolve the issue on its own. In these cases, the database is considered corrupted.

Identifying a corrupted database

There are many reasons why a database might become corrupted. The database might have encountered errors while writing data, table definitions might have been degraded over time, some VBA code or macro might have caused a fatal error, and so on. Because corruption can be caused by a wide range of nebulous issues, the signs and symptoms of a corrupted database are just as expansive and just as nebulous. You'll never see a message explicitly stating that your database is corrupt. So, the question is: How do you know if your database has been corrupted?

Databases that fall victim to corruption can generally be separated into two categories: those that you can open and work with, and those that will not open at all.

The dangerous thing about corrupted databases that are still usable is that you may never know that you're working with a corrupted database. Spotting the signs of this type of corruption can be quite difficult. That said, there are some reasonably clear indicators that strongly suggest corruption:

- You get an `Invalid field data type` error message when trying to open a table in either Data view or Design view or when viewing the Relationships window.
- You get a `Could not find field Description` error message when trying to compact and repair the database.
- When you try to open a table, query, form, report, or data access page, you get one of the following similar messages:
  - `MSAccess can't open the table in Datasheet view`
  - `Record is deleted`
  - `Unable to carry out the command`
  - `There was an error executing the command`
- You get a `Table 'TempMSysAccessObjects' already exists` error message when trying to compact and repair the database.
- Nothing happens when you try to open or delete a linked table.
- Access unexpectedly closes and then tries to send an error report.
- You get an error message *falsely* stating the following: `The changes you requested to the table were not successful because they would create duplicate values in the index, primary key, or relationship.`

C

- `#DELETED#` starts appearing in your tables.
- Access starts to drop records randomly.
- You get an `Invalid argument` error message when clicking on a record.
- All fields for a specific record show `#Error` when you run a query against that record or view it in a form.

Recovering a corrupted database

If you've determined that your database is, indeed, corrupt, there are actions you can take to attempt recovery. Keep in mind that your ability to fix a corrupted database depends on the nature and extent of the corruption. The idea is to follow these steps until your issue is resolved.

1. **Make a backup copy of the corrupt database.** Any recovery attempts come with the possibility of permanently disabling the database. You'll definitely want a backup in case this happens.
2. **Try working in another environment.** Try opening and using the database on several local machines (especially if you're working with the database through a network). If this resolves your issue, the problem is probably not a corruption issue. Look for other hardware or software issues.
3. **Delete the LACCDB file associated with the database.** When you open an Access database, an LACCDB file is created. This file is the mechanism that allows for multi-user operations. Deleting the associated LACCDB file will ensure that no rogue instances of the database are left hanging around. If you can't delete the file, use the Windows Task Manager and end all instances of Access and/or any other process that could be logged into the database. In some cases, this action can actually resolve your issue.
4. **Import your database into a fresh ACCDB file.** Start a new database and try to import your tables, queries, forms, reports, macros, data access pages, and modules from the corrupted database. In most cases, all your data and code can be salvaged using this method.
5. **Restore the database from a previously backed up version.** If you have a backup of your database, you might want to use it to help restore some of the data you've lost.
6. **Use an Access repair service.** The last resort is to use an Access repair service. These services use specialized software to restore databases, with a success rate close to 99 percent. This service will cost you between $50 and $200, depending on the company you use and the complexity of your issue. You can find a plethora of Access repair services by searching on *corrupt Access database* with your favorite search engine.

Preventing database corruption

Unfortunately, there isn't a clear set of warnings alerting you to the fact that your database is on the verge of corruption. By the time you know that you have a corrupted database, it's too late. Get into the habit of taking a few simple measures that will minimize the chance of corruption and prepare you for the event of a corrupted database.

Back up your database regularly

Having a backup of your database is like having a spare tire. There is no better safeguard against losing data than having a spare copy of it stored away. When you choose a backup plan, you'll want to consider two questions:

- **When should you back up your database?** Choose a backup schedule that directly relates to your threshold of data loss. For example, if you can't lose more than one day's worth of data, make a backup of your database every day. If daily backups are excessive, make a weekly backup.

CAUTION

Never back up your database while it's being used. You'll run the risk of the backup being in an incomplete state.

- **Where should you back up your database?** Choose a location that's safe, accessible, and not in the same folder as your working database.

Compact and repair your database regularly

Certain things happen through the natural course of using a database. For example, the data blocks in the database become fragmented, the table statistics become outmoded, and the database grows in size. Although none of these occurrences directly leads to a corrupt database, they can contribute to one if left unchecked. Many Access users think that the compact and repair utility simply releases disk space, but several important actions are performed with a compact and repair procedure.

The compact and repair utility

- Reclaims disk space and ensures the prevention of database bloat
- Defragments the blocks of data that make up table pages, improving performance and making efficient use of the read ahead cache
- Resets AutoNumber fields, ensuring that the next value allocated will be one more than the highest value in the remaining records
- Regenerates table statistics used by the query optimizer to create query execution strategies
- Flags all queries, indicating a recompile the next time the query is executed

These actions can play a big part in keeping your database streamlined and efficient.

To compact and repair your database, follow the steps in "Compacting and repairing your database regularly," earlier in this chapter.

Avoid interruption of service while writing to your database

The most common cause of corruption is interruption while writing to your database. Interrupted write processes can lead to a host of issues, from incomplete table definitions to lost indexes. In that vein, be sure to avoid any type of abnormal or abrupt termination of Access.

Following these general guidelines will help you avoid corruption due to interrupted processes:

- Always wait until all queries, macros, and procedures have completed execution before closing Access.
- Avoid using the Task Manager to shut down Access.
- Never place your Access database on a file server that is regularly shut down or rebooted.
- Avoid power loss while working with your database. If your database is on a file server, make sure the server has protection against power surges or power outages.

Never work with a database from removable media

When you work with an Access database, additional disk space is needed for the LACCDB file and for the normal database bloat that comes with using Access. If you open an Access database on removable media such as a memory stick or a zip disk, you run the risk of corruption due to disk space errors. A generally good practice is to copy the database to your hard drive, work with the database there, and then copy it back to the removable media when you're done.

APPENDIX

D

Function Reference for Data Analysts

IN THIS APPENDIX

Looking at functions commonly used in data analysis

Familiarizing yourself with a variety of functions

This appendix is designed to provide a solid reference to the functions that are most relevant to the realm of data analysis. Several of these functions are covered in detail throughout this book.

TIP

You can learn more about the functions that are not covered in this book by using the Access Help system.

Abs

Purpose: The `Abs` function is a math function that returns a value that represents the absolute value of the number (that is, the magnitude of the number without the positive or negative sign). For example, `Abs(-5)` would return `5`.

Arguments:

```
Abs(Number)
```

Number (required): This is the numeric expression you're evaluating. In a query environment, you can use the name of a field to specify that you're evaluating all the row values of that field.

Asc

Purpose: The `Asc` function is a conversion function used to convert a string to its ASCII code. For example, `Asc("A")` would return `65` because 65 is the ASCII code for the uppercase letter *A*. If you pass a whole word to the `Asc` function, it will return only the ASCII code for the first letter of the word.

Arguments:

```
Asc(String)
```

String (required): This is the string you're evaluating. If the string you're passing to the function contains no characters, the function will fail and produce a runtime error.

Atn

Purpose: The `Atn` function is a math function that allows you to calculate the arctangent of a number.

Arguments:

```
Atn(number)
```

Number (required): This is the numeric expression you're evaluating.

Choose

Purpose: The `Choose` function is a program flow function that allows you to return a value from a list of choices based on a given position. For instance: `Choose(3, "Microsoft", "Access", "Data", "Analysis")` would return `Data`. This is because the word *Data* is in the third position in the list of values.

Arguments:

```
Choose(PositionNumber, List of Values Separated by Commas)
```

PositionNumber (required): This is the numeric expression or field that results in a value between 1 and the number of available choices. If this argument's value is less than 1 or greater than the number of choices in the function, a `Null` value will be returned. This argument must be a whole number.

List of Values Separated by Commas (required): This is a variant expression that contains a list of one or more values.

Chr

Purpose: The `Chr` function is a conversion function that is used to convert a string to its associated ASCII code. For example, `Chr(65)` would return `A`.

Arguments:

```
Chr(Number)
```

Number (required): This is the number value that represents an ASCII character code. If the number you're passing to the function is not a valid ASCII character code, the function will fail and produce a runtime error.

Cos

Purpose: The `Cos` function is a math function that allows you to calculate the cosine of an angle.

Arguments:

```
Cos(Number)
```

Number (required): This is the numeric expression that represents an angle in radians.

Date

Purpose: The `Date` function returns today's date based on your computer's current system date. The `Date` function is key to performing any analysis that involves a time comparison in relation to today's date.

Arguments: There are no required arguments for this function; to use it, simply enter **Date()**.

DateAdd

Purpose: The `DateAdd` function returns a date to which a specified interval has been added. In other words, the `DateAdd` function allows you calculate a date by adding 30 days to it, subtracting three weeks from it, adding four months to it, and so on. For example,

- `DateAdd("ww",1,#11/30/2004#)` adds one week, returning `12/7/2004`.
- `DateAdd("m",2,#11/30/2004#)` adds two months, returning `1/30/2005`.
- `DateAdd("yyyy",-1,#11/30/2004#)` subtracts one year, returning `11/30/2003`.

D

Arguments:

```
DateAdd(Interval, Number, Date)
```

Interval (required): This is the interval of time you want to use. The intervals available are

- `"yyyy"`: Year
- `"q"`: Quarter
- `"m"`: Month
- `"y"`: Day of year
- `"d"`: Day
- `"w"`: Weekday
- `"ww"`: Week
- `"h"`: Hour
- `"n"`: Minute
- `"s"`: Second

Number (required): This is the number of intervals to add. A positive number will return a date in the future; a negative number will return a date in the past.

Date (required): This is the date value with which you're working. In a query environment, you can use the name of a field to specify that you're evaluating all the row values of that field.

DateDiff

Purpose: The `DateDiff` function returns the difference between two dates based on a specified time interval. For example, `DateDiff('yyyy', #5/16/1972#, #5/16/2005#)` returns `33` because there is a difference of 33 years between the two dates.

Arguments:

```
DateDiff(Interval, Date1, Date2, FirstDayOfTheWeek, FirstWeekOfTheYear)
```

Interval (required): This is the interval of time you want to use. The intervals available are

- `"yyyy"`: Year
- `"q"`: Quarter
- `"m"`: Month
- `"y"`: Day of year
- `"d"`: Day

- `"w"`: Weekday
- `"ww"`: Week
- `"h"`: Hour
- `"n"`: Minute
- `"s"`: Second

Date1 (required): This is one of the two dates you want to calculate the difference between. In a query environment, you can use the name of a field to specify that you're evaluating all the row values of that field.

Date2 (required): This is one of the two dates you want to calculate the difference between. In a query environment, you can use the name of a field to specify that you're evaluating all the row values of that field.

FirstDayOfTheWeek (optional): This specifies which day you want to count as the first day of the week. Enter **1** in this argument to make the first day Sunday, **2** to make it Monday, **3** to make it Tuesday, and so on. If this argument is omitted, the first day is a Sunday by default.

FirstWeekOfTheYear (optional): This specifies the first week of the year. In most cases, you would omit this argument. This uses the first week that includes January 1 as the default. However, you can alter this setting by using one of the following values.

- `0`: Use the National Language Support (NLS) API setting.
- `1`: Use the first week that includes January 1.
- `2`: Use the first week that has at least four days.
- `3`: Use the first week that has seven days.

DatePart

Purpose: The `DatePart` function allows you to evaluate a date and return a specific interval of time represented in that date. For example, `DatePart("q",#6/4/2004#)` returns `2` (as in second quarter), which is the quarter that is represented in that date.

Arguments:

```
DatePart(Interval, ValidDate, FirstDayOfTheWeek, FirstWeekOfTheYear)
```

Interval (required): This is the interval of time you want to use. The intervals available are

- `"yyyy"`: Year
- `"q"`: Quarter
- `"m"`: Month

D

- `"y"`: Day of year
- `"d"`: Day
- `"w"`: Weekday
- `"ww"`: Week
- `"h"`: Hour
- `"n"`: Minute
- `"s"`: Second

ValidDate (required): This is the date value with which you're working. In a query environment, you can use the name of a field to specify that you're evaluating all the row values of that field.

FirstDayOfTheWeek (optional): This specifies which day you want to count as the first day of the week. Enter **1** in this argument to make the first day Sunday, **2** to make it Monday, **3** to make it Tuesday, and so on. If this argument is omitted, the first day is a Sunday by default.

FirstWeekOfTheYear (optional): This specifies the first week of the year. In most cases, you would omit this argument. This uses the first week that includes January 1 as the default. However, you can alter this setting by using one of the following values.

- `0`: Use the NLS API setting.
- `1`: Use the first week that includes January 1.
- `2`: Use the first week that has at least four days.
- `3`: Use the first week that has seven days.

DateSerial

Purpose: The `DateSerial` function allows you to construct a date value by combining given year, month, and day components. This function is perfect for converting disparate strings that, together, represent a date, into an actual date. For example, `DateSerial(2004, 4, 3)` would return `April 3, 2004`.

Arguments:

```
DateSerial(Year, Month, Day)
```

- **Year (required):** Any number or numeric expression from 100 to 9999
- **Month (required):** Any number or numeric expression
- **Day (required):** Any number or numeric expression

DateValue

Purpose: The `DateValue` function allows you to convert any string or expression that represents a valid date, time, or both into a date value. For example, `DateValue ("October 31, 2004")` would return `10/31/2004`.

Arguments:

```
DateValue(Expression)
```

Expression (required): Any string or valid expression that can represent a valid date, time, or both.

Day

Purpose: The `Day` function is a conversion function that converts a valid date to a number from 1 to 31, representing the day of the month for a given date. For example, `Day(#5/16/1972#)` would return `16`.

Arguments:

```
Day(ValidDate)
```

ValidDate (required): This is any value that can represent a valid date. In a query environment, you can use the name of a field to specify that you're evaluating all the row values of that field.

DDB

Purpose: The `DDB` function is a financial function that calculates the depreciation of an asset for a specific period using the double-declining balance method or anther specified method.

Arguments:

```
DDB(Cost, Salvage, Life, Period, Factor)
```

Cost (required): This is the initial cost of the asset. It must be a positive number.

Salvage (required): This is the value of the asset at the end of its useful life. It must be a positive number.

Life (required): This is the length of the useful life of the asset.

Period (required): This is the period for which asset depreciation is calculated.

Factor (optional): This is the rate at which the balance declines. The default setting for this argument is the double-declining method (a factor of 2).

Domain Aggregate Functions

Purpose: Domain aggregate functions allow you to extract and aggregate statistical information from an entire dataset (a domain). These functions differ from an aggregate query in that an aggregate query will group data before evaluating the values, whereas a domain aggregate function will evaluate the values for the entire dataset. There are 12 domain aggregate functions, but they all have the same arguments.

- **DSum:** The `DSum` function returns the total sum value of a specified field in the domain. `DSum("[Sales_Amount]", "[TransactionMaster]")` would give you the total sum of sales amount in the table.
- **DAvg:** The `DAvg` function returns the average value of a specified field in the domain. `DAvg("[Sales_Amount]", "[TransactionMaster]")` would give you the average sales amount in the `TransactionMaster` table.
- **DCount:** The `DCount` function returns the total number of records in the domain. `DCount("*", "[TransactionMaster]")` would give you the total number of records in the `TransactionMaster` table.
- **DLookup:** The `DLookup` function returns the first value of a specified field that matches the criteria you define within the `DLookup` function. If you don't supply a criteria, the `DLookup` function returns a random value in the domain. `DLookup` functions are particularly useful when you need to retrieve a value from an outside dataset. `DLookUp("[Last_Name]","[Employee_Master]","[Employee_Number]='42620' ")` would return the value in the `Last_Name` field of the record where the `Employee_Number` is '`42620`'.
- **DMin, DMax:** The `DMin` and `DMax` functions return the minimum and maximum values in the domain, respectively. `DMin("[Sales_Amount]", "[TransactionMaster]")` would return the lowest sales amount in the `TransactionMaster` table while `DMin("[Sales_Amount]", "[TransactionMaster]")` would return the highest.
- **DFirst, DLast:** The `DFirst` and `DLast` functions return the first and last values in the domain, respectively. `DFirst("[Sales_Amount]", "[TransactionMaster]")` would return the first sales amount in the `TransactionMaster` table while `DLast("[Sales_Amount]", "[TransactionMaster]")` would return the last.
- **DStdev, Dstdevp, DVar, Dvarp:** You can use the `DStdev` and the `DStdevp` functions to return the standard deviation across a population sample and a population, respectively. The `Dvar` and `Dvarp` functions similarly return the variance across a population sample and a population, respectively.

Arguments: All the domain aggregate functions have the same arguments:

```
("Field Name]","[Dataset Name]", "[Criteria]")
```

Field Name (required): This expression identifies the field containing the data with which you are working. This argument must be in quotes.

Dataset Name (required): This expression identifies the table or query you're working with, also known as the domain. This argument must be in quotes.

Criteria (optional): This expression is used to restrict the range of data on which the domain aggregate function is performed. If omitted, the domain aggregate function is performed against the entire dataset. This argument must be in quotes.

Exp

Purpose: The `Exp` function is a math function that raises the base of natural logarithms (2.718282) number to a power you specify.

Arguments:

```
Exp(Number)
```

Number (required): This is the numeric expression that is used as the power to raise 2.718282.

FormatCurrency

Purpose: The `FormatCurrency` function is a conversion function that converts an expression to a currency using the currency symbol defined by your computer's regional settings.

Arguments:

```
FormatCurrency(Number, TrailingDigits, LeadingDigits, NegativeParens, Group)
```

Number (required): This is the number value you want to convert. In a query environment, you can use the name of a field to specify that you're evaluating all the row values of that field.

TrailingDigits (optional): This is the number of digits to the right of the decimal you want displayed.

LeadingDigits (optional): This indicates whether a leading zero is displayed for fractional values. The settings for this argument are `-1` for True, `0` for False, or `-2` to use the computer's regional/default settings.

NegativeParens (optional): This specifies if negative values should be wrapped in parentheses. The settings for this argument are `-1` for True, `0` for False, or `-2` to use the computer's regional settings.

Group (optional): This indicates whether numbers are grouped using the group delimiter specified in the computer's regional settings. The settings for this argument are `-1` for True, `0` for False, or `-2` to use the computer's regional settings.

FormatDateTime

Purpose: The `FormatDateTime` function is a conversion function that converts an expression to a date or time.

Arguments:

```
FormatDateTime(Date, NamedFormat)
```

Date (required): This is the date/time expression you want to convert. In a query environment, you can use the name of a field to specify that you're evaluating all the row values of that field.

NamedFormat (optional): This is the format code specifying the date/time format you would like to use. The settings for this argument are as follows:

- `0`: Display date as a short date and time as a long time.
- `1`: Display a date using the long date format specified in your computer's regional settings.
- `2`: Display a date using the short date format specified in your computer's regional settings.
- `3`: Display a time using the time format specified in your computer's regional settings.
- `4`: Display a time using the 24-hour format (hh:mm).

FormatNumber

Purpose: The `FormatNumber` function is a conversion function that converts a numeric expression to a formatted number.

Arguments:

```
FormatNumber(Number, TrailingDigits, LeadingDigits, NegativeParens, Group)
```

Number (required): This is the number value you want to convert. In a query environment, you can use the name of a field to specify that you're evaluating all the row values of that field.

TrailingDigits (optional): This is the number of digits to the right of the decimal you want displayed.

LeadingDigits (optional): This indicates whether a leading zero is displayed for fractional values. The settings for this argument are `-1` for True, `0` for False, or `-2` to use the computer's regional/default settings.

NegativeParens (optional): This specifies if negative values should be wrapped in parentheses. The settings for this argument are `-1` for True, `0` for False, or `-2` to use the computer's regional settings.

Group (optional): This indicates whether numbers are grouped using the group delimiter specified in the computer's regional settings. The settings for this argument are `-1` for True, `0` for False, or `-2` to use the computer's regional settings.

FormatPercent

Purpose: The `FormatPercent` function is a conversion function that converts a numeric expression to a formatted percentage with a trailing percent (`%`) character.

Arguments:

```
FormatPercent(Number, TrailingDigits, LeadingDigits, NegativeParens, Group)
```

Number (required): This is the number value you want to convert. In a query environment, you can use the name of a field to specify that you're evaluating all the row values of that field.

TrailingDigits (optional): This is the number of digits to the right of the decimal you want displayed.

LeadingDigits (optional): This indicates whether a leading zero is displayed for fractional values. The settings for this argument are `1` for True, `0` for False, or `2` to use the computer's regional settings.

NegativeParens (optional): This specifies if negative values should be wrapped in parentheses. The settings for this argument are `1` for True, `0` for False, or `2` to use the computer's regional settings.

Group (optional): This indicates whether numbers are grouped using the group delimiter specified in the computer's regional settings. The settings for this argument are `1` for True, `0` for False, or `2` to use the computer's regional settings.

FV

Purpose: The `FV` function is a financial function that allows you to calculate an annuity's future value. An annuity is a series of fixed cash payments normally made against a loan over a period of time.

Arguments:

```
FV(Rate, PaymentPeriods, PaymentAmount, PresentValue, Type)
```

Rate (required): This is the average interest rate per period.

PaymentPeriods (required): This is the total number of payment periods in the annuity.

PaymentAmount (required): This is the payment amount, usually consisting of principal and interest.

PresentValue (optional): This is the present value of future payments. If omitted, `0` is assumed.

Type (optional): This argument specifies when payments are due. A value of `0` means that payments are due at the end of the payment period, while a value of `1` means that payments are due at the beginning of the payment period. If omitted, `0` is assumed.

Hour

Purpose: The `Hour` function is a conversion function that converts a valid time to a number from 0 to 23, representing the hour of the day. For example, `Hour(#9:30:00 PM#)` would return `21`.

Arguments:

```
Hour(ValidTime)
```

ValidTime (required): This is any combination of values that can represent valid time. In a query environment, you can use the name of a field to specify that you're evaluating all the row values of that field.

IIf

Purpose: The `IIf` function is a program flow function that allows you to create an `If…Then…Else` statement, returning one value if a condition evaluates to true and another value if it evaluates to false.

Arguments:

```
IIf(Expression, TrueAnswer, FalseAnswer)
```

Expression (required): This is the expression you want to evaluate.

TrueAnswer (required): This is the value to return if the expression is true.

FalseAnswer (required): This is the value to return if the expression is false.

InStr

Purpose: The `InStr` function is a text function that searches for a specified string in another string and returns its position number. For example, `InStr("Alexander, Mike","x")` would return `4` because the `"x"` is character number 4 in this string.

Arguments:

```
InStr(Start, SearchString, FindString, Compare)
```

Start (optional): This is character number to start the search; default is `1`.

SearchString (required): This is the string to be searched.

FindString (required): This is the string to search for.

Compare (optional): This specifies the type of string comparison. The `Compare` argument can have the following values

- `-1`: Performs a comparison using the setting of the Option Compare statement.
- `0`: Performs a binary comparison.
- `1`: Performs a textual comparison.
- `2`: Microsoft Access only. Performs a comparison based on information in your database.

InStrRev

Purpose: The `InStrRev` function is a text function that searches for a specified string in another string and returns its position number from the end of the string.

Arguments:

```
InstrRev(SearchString, FindString, Start, Compare)
```

SearchString (required): This is the string to be searched.

FindString (required): This is the string to search for.

Start (optional): This is the character number to start the search; default is `1`.

Compare (optional): This specifies the type of string comparison. The `Compare` argument can have the following values:

- `-1`: Performs a comparison using the setting of the Option Compare statement.
- `0`: Performs a binary comparison.
- `1`: Performs a textual comparison.
- `2`: Microsoft Access only. Performs a comparison based on information in your database.

IPmt

Purpose: The `IPmt` function is a financial function that allows you to calculate the interest paid within a specified period during the life of an annuity. An annuity is a series of fixed cash payments normally made against a loan over a period of time.

Arguments:

```
IPmt(Rate, Period, PaymentPeriods, PresentValue, FutureValue, Type)
```

Rate (required): This is the average interest rate per period.

Period (required): This is the specified payment period in question.

PaymentPeriods (required): This is the total number of payment periods in the annuity.

PresentValue (required): This is the present value of future payments.

FutureValue (optional): This is the future value or final balance on a loan or an investment upon making the last payment. If omitted, `0` is assumed.

Type (optional): This argument specifies when payments are due. A value of `0` means that payments are due at the end of the payment period, while a value of `1` means that payments are due at the beginning of the payment period. If omitted, `0` is assumed.

IRR

Purpose: The `IRR` function is a financial function that calculates the internal rate of return based on serial cash flow, payments, and receipts.

Arguments:

```
IRR(IncomeValues, Guess)
```

IncomeValues (required): These values make up an array that represents the periodic cash flow values. Within this array, there must be at least one negative number and one positive number.

Guess (optional): This argument allows you to estimate the percent of total investment that will be returned. If this is omitted, 10 percent is used.

IsError

Purpose: The `IsError` function is an inspection function that determines if an expression evaluates as an error. This function returns a `True` or `False` answer.

Arguments:

```
IsError(Expression)
```

Expression (required): This is any value or expression. In a query environment, you can use the name of a field to specify that you're evaluating all the row values of that field.

IsNull

Purpose: The `IsNull` function is an inspection function that determines if a value contains no valid data. This function returns a `True` or `False` answer.

Arguments:

```
IsNull(Expression)
```

Expression (required): This is any value or expression. In a query environment, you can use the name of a field to specify that you're evaluating all the row values of that field.

IsNumeric

Purpose: The `IsNumeric` function is an inspection function that determines if an expression evaluates as a numeric value. This function returns a `True` or `False` answer.

Arguments:

```
IsNumeric(Expression)
```

Expression (required): This is any value or expression. In a query environment, you can use the name of a field to specify that you're evaluating all the row values of that field.

LCase

Purpose: The `LCase` function converts a string to lowercase letters.

Arguments:

```
LCase(String)
```

String (required): This is the string to be converted. In a query environment, you can use the name of a field to specify that you're converting all the row values of that field.

Left

Purpose: The `Left` function returns a specified number of characters starting from the leftmost character of the string. For example, `Left("Nowhere", 3)` would return `Now`.

Arguments:

```
Left(String, NumberOfCharacters)
```

String (required): This is the string to be evaluated. In a query environment, you can use the name of a field to specify that you're evaluating all the row values of that field.

NumberofCharacters (required): This is the number of characters you want returned. If this argument is greater than or equal to the number of characters in the string, the entire string is returned.

Len

Purpose: The `Len` function returns a number identifying the number of characters in a given string. This function is quite useful when you need to dynamically determine the length of a string. For instance, `Len("Alexander")` would return `9`.

Arguments:

```
Len(String or Variable)
```

String or Variable (required): This is the string or variable to be evaluated. In a query environment, you can use the name of a field to specify that you're evaluating all the row values of that field.

Log

Purpose: The `Log` function is a math function that calculates the natural logarithm of a number.

Arguments:

```
Log(Number)
```

Number (required): This is the numeric expression that is to be evaluated; it must be greater than zero.

Mid

Purpose: The `Mid` function returns a specified number of characters starting from a specified character position. The required arguments for the `Mid` function are

- The text you're evaluating
- The starting position
- The number of characters you want returned

For example, `Mid("Lonely", 2, 3)` captures three characters starting from character number two in the string, returning `one`.

Arguments:

```
Mid(String, StartPosition, NumberOfCharacters)
```

String (required): This is the string to be evaluated. In a query environment, you can use the name of a field to specify that you're evaluating all the row values of that field.

StartPosition (required): This is the position number of the character you want to start your capture.

NumberofCharacters (optional): This is the number of characters you want returned. If this argument is greater than or equal to the number of characters in the string, the entire string is returned. If this argument is omitted (or is larger than the length of the string), it takes all characters from the `StartPosition` to the end of the string.

Minute

Purpose: The `Minute` function converts a valid time to a number from 0 to 59, representing the minute component of the time value. For example, `Minute(#9:30:00 PM#)` would return `30`.

Arguments:

```
Minute(ValidTime)
```

ValidTime (required): This is any combination of values that can represent valid time. In a query environment, you can use the name of a field to specify that you're evaluating all the row values of that field

D

MIRR

Purpose: The `MIRR` function is a financial function that calculates the internal rate of return based on serial cash flow, payments, and receipts that are financed at different rates.

Arguments:

```
MIRR(IncomeValues, FinanceRate, ReinvestRate)
```

IncomeValues (required): These values make up an array that represents the periodic cash flow values. Within this array, there must be at least one negative number and one positive number.

FinanceRate (required): This is the interest rate paid as the cost of investing. The values of this argument must be represented as decimal values.

ReinvestRate (required): This is the interest rate received on gains from cash reinvestment. The values of this argument must be represented as decimal values.

Month

Purpose: The `Month` function converts a valid date to a number from 1 to 12, representing the month for a given date. For example, `Month(#5/16/1972#)` would return `5`.

Arguments:

```
Month(ValidDate)
```

ValidDate (required): This is any value that can represent a valid date. In a query environment, you can use the name of a field to specify that you're evaluating all the row values of that field.

MonthName

Purpose: The `MonthName` function converts a numeric month designation (1 to 12) to a month name. For instance, `MonthName(8)` would return `August`. Values less than 1 or greater than 12 will cause an error.

Arguments:

```
MonthName(NumericMonth, Abbreviated)
```

NumericMonth (required): This is a number from 1 to 12 that represents a month. The number 1 represents January, the number 2 represents February, and so on.

Abbreviated (optional): This specifies whether the month is abbreviated or not. If this argument is omitted, the month is not abbreviated. Enter **1** to return abbreviated months.

Now

Purpose: The `Now` function returns today's date and time based on your computer's current system date and time.

Arguments: There are no required arguments for this function; to use it, simply enter **Now()**.

NPer

Purpose: The `NPer` function is a financial function that specifies the number of periods for an annuity based on periodic, fixed payments at a fixed interest rate. An annuity is a series of fixed cash payments normally made against a loan over a period of time.

Arguments:

```
NPer(Rate, PaymentAmount, PresentValue, FutureValue, Type)
```

Rate (required): This is the average interest rate per period.

PaymentAmount (required): This is the payment amount, usually consisting of principal and interest.

PresentValue (required): This is the present value of future payments and receipts.

FutureValue (optional): This is the future value or final balance on a loan or an investment upon making the last payment. If omitted, `0` is assumed.

Type (optional): This argument specifies when payments are due. A value of `0` means that payments are due at the end of the payment period, while a value of `1` means that payments are due at the beginning of the payment period. If omitted, `0` is assumed.

NPV

Purpose: The `NPV` function is a financial function that calculates the net present value or the current value of a future series of payments and receipts based on serial cash flow, payments, receipts, and a discount rate.

Arguments:

```
NPV(DiscountRate, IncomeValues)
```

DiscountRate (required): This is the discount rate received over the length of the period. The values of this argument must be represented as decimal values.

IncomeValues (required): These values make up an array that represents the periodic cash flow values. Within this array, there must be at least one negative number and one positive number.

D

NZ

Purpose: The `NZ` function allows you to tell Access to recognize `Null` values as another value, preventing your `Null` values from propagating through an expression.

Arguments:

```
NZ(Variant, ValueIfNull)
```

Variant (required): This is the data you're working with.

ValueIfNull (required in the query environment): This is the value you want returned if the `Variant` is `Null`.

Partition

Purpose: The `Partition` function is a database function that identifies the particular range in which a number falls and returns a string describing that range. This function is useful when you need to create a quick and easy frequency distribution.

Arguments:

```
Partition(Number, Range Start, Range Stop, Interval)
```

Number (required): This is the number you're evaluating. In a query environment, you typically use the name of a field to specify that you're evaluating all the row values of that field.

Range Start (required): This is a whole number that is to be the start of the overall range of numbers. Note that this number cannot be less than zero.

Range Stop (required): This is a whole number that is to be the end of the overall range of numbers. Note that this number cannot be equal to or less than the `Range Start`.

Interval (required): This is a whole number that is to be the span of each range in the series from `Range Start` to `Range Stop`. Note that this number cannot be less than one.

Pmt

Purpose: The `Pmt` function is a financial function that calculates the payment for an annuity based on periodic, fixed payments at a fixed interest rate. An annuity is a series of fixed cash payments normally made against a loan over a period of time.

Arguments:

```
Pmt(Rate, PaymentPeriods, PresentValue, FutureValue, Type)
```

Rate (required): This is the average interest rate per period.

PaymentPeriods (required): This is the total number of payment periods in the annuity.

PresentValue (required): This is the present value of future payments and receipts.

FutureValue (optional): This is the future value or final balance on a loan or an investment upon making the last payment. If omitted, `0` is assumed.

Type (optional): This argument specifies when payments are due. A value of `0` means that payments are due at the end of the payment period, while a value of `1` means that payments are due at the beginning of the payment period. If omitted, `0` is assumed.

PPmt

Purpose: The `PPmt` function is a financial function that allows you to calculate the principal payment for a specified period during the life of an annuity. An annuity is a series of fixed cash payments normally made against a loan over a period of time.

Arguments:

```
PPmt(Rate, Period, PaymentPeriods, PresentValue, FutureValue, Type)
```

Rate (required): This is the average interest rate per period.

Period (required): This is the specified payment period in question.

PaymentPeriods (required): This is the total number of payment periods in the annuity.

PresentValue (required): This is the present value of future payments and receipts.

FutureValue (optional): This is the future value or final balance on a loan or an investment upon making the last payment. If omitted, `0` is assumed.

Type (optional): This argument specifies when payments are due. A value of `0` means that payments are due at the end of the payment period, while a value of `1` means that payments are due at the beginning of the payment period. If omitted, `0` is assumed.

D

PV

Purpose: The PV function is a financial function that allows you to calculate an annuity's present value. An annuity is a series of fixed cash payments normally made against a loan over a period of time.

Arguments:

```
PV(Rate, PaymentPeriods, PaymentAmount, FutureValue, Type)
```

Rate (required): This is the average interest rate per period.

PaymentPeriods (required): This is the total number of payment periods in the annuity.

PaymentAmount (required): This is the payment amount, usually consisting of principal and interest.

FutureValue (optional): This is the future value or final balance on a loan or an investment upon making the last payment. If omitted, 0 is assumed.

Type (optional): This argument specifies when payments are due. A value of 0 means that payments are due at the end of the payment period, while a value of 1 means that payments are due at the beginning of the payment period. If omitted, 0 is assumed.

Rate

Purpose: The Rate function is a financial function that allows you to calculate the interest rate per period for an annuity. An annuity is a series of fixed cash payments normally made against a loan over a period of time.

Arguments:

```
Rate(Periods, PaymentAmount, PresentValue, FutureValue, Type, Guess)
```

Periods (required): This is the total number of payment periods in the annuity.

PaymentAmount (required): This is the payment amount, usually consisting of principal and interest.

PresentValue (required): This is the present value of future payments and receipts.

FutureValue (optional): This is the future value or final balance on a loan or an investment upon making the last payment. If omitted, 0 is assumed.

Type (optional): This argument specifies when payments are due. A value of 0 means that payments are due at the end of the payment period, while a value of 1 means that payments are due at the beginning of the payment period. If omitted, 0 is assumed.

Guess (optional): This argument allows you to estimate the percent of total investment that will be returned. If omitted, 10 percent is used.

Replace

Purpose: The `Replace` function allows you to replace a specified substring with another substring. This function has the same effect as the Find and Replace functionality. For example, `Replace("Pear", "P", "B")` would return `Bear`.

Arguments:

```
Replace(String, Find, Replace, Start, Count, Compare)
```

String (required): This is the full string you're evaluating. In a query environment, you can use the name of a field to specify that you're evaluating all the row values of that field.

Find (required): This is the substring you need to find and replace.

Replace (required): This is the substring used as the replacement.

Start (optional): This is the position within the substring to begin the search; the default is `1`.

Count (optional): This is the number of occurrences to replace; the default is all occurrences.

Compare (optional): This is the kind of comparison to use. The `Compare` argument can have the following values:

- `-1`: Performs a comparison using the setting of the Option Compare statement.
- `0`: Performs a binary comparison.
- `1`: Performs a textual comparison.
- `2`: Microsoft Access only. Performs a comparison based on information in your database.

Right

Purpose: The `Right` function returns a specified number of characters starting from the rightmost character of the string. For example, `Left("Nowhere", 4)` would return `here`.

Arguments:

```
Right(String, NumberOfCharacters)
```

String (required): This is the string to be evaluated. In a query environment, you can use the name of a field to specify that you're evaluating all the row values of that field.

NumberofCharacters (required): This is the number of characters you want returned. If this argument is greater than or equal to the number of characters in a string, the entire string is returned.

D

Rnd

Purpose: The `Rnd` function is a math function that generates and returns a random number that is greater than or equal to 0 but less than 1.

Arguments:

```
Rnd(number)
```

Number (optional): This numeric expression determines how the random number is generated. The `Rnd` function follows these rules:

- If the `Number` argument is omitted from the function, the next random number in the sequence is generated.
- If the `Number` argument is less than zero, the same number is generated every time.
- If the `Number` argument is greater than zero, the next random number in the sequence is generated.
- If the `Number` argument equals zero, the most recently generated number is returned.

Round

Purpose: The `Round` function is a math function that allows you to round a number to a specified number of decimal places. For example, `Round(456.7276)` returns `456`.

Arguments:

```
Round(Number, DecimalPlaces)
```

Number (required): This is the numeric expression you want to evaluate. In a query environment, you typically use the name of a field to specify that you're evaluating all the row values of that field.

DecimalPlaces (optional): This is the number of places to the right of the decimal that are included in the rounding. If omitted, the `Round` function returns an integer with zero decimal places.

Second

Purpose: The `Second` function converts a valid time to a number from 0 to 59, representing the second of the minute. For example, `Second(#9:00:35 PM#)` would return `35`.

Arguments:

```
Second(ValidTime)
```

ValidTime (required): This is any combination of values that can represent valid time. In a query environment, you can use the name of a field to specify that you're evaluating all the row values of that field.

Sgn

Purpose: The `Sgn` function is a math function that returns an integer code associated with the sign of a given number. If the given number is less than zero (has a negative designation), the `Sgn` function returns `-1`. If the given number equals zero, the `Sgn` function returns `0`. If the given number is greater than zero (has a positive designation), the `Sgn` function returns `1`.

Arguments:

```
Sgn(number)
```

Number (required): This is the numeric expression you're evaluating.

Sin

Purpose: The `Sin` function is a math function that allows you to calculate the sine of an angle.

Arguments:

```
Sin(Number)
```

Number (required): This is any numeric expression that expresses an angle in radians.

SLN

Purpose: The `SLN` function is a financial function that calculates the straight-line depreciation of an asset for one period.

Arguments:

```
SLN(Cost, Salvage, Life)
```

Cost (required): This is the initial cost of the asset; it must be a positive number.

Salvage (required): This is the value of the asset at the end of its useful life; it must be a positive number.

Life (required): This is the length of the useful life of the asset.

Space

Purpose: The `Space` function allows you to create a string with a specified number of spaces to a string. This function comes in handy when you need to clear data in fixed-length strings. For example, you can use the `Space` function within an expression such as `Space(5) & "Access"`. This would change the string `"Access"` to `"     Access"`.

Arguments:

```
Space(Number)
```

Number (required): This is the number of spaces to include in the string.

SQL Aggregate Functions

Purpose: SQL aggregate functions are the most commonly used functions in Access. These functions perform either mathematical calculations or value evaluations against a given expression. These functions are typically used in a query environment where the `Expression` argument refers to a field in a table where you're evaluating all the row values of that field.

- **Sum(Expression):** `Sum` calculates the total value of all the records in the designated field or grouping. This function will only work with the following data types: AutoNumber, Currency, Date/Time, and Number.
- **Avg(Expression):** `Avg` calculates the average of all the records in the designated field or grouping. This function will only work with the following data types: AutoNumber, Currency, Date/Time, and Number.
- **Count(Expression):** `Count` simply counts the number of entries within the designated field or grouping. This function works with all data types.
- **StDev(Expression):** `StDev` calculates the standard deviation across all records within the designated field or grouping. This function will only work with the following data types: AutoNumber, Currency, Date/Time, and Number.
- **Var(Expression):** `Var` calculates the amount by which all the values within the designated field or grouping vary from the average value of the group. This function will only work with the following data types: AutoNumber, Currency, Date/Time, and Number.

- **Min(Expression):** `Min` returns the value of the record with the lowest value in the designated field or grouping. This function will only work with the following data types: AutoNumber, Currency, Date/Time, Number, and Text.
- **Max(Expression):** `Max` returns the value of the record with the highest value in the designated field or grouping. This function will only work with the following data types: AutoNumber, Currency, Date/Time, Number, and Text.
- **First(Expression):** `First` returns the value of the first record in the designated field or grouping. This function works with all data types.
- **Last(Expression):** `Last` returns the value of the last record in the designated field or grouping. This function works with all data types.

Sqr

Purpose: The `Sqr` function is a math function that calculates the square root of a given number.

Arguments:

```
Sqr(Number)
```

Number (required): This is the numeric expression you're evaluating.

Str

Purpose: The `Str` function is a conversion function that converts a numeric value into a string representation of the number. For instance, `Str(2304)` would return " `2304`." Note that positive numbers converted with `Str` always have a leading space to represent the positive sign. Negative numbers have a negative sign as the leading character.

Arguments:

```
Str(Number)
```

Number (required): This is the number you want to convert to a string. In a query environment, you can use the name of a field to specify that you're evaluating all the row values of that field.

D

StrConv

Purpose: The `StrConv` function allows you to convert a string to a specified conversion setting such as uppercase, lowercase, or proper case. For example, `StrConv("my text",3)` would be converted to proper case, reading `My Text`.

Arguments:

```
StrConv(String, ConversionType, LCID)
```

String (required): This is the string to be converted. In a query environment, you can use the name of a field to specify that you're converting all the row values of that field.

ConversionType (required): The conversion type specifies how to convert the string. The following constants identify the conversion type.

- `1`: Converts the string to uppercase characters.
- `2`: Converts the string to lowercase characters.
- `3`: Converts the first letter of every word in the string to uppercase.
- `64`: Converts the string to Unicode using the default system code page.
- `128`: Converts the string from Unicode to the default system code page.

LCID (optional): This is the LocaleID you want to use. The system LocaleID is the default.

String

Purpose: The `String` function allows you to return a character string of a certain length. For example, `String(4, "0")` would return `0000`.

Arguments:

```
String(LengthOfString, StringCharacter)
```

LengthOfString (required): This is the number of times you want to repeat the `StringCharacter`.

StringCharacter (required): This is the character that will make up your string. If you enter a series of characters, only the first character will be used.

StrReverse

Purpose: The `StrReverse` function returns an expression in reverse order. For instance, `StrReverse("ten")` returns `net`. This works with numbers too; `StrReverse(5432)` returns `2345`.

Arguments:

```
StrReverse(Expression)
```

Expression (required): This is the expression that contains the characters you want reversed.

Switch

Purpose: The `Switch` function is a program flow function that allows you to evaluate a list of expressions and return the value associated with the expression determined to be true. To use the `Switch` function, you must provide a minimum of one expression and one value.

Arguments:

```
Switch(Expression, Value)
```

Expression (required): This is the expression you want to evaluate.

Value (required): This is the value to return if the expression is true.

To evaluate multiple expressions, simply add another Expression and Value to the function — for example, `Switch(Expression1, Value1, Expression2, Value2, Expression3, Value3)`.

When the `Switch` function is executed, each expression is evaluated. If an expression evaluates to true, the value that follows that expression is returned. If more than one expression is true, the value for the first true expression is returned.

SYD

Purpose: The `SYD` function is a financial function that calculates the sum-of-years' digits depreciation of an asset for a specified period.

Arguments:

```
SYD(Cost, Salvage, Life, Period)
```

Cost (required): This is the initial cost of the asset; it must be a positive number.

Salvage (required): This is the value of the asset at the end of its useful life; it must be a positive number.

Life (required): This is the length of the useful life of the asset.

Period (required): This is the period for which asset depreciation is calculated.

Tan

Purpose: The `Tan` function is a math function that allows you to calculate the tangent of an angle.

Arguments:

```
Tan(number)
```

Number (required): This is any numeric expression that expresses an angle in radians.

Time

Purpose: The `Time` function returns today's time based on your computer's current system time. This function is ideal for time stamping transactions.

Arguments: There are no required arguments for this function; to use it, simply enter **Time()**.

TimeSerial

Purpose: The `TimeSerial` function essentially builds a time value based on the given hour, minute, and second components. Keep in mind that this function works on a 24-hour clock, so the expression `TimeSerial(18,30,0)` would return `6:30:00 PM`. This function is perfect for converting disparate strings that represent a time when combined into an actual time.

Arguments:

```
TimeSerial(Hour, Minute, Second)
```

Hour (required): This is any number or numeric expression that has a value between 0 and 23, inclusive. In a query environment, you can use the name of a field to specify that you're evaluating all the row values of that field; this is true for all the arguments in this function.

Minute (required): This is any number or numeric expression. If the number specified for this argument exceeds the normal range for minutes in an hour, the function increments the hour as appropriate. For instance, `TimeSerial(7,90,00)` would return `8:30:00 AM`.

Second (required): This is any number or numeric expression. If the number specified for this argument exceeds the normal range for seconds in a minute, the function increments the minutes as appropriate. For instance, `TimeSerial(7,10, 75)` would return `7:11:15 AM`.

TimeValue

Purpose: The `TimeValue` function converts a string representation of a time to an actual time value. For instance, `TimeValue("4:20:37 PM")` would return `4:20:37 PM`.

The function also works on a 24-hour clock.

Arguments:

```
TimeValue(String)
```

String (required): This is any string or expression that represents a time ranging from 0:00:00 to 23:59:59. The string can be either a 12-hour clock entry or a 24-hour clock entry. In a query environment, you can use the name of a field to specify that you're evaluating all the row values of that field.

Trim, LTrim, RTrim

Purpose: The `Trim` function effectively removes both the leading and trailing spaces from a string. The `LTrim` function removes only the leading spaces, while the `RTrim` function removes only the trailing spaces. These functions come in handy when cleaning up data received from a mainframe source.

Arguments:

```
Trim(String)
LTrim(String)
RTrim(String)
```

String (required): This is the string you're working with. In a query environment, you can use the name of a field to specify that you're evaluating all the row values of that field.

TypeName

Purpose: The `TypeName` function is an inspection function that returns the type information of a variable. For instance, `TypeName("Michael")` would return `String`.

Arguments:

```
TypeName(Variable)
```

Variable (required): This is the variable you want to evaluate. In a query environment, you can use the name of a field to specify that you're evaluating all the row values of that field.

The string returned by the TypeName function can be any one of the following:

- `Object type`: An object whose type is ObjectType
- `Byte`: A Byte value
- `Integer`: An Integer type
- `Long`: A Long integer type
- `Single`: A Single-precision floating-point number
- `Double`: A Double-precision floating-point number

D

- `Currency`: A Currency value
- `Decimal`: A Decimal value
- `Date`: A Date value
- `String`: A String type
- `Boolean`: A Boolean value
- `Error`: An error value
- `Empty`: Variable has not been initialized
- `Null`: Variable contains no valid data; a `Null` value
- `Object`: An object
- `Unknown`: An object whose type is unknown
- `Nothing`: An Object variable that does not refer to an object

UCase

Purpose: The UCase function converts a string to uppercase letters.

Arguments:

```
UCase(String)
```

String (required): This is the string to be converted. In a query environment, you can use the name of a field to specify that you're converting all the row values of that field.

Val

Purpose: The Val function is a conversion function that extracts the numeric part of a string. For instance, `Val("5400 Legacy Drive")` would return `5400`. One caveat to the `Val` function: It stops reading the string as soon as it hits a textual character. Therefore, the number you're extracting needs to be at the beginning of the string.

Arguments:

```
Val(String)
```

String (required): This is the string you want to evaluate. In a query environment, you can use the name of a field to specify that you're evaluating all the row values of that field.

VarType

Purpose: The `VarType` function is an inspection function that returns the subtype code associated with a variant's character type. For instance, `VarType("Michael")` would return `8` because this is the subtype code for a string.

Arguments:

```
VarType(Variant)
```

Variant (required): This is the variant you want to evaluate. In a query environment, you can use the name of a field to specify that you're evaluating all the row values of that field.

The following is a list of the subtype codes that the `VarType` function can return.

- `0`: Empty (uninitialized)
- `1`: Null (no valid data)
- `2`: Integer
- `3`: Long integer
- `4`: Single-precision floating-point number
- `5`: Double-precision floating-point number
- `6`: Currency value
- `7`: Date value
- `8`: String
- `9`: Object
- `10`: Error value
- `11`: Boolean value
- `12`: Variant (used only with arrays of variants)
- `13`: A data access object
- `14`: Decimal value
- `17`: Byte value
- `36`: Variants that contain user-defined types
- `8192`: Array

Weekday

Purpose: The `Weekday` function returns a number from 1 to 7 representing the day of the week for a given date. The number `1` represents Sunday, `2` represents Monday, and so on. For example, `Weekday(#12/31/1997#)` will return `4`.

Arguments:

```
Weekday(ValidDate,FirstDayOfTheWeek)
```

ValidDate (required): This is any value that can represent a valid date. In a query environment, you can use the name of a field to specify that you're evaluating all the row values of that field.

FirstDayOfTheWeek (optional): This specifies which day you want to count as the first day of the week. Enter **1** in this argument to make the first day Sunday, **2** for Monday, **3** for Tuesday, and so on. If this argument is omitted, the first day is a Sunday by default. If Sunday is not the first day of the week in your part of the world, you can use this optional `FirstDayOfWeek` argument.

WeekdayName

Purpose: The `WeekdayName` function converts a numeric weekday designation (1 to 7) to a weekday name. For instance, `WeekdayName(7)` would return Saturday. Values less than 1 or greater than 7 will cause an error.

Arguments:

```
WeekdayName(WeekdayNumber, Abbreviated, FirstDayOfTheWeek)
```

WeekdayNumber (required): This is a number from 1 to 7 that represents a weekday. The number 1 represents Sunday, 2 represents Monday, and so on.

Abbreviated (optional): This specifies whether the weekday is abbreviated or not. If this argument is omitted, the weekday is not abbreviated. Enter **1** for this argument to return abbreviated weekdays.

FirstDayOfTheWeek (optional): This specifies which day you want to count as the first day of the week. Enter **1** in this argument to make the first day Sunday, **2** for Monday, **3** for Tuesday, and so on. If this argument is omitted, the first day is a Sunday by default.

Year

Purpose: The `Year` function returns a whole number representing the year for a given date. For example, `Year(#5/16/1972#)` would return `1972`.

Arguments:

```
Year(ValidDate)
```

ValidDate (required): This is any value that can represent a valid date. In a query environment, you can use the name of a field to specify that you're evaluating all the row values of that field.

Index

SYMBOLS AND NUMERICS

Index

B

C

F

H

I

J

K

L

M

N

O

Q

R

Index

S

U

X

Y

Z